The Practice of Management

JOHN B. MINER
Georgia State University

with
TIMOTHY M. SINGLETON
University of Houston/Clear Lake City

and
VINCENT P. LUCHSINGER
University of Baltimore

Charles E. Merrill Publishing Company
A Bell & Howell Company
Columbus Toronto London Sydney

Published by Charles E. Merrill Publishing Company
A Bell & Howell Company
Columbus, Ohio 43216

This book was set in Garamond.
Production Coordination and Text Design: Martha Morss
Cover Design: Cathy Watterson

Photo Credits: Part One, courtesy of ROLM Corporation, Santa Clara, California; Part
Two, Nationwide Insurance Company; Part Three, Xerox Corporation; Part Four,
Courtesy of AT&T; Part Five, © Freda Leinwand; Part Six, The Firestone Tire and
Rubber Company; Part Seven, Bell & Howell Company.

International Standard Book Number: 0–675–20388–0
Library of Congress Catalog Card Number: 84–61745
1 2 3 4 5 6 7 8 9—90 89 88 87 86 85
Printed in the United States of America

To Barbara
with love and appreciation for her help

Preface

This book surveys the field of management as a whole, drawing upon sound scholarship and tying the material as closely as possible to practice. Our objective is to provide a comprehensive introduction to the field of management and to the context of actual management practice. We have sought to provide the detail management majors need to be equipped to assume managerial positions, and also to give the general overview required by students who need only a working knowledge of the field. In this way, the book provides breadth of coverage so that students can understand what the management field is about in general. It will serve both the students who will not take additional courses in the field and those who need preparation for more advanced work.

The order in which the subject matter is presented is not intended to be binding. Part One, dealing with the meaning of management, provides certain background information upon which all of the other parts build. Chapter 1 surveys the ways mangement courses and curricula have been organized and how the book may be used to follow a particular approach. Beyond this, each part is relatively self-contained, so the order of coverage can be varied. For example, a somewhat more traditional approach might take up Part Four, dealing with planning and management policy/strategy, immediately after the initial three chapters. Any number of patterns in covering the material are feasible, depending upon the approach a professor wishes to take in the course. The instructor's manual that accompanies the text discusses alternate course organizations in detail.

The flexible format of the text provides complete coverage of the traditional management framework along with less-established systems today's student needs to recognize and understand. Management skills are covered according to the hierarchy in which they are used. Examples and applications simulate actual business practice, providing an authentic feel for the situations managerial personnel face and the skills they must possess. Appropriate attention is paid to topics that have been stressed by the AACSB, such as production/operations management, policy management, social responsibility, international management, and others.

Integrated into the text are a number of pedagogical features designed to enhance learning. For instance, chapters begin with outlines and objectives to provide a preview of what should be learned from reading each section. Articles from major management publications, executive profiles, case studies, and readings are all designed to introduce students to influential literature of the field, reinforce text materials, and highlight contemporary management topics. Many students will find such features as chapter summaries, notes and sources, review questions, cases, problems, and reading particularly helpful in evaluating what they have learned and in applying their knowledge.

Accompanying the text is an instructor's manual prepared by Timothy M. Singleton and Louis P. White. The manual provides additional information, outlines, lecture and case discussions, and answers to discussion questions. A student study guide prepared by Larry Wall and Douglas Naffziger is designed as a self-study vehicle to enhance student retention and understanding of the material. A test bank prepared by Shelby Morton includes objective and essay examination questions. It can be obtained in print form and on diskette for the IBM–PC, Apple II, and TRS–80.

The division of labor in writing this book was as follows: John B. Miner wrote Parts One through Five and Part Seven in their entirety; he also selected the readings and prepared the executive profiles. Timothy Singleton prepared the case section at the end of the book (Part Eight). Vincent P. Luchsinger wrote Chapters 16 and 17 in Part Six.

Developing this book to its present form has been a lengthy process. Ideas have been continually tried out, tested against the opinions of teachers in the field, and then either accepted, refined, or rejected. The final product reflects the views and contributions of over 100 teachers of management. It is not possible to acknowledge all who have exerted an influence in this manner. We wish to thank those who reviewed the manuscript extensively and provided valuable suggestions: Allen C. Bluedorn of the University of Missouri at Columbia, Earl Brooks of Cornell University, Marvin Karlins of the University of South Florida at Tampa, Steven E. Markham of Virginia Polytechnic Institute, Wilban Terpening of the University of Notre Dame, and Lyman Porter of the University of California at Irvine.

In addition, thanks are due to Barbara Miner, to whom this book is dedicated, Martha Giardina for secretarial and research help, and a host of people at Charles E. Merrill Publishing Company, including Gary Bauer and Steve Smith.

Contents

PART ONE
THE MEANING OF MANAGEMENT

Chapter 1
What Is Management?   2

The Management Process Framework   4

    The Concept of Management Functions □
Research on Management Functions □ Definitions
of the Management Functions □ Alternative Interpretations □ Managerial and Nonmanagerial
Work □ Strengths and Weaknesses of the Management Process Framework

The Subdisciplines within Management
Framework   10

    Definitions of the Subdisciplines □ Additional
Considerations □ Strengths and Weaknesses of the
Subdisciplines Framework

The Structure of This Book   16

    The Major Parts □ Other Management Func-
tions □ Other Components of the Management
Subdisciplines Framework □ Readings, Profiles,
and Cases

Chapter 2
Why Is the Study of Management
Useful?   24

Jack L.: Satisfactions and Frustrations of a
Management Career   26

Managerial Careers   28

    Aspects of Management Potential □ Supply and
Demand Considerations

Careers in the Functional Areas of Organizations   37

    Personnel and Human Resources Careers □
Careers in Production/Operations

Professional Careers in Management   44

    Management Consulting □ Faculty Careers □
Research and Development

Chapter 3
The Origins of Management
Knowledge   54

The Five Conceptual Building Blocks   57

The "Schools" Approach □ Taylor and Scientific Management □ Fayol and Classical Management □ Weber and Bureaucracy □ Mayo, Roethlisberger, and Human Relations □ Barnard, Simon, and Decision Making □ The Test of Time

Origins of the Functional Subdisciplines   72

The Diverse Heritage of Personnel Management □ Origins of Production/Operations Management

Scientific Origins   76

Nonscientific Ways of Knowing □ The Nature of Science □ Management and Science

Readings and Profiles   85

Today's Young Managers: They Can Do It, but Will They?   86
Ranking Corporate Reputations   94
John A. Young and Hewlett-Packard Company   104

PART TWO
INFLUENCING AND ORGANIZATIONAL BEHAVIOR

Chapter 4
Performance in Organizations   110

What Is Performance?   112

Organizational Goals □ Dimensions of Performance

Individual Influences on Performance   116

Intelligence and Learning □ Motivation and Values □ Feelings, Stress, and Satisfaction □ Physical Factors

Environmental Influences on Performance   124

The Open Systems View □ The Internal Organizational Environment □ The External Environment

Controlling Performance   130

The Open-Loop Control Model □ The Timing of Control

Chapter 5
Motivation in Organizations   140

Ways of Thinking about Motivation   142

Views Regarding Human Needs □ Views Regarding Equity □ Expectancy Views □ Behavior Modification and Operant Learning

Goal Setting and Job Design Applications   154

Locke's Concept of Goal Setting □ Management by Objectives (MBO) □ Work Redesign and Job Characteristics Theory □ Work Redesign and Motivation-Hygiene Theory

Attachment, Commitment, and the Role of Values   160

Attachment and Behavioral Commitment □ Attitudinal Commitment □ The Role of Values

Chapter 6
Groups, Leadership, and Supervision   172

Jim Thomas: Lessons for Management Practice from the Football Field   174
Views of Groups in Group-Based Systems   175

What Is a Group? □ Suppose We Took Groups Seriously □ Likert's Ideas Regarding Groups □ Sociotechnical Theory and Autonomous Work Groups

Aspects of Group Functioning   183

Formal and Informal Groups □ Group Cohesiveness □ International Comparisons

Leadership and Supervision   187

Theory X and Theory Y □ Contingency Views of Leadership □ Consideration and Initiating Structure □ Path-Goal Views of Leadership □ Decision Tree Concepts of Participation □ Vertical Dyad Linkages

Readings and Profiles   204

Small Group Activity at Musashi Semiconductor
     Works   205
How to Build Employee Trust and Productivity   216
Lee L. Morgan and Caterpillar Tractor
     Company   221

**PART THREE
ORGANIZING AND ORGANIZATIONAL
PROCESS AND STRUCTURE**

**Chapter 7
Using Power and Communicating in
Organizations   226**

Power and Authority   228

     Formal Versus Acceptance Views of Authority □
     Bases of Power and Authority □ Strategic Contin-
     gencies and Power

Bargaining and Organizational Politics   232

     Factors in Bargaining □ Organizational Politics

Organizational Communication   240

     Communication and Organizing □ Informal Sys-
     tems and the Grapevine □ Management Informa-
     tion Systems □ Individual Communication Skills

**Chapter 8
Coordinating and Controlling
Organizational Components   254**

Conflict and Coordination   256

     Nature and Sources of Conflict □ Achieving Coor-
     dination □ Guidelines for Coordinating

Organizational Control   265

     Aspects of Control Systems □ Conducting
     Audits □ Major Types of Accounting Control
     Systems □ Human Asset Accounting □ Effective-
     ness of Organizational Control

**Chapter 9
Designs for Organizations   278**

Open Systems Formulations   280

     Katz and Kahn's Social Psychological Approach
     □ Sociotechnical Systems Theory □
     Thompson's Sociological Approach

Contingency Views of Organization   290

     The Technological Imperative □ Differentiation
     and Integration under Uncertainty □ Growth
     Strategy and Structure

Bureaucratic Theory and Professional Systems   301

     Evidence on the Value of Bureaucratic Struc-
     tures □ The Nature of Professional Systems

**Chapter 10
Organizational Change and
Development   312**

Bureaucracy and Change   314

     Direct Hierarchic Change □ Consultant-Initiated
     Change □ The Role of Change Units □
     Resistance to Change

Organization Development   320

     Definitions and Values □ Origins in Sensitivity
     Training and T-Groups □ Sociotechnical Systems
     Design □ The Contingency Approach to Organiza-
     tion Development □ The Survey Feedback Ap-
     proach □ Quality Circles

Growth and Decline   333

     Reasons for Growth □ Stages of Growth □
     Problems of Decline

Readings and Executive Profiles   345

Looking Back at Topeka: General Foods and the
     Quality-of-Work-Life Experiment   346
Conversation with Charles L. Brown   358
Ruben F. Mettler and TRW Inc.   364

PART FOUR
PLANNING AND MANAGEMENT
POLICY/STRATEGY

Chapter 11
Planning and Formulating
Policy/Strategy   370

Strategic Management   372

Terms and Definitions □ Types of Policies and
Strategies □ The Atlantic Refining Co. (ARCO):
Strategy in Action

Strategic Planning   379

The Planning Process □ The Organization of Planning □ Contributions and Problems

Identifying and Evaluating Policies and
Strategies   389

Specific Approaches □ Forecasting

Chapter 12
Organizational Decision Making   402

How Decisions Are Made   404

The Importance of Decision Making □ Bounded
and Full Rationality □ Incremental Decision
Making □ Variations With Decision Circumstances □ Decision Making in the Boardroom □ The Top Level Decision Hierarchy

Individual Decision Making   414

Entrepreneurial Decision Making □ Factors
Influencing Individual Decisions □ Creative
Decisions

Group Decision Making   421

Creativity in Groups □ Special Problems with
Group Decisions □ Diversity and Size Considerations

Chapter 13
Social Responsibility and Ethics   434

Whistle-Blowing at the Bay Area Rapid Transit
System (BART)   436
Concepts of Social Responsibility   438

Conflicting Views of Social Responsibility □
Humanism and Quality of Work Life □ Ethics,
Morality, and the Law □

Corporate Responses to Social Expectations   449

Types of Response □ Policies and Their Implementation □ Social Auditing

Representing and Public Relations   457

The Scope of Activities □ Influencing the Corporate Image

Readings and Executive Profiles   468

Conversation with Reginald H. Jones and Frank
    Doyle   470
Top Management's Role in Strategic Planning   475
The Impact of Consumer Trends on Corporate
    Strategy   480
James E. Burke and Johnson & Johnson
    Company   488

PART FIVE
STAFFING AND PERSONNEL/HUMAN
STAFFING RESOURCES MANAGEMENT

Chapter 14
Organizations   496

Major Constraints: Resource Availability, Laws, and
Labor Unions   498

Availability of Needed Human Resources
□ Personnel/Human Resources Laws
□ Labor Union Activities

Job Analysis and Human Resource Planning 506

The Role and Nature of Job Analysis □ Approaches in Human Resource Planning

Recruiting and Selection 511

The Logic of Selection □ Recruiting □ Selection Methods

Training and Development 519

The Logic of Training and Development □ Training and Development Methods

Chapter 15
Maintaining an Effective Work Force 530

Performance Appraisal 532

Management Appraisal □ Problems in Evaluation Systems

Compensation 539

Wage and Salary Administration □ Incentive Systems □ Executive Compensation □ Employee Benefits

Personnel Communications 547

The Choice of Media □ Company Publications □ Employee Attitude Measurement □ Suggestion Programs

Health, Safety, and Performance Control 555

Preventive Medicine □ Safety Management □ Reassignment, Discipline, and Counseling

Readings and Profiles 568

Managing Turnover Strategically 569
A Radical Experiment Cuts Deep Into the
   Attractiveness of Unions 576
David C. Garrett and Delta Airlines Inc. 579

PART SIX
MANAGEMENT PROCESS AND PRODUCTION-OPERATIONS MANAGEMENT

Chapter 16
Production-Operations Management Systems 584

Production-Operations Management 586

Major Concepts of Production-Operations Management □ Systems Approach to Operations Management □ Importance of the Operations Approach □ Operations and Outputs □ Operations Systems

Managing Operations 591

A Strategic Emphasis □ Jobs in Operations □ Operations and the Environment □ Operations and Other Functions □ Managing Operations Functions

Operations Management and Technology 598

Definition and Concepts □ Technology and the Manager □ Technology and Society □ Managing Technology □ Technology Available for Choices □ Managing Technological Change

Productivity 604

The Nature of Productivity □ Trends in Productivity □ Factors Influencing Productivity □ Managing Productivity in Operations □ Operations Management and the Future

Chapter 17
Designing, Planning, and Controlling Operating Systems 614

Design of Operating Systems 616

Strategic Aspects of Design □ Decisions in Design of Operating Systems

Planning and Control of Operations 624

Aggregate Planning □ Resource Allocation □ Activity Scheduling

Inventory Planning and Control 628

Inventory Economics □ Inventory Planning □ Economic Order □ Inventory Systems

Quality Control 632

Planning for Quality Control □ Types of Quality Control □ Quality Control Circles

Readings and Profiles 642

The New Industrial Competition 643
The Rescue and Resuscitation of Chrysler 658
Thornton A. Wilson and the Boeing Company 662

PART SEVEN
THE EXPANDING ARENA

Chapter 18
Management in International Perspective 668

Dow Chemical Company's International Development Process 670
National and Cultural Variations 671

Educational Characteristics □ Sociological Characteristics □ Political and Legal Characteristics □ Economic Characteristics

Multinational Corporations 675

Organizing Multinational Operations □ Independence of Decision Making □ Strategies for Dealing with National Contexts

The Japanese 680

Evidence of Success □ Alternative Interpretations □ Research Studies of the Japanese □ The Transferability Question

Readings and Profiles 694

The Corporate Culture Vultures 695
HP-Grenoble: Case Study in Technology Transfer 702
John F. Bookout and Shell Oil Company 711

PART EIGHT
CASES

Case 1
Jack Powers' Morning C2
Ron Thorn

Case 2
Choosing a Computing Center Supervisor: Six Candidates C4
John B. Miner

Case 3
Predicting the Future C9
Richard M. Hodgetts

Case 4
ABC Mud Engineering Company C12
Louis P. White and Dorothy N. Harlow

Case 5
Professor Zanuli Goes to Germany C17
Roland B. Cousins

Case 6
Bendix Corporation "As the Boardroom Turns" C20
Timothy M. Singleton

Case 7
Rodman Motors C27
George Eddy and Kenneth Olm

Case 8
Wade Jones Company of Illinois C35
William E. Wright

Case 9
Who's on First?   C41
George Eddy

Case 10
AT&T's Entrepreneur   C48
Monica Langley

Case 11
Texas Air Corporation: Peanuts and
Profits   C52
*Timothy M. Singleton and Robert
McGlashan*

Case 12
The Love Canal Incident   C61
*Timothy M. Singleton and Robert
McGlashan*

Case 13
A Thermos of "Tea" at KWC   C68
*William V. Rice, Jr., Robert McGlashan,
and Gerard V. Hayden*

Case 14
Survey at Venture Manufacturing   C72
James L. Harbin

Case 15
Internal Theft at Kline's   C77
Stephen L. Payne

Case 16
The Road to Hell . . .   C81
Gareth Evans

Case 17
Production Control at Carbide Products,
Inc.   C86
Taylor Cox, Jr.

Case 18
Tower Motor and Machine Company   C94
Roy H. Williams and Thomas R. Miller

Case 19
John Lockley   C99
Ruel Kahler

Case 20
Which Company Is Truly Multinational?
C102
Warren J. Keegan

Author Index   I1

Subject Index   I5

The Practice of Management

The Meaning of Management

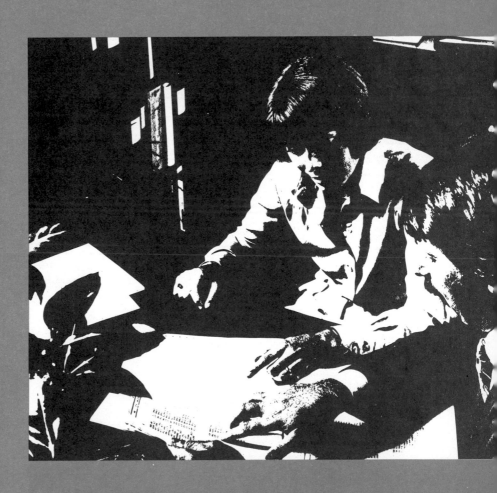

Students starting out in a new course of study often have a number of questions about what they are getting into. What kind of subject matter will be covered? Is this material likely to be interesting? How difficult to understand is this type of subject matter? What is the potential return on the investment in learning about the field—in terms of both personal development and subsequent career achievement? How does this field relate to other areas and courses? What are the sources of the material covered, and how much can one really rely on what is learned?

In these first three chapters we will consider answers to these types of questions. To a large extent these answers depend on the characteristics of individual students—their interests, abilities, prior learning, career aspirations, and the like. But whether learning about management is interesting or dull, difficult or easy, useful or a waste of time depends on a set of relationships between aspects of the subject matter itself and the individual student. The goal here, at the beginning, is to provide the kinds of information needed for students to answer their own questions.

Chapter 1 deals with the various dimensions of the management field. This is an unusually wide-ranging discipline, and it is important to view it in its entirety. Chapter 2 is concerned with how a knowledge of management subject matter applies to jobs and careers, opportunities, and practical usefulness to the student. Just as management knowledge is wide-ranging in its coverage, the kinds of jobs and careers that require this type of knowledge are diverse as well. Chapter 3 considers the origins of the management field from three interrelated perspectives. The initial focus is on the historical origins of the management and organization field, a second concern is with the origins of personnel and production management, and the third is with the degree to which management knowledge has its origins in the research methods of the social sciences.

CHAPTER 1

What Is Management?

CHAPTER OUTLINE

The Management Process Framework
The Concept of Management Functions
Research on Management Functions
Definitions of the Management Functions
    Planning
    Organizing
    Staffing
    Influencing
    Controlling
    Coordinating
    Representing
    Decision Making
    Communicating
    Bargaining
Alternative Interpretations
Managerial and Nonmanagerial Work
Strengths and Weaknesses of the Management
    Process Framework

**The Subdisciplines Within Management
Framework**
Definitions of the Subdisciplines
    Organizational Behavior
    Organizational Process and Structure
    Management Policy and Strategy
    Personnel/Human Resources Management
    Production/Operations Management
Additional Considerations
    Management Courses
    Professional Associations
Strengths and Weaknesses of the Subdisciplines
    Framework

The Structure of This Book
The Major Parts
    Influencing and Organizational Behavior
    Organizing and Organizational Process and
        Structure
    Planning and Management Policy and Strategy
    Staffing and Personnel/Human Resources
        Management
    Management Process and Production/
        Operations Management
Other Management Functions
Other Components of the Management
    Subdisciplines Framework
Readings, Profiles, and Cases

OBJECTIVES

To describe and evaluate the management process approach to structuring the management field.

To describe and evaluate the subdisciplines approach to structuring the management field.

To present the combined approach to structuring the management field used in this book.

W e live increasingly in a world of organizations, where people combine their efforts to achieve goals that no individual could possibly achieve alone. These organizations come in a variety of sizes and types—schools, companies, governments, hospitals, and so on—and they serve a wide range of functions. They are important for all of us because we must deal with them continually, because we typically earn our livelihoods as organization members, and because organizations are the units out of which society is constructed.

The field of management deals with these organizations—how people behave in them, how they are designed, and how they function. Management is concerned with people in organizations primarily and thus with *human resources,* as opposed to the concern with monetary resources in fields like finance and accounting or with material resources (products), as in purchasing and marketing. As we will see, there is something more to management than its focus on human resources. Historically, management has extended into the areas of production and manufacturing as well, and thus has become concerned with material resources in organizations. But the predominant thrust remains the study of people and their actions.

A distinction must be made between the field of management and *managing.* The things people do in the process of managing in an organization certainly constitute a large part of what the management field is all about. Those who perform management functions are among the most important human resources that organizations have. However, strange as it may seem, management as a discipline—a field of study, a body of knowledge—is not restricted to the study of managing. To fully understand this point, to understand what the management field is and is not, it is necessary to take a closer look at the way it is structured. Two different frameworks or models predominate: the management process approach and an approach based on the subdisciplines within management. Both have held a strong position in the field for a number of years.

THE MANAGEMENT PROCESS FRAMEWORK

The question of what managers do has been the subject of a great deal of speculation and research over the years. If we are to develop a useful body of knowledge about managerial jobs it is important to start with some conception of what the process of managing is. The management process framework has emerged out of thinking and research in this area. It divides managing into a number of functions. In this view, management as a field and the process of managing *are* defined as being the same thing. As we will see, this may have been true once, but it is true no longer.

The Concept of Management Functions

Exhibit 1.1 presents the views of three widely respected early theorists: Fayol, Davis, and Barnard.[1] Fayol and Barnard wrote from their experiences as chief executives of corporations, the former with a major mining firm in France and

EXHIBIT 1.1 The elements of management as set forth by early theorists

Henri Fayol (1916)	Ralph C. Davis (1934)	Chester Barnard (1937)
Planning	Planning	Providing a system of communication
Organizing	Organizing	Securing essential efforts
Command	Controlling	Formulating and defining purpose
Coordination		
Control		

NOTE: The dates noted are those of first statement.

the latter with New Jersey Bell Telephone Company in the United States. Davis, although a professor at Ohio State University throughout much of his career, developed his ideas from his considerable experience in industry. Although these views share similarities, the functions of management noted are not the same.

In Exhibit 1.2, recent thinking in this area is presented in the form of lists of functions used to organize management textbooks. These texts have been published in a number of successive editions, and their major authors have all been influential in the field for many years.[2]

The extent of agreement remains well short of perfect, although all include certain functions: planning, organizing, and controlling. These writers are university professors who draw their conclusions primarily from theory and research in the field, rather than from personal executive experience. All of these lists have changed somewhat from one edition of the book to another. Thus, not only is there disagreement between different authors, but over time the same authors often have not agreed with themselves. Nevertheless, practicing managers have tended to use concepts such as these for many years in discussing their work, and major consulting firms, such as McKinsey and Company, have long used them in designing managerial jobs.

EXHIBIT 1.2 The elements or functions of management as set forth by recent writers

Harold Koontz, Cyril O'Donnell, and Heinz Weihrich (1980)	William Newman, Kirby Warren, and Jerome Schnee (1982)	Dalton McFarland (1979)	Theo Haimann, William Scott, and Patrick Connor (1982)
Planning	Planning	Planning	Planning
Organizing	Organizing	Organizing	Organizing
Staffing	Motivating	Staffing	Staffing
Leading	Leading	Leadership and supervision	Influencing
Controlling	Controlling	Control	Controlling
		Coordinating	
		Decision making	

A number of studies have been conducted in a variety of settings to identify what the management functions really are. Rarely has a study considered all of the functions noted in Exhibits 1.1 and 1.2, and most of the research has been conducted in a single organization or in several organizations very similar in nature. Yet it is possible to construct a coherent whole out of this patchwork.[3] Managing in one organization may not be the same as managing in another; and, as noted in Exhibit 1.3, management jobs at different levels may differ considerably. Yet certain activities do appear to absorb a disproportionately large amount of the time of those holding management positions in organizations having a number of levels from top to bottom (hierarchy).

Planning, staffing, influencing, controlling, and coordinating are functions in which managers spend much of their time. The function of organizing tends to occupy the time of only a small group of managers at the top, and then only infrequently. In addition, representing the organization outward to its publics emerges as important, even though the lists in Exhibits 1.1 and 1.2 do not contain this function.

To these seven functions it is necessary to add three more that can be equally important but operate in a different manner, cutting across the others and in fact becoming an aspect of each of them. In this respect these three serve as linking functions. They are decision making, communicating, and bargaining (or negotiating).

EXHIBIT 1.3 Proportion of managers at various levels best described as planners, generalists and supervisors

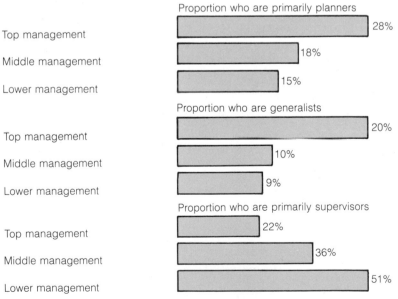

Proportion who are primarily planners

Top management — 28%
Middle management — 18%
Lower management — 15%

Proportion who are generalists

Top management — 20%
Middle management — 10%
Lower management — 9%

Proportion who are primarily supervisors

Top management — 22%
Middle management — 36%
Lower management — 51%

Adapted from Thomas A. Mahoney, Thomas H. Jerdee, and Stephen J. Carroll, "The Job(s) of Management," *Industrial Relations* (February 1965):109.

These ten types of activities are double the number proposed by Fayol. Few authors have suggested a list nearly as long. However, the research evidence indicates that managerial work is much more diversified than was originally believed. To understand the management process framework, and thus the way managers talk about their jobs as well as much of the discussion in this book, it is necessary to understand these ten functions.

Definitions of the Management Functions

Planning   Although planning can occur in any management position, its major manifestation is at the top—in the formal strategic planning that extends out into the organization's environment. Plans often are based on forecasts of future events. They typically result in policies and procedures (*role prescriptions*) which guide the behavior of those who implement the plans.

Organizing   Organizing involves designing both the structural flow of authority and the prescribed patterns of communication in organizations. It is a form of planning and thus a method of establishing role prescriptions for organization members, but unlike planning it extends inward into organizational operations only.

Staffing   Staffing as a management function actually deals with filling management positions—recruiting, hiring, and the like. In the literature, staffing sometimes has been extended to include management development, executive compensation, management appraisal, and even some other personnel activities at the managerial level.

Influencing   Influencing is an activity with many names. We have chosen the word influencing rather than directing, supervising, or leading because it is more comprehensive. In hierarchical systems this means the use of any method to get subordinates to do what they are supposed to do in terms of the role prescriptions for their jobs. Although influencing can refer to restoring effective performance among those who have failed to achieve it or to maintaining existing performance levels, influencing chiefly involves helping subordinates achieve their highest level of performance.

Controlling   In the research on managerial jobs, controlling often is broken down into investigating and evaluating, each of which has been established as an important aspect of managerial work. Controlling attempts to identify, determine the causes of, and correct deviations from acceptable standards of performance that have been established by role-making activities such as planning and organizing.

Coordinating   Coordinating is concerned with adjusting the relationships between individuals and groups in an organization so that frictions do not develop among them which might sap the potential effectiveness of the organization as a whole. Managers are coordinating when they attempt to prevent misunderstandings, conflict, and controversy from disrupting needed interdependence between units; adjusting manufacturing department production to marketing department estimates of demand would be an example.

Representing   Representing focuses on efforts to influence external forces—such as laws, societal values and ethics, resources, and customer or client attitudes—with a view to creating a favorable climate for the organization to operate in. Although representing has rarely been treated as a separate function, the research literature supports its inclusion as a management function. Also, it makes sense to include representing (involving public relations), which deals with external relations, if one is to include staffing (involving employee relations), which deals with internal relations.

Decision making   Decision making is the first of the three types of activities that we have designated linking functions. In one sense they are not separate functions, but rather aspects of the others. Decision making is often considered in relation to planning, but it certainly can be involved in any of the other types of activities as well. In fact, some theories view decision making as *the* central process in organizational functioning. Clearly it is a very significant one.

Communicating   Like decision making, both oral and written communication are involved in all of the other functions. Communication is a necessary precondition for reaching decisions and must follow decisions if they are to be implemented. In the management literature communicating is often associated closely with influencing, and downward communication to subordinate levels is emphasized. However, communication can flow in any direction within an organization or across its boundaries, as in representing.

Bargaining   Of the three linking functions, bargaining or negotiating has received the least attention in the management literature. Bargaining is closely associated with the distribution of power in organizations. Only recently has its importance been fully recognized, largely because for many years bargaining was assumed to be inconsistent with the workings of authority systems in hierarchical organizations. However, planning and organizing, and even influencing and controlling, often occur against a background of substantial bargaining among interested parties.

Alternative Interpretations

The concept of managerial work that emerges from the research is far more varied than what Fayol or Davis or Barnard envisioned (see Exhibit 1.1). Yet the ten functions do build in a general way upon what these early theorists proposed. Other views have been set forth as alternatives, based on the supposition that the idea of management functions is inadequate for understanding what managers do. An example of such an alternative approach is given in Exhibit 1.4.

In the *managerial work roles* approach of Exhibit 1.4, different roles are important in different managerial jobs, paralleling the findings for management functions.[4] For example, the liaison role is unique to top management, and the monitor role is strong in accounting management. There are also major differences related to the particular organization and the problems it faces. Studies to date have had some difficulty in establishing the figurehead, disseminator, disturbance handler, and negotiator roles as clearly distinct from the others.[5]

The managerial work roles approach actually may be less different from the management process approach, or at least that version of it supported by the research, than was originally believed. The importance that both assign to communicating and decision making is certainly not inconsistent between the two,

EXHIBIT 1.4 The managerial work roles approach to managing

Informational Roles	Decisional Roles
Figurehead—symbolic head; performs routine duties of a legal or social nature	*Leader*—responsible for motivation of subordinates and for staffing and training them
Liaison—maintains network of outside contacts to obtain favors and information	*Monitor*—seeks and receives information to obtain thorough understanding of organization and environment
Disseminator—transmits information received from other organization members	*Entrepreneur*—initiates and supervises design of organizational improvement projects as opportunities arise
Spokesman—transmits information to outsiders on organization plans, policies, and actions	*Disturbance handler*—responsible for corrective action when organization faces unexpected crises
	Resource allocator—responsible for allocation of human, monetary, and material resources
	Negotiator—responsible for representing the organization in bargaining and negotiations

Adapted from Henry Mintzberg, *The Nature of Managerial Work* (New York: Harper & Row, 1973); Zur Shapiro and Roger L. M. Dunbar, "Testing Mintzberg's Managerial Roles Classification Using an In-basket Simulation," *Journal of Applied Psychology* (February 1980):93.

and a number of the roles have much in common with certain functions. Yet there are differences as well. Clearly, the management process approach is not the only way of looking at managerial jobs.

Managerial and Nonmanagerial Work

Management positions may involve a sizable amount of nonmanagerial work. Fayol recognized this point, and his early statements on the subject have some validity today.[6] Exhibit 1.5 sets forth Fayol's views regarding the ability requirements of various positions in a manufacturing hierarchy, based on his experience over many years with a French mining company. At the lower levels the various nonmanagerial abilities, especially those of a technical nature, are primary; a larger proportion of the work requires abilities other than those of a managerial nature. As one moves up the chain, technical considerations decline and managerial requirements increase substantially. Certainly there is no firm basis for accepting the particular percentage values Fayol specified, but the trends involved are worthy of note. Success in management, even at relatively high levels, involves more than merely being able to perform the managerial functions or working roles well.

Strengths and Weaknesses of the Management Process Framework

The things that managers do are important in the overall picture of the management field; at the present time the field contains more information in this area than in any of the others. The major advantage of the management process framework is that it effectively integrates this information on managerial tasks, and up

EXHIBIT 1.5 Hypothesized ability requirements at various hierarchical levels

	Abilities Required					
	Managerial	**Technical**	**Commercial**	**Financial**	**Security**	**Accounting**
General manager	50%	10%	10%	10%	10%	10%
Plant manager	40%	15%	15%	10%	10%	10%
Superintendent	25%	45%	5%	0	10%	15%
Foreman	15%	60%	5%	0	10%	10%
Production worker	5%	85%	0	0	5%	5%

Adapted from Henri Fayol, *General and Industrial Management* (London: Pitman, 1949), p. 8.

until recently it has served well as the approach to structuring introductory textbooks.

Yet there are problems also. Disagreement and uncertainty persist as to what the management functions are. There are alternative ways of analyzing managerial jobs, and in any event managers often do many of the same things that nonmanagers do. Questions have been raised for some time as to whether the management process approach is the best type of looking glass through which to view managerial work. If it is not, then using it to view the whole field of management only compounds the error.

Increasingly the management field has come to include subject matter that does not fit well in the management process framework. For example, some organizations or parts of organizations are not managed traditionally (such as groups of professionals, voluntary associations, commissioned sales forces and manufacturers' representatives, and autonomous work groups). These types of organizational systems are being studied extensively now, and knowledge about them is being added to the management field. Knowledge also is accumulating in two areas that are usually considered part of the management field but are in fact specialized areas of organizational functioning: personnel/human resources management and production/operations management. Information about these areas is not just of interest to managers; it is equally relevant for specialists below the managerial level.

In short, a framework which at one time did come close to encompassing the management field has now become somewhat outmoded, even though it is still widely used and thus important to understand. As we will see in chapter 3, the classical theory that contributed this framework has also lost a good deal of its usefulness. The management process framework alone is not sufficient to comprehend the whole of the field of management.

THE SUBDISCIPLINES WITHIN MANAGEMENT FRAMEWORK

The second framework for structuring the management field has rarely been used to organize introductory textbooks, but it is used in establishing courses and major areas of concentration and in structuring professional associations of professors and practitioners. This framework divides the discipline into a number of subdisciplines or areas of specialization. Those who teach or do research, and to some extent practitioners as well, concentrate their efforts within one, or occasionally several, of these subdisciplines.

At the present time management is separated into five major subdisciplines, plus several others that cut across or enter into the basic five, such as management history or research methods. There may not be total agreement on the status of these five subdisciplines, but a consensus has emerged in recent years. The most common departure would be in breaking the field down into more parts. It is important to note that the first three subdisciplines mirror the management hierarchy, focusing on lower, middle, and top management activities.

Definitions of the Subdisciplines

Organizational Behavior   The area of organizational behavior is concerned with characteristics and behaviors of organization members and with relationships among the individuals in a work group. In actual practice the greatest concerns have been with the relationship between motivation and performance of individuals and with leadership and supervision at the group level, although such topics as perception, learning, abilities, and group dynamics also are important. This area is grounded in individual and social psychology. Frequently noted topics are human behavior, human relations, interpersonal dynamics, group processes, and leadership.

Organizational Process and Structure   The area of organizational process and structure covers relationships extending beyond the bounds of the single work group, including: coordination among groups, designing or structuring the organization as a whole, developing and operating organizational control processes, introducing various kinds of interventions aimed at organization development, and other types of processes that include more than one work group. Considerable attention has been devoted to both the technologies the organization uses and aspects of the external environment surrounding the organization as they relate to structures and processes. Organizational process and structure is often described as dealing with the macro level of organization, in contrast with the micro level that is of concern for organizational behavior. Historically, this has been an area to which sociologists have made substantial contributions. Frequently noted topics are organization development, organization theory, organizational design, and organizational change.

Management Policy and Strategy   The policy and strategy area deals with top level processes, especially the activities of the chief executive officer. Concerns include strategic management and strategic planning, as distinct from operating management, which characterizes lower organizational levels. The emphasis on strategy vis-à-vis competitors, government regulations, and the like leads to a major focus on societal and other environmental factors that can or do influence what happens to the organization; hence the inclusion of topics such as social responsibilities, ethics, and the organizational environment. Because strategy formulation is in essence decision making, organizational decision processes often become part of this area as well. Entrepreneurship, which deals with the founding of small firms and the course of their development, is important in providing a perspective on the emergence of strategic management and the patterns of growth in policy formation. Initially this area was concerned only with business firms and was influenced strongly by the field of economics. However, management policy and strategy now encompasses the processes of other types of organizations, particularly governmental, and has moved beyond strictly economic concepts. Frequently noted topics are social issues, entrepreneurship, business and society, policy formation, decision making, planning, and relations between business and government.

Personnel/Human Resources Management   The personnel management function covers a wide range of activities concerning an organization's human resources—bringing employees into the organization, retaining them, influencing their performance and morale, and dealing with their departure. All of these activities are subject to constraints introduced by relevant laws and by agreements with labor unions. Personnel and human resources subject matter deals with the major organizational function devoted to human beings, as employees of organizations. Personnel management is a composite of influences from a wide range of disciplines and professions, yet it is also a field of specialization and practice in its own right. Frequently noted topics are management education and development, career development, labor relations, selection, compensation, staffing, collective bargaining, and equal employment opportunity.

Production/Operations Management   Like personnel management, production/operations management is a specific function of certain organizational units. It is concerned with the conversion or transformation of primarily material inputs into products and services by accumulating the resources needed, designing and installing conversion or manufacturing processes, and operating these processes to produce goods and services. There are close ties to engineering, particularly industrial engineering. Also, the area has come to rely increasingly on quantitative mathematical techniques. Production/operations management has long-standing ties to the management discipline and its courses usually are housed in the management department, but it may be located in other parts of a business college. Frequently noted topics are methods and standards, factory design, operations planning and control, management systems, research and development management, project management, and quantitative techniques in production.

Additional Considerations

As noted previously, other subareas are included in the subdisciplines within management framework that enter into or overlap the basic five. Thus, as we will see in chapter 3, all five subdisciplines have historical origins, although they are not the same. All five also have a body of knowledge regarding appropriate research techniques, and they have extended beyond one country to develop a comparative, international knowledge base. Some information has also accumulated in each of the subdiscipline areas regarding the process of consulting with client organizations. These common threads running through the subdisciplines—history, research, international, and consulting—may be treated as separate areas of study in their own right; when one hears of management history, management research, international management, and managerial consultation, this is what is meant.

The management field sometimes is explicitly expanded beyond the business domain to include other types of organizations. Thus, the subdisciplines framework can incorporate health care administration, public administration, and perhaps other areas. In such cases, subject matter from organizational behavior, organizational process and structure, management policy and strategy, and personnel management is focused on a particular type of organization. Production/operations management could contribute in the same manner, but in practice it rarely does, being primarily restricted to business organizations.

Management Courses We have noted that the subdisciplines within management structure have been widely used in splitting up the subject matter of the field so that it may be taught in individual courses. Exhibit 1.6 lists a number

EXHIBIT 1.6 Typical courses in the management field in relation to the subdisciplines within management framework

Course Titles	Subdisciplines within Management				
	Organizational Behavior	Organizational Process and Structure	Management Policy and Strategy	Personnel Management	Production/ Operations Management
Human behavior in organizations	X				
Introduction to organizational behavior	X				
Interpersonal dynamics	X				
Group processes in organizations	X				
Theories of leadership	X				
Human relations	X				
Organization development		X			
Organization theory and practice		X			
Organizational design and environment		X			
Organizational change and development		X			
Theory of organization		X			
Introduction to organizational communication		X			
Administrative policy			X		
Entrepreneurship			X		
Business and society			X		
Policy and planning			X		
Strategic management			X		
Business policy			X		
Social issues in management			X		
Problems of personnel administration				X	
Personnel selection				X	
Compensation administration				X	
Personnel research				X	
Staffing				X	
Labor legislation				X	

(continued)

EXHIBIT 1.6 (continued)

Course Titles	Subdisciplines within Management				
	Organizational Behavior	Organizational Process and Structure	Management Policy and Strategy	Personnel Management	Production/ Operations Management
Collective bargaining				X	
Management training in industry				X	
Human resources				X	
Operations planning and control					X
Factory design					X
Methods and standards					X
Project management					X
Management in manufacturing					X
Quantitative techniques in production					X
Design of operating systems					X
History and philosophy of management	X	X	X	X	X
International business operations	X	X	X	X	X
Management research	X	X	X	X	X
Nonprofit organization management	X	X	X	X	

of course titles taken from university catalogs; these listings are under a management department (or perhaps a department with a somewhat different name that deals with the same material). These courses need not be considered either typical or the most desirable, but we have attempted to be comprehensive. The courses arrange themselves rather easily within the five major subdisciplines. Beyond this, there are the courses such as those in history, research methods, and the like that enter into multiple subdisciplines. Courses dealing with management consulting are not listed because very few universities have them at the present time.

Professional Associations Another instance of the use of a subdisciplines framework is in the professional associations of the management field. Exhibit 1.7 has been developed to parallel Exhibit 1.6. It lists the current major groupings within the Academy of Management, an organization made up largely of university professors with an interest in management but also including some individuals from other organizational contexts: consultants, business managers, and others.

Strengths and Weaknesses of the Subdisciplines Framework

The primary advantage of the subdisciplines approach is that it is broad enough to take in practically all of the subject matter of the management field. There seems to be considerable agreement on what the basic parts are, although that has been true only recently and is not entirely true even today. Accordingly, the number and nature of the subdisciplines could change in the future. Nevertheless,

EXHIBIT 1.7 Structure of the Academy of Management (divisions and interest groups) in relation to the subdisciplines within management framework

Academy of Management Divisions and Groups	Subdisciples within Management				
	Organizational Behavior	Organizational Process and Structure	Management Policy and Strategy	Personnel Management	Production/ Operations Management
Organizational behavior	X				
Organization and management theory		X			
Organizational development		X			
Organizational communication		X			
Business policy and planning			X		
Social issues in management			X		
Entrepreneurship			X		
Management education and development				X	
Personnel/human resources				X	
Women in management				X	
Careers				X	
Production/operations management					X
R and D/technology/innovation					X
Management history	X	X	X	X	X
Managerial consultation	X	X	X	X	X
International management	X	X	X	X	X
Health care administration	X	X	X	X	
Public sector	X	X	X	X	

this structure is capable of handling those parts of the management field that extend beyond managing in hierarchical organizations. It also may be attractive to students because it is essentially the same type of structure found in most other disciplines studied in colleges and universities.

However, the subdisciplines within management approach suffers from one major weakness: to a considerable extent its parts are arbitrary, unrelated groupings created because the management field is too large to deal with as a whole. The parts often are not logically tied together and integrated. The three subdisciplines of organizational behavior, organizational process and structure, and management policy and strategy do move sequentially up the organizational hierarchy, and each encompasses a larger whole; for these subdisciplines there is an internal logic that makes considerable sense. When one shifts to personnel management and production/operations management, however, the basis for grouping becomes instead the department structure or organizational functions carried out by a firm. Furthermore, one of these subdisciplines deals primarily with material rather than human resources and is separated from marketing, with which it would seem to have the closest ties. In short, when looked at this way, the management field appears to lack coherence and internal logic.

Both the management process and subdisciplines frameworks have their strengths and weaknesses. Although they appear on the surface to have little in common, on closer examination certain parallels or correlations emerge. It is possible, therefore, to develop a framework that combines the two and thus draws upon the strengths of both. Such a framework provides the overarching structure for this book.

✗ The Major Parts

Influencing and Organizational Behavior   One of the correlations between the two frameworks is that between the influencing function and the organizational behavior subdiscipline. As indicated in Exhibit 1.3, managers at the lower levels tend to spend a large part of their time functioning as supervisors. Organizational behavior also focuses on the work group level and managerial activities occurring there. Influencing may extend beyond supervising to include whatever is done to get people to contribute to organizational tasks (whether in the role of a manager or not), but it does not cover all of the ground that organizational behavior does. Similarly, influencing may be important higher up in the organization, above the level at which organizational behavior concentrates, although this becomes less and less likely as one goes up the hierarchy. Yet the overlap is such that the two subjects can logically be considered together, as is done in part 2.

Organizing and Organizational Process and Structure   The next point at which the two frameworks come together involves the organizing function and the organizational process and structure subdiscipline. In this case organizing as a management activity falls completely within the bounds of the subdiscipline, but the latter is broader, concerning itself in particular with the processes of communication, coordination, and control (which are not part of designing an organization's structure per se). These processes are closely allied to organizing and exert considerable influence on it. Organizing and organizational process and structure are considered together in part 3.

Planning and Management Policy Strategy   Planning occurs in any part of an organization, but the planning that counts the most and exerts the most influence is done at the top. It is called strategic planning. For many years the practice has been to link planning and policy formulation together. Thus, although management policy and strategy is certainly more than strategic planning, and planning can and does occur other than at the top level, it makes sense to treat the two together; this is done in part 4.

Staffing and Personnel/Human Resources Management   The close ties between staffing and personnel/human resources management already have been noted. Staffing is by no means the whole of this subdiscipline—it does not include labor relations, for instance—but staffing does fall entirely within it and occupies a very important role. Furthermore, much of what we know about personnel management applies equally at the managerial level and below it. Part 5 discusses staffing in the context of the personnel subdiscipline.

Management Process and Production/Operations Management   No one management function aligns itself easily with the production/operations management subdiscipline, as in the other four instances. Rather, several functions

16   Chapter 1

appear to assume major roles, although all of these enter strongly into other subdisciplines as well. One formulation emphasizes the primary roles of planning, organizing, and controlling in the production/operations area.[7] Operations planning and control systems represent a major thrust within the field; so too does the designing (organizing) of systems, plants, facilities, and the like. We have already seen that planning is most closely allied to the policy and strategy area, and organizing to process and structure. Controlling, as we will see, is of significance to all subdisciplines. Furthermore, production/operations management is not totally covered by even these three functions. The many overlaps between the management process and this subdiscipline are considered in part 6.

Other Management Functions

In attempting to relate the management process and subdisciplines frameworks, we have found four major correlations involving influencing, organizing, planning, and staffing. The other management functions do not have such obvious counterparts in the subdisciplines; many of these functions appear roughly equally in all the areas and are treated in several different ways in this book.

Controlling is a significant aspect of production/operations management, and accordingly it is stressed in part 6. Yet it is equally important for other subdisciplines. Some of the basic aspects relating to individual performance are considered in part 2, on influencing and organizational performance, and are elaborated in part 3, on organizing and organizational process and structure. The remaining parts deal with controlling at various points as appropriate to the context.

Communicating is an important factor in individual performance and thus is discussed in part 2, but it is also tied closely to structural factors and is emphasized in this light in part 3. Within management planning and policy and strategy, communicating relates to acquiring information and implementing decisions and strategies. In the context of part 5 it relates to company newspapers, magazines, and the like, and in part 6 to management information systems.

Coordinating comes in primarily in relation to organizing and organizational process and structure in part 3, since it assumes more than one organizational unit. Additional discussions occur at various points in the remaining parts.

Bargaining is most relevant initially within the context of organizing and organizational process and structure, and that is where the major treatment of the subject occurs. Yet bargaining is also important for planning and policy and strategy and thus enters into the discussions of part 4 at various points. In part 5 it becomes of major importance in reference to labor unions (in the form of collective bargaining).

Decision making permeates all areas, exerting a strong influence on individual performances of an intellectual nature (considered in part 2) and on organizational structuring (as discussed in part 3). However, its major treatment is in relation to planning and management policy and strategy, because this is the point at which the most wide-ranging decisions are made. Part 6 gives additional consideration to certain mathematical approaches for rational decision making in the production/operations area.

Similar to the relationship between staffing and personnel/human resources management, *representing* is closely tied to the field of public relations. Public relations, however, has become largely detached from the field of management and even from business administration as a whole; its closest ties are with journalism and communications, wherever these may reside in the university. In this book, representing and public relations are considered primarily within part 4, on planning and management policy and strategy, because it is here that the organization's interface with its environment becomes most important.

Other Components of the Management Subdisciplines Framework

Management history is treated as a whole in chapter 3, because without some historical perspective it is difficult to understand the meaning of management. Management consulting is considered at points throughout the book, but it is not treated at great length, simply because a solid knowledge base is only just beginning to develop in this area; currently very few courses focus on consulting. Careers in the area are discussed in chapter 2.

International management is of considerable importance and is discussed at length. However, the subject matter that is involved when one considers international comparisons in the context of organizational behavior differs sharply from the material in the personnel area, for instance. Given this situation the international area is broken up, and relevant subjects are treated in each part of the book as appropriate. The final chapter of the book uses an international perspective to survey the management field as a whole and accordingly provides the most extensive treatment of international management.

Quantitative research methods largely are beyond the scope of this book. We will be concerned repeatedly with the findings from research, but rarely with the underlying statistical and mathematical methods, experimental designs, and measurement properties. These are advanced subjects, and they require extensive treatment to have much meaning; accordingly, they are best left to the more advanced courses in the field. Chapter 3 does present a discussion of the relationship of scientific method, theory, and research to the management field, and some of the more important quantitative techniques are outlined in part 6.

This book primarily deals with business organizations, and indeed we have much more comprehensive knowledge of such organizations than of other types in all areas of management. Yet other types are important and significant information has accumulated regarding them, particularly governmental organizations. Where relevant, this knowledge is considered throughout the book. In general the focus is also on larger businesses rather than small ones. This is not because small business is unimportant; part 4 takes up the founding of such organizations (entrepreneurship) at some length. The reason for emphasizing larger businesses is that they are more complex and a more varied range of phenomena are to be found there. Certain activities that need to be discussed do not occur in small companies at all, or only at a very simplified level. If one's objective is to consider the management field in all its diversity, the larger corporations provide many more examples.

Readings, Profiles, and Cases

While the major approach to learning used in this book is through the text material, this is not the only approach. Readings are provided at the end of each part, as are profiles of successful top executives. At the end of each chapter are problems based on short cases, and a number of longer cases appear at the end of the book.

Readings have been selected with several objectives in mind. The primary intent is to provide greater depth on subjects not fully covered elsewhere. We also wish to expose readers to the types of articles appearing in the major business and management publications. Many of the articles feature practical applications of topics considered in the text. We have attempted to limit the selections to those that are well-written and readable.

The executive profiles provide information on the careers of chief executives of major corporations and on those corporations themselves. In this way it is possible to see how people and companies come to fit each other. The objective in presenting these profiles is to give a picture of the career paths that successful managers follow, and thus to introduce a greater element of reality for those contemplating a managerial career. Most of the executives have moved over time from the bottom to the very top of the companies they now head, and those companies are acknowledged to be the most successful in their industries.[8]

Cases serve two useful purposes: they provide examples, thus supplementing the text in important ways and contributing to learning, and they provide an opportunity to develop one's problem-solving and decision making skills. The cases that appear at the end of each chapter focus on specific issues considered in the chapter text. They supplement the discussion and review questions by providing an opportunity to apply what has been learned in a real-life context. These cases are short, but they have been developed to cover as wide a range of organizational contexts and situations as possible. The cases at the end of the book serve similar purposes, but the approach is different. Although not long by the standards of the usual policy and strategy case, they are longer than the end-of-chapter cases. Thus it is possible to introduce much richer detail. These cases may well bridge several chapters within the same part of the book, thus providing an opportunity to integrate knowledge from different sources. Yet the focus remains entirely within the field of management and on the material covered in this book. Complex financial analyses and quantitative applications are the material of more advanced courses and thus are not included in the cases used.

Summary

Of the two major approaches to structuring the management field, the management process framework has the longer history. It emerged from the period when the management field was synonymous with managing hierarchical organizations, and it has remained the primary method of structuring introductory textbooks. Research has provided some support for the management process approach as a way of viewing and talking about managerial work, although the number of functions needed to achieve comprehensiveness is greater than previously believed. This approach is not, however, the only one; the managerial work roles view represents a viable alternative. Yet many of the management functions are widely used as management practitioners seek to understand and describe their work.

The second, subdisciplines framework achieved its present form only recently, and it has been employed widely in structuring university curriculums as well as professional associations in the field. Some of its components, such as personnel management and production/operations management, have been reflected directly in company practice for years. Management policy and strategy has only recently taken on this role, as it has become differentiated from operating management. Organizational behavior and organizational process and structure also have counterparts in organizational practice, but they are somewhat fewer in number.

The two frameworks have different strengths. Management process is well integrated, but the subdisciplines approach is not. The subdiscipline concepts provide broad coverage of the field, but the management process does not. Historically, management process has suffered from fluctuations in the definition of its major components; the subdisciplines have not, but this may simply be a function of their recent emergence. Other problems relate to theoretical origins. Both frameworks have firm roots in the practice of management. Given these considerations, a marriage of the two frameworks appears the best solution to characterizing the management field at the present time.

Influencing, organizing, planning, and staffing fall easily within the domains of various subdisciplines. Production/operations management requires a more diverse array of management functions, and many management functions relate to numerous subdisciplines. Topics such as management history, international management, management research, and consulting, as well as the various sector-based topics (such as public and health care administration), may relate to all of the management functions.

Exhibit 1.8 utilizes an input-output systems model, developed primarily for manufacturing organizations, to place the field of management in its practical

---

EXHIBIT 1.8 The position of the field of management in business organizations

Organizational Inputs	Input Processes	Transformation or Mediating Processes	Organizational Outputs
Monetary resources	Financing—stock issues, reinvested profit, borrowing (debt)	Auditing, credit, tax, budget, accounts receivable, cash management, cost accounting, etc.	Profit or loss evaluated by income statements, return on investment, etc.
Material resources	Purchasing Exploration and prospecting Real estate acquisition	Production/operations management processes as appropriate to the particular firm	Sales of products and services evaluated by market share, sales volume, etc.
Human resources	Recruiting Selection	Training, compensation, safety, labor relations, job analysis employee communications, etc.	Job performance evaluated by performance appraisals

All this is managed at one level or another with the following functions being performed:

Influencing	Organizing
Controlling	Planning
Communicating	Decision making
Coordinating	Representing
Bargaining	Staffing

NOTE: Boxed areas represent aspects of the management field.

organizational perspective. The student will recognize other components of the business curriculum outside the boxes which bound the various aspects of the management field, including finance, accounting, and marketing. Nevertheless, it is apparent that management covers a large part of the organizational landscape. Indeed it covers the human resource-related aspects in their entirety, and part of the material resource chain as well. In a very real sense, it is the study of human organizations.

What Have You Learned?

1. Distinguish between the process of managing and the field or overall discipline of management. How does one relate to the other?
2. In what respects are the ten management functions derived from research different from the ten managerial work roles proposed by Mintzberg? In what respects are they the same?
3. How does the mix of managerial and non-managerial work requirements vary with managerial level?
4. Various writers have presented lists of management functions. What are some of these lists? How do the more recent lists compare with those of the early period?
5. What are the advantages and disadvantages of the subdisciplines within management framework?
6. In what ways can cases contribute to studying the management field?
7. What does the research on management functions tell us? Does theory and speculation yield the same result as the research?
8. How do the management process and subdisciplines frameworks differ? In what ways are they the same?
9. What are the advantages and disadvantages of the management process framework?
10. How do the various frameworks considered relate to course offerings in management and the structuring of professional associations?

How Well Can You Apply Your Knowledge?

Problem 1. A manufacturing firm has experienced considerable turnover in its management ranks recently, largely because its salary scales and benefits have been below industry levels. For years the industry was relatively stable in makeup and new opportunities were few in number; as a result, movement of management personnel was minimal. Now, however, with the entry of several new firms into the industry, the picture has changed drastically, and the company finds itself with a serious problem.

Although a number of the openings can be filled immediately by promotions from within, for several positions this is not the case. The company had seen little reason to invest in managerial resource planning; as a result, the lack of qualified backup personnel for some of the positions that have been vacated was not previously evident. Accordingly, there seems no alternative but to go into the outside market. This, of course, requires a sizable increase in compensation levels to attract good people and a general readjustment upward of management compensation levels. The company has accepted this and has taken the appropriate steps. It has also engaged a management recruiting firm to help locate candidates for the vacant positions.

In the first discussions with representatives from the recruiting firm, it has become evident that managerial position descriptions are needed to help guide the search. Like managerial resource planning in general, this had been neglected in the past largely because in a highly stable staffing situation the need did not manifest itself very often.

What is needed now is a statement of how the managers will spend their time; what are major activities and what are less important ones, and roughly what kinds of abilities are needed? Given existing priorities, the greatest need is to get descriptions of the following three positions to the recruiting people as quickly as possible: a vice-president of manufacturing for one of the major divisions, a quality control supervisor for a plant with serious problems in maintaining production quality, and an industrial relations manager whose first assignment is to handle the renegotiation of several union contracts coming up for renewal.

Questions

1. How would you approach the problem of writing these three management position descriptions? What categories would you use in looking into the jobs?
2. Try to draft position descriptions of the kind needed for purposes of recruiting. What would you emphasize and what would you deemphasize with regard to each position? Be as detailed as you can.

Problem 2. For many years, a small private college in the Midwest had provided a good liberal arts education to students drawn primarily from the surrounding area. The college was heavily dependent on tuition income and over a period of years had experienced a gradual decline in enrollments which now threatened the college's survival. Initially this decline had been predominantly among the male students, but in recent years female enrollments had fallen off also.

Investigation indicated that the college's failure to offer business courses was a major source of the difficulty. A state college nearby that did offer business courses was experiencing significant growth in that area, particularly among female students; sons and daughters of alumni, who otherwise would have attended the college, apparently were not enrolling because they wanted to major in business.

After lengthy deliberations, and over substantial faculty opposition, the college's administration decided to initiate a new program in business administration at the undergraduate level. An individual was hired to head up the program, and she in turn brought in department chairpersons in the fields of accounting, finance, management, data processing and quantitative methods, and marketing. These department administrators were responsible for developing the curriculums in their fields and providing justifications for all courses proposed. The head of the program was concerned about any proliferation of courses beyond what was absolutely essential, because of the cost of hiring additional qualified faculty.

Questions

1. If you were the person in charge of the management area, what courses would you propose and what would be your written justification for each?
2. Describe briefly the subject matter that would be included in each of these courses, drawing upon your own undergraduate catalog if you wish. To what degree does your proposed curriculum cover the entire field of management?
3. Which of the courses would you require of all management majors, and which would be electives?

Additional Sources for More Detailed Study

Biddle, Bruce J. *Role Theory: Expectations, Identities, and Behaviors.* New York: Academic Press, 1979.

Campbell, John P.; Dunnette, Marvin D.; Lawler, Edward E.; and Weick, Karl E. *Managerial Behavior, Performance, and Effectiveness.* New York: McGraw-Hill, 1970.

Gordon, Robert A., and Howell, James E. *Higher Education for Business.* New York: Columbia University Press, 1959.

Holden, Paul E.; Pederson, Carlton A.; and Germane, Gayton E. *Top Management.* New York: McGraw-Hill, 1968.

Katz, Daniel, and Kahn, Robert L. *The Social Psychology of Organizations.* New York: Wiley, 1978.

Mahoney, Thomas A.; Jerdee, Thomas H.; and Carroll, Stephen J. *Development of Managerial Performance: A Research Approach.* Cincinnati: Southwestern, 1963.

McGuire, Joseph W. *Contemporary Management: Issues*

and Viewpoints. Englewood Cliffs, N.J.: Prentice-Hall, 1974.

Pierson, Frank C. *The Education of American Businessmen.* New York: McGraw-Hill, 1959.

Stewart, Rosemary. *Choices for the Manager.* Englewood Cliffs, N.J.: Prentice-Hall, 1982.

Urwick, Lyndall F. *The Elements of Administration.* New York: Harper & Row, 1943.

Wortman, Max S., and Sperling, JoAnn. *Defining the Manager's Job.* New York: Amacom, 1975.

Notes

1. Henri Fayol, *General and Industrial Management* (London: Pitman, 1949); Ralph C. Davis, *The Fundamentals of Top Management* (New York: Harper & Row, 1951); Chester I. Barnard, *The Functions of the Executive* (Cambridge, Mass.: Harvard University Press, 1938).

2. Harold Koontz, Cyril O'Donnell, and Heinz Weihrich, *Management* (New York: McGraw-Hill, 1980); William H. Newman, E. Kirby Warren, and Jerome E. Schnee, *The Process of Management* (Englewood Cliffs, N.J.: Prentice-Hall, 1982); Dalton E. McFarland, *Management* (New York: Macmillan, 1979); Theo Haimann, William G. Scott, and Patrick E. Connor, *Management* (Boston: Houghton Mifflin, 1982).

3. John B. Miner, *Management Theory* (New York: Macmillan, 1971); *The Management Process* (New York: Macmillan, 1978).

4. Larry D. Alexander, "The Effect Level in the Hierarchy and Functional Area Have on the Extent Mintzberg's Roles are Required by Managerial Jobs," *Academy of Management Proceedings,* August 1979; John J. Morse and Francis R. Wagner, "Measuring the Process of Managerial Effectiveness," *Academy of Management Journal,* March 1978.

5. Morgan W. McCall and Cheryl A. Segrist, *In Pursuit of the Manager's Job: Building on Mintzberg* (Greensboro, N.C.: Center for Creative Leadership, 1980).

6. John B. Miner, *Theories of Organizational Structure and Process* (Hinsdale, Ill.: Dryden, 1982).

7. Everett E. Adam and Ronald J. Ebert, *Production and Operations Management—Concepts, Models and Behavior* (Englewood Cliffs, N.J.: Prentice-Hall, 1982).

8. Claire Makin, "Ranking Corporate Reputations," *Fortune,* January 10, 1983.

CHAPTER 2

Why Is the Study of Management Useful?

CHAPTER OUTLINE

Jack L.—Satisfactions and Frustrations of a Managerial Career

Managerial Careers
Aspects of Management Potential
    Intellectual Capabilities
    The Role of Knowledge
    Personality Characteristics
    Motivation to Manage
Supply and Demand Considerations
    Population and Employment Trends
    Intellectual Supplies
    Motivational Supplies
    Calculating the Balance

Careers in the Functional Areas of Organizations
Personnel and Human Resources Careers
    The Nature of the Work
    Opportunities
    Factors in Success
    Managerial Talent Supplies
Careers in Production/Operations
    The Role of Production/Operations
        Management
    Career Opportunities

Professional Careers in Management
Management Consulting
    Management Consulting Firms
    Career Opportunities
Faculty Careers
    The Nature of the Work
    Requirements for Success
    Prospects and Opportunities
Research and Development

OBJECTIVES

To provide an understanding of the individual characteristics that make for a successful managerial career, and to relate these characteristics to the opportunities for managerial jobs.

To provide information on careers in the two functional areas of organizations covered by the management field.

To outline the various professional careers available in the management field.

JACK L.—SATISFACTIONS AND FRUSTRATIONS OF A MANAGERIAL CAREER

Jack L. had been one of the toughest kids in one of the roughest areas of Los Angeles. A poor student in his elementary school days, he came under the influence of a very strong willed teacher when he entered high school. This teacher opened the world of achievement and occupational aspiration to him by exposing him to various "role models." These were people from Jack's background who had achieved considerable status and wealth. Frequently, also, Jack and the teacher would discuss the benefits of such wealth and status and how they could be achieved. Looking back now, it can be said that Jack's experiences with this teacher really laid the foundation for Jack's life and became the cornerstone upon which he built his career.

From that time of high school until the present, Jack's life has been marked by hard work and ambition. For him, college consisted of full-time evening employment in a restaurant after a regular schedule of classes at one of the more challenging local institutions. Upon graduation, Jack went to work in the restaurant industry on a managerial level, reasoning that (1) competition with the new graduates would be less since few people his age would be willing to work the evenings and weekends necessary and (2) the financial rewards would be great if he were successful. Although his assumptions, particularly the first, might have been questionable, his success was not. He did so well that within a few years Jack became a district manager for the corporation which owned, among its many subsidiaries, the restaurant he had worked in while attending college. His record as district manager was so outstanding that eventually he moved into a position with a large corporation which was one of his firm's major suppliers. This move was a sign to him that his ambition and willingness to work seven days a week, if need be, had paid off and would bring him even more rewards in the future if he continued this type of work and career commitment.

Jack's career with the new company was, therefore, similarly successful. Over a period of years Jack moved through a series of positions, each one higher than the last and each involving a geographic move for his family. Eventually, he moved into the position that had been his goal—executive vice-president of sales and marketing.

It was also as a result of this last promotion that Jack was able to build a very impressive home. Five houses and five communities after joining the company, Jack had his dream house. Set on a large lot in a beautiful area of town, the house was truly a showcase for the small city in which the corporate headquarters were located. Jack and the architect had worked side by side in its design and the result was an excellent example of good taste and attractiveness.

It was apparent, however, that Jack's interest in the house and his satisfaction with it were not shared by his wife or his children. Elizabeth, Jack's wife, had changed considerably from the withdrawn, rather traditional girl he had married before he began his corporate climb. A trained teacher, she complained bitterly about their frequent moves and had refused to take any part in planning or decorating their latest home. Perhaps even more significant, she was now showing a lack of interest in Jack's career and the problems he was facing at work. This was something new to Jack and a great loss to him since he had, during the course of their marriage, come to rely greatly on her calmness and on her stability of judgment. Now, when he needed her greatly as a result of some of the severe problems he was facing, she was refusing to help. Instead, she was withdrawing more and more from his particular needs and asserting herself more and more in ways that Jack found disconcerting. She talked of a career of her own and of developing a more independent life for herself. She was also showing a lack of interest in the problems their children were facing, a fact that Jack also found distressing and very surprising considering her great interest in their children during their growing years. Now, as they had attained young adulthood and were still having problems, his wife was withdrawing and leaving him to handle the situation.

Perhaps Jack would not be so upset if his job were not causing him difficulties. But this is not the case. There are several very difficult problems demanding his attention. One of these concerns the extramarital exploits of one of his key managers. Although Jack prides himself on keeping out of the personal lives of his employees, this particular manager is taking few precautions in his affairs and his activities are the talk of the plant. In addition, the man's wife has taken it upon herself to write letters to the company president detailing her anger and bitterness but at the same time insisting that her husband be kept on his job to protect her financial security. Jack, himself, is bothered by the matter on several grounds. First, he is perceptive enough to realize that he is threatened because his own marriage is having difficulties. Second, he believes strongly that a man's private life is his own affair. As long as a person does his job, it is not the business of the company to interfere. However, he sees that the man's activities are having a detrimental effect on his job performance, although he cannot prove it in an objective manner. Jack is feeling inordinately pressured because the company president has tossed the matter into his lap without any specific recommendation. Jack does not feel that this is fair.

Jack is also dealing with the possibility of a major sales and marketing reorganization. He has to determine whether certain product distribution patterns are overextended and whether the company should decrease the size of its marketing area for these goods. On the one hand, Jack feels that there is good reason to follow this approach because of the general weakness of some of their sales force and the fact that personnel could be shifted into more efficient working units in order to develop a stronger overall presence. However, Jack is also constantly being faced with the demands of the company president that sales volume be increased. He is also upset by the idea that some employees would be let go by the changes. Jack feels that he is being put into an impossible bind here also.

Until a few years ago, almost to the time of their most recent move, Jack had been able to talk to his wife about these matters. Now, however, she is angry most of the time. She complains bitterly about the fact that they are living in "his house" in a community to which "his job" has taken them. She talks continually about the loss of her own opportunities for growth and the fact that life holds nothing for her. Although Jack does not respond to these attacks, he believes she is being unfair. He feels that he has been a good husband and that his hard work over the years has been as much for her and for the children as for himself. They live in the house as much as he does and the overwhelming amount of his income is spent on them. He believes that he allows Elizabeth great discretion in running the household and that he makes few demands as to how the money should be spent. It is unfair, he feels, for his wife to complain in the late 1970s that he did not behave in the 1960s the way he would probably behave today if they were starting over again. He also feels that she bears at least part of the responsibility for the course of her life and that it is not fair for her to blame him for all her failures and disillusionments and not give him credit for the fine life he provides her.

Jack is also somewhat disillusioned as far as his children are concerned. His son, now 21, shows little interest in anything that promises career advancement. He is working as a cabdriver in Chicago and refuses to listen to his father's entreaties that he return to the college he left at 19. In fact, communication between Jack and his son is almost nonexistent at this point.

The situation is slightly better with his daughter, but there are problems here also. At 20, she has already been through one marriage and shows few signs of having learned much. She is an infantile person who looks to her father for guidance more than he believes she should. Although he is aware that he may have encouraged this dependency when she was younger, he feels that his wife is now partially to blame because of her increasing withdrawal and her anger toward him. He is trying to convince his daughter to return to school and may succeed.

Increasingly, however, he wishes that Elizabeth would handle these family matters so that he could concentrate on his job problems. Recently, he has begun to think about his old interests in architecture and construction. Although he does not want to go back to school, he now finds himself day-

Why Is the Study of Management Useful?

dreaming about opening a construction firm specializing in custom-built homes similar to his own. He realizes, however, that his material comforts are important to him and that he would have great difficulty in adjusting to the reduced income that would be involved in this type of job change.[1]

J ack L.'s experiences are not necessarily typical, but they do point up the fact that a successful managerial career, for either a man or a woman, may come at some cost—both in terms of job stresses and family conflicts. With forethought it may be possible to reduce these kinds of problems, but it seems unlikely that they can be completely eliminated without damaging the chances for success itself.

A major reason for studying in the field of management is to prepare oneself so as to experience some sense of accomplishment and satisfaction in this career, and to make a worthwhile contribution. In spite of his misgivings and current problems, Jack L. has had a successful career. Among other things he wanted very much to make money and obtain material comforts, and he has achieved both. In this chapter we consider what it takes to obtain this kind of success and other kinds that utilize knowledge from the management field. Why, and for what, is the study of management useful? What opportunities are opened? What chances do different kinds of people have of obtaining success via this route? And ultimately, for the individual student, are any of the possible careers to which the study of management leads attractive enough to warrant a major concentration of effort in this area?

MANAGERIAL CAREERS

As the example of Jack L. indicates, managerial careers typically extend through a number of positions. Each of these positions often is at a successively higher level in the organizational hierarchy. However, lateral moves, and even demotions, may be interspersed. A manager likely will move around the country, and perhaps around the world also. There may be changes from one organization to another as well.

All of these possibilities are true whether one manages in business, in government, in the educational world, or elsewhere. In fact, the differences between management positions in two different business firms can be greater than those between business and government employment. What is different about business is that if one achieves a position toward the top of the managerial hierarchy, the financial rewards can be very sizable. As of this writing, the total yearly compensation packages (salary plus bonus) of certain corporate officers extend into the millions of dollars. On the other hand, if one's managerial career turns out to be only moderately successful, the relative financial benefits of business as opposed to other types of career settings are not nearly so great.

Aspects of Management Potential

Individuals differ from one another in a large number of respects, many of which have very little if anything to do with success in a managerial career. A number of studies have been conducted comparing aspects of individuals with information about their relative performance in managerial work, promotion rates, salary progression, and the like. This research has yielded certain solid indications of what constitutes potential for managerial success. The characteristics identified may be grouped logically into those of an intellectual and personality (or motivational) nature.

Intellectual Capabilities *Intelligence* may be defined as the degree or extent to which an individual is ready to learn new things rapidly and solve problems (reason) correctly—the developed capacity to group, relate, and use concepts. Intelligence thus defined may be differentiated into a number of special abilities; considered from this viewpoint, it becomes the total complex of these special abilities as they exist in the individual. The intellectual abilities that are important in job performance are set forth in Exhibit 2.1. For managerial work and for many other higher-level occupations, *verbal ability* is the most important component because of its central role in communication. The other special abilities are of varying significance depending on the specific nature of the managerial position.

Studies repeatedly have shown that intelligence is of prime importance to rising in the managerial hierarchy and to staying there once one reaches the upper levels.[2] Research conducted in the country's largest corporations—such as American Telephone and Telegraph (AT&T), Sears, Roebuck, and Exxon—has consistently found that intelligence is a major component of management potential.

Data on the relationship between intelligence and occupational level are given in Exhibit 2.2. At each successively higher level of occupation, the average intelligence level increases, and the bare minimum at which one can get by increases also. Level 1 occupations in Exhibit 2.2 include corporate top executives; when such individuals are considered separately they stand out as an extremely high intelligence group.

One reason that the intelligence requirements of managerial positions rise further up the hierarchy is that managing occurs in a competitive context, both externally with other firms and internally with other managers. To the extent that a person can learn rapidly and use large amounts of information to make reasoned choices among alternatives, that person has a competitive advantage, does

---

EXHIBIT 2.1   Intellectual abilities important in job performance

Verbal Ability	Numerical Ability	Mechanical Ability	Spatial Ability
A knowledge of words, and skill in their use.	Skill in manipulating numbers.	A capacity for dealing with mechanical objects and a knowledge of the principles which govern their operation.	Skill in visualizing and relating objects in accordance with their shape and position.

Importance for Managerial Performance

High ←——————————————————————————————————→ Low

EXHIBIT 2.2 Average intelligence of corporate top executives in comparison with various other occupational levels

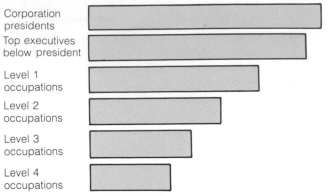

Relative Intelligence

Level 1: Higher-level professional workers, executives, those involved in the more technical and complex clerical and sales work, large-scale farmers

Level 2: Most retail managers, the more highly skilled workers, skilled clerical workers, foremen, wholesale salespersons, technicians, lower-level professional workers, relatively large-scale farmers

Level 3: Lower-level skilled workers, the semiskilled, routine clerical workers, retail sales clerks, most farmers, proprietors of relatively simple businesses

Level 4: Primarily unskilled workers

ambition perhaps

SOURCE: John B. Miner, *Intelligence in the United States* (Westport, Conn.: Greenwood Press, 1973), 128, 165–69.

a better job, and is more likely to be promoted. Furthermore, the higher level positions present management with a more complex and demanding environment; high intelligence is needed just to cope.

The Role of Knowledge Intelligence is important in managerial work because it contributes to decision making in all areas and thus to the process of reasoning through to a rational course of action. But for intelligence of this kind to work effectively, it must operate in a context of knowledge. Managers must know what they need to know to deal with a question at hand, or they must be able to put their hands on the relevant information very quickly. This, too, is an aspect of intellectual capability.

In years past this kind of knowledge was acquired almost entirely "on the job." For this reason companies often gave preference in hiring to intelligent, broadly educated young people who had little previous exposure to business and business subject matter. "We'll teach them what they need to know about business" was a frequently heard explanation. Certainly, there still is a great deal of needed knowledge that is of this kind, knowledge often referred to as coming from *experience*. Information that is unique to a particular position, company location, or firm—such things as the names of local suppliers and the towns where company plants are located—has to be learned this way.

Increasingly, however, there is another kind of knowledge—of accounting, marketing, finance, engineering, law, and management—which is important and which applies to a large number of positions across many organizations. It is feasible to bring this information together in courses as part of formal education, and to have those courses taught by experts in a specialized area; in short, to utilize the expertise of professors in professional schools of business, engineering, law, and the like.

Knowledge relevant to managing is expanding at a very rapid rate, and the old "learn it on the job" approach is no longer adequate. As a result companies now are looking for young people—accountants, M.B.A.s, computer specialists, and the like—who can bring needed knowledge with them. Managers for the future must have an education which permits them to provide employers with significant input, including knowledge of organizational behavior, organizational process and structure, and management policy and strategy.

Yet in almost every company, large numbers of managers, many of them good managers in certain respects, have been caught unawares by the information explosion. They do not have the training needed because in their day, it was neither necessary nor available; they have not acquired the knowledge since, because it cannot be obtained on the job. Many practicing managers are badly lacking in the kind of knowledge that an up-to-date formal education in the area of specialization would provide.[3]

This situation of rapid change in knowledge requirements has created considerable potential for conflict. Often the result is that available, relevant knowledge is not utilized, as the following quote illustrates:

> As a result of corporate pressures, an increasing number of young managers and executives with MBA-level training have joined the company. This has created a managerial force consisting of two very different types of managers: the new, younger people and the oldtimers who date back to preacquisition days. There is now conflict in the company as these mutually antagonistic groups work together. Open hostility at staff meetings and nasty backbiting are common. One illustration of the problem is that despite the fact that an expensive computer system has been introduced, it is not being utilized at maximum effectiveness because of the antipathy of the two groups toward each other. The old line sales-marketing executives are unwilling to work with the young manager in charge of the electronic data processing facility. Throughout the company similar conflicts to these are taking place.[4]

Personality Characteristics We have considered the various intellectual capabilities associated with success in a managerial career, including intelligence and job-related knowledge (ranging from knowing the name of one's immediate superior to the content of formal degree programs). A second major aspect of management potential has to do with personality—the attitudes, interests, values, traits, and motives that make for success.

The characteristics that make for success in one firm often do not prove equally valuable in another. Yet certain generalizations appear to hold across organizations, or at least across those in the business sector. In terms of *interests,* managerial success is related to those of a persuasive and verbal or literary nature, and not to interest in scientific pursuits or in occupations below the managerial level. Successful managers find the business world per se and business occupations attractive, particularly the task of supervising others. This interest in supervision and leadership often extends back to an early period in high school or before.

Characteristics such as a desire for personal dominance and to exercise power over others seem to contribute not only to the choice of a managerial career but to success in it as well. Also important are a desire for upward mobility, independence, a certain amount of self-esteem or self-assurance, and decisiveness. This is not all a matter of possessing "good" qualities, and no bad ones; successful managers can be so intent on exercising power that they appear domineering to others, and their desire to move upward in both social standing and the organizational hierarchy can lead to their being viewed as somewhat snobbish. Female managers with these qualities may be criticized as excessively pushy and unfeminine. The point is that these qualities make for a successful managerial career, not necessarily for wide popularity and approval on other grounds. In the case of Jack L., career success came at the cost of considerable disapproval on the part of his family.

With regard to *values,* successful managers tend toward those of a pragmatic, dynamic, achievement-oriented nature; less successful managers, whose compensation levels have risen less rapidly, place greater value on passivity, security, and the status quo. Specific data for United States managers are given in Exhibit 2.3. Similar values make for success in other countries as well, but there are in addition pervasive values that characterize whole cultures that must be taken into account: tactful acquisition of influence and due regard for others (United States); deference to superiors and company commitment (Japan); personal forcefulness

---

EXHIBIT 2.3 Concepts valued by successful and less successful managers

Managers Who Value These Concepts:	Make More Than Five Times as Much as	Managers Who Value These Concepts:
Profit maximization		Organizational stability
Their subordinates		Obedience
Labor unions		Trust
Ability		Loyalty
Achievement		Cooperation
Influence		Conformity
Power		Leisure
Success		Dignity
Change		Security
Risk		Caution
		Equality
		Religion

Adapted from George W. England, *The Manager and His Values: An International Perspective* (Cambridge, Mass.: Ballinger, 1975), pp. 65–66.

and aggressiveness with low recognition of effects on others (Korea); a highly centralized, personal, and rigid social structure (India); a low-keyed approach to management involving high concern for others (Australia); and so on.[5]

Motivation to Manage   Much of what has been said about personality characteristics may be summarized in terms of the motivation to manage concept (see Exhibit 2.4). Managers with high levels of motivation to manage, and thus with the various attitudes and motives which compose it, have been found consistently to perform better on the job and to progress more rapidly and further up the management hierarchy.[6]

Motivation to manage is one of the most important considerations in the choice of a managerial career. A highly intelligent person with a fine business education, and perhaps also several years of solid experience with a company in a nonmanagerial role such as selling, still is unlikely to succeed when promoted into management if he or she lacks managerial motivation. People can want to be managers because of the pay, or the social standing in the community, or because their parents want them to be managers, or for many other reasons, without possessing motivation to manage. What is important is that one obtain a real sense of personal satisfaction from doing the things that managers do. Such a person would rather be managing than doing almost anything else, because this is the type of activity that satisfies certain very strong needs. In other words, managing is fun.

Supply and Demand Considerations

The prospects for a successful and satisfying managerial career depend not only on possessing or acquiring the necessary intellectual capabilities and personality characteristics, but also on the extent to which opportunities (openings) become

---

EXHIBIT 2.4   Elements of the motivation to manage

1. *Positive attitudes toward authority*. In a hierarchical system there must be communication and interaction with superiors; a manager must be able to represent his/her group upward and obtain support for activities at higher levels.

2. *Competitive motivation*. In a hierarchy, rewards including promotion to higher levels and large salaries are unequally distributed; it thus becomes necessary to distinguish oneself from peers.

3. *Assertive motivation*. In a hierarchy the managerial role has much in common with the traditional parental role in a family. Accordingly, a degree of assertiveness and a "take charge" attitude are required.

4. *Power motivation*. In a hierarchy, manipulation of sanctions and downward supervision are essential; managers must guide the behavior of subordinates in support of organizational objectives.

5. *Motivation to stand out from a group*. In a hierarchy, managers must assume a highly visible position that is clearly differentiated from the subordinate group in terms of what is done.

6. *Motivation to assume routine administrative responsibilities*. In a hierarchy it is essential that various routine decision-making and communication tasks be carried out.

Why Is the Study of Management Useful?

available. The ideal from the viewpoint of a qualified student is the situation where there are lots of jobs (demand is high) and very few people available to fill the jobs (supply is low). To what extent is this ideal situation likely to prevail in the years to come?

Population and Employment Trends   Projecting the demand for managers in hierarchical organizations is a risky business. Ten years ago the projections indicated a continuing and large growth in demand; a few short years later these optimistic forecasts were tempered substantially and there was increasing concern about an oversupply of managerial talent.[7] Forecasting becomes complicated (or even meaningless) when one adds in considerations such as the extent of growth of alternative organizational forms, which do not employ hierarchy and thus do not need managers in the sense we are using the term, and changes in the typical retirement age of managers.

Nevertheless, given that we are a society of large organizations, many of which are getting larger still, we can anticipate some continuing growth in the demand for managers at all levels. At the same time managing occurs in organizations that are shaped like a pyramid (see Exhibit 2.5) in which there are lots of managers at the bottom and very few at the top. A successful career in management means moving well up that pyramid, to a point where opportunities tend to be scarce. It takes a very rapid expansion of the economy and a rapid growth in the number of firms before the demand for upper-middle and top managers becomes very great. Assuming that this kind of growth period is behind us in the United States, this demand can be expected to increase only moderately.

Another important population trend involves the number of individuals in various age groups. As a consequence of the post-World War II increase in the birth rate, the number of people in the 25–44 age bracket is now expanding rapidly. This is the age group from which new managers come. On the evidence from population statistics alone, the supply of potential managers should increase the competition and thereby decrease the chance for a successful managerial career for some time to come. The labor force also has expanded substantially because increasing numbers of women have entered

---

EXHIBIT 2.5   Demand for managers at different levels of the organizational hierarchy

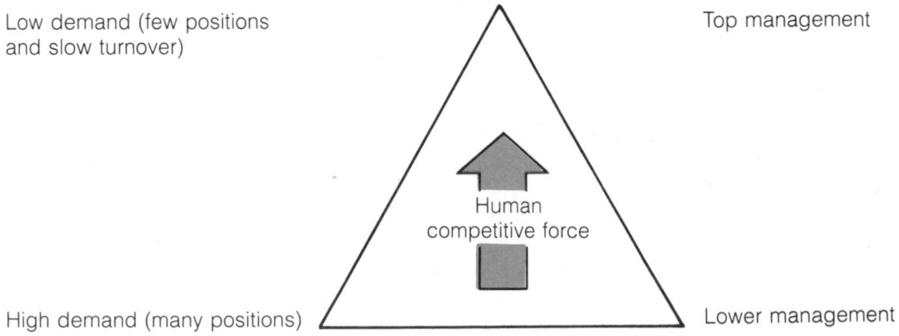

Low demand (few positions and slow turnover)

Top management

Human competitive force

High demand (many positions)

Lower management

and stayed in it longer. More women and minority group members want and can have a successful managerial career. As the supply pool gets bigger, the competition gets tougher. These kinds of considerations have led to the contention that the market is approaching an oversupply of managerial talent.

Intellectual Supplies   We hear a lot about declining college enrollments these days, because the college age group is decreasing in size within the population. But enrollments in both undergraduate and master's programs which produce the knowledge base for managerial work, such as business administration, are up substantially. Particularly noteworthy is that the number of females taking business coursework has expanded substantially in the past few years.

However, average scores on various intelligence tests taken by college students declined steadily, in all population groups, over a twenty-year period during the 1960s and 1970s.[8] Consistent with the idea that intelligence reflects an ability to learn, achievement levels in a variety of areas have declined also. One could hope that the relative intelligence deficiencies would correct themselves over time, and in fact there is reason to believe that intelligence, particularly verbal ability, does tend to increase in managerial and professional people at least until age 50 and perhaps beyond.[9] But the kind of sharp increase that would be necessary to compensate for a lower starting point seems unlikely. There has been a slight improvement in average college student scores very recently, but not enough to mean a great deal as yet.

In summary, increasing numbers of students who enter the business world bring some useful business knowledge to it. Fewer students now have the intelligence to move well up the management hierarchy, using current standards, and many students do not start their work in organizations with as much relevant information as they might. They are more likely than in the past to bring business knowledge, but because of their lesser intelligence they have learned less of that to which they have been exposed. Opportunities for those with above average intelligence, and for those who have absorbed more than their share of knowledge in college, are much greater than employment statistics would indicate.

Motivational Supplies   Among the various personality characteristics, the most extensive information on trends is available for motivation to manage. The overall pattern is one of decline, starting in the early to mid-1960s, plateauing some ten years later, and remaining at the same low level since that time. Both intelligence and motivation to manage thus have decreased, but the two changes appear to be unrelated. Among business administration students, both the males and the females of today are less motivated toward managerial activities than students of the past, but the rate of change has been less pronounced for the females (see Exhibit 2.6). As a result what was once a major gap favoring the males has disappeared; the sexes are now at essentially the same level. Liberal arts majors have consistently had less managerial motivation on the average than the business administration majors, and engineering students roughly the same amount or perhaps slightly more.[10]

The decline in managerial motivation has not affected all aspects of motivation equally. Decreases are noted in positive attitudes toward authority, competitive motivation, assertive motivation, and motivation to assume routine ad-

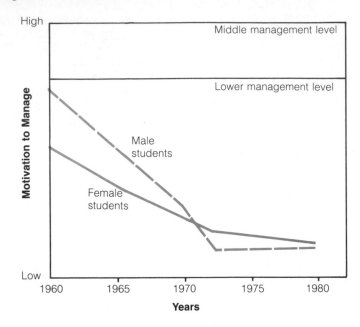

EXHIBIT 2.6 Overall motivation to manage of male and female business students compared with managers

ministrative responsibilities; in all of these cases the patterns are much the same for males and females. But there is no evidence of consistent changes for either group in power motivation or motivation to stand out from a group (these latter two motives have consistently been at a level below that of even first-line supervisors throughout the twenty-year period for which data are available).

Many students of the 1970s and the 1980s do not have a strong desire for a managerial career, in the sense of wanting to do the things managers do. Their motivation is well below the existing standards not only for middle managers but for lower level managers as well. Recent data show that when these individuals accept management trainee positions or actually move into management, they are just as dissatisfied and unmotivated as the student data would suggest.[11] Many such people simply will not seek a management level position even though they may enter upon business employment; others will move into management only to leave it at the first opportunity; and still others will stick it out for a variety of reasons, turning in mediocre performances and experiencing marginally successful careers at best.

However, as with intelligence, today's college students display a wide range of managerial motivation. Although the supply of motivational talent has decreased, for those with well above average levels of motivation to manage—something more akin to the levels prevailing in the early 1960s—there are increased opportunities for a successful managerial career.

Calculating the Balance In Exhibit 2.7, the various factors we have been considering are weighed as they might be expected to operate during the period when today's college students work their way up to the management ranks and then on up in the hierarchy. Although the prospects are not what they would be in a rapid growth economy, where demand constantly outstrips supply, they appear very promising for those who have the managerial talent. Projections of managerial oversupply, based on population data alone, appear unbalanced when matched against the total picture in Exhibit 2.7. For students, then, a decision to study management with the objective of pursuing a managerial career seems sensible and consistent with the opportunities expected to become available.

CAREERS IN THE FUNCTIONAL AREAS OF ORGANIZATIONS

We have been considering careers in managing generally, in any part of the organization; our focus has been on vertical differences in level. Now we turn to a different type of division, one that separates the organization into functions horizontally. Within the field of management there are two such functional areas: personnel/human resources, and production/operations. These two join other functional areas, such as accounting, marketing, purchasing, and the like (specializations that are not part of management) to constitute a total organization.

EXHIBIT 2.7 Opportunity outlook derived from weighing supply and demand factors

Factors Influencing Demand		Factors Influencing Supply	
Increase	**Decrease**	**Increase**	**Decrease**
Growth in the size and number of organizations	Growth in the use of alternatives to hierarchy that do not require managers	Expansion of the 25–44 age group	Declines in overall college enrollments
	Present managers work longer before retiring	Women and minorities available as candidates in increasing numbers	Intelligence levels lower
		Growth in business school enrollments	Motivation to manage levels lower
Expected Net Consequence		**Expected Net Consequence**	
Moderate growth in demand at all levels		Some overall decrease in supply, especially at the upper management levels	
Expected Net Opportunities			
Good to very good, with the prospects for a successful managerial career particularly strong for those with high intellectual and motivational potential			

Why Is the Study of Management Useful?

The functional areas include both managerial and nonmanagerial jobs. Careers typically start below the managerial level and involve movement upward over time. Whether promotion into management actually involves much managing, or at least supervising, depends in large part on the nature of the specialty. Most personnel jobs, for instance, are structured so that the managers have relatively few subordinates reporting to them; much of the work involves the direct application of specialized knowledge to particular problems. In such cases the knowledge gained through education is a very important factor in career success.

Personnel and Human Resources Careers

Personnel management involves the development, application, and evaluation of policies, procedures, and programs concerning the individual in the organization. It includes all the activities dealing with the human resources of the organization, as opposed to material or financial resources.

The Nature of the Work An expanded picture of what personnel specialists and managers do is contained in Exhibit 2.8. They bring employees into the

EXHIBIT 2.8 Activities carried out by personnel departments

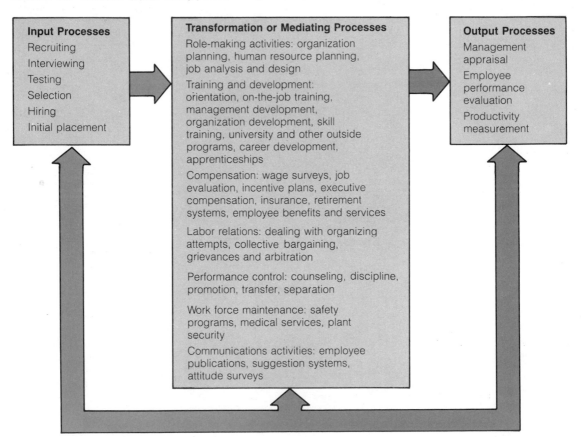

Input Processes
Recruiting
Interviewing
Testing
Selection
Hiring
Initial placement

Transformation or Mediating Processes
Role-making activities: organization planning, human resource planning, job analysis and design
Training and development: orientation, on-the-job training, management development, organization development, skill training, university and other outside programs, career development, apprenticeships
Compensation: wage surveys, job evaluation, incentive plans, executive compensation, insurance, retirement systems, employee benefits and services
Labor relations: dealing with organizing attempts, collective bargaining, grievances and arbitration
Performance control: counseling, discipline, promotion, transfer, separation
Work force maintenance: safety programs, medical services, plant security
Communications activities: employee publications, suggestion systems, attitude surveys

Output Processes
Management appraisal
Employee performance evaluation
Productivity measurement

organization, carry out a host of activities designed to keep the total work force contributing to achieving organizational goals as much as possible, and monitor and evaluate employee performance. This latter activity then feeds back and influences the way that both input and mediating activities are carried out. All of these activities may be influenced by a personnel research function and by an employee records management process, which often incorporates some kind of computerized employee information system.

To complete the picture of the kinds of things that people in personnel deal with and must take into account in their decisions, we should add the various internal and external forces that surround Exhibit 2.8. External forces include characteristics of the cultural (international), physical (geographical), and organizational (industry) environment in which the organization operates. They also include applicable labor relations and employment laws, which have exerted a far greater impact on personnel decisions in recent years, and characteristics of the external labor force. Internal forces in the organization are such factors as existing company plans and policies, union contracts, and characteristics of the internal labor force (individual differences).[12]

Not all organizations deal with all of the matters described in Exhibit 2.8. If there is no union, for instance, collective bargaining does not occur, although there may be other labor relations activities, such as dealing with attempts to organize a union. In general, smaller firms tend to invest less in the personnel area, and firms that are having financial difficulties often cut back, not only in their total labor force but also in activities such as training and development, communication, and planning. The Curtis Publishing Company, a major magazine publisher, practically abolished its personnel department in the years before the business finally failed.

Opportunities Personnel occupations have been a major growth area for a number of years, but there is now some indication that the demand is leveling off. Nevertheless, the U.S. Department of Labor projects that jobs for people with specialized knowledge in personnel will continue to grow at roughly the same rate as the labor force as a whole.[13] Furthermore, the field is attractive on a number of other counts:

> For the man or woman who has the talent, the discipline, and the exposure, the opportunities in personnel are excellent and growing. Money, status, and other ego-satisfying factors will come faster and in greater quantity. More importantly, the person who chooses personnel administration has a greater opportunity than most to affect the way in which people live and work together in a world whose potential for strife grows in proportion to its increasing complexity.[14]

At one time, not too long ago, personnel managers were not well paid relative to managers in other areas, and the function was headed by an individual who had not yet been admitted to the ranks of top management. At present, starting salaries are equal to those for other types of business administration graduates; compensation levels now much higher, although still below the top salaries in some other functional areas. Companies of all sizes now consistently award the top personnel executive a vice-presidential title and in many cases election to the board of directors.

Factors in Success Intelligence, a strong desire to supervise others, initiative, and a need to move upward in the organization are just as important in the personnel field as elsewhere.[15] So too are certain aspects of motivation to manage. Overall managerial motivation is higher among the upper-level, better-paid personnel managers, and positive attitudes toward authority, competitive motivation, and assertive motivation also are important for success.

In the corporate world, success is associated with rising to the top of the personnel pyramid, which often is not a very tall one; this success is achieved by combining considerable specialized knowledge of the field with the intellectual and motivational talents of a manager. Some people are attracted to personnel work initially because they "like people" and want to help them. Such motives, although admirable (and consistent with certain origins of the personnel field, as will be considered in chapter 3), do not appear to be the prime ingredients for success at the present time, at least in the corporate environment.

Managerial Talent Supplies A very important consideration for the student anticipating a career in personnel is the extent to which the field attracts the type of managerial talent it needs. Exhibit 2.9 is very revealing on this point: personnel managers frequently fall below other managers on the various aspects of managerial talent. Both trees are strongly overbalanced to the left, in a negative direction. This pattern is characteristic at the lower levels of personnel management also, not just at the top and in the middle. Clearly, the personnel field has not been attracting its share of managerial talent.

The consequence is that this is an area of unusual opportunity for those who do possess the characteristics required for success. Because managerial motivation has been low among students over the past few years and current managers in personnel generally show relatively low levels of this type of motivation, the level of competition is lower. Those who want to rise to the top should have a good chance of doing so rapidly in the personnel area for some time to come.

Careers in Production/Operations

The production/operations field is in ferment at the present time. After a long period of neglect it is an increasingly important factor in management curriculums. Yet there is considerable controversy over what the major thrust of the new courses should be.

A major difficulty has to do with the nature of the production/operations curriculum vis-à-vis company practice. Historically the field was concerned with manufacturing, but this was a function dominated by engineering; also, many people rose to the top through the ranks of line management with little formal education. Where did production/operations students from a business school fit in?

The Role of Production/Operations Management In the early years, production/operations was closely allied with industrial engineering and with the use of various techniques of work-study and design. This technical emphasis has continued, but production now includes a wide range of quantitative procedures. Some of these techniques are well established, as indicated in Exhibit

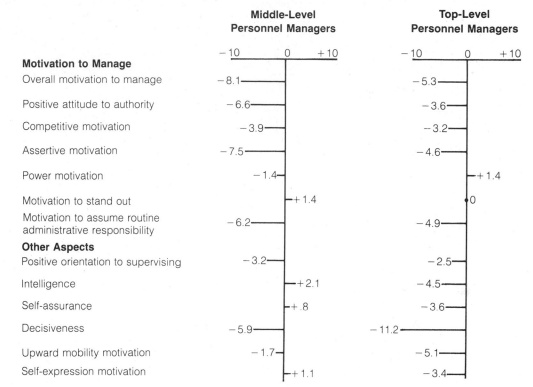

	Middle-Level Personnel Managers	Top-Level Personnel Managers
Motivation to Manage		
Overall motivation to manage	−8.1	−5.3
Positive attitude to authority	−6.6	−3.6
Competitive motivation	−3.9	−3.2
Assertive motivation	−7.5	−4.6
Power motivation	−1.4	+1.4
Motivation to stand out	+1.4	0
Motivation to assume routine administrative responsibility	−6.2	−4.9
Other Aspects		
Positive orientation to supervising	−3.2	−2.5
Intelligence	+2.1	−4.5
Self-assurance	+.8	−3.6
Decisiveness	−5.9	−11.2
Upward mobility motivation	−1.7	−5.1
Self-expression motivation	+1.1	−3.4

NOTE: A score of 0 on the scale represents the average value for managers in general working at that particular level.
SOURCE: John B. Miner, "Managerial Talent in Personnel," *Business Horizons* (December 1979):13.

2.10; others should increase in use, according to manufacturing vice presidents. Numerous techniques other than those of Exhibit 2.10 are part of the knowledge base of the production/operations field, and it is the sum of these techniques that gives the field its unique strength.

There are several ways to become a production/operations manager, but following the route from business school study provides a very different experience than pursuing engineering or rising through the technical ranks. The advantage of studying production/operations in a business school is in acquiring techniques, particularly quantitative techniques. This strength can yield jobs as foreman, general foreman, superintendent, plant manager, or vice-president of manufacturing. Coursework covers certain concepts and techniques, of the kind noted in Exhibit 2.11, that provide a particular capability in areas such as assembly line balancing, facilities management and layout, inventory control, quality control, project management, manufacturing purchasing, and

EXHIBIT 2.10 Use of quantitative techniques from the production/operations area in the manufacturing operations of large companies

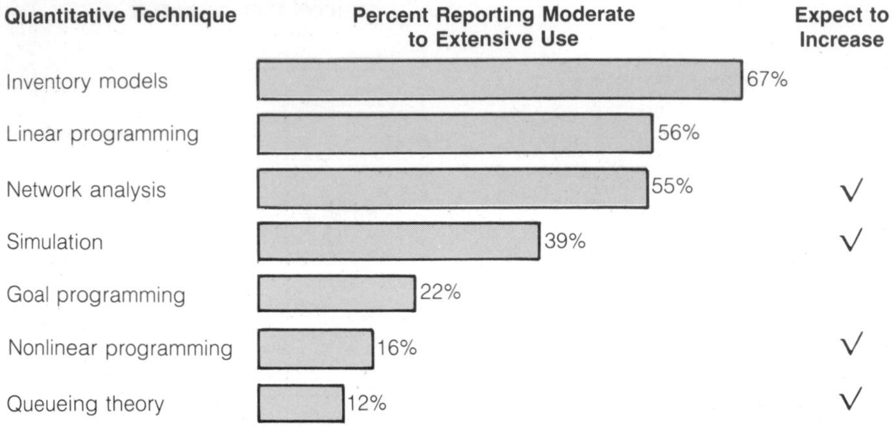

Quantitative Technique	Percent Reporting Moderate to Extensive Use	Expect to Increase
Inventory models	67%	
Linear programming	56%	
Network analysis	55%	✓
Simulation	39%	✓
Goal programming	22%	
Nonlinear programming	16%	✓
Queueing theory	12%	✓

Adapted from Thad B. Green, Walter B. Newsom, and S. Roland Jones, "A Survey of the Application of Quantitative Techniques to Production/Operations Management in Large Corporations," *Academy of Management Journal* (December 1977): 671–72.

the like. Entry jobs may be in specialized groups created for these various purposes or in line management itself.

Recently there has been a push, with the growth of employment in the service sector, to extend the application of production/operations management techniques beyond the manufacturing sector. Certainly there are close parallels between manufacturing operations and many service functions; Exhibit 2.12 displays these parallels, using the service activities of a college of business administration

EXHIBIT 2.11 Content of a production/operations course

Principles and Concepts	Techniques and Tools
Types of productive systems	Forecasting
Selection of product specification	Standards
Quality determination and control	Financial analysis
Planning: capacity, people, material	Program evaluation and review techniques
Equipment selection	
Plant location and layout	Simulation
Master scheduling	Learning curve
Materials and information flow	Waiting lines
Control	Wage determination
	Performance evaluation

NOTE: The course is designed to teach the general principles of and concepts of sound deliberation, and the techniques and tools of decision making and implementation.

SOURCE: Jerry V. Novak, "Management of Work," *Academy of Management Proceedings,* 1979, p. 168.

EXHIBIT 2.12 Parallels between manufacturing production/operations and a college of business administration

Manufacturing Activities	Comparable College of Business Activities
Material procurement	Recruiting students
Resource planning and development	Recruiting faculty
Supplies procurement	Faculty research and study
Facilities planning and development	Facilities planning and development
Product and process planning	Curriculum planning
Process planning	Instructional methods planning
Flow scheduling	Class scheduling
Material transformation	Instruction
Quality control	Examinations and awarding of credits
Resource maintenance	Instructor evaluation
Marketing	Placement
Delivery	Graduation

Adapted from Eugene C. Bell, "A College of Business Administration as a Production System," *Academy of Management Journal* (June 1974):310.

as an example. Potentially, at least, applications beyond the manufacturing sector are both feasible and promising. Nevertheless, at the present time, service organizations do not represent a major source of production/operations employment.

Career Opportunities The major strength of a person trained in the production/operations area is the possession of scarce knowledge regarding the nature and use of the tools and techniques of the field. When organizations do not have such knowledge already, and know they need it, they tend to hire it from the outside; the result has been a tremendous opportunity for those skilled in the production/operations area, and this world of opportunity gives every prospect of continuing. Pay levels are high and should remain so.

Opportunities are greatest in manufacturing, even though manufacturing employment overall is declining. Numerous opportunities are developing outside manufacturing, which has been the traditional home of the field in the United States. Growth in employment in nontraditional contexts, such as banking, transportation, communications, agriculture, and the like—in the service sector generally—seems likely to expand; it is not possible to say when this type of employment will represent a significant factor in the field, however. Furthermore, major opportunities are beginning to appear around the world, especially in the developing countries of Africa, South America, and Asia. These countries are attempting to move through the industrialization process at an accelerated rate, and production/operations management is a major force to that end.

It is also likely that developments in the computer area will create opportunities for the expanded use of production/operations techniques and for their use in organizations where they were not previously feasible:

Perhaps the most significant change in the future in operations will be the use of information processing. As information processing becomes available cheaply to even small organizations, functions such as inventory control and production scheduling may become more sophisticated in small organizations. As optical scanning becomes available, good perpetual-inventory systems will be available to help reduce inventory. Soon, computers will have interface compatibility with each other on a large scale, and automatic orders can go from a customer to its major suppliers, with promised delivery dates being sent back immediately. The increased visibility into orders and inventory will help reduce but not eliminate variability of forecasting and of scheduling.[16]

Knowledge is important for success in all areas, but its role in a production/operations career seems particularly crucial. Verbal ability continues to be a necessary ingredient for success but it is now joined more closely by the other abilities—numerical in particular, but also mechanical and spatial.[17] Motivation to manage remains a significant factor to the degree a successful career involves movement into the better paying, middle- and upper-level management positions. But the competitive advantage that a person with high motivation to manage has in the personnel area cannot be anticipated in production/operations. Manufacturing managers above the first level of supervision tend to possess strong motives of a managerial nature, and the engineering schools have maintained relatively high levels of motivation to manage among their students.

When all factors are considered, the prospects for students who major in production/operations are at least equal to those for students in the personnel area, and probably are somewhat better. However, the mix of factors that creates opportunity in the two fields differs substantially—just as the work to be performed does.

<table>
<tr><td>

PROFESSIONAL CAREERS IN MANAGEMENT

</td><td>

A *profession* is characterized by (1) the existence of a set of specific techniques supported by a theoretical underpinning, (2) the development of individual careers influenced by an association of colleagues—the professional association, (3) the presence of some agreement within society that professional status applies, and (4) the existence of a set of professional norms or ethics. Typically, the specialized techniques needed to practice the profession are learned through enrollment in a professional school and through the completion of a specified degree program, as with medical or law school.

Within the management field the criteria for a true profession are not met in the process of organizational management, nor are they met in the functional areas of personnel and production/operations. Although some movement toward professionalization has occurred in all of these areas, it has been limited. Probably this is a good thing. Controlling entry to careers in management and the functional areas through professional school requirements, licensing, and the like may not be in the best interests of society.

Other careers based on the acquisition of knowledge in the management field do qualify as professional. These include faculty employment in colleges and universities, research appointments, and certain types of management consulting. Although not large in terms of numbers, these professions are very important to the survival and growth of the field.

</td></tr>
</table>

Consultants are specialists retained by organizations to provide services either not otherwise available or for which the hiring of a permanent staff would be too costly. The term *management consultant* actually embraces much more than the provision of services based on the knowledge of the management field; in fact it covers any consulting service to management. The concern here is with the wide range of services available from people who are expert in one or more of the areas that constitute the management field.

Management consulting may be a part-time activity (as with university faculty members), or it may be a full-time private practice, or one may be employed by or be a partner in a consulting firm. Such firms vary in size from small groups of individuals with a common interest to a large firm with offices all over the world. The degree to which management consulting is a profession varies considerably. For those with a doctoral degree providing highly specialized services to clients on an individual basis, it clearly is a profession. Within the major consulting firms—such as Booz, Allen and Hamilton, McKinsey & Co., A. T. Kearney & Co., and Cresap, McCormick and Paget—the doctorate is not required; in fact, the most typical degree is an MBA. These firms are organized and operate in much the same manner as the large law firms primarily serving corporate clients. Thus, they function as professional organizations.

Management Consulting Firms   The nature of consulting work can be illustrated with reference to these large international firms (see Exhibit 2.13). Typically when such a firm is engaged, a group of consultants works on the assignment. Usually the engagement starts with the consultants interviewing company management and analyzing company data such as financial figures. Based on these interviews, financial analyses, and other considerations, a report and recommendations eventually are developed. The company may or

EXHIBIT 2.13   Major focus of a sample of client engagements carried out by McKinsey & Company

Executive and sales compensation	19%
Organization planning	18%
Market planning	10%
Strategic planning regarding industry position	10%
Data processing and management information systems	9%
General consultation with individual executives	8%
Cost reduction	7%
Product marketing	4%
Acquisitions and mergers	3%
Inventory management and control	3%
Facilities planning	2%
Management controls	2%
Production planning and control	2%
Others	3%

may not accept the recommendations, but even if they are accepted the consultants rarely are involved in implementing them. Consultants are essentially problem solvers and planners, not doers.

Engagements to deal with a specific problem of a particular client may last from a month or so to over two years. Usually four or five consultants are involved in any such engagement, but there may be only a single partner offering advice to a chief executive, and the engagement team can well expand to fourteen or fifteen members. These are not full-time assignments, however; consultants shift back and forth from one engagement to another as client needs require.

Consulting firms use what is known as an up-or-out hiring policy. New consultants are brought in directly from advanced degree programs or after relevant business experience. They are paid well for their age and level, but they have no guarantee of permanent employment. The average person lasts three or four years; only a small minority survive to become partners in the firm. In this way costs are kept down because most of the actual consulting is done by junior personnel. The relatively few who make it to partnership ultimately are paid very well, in the hundreds of thousands. They achieve this position because they can bring in new clients and serve them well, thus retaining them for the consulting firm.

Success in this type of work requires more of a planner and thinker than a manager. Such people enjoy interaction with the leaders of the business world and elite associations in general; they like to spend their time with those in authority, yet they do not have strong motivation to manage. They are independent and intelligent, and they exhibit sound practical judgment. Generally they have exhibited upward mobility, beyond the educational and occupational levels of their mothers and fathers, since their early years.

Career Opportunities   The demand for consulting services has been expanding for a number of years. Presently, some 75 to 80 percent of all firms of substantial size use consultants. However, employment is highly responsive to changes in the economy. Companies whose profits are down tend to forgo the use of consultants, whose fees often are substantial. Some management consultants, especially partners in the major firms, make a very good living; many in private practice must spend much of their time in unpaid prospecting for clients and are not well compensated at all. In short, management consulting covers a wide range of activities, employment contexts, and income levels, and accordingly a career in the field can mean a great many different things.

Faculty Careers

Although in the past a doctoral degree was not always required for a faculty position at the college level, in the management field it now is almost a necessity. Many doctoral students also teach during the period when they are obtaining their degree, and at the junior college level a master's degree may be sufficient. Generally it takes at least four or five years after the undergraduate degree to earn the doctorate, which may be either a D.B.A. (Doctor of Business Administration) or more probably now a Ph.D. (Doctor of Philosophy). In most cases this degree is obtained from a management department, but individuals with degrees from other parts of the university may serve on a management faculty as well.

The Nature of the Work A faculty position involves teaching—conveying knowledge to students (clients) in the classroom. But there are many other aspects of the work also, even though teaching students is primary. For instance, information may be presented to students in written form via textbook writing. It may be conveyed to existing managers to combat obsolescence via management development programs. It may be used to solve organizational problems via a consulting relationship with a client company. At a more basic level, knowledge in the management field must be created and expanded through theory construction and research. Other activities include those concerning the operation of the university organization, including administration responsibilities. The job is a mixture of many activities, and the exact nature of the mix is largely up to the individual.

Requirements for Success Admission to a doctoral program primarily requires a demonstration of intellectual capabilities. One must attain high scores on measures of verbal and numerical ability and must have achieved good grades in prior academic work.

A successful career in the management field as a faculty member also depends on *professional motivation,* which is in many ways analogous to motivation to manage in the managerial sphere. The elements of professional motivation are listed in Exhibit 2.14. These motives have been found to be strongly related to various indexes of success in a professional career, while the motives that make up managerial motivation have not. Clearly, the kind of person who achieves success in the academic world is not necessarily the same kind of person who succeeds in the corporate world. Exhibit 2.15 presents information on how professional motivation relates to success as a management faculty member. The data are for more than 100 faculty members of the Academy of Management. To have a successful professional career in the management field requires not only strong intellectual capabilities but a type of motivation that is basic to professional work generally.

EXHIBIT 2.14 Elements of professional motivation

1. *Motivation to acquire knowledge.* Technical expertise and knowledge must be developed, transmitted, and used in the service of clients.
2. *Independence motivation.* There is a private and personally responsible relationship with clients of a kind that typically requires autonomous action based on individual judgment.
3. *Status motivation.* A necessary condition for practice is that clients recognize the existence of expert status. The desire for status relates to attracting and retaining clients so that available services are utilized.
4. *Motivation to provide help.* The client–professional relationship is crucial, and within that relationship clients must be helped to achieve what is in their best interest.
5. *Professional commitment.* There should be a strong tie to the profession that makes people responsive to ethics and norms, as well as keeping them from leaving the profession.

EXHIBIT 2.15 Contributions of professional motivation to success as a management faculty member

Success Indexes	Overall Professional Motivation	Motivation to Acquire Knowledge	Independence Motivation	Status Motivation	Motivation to Provide Help	Professional Commitment
Total professional compensation	√	√	√	√	√	√
University salary	√	√	√	√	√	√
Income from management development teaching	√		√	√	√	
Income from consulting	√		√		√	
Higher academic rank	√		√	√	√	√
Number of books published	√		√	√	·√	√
Number of professional journal articles	√	√	√	√	√	√
Movement to an administrative position	√	√	√	√	√	√

Adapted from John B. Miner, "The Role of Managerial and Professional Motivation in the Career Success of Management Professors," *Academy of Management Journal* (September 1980): 502.

Prospects and Opportunities   As of this writing enrollments in colleges and universities are down, but they are up in business schools and management departments. Doctoral programs in management are producing fewer graduates than in the past. In contrast to other areas of the university, therefore, opportunities in the management field are good. Whether or not this optimistic picture will hold in years to come is anyone's guess, but the generally positive employment outlook for management graduates—as managers, in personnel, in production/operations—augurs well for the employment of management professors as well.

The fact that starting college and university salaries typically do not measure up to those in the business world often is cited as a factor that diverts talented individuals from academic work. It should not do so. One consideration is the relative strength of a person's managerial and professional motivation: if an individual wants to do professional and not managerial things, letting starting salaries divert one into a dead end is foolish. Also, although university *salaries* often are not the equal of those in business, income is another matter. University professors are professionals and many types of clients seek their services, as Exhibit 2.15 indicates. Thus, professors of management can structure the mix of their activities to achieve total incomes that equal those of many managers.

Research and Development

Research and the publication of research results are important aspects of university faculty work. In addition, there are a limited number of employment opportunities in full-time research positions in universities, or in government, or in independent organizations established specifically for research purposes. Such opportunities also may exist within a company, such as the personnel research units that many of the larger corporations maintain.

This type of employment requires a doctoral degree and a solid grounding in research techniques. Opportunities of this kind have not been widely available to individuals in the management field in the past, but some modest growth can be anticipated. Salaries are variable, depending on the nature of the employing organization. Probably the major attraction is the nature of the work. Carrying out original, creative research can be a very personally satisfying activity for certain kinds of people.

Summary

This chapter has examined the different types of careers in the management field. Whether or not a student should prepare for one of these careers depends on (1) whether the student possesses the characteristics that make for success in the career; (2) whether the career is attractive in terms of the nature of the work, compensation levels, and the like; and (3) whether employment opportunities will be available.

Characteristics making for success include job-related knowledge, intelligence, values, motivation to manage, and professional motivation. The nature of the work varies considerably across the management careers, although, with the exception of the production/operations area, all tend to be concerned with human resources predominantly. Compensation levels generally are good, especially in the upper levels of corporate management and for partners in the larger consulting firms. Almost without exception the management careers present a picture of expanding opportunity in years to come. There appear to be many good practical reasons for devoting oneself to the study of management.

What Have You Learned?

1. How do formal education and experience differ as sources of knowledge, and how can these differences lead to conflicts within a company?

2. Production/operations specialists and managers do a number of different types of things and work in a variety of contexts. What are the different types of employment opportunities now and in the expected future?

3. How do professors of management prepare for their careers, and what else may they do in addition to teaching?

4. What are the major aspects of the personnel function, and how do they interrelate?

5. How do trends in the supply of intellectual and motivational talent serve to offset population and employment trends in determining future opportunities for someone seeking a career as a manager?

6. What are the characteristics of supply and demand that make the fields of personnel and production/operations a better opportunity at the present time?

7. What is intelligence, what are the major abilities involved, and how do they relate to the various management careers?

8. Both motivation to manage and professional motivation are important in career success.

What are these two types of motivation, and how exactly do they relate to success?

9. What are the criteria of a profession, and how do the various careers in the management field measure up against them?

10. Management consulting takes a variety of forms. What are these forms, and what are the chances of having a successful career in each of them?

How Well Can You Apply Your Knowledge?

Problem 1. Sitting in a professor's office waiting to go over an examination with him, a young student idly picked up a copy of the *Academy of Management Journal* dated September 1979. Glancing down the table of contents he saw titles such as "Issues in the Creation of Organizations: Initiation, Innovation, and Institutionalization"; "Impacts of Perceived Environmental Variability on Patterns of Work Related Communication"; "The Impact of Comprehensive Planning on Financial Performance"; and "Characteristics of Career Planners in Upwardly Mobile Occupations." That last one made him stop and think. He flipped to page 539 and read the abstract:

> Career variables of 277 municipal employees of a large southwestern city in upwardly mobile occupations were surveyed with a questionnaire instrument. Analysis of the collected data revealed that individuals with the most effective careers reported more extensive career planning. These results are discussed in the light of the current literature.

The article was by Sam Gould at the University of Texas, San Antonio.

The student started reading the article and found it pretty difficult to understand, especially the tables and statistics (rotated factor matrix, means and standard deviations, zero order correlations, stepwise multiple regression), but the discussion section helped some. What the article seemed to say was that people who had planned their careers—collected relevant information, figured out what they wanted to do, and developed strategies for getting there—actually did have more successful careers, in terms of movement to higher managerial levels, larger salaries, and a greater sense that their work was worthwhile.

Thinking about himself, the student realized that he probably had never devoted more than ten minutes to planning what he would do and how he would get there. He was a management major because he had to major in something and because managing seemed a little glamorous, and he had been told it paid well. That really was not much of a planning process. He decided he had better give a good deal more thought to his career objectives before he got so far committed to something he might not want that he could not get out.

Questions

1. If you were this student, how would you go about reevaluating your initial choice of a career as a manager? What factors would you take into account, and how would you weight them in reaching a decision?

2. How does the case of Jack L. at the beginning of this chapter relate to this matter of the value of early career planning for career success? Should such planning take into account non job-related factors, such as family considerations?

Problem 2. Let us work through some questions with your own situation in mind and reach some tentative conclusions regarding your future.

Questions

1. What things that people in the management field do are particularly attractive to you? In this connection, you might want to review chapter 1 and look at Exhibits 2.8, 2.10, 2.11, 2.13, and 2.15 in this chapter.

2. How do you think you stack up on the various characteristics that make for success in the careers in management? Refer to Exhibits 2.1, 2.3, 2.4, and 2.14.

3. What are the various supply and demand relationships that affect your own opportunity for

the different careers in management? Review Exhibits 2.6, 2.7, and 2.9.

Make up a table along the following lines to record the answers to these three questions:

Careers in Management

	Negative				Positive	
	1	2	3	4	5	6
Attractiveness						
Capabilities						
Opportunity						

4. At the present time how would you put this all together to reach a conclusion? Do any of the careers make sense for you, or should you look beyond the management field? If there are some that make sense, rank them. Can you combine these careers in any way? What is your tentative decision?

It is too early now to commit yourself. Wait at least until you have finished this course and read this book. But keep your tentative decision in mind as you move on.

Additional Sources for More Detailed Study

Dill, William R.; Hilton, Thomas L.; and Reitman, Walter R. *The New Managers: Patterns of Behavior and Development.* Englewood Cliffs, N.J.: Prentice-Hall, 1962.

Fernandez, John P. *Black Managers in White Corporations.* New York: Wiley, 1975.

Hall, Douglas T. *Careers in Organizations.* Pacific Palisades, Calif.: Goodyear, 1976.

Jewell, Donald O. *Women and Management: An Expanding Role.* Atlanta: College of Business Administration, Georgia State University, 1977.

Kaufman, Harold G. *Career Management: A Guide to Combating Obsolescence.* New York: Institute for Electrical and Electronics Engineers Press, 1975.

Kotter, John P.; Faux, Victor A.; and McArthur, Charles C. *Self Assessment and Career Development.* Englewood Cliffs, N.J.: Prentice-Hall, 1978.

Kubr, M. *Management Consulting: A Guide to the Profession.* Geneva, Switzerland: International Labour Office, 1976.

Larwood, Laurie, and Wood, Marion M. *Women in Management.* Lexington, Mass.: D.C. Heath, 1977.

London, Manuel, and Stumpf, Stephan A. *Managing Careers.* Reading, Mass.: Addison-Wesley, 1982.

Miner, John B. *Studies in Management Education.* Atlanta: Organizational Measurement Systems Press, 1965.

———. *Motivation to Manage: A Ten-Year Update on the "Studies in Management Education" Research.* Atlanta: Organizational Measurement Systems Press, 1977.

Schein, Edgar H. *Career Dynamics: Matching Individual and Organizational Needs.* Reading, Mass.: Addison-Wesley, 1978.

Tyler, Leona A. *Individuality: Human Possibilities and Personal Choice in the Psychological Development of Men and Women.* San Francisco: Jossey-Bass, 1978.

Watson, Tony J. *The Personnel Managers: A Study in the Sociology of Work and Employment.* London: Routledge and Kegan Paul, 1977.

The following books should prove particularly useful for the practical guidelines they contain on how to manage well.

Adizes, Ichak. *How to Solve the Mismanagement Crisis.* Homewood, Ill.: Dow Jones-Irwin, 1979.

Bonoma, Thomas V., and Slevin, Dennis P. *Executive Survival Manual: A Program for Managerial Effectiveness.* Boston: CBI, 1978.

Filley, Alan C. *The Compleat Manager: What Works When.* Champaign, Ill.: Research Press, 1978.

McFarland, Dalton E. *Action Strategies for Managerial Achievement.* New York: AMACOM, 1977.

See also *Business Week's Guide to Careers,* first published in March 1983 and now appearing with four issues per year, for up-to-date career information.

Notes

1. Abraham K. Korman and Rhoda W. Korman, *Career Success/Personal Failure,* ©1980, pp. 119–23. Reprinted by permission of Prentice-Hall, Inc., Englewood Cliffs, N.J.

2. Edwin E. Ghiselli, "The Validity of Aptitude Tests in Personnel Selection," *Personnel Psychology* (Winter 1973); John P. Campbell, Marvin D. Dunnette, Edward E. Lawler, and Karl E. Weick, *Managerial Be-*

havior, Performance and Effectiveness (New York: McGraw-Hill, 1970).

3. Martin J. Gannon, "Managerial Ignorance," *Business Horizons* (May/June 1983).

4. Abraham K. Korman and Rhoda W. Korman, *Career Success/Personal Failure* (Englewood Cliffs, N.J.: Prentice-Hall, 1980), p. 125.

5. William Whitely and George W. England, "Variability in Common Dimensions of Managerial Values Due to Value Orientation and Country Differences," *Personnel Psychology* (Spring 1980).

6. John B. Miner, "Sentence Completion Measures in Personnel Research: The Development and Validation of the Miner Sentence Completion Scales," in *Personality Assessment in Organizations,* ed. H. J. Bernardin and D. Bownas (New York: Praeger, 1985).

7. John B. Miner, *The Human Constraint: The Coming Shortage of Managerial Talent* (Atlanta: Organizational Measurement Systems Press, 1974); Arch Patton, "The Coming Flood of Young Executives," *Harvard Business Review* (September 1976); William H. Newman, *Managers for the Year 2000* (Englewood Cliffs, N.J.: Prentice-Hall, 1978).

8. Arthur Levine, *When Dreams and Heroes Died: A Portrait of Today's College Student* (San Francisco: Jossey-Bass, 1980); College Board, *National College-Bound Seniors* (New York: College Board, 1982).

9. John B. Carroll and Scott E. Maxwell, "Individual Differences in Cognitive Abilities," *Annual Review of Psychology* (1979).

10. John B. Miner and Norman R. Smith, "Decline and Stabilization of Managerial Motivation Over a 20-Year Period," *Journal of Applied Psychology* (May 1982); Richard P. Butler, Charles L. Lardent, and John B. Miner, "A Motivational Basis for Turnover in Military Officer Education and Training," *Journal of Applied Psychology* (May 1983).

11. Ann Howard and Douglas W. Bray, "Today's Young Managers: They Can Do It, But Will They?" *Wharton Magazine* (Summer 1981); Opinion Research Corporation, *Strategic Planning for Human Resources: 1980 and Beyond* (Princeton, N.J.: Opinion Research Corporation, 1980).

12. John B. Miner, *Personnel and Industrial Relations: A Managerial Approach* (New York: Macmillan, 1985).

13. U.S. Department of Labor, *Occupational Outlook Handbook, 1982–1983 Edition* (Washington, D.C.: Government Printing Office, 1982).

14. Dale Yoder and Herbert G. Heneman, *American Society for Personnel Administration (ASPA) Handbook of Personnel and Industrial Relations Volume VIII—Professional PAIR* (Washington, D.C.: Bureau of National Affairs, 1979), p. 17.

15. Edwin E. Ghiselli, *Explorations in Managerial Talent* (Pacific Palisades, Calif.: Goodyear, 1971); John B. Miner and Mary G. Miner, "Managerial Characteristics of Personnel Managers," *Industrial Relations* (May 1976).

16. John O. McClain and L. Joseph Thomas, *Operations Management: Production of Goods and Services* (Englewood Cliffs, N.J.: Prentice-Hall, 1980), p. 501.

17. See chapter 8, "Production Managers," of Thomas W. Harrell, *Managers' Performance and Personality* (Cincinnati: Southwestern, 1961).

CHAPTER 3

The Origins of Management Knowledge

CHAPTER OUTLINE

The Five Conceptual Building Blocks
The "Schools" Approach
Taylor and Scientific Management
    Contributions to Engineering and Production
      Management
    Concepts and Principles
    Gantt, the Gilbreths, and Other Disciples
Fayol and Classical Management
    Essential Activities
    Principles of Management
Weber and Bureaucracy
    Rational-Legal Authority
    The Concept of Bureaucracy
Mayo, Roethlisberger, and Human Relations
    The Hawthorne Studies
    Organizations as Social Systems
Barnard, Simon, and Decision Making
    Functions of the Executive
    Administrative Behavior
The Test of Time

Origins of the Functional Subdisciplines
The Diverse Heritage of Personnel Management
    The Law and the Courts
    The Labor Movement and Labor Relations
    Welfare Secretaries and Social Work
    Industrial Psychology
    Personnel and Employment Management
    Additional Disciplines
Origins of Production/Operations Management
    The Industrial Management Period
    Mathematics and Computers

Scientific Origins
Nonscientific Ways of Knowing
The Nature of Science
    Structure
    Goals
    Methods
Management and Science

OBJECTIVES

To identify and discuss the pioneers of the management field.

To identify and discuss the major forces, disciplines, and individuals contributing to the historical development of the subdisciplines.

To indicate the extent to which the management discipline meets scientific criteria in establishing its knowledge base.

number of years ago some members of the Academy of Management came up with the idea of having major pioneers in the field memorialized on a series of U.S. postage stamps. The intent was to tie the series to the American Bicentennial celebration, and thus only Americans could be included. Furthermore, the Postal Service requires that those honored in this way no longer be living. With these limitations in mind, a survey was conducted among knowledgeable individuals to develop a list of people to recommend. Exhibit 3.1 presents the twelve pioneers with the most votes, along with some information about them. Two Europeans who without question would have been toward the top of the list, had their names been available for consideration, have been added.

Exhibit 3.1 says several things about the origins of the management field. First, the field is not very old; the earliest date noted is 1900, although several of these individuals were developing their ideas in some form well before that date. Second, most of these pioneers were associated primarily with companies or served as consultants; only four had university careers: Mayo, Maslow, Roethlisberger, and Weber. Third, in the early period the concepts of *scientific management,* initially associated with the name of Frederick Taylor, played an important role; in addi-

EXHIBIT 3.1 Pioneers of management thought and practice

American Pioneers as Ranked by Members of the Academy of Management and Business History Conference

Name	Decade of Major Contribution	Major Institutional Affiliation
1. Frederick W. Taylor	1900s	Midvale Steel
2. Chester I. Barnard	1930s	New Jersey Bell Telephone
3. Elton Mayo	1930s	Harvard University
4. Frank B. Gilbreth	1900s	Whidden and Company
5. Lillian M. Gilbreth	1910s	Independent consultant
6. Alfred P. Sloan, Jr.	1920s	General Motors
7. Mary Parker Follett	1920s	Independent consultant
8. Henry Ford	1910s	Ford
9. Abraham H. Maslow	1940s	Brandeis University
10. Fritz J. Roethlisberger	1930s	Harvard University
11. Henry L. Gantt	1900s	Midvale Steel
12. Joseph Wharton	1900s	Bethlehem Steel
Additional European Pioneers		
Henri Fayol (France)	1910s	S. A. Commentary-Fourchambault-Décazeville
Max Weber (Germany)	1900s	University of Heidelberg

Adapted from Daniel A. Wren and Robert D. Hay, ''Management Historians and Business Historians: Differing Perceptions of Pioneer Contributors,'' *Academy of Management Journal* (September 1977):476.

tion to Taylor, the Gilbreths, Gantt, and Wharton were all concerned with this approach.

If one searches the list set forth in Exhibit 3.1 for the major thought leaders—those who introduced a way of looking at the management field that has had a major impact since—the names that emerge are the following, in order of contribution:

1. Frederick Taylor and scientific management
2. Henri Fayol and classical management theory
3. Max Weber and the concept of bureaucracy
4. Elton Mayo and Fritz Roethlisberger and the human relations movement
5. Chester Barnard (in conjunction with Herbert A. Simon, who is not included in Exhibit 3.1 because he is still living) and the decision-making approach.

In this chapter we will focus on these five sources or origins of the management field.

THE FIVE CONCEPTUAL BUILDING BLOCKS

A few words are in order regarding the individuals in Exhibit 3.1 who are neither associated with scientific management nor originators of one of the five building blocks of the field. Alfred P. Sloan was for many years chief executive officer of General Motors, where he originated a widely copied system of decentralized structure and more centralized control processes. Henry Ford, also a chief executive, was instrumental in developing the moving assembly line and one of the early personnel departments. Mary Parker Follett was an early management philosopher whose emphasis on coordination in handling conflict antedated the human relations movement. Abraham Maslow was a psychologist who contributed substantially to the development of human relations ideas, especially in the area of motivation. Joseph Wharton was a sponsor not only of scientific management but also of the first business school, at the University of Pennsylvania. These individuals and the others noted in Exhibit 3.1 will be discussed further.

The "Schools" Approach

It is common practice to consider the origins of the management field not in terms of the contributions of specific individuals, but in terms of the approaches taken by so-called schools. Schools are groups of individuals who think along the same lines and tend to emphasize common factors. One of the problems with this approach is that agreement on what the important schools are is almost impossible to obtain; two different classification systems may well assign the same pioneer to different schools.

One well-known schools approach is depicted in Exhibit 3.2. Five completely new schools were added over a roughly twenty-year period, and one of the preexisting schools was split into two parts. The six schools noted in 1961 have very little relationship to the five conceptual building blocks noted previously, and it is very difficult to match the schools with the individual pioneers of Exhibit 3.1. Students should be aware that the schools approach exists, but as an aid to understanding the origins of the management field it has often contributed little but confusion. It is indeed apt that these schools have been referred to as a "jungle," even by proponents of the approach.

EXHIBIT 3.2 The management theory jungles—1961 and 1980

Management Schools—1961	Management Schools—1980
1. *Empirical*	1. *Empirical or case*—emphasizes the study of managerial successes and failures in individual cases.
2. *Human Behavior*	2. *Interpersonal behavior*—emphasizes individuals and their motivations.
	3. *Group behavior*—emphasizes behavior of people in groups.
3. *Social Systems*	4. *Cooperative social systems*—emphasizes human relationships within cooperative social systems.
	5. *Sociotechnical systems*—emphasizes harmonizing social and technical systems.
4. *Decision Theory*	6. *Decision theory*—emphasizes the central role of decision making.
	7. *Systems*—emphasizes the systems view of organizations as an assemblage of interconnected or interdependent parts forming a complex unity.
5. *Mathematical*	8. *Mathematical or management science*—emphasizes mathematical processes, concepts, symbols, and models.
	9. *Contingency or situation*—emphasizes the idea that what managers do depends on a given set of circumstances.
	10. *Managerial roles*—emphasizes roles developed from observation.
6. *Management Process*	11. *Operational*—emphasizes concepts, principles, theory, and techniques underpinning practice.

Adapted from Harold Koontz, "The Management Theory Jungle," *Academy of Management Journal* (December 1961); idem, "The Management Theory Jungle Revisited," *Academy of Management Review* (April 1980).

Taylor and Scientific Management

Frederick W. Taylor began developing his ideas at the Midvale Steel Company in Philadelphia, primarily during the 1880s. During this period he also obtained a degree in mechanical engineering. Subsequently he became an independent consultant, but it was in the period from 1901 to 1915, when he died, that Taylor's ideas became widely known. During this period he devoted himself to publicizing and promoting scientific management.[1] Taylor's ideas were developed out of his experiences on the shop floor and as a manufacturing manager. He took out a number of patents for his inventions and largely supported himself from them from 1900 on. He did major research on the cutting of metals, and he served as president of the American Society of Mechanical Engineers in 1906.

Contributions to Engineering and Production Management Although he would have preferred that his ideas be taught as part of an engineering curriculum, Taylor helped to introduce them into the business schools of the time and thus was instrumental in starting production/operations management courses. Much of current practice in areas such as labor simplification, work measurement, and plant scheduling is based on Taylor. No other individual has had as much influence on the development of production/operations.

Concepts and Principles The four principles of management most widely cited as reflecting Taylor's views are:

1. Develop a science for each person's work: a one best way.
2. Scientifically select the best person for the job and train that person in the procedures to be followed.
3. Cooperate with the workers to insure that the work is done in the way prescribed. This should include, but not be limited to, providing for increased earning by those who follow the prescribed way most closely.
4. Divide the work so that activities such as planning, organizing, and controlling are the responsibility of management, not of the individual worker.

The first principle provided an underpinning for methods engineering and work measurement. The second and third principles provided an impetus for the personnel function, even though Taylor himself gave little direct attention to that activity. The fourth exerted a strong influence on the way factory work is organized. Taylor advocated that planning be separated from the work itself and carried out on a centralized basis. He also advocated *functional foremanship,* whereby a worker would report to a different foreman depending on the particular aspect of the work involved. As shown in Exhibit 3.3, the worker can have as many as eight bosses, if several activities are not combined in a single person.

EXHIBIT 3.3 Taylor's functional foreman concept

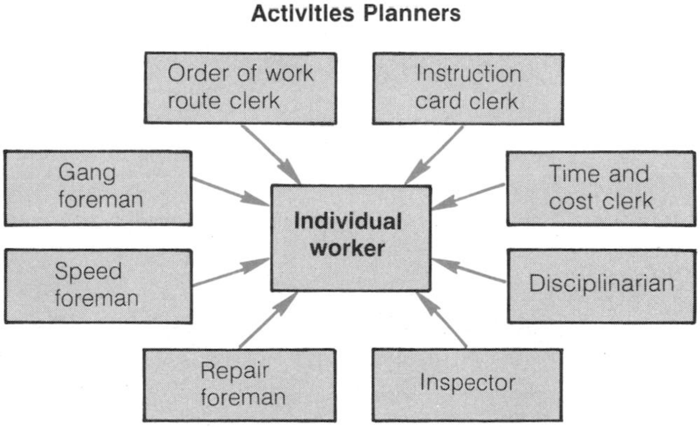

Activities Planners

Adapted from Frank B. Gilbreth and Lillian M. Gilbreth, *Applied Motion Study* (New York: Sturgis and Walton, 1917).

Another important concept was the *exception principle*. Once production standards and procedures are established through precise measurement, management should focus attention on those cases where standards either are not met or are exceeded to a sizable degree, and on instances where established procedures either are not or cannot be followed. The implication is that individuals should be dealt with one at a time. On the other hand, Taylor was well aware of how work groups can combine to restrict the productive output of individual members, a topic we will return to in considering the ideas of Mayo and Roethlisberger.

The adjective *scientific* as applied to Taylor's approach is by no means a misnomer. He advocated research and experiment in management, conducted numerous studies to establish how various jobs should be performed, and developed techniques for the controlled observation and measurement of behavior. In fact, his emphasis on studying jobs and work scientifically and measuring them precisely appears to be Taylor's greatest contribution.

Gantt, the Gilbreths, and Other Disciples A number of disciples served to spread Taylor's ideas and in some cases to develop and expand upon them as well. In most instances these individuals worked as consultants; as so often happens in such situations, many of them ultimately broke with Taylor over some matter, either personal or professional. These relationships often were strained by Taylor's tendency to elaborate upon events in order to present his theories in the most favorable light, and to use the work of disciples without giving them the appropriate credit.[2]

Henry Gantt worked with Taylor at Midvale Steel Company and was an early proponent of scientific management. He devoted more attention to personnel matters than Taylor did, particularly in the development of incentive pay plans and training methods. He also developed a variety of charts and graphic displays to depict various aspects of production, most notably scheduling. His charting methods for showing how progress toward a goal relates to planned schedules and costs are the basis for much practice today. Also, toward the end of his career, Gantt became heavily involved in formulating the social role of industry.

Like Taylor at Midvale, Frank Gilbreth rose through the ranks of Whidden and Company, starting as an apprentice bricklayer and then achieving considerable success as an independent contractor and later as a management consultant. He developed techniques for studying the motions involved in work and then reducing them, and for the investigation of fatigue. His work-study procedures included the use of motion pictures. Although the early studies on bricklaying were carried out independently of Taylor, Gilbreth later became strongly identified with the scientific management movement.

Lillian Gilbreth became Frank's wife in 1904 and joined him in his studies. She received a Ph.D. in psychology in 1915 and became one of the very early contributors to the emerging field of industrial psychology. Much of the research on fatigue was Lillian's. In addition she contributed directly to the understanding of management, including the view that the role of management is to develop individuals to their full potential. The result was a considerable humanization of scientific management. Lillian Gilbreth survived her husband (who died in 1924) by many years and subsequently applied the principles and techniques of scientific management to the homemaker role.

Fayol and Classical Management

Although Taylor's ideas had their greatest impact in the production/operations area, by focusing on the individual worker and the immediate work situation they also had considerable relevance for organizational behavior. Henri Fayol, in contrast, looked at the total organization from the top down, as a chief executive officer. His views are most relevant for organizing and organizational process and structure. In chapter 1 we considered Fayol's thinking on management functions and the mix of managerial and nonmanagerial work.

Fayol was educated as a mining engineer in France, and he conducted research in that field over a number of years. He rose through the ranks of a large coal and iron combine and became chief executive in 1888. However, his contributions to the management field came much later. His major publication appeared in 1916, when he was 75.[3] His interest in management subjects continued until his death in 1925.

Fayol's major objective in writing about management was to develop a body of theory, which he considered to be a necessary condition for instituting programs of management education. He felt that education of this kind was badly needed to supplement technical education, such as his own training in engineering. Given this early emphasis, it is rather surprising that French business education (and European education of this kind generally) developed much more slowly than in the United States.

Essential Activities   Fayol envisioned two types of theory. The first kind covered what industrial organizations and managers do; it dealt with the activities considered to be essential to the functioning of a business. The second type of theory was much more prescriptive, setting forth principles intended to guide the behavior of managers.

The essential activities of industrial organizations were six in number: technical, commercial, financial, security, accounting, and managerial. As noted in chapter 1, Fayol was concerned particularly with the managerial functions, of which five were considered primary. *Planning* was understood to include forecasting; *organizing* included staffing the structure created and evaluating performance, especially of managers; *command* involved knowing the management principles and applying them with skill; *coordination* included scheduling; and *control* included inspection.

Principles of Management   Fayol's principles of management were more extensive than Taylor's, and in some respects they appear to conflict with Taylor's views (see Exhibit 3.4). Functional foremanship, for instance, would make unity of command (principle 4) difficult, if not impossible, to achieve. Fayol, who appears to have been quite familiar with Taylor's ideas, at first seemed somewhat negative toward them; later on, he came to view the two theories as complementary, which to a large degree they are.

Initially, also, Fayol considered his ideas to be applicable across all types of organizations. However, after several frustrating experiences working in a consulting role with components of the French government, he came to question the value of these ideas in highly political, governmental contexts. Neverthe-

EXHIBIT 3.4 Fayol's principles of management

1. *Division of work.* There should be division of labor or specialization to reduce the number of objects to which attention must be given; division of work should not be carried too far, however.
2. *Authority and responsibility.* Managers should have a degree of authority based on both their positions and personal skills; they should be held responsible for outcomes in proportion to this authority.
3. *Discipline.* Discipline should prevail throughout the organization, and it should be maintained by good leadership, clear and fair agreements with employees, and appropriate penalties.
4. *Unity of command.* There should be unity of command so that a person receives orders regarding an action from one source only.
5. *Unity of direction.* There should be only one person in charge and only one plan of action, when a group of activities have the same objective; this is a principle of organization.
6. *Subordination of individual interest to general interest.* The interests of the organization should take precedence over those of individual members; means to achieve this are firmness, fair agreements with employees, and constant supervision.
7. *Remuneration of personnel.* There should be a system of payment that is fair, rewards good performance, and does not exceed reasonable limits.
8. *Centralization.* Authority should be centralized to the degree appropriate to the circumstances; moderating circumstances are firm size, aspects of the manager, reliability of subordinates, and condition of the business.
9. *Scalar chain.* There should be a chain of authority and communication up and down the hierarchical pyramid; horizontal communication between managers at the same level may be necessary when speed is essential, but it should be authorized by managers at the next higher level.
10. *Order.* Material order should prevail so that everything is in an appropriate place, and social order so that people are positioned appropriately for the task; the latter means that suitable positions should be established and documented with an organization chart, and the right people selected to fill them.
11. *Equity.* There should be kindliness and justice in the treatment of individuals throughout the organization, with the objective of obtaining loyalty and devotion in return.
12. *Stability of tenure of personnel.* Employment should be stable both in a given position and within the organization; there can be too much stability, however.
13. *Initiative.* There should be freedom to think out plans and execute them at all levels; such initiative provides a source of satisfaction and a means of motivation and is very important in difficult times.
14. *Esprit de corps.* Harmony should be encouraged continually rather than conflict and dissension; in this regard oral communication is far superior to written because it is two-way.

Adapted from Henri Fayol, *General and Industrial Management* (London: Pitman, 1949), pp. 20–41.

less, those who have followed Fayol and have spread his ideas usually claim that they can be applied universally.

Weber and Bureaucracy

Max Weber was educated in Germany as a lawyer and contributed to a number of the social science disciplines. However, he is primarily identified with sociology, a field in which he wrote widely. Our concern is with his theories of bureaucracy and organizations. Weber's views in this regard constitute a major underpinning of the subdiscipline of organizational process and structure; they were in fact the major impetus to sociological development in that area.

Weber wrote in essentially the same time period as Taylor and Fayol; he died in 1920 at age 56. Yet there is no evidence that he was aware of Fayol's ideas, or Fayol of his. Weber did know about scientific management and considered it to be highly consistent with the goals of bureaucracy as he defined it. Yet, because of the micro-level focus of scientific management, as opposed to Weber's macro-level concern, Taylor's ideas exerted no identifiable influence on bureaucratic theory. Weber's writings were translated from the original German only fragmentarily until the late 1940s.[4] Thus, they came to the United States at the same time as Fayol's, over thirty-five years after Taylor's major publications.

Rational-Legal Authority   A cornerstone of Weber's thinking is the concept of authority, and he describes various ways in which authority may be legitimized or receive its force. Chief among these is an appeal to rational-legal rules, as in our system of courts and laws. Rational-legal authority underlies the form of organization called bureaucracy (see Exhibit 3.5).

Rational-legal authority is contrasted with two other types. *Traditional* authority is personal, rather than being attached to an impersonal position, and is associated with a common upbringing of leader and follower which teaches them both to respect it. It occurs often when positions of power are filled through family membership, as in kingdoms and family-owned businesses. *Charismatic* authority is also personal, but it is based on the current interaction of leader and follower personalities, not long-standing tradition. Exceptional

---

EXHIBIT 3.5   Categories of rational-legal authority

1. A continuous rule-bound conduct of official business.
2. A specific sphere of competence (jurisdiction). This involves:
   a. A sphere of obligations to perform functions which have been marked off as part of a systematic division of labor.
   b. The provision of the incumbent with the necessary powers.
   c. That the necessary means of compulsion are clearly defined and their use is subject to definite conditions.
3. The organization of offices follows the principle of hierarchy; that is, each lower office is under the control and supervision of a higher one.
4. The rules which regulate the office may be technical rules or norms.
5. The members of the administrative staff should be completely separated from ownership of the means of production. . . . There exists, furthermore, in principle complete separation of the organization's property and the personal property of the official.
6. There is also a complete absence of appropriation of his official position by the incumbent.
7. Administrative acts, decisions, and rules are formulated and recorded in writing.
8. Legal authority can be exercised in a wide variety of different forms.

SOURCE: Max Weber, *Economy and Society,* trans. Guenther Roth and Claus Wittich (New York: Bedminster Press, 1968), pp. 218–19.

or even supernatural powers often are attributed to the leader, and the devotion of followers is complete. Examples include certain religious groups and communes where emotional ties to the leader are strong; a horrible but striking instance is the mass suicides that occured a few years ago in Guiana at the behest of the Reverend Jim Jones.

The Concept of Bureaucracy Weber devoted himself to the description of bureaucracy as a method of structuring and operating organizations; some of its characteristics are inherent in rational-legal authority. He believed that in its pure form, undiluted by other types of authority and forms of organization, bureaucracy represents the most efficient organization possible. He viewed it as a machine—precise, rapid, unambiguous, relatively free from friction, continuous in operation. He did not say that people would be happier in a bureaucracy (in fact, Weber appears at times to be slightly in awe of his creation), but when done right, bureaucracy works very well indeed.

A bureaucracy is a set of areas of jurisdiction, operated according to rules. Activities that the organization needs to engage in are assigned to jurisdictions in the form of duties. Authority to get subordinates to carry out these duties is strictly limited. There is a clear hierarchy, as with Fayol's scalar chain. Management positions presuppose thorough training in a specialized area and comprehensive knowledge of the organization's rules. After being hired, the individual enters on a career in the organization expecting to rise in the hierarchy; such appointments are made by superior authority. Certain rights of office go with a position, and these serve to protect the individual against arbitrary, personal actions by superiors. The climate is one of impersonality—in Weber's words, "without hatred or passion and hence without affection or enthusiasm." Above all else, such systems dominate through knowledge, and that is what gives them their rationality.

Mayo, Roethlisberger, and Human Relations

George Elton Mayo received a master's degree in philosophy from the University of Adelaide in Australia and later studied medicine, without obtaining a degree, in Scotland. Not long after coming to the United States he gravitated to Harvard in 1926; subsequently he became involved in research being conducted at the Hawthorne works of the Western Electric Company near Chicago. His major publications were related to this research.[5]

Fritz J. Roethlisberger was originally educated as an engineer and received a master's degree from Harvard in 1925. He joined the same research unit with Mayo and ultimately became involved in the Hawthorne studies as well. He, too, published on this subject.[6]

The work of both Mayo and Roethlisberger is generally characterized as sociological in nature, although Mayo had a strong psychiatric orientation and the Hawthorne studies proved to be a major underpinning for the organizational behavior area (to which psychologists were predominantly attracted). Both remained at Harvard throughout their careers and made major contributions to the evolving human relations movement. Mayo died in 1949 and Roethlisberger in 1974.

The Hawthorne Studies In the tradition of scientific management, the initial research attempted to determine the effects of variations in illumination on worker productivity. The results were inconclusive but indicated that something other than lighting was causing the productivity changes that did occur.

At the end of this phase of the research the studies shifted to emphasize fatigue, rest pauses, and hours of work. As indicated in the chronology (Exhibit 3.6), the Relay Assembly Test Room research was the result.

Exhibit 3.7 contains results from this study of working conditions. The striking finding is that output went up steadily. Even when there was a return to prior conditions and rest periods were reduced or hours increased, productivity did not drop back to what it was at the beginning, and for some operators it did not drop at all (see results for periods 10 and 12). Subsequent studies with a second relay assembly group and in a mica splitting test room, designed to determine whether payment procedures might account for these results, were interpreted by the researchers as evidence to the contrary. Everything pointed to the importance of social considerations—employee attitudes, the attention given the operators under experimental conditions, being given more opportunity to influence decisions, and receiving less direct supervision. This interpretation led to an extensive interviewing program designed to study attitudes throughout the plant and, much later, to a long-term employee counseling program.

The last of the original Hawthorne studies was conducted in a bank wiring room and was purely observational; no experimental changes in the circum-

EXHIBIT 3.6 Chronology of the Hawthorne Studies

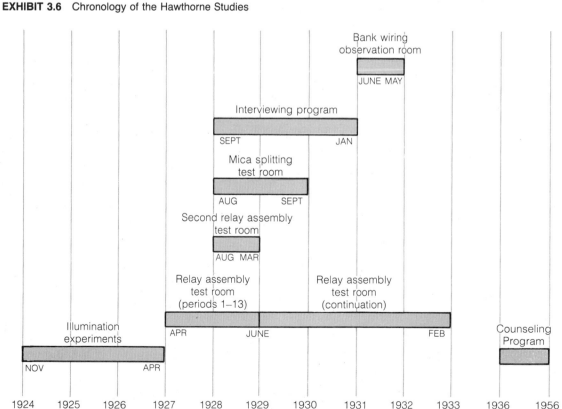

The Origins of Management Knowledge

EXHIBIT 3.7 Average hourly output per week for operators in the relay assembly test room at the Hawthorne plant

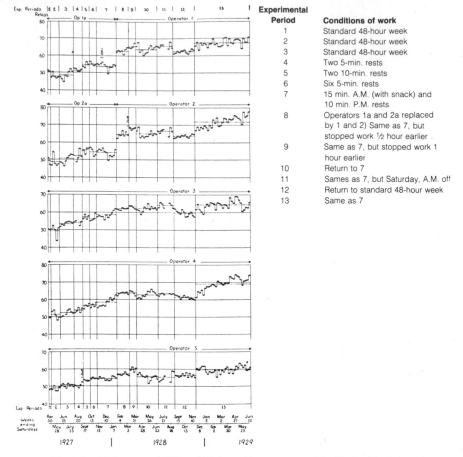

Experimental Period	Conditions of work
1	Standard 48-hour week
2	Standard 48-hour week
3	Standard 48-hour week
4	Two 5-min. rests
5	Two 10-min. rests
6	Six 5-min. rests
7	15 min. A.M. (with snack) and 10 min. P.M. rests
8	Operators 1a and 2a replaced by 1 and 2) Same as 7, but stopped work ½ hour earlier
9	Same as 7, but stopped work 1 hour earlier
10	Return to 7
11	Sames as 7, but Saturday, A.M. off
12	Return to standard 48-hour week
13	Same as 7

SOURCE: Fritz J. Roethlisberger and William J. Dickson, *Management and the Worker* (Cambridge, Mass.: Harvard University Press, 1967), p. 76. Reprinted by permission.

stances of work were introduced. Again, major social and group processes were found. The researchers "discovered" a tendency for groups to force individual members to hold down production to a group norm—to protect the less capable members and to keep management from raising standards. Actually this practice of output restriction had been a major concern of Taylor's and had been discussed widely in the scientific management literature for some time. The researchers also found certain sociometric relationships within the larger group—informal cliques, isolates, and the like—that related to productivity.

Organizations as Social Systems Mayo and Roethlisberger proposed that the social factor had been badly overlooked, and that a full understanding of factory work required going beyond the considerations emphasized by scientific management to matters such as employee attitudes, social motives, and group processes (especially informal processes). Thus the human relations movement was born, and a major part of the foundation for the organizational behavior subdiscipline was put in place. A number of the larger companies soon instituted human relations training programs for supervisors, as well as attitude surveys (the Hawthorne interviewing program was one such approach) and counseling programs designed to improve employee attitudes.

Mayo and Roethlisberger, writing independently, emphasized the importance of social needs and sentiments, in addition to economic needs, in work and productivity. They stressed the role of informal groups and organizations and the need for equilibrium between these and the technical and formal organizations. Roethlisberger, in particular, was concerned with problems of communication, especially interpersonal communication (as between supervisor and worker). Communication and listening skills were stressed as crucial to effective managing.

The idea that industrialization had disrupted traditional social relationships was important in Mayo's thinking. Workers were frustrated in a social sense; informal groups, restriction of output, and the like represented their attempts to deal with social frustration. A new social code had to be reestablished to facilitate collaboration in industrial organizations. Without it workers would continue to experience social deprivation and a kind of social pathology; productivity would suffer as a result.

Barnard, Simon, and Decision Making

Chester I. Barnard attended Harvard and majored in economics. He went on to a distinguished managerial career with Bell Telephone, as noted in chapter 1, and also held a number of high positions in government, as well as serving as president of the Rockefeller Foundation. He was strongly influenced by and himself influenced the work of Mayo, Roethlisberger, and others at Harvard. Although it has been common practice to consider his ideas, and those of Mary Parker Follett, in conjunction with the human relations movement, both Follett and Barnard were influenced by other sources as well and made independent contributions to management thought. Follett, for instance, was strongly influenced by scientific management; Barnard read Weber in the German long before Weber's writings were translated into English, and this influence shows.

Barnard's ideas are most distinctive concerning formulating purpose for the organization, decision making, and the implementation of decisions. In this regard he was closer to the management policy and strategy subdiscipline than any of the other pioneers. Barnard published his major book in 1938.[7] This book and subsequent contacts up until Barnard's death in 1961 influenced Herbert Simon in numerous ways; the Barnard-Simon formulations initiated a continuing emphasis in the management field on understanding organizations through a study of their decision-making processes. Simon received his Ph.D. in political science and has been on the faculty at Carnegie-Mellon University for many years, currently with appointments in psychology and computer science. He has received a Nobel prize in economics. Although Simon has written widely, we are concerned here with historical origins and thus with that part of his work most closely tied to Barnard.[8]

Functions of the Executive   Barnard's concept of the organization extended beyond the traditional boundaries to include investors, customers, suppliers, and the like. He utilized an *open systems* approach, wherein the organization is seen as being in constant interaction and exchange with its environment. Decisions must be made in order to adjust to this environment and thus to maintain a stable equilibrium between the organization and the environment. Here Barnard seemed to be talking about strategy formulation of a kind that has now become a major concern in management policy and strategy.

Organizations are effective primarily because they can achieve *cooperative* efforts from a number of individuals who, as a total, integrated system, represent more than the sum of the individual efforts. Individuals are induced to contribute to such a cooperative system through the use of various incentives, including pay. One of the things they give is a willingness to follow authority. Thus Barnard's view of authority is bottom up, and by the consent of the governed. Individuals decide what range of authority they will let the organization exercise over them, and within this range they will do whatever they are told—the *zone of indifference*. The size of this zone is influenced by the inducements offered: the more the organization gives, the wider the range of personal discretion the individual is willing to give up.

How this so-called *acceptance* theory of authority and the zone of indifference work may be illustrated from the consulting field. A consultant working for a large firm expects to be away from home overnight during the regular work week, and it is a matter of indifference whether this involves being sent to Seattle, St. Louis, or San Antonio. However, spending weekends away from home is another matter; such a requirement would meet with considerable resistance. But a change in inducements—perhaps the offer of a partnership in the firm—could shift the balance in this regard so that contributing weekends away from home, when requested by the managing partner, might well be accepted with no questions at all.

When organizational authority is viewed in this way, maintaining authority becomes a difficult and important problem, and communication plays a significant role in solving this problem (see Exhibit 3.8). The goal is to structure the communication system so that individuals decide to accept formal authority, with the result that a cooperative organization is fostered.

Decisions involve choices among alternatives, and Barnard strongly emphasized the role of intuition and nonlogical processes in these choices; in this he appears to have been influenced by his association with the Hawthorne researchers. Simon, on the other hand, has consistently advocated a more rational, logical approach to decision making while recognizing that most decisions necessarily fall short of full rationality.

Administrative Behavior   Simon develops decision making as the key to understanding organizations much more explicitly than Barnard. Simon draws heavily on Barnard's ideas with regard to inducements, contributions, authority, and the zone of indifference, while rejecting certain others (such as nonlogical processes). But Simon's views on the role of decisions appear to be his own.

Simon's argument is that the all-knowing, rational decision maker as conceptualized in economic theory is a figment of economists' imaginations. This argu-

EXHIBIT 3.8 Barnard's principles of organizational communication systems for maintaining formal authority

Premises
1. A communication has the presumption of authority when it originates at sources of organization information—a communications center—better than individual sources. . . . This is the authority of *position*.
2. Some people have superior ability. Their knowledge and understanding regardless of position command respect. . . . This is the authority of *leadership*.

Accordingly
3. When the authority of leadership is combined with the authority of position, people who have an established connection with an organization generally will grant authority, accepting orders far outside the zone of indifference.

Principles
1. Channels of communication should be definitely known.
2. Objective authority requires a definite formal channel of communication to every member of an organization.
3. The line of communication must be as direct or short as possible.
4. The complete line of communication should usually be used.
5. Competence of the persons serving as communication centers, that is, officers, supervisory heads, must be adequate.
6. The line of communication should not be interrupted during the time the organization is to function.
7. Every communication should be authenticated . . . the person communicating must be known actually to occupy the "position of authority" concerned; the position includes the type of communication concerned—that is, it is "within its authority"; and it actually is an authorized communication from this office.

Adapted from Chester I. Barnard, *The Functions of the Executive* (Cambridge, Mass.: Harvard University Press, 1968), pp. 173–81.

ment is set forth in Exhibit 3.9 along with Simon's concept of *satisficing* and administrative man. Within an organization the decision process follows a set course:

1. *Substantive planning,* which involves broad decisions regarding values, methods to obtain them, and the necessary knowledge and skills.
2. *Procedural planning,* which involves decisions regarding ways of directing attention and channeling information to conform to the substantive plan.
3. *Execution* based on day-to-day, operating decisions.

These steps serve to increasingly restrict alternatives, consistent with the idea of bounded rationality. Toward this end the work is divided up among individuals, standard practices are established, decisions are communicated through the organization, and people are trained as appropriate to their particular decision-making jurisdiction. Using this decision-making approach, Simon deals with many aspects of organizational structure and process. The result is a way of looking at organizations in their entirety.

EXHIBIT 3.9 Economic man and administrative man—the line of argument

Economic Man—Full Rationality	Administrative Man—Bounded Rationality
1. Economic man maximizes—selects the best alternative from among all those available to him.	1. Administrative man satisfices—looks for a course of action that is satisfactory or "good enough."
2. Economic man deals with the "real world" in all its complexity. (He is rational.)	2. Administrative man recognizes that the world he perceives is a drastically simplified model of the buzzing, blooming confusion that constitutes the real world.
3. Rationality requires a complete knowledge and anticipation of the consequences that will follow on each choice.	3. Knowledge of consequences is always fragmentary. Since these consequences lie in the future, imagination must supply the lack of experienced feeling.
4. Rationality requires a choice among all possible alternative behaviors.	4. In actual behavior only a very few of all possible alternatives ever come to mind.

Resolution in Favor of Satisficing, Administrative Man

1. It is impossible for the behavior of a single, isolated individual to reach any high degree of rationality. The number of alternatives he must explore is so great, the information he would need to evaluate them so vast that even an approximation to objective rationality is hard to conceive.
2. Administrative man is able to make his decisions with relatively simple rules of thumb that do not make impossible demands upon his capacity for thought. . . . He makes his choices using a simple picture of the situation that takes into account just a few of the factors that he regards as most relevant and crucial.

Adapted from Herbert A. Simon, *Administrative Behavior* (New York: Free Press, 1947 and 1957), pp. xxv, xxvi, 79, 81.

The Test of Time

We have considered a number of propositions about how organizations should be structured and should operate. These formulations span some fifty years, but over thirty-five years have elapsed since the last of them, and in most cases the intervening span is considerably longer than that. These have been busy years for the field of management and new knowledge has accumulated at a rapid rate. Accordingly the student is cautioned not to accept the ideas of Taylor, Fayol, Weber, and the others uncritically. These ideas are important because they set the tone and direction for what followed, not because they have weathered the test of time and stand as strong as when first proposed. Several of these ideas have not survived very well at all.

Taylor's ideas have influenced practice in many respects, but their impact often has been muted and uneven.[9] Functional foremanship has not proved to be very effective. Incentive compensation for factory workers has been found to exert an overall positive impact on productivity, but it does not eliminate group norms that restrict output. The idea of "one best way" fails to take into account individual differences, and recent work on job redesign and enlargement has superseded many of Taylor's views in this regard. Under certain circumstances considerable planning, organizing, and controlling should be left to the individual worker. Taylor's formulation of employee motivation in essentially economic terms has proved to be a major oversimplification. In short, the current status of scientific management, while remaining strong in the engineering and production management areas from which it came, is much weaker in other areas of management. Within the organizational behavior subdiscipline, with which it is clearly allied, scientific management is now largely outdated.

We have already contrasted Fayol's views on management functions with the research findings regarding them in chapter 1 and have noted some of the problems in this area. Fayol's other ideas, especially his principles of management and the original claims to universality of application across all types of organizations, have come under considerable attack, often with justification. Simon begins his book *Administrative Behavior* with a critique of classical management theory as logically inconsistent, ambiguous, and lacking in research support. Others in the human relations tradition have emphasized a failure to consider the human element in organizations. As guides to practice, Fayol's ideas now appear to be of very limited value.[10] The following quote provides a good perspective:

> Inevitably the debt we owe to Fayol diminishes as time and greater complexity make his day and age seem more and more remote. At the time his attempt, the only one of its kind, to build a basic theory of management was invaluable. It was incomplete . . . too narrow . . . , but there was a great deal of value in it . . . there are, for those who can separate the wheat from the chaff, principles and guidelines in Fayol's work which we would do well to remember today.[11]

In a number of respects Weber's concept of bureaucracy has survived the test of time rather well. Problems include (1) the role of professionals within bureaucratic systems; (2) some of the aspects of organization that define bureaucracy (such as the degree to which authority is centralized); (3) the lack of comprehensiveness and somewhat outdated nature of the treatment of authority; (4) certain negative consequences of bureaucracy, such as restriction of output; and (5) disagreements about what Weber actually said.[12] Nevertheless, much of the current thinking regarding organizational process and structure still comes straight from Weber.

Recently, extensive statistical analyses have been carried out on the original Hawthorne data, using techniques not available at the time of the studies themselves. The findings indicate that much of the change in productivity can be traced to factors such as the replacement of operators 1a and 2a by operators 1 and 2 (see Exhibit 3.7), the advent of the Depression and its continuing effects over the latter years of the relay assembly test room study, the reduction of fatigue through opportunities for rest, and the use of pay incentives.[13] These findings cannot rule out the effects of social factors entirely, since these factors were never measured directly, but they leave much less room for their influence than Mayo and Roethlisberger posited. Thus, a major cornerstone of the human relations approach now appears to be very shaky indeed. The Hawthorne studies did lead to increasing concern over individual attitudes, social motivation, work group processes, and the like; this concern is an important, continuing contribution, even though the research itself appears to have been largely misinterpreted by Mayo, Roethlisberger, and many others.

The views of Barnard and Simon overlap so much that subsequent evaluations have tended to treat them as a whole. However, Simon's advocacy of the pursuit of rationality, to the degree possible, has withstood the test of time better than Barnard's championing of nonlogical processes and intuition. The formulations regarding administrative and economic man, satisficing, and bounded rationality have been found to be valid as far as they go, but these concepts are no longer sufficient to deal with the full complexity of organizational decision making. Inducements-contributions, the zone of indifference, and the acceptance theory of authority have proved to be useful concepts; so too has Barnard's stress on the importance of the organizational environment. Like Weber's, the ideas of Barnard and Simon have survived into the present reasonably intact.

ORIGINS OF THE FUNCTIONAL SUBDISCIPLINES

In the previous section we touched at various points on historical developments related to personnel management and production/operations management. We will now explore the many aspects of the evolution of these areas.

The Diverse Heritage of Personnel Management

Of the pioneers considered, Taylor and certain of his disciples and the Hawthorne researchers contributed most to the development of personnel management. Yet neither group moved far toward establishing this human resources activity as a separate unit. The scientific management people stressed selection and placement as well as incentive compensation and employee training, but in practice they did little in any area except compensation. Taylor's disciplinarian role could have served as the beginning of a personnel department, but because functional foremanship was rarely implemented this was not the way the personnel departments started. The Hawthorne researchers stressed attitude study and employee counseling, as well as human relations training for supervisors, but they ignored labor unions completely; they contributed primarily a philosophy and a handful of techniques to the development of the personnel area.

Exhibit 3.10 sets forth an abbreviated chronology of the forces contributing to the emergence of the personnel area.

The Law and the Courts   As is evident in Exhibit 3.10, court cases and both state and federal legislation have played an important role in the development of personnel work. Initially the emphasis was on legal matters related to unions and their recognition as bargaining agents. This concern with labor law has continued, but other aspects of employment law have developed. In the early period, child labor, the minimum wage, hours of work, safety, and worker's compensation were of major concern; the range has increased rapidly in recent years, especially with the passage of equal employment opportunity laws. From a very early time, labor and employment lawyers have exerted a strong influence on the ways in which the personnel function has developed.

EXHIBIT 3.10 Selected chronology of the development of personnel management

1842	In the case of *Commonwealth vs. Hunt* the state of Massachusetts finds that unions are not an illegal conspiracy.
1880	The Yale and Towne Manufacturing Company initiates a suggestion system.
1884	A Bureau of Labor is established in the federal government.
1886	Formation of the American Federation of Labor (AFL), headed by Samuel Gompers.
1888	The first federal labor law is passed regulating the railroad industry.
1889	Welfare secretaries appear in U.S. industry providing social work services to employees.
1890	James McKeen Cattell, one of the early psychologists, begins his work on mental tests.
1898	The Erdman Act further defines labor relations in the railroad industry.
1900	B. F. Goodrich Company establishes an employment department.
1902	National Cash Register Company establishes a labor department.
1912	Massachusetts enacts a minimum wage law; personnel departments in the modern mode begin to appear; first employment managers association is formed in Boston.
1913	The U.S. Department of Labor is established; Hugo Muensterberg publishes the first major work in industrial psychology.
1914	The Clayton Act furthers the development of unions; Lillian Gilbreth publishes *The Psychology of Management*.
1915	Dartmouth College introduces the first training program for employment managers.
1916	Federal legislation on child labor is passed; army psychological tests are developed to screen recruits; the *Journal of Applied Psychology* is established.
1919	The first personnel consulting firm is created: the Scott Co.
1920	The first personnel management text is published: *Personnel Administration* by Ordway Tead and Henry C. Metcalf.
1923	First vice-president of personnel is appointed at A.T.&T.
1926	Railway Labor Act is passed.
1931	The Davis-Bacon Act provides for paying prevailing wages on federal construction contracts.
1932	The Norris-LaGuardia Act furthers the development of unions.
1935	Social Security is initiated; the Wagner Act makes unions a stable reality in U.S. industry.
1937	The U.S. Supreme Court holds the Wagner Act to be constitutional.

Based in large part on a chronology in Wendell L. French, *The Personnel Management Process* (Boston: Houghton Mifflin, 1982), pp. 650–56.

The Labor Movement and Labor Relations   Exhibit 3.10 also reveals the growth of the labor movement, often in close association with legal developments. Personnel departments were often formed to protect the company against legal claims and against the demands of unions. Although unions existed back into the 1700s and there were strikes then, the law of the times viewed unions as conspiracies against society, and accordingly unions tended to be localized and weak. Subsequently there were numerous attempts to establish national and international organizations, but periodic depressions thwarted these efforts again and again. It was not until the late 1800s that the demands of organized labor became loud enough to warrant management attention on a substantial scale. From then on, companies increasingly employed labor relations specialists to deal with and bargain with the unions.

Welfare Secretaries and Social Work   Another response to unionization was the employment of what became known as welfare or social secretaries who were to identify with the workers and help them with housing, legal matters, medical care, education, and recreational activities, as well as suggesting improvements in the conditions of work. Typically the objective was to supplant a union and leave it with no viable role. Increasingly these individuals engaged in counseling; the first full-scale department for this purpose was introduced by Henry Ford in 1914. Thus, the social welfare tradition in personnel management began, a tradition which has subsequently proved hard to live down. Even today, personnel managers sometimes find themselves accused of being "bleeding hearts" and worker advocates, rather than loyal contributors to management goals. In any event the ranks of labor lawyers and labor relations specialists were now joined by the social workers.

Industrial Psychology   At roughly the same time, psychologists became increasingly interested in problems of work and employment. Important in the early period, as noted in Exhibit 3.10, were Lillian Gilbreth, in the tradition of scientific management; James McKeen Cattell at Columbia University, with his studies of psychological testing; and Hugo Muensterberg at Harvard, who significantly advanced the application of psychological techniques to employee selection. From these beginnings came the profession of industrial psychology, which now staffs most personnel research units in the larger companies.

Personnel and Employment Management   The final factor noticeable in Exhibit 3.10 is the rise of more generalized personnel management itself. Personnel departments spread rapidly between 1900 and World War I, and associations of personnel managers were formed in local areas. The scope of the early departments was not great by modern standards, and the focus was almost entirely at the worker level, not management. Nevertheless, activities concerning compensation, selection, working conditions, grievances, training, and record keeping were brought together under one roof, and a new organizational function was born.

Additional Disciplines   Exhibit 3.10 highlights the origins of personnel in law, labor relations, social work, and psychology and notes the gradual emergence of the personnel area itself as a separate entity. A number of other disciplines also contributed to the unusually diversified heritage of the field. In many respects personnel management has been, and still is, a collection of varied professions and specialties rather than a single entity.

From a relatively early time physicians have been concerned with health hazards in industry, and industrial medicine is a recognized medical specialty, usually practiced within the personnel department. Safety management is also a component of personnel to which safety engineers have been the major contributors. The field of education, and industrial education in particular, has had a long-standing impact on the development of training techniques and programs, including apprenticeship systems. Economists have been particularly concerned with human resource planning and wage and salary administration. Accountants have been actively involved in benefits and retirement planning, and thus increasingly in labor relations activities, as these have become bargaining issues. Journalists have been employed in industry for many years to write and produce employee publications.

Its diverse origins have made personnel work a stimulating and dynamic activity, but as so often happens, they have also contributed to the internal conflicts that have plagued the evolution of the area. Perhaps a more homogeneous heritage would have made the developmental path a little less rocky.

Origins of Production/ Operations Management

The Industrial Management Period Exhibit 3.11 outlines the development of the production function. The early years dealt essentially with the evolution of the factory system and the role of both specialization of work assignments and technology. There is little here that relates directly to modern production/operations management; this subdiscipline really began with scientific management. In its heyday, traveling under the title of industrial management, and

---

EXHIBIT 3.11 Selected chronology of the development of production management

1776	Adam Smith discusses division of labor in manufacturing.
1798	Eli Whitney develops and engineers the idea of interchangeability of parts.
1800	The growth of the factory system with the aid of steam power reaches the proportions of an *industrial revolution* in England.
1832	Charles Babbage extends Adam Smith's views on the advantage of specialization in manufacturing.
1900	The ideas of Frederick Taylor begin to have increasing impact, and scientific management is born.
1913	The moving assembly line is introduced by Henry Ford based on principles of interchangeability and synchronization.
1915	F. W. Harris develops an economic lot size model for inventory control.
1931	Statistical quality control is invented by Walter Shewhart.
1934	L. H. C. Tippett applies statistical sampling procedures to work measurement.
1935	H. F. Dodge and H. G. Romig extend statistical sampling in quality control and inspection.
	Walter Rautenstrauch invents the break-even chart.

riding on the scientific management balloon, the production area was synonymous with the management field as a whole. One textbook as late as 1947, entitled *Industrial Management,* dealt with:

Fundamental Considerations in Industry

Organization Structure

The Plant and Equipment

Motion and Time Study

Wage Payment

Buying, Selling, and Transportation

Material and Production Control

Personnel Administration and Management[14]

This comprehensive concept has increasingly been eroded to produce the very different picture of the management field set forth in chapter 1. Production management, or industrial management, has moved from center stage to share its position with a number of other areas.

Mathematics and Computers   As we move beyond the Taylor era in Exhibit 3.11, what emerges is a marked emphasis on the development of quantitative techniques having origins in statistics, economics, and engineering. Even the addition of the term *operations management* in the 1950s reflected the significant role operations research techniques now played in dealing with production problems.

The history and origins of the production/operations management area are clearly quite different from what we found in personnel management. In contrast to the diversity and breadth of the latter area, production/operations has narrowed its emphasis and focused on a set of quantitative techniques, augmented in recent years by the expansion of computer technology. Both areas have achieved success, but out of very different origins and following completely different paths.

SCIENTIFIC ORIGINS

A question often raised is whether the field of management has its origins in science. Is the practice of management, either as a manager or as a specialist in one of the functional areas of organization, solidly grounded in scientific theory and research, as for example is the case with medicine? To answer this question we must consider alternative ways of knowing things, other than through science, and develop a definition of science.

Nonscientific Ways of Knowing

Beliefs can be established or defended in three ways that are not scientific in nature.[15] One is *tenacity:* something is accepted as fact on faith, simply because it always has been believed to be true. Habit plays an important role here, and contradictory evidence is ignored. One problem with tenacity as a way of knowing is that people can hold contradictory versions of the "facts" for long periods of time without a resolution, because there is no way of determining which tenaciously held view is to win out.

Another way of knowing something is because some highly respected *authority* held it to be true. Thus, for many years Fayol's views were perpetuated in practice simply on the grounds that "Fayol said so." Once again, two authorities may say different things, as Fayol and Taylor appeared to do on the subject of functional foremanship, and no method of resolution is readily available.

Third, one may know based on *intuition:* something is true because it is so obvious and self-evident that it could not be false. This is the approach to managerial decision making that Barnard favored and Simon did not. Again, one person's intuition may not be the same as another person's, and no basis exists for deciding between the two.

The Nature of Science

A problem with tenacity, authority, and intuition as sources of knowledge is that they are inherently subjective—truth is defined within some individual. Science, on the other hand, seeks objectivity—something beyond individual opinion—through reliance on data, observations, experiments, and the like. Scientific method, accordingly, is a way of approaching the world objectively in order to resolve differences of opinion and move closer to truth.

Science is defined in part by its methods, the ways in which scientific inquiry is conducted. It is also defined by its structure and its goals.

Structure   Science is structured in terms of a number of disciplines which seek its goals and utilize its methods. Often a distinction is made between social sciences (such as economics, sociology, and psychology) and physical sciences (such as chemistry, physics, and engineering). Each of these sciences seeks to provide a set of internally (logically) consistent hypotheses, principles, laws, and theories dealing with some aspect of knowledge. Many of the physical sciences meet this criterion and thus may be said to be mature. Many of the social sciences only approximate such a logically interrelated body of knowledge; this, however, does not make them any less sciences. In contrast with disciplines in the humanities and arts, they do seek the goals and utilize the methods of science.

The management discipline, at the present time, appears to be one of the social sciences. Its historical origins, however, are distinctly mixed, as are those of almost every other science. Its pioneers include engineers such as Taylor, Fayol, and Roethlisberger, but also social scientists such as Weber and Simon. In addition, some early contributors were not trained in science or did not complete the usual requirements to qualify as scientific professionals—Mayo and Barnard, for instance. At one time, much of the writing in the field of management was more philosophical than scientific. This is no longer true; anyone who might question this conclusion should spend a few hours browsing through some of the major journals in the field: the *Academy of Management Journal, Academy of Management Review, Administrative Science Quarterly, Organizational Behavior and Human Performance, Industrial Relations,* and the like.

Goals   A science seeks to describe and explain some area of knowledge and thus to gain *understanding.* The Hawthorne studies, for instance, were an attempt to understand what might account for differences in productivity. Another goal of science is *predicting* events in the future. Much personnel research, for example, is devoted to finding selection procedures that can be used at hiring to predict performance levels later, on the job. In an applied science, understanding and prediction are joined by the goal of *influencing* or managing the future. Fayol's principles of management, whatever their shortcomings, were intended to provide a means of organizing and operating an organization to achieve a high level of effectiveness. Thus, he sought to provide ways for a company to control its movement toward achieving its goals.

Methods   Scientific method consists of theorizing and research. A model of the process involved is given in Exhibit 3.12. These steps are carried out according to the rules of science. One of the important rules is to define concepts clearly in terms of the procedures used to measure them. In this way research can be repeated (replicated), so that others may duplicate the research and agree that the findings are indeed objectively true. In the first relay assembly study of the Hawthorne research, for instance, the substitution of operators 1 and 2 for la and 2a occurred without sufficient information to permit doing exactly the same thing over again, and thus the productivity findings would be hard to repeat.

Another rule is to control observations so that causation can be attributed correctly. This is what experimental design seeks to achieve. Again, the relay assembly room research may be used as an example. If the study had been conducted in the original manner but had also used a second group, a *control group*—in which everything was identical except that no experimenter-observer was present and changes in experimental conditions (rest pauses, hours of work, and so on) were merely flashed on a screen rather than discussed extensively—then the effects of various social factors could have been determined directly by comparing the two circumstances.

Third, science is concerned with generalizing beyond the immediate situation in which the research is conducted, and this requires appropriate sampling. In the Hawthorne studies, more people should have been studied (a number of relay assembly test rooms, for instance), and the people themselves—the research *subjects*—should have been selected at least to be typical of people doing this kind of work in the particular plant. These circumstances, too, were not present. Accordingly, it is not possible to say even that the findings apply to the whole Hawthorne works of the period 1927–1933.

Finally, insofar as possible, the theorizing that underlies research must be "good" in and of itself. Good theory is testable, is logically consistent within itself, and has clearly stated boundaries within which it applies.

Management and Science

In its historical origins the management discipline fulfills our criteria of science in various ways, but there are wide disparities as well. Often the origins we have considered represent subjective opinion more than objective fact, and philosophical speculation more than scientific theory. Such a beginning is not all that surprising, given the histories of other scientific disciplines.

Importantly, the field has increasingly moved in the direction of science. At present its goals and methods are consistent with the criteria we have considered, and the management discipline now occupies a niche within the scientific structure.

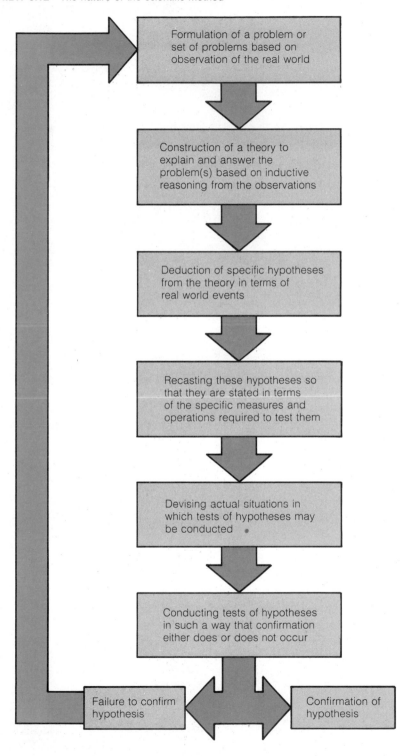

EXHIBIT 3.12 The nature of the scientific method

Formulation of a problem or set of problems based on observation of the real world

Construction of a theory to explain and answer the problem(s) based on inductive reasoning from the observations

Deduction of specific hypotheses from the theory in terms of real world events

Recasting these hypotheses so that they are stated in terms of the specific measures and operations required to test them

Devising actual situations in which tests of hypotheses may be conducted

Conducting tests of hypotheses in such a way that confirmation either does or does not occur

Failure to confirm hypothesis

Confirmation of hypothesis

EXHIBIT 3.13 Parts of this book and the related origins

Origins	Parts of This Book				
	2 Influencing and Organizational Behavior	3 Organizing and Organizational Process/Structure	4 Planning and Management Policy/Strategy	5 Staffing and Personnel/Human Resources Management	6 Management Process and Production/Operations Management
Taylor and Scientific Management	✓			✓	✓
Fayol and Classical Management		✓			
Weber and Bureaucracy		✓			
Mayo, Roethlisberger, and Human Relations	✓			✓	
Barnard, Simon, and Decision Making		✓	✓		
Law, Labor Relations, Social Work, Psychology, etc.				✓	
The Factory System and Quantitative Methods from Economics, Engineering, etc.					✓

Summary   The major pioneers of the management field have contributed five conceptual building blocks. Exhibit 3.13 lists these building blocks and those of the two subdisciplines concerned with functional areas of organization, along with the parts of this book for which they are relevant. This approach to understanding the historical origins of the management discipline appears preferable to a "schools" approach, because of the ambiguities inherent in the latter. In considering historical origins, one must recognize that yesterday's truths may not be lasting. Old theories often are superseded by new, and this typically has been the case in the management field.

Personnel/human resources management and production/operations management have developed in very different ways. The former has been characterized by great diversity throughout its history, while the latter has narrowed increasingly to focus on quantitative techniques. Yet both have contributed an abundance of useful knowledge and effective guidelines for practice.

The pioneers and sources contributing to the development of the management field are extremely diverse. Although some sought scientific goals and utilized scientific methods, others did not. Each theory appears "good" by some criteria, and not so good by others. But over time the management discipline has come to conform to the criteria of a science, and it now has as legitimate a claim to that title as any other of the social sciences.

What Have You Learned?

1. What are the structure, goals, and methods of science?

2. In what ways do Herbert Simon's early views go beyond those of Chester Barnard? In what ways are they the same? Where do the two disagree?

3. What are the multiple heritages of the personnel area, and what specific personnel activities have been influenced most by each of these forces or disciplines?

4. What are Henri Fayol's principles of management, and what is their current status?

5. What advantages result from the use of a scientific approach to knowing, as contrasted with various other ways of knowing?

6. What is the schools approach to the origins of management, and what problems exist in using it?

7. How have recent analyses and critiques of the Hawthorne studies altered the interpretation of them? What problems in the design and conduct of these studies make them difficult to interpret?

8. How has the development of production/operations management differed from that of personnel management? What have been the consequences of these differences for the role of production/operations in the management field as a whole?

9. What is rational-legal authority as contrasted with other types, and how does it relate to Max Weber's concept of bureaucracy?

10. What are the major features of Frederick Taylor's scientific management, and how well have they withstood the test of time?

How Well Can You Apply Your Knowledge?

Problem 1.   The year is 1912. The president of a large steel fabricating firm has just made a visit to Frederick Taylor's home in Germantown, Pennsylvania, spent the night there, and during the next morning listened enthusiastically to Taylor's presentation of the virtues of scientific management. At the end of the presentation, Taylor and the president discussed how scientific management might be implemented in the company's plants, and a decision was made to start at a location nearby, in the Philadelphia area. Taylor has suggested that a colleague of his, who has had extensive experience in such matters and whom he personally considers one of the best engineering minds in the country, be brought in as a consultant to assist in the lengthy process of converting the plant to scientific management. The president has agreed, and subsequently, he and the consultant have arranged a meeting at the pilot plant location. There the consultant outlines what is involved in making the plant a model of scientific management.

Question

If you were this consultant, what would you propose to the president? What procedures would you advocate introducing, and what steps to introduce them?

The year is 1938. The president of the same steel fabricating company has contacted a consulting firm known to have a large practice in the personnel area to see if anyone on their staff can tell him about the work on employee productivity done in the Western Electric Company a few years back. He is interested in doing anything he can to improve productivity. The company introduced scientific management techniques some twenty-five years ago, and many vestiges of that effort still remain, but over the years the approach has not accomplished as much as many had hoped. A friend at Harvard seems to think the Western Electric experiment might provide some insights into why scientific management has not worked out better, and what can be done about it.

The consulting firm has put one of their people in touch with the president. This particular individual has been employed at the Hawthorne Works up until recently and is thoroughly familiar with the studies there and with the recently initiated counseling program. He knows Elton Mayo and Fritz Roethlisberger and has discussed their views with them at considerable length. The consultant and the president spend a good deal of time together, and the president gradually becomes convinced that the Hawthorne studies have major implications for his firm. He asks the consultant to outline what would be involved in putting the ideas from Hawthorne to work to improve the productivity of his Philadelphia plant.

Question

If you were this consultant, what would you propose to the president? What procedures would you advocate introducing, and what steps to introduce them?

The year is 1983. At another company's board of directors' meeting, the president of the same steel fabricating firm has gotten into a discussion with a business school dean whose specialty is organizational behavior. The president recounts his firm's experiences with scientific management and a human relations approach over some sixty years and wonders why neither has been entirely successful.

Question

If you were the dean, how would you answer the president?

Problem 2. A young psychologist who had just joined the personnel staff of one of the major oil companies almost immediately was contacted by the man in charge of management development about the possibility of conducting a program for the managers in research and development (R & D). There was a serious problem: a number of top scientists moved up into management, primarily to make it possible to pay them enough so they would not be pirated away by other oil companies. Often these individuals knew practically nothing about management and cared even less. As far as they were concerned their satisfactions and rewards came from scientific research, not their "phony" management positions. The problem was that they had subordinates who needed supervision, and they had numerous other managerial responsibilities as well. Could a management development program be devised that would help solve this problem?

The psychologist believed that something could be done, but he and the director of management development encountered considerable skepticism on the part of top-level R & D management; they recognized the problem, but they were not at all sure that management development was the solution. Finally, the R & D vice-president agreed to a pilot program for fifteen of his managers whose judgment he particularly respected. There would be one session a week on Tuesday afternoon, lasting about two hours, and if all went well the program would extend for ten weeks. If the program appeared promising, in the opinion of this initial group, it would be extended to additional groups of R & D managers as quickly as possible. The psychologist was given a clear message that he was very much on trial with the initial group.

The first session went very well up to the lecture part and during the question-and-answer period. Then a chemist who had a long string of patents to his credit and whose research was widely respected by the group began to raise a series of questions about the scientific validity of what the psychologist was saying. His point was that the field of management is not a "real science," is not grounded in research, and has its origins in "company folklore" and "armchair philosophizing." At least this was the impression he had gained, and he wondered if the psychologist would like to comment on this. The others seemed to have similar feelings, and it became apparent that this particular group would be impossible to influence unless it could be established that management subject matter is grounded in science. The psychologist recognized that he was on the spot and that his whole program might be in jeopardy.

Questions

1. How would you answer the chemist regarding the status of management as a "real science"? How would you relate management as a science to his own field of chemistry?

2. What points would you make in answer to the chemist's claim that the field of management has its origins in "company folklore" and "armchair philosophizing"? What early pioneers in management would you emphasize?

3. In dealing with such a crisis, how important is it to convey to the group that you fully understand what a science is, what it seeks to accomplish, and what its methods are?

Additional Sources for Detailed Study

Cass, Eugene L., and Zimmer, Frederick G. *Man and Work in Society*. New York: Van Nostrand Reinhold, 1975.

Dansereau, Fred; Alutto, Joseph A.; and Yammarino, Francis J. *Theory Testing in Organizational Behavior: The Varient Approach*. Englewood Cliffs, N.J.: Prentice-Hall, 1984.

Dubin, Robert. *Theory Building*. New York: Free Press, 1969.

Kakar, Sudhir. *Frederick Taylor: A Study in Personality and Innovation*. Cambridge, Mass.: M.I.T. Press, 1970.

Koontz, Harold. *Toward a Unified Theory of Management*. New York: McGraw-Hill, 1964.

Ling, Cyril C. *The Management of Personnel Relations: History and Origins*. Homewood, Ill.: Irwin, 1965.

Merrill, Harwood F. *Classics in Management*. New York: American Management Association, 1970.

Milton, Charles R. *Ethics and Expediency in Personnel Management: A Critical History of Personnel Philosophy*. Columbia: University of South Carolina Press, 1970.

Miner, John B. *Theories of Organizational Structure and Process*. Hinsdale, Ill.: Dryden, 1982. (See chapter 11—Barnard, Simon; chapter 12—Fayol; and chapter 13—Weber.)

Nash, Allan N., and Miner, John B. *Personnel and Labor Relations: An Evolutionary Approach*. New York: Macmillan, 1973.

Natemeyer, Walter E. *Classics of Organizational Behavior*. Oak Park, Ill.: Moore, 1978.

Nelson, Daniel. *Frederick W. Taylor and the Rise of Scientific Management*. Madison: University of Wisconsin Press, 1980.

Shafritz, Jay M., and Whitbeck, Philip H. *Classics of Organization Theory*. Oak Park, Ill.: Moore, 1978.

Sloan, Alfred P. *My Years with General Motors*. Garden City, N.J.: Doubleday, 1963.

Stone, Eugene. *Research Methods in Organizational Behavior*. Santa Monica: Goodyear, 1978.

Wolf, William B. *The Basic Barnard*. Ithaca: New York State School of Industrial and Labor Relations, Cornell University, 1974.

Wren, Daniel A. *The Evolution of Management Thought*. New York: Wiley, 1979.

Zedeck, Sheldon, and Blood, Milton R. *Foundations of Behavioral Science Research in Organizations*. Monterey, Calif.: Brooks/Cole, 1974.

Notes

1. Frederick W. Taylor, *Shop Management* (New York: Harper & Row, 1903); idem, *The Principles of Scientific Management* (New York: Harper & Row, 1911).

2. Charles D. Wrege and Amedeo G. Perroni, "Taylor's Pig-Tale: A Historical Analysis of Frederick W. Taylor's Pig-Iron Experiments," *Academy of Management Journal* (March 1974); Charles D. Wrege and Anne M. Stotka, "Cooke Creates a Classic: The Story Behind F. W. Taylor's Principles of Scientific Management," *Academy of Management Review* (October 1978).

3. Henri Fayol, *General and Industrial Management,* trans. Constance Storrs (London: Pitman, 1949).

4. Max Weber, *From Max Weber: Essays in Sociology,* trans. H. H. Gerth and C. Wright Mills (New York: Oxford University Press, 1946); idem, *Max Weber: The Theory of Social and Economic Organization,* trans. Talcott Parsons and A. M. Henderson (New York: Free Press, 1947).

5. Elton Mayo, *The Human Problems of an Industrial Civilization* (New York: Macmillan, 1933); idem, *The Social Problems of an Industrial Civilization* (Boston: Graduate School of Business Administration, Harvard University, 1945).

6. Fritz J. Roethlisberger and William J. Dickson, *Management and the Worker* (Cambridge, Mass.: Harvard University Press, 1939); William J. Dickson and Fritz J. Roethlisberger, *Counseling in an Organization* (Boston: Graduate School of Business Administration, Harvard University, 1966).

7. Chester I. Barnard, *The Functions of the Executive* (Cambridge, Mass.: Harvard University Press, 1938).

8. Herbert A. Simon, *Administrative Behavior: A Study of Decision-Making Processes in Administrative Organization* (New York: Free Press, 1976).

9. Daniel Nelson, *Managers and Workers: Origins of the New Factory System in the United States—1880–1920* (Madison: University of Wisconsin Press, 1975).

10. Richard G. Brandenburg, "The Usefulness of Management Thought for Management," in *Contemporary Management: Issues and Viewpoints,* ed. Joseph W. McGuire (Englewood Cliffs, N. J.: Prentice-Hall, 1974).

11. Harold R. Pollard, *Developments in Management Thought* (New York: Crane, Russak, 1974), p. 99.

12. Peter M. Blau, *On the Nature of Organizations* (New York: Wiley, 1974).

13. Richard H. Franke and James D. Kaul, "The Hawthorne Experiments: First Statistical Interpretations," *American Sociological Review* (October 1978); Richard H. Franke, "Worker Productivity at Hawthorne," *American Sociological Review* (December 1980). See also Ronald G. Greenwood, Alfred A. Bolton, and Regina A. Greenwood, "Hawthorne a Half Century Later: Relay Assembly Participants Remember," *Journal of Management* (Fall 1983).

14. William R. Spriegel and Richard H. Lansburgh, *Industrial Management* (New York: Wiley, 1947).

15. Morris Cohen and Ernest Nagel, *An Introduction to Logic and Scientific Method* (New York: Harcourt, Brace, 1934).

READINGS AND PROFILES

Today's Young Managers: They Can Do It, But Will They?
Ann Howard and Douglas W. Bray
The Wharton Magazine

Ranking Corporate Reputations
Claire Makin
Fortune

John A. Young and Hewlett-Packard Company

The selections that follow were chosen to illustrate the meaning of management. More specifically, they deal with managing in hierarchical business organizations and with the factors that make for success (and failure) as a manager.

The Howard and Bray article compares today's crop of young managers with those of the past and provides a vivid picture of the consequences of declining motivation to manage. The setting is AT&T and the Bell System in a period prior to the breakup of the company by court order.

Makin describes the results of a survey designed to evaluate the 200 largest U.S. corporations. The article provides a good illustration of the factors that serve to make some companies successful and others less so. It also provides interesting thumbnail sketches of a number of this country's large, and often better known, companies.

The executive profile of John Young and his company, Hewlett-Packard, deals with a firm that, according to *Fortune's* survey, ties IBM for the top position. Hewlett-Packard is the most admired company in the precision instruments industry, but it is of particular interest here because it is rated number one in ability to attract, develop, and keep talent. It is just behind IBM in quality of management and long-term investment value. It comes in third overall in quality of products and innovativeness. Hewlett-Packard has remained one of the country's best-managed firms for many years, and John Young rose to his present position through the management ranks of that company.

Today's Young Managers: They Can Do It, But Will They?

Ann Howard and Douglas W. Bray

A quarter century ago, the Bell System began its first longitudinal study of first-level managers in its operating companies. Called the Management Progress Study (MPS), this undertaking has yielded many important revelations concerning who gets ahead and why, as well as changes over time in managers' personalities and values (see *The Wharton Magazine,* Winter 1979). And such data are still forthcoming as the study continues.

In the mid-1970's the question was raised as to whether the MPS findings would be equally applicable to the generation of college graduates currently being hired. Such concerns led us to initiate in 1977 a new longitudinal study (the Management Continuity Study), similarly dedicated to following and analyzing managers' careers.

Although data on the progress of these new managers within the Bell System are just beginning to come in, initial testing and assessment of this group showed them to be significantly different in several major respects from their counterparts of a generation ago. These differences (as well as some similarities) and their implications will be the subject of this article.

The sample of new first-level managers (204 people who underwent initial assessment in the period 1977–1979) was matched with a subsample (274 people, initially evaluated in 1956–1960) of the earlier group. As a result, all participants were college graduates newly hired into first-level general management jobs. Although managers in the original study were selected from only six telephone companies, the newer managers came from a broader range of thirteen Bell operating companies. The average age of the 1950's participants was 24; for the new recruits, it was 25. The new sample was better educated, in that 45 percent had postgraduate training, compared with only 11 percent of the earlier group.

Dr. Ann Howard is manager, and Dr. Douglas W. Bray director, of basic human resources research at AT&T. They are the principal researchers of both the Management Continuity Study and the Management Progress Study.

Reprinted from *The Wharton Magazine* (Summer 1981): 23–28.

There were major differences in the racial and sexual makeup of the two samples. Back in the 1950's, when the quest was for young managers expected to rise to middle management, the most probable candidates were white males. In recent years, due to equal employment efforts, this is not at all the case. Consequently, whereas the 1950's group consisted entirely of white men, half of the 1970's participants were women, and one-third were members of various minority groups.

Both longitudinal studies began data collection at a three-day assessment center. In an off-the-job setting, participants were evaluated by a team of assessors after completing a variety of exercises. The exercises included ability tests; personality, motivation, and attitude questionnaires; simulations of work situations; group discussions; interviews; and projective tests. The assessors rated each participant on 26 dimensions (for example, "inner work standards," "need for superior approval," and "need for advancement") representing critical managerial abilities and motivations. In addition, predictions were made as to whether each participant had the potential for middle management and whether he or she would remain with the Bell System for a normal career life.

We were gratified to find that the average ability level of the new generation of managers was on a par with that of the previous generation. On the dimension "general mental ability," the 1950's group and the 1970's group each received an average rating from the assessors of 3.0, on a scale of 1-5. Their respective ratings on "planning and organizing" were 2.9 and 2.8; on "decision-making," 2.7 and 2.6; and on "leadership skills," 2.7 each. (The slight differences in the two sets of average ratings were not statistically significant.)

For both groups, the mental ability rating was based primarily on performance on the School and College Ability Test, as well as on responses in a general information test and performance on cognitive tasks in the simulations. The ratings for planning and organizing and for decision-making were based largely on the participants' handling of situations presented in a simulation of a middle manager's "In-Basket," while leadership skills were judged from performance in group discussions or management games.

For some aspects of motivation, there was also an underlying continuity between our two generations of managers. What might be called motivation for accomplishment was gauged, in part, by the Edwards Personal Preference Schedule, a "forced-choice" questionnaire that measures a variety of motivations. On the questionnaire's so-called Need for Achievement scale, respondents indicate their degree of preference for such goals as accomplishing something of great significance or doing a difficult job well; the focus here is on mastery of challenging tasks, with no assumptions about extrinsic rewards that might accompany such accomplishments. A comparison of the 1950's and 1970's groups showed no significant difference in the average scores on this scale; both groups scored near the 60th percentile at their original assessments.

After the staff assessors had heard all data from various exercises indicating motivation for accomplishment, they rated the incoming managers on "inner work standards," or the extent to which the individual would want to do a good job even if a not so good one was acceptable to the boss and to others. Here, too, there was no difference in average ratings between the two groups. Thus, to the extent that a management job provides challenge and a sense of accomplishment, the new groups of recruits should be as motivated to perform it as the last.

Differing Expectations

There are, of course, other aspects to managerial motivation besides enjoyment of task accomplishment. In fact, this particular motivational quality is perhaps more important for the technical specialist than the general manager. What differentiates the manager is that he or she expects to rise to higher and higher levels, directing and coordinating the efforts of others toward the accomplishment of group and organization goals, not just individual task goals. The management trainee, then, should want to rise to high places, deriving satisfaction from managing and motivating those below.

It is here that our story stumbles into discontinuity, disjunction, and disappointment. One of the motivational exercises used in our assessment centers was a short questionnaire measuring desire for upward mobility, or drive to attain powerful, high-status, and well-paying positions. The average score for the 1950's group on this questionnaire was at the 52nd percentile, whereas for the 1970's generation, the average was at the 29th percentile, a statistically significant difference.

The eighteen items on this upward-mobility questionnaire can be roughly divided into three groups: nine general items having to do with looking toward the future and striving toward ambitious goals, four items that specifically relate to financial progress, and five that focus on personal advancement. The 1970's participants scored significantly lower than their 1950's counterparts on half of the general and money-related items—and on *all* the advancement items. As much as we might prefer to blame the lower scores on affluent upbringings or a stagnant economy, the main message seems to be that the 1970's group just isn't as interested in advancing up the corporate ladder. And as Andrew Carnegie put it, "You cannot push anyone up the ladder unless he is willing to climb himself."

More fuel was added to our fires of discontent when we observed the new recruits' responses to another questionnaire, called the Expectations Inventory. In this questionnaire, the recruits were asked to speculate on their lives five years in the future, indicating for a variety of situations what they expected to be true or false. The items concerned not only advancement and salary but also more generalized aspects of managerial life, such as intellectual stimulation from peers, access to company information and resources, and geographical desirability of work location. The average score of the 1970's recruits was only at the 17th percentile; for the 1950's group, it was again at the 52nd.

The new generation's score should not be interpreted as reflecting unbridled negativism, but rather a dampened optimism toward many aspects of work life. The new recruits believe the future has much less to offer. For example, while 69 percent of the 1950's sample strongly affirmed that in five years they would have a challenging job with many opportunities to learn and do new things, only 45 percent of the 1970's group was this positive. Regarding the expectation that the company would make a strong effort to provide all the re-

sources needed to do a good job, 58 percent of the 1950's group was strongly positive, compared with only 27 percent of the new recruits. Even with respect to having deep friendships with at least two or three work associates, 75 percent of the last generation had the highest hopes, compared with only 46 percent of the current one.

When the assessment participants were asked to list which of the Expectations Inventory items they most hoped would be true, about the same proportion of each group wanted a challenging job and one that would pay at least a middle manager's salary. But 54 percent of the 1950's sample also chose advancing to middle management as something they most wanted to happen, while only 34 percent of the 1970's sample chose that item. With respect to a managerial career, the new generation doesn't want as much and doesn't expect as much.

Further evidence about both task accomplishment and career advancement comes from the responses of both groups to projective techniques, which are more indirect than questionnaires and used to determine underlying motivations. A clinical psychologist analyzed the responses from both samples and concluded that the new recruits were less involved with and concerned about advancement, although equally as interested in individual task accomplishment as the 1950's group. They were also less committed to a business career, which perhaps coincides with the pessimism expressed on the Expectations Inventory. In personal interviews, many of the new recruits expressed the intention of returning to graduate school, indicating that neither their formal education nor their career plans had as yet been finalized.

Exactly what is less attractive about a high-level management career these days is not completely clear. These young people have never known an economic depression or, excepting many of the nonwhites, financial deprivation, but rejection of financial gains is not at all clear from this sample. If the bête noire is not dirty money, then perhaps it is power.

An unavoidable characteristic of a managerial job is the necessity to lead and direct others. And a hierarchial organizational structure requires that fewer and fewer managers at higher levels be responsible for greater and greater numbers of managers and workers at lower levels. It is therefore imperative that an upwardly mobile manager appreciate, respond to, indeed thrive on leadership responsibilities.

One measure of motivation toward leadership comes from the Dominance scale of the Edwards Personal Preference Schedule. Respondents indicate on this scale their degree of preference for such activities as leading and directing others, being a leader in groups to which they belong, and persuading and influencing others to do what they want. The 1970's group tested at the assessment center was much less favorable toward these items than the 1950's managers had been, their average score being only at the 22nd percentile, compared with the 49th percentile for the 1950's group.

But, some might protest, that's just the influence of the women in the sample. True, the females did score significantly lower than the males, but the average score on the Dominance scale for the males among the 1970's recruits was only at the 28th percentile, still depressingly low from our point of view.

The desire to lead and direct others expressed on the Dominance scale by the 1950's group should not be construed as a preference for an authoritarian, rule-oriented, inflexible use of power. In fact, on another questionnaire, aimed at measuring authoritarianism, the 1970's recruits were not significantly less rigid and dogmatic than their peers of the previous generation. The new managers appear to be rejecting leadership roles regardless of leadership style.

Nor does their rejection of leadership symbolize a preference for followership. On the Edwards scale of Deference, indicating a tendency to follow instructions, follow the lead of others, and defer to if not revere those in higher positions, the 1970's managers again scored lower than their 1950's counterparts, although this difference (36th percentile versus 43rd) was not nearly so pronounced as that on the Dominance scale. More convincing evidence of a lack of deference among the new group came from the interviews and projective tests, so that the ratings of the assessors on the recruits' "need for superior approval" showed a marked discrepancy between the two generations. While 68 percent of the 1950's participants had

been given high ratings, only 37 percent of the 1970's participants were so judged.

"The hierarchy be damned" is the overall message here. The new managers simply pay less homage to higher-level positions. They neither aspire to those jobs nor defer to those who have them. They don't want to lead; they don't want to follow.

What kind of relationships do these new managers want with others in the organization, then? Since the Edwards Personal Preference Schedule is a forced-choice questionnaire, lower scores on some scales are necessarily counterbalanced by higher scores on others. Two scales on which the new managers scored notably higher than their 1950's counterparts both have to do with emotional support. The so-called Nurturance scale measures the desire to assist others less fortunate, treat others with kindness and sympathy, and be generous to others. The average score of the 1970's recruits was at the 74th percentile, compared with the 49th for the previous generation. If this nurturing predilection is a substitute for leading and directing others, we might expect the 1970's managers to be more intrigued by their subordinates' personal problems than by their approach to solving the problems of the business. There were no sex differences on this scale, so the results are not attributable to a "feminizing" of the work force.

High Scores on Emotional Support

The new managers apparently want to receive as well as give emotional support. This is reflected in the Edwards Succorance scale, which measures the desire to receive help from others in times of trouble, seek encouragement from others, and have others be sympathetic and understanding about personal problems. Again, the 1970's managers scored high compared with those in the past, their average score topping the 80th percentile, as against the 66th percentile for the 1950's group. As on the Dominance scale, there was a significant sex difference in the scores of the 1970's recruits, but it did not account for the generation difference. The 1970's males logged an average score at the 76th percentile, a significant increase over the males of the previous generation.

The message from the new generation of managers now reads, "Love me, don't lead me." Furthermore, "I'll do the same to you." With all due respect to the virtues of human warmth and kindness, who is going to run our corporations in the future?

The trend of these various scores points to significant changes over the last two decades in the values of new college graduates. In an effort to pin down these changes more specifically, the 1970's group was administered a more direct measure of fundamental beliefs, the Rokeach Survey of Values. Unfortunately, this exercise was not available for the 1950's recruits, but comparisons can be made with a sample of 71 successful middle managers who went through a Bell Advanced Management Program (abbreviated BAMP) in 1978. These managers were fifteen years older, on the average, than the 1970's recruits, so that age effects confound the data here. Nevertheless, the trends are provocative and consistent with what has already been shown.

The first section of the Rokeach Survey asks respondents to rank eighteen goals in order of their importance to them as guiding principles in their lives. The older, successful BAMP managers gave significantly higher ranks to "a sense of accomplishment," "freedom," and "an exciting life"—all goals with dynamic intimations. The 1970's groups gave higher ranks to "inner harmony," "wisdom," and "true friendship"—all quiescent in tone. The BAMP managers value doing; the new managers value "being." However, they apparently don't value being higher-level managers.

But what of the women and minority-group members entering the managerial ranks—the type of people deprived of important management positions in the past but now, through affirmative action programs, finally getting their day in the sun? The whole idea behind affirmative action was to give them opportunities they never had before, to take the "White Males Only" label off the most powerful, lucrative, and desirable jobs corporations had to offer. Will these newly admitted groups surge ahead, fulfilling their long-denied destinies?

Looking first at the 100 women in our sample of 1970's recruits, we see that their assessment ratings establish from the outset that their managerial abilities are decidedly up to those of the men of either yesterday or today. The assessors judged 45 percent of the women to have middle management potential, compared with 39 percent of the men in the 1970's group. Where sex differences appeared in average ratings on dimensions of general ability, they nearly always favored the women, who demonstrated better written communication skills and creativity than did the men and had higher personal standards for work quality. A greater sensitivity among the women was also reflected in higher average ratings on the dimensions "perception of threshold social cues" (that is, the ability to perceive minimal cues in the behavior of others toward them) and "social objectivity" (freedom from prejudices against racial, ethnic, socioeconomic, educational, and other kinds of groups).

In terms of skills, then, the Bell System might actually do better if women with leadership and advancement ambitions preempted men now lacking such drives. But the data offer no encouragement that such ambitions prevail. As was previously noted, the women among the 1970's recruits were even less inclined than the men to direct others, with their average scores being quite low on the Edwards Dominance scale (16th percentile) and quite high on the Succorance scale (83rd percentile). As for career advancement, on both the Expectations Inventory and the questionnaire measuring motivation for upward mobility, the women's average scores were almost an exact replica of the men's—and much lower than those of the 1950's sample.

Moreover, on several career-oriented dimensions, assessors gave average ratings to the women that were no higher than those of their male peers. And on one dimension—"goal flexibility"—a difference showed up that was *not* favorable to the women. The females were rated as more flexible, meaning they were more likely to change their life goals in accordance with opportunities. In addition, the assessors concluded that twice as many women as men in the 1970's sample could be expected to leave the Bell System voluntarily (32 percent versus 15).

What these differences indicate is that the women were far less dedicated to a lifetime career with the corporation. Many will not reach positions of leadership because they won't be around long enough. Previous assessment center projections of turnover have turned out to be underestimates, and there is every reason to believe that the 32 percent figure will be as well. Many, perhaps most, of the women assessed had not yet resolved expected family/career conflicts. Most, it would seem, had not even faced them, since three-quarters of the women assessed were single.

A Look at Minorities

Let us turn, then, to the minorities. In the 1970's sample, "minorities" stood for 72 managers, 92 percent of whom were black. At first glance, their assessment results gave grounds for encouragement. On the upward mobility questionnaire, for example, the minorities scored significantly higher than the whites. In fact, their average score—at the 42nd percentile—was only ten points below that of the 1950's sample, while the whites dawdled at the 22nd percentile. In light of all the past racial discrimination in our culture, what fitting irony if we discovered that Horatio Alger is now black!

Further examination of the items in this questionnaire somewhat restrained our enthusiasm, however. The minorities scored significantly higher than the 1970's whites on six of the eighteen items, including all four relating to money. Compared to the 1950's sample, they scored higher on two money items and lower on two personal advancement items. If the minorities showed more interest in rising to the top of the corporate ladder, it appeared to be primarily because of the financial rewards dwelling there. This impression was confirmed in the interviews and other assessment exercises.

But let us not be snobs in this matter. What if minority-group members are motivated to seek higher-level positions because of extrinsic, financial rewards? What difference does it make *why* they want them *if* they perform well in them? The potential difficulty lies with the "if," not the "why." For one thing, the assessment results indicated that the nonwhites were less motivated than the whites for task accomplishment; on two measures of achievement motivation, the minorities had lower scores. The differences were not great, but they raised some doubts as to whether the minorities will combine sufficient drive to perform tasks well with their desires for upward mobility.

Another problem is that, on the average, their ability levels were not up to those of the whites in the 1970's sample. Although interpersonal tasks usually presented the minorities with no problems, the more closely the assessment exercises resembled schoolwork, the more difficulty they had with them. It has been hypothesized that one of the reasons for blacks' relatively poor school performance is a failure to associate accomplishing the task at hand with dreams of future success. Perhaps a similar lack of association is operating here.

Putting all the information together for the sex and race groups, we find no reason either to fear that affirmative action has torn the house down or to hope that it will be a salvation from the motivational problems observed in the new generation. The women showed they have the ability for higher-level management jobs, but their degree of ambition was as low as that of their male peers rather than as high as that of (male) managers of the previous generation. Moreover, their lack of resolution of anticipated role conflicts makes their tenure uncertain and the corporation vulnerable to their desertion. As for the nonwhites, their generally greater ambition may be geared more to financial rewards than to a philosophy of working hard to achieve present and future goals. Moreover, various ability deficiencies may mean they need to spend a little longer mastering jobs at lower levels before being promoted within the organization.

Individualists Abound

Although we have talked of the problems and priorities of women, men, whites, or nonwhites as a group, one critical observation must be made: the managers in the current generation are a highly individualistic lot, much more so than our 1950's generation of managers. The photographs of that earlier group almost always show crew cuts, clean-shaven faces, and skinny ties trimly adorning pressed, white shirts. It seemed as if most of these men were political conservatives who wanted a homemaker wife, children, and to be "Mr. Telephone" in their local communities. Off the job, they fished and went to church.

By comparison, the new generation explodes with diversity—and not just because the group includes women and blacks. Men are just as likely to be bearded as clean shaven. Wildly colorful informal dress is just as common as traditional business suits. Our new managers may be right-wingers, or Marxists, or disgusted with the whole idea of politics. The group includes women who want to be president and men whose hobby is home decorating. Others may aspire to running for the state legislature or returning to school for a degree in speech pathology. In short, these are children born to conflicting values in a confused and confusing culture.

So much diversity makes generalizations about the 1970's generation oversimplifications at best. It also means these people will inevitably be difficult to manage. Our impressions are that the older Bell System managers have adapted to their subordinates' diversity but are troubled by their lack of deference. Yet, what none of us may be able to tolerate is the paucity of upwardly mobile, capable managers to run businesses and other organizations in the future. If the 1970's Bell System recruits are representative of trends elsewhere in the country, and we have some reasons to believe they are, U.S. organizations may be headed for trouble. Our previous research has shown that desiring advancement, preferring a leadership role, and having high career expectations are predictive of future managerial success. In fact, original assessment ratings of our 1950's men on the dimension "need for advancement" still correlated significantly with management level achieved after a span of twenty years. The motivation—or lack of it—of young managers is an issue we must face now if we are to be prepared for the decades ahead.

Possible Solutions

We have formulated several possible solutions to the problem. One approach may be to select, from among the diverse candidates on the college campuses, those that are more "our kind of people." This does not mean picking only men with a white face, a crew cut, a skinny tie, and a traditional wife. It does mean trying to find people who genuinely desire leadership positions and aspire to higher levels of management.

Selecting the best always puts one organization in competition with others looking for the same characteristics. Winning the competition in a big way would take a lot of time, effort, and money. It is certainly possible to do a more thorough job of selecting candidates from the campus population—by preemployment assessment, for example. But the logistics and financial problems involved in such an ambitious undertaking militate against running headlong in that direction. It would no doubt also be necessary to spend more on staff development programs and salaries to attract and keep the "cream of the crop." In addition to wondering whether an organization can afford this solution, one must also question whether it is possible for such an approach to suceed at all. There may not be enough college graduates of the kind we are looking for to go around—even for just a few top organizations.

A second possibility, then, is to try to increase the number of people willing to consider management jobs in business and industry. Perhaps other types of organizations, such as government agencies, universities, or charitable foundations, appeal more to the values of the new graduates. If so, the image of business and industry may need to be improved. Yet, there is no direct evidence that the best people are lost to other types of organizations. A more likely hypothesis is that the self-preoccupied young people of today's "me generation" are as little interested in responsible, leadership positions in other types of organizations as they are in top-management jobs in business and industry. Furthermore, some studies have indicated that reported disillusionment with the business establishment is part of a generalized cynicism and pessimism permeating all segments of society.

Another possible solution counts on nature to take its course, with a little assist from a clever corporation. One finding of the Management Progress Study initiated in the 1950's was that managers, early in their careers, got "hooked" on their jobs. Their achievement motivation increased, and work became one of the most important things in their lives, especially for those who were successful at it. The 1970's managers have already shown, at the assessment center, a comparable initial level of achievement motivation. If the company can tie the challenge of task accomplishment to the carrot of promotion, the new generation may yet learn to yearn for advancement. They will have to come to perceive that, in order to have a job that is sufficiently challenging, one must advance to higher and higher levels of management. If this occurs, then the motivational crisis may be but a temporary lag of direction and spirit.

Others have argued that these solutions are regressive and old-fashioned, that organizations will have to adapt to the new breed, not vice versa. The hierarchy, they say, will have to be flattened, with matrices and committees replacing bosses and leaders. Aside from questioning whether this approach will work at all, we certainly wonder whether it makes sense for the coming years as organizations strive to meet the turbulence, ambiguity, and constant change expected in the 1980's. A period when emergencies and crises predominate seems like exactly the wrong time to pull down the hierarchical command structure, to sponsor group rather than individual decisions. How will our increasingly urgent business decisions be made if the "boss" becomes an emotionally supportive but conflicted committee that can't make up its collective mind what to do?

In conclusion, then, our studies of Bell System managers point to a potential crisis brewing as the next generation meets and replaces the last. A generally reassuring continuity in managerial abilities is matched by a disturbing discontinuity in managerial motivation. For the sake of our organizations, our economy, and our country, we hope a solution can be found.

Ranking Corporate Reputations

Claire Makin

ortune's survey, completed in September, drew responses from 51% of those polled—an unusually good return, according to polling professionals. The respondents in 20 groups, one for each industry, were asked to rate only companies in their own industry (or, in the case of security analysts, an industry they follow), using a scale of 0 (poor) to 10 (excellent). The industries represented in the survey are the largest in *Fortune's* directories of U.S. industrial and non-industrial corporations.

The companies in each industry group were rated on eight key attributes of reputation: quality of management; quality of products or services; innovativeness; value as a long-term investment; financial soundness; ability to attract, develop, and keep talented people; community and environmental responsibility; and use of corporate assets. The companies that rated highest and lowest among the 200 for each attribute are listed in Exhibits 1 and 2. Exhibit 3 shows how each company

ranks within its industry; the overall score for each company is the average of its ratings on all eight attributes.

Hewlett-Packard and IBM each emerged with an average score of 8.26 out of the possible 10—higher than any of the other companies in the survey. But there was a tie breaker. IBM was accorded the top spot because it rated higher than Hewlett-Packard in five of the eight measures of reputation, most notably in perceptions of financial soundness, in which IBM scored a remarkable 9.21. That was the closest any company came to a 10 for any attribute.

Fortune's survey was conducted before someone packed cyanide into Tylenol capsules in Chicago, killing seven people. But the incident seems unlikely to have any lasting effect on the reputation of Johnson & Johnson, Tylenol's maker. One indicator: after an initial seven-point drop, Johnson & Johnson's stock returned to pre-crisis levels and in early December reached $49 a share, a record high.

Well-thought-of companies generally do well in financial terms too, and those with poor reputations do poorly. Four companies on the honor roll—IBM, GE, Merck, and AT&T—have triple-A bond ratings. Three others—SmithKline Beckman, General Mills, and Digital Equipment—are rated double-A. (Hewlett-Packard, Johnson & Johnson, and Eastman Kodak carry little debt.) The median return on shareholders' equity of the ten most-ad-mired companies was an impressive 18.2% in 1981, vs. 4.5% for the ten least admired. The 1981 median for the *Fortune* 500 was 13.8%.

The most-admired companies' median net profit margin in 1981 was 10.7 of sales, more than double the *Fortune* 500 median of 4.6%. The least-admired companies had a melancholy median net profit margin of 0.9%. Price-earnings multiples followed the same pattern—a median hovering around 12 for the stocks of companies at the top and under 5 for their poor relations, only five of which are expected to turn a profit in 1982.

EXHIBIT 1 At the top and bottom of the 200 companies

THE MOST ADMIRED	Rank	Company	Industry Group	Score
The 200 corporations in *Fortune's* survey were rated by their peers—executives and outside directors in their industries—and those who peer at them—financial analysts specializing in their industries. The scores are averages of each company's ratings on eight key attributes of reputation.	1	IBM	Office equipment, computers	8.26[1]
	2	Hewlett-Packard	Precision instruments	8.26[1]
	3	Johnson & Johnson	Pharmaceuticals	8.14
	4	Eastman Kodak	Precision instruments	8.02
	5	Merck	Pharmaceuticals	7.92
	6	AT&T	Utilities	7.91
	7	Digital Equipment	Office equipment, computers	7.70
	8	SmithKline Beckman	Pharmaceuticals	7.66
	9	General Electric	Electronics, appliances	7.54
	10	General Mills	Food	7.52

THE LEAST ADMIRED	Rank	Company	Industry Group	Score
Most of the companies at the bottom of the 200 have the bad luck to be in troubled industries, such as motor vehicles, steel, or forest products. But how their peers see their financial soundness and management quality has a lot to do with the ratings.	200	International Harvester	Motor vehicles and parts	2.62
	199	A&P	Retailing	3.17
	198	American Motors	Motor vehicles and parts	3.78[2]
	197	Pan Am	Transportation	3.78[2]
	196	F.W. Woolworth	Retailing	4.09
	195	Crown Zellerbach	Forest products	4.32
	194	RCA	Electronics, appliances	4.50
	193	Republic Steel	Metal manufacturing	4.57
	192	Tesoro Petroleum	Diversified services	4.59
	191	National Steel	Metal manufacturing	4.62

[1]Tie. IBM scores higher than Hewlett-Packard in five of eight attributes.
[2]Tie. American Motors scores lower than Pan Am in five of eight attributes.

EXHIBIT 2 Eight key attributes of reputation

Quality of Management

Most Admired	Score	Least Admired	Score
IBM	8.86	International Harvester	2.58
Hewlett-Packard	8.76	A&P	3.44
Johnson & Johnson	8.48	RCA	3.99

Quality of Products or Services

Boeing	9.09	F.W. Woolworth	4.47
Caterpillar Tractor	9.04	American Motors	4.66
Hewlett-Packard	8.77	A&P	4.86

Innovativeness

Citicorp	8.61	A&P	2.92
Merrill Lynch	8.56	International Harvester	3.43
Hewlett-Packard	8.46	F.W. Woolworth	3.62

Long-term Investment Value

IBM	8.11	International Harvester	1.58
Hewlett-Packard	7.99	American Motors	2.50
Johnson & Johnson	7.87	Pan Am	2.66

Financial Soundness

IBM	9.21	International Harvester	0.60
American Home Products	8.88	Pan Am	2.07
Johnson & Johnson	8.78	Chrysler	2.15

Ability to Attract, Develop, and Keep Talented People

Hewlett-Packard	8.29	International Harvester	1.71
IBM	8.15[1]	A&P	2.45
Merck	8.15[1]	American Motors	3.11

Community and Environmental Responsibility

Eastman Kodak	8.32	A&P	3.45
IBM	7.85	International Harvester	3.98
Johnson & Johnson	7.76	F.W. Woolworth	4.50

Use of Corporate Assets

Johnson & Johnson	8.02	International Harvester	1.91
IBM	7.96	A&P	2.93
Abbott Laboratories	7.88	Pan Am	3.30

[1]Tie.

Only in total return to investors, a measure combining price appreciation and dividend yield and therefore important to shareholders, did the highly regarded companies fail to perform outstandingly well. Their average annual ten-year median was 7.19%—surprisingly lower than the ten-year median of 8.52% for the *Fortune* 500. But the companies with poor reputations came in with a dismal *negative* return of 1.87% for the ten years.

In financial performance, SmithKline Beckman (1981 sales: $2 billion) is the brightest of the stars, with a 1981 return on equity of 30.2%, a profit margin of 18.6%, and a ten-year total return to investors of 20.18% annually. Pan Am was the overall loser here; it was in the red in 1981 and had a ten-year total return of minus 15.74%.

A strong position in a high-growth market naturally adds points to a company's reputation, whether the market is health care products or computers. Comments Chief Executive John Opel of IBM, "Certainly we chose the right industry to be in."

All the companies on the honor roll have chief executives who have been with their companies at least 20 years. In sharp contrast, eight of the ten companies rated lowest have hired, fired, or otherwise rearranged top managements in the past 18 months. Respondents in *Fortune's* survey seemed to equate poor corporate performance with poor management—although sometimes it's hard to establish which comes first. Wonders a Wall Street analyst who follows the ailing forest products industry, "Can shuffling the deck achieve anything in a capital-intensive industry?"

Almost all the high-rated companies stress motivating—and retaining—their most promising managers by allowing them freedom to make decisions within a few broad policy guidelines. Six of the companies—GE, Digital Equipment, Hewlett-Packard, Johnson & Johnson, SmithKline Beckman, and General Mills—pride themselves on being decentralized. "Decentralization is terribly important," says Bruce Atwater, chief executive of General Mills. "Good people won't work within a highly structured system—you've got to give them rein."

Corporations at the top of the list rank high in all eight key attributes—a company well respected for one is likely to get good marks across the board:

IBM was accorded the highest rating for quality of management, 8.86, given any company in the survey. It was also No. 1 for value as a long-term investment and for financial soundness, while ranking second in ability to attract, develop, and keep talented people; community and environmental responsibility; and wise use of corporate assets. In quality of products and innovativeness IBM fell from the top rank; in those categories it ranked eighth and 18th respectively.

Hewlett-Packard, No. 2, scored 8.29 for its way with people, the only attribute for which it scored first among the 200. But it ranked among the top three companies for four other attributes. For innovativeness, the $4.3-billion-a-year manufacturer of minicomputers and precision instruments rates higher than any other industrial company—8.46. (Citicorp and Merrill Lynch, both non-industrials, scored higher.) Hewlett-Packard's highest score was for quality of products, though Boeing and Caterpillar Tractor came out slightly better in this respect. Hewlett-Packard also has a sterling reputation for management (8.76) and for investment value (7.99). In both respects it was regarded as second only to IBM.

Johnson & Johnson, No. 3, ranks just behind Hewlett-Packard in quality of management and value as a long-term investment. The company was also judged among the top three for use of corporate assets, financial soundness, and community and environmental responsibility.

Eastman Kodak attained the No. 4 spot while scoring first among the 200—with a rating of 8.32—only for community and environmental responsibility. The company's highest rating, 8.69, was for the quality of its products; it just missed being among the top three for this attribute.

Merck, No. 5 overall, earns higher marks for innovativeness—7.61—than any other pharmaceutical company; it is renowned as one of the heaviest R&D investors among the big-spending drug manufacturers. The company ties IBM in reputation for dealing with employees, scoring 8.15.

EXHIBIT 3 How they rank in 20 industries

AEROSPACE
Boeing topped the 200 for product quality, but United Technologies bested Boeing in financial soundness and use of assets. The industry groups are based on OMB categories. Each company is assigned according to the business that contributed most to 1981 sales (or assets, for some financial companies).

CHEMICALS
The chemical companies are a homogeneous bunch. Lowest-ranked Celanese is not many strides behind top-rated Du Pont.

Rank	Aerospace	Score	Chemicals	Score
1	Boeing	7.47	Du Pont	6.84
2	United Technologies	7.20	Dow Chemical	6.63
3	Northrop	6.83	Monsanto	6.29
4	Rockwell International	6.80	Union Carbide	6.02
5	Martin Marietta	6.60	PPG Industries	5.82
6	McDonnell Douglas	6.44	NL Industries	5.81
7	General Dynamics	6.32	W.R. Grace	5.80
8	Lockheed	6.08	American Cyanamid	5.57
9	Grumman	5.76	Allied	5.46
10	Fairchild Industries	5.46	Celanese	5.36

COMMERCIAL BANKING
Staid J.P. Morgan, which does little retail business, outclassed all other banks in every attribute except community responsibility and innovativeness. Trend-setting Citicorp beat all 99 other companies for innovativeness.

DIVERSIFIED FINANCIAL
Fannie Mae (1981 assets: $62 billion), a private corporation with government backing, is the largest of these companies. But it ranks below the others for use of corporate assets and management.

Rank	Commercial Banking	Score	Diversified Financial	Score
1	J. P. Morgan	7.47	Merrill Lynch	7.44
2	Citicorp	7.09	American Express	7.41
3	BankAmerica	6.37[1]	First Boston	6.80
4	First Interstate Bancorp	6.37[1]	Aetna Life & Casualty	6.59
5	Bankers Trust New York	6.36	Travelers	6.18
6	Chemical New York	5.97	INA[2]	6.04
7	Manufacturers Hanover	5.94	Loews	5.87
8	First Chicago	5.72	Great Western Financial	5.22
9	Chase Manhattan	5.45	Fannie Mae	5.19
10	Continental Illinois	5.16	H. F. Ahmanson	5.12

DIVERSIFIED SERVICES
American Hospital Supply scored highest in this group for all but three attributes. Phibro-Salomon, a commodities and securities trading company, was first for innovativeness and way with people. Halliburton was most admired for the quality of its oil-field products and services.

ELECTRONICS, APPLIANCES
GE outshone all others in its group, particularly for management. RCA was last except in community and environmental responsibility, for which ITT was rated lower.

Rank	Diversified Services	Score	Electronics, Appliances	Score
1	American Hospital Supply	7.30	General Electric	7.54
2	Phibro-Salomon	7.08	Emerson Electric	6.93
3	Halliburton	6.96	Western Electric[3]	6.86
4	Super Value Stores	6.66	Raytheon	6.74
5	Fluor	6.40	Texas Instruments	6.69
6	Fleming Companies	6.29	Motorola	6.61
7	Foremost-McKesson	5.94	Westinghouse Electric	5.45
8	CBS	5.82	Litton Industries	5.38
9	Agri Industries	5.68	ITT	5.28
10	Tesoro Petroleum	4.59	RCA	4.50

[1]Tie. BankAmerica leads all banks in one attribute (community responsibility), First Interstate in none.
[2]INA has merged with Connecticut General to form Cigna Corp.
[3]Wholly owned by AT&T.

EXHIBIT 3 (continued)

	Rank	Food	Score	Forest Products	Score
FOOD	1	General Mills	7.52	Kimberly-Clark	6.79
Almost everyone's favorite in the food industry is General Mills, which scored highest on all eight attributes. Greyhound—which gets more revenues from Armour, a food subsidiary, than from its buses—was at the bottom in every category.	2	Nabisco Brands	6.63	Weyerhaeuser	6.50
	3	CPC International	6.49	Boise Cascade	6.14
	4	Dart & Kraft	6.46	Georgia-Pacific	6.02
	5	General Foods	6.21	International Paper	6.01
	6	Beatrice Foods	6.02	Champton International	5.58
	7	Ralston Purina	5.94	St. Regis Paper	5.52
	8	Borden	5.71	Mead	5.38
FOREST PRODUCTS	9	IC Industries	5.47	Scott Paper	5.00
In this recession-weary industry, Kimberly-Clark was first in five of the eight attributes; its highest score was for product quality. Crown Zellerbach was rated lowest in all categories.	10	Greyhound	4.92	Crown Zellerbach	4.32

	Rank	Industrial/Farm Equipment	Score	Life Insurance	Score
INDUSTRIAL/FARM EQUIPMENT	1	Caterpillar Tractor	7.48	Northwestern Mutual	7.15
In an industry well sprinkled with conglomerates, Caterpillar Tractor and its earth-moving equipment still rank first. Deere leads this group for innovativeness and community responsibility.	2	Deere	7.27	Aetna Life[4]	7.12
	3	Cooper Industries	6.97	Prudential	6.95
	4	Dresser Industries	6.61	Connecticut General Life[5]	6.93
	5	Combustion Engineering	6.55	Teachers Ins. & Annuity	6.36
	6	Borg-Warner	6.30	Travelers[6]	6.34
	7	Teledyne	6.17	John Hancock Mutual	5.88
LIFE INSURANCE	8	FMC	5.93	Equitable Life	5.79
Northwestern is first overall and for four attributes, including quality of services and management. All but Aetna, Connecticut General, Travelers, and Teachers are mutual companies, for which investment value is not applicable.	9	Ingersoll-Rand	5.88	New York Life	5.78
	10	Kidde	5.61	Metropolitan	5.55

	Rank	Metal Manufacturing	Score	Metal Products	Score
METAL MANUFACTURING	1	Alcoa	6.49	Gillette	7.09
Most of these companies are out of favor, especially for long-term investment value. Top-ranked Alcoa as rated highest for management and quality of products, from bottle caps to car bumpers.	2	Armco	6.13	Textron	6.50
	3	Northwest Industries	5.71	Continental Group	6.36
	4	Inland Steel	5.43	Whittaker	6.20
	5	Reynolds Metals	5.25	Foster Wheeler	6.15
	6	LTV	5.22	McDermott	5.95
METAL PRODUCTS	7	Bethlehem Steel	5.05	Gulf & Western	5.81
Gillette is here because the company gets more revenues from razor blades than any other product. With only security analysts as judges Whittaker would have been second, but industry executives and directors preferred Textron.	8	U.S. Steel	4.97	National Can	5.47
	9	National Steel	4.62	American Can	5.38
	10	Republic Steel	4.57	Chromalloy American	5.13

[4]Wholly owned by Aetna Life & Casualty.
[5]Connecticut General has merged with INA to form Cigna Corp.
[6]Wholly owned by Travelers Corp.

EXHIBIT 3 (continued)

MOTOR VEHICLES AND PARTS

TRW is champ of its industry in all respects except financial soundness, for which Bendix ranks first. The survey was made while Bendix and Martin Marietta were still dueling. Only Ford, AMC, and International Harvester rated lower than Bendix for management.

OFFICE EQUIPMENT, COMPUTERS

IBM tops the ranking for all attributes except innovativeness: Wang comes in first for its word-processing systems.

Rank	Motor Vehicles and Parts	Score	Office Equipment, Computers	Score
1	TRW	7.27	IBM	8.26
2	Dana	6.48	Digital Equipment	7.70
3	Eaton	6.47	Wang Laboratories	7.35
4	General Motors	6.31	Storage Technology	6.40
5	Bendix	6.29	Control Data	6.12
6	Signal Companies	5.85	NCR	5.76
7	Ford Motor	5.33	Honeywell	5.67
8	Chrysler	4.85	Pitney Bowes	5.24
9	American Motors	3.78	Burroughs	5.05
10	International Harvester	2.62	Sperry	4.93

PETROLEUM REFINING

Analysts gave companies in this group lower ratings than did the executives and directors polled, probably because oil stocks haven't been too slick lately. Both groups agreed, however, that Shell's greatest strength is management. Exxon rated third from last for use of assets.

PHARMACEUTICALS

The three top-rated drug companies are also among the ten most-admired corporations. Abbott just missed a place on that honor roll, but ranks third among the 200 for use of assets.

Rank	Petroleum Refining	Score	Pharmaceuticals	Score
1	Shell Oil	7.26	Johnson & Johnson	8.14
2	Atlantic Richfield	7.17	Merck	7.92
3	Standard Oil (Indiana)	7.11	SmithKline Beckman	7.66
4	Standard Oil of Calif.	6.77	Abbott Laboratories	7.50
5	Exxon	6.42	Bristol-Myers	7.41
6	Mobil	6.35	Pfizer	7.33
7	Phillips Petroleum	5.77	Eli Lilly	7.14
8	Tenneco	5.62	American Home Products	7.10
9	Gulf Oil	5.53	Upjohn	6.33
10	Texaco	5.20	Warner-Lambert	5.46

PRECISION INSTRUMENTS

There are many well-regarded companies in this industry group, starting with Hewlett-Packard. But two high-fliers of yesteryear, Xerox and Polaroid, landed near the bottom. Polaroid takes last place for long-term investment value.

RETAILING

Federated and Kroger, both Cincinnati based, vie for top spot among the retailers. Federated rates highest for financial soundness, but Kroger was judged the best bet for investment value.

Rank	Precision Instruments	Score	Retailing	Score
1	Hewlett-Packard	8.26	Federated	6.93
2	Eastman Kodak	8.02	Kroger	6.90
3	3M	7.46	J.C. Penney	6.59
4	Perkin-Elmer	6.78	Lucky Stores	6.15
5	Tektronix	6.43	Sears Roebuck	5.95
6	Becton Dickinson	6.32	Safeway Stores	5.91
7	General Signal	6.30	American Stores	5.71
8	Xerox	6.22	K mart	5.52
9	Polaroid	6.04	F.W. Woolworth	4.09
10	Lear Siegler	5.75	A&P	3.17

EXHIBIT 3 (continued)

TRANSPORTATION	Rank	Transportation	Score	Utilities	Score
Railroads have overtaken airlines, especially in	1	Delta Air Lines	7.25	AT&T	7.91
perceptions of financial	2	United Parcel Service	6.91	Texas Utilities	7.16
soundness. Delta is the only	3	CSX	6.34	Southern Calif. Edison	6.59
airline that reached the	4	Santa Fe Industries	6.30	GTE	6.57
stratosphere. Pan Am barely	5	Burlington Northern	6.00	Commonwealth Edison	6.27
got off the ground.	6	American Airlines	5.85	American Electric Power	6.19
UTILITIES	7	UAL	5.67	Pacific Gas & Electric	6.01
The experts who rated them	8	Trans World	5.21	Southern Co.	5.87
agreed that all the largest	9	Eastern Air Lines	4.67	Consolidated Edison	5.82
utilities are well managed and	10	Pan Am	3.78	Middle South Utilities	5.76
provide excellent service. AT&T and Texas Utilities scored especially high for long-term investment value and financial soundness. Ma Bell is the only non-industrial among the ten most admired corporations.					

AT&T, No. 6, achieved its highest rating, 8.63, for quality of service. Thanks to Bell Laboratories, AT&T was rated 8.01 for innovativeness. Once a lead-footed behemoth in a monopolistic world, the company is trying to dance to the tune of competition, and *Fortune's* respondents rate AT&T's management highly, at 8.27.

Digital Equipment, No. 7, ranks second only to IBM in the office equipment group. "Digital is perceived," says Michael Geran, vice president and computer-industry analyst at E.F. Hutton, "as the company that founded and continues to dominate the minicomputer market." For innovativeness, Digital gets a 7.86, eighth among the 200 companies surveyed. It was rated 8.18 for management and 8.13 for products, both outstanding scores.

SmithKline Beckman, No. 8, was once just lackluster Smith Kline & French. But the company's ulcer remedy, Tagamet, introduced in the U.S. in 1977, has made it golden. The drug's 1982 sales, estimated at over $800 million, about equaled SmithKline's entire 1977 revenues. Tagamet accounts for some 60% of profits. A merger in early 1982 with Beckman Instruments, a manufacturer of medical diagnostic equipment, further polished the company's reputation. Pharmaceutical companies all rate highly for the soundness of their financial positions; SmithKline rated 8.54, fourth among the 200.

General Electric, No. 9, was beaten out, though just barely, by IBM, Hewlett-Packard, Johnson & Johnson, and J.P. Morgan in the ranking for management. GE's rating was 8.42. That verdict is a little surprising: former Chief Executive Reginald Jones was chosen best C.E.O. and GE the best-managed company in a poll of *Fortune* 500 chief executives (see "C.E.O.s Pick the Best C.E.O.s," *Fortune,* May 4, 1981). Jones's successor, Jack Welch, is faced with the challenge of retaining the company's reputation for financial stability—it got an excellent rating of 8.32—while moving GE ahead in high-growth markets such as microelectronics. This effort might perk up the company's reputation for innovation, a run-of-the-mill 6.77. Welch feels GE doesn't always get the credit it deserves: "My inward feeling is that we are leaner, more demanding, and more agile than we are perceived to be from the outside."

General Mills, No. 10, is one of the top-ranked companies that was not rated first among the 200 for any single attribute of reputation. (The others: Merck, AT&T, Digital Equipment, SmithKline Beckman, GE.) The $5.3-billion-a-year packaged-foods giant stays ahead of the competition by plowing back cash generated by such brands as 103-year-old Gold Medal flour into high-growth cash users like its Red Lobster restaurant chain. The maker of Wheaties, "Breakfast of Champions," rates 7.64 for financial soundness, ahead of 181 of the companies in the survey.

Least-admired big companies are ruled by uncertainty—about management, markets, and earnings. *International Harvester's* ranking as No. 200 is probably predictable, given its lingering flirtation with bankruptcy. The company's management changed in May, when Archie McCardell was replaced as chief executive, but it still gets a dismal rating of 2.58. This is a good deal better than Harvester's score for financial soundness, a barely perceptible 0.6.

Great Atlantic & Pacific Tea, No. 199, has been staggering for years. A&P last paid a dividend in 1978. Managements changed and so did ownership. The huge chain (1981 sales: $7 billion) is now controlled by the Tengelmann Group, a German retailer. A&P landed among the three lowest-rated companies in all eight of the attributes of reputation surveyed except long-term investment value and financial soundness, in both of which it came in fourth from last. Trimming unprofitable stores and a third of its work force may have put A&P in the black in 1982 for the first year since 1977.

American Motors, No. 198, was slow to upgrade the fuel efficiency of its cars, though it had been the first major U.S. carmaker to trumpet the thought that small is beautiful. The company ranks a low 4.66 for product quality. (*Chrysler,* No. 189 overall, with an average score of 4.85, just escaped a place among the ten least-admired companies.)

Pan Am, No. 197, which had the same overall score as American Motors, 3.78, rated higher than the automaker on five attributes; that was the tie breaker. Pan Am's lowest rating, 2.07, was for financial soundness; it has been selling off everything from its Manhattan building ($400 million) to Intercontinental Hotels ($500 million) in a desperate effort to stay airborne. The company also falls among the lowest scorers for use of assets and long-term investment value.

F.W. Woolworth, No. 196, is the only retailer other than A&P among the least-admired corporations. Just five companies rate lower for management than Woolworth's 4.39. In September, a few weeks before his sudden death, Chief Executive Edward F. Gibbons resolved the company's identity crisis by deciding to close down 336 money-losing

Woolco discount stores and concentrate on variety and specialty stores, including shoe stores. (See "Ed Gibbons's Legacy to Woolworth," *Fortune,* November 29.) Of the 200 companies, Woolworth scored lowest for product quality—4.47.

Crown Zellerbach, No. 195, did not rank lowest or very high either for any one attribute. Perceived as the high-cost producer in its industry, the forest products company has achieved an average annual total return to investors of only 3.55% over the past ten years vs. an industry median of 8.12%. Its highest score was 5.64 for product quality, and its lowest, 3.43, was for long-term investment value.

RCA, No. 194, drained its coffers by diversifying away from electronics and entertainment in the 1960s and 1970s, and the company's lowest rating—3.74—is for use of assets. The door of RCA's executive suite has been revolving—four chief executives in six years—and the company received an unimpressive 3.99 for management.

Operating levels in the steel industry are below 40% of capacity, lowest since the Depression, and two steelmakers are among the least admired. *Republic,* No. 193, has continued to pour dollars into a broad modernization program, and its value as a long-term investment was rated at 3.83—lowest in the metal manufacturing group. *National Steel,* No. 191, beset by weakness in its savings and loan and aluminum businesses as well as steel, is facing an estimated 1982 deficit of over $200 million.

Perhaps the least-known company on the list of the poorly regarded is *Tesoro Petroleum,* No. 192. Its low overall rating has little to do with the state of its industry, petroleum refining and marketing. Unlike some other companies rated low, Tesoro (1981 sales: $3 billion) is not awash in red ink—it made $80.2 million in 1981—and has not been realigning top management: Chief Executive Robert V. West Jr. founded the company in 1964. Tesoro's problem is uncertainty even in its industry about just what it's up to. In 1975 the company made an investment in Commonwealth Oil Refining that went sour when Commonwealth developed acute financial problems; the investment was written off in March. Tesoro's lowest rating—4.12—was for use of assets.

Reputation can assume as many shapes as Proteus, the Greek sea god, and be as difficult to pin down. But when Michael Geran of E.F. Hutton was asked why IBM is so well thought of, he replied that the company's reputation rests on accomplishment. "Perception is reality," he says. *Fortune's* survey suggests that this claim, argued by philosophers through the ages, isn't far off the mark.

The best recipe for a golden reputation seems to be fast growth and few surprises—not an easy combination to sustain. Ten years ago, for example, Polaroid and Xerox would almost certainly have been high on anyone's list of well-regarded companies; in this survey both ranked in the midrange. Investors should note that except for fast-growing stars like SmithKline Beckman and Hewlett-Packard, the most admired companies weren't the best buys in the 1971-81 decade. But recently most of their stocks have outperformed the indexes. The market apparently shares the view of our respondents that these companies have positioned themselves adroitly for the Eighties.

Note: The January 9, 1984, issue of *Fortune* featured an update of this article entitled "America's Most Admired Corporations" by Nancy J. Perry. The new data introduced additional firms and industries and thus some variations. Yet in 16 of the 20 industries originally considered, the leaders retain their superiority. Three previous industry leaders dropped to second place, and the fourth is no longer ranked in the survey. In short, the article by Claire Makin continues to provide a solid picture of U.S. business leadership. Nevertheless, the reader may find Perry's article of interest.

John A. Young and Hewlett-Packard Company

Hewlett-Packard was founded by William Hewlett and David Packard, who between them headed the company for 40 years. John Young became chief executive officer in 1978 as the two founders moved into semiretirement. In the early years the company developed a strong position in the field of precision electronic instruments. Since 1966 it has moved ahead in computers as well. Currently the major product categories are computers and calculators, test and measuring instrumentation, medical electronic equipment, and instrumentation for chemical analysis. Originally a West Coast company and still headquartered in Palo Alto, California, Hewlett-Packard has extended its operations throughout the world. However, the greatest part of its international business is concentrated in Europe.

Company growth largely has been internally financed. There is a strong emphasis on new product development, and R & D expenditures are substantial. Often, new products are launched by new divisions created for that purpose. Currently there are forty-four different product divisions; most are small, and they operate with considerable autonomy. A strong value is placed on personal development—giving people the freedom to show what they can do and rewarding them accordingly. With a large number of professional employees the management style has tended to be informal and participatory. The goal is to encourage productive motivation, entrepreneurial enthusiasm, and research creativity.

Although Hewlett-Packard has been enormously successful, particularly in the precision instrument field, it now faces new problems. Growth has brought difficulties of coordination. The many small divisions have fostered an entrepreneurial spirit, but they have also created a fragmented, somewhat unplanned approach in the marketplace. For instance, the computer hardware and software produced by two separate divisions may not be entirely compatible. Products are often overlapping. The founders and many older managers are clearly more comfortable with the instrumentation part of

John Young of Hewlett-Packard

turned upon obtaining the degree and has been there since. Beginning on the marketing planning staff, he subsequently served as a regional sales manager, member of the corporate finance staff, marketing manager for the Microwave Division, and later as general manager of that division. The great majority of his experience was in marketing. As he moved on up to become chief executive in 1978, he served for several years as head of the developing computer systems group and thus gained a type of experience badly needed for company leadership. He served successively as vice-

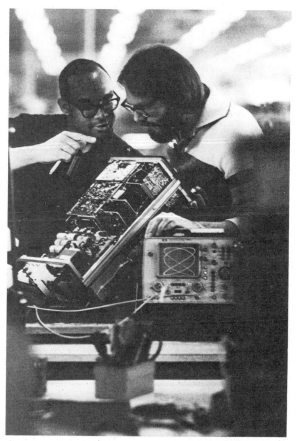

Hewlett-Packard technician Julius Moran (left) and assembler Don Schmier were part of a two-year Productivity Improvement Plan at Hewlett-Packard's oscilloscope manufacturing operation. The plan included raising quality expectations, better utilizing assets and employing current technology to reduce production-cycle times, space requirements, and inventory and rework costs.

the business; not surprisingly, the company has been somewhat less successful in the computer field to date. Finally, the entrepreneurial training provided through introduction of new products and divisions has recently proved to have its negative side as well. With the flow of venture capital into the San Francisco Bay area, many talented individuals have been leaving Hewlett-Packard to start their own firms.

The person now attempting to deal with these problems, John Young, has spent his entire career with the company. He, like the company, is a West Coast product—born in Idaho; raised in Oregon, where he obtained a degree in electrical engineering from Oregon State; and educated further at Stanford University, where he earned an M.B.A. degree in 1958.

John Young started with the company in a summer job while working toward his M.B.A. He re-

president, executive vice-president, and president during the late 1960s and 1970s.

The job of maintaining entrepreneurial enthusiasm and creativity while at the same time achieving market planning and coordination, especially within the computer business, is not an easy challenge. With too much emphasis on planning and coordination, turnover of talented personnel will become a major problem. With too much emphasis on independent entrepreneurship, sales as well as profits may decline as customers become disillusioned. It is apparent, however, that John Young was selected for his position because he had the type of knowledge and company experience that this challenge seemed to require. He is generally acknowledged to be an outstanding manager.

Chemical analysis of industrial effluent is one application for the Hewlett-Packard lab automation system at the environmental testing and certification corporation in Edison, New Jersey.

Organizational Behavior and Influencing

Part 2 examines individual employees and the forces that influence their behavior in organizations, including group processes and supervision.

These matters are important at any level of organization and throughout a managerial career, but they are most important—and absorb the greatest amount of time—at the beginning, as a person moves into the first level of supervision with responsibility for the performance of a number of employees. If people do not learn to cope with individual employees and work group dynamics effectively at this point, their managerial careers may very well be short lived; certainly their prospects for moving on up to higher levels and more diverse functions would be dim.

Much of this discussion, then, focuses on what is described in the management literature as supervising, directing, commanding, leading, motivating or activating—what we have chosen to call influencing. We also will touch upon aspects of other functions, such as controlling, decision making, and communicating. To place influencing and organizational behavior in context, it is important to keep in mind that the parts of this book dealing with organizing and organizational process and structure and with planning and management policy and strategy move successively further along the managerial career path, considering the functions that predominate at increasingly higher levels of an organization. Our concern is with bureaucratic organizations containing a number of levels of managerial hierarchy (the kind of organizations Max Weber described), unless specific reference is made to some other type of organizational system.

Although the orientation to influencing and organizational behavior is decidedly managerial, students should recognize that other approaches do exist. These may well become evident in pursuing the additional sources for more detailed study at the end of the chapters. Some writers, for instance, identify primarily with individual employees below the managerial level or with groups of such employees, and focus on personal and group development and maturity. Others are concerned with an understanding of organizational behavior for its own sake, with little reference to how this understanding is applied. Although these orientations to the field are important—for vocational guidance and for pure social science, for instance—they are not congruent with either the nature of the management discipline or the objectives of this book; thus they are not emphasized here.

Chapter 4 provides a general discussion of organizational behavior and performance, with special reference to the wide range of factors that may influence performance. Attention is given to the ways in which a knowledge of the factors determining performance may be used to supervise more effectively. This chapter introduces a framework for part 2 as a whole. In chapter 5 one particularly important factor is developed in detail: motivation. Chapter 6 examines the work group and its leadership or supervision; this chapter is the one most directly concerned with the influencing function.

Performance in Organizations

CHAPTER OUTLINE

What is Performance?
Organizational Goals
    Official Goals
    Operative Goals
    From Goals to Positions
    From Positions to Performance
Dimensions of Performance

Individual Influences on Performance
Intelligence and Learning
    Learning
    Cognitive Style
Motivation and Values
Feelings, Stress, and Satisfaction
    Stress and Performance
    Job Satisfaction
Physical Factors

Environmental Influences on Performance
The Open Systems View
The Internal Organizational Environment
    Work Groups
    Hierarchical Structure Within Groups
    Decisions at Higher Levels
    Communication
The External Environment
    Family Influences
    Physical, Economic, and Cultural Environments

Controlling Performance
The Open-Loop Control Model
    Setting Standards
    Measuring Negative Deviations
    Diagnosing Causes
    Taking Corrective Action
The Timing of Control

OBJECTIVES

To explain the nature of individual performance and how the goals of organizations influence definitions of performance.

To show how aspects of the individual influence performance in different jobs.

To provide a framework for considering how the environment influences performance.

To describe the process of control and how it may be used to identify and correct unacceptable performance.

A young secretary who had had no prior business employment experienced a good deal of difficulty in her first few months on the job. She put in the required hours and more, but she often made mistakes with regard to paperwork procedures that elicited negative comments from people in other parts of the company and necessitated her having to do the work over. Also, she seemed to enjoy talking with the other secretaries near her—so much so that she was often behind in her own work, and as a consequence of her talkativeness so were the other secretaries. Then, as a result of a divorce, the young secretary's need for work increased dramatically; at the same time high unemployment in the area made it very unlikely that she could obtain other employment. Also she found, contrary to her initial impression, that she really liked her boss and came to enjoy talking with him about a whole host of job-related matters that the two really should have been talking about all along. By the end of the first year the initial difficulties had disappeared and her performance ratings were very favorable.

This description obviously relates to various aspects of performance—such as amount and quality of work output and effects on the work of others—and to changes in performance level. It also suggests that the early difficulties were caused by a combination of factors, including a lack of business knowledge, misdirected social motivation, and a lack of strong monetary incentive, coupled with a particular set of job requirements and circumstances of the work group environment, family context, and the labor force. The important points are that (1) performance is multifaceted, so that people can do well in one area and not in another; (2) performance is typically a composite result of a number of forces within and outside the individual; and (3) changes in either individual characteristics or relevant outside forces may bring about a change in performance.

WHAT IS PERFORMANCE?

To fully understand what the concept of performance means, it is necessary to start at a point far removed from individual employees such as the young secretary: the goal structure of the organization.

Organizational Goals

The idea of organizational goals has a long history in economics, in which the classic position posits an entrepreneur or ownership group which in turn establishes the goals of the firm. Alternatively, these goals may represent a consensus arrived at by all members of the organization. Views such as these have proved more useful in the field of economics than in the management field.

An approach that is useful distinguishes between official goals, which closely parallel public expectations for the organization, and operative goals, which approximate the organization's actual guiding policies and strategies. Operative goals serve as constraints or limitations that channel high-level decisions, and often lower-level ones too, in certain directions and not others.[1]

Official Goals Society as a whole tends to have certain expectations for what organizations operating in various sectors should and should not do. Banks should lend money, universities should provide knowledge, hospitals should treat the sick, and so on; often there are clear legal statements of how these things should be done, as well as pressures to maximize production of goods and services. In essence the society establishes role prescriptions to guide the actions of organizations; typically organizations at least pay lip service to these official goals in their charters, annual reports, press releases, and in statements by top executives. For example, Hewlett-Packard's annual report contains a whole section on how it has met societal expectations in such areas as philanthropy, environmental health and safety, energy conservation, and equal employment opportunity.

Operative Goals   Usually the actual goals of an organization follow the official ones closely, yet the match need not be perfect and on occasion the gap can become sizable. In the latter instance, a company may suffer considerably as a result of court suits, loss of consumer confidence, and the like. Firms may fail to understand the official goals fully, may lack the know-how to make them operative, or may simply wish to pursue other, conflicting goals. Simon's ideas of satisficing and bounded rationality are relevant here: administrative man may fall short of official expectations and settle for what is "just good enough." Yet in departing from a fully rational, maximizing approach he may miscalculate, exceed the limits of society's zone of indifference, and incur heavy sanctions for his company.

Operative goals can vary substantially among companies, even within the same industry. If one looks outside the United States, it becomes apparent that cultural values also exert a very important influence. Exhibit 4.1 demonstrates the expansionist, productivity-oriented thrust of Japanese industry in recent years; it also indicates that Indian firms purposefully sacrifice profits to employee welfare, whereas U.S. and especially Japanese firms do not.

Finally, operative goals may function without ever being outwardly stated by anyone—or at least without such statements moving beyond the boundaries of a very small group. Companies can have goals such as liquidation, manipulating stock to maximize earnings for top executives, providing well-paying jobs for members of a controlling family, and the like. Widespread recognition of these goals might well thwart their achievement. It is not always easy, therefore, to establish what a company's operative goals really are. Organized crime provides a good example. Often established businesses are used as a front to cover operative goals which differ sharply from the apparent, socially accepted official goals of the company. The basic criminal intent in such cases may be very hard to establish.

From Goals to Positions   Because human capabilities are limited, the work that must be done to achieve operative goals is divided up horizontally, and in bureaucratic systems vertically as well, to create a hierarchy. The result is a range of positions, small in number at first, but increasing as organizations grow. To maintain order among these positions and orient them toward goals, role prescriptions are established indicating the activities each position entails; thus, jurisdictions are created.

Ideally, position requirements will be established so that they maximize the attainment of the operative goal structure taken as a whole. But for the same

EXHIBIT 4.1 Manager's operative goals in different countries

Goals   **Percent of Managers Endorsing**

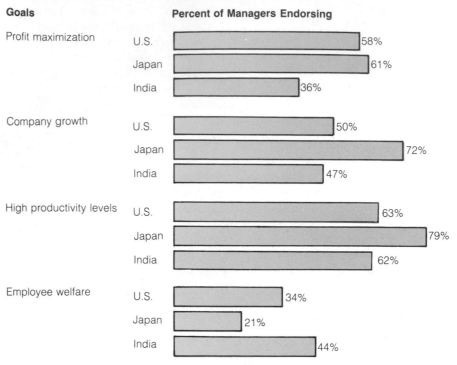

Profit maximization
U.S. — 58%
Japan — 61%
India — 36%

Company growth
U.S. — 50%
Japan — 72%
India — 47%

High productivity levels
U.S. — 63%
Japan — 79%
India — 62%

Employee welfare
U.S. — 34%
Japan — 21%
India — 44%

Adapted from George W. England, *The Manager and His Values: An International Perspective* (Cambridge, Mass.: Ballinger, 1975), p. 30.

kind of reasons that operative goals do not always match official ones, position requirements may not be perfectly congruent with operative goals. Again, if this disparity becomes too great, the organization will lack integration behind its goals—just like a football team that does not understand, or remember, or want to follow, or even have, a set of plays. Both the team and the company are likely to fail under such circumstances.

From Positions to Performance Positions may be vaguely or improperly designed; people may not really know what to do, or they may be very clear about doing things that will be disastrous for the company. Assuming a reasonable degree of congruence on up the line—from position to operative goals to official goals—widespread and large disparities between position requirements and performance can become a source of organizational failure, just as in the previous instances. But this disparity can also become a source of individual failure. If individual performance moves beyond the organization's zone of indifference, the employee becomes ineffective, and that is true for any level position—from chief executive officer to unskilled labor.

Performance, then, is what one does within the limits of a position created by an organization to achieve goals. Performance is good to the extent that it approximates the role prescriptions for the position; performance is bad to the

EXHIBIT 4.2 The flow from organizational goals to individual performance

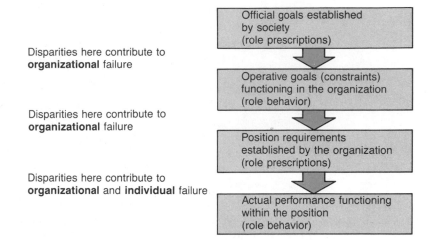

Disparities here contribute to
organizational failure

Disparities here contribute to
organizational failure

Disparities here contribute to
organizational and **individual** failure

Official goals established
by society
(role prescriptions)

Operative goals (constraints)
functioning in the organization
(role behavior)

Position requirements
established by the organization
(role prescriptions)

Actual performance functioning
within the position
(role behavior)

extent that it departs from them. At some point this departure can become excessive, so that performance failure occurs.

The processes we have been considering are outlined in Exhibit 4-2.

**Dimensions of
Performance**

Four general dimensions appear to encompass most of what is considered to be performance:

1. *Quality*—mistakes, errors, waste, accuracy.
2. *Quantity*—amount, productivity, profit and loss.
3. *Time at work*—absenteeism, lateness, lost-time accidents, premature turnover, long service, overtime.
4. *Cooperation* toward goal attainment, including—positive and negative effects on the performance of others and on goal attainment: theft, sabotage, incurring of costs, squandering resources, contributions.

People may be judged on a variety of other factors, from the color of their skin to their drinking habits off the job to their political activities. But if such factors cannot be derived in some logical manner from official goals, and thus shown to be a matter of business necessity, they are not a legitimate part of the position requirements. Neither are they included in the balance of company inducements vs. individual contributions, and thus they are not a component of the performance concept. Social legislation passed over the last 30 years has done much toward clarifying official goals in this regard.

The four dimensions of performance noted are neither mutually exclusive nor unrelated in practice. Efficiency, as it relates to the best utilization of resources, is a concept that includes both quality and quantity. Time at work, although a discrete dimension, has potential consequences for both quantity and quality. (It is often difficult to specify when turnover is premature, but at the very least separation should not occur before all costs of employment, including training, have been recovered; one company explicitly uses the term *hiring error* to denote this source of failure.) Cooperation affects quality and quantity—for example, consider

Performance in Organizations

the effect of the young secretary discussed at the beginning of this chapter on the work of other secretaries, and the positive and negative effects managers can have on those who work for them. Cooperation also can influence time at work, as when one employee saves another from serious injury, and it can on occasion affect goals such as profit directly.

INDIVIDUAL INFLUENCES ON PERFORMANCE

How can we account for differences in the performance of individuals? There is a marked tendency to attribute these differences to aspects of the person. One employee is lazy, another is a creative genius, and yet another is a real self-starter. These differences are important; they do affect performance. But so do aspects of the environment outside the individual, such as the young secretary's increased need for money as a result of family changes (a divorce) and the effects of a high unemployment level on her desire to keep her present position.

The aspects of the individual that are important for performance can be distinguished as intellectual, motivational, emotional, and physical. Although they have prevailed within the fields of organizational behavior and psychology for many years, these categories are somewhat arbitrary. For example, intelligence is subject to motivational and emotional influences, and emotional factors exert a strong effect on both physical functioning and motivation.

Intelligence and Learning

As noted in chapter 2, the occupational level at which people can function effectively—like the educational level they can realistically attain—is influenced primarily by their general intelligence, usually measured as verbal abilities. When we say that people have gotten over their heads in a job, this often means that the job requires more of such intelligence than they can bring to it. But having much *more* intelligence than a job requires need not affect performance, although it may prove personally frustrating.

Once a person achieves a position that is not too demanding in a general intellectual sense, other kinds of intellectual factors become important. Whether the individual does well or not depends on the extent to which he or she can apply knowledge relevant to the job; this in turn is a function of opportunity and ability to acquire this knowledge. Some jobs require more numerical ability, some more mechanical, some more spatial, and so on. Having these requisite abilities makes it easier not only to learn what the job requires but also to continue to perform in the job as well.

Learning is an important concept for management, and certain ways of considering employee motivation draw heavily upon it. In addition, some researchers are developing formulations of organizational learning—the process whereby organizations as a whole acquire usable knowledge.[2] One study, for instance, has examined how the companies in the tobacco industry have learned to deal with the problems created by adverse research findings regarding the effects of smoking on health. However, the field of management has developed little in the way of new theories of learning for its purposes, as it has in the areas of employee motivation and work group dynamics. The tendency has been to rely on the rather fragmented theoretical structure of the field of psychology.

A definition of learning that emphasizes aspects important for performance is as follows: *Learning* is a change in behavior of some permanence resulting from experience. The change produced need not contribute to improved performance. Learning also can (and often does) yield myths, fictions, folklore, and illusions on the job. Changes that fail to achieve any status in memory have no meaning for performance; performance is ongoing, and any learning that affects it must be also. Some type of practice or experience is necessary for learning to occur. In many cases this entails actually doing what is to be learned, but it may also involve mental rehearsal only.

Cognitive Style The way in which individuals use their intelligence in approaching specific problems and decisions is called their *cognitive style.* This concept is important not only for upper-level management, but in many other jobs as well: research positions, advertising, human resource planning, and so on. Exhibit 4.3 presents one of the most fully developed and researched approaches to this matter of cognitive style.

EXHIBIT 4.3 Types of cognitive styles

Amount of Information Used in Decisions

	Rather Low (Satisficing)	High (Maximizing)
One	**Decisive Style** Tends to use just enough data to reach a good enough decision. This decision is final, and there is no going back. Example: Harry Truman Values emphasized: efficiency, speed, and consistency Planning is based on little data, is short range, and is tight.	**Hierarchical Style** Tends to use all available data to reach the one best solution. This decision is implemented based on precise and often elaborate planning. Example: Richard Nixon Values emphasized: quality, rigorous method, and system Planning is based on much data, is long range, and is tight.
Many	**Flexible Style** Tends to use just enough data, but decisions are continually reconsidered and new solutions produced as the situation changes. Example: Franklin D. Roosevelt Values emphasized: adaptability, speed, and getting along with others Planning is based on little data and tends to be intuitive.	**Integrative Style** Tends to use all available data but produces a number of possible solutions, all of which are implemented. Example: Adlai Stevenson Values emphasized: creativity, information, and empathy Planning is based on much data, is long range, and adaptive.

Number of Possible Solutions Produced

Adapted from Michael J. Driver, "Individual Decision Making and Creativity," in *Organizational Behavior,* ed. Steven Kerr (Columbus: Grid, 1979), pp. 86–88; Michael J. Driver and Alan J. Rowe, "Decision-Making Styles: A New Approach to Management Decision Making," in *Behavioral Problems in Organization,* ed. Cary L. Cooper (Englewood Cliffs, N.J.: Prentice-Hall, 1979), pp. 151–52.

Although individuals tend to use one of these four styles under most circumstances, they usually shift to another, backup style when pressures from their environment become either very high or very low. The major exception occurs with the decisive style, which tends to be retained irrespective of what happens. Also, it appears that the best style for performance is contingent on the situation. In the insurance industry, a decisive style was best in entry-level claims adjuster positions, but in more advanced adjuster work the hierarchical style was best, and underwriters did better with an integrative style. Integrative styles also appeared to help under the uncertain conditions prevailing in the aerospace industry, but a hierarchical style was more appropriate to the highly regulated airlines.

Motivation and Values

Although they differ in connotation, terms such as interests, needs, wishes, impulses, drives, wants, intentions, motives, desires, attitudes, and values all refer to human motivation. So too do many personality traits, such as conformity and sociability. In large part people bring these motivational constellations with them to an organization, but some may be developed during employment. Motivation energizes or activates the human structures called organizations, just as electricity provides the energy that makes a machine run. Because of its essential energizing function, motivation is an extremely important consideration in the study of management.

For performance to be at its best, the motivation of the individual and the role prescriptions of the organization should mesh perfectly. If a person has strong needs that are constantly frustrated by the requirements of a position, or the position calls for certain motives which the individual lacks to any meaningful degree, performance will suffer.

A wide range of theories—many of them well supported by research—have been advanced to explain motivation in an organizational context and to improve the fit between the individual and the work. These theories may focus on different aspects of motivation, or they may apply to certain kinds of jobs but not others. We have seen that the theories of motivation to manage and professional motivation as stated in Exhibits 2.4 and 2.14 are job specific in this sense. Chapter 5 examines a number of other important ideas about motivation, and it also deals with the role of values in performance. A value may be defined as:

> An enduring . . . belief that a specific mode of behavior or end-state of existence is preferred to an opposite mode of behavior or end-state. This belief transcends attitudes toward objects and toward situations; it is a standard that guides and determines action, attitudes . . . , ideology, presentations of self to others, and attempts to influence others.[3]

Values are extremely powerful motivational forces and very resistant to change. On occasion they are much like other motives, but more frequently they derive from a whole culture and are widely shared within that culture. Changes in individual values of this kind are very unlikely without a preceding cultural change. For example, values regarding the employment of women remained consistently negative in this country until the demands of a wartime economy during World War II brought about a substantial shift in the culture itself.

Feelings, Stress, and Satisfaction

Feelings, or emotions, range from positive to negative: joy, happiness, and love; excitement, anger, hatred, and jealousy; anxiety, fear, shame, guilt, and depression.

Most of these emotions do not have a consistent impact on performance. Emotions in healthy people are transistory, and we would not expect them to exert the effects that motives and values do. Yet some important effects have been found, usually when for some reason an emotional state becomes both intense and sustained.

Stress and Performance Exhibit 4.4 sets forth some of the consequences of high and continuing stress levels. Stress causes emotional arousal, which in turn can produce a wide range of physiological changes. Thus, continuing stress can place excessive demands on certain bodily processes.[4] It also can contribute to emotional disorders and to impaired physical health.

Stress results from an interaction between a particular situation and a negative emotional reaction in the individual. This interaction appears to be learned in some manner, often early in life. The factors which interact to produce emotional and physical symptoms that can affect performance are as follows:

1. A set of situations such as airplane travel, oral presentations before groups, interactions with superiors, and the like that are seen as directly threatening and that arouse strong negative feelings. The more such situations there are, the greater the likelihood of continuing exposure to stress.
2. The frequency and duration of actual exposure to these situations, perhaps as necessitated by the role prescriptions for a job. Anticipation of exposure also may set off stress reactions in many people.
3. The intensity of the emotional reaction caused by these situations. In general the more intense the reaction the more far-reaching the consequences, but differences do exist between people in what is called *ego strength*—the capacity to withstand intense emotion without overreaction.

To the extent these factors lead to avoidance of situations and behaviors that are part of the job, a person's performance in its various dimensions will be influenced directly. Alternatively, reactions of the kind noted in Exhibit 4.4 may occur that in turn have negative effects on performance. This is not to imply that performance is always harmed by emotion, or even by negative feelings; up to a point, arousal tends to have positive effects. Beyond this the emotions become stressful and distracting. Routine, automatic work is less likely to be disrupted, however.[5] Thus, lower-level job performance can go uninfluenced by stress reactions that are highly disruptive of performance in more skilled and managerial positions.

The literature on job stress has expanded sharply in the past few years, and so have programs designed to reduce this stress, from meditation to exercise programs to time management. There has also been substantial discussion, and some research, dealing with the *Type A* personality (a stress-prone type of person likely to develop coronary heart disease) and with *job burnout* (a reaction to stress characterized by exhaustion, depression, and disengagement, frequently found among professionals).[6] The basic idea is that stress reflects a lack of fit between aspects of the person and aspects of the job.

Job Satisfaction Feelings of anxiety at work are closely associated with greater perceived job stress and with more health problems. They are also related to less overall job satisfaction.[7] Job satisfaction refers to the feelings

EXHIBIT 4.4 Possible effects of stress

Subjective
Anxiety
Aggression
Apathy
Boredom
Depression
Fatigue
Frustration
Guilt
Shame
Irritability
Moodiness
Low self-esteem
Threat
Nervousness
Loneliness

Behavioral
Accident proneness
Drug use
Emotional outburst
Excessive eating
Loss of appetite
Excessive drinking
Excitability
Impulsive behavior
Impaired speech
Nervous laughter
Restlessness
Trembling

Cognitive
Inability to make decisions and concentrate
Frequent forgetfulness
Sensitivity to criticism
Mental blocks

Physiological
Increased blood and urine
  catecholamines and corticosteroids
Increased blood glucose
Increased heart rate and blood
  pressure
Dryness of the mouth
Sweating
Dilation of pupils
Difficulty in breathing
Hot and cold spells
Lump in the throat
Numbness in the limbs

Health
Asthma
Amenorrhea
Dyspepsia
Frequent urination
Psychosomatic disorders
Diabetes mellitus
Chest or back pains
Coronary heart disease
Diarrhea
Faintness and dizziness
Headache or migraine
Neurosis or psychosis
Nightmares
Insomnia
Skin rash
Ulcers
Loss of sex drive
Weakness

Organizational
Absenteeism
Poor industrial relations
Poor productivity
High accident rates
High labor turnover
Poor organizational climate
Antagonism at work
Job dissatisfaction

Adapted from T. Cox, *Stress* (Baltimore: University Park Press, 1978).

people have in evaluating their jobs or job experiences. This evaluation typically is made relative to some standard of expectation, value, or desire; it results in emotions such as pleasure, anger, unhappiness, or depression.

Although job satisfaction often is spoken of and measured as applying to the job as a whole, this is somewhat misleading. People are more or less satisfied with different aspects of the work at different times. Because role prescriptions vary according to the position, the aspects of the work that are important for satisfaction can vary too. Exhibit 4.5 lists aspects found to be important in job satisfaction in two different occupational groups in two countries. As Exhibit 4.5 shows, a wide range of factors can elicit feelings about one's job.

Exhibit 4.6 derives from a study of a national sample of the United States labor force and provides some idea of what bothers people in this country most about their work. It is important for what it says about things a company can do to improve satisfaction.

The matter of how job satisfaction relates to performance has intrigued social scientists for years, and a large body of research has been developed in this area. For some time it was thought to be almost axiomatic that the more satisfied a person is on the job, the better the quantity and quality of performance. In the early years this was the basic rationale for the human relations movement which developed out of the Hawthorne studies. However, in many

---

EXHIBIT 4.5 Aspects of determining job satisfaction in the U.S. and Great Britain

U.S. Accountants and Engineers	British Electronics Industry Production Workers
Recognition	Pay
Achievement	Self-actualization
Possibility of growth	Induction to the job
Advancement	Recognition
Salary	Training
Interpersonal relations with supervisor	Physical effort and conditions
Interpersonal relations with subordinates	Supervision
Interpersonal relations with peers	Working conditions
Technical supervision	Mental as opposed to physical work
Responsibility	Self-control of work as opposed to required output
Company policy and administration	Social peer relations
Working conditions	Responsibility for quality
The work itself	
Factors in personal life	
Status	
Job security	

SOURCE: U.S. data: Frederick Herzberg, Bernard Mausner, and Barbara S. Snyderman, *The Motivation to Work* (New York: Wiley, 1959), p. 60; Great Britain data: Ray Wild and J. A. Dawson, "The Relationship of Specific Job Attitudes with Overall Job Satisfaction and the Influence of Biographical Variables," *Journal of Management Studies* (April 1972):152.

EXHIBIT 4.6 Work-related problems of U.S. workers

Problem	Percent Reporting
Exposed to safety and health hazards	78
Difficult to get work days changed	77
Difficult to get work hours changed	72
Desire for improvement of present fringe benefits	58
Inadequate time for leisure activities	55
Desire for additional fringe benefits	55
Shortage of jobs in worker's line of work	54
Difficult to get duties changed	54
Stake in present job too great to change jobs	48
Difficult to find another job with similar pay	42
Feeling that time drags at work	40
Earns less than deserved compared to others doing similar work	39
Transportation problems	38
Unpleasant work environment	37
Skills underutilized in present job	36

Adapted from G. L. Staines and R. P. Quinn, "American Workers Evaluate the Quality of Their Jobs," *Monthly Labor Review* (January 1979):6.

contexts the more satisfied employees are not the most productive—in fact, they can be the least productive. Productivity depends on a wide range of contingencies, although there does appear to be a slight tendency for satisfaction and productive output to move together. Even this does not imply a causal effect of satisfaction on performance; often the process is reversed, with satisfaction (or the lack of it) being a consequence of how well the person is performing. Or some other factor, such as high pay, may yield both good performance and high satisfaction.

One consistent finding is that satisfaction level is related to time at work.[8] More specifically, those who are most likely to leave an organization or to be absent frequently are people who feel considerable dissatisfaction. The processes through which turnover may come about are outlined in Exhibit 4.7. Many instances of uncooperative performance also appear to be a consequence of low satisfaction levels.

Overall, then, whether job satisfaction is an important determinant of performance depends almost entirely on which aspect of performance one has in mind—for some dimensions it is a very powerful factor. Strikes, such as the recent walkouts by employees at Greyhound Corporation and Continental Airlines, often are triggered by substantial dissatisfaction. From a managerial viewpoint, the relationship between job satisfaction and the quality and quantity of performance does not appear to be strong enough or well enough understood to provide much of a guide for action. This is not true of the other aspects of performance, however.

EXHIBIT 4.7 The employee turnover decision process

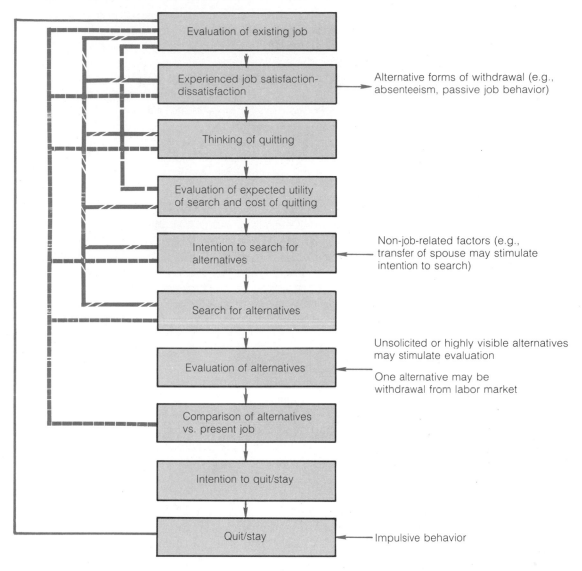

SOURCE: William H. Mobley, "Intermediate Linkages in the Relationship between Job Satisfaction and Employee Turnover," *Journal of Applied Psychology* (April 1977):238. Copyright 1977 by the American Psychological Association. Reprinted by permission of the author.

Physical Factors

Completing our list of individual influences on performance are certain physical factors, ranging from illness to bodily proportions to various motor and sensory skills and dexterities. These factors have not typically been the subject of special study within the framework of the management field; what is known about them derived almost entirely from medicine and psychology.

One type of factor that may influence performance is physical well-being, whether associated with emotional factors or not. The major effects are on absenteeism, but work quality and quantity can suffer as well. Research on the effects of high bodily temperatures and feverish conditions indicates that although performance suffers more the higher the temperature, the point at which a significant performance effect occurs varies considerably; some people's work is affected very little even when they are quite ill.[9]

Physical handicaps have consequences for job performance that vary according to the nature of the handicap and the nature of the position. When the fit is an appropriate one, turnover tends to be low and the quantity and quality of performance are unaffected. Neither absenteeism nor accidents present special problems, although the time lost when accidents do occur is often greater than for those who are not disabled.[10] The important consideration is to get physically handicapped employees into positions where the specific disability is least relevant for the work.

Another set of physical factors has to do with bodily aspects, many of which are in large part determined at birth: proportions, attractiveness, strength, muscular and sensory skills and dexterities. Again, relevance for performance depends on the nature of the job. Height is important for professional basketball players and attractive physical proportions for models; in many other types of work such factors matter not at all. Designing equipment to adapt it to the characteristics of human operators is an important consideration here and is a concern of the field of human engineering.

Muscular skills and dexterities are strongly influenced by training, although underlying physical abilities affect the speed and extent of learning. Thus, men typically outperform women in sheer strength, but in manipulative dexterity of the kind required in many assembly jobs, women excel over men. Among the sensory and perceptual capabilities, those of a visual and auditory nature are most relevant for performance. Perceptual speed is important in a variety of clerical and inspection tasks in which numerical data or mechanical assemblies must be checked rapidly. On occasion this requirement extends into the muscular area as well (perceptual-motor speed)—for instance, when certain actions must be taken if errors are noted.

| ENVIRONMENTAL INFLUENCES ON PERFORMANCE | We have already noted that performance is in part a function of the way positions are defined and structured within an organization. However, numerous other forces both within the organization and beyond its boundaries can boost or weaken performance. This whole process is best understood within the framework of an open systems model. |

| The Open Systems View | The open systems approach emphasizes two major aspects of organizational behavior: (1) its *system* character, such that movements or actions in one part of the organization lead in predictable ways to movements or actions in other parts; and (2) its *openness* to environmental forces, with the result that the behavior is continually in a state of flux.[11] The manner in which this process operates is outlined in Exhibit 4.8. Aspects of the individual—intellectual, motivational, emotional, and physical—do not yield one-to-one relationships with performance; they are conditioned by forces within the organization that may maximize the return on the |

EXHIBIT 4.8 The role of the environment in an open systems view of performance

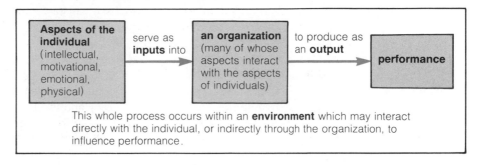

human input or obliterate it, depending on the particular mix of human inputs and organizational forces involved. Also, the environment beyond the boundaries of the organization itself can influence not only the ways in which the various organizational forces operate, but more important for our purposes, it can interact directly with aspects of the individual to affect performance.

Exhibit 4.8 does not contain a statement of the specific organizational forces that are important for performance, nor does it indicate the parts of the organization these forces usually come from. The exhibit is also incomplete in its statement of important forces outside the organization. These are intentional omissions, designed to make the open systems concept easier to understand. The discussions that follow are intended to fill in these blanks.

The Internal Organizational Environment

Organizations influence performance implicitly in how they create positions and establish role prescriptions—how they structure the work in relationship to organizational goals. If a job in financial planning calls for extensive numerical calculations, often with the aid of computer programs, and the person in the job has both high numerical ability and the relevant mathematical and computer knowledge, job success is a function not only of individual characteristics but also of how the job was structured by the organization. If either the individual capabilities or the organizational requirements should change, performance could well suffer. As will be discussed in part 5, position requirements often are determined in a personnel department, but under certain circumstances they may be created directly at the work group level or even in part by the individual performing the job. At higher management levels and in certain technical areas it has been common for individuals to "write their own job descriptions" in terms of their unique capabilities. As we shall see in the next chapter, this approach is now finding its way into many other positions—with both added benefits and new problems of coordination.

Work Groups Typically, work groups have been thought of as consisting of the people who report to a first-line supervisor and that supervisor. This is an overly narrow view, however. Committees and boards are work groups; so are special project teams created to carry out certain functions, such as research efforts or the evaluation of a particular activity. The managers at higher levels who all report to the same manager may or may not be part of the same work group. Whether a number of regional sales managers across the country represent a group depends on whether their superior treats them as such or instead deals with them one-on-one, and on how they relate to one another.

Most people in the business world perform at least part of the time in a group environment, and many are members of several groups. These groups can condition performance in numerous ways. Groups can operate to enforce their own norms restricting output, as Frederick Taylor and the Hawthorne researchers observed; they can also serve to support and help their members, in the manner of many military squads under combat conditions. This important aspect of organizational behavior is considered at length in chapter 6.

Hierarchical Structure Within Groups   Chapter 6 also gives detailed attention to the roles and behaviors of those people who come to be in charge of groups, through election, appointment, or other means. It is common practice to fire managers, whether of company units or athletic teams, even chief executive officers, when things are not going well. Behind such actions is the clear expectation that how a manager behaves causes either poor or good performance in a group, and therefore it is reasonable to hold managers accountable for group results. By replacing the manager, it should be possible to turn a group or a company around and get back on the right track. Anyone who has worked in business for very long will have observed that there are tremendous differences among managers in how they act; it is only natural to assume that these differences are directly reflected in the level of subordinates' performance.

Research indicates that influencing does make a difference.[12] But under normal circumstances it probably does not make nearly as much difference as is commonly assumed. Many lower-level supervisors operating within the confines of company policies, union contracts, and preprogrammed machines do not have enough discretion to influence the performance of those who work for them; two supervisors can behave quite differently and it matters very little. Similarly, when a work group consists entirely of experienced employees who know their jobs well, supervisory effects on performance typically are small.

The behavior of subordinates, particularly the level of their performance, and the complexity of the work to be done exert as much influence on the behavior of supervisors as the supervisors' behavior does on subordinate performance. Many of the differences we note among supervisors are simply reactions to the particular problems they are facing, rather than reflections of their own established styles. Given all these considerations it is not too surprising that replacing the manager of a poorly performing basketball or baseball team often has very little long-term effect at all. Influencing is important, but so are many other things. Even at higher levels, influencing may fail to achieve its goals. During the period of the Cuban missile crisis President Kennedy repeatedly ordered the removal of United States missiles from our bases in Turkey. Yet they remained firmly in place.

Decisions at Higher Levels   In bureaucratic systems, what happens at the top of the pyramid can have a sizable impact down through the system, and this is particularly true for performance. Top-level decisions often are in the form of policies that direct actions throughout the organization. A policy of promotion from within, for instance, may result in the identification of an ideal candidate for a management position who otherwise might have been overlooked; alternatively, it may cause the promotion of a manager into a position where he or she is clearly underqualified. Decisions at the top need not be formulated as policy, however. Often, special cases are forwarded to higher levels for decision: how to handle a younger member of a family that owns a large block of company stock, what decision to make in a discipline case that the union is sure to take all the way to arbitration.

Exhibit 4.9 contains examples of ways in which decisions at higher levels within the organization may influence performance. As these examples show, a

---

EXHIBIT 4.9 Top-level decisions and their effect on performance

1. Variations in the extent to which investments are made in different types of organizational actions.
   Positive example: An experienced manager has a drinking problem and is restored to an effective performance level through a company-sponsored treatment program.
   Negative example: A clerk-typist does not type well because of poor training before coming into the company, and this situation continues because the company has decided not to invest in training of this kind.

2. Variations in how effectively placement decisions match individuals with positions.
   Positive example: Detailed medical information is obtained on a person who has suffered from infantile paralysis (poliomyelitis), and in accordance with existing policies regarding the hiring of handicapped people the individual is employed and appropriately placed.
   Negative example: A young Ph.D. chemist finds herself working on the production floor the first day at work because "everyone has to learn the business from the bottom up"; she resigns at the end of the first week.

3. Variations in the company's permissiveness with regard to performance-related matters.
   Positive example: An employee receives a three-day suspension without pay for fighting, in accordance with company policy and the terms of the union contract. He understands that a subsequent infraction will result in discharge and does not fight again.
   Negative example: The company prides itself on a particularly liberal sick leave policy and makes no effort to check on the status of employees who call in sick. This company has the greatest absenteeism problem in its industry.

4. Variations in the number of subordinates permitted to work for a single supervisor (span of control).
   Positive example: A sales region containing twenty districts is performing very poorly. The region is split into two so that each regional manager may devote more time to working with the district managers, and sales improve.
   Negative example: In the interest of maintaining low administrative overhead, a company assigns a large number of employees to each first-level supervisor. As a consequence there is a complete breakdown of the quality control function in a unit that has experienced high turnover and has a large number of "green" employees who need supervisory assistance.

large proportion of the higher-level decisions that relate to performance fall in the personnel area. Policy formulation, decision making, and policy implementation on these matters may be assigned in part to the department that handles this function.

Communication   When certain information is necessary for a person to perform effectively and a communication breakdown occurs, with the result that the information does not get where it is needed when it should, performance suffers. Similarly, effective communication processes that do not contain blocks—so that the sender sends, the transmission process transmits, and the receiver receives—contribute to good performance. To some extent this is a matter of technical effectiveness in telecommunications, computerized information systems, and the like, but there are additional considerations that extend beyond the purely technical.

Many communications simply are lost—people do not recall receiving them, even a few hours later. Of those that definitely are received, only some 50 percent would be fully recognized if they were fed back again to the sender; in other words, virtually half of all actual communications received do not contain the sender's full intent. Various procedures have been developed to reduce errors in communication. One is *redundancy*—the message is sent several times in various forms, as when an item of information is read in a textbook, heard in a lecture, and also included in an examination question. Another approach involves *feedback* with verification: the receiver reports back what he or she has understood and is then corrected, until complete mutual agreement has been achieved between sender and receiver. Redundancy and the two-way communication required for feedback are time consuming and costly, but they can contribute to improved performance.[13]

In most companies, downward communication appears to work relatively well (at least with really important information), largely because bureaucratic systems facilitate the process. The major problems occur in upward communication, because bureaucracies were not really designed for this purpose. Managers at higher levels may not receive information that they need to make good decisions—information that is available at lower levels. Distortions and blocks in the upward movement of information are greater (1) the larger the differential is in the status of sender and receiver, (2) the more influence the higher-level person has on promotion decisions related to the lower-level sender, (3) the less the lower-level person trusts the superior, and (4) the more insecure the subordinate is. In other words, subordinates tend to filter the information they send up the line to protect themselves and foster their own interests. As a result, the performances of those at higher levels suffer for lack of valid information. Upward communication is one of the major problems in bureaucratically organized systems. However, computerized information systems that can effectively bypass many hierarchical levels have provided a partial solution to this problem in recent years. Once information gets into a computer memory, it is available to anyone who can tap the computer system.

A final performance-related problem in communication is overload: individuals receiving more information than they can process effectively. Redundancy and feedback can contribute to overload. Also, the mass of information stored in computers can produce a maze of printouts beyond the capacity of any human being to absorb. Overload is a major source of job stress. A variety of means of dealing with information overload exist, each with its own advantages and disadvantages; nevertheless, overload is a major cause of performance problems, especially at higher organizational levels in which multiple communication channels come together.

The External Environment

A number of important theories of an open systems nature deal with how environmental forces beyond the organization's boundaries can influence its structures and functioning. These structures and processes (such as spans of control and personnel policies) in turn can have an impact on the performance of individuals, as we have just noted. More important for present purposes than these indirect effects of the external environment on individual performance, however, are certain direct effects stemming largely from family events and from the physical, economic, and cultural work context.

Family Influences   In general, family influences stem from either the nuclear family into which a person is born or the family created by marriage. However, many significant families extend to include other relatives, and close personal bonds can create a quasi-family even without the formalization of marriage. Family influences can exert strong positive or negative pressures on work performance. Some of the ways in which this may happen include the following:

1. Family crises such as divorce, death, severe illness, and the like produce emotional stress that disrupts work performance. *Example:* An individual responds to the death of a parent with severe grief and is so depressed that she is unable to work. Alternatively, the lack of such crises in an individual's life may provide the conditions for productive work.
2. Separation from significant family members and the support they provide produces separation anxiety or homesickness that disrupts work performance. *Example:* A management consultant is required to spend long periods away from his wife and family, much of the time in Europe. He feels extremely upset and helpless during these periods, cannot concentrate on his work, and spends an inordinate amount on telephone calls to his home. Alternatively, being able to return home to a supportive family every evening may enable an individual to work effectively.
3. Demands and competing pressures stemming from a family may reduce the time an individual spends at work or otherwise may interfere with performance. *Example:* A mother of two small children is not able to make satisfactory arrangements to have her children cared for while she works, in part because the children are sick a lot. Consequently she misses an excessive amount of time and often has to leave work during the day to care for her children. Alternatively, a family may provide strong support and approval of work activities, with the result that performance is strengthened.

For many people, however, it is possible (and preferable) to maintain a separation between job and family, in much the same manner as the U.S. Constitution provides for the separation of church and state.

Physical, Economic, and Cultural Environments   The range of factors that may be included here is large, but it is possible to provide a general idea of how performance might be affected. For example, aspects of the climate and topography of a region can combine with either emotional or physical factors to influence performance. Certain individuals react to the prevailing rain and dampness in the Pacific Northwest with low-grade depression and chronic bronchial problems, but many long-term residents thrive on the climate and look forward to the rainy season. Other aspects of a geographic location that can make a difference in performance are the degree of isolation of the environment and its novelty or strangeness. Work in the arctic region with the oil companies, for instance, appears to be influenced more by these factors than by the climate itself.

Noise, lighting, temperature, and other conditions in the workplace, of the kind the Hawthorne researchers originally set out to study, can be important. So too can the design and operating condition of equipment and machinery used in carrying out the work. Health and accident hazards not only can result in excessive absenteeism but also can produce enough anxiety to disrupt the quantity and quality of output.

Aspects of the economic environment that affect performance include (1) competitive pressures that make it impossible for a salesperson to sell a product; (2) union activities that cause a number of union members to go out on strike; and (3) business cycles that in times of recession and high unemployment stimulate employees to do everything they can to hold onto their jobs. The economic environment can provide both positive and negative forces. Economic competition within an industry can stimulate the efforts and performance of certain people, and union actions can contribute to a more secure and productive work environment.

The cultural environment and its values can stimulate or depress performance generally within a society. There is considerable evidence that the more industrialized societies have been characterized by strong achievement values during the periods of their greatest development.[14] Similarly, individuals may selectively uphold certain strong values of their culture or subculture, and the effect on performance can be either positive or negative. During wartime it is common practice to excuse conscientious objectors from combat duty because of their religious values. But many others with similar values enter combat units and fail to perform their jobs effectively, either because they do not fire their weapons or because they deliberately miss.

Societies also create legal sanctions and other pressures to enforce compliance with values. Such forces may lead an individual to decide against stealing from an employer when an easy opportunity presents itself. They may also lead to the imprisonment of an employee for something done outside of work, although at work he or she may have been a model performer; such imprisonment can result in lengthy, enforced absenteeism that represents a performance problem for the company, whether or not the individual ever returns to work.

CONTROLLING PERFORMANCE

We have reviewed a large number of factors that interact in an open systems model to produce individual performance. The result may be anything from outstanding performance to total failure, depending on what factors interact and in what manner. One way in which managers can use this information about performance is by understanding how the process of control operates.

The Open-Loop Control Model

Exhibit 4.10 outlines the flow of the control process. Control involves comparing events, in this case performance, against previously established standards with a view to introducing corrective action when there is an unacceptable deviation. As long as performance is within an acceptable range, even when there is considerable room for improvement, the control model prescribes no action. Thus, controlling focuses on what are or what might become the worst cases. Under some circumstances, perhaps a very wide span of control, this is all that a manager can accomplish. At other times controlling may represent a satisficing approach to the job, in the worst sense of that term; efforts beyond merely controlling should aim to move acceptable performance to higher levels whenever possible.

The model of Exhibit 4.10 is described as open loop because it contains a diagnostic, decision-making step between the identification of a problem and action to correct it. This diagnostic process can cover a considerable period of time, as when medical or psychological tests are introduced as aids to identify causes. It appears to be inevitable when dealing with human performance as opposed to machinery. A closed-loop control system, in contrast, does not require any diagnosis.[15] The discovery of an unacceptable deviation automatically triggers a predetermined corrective action which feeds back to performance. Computer-based control systems, such as those used in chemical manufacturing or petroleum refining, are closed loop in this sense.

EXHIBIT 4.10   An open-loop control model

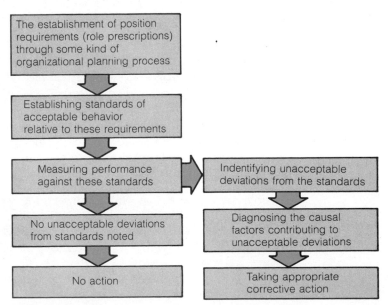

Performance in Organizations

Setting Standards First, standards must establish a minimally acceptable level of performance on the various dimensions—quality, quantity, time at work, and cooperation. These standards typically are developed by an immediate superior or by organizational units assigned this task: personnel, budget, methods and standards, industrial engineering, quality control, and the like. Standards ideally should be clearly established numerical cutting points—number of units rejected as below standard, proportion of work days on which the employee is absent, and so on—but often they are the highly subjective feelings of individual supervisors. Once established, standards serve to trigger control processes.

In recent years there has been an increasing tendency to include the individuals performing the work in the standard-setting process. This is particularly characteristic of certain management-by-objectives programs, where goals or standards are set in advance and subsequently are used to measure performance. Within such programs, performance appears to be little affected by whether or not the individual participates in the establishment of personal work standards.[16] Nevertheless, the existence of some kind of standard-setting or goal-setting procedure does make a difference. As we shall see in the next chapter, goal setting is an important contributor to performance outcomes.

Measuring Negative Deviations Once standards are set, the performance of an individual must be measured against them. Again, the ideal is an objective, numerical measure applied against an objective, numerical standard. But this may not be feasible for important aspects of the work, and subjective measures often are employed.

Since performance contains a number of dimensions, a question arises as to how they may be used in defining performance failure. The answer is that below-standard performance on any dimension considered relevant should activate the control process. Obviously if two or three or four dimensions are involved, the problem is greater than if only one aspect of performance yields an unacceptable label.

Diagnosing Causes Rarely if ever is performance failure a result of a single cause; individual and environmental interactions are typical. Exhibit 4.11 presents one type of diagnostic schema that has been used in determining why people fail to meet established performance standards. This schema parallels much of the preceding discussion. Percentage estimates of occurrence of performance problems are provided for the major groupings. In individual cases of unacceptable performance deviations, the number of causes found to be operating (out of the thirty-five noted) range up to seven. On the average there are about 3.5 causal factors in each instance of failure.

Taking Corrective Action In applying corrective action it is essential to look at the causes established during diagnosis to determine which can be changed and which cannot. Of those that can be changed, which can be changed most easily, at the least cost, and with the greatest likelihood that acceptable performance will result? One possible corrective action is to revise existing standards downward to make them more appropriate to employee capabilities, analogous to revising budget figures to fit more recent data.

EXHIBIT 4.11 Schema of possible causes of negative performance

Individual Influences

Problems of Intelligence and Job Knowledge (25%)

1. Insufficient verbal ability
2. Insufficient special ability
3. Insufficient job knowledge
4. Defect of judgment or memory

Emotional Problems (60%)

5. Frequent disruptive emotion (anxiety, depression, anger, excitement, shame, guilt, jealousy)
6. Neurosis (with anxiety, depression, anger, and so on, predominating)
7. Psychosis (with anxiety, depression, anger, and so on, predominating)
8. Alcohol and drug problems

Motivational Problems (62%)

9. Strong motives frustrated at work (pleasure in success, fear of failure, avoidance motives, dominance, desire to be popular, social motivation, need for attention, and so on)
10. Unintegrated means used to satisfy strong motives
11. Excessively low personal work standards
12. Generalized low work motivation

Physical Problems (10%)

13. Physical illness or handicap, including brain disorders
14. Physical disorders of emotional origin
15. Inappropriate physical characteristics
16. Insufficient muscular or sensory ability or skill

Environmental Influences

Family Related Problems (20%)

17. Family crises (divorce, death, severe illness, and the like)
18. Separation from the family and isolation
19. Predominance of family considerations over work demands

Problems Caused in the Work Group (33%)

20. Negative consequences associated with group cohesion
21. Ineffective management
22. Inappropriate managerial standards or criteria

Problems Originating in Company Policies and Higher-Level Decisions (90%)

23. Insufficient organizational action
24. Placement error
25. Organizational overpermissiveness
26. Excessive spans of control
27. Inappropriate organizational standards and criteria

Problems Stemming from Society and Its Values (12%)

28. Application of legal sanctions
29. Enforcement of societal values by means other than the law (including the use of value-based inappropriate criteria)

(continued)

EXHIBIT 4.11 (continued)

30. Conflict between job demands and cultural values (equity, freedom, moral and religious values, and so on)

Problems Growing Out of the Work Context and the Work Itself (30%)

31. Negative consequences of economic forces
32. Negative consequences of geographic location
33. Detrimental conditions in the work setting
34. Excessive danger
35. Problems in the work itself

SOURCE: John B. Miner, *The Challenge of Managing* (Philadelphia: Saunders, 1975), pp. 330–31.

Appropriate corrective action can include the following:

Job redesign and changed role prescriptions
Promotion, transfer, or demotion
Management development and training
Changes in supervision (either the style or person)
Changes in compensation
Personnel policy modification (or making exceptions)
Threats and disciplinary action
Counseling and psychotherapy
Medical treatment
Alcoholics Anonymous[17]

The Timing of Control

Ideally, corrective actions would be introduced to prevent unacceptable deviations from happening at all. For example, if a manager was absolutely sure that a particular individual would respond negatively to being away from home over an extended period, the manager could take steps to ensure that this individual did not ever receive assignments involving extensive travel. Whether this is actually control at all or merely preventive action is something of an open question; in any event, this kind of action requires the capacity to forecast accurately, which may be very costly or perhaps impossible. Also, it is often difficult to convince others, such as those who must travel because the one individual does not, that an action is appropriate when there is not yet any evidence that a problem exists.

Most managers do face numerous control situations which have moved beyond the preventive stage. Sometimes controls may be initiated early, but in the case of performance it is usually necessary to wait until departures from standards are clearly established. *Steering* controls are introduced long before a process is completed, based on measurements of relatively small deviations and predictions of what these deviations could develop into if left uncorrected. Much supervisory coaching of new employees has this quality. *Yes–no* controls are designed to ensure that preliminary steps in a process are performed up to standard before subsequent steps are initiated. This approach can often be used in training: learning and performance on one part of a job must reach a certain level before the individual can move on to the next part.

With experienced employees, control that occurs well after the action often is all that is feasible. Managers must actually overspend their budgets, employees must in fact be absent more than they should within a given time period, workers must show a continuing inability to produce up to standard, and so on. Without waiting for these final results to come in, a manager simply may not be able to legitimize corrective action and accordingly may face overwhelming resistance from either the employee or others who are affected.

Summary

We have been concerned with understanding the nature of performance and how a wide range of individual and environmental factors may combine to influence individual performance. The primary focus has been on the causation of performance, because that is what managers must concern themselves with in their jobs. However, important concepts such as the nature of organizational goals, the open systems view, and the control model also have been introduced.

If one evaluates managerial performance in terms of results achieved, and most companies do, then the performance of subordinates is just about the most important thing a manager has to deal with. In an ideal world managers do all they can to maximize the performance of subordinates; managers try to employ the best possible people for the jobs to be done, to influence these people to achieve their full potential, and to influence their environments so that this will be possible.

Yet there are a great many things about the individual employee and the environment that a manager cannot influence, especially in the first level of supervision. Furthermore, not all managers are perfect. Many managers will often find themselves operating in a preventive mode, devoting their major energies to heading off problems and keeping performance levels at least from falling into the unacceptable zone. All too often this does not work and the manager faces certain clear instances of ineffective performance. At this point, managing becomes a matter of controlling with the objective of moving performance levels up to an acceptable level.

Whether concerned with maximizing, taking preventive action, or controlling in dealing with performance, managers encounter (1) a set of factors in the individual—intellectual, motivational, emotional, and physical; (2) a set of factors in the organizational environment itself—groups and the exercise of power within them, higher-level decisions, communication processes; and (3) a set of factors beyond the organization's boundary—family considerations, the geographic and physical environment, economic circumstances, and culture. Exhibit 4.11 lists some of these determinants of performance. The more one knows about these determinants, the more one can control—and improve—the performance of subordinates. Ultimately, this means becoming a better manager.

What Have You Learned?

1. How do aspects of the individual and the situation interact to produce stress and emotional symptoms? How does stress affect performance?

2. How is the control model utilized in dealing with individual performance? How are corrective actions selected?

3. What are redundancy and feedback, and why

are they used in communication? How do they relate to overload?

4. What are the various aspects or dimensions of performance?

5. What can be said about how job satisfaction relates to performance?

6. How do aspects of the external environment influence performance in organizations? Note some examples.

7. How may official and operative goals differ? In what ways do these goals relate to performance?

8. In what ways are open- and closed-loop control systems the same, and in what ways are they different?

9. Verbal ability, or general intelligence, appears to play a somewhat different role in performance than other cognitive abilities and specific job knowledge. Explain.

10. What is the open systems view, and how does it assist in understanding performance?

How Well Can You Apply Your Knowledge?

Problem 1. The Brazilian subsidiary of a large American company has hired a new manager as a potential replacement for the person currently in charge of accounting activities, who is expected to retire shortly. The new manager has substantial experience in foreign assignments and a good background in accounting, but he has never managed before. He is expected to gradually assume more responsibility for the accounting department as he learns about the company and becomes proficient in Portuguese.

An initial review of the manager's progress after several months indicates that he has been doing very well in learning the company's accounting procedures and familiarizing himself with existing data. However, there are some problems. He continues to function more as an accountant than a manager. He does not communicate well with other members of the department. Conversations with others are brief, if they occur at all, and subordinates usually go away unsure of what is desired of them. Memos are poorly written and short; most are late. Furthermore, the new manager has failed to develop contacts inside the company or in the city. He rarely speaks to anyone unless approached first. After some prodding he did sign up for a company-sponsored course to learn Portuguese; however, after what appears to have been a real effort at first, which has produced little in results, he seems to have lost interest and is no longer doing anything in this area.

The outgoing accounting department manager wants to retire on schedule but feels she cannot until her replacement is firmly in place. Several talks with the new man regarding his communication problems unearth a few bits of information. He was brought up strictly and was continually admonished as a child "not to speak unless spoken to." The family was poor and his parents were uneducated; their home contained few books. He had always done well in school in courses dealing with arithmetic and mathematics, and later in college in accounting. His grades in these courses offset his poor performance in courses in English, literature, composition and the like. He rarely reads a book now or even looks at a magazine.

Although these discussions have produced some relevant information, they do nothing to solve the new manager's performance problems. There is a serious question as to whether he will be ready to take over from the retiring manager when the time comes to do so.

Questions

1. What do you believe are the causes of the new accounting manager's problems? What aspects of the situation lead you to these conclusions?

2. If you were the retiring manager, would you recommend a promotion? If not, what would you do in this situation? Why?

Problem 2. A woman in her early thirties has been hired as a sales clerk by a local department store. She had been out of the labor force for several years, but she did have prior sales experience. She left college before graduating to get married but still hoped to get her degree. Her performance on the various selection tests administered by the personnel department was quite good, and there was some thought that she might eventually move up into supervision. She and her husband have two young children of their own, and her husband's daughter from a previous marriage also lives with them. Her mother-in-law will be taking care of the children while she is at work.

For approximately a year things went well, and the department manager was quite pleased with the clerk's performance. Then, unexpectedly, her mother-in-law became seriously ill. The sales clerk began to lose considerable time from work because of problems concerning both the care of the children and her mother-in-law also, whose condition had worsened. When the mother-in-law died, it was two weeks before the sales clerk returned to work; she now appears to be a changed person.

It now takes her a long time to wait on each customer, with the result that many become quite irritated. She appears preoccupied and spends considerable time standing around looking unhappy and morose. Unless customers ask for service, she ignores them. When they ask for advice, she conveys the impression that she does not consider herself worthy of giving it. If they become angry with her, she tends to react with self-criticism. Absenteeism continues to be a problem; on one occasion she cut herself rather severely while displaying a food processor to a customer. There are continuing problems with the care of the children, and the department manager suspects that the clerk's husband travels a good deal, with the result that she has to cope pretty much on her own. At least insofar as her job is concerned, it is apparent that she is not coping very well.

The department manager now realizes that not only does her sales clerk have a problem, but she herself has a problem too: the situation has not gone totally unnoticed by the top levels of management in the store.

Questions

1. What factors seem to have converged to produce the sales clerk's problems? What aspects of her performance are affected?
2. What action would you take as the department head? To what extent would top management's involvement be a factor in your decision?

Additional Sources for Detailed Study

Becker, Franklin D. *Workspace: Creating Environments in Organizations*. New York: Praeger, 1981.

Brief, Arthur P.; Schuler, Randall S.; and Van Sell, Mary. *Managing Job Stress*. Boston: Little Brown, 1981.

Cummings, L.L., and Schwab, Donald P. *Performance in Organizations: Determinants and Appraisal*. Glenview, Ill.: Scott, Foresman, 1973.

England, George W.; Negandhi, Anant R.; and Wilpert, Bernhard. *The Functioning of Complex Organizations*. Cambridge, Mass.: Oelgeschlager, Gunn, and Hain, 1981.

Filley, Alan C.; House, Robert J.; and Kerr, Steven. *Managerial Process and Organizational Behavior*. Glenview, Ill.: Scott, Foresman, 1976.

Gruneberg, Michael M. *Job Satisfaction*. New York: Wiley, 1976.

Hellriegel, Don; Slocum, John W.; and Woodman, Richard W. *Organizational Behavior*. St. Paul: West, 1983.

Ivancevich, John M., and Matteson, Michael T. *Stress and Work: A Managerial Perspective*. Glenview, Ill.: Scott, Foresman, 1980.

Jabes, Jak. *Individual Processes in Organizational Behavior*. Arlington Heights, Ill.: AHM, 1978.

Kahn, Robert L. *Work and Health*. New York: Wiley, 1981.

Kerr, Steven. *Organizational Behavior*. Columbus: Grid, 1979.

Korman, Abraham K. *Organizational Behavior*. Englewood Cliffs, N.J.: Prentice-Hall, 1977.

Newman, William H. *Constructive Control: Design and Use of Control Systems*. Englewood Cliffs, N.J.: Prentice-Hall, 1975.

Porter, Lyman W.; Lawler, Edward E.; and Hackman, J. Richard. *Behavior in Organizations*. New York: McGraw-Hill, 1975.

Schroder, Harold M.; Driver, Michael J.; and Streufert, Siegfried. *Human Information Processing*. New York: Holt, Rinehart, and Winston, 1967.

Steele, Fred I. *Physical Settings and Organization Development.* Reading, Mass.: Addison-Wesley, 1973.

Szilagyi, Andrew D., and Wallace, Marc J. *Organizational Behavior and Performance.* Glenview, Ill.: Scott, Foresman, 1983.

Walter, Gordon A., and Marks, Stephen E. *Experiential Learning and Change: Theory, Design and Practice.* New York: Wiley, 1981.

The following books should prove particularly useful for the practical guidelines they contain on dealing with performance problems:

Miner, John B. *The Challenge of Managing.* Hinsdale, Ill.: Dryden, 1975.

Roseman, Edward. *Managing the Problem Employee.* New York: AMACOM, 1982.

Steinmetz, Lawrence L. *Managing the Marginal and Unsatisfactory Performer.* Reading, Mass.: Addison-Wesley, 1969.

Stewart, Valerie, and Stewart, Andrew. *Managing the Poor Performer.* Aldershot, Great Britain: Gower, 1982.

Notes

1. Charles Perrow, "The Analysis of Goals in Complex Organizations," *American Sociological Review* (April 1961); Herbert A. Simon, "On the Concept of Organizational Goal," *Administrative Science Quarterly* (June 1964).

2. James G. March and Johan P. Olsen, *Ambiguity and Choice in Organizations* (Bergen, Norway: Universitetsforlaget, 1976); Robert H. Miles, *Coffin Nails and Corporate Strategies* (Englewood Cliffs, N.J.: Prentice-Hall, 1982).

3. Milton Rokeach, *The Nature of Human Values* (New York: Free Press, 1973), p. 25.

4. George C. Curtis, "Psychophysiology of Stress," in *Mental Health and The Economy,* ed. Louis A. Ferman and Jeanne P. Gordus (Kalamazoo: Upjohn Institute for Employment Research, 1979).

5. Christopher Poulton, "Skilled Performance and Stress," in *Psychology at Work,* ed. Peter B. Warr (Baltimore: Penguin, 1971).

6. Karen A. Mathews, "Psychological Perspectives on the Type A Behavior Pattern," *Psychological Bulletin* (March 1982); Whitton S. Paine, *Job Stress and Burnout: Research, Theory and Intervention Perspectives* (Beverly Hills: Sage, 1982).

7. Alan McLean, "Occupational Stressors," in *Man and Work in Society,* ed. Eugene L. Cass and Frederick G. Zimmer (New York: Van Nostrand Reinhold, 1975).

8. Richard T. Mowday, Lyman W. Porter, and Richard M. Steers, *Employee–Organization Linkages: The Psychology of Commitment, Absenteeism, and Turnover* (New York: Academic, 1982).

9. Glynn D. Coates et al., "Behavioral Effects of Infectious Diseases: Phlebotomus Fever in Man," *Journal of Applied Psychology* (June 1972).

10. G. N. Wright and A. B. Trotter, *Rehabilitation Research* (Madison: University of Wisconsin, 1968).

11. Daniel Katz and Robert L. Kahn, *The Social Psychology of Organizations* (New York: Wiley, 1978), p. 3.

12. Bernard M. Bass, *Stogdill's Handbook of Leadership* (New York: Free Press, 1981).

13. Otis W. Baskin and Craig E. Aronoff, *Interpersonal Communication in Organizations* (Santa Monica: Goodyear, 1980).

14. David C. McClelland, *The Achieving Society* (Princeton: Van Nostrand, 1961).

15. Norton M. Bedford, "Managerial Control," in *Contemporary Management: Issues and Viewpoints,* ed. Joseph W. McGuire (Englewood Cliffs, N.J.: Prentice-Hall, 1974).

16. Stephen J. Carroll and Henry L. Tosi, *Management by Objectives: Applications and Research* (New York: Macmillan, 1973).

17. John B. Miner and J. Frank Brewer, "The Management of Ineffective Performance," in *Handbook of Industrial and Organizational Psychology,* ed. Marvin D. Dunnette (Chicago: Rand McNally, 1976).

CHAPTER 5

Motivation in Organizations

CHAPTER OUTLINE

Ways of Thinking About Motivation
Views Regarding Human Needs
    Need Hierarchy Theory
    Achievement Motivation Theory
    Power and Affiliation Needs
Views Regarding Equity
    The Adams Theory
    Significance for Managing
Expectancy Views
    Outline of the Theory
    Zone of Application
Behavior Modification and Operant Learning
    From Learning to Performance
    Significance for Management

Goal Setting and Job Design Applications
Locke's Concept of Goal Setting
    Goal Setting in Practice
    Parkinson's Law
Management by Objectives (MBO)
Work Redesign and Job Characteristics Theory
    How to Redesign Jobs
    Does It Work?
Work Redesign and Motivation-Hygiene Theory

Attachment, Commitment, and the Role of Values
Attachment and Behavioral Commitment
Attitudinal Commitment
    Professional Commitment
    Obtaining Commitment
The Role of Values
    International Comparisons
    Business Ethics and Values

OBJECTIVES

To present and evaluate some of the better-known and potentially useful views regarding motivation in organizations.

To describe some of the motivational techniques or programs that are currently in vogue and assess their value.

To explain the motivational roles of various types of commitments and values.

Motivation is the force that makes organizations dynamic, acting systems rather than static structures. For the organization to achieve its goals, it is essential that employees channel the motivational potential they bring to an organization toward goal attainment. This potential should not lie dormant, but rather should be activated or stimulated so that organizations receive the maximum possible energy from employees.

If one considers all this from the viewpoint of a group of managers or even of a single entrepreneur, trying to channel and maximize the motives of employees toward a company's operative goals without regard for the welfare of the employees themselves looks very much like manipulation. Many unions hold this view, and so do certain well-known authors in the field of organizational behavior.[1] Looking at the situation this way, even concerning oneself with matters of employee motivation is more than a little unethical.

But what if the goals sought are not self-serving but organization serving and closely aligned with society's official goals for the organization? What if there is regard for the welfare of the employee and a full understanding that stressing a person too much does not maximize motivation? What if the employees are not being "used" to achieve someone else's goals, but instead identify with and want to channel their efforts toward operative goals? What if the employees own the organization and share its profits?

Nothing about studying and understanding motivation in organizations is unethical in and of itself. Like any other kind of knowledge, knowledge of motivation can be misused; it can be put in the service of manipulation for the personal gain of a few people. In such cases labor unions and certain other types of employee response appear entirely justified. However, an understanding of motivation can also serve society, the organization as a whole, and individual employees. It is with these latter types of objectives in mind that we consider the subject here.

WAYS OF THINKING ABOUT MOTIVATION

The field of management has produced a number of broadly applicable ways of thinking about motivation that are concerned primarily with employees who are neither managers nor professionals. For the scientist these are theories to be tested by research; for the manager they are sets of working hypotheses that are useful in varying degree for understanding and influencing employee performance. To a large extent it is the scientist's research that determines whether these ideas can be useful to a manager. The ways of thinking about motivation that we consider have been the subject of considerable research and appear to be at least partially correct. Some of the concepts involved are quite complex and should not be treated in great detail in an introductory course. Yet these ideas can provide useful guidelines for handling employee performance.

Views Regarding Human Needs

One long-standing view in psychology is that human behavior is a consequence of various relatively stable needs established in part through the processes of genetic inheritance, but more importantly through learning that occurs at an early age. Over the past thirty years, the field of management has absorbed and expanded upon ideas of this kind. Applying need theories to understanding performance has been the subject of criticism, even to the point of recommending that these theories be completely abandoned; yet some researchers have responded to these criticisms, and in one form or another this approach to motivation has been remarkably resilient.[2] Two such views that have been particularly durable are generally known as need hierarchy theory and achievement motivation theory.

Need Hierarchy Theory   Need hierarchy theory originally was developed by Abraham Maslow as a general view of motivation. It moved into the management field primarily through the efforts of Douglas McGregor, and later Maslow himself.[3] The basic elements of the theory are given in Exhibit 5.1. The first hierarchy (I) of five levels has been of by far the greatest concern in influencing and organizational behavior. Within this hierarchy it is proposed that to the extent lower-level needs—physiological and then safety—are satisfied in the workplace, higher-level needs emerge in ascending order to govern behavior. At some point in time most workers are largely satisfied at the physiological level, but very little satisfied at the level of self-actualization. In a healthy person, physiological needs are satisfied in infancy, safety needs in childhood, love needs in adolescence, and self-esteem needs in adulthood. Self-actualization thus becomes a meaningful factor in motivation only rather late in life.

The other components of Exhibit 5.1 (II and III) are the aesthetic needs and the cognitive hierarchy, in which needs to understand supersede needs to know once the latter have been satisfied. Motives of this kind are important and probably should be given greater attention than they have received.

One of the most interesting—and controversial—aspects of need hierarchy theory is the idea of self-actualization. Exhibit 5.2 lists the characteristics and values of self-actualizing people, as well as the circumstances that impinge on these values. In addition to having the kinds of values noted, self-actualizing people:

Accept themselves, others, and the realities of life

Are spontaneous and natural

Focus on real problems outside themselves

Have a quality of detachment and a need for privacy

Experience continued freshness of appreciation

Have frequent mystic experiences

Feel sympathy and affection for mankind

Have a democratic character structure

Are creative

Have a capacity to resolve dichotomies

Experience deep and profound relationships with others

Among other reasons, need hierarchy theory is attractive because it is concerned with humanity in general. Except perhaps for the relatively rare self-ac-

EXHIBIT 5.1 Maslow's hierarchy of need

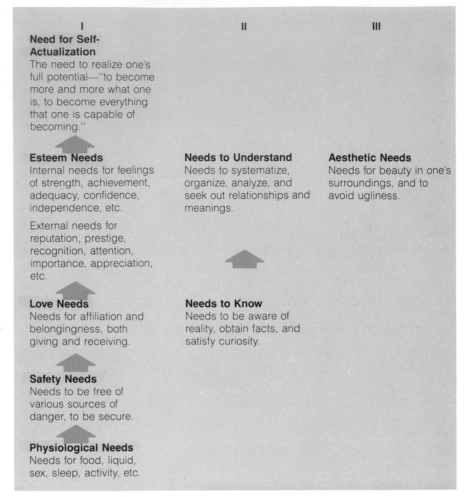

Based on Abraham H. Maslow, "A Theory of Human Motivation," *Psychological Review* (July 1943); idem, *Motivation and Personality* (New York: Harper & Row, 1954).

tualizer, it deals not with individual differences but with large groups of employees at different levels of need satisfaction. Consequently it fits well with the idea of developing human resource policies for broad categories of employees, which is the prevailing mode in the business world today.

Yet research on the theory gives only limited support. It does appear that when lower level physiological and safety needs are denied, a preoccupation with such matters is characteristic. Once certain primary needs are satisfied, however, any one of a wide range of motives may dominate behavior depending upon individual developmental experiences. This makes policy formulation more difficult. Yet we cannot dismiss the lower level needs as unimportant. There are people such as low-pay, low-seniority, low-skill family breadwinners in industries characterized by major economic swings, working in regions with high unemployment from

EXHIBIT 5.2   Values of self-actualizing people

These Values Typical of Self-actualizing People. . .	Become Deprived or Denied by These Conditions
Truth	Dishonesty, disbelief, distrust
Goodness	Evil, utter selfishness
Aliveness	Deadness, emptiness, robotizing
Uniqueness	Sameness, uniformity
Perfection	Sloppiness, poor workmanship
Completion	Incompleteness, cessation of striving
Justice	Injustice, lawlessness
Order	Chaos, breakdown of authority
Effortlessness	Fatigue, strain, gracelessness
Playfulness	Grimness, depression
Self-sufficiency	Dependence, contingency
Meaningfulness	Meaninglessness, despair

Adapted from Abraham H. Maslow, "A Theory of Metamotivation: The Biological Rooting of the Value Life," *Journal of Humanistic Psychology* (Fall 1967):108–9; idem, *Motivation and Personality,* (New York: Harper & Row, 1954).

which the individual (female, minority?) cannot move because of family or cultural pressures. For such people lower level needs are very important.

In short, management should recognize that deprivation of the lower level physiological and safety needs and preoccupation with such matters do occur, even in highly advanced, industrialized societies.[4] Need hierarchy theory suggests important motives that can influence performance, even if the idea of a fixed hierarchy is not valid, and the concept of self-actualization is an intriguing and sometimes revealing way of viewing certain individuals. Maslow provides some important ideas that can contribute to a managerial working theory of motivation.

Achievement Motivation Theory   According to David McClelland, people who exhibit a strong need for achievement—whose motivational hierarchies place achievement striving close to the top—are particularly responsive to certain types of work environments. These are situations where one can attain success through one's own efforts rather than by chance; where the difficulty level and risk inherent in the work is neither too great nor too small; and where there is clear feedback on results, so that one knows whether he or she has been successful. Among those expected to desire and seek out such environments are entrepreneurs, and in fact achievement motivation theory is largely a theory of entrepreneurship and the means by which businesses are founded or rapidly expanded. Thus, the theory is important because it tells us something about the kinds of people who operate in an entrepreneurial role in the business world.

The theory also is applied to the economic development of a country. Countries whose cultures include achievement motives and achievement values, so that large numbers of people have high achievement needs, are expected to experience more rapid economic development. This appears to be true.[5] For

Motivation in Organizations

example, countries such as India and Israel have high achievement motivation levels and also have exhibited more rapid growth. Yet there are exceptions—France has not shown the economic growth that its achievement motivation level would seem to warrant, and Russia has outperformed expectations in this regard. Although other factors also are involved in economic development, achievement motivation theory is useful in examining the developing countries of the world.

Power and Affiliation Needs   Research in the area of achievement needs has extended to related concerns, such as fear of failure and fear of success.[6] In addition there has been increasing interest, especially on the part of David McClelland, in two other needs: for power and for affiliation (akin to Maslow's love needs). The reason for focusing on these two needs is that they appear to play a significant role in effectively managing large bureaucratic systems; in contrast, creating such systems is primarily a matter of achievement motivation.

McClelland views affiliation motivation as a negative factor in managerial performance. It tends to make a manager too subjectively concerned with individuals and thus interferes with the objectivity and rationality (without hatred or passion and hence without affection or enthusiasm) that should prevail, according to Weber's bureaucracy. Power motivation, on the other hand, is a positive factor.

The role of power motivation is outlined in Exhibit 5.3. Power motivation

---

EXHIBIT 5.3   Development of power motivation and consequences for managerial performance

Early to Mature Motivational Patterns	Implications for Management
1. A sense of power derives from attaching oneself to strong people. The desire to influence others is low.	Not assertive enough to manage well
2. A sense of power derives from being oneself and "doing one's own thing." Influencing others is not involved.	Not related to managing
3. A sense of power derives from dominating others and demonstrating their weakness by establishing a helping relationship over them.	
a. High need for power, low inhibition, low need for affiliation	The conquistador pattern, the feudal lord
b. High need for power, high inhibition, low need for affiliation	The imperial pattern, personalized power shades into socialized
4. A sense of power derives from influencing others for some greater good, such as company success; high inhibition, low need for affiliation	Selfless leadership and efficient organizational management

Adapted from David C. McClelland, *Power: The Inner Experience* (New York: Irvington, 1975), chapter 7, p. 264.

moves through the four stages in a gradual process of development, although people often do not get all the way to the mature, socialized power need that makes for effective managing. Accordingly, many people are not likely to do well in management positions. These views on the role of power motivation in managerial success are supported by studies at AT & T that track promotion rates of managers with different motive patterns.[7] Research on the motivation to manage (see chapter 2) also is consistent with McClelland's ideas. Both approaches consider power motivation as important for a manager, but it is one among several motivational factors.

Achievement motivation, power motivation, and motivation to manage all can be increased through the use of certain procedures for management development. People with strong needs of this kind should be placed in an appropriate entrepreneurial or managerial work context and "given free rein." Their intrinsic needs will motivate them sufficiently. Where these types of needs are low, however, other kinds of motivational theories should guide supervision.

Views Regarding Equity

Although a number of views regarding the motivating effects of unfairness, injustice, and inequity have been proposed, the ideas developed by Stacy Adams while he was with General Electric have proved to be most significant for the study of organizational behavior.[8] In this view the perception of unfairness is one of the most powerful forces in the organizational world. The truth of this position is attested to by the appeals and success of the labor movement; it is a rare picket line that does not include someone carrying a placard with the words "management unfair."

The Adams Theory   The major motivating force in this theory is a striving for equity, which emerges only after some inequity or unfairness is perceived. The starting point is an exchange in which the individual gives something (an input) and then receives something (an outcome). This is much like the idea of contributions countered by inducements that Barnard (and later Simon) proposed. If the ratio of input to outcome does not match well with the ratio perceived for some reference source (such as a coworker or the profession in general), then people experience inequity. They feel that they have gotten either too little or, on occasion, too much. Either way, a desire emerges to return to equitable circumstances, and a strong motivational force arises. The elements and results of this process are outlined in Exhibit 5.4.

What, then, would a person be expected to do to restore equity, given that there is a feeling of anger when reward is perceived as too little relative to others, or a feeling of guilt when reward is perceived as too great? The possibilities are as follows:

1. Change input either up or down to achieve equity—that is, work harder or less hard.
2. Attempt to change outcomes either up or down to achieve equity—that is, get more pay or reduce one's pay.
3. Distort input or outcome toward equity—for example, overstate skill level or the intrinsic satisfactions from the work.
4. Avoid the inequitable situation (seek a transfer or leave the company).
5. Attempt to influence reference sources by distortion, by actually changing

their input or outcome, or by forcing them out of the environment (misstating a coworker's effort, or forcing him or her to restrict output, or harassing him or her into quitting).

6. Shift reference source (for example, compare oneself with immediate coworkers rather than with a craft group as a whole).

Adams and others have attempted to establish guidelines stating when one or another of these reactions will occur. However, this is not one of the strongest aspects of the theory, and managers would do best to figure out which of the various possible reactions are most likely to occur in their own particular context. Usually, environmental forces minimize the number of alternatives actually available in a given context.

Significance for Managing   In general the research indicates that equity theory is a valid and valuable way of looking at human work. Much of this research has focused on pay differentials, but studies do deal with other outcomes as well. Just as managers will have to study a particular situation to determine employees' reactions to perceived inequity, they will also have to establish on their own what reference sources are being used. The theory is not very helpful in these areas. Also, people differ greatly in the ways and extent to which they experience inequity. Such factors as insecurity, sense of responsibility, maturity and the like affect responses to inequity. Some people have a low inequity threshold and experience frequent feelings of discrimination; others may react very differently to the same situation.

There even appear to be major differences between cultures. In one study comparing Dutch and American workers, the Dutch were found to be less

---

EXHIBIT 5.4   Key factors in the Adams theory and their relationship to perception of inequity

KEY FACTORS

Input	Outcome	Reference Source
Education	Pay	Coworkers
Intelligence	Intrinsic satisfaction of strong motives	Relatives
Experience	Fringe benefits	Neighbors
Skill	Status	Craft group
Seniority	Working conditions	Profession
Job effort	Relations with others	Industry patterns
Health		

INEQUITY PERCEIVED

Individual's Input vs. Outcome	Reference Source's Input vs. Outcome			
	Low/High	High/Low	Low/Low	High/High
Low/High	0	Great	Some	Some
High/Low	Great	0	Some	Some
Low/Low	Some	Some	0	0
High/High	Some	Some	0	0

motivated by equity considerations and more concerned with their own input than the outcomes they received.[9] Accordingly in the course of day-to-day events, managers in the Netherlands would normally be less involved with this type of motivation than American managers. In this country perceived inequity is of major concern, and it is important that managers be aware of it.

Most managers will encounter overreward inequity—when workers feel their outcomes exceed their input and thus are motivated in their work by feelings of guilt or shame—rather infrequently. This kind of motivation tends to be activated less easily than underreward inequity (input exceeds outcomes), and it often dissipates rather quickly over time. The impact of overpayment on performance, for instance, would be expected to be short lived. However, when a great burst of effort is needed to meet an emergency situation, overpayment can be a useful strategy.

Expectancy Views

Like many of the other theories, expectancy views come in a wide range of forms and also originate in psychology. Basically the approach operates on the assumption that motivation to perform a job well is a consequence of (1) a belief that the effort put into a job can be converted into performance results and (2) the net total attractiveness of the outcomes perceived to result from good performance.

Outline of the Theory The essential elements of the expectancy view and their relationship are given in Exhibit 5.5. Here outcomes are to be understood much as they were in the discussion of equity theory, and as illustrated in Exhibit 5.4. The $E \longrightarrow P$ expectancy is a person's internal belief regarding the likelihood that he or she can perform at a given level, or that effort will lead to successful performance. This perceived probability is influenced by the situation and by prior experience in such situations. The $P \longrightarrow O$ expectancy is a person's internal beliefs regarding the likelihood that successful performance will lead to certain outcomes. The greater the perceived probability that performance will lead to desired consequences, the more likely the person is to try to perform at the required level. *Valence* is the value or attractiveness of various outcomes to the person. Some outcomes take on valence for a person because they have direct value or attractiveness. Other outcomes take on valence because they lead to other (second-level) outcomes that are viewed as valuable or attractive. *Instrumentality* is the internal belief (perceived probability) that a first-level outcome will lead to a second-level outcome, which carries the true valence for a person. *Extrinsic outcome* is an outcome of performance that is provided or mediated by external factors, such as the organization, a supervisor, and the like. Pay, recognition from others, and promotions are examples. An *intrinsic outcome* is one that occurs as a direct result of performing the task itself and that people accordingly give to themselves. Examples include feelings of accomplishment, need satisfactions, and the enjoyment of managerial work that people with high motivation to manage experience.

The level of motivation may be calculated as follows, using the symbolism of Exhibit 5.5:

Motivation = $E \longrightarrow P$ × the sum of all ($P \longrightarrow$ Os × their valences)

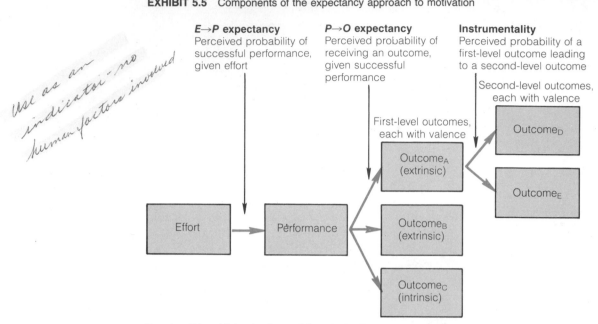

EXHIBIT 5.5 Components of the expectancy approach to motivation

E→P **expectancy**
Perceived probability of successful performance, given effort

P→O **expectancy**
Perceived probability of receiving an outcome, given successful performance

Instrumentality
Perceived probability of a first-level outcome leading to a second-level outcome

Second-level outcomes, each with valence

First-level outcomes, each with valence

Effort

Performance

Outcome$_A$ (extrinsic)

Outcome$_B$ (extrinsic)

Outcome$_C$ (intrinsic)

Outcome$_D$

Outcome$_E$

use as an indicator - no human factors involved

Based on Edward E. Lawler, *Pay and Organization Development,* © 1981, Addison-Wesley, Reading, Massachusetts. p. 231. Reprinted with permission.

In this formula, first-level outcomes subsume second-level outcomes and their valences. This would occur if, for instance, pay (a first-level outcome) was relatively unimportant in its own right, but was important because it was instrumental to attaining some other high-valence (second-level) outcome, such as keeping a special car that had been bought on credit or paying for drugs when a person has a bad drug habit. Motivation activated in this manner leads to job-related efforts, which in turn contribute to performance.

Zone of Application A number of questions have been raised about expectancy theory.[10] For one thing it does not deal effectively with any kind of self-punitive behavior, such as some of the reactions to guilt that occur in the presence of overreward inequity. Also, expectancy theories without exception assume a desire to maximize satisfaction, yet we know that human beings do not always maximize satisfaction.

These theories face many of the same problems that the "economic man" theory of decision making does (see chapter 3). Human beings do not consider all possible alternatives in a highly rational, conscious fashion, in part because they often do not want to but also because of the limitations of human mental capacity. The result is satisficing. Similarly, people cannot evaluate all possible outcomes, and then second-level outcomes, in terms of specific probabilities and valences and then make conscious choices among them. At best they approximate such a process. Furthermore, not all human motives are conscious. Need theories have no problem dealing with motivation of which a person is not aware, but expectancy theories are not applicable outside of conscious, rational processes.

All this suggests that expectancy theories have a zone of application in which they work reasonably well, but they cannot predict many aspects of organizational behavior. Research supports this conclusion. For the theory to work, people must have in their minds the idea that desirable outcomes, such as more pay, are linked to or are contingent upon effective job performance. Some organizations build these performance–reward contingencies into their employees, but others do not.

The kind of organization in which expectancy theory works has the following characteristics:

1. People are rewarded according to the excellence of their performance.
2. Merit increase percentages are an accurate reflection of relative performance.
3. The promotion system helps the best person to the top.
4. Salary increases are viewed as based on performance.
5. Reward and recognition are given for good work.
6. People with ability have a promising future.

Within its zone of application, expectancy theory provides one of the most powerful ways of understanding work behavior currently available to us. Unfortunately it is somewhat cumbersome for managers to apply in practice, and little has been done to assist managers in using it. Yet if one really wants to operate an organization, or a part of one, in such a way as to achieve the closest thing possible to maximum performance, expectancy views provide the best guidelines available for this purpose.

Behavior Modification and Operant Learning

According to organizational behavior modification theory, behavior is entirely a function of its consequences. Unobservable states such as achievement motivation, self-actualization, valence, expectancy, anger over inequity, guilt, and the like have no theoretical relevance. Accordingly, the idea of motivation as a cause of performance is rejected. Performance results from learning, not motivation. Yet the result is performance, and consequently this type of theory is important for our purposes. Exhibit 5.6 shows the way in which this theory merged into the field of management.

From Learning to Performance   The theory starts with a definition of learning, much the same as the one discussed in chapter 4. Behaviors are viewed as occurring randomly in the beginning. Reinforcers are then applied selectively to those behaviors. Behaviors are learned as consequences accrue in the forms of rewards and punishments. These reinforcers are applied contingent upon whether or not desired behaviors result.

In organizational behavior modification, the role of a supervisor is to orchestrate reinforcements to yield desired behaviors at a high frequency, thus improving performance. To achieve this end, supervisors should follow these rules:

1. Do not give the same level of reward to all, but rather differentiate according to the level of performance.

EXHIBIT 5.6   Roots of organizational behavior modification in learning theory and the Hawthorne studies

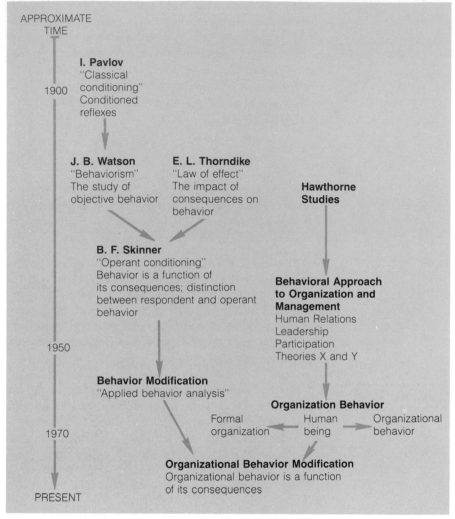

SOURCE: Fred Luthans and Robert Kreitner, *Organizational Behavior Modification* (Glenview, Ill.: Scott, Foresman, 1975), p. 31.

2. Failure to respond to a behavior has reinforcing consequences, which should be recognized, and accordingly both nonactions and actions should be adapted to the ends desired.

3. Tell a person what behavior is to be reinforced and reinforce it.

4. Tell people what they are doing wrong.

5. Punishment should be used sparingly and not in front of others, in order to avoid negative side effects.

6. Make the consequences equal to the behavior—that is, adjust rewards to make them fully contingent on performance.

As indicated in Exhibit 5.7, the focus of the operant learning approach is on the ways supervisors can orchestrate contingencies of reinforcement—positive, negative, extinction, punishment—to obtain desired performances. In this view influencing really does make a difference, but for that to happen the supervisor must have substantial control over the work environment.

In formal applications, where a company has undertaken a program designed to utilize organizational behavior modification techniques, this approach involves considerable measurement and following a series of steps:

1. Identify performance-related behaviors that can be reduced to observable events, counted, and exactly specified.
2. Measure to establish baseline frequencies of behaviors, using tally sheets and time sampling.
3. Identify existing contingencies of reinforcement to determine where the behavior takes place and what its consequences are.
4. Carry out an intervention in the existing behavior patterns by (1) developing an intervention strategy, (2) applying the strategy with appropriate types of contingencies, (3) measuring to determine frequencies of postintervention behaviors, and (4) maintaining the behavior with appropriate reinforcements.
5. Evaluate the overall impact on performance.[11]

Obviously, to be able to do this well, managers need to learn a great deal themselves. Yet there are numerous reports of companies that have made such an approach work; Emery Air Freight is among the best known.

Significance for Management   When interventions of this kind are carried out systematically, they do influence performance, particularly the quantity of out-

---

EXHIBIT 5.7   Contingencies of reinforcements

1. *Positive Reinforcement*
   An existing set of circumstances ⟶ a particular behavior ⟶ the contingent positive consequence ⟶ increase in the frequency of the behavior.

2. *Negative (avoidance) Reinforcement*
   An existing set of circumstances ⟶ a particular behavior ⟶ contingent termination or withdrawal of an unpleasant consequence ⟶ increase in the frequency of the behavior.

3. *Extinction*
   An existing set of circumstances ⟶ a particular behavior ⟶ the contingent positive consequence is withheld ⟶ decrease in the frequency of the behavior.

4. *Punishment*
   An existing set of circumstances ⟶ a particular behavior ⟶ the contingent negative consequences ⟶ decrease in the frequency of behavior.

Based on W. Clay Hamner, "Reinforcement Theory and Contingency Management in Organizational Settings," in *Organizational Behavior and Management: A Contingency Approach,* ed. Henry L. Tosi and W. Clay Hamner (Chicago: St. Clair, 1974), pp. 86–112.

put and absenteeism levels. The approach requires considerable control over the work situation of the kind often found in production units at the bottom of bureaucratic hierarchies and in small businesses. Given this kind of control and supervisors who are proficient in the use of these techniques, the results can be sizable, at least initially. However, there is some tendency for the effects to diminish over a period of several years.

Whether a behavior modification view of performance is preferable to other views is largely a matter of individual orientation and preference. The theory overlaps with various theories of motivation (expectancy theory, for instance) in numerous respects; in these areas the other theories do at least as well, and probably better, in predicting performance. Also, strictly behavioral approaches ignore important motivational processes, such as intrinsic motivation. In any event, to use organizational behavior modification it is necessary to control reinforcements and know what they mean. Supervisory praise, for instance, is usually a positive reinforcer, but in the hands of a person who is not generally respected it may lose its positive force and even take on negative valence.

More than any of the other approaches considered in this chapter, behavior modification has been attacked as unethical. In this view the approach puts too much power in the hands of management, makes employees too dependent, is essentially totalitarian, and violates individual rights. These characteristics are particularly pronounced when punishment and avoidance learning are involved. Theories of this kind tend to produce a picture of mindless obedience, with human robots responding unthinkingly to slight pulls on managerially manipulated strings. Actually, behavior modification is not inherently more unethical than the other theories—it all depends on how a theory is used. But the theory's denial of a role for internal thought and choice does create image problems (robots?). Accordingly, some managers may be uncomfortable using behavior modification and operant learning views in their working theories for understanding employee performance.

GOAL SETTING AND JOB DESIGN APPLICATIONS

Two additional motivational approaches that have achieved considerable significance are important more for the programs or techniques they espouse than for their theoretical underpinnings. This is not to say that they lack a theoretical base; for one reason or another, practice has taken on a more important role than the underlying theory. Thus, for a manager these approaches more often provide useful techniques than important conceptual working theories of human motivation.

Locke's Concept of Goal Setting

Although the idea that explicit goal setting is an important motivational force has been apparent for a long time, Edwin Locke has done the most to provide guidelines for the use of this approach. His view of the goal-setting process and an example from the classroom are outlined in Exhibit 5.8. The effectiveness of goals depends on how explicit and specific they are and on how difficult they are to achieve. However, to influence performance, goals must be accepted and internalized; a goal can be so difficult that aspiring to it is considered unrealistic.

EXHIBIT 5.8 The goal-setting process

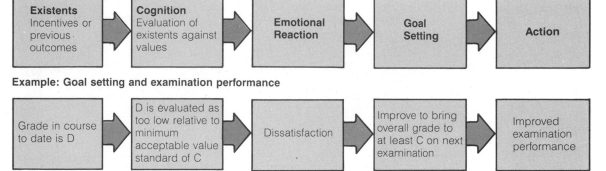

Example: Goal setting and examination performance

Based on Edwin A. Locke, Norman Cartledge, and Claramae S. Knerr, "Studies of the Relationship Between Satisfaction, Goal Setting, and Performance," *Organizational Behavior and Human Performance* (March 1970).

Goal Setting in Practice   The initial research on goal setting, although supporting Locke's views, was carried out in such highly controlled laboratory settings that its practical usefulness was uncertain. Now, however, the research has extended into numerous actual work situations. It is apparent that setting specific, quantitative goals of some difficulty can improve performance. A number of studies have been conducted in the wood products industry dealing with timber cutting, the loading of logging trucks, and the like. Exhibit 5.9 presents the results of goal setting by students prior to taking a history course. Note that no matter how the goal was established—the grade hoped for, expected, considered minimally acceptable, or actually tried for—the more difficult the goal, and thus the higher the grade aspired to, the higher the actual grade obtained in the course.

As long as the source of a goal is viewed as legitimate, it does not matter much whether goals are set by an outside authority or by the individuals themselves. However, in this regard as in other aspects of goal setting, individual differences emerge: some people are more responsive to goal setting than others, and some need to set the goals themselves.

For a manager, goal setting is a particularly attractive motivational approach. However, one caution should be recognized. There is evidence that when the work requires coordination of effort among several individuals, individual goal setting can have negative consequences.[12] Goal setting tends to reduce the necessary communication with others and individuals focus on their own goals. Teamwork suffers, and so does performance. Almost without exception, positive results from goal setting occur under conditions of individualized, self-contained performance.

Parkinson's Law   Locke has employed the concept of goal setting to explain the effectiveness of a number of other motivational procedures, such as feedback of results and monetary incentives. One of the most interesting of these extensions of his views is their application to Parkinson's Law—the idea that

EXHIBIT 5.9 Influence of goals on grades obtained in a history course

Grade Goals Set at the Beginning of the Course	Average Grade Actually Obtained
Students hope to obtain a grade of	
C	C
B	C+
A	B
Students expect to obtain a grade of	
D	C−
C	C+
B	B−
A	B+
Students set the minimum grade they would be satisfied with as	
D	C
C	C+
B	B
A	B
Students actually tried for a grade of	
C	C+
B	C+
A	B

Adapted from Edwin A. Locke and Judith F. Bryan, "Grade Goals as Determinants of Academic Achievement," *Journal of General Psychology* (October 1968):225.

work expands to fill the time available for its completion, or more generally that the amount of effort exerted is adjusted to the difficulty of the task at hand.[13] Locke argues that once people size up a job to be done they establish goals for themselves accordingly, and this is what mediates the amount and timing of the effort they expend. Furthermore, he presents research evidence that goal setting does make a difference in this process.

Management by Objectives (MBO)

Locke's ideas about goal setting typically have been applied in a one-to-one context involving supervisor and subordinate. Management by objectives (MBO) is similar in its emphasis on goal setting but is more programmatic in nature; a formalized goal setting and monitoring process is implemented throughout a company or a major segment of it. The current popularity of MBO programs dates back to the 1950s, preceding Locke's initial contributions by a decade.[14]

Although programs in different companies vary considerably, the process described in Exhibit 5.10 starting with top management planning is representative. As indicated in the final step of the exhibit, a variety of personnel and human resources activities may be telescoped into an MBO effort. Among these activities management appraisal applications are often emphasized, but this is far from being the only one. For example, compensation is often tied to attaining objectives, and training may be given to facilitate attaining them.

Research on company MBO programs does not yield nearly as positive a picture as for more individualized goal setting. Studies of this kind have been carried

EXHIBIT 5.10 Steps in management by objectives

1. Formulate long-range goals and strategic plans at the top of the organization.
2. Develop specific objectives to be achieved within a given time period.
3. Establish derivative objectives and subobjectives for major departments and subunits.
4. Set realistic and challenging objectives and standards of performance for members of the organization.
5. Formulate action plans for achieving the objectives.
6. Implement and take corrective action as required to ensure the attainment of objectives.
7. Review individual and organizational performance in terms of established goals and objectives.
8. Appraise overall performance, reinforce behavior, and strengthen motivation through effective management training and development, compensation, and career planning.

Based on Anthony P. Raia, *Managing by Objectives* (Glenview, Ill.: Scott, Foresman, 1974), pp. 18–22.

out at General Electric, Purex Corporation, the Black and Decker Company, and elsewhere. It appears to be difficult to install a program that really works as it is supposed to, and in particular it is difficult to ensure widespread goal acceptance. When a clear-cut impact on performance is obtained, it is typically short lived. MBO programs have a tendency to wither away, and effects on performance cannot be counted on to continue.

As with goal setting generally, individual differences in responsiveness to MBO are characteristic; in particular, people with a strong need for achievement tend to respond with improved performance.[15] One of the major problems in MBO is that applying goal setting to the whole range of management jobs, where many of these jobs are interlocking and require interdependent efforts, can easily be self-defeating. Under such circumstances, it becomes very difficult to achieve co-ordination without stifling the goal-setting process; managers tend to move off in pursuit of their own specific goals, with insufficient attention to what others are doing. Yet organizational performance suffers if coordination is not achieved, and in the end the MBO program loses its legitimacy and thus the support of those who must implement it. For most companies, training supervisors in individual goal-setting techniques is likely to prove more fruitful than installing a comprehensive MBO program.

Work Redesign and Job Characteristics Theory

One way to achieve greater energy input from employees is to design jobs so as to elicit greater motivation. Many jobs at lower levels in bureaucratic systems have been designed more with an eye to specialization and formalization of work than to their motivating properties. If these jobs can be enriched by drawing into them role prescriptions from elsewhere in the organization—inspection and quality control units, planning units, higher management and the like—they can be expected to have greater motivating potential. Job characteristics theory provides one approach to redesigning jobs in this manner.

How to Redesign Jobs   As indicated in Exhibit 5-11, increasing the motivating potential of a job requires changes in five core aspects. In the formula, three of these—skill variety, identity, and significance—are simply averaged; these three all contribute to a sense of meaningfulness. This average is then multiplied with autonomy and feedback to calculate how much the motivating potential of the job has changed—how much enrichment has occurred. Questionnaires have been designed to measure these changes.

In going about enriching jobs along these lines, one should:

Form natural work units to increase task identity and task significance.

Combine tasks to increase skill variety and task identity.

Load the job vertically with role prescriptions formerly allocated to management to increase autonomy.

Establish client relationships with the ultimate user to increase skill variety, autonomy, and feedback.

Open feedback channels, especially those inherent in the job itself, to increase feedback.[16]

Once jobs are changed in this way they should produce certain psychological states in people who work at them and subsequently the outcomes indicated in Exhibit 5.11. These outcomes are more likely to occur (1) the greater the person's job-relevant knowledge and skill; (2) the greater the person's growth need strength (esteem needs that are self-confirmed and self-actualization from the Maslow hierarchy); and (3) the greater the person's satisfaction with job security, pay, coworkers, and supervision. This process cannot be expected to succeed for everyone. It will not produce the desired results if a person lacks the competence

EXHIBIT 5.11   Job characteristics theory of work redesign

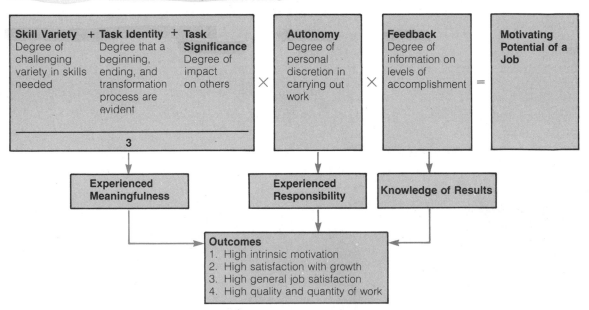

Based on J. Richard Hackman and Greg R. Oldham, *Work Redesign* (Reading, Mass: Addison-Wesley, 1980), pp. 77–94.

to do the work well, or does not possess the kind of motivational patterns that mesh well with these kinds of role prescriptions (defined as *growth* needs), or is bound up in problems, conflicts, and dissatisfactions within the work context. Thus, job redesign along the lines indicated is not for everyone. People should be selected for this purpose, taking into account individual differences.

Does It Work? Job enrichment carried out in accordance with job characteristics theory can work, but many projects of this kind fail to achieve their objectives, for a variety of different reasons. Also, as with MBO, there is a tendency for initial effects to dissipate over time, so that performance returns to its prior state. Overall, measures of intrinsic motivation and job satisfaction are more likely to improve than the actual quality and quantity of job performance.

Travelers Insurance Company and Bankers Trust Company clearly have had favorable experiences. In the latter instance, the reported results were as follows:

1. Forgeries paid dropped 56 percent.
2. Misfiled items decreased 19 percent.
3. Complaints from branch banks decreased approximately 25 percent.
4. Staffing levels were reduced 16 percent even though work volume increased.
5. A productivity level of 110 was attained, as against a 98 standard.[17]

Job redesign tends to have positive consequences with some individuals and not others. Achievement motivation plays an important role in this regard, and it appears to be the most relevant aspect of "growth need strength." People with strong needs to achieve do respond well to enriched jobs, just as they do to management by objectives. However, in many organizations there may be only a few such people who really want what job enrichment has to offer. For these individuals, the addition of skill variety, task significance, autonomy, and feedback to their work appears desirable; the research provides little support for task identity in this regard.

Work Redesign and Motivation-Hygiene Theory

A second approach to work redesign has a different theoretical base from that of job characteristics theory. Motivation-hygiene theory, as developed by Herzberg and others, utilizes the sources of job satisfaction noted in Exhibit 4.6. Certain of these are considered sources of dissatisfaction only—that is, their absence can have a negative impact, but their presence does not contribute to positive consequences. Other job factors are essentially positive in nature and can contribute to strong performance-oriented motivation but not to dissatisfaction. It is these positive factors—responsibility, achievement, recognition, possibility of growth and advancement—that must be engaged if job enrichment is to be successful.[18]

Motivation-hygiene theory itself, with its dichotomized approach to work motivation, has not proved to be very valid. But the job enrichment approach that grew out of it, which has much in common with the approach derived from job characteristics theory, is much more promising. There have been positive applications at AT & T and in the U.S. Air Force, for instance. It is unlikely that these have occurred for the exact reasons motivation-hygiene theory indicates, but nevertheless they have occurred. This approach has spawned its share of unsuccessful efforts as well; once again, some people respond to job enrichment while others do not. In contrast to job characteristics theory, job enrichment approaches based on motivation-hygiene theory have no way of dealing with individual differences, and this presents a special problem for this type of job enrichment program.

Viewing the job enrichment strategy for sparking motivation as a whole, it appears that at a particular point in time people have a scope or range of work that is ideal for them in terms of their capabilities and motivational patterns. Accordingly, individual differences can be very important. Jobs can be too enriched or too simplified, depending on the person. Some jobs put people over their heads—intellectually, emotionally, or motivationally. Others do not arouse and satisfy strong motives sufficiently (achievement motivation is relevant in this regard), so that enrichment can provide an important contribution in these cases. The need is to provide a good matching of people with jobs; as noted in part 5, that is what personnel selection, placement, and job analysis are all about.

ATTACHMENT, COMMITMENT, AND THE ROLE OF VALUES

The theories and approaches considered to this point have focused more on motivation, as it relates to the quality and quantity of output aspects of performance, than on time spent on the job and cooperation with others in attaining organizational goals. Actually, the general thrust of thinking in the area of motivation has been largely toward productivity considerations; absenteeism, turnover, and the like have been viewed more in relation to the emotional factors of satisfaction and dissatisfaction. Ideas involving commitment and the role of values in organizations are useful primarily in understanding the motives underlying aspects of performance other than those of quality and quantity of output. These are the kinds of ideas to which we now turn.

Attachment and Behavioral Commitment

One way in which people become attached to organizations is by investing something of themselves in a particular source of employment—something that would be hard to get back if they were to voluntarily leave or be forced to leave. This investment typically involves a decision and a behavioral commitment from which other decisions and actions follow. When a graduating senior makes a decision to take a job with a particular company and actually goes to work for that company, that is a behavioral commitment. Having made that commitment, the individual then spends time in a company training program dealing with many topics that are specific to this company. Jobs follow in which much of the content is also unique to the company. The individual builds seniority. Gradually, through a series of decisions and actions that seem to flow easily from one to another, the person becomes attached to that particular company.

In these cases the final outcome—an attachment so strong that a person wants to stay with the company if at all possible—occurs without the individual's having made a single overarching decision to get into this situation. A series of seemingly small decisions gradually escalate to the point of attachment. Behavioral commitments of this kind can produce very strong motivational forces.[19] Not only do they lead people to stay with the same employer, even in the face of attractive outside offers, but they also serve to motivate a level of performance calculated to ensure that the company will not terminate the relationship. Attachments based on this kind of commitment do not necessarily lead to outstanding performance, but they also are unlikely to produce ineffective performance. They can exert an influence even when a person is not very happy with an employment situation.

Numerous examples can be cited of attachments based on behavioral commitments. When one undergoes the initiation rights of a sorority or fraternity, an investment is made that fosters attachment. If one packs up, moves one's family, and sells and buys a house in order to take a job across the country, the behavioral commitment is greater than if employment is obtained in one's present locale. The professions, such as medicine, achieve life-long attachments in the same manner: premedical courses lead to medical school, an internship, a residency, board specialization, and the development of a good practice. In the end it is very difficult to change the course of one's life; few if any equally attractive alternatives remain available.

Attitudinal Commitment

Another kind of commitment is more a matter of attitude toward an organization. It has much in common with loyalty. Attitudinal commitment has many of the same performance consequences as behavioral commitment, but the motivational processes differ. This kind of commitment may be characterized as follows:

1. A feeling of identification with organizational objectives such that individual and organizational goals and values are closely aligned.
2. A feeling of involvement and immersion in one's work such that one is willing to exert high levels of effort on behalf of the organization and enjoys working there.
3. A feeling of loyalty and possibly affection toward the organization such that the person has a strong desire to spend time in and continue to be employed by that organization.[20]

Commitment is not a subject that has been studied extensively. In fact, its importance for organizations has begun to be appreciated only relatively recently. It is apparent that different organizations tend to affect their members differently in this regard. Generally speaking, governmental employees bring a rather low level of commitment to their work, while many corporations obtain a much greater amount, at least at the management level. Unions also can achieve rather high levels of attitudinal commitment, often based on a meshing of individual and organizational values. Exhibit 5.12 provides information on some of the characteristics that distinguish low- and high-commitment organizations.

Commitment typically is greater among older, more senior employees who have worked themselves up in the organization. Attitudinal commitment is likely to be high when (1) the organization is considered dependable and fair; (2) the management ranks above are viewed as trustworthy; and (3) the work has some meaning, probably with a certain amount of decentralization of authority to lower levels. Often, high-commitment employees are not the most educated.

High commitment appears to result in less absenteeism and turnover; people do indeed want to spend time at work. It also provides a reservoir of potential energy that can be drawn upon in times of organizational need, even though on a day-to-day basis it typically does not yield better quality and quantity of output.

EXHIBIT 5.12   Differences between low-commitment government agencies and high-commitment corporations

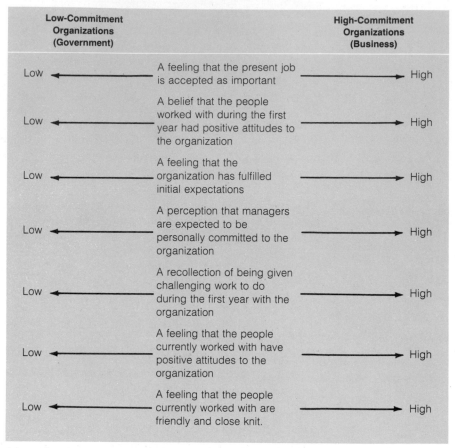

Low-Commitment Organizations (Government)		High-Commitment Organizations (Business)
Low ←	A feeling that the present job is accepted as important	→ High
Low ←	A belief that the people worked with during the first year had positive attitudes to the organization	→ High
Low ←	A feeling that the organization has fulfilled initial expectations	→ High
Low ←	A perception that managers are expected to be personally committed to the organization	→ High
Low ←	A recollection of being given challenging work to do during the first year with the organization	→ High
Low ←	A feeling that the people currently worked with have positive attitudes to the organization	→ High
Low ←	A feeling that the people currently worked with are friendly and close knit.	→ High

Adapted from Bruce Buchanan, "Building Organizational Commitment: The Socialization of Managers in Work Organizations," *Administrative Science Quarterly* (December 1974):539–40.

Finally, because commitment involves identification with the goals of an organization, it contributes to the implementation of strategies and policies.[21] High-commitment people have no problem doing whatever is necessary to carry out company policies.

Professional Commitment   Just as organizations can obtain commitment, so can professions. In fact the process appears to be very much the same. Professional commitment is discussed in chapter 2 as a component of professional motivation. Although there has been some speculation that commitment to a profession might divert professionals from commitment to an organization, this does not appear to be true. The various types of attitudinal commitment involving different sources appear to be closely related; this extends even to company and union.[22] People who are able to develop strong commitments apparently have no difficulty attaching these motives to several sources. Thus the development of a strong professional identification need not keep a corporate lawyer from being equally committed to the company as well.

Obtaining Commitment   Having a large number of strongly committed employees can create a heavy burden of responsibility for a company. It can make getting rid of people—either because of their own deficiencies or because of a need for organizational retrenchment—very difficult. It can exert an influence toward rigidity and lack of adaptability to changing environmental influences. Yet, overall, organizational commitment appears to be desirable. The question then becomes, how does one get it?

One factor appears to be the extent to which the work is made challenging and directly relevant to organizational goals. Overstaffing and make-work reduce commitment. Raising expectations too high at the time of initial hiring should be avoided; subsequent disillusionment can do more harm than the benefits that early expectations could ever contribute. Top-level managers should avoid actions that are clearly in their own self-interest, particularly those that might prove to be at the expense of the firm's interests. Expecting commitment from those at lower levels means very little if the same commitment is clearly not present at the top.

Commitment can thrive only in an equitable environment in which people can state their concerns, raise issues, and achieve a fair hearing for their views. Open communication channels and kept promises do a lot to foster the trust and feelings of equity that in turn lay the groundwork for developing attitudinal commitment.

Finally, it is important to recognize that individual differences play an important role. Some people want to develop commitments; others feel uncomfortable doing so. Values can play an important role here. Conflicts between personal values and organizational objectives virtually guarantee low commitment levels. Pacifists in the defense industry, vegetarians in meat packing, environmentalists in wood products simply may experience too much strain to be able to achieve commitment to their employing organizations. Some people hold values that yield similar problems in any profitmaking organization within a free enterprise society. The answer is clear: to the extent possible, hire people who can develop commitment to the company and avoid those who cannot.

The Role of Values

We have touched on the role of values as motivational factors in chapters 2 and 4 and at certain points in this chapter. These values are very important and permeate much of our lives. Although knowledge regarding the role of values in performance is not as complete as might be desired, values probably have their greatest effects with regard to the conditions and organizations within which people will seek work or continue to work, and the kind of behaviors viewed as ethical. Thus, values may influence time spent on the job and cooperation with others in attaining organizational goals. In any event, values do relate to indexes of career success.

International Comparisons   As Exhibit 5.13 shows, certain values are associated with success, as measured by a rapid rate of movement up the management hierarchy, across a wide range of countries. The findings of Exhibit 5.13 were drawn from studies that dealt with managers in the United States, Great Britain, the Netherlands, Belgium, Germany, Austria, Scandinavia, France, Italy, Spain, Portugal, and Latin America. Variations may occur from country to country, but these variations are not so great as to preclude any overall relationships. Those who possess the value pattern set forth in Exhibit 5.13 should be particularly suited to multinational careers. They are most likely to prove successful when transferred from position to position in a number of different countries.

The extent to which societies can differ in their values—this time at the level of the worker—is vividly portrayed in Exhibit 5.14. These results are based on large groups of employees in the United States and Japan. Clearly, American and Japanese workers differ substantially on what they feel they should do, perhaps much of what they will do, as well as on how they evaluate the behavior of others around them. Managers who fail to develop an understanding of these cultural differences, when working outside their native environment, run the risk of being seriously misunderstood.

Business Ethics and Values   Values have a great deal to do with what is considered ethical and what is not. Since values differ from society to society, and within societies among individuals, widespread ethical variations can be expected. Some individuals view the payment of bribes by top corporate management as absolutely reprehensible; others consider it a normal part of business dealing, or even a desirable method of sharing the wealth. Similarly, some

---

EXHIBIT 5.13   Values related to advancement in many countries throughout the world

Values of Managers Who Move Up Fast	Values Less Favored by Rapidly Promoted Managers Than by Relatively Unsuccessful Managers	Values Unrelated to Managerial Advancement
Leadership—becoming an influential leader, organizing and controlling others, achieving community or organizational goals	*Affection*—obtaining and sharing companionship and affection through families and friends	*Service*—contributing to the satisfaction of others, helping others who are in need
Expertness—becoming an authority on a subject, persevering to reach an expert level of skill and accomplishment	*Security*—achieving a secure and stable position in work and financially	*Wealth*—earning a great deal of money, building a large financial estate
Prestige—becoming well known, obtaining recognition and the award of high social status	*Self-realization*—optimizing their own personal development, realizing their full creative and innovative potential	*Independence*—having an opportunity for freedom of thought and action, being one's own boss
Duty—dedicating themselves totally to the pursuit of ultimate values, ideals, and principles	*Pleasure*—enjoying life, being happy and content, having the good things in life	

Adapted from Bernard M. Bass and Philip C. Burger, *Assessment of Managers: An International Comparison* (New York: Free Press, 1979), pp. 56, 174.

EXHIBIT 5.14 Values of American and Japanese production workers

Topic of Concern	American Response	Japanese Response
Deciding about promotions to supervisory levels	Management should decide based on its judgment (68%)	Management should secure agreement from subordinates affected (38%)
Decisions about promotion, transfer, wage increases, and hours of work	Should be based on previously established written policy (60%)	Should be based on discussions concerning each problem when it arises (49%)
Action to take with willing but unqualified workers	Management should continue employment for 3 months so they may seek employment elsewhere (38%)	Management should continue employment until they retire or die (55%)
The source of workers' willingness to work hard	A feeling of responsibility to the company and coworkers that they should do what is assigned (61%)	A feeling that they should live up to the expectations of family, friends, and society (41%)
What to do when an immediate supervisor enters a crowded bus on which one has a seat	One should remain seated in accordance with "first come, first served" (68%)	One should offer the seat, unless you feel ill (44%)
What to do when a worker wishes to marry	Supervisor should not get involved in such personal matters (60%)	Supervisor should offer personal advice if requested (70%)

Adapted from Arthur M. Whitehill and S. Takezawa, *The Other Worker* (Honolulu: East-West Center Press, 1968).

workers consider stocking their tool chests at home with items from the shop floor as theft, pure and simple; others believe that this is a normal right of workers, a part of their just remuneration, and would feel offended if management should question the practice.

The point in giving these examples is not to argue for ethical relativism. Rather, it is to demonstrate that values do differ; they influence both ethics and behavior, and thus wide ranges of ethical behavior should be expected. Managers should be aware of this, especially if they are to work in an international environment. A study conducted with M.B.A. students makes this point well.[23] The students were faced with a simulated situation in which continuing company profitability seemed to depend on paying kickbacks to the purchasing agents they dealt with. Having high or low theoretical, political, artistic, social, or religious values did not seem to influence the decision reached, but economic values did. Those who placed a high value on economic outcomes were more likely to decide in favor of the kickbacks. When the students who were United States citizens were compared with those who were foreign nationals, the latter were more likely to endorse kickbacks. Undoubtedly this was because a number of them came from cultures in which such behavior, if not positively valued, is at least not considered unethical. Once again we see that values can exert a strong motivational force and can influence many very important decisions and behaviors.

EXHIBIT 5.15 Contributions of various motivational concepts and approaches

Source	Major Contribution
Need hierarchy theory	Asserting the prepotency of lower-level physiological and safety needs and the importance of many other needs in job performance
Achievement motivation theory	Relating achievement motivation to entrepreneurship and pointing out the importance of power and affiliation motivation in management
Equity theory	Explaining why motivation from inequity is important and how it operates, especially underreward inequity
Expectancy theory	Facilitating understanding of conscious, rational, maximizing motivation under organizational circumstances that foster this type of motivation
Behavior modification and operant learning	Providing insights into how learning processes may influence performance and into the roles of contingencies of reinforcement
Individual goal setting	Specifying a valuable technique for activating strong motivation
Management by objectives	Specifying a program for applying goal setting throughout an organization, which can prove useful, although it is difficult to implement effectively
Work redesign and enrichment	Specifying certain techniques which can be used effectively with some people to increase work motivation
Organizational commitment	Describing how behavioral and attitudinal processes influence turnover, absenteeism, and policy implementation
Cultural and personal values	Describing how people come to have different views of what is right and exhibit differing ethical behaviors; particularly important for multinational management

Summary   A wide range of theories, hypotheses, concepts, techniques, and programs exist in the area of organizational motivation. Those that have been considered in this chapter are noted in Exhibit 5.15 along with a statement of their potential value for a manager. Some are useful for one purpose, some for another; some help with one person, some help with another. There is no single, all-purpose theory at the present time that can guide managers' actions with regard to employees. Managers must develop their own working theories, using some mix of the approaches noted in Exhibit 5.15 as appropriate to the particular problems they face. Whatever the nature of this mix, however, managers must get to know their employees—what they want, how they think, how they react to differing events. The fact of individual differences is the most pervasive aspect of motivation in organizations.

What Have You Learned?

1. In what ways are individual goal setting and management by objectives (MBO) the same, and in what ways are they different? Which appears more effective?
2. Why is an understanding of differing values important in multinational management? Give some examples.
3. How do various needs relate to each other in need hierarchy theory, and what is the research support for this theory?
4. What exactly is the exchange process, as stated by equity theory? What are the possible responses to inequity?
5. What is the nature of job characteristics theory, and how is it used to redesign jobs?
6. How does behavior modification work, and why is it particularly susceptible to charges of unethical manipulation?
7. In what ways do achievement, power, and affiliation needs relate to performance in different types of organizations?
8. How do expectancies, valences, outcomes, and instrumentalities operate in expectancy theories? When does the theory hold?
9. How do behavioral commitment and attitudinal commitment operate, and how do they influence performance?
10. What are the ethical implications of studying motivation in organizations?

How Well Can You Apply Your Knowledge?

Problem 1.   The board of directors of a large corporation has decided to expand its investment in research and development, with a view to generating a number of new products internally. In implementing this decision, the personnel department has moved actively into the recruiting of new Ph.D.s in the sciences from major universities, while at the same time initiating contacts with several more experienced individuals in the industry. Qualified people definitely are in short supply, and acquiring them respresents a major recruiting challenge.

One of the people contacted is a young woman just finishing her doctoral dissertation. This dissertation research is in an area in which the company has a particular interest, and a strong effort to hire the young scientist is initiated. The company's situation has been presented in very attractive terms. There will be a lot of opportunity in an expanding research effort, new senior scientists with international reputations will be available to work with, a new research center is to be built, and major equipment purchases are scheduled. The pay offered is good, although not exceptional, but the scientist will be given every opportunity to conduct research in her area of major interest, including one day a week to work on her own rather than on company priority projects. The picture painted is that of a creative research environment with considerable freedom to pursue new and exciting ideas.

To the young scientist this appears an ideal opportunity, and she accepts the company's offer. Over time, however, it appears increasingly that this was a mistake on her part. The expanded research effort is somewhat underbudgeted; recruiting has not gone well, especially at the more senior levels; and there seems to be some uncertainty within R & D management as to what direction it should take. As a result of these factors, the young scientist is assigned initially to a high-priority development project staffed primarily with engineers. Because of the emphasis on application rather than basic research, people on this project are not given time to pursue their own projects, not even one day a month. Any effort to conduct research in the area of her dissertation will have to wait. For some reason the construction of a new research facility has been delayed indefinitely. Also, the company has decided that the development project work is not at a level to justify the initial hiring salary. They will stick by their commitment to pay that salary, but all raises will have to be deferred until her compensation level is more in line with the job being performed.

The young scientist becomes increasingly hurt and angry. Finally she begins to talk to the people back at the university about finding another job. She does not speak very well of her present employer.

Questions

1. How do the various ways of considering motivation, as discussed in this chapter and summarized in Exhibit 5.15, provide an understanding of the young scientist's reactions?
2. Using the motivational concepts we have been considering, what would have to be done in order to retain the scientist?

Problem 2. The company faces a very difficult problem. A salesman was hired originally because his father had called the company president and asked about a position for him. The father's firm has been a major purchaser of the company's products for years, and the president felt that he had little choice but to hire the son. The family is socially prominent in the area, and the business relationship has been a profitable one for the company. The problem is that the son is performing very poorly on the job, and apparently not much can be done about it. If it were not for the circumstances of his employment, he would have been fired some time ago.

The president has a reasonably good picture of the situation. The salesman and his wife are ardent golfers who entertain frequently. They both come from wealthy backgrounds and have been treated generously by their families. The salesman's income from his job is not a significant factor in their finances. Furthermore, although it is by no means certain how the father would react toward the company if the salesman were terminated, it is generally known that family pressures would force him to employ his son in his own firm if other employment were not available. The family is unlikely to permit one of its members to carry the social stigma of unemployment.

It was evident from the beginning that the company did not acquire a very good salesman. The problem is not the man's incapacity, but simply laziness. He is absent from work often, in most cases to play golf. This probably would be excusable if his sales figures were good, but they are not. The territory is way off the business it had produced previously. The company utilizes a system of objectives with its sales force covering calls made, volume of business generated, and the like. The salesman has never met any of these objectives. Increasingly, customers have become angry because they cannot locate the salesman when they need him, or he fails to keep appointments, or he does not file orders promptly. He is often not up to date on product information. He has a particularly annoying tendency to go to sleep in the waiting room when a purchasing agent cannot see him immediately. As a result of all of this, his sales manager has been spending much of his own time putting out fires that the salesman had kindled. The sales manager's justified anger and frustration at not being able to do anything about the situation add to the gravity of the problem. Repeated talks with the man about his performance have accomplished nothing.

Questions

1. What insights into this problem can be gained by viewing it in terms of the various motivational concepts? Which theories are most applicable?

2. Any action clearly must be initiated by the president. What should the president do? Why?

Additional Sources for More Detailed Study

Aldag, Ramon J., and Brief, Arthur P. *Task Design and Employee Motivation.* Glenview, Ill.: Scott, Foresman, 1979.

Alderfer, Clayton P. *Existence, Relatedness, and Growth: Human Needs in Organizational Settings.* New York: Free Press, 1972.

Carroll, Stephen J., and Tosi, Henry L. *Management by Objectives: Applications and Research.* New York: Macmillan, 1973.

Chung, Kae H. *Motivational Theories and Practices.* Columbus: Grid, 1977.

Deci, Edward L. *Intrinsic Motivation.* New York: Plenum, 1975.

England, George W. *The Manager and His Values: An International Perspective from the United States, Japan, Korea, India, and Australia.* Cambridge, Mass.: Ballinger, 1975.

Goldstein, Arnold P., and Sorcher, Melvin. *Changing Supervisor Behavior.* New York: Pergamon, 1974.

Hackman, J. Richard, and Suttle, J. Lloyd. *Improving Life at Work: Behavioral Science Approaches to Organizational Change.* Santa Monica: Goodyear, 1977.

Hamner, W. Clay. *Organizational Shock.* New York: Wiley, 1980.

Lawler, Edward E. *Motivation in Work Organizations.* Monterey, Calif.: Brooks/Cole, 1973.

Miner, John B. *Theories of Organizational Behavior.* Hinsdale, Ill.: Dryden, 1980.

Mowday, Richard T.; Porter, Lyman W.; and Steers, Richard M. *Employee–Organization Linkages: The Psychology of Commitment, Absenteeism and Turnover.* New York: Academic Press, 1982.

Naylor, James C.; Pritchard, Robert D.; and Ilgen, Daniel R. *A Theory of Behavior in Organizations.* New York: Academic Press, 1980.

Odiorne, George S. *MBO II: A System of Managerial Leadership for the 80s.* Belmont, Calif.: Fearson Pitman, 1979.

Porter, Lyman W., and Lawler, Edward E. *Managerial Attitudes and Performance.* Homewood, Ill.: Irwin, 1968.

Steers, Richard M., and Porter, Lyman W. *Motivation and Work Behavior.* New York: McGraw-Hill, 1983.

Vroom, Victor H. *Work and Motivation.* New York: Wiley, 1964.

Weiner, Bernard. *Theories of Motivation: From Mechanism to Cognition.* Chicago: Markham, 1972.

Notes

1. See, for example, Chris Argyris's books, *Personality and Organization* (New York: Harper & Row, 1957) and *Integrating the Individual and the Organization* (New York: Wiley, 1964).

2. For example, see Gerald R. Salancik and Jeffrey Pfeffer, "An Examination of Need-Satisfaction Models of Job Attitudes," *Administrative Science Quarterly* (September 1977); and Clayton P. Alderfer, "A Critique of Salancik and Pfeffer's Examination of Need-Satisfaction Theories," *Administrative Science Quarterly* (December 1977).

3. Douglas McGregor, *The Human Side of Enterprise* (New York: McGraw-Hill, 1960); Abraham H. Maslow, *Eupsychian Management* (Homewood, Ill.: Irwin, 1965).

4. Yoel Yinon, Aharon Bizman, and Martha Goldberg, "Effect of Relative Magnitude of Reward and Type of Need on Satisfaction," *Journal of Applied Psychology* (June 1976).

5. David C. McClelland, *The Achieving Society* (Princeton, N.J.: Van Nostrand, 1961).

6. Norman T. Feather, *Expectations and Actions* (Hillsdale, N.J.: Lawrence Erlbaum, 1982).

7. David C. McClelland and Richard E. Boyatzis, "Leadership Motive Pattern and Long-Term Success in Management," *Journal of Applied Psychology* (December 1982).

8. J. Stacy Adams, "Toward an Understanding of Inequity," *Journal of Abnormal and Social Psychology* (November 1963); idem, "Inequity in Social Ex-

change," in *Advances in Experimental Social Psychology,* vol. 2, ed. Leonard Berkowitz (New York: Academic Press, 1965).

9. Karl E. Weick, Michael G. Bougon, and Geoffrey Maruyama, "The Equity Context," *Organizational Behavior and Human Performance* (February 1976).

10. Edwin A. Locke, "Personnel Attitudes and Motivation," *Annual Review of Psychology* (1975).

11. Fred Luthans and Robert Kreitner, *Organizational Behavior Modification* (Glenview, Ill.: Scott, Foresman, 1975).

12. John V. Baumler, "Defined Criteria of Performance in Organizational Control," *Administrative Science Quarterly* (September 1971).

13. C. Northcote Parkinson, *Parkinson's Law and Other Studies in Administration* (Boston: Houghton-Mifflin, 1957); Judith F. Bryan and Edwin A. Locke, "Parkinson's Law as a Goal Setting Phenomenon," *Organizational Behavior and Human Performance* (August 1967).

14. Peter F. Drucker, *The Practice of Management* (New York: Harper, 1954); Douglas McGregor, "An Uneasy Look at Performance Appraisal," *Harvard Business Review* (May 1957).

15. Richard M. Steers, "Task–Goal Attributes, Achievement, and Supervisory Performance," *Organizational Behavior and Human Performance* (June 1975).

16. J. Richard Hackman, "Work Design," in *Improving Life at Work: Behavioral Science Approaches to Organizational Change,* ed. Richard Hackman and J. Lloyd Suttle (Santa Monica: Goodyear, 1977).

17. W. Philip Kraft and Kathleen L. Williams, "Job Redesign Improves Productivity," *Personnel Journal* (July 1974).

18. Frederick Herzberg, *The Managerial Choice: To Be Efficient and To Be Human* (Homewood, Ill.: Dow Jones-Irwin, 1976).

19. Gerald R. Salancik, "Commitment and the Control of Organizational Behavior and Belief," in *New Directions in Organizational Behavior,* ed. Barry M. Staw and Gerald R. Salancik (Chicago: St. Clair Press, 1977).

20. Bruce Buchanan, "To Walk an Extra Mile—The Whats, Whens and Whys of Organizational Commitment," *Organizational Dynamics* (Spring 1975); Lyman W. Porter, William J. Crampon, and Frank J. Smith, "Organizational Commitment and Managerial Turnover," *Organizational Behavior and Human Performance* (February 1976).

21. George A. Steiner and John B. Miner, *Management Policy and Strategy* (New York: Macmillan, 1982), chapter 15.

22. Kathryn M. Bartol, "Professionalism as a Predictor of Organizational Commitment, Role Stress, and Turnover: A Multidimensional Approach," *Academy of Management Journal* (December 1979); Theodore V. Purcell, *Blue Collar Man: Patterns of Dual Allegiance in Industry* (Cambridge, Mass.: Harvard University Press, 1960).

23. Henry P. Sims and W. Harvey Hegarty, "Policies, Objectives, and Ethical Decision Behavior: An Experiment," *Academy of Management Proceedings* (1977).

CHAPTER 6

Groups, Leadership, and Supervision

CHAPTER OUTLINE

Jim Thomas—Lessons for Management Practice from the Football Field

Views of Groups in Group-Based Systems
What is a Group?
    Reference Groups
Suppose We Took Groups Seriously
Likert's Ideas Regarding Groups
    The Nature of System 4
    Research on Participative Management
Sociotechnical Theory and Autonomous Work
        Groups
    The Nature of Autonomous Groups
    Effects on Performance

Aspects of Group Functioning
Formal and Informal Groups
    Natural and Artificial Systems
    Types of Groups
    Groups and the Manager
Group Cohesiveness
    Work Groups and Cohesion
    Cohesiveness and Performance
International Comparisons

Leadership and Supervision
Theory X and Theory Y
    The McGregor and Miles Approaches
    Problems with Stereotyping
Contingency Views of Leadership
    The LPC Score
    Overall Evaluation
Consideration and Initiating Structure
Path-Goal Views of Leadership
    Leader Behavior
    Overall Evaluation
Decision Tree Concepts of Participation
    Early Views
    Vroom's Theory
Vertical Dyad Linkages

OBJECTIVES

To demonstrate how group-based systems operate in the business world and how effective these team approaches can be

To provide an understanding of various kinds of group phenomena and how they relate to performance

To discuss and evaluate the usefulness of various ideas regarding leadership and supervisory processes, and thus in an overall sense influencing

JIM THOMAS—LESSONS FOR MANAGEMENT PRACTICE FROM THE FOOTBALL FIELD

1. Some individuals have never really learned what their assignments are, particularly for certain plays or situations.
2. Some are afraid of the coach, so they pretend to know things that they should be asking questions about.
3. Some want to do things "the old way," while others feel that more modern methods are needed.
4. Factions and cliques quarrel and fight among one another.
5. The whole unit has not come together to develop common goals to which everyone is committed.
6. Decisions are made by someone, but some people either don't "get the word" or they disagree with the decision and drag their feet.
7. There is jealousy between units and a lack of playing together.
8. Even when people are aware of a problem, they don't know exactly what to do about it.

Teams are collections of people who must rely on group collaboration if each member is to experience the optimum of success and goal achievement. It is obvious that in order to score touchdowns (and prevent the opponent from scoring) a football team has to play together. It should be just as obvious that a work unit or a management group must also work together to ensure success. A football team practices over and over again how it will execute its plays. The team has "skull" practice—they talk over plans and strategies. They review films of past games, identify mistakes, set up goals for the next week. Unfortunately, Jim Thomas's management group does not engage in any similar type of activities. They do not review their past actions and they do not really plan new strategies. They do not come together to learn from their mistakes, nor do they practice or get coaching on new methods, set new goals, or build up their team "spirit." Jim Thomas can spot the absence of teamwork on the playing field, but cannot see similar symptoms in the work plant.

Jim Thomas is manager of the Mountain Side plant of the National Alloys Company. He has a tough production schedule that demands solid performance from all of his people, in all areas of the plant. Jim wants to do a top-flight job and becomes concerned when production drops, when problems go unsolved, or when morale sags.

After his job and his family, Jim's greatest interest is pro football—particularly as played by the Dallas Cowboys. Being a native Texan, Jim has followed the Dallas team from its inception. He gets to attend an occasional game and watches them regularly on TV or listens to them on the radio. When the game is over, Jim can give a clear, detailed accounting for the team's success or failure.

What raises Jim's boiling point higher than anything is to watch his team fail to play together. He can spot in an instant when someone misses a block, loafs on the job, fails to pass on obvious information to the quarterback, or tries to "shine" at the expense of the team. He can diagnose the Cowboys' areas of weakness, and, if the coach could only hear him, he would tell him what to do to remedy the situation. But with all of his insight about teamwork and football, Jim fails to see the parallels between what is needed to improve the Dallas Cowboys and what is needed to shape up the management team at National Alloys. Many of the problems are exactly the same.[1]

T he message from this case is that Jim Thomas should deal with his managers as a group, or team, and that his role should be that of a group leader, or coach. Although by no means universally accepted, this is an important way of looking at a number of aspects of the management job. Furthermore, groups clearly do form within organizations, whether intended or not. It therefore is important to understand groups—how they function and how they influence performance. It is also important to recognize the various types of leadership that may be exercised in these groups, and in particular how leadership shades into supervision within bureaucratic systems.

A number of views emphasize the role of groups as essential building blocks in organizations, taking positions similar to that expressed in the case of Jim Thomas. We will consider these approaches involving groups at some length. However, these newer approaches should be contrasted with a more traditional emphasis on the individual as the cornerstone of organizations. This latter (individual) approach is generally more consistent with the views of Frederick Taylor, Henri Fayol, and Max Weber as discussed in chapter 3. Weber did recognize the power of the group in his "law of the small number," however—a concept he applied only to the top management level:

> The ruling minority can quickly reach understanding among its members . . . to initiate that rationally organized action which is necessary to preserve its position of power. . . . Another benefit . . . is the ease of secrecy as to the intentions and resolutions of the rulers and the state of their information.[2]

What Weber did not recognize is that groups at other levels of the organization also can achieve a degree of power in the same manner, simply by virtue of being groups.

VIEWS OF GROUPS IN GROUP-BASED SYSTEMS

Let us start with some of the positions favoring a major formal role for groups in organizations. Against this background it will be easier to look at the functioning of groups in more traditional organizations and to understand important aspects of group dynamics.

What Is a Group?

Simple as it may seem, the concept of "group" has presented a number of difficulties in definition. Writers on the subject have not been in agreement, largely because they have considered groups from different perspectives that emphasize certain aspects and not others.

Cartwright and Zander's definition places primary emphasis on interdependence—the idea that members are dependent on one another to achieve goals; they do not or cannot "go it alone":

> A group is a collection of individuals who have relations to one another that make them interdependent to some significant degree. . . . When a set of people constitutes a group, one or more of the following statements will characterize them:
>
> a. They engage in frequent interaction.
> b. They define themselves as members.
> c. They are defined by others as belonging to the group.
> d. They share norms concerning matters of common interest.
> e. They participate in a system of interlocking roles.
> f. They identify with one another . . . .
> g. They feel the group to be rewarding.
> h. They pursue promotively interdependent goals.
> i. They have a collective perception of their unity.
> j. They tend to act in a unitary manner toward the environment.[3]

Cartwright and Zander list a number of characteristics taken from other definitions that have some credibility in the field. Their position is that, although others have viewed certain of these (in various combinations) as essential to the existence of a group, no one characteristic is absolutely necessary. Collectively, it might be useful to treat Cartwright and Zander's characteristics as a checklist: the larger the number of statements that can be endorsed, the greater the "groupness" present. Using this approach, Schein's definition can be viewed as a short checklist focusing on several of the most important characteristics: "A psychological group is any number of people who (1) interact with one another, (2) are psychologically aware of one another, and (3) perceive themselves to be a group."[4]

Alderfer contributes a third definition of a group:

A human group is a collection of individuals:

1. Who have significantly interdependent relations with each other.
2. Who perceive themselves as a group by reliably distinguishing members from nonmembers.
3. Whose group identity is recognized by nonmembers.
4. Who have differentiated roles in the group as a function of expectations from themselves, other group members, and nongroup members.
5. Who, as group members acting alone or in concert, have significantly interdependent relations with other groups.[5]

This definition adds an additional important dimension, particularly in its fifth component. This dimension is the open systems character of groups, the idea that factors in the environment of a group play an important role in its functioning. In particular, other groups in the environment—within or even outside the organization—are important. Alderfer's views in this regard have particular significance for groups functioning in large organizations.

The concept of group emphasized here is not one of yes or no; it is that a "bunch" of people becomes more and more of a group to the extent it possesses characteristics of the kind listed in these definitions. The more of each characteristic there is and the more statements that can be endorsed at all, the more groupness we have. In short, the idea of group is viewed as a variable, not a distinct category.

Reference Groups   Reference groups are groups to which people relate their attitudes. Such groups are important in developing feelings of equity and inequity, as discussed in chapter 5; they also are important for a number of other aspects of organizational behavior, particularly the feelings of status that people develop. For instance, management may be a positive reference group, or perhaps top management, but at the same time the inhabitants of a poor and rundown neighborhood from which one wishes to escape may constitute a negative reference group (as in the case of Jack L. in chapter 2).

In the following discussions we will be concerned primarily with membership groups, which very well may serve as positive reference groups. But reference groups are not necessarily the same as membership groups. A person may use a membership group as a reference group, as when a manager uses his own company's management in this manner, but a part-time mail boy in the same company who is still attending high school might also use the same management as a reference group. Whether and how people refer their attitudes toward various groups seems to depend on their orientation to membership, not whether they are actually members. If a person wants to be (or stay) a member of a group, there is a tendency to use it as a positive reference group and to become similar to known members in those ways that distinguish them as members. If a person wants to avoid membership or identification with a group, the natural tendency is to maximize differences from group members.

Suppose We Took Groups Seriously

Harold Leavitt has advocated that organizations be constructed using groups rather than individuals as the basic building blocks. This is the ultimate extension of the ideas generated at the Hawthorne works of the Western Electric Company many years ago (see chapter 3). It is congruent with the team approach as recommended for Jim Thomas, with the various organization development methods considered in chapter 10, and with so-called participative management. It has much in common with the way many Japanese firms operate. At the same time, this concept is at variance with the individualistic ethic that has permeated American society for so many years. Leavitt advances a number of arguments in favor of taking groups seriously:

Small groups are good for people, in that they satisfy important needs, provide a range of activities for members, provide support in times of stress and crisis, and are settings in which people can learn to be trusting and helpful to one another.

Groups are good problem finding tools, useful in promoting innovation and creativity.

Groups make better decisions than individuals in a certain range of situations.

Groups are great tools for implementing decisions in that they gain commitments from members so that group decisions are likely to be carried out.

Groups can control and discipline members in ways that bureaucratic systems find difficult.

Small groups are valuable in fending off the negative consequences of large organizational size; they prevent such things as too-long communication lines, too steep hierarchies, and the individual getting lost in the crowd.

Groups are natural phenomena and facts of organizational life; since groups are inevitable in any event, they might best be planned for, so that they become part of the formal rather than informal system. (Put otherwise, groups in individualized systems represent pesty weeds that will not go away. Better to beautify the landscape by treating them as flowers, thus amplifying the aesthetic qualities of the organizational garden.)[6]

Using groups as the primary unit of analysis would mean certain things that at present are encountered only rarely in this country. Thus, one would hire groups, train groups, pay groups, promote groups, design jobs for groups, fire groups, and so on. The whole gamut of activities normally carried out to obtain and utilize human inputs is applied at the group rather than individual level. Actually, some approaches to constructing organizations or at least parts of them this way have been proposed and even put into practice. Let us see how groups operating in these group-based systems actually look.

One person who took groups seriously at an early point was Rensis Likert. Along with a number of coworkers at the University of Michigan, Likert not only developed a detailed theory of group-based systems but also initiated extensive research on the subject.

The Nature of System 4   Likert viewed organizational systems as extending from system 0, in which operations are so permissive and laissez-faire that there is hardly any organization at all, to system 5—a hypothesized future state in which hierarchy will be entirely replaced by overlapping group relationships.[7] In between are system 1—exploitive authoritative, system 2—benevolent authoritative, system 3—consultative, and system 4—participative group. The larger the system number, the greater the hypothesized effectiveness of performance in every respect. Only the system 1 to 4 continuum has been worked out in detail. Exhibit 6.1 describes system 4, the participative system

EXHIBIT 6.1   Selected characteristics of Likert's system

System 1: Exploitive Authoritative	System 4: Participative Group
Low Performance Effectiveness ⟵————————⟶ High Performance Effectiveness	
Taps motives of security and status	Taps all motives, including group
Uses fear and punishment to motivate	Uses participation and involvement to motivate
Subservient and hostile attitudes	Favorable and cooperative attitudes
Overall dissatisfaction	High satisfaction
Very little communication	Much communication
Communication inaccurate	Accurate communication
No cooperative teamwork	Substantial cooperative teamwork
No subordinate influence	A great deal of member influence
Downward influence structure	Influence flows in all directions
No subordinate-superior trust	Complete member-leader trust
Subordinate ideas seldom used	Member ideas always used
Subordinates not involved in decision making	Members fully involved in decision making
Decision making is at the top	Decision making is at all levels
Decision making pattern is person-to-person	Decision making pattern is largely group
Goal setting via orders	Goal setting by group participation
Goals covertly resisted	Goals fully accepted
Informal organization opposes formal	Informal and formal organization are one
Quality control is necessary	Quality control used for self-guidance

Based on Rensis Likert, *New Patterns of Management* (New York: McGraw-Hill, 1961), pp. 223–33; Rensis Likert, *The Human Organization* (New York: McGraw-Hill, 1967), pp. 197–211.

Likert advocated, and contrasts it with system 1, the authoritarian system he deplored.

The theory also contains an extensive discussion of the groups in system 4. This discussion is summarized in Exhibit 6.2. The idea is that everyone in the organization will be a member of at least one work group—each with strong group loyalty, skilled interactions, and high performance goals. The groups are brought together by people with dual memberships who perform a *linking pin* function, as described in item 6 of Exhibit 6.2. These dual members need to exert influence in both groups. Typically a leader in one group will be a member of another group. Groups are linked in this manner both vertically and horizontally throughout the organization.

Research on Participative Management The research dealing with system 4 yields a decidedly mixed picture. There are favorable results, but in almost every case one cannot be sure from the way the study was carried out that groupness is what caused those results. There are unfavorable results also; aspects of satisfaction often increase when system 4 is introduced, but performance effects are another matter.

Exhibit 6.3 provides a case in point. In that study, which has become something of a classic in the field, some units in the company were deliberately moved toward system 4 and others toward system 1. When the results were measured, the system 4 units experienced a somewhat greater movement of decision making into the work groups as anticipated, and some degree of improvement in certain aspects of satisfaction. Productivity improved under both systems, but it improved *more* under system 1. Likert later contended that this situation would have reversed itself if the experiment had continued over a longer time span. It is quite possible that this is true, but there is no way we can be sure the system 4 units would have been more productive in the end.

A major problem with the research on the Likert theory is that to the extent it has produced any positive results at all, it was carried out with lower-level work groups housed in organizations that were still in an overall sense bureaucratic. In no case was the group-based system extended throughout the organization using the linking pin concept. This may merely mean that group systems have trouble achieving their full potential within a bureaucratic environment; perhaps the research has not gone far enough. Weber anticipated that well-designed and well-operated bureaucracies would be exceedingly powerful, and in fact nonbureaucratic systems generally do tend to have difficulties surviving within them. In any event it is clear that participative management does not work everywhere. One major factor on which results are contingent is the composition of the groups involved.[8] Not everyone functions well in a group-based system; for some this is a very unpleasant way to work. But for others it appears to be ideal.

Sociotechnical Theory and Autonomous Work Groups

Sociotechnical systems theory is in a sense the European counterpart of system 4 theory. Both approaches take groups very seriously, but they do this in somewhat different ways. Both give relatively little attention, especially in their research studies, to organizational components other than basic production units.

Sociotechnical theory arose out of a series of studies of coal mining in Great Britain; these studies serve to illustrate aspects of the theory. Historically, mining

EXHIBIT 6.2 Characteristics of highly effective groups within Likert's theory

1. Members are skilled in the various leadership and membership roles and functions required for interaction.
2. The group is in existence long enough to have established stable, relaxed working relationships.
3. Members are attracted to the group and are loyal to one another.
4. Members and leaders are confident in and trusting of each other.
5. Group values and goals are shaped by the members and satisfy their needs.
6. Members who are also members of other groups try to harmonize the various values and goals of these groups.
7. There is greater member acceptance of the most important group values.
8. Members are motivated to abide by major group values and achieve important goals.
9. A supportive atmosphere characterizes group interactions and decision making; individual egos are subordinated to the group.
10. Leaders create a supportive atmosphere and emphasize cooperation over competition.
11. Members help each other develop to their full potential by providing technical knowledge and training in interpersonal skills.
12. Group goals are accepted by members without resentment; goals are high but remain realistic.
13. Expectations stretch members to the maximum to foster growth, but must be tempered as necessary to avoid feelings of failure.
14. Members provide mutual help to each other.
15. Creativity is stimulated by the supportive atmosphere and by values favoring creativity over conformity.
16. Constructive conformity in mechanical and administrative matters is valued, but without adversely affecting creativity.
17. There is full and open communication of relevant information within the group.
18. Communication processes are used to serve the goals of the group.
19. High motivation both to communicate and to receive communications characterizes group members.
20. High motivation both to influence others and to be influenced characterizes group members.
21. Leaders are strongly influenced by members and are provided with considerable information as a consequence of group processes.
22. Flexibility and adaptability are fostered by the existing capacity for influence but are tempered by the steadying influence of group goals and values.
23. Members feel secure in making decisions themselves, thus fostering initiative, because they understand the overall constraints of group philosophies and goals.
24. Leaders are selected carefully and are those who would emerge as leaders anyway; peer nominations and related methods are used to this end.

The *principle of supportive relationships* operates within all of these characteristics, with the result that the effective group ensures "a maximum probability that in all interactions and all relationships with the organization each member will, in the light of his background, values and expectations, view the experience as supportive and one which builds and maintains his sense of personal worth and importance" (p. 103).

Based on Rensis Likert, *New Patterns of Management* (New York: McGraw-Hill, 1961), pp. 103, 166–69.

EXHIBIT 6.3 Changes in various factors over 18 months—system 4 and system 1 units

Factor	Amount of Change	
	System 4 Units	System 1 Units
Employee perceptions of the level at which decisions are made on a 9-point scale (1 = low, 9 = top)	− 1.8	+ .6
Perceived self-actualization on a 5-point scale (1 = low, 5 = high)	+ .1	− .1
Satisfaction in relations with higher level management on a 5-point scale (1 = low, 5 = high)	+ .2	− .5
Satisfaction with higher level management as representatives of employees on a 5-point scale (1 = low, 5 = high)	+ .4	− .4
Satisfaction with the company on a 5-point scale (1 = low, 5 = high)	+ .2	− .3
Productivity measured on a scale of 100, with higher values indicating greater productivity	+ 10.0	+ 14.1

Adapted from Nancy C. Morse and Everett Reimer, "The Experimental Change of a Major Organizational Variable," *Journal of Abnormal and Social Psychology* (January 1956): 123–28.

had been carried out with considerable reliance on group-based systems. However, with the introduction of a new technology, the longwall method, the groups were broken up and tasks of a highly specialized nature were introduced. This approach did not yield the performance levels that the new technology appeared to warrant. According to sociotechnical theory this was because the appropriate match or balance between technology and social group needs had been lost.[9]

Studies dealt with the consequences of reinstituting group-based systems in the context of the new longwall technology, and with the introduction of multiskilling. With multiskilling, workers learn a number of different jobs performed in the work group, perhaps all of them. Consequently a degree of job enrichment is achieved and bottlenecks caused by the need for certain skills in particular phases of the work are avoided.

In most cases changes based on sociotechnical theory did yield improvements, especially increased productivity and reduced absenteeism.[10] But there were instances in which the miners strongly resisted the autonomous work groups; these appeared to be situations in which a tradition of group-based operation did not exist.

A major feature of sociotechnical theory is its emphasis on group-based job enrichment. Much of what is involved directly parallels the discussion of this subject in chapter 5. Approaches used include job rotation based on multiskilling, the creation of closely interlocking tasks, placing workers in close physical proximity to one another, making information for self-control available to production workers, and using meetings to foster group formation.

The Nature of Autonomous Groups The role of leadership and supervision can vary considerably, but in the more truly autonomous situations leadership emerges from the group, based on implicit or explicit election; it is not achieved by appointment at the hands of higher level authority. Under these circumstances leadership tends to be very fragile. The power of appointment and recall remains in the group. Any decisions the leader makes are severely limited by group norms, values, and goals. In large part the leader role becomes one of communication, coordinating the group with the resources and objectives of the larger organization. This role may be rotated among members.

In different applications the degree of work group autonomy vis-à-vis the larger organization (the bureaucracy) has varied substantially. Exhibit 6.4 shows an ascending scale of autonomy or group power, and at the same time provides a picture of what taking groups seriously can involve.

Effects on Performance Applications of sociotechnical theory have expanded from the original source in Great Britain to most of the countries of Europe, to the United States and Canada, to India, and elsewhere. Understanding the effects of these applications is plagued with many of the same problems noted with regard to system 4. Was it really the existence of autonomous groups that caused an improvement in performance, or was it something else, such as increased pay or the initiation of goal setting? Also performance is not always improved by any means, and autonomous groups tend to revert back to bureaucratic systems under certain circumstances.

Yet the performance results are encouraging, although it is very difficult to predict what the outcome will be—better quality, higher quantity, less absenteeism, reduced turnover, or fewer accidents. Multiskilling and other factors tend to reduce the number of people needed to do the work, and the way in which leadership is handled can reduce the number of managers needed. The

---

EXHIBIT 6.4 Increasing degrees of group autonomy

Level of Autonomy	Powers of the Work Group
Low	Determines only how work operations are to be performed
	Decides whether it wants a leader to deal with internal questions, and if it does, who
	Decides on who will be admitted to membership
	Determines how the total group task is to be divided up among members
	Makes decisions regarding the choice of production methods
	Can decide when it will work
	Can govern its performance above and beyond where and when to work
	Decides whether it wants a leader to deal with conditions at the boundary between itself and the rest of the organization, and if it does, who
	Can influence the formulation of its quantitative goals
High	Can influence the formulation of its qualitative goals

Adapted from Jon Gulowsen, "A Measure of Work Group Autonomy," in *Design of Jobs,* ed. Louis E. Davis and James C. Taylor (Baltimore: Penguin, 1972), pp. 376–78.

result is typically a sizable decrease in labor costs, even though individual workers earn more. In the United States autonomous groups have proved to be very resistant to organizing attempts by the unions.

As noted previously, group-based systems are not for all. In some situations the workers themselves have strongly resisted them. A history of group work, as in many of the British coal mines, or supporting cultural values, as found in Sweden, can ensure a sizable pool of group-motivated workers. In other contexts it may be best to rely on volunteers to avoid the inclusion of people who might view the extensive forced social interaction with distaste. Success appears most likely when there is:

1. A small-town environment
2. A rather small work force, say below 100
3. A new factory or startup situation
4. Geographic separation from the rest of the company
5. The use of outside consultants
6. A long lead time for planning and training
7. The absence of a union or a very favorable union climate.[11]

Under these circumstances the autonomous groups can best maintain themselves in the face of the almost inevitable bureaucratic pressures—from both company and unions.

Although sociotechnical programs and the introduction of autonomous work groups had origins quite different from much of organization development, there has been an increasing tendency to bring the sociotechnical approach in under the umbrella of organization development. This is reflected in the discussion in chapter 10 dealing with sociotechnical systems design. Thus, many of the applications at General Foods, General Motors, Mead Corporation, Volvo in Sweden, and elsewhere are now viewed as being of an organization development nature.

ASPECTS OF GROUP FUNCTIONING	System 4 and the sociotechnical approach represent some of the more extreme circumstances involving groups. In most organizations, individuals rather than groups remain the building blocks. But groups are a distinct and everpresent reality—sometimes because management's actions encourage a degree of groupness, and sometimes despite management's efforts to discourage groups. Either way, dealing with groups is something managers need to know about.

Formal and Informal Groups

For a variety of reasons managers may take steps, such as calling meetings and emphasizing group goals, in order to encourage a degree of groupness among subordinates. The boundaries of these groups are defined by existing organizational charts, position descriptions, and other indicators of organizational structure. They are *formal groups,* and in bureaucratic systems how much of a group they are depends in large part on the manager in charge. If considerable groupness exists and the manager has actually become the leader of a team, this may be for all practical purposes the only group that is present.

In certain situations, as exemplified by the Hawthorne studies, another type of group develops that does not include representatives of management in most cases. These *informal groups* form for different reasons. They may represent a reaction to a lack of groupness created along formal lines, or an attempt to cope with the impersonal nature of bureaucratic process. They may arise in reaction to the autocracy or arbitrariness of an individual manager. Historically they have been found often in conjunction with incentive pay systems and engineered production standards. In such cases the informal groups seek to restrict output out of a fear that standards will be raised otherwise, and members will have to work harder for less pay.

Natural and Artificial Systems   Victor Thompson has provided a view of informal groups as the natural system of organization, with bureaucratic structures and processes constituting an artificial overlay.[12] In contrast to the rationality of this artificial system, natural systems are not concerned with being rational. They are inevitable wherever bureaucracy exists, and they foster survival-oriented adaptation to the artificial system. The informal groups of the natural system emerge spontaneously and serve only themselves. Basically the two systems have conflicting interests, although on occasion they may complement each other. In particular the natural system may contribute needed flexibility and innovation.

Types of Groups   Writers such as Leavitt and Thompson assume that informal groups are inevitable. However, there was a time in the United States when many companies tried very hard to keep such groups from forming in the hope that by doing so they could forestall union organization. Presumably, these managements did not view informal groups as inevitable. They instituted rules against talking on the job, staggered rest periods, and the like to reduce communication among employees and thus prevent group formation.

Informal groups can vary substantially in their degree of groupness, and thus in their potential for exercising power and their behavior as it relates to the objectives of management. The results obtained from a study of 300 work groups in thirty plants are summarized in Exhibit 6.5. The *apathetic* groups had few grievances, used few pressure tactics, lacked clear leadership, had internal disunity and conflict, and showed considerable suppressed discontent. Generally they were passive. Typically these were mixed units with no concentrations of workers doing identical tasks or very long assembly lines. In contrast, the *erratic* groups were engaged in crew operations with members performing similar work or short assembly lines. Their behavior was unstable and demonstrative; they were easily inflamed, used poorly controlled pressure tactics, exhibited quick conversions to good relations with management, had highly centralized leadership, and were active in the union.

In contrast to the apathetic and erratic groups, management generally looked favorably on the other two types. *Strategic* group members usually performed individual operations, and their jobs were more desirable and often more skilled than those of the previous two groups. The groups exhibited persistent self-interest, exerted continuous pressure on management, had a well-planned and consistent grievance activity, were internally unified, participated in the union on a sustained basis, and had relatively good production records. The *conservative* groups also performed individual operations, often in scattered locations. They maintained restrained pressure for very specific objectives, exhibited moderate internal

EXHIBIT 6.5 Characteristics of different types of informal work groups

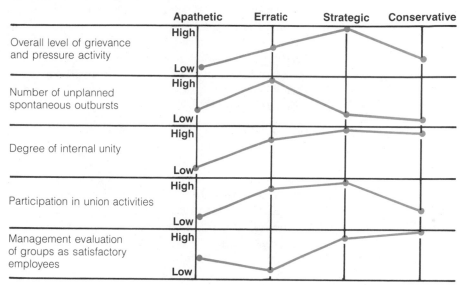

SOURCE: Leonard L. Sayles, *Behavior of Industrial Work Groups: Prediction and Control* (New York: Wiley, 1958), p. 39.

unity and self-assurance, varied in their degree of union and grievance activity from time to time, and overall were very stable.

This study and others suggest that the nature of the work and the types and degree of communication it fosters can be factors in the behavior of informal groups. Groups can differ a great deal, and in ways that make considerable difference to management.

Groups and the Manager Informal groups can constitute "weeds," as Leavitt put it, from a managerial perspective. In many cases they may be very resistant to weed killers and may sprout up again very quickly even when the weed killers do work. One appeal of taking groups seriously as the building blocks of organization is that formal and informal groups are fused, thus turning the former weeds into flowers. An alternative, however, is to accept informal groups of some kind while trying to minimize their negative consequences for organizational goal attainment. This can take various forms. To the degree the groupness of the formal group is increased, the groupness of the informal group is likely to decrease. Informal group leaders can be separated from their groups, as occurs in the not infrequent practice of promoting union stewards into management. Certain types of groups—perhaps strategic or conservative—may be fostered. Perhaps some kinds of weed killers will work.

It is important to recognize that group motivation can operate on individual members as a major force for superior performance. People can lose themselves in a group, take great pride in it, and work very hard for group success. These are very positive forces; if they can be harnessed behind an organization's goals, the organization certainly will benefit.

Group cohesiveness is determined by the extent to which members desire to remain members. Accordingly, highly cohesive groups exert considerable power over their members, they are not very tolerant of members who transgress group norms, and they tend to be quite harmonious. Such groups can and do act essentially as a unit, unlike apathetic groups for instance. Members value their membership and do not want to risk losing it by violating the norms of their group. The problem is that informal groups primarily serve their members, and cohesive informal groups do so particularly well. What does this imply for the attainment of organizational goals?

Work Groups and Cohesion A number of factors that characterize most business organizations automatically reduce cohesiveness. Members and leaders are usually appointed, and thus the membership does not control certain crucial aspects of group functioning. Work group members are members of other strong groups—families, social clubs, various reference groups, and the like. Because the employer does not usually exercise twenty-four-hour surveillance (as do the military and prisons, for example), these other groups can represent strong competitors for work group cohesiveness. To the extent that work groups satisfy strong, often social needs, provide emotionally for their members, and achieve a sense of commitment to a common goal, they can become very cohesive. But in the present corporate environment this probably does not happen very often. It does happen in group-based systems and in organizations or their components composed of high-status professionals. Yet even within the typical corporate structure, some managers do seem to create a high degree of cohesiveness.

Cohesiveness and Performance What does cohesiveness mean for performance? Overall it is a mixed blessing. It can help in solving certain kinds of problems, while increasing others. By their nature, cohesive groups reduce separations and absenteeism; members want to be with the group. Cohesive groups support their members, thus reducing stress, providing needed training, and offering other antidotes to performance failure that might hurt the group and force a member to leave it. In emergency situations these groups can utilize their norms to get everyone behind a strong group effort.

But quantity and quality of output depend on how group norms and values relate to organizational goals. They may not relate very well: there may be fear of management, or distrust, or simply a desire to take the company for all it is worth. A high degree of commitment throughout a group, however, may result in both cohesiveness and a favorable orientation to the company. Cohesiveness produces a degree of protectiveness toward group members that may serve to cover up personal problems until they become so extreme that little can be done about them. Alcoholics, for instance, are often hidden by a group to a point where no one can protect them, or help them either. Such pressures can extend to supervisors also. The net effect, ultimately, is bad for both the individual and the organization.

Finally, the boundaries of formal and informal groups may not be identical. This is a frequent problem for utility workers who shift from unit to unit depending on vacation schedules, absenteeism, hiring difficulties, and the like. Such individuals often find it hard to gain acceptance in the various groups of which they are temporary members, at least formally. The potential is great for ostracism, with its characteristic threat to self-esteem. Individuals also may be ostracized by the only group in which they could possibly achieve membership, for reasons that have much to do with group norms, values, and goals but little to do with performance and organizational goals.

The effects of informal group ostracism can be sizable. Some years ago the Atlantic Refining Company, which had not previously hired people with M.B.A. degrees, decided to do so on an experimental basis to bolster its supply of managerial talent in a particular department. The twelve individuals hired were to rotate through various functions for training and then were slated for "fast track" promotions into middle management. Yet three years later, eleven had left the company and the one who remained was working in another department. The young M.B.As had been consistently ostracized by the existing lower- and middle-management group. They were referred to contemptuously as "the prima donnas" by the much less educated old-timers. Some quit out of frustration; others were so upset by their unexpected reception that they failed to perform acceptably and were fired. Overall the company experienced a sizable loss on its hiring and training investment, and the individuals suffered considerable career damage.

International Comparisons

We have noted that sociotechnical theory has had widespread application around the world. The evidence from these studies suggests that group-based systems can function effectively in a wide range of cultures. Group phenomena and the processes we have been considering are not culture bound. Autonomous work groups have been found to operate well in highly authoritarian societies such as India as well as in more socially or group-oriented countries like Sweden. Yet it is also true that getting such groups started and maintaining them appears to be much easier in an environment of the kind Sweden provides.

A wide range of studies supports the view that the kinds of group processes discussed—conformity to group norms, cohesiveness, ostracism of deviates, and the like—are worldwide in scope.[13] Yet there are cultural variations too. Thus it has been found rather consistently that group conformity pressures are particularly effective in France and Norway. They are less effective in Great Britain and Germany, but this is not to say that group pressures do not influence people in these countries also. The data indicate that people who are highly responsive to groupness can be found almost everywhere, but that in certain cultures they are easier to find because early socialization processes have produced more of them.

LEADERSHIP AND SUPERVISION

Leadership is a term that has often been associated with studies of small groups—sometimes groups of strangers brought together in a laboratory setting, less often groups of coworkers in ongoing work contexts. The term clearly is applicable to the kinds of structuring that emerge in informal groups and in group-based systems. *Supervision,* on the other hand, is a term from the world of formal management and hierarchical systems. It assumes some type of authority based on the ability to influence rewards and punishments; it also assumes a bureaucratic context. *Influencing* covers both leadership and supervision.

In actual practice these terms—leadership, supervision, and influencing—tend to get thoroughly confused. Some people view leadership as an aspect of supervision, and some view supervision as a type of leadership. Influencing can mean almost anything. Although disentangling this confusion is hardly possible here, it is important to recognize that the concept of leadership relates primarily to small groups and their dynamics, while supervision is more closely allied with the management of bureaucracies.[14]

Theory X and Theory Y

Theory X and theory Y are not scientific theories of leadership and supervision but rather working theories or assumptions about subordinates and their managers. Douglas McGregor, the originator of this approach, considers theory X to be by far the more common. However, theory Y is favored on grounds of both practical efficiency and McGregor's own humanitarian values.

The McGregor and Miles Approaches   Exhibit 6.6 displays the nature of the two sets of assumptions. Theory X is considered to be oriented toward Maslow's lower level needs (see chapter 5). Since it is assumed that most people have satisfied those needs and are functioning at a higher level, theory X misses the mark. What is needed is a theory Y type of approach to supervision. But most managers have not made the conversion.

EXHIBIT 6.6   Two types of working assumptions held by managers

Theory X	Theory Y
1. Management is responsible for organizing the elements of productive enterprise—money, materials, equipment, people—in the interest of economic ends.	1. Same assumption as in theory X.
2. With respect to people this is a process of directing their efforts, motivating them, controlling their actions, modifying their behavior to fit the needs of the organization.	2. The essential task of management is to arrange organizational conditions and methods of operation so that people can best achieve their own goals by directing their own efforts toward organizational objectives.
3. Without this active intervention by management, people would be passive—even resistant—to organizational needs. They must therefore be persuaded, rewarded, punished, controlled—their activities must be directed.	3. People are not by nature passive or resistant to organizational needs. They have become so as a result of experience in organizations.
4. The average person is by nature: a. indolent and works as little as possible, b. lacking in ambition and prefers to be led, c. inherently self-centered and indifferent to organizational needs, d. resistant to change, and e. gullible and not very bright.	4. The motivation, the potential for development, the capacity for assuming responsibility, the readiness to direct behavior toward organizational goals are all present in people. Management does not put them there. It is a responsibility of management to make it possible for people to recognize and develop these human characteristics.

Based on Douglas McGregor, "The Human Side of Enterprise," *Management Review* (November 1957): 23, 88, 89.

A somewhat expanded version of this approach is given in Exhibit 6.7. In this view the traditional theory is more closely allied with theory X. The human relations theory is closer to theory X than to theory Y; McGregor would view this as pseudoparticipation and thus not a genuine theory Y approach. Miles, the author of the three-way categorization, considers the human relations theory to be the most frequently held, even though a human resources type of theory is preferable.

The data available on these approaches do not indicate that theory Y and human resources assumptions are strongly related to performance as a manager. Nor is the underlying need hierarchy theory very valid. However, working theories like theory X or human relations theory are widely held in management. The specific pattern that appears most frequently is demonstrated in Exhibit 6.8, which was developed from the responses of 3,600 managers in fourteen countries. A close look at that exhibit indicates a tendency for theory X's rather negative assumptions about the capabilities and motives of subordinates to be combined with more favorable attitudes toward theory Y-based administrative practices—sharing information needed for decision making with subordinates, having subordinates participate in decisions, and fostering subordinates' self-control of their own work. In Sweden, for instance, the generally very favorable orientation to theory Y practice, which one would anticipate from previous discussions, is coupled with a strong theory X view of the subordinates to whom these practices are applied. Throughout the fourteen countries the trend of the data is consistently

EXHIBIT 6.7 Three-way categorization of managers' working assumptions

Traditional Theory	Human Relations Theory	Human Resources Theory
1. Work is inherently distasteful.	1. People want to feel useful and important.	1. Work is not inherently distasteful. People want to contribute to goals they have helped establish.
2. What workers do is less important than what they earn.	2. People desire to belong and be recognized.	
3. Few want or can do work that requires creativity, self-direction, or self-control.	3. Money is not as important in motivating people as the needs noted above.	2. Most jobs demand less creativity, self-direction, and self-control than people are capable of.
4. The basic managerial task is to closely supervise and control subordinates.	4. The basic managerial task is to make each worker feel useful and important.	3. The basic managerial task is to make use of untapped human resources.
5. Tasks must be broken into simple, repetitive, easily learned operations.	5. A manager should keep subordinates informed and listen to their objections.	4. Managers should create an environment in which members contribute all they can.
6. Managers must establish detailed work routines and enforce them firmly but fairly.	6. At least on routine matters, managers should allow subordinates to exercise self-direction and self-control.	5. Managers should encourage full participation on important matters.

◄──────────── **Theory X / Theory Y** ────────────►

Based on Raymond E. Miles, *Theories of Management: Implications for Organizational Behavior and Development* (New York: McGraw-Hill, 1975), p. 35.

EXHIBIT 6.8 Theory X and theory Y assumptions among managers in different countries

Ranking of Countries on Attitude Toward Subordinates	Relative Position (X or Y) on Attitude Toward Administrative Practices		
	Sharing Information with Subordinates	Subordinate Participation	Fostering Subordinates' Self-Control
Theory X Assumptions			
Sweden	Y	Neutral	Y
Belgium	Neutral	Y	Neutral
Germany	X	Neutral	Y
France	Y	Y	Neutral
Italy	Neutral	X	Neutral
Denmark	X	Y	Y
Norway	Y	Neutral	Y
Spain	Neutral	Y	Neutral
Argentina	X	X	Neutral
England	Y	Neutral	Neutral
Chile	X	X	Neutral
India	X	Neutral	X
Japan	Neutral	Y	Neutral
United States	Y	Neutral	Neutral
Theory Y Assumptions			

Adapted from Mason Haire, Edwin E. Ghiselli, and Lyman W. Porter, *Managerial Thinking: An International Study* (New York: Wiley, 1966), p. 22.

toward more theory X assumptions coupled with more theory Y practices, although in countries like Japan and the United States the disparities are smaller.

Problems with Stereotyping In large part approaches such as those considered here have given way to more fully developed views such as system 4, autonomous work groups, and the like. As the field has moved on, however, theory X and theory Y have become very much part of our vocabulary; it is important to understand what they mean.

Another reason for studying such concepts is to recognize that working theories of this kind are stereotypes. Managers do appear to think in these ways frequently, but there is a serious question about whether they should. Throughout this book, the discussions emphasize that people come in all varieties of individual differences. An effective manager will recognize these variations and deal with each person as he or she really is, rather than grouping subordinates together in some grossly oversimplified category. To do otherwise is to perceive almost every subordinate incorrectly in some aspects, and to distort some by a very large degree. In this view theory Y is just as wrong as theory X, and human resources theory just as wrong as the human relations and traditional views—simply because all are stereotypes, and stereotypes by their nature are wrong. Studying theories X and Y is a good way to understand and learn this point.

A contingency approach means that whether a particular kind of person will prove to be effective in an influencing position depends on the nature of the situation in which the person operates. The same person behaving in the same way can be effective or ineffective; what makes this so is the context surrounding the behavior. An outline of the view most widely associated with the contingency concept is given in Exhibit 6.9. This view, developed by Fred Fiedler, has a long history, has undergone a variety of changes over the years, and despite considerable research remains the subject of much controversy.

The LPC Score   One of the major problems relates to the motivational characteristic of the leader that is at the heart of the theory. A measure was developed some years ago called the least preferred coworker (LPC) score. This measure asks an individual to "think of the person with whom you can work least well . . . the person with whom you had the most difficulty in getting a job done."[15] Then a series of adjective pairs is presented (helpful–frustrating, cooperative–uncooperative, efficient–inefficient, etc.) and the individual is to mark on an eight-point scale which adjective best describes the person. A higher score goes with a more favorable view of the person who is hard to work with.

This LPC score has been a measure in search of a meaning ever since it was created. Fiedler himself and others have advocated a number of interpretations at different times. In a recent article, the originator of the theory emphasizes "the leader's motivational structure, that is whether he or she is primarily motivated by task accomplishment or by good interpersonal relations."[16] A high LPC score means good interpersonal relations; a low score, a primary desire for task achievement. Although this interpretation of the score is not entirely consistent with either the research or prior theoretical statements, it is used in Exhibit 6.9 for lack of a clearly superior alternative.

EXHIBIT 6.9   The contingency view of leadership

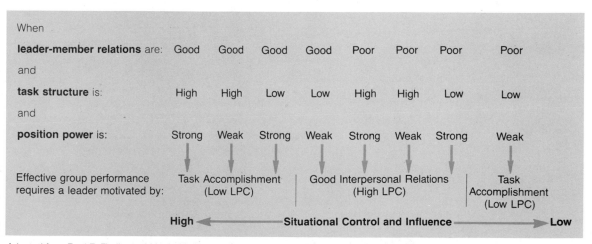

When								
leader-member relations are:	Good	Good	Good	Good	Poor	Poor	Poor	Poor
and								
task structure is:	High	High	Low	Low	High	High	Low	Low
and								
position power is:	Strong	Weak	Strong	Weak	Strong	Weak	Strong	Weak

Effective group performance requires a leader motivated by:

Task Accomplishment (Low LPC)   Good Interpersonal Relations (High LPC)   Task Accomplishment (Low LPC)

High ◄──────── **Situational Control and Influence** ────────► **Low**

Adapted from Fred E. Fiedler and Martin M. Chemers, *Leadership and Effective Management* (Glenview, Ill.: Scott, Foresman), 1974, p. 80.

Three aspects of the situation determine whether high or low LPC is preferred in a leader. *Leader-member relations,* the most important consideration, is concerned with the degree to which subordinates are supportive, loyal, and accepting, and a positive group atmosphere exists. *Task structure* refers to the extent to which rules, regulations, job descriptions, and policies define the goals, methods, and standards of performance, so that it is easy to establish performance levels. In contrast with leader-member relations, task structure tends to extend out into an organization beyond the work group. So too does *position power,* which involves such things as the amount of legitimate authority available, the degree to which rewards and punishments can be brought to bear, and thus the extent to which hierarchy can be mobilized behind one's leadership (or, perhaps more correctly, supervision). These three situational factors combine to determine the favorableness (or, as stated more recently, the situational control and influence) available to the leader, extending from maximal on the left side of Exhibit 6.9 to minimal on the right. However, Fiedler has noted other contingency variables, such as stress levels and cultural factors, that should enter into these calculations as well. In any event when the contingencies are positive, supervisors face relatively little uncertainty; when they are negative, they face a great deal.

Overall Evaluation Do LPC scores combine with the various situational contingencies to produce effective subordinate group performance in the manner indicated? Problems of changing measures, changing theories, and changing interpretations make this a very difficult question to answer, in spite of a sizable amount of research. The theory seems to be correct at the extremes: good leader-member relations, high task structure, and strong position power, as well as the lack of all three require a low LPC score and thus presumably something approximating a desire for task accomplishment. Also, the theory appears to work in the middle zone: good leader-member relations, low task structure, and weak position power or, conversely, poor leader-member relations combined with positive values on the other two factors both require a high LPC and thus perhaps a strong desire for good interpersonal relations. The other four hypotheses simply do not hold up under research investigation. In any event what is apparent—and in this, contingency views have made a major contribution—is that various aspects of the influencing context combined with personality characteristics of the leader can be important considerations in subordinate performance effectiveness. Exactly how this whole process works awaits further theoretical developments.

Consideration and Initiating Structure

One of the early views on leadership concerned the concepts of consideration and initiating structure, as described in Exhibit 6.10. These concepts are not unlike what Fiedler has in mind when he associates good interpersonal relations and task accomplishment with high and low LPC scores, respectively. The major differences are that consideration and initiating structure are two separate dimensions of behavior, rather than opposite ends of a single motivational factor. A number of research studies have used several measures of both dimensions that were developed utilizing information from supervisors themselves and from their subordinates.

Despite certain problems with the way they have been measured, consideration and initiating structure are important ways of thinking about leader behavior.

EXHIBIT 6.10   The roles of leader consideration and initiating structure

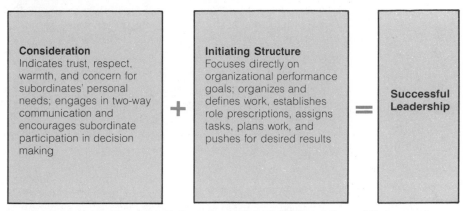

Based on Ralph M. Stogdill and Alvin E. Coons, *Leader Behavior: Its Description and Measurement* (Columbus: Bureau of Business Research, Ohio State University, 1957), pp. 153–62.

However, the original theory as outlined in Exhibit 6.10 turns out to be a major oversimplification. We noted in chapter 4 that how subordinates behave can influence leader behavior as much as leader behavior influences subordinate performance; this has been a problem for the theory. Also, one or the other factor may be important in different situations, but rarely are both equally important.

There are certain circumstances in which consideration behavior does produce positive results and others in which it does not; the same is true for initiating structure. Thus, in one study it was found that professors who were perceived to exhibit initiating structure behavior in the classroom were subsequently given low ratings by freshman and sophomore students, but initiating structure made no difference in the teaching evaluations of upper division and graduate students.[17]

Although they have limitations, the consideration and initiating structure concepts have provided a basis for several theories that have achieved considerable popularity and have been used widely in connection with management development programs. This is true, for instance, of the managerial grid approach to leadership, and also of what was originally called the life cycle theory of leadership, now known as the situational leadership theory.[18] Views such as these have not been the subject of much quantitative research, but they appear to suffer from much the same problems as other applications of their underlying constructs—consideration and initiating structure.

Path-Goal Views of Leadership

One view that builds upon expectancy theories of employee motivation, as considered in chapter 5, attempts to deal with many of the deficiencies that have appeared in the original formulations of consideration and initiating structure. Unlike the contingency views of Fiedler, this path-goal approach assumes that a single individual can adopt different behavior patterns—be primarily considerate or primarily structuring, for instance—depending on what is needed at a point in time.

Leader Behavior   Leader behaviors are the inputs to the overall leadership process considered in path-goal theory. Initially these were stated in terms of the consideration and initiating structure categories, but more recent statements of the theory have extended the varieties of behaviors beyond this base.[19] Furthermore, evidence is beginning to accrue that these new behaviors are important.[20] The stated outputs or consequences of behaviors are that (1) the leader is accepted by subordinates, (2) subordinates experience job satisfaction, and (3) subordinates are motivated to perform. The role of the leader is to recognize and arouse subordinate desires for outcomes that the leader is in a position to provide, to get subordinates moving down appropriate paths toward performance goals, and to provide the desired outcomes contingent on effective performance.

How these things may be achieved is best described in the basic propositions of the theory:

1. Leader behavior is *acceptable* and *satisfying* to subordinates to the extent that the subordinates see such behavior as either an immediate source of satisfaction or as instrumental to future satisfaction.
2. Leader behavior will be *motivational* to the extent that a) such behavior makes satisfaction of subordinates' needs contingent on effective performance and b) such behavior complements the environment of subordinates by providing the coaching, guidance, support and rewards necessary for effective performance.
3. The *motivational* functions of the leader consist of increasing the number and kinds of personal payoffs to subordinates for work goal attainment and making paths to these payoffs easier to travel by clarifying the paths, reducing road blocks and pitfalls, and increasing the opportunities for personal satisfaction en route.[21]

What kind of behavior the leader should use depends on a number of considerations. Path-goal theory has more contingency factors than the primary three of Fiedler's theory, but details of operation have not been fully worked out in all cases. Such factors include aspects of the task, such as the task structure dimension in contingency theory; aspects of the subordinates themselves, such as their abilities; and the nature of the group in which a subordinate works. Exhibit 6.11 provides an example of how the theory operates, using task structure as a contingency source. Consideration is prescribed for more structured (routine) tasks because more structuring behavior, of the kind really needed for unstructured (nonroutine) tasks, would be viewed as overkill and excessively close supervision by subordinates, and therefore would lessen their motivation. Initiating structure is appropriate when subordinates are of low ability, when they are rather authoritarian in personality, when they do not view events as under their own control, as well as when the task is less structured.

Overall Evaluation A major problem with path-goal theory as a source of managerial working hypotheses is that specific guidelines for management action have not been developed. No training programs are available in the use of the approach, as there are for the contingency theory of leadership for instance, and the complexity of the path-goal views makes them hard to use without training.

Research on the theory itself is promising but incomplete. There are no comprehensive tests of its propositions, only piecemeal considerations. Its grounding in expectancy views of motivation is a decided plus, in contrast with the grounding of theory X and theory Y in Maslow's need hierarchy concepts.

EXHIBIT 6.11 An example of how the path-goal approach works

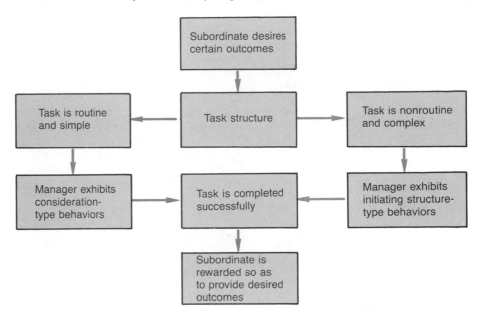

But expectancy theories are not easy to apply in practical situations, either. All the positive and negative considerations noted for expectancy views in chapter 5 apply equally well to the path-goal approach.

Path-goal theory does not appear to be ready for application yet. However, the emphasis on guiding and coaching subordinates, the expanded view of contingency processes, and the advocacy of managerial flexibility in dealing with different individuals all represent important advances. It has been shown that a marriage of expectancy concepts and influencing can produce useful results. Now the need is to make this marriage a truly successful one.

Decision Tree Concepts of Participation

In contrast to the preceding approaches to influencing, a number of theories focus on relatively narrow issues that are nevertheless of considerable importance. An area that has received sizable attention in this regard is the sharing of decisions with subordinates by managers; several formulations of this kind have been developed.

Early Views Exhibit 6.12 sets forth one of the first views regarding a participative approach to decision making. Seven different types of behavior are considered, involving subordinates to increasing degrees in the decision process. Such an approach does not say that participation is desirable under all circumstances, as does system 4 for instance; it all depends on aspects of the situation, as noted in Exhibit 6.12.

Although they represented a major advance in the understanding of the practical realities that managers face, these early views did not provide specific guidelines for the use of participation in decision making. When should the various types of managerial, subordinate, and situational contingencies be considered, and in what order? Obviously a more precise approach was needed.

EXHIBIT 6.12 How to choose a leadership pattern

Boss-centered leadership

The manager makes and announces the decision.

The manager sells a decision to subordinates.

The manager presents ideas and invites questions.

The manager presents a tentative decision subject to change.

The manager presents a problem, invites suggestions, and decides.

The manager defines the limits of a decision the group makes.

Subordinate-centered leadership

The manager permits subordinates to function within limits imposed by the manager's superior.

Which behavior is selected depends on:

1. Managerial factors: the manager's value system, confidence and trust in subordinates, inclinations toward directive or team leadership, security in delegating.
2. Subordinate factors: the subordinates' independence, readiness to assume responsibility, tolerance for ambiguity, interest in the problem, understanding of and identification with organizational goals, knowledge and experience, expectations regarding decision sharing.
3. Situational factors: the type of organization including values toward participation and size, smoothness of work group functioning, problem nature, time pressures for a solution.

Based on Robert Tannenbaum and Warren H. Schmidt, "How to Choose a Leadership Pattern," *Harvard Business Review* (March–April 1958).

Vroom's Theory   The needed precision was introduced by Victor Vroom and others working with him in the form of specific decision trees (see Exhibit 6.13). The decision tree presented is intended for use in situations where it might be appropriate to share a decision with a group of subordinates. The actions noted in Exhibit 6.13 are those recommended where the decision must be made as quickly as possible. Other alternatives can be used with some of the end points if time is not a consideration and a manager desires to engage in participative decision making in order to develop subordinates. Thus, for endpoint 1 in the decision tree, all five alternatives (*a* through *e*) are feasible, but as one goes down the list the time needed to reach a decision increases, with *e* being the most time consuming.

The decision tree approach also has been applied to instances where a manager might be in a position to share decisions with a single subordinate. The available alternatives for action are of course somewhat different from those noted in Exhibit 6.13, including total delegation of responsibility for the decision to the subordinate, but the overall approach is much the same. (Step 7, involving conflict among subordinates, would not be applicable.)

Is this an approach that a manager might want to use in making decisions about how to decide? On the surface the procedures involved appear overly complex and cumbersome. Yet the decision tree approach simplifies the overall process by asking questions in a step-by-step manner, and training programs in the use of the technique are available. It may well be that characteristics of the subordinates themselves relating to their desire and ability to function in group-based

EXHIBIT 6.13   Decision tree for participation

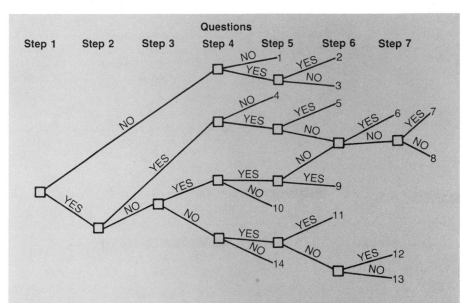

Managers should ask themselves these questions:

At step 1   Is there a quality requirement such that one solution is likely to be more rational than another?

At step 2   Do I have sufficient information to make a high-quality decision?

At step 3   Is the problem structured?

At step 4   Is acceptance of the decision by subordinates critical to effective implementation?

At step 5   If I were to make the decision by myself, is it reasonably certain that it would be accepted by my subordinates?

At step 6   Do my subordinates share the organizational goals to be attained in solving the problem?

At step 7   Is conflict among subordinates likely in preferred solutions?

If through this process the endpoint reached is:

(a) 1, 2, 4, or 5, to minimize time managers should solve the problem or make the decision themselves, using information available at the time.

(b) 9 or 10, to minimize time managers should obtain the necessary information from subordinates, then decide the solution to the problem themselves.

(c) 8, to minimize time managers should share the problem with the relevant individual subordinates, getting their ideas and suggestions without bringing them together as a group, and then make the decision themselves.

(d) 7, 11, 13, or 14, to minimize time managers should share the problem with subordinates as a group, obtaining their collective ideas and suggestions, and then make the decision themselves.

(e) 3, 6, or 12, to minimize time managers should share the problem with subordinates as a group, serve in a role much like a chairperson in attempting to reach a consensus on a solution, and be willing to accept any solution that has the support of the group.

Based on Victor H. Vroom and Philip W. Yetton, *Leadership and Decision-making* (Pittsburgh: University of Pittsburgh Press, 1973).

systems should be considered, but the manager can take such factors into account. The basic question, then, is whether the theory is essentially correct.

The answer is a qualified yes. The research indicates that managers do tend to make decisions along the lines indicated by the theory, although to follow the theory explicitly they would have to spread their actions over a greater range, depending on the situation; thus, they would both make decisions themselves and let the group decide more frequently than they do at present. There is also some indication that the decisions emerging out of the use of these procedures are better decisions.[22] In any event, in deciding whether or not to share decisions, a manager should at least take into account the considerations noted in steps 1 through 6 in Exhibit 6.13. Beyond this it would probably be best to await further elaborations of the theory.

Vertical Dyad Linkages

A vertical dyad consists of a superior and a single subordinate. The linkages between the superior and different subordinates may vary in type or quality, a fact that has been the focus of a very intriguing series of studies by George Graen and coworkers.[23] First, there are linkages with some subordinates that are of an in-group nature, of high quality, and that involve leadership on the part of the superior. Here there is considerable participative decision making and job enrichment as well. The leader provides help and guidance, the relationship is characterized by support and trust, and formal authority is replaced by interpersonal exchange and negotiation. To a great extent the leader's position is like that of the leader in an informal group or any other group-based system. Under such circumstances the leader becomes less powerful but gains considerable subordinate loyalty; the subordinate gains power vis-à-vis the leader, but can no longer rely on the impersonal safeguards of the bureaucratic systems. A perhaps somewhat unusual, but nevertheless instructive, example of this type of relationship involved William Agee, chairman at Bendix Corporation, and Mary Cunningham, his vice-president for strategic planning. Ms. Cunningham subsequently married Mr. Agee.

A second type of linkage, probably more frequent, is of an out-group, low-quality nature and is best characterized as involving supervision rather than leadership. The supervisor does not extend much negotiating latitude to the subordinate and gives less individualized assistance. The whole relationship is more formal, with subordinates accepting legitimate authority in exchange for pay and benefits. An essentially bureaucratic system governs the linkage.

The theory predicts that where the vertical dyad linkage is of the in-group type the subordinate's job performance ratings will be better, job satisfaction will be higher, and there will be fewer problems with supervision; there is also less likelihood of turnover. These predictions tend to be accurate, although there is a need for more applications of this approach in corporate settings. It should be noted, however, that each superior is assumed to have both types of linkages with members of the subordinate group as a whole, and the contrasts involved may well enhance the quality of in-group linkages. Also it seems likely that certain kinds of people are more prone to engage in an in-group relationship with a superior, just as certain people are more suited to group-based systems generally. There is no implication from the theory that leadership can be extended to everyone and supervision abolished.

Summary

The theories and ideas considered in this chapter return repeatedly to the issue of group-based systems, in which leadership is important, versus bureaucratic systems, in which supervision is important—thus reinforcing the need for a concept such as influencing, which embraces both. System 4, sociotechnical systems, informal groups, theory Y, consideration and similar concepts lean heavily in the direction of group leadership. Other contingency views contain both leadership and supervision within their boundaries, often portraying a single manager as playing both roles depending on the individuals involved and the circumstances of interaction.

An outline of the various ideas we have been considering is provided in Exhibit 6.14. To use these ideas effectively, managers must first determine whether they are to behave in the leadership mode or a supervisory one. These ideas are not all the alternatives available; for instance, professional systems contain important differentiations based on professional status and expertise which involve neither leadership nor supervision. However, theory and research have focused on group-based and bureaucratic systems, and accordingly these are the areas where management knowledge has the most to contribute.

One might ask whether leadership or supervision yields superior performance, given that each operates in an optimal environment for its purposes. As we have seen in this chapter there are many who would endorse leadership in this regard. Historically, if one goes back to origins (as in chapter 3), the vote behind supervision becomes stronger. Unfortunately, the experiment that would answer this question once and for all has not yet been conducted. It is entirely possible that when research of this kind is carried out, it will indicate that both are equally effective—that the most important thing is to obtain a fit with the characteristics of the system, the situation, and the people involved, thus carrying out the influencing function in a manner appropriate to the existing circumstances.

What Have You Learned?

1. In what ways do reference and membership groups differ from each other? When might the two overlap?

2. How do the concepts of leadership and supervision differ in vertical dyad linkage theory, and what are the consequences for the power of the superior?

3. Leadership and multiskilling are important concepts in sociotechnical theory. How is each involved in autonomous work groups?

4. One problem with theory X and theory Y and derivatives of this approach is that they are stereotypes. How does the concept of individual differences challenge such theories?

5. How does group cohesiveness relate to performance in its various aspects?

6. What are the major characteristics of the decision tree approach to participation, and how do the recent ideas of Vroom represent an advance over early statements?

7. Why is it preferable to consider the degree of groupness rather than group and nongroup? What factors determine the degree of groupness?

8. What are the various contingency factors in Fiedler's theory, and how do they relate to LPC?

9. What are the pros and cons of informal group formation in an organization? What can management do to foster or hinder this process?

10. How do groups operate in Likert's system 4, and what is the role of the linking pin's function in the theory?

EXHIBIT 6.14 Contributions of ideas on groups and leadership

Source	Major Contributions
System 4 theory	Explanation of what a group-based system might look like and fostering active study of the participative management alternative to Weber's bureaucracy
Sociotechnical theory	Further elaboration of the nature of group-based systems that can, under appropriate circumstances, contribute very effective performance to an organization
Informal groups and natural systems	An understanding of how group-based systems may permeate bureaucratic organizations even though not intended, may come to exercise power, and may influence organizational goal achievement
Group cohesiveness	An understanding of what makes groups pull together and of their effects on stress reduction, decreased turnover, reduced absenteeism, but also certain negative performance outcomes, such as those associated with ostracism
Theory X and theory Y	Insight into the ways managers often think about subordinates, even though they should not
Contigency theory of leadership	Demonstration that aspects of the supervisory context and of the supervisor's personality influence subordinate performance
Path-goal theory	An expanded understanding of the role of contingency factors in leadership, extension of expectancy theory of motivation to include leadership, and insight into the importance of supervisory guidance and coaching
Decision tree theory	Specification of important factors in deciding whether to share decisions with subordinates, and provision of a method of combining these factors to make a choice
Vertical dyad linkage theory	Explanation of the differences between in-group and out-group superior–subordinate relationships and consequences of each

How Well Can You Apply Your Knowledge?

Problem 1. A production foreman assumed his current position after many years working in the group he now supervises. The promotion was decided upon because of his seniority, experience as a vacation replacement for the previous foremen who had retired, and widespread popularity in the plant as well as within his own work group. It was an easy choice to make. Although there was some fall-off in production after the new foreman took charge, despite a certain amount of increased overstaffing according to company manning tables, both effects could be attributed to the fact that the equipment used was old and continually in need of repair. On the plus side was a decrease in grievances and disciplinary actions to an all-time low level.

Late one afternoon a maintenance foreman reports a rather strange situation to his superior. A crew was working on the old equipment again and finished up about mid-afternoon. The operators of this particular equipment were not around at the time the maintenance work was finished, but a check of their time cards indicated they were in the plant. The production foreman says he will handle the situation. For various reasons the maintenance foreman has to go back into the area several times during the remainder of the afternoon. He never is able to locate the missing operators, but does note that they were punched out as of five o'clock.

When the plant manager hears about this situation he verifies the time card information and then starts a thorough investigation. How could the missing operators have punched out their time cards when no one had seen them in the plant that afternoon? The answer that finally comes out is that *they* had not punched out; their foreman did it for them. Actually the operators had left the plant and headed for the nearest bar when their equipment broke down. By the time they should have returned they were in no state to do so. The production foreman decided to cover up for his crew. Apparently this is not the first time he has faced this kind of situation, and he was well aware of what had happened.

Faced with this information, the production foreman's defense is that he had only intended to protect his crew so they would not get in trouble. To do otherwise might make them unhappy, and his other subordinates too. A foreman has to get along with his people and be one of the gang. Without this, he is bound to fail; he needs to be able to count on them. He helps them and they help him; this is the way the system works. What he had done was intended to prevent trouble and maintain morale at a high level. He has not only tried to keep these particular operators from getting into difficulties but has held his work group together, has headed off a potential problem with the union, and in general has done the company a real service. If anything he should be praised for what he has done, not criticized. The plant manager gradually becomes convinced that his production foreman really believes what he is saying. It is not as easy a situation to deal with as it had seemed at first.

Questions
1. What is going on here? How can the ideas and concepts considered in this chapter help to explain the situation?
2. If you were the plant manager what would you do? Would you reward the production foreman for his actions or would you punish him? The maintenance people seem to think he should be fired. Would you as plant manager support such a decision?

Problem 2. The manager in charge of an accounts receivable section for a large company has one of the most experienced units in the whole accounting department. The work is reasonably straightforward, the people know their jobs, and there is very little variation from day to day in what has to be done. Even when a new and inexperienced employee does come on board, which is not common, the work is simple enough to learn so that people usually are able to get up to speed in a short period of time.

From the manager's viewpoint there is one major problem. When errors do occur everyone seems to know about it and she becomes the center of a great deal of criticism. Customers become irate because their bills are wrong, the credit and collections people become upset, and often higher level management becomes involved as well. In order to prevent such unpleasant episodes, the manager decides to work more closely with her people and try to train them better. She starts explaining exactly what she wants done and maintains a constant check to see that it is done. When she detects an error she makes it a point to criticize the employee in front of the others to set an example. And she does not hesitate to say what she thinks. She never leaves the work area if she can possibly help it. She makes it very clear to everyone that she is not going to put up with errors and suffer criticism from everyone else in the company just because one of her employees makes a mistake.

The results of this treatment are not exactly as expected. Somehow, despite the manager's best efforts, the error rate in the section (which never was really high), remains pretty much the same. The employees begin to almost ignore their man-

ager. They listen, but then go ahead as before. There is a good deal of complaining about little things that should not matter; people are increasingly unhappy, and this shows in increasing incidences of coming in late for work and being absent. Several good employees who have been with the company for a while obtain lateral transfers to other units. A few quit. The net effect is that the section's output begins to fall off, to the point where the work assigned is not being processed on schedule. This has never happened before.

Questions

1. How do the various ideas regarding leadership and supervision considered in this chapter help to explain the consequences of the manager's new leadership style? Could these consequences have been predicted from any theory?

2. What type of leadership style would be more appropriate in this situation? What personality characteristics of the manager appear to make it difficult for her to adopt a more appropriate style?

Additional Sources for More Detailed Study

Bass, Bernard M. *Stogdill's Handbook of Leadership.* New York: Free Press, 1981.

Heller, Frank A. *Managerial Decision-making: A Study of Leadership Styles and Power-sharing Among Senior Managers.* London: Tavistock, 1971.

————, and Wilpert, Bernhard. *Competence and Power in Managerial Decision-Making: A Study of Senior Levels of Organization in Eight Countries.* New York: Wiley, 1981.

Hinton, Bernard L., and Reitz, Joseph. *Groups and Organizations: Integrated Readings in the Analysis of Social Behavior.* Belmont, Calif.: Wadsworth, 1971.

Homans, George C. *The Human Group.* New York: Harcourt, Brace, Jovanovich, 1950.

Hunt, James G.; Sekaran, Uma; and Schriesheim, Chester A. *Leadership: Beyond Establishment Views.* Carbondale, Ill.: Southern Illinois University Press, 1982.

Hyman, Herbert H., and Singer, Eleanor. *Readings in Reference Group Theory and Research.* New York: Free Press, 1968.

Jacobs, T. O. *Leadership and Exchange in Formal Organizations.* Alexandria, Va.: Human Resources Research Organization, 1971.

Kiesler, Sara. *Interpersonal Processes in Groups and Organizations.* Arlington Heights, Ill.: AHM, 1978.

McGregor, Douglas. *The Human Side of Enterprise.* New York: McGraw-Hill, 1960.

Miner, John B. *Theories of Organizational Behavior.* Hinsdale, Ill.: Dryden, 1980.

Pasmore, William A., and Sherwood, John J. *Sociotechnical Systems: A Sourcebook.* La Jolla, Calif.: University Associates, 1978.

Steiner, Ivan D. *Group Process and Productivity.* New York: Academic Press, 1972.

Whyte, William F. *Money and Motivation: An Analysis of Incentives in Industry.* New York: Harper & Row, 1955.

Yukl, Gary A. *Leadership in Organizations.* Englewood Cliffs, N.J.: Prentice-Hall, 1981.

Zander, Alvin. *Making Groups Effective.* San Francisco: Jossey-Bass, 1982.

Notes

1. William G. Dyer, *Team Building: Issues and Alternatives,* © 1977, Addison-Wesley, Reading, Massachusetts. Pp. 3–4. Reprinted with permission.

2. Max Weber, *Economy and Society,* trans. Guenther Roth and Claus Wittich (New York: Bedminster, 1968), p. 952.

3. Dorwin Cartwright and Alvin Zander, *Group Dynamics: Research and Theory* (New York: Harper & Row, 1968), pp. 46, 48.

4. Edgar H. Schein, *Organizational Psychology* (Englewood Cliffs, N.J.: Prentice-Hall, 1980), p. 145.

5. Clayton P. Alderfer, "Group and Intergroup Relations," in *Improving Life at Work: Behavioral Science Approaches to Organizational Change,* ed. J. Richard Hackman and J. Lloyd Suttle (Santa Monica; Goodyear, 1977), p. 230.

6. Harold J. Leavitt, "Suppose We Took Groups Seriously . . . ," in *Man and Work in Society,* ed. Eugene L. Cass and Frederick G. Zimmer (New York: Van Nostrand Reinhold, 1975), pp. 69–70.

7. Rensis Likert and Jane G. Likert, *New Ways of Managing Conflict* (New York: McGraw-Hill, 1976).

8. John B. Miner, *Theories of Organizational Structure and Process* (Hinsdale, Ill.: Dryden, 1982).

9. Eric L. Trist and K. W. Bamforth, "Some Social and Psychological Consequences of the Longwall Method of Coal-Getting," *Human Relations* (January 1951).

10. Eric L. Trist *et al., Organizational Choice: Capabilities of Groups at the Coal Face Under Changing Technologies* (London: Tavistock, 1963); Fred E. Emery and Einar Thorsrud, *Democracy at Work* (Leiden, the Netherlands: Martinus Nijhoff, 1976).

11. Richard E. Walton, "Innovative Restructuring of Work," in *The Worker and the Job: Coping with Change,* ed. Jerome M. Rosow (Englewood Cliffs, N.J.: Prentice-Hall, 1974), pp 145–76.

12. Victor A. Thompson, *Bureaucracy and the Modern World* (Morristown, N.J.: General Learning Press, 1976).

13. Leon Mann, "Cross-Cultural Studies of Small Groups," in *Handbook of Cross-Cultural Psychology,* vol. 5, ed. Harry C. Triandis and Richard W. Brislin (Boston, Mass.: Allyn & Bacon, 1980), pp. 155–209.

14. See John B. Miner, "The Uncertain Future of the Leadership Concept: Extensions and Clarifications," *Journal of Applied Behavioral Science* (October 1982).

15. Fred E. Fiedler, *A Theory of Leadership Effectiveness* (New York: McGraw-Hill, 1967), p. 41.

16. Fred E. Fiedler and Linda Mahar, "The Effectiveness of Contingency Model Training: A Review of the Validation of Leader Match," *Personnel Psychology* (Spring 1979): 45.

17. Bat-sheva Lahat-Mandelbaum and David Kipnis, "Leader Behavior Dimensions Related to Students' Evaluations of Teaching Effectiveness," *Journal of Applied Psychology* (October 1973).

18. Robert R. Blake and Jane S. Mouton, *The New Managerial Grid* (Houston: Gulf, 1978); Paul Hersey and Kenneth H. Blanchard, *Management of Organizational Behavior* (Englewood Cliffs, N.J.: Prentice-Hall, 1982).

19. Alan C. Filley, Robert J. House, and Steven Kerr, *Managerial Process and Organizational Behavior* (Glenview, Ill.: Scott, Foresman, 1976); Martin G. Evans, "Leadership," in *Organizational Behavior,* ed. Steven Kerr (Columbus: Grid, 1979), pp. 207–39.

20. Janet Fulk and Eric R. Wendler, "Dimensionality of Leader-Subordinate Interactions: A Path-Goal Investigation," *Organizational Behavior and Human Performance* (October 1982).

21. Robert J. House and Terence R. Mitchell, "Path-Goal Theory of Leadership," *Journal of Contemporary Business* (Fall 1974): 84–85.

22. R. H. George Field, "A Test of the Vroom-Yetton Normative Model of Leadership," *Journal of Applied Psychology* (October 1982).

23. Fred Dansereau, George Grean, and William J. Haga, "A Vertical Dyad Linkage Approach to Leadership Within Formal Organizations: A Longitudinal Investigation of the Role Making Process," *Organizational Behavior and Human Performance* (February 1975); George Graen and James F. Cashman, "A Role-Making Model of Leadership in Formal Organizations: A Developmental Approach," in *Leadership Frontiers,* ed. James G. Hunt and Lars L. Larson (Kent, Ohio: Kent State University Press, 1975); George Graen and William Schiemann, "Leader–Member Agreement: A Vertical Dyad Linkage Approach," *Journal of Applied Psychology* (April 1978).

READINGS AND PROFILES

Small Group Activity at Musashi Semiconductor Works
William H. Davidson
Sloan Management Review

How to Build Employee Trust and Productivity
Thomas H. Melohn
Harvard Business Review

Lee L. Morgan and Caterpillar Tractor Company

The selections focus on problems and methods of dealing with productivity, primarily at the shop floor level. How can employees be influenced to be more productive? This has become the number one problem in the United States with the inroads of foreign competition. The Japanese in particular have been very successful in obtaining substantial increases in productive output while maintaining compensation levels well below those in the United States.

Davidson provides a particularly insightful analysis of the group-based systems developed in Japan to obtain the productive advantages of small unit size. This discussion supplements those on system 4 and the sociotechnical approach in the text. The distinctive aspects of the Japanese management system are elaborated further in various chapters of this book, particularly chapter 18.

The short article by Melohn describes one small but very successful company's experiences in attempting to influence employee productivity. In part it serves to emphasize the advantages small firms have in this area, just because of their size. But it is also true that the company has done a very effective job (although probably unwittingly) of drawing upon the various views regarding employee motivation and influencing discussed in the preceding chapters.

The executive profile of Lee Morgan at Caterpillar provides a striking example of the productivity/cost binds that have hit American industry as a result of foreign competition—in American markets, but around the world as well. Unlike many other American companies, Caterpillar still holds a very strong position in world markets. It is rated at the top of the industrial/farm equipment industry group in the *Fortune* survey and second only to Boeing Aircraft in overall quality of goods and services among the 200 firms. Yet even Caterpillar is concerned; in the early 1980s it showed its first losses since the Depression year of 1932.

Small Group Activity at Musashi Semiconductor Works

William H. Davidson

Musashi Semiconductor Works is Hitachi Corporation's oldest and largest semiconductor factory. Located less than one mile from Hitachi's central research laboratory in the suburbs of Tokyo, the present facility grew out of a small transistor research center and pilot plant created in 1958. Today Musashi employs 2,700 workers and manufactures semiconductor memory and logic devices, microcomputers, and computer boards.

Musashi is an independent profit center within Hitachi's semiconductor division. This division, one of twenty within the parent company, accounted for 9.8 percent of Hitachi's total 1980 sales of $13.4 billion. In addition to the Musashi Works, the division operates three other factories in Japan as well as factories in Malaysia, Hong Kong, West Germany, and the United States. The semiconductor division is the fourth largest vendor in its worldwide industry.

Musashi's semiconductor manufacturing technology generally follows standard industry proce-

dures. Semiconductor fabrication is a multistage process with many distinct process steps and work areas. Some of the principal production stages for semiconductors are circuit design, photomask preparation, wafer creation, polishing, diffusion, photolithography, and numerous assembly and testing tasks.[1] Clinical sterility is required to avoid contamination of materials during the process. Despite a rapid trend toward automation of the pro-

William H. Davidson is Associate Professor of Business at The Colgate Darden School, University of Virginia. Dr. Davidson holds the A.B. degree from Harvard College and the M.B.A. and D.B.A. degrees from the Harvard Business School. His current research interest is the Japanese information technology sector, which is being developed in a book entitled *Studies in Strategy: Japan and the U.S. in the Information Age.* Dr. Davidson is the author of *Global Strategic Management* and *Experience Effects in International Investment and Technology Transfer.*

Reprinted from "Small Group Activity at Musashi Semiconductor Works," by William H. Davidson, *Sloan Management Review,* Volume 23, Spring 1982, pp. 3–14, by permission of the publisher. Copyright © 1982 by the Sloan Management Review Association. All rights reserved.

duction process, semiconductor design and fabrication demand a highly trained and skilled work force.

Semiconductor manufacturing, especially for logic chips, closely corresponds to a multistation, job-shop type of production system. Distinct and customized operations are performed on the silicon wafer at a number of discrete work stations. Despite the level of computer-aided manufacturing (CAM) systems used in the production process, semiconductor manufacturing remains a highly labor-intensive process. Labor costs and productivity, measured in terms of effective yield, are critical determinants of success in this industry. The nature of the manufacturing process lends itself well to the application of small group activity programs.

Small Group Activity

Small group activity programs are widely employed throughout Japanese industry. All of Hitachi's twenty-seven Japanese factories employ formal small group activity programs. These programs must be differentiated from the prevailing U. S. concept of the quality circle. The Japanese concept of small group activity encompasses a much broader range of activities than that normally associated with quality circles. Quality circles, or small groups whose purpose is to improve and control product quality, account for about 29 percent of all small group activity within Hitachi. Another 4 percent of all small groups are principally concerned with worker safety: the remainder focus on what are called management improvement (MI) activities.[2] The focus of MI groups can be broadly described as operations management and refinement. It is important to note that small group activity in Japan encompasses not only production workers but also clerical, support, and certain managerial personnel. Regardless of the area of activity, MI groups play an important role in designing and refining operating, administrative, and organizational systems.

The Origins of Small Group Systems

The origins of Japanese small group systems are widely attributed to Professors W. E. Deming and J. M. Juran.[3] These American experts in statistical quality control were instrumental in stimulating the use of small group systems for quality control purposes in Japan. Following Deming's and Juran's initial visits to Japan in the early 1950s, the use of small group programs was promoted by the Union of Japanese Scientists and Engineers (JUSE), a private organization. Since the initial experimental adoption of such systems by private industry in the 1960s, their use has expanded dramatically. Over eight million Japanese workers are now estimated to be active in small group programs.[4] The range of activities of small group systems has also flourished, extending well beyond quality control purposes.

Although the origin of small group systems can be traced directly to American statistical quality control and Scanlon Plan technology, other factors influencing the development of these systems are distinctly Japanese.[5] Perhaps the most important indigenous base for such systems can be found in the tradition of the *habatsu*. The Japanese word *batsu* means group. The habatsu is an ancient Japanese unit of military organization. An habatsu unit typically consisted of six men who lived and fought together as a "fighting clique." These units have been the basis of military organization and strategy in Japan for centuries. This tradition, in combination with other well-known Japanese cultural qualities, provided a firm foundation for the adoption of small group systems. Examination of small group activities at Musashi Semiconductor Works provides insight into the distinctly Japanese nature of these systems.

Implementation of a Small Group Program

The implementation of a small group program at Musashi began in 1971. Hitachi Corporation had already initiated programs at fourteen other factories, and procedures for designing and implementing small group systems at the plant level had been well established. There are two distinct phases of implementation. The first phase focuses on management orientation and development of the philosophy and values underlying small group programs. The second phase focuses on introducing the program at the worker level.

The initial stage of implementation at Musashi, which occurred between 1971 and 1975, is called the enlightenment period. This period focused almost entirely on the orientation of management: Musashi managers were trained and oriented in the philosophy, principles, structure, and function of small group activities. In general, formal education programs play a key role in management orientation. Distinct programs are held for each level of management. Exhibit 1 provides an example of how the education support program is scheduled in a typical Japanese company. These programs are often conducted at remote sites. In most cases, the instructors are corporate personnel. In some companies, members of the corporate board of directors play key roles as instructors. Although individual courses can last up to six months, most of them generally last less than one month. In the case of Musashi, it took over three years to complete the entire management orientation program.

The small group concept was introduced by management to the rest of the organization in 1975. At the worker level, the small group program was implemented as part of a broader campaign designed to improve dramatically the status and productivity of Musashi Works. This broader program, called the MMM movement, entailed no specific organization or managerial innovations. It was intended to provide continuing themes, rallying points, and broad goals throughout the process of initiating the small group program. The MMM movement refers to three words: muda, mura, muri. These words were used to symbolize a new guiding theme for Musashi Works. They can be translated respectively as waste, inconsistency, and

---

EXHIBIT 1   Education support program for small group systems implementation

Position in Plant Hierarchy	
General managers	**Top Management Course (O)** Motivation seminar Leadership seminar
	Small Group Course (O) Group structures seminar
Department heads	**Management Course (O)**
	Small Group Course (H) Planning methods seminar
Section heads	**Middle Management Course (O)**
	Small Group Seminar (H) Statistical analysis technique seminar
Senior supervisors (Engineers and subsection managers)	**Small Group Course (H)** Group management training seminar Auditing seminar
Foremen	**Lower Management Course (P)**
Workers	**Orientation (P)**

Key:
(O)—Course held outside the company
(H)—Held at parent headquarters
(P)—Held at plant

Time

fear of the impossible. The theme of the MMM movement is to eliminate these three evils from Musashi Works.

Several phases of the MMM movement at Musashi can be identified. In the first phase, between 1975 and 1976, the focus of the MMM movement was on achieving higher quality in manufacturing through reduction of the three evils. In the second phase, between 1976 and 1977, MMMII's theme stated that by reducing the three evils, Musashi could spring forward to become a factor in world industry. The objective of the third phase, between 1977 and 1978, was more specific: the MMM20 campaign was designed to increase efficiency in terms of output per worker by 20 percent in six months. After this specific objective had been met, another general objective was introduced: the MMM80 campaign, between 1978 and 1980, sought to challenge and defeat the top-line brands of the world through reduction of the three evils. In 1981, a new theme with a specific objective was introduced: the MMM200 UP program intends to double chip output in two years.

The MMM movement appears to have been an important instrument in introducing small group activity at the worker level. However, the MMM movement is only the very tip of the iceberg. Underlying this program is a complex and sophisticated organization built around the small group unit.

Small Group Organization and Administration

The 2,700 workers at Musashi are organized into 360 groups. A typical group numbers 8 to 10 people. Group membership is determined largely by work stations, although some self-selection is possible in certain work areas. Group members typically hold the same rank or position in the company, but groups are often of mixed sex and age. Small group systems are highly democratic at the group level, with each group electing a leader from among its members.

Immediately above the small group level, a formal hierarchy is developed to administer group activities. This hierarchy is composed of councils, and it closely parallels the overall formal structure of the Musashi organization. Each of the twenty de-

partments within Musashi has its own department council, which is chaired by the department manager and which includes senior departmental managers as members. Further, each department contains between two and ten sections. Separate councils are formed for each of these sections, with participants drawn from the full range of the departmental hierarchy. This range includes senior departmental managers as well as foremen and workers. Section councils thus serve as the most important forum for information exchange: they facilitate communication between all levels of the organization. Exhibit 2 shows the structure of the small group system.

Hitachi views these section councils as a means of communicating policies and objectives from management to the rest of the organization, particularly to the group level. Section councils set specific objectives and themes for individual groups and review each group's performance on a monthly basis. However it is very important to emphasize that communication between a council and a worker is a bilateral exchange.

Worker groups are assigned objectives and themes by their section council, but they also choose a parallel theme for themselves. These groups have a great deal of latitude, self-direction, and autonomy in Hitachi's program. The sole constraint on group activities is that they be broadly consistent with the objectives of the divisional management and Hitachi Corporation. Within the framework of the MMM movement at Musashi, worker groups are given equal footing with management in that both are equally responsible for submitting management improvement suggestions. The conceptual framework for the overall small group activities movement is presented in Exhibit 3.

The task force projects cited in Exhibits 2 and 3 are an important element in small group programs. Although the primary focus of small group programs is on generating self-selected proposals from worker groups, management also has mechanisms to direct group efforts toward specific projects. Following the establishment of channels for submission of group proposals, department and section councils identify special areas and projects for specific attention. A committee structure is used to

EXHIBIT 2 Structure and staffing of a small group system

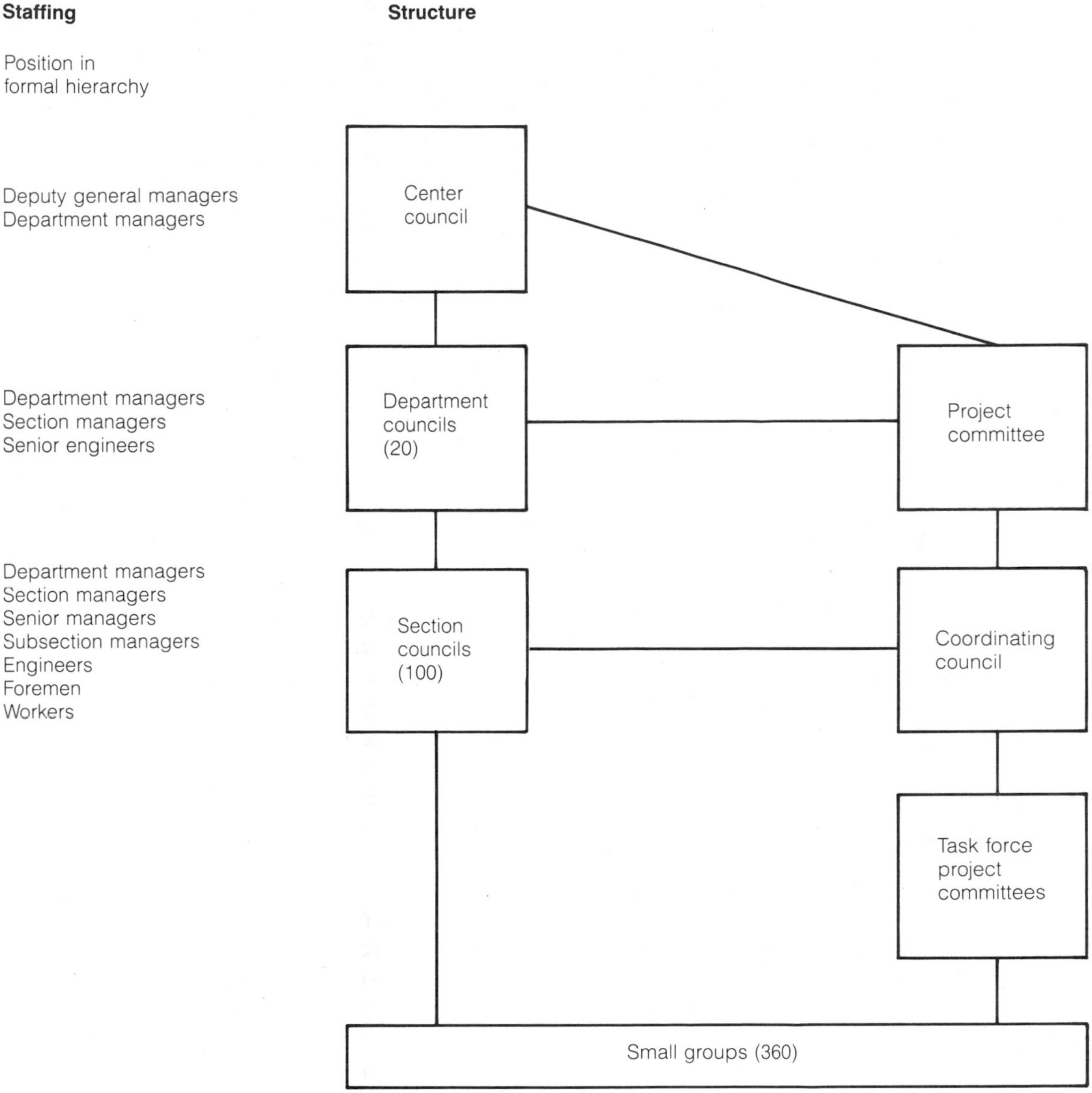

Staffing   **Structure**

Position in
formal hierarchy

Deputy general managers   Center
Department managers   council

Department managers   Department
Section managers   councils   Project
Senior engineers   (20)   committee

Department managers
Section managers
Senior managers   Section
Subsection managers   councils   Coordinating
Engineers   (100)   council
Foremen
Workers

                                                       Task force
                                                       project
                                                       committees

                        Small groups (360)

manage these special project activities. Depending on the priorities established in the center council, an individual group could find itself working primarily with a Project Task Force Committee, which is composed primarily of aggressive junior managers, rather than on self-selected improvements. These specific projects are defined and initiated by management, and implemented through the pro-

ject committee shown in Exhibit 2. Since many task force projects involve multiple worker groups, sections, and departments, a coordinating council is used to promote cooperative efforts in such projects.

In addition to communicating policies and objectives from management to workers, Hitachi describes the section councils as a means of achiev-

EXHIBIT 3 A conceptual framework of small group activities

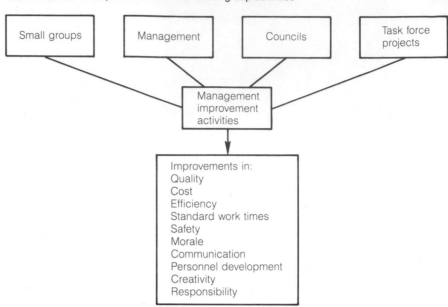

ing "technology transfer" from small groups to the management level. The vehicle for transferring technology, and indeed the focal point of the entire small group program, is called the improvement proposal.

Improvement Proposals

Improvement proposal generation, evaluation, and implementation within a small group activity program are part of an extremely sophisticated process having far-reaching implications. An improvement proposal is first submitted formally by a group to a section council. The proposal includes a statement of the problem, a proposed solution, and, in many cases, a description of actual results achieved under the new method. Proposals need not be approved before they are executed unless they involve major capital expenditures or adjustments at other work stations. If adjustments are required at other stations, section and departmental approval is required, and implementation is overseen by the coordinating council.

The first improvement proposals were filed within Musashi Works in 1977, six years after the program began. Initially, small groups were encouraged to identify areas within their work sta-

tions that could be improved to further the MMM movement. Thus, the first improvement proposals were voluntary. Over time, the scope of self-selected improvement activities was broadened significantly. By 1980, section councils were asking groups to commit themselves to filing a certain number of improvement proposals each month. The targeted number of proposals was negotiated individually with each group, but competition and peer pressure clearly played a role in this process.

Improvement proposals are typically filed on hand-written sheets of paper. A translated example of a proposal appears in Exhibit 4. In this case, the proposal suggests a change in the design of work stations and work flow in the large scale integrated (LSI) chip sealing process. The proposal involves reduction of the number of work steps and the elimination of one employee per station.

Each group also submits a monthly review of its activities in addition to submitting individual proposals. These monthly reviews serve as the principal vehicle for control and feedback from management. Reviews are presented on poster-sized paper and often contain interesting and creative artwork. These documents provide perhaps the best insight into the inner workings of the small group system.

EXHIBIT 4 Translation of an improvement proposal

Sec-tion	Item	Improvements of Heat Sealing Process for LSI Semiconductors					Name of Group Leader	K. Sukiya	Unit	Department AB: Prototype Development	Group Name	H&S	Tel.	683
No.	Date	The 10th Month of the 55th Year of Emperor Hirohito's Reign (1980)	Cost Savings	¥140,000 Per Month	Capital Invested	¥3 (Mill.)	Area Involved in Application	Prototype Design		Engineering Application			MD Activities	

Before Improvement

In the sealing process for final LSI preparation, the following problems occur:
1. The efficiency of the sealing oven is low because of the need to space units entering it (see flow chart).
2. Two people are required for inserting and removing units from the oven. Each has to wait in between units because of spacing requirements.

Sealing Process Flow Chart

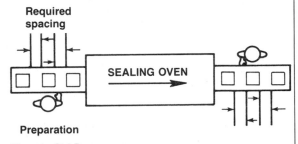

Steps in Old Process:
1. Preparation: manually place units in staging area.
2. Manually place units on oven conveyor belt.
3. Wait for proper spacing of next unit.
4. Place next unit on conveyor belt.
5. Sealing takes place within the oven.
6. Manually remove unit from oven.
7. Place unit in box for transport to final packing area.
8. Wait.
9. Remove next unit.

After Improvement

By analyzing the thermal requirements and characteristics of the sealing process, it was possible to develop a temperature and time cycle that eliminates the need for spacing. This results in an increased speed of production, and it permits automation of the insertion and removal of units from the oven (see flow chart).

Sealing Process Flow Chart

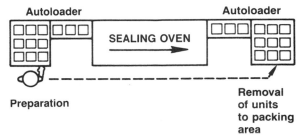

Steps in New Process.
1. Preparation: manually place units in staging area.
2. Insertion into oven done by autoloader.
3. Sealing takes place.
4. Removal done by autoloader.
5. Place units in box for transport to packing area.

The Bandits. Exhibit 5 offers insight into the dynamics of the small group system. As the figure shows, this group of three men and three women work in the photolithography section of the integrated circuits (IC) production department. Their job is to transfer circuitry from master photomasks to photosensitized silicon wafers. The box in the upper right-hand corner gives the department and section, the group leader's name, and the chosen name of the group—The Bandits.

The long rectangular box at the top gives the group's theme and goal: improvement of photolithography management and an increase in chip yield at this stage from 80 percent to 88 percent. Below the rectangle, the group introduces itself. It says it is a group with strong personalities, but the mem-

EXHIBIT 5   The Bandits

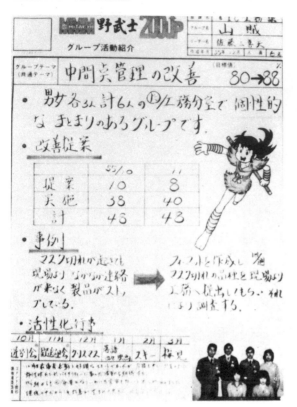

The bottom area of this poster includes the group's plans for joint activities along with supervisor comments. The group held a farewell party in October, a welcome party in November, and a Christmas party in December; they are planning a show or movie in January, a skiing trip in February, and a Plum Blossom picnic in March. At the very bottom are the supervisor's comments: "Your group was announced to be the best group in October. I am expecting this group to continue its energetic activities. For the last half of this year, your group will stay on the Special Project Team (i.e., report to a Project Task Force Committee). I know it is very hard to work on Special Projects, but very important improvements will result. Good luck."

The Ten Philosophers. One further example of a monthly review is useful in understanding how the small group system works. Exhibit 6 presents another group called The Ten Philosophers. The group's statement is presented in the same general

EXHIBIT 6   The Ten Philosophers

bers work well together. The numbers in the box show the group's level of improvement proposal activity in the tenth and eleventh months of the fifty-fifth year of Emperor Hirohito's reign. In October, the group submitted ten suggestions for discussion and implemented thirty-eight improvements. In November, the group submitted eight proposals and implemented forty improvements. Below the box an example of one of their proposals is cited. The example states that mask deterioration is often not noticed until after chip output is affected. Implanted impurities accumulate as photomasks are used, resulting in defects on individual integrated circuits and reducing yields. The group developed a new format in conjunction with the photomask department to test masks weekly for impurities to reduce this problem.

format as The Bandits' in Exhibit 5. The group comes from the wafer processing section of the IC memories manufacturing department. Their theme and objective is reduction of foreign matter (e.g., dust) in ICs. Below the theme box is a circle. The words inside the circle ask: What is a philosopher? The answer is given in four parts. First, he is a person who knows the world and what we should and shouldn't do. Second, he is a person who deserves respect. Third, he is wise. Finally, he is a master of distorted logic. The caption concludes: "Therefore, we must be weirdos, no?"

Parallel to the photograph is an introduction to the group that states: "We are ten philosophers, like our name says. We are young, human, and enthusiastic personnel." Under the striped lines on the left is an example of an actual improvement that was implemented by the group. The pie chart shows that the areas of highest probability of wafer contamination are in the deposition of thin insulating and conducting films through chemical-vapor deposition (CVD) or evaporation processes. Impurities introduced in these processes can become implanted in the silicon, destroying the integrity of circuits and causing reduction in chip yield. Introduction of impurities is not the only problem. The diffusion process, where wafers are exposed to gases such as aluminum, boron, or arsenic dopants to create positive and negative charged areas in the silicon, also represents a major area of contamination. Diffusion can cause the migration of previous layers of dopants, or the migration of contaminants. This problem, called autodoping, is a major cause of chip defects.[6] As Exhibit 6 points out, these contaminants can circulate freely in the gas chamber, and they can recirculate back onto the wafer surface. However, as a result of this group's implementing a new system, gases pass through filter screens to reduce the possibility of contamination.

To the right of the improvement example is a statement along with some artwork created by the group. It states: "Our key phrase is drinking makes everyone friends. Therefore we drink and sing a lot to improve our group. In addition, we have other activities once a month." Below this statement are the supervisor's comments. He states: "By focusing on communication, you are trying to im-prove group unity. In most respects, your performance is double that of other groups. In the future, try to improve your contact with other groups. You should be an example for other groups and teach them."

Mechanisms for Achieving Management Objectives. The improvement proposal submitted by individual groups is the key mechanism for achieving management objectives as outlined in the MMM movement. Based on themes suggested by management, small groups propose improvements that are then translated into specific projects. Thus, management support of the small group program, coupled with what Hitachi calls total employee participation, creativity, and aggressive spirit, leads to specific benefits in morale, quality, and efficiency, including improvements in inventory levels and standard production times.

Improvement proposals are the core of the small group programs, but these programs contain two other pathways for achieving management objectives. The first is called direct employee action. In the case of Musashi, introduction of the broad MMM theme stimulated better morale and directly resulted in cleaner facilities and higher efficiency. This result might be correlated with the widely discussed Hawthorne Effect known to U.S. managers. Second, the project committee mechanism for implementing management-initiated improvements also plays a critical role in achieving specific management objectives (see Exhibit 7).

Results of the Small Group Activity Program

The first formal improvement proposals were filed at Musashi Works in 1977. In 1978, 26,543 specific proposals were filed. Since that time, the number of proposals has increased dramatically. In the first half of 1979, 47,347 proposals were submitted. In the second half of 1980, 112,022 proposals were submitted by the 360 worker groups within the Musashi factory. Of this total, 98,347 improvements were implemented by the end of the year. The average group completed about 45 improvements per month between July and the end of December 1980.

EXHIBIT 7 Mechanisms for achieving management objectives

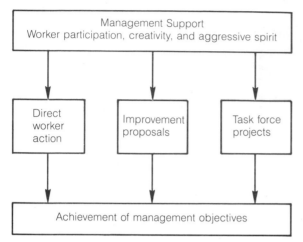

Aishin Seiki workers submitted 56 proposals per worker;

Aishi Warner workers submitted 44 proposals per worker;

Fuji Electric workers submitted 99 proposals per worker;

Pentel workers submitted 43 proposals per worker.

As a whole, Hitachi Corporation received an average of 39 proposals per worker.

Conclusion

As the example of Musashi Works demonstrates, Japanese small group activity systems are painstakingly and patiently nurtured into a highly sophisticated and powerful structure for achieving specific and general management objectives. Worker participation is encouraged through peer pressure, group affiliation benefits, and the intergroup competition inherent in the system. The group structure is used to formalize specific objectives and commitments consistent with overall management strategy at all levels of the organization.

The Musashi example suggests that managerial support and respect for the group system is critical in achieving success with such programs. Management orientation is the first step in the process of implementing a small group system within Hitachi Corporation. Hitachi management permits the group system to exist outside of the formal hierarchy in order to increase its effectiveness. Linkages between the group structure and the formal hierarchy are strong and sophisticated, however, to insure monitoring and control of group activities.

The record of small group activities at Musashi Works indicates the tremendous potential of such programs in improving operating results. These activities systematize and accelerate the realization of learning curve benefits in all aspects of operations. As a force for improved efficiency and quality, small group activity represents one of the most important competitive advantages of the Japanese industrial system. Such activities are particularly important in industries such as the semiconductor industry, where technical change is frequent and process evolution is rapid.

The completed improvements can be broken down into several categories. Of the 98,347 improvements completed, 26 percent resulted in a reduction of standard times at individual work stations. An additional 27 percent resulted in the reduction of inventory. Safety improvements and overhead cost savings each accounted for 6 percent of the completed improvements. Efficiency improvements in office and clerical functions were the focus of 24 percent of the completed proposals, which reflected small group activity away from the factory floor. The remaining proposals were largely devoted to increasing yields at various stages of production.

Although the level and intensity of small group activity appear remarkable by Western standards, Musashi only achieved the average level of activity for Hitachi as a whole in 1980. Activity in this case is measured in terms of the annual number of proposals completed per worker. Although Hitachi is a leading user of small group systems, activity levels at Hitachi should not be viewed as unrepresentative of Japanese industry. In 1979, a number of Japanese companies exhibited higher levels of small group activity. The following is a list of some of these companies and the number of proposals submitted by each worker:

The applicability of small group systems in foreign settings remains to be seen.[7] Although widely used in the United States, American versions of such activities rarely approach the scope of Japanese programs. The power of parallel group-oriented structures has yet to be harnessed by American industry.

References

1. A description of production processes for semiconductors can be found in: W. G. Oldham, "The Fabrication of Microelectronic Circuits," *Scientific American,* September 1977, pp. 110–128; R. L. Boylestad, *Electronic Devices and Circuit Theory* (Englewood Cliffs, N.J.: Prentice-Hall, 1982).

2. For a similar discussion of the nature and composition of small group activities within the Nippon Steel Corporation, see, *Productivity and Quality Control* (Tokyo: JETRO, 1980), pp. 19–22.

3. The origins of statistical quality control predate World War II. For example, see W. A. Shewhart and W. E. Deming, *Statistical Methods from the Viewpoint of Quality Control* (Washington, D.C.: Department of Agriculture, 1939). For a more recent view, see J. M. Juran, *Quality Planning and Analysis,* 2d ed. (New York: McGraw-Hill, 1980).

4. See "Quality Control: Industrial Democracy in Action," *Dentsu Japan,* Spring-Summer 1982, p. 6.

5. Scanlon Plan programs were widely used in the United States prior to World War II. See F. G. Lesieur, ed., *The Scanlon Plan: A Frontier in Labor-Management Cooperation* (New York: John Wiley & Sons, 1958).

6. This problem is described in R. W. Atherton, "Fundamentals of Silicon Epitaxy," *Semiconductor International,* November 1981, pp. 117–130.

7. Quality circles have been adopted by over 400 U.S. firms. For example, see F. K. Plous, "The Quality Circle Concept: Growing by Leaps and Bounds," *World of Work Report,* April 1981. However, R. E. Cole notes that "most of the experiences of these (U.S.) companies have been quite shallow. Thus it would be premature to make assessments as to their suitability to the American Environment." See R. E. Cole, "QC Warning," *World of Work Report,* July 1981. The ability of Japanese firms to apply successfully small group systems in the U.S. is also subject to debate. Johnson and Ouchi found that Japanese plants in the U.S. were more efficient than similar U.S.-owned plants. They attributed the difference partially to Japanese labor relations systems. See R. Johnson and W. Ouchi, "Made in America under Japanese Management," *Harvard Business Review,* September-October 1974. Later studies show that subsidiaries often fail to implement successfully Japanese systems. See: W. Ouchi, "Success and Failure of Japanese Subsidiaries in the U.S.," *Columbia Journal of World Business,* Spring 1977; "Japan's U.S. Plants Go Union," *Business Week,* 5 October 1981, pp. 70–76.

How to Build Employee Trust and Productivity

Thomas H. Melohn

When the author and his partner acquired North American Tool & Die, Inc. four and a half years ago, it was not unlike many smaller manufacturers—marginally profitable, its work force unenthusiastic. Nor did the future look especially bright, since a number of long-time employees were exploring greener pastures. Today, the situation is much different. The company's sales are triple, and profits six times what they were three years ago. Moreover, turnover among its 70 employees has dropped sharply. A few employees told a visitor recently during a plant tour that they never imagined the company could become such a challenging and exciting place to work. The author argues that the connection between financial results and employee morale is far from casual. Indeed, he fully credits a carefully considered strategy of building trust between employees and owners for North American Tool's impressive earnings record.

Take a moment to ask yourself a few questions and consider some management problems. If you're at the top, try these:

Why is it I'm the only one to initiate new ideas?

Why do our people avoid facing up to the tough situations affecting our business? All I hear or read are platitudes—"That's under constant review," "let's hold that in abeyance just for now," "perhaps we should appoint a task group to study it."

Is our corporation any different from the government's bureaucracy? Middle managers always seem to resist innovation.

Why are our employees cleaned up and ready to leave 15 minutes early, and why is our productivity failing to improve or even declining?

Why is our sales force unwilling to make those extra calls? Is cutting prices the only way it knows how to sell?

What's happened to company loyalty? For a few extra bucks, employees leave, after all we've done for them.

Reprinted by permission of the *Harvard Business Review*. "How to Build Employee Trust and Productivity" by Thomas H. Melohn (January/February 1983). Copyright © 1983 by the President and Fellows of Harvard College; all rights reserved.

Mr. Melohn is president, chief executive officer, and half owner of North American Tool & Die in San Leandro, California. Garner Beckett, Jr., the other owner of NATD, is vice president, finance. Prior to purchasing the company in 1978, Mr. Melohn was a marketing official with a number of large corporations, including C&H Sugar, Swift & Company, and Pet Incorporated.

Now try the same quiz, but from the vantage point of the person looking up from lower down in the company hierarchy:

Why won't they ever listen? After all that extra work, my new idea gets a brush-off or a put-down.

Why won't they level with me? Meeting after meeting, and no real decisions made. Report after report, study on study.

How is it that my job has become so boring, a means to an end rather than an end in itself? I can't wait till I'm out of here tonight so that I can work on my car, build that extra room, read that good book.

What's company loyalty? For 30 years I've kept quiet and done my job, and for what? A watch, a phony ceremonial dinner, and out to the trash heap.

The Most Important Asset

The tragedy here is that both parties do care a great deal. Yet, these misunderstandings exist in company after company across the United States. Many are grasping at any possible solution to their problems—including reindustrialization, quality circles, protective import constraints, and government subsidies.

The article outlines a more old-fashioned philosophy that has worked for our company—the belief that a company's most important asset is its employees.

With the conviction that people make the difference between success and failure, my partner, Garner Beckett, Jr., and I set three objectives when we bought North American Tool & Die, a computer components contract manufacturer in San Leandro, California, in June 1978. First, we planned to steadily expand the company and raise profits. Our second goal was to share whatever wealth was created. Third, we wanted everyone to feel satisfaction and even have fun on the job. The only way to achieve these goals, we decided, was to create an atmosphere of complete trust between us, the owners, and *all* our employees.

To summarize the last three years, our sales have gone from $1.8 million to over $6 million, our pretax earnings have increased well over 600%, our stock appreciated 36% in 1980 and again in 1981, our customer reject rate has declined from 5% to 0.3%, our productivity has doubled, our turnover has dropped from 27% to 6%, and we've all had a good time.

To guide this kind of progress appears deceptively simple. We have no proprietary product, nor do we have any geographic advantage in our distribution pattern to add to our marketing ability. Instead, our primary strength is our employees.

Before I recount the steps Beckett and I took to create an atmosphere of trust, one admonition: you've got to really mean it when you say you want such an atmosphere. You truly have to believe in it. Then you've got to work at improving relations every day in every situation. Otherwise, your employees will sense the hypocrisy and all will be for naught.

Growth & Profits

In the analysis of our marketplace before we bought NATD, several marketing and competitive factors stood out. Total computer sales growth was quite impressive—up about 30% annually. With that growth rate and the inherent complexity of product design, we concluded that there had to be an ever-increasing customer need for quality and prompt delivery. Yet our assessment of potential competition suggested generally lax quality control and attention to delivery. Our competitive points of difference became apparent—quality and service.

Our potential competitors tended to be technically skilled entrepreneurs who were often only semi-skilled as managers. Our business could then employ professional management skills and thereby position itself as a growing company rather than as just a two-person venture. That approach would be helpful as the big computer manufacturers got bigger. Their suppliers would also have to grow disproportionately. A cottage industry of regional suppliers will soon be an anachronism. The vendors who succeed over the long term will be those with the best organizational skills and employee motivation.

Such observations are relatively easy to come by. Making everything happen is tough.

We bought a job shop with a reputation for acceptable but not outstanding quality. The only way our quality would improve would be if our employees improved it—every day, on every job, on every part.

Ours is a highly technical business. We produce hundreds of different kinds of parts with a tolerance of ±19.001 of an inch. That's about one-fourth the thickness of a human hair. Such minute tolerances require much skill and dedication. NATD manufactures each of those different parts by the thousands each year. Thus, the company's well-being depends entirely on employees caring a great deal about their performance.

Of course, truly good people want to do a good job. We spread the gospel of quality and repeatedly recognize their efforts to eliminate all rejects.

Each month, there's a plantwide meeting—on company time—with a threefold purpose. First, we recognize one employee (no supervisors allowed) who has done a super job of producing good quality during that month. A check for $50 is just a token of what we give. Of much greater import is the "Super Person of the Month" plaque. The employee's name is engraved on the plaque, and it is prominently and permanently displayed in the plant. Second, each employee is given a silver dollar for every year of service if his or her employment anniversary occurs during the month of the meeting. Finally, we share with our "family" where we've been, where we are, and where we're going—in percentages when appropriate. In that way, each employee knows firsthand what's going on at his or her company.

Every time we get a compliment from one of our customers, we tell our employees about it in detail at that meeting. Recently NATD won a supplier excellence award from one of our major customers. The morning after the awards banquet, we gave the plaque to our department heads because they had earned it. We conveyed our pride to all our employees at the next monthly Super Person meeting, and we put their plaque up on the wall of the plant. No, it's not in the office to impress other customers. It's in the plant to remind our employees each day—each shift—that they are good.

Sharing the Wealth

We share ownership primarily through our employee stock ownership plan (ESOP). We give each employee shares of NATD stock each year, according to three simple selection criteria. The employee must be at least 24 years old, work a minimum of 1,000 hours a year, and be on the payroll at year end. In our judgment, our people have earned the right to be given company stock without any cash outlay of their own. It's not a warrant, a reduced-price purchase plan, matching dollars, an option, or phantom stock. It's free.

By the way, my partner and I waived our rights to participate in this program. We wanted the number of shares allotted for our employees to be that much larger, that much more meaningful. The shares we grant annually are newly issued—we do not realize any gain by selling our own. NATD's ESOP program has also been instrumental in lowering our rejection rates from customers and improving our productivity and delivery time.

We also try to stress fair and equitable compensation as a motivational tool. We hold compensation reviews twice annually. This is not a rubber stamp operation. Each employee has a one-on-one performance review with his or her boss. Here's where you're doing well, and here's where you need to improve, and here's what the company can do to help.

Finally, we use cash bonuses to reward innovative employees. In recent months, several employees have taken action to help the company and win cash. In one instance, a young employee decided on his own to develop a means of both multiply riveting a very difficult part and automating the entire process. In another, a department foreman who saw that our labor cost for an important job was too high devised a new method of doing ten operations at one time. He challenged his young associate to "top this" and soon found the entire production step completely automated. Our labor costs were reduced 80%.

In a third instance, our chief engineer decided on his own to satisfy NATD's need for a much larger punch press than we had. After getting input from two other departments at NATD, he developed the specs, selected the top two choices of machines, arranged for demonstrations, identified additional required options, and purchased the entire package. My role was merely to sign the purchase order.

Satisfaction & Fun

With our strong belief in the importance of our employees, it's axiomatic that NATD hires only the best. We hire a certain kind of person—a decent person who cares about himself, his family, and his company. The person must be honest, willing to speak up, and curious, be it as a sweeper, machine operator, plant foreman, or office manager. That's why I interview each prospective employee myself. My purpose is to determine if the candidate will fit into the NATD family. Perhaps that concept seems old-fashioned, but to us it's pivotal. This process of lengthy evaluation and interviewing is a lot of work, but the results are well worth it.

Let's face it, the traditional adversary role between management and employees is not productive. In encouraging employee satisfaction at NATD, we follow the tenet that our employees deserve the same treatment we expect from them. They want to know about their future compensation, their potential career paths, how they are contributing, and what they can do to grow. To keep people involved and caring, we work at giving out real compliments—not just the perfunctory "Good job, Smith" but statements of sincere appreciation for each person's special efforts and accomplishments.

Compliments don't cost a company anything. We all need them and even crave them. Recognition—both personal and professional—is a major motivating factor. At least two or three times a week, we go through the plant chatting with each employee and complimenting those who've worked well.

Employees care deeply about their work. If you can tap this well of concern and mesh it with the goals of your corporation, the results will truly stun you.

Besides handing out compliments, we work at trying to promote our employees' best interests. Sounds out of place in today's cynical work environment, doesn't it? All we can say is that it works. At NATD we care about our people, not just as employees, but as human beings, as friends, and we try to help them in any way we can. Let me give you some examples:

One outstanding Korean employee suffered a sudden weight loss but was having difficulty communicating this problem to his doctor. My partner searched the entire San Francisco area and finally found a Korean-speaking physician. The problem is now being resolved.

NATD lends its employees company trucks on weekends for moving purposes—at no charge. Any employee can also borrow one week's pay—at no interest—in an emergency.

We sometimes arrange flex hours, as we did for one employee who was going through some marital problems. Now they are happily resolved.

Another employee didn't get all the maternity benefits to which she was entitled. NATD pestered our insurance carrier for over six months and finally rectified this oversight.

NATD sends flowers to every employee or spouse who is in the hospital, and each employee gets a check from the company as a wedding present.

Each month, the owners buy donuts for the entire plant to celebrate payday—Friday—and the end of the month. We also make four free season tickets to National Football League games available to our employees.

We're even occasionally silly enough to send our employees home early on a beautiful day to enjoy it, but with a full day's pay.

By now, I'm sure you're thoroughly convinced my partner and I are deranged. I can almost hear the talk: "You're running nothing but a country club!" "You're squandering company assets!"

Well, perhaps, but the results outlined earlier seem to belie these observations. A happy employee is a productive employee. Output increases, rejects fall, attitude improves, and turnover drops. Besides, it's more fun to work in a happy shop.

Effective Implementation

My job as CEO is to outline the company's objectives and the strategies to attain those goals. To achieve them, we place heavy emphasis on true delegation of responsibility.

We believe that our managers really want to manage, but we realize that certain conditions must first be met. First, we work with managers to be sure the goals are clear and in fact attainable. Second, we give our employees the tools to reach our goals. Finally, we let our managers alone and allow them flexibility. The last thing any manager needs is a second-guessing or a preemptive superior.

Each foreman is responsible for on-time production with no rejects and at maximum efficiency. How he does it is totally up to him.

We then make sure our managers and employees get credit for their successful accomplishments—from us, from their peers, and in their paychecks.

Incidentally, we attach no blame to failure. If we have given a job "our best shot," there's no problem. If our people are inhibited by the fear of failure, they won't dare to try. If we don't try the unexplored and the untested, then our growth rate and profitability will suffer. And that's no fun.

Once your managers are truly managing, your job as CEO becomes much easier. Decisions stop drifting to the CEO, and you are able to concentrate on the issues that will affect the corporation's growth.

Von Clausewitz, the great Prussian military strategist (1780–1831) devised theories that were honed in battle and later brilliantly set forth in his book *On War*. One of his important concepts that's particularly applicable to business is to divide any problem into progressively smaller and thereby more manageable parts. To me, this reference to military strategy is frighteningly appropriate for American industry today because we're in a battle for long-term economic survival.

Lee L. Morgan and Caterpillar Tractor Company

Lee Morgan has been chairman and chief executive officer at Caterpillar since 1977. The company is headquartered in Peoria, Illinois, and has three basic product lines: earth-moving equipment, materials-handling devices such as lift trucks, and engines. None of these is a high growth area, although of the three the engine business has been expanding most rapidly and should continue to do so. These engines power boats, oil field equipment, trucks, and electrical generators, as well as the firm's own vehicles. Over half the company's business is done outside the United States, with the heaviest concentrations being in Africa, the Middle East, and Europe. Manufacturing is worldwide but in proportion to sales tends to be more heavily concentrated in the United States.

The company's greatest strength is its dealer network. Numbering 239, 135 of them outside the U.S., these dealerships are independently owned and typically very profitable. All products are sold through a single dealer network. Caterpillar has been very successful in developing dealer loyalty through training programs, efficient parts distribution, and above all a strong emphasis on product quality. Constant feedback regarding product performance is maintained from customers and dealers. Although quality circles have been introduced in the plants recently, the company has maintained an outstanding reputation for quality for years through more traditional means.

Caterpillar tends to be an inbred organization with a management that has learned the values of meeting customer needs and product quality through many years of company service. Most start at the bottom, just out of college, and learn on the job. Because acquisitions are rare, new products are developed internally (usually over considerable periods of time), and product lines are both few in number and closely related, the result has been a very effective management team that knows its business very well.

If there is any weakness in the company it is in the efficiency of production relative to competitors. In the plants, at the blue collar level, there are some problems, and these are compounded by competitor pressure. Although Caterpillar has a strong market position with all its product lines and clearly dominates its domestic competitors, it is vulnerable to foreign competition. Komatsu of Japan is expanding rapidly worldwide and can underprice Caterpillar by 10 percent in the U.S. market. There are strong German and Italian competitors as well. To cut costs and meet price competition, Caterpillar has reduced its work force and closed several plants because of overcapacity. Lift truck production has been shifted in part to Korea, where labor costs are lower. Attempts to contain labor costs in the United States (which are double those in Japan) have included pay reductions for managerial and salaried employees and attempts to obtain more favorable contract terms from the major union—the United Auto workers. Workers have been replaced by automated procedures and robots in certain instances.

Like so many other firms manufacturing in the United States, Caterpillar feels it must get more productive output from its workers relative to the costs of production in order to meet foreign competition, particularly Japanese. Yet the steps taken to date have had a demotivating effect. There was a bitter strike of production workers lasting up to

This 227 Logger is working in the woods of the Pacific Northwest, near Seattle, Washington. Despite decreased activity in the forest industry, Caterpillar forestry products have achieved increased acceptance by users.

Lee Morgan

eleven weeks in 1979, and when that contract came up for renewal in 1982 the workers walked out again—this time for seven months. Production was slow returning to prestrike levels and it appears that management was forced to settle for fewer cost savings than desired because of depleted inventories. Company commitment among production workers is low.

The person ultimately responsible for dealing with these problems, Lee Morgan, is very much a product of this company and its values. He was born in a small town in Illinois and graduated from the University of Illinois with a degree in agriculture. After serving in the Army during World War II, he joined Caterpillar as a district sales representative. He has never worked for any other firm. Rising through various marketing positions, he became manager of the Sales Development Department in 1958. Three years later he moved into general management as vice-president in charge of the Engine Division—the major source of company growth. Gradually he continued his upward progress: executive vice-president, president, and finally chairman and CEO. It is characteristic of the company and its deliberate approach to manager development, which makes for few prima donnas, that it took Lee Morgan thirty-one years to reach the top, at the age of 57.

Bicyclist stops to watch Caterpillar crawler and off-highway tractors at site of world's largest lignite mine near Neyveli, India. Some eighty Cat machines are at work there.

Organizing and Organizational Process and Structure

Part 3 focuses on subject matter that is of primary importance at the second phase of successful managerial careers, after promotion has occurred. The concern is with intergroup relations, organizationwide concepts, and organization–environment interactions. Here a broad range of management functions take the spotlight, although organizing is the most central.

Organizational process and structure by definition involve at least two basic work units. Organizing, bargaining, communicating, coordinating, controlling and the like at the organizational level are functions that extend upward from the second level of supervision into middle management. Yet they do not encompass the strategic considerations of top management planning and policy/strategy. For the student who expects to start at the bottom and work up, the issues considered in part 3 are not of as immediate concern as those convered in part 2. But they are important nevertheless—partly because with any degree of success the student can realistically expect to rise above the first level of management, and partly because even at the first level, organizational processes and structures create the broader organizational environment one must operate in and interact with continually.

Another way of considering the subject matter covered in this part relates to implementing plans, policies, and strategies developed at the top levels of hierarchical organizations. To a large extent, organizing and the other functions considered are aimed at putting into action decisions made previously at the top. Yet not all of what we will treat within the context of organizing and organizational process and structure fits this type of formulation. Certain techniques in organization development discussed in chapter 10, for instance, attempt not to implement in a top-down manner but rather to plan and implement from the bottom up.

Chapter 7 deals with several topics that are significant for organizational functioning: power, authority, bargaining, organizational politics and how these factors combine to facilitate or impede the flow of communication. Chapter 8 considers how coordinating processes handle interdependencies and conflicts between and among units, as well as how control processes operate at a more comprehensive level than that of individual performance. In chapter 9 a number of these same concepts are applied to the designing or structuring of an organization and thus specifically to the matter of organizing. Particular attention is given to the major sociological and social psychological views of organization. Chapter 10 discusses change, innovation, growth and decline, especially the more important approaches in what has come to be called organizational development.

CHAPTER 7

Using Power and Communicating in Organizations

CHAPTER OUTLINE

Power and Authority
Formal Versus Acceptance Views of Authority
Bases of Power and Authority
    The Use of Power
    Mindless Obedience
Strategic Contingencies and Power

Bargaining and Organizational Politics
Factors in Bargaining
    Personality Factors
    Others in the Relationship
    Locations and Communications
    Intangible Issues
    Strategies

Organizational Politics
    Political Tactics
    Ethics and Legitimacy

Organizational Communication
Communication and Organizing
    Structural Responses to Overload
    Communication Networks
Informal Systems and the Grapevine
Management Information Systems
    Communication Problems
Individual Communication Skills
    Writing
    Speaking
    Listening

OBJECTIVES

To consider the nature of power and authority and how they operate within organizations.

To understand the nature of effective bargaining and how organizational politics, often involving bargaining, operate.

To explain the nature of organizational communication and the factors that may make it more or less effective.

A sales manager, believing he has the right to do so, makes an agreement with a customer to deliver a certain quantity of product at a given price. As has always been the case in the past, the agreement is made over the telephone. Subsequently the sales manager's superior indicates that the price quoted is too low, and that the sales manager must somehow get out of his previous commitment and establish a higher price. The sales manager then calls the customer back, denies that he ever made the original price quotation, and indicates the current terms of sale.

A city government manager offers a position to an applicant during an interview. Subsequently she learns that because tax revenues are down a freeze has been placed on all hiring; she is ordered to rescind the offer, even though she had no knowledge of the freeze when she made it. She calls the applicant and withdraws the offer verbally, while at the same time following up with a written statement that she was wrong and had no right to make the offer.

An editor with a publishing house makes an agreement, after lengthy discussions with an author, to pay a certain royalty and to provide a sizable advance against royalties subsequently earned. The vice-president in charge turns down the advance, on the grounds that it exceeds the amount authorized by existing policy guidelines, and refuses to issue the check to the author. The editor tells the author what has happened, says he is sorry, and offers a substantially smaller advance that is within guidelines.

These are examples of the exercise of power and bureaucratic authority; they are real. The examples differ in the extent to which the subordinate manager may have overstepped the existing bounds of authority and in the manner in which the same manager deals with the problem. But what is common to all three episodes is that the subordinate manager responds to superior power, irrespective of the circumstances.

POWER AND AUTHORITY

Let us start by making some definitional distinctions. At the broadest level there is *influence*—any behavior on the part of one person that alters the behavior, attitudes, feelings and the like of another. Influence takes several forms, including controlling rewards and punishments, persuasion, playing upon existing attitudes and values, exercising control over significant aspects of the environment, and resulting from an exchange agreement. The examples we began with all represent influence, but so too does an effective advertising campaign or a successful attempt to convince a long-term boyfriend or girlfriend to take the final step into marriage. The applications of influencing at lower organizational levels are considered in part 2.

Power is the potential to exert influence, and it can exist even though no influencing attempt actually occurs. Usually power arises from a capacity to dispense rewards and punishments. The subordinate managers in our examples may have thought about such things as losing raises and promotions, or even about being fired, when they decided to be governed by the power of their superiors.

Authority is institutionalized power, legitimized by the existing system. It is inherent in role prescriptions and viewed as right and proper by organization members. Examples are rational-legal, traditional, and charismatic authority as described by Weber and considered in chapter 3. The episodes described at the beginning of this chapter involve the use of hierarchical authority within bureaucratic systems.

Formal versus Acceptance Views of Authority

The classical view of authority going back to Fayol is that there is a delegation of rights to decide and command on down the hierarchy. At each lower level certain areas of authority are specified. At the same time, higher-level managers are responsible for what they delegate. If the lower-level manager fails to use authority effectively, the higher-level manager remains responsible for the outcome. Why? Because the authority was delegated in the first place.

This kind of theory allows no room for such concerns as subordinate acceptance, bargaining, and the like. Authority is in fact never questioned. Indeed, classical theory has never recognized bargaining as a legitimate management function. Yet we know that things do not always happen as the formally established flow of authority would lead one to predict. The data on informal groups and natural systems provide some support for this conclusion. Exhibit 7.1 indicates that even within management, formal authority structures are not followed perfectly. Members of the two Air Force wings, which were supposed to be organized on exactly the same basis, were asked to indicate where the power really resided. The results indicate that either one wing or the other (or maybe both) was not functioning in accordance with formal expectations. Furthermore, neither wing awarded the squadron commanders the level of authority they were supposed to have. Formal, classical concepts of authority may indicate how authority should be allocated, but they say much less about how it is allocated. That is because bargaining can become a factor in the authority relationship and the bases or sources of authority can extend far beyond what is specified by legitimate, rational-legal concepts.

Bases of Power and Authority

Exhibit 7.2 sets forth the three bases of authority noted by Weber, plus a fourth alternative proposed in a similar vein to cover authority in professional organizations. Several additional formulations regarding the bases of power and authority

---

EXHIBIT 7.1 Rank order of power in two identically structured Air Force wings

Position	Wing A	Wing B
Director of Operations	1	1
Deputy Wing Commander	2	3
Director of Materiel	3	2
Director of Personnel	4	5
Commander, Squadron A	5	7
Commander, Squadron B	6.5 tied	7 tied
Commander, Squadron C	6.5	7
Executive Officer	8	9.5
Maintenance Control Officer	9.5 tied	4 tied
Intelligence Officer	9.5	9.5

Based on James D. Thompson, "Authority and Power in 'Identical' Organizations," *American Journal of Sociology* (November 1956): 294.

Using Power and Communicating in Organizations

EXHIBIT 7.2 Views of the bases of power and authority

Max Weber

1. *Rational-legal authority*—Based on the enactment of laws or rules.
2. *Traditional authority*—Based on the sacredness of the social order.
3. *Charismatic authority*—Based on the affectual and personal devotion of subordinates.
   Value-rational authority (Satow)—Based on the power of ideological or professional norms.

French and Raven

1. *Reward power*—The person can give or withhold something desired.
2. *Coercive power*—The person can apply punishments.
3. *Legitimate power*—The person who exercises power is viewed as right in terms of the values of the one influenced.
4. *Referent power*—The individual influenced desires to model his or her behavior on the person.
5. *Expert power*—The person has the status of an expert and thus is likely to be accurate.

Filley and Grimes

1. *Formal authority*—The person is viewed as having a legitimate right by virtue of level of position.
2. *Authority of responsibility and function*—The person is viewed as responsible for matters of the type at hand.
3. *Manipulation*—The person is viewed as being capable of getting the job done in a desired manner.
4. *Authority by default*—The person is available and will deal with the matter.
5. *Authority of expertise*—The person has superior knowledge of the subject.
6. *Authority from control of resources*—The person controls needed money and information.
7. *Authority by virtue of rules*—The person is legitimized by existing rules, policies, customs, or traditions.
8. *Collegial authority*—A group of peers is viewed as having a legitimate right to know and to exert influence.
9. *Authority from friendship*—The person is liked and a positive relationship exists.
10. *Authority of equity*—The person is viewed as generally equitable and fair.

Based on Max Weber (see chapter 3); Roberta L. Satow, "Value-Rational Authority and Professional Organizations: Weber's Missing Type," *Administrative Science Quarterly* (December 1975); John R. P. French and Bertram Raven, "The Bases of Social Power," in *Studies in Social Power,* ed. Dorwin Cartwright (Ann Arbor: Research Center for Group Dynamics, University of Michigan, 1959); Alan C. Filley and A. J. Grimes, "The Bases of Power in Decision Processes," *Academy of Management Proceedings* (1967).

are presented as well. The result is a reasonably comprehensive statement of why people respond to the power and authority of others. Much of this is consistent with the formulations of bureaucratic theory, but there are exceptions also. Even within bureaucratic systems some sources of power are not part of the system. The result can be bargaining as to the scope of bureaucratic authority, and major departures from formal expectations.

Typically the bases covered by such terms as rational-legal authority, legitimate power, formal authority, and authority of responsibility and function do predominate in bureaucratic organizations. Similarly bases such as value-rational authority, expert power, and authority of expertise are characteristic in professional systems involving physicians, lawyers, college professors, and like. There is some evidence that referent and expert types of power yield the least dissatisfaction and produce the most positive performance outcomes in terms of quantity and quality of output. The problem is that one is not always in a position to effect these types of power bases. Especially when dealing with problems of attitude and cooperation, a manager may be forced to draw upon other sources and types of power and authority that, although less popular, remain more effective than doing nothing at all.

The Use of Power   There is considerable evidence that "doing nothing at all," even when power is available to deal with a problem, happens not infrequently. Inexperienced managers in particular and those who lack self-confidence tend to avoid using power, preferring to pass problems with difficult employees and the like to others if at all possible. A study conducted in various federal government agencies identified a widespread tendency to avoid receiving information on subordinate noncompliance with directives, because if the manager did receive this information, it might very well be necessary to exercise power over the subordinate.[1]

Failure to use power and authority that is readily available does not make for an effectively functioning system. The organizational consequences become increasingly pronounced toward the top of a company because in hierarchical systems abdications of authority have effects all the way down the line. Yet trying to use power that one does not have (because of legal constraints, for instance) can be equally detrimental. Again and again managerial actions with regard to employees are reversed by Labor Relations Board decisions, the courts, arbitrators, and the power of public pressure, at considerable cost to the company. The judicious and effective use of power is one of the most difficult lessons a manager has to learn.

Mindless Obedience   A widely publicized series of studies dealing with the willingness of one person to administer shock to another when told to do so by an experimenter produced results that were summarized as follows:

> Many subjects will obey the experimenter no matter how vehement the pleading of the person being shocked, no matter how painful the shocks seem to be, and no matter how much the victim pleads to be let out. This was seen time and again in our studies. . . . It is the extreme willingness of adults to go to almost any lengths on the command of an authority that constitutes the chief finding of the study.[2]

Findings such as these raise such concerns as brainwashing, the atrocities of the Nazi concentration camps, and mindless obedience in general. That this kind of obedience decreased sharply in the studies when two authorities disagreed, when any disobedience was not immediately obvious, and when others also resisted authority is not an entirely satisfactory solution. There are many cases in the business world, especially within the middle ranks of management, where such limiting forces on the impact of authority are not present. Authority legitimized by a large organization or a profession can be a very strong motivating force. It can be abused, and it can produce mindless obedience. How often such events occur we do not know, but the potential is there and it is well that we all be aware of that fact.

Strategic Contingencies and Power

An important issue with regard to power in organizations involves the conditions under which power accrues to individuals and the units of which they are members. We know that legitimate authority has an influence, but what about units at the same hierarchical level and the kind of nonlegitimized power differences noted in Exhibit 7.1? One view that appears useful, and has been the subject of research, states that power will be greatest where there is the greatest capacity to cope with problems and sources of uncertainty facing the organization as a whole.[3] This is the strategic contingencies concept. An individual or a group has power to the extent it is perceived as being in a unique position to help others solve their problems. The extent of power depends on what the problems are and who has the capacity to deal with them.

The strategic contingencies view may be illustrated with reference to a very important decision that Bethlehem Steel Company faced a few years ago. Lewis W. Foy, chairman and chief executive officer, was retiring, and the company faced a host of problems (like the U.S. steel industry in general). One problem was to modernize old and inefficient plants and thus was of a manufacturing nature. A second problem was to raise money for the purpose of expanding and diversifying and thus was essentially financial in nature. A third problem was to improve governmental lobbying and achieve more favorable treatment in competing with foreign steel and thus was of a government relations nature. Congruent with these problem areas were the three candidates for the position being vacated by Lewis Foy: Walter Williams, who had come up through operations; Donald Trautlein, who had been a partner in the Price, Waterhouse accounting firm before joining the company; and Richard Schubert, who had been Labor Undersecretary in the Nixon administration. According to the strategic contingencies view, the greatest power—and thus the promotion to CEO—should go to the individual most able to solve the problems of the company as a whole.[4]

Not surprisingly, Donald Trautlein became CEO. Unless the company could solve its financial problems and raise new capital it could neither construct new plants nor diversify. Thus, the financial problem appeared to subsume the manufacturing one. Government relations, on the other hand, appeared to be more of a holding action than a long-run solution to the company's problems.

BARGAINING AND ORGANIZATIONAL POLITICS

In considering Barnard's ideas in chapter 3, we noted that people either explicitly or implicitly establish a contract with the employing organization. A balance is set up between inducements and contributions in which the contribution is a willingness to follow authority within a zone of indifference. The limits of this zone and the nature of the inducements from the organization are determined by bargaining. Typically neither the inducements nor the contributions are defined with great precision at the time of employment. Thus, bargaining continues to settle unresolved issues over time. It is for these reasons that matters of power and authority are closely intertwined with bargaining; one can hardly talk about one without considering the other. In collective bargaining and labor–management negotiations, for instance, the issue of management rights (authority) is always a central concern. In these and other contexts, *bargaining* may be defined as a process in which at least two parties attempt to establish through some type of transaction what each shall give and take, or perform and receive.

In the same way that the use of power and authority in bureaucratic systems often is constrained by bargaining, managers at the same or similar levels may find themselves forced into bargaining relationships in order to deal with mutual problems. It is not uncommon that industrial relations managers must bargain with line production or sales managers to determine who will exert the primary influence, prior to engaging in collective bargaining with a union. Bargaining permeates organizations—vertically, horizontally, and diagonally. The literature on these relationships and their outcomes provides a good deal of useful information for the manager.[5]

Factors in Bargaining

When may bargaining of this nature be said to occur? This is a matter of defining the characteristics of a bargaining relationship. A useful approach in this regard is the following. Bargaining occurs when:

1. At least two parties are involved.
2. The parties have a conflict of interest with respect to one or more different issues.
3. Regardless of the existence of prior experience or acquaintance with one another, the parties are at least temporarily joined together in a special kind of voluntary relationship.
4. Activity in the relationship concerns
   a. The division or exchange of one or more specific resources
   b. The resolution of one or more intangible issues (such as saving face) among the parties or among the parties whom they represent.
5. The activity involves the presentation of demands or proposals by one party, evaluation of these by the other, followed by concessions and counterproposals. The activity is thus sequential rather than simultaneous.[6]

Personality Factors Some people are more effective bargainers than others. Exhibit 7.3 provides data on four characteristics thought to be related to bargaining. It is interesting to note that American managers are at the extreme on three of the four characteristics; they are more prone to take risks, have a stronger belief in self-determination, and are more trusting than managers in other countries. Actually, of the four characteristics, only two were found to be closely related to bargaining behavior. Those who prefer to avoid risks and those who believe in self-determination seek the most initially in bargaining relationships, utilize tougher strategies, and tend to emerge as winners more often. The two other personality factors, although seemingly important in bargaining, did not prove to be so.

Another factor that relates to being an effective bargainer is aspiration level. One might think that hard goals would be related to better bargaining outcomes. This is true; people who are motivated by the difficult goals they set for themselves going into a situation are more likely to succeed in bargaining.

Others in the Relationship When managers bargain across the boundaries of a company—as the company's representative in a sales or purchasing capacity, as a labor relations negotiator, or whatever—there are others in the relation-

EXHIBIT 7.3 Ranking of countries on personality characteristics expected to be related to bargaining

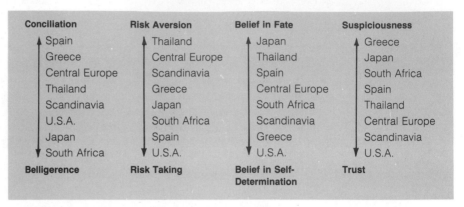

Conciliation	Risk Aversion	Belief in Fate	Suspiciousness
↑ Spain	↑ Thailand	↑ Japan	↑ Greece
Greece	Central Europe	Thailand	Japan
Central Europe	Scandinavia	Spain	South Africa
Thailand	Greece	Central Europe	Spain
Scandinavia	Japan	South Africa	Thailand
U.S.A.	South Africa	Scandinavia	Central Europe
Japan	Spain	Greece	Scandinavia
↓ South Africa	↓ U.S.A.	↓ U.S.A.	↓ U.S.A.
Belligerence	**Risk Taking**	**Belief in Self-Determination**	**Trust**

NOTE: Central European countries included are Belgium, France, Switzerland, and England; Scandinavian countries included are Denmark and Finland.

Based on Donald L. Harnett and Larry L. Cummings, *Bargaining Behavior: An International Study* (Houston: Dame, 1980), pp. 122–24.

ship. It is not just a matter of two people bargaining. The same is true within the company when managers represent work units, cliques, political coalitions, and the like. When they represent constituencies, bargainers tend to get tougher in their demands and push harder for results, particularly if members of the constituency are actually present to observe the bargaining process. The result can be antagonism, hardening of the other party's position, and eventual deadlock. If the bargainer feels trusted by the constituency this effect is reduced, because the need to prove one's loyalty is less. Many experienced bargainers try to work within the limits prescribed by the group they represent and then get away somewhere where there will be no witnesses to do the actual bargaining. This frees them up in the use of strategies, and they need be judged only on the final result.

Others may also be involved in the bargaining relationship when there is someone attempting to mediate a resolution or someone who will arbitrate if a deadlock occurs. In labor relations these are common features, but often within companies too a higher-level manager assumes a mediator or arbitrator role as two subordinate managers try to work out their differences. Usually when it is known that someone with the authority to do so will make a decision and thus arbitrate if they do not reach an agreement, bargainers will concede more and come to some resolution on more issues—provided it is apparent that one or the other's position will be accepted in total. They simply do not want to lose control of the situation so that what happens is completely out of their hands and left to an arbitrator who can make them lose completely. However, if it is likely that the arbitrator will split the difference so that everybody wins a little, then a chilling effect on bargaining occurs and many issues tend to be left unresolved—to be handled by the arbitrator. The prospect of mediation, where a third party advises and tries to help the parties to reach agreement, also has this chilling effect.[7] For many people it is more face saving to go along with the recommendations of a mediator than to give in to an opponent.

Locations and Communications   In sports there is something known as "the home field advantage." This turns out to be a reality in bargaining as well. A manager holding a committee meeting in her own office, a purchasing agent who has sales representatives come to see him, a bank loan officer who negotiates a business loan at the bank has an advantage. People bargaining on their own territory tend to be more secure and more assertive, and they get more.

Similarly, bargaining tends to be facilitated by open communication channels where the people involved can see and hear each other clearly. Bargaining is a verbal process. It becomes difficult if people only partially understand each other's language or have to work through an interpreter. These are major problems in multinational business dealings. Also when bargaining teams are involved, agreement is hampered by people leaving the room intermittently to take telephone calls and the like. Open and full communication, and physical arrangements that contribute to that end, do not guarantee a satisfactory result, but without them antagonisms can easily be intensified.

Intangible Issues   At times in bargaining people seem to get off the track. A parent and child discussing the size of an allowance may get into who does or does not love whom. A manager and subordinate discussing a raise may get into issues of appreciation for effort expended and loyalty. These intangible issues often involve loss of honor, public image, face, self-esteem, and the like; there is a feeling on one side or the other of being "put down," and personalities rather than tangible issues become the focus of discussion.

In these cases there is a real risk that the ultimate trade-off will be self-esteem for tangible accomplishment. One side wins whatever was at issue originally and the other gets in return the retention or regaining of a threatened self-esteem. For individuals such trade-offs may be entirely acceptable, even desirable; but when there are groups or constituencies involved, maintaining a bargaining representative's self-esteem may not be a very high priority. Accordingly bargainers who get bogged down in intangible issues usually are not considered to be very effective. Bargaining therefore is best done by people with relatively high self-esteem, who do not have a great need for social acceptance and whose power motivation has developed to a mature level.

Strategies   Obviously the bargaining strategy most likely to work will vary with the circumstances. However, two generalizations are possible:

1. Although tough bargaining often gets results, there is a point beyond which toughness merely leads to deadlock. Accordingly, the toughness of one's position should be adjusted to an evaluation of the consequences of deadlock.
2. Bargainers on both sides invariably expect concessions at intervals throughout the bargaining process. Accordingly it is desirable to start at a high enough initial level to leave room for certain concessions, unless one's power position is very strong.

This means that opening with an extreme demand and then adjusting downward as one learns about the other's position and evaluates the consequences and probabilities of deadlock is usually a sound approach. It is important, however, to know what the other side really wants. One can make a concession of little value and get practically nothing in return. One can also give much more than is needed, because one does not understand the opposing values. This is why experienced bargainers spend so much time in what looks like fruitless sparring. They are learning the value of the various considerations at issue, so that when they make a concession it will be the right one and appropriate in degree.

Much bargaining is by nature or because of the predispositions of those involved of a win–lose type. There is a fixed pie, and what one side gets the other loses. It is well to recognize, however, that more creative solutions may be available. Bargainers can work together to find a way to expand the size of the pie so that both end up winning to some degree. Or attitudes and understandings can change during the bargaining process so that a pie that was originally viewed as almost inedible become much more enticing. The point is that bargaining typically permits a wide range of solutions, and a strategy that emphasizes a creative search for alternatives often can be very rewarding.

Organizational Politics

Organizational politics relates to behaviors that are outside those on which the organization has taken a specific position for or against; the behaviors are intended to obtain selfish, individual ends that are opposed to the ends of others in the organization. Organizational politics may focus on the goals of groups as well as individuals, and they may well involve behaviors that are harmful to the organization as a whole. They appear to be inevitable, but at the same time there are wide variations from organization to organization. Ethical issues often come to the fore, and bargaining is an important consideration in organizational politics.

Organizational politics create very ambivalent responses—people view the whole process both negatively and positively, depending on the particular perspective they have in mind. Overall, however, those who are successful in organizational politics tend to be viewed favorably, perhaps because they are successful competitors in other respects as well.

Research indicates that political matters of this kind are a frequent topic of conversation and that the most frequent issues are interdepartmental coordination, delegation of authority, and promotions or transfers.[8] A common concern is the promotion of a less competent person based on "pull" or friendship (that is, political effectiveness). Inherent in this and many other politicized situations are the influencing of performance evaluations, positively for oneself and negatively for competitors, and the influencing of authority allocations, as between one work unit and another or between supervisor and subordinate.

Organizational politics become more prevalent and more important for the individual at each higher level of management—in short, as the competition gets rougher. As Exhibit 7.4 suggests, the tactics used also change with management level, and the kinds of people who are effective politicians are somewhat different. There is ample evidence that strategic decisions at the top levels of corporations may well be politically influenced.[9] For instance, new company locations may be influenced by the desires of top people regarding where they would like

EXHIBIT 7.4 Ranking of tactics and characteristics of good politicians

	Ranking of Frequency of Mention		
Tactical Approaches	**Chief Executive Officers**	**High-Level Staff Managers**	**First-Level Supervisors**
Attacking or blaming others; scapegoating	1	2	2
Withholding, distorting or overwhelming with information	2	1	3
Developing a base of support for one's ideas	3	4	7
Creating a favorable image; impression management	4	3	1
Developing strong allies and forming power coalitions	5	7	5
Praising others; ingratiating oneself with others	6.5 } tie	6	4
Associating with influential people	6.5 ⌋	5	8
Creating obligations and a basis for reciprocity	8	8	6

	Frequently Noted Characteristics of Good Politicians		
	Sensitive	Sensitive	Competent
	Articulate	Articulate	Popular
	Ambitious	Ambitious	Aggressive
	Intelligent	Socially adept	Devious
	"Organization man"	Competent	
		Self-confident	
		Logical	

Adapted from Robert W. Allen et al., "Organizational Politics: Tactics and Characteristics of Its Actors," *California Management Review* (Fall 1979): 79–80.

to live or visit. It appears that Dow Chemical Company located its headquarters in Midland, Michigan largely for such reasons.

Political Tactics Exhibit 7.4 provides an idea of the types of political tactics in widespread use. All eight approaches are among the most frequently used, but there are sizable differences among them nevertheless. Interestingly, attacking or blaming others is noted by at least 50 percent of the managers in all three categories; competition is clearly a prime force in organizational politics. Furthermore, a number of the approaches involve establishing a strong bargaining position.

Exhibit 7.5 notes some of the political tactics proposed to achieve a competitive advantage. These tactics have their origins in practical experience. Nevertheless, a number of them fit well with what has been learned from research on bargaining. Whatever their value, these are the kinds of strategies people often follow in bureaucratic organizations.

Exhibit 7.6 presents a somewhat different view via the medium of a questionnaire. It is presented here not because it represents a well-researched, standardized measure, but because the questions provide a further indication of what organizational politics are all about. The questionnaire is normally scored by giving one point for each "mostly agree" answer. It takes a score of sixteen or more to conclude that a strong inclination toward playing politics exists.

EXHIBIT 7.5 Some suggested political tactics

1. Exert influence over the time and place of your bargaining efforts so that these conditions are selected to support your goals; thus in many cases it is advisable to bargain in your home territory.
2. It is a desirable bargaining tactic to disguise your true interests for as long as possible; to be overly eager for a given outcome may leave you at a distinct disadvantage with regard to other, related considerations.
3. Shoot for the moon initially so that you can then settle for less, but do not use this tactic too often with the same person.
4. Identify any weaknesses that adversaries may have and continually work on and publicize them.
5. Where the opposition consists of a loosely assembled coalition, try to point up the differences within the coalition and any common interests you have with each member; thus, attempt to divide and conquer.
6. Establish alliances with superiors, peers, and subordinates so that when needed they can be counted on to be on your side.
7. Select subordinates who are not only competent but reliable, dependable, and above all else loyal.
8. Do not get yourself in a position of relying on an adversary's expertise; if you are not knowledgeable in an area, secure your own expert and take steps to establish his or her credibility.
9. Do not injure another person who is or might well be in a position to take revenge.
10. Do not do anything to alienate or anger former colleagues when leaving a position; bridges that have been burned may be needed unexpectedly later on.
11. If a proposal developed by an adversary is unattractive but cannot be thwarted immediately, attempt to refer it to a committee to delay it and widen the bargaining area.
12. If the outcome is uncertain it is often desirable to support the aggressive efforts of someone else, rather than take the lead oneself; that way it may be easier to get off the ship early, if it begins to sink.
13. In dealing with an adversary try to leave the door open so that communication is not closed off and differences can still be resolved if necessary.
14. Avoid dealing in personalities, never attack the adversary personally, and focus on the real facts and issues.
15. Choose when and under what circumstances a vote should be used to settle an issue; let matters go to a vote for resolution only when you know you have a majority.

Based on Richard H. Buskirk, *Handbook of Managerial Tactics* (Boston: Cahners, 1976); Robert N. McMurry, "Power and the Ambitious Executive," *Harvard Business Review* (November–December 1973).

Ethics and Legitimacy Without question, the contents of Exhibits 7.5 and 7.6 raise questions regarding what is ethical and legitimate in terms of the goals of the organization involved. Whether a certain type of political behavior can be viewed as ethical must be judged against some model or criterion.[10] Behavior may be evaluated in terms of a utilitarian model (the greatest good for the greatest number), a rights model (an individual's rights should not be violated), or a justice model (there should be a fair and equitable distribution of benefits and burdens). Ideally all three models should be applied, and behavior should meet all three tests to be considered ethical. Yet there are cases

EXHIBIT 7.6 Political orientation questionnaire

Directions: Answer each question "mostly agree" or "mostly disagree," even if it is difficult for you to decide which alternative best describes your opinion.

	Mostly Agree	Mostly Disagree
1. Only a fool would correct a boss's mistakes.	____	____
2. If you have certain confidential information, release it to your advantage.	____	____
3. I would be careful not to hire a subordinate with more formal education than myself.	____	____
4. If you do somebody a favor, remember to cash in on it.	____	____
5. Given the opportunity, I would cultivate friendships with powerful people.	____	____
6. I like the idea of saying nice things about a rival in order to get that person transferred from my department.	____	____
7. Why not take credit for someone else's work? They would do the same to you.	____	____
8. Given the chance, I would offer to help my boss build some shelves for his or her den.	____	____
9. I laugh heartily at my boss's jokes, even when they are not funny.	____	____
10. I would be sure to attend a company picnic even if I had the chance to do something I enjoyed more that day.	____	____
11. If I knew an executive in my company was stealing money, I would use that against him or her in asking for favors.	____	____
12. I would first find out my boss's political preferences before discussing politics with him or her.	____	____
13. I think using memos to zap somebody for his or her mistakes is a good idea (especially when you want to show that person up).	____	____
14. If I wanted something done by a coworker, I would be willing to say "If you don't get this done, our boss might be very unhappy."	____	____
15. I would invite my boss to a party at my house, even if I didn't like him or her.	____	____
16. When I'm in a position to, I would have lunch with the "right people" at least twice a week.	____	____
17. Richard M. Nixon's bugging the Democratic Headquarters would have been a clever idea if he wasn't caught.	____	____
18. Power for its own sake is one of life's most precious commodities.	____	____
19. Having a high school named after you would be an incredible thrill.	____	____
20. Reading about job politics is as much fun as reading an adventure story.	____	____

SOURCE: Andrew J. Dubrin, *Human Relations: A Job-Oriented Approach,* 1978. Reprinted with permission of Reston Publishing Company, a Prentice-Hall company, 11480 Sunset Hills Road, Reston, VA 22090.

Using Power and Communicating in Organizations

EXHIBIT 7.7 Types of political behavior

Direction of Political Exchange	Internal to the Organization		External to the Organization	
	Legitimate Behavior	**Illegitimate Behavior**	**Legitimate Behavior**	**Illegitimate Behavior**
Vertical (up and down the hierarchy)	Direct voice Complain to supervisor Bypassing chain of command Obstructionism so that policies are not implemented	Sabotage Symbolic protests Mutinies Riots	Lawsuits against the firm	Whistle blowing to the public regarding organizational misconduct
Horizontal (across the hierarchy)	Coalition formation Exchange of favors Reprisals	Physical threats	Talks with a counter-part from another organization Outside professional activity	Defections to competitors Organizational duplicity, such as spying

Adapted from Dan Farrell and James C. Petersen, "Patterns of Political Behavior in Organizations," *Academy of Management Review* (July 1982):407.

where conflicts occur or information is limited so that it is not entirely clear what is ethical. Chapter 13 deals with these matters in greater detail.

A somewhat different consideration is whether the behavior involved is considered as within or outside the organization's normal and acceptable range. Where certain political behaviors are viewed as illegitimate, severe sanctions may be brought to bear against those who engage in them. Exhibit 7.7 provides a way of looking at political behaviors, and a method of distinguishing between what are likely to be considered legitimate and illegitimate activities.

ORGANIZATIONAL COMMUNICATION

Bargaining and organizational politics rely on communication; so too does the use of power and authority, as Chester Barnard argued so convincingly (see Exhibit 3.8). In fact communication—one-on-one discussions, group meeting, telephone conversations, speeches, computer interaction, memoranda, position papers, reports, letters, and the like—permeates almost every aspect of organizational functioning. Managers spend a very high proportion of their time in communication, especially oral communication. Despite bureaucratic theory's emphasis on the importance of written records and the files, and legalistic arguments for "getting it in writing," a high proportion of organizational communication occurs face-to-face and over the telephone, and most managers appear to prefer it that way. The savings in time and effort often are sizable.

Exhibit 7.8 provides a picture of what communication is and the role of organizational communication within it. Organizational communication is much less concerned with the performance of individuals and groups than with communication flows and channels running across major segments of the organization.

EXHIBIT 7.8   Nature and aspects of organizational communication

Definition   Communication is the exchange of information between sender and receiver and the inferring of meaning among those involved.

Levels of Analysis for Communications

1. Intraindividual—how the individual takes in, processes, and produces communications.
2. Interpersonal—how communication occurs between people and within small groups.
3. Intraorganizational—how communications flow within the boundaries of organizations.
4. Extraorganizational—how communications operate across the organizational boundary to and from the environment.
5. Technical—how communication technology (in particular involving computers) relates to communication processes.

Organizational Communication

Functions of Organizational Communication

1. To provide information for decisions.
2. To establish tasks, duties, authority and responsibility.
3. To achieve cooperation and action toward goals.
4. To instruct and change.
5. To provide feedback to a source.

The Flow of Organizational Communication Systems

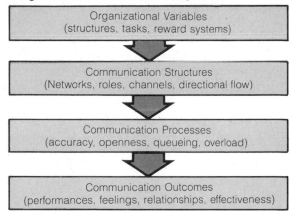

Organizational Variables
(structures, tasks, reward systems)

Communication Structures
(Networks, roles, channels, directional flow)

Communication Processes
(accuracy, openness, queueing, overload)

Communication Outcomes
(performances, feelings, relationships, effectiveness)

Based on Charles A. O'Reilley and Louis R. Pondy, "Organizational Communication" in *Organizational Behavior*, ed. Steven Kerr (Columbus: Grid, 1979), pp. 121–22, 129.

Communication and Organizing

In one sense an organization's structure (as reflected in charts, for instance) is a diagram for communication flow. It indicates desired channels and directions, and thus who should communicate with whom. Yet when the flow of organizational communication systems in Exhibit 7.8 is considered, there is no intention of implying that communication structures will, or even should, match the organizational variables perfectly.

Organizational patterns do not match communication flows perfectly because under most circumstances organizations do not exercise continual surveillance over members. People in a car pool, members of the same club, and individuals who meet by chance on the elevator can and do engage in organizationally relevant communication irrespective of prescribed channels. Typically the organization cannot stop these types of communication flows and does not try. Organizational structure does not operate like the water pipes in a house that rigidly control the flow of water. Rather it facilitates communication flow up and down the hierarchy, horizontally across it, or even diagonally, depending on how the structure is designed.

Hierarchical systems tend to facilitate vertical flow, but typically there are also structural or other types of approaches to facilitate other kinds of flows as well. As noted in chapter 3, Fayol's scalar chain principle included a "gangplank" or bridge created between two managers at the same level in the hierarchy by virtue of the fact that their superiors authorize communication.

Communication flows other than strictly vertical are facilitated by the creation of specialized staff groups, such as those dealing with personnel and human resources. Staff units provide advice, control, administrative services, specialized programs, and troubleshooting across the organization. Their power is based largely on expertise. Staff managers and representatives communicate directly with the line organization (usually consisting of production and sales personnel) and with other staff units regarding matters within their domain of expertise. In this way, specialized knowledge flows throughout the organization, not just up and down a hierarchy.

Other ways of facilitating nonvertical communication are to design committees for this purpose and to introduce liaison positions and groups that serve to bring together various units in a horizontal relationship to one another. A committee to coordinate management compensation levels across departments might comprise representatives from all units headed by a vice-president. Companies often create product or project manager positions to mediate needed communication from research through manufacturing to sales and marketing.

Even within the vertical hierarchy, methods of facilitating flows may be introduced to speed up communication or to circumvent possible blockages. Typically these needs are greatest with regard to upward communication, and the approach taken serves to skip over levels in the hierarchy. Upper-level managers may utilize an "open door" policy to encourage communication with lower-level employees. Such is the case at Caterpillar Tractor, for instance, although the open door is used primarily by long-time employees who worked with the top managers back when they were at lower levels. Attitude surveys, suggestion systems, employee meetings, and counseling programs also can be used to bypass levels in the hierarchy. In all of these cases it is important to establish the legitimacy of the approach with all concerned. If this is not done, those who are left out of the flow of communications can react with resentment and attempt to disrupt the flow.[11]

Structural Responses to Overload Communication channels can become overloaded and clogged, with the result that important information does not get through and therefore is not used. In hierarchical systems this occurs most often toward the top. High-level staff managers are particularly likely to face this problem because they have multiple communications contacts, and therefore flows come from all directions.[12] However, the most common instance of communication overload is the office of the chief executive officer.

Organizations cope with overload by attempting to reduce flows in a particular channel or by structuring the flows so that what needs to get through does. One approach is to delegate and decentralize, thus substituting several individuals for one,·setting up more channels, and decreasing the load on any one channel. Communications go only to those who will need them to deal with their particular role requirements. A top executive may create subordinate positions to handle certain matters and may specify that communications should move on up to the top only under unusual circumstances—when expenditures will be in excess of a particular amount, for instance.

Another approach is to select communication channels that have proven effective in the past and essentially ignore others, in effect restructuring the communication system. In this way a manager may come to spend much more time with some subordinates than others, read certain publications but not others, receive calls and communications from particular outsiders while ignoring others, and so on. The trusted and true sources become "gatekeepers" for communication flows. Obviously, the success of this approach depends on the validity of the channel selection process.

A frequent solution is to introduce methods of queueing and filtering communications so that really important items get through immediately, while others are delayed as appropriate to their urgency or content and many are buffered out completely. Positions may be created in a manager's office solely for this purpose. One or more individuals may be given "assistant to" titles and assigned duties involving the filtering and queueing of certaing types of information. Or such matters may become the concern of a general staff, analogous to the White House staff created by various American presidents in recent years. Under this system, information flows to a group of individuals who sort and compress it for the president, presenting it in briefing sessions or papers.

Communication Networks Starting in the 1950s, a series of studies was conducted in small-group, laboratory settings with a view to determining whether certain communication patterns are inherently superior to others.[13] Groups whose communications channels were forcefully predetermined, like the water system of a house, were compared in their capacity to solve problems. Exhibit 7.9 provides examples of the patterns or networks used. Results generally supported the use of the wheel network, featuring one central information processor, in dealing with relatively simple tasks. As the problem becomes more complex the skills of all are needed, and more decentralized networks—the circle and even the all-channel—become preferable.

These results do have implications for communication in organizations, but one should apply them with caution. Five-person groups of former strangers are not the same as large managerial components with long histories of working together. Furthermore, organizations have much more porous communication systems than those in the studies. What might appear to be a highly centralized wheel network in a company may well turn out, on closer observation, to have much more of an all-channel nature. Also the communication network research has focused on decision making, but not decision implementation; organizations do both. Thus, the findings from this research should be considered only as information to take into account in reaching conclusions about organization communication flows, not specific guidelines.

EXHIBIT 7.9 Structures used in communication network research

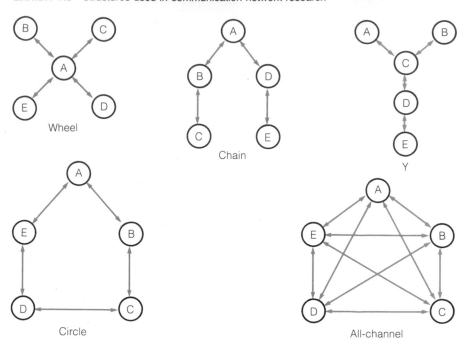

Wheel

Chain

Y

Circle

All-channel

Informal Systems and the Grapevine

Where the communication structure (see Exhibit 7.8) is not congruent with organizational variables, nonformal communication exists. Conceivably this might involve unanticipated direct communication with management from members of a lower-level, group-based system. More typically today it involves communication across the hierarchical organization outside formally established channels. In either case communication occurs in ways that are not among those facilitated by the organization. Historically this type of communication has been considered in relation to informal groups and natural systems of the kind discussed in chapter 6. It also has been considered as the grapevine, scuttlebutt, or rumor.

However described, communication of this kind can serve certain purposes. It integrates people into the organization and may well contribute to commitment, it tends to inform people regarding matters that although important are not of a public nature, and it can achieve communication between people who have not yet been linked formally even though the work indicates they should be. Yet overall it does not function very effectively, and the same needs could in all likelihood be accomplished better by the institution of more formal channels.

Channels such as the grapevine do not transmit very accurately, fail to reach many individuals, and are often perceived negatively by employees, even though they can be influential.[14] There is a tendency for only very few individuals to transmit, even though many more receive. Even so, many people (and even whole groups) can lie outside nonformal channels; this is particularly true of lower-level production and marketing units. Among those who do receive, there are a number who have so little trust in this type of communication that they pay practically no attention to it. In short, informal systems and the grapevine are not an adequate substitute for appropriately designed channels. In fact, their growth may well be a reflection of the inadequacies of organizationally facilitated flows. Also, they are often highly subject to distorting influences originating in organizational politics.

Management information systems operate primarily at the technical level insofar as communication is concerned; they rely heavily on computers. Furthermore, they are relevant not only to communication but also to many other areas of management, including decision making, planning, controlling, and the performance of personnel/human resources and production/operations functions. Exhibit 7.10 shows one way that computerized systems can mesh with other factors in a total management information system.

Let us start by differentiating among three terms. *Data* are facts organized in some manner to facilitate retrieval. *Information* is data organized around a particular problem; it serves to provide understanding of some situation. *Intelligence* is information that has been analyzed in such a way as to provide a preferred course of action among alternatives. Clearly, as one moves to computerized systems that provide intelligence, the concern is no longer just with communication but with decision making as well.

Another important concept is that of the *data base*. Exhibit 7.11 diagrams such a system. Data base systems are companywide, drawing data from production, personnel, accounting, purchasing, marketing, and the like while eliminating any duplications that might exist in separate systems. Systems of this kind permit the interrelating of data from various functional areas and thus types of information that might not otherwise be available. Output may be in the form of standardized information reports, programmed for production at certain intervals, or responses to ad hoc inquiries initiated because a particular problem has arisen.

Communication Problems A management information system that captures data from many sources throughout the organization could be structured so that it is directly integrated into existing structures and facilitated communication flows. Typically, however, this is not the case; data are captured wherever they first become available. The result can be a very efficient and rapid communication system, if this approach is widely accepted and legitimized. If it is not, those who believe they have been unfairly removed from the communication process may well react in ways that jeopardize the validity of the information output. Potential users may come to mistrust the information they receive, or they may be reluctant to use it because of extensive internal resistance to its source. Obtaining information from computerized systems that have not acquired widespread acceptance may not hamper the decision-making process; in fact, that process can well be facilitated. But implementation of the decision may prove to be impossible. This is one reason that management information system technology far exceeds the level of actual use in most companies.

A related problem is that people lose control over the use of data once they put it into a data base system. They no longer are crucial sources of expertise others must go to for information; they lose power and become expendable.

EXHIBIT 7.10 The manager in a management information system

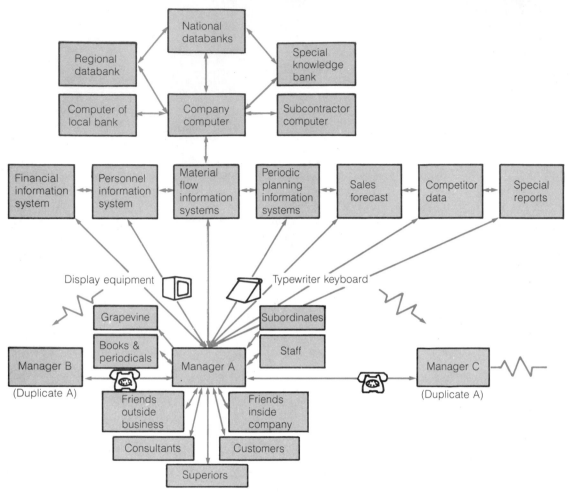

SOURCE: Reprinted with permission of The Free Press, a division of Macmillan, Inc. From *Top Management Planning* by George A. Steiner, p. 508. Copyright © 1969 by The Trustees of Columbia University in the City of New York.

EXHIBIT 7.11 Structure of a data base system

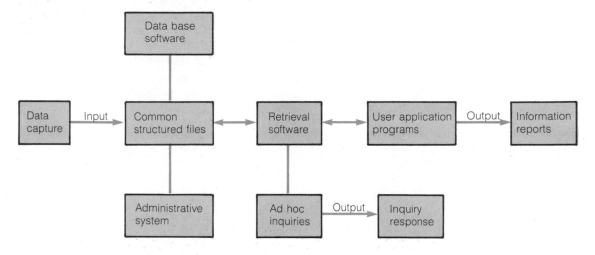

Furthermore, once the data are in the computer it is difficult to know who might obtain them. Secrecy cannot be assured, and one of the primary tactical approaches in organizational politics (see Exhibit 7.4) is no longer available. It is not surprising that many managers tend to hold data out of computerized communication systems or openly attack their development and use.

A good example of what can happen is provided by the introduction of a work measurement information system at the U.S. Postal Service. The system was constantly delayed with the result that it became operative two years later than planned and cost twice as much. When it did start operating, the surprising consequences were that it required more rather than fewer people, produced an increase in errors, cost more, and produced many reports that no one used. All this appears to have been caused by negative reactions on the part of users and those who supplied data. Resistance took such forms as deliberate input errors and sabotage so that the system could not operate effectively. The computer was blamed for a wide range of problems totally unrelated to the management information system. Results of this kind are not inevitable, and some projects of this kind have worked out very well.[15] It is important to be aware of the potential communications problems, however.

Individual Communication Skills

Organizational communication between individuals is inevitably influenced by the skills those individuals have in sending and receiving. Sending is typically in verbal form—the written or spoken word. This does not deny a role to nonverbal communication, such as facial expressions, body language, dress and the like. Yet these nonverbal modes are difficult to change and often supplement or reinforce the verbal forms. Receiving is primarily through seeing or listening, although other senses may be involved on occasion. Listening, in particular, is likely to be a source of communications problems. In contrast to reading, there may be no opportunity to go back and check one's initial perception. Thus, errors are more probable when oral communication is involved.

Writing   People in the business world do evaluate letters, reports, memos, and the like in terms of how well they are written and how effectively they communicate. In fact, most managers become very sensitive in this regard and are quite accurate in distinguishing a well-written piece from a less well-written one.[16] Various proposals have been put forth regarding what constitutes effective written communication, in the sense that the intended message and meaning are likely to get through to the receiver. The following listing is reasonably comprehensive. Organizational communications should be:

Readable—It should be understandable to the intended audience, both in terms of the words used and the style of writing.

Tactful—It should not arouse negative emotional reactions (be offensive or demeaning).

Personal—It should focus on the individual needs of the reader.

Mechanically sound—It should not distract from the primary objective as a result of grammatical errors or inappropriate format.

Active—It should use the active voice rather than passive for emphasis.

Unified—Consistent with its variation in sentence structure, it should contain single themes in each sentence and paragraph.

Coherent—It should contain sentences and paragraphs that stick together and are not subject to multiple interpretations.

Clear—Words should be chosen carefully, topic sentences should be used at the beginning of paragraphs, and ideas should be thought through before writing starts, perhaps by outlining.

Concise—It should convey the intended meaning in the fewest possible words.

Positive—The tone of the communication should be positive rather than negative.[17]

A final point relates to jargon or technical terms. Whether a given word is jargon or not depends on the intended receiver. What is jargon to the uninformed may be effective communication to another individual in the appropriate occupational area. Technical terms are necessary to describe phenomena not otherwise describable. The problem becomes particularly acute as new entrants learn about an area, such as management. What is jargon at one point becomes effective technical communication at another, as one moves from neophyte to journeyman practitioner.

Speaking   Oral communication most frequently is ineffective because anxiety enters in and jumbles the communication process or blocks it completely. Often this occurs in public speaking in the form of stage fright, but it can occur as well in interpersonal discussions, as with a superior. One solution is to prepare well in advance so that one knows what is to be said. This may not make for entirely effective communication, but it is likely to forestall complete breakdown as a result of panic. Another consideration is to gear the presentation closely to the values, interests, and capabilities of the audience. That way it becomes possible to obtain an initial positive reaction, a major step toward achieving speaker confidence.

It is important to determine in advance whether the major objective is to inform, to persuade, or to entertain, and to act accordingly. Presentations, whether face-to-face or to large audiences, differ in these respects, and some people are better at one or another. To the extent choice is possible, it is best to focus on the particular objective among the three that one finds most comfortable. In any event the major barrier to effective speaking is interpersonal anxiety.

Listening   People seem to hear, or at least recall immediately, only about 50 percent of what they are told. Listening as a receiving process is often not very effective, and communication suffers accordingly. People may be distracted, or they may filter what is sent in terms of their needs and interests, or their emotions may blot out messages. Therefore, it is not necessarily true that the best of communications will result in complete, undistorted reception by an intended audience. Communication after all is a two-part process. The receiver simply may not listen very well.

This problem may be overcome by redundant communication—what is not heard the first time may be heard the second. It may also be overcome through a two-way process, in that questions and answers gradually elicit understanding. It may be overcome, as well, by communication training which teaches listening skills. Finally, note taking may serve to foster both listening and retention. The best solution is an individual matter.

Summary

The various organizational processes we have been considering are intimately intertwined; it is almost impossible to discuss one without invoking others. Although numerous writers do treat power, authority, bargaining, political processes and communication as distinct entities, doing so makes for an incomplete consideration. All of these processes are methods of tying an organization together and integrating it toward (or perhaps, under certain circumstances, away from) the pursuit of operative goals.

The ways in which power and authority are used are inevitably influenced by bargaining in the context of the inducements–contributions balance. Authority structures and communication structures, although not identical, typically share much common ground. Bargaining is a frequent factor in establishing structures and approaches for communication, particularly if some violation of existing legitimized practice is concerned. Thus approaches which can bypass large segments of the hierarchy, such as management information systems, are particularly likely to become enmeshed in organizational politics and bargaining.

Some of the approaches discussed are more effective than others—certain bases of power, conditions for bargaining, political tactics, communications procedures and media. Yet all of the approaches considered are part of what happens in organizations, and all are closely interrelated. This extends to coordination and control as considered in the next chapter as well. Here, too, power, authority, bargaining, political processes and communication play an important role.

What Have You Learned?

1. What approaches may be used to deal with communication overload? How effective are they?
2. Under what circumstances is it most likely that a manger will emerge as a winner from a bargaining situation? When is a deadlock likely to occur?
3. What is meant by the following:
   a. intangible issues in bargaining
   b. a wheel network
   c. referent power
   d. information
   e. mediation
4. It is often said that bureaucracies are vertical communication systems only and that they operate slowly because each step in the hierarchy must be touched. What are some approaches that negate these conclusions?

5. What is the strategic contingencies view of unit power in an organization?
6. What guidelines exist for communicating effectively in writing? Explain.
7. How are influence, power, authority and bargaining related?
8. In what ways may power be abused or mishandled in organizations? Provide examples.
9. What are organizational politics, and what are some of the common tactics used? How may the ethics of such behavior be judged?
10. Computerized management information systems have been the subject of much controversy. What advantages do they offer, and what sources of difficulty have they encountered?

How Well Can You Apply Your Knowledge?

Problem 1. Faced with the prospect that its teachers might join a union, a city school system undertakes a communication audit to determine if defects of communication structure and flow might be a contributing factor in the teachers' discontent. The audit is conducted by outside consultants who administer a survey questionnaire to a sizable sample of school system personnel and also conduct in-depth interviews with a much smaller group.

The consultants' conclusion is that the school district's communication system suffers from certain defects and blockages which might well contribute to unionization, and that these problems, if not corrected, almost certainly will impede any efforts to present the school board's position on this matter to employees. The following conclusions are derived from an analysis of the survey questionnaire responses:

1. School system personnel receive adequate information regarding individual jobs, but inadequate information regarding school board or district-level decisions in areas such as school finances, job security, policies, salaries and the like. Essentially, downward communication from the top of the school system is felt to be insufficient or ineffective.
2. While personnel perceived adequate opportunity for upward communication (complaints, requests for information, suggestions, etc.), they perceived inadequate follow-up. Essentially, upward communication channels appeared open, but downward feedback to upward-initiated communication was felt to be lacking.
3. Information sources closest (hierarchically) to employees were perceived as highly satisfactory. In contrast, upper-level information sources (School Board, District Level Administration) were perceived as highly unsatisfactory. In short, proximity affected satisfaction with known information sources.
4. Quality of information from colleagues and immediate supervisors was perceived as high in terms of timeliness, clarity, and credibility. In contrast, quality of information from top administrative levels was perceived as low, particularly in terms of its timeliness.
5. Channels of communication (written, face-to-face, telephone, closed-circuit television, etc.) were perceived as operating satisfactorily.
6. Communication relationships were perceived as satisfactory within one's immediate work environment

(high degrees of trust, openness, warmth, friendliness, candor). In contrast, personnel at district and school board levels were perceived as insincere, low in trust, and impersonal. Further, communication relationships between segments of the system (school to school) were perceived as unsatisfactory; suggesting an inadequate *horizontal* flow of information.

7. Physical constraints (room locations, employees' proximity to one another, architectural design, etc.) were not perceived as impediments to communication.

In addition the consultants reported the following based on the depth interviews:

1. Most respondents praised the superintendent's attempt to improve the communication climate of the system. (The audit itself was appreciated by interviewees for its implicit indication of concern for improvement.)

2. Interviewees were concerned about the inability of the administration to separate "politics" from effective management of the school system. References to the School Board's and Administration's "secrecy," "political expediency," and "cronieism," were frequent.

3. General consensus was that the downward communication system needs serious re-evaluation. Important information is oftimes lost, distorted, or "blocked." Distortions and blockages in information flow were perceived as intentional in the majority of instances.

4. Regarding upward information flow, interviewees were in agreement that, while the opportunity for "input" had recently increased, lack of response to such input by the Administration discouraged upward communication efforts.

5. Multi-level committees (usually formed on an "ad hoc" basis) were seen as ineffective. Interviewees felt that these are usually "window dressing" groups whose conclusions have been pre-determined or whose "charge" does not permit adequate time for data-gathering and intelligent decision-making.

6. Horizontal communication was perceived as inadequate. Insufficient lead notice of committee meetings and physical distance between parties were viewed as major obstacles to effective horizontal irelationships.[18]

Questions

1. If you were the superintendent of this school system, what steps would you take to improve communications based on the consultants' con-

clusions? What specific approaches would you introduce, and how would you introduce them?

2. How do your recommendations relate to the specific problems identified by the consultants? What particular problem is each recommendation intended to overcome?

Problem 2. The dean of arts and sciences at a large state university has been notified of his probable selection to serve as the new vice-president for academic affairs. The promotion has cleared the university itself but must be acted upon by the Board of Regents for the university system as a whole. Normally approval at this level is automatic, but it can take some time. In the meantime the dean wants to take steps to name his own successor, since that person would be reporting directly to him in his new position. The problem is that the successor will be picked by a search committee composed of faculty and administrators, and he is not at all sure he can control the actions of that committee. It seems almost certain that the successful candidate will come from inside the university, since a number of strong candidates are available.

Among these candidates is one whom the dean favors; in fact, this is the person he strongly prefers for the job. As a strategy to achieve his ends, the dean decides to utilize the upcoming round of performance evaluations. All the candidates are department heads, and he will be evaluating all of them. His idea is to evaluate his preferred candidate very positively, the other candidates negatively, and to put these evaluations in the respective personnel files. The forms will be presented to the dean search committee at the appropriate time. Since the department heads have to sign their evaluations, there is an implication that they accept what is said there. Some of them might even decide not to let themselves be considered for the deanship for fear the negative evaluations will come out.

The strategy goes very well through the preferred candidate and most of the others. Everyone signs the evaluation form as originally presented, although there are some very unhappy people. Only the discussion with the chemistry department chairperson remains, and that is where the trouble starts. The woman simply will not sign the form. She contends that charges such as that she spends too much time in the research laboratory rather than in the departmental office, is not available to students, does not get needed papers in on time, and the like simply are not true. The dean agrees to revise the evaluation to make it more palatable, and they will meet again.

This second round goes no better; in fact, it is worse. The evaluation remains quite negative, although somewhat toned down. The department chairperson says she has been talking with some of the other people, and there is a strong feeling that the performance evaluation process is being misused. They have seriously considered going up to see the university's president about the matter; that could very well still happen. The dean agrees to make another try at drafting an acceptable evaluation document.

The next meeting produces a new problem. After looking over the revised performance statement, which again has shifted to a slightly less negative view, the department chairperson produces a formal letter requesting that the whole matter be placed before the Committee on Faculty Evaluation, Compensation, and Tenure for a public hearing. She indicates that if this appeal fails she might very well have to take the whole matter to the courts for resolution. In any event under existing regulations the dean is required to put her case in the hands of the committee within 48 hours—unless they can come to a mutual agreement on the performance evaluation document, in which case she will withdraw the appeal. Given the fact that the dean's promotion itself is not yet final, this turn of events has him a little worried.

Questions

1. Which among the concepts and processes discussed in this chapter are represented in this situation? Provide specific examples from the case.
2. If you were the dean, how would you handle the situation? Why?

Additional Sources for More Detailed Study

Athos, Anthony G., and Gabarro, John J. *Interpersonal Behavior: Communication and Understanding in Relationships.* Englewood Cliffs, N.J.: Prentice-Hall, 1978.

Bacharach, Samuel B., and Lawler, Edward J. *Power and Politics in Organizations.* San Francisco: Jossey-Bass, 1980.

Baskin, Otis W., and Aronoff, Craig E. *Interpersonal Communication in Organizations.* Santa Monica: Goodyear, 1980.

Hatch, Richard. *Business Communication: Theory and Technique.* Chicago: Science Research Associates, 1983.

Huber, George. "Organizational Information Systems: Determinants of Their Performance and Behavior." *Management Science* (February 1982).

Jay, Antony. *Management and Machiavelli: An Inquiry into the Politics of Corporate Life.* New York: Bantam Books, 1974.

MacMillan, Ian C. *Strategy Formulation: Political Concepts.* St. Paul: West, 1978.

Miles, Robert H. *Macro Organizational Behavior.* Santa Monica: Goodyear, 1980.

Mintzberg, Henry. *Power In and Around Organizations.* Englewood Cliffs, N.J.: Prentice-Hall, 1983.

Phillips, Gerald M. *Communicating in Organizations.* New York: Macmillan, 1982.

Pruitt, Dean G. *Negotiation Behavior.* New York: Academic Press, 1981.

Sprowls, R. C. *Management Data Bases.* Santa Barbara: Wiley/Hamilton, 1976.

Strauss, Anselm. *Negotiations: Varieties, Contexts, Processes, and the Social Order.* San Francisco: Jossey-Bass, 1978.

Timm, Paul R. *Managerial Communication—A Finger on the Pulse.* Englewood Cliffs, N.J.: Prentice-Hall, 1980.

Walton, Richard E., and McKersie, Robert W. *A Behavioral Theory of Labor Negotiations.* New York: McGraw-Hill, 1965.

Zaleznik, Abraham, and Kets de Vries, Manfred F. R. *Power and the Corporate Mind.* Boston: Houghton Mifflin, 1975.

The following books should prove particularly useful for the *practical* guidelines they contain on how to practice organizational politics:

Buskirk, Richard H. *Handbook of Managerial Tactics.* Boston: Cahners, 1976.

Cox, Allan. *The Cox Report on the American Corporation.* New York: Delacorte Press, 1982.

Kennedy, Marilyn M. *Office Politics: Seizing Power, Wielding Clout.* Chicago: Follett, 1980.

Kotter, John P. *Power in Management.* New York: AMACOM, 1979.

Notes

1. Herbert Kaufman, *Administrative Feedback: Monitoring Subordinates' Behavior* (Washington, D.C.: Brookings Institution, 1973).
2. Stanley Milgram, *Obedience to Authority* (New York: Harper and Row, 1974), p. 5.
3. C. R. Hinings et al., "Structural Conditions of Intraorganizational Power," *Administrative Science Quarterly* (March 1974), Carol S. Saunders and Richard Scamell, "Intraorganizational Distributions of Power: Replication Research," *Academy of Management Journal* (March 1982).
4. Jeffrey Pfeffer, *Power in Organizations* (Boston: Pitman, 1981).
5. W. Clay Hamner, "The Influence of Structural, Individual, and Strategic Differences," in *Bargaining and Behavior: An International Study,* ed. Donald L. Harnett and Larry L. Cummings (Houston: Dame, 1980), pp. 21–80; Fred C. Ikle, "Bargaining and Communication," in *Handbook of Communication,* Ithiel des. Pool and William Schramm (Chicago: Rand McNally, 1973), pp. 836–43.
6. Jeffrey Z. Rubin and Bert R. Brown, *The Social Psychology of Bargaining and Negotiation* (New York: Academic Press, 1975), p. 18.
7. David W. Grigsby and William J. Bigoness, "Effects of Mediation and Alternative Forms of Arbitration on Bargaining Behavior: A Laboratory Study," *Journal of Applied Psychology* (October 1982).
8. Jeffrey Gandz and Victor V. Murray, "The Experience of Workplace Politics," *Academy of Management Journal* (June 1980).
9. V. K. Narayanan and Liam Fahey, "The Micro-Politics of Strategy Formulations," *Academy of Management Review* (January 1982).
10. Manual Velasquez, Dennis J. Moberg, and Gerald F. Cavanagh, "Organizational Statesmanship and Dirty Politics: Ethical Guidelines for the Organizational Politician," *Organizational Dynamics* (Autumn 1983).
11. Monroe M. Bird, "Gains and Losses from an Open Line Program as Perceived by By-passed Managers: A Case Study," *Academy of Management Journal (June 1973).*
12. Lyman W. Porter and Karlene H. Roberts, "Communication in Organizations," in *Handbook of Industrial and Organizational Psychology,* ed. Marvin D. Dunnette (Chicago: Rand McNally, 1976), pp. 1553–89.
13. Ronald J. Ebert and Terence R. Mitchell, *Organizational Decision Processes: Concepts and Analysis* (New York: Crane, Russak, 1975).
14. See Rexford Hersey, "The Grapevine . . . Here to Stay But Not Beyond Control," *Personnel* (January 1966); John W. Newstom, Robert M. Moncza, and William E. Reif, "Perceptions of the Grapevine: Its Value and Influence," *Journal of Business Communication* (Spring 1974).
15. Paul H. Cheney and Gary W. Dickson, "Organizational Characteristics and Information Systems: An Exploratory Investigation," *Academy of Management Journal* (March 1982).
16. William R. Morrow and Geula Lowenberg, "Evaluation of Business Memos: Effects of Writer Sex and Organizational Position, Memo Quality, and Rater Sex," *Personnel Psychology* (Spring 1983).
17. Richard C. Huseman, James M. Laiff, and John D. Hatfield, *Business Communication: Strategies and Skills* (Hinsdale, Ill.: Dryden, 1981).
18. Gary M. Richetto and Harry S. Dennis, "A Communication Audit of a Public School System," *Academy of Management Proceedings* (1976): 423–24.

CHAPTER 8

Coordinating and Controlling Organizational Components

CHAPTER OUTLINE

Conflict and Coordination
Nature and Sources of Conflict
    Conflict in Cleveland City Government
    Conflict and Performance
    Intergroup Conflict
    Conflict at the Boundaries
Achieving Coordination
    Coordination by Hierarchy
    Horizontal Integration
    Using Role Prescriptions
    Appeal to Superordinate Goals
    Rational Confrontation
    Improved Communication
Guidelines for Coordinating

Organizational Control
Aspects of Control Systems
    Standards
    Measures
    Corrective Actions
Conducting Audits
Major Types of Accounting Control Systems
    Budgets
    Responsibility Accounting
    Standard Cost Systems
Human Asset Accounting
Effectiveness of Organizational Control
    Controls and Company Success
    Dysfunctions of Control Systems
    Views of Good and Poor Control

OBJECTIVES

To provide information on the value and use of various approaches to coordination in organizations.

To describe different types of organizational control systems with emphasis on positive features and potential problems.

O rganizations by their very nature must split up the work to be done and allocate it to smaller, more specialized components. The components are to some degree arranged along a vertical dimension, ranging from the board of directors, the executive committee, and the top management team at one end to shop-floor production units and sales districts at the other. They are also differentiated horizontally. There may be a large number of shop-floor production units, some of which do the same things while others have different tasks. Sales districts may well be spread all over the country, with each one doing essentially the same things as the others but in a different geographical location.

For the organization to function effectively, all these small components have to be orchestrated and integrated so that they work together toward the achievement of operative goals. They cannot be going off at cross-purposes, and one unit cannot be allowed to use up the organization's resources so that insufficient resources remain for other units to operate effectively. The processes by which the needed integration of components is achieved are referred to as coordinating and controlling; we consider both in this chapter.

CONFLICT AND COORDINATION

Coordination involves adjusting the relations among individuals and groups so that frictions do not develop that might undermine organizational effectiveness. These frictions may be associated with overt, conscious conflict and controversy, where the parties view each other as the enemy. Coordination also comes into play when the parties perform work which by its nature is interdependent (as when production units must adjust output to sales performance), and integration of effort must be achieved. In instances of the latter type there may be friction in the system, but it may not be caused by intentional conflict.

Coordination can well require that a manager use power and authority. It may be achieved by bargaining between the parties. It typically involves both vertical and horizontal communication. Thus, coordination is an organizational process that builds upon the various processes considered in chapter 7.

Nature and Sources of Conflict

Conflict within an organization frequently brings forth the need for coordination. Which approach to coordination should be taken often is determined by the nature and source of the conflict. Accordingly it is important to start with a consideration of conflict itself. The following example provides a demonstration both of what conflict looks like and of its consequences.

Conflict in Cleveland City Government

On December 15, 1978, the City of Cleveland defaulted on payment of $15.5 million in short-term notes held by six local banks. The city thus achieved the dubious distinction of being the first major American city to default on its notes since the Depression, though others—notably New York— had only missed that title by a whisker. Observers suggested that the consequences of Cleveland's default might include state control over the city's finances, seriously restricted access to municipal bond markets (at a time when the city was in dire need of capital for rebuilding its deteriorating physical plants), layoffs of public employees and reductions of already inadequate municipal services, and wholesale exodus of the city's remaining business and industrial firms. Default was not seen as a desirable event by anyone.

Cleveland's financial crisis sprang from many sources. Long-term out-migration of upper- and middle-income families left a central city populated by poor ethnic whites on the West Side and poor blacks on the East Side. Deteriorating city services, strong unions, and obsolete technical installations encouraged business and industry departures that further eroded the city's tax base. Voter resistance to income tax increases led to discrepancies between tax revenues and the city's operating expenses. To cover operating costs, city administrations surreptitiously dipped into capital improvement funds to meet current expenses. Shortly before the crisis, the incumbent Administration revealed that the capital investment funds were short $40 million because of these invasions.

In the shorter term, the city's gloomy financial picture was complicated by several other factors. The incumbent Administration had negotiated a settlement with public employee unions characterized by some City Councilmen as a "budget-buster." The city's Municipal Light Plant could not compete with private suppliers of power, and required heavy subsidies from the city. Opinions differed as to the potential future profitability of the Plant, but the Mayor had taken a strong stand against an agreement to sell the Plant negotiated by his predecessor.

The Mayor had been a City Councilman from a white ethnic ward, and he challenged "Big Business" interests vociferously in his campaign. He campaigned vigorously against tax increases and the sale of the Municipal Light Plant, a transaction he described as a deal to benefit business interests at the expense of the poor. The Mayor's staff and close associates were on the whole young and inexperienced in municipal management.

The Cleveland City Council was roughly half black and half white. The President of the Council was a black councilman who had opposed the new Mayor on a variety of issues for years. The Council President favored the sale of the Municipal Light Plant.

Publicity about the missing capital improvement funds and charges of financial mismanagement at City Hall contributed to lowered ratings of the city's bonds on national markets. The six local banks holding the city's notes informed the Administration that they could not responsibly renew the city's notes without evidence of improved financial control over the city's funds.

Several days before the notes were due, the Mayor made a dramatic televised appeal for a tax increase (whose burden, he argued, would be largely borne by Big Business and suburban residents) and for retention of the Municipal Light Plant. The banks avoided public reference to the Plant, but some observers suggested that "fiscal responsibility" required its sale. Conferences between the Mayor, the Council President, and bank representatives were spotlighted by intense media interest as the deadline drew nigh. Credible response to the banks required agreement by both Mayor and Council. A few hours before midnight the Council President pushed a resolution through the Council supporting a tax increase referendum *and* the sale of the Light Plant. The Mayor rejected the resolution. A counter-resolution for the tax referendum without selling the Light Plant was killed in the Council shortly before midnight. The Council adjourned at midnight. Cleveland was in default.[1]

It is apparent that the conflicts here are intense—between the labor unions and city management, between the Mayor's office and the City Council, and probably between other groups as well. It is also apparent that conflict can lead to deadlock, where everybody loses.

Conflict and Performance Conflict typically yields negative consequences within an organization in part because it deflects energy away from performance. This is obvious with regard to labor–management conflict that results in slowdowns or strikes, but it is equally true of other types of conflict. All aspects of performance can be affected. As people focus on an internal conflict and neglect their work, quality and quantity suffer. The situation may become so unpleasant that absenteeism increases, and turnover can well be an eventual outcome. As the parties become increasingly involved, each causes the other to devote less time and effort to the work. At high levels within an organization dissension can become so acute that a company dissolves into pieces. This appears to occur frequently in professional organizations such as consulting and law firms; partners finally leave to form their own organizations. Similar high levels of conflict at top levels plagued Chrysler Corporation for many years and nearly brought it to bankruptcy.

As indicated in the case of the city of Cleveland, conflict can also affect performance and the effectiveness of an organization by producing deadlocks, so that nothing is done even though it is apparent to all involved that something needs to be done. Under such circumstances the fate of the organization often is no longer in its own hands, and external forces take control. The banks in the case of Cleveland government provide an example.

Finally, conflict can introduce a degree of uncertainty into a situation to the point where no one is sure what will happen next. Under such conditions decisions become problematic at best and may well turn out to be completely wrong. Individual and organizational performance can suffer accordingly.

Although conflict itself is most likely to have negative consequences, it is important to understand that it can be closely tied to other organizational processes which yield positive outcomes. Competition, for instance, can be a strong positive motivational force among managers in bureaucratic systems, and if it operates much like a race there is no conflict. But the temptation to trip a fellow manager while playing the game of organizational politics can become overpowering, and then figuratively, if not factually, a fight is likely to break out. Similarly, creative accomplishment, organizational innovation, the addition of women and minorities to a previously white male employment context (in fact, any bringing together of people from diverse backgrounds or origins) can well carry along with them a tendency toward conflict. In such instances the conflict may detract from the otherwise positive effects. Here the essential skill of coordination is to defuse the conflict without "throwing the baby out with the bath." If one makes the mistake, as some have, of confusing the organizational good with its byproduct, then it is possible to conclude that conflict itself is desirable. Doing this makes it very difficult to achieve coordination.

Intergroup Conflict Conflict is particularly likely to occur in a number of circumstances. These are by no means mutually exclusive. In fact, it is characteristic for two or more factors to operate simultaneously. Typically the result is that groups, units, or large components of the company and the managers who head them come into conflict with each other. Some of the conditions are as follows:

1. The presence of individuals who are particularly prone to the expression of aggression or who because of their nonconformity, creativity, and the like tend to elicit aggression in others
2. The presence of individuals who are experiencing major dissatisfactions with aspects of their roles in the organization
3. Interdependence between the work of individuals and groups requiring that *decisions be made jointly*. Examples are two units using a common service unit, such as a maintenance department, or one production unit dependent on another unit for its input, creating a need for mutual decisions on scheduling.
4. Sharp competition between groups having *differing objectives or goals*
5. Individuals and groups possessing *differing perceptions* regarding aspects of the work situation, especially if these perceptions are rooted in strongly held values
6. Considerable loose-lying power with the result that authority allocations are not well established and there is considerable ambiguity regarding roles

Thus, individuals who frequently are surrounded by controversy tend to acquire constituencies, either along formal organizational lines or in terms of informal networks of individuals, who are of like mind. Dissatisfaction, if it spreads, has often been the basis for unionization or for more militant labor–management relations when a union is already on the scene. In joint decision-making situations, the conflicts are almost invariably between units and their managers. Under such circumstances there is a tendency for the parties to overstate needs for resources and to create something of a crisis atmosphere surrounding the decision process. Not unexpectedly the result is that a smoldering fire breaks into open flame.

When one unit consistently dominates another so that its viewpoint prevails even in the face of rational arguments to the contrary, conflict tends to be continually fanned. This situation has often been a source of difficulties between line and staff components. It is not unknown, for instance, for manufacturing managers to reject highly qualified candidates for employment recommended by personnel, simply to establish dominance over the decision processes involved. That emotions may run high at such times is not very surprising. However, where power differentials are legitimized and accepted, this type of conflict need not arise; manufacturing, for instance, would have no need to dramatize its dominance.

Research has revealed a number of patterns of behavior related to intergroup competition.[2] Within the competing groups, one finds:

Members tend to compete with each other less, becoming more loyal to the group and more responsive to group norms.

A greater degree of formality and structure emerges, coupled with more acceptance of leader dominance and a greater emphasis on task accomplishment.

Individuals tend to become submerged in the group.

Between the groups there is:

A marked tendency to view members of the other group as enemies, with the result that communication between groups declines.

Perceptual distortions appear which exaggerate and perpetuate conflict.

Groups overevaluate their own contributions and products and view their own solutions to problems as better.

The same type of stereotyping serves to downplay the efforts of the competing group.

The importance of perceptual factors may be illustrated by a situation in which managers from different departments were to propose solutions to the same case.[3] The sales managers almost invariably emphasized sales problems and solutions. Faced with the same situation, production managers stressed the need to clarify organizational structures, and personnel managers saw the problem as essentially of a human relations nature. Exhibit 8.1 diagrams how conditions 3, 4, and 5 may serve to produce conflict.

Conflict at the Boundaries   The phenomena of loose-lying power and ambiguity of roles frequently are found in professional organizations. Within companies they often occur in boundary positions requiring interactions with clients, customers, suppliers, government personnel, bankers, and the like. Be-

EXHIBIT 8.1   Flow of factors in intergroup conflict

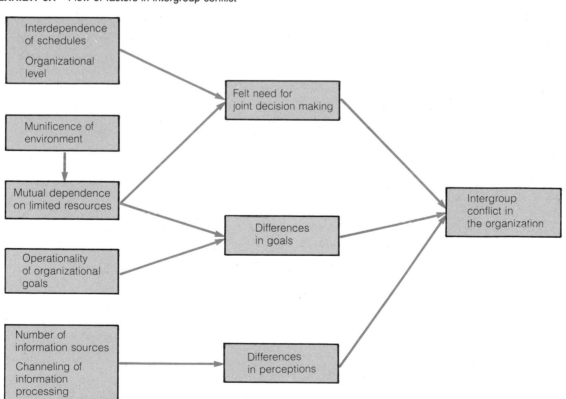

Adapted from James G. March and Herbert A. Simon. *Organizations* (New York: Wiley, 1958), p. 128.

cause it is usually not predictable what these outsiders will do and the company has little control over them, it is difficult to establish definite role requirements for those who deal with them. Often quite different perceptions of relative power and authority arise out of the prevailing uncertainty, as between those in the boundary positions and others in the company. Conflicts often result as struggles for loose-lying power break out. Thus, sales and production may struggle to gain power over questions of product design and purchasing and engineering over decisions on equipment specifications.

Achieving Coordination

To a very large extent coordination is concerned with preventing conflicts and other frictions among the parts of an organization before they occur. Bargaining can be an important means of coordination, as we have seen in chapter 7. Probably its contribution is much greater than is usually recognized since so much bargaining within hierarchical systems is implicit rather than explicit. Yet there are numerous other coordination approaches as well.

Coordination by Hierarchy   In bureaucracies, the traditional approach to coordination has been that the lowest level common superior to the parties in conflict brings about a resolution through the use of authority, or an indication that authority might be invoked. In the former instance the higher-level manager acts as an arbitrator or judge. In the latter case there is some mediation involved, but with the implication that if mediation does not work the next step will be compulsory. Many chief executive officers spend much of their time in this sort of coordination. Formal grievance and appeal systems of a quasi-judicial nature also represent a type of coordination by the direct use of hierarchy.

A somewhat different type of hierarchical coordination is achieved by bringing sanctions to bear against the fact of conflict itself. Here the superior manager does not resolve the conflict so much as indicate that if it is not resolved directly by those involved they will suffer in some manner, or alternatively, that if it is resolved they will gain. Approaches of this kind often are used as preventatives to conflict with the result that open manifestations are suppressed. Unfortunately the use of hierarchy to make conflict itself undesirable, irrespective of cause, may serve only to drive the whole process underground. It may also entirely negate any positive features, such as creative ideas, with which conflict is associated.

Horizontal Integration   Another structure-based approach is to set up some mechanism for tying together and thus coordinating units at essentially the same level. A product manager may coordinate a given product all the way from research and development through manufacturing to marketing. Or coordinating committees made up of members from all units involved may serve the same purpose. Sometimes in the so-called matrix structure, people from the different functional areas (R&D, production, marketing) actually are assigned to a unified project structure, while at the same time retaining their functional assignments as well. Thus coordination is achieved by placing an overlay across the organization. Another approach—one that is most useful when conflict has actually broken out between interdependent units that must engage in joint decision making—is to interpose a unit between the two and require all communications to flow through this liaison unit. Thus friction is buffered and conflict defused.

These various approaches serve to tie units of the organization together and thus integrate them into the larger whole. Communication is facilitated. That this kind of integration can make a difference in company effectiveness is apparent from the first and second columns of Exhibit 8.2.

Using Role Prescriptions If clear and specific role prescriptions are established in company policies, organization structures, and job descriptions at an early point, so that everyone knows who has jurisdiction over what, this can serve to head off future conflicts. Later, should conflict become likely, it is possible to appeal to these role prescriptions, which were previously accepted by all and before emotions began to heat up, as a basis for resolution. In many instances variants of this approach can even be used·to advantage in dealing with loose-lying power at organizational boundaries. Planning, rules, routines, and scheduling all are methods of establishing role prescriptions in this manner.

Role prescriptions reduce the need for joint decision making, since they establish which unit is to handle a particular question and thus make units more independent of one another.[4] Thus, if the industrial relations department has been given major responsibility for handling union negotiations, a later claim by another department in the heat of bargaining over a new contract—that it should exert primary influence on matters affecting its interests—can be handled as a repudiation of prior commitments and established procedures.

Appeal to Superordinate Goals The risks in the approaches to coordination we have been considering are that unless one is very careful, conflict will merely be suppressed to erupt again in another context, and important, innovative ideas may be suppressed along with the conflict. This is less likely if an overarching goal can be identified that will pull conflicting groups together to achieve a course of action in the best interest of the whole. Superordinate goals can serve to coordinate groups very effectively, provided it is possible to

EXHIBIT 8.2 Overall effectiveness related to use of integrating methods and of rational confrontation in six plastics firms

	Rank Order of Effectiveness	Rank Order of Integration	Rank Order of Use of Confrontation	
Firm A	1	2	1	**High**
Firm B	2	1	2	↑
Firm C	3	3	3	
Firm D	4	4	4	↓
Firm E	5	6	5	
Firm F	6	5	6	**Low**

Adapted from Paul R. Lawrence and Jay W. Lorsch, *Organization and Environment: Managing Differentiation and Integration* (Boston: Graduate School of Business Administration, Harvard University, 1967), pp. 40, 77.

get all parties to accept them.[5] An example would be where a company's market share for a given product is being badly eroded by aggressive competition from foreign firms. It might be possible here to persuade previously warring factions within the company to "bury the hatchet" in order to combine their energies in a major cost-cutting effort aimed at driving out the common adversary. The superordinate goal is to drive the "outsiders" from the company's market, through more competitive pricing policies.

Rational Confrontation   Confrontation operates in clear distinction from coordination by hierarchy. In the latter instance, conflicts tend to be smoothed over and thus suppressed, or there is a forced resolution from the top downward. In confrontation, differences are aired openly and the parties discuss them. Steps are taken, often through the use of an outside consultant, to mediate the conflict and prevent communication breakdown as well as excessive nonrational emotionality. Varying objectives, values, and perceptions are brought out so that they may be recognized and dealt with. The prevailing climate is one of open discussion and rational argument. To the extent this kind of climate exists in an organization, and rational confrontation is widely used, companies are very likely to be effective, as the third column in Exhibit 8.2 shows. Yet it may not be easy to create a climate in which confrontation approaches to coordination will thrive. When they do thrive, however, joint decision making really does work and problem solving is very likely.

Improved Communication   Confrontation and other coordination procedures bring about increased communication in relevant channels. Although communication per se does not guarantee that effective coordination will result, it does permit valid information to flow and incorrect perceptions to be altered. Legitimized management information systems can be an important factor in this process.

Another role that communication can play is to make the consequences of decisions more visible to everyone. With this type of information available, cost-benefit relationships can be identified. It becomes impossible to hide the fact if a given action does not contribute to attainment of organizational goals. Visibility of consequences through improved, open communication takes decisions out of an environment of conflict and intangible issues and places them in a rational, problem-solving context. Research evidence suggests that improved organizational effectiveness results.[6]

Along with bargaining and the use of power and authority, communication is a very important factor in coordination and conflict resolution.

Guidelines for Coordinating

When conflict becomes very intense and steps have not been taken to deal with it, bureaucratic systems tend to mobilize coordination by hierarchy. For instance, when "Bunkie" Knudsen was brought in from General Motors to head up Ford operations, an increasing escalation of conflict occurred partly as a consequence of individual personalities and partly on political grounds. The conflict became so intense that Henry Ford was forced to use his authority to resolve it. The consequence was that Knudsen left the company. In other instances persuasion, rather than direct authority, has been used, usually with reference to superordinate goals.

Coordinating and Controlling Organizational Components

EXHIBIT 8.3 Types of interdependence among the units of an organization

Pooled interdependence—Each unit makes a separate contribution to the total organization and is in turn supported by the organization as a whole.

Example: "The Tuscaloosa branch of an organization may not interact at all with the Oshkosh branch, and neither may have contact with the Kokomo branch. Yet they may be interdependent in the sense that unless each performs adequately the total organization is jeopardized."

Appropriate method of coordination: Standardization through the establishment of *rules* and *routines*

Sequential interdependence—One unit must act before another unit can act.

Example: "The Keokuk plant producing parts which become inputs for the Tucumcari assembly operation . . . Keokuk must act properly before Tucumcari can act; and unless Tucumcari acts, Keokuk cannot solve its output problem."

Appropriate method of coordination: Planning and scheduling

Reciprocal interdependence—The relationship between units runs both ways, so that the outputs of each unit are inputs to the other.

Example: "The airline which contains both operations and maintenance units. The production of the maintenance unit is an input for operations, in the form of serviceable aircraft; and the product (or byproduct) of operations is an input for maintenance, in the form of an aircraft needing maintenance."

Appropriate method of coordination: Mutual adjustment and *feedback,* often involving horizontal *information flow* and *bargaining*

Based on James D. Thompson, *Organizations in Action* (New York: McGraw-Hill, 1967), pp. 54–56.

However, these types of authority are more approaches of last resort than ideals. In general the more programmed approaches to coordination—rules, schedules, predetermined uses of authority—work well when conflict and uncertainty are relatively low. When uncertainty and conflict are higher, the best methods of coordination usually involve mutual adjustments and autonomous actions by the units involved—in short, freedom to bargain and confront.[7]

Another view of the appropriate strategies for coordinating is given in Exhibit 8.3. Here the best approach to coordination depends on how the units relate to each other—on the mandates embedded in the basic technology itself. If the work is split up in separate segments, as with geographically organized sales districts, rules and routines serve to coordinate the contributions of each component to the whole. If the work is split up on a sequential basis, as for instance where manufacturing must produce a product before marketing can sell it, coordination should be by planning and scheduling, so that neither too much nor too little product is available relative to market demand. Finally, if the work is split up to require interactions flowing both ways, as when maintenance keeps the machines running and broken machines keep maintenance running, there should be mutual adjustment involving full communication and bargaining.

Other guidelines beyond those considered might be noted.[8] However, those indicated appear to have the most secure grounding in research.

Organizational control involves the same processes as the control of individual performance considered in chapter 4. In broad outline the model of Exhibit 4.10 is appropriate. But with organizational control it is the performance of units and major components of the organization that is important, not just the performance of individuals. Furthermore, the planning function that initiates the control process covers a much broader range of activities than organization structuring and establishing position requirements that govern at the level of individual performance control. Exhibit 8.4 points up these differences.

Aspects of Control Systems

Organizational control systems vary in the types of standards established to define contributions to organizational goals, the measures used to obtain evaluations, and the corrective actions taken. In particular, corrective actions vary in the extent to which they are based on an open-loop concept.

EXHIBIT 8.4   An organizational open-loop control model

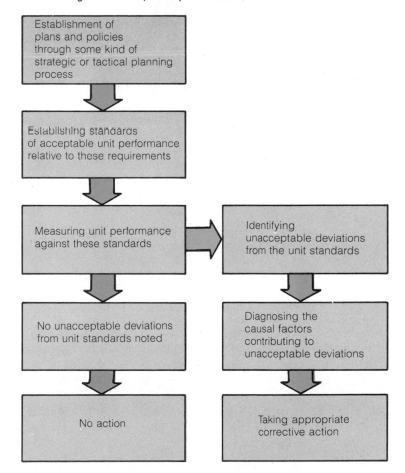

Standards Chapter 4 considers unidirectional controls in that only a minimum standard is used. It is also possible to have bidirectional controls, however, which set both a minimum and maximum. Inventory controls are typically of this kind, and so too are some product quality standards. In the latter case too low a quality might make the product unsaleable, but too high quality might drive costs well beyond the point where they could be recovered in a competitive market.

It is also possible to use complex multidirectional controls that combine a number of variables and set standards for each. These and variance controls are most common in manufacturing. In variance control, statistical sampling techniques are used; standards are considered exceeded not in each instance of unacceptable variation, but when the total pattern of results varies from expectations based on past performance consistently enough to reject chance fluctuation as an explanation. Such a departure from statistical standards might arise because of some defect that has cropped up in the training of new employees, or because of a failure to program a new computerized inventory system correctly.

Measures Control measures are often of a monetary nature such as budgets and the various financial ratios, but they can be of almost any kind. Generally there is a preference for objective, numerical measures because they are more difficult to argue with and to falsify. But it is not always true that numerical measures cover all the factors that need to be covered if the control system is to be comprehensive. Thus a department store may utilize numerical measures that get at sales volume and mark-up but fail to measure customer goodwill, because it is difficult to quantify. Yet leaving customer goodwill out of the control system can shift the behavior of sales personnel to emphasize approaches that are not in fact what the company's top management desires. Usually a balanced control system will need to incorporate a variety of types of measures, some of which are quite subjective and utilize numbers only in a rather arbitrary sense.

However, control measures may proliferate to the point where the organizational control process is more costly than the results it can possibly yield. Developing measures and using them constantly to obtain control information can become a very expensive process in and of itself. For this reason it is essential that measures be designed to get at organizationally important factors only. Controlling things that matter very little may keep controllers busy, but it can have many other negative consequences.

Corrective Actions The typical approach used when standards are exceeded is to bring authority to bear, usually in a punitive sense. Those who overspend their budgets, fail to meet profit goals, or do not maintain adequate inventory are penalized in some manner—often through withholding of bonus payments, sometimes through managerial transfer or separation. Where punitive action is inevitable the control system is more closed loop than open loop. Yet it is entirely possible to employ open-loop concepts which involve a diagnosis of why the failure to meet standards occurred and then the application of an appropriate corrective action. In such cases a variety of corrective actions may be applied to both organizational units and their managers.

The basic control model assumes an ongoing process of information collection. In contrast, audits utilize data for an extended period but are themselves conducted in a relatively brief interval. Usually we think of financial audits carried out by a unit within the company or by an accounting firm. But there are many other types of audits—to determine the effectiveness of communication flows, the quality of management, the usefulness of personnel systems, the nature of company social responsibility, and so on. Such audits may be carried out on a one-time, troubleshooting basis or at regular intervals. They may focus on results obtained or on the extent to which established procedures are followed.

Audits are important, in part because legislation requires them. They represent an investigative, analytic, comparative process that can be applied to any activity that is important for company success. Yet audits are not always an effective method of control. For one thing they tend to elicit considerable defensiveness and efforts to conceal information, especially in the face of excessive auditing. Perhaps more important is the fact that the long-time intervals between audits permit considerable error to spread out over extended periods. Continuous control systems tend not only to be more effective contributors to goal attainment but also to achieve greater acceptance.

Historically, accounting control systems have been the primary methods of control used in organizations. They deal with measuring, processing, and reporting information that can be expressed in monetary terms, although recently there has been some resort to quantitative approaches of other types also. Accounting controls generally fall into three categories: budgets, responsibility systems, and systems based on standard costs.

Budgets Budgets derive from organizational goals and plans to achieve them. The system as a whole includes the process of establishing numbers for revenues, expenses, profits, or whatever is being budgeted and a set of reports used to indicate whether standards are being met. The numbers and standards may be developed either with considerable participation on the part of those who will be affected by the budget or unilaterally by someone with this authority. Budgets typically include a time span of application, often one year.

Fixed budgets are based on a single set of assumptions. Thus, a sales forecast which is considered to be the best available would underlie a manufacturing budget. Alternatively, budgets may be flexible or contingent with different values and standards attached to different levels of anticipated sales. The version used then depends on how sales actually develop.

Responsibility Accounting Under responsibility systems, units and their managers are assigned responsibility for certain financial activities, performance is measured, and the results are fed back to those responsible and their superiors. The extent of the responsibility depends on the types of financial activities that are subject to influence. Three alternatives may be defined:

1. Investment center—An organizational unit in which those responsible have control (that is, authority to make decisions) over revenues, costs, and capital investment. For example, the General Electric Corporation as a whole may be viewed as an investment center, but some of its divisions may not, since they do not have authority over capital expenditures (investment).

2. Profit center—An organizational unit that has control over both revenues and expenses but not investment. For example, the Chevrolet Division of General Motors could be termed a profit center (but not an investment center) if it controls revenues and expenses but not capital investment.
3. Cost center—An organizational unit that has control over costs but not revenues or expenses. Thus, a plant manufacturing products based on orders from an independent sales unit is a cost center; it controls its manufacturing costs but not revenues.[9]

Standard Cost Systems A standard cost is an indication of what something ought to cost under certain specified conditions. These costs are usually established based on engineering or accounting analyses and calculations; rarely do those who will be controlled by them participate in the process. Control systems of this kind involve determining the standard costs, using these costs as standards, measuring actual cost performance, and comparing actual with standard costs. Variations from standard then become the basis for corrective action. Standard costs may be developed for extended operations involving large numbers of people.

Human Asset Accounting

Accounting systems traditionally have limited their treatment of assets to those of a physical and financial nature. Human assets of the kind noted in Exhibit 8.5 usually are handled as operating expenses and are not included in the capital budget. This is a good example of the type of misdirection of effort and deflection from goals that control systems can produce when they focus on easily measured factors. It is relatively easy to quantify physical and financial assets. In contrast human assets have proved much more resistant to measurement, although some useful approaches have been developed. The result is that firms are likely to squander human assets. The control system encourages managers to emphasize physical and financial factors and to give only very limited attention to human factors. As a result talented employees with needed skills may be permitted to

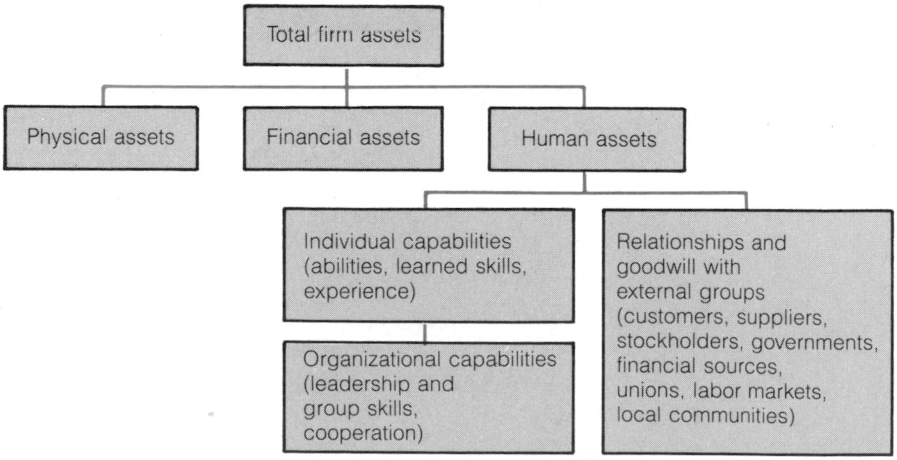

EXHIBIT 8.5 Relation of human assets to total firm assets

leave the company when profits are down simply to recover their high salaries. That long-term assets are thus being liquidated is not reflected anywhere in the accounting control system.

This problem was recognized at an early point by Rensis Likert and those who worked with him.[10] Various approaches to human asset accounting were proposed in conjunction with the development of system 4 (see chapter 6). Likert was particularly concerned that authoritarian management, as in system 1, would produce short-term results in terms of improved productive output, but would generate so much negative feeling that good employees would either leave eventually or fail to invest much effort in their work; either way, productivity would suffer in the long run. Control systems that incorporate a valuation of human assets are seen as a way of preventing this and helping to move companies toward the group-based system 4.

Effectiveness of Organizational Control

Does the widespread utilization of organizational control systems contribute to more effective organizational functioning? To answer this question it is necessary to look first at some research which relates the presence of controls to profits and growth, and then to consider some data on possible dysfunctions of organizational control.

Controls and Company Success Although research relating aspects of the control process to company success is not extensive, it is sufficient to reach some conclusions.[11] It appears that higher profits do not necessarily result from having a large number of control systems such as the following:

1. Statistical quality control of production
2. Standard costs and cost variance analysis
3. Flexible budgets
4. Evaluating investments on the basis of internal rate of return or present value
5. Inventory control and production scheduling by using operations research techniques
6. Marginal costing for pricing decisions and decisions whether to make or buy components
7. Internal auditing
8. Performance audits by outside auditors
9. Systematic performance appraisal

However, controls of these kinds are more characteristic in companies that have grown to large size.

If one takes into account the qualifications of those who install and operate these kinds of control systems and how well the controls are working, the picture is much more favorable. Well-designed control systems can represent a positive factor in company operations, but merely having the controls in place does not necessarily accomplish anything. As with so many other things, one has to do it right to reap the benefits.

Dysfunctions of Control Systems The problem is that control systems can elicit strong negative reactions from those affected by them, and these reactions can in turn motivate behavior which makes the systems less than maximally effective. As noted in Exhibit 8.6, control systems can elicit overcompliance, resistance, or the introduction of invalid data, depending on the exact conditions that are present.

A major source of difficulty appears to be the fact that many control systems are introduced and operated by higher authority in a manner that carries the message, "You are not to be trusted." Often those affected do not accept this view of themselves. They resent being continually monitored and evaluated against stan-

---

EXHIBIT 8.6 Dysfunctional responses to organizational control

A rigid *overcompliance,* involving following the rules to the last letter without taking into account their intent, can be expected when:

1. The control measures are not inclusive of everything that should be measured or do not adequately reflect goals.
2. The standards are too high and have been established without participation.
3. The comparison against standards is made by a person who can bestow and withhold rewards.
4. Information from the control system goes to a person who can bestow and withhold rewards.
5. The individuals subject to the control system want the rewards.
6. Organizational goals are characterized by ambiguity or poor acceptance.
7. Strong identification with units or groups exists.

Overt or covert *resistance* to the control system, with the result that it becomes only partially operative or does not operate according to plan, can be expected when:

1. The control measures relate to some new area of endeavor.
2. The control system has replaced a former system in which the people involved had invested much.
3. The standards have been established without participation.
4. There is no direct feedback of results to the people involved.
5. Results of control comparisons go directly to superiors who then use them as a basis for bestowing or withholding rewards.
6. The individuals subject to the control system are satisfied with the status quo and feel commitment to the company.

Introduction of *invalid data* into the control system, so that its contribution to attaining company goals is sabotaged, can be expected when:

1. The control measures are in large part subjective.
2. The control measures directly reflect upon the competence of the individual.
3. The standards are considered unreasonable and have been established without participation.
4. Gathering control information and comparing against standards are activities subject to influence by the individual.
5. Information generated by the control system goes to superiors who use it as a basis for bestowing or withholding rewards.
6. The individuals subject to the control system want the rewards and feel alienated.
7. The control process is characterized by ambiguous outcomes and measurement difficulties.
8. The activity involved is not an essential aspect of the company's functioning.

Based on Edward E. Lawler, "Control Systems in Organizations," in *Handbook of Industrial and Organizational Psychology,* ed. Marvin D. Dunnette (Chicago: Rand McNally, 1976), pp. 1259, 1264–65, 1274.

dards imposed from on high by people who they believe know less about the work than they do. In short, they want to move the control system away from the hierarchical authority structure and introduce an element of bargaining into the development of measures, setting of standards, and application of corrective actions. The desire is for increased participation by those affected, but the reason for participation is so that some element of bargaining can occur. It appears that introducing bargaining into the organizational control process in this mannter (assuming that expert power dominates) often can make for more effective control systems.

Views of Good and Poor Control   A number of proposals have been widely disseminated dealing with the characteristics of good control systems. A summary of these views is given in Exhibit 8.7. Generally these hypotheses make good sense, although they have rarely been subjected to research study. Yet they are logically consistent with the basic idea of control.

Perfect control is unlikely, simply because unforeseen events are inevitable. Good control, however, means that a reasonable, informed person could be confident that unpleasant surprises are unlikely. In this connection it is important to keep in mind that:

1. Control is oriented toward the future; the goal is to have no unpleasant surprises in the future.
2. Control is multidimensional, and good control cannot be established over an activity with multiple objectives unless performance on all significant dimensions has been considered; control of a production department can-

---

EXHIBIT 8.7   Characteristics of good control

1. *Relevance, and thus tailored to plans and people*—The control system should be adapted to the specific plans, positions, and people to which it applies; no one system effectively controls every activity under all situations.
2. *Flexibility*—Controls should be capable of change to deal with new plans, changed environmental circumstances, and shifts in personnel.
3. *Focus on critical points*—Control systems should be applied at strategic points that are crucial to the final outcome.
4. *Timeliness and reporting speed*—The better control systems warn of deviations immediately so that corrective action can be taken before the deviation continues to grow.
5. *Simplicity and clarity*—For control systems to work well, those who apply them must understand them including the standards, measures, corrective actions, and nature of operation.
6. *Cost effectiveness*—Controls should produce savings at least the equal of their costs.
7. *Suitability for corrective action*—Control systems should be designed not only to identify deviations from standard but to point up appropriate corrective actions; in closed-loop systems this means an appropriate feedback loop; in open-loop systems it means providing information needed for diagnosis.

not be considered good unless quality, efficiency, and asset management all are controlled.

3. The assessment of whether good performance assurance has been achieved is difficult and subjective; judgment is subject to error because adequacy must be measured against a future that can be very difficult to assess.

4. Better control is not always economically desirable; control tools are costly and should be implemented only if the expected benefits exceed the costs.[12]

Although it is much more common practice to talk about the characteristics of good than of poor control, the latter does occur. The dysfunctions noted in Exhibit 8.6 clearly appear when control systems are not working well. But there are other indications of poor control as well.[13]

One source of problems is poor objectives and standards emanating from the planning process. Unmeasurable, ambiguous objectives make effective control impossible. A second difficulty arises out of insufficient or faulty information processing, so that desired and actual performance cannot be compared in a meaningful way. If the needed data cannot be marshaled or the data that are marshaled are inaccurate or incomplete, then controls may as well not exist at all. Third, an exclusive emphasis on negative deviations—mistakes—can ultimately backfire. Control of this kind needs to be coupled with efforts at prevention and stimulation of maximum unit performance. Positive as well as negative deviations need to be identified, and the former rewarded just as the latter are corrected (punished). Fourth, poor unit control systems often reflect poor or nonexistent individual performance control. After all, unit results are built out of the performances of individuals. Thus there should not be inadequate evaluations and corrective actions at the individual level. Additional problems that may emerge in control systems could be noted. The important point is that having controls in place is one thing; making them operate well to achieve more effective component performance in relation to the total organization is quite another.

How control systems may go wrong when applied in the wrong context can be illustrated with reference to an equipment control procedure used by the U.S. Army. The procedure was developed for use in a barracks situation on a military post where the equipment assigned to a company stayed largely in a single, circumscribed space. It involved issuing articles such as weapons, communications equipment, field kitchen equipment, vehicles and the like to a company; maintaining books on items issued, returned for repair, replaced, and so on; and carrying out periodic, in-person audits to see that what was carried on the books actually was present. If deviations occurred the company commander could be held financially accountable.

In the aftermath of World War II among units being gradually demobilized, this control system was modified only to permit combat losses to be written off, and that only for a brief period. After the war in Europe ended, however, procedures for establishing combat losses were not well worked out; many units later found articles that had been written off (and thus actually developed excesses), while at the same time certain articles not written off subsequently turned out to be missing. Thus, the books and reality often deviated sharply. These deviations became larger over time as items were lost during frequent moves, and because of thefts by both military personnel and German and Austrian civilians.

Audits might well have revealed the discrepancies, but it was almost impossible to conduct audits effectively because units and equipment were dispersed over large areas in which local civilian populations lived, and the personnel needed to conduct audits were not available because of the rapid demobilization. Furthermore, frequent turnover in many positions—including that of company commander—made it very difficult to hold individuals accountable. No one knew when the discrepancies had first occurred. It is safe to say the control system was "out of control."

This all came to a head as units were required to turn in their equipment at the time when most of their personnel had been returned to the U.S., and thus the unit's existence was to be discontinued. Under the control system the company commander could have faced some very sizable charges. That rarely happened. Instead, captured German equipment, articles from the civilian society, parts of various items, and articles obtained by exchange with other companies who had excesses were used to fill the gaps. Officially the integrity of the control system was maintained; in actuality, it had long lost its usefulness to achieve the intended objectives.

Summary

Coordinating and controlling are closely intertwined with such things as the use of power, authority, bargaining, and communication—as discussed in chapter 7—as well as with each other. Power and authority have much to do with achieving coordination and introducing corrective actions in control systems. Bargaining often permeates the coordination process, and to the extent participation is used it becomes an important factor in the control process—particularly in establishing standards and measures.

Improved communication can make significant contributions to the handling of conflict, as in coordinating intergroup conflict by rational confrontation. By their very nature, control systems rely heavily on communication flows, especially written flows, to obtain and utilize data. Finally, coordination and control become essentially the same thing when a control system operates to correct conflicts that have escalated beyond some acceptable level. Thus a company may establish a standard for the number of days a strike can last in its plants before some type of corrective action is taken; in such cases both coordination and control are involved.

Coordination becomes necessary when there is some friction between organizational components so that they are not operating well together. Often the friction is a result of conflict, and this conflict can in turn have negative consequences for both individual and organizational performance. Conflict between units is particularly likely when decisions must be made jointly, differing objectives or goals exist, and differing perceptions are present. A number of procedures have been developed to reduce or eliminate the negative effects of conflict and to coordinate units. From the research it appears that there is no single best approach; it depends very much on aspects of the situation.

Control may be considered as it operates on individual performance, as it affects the operation of machinery, and as it influences the performance of organizational components. The latter is of primary concern here. The different types of control systems that have been developed generally are viewed rather negatively by those who owe allegiance to the human relations tradition of Roethlisberger and Mayo; such people tend to emphasize the dysfunctions of controls. Others in the tradition of Taylor, Fayol, and Weber note the positive motivational effects. Out of these differing views has come (a) a lively dialogue which has extended into the accounting field as well, (b) some research, and ultimately (c) a much better understanding of both the pluses and minuses of various types of control systems.

What Have You Learned?

1. How are audits used, and what problems do they face as methods of control?
2. What are some of the various ways that bargaining may enter into both coordination and control processes? When does bargaining appear to be desirable?
3. What is meant by the following:
   a. Variance control
   b. Human asset accounting
   c. Standard costs
   d. Flexible budgeting
   e. Profit centers
4. Various guidelines have been developed for how and when various control procedures should be used. What are these guidelines, and what type of evidence exists to support their use?
5. Under what circumstances is conflict most likely to break out in an organization? Which would appear more likely in a very small business?

6. How exactly do standards, measures, and corrective actions enter into the control process? Do they operate differently under open-loop and closed-loop conditions?
7. What approaches may be used to foster coordination? What are some of the problems associated with these approaches?
8. Why do control systems tend to produce dysfunctional consequences? What are these consequences?
9. What is known about the circumstances under which various types of coordination are most appropriately used?
10. How is the success of a company likely to be affected if conflict becomes rampant? Give examples of the various consequences that may occur.

How Well Can You Apply Your Knowledge?

Problem 1. The industrial relations department of a large oil company is organized with a vice-president at its head and two managers, both of whom are at the same hierarchical and pay levels, reporting to him. One of these managers has responsibility for the operating personnel units. There are separate units of this kind to handle personnel activities for exploration and production, manufacturing and the refineries, marketing, and office employees such as those in accounting. The other manager has responsibility for a variety of staff units within the industrial relations function that are concerned with such matters as preparing for collective bargaining with the unions, conducting training and management development programs, studying jobs to determine whether compensation levels should be changed, administering equal employment opportunity matters, conducting personnel research studies primarily related to selection and hiring, and the like.

Not surprisingly, there is considerable conflict between the two managers, each of whom has been with the company for some time and each of whom wishes eventually to move up to the vice-presidency. This conflict has very little visible effect at the level of the individuals involved, primarily because the vice-president has taken active steps to maintain an equal power balance between them. On down the line, however, there are major effects. Each manager places a strong emphasis on loyalty among subordinates so that the department as a whole is split into two camps. Communication within camps is frequent; between camps it occurs only when absolutely necessary. Promotions and transfers occur almost entirely within camps, since neither manager wants to take on a person who might not prove loyal.

The most difficult problem, however, has developed gradually and threatens to disrupt even the power balance at the top. Since the operating personnel units serve as gateways and control access to other components of the company, they can in essence keep the staff units from doing their jobs. This is particularly true when the staff unit operates on a project-by-project basis—a personnel research study, a particular training program, a needed job restudy, an investigation of possible employment discrimination. Also the operating personnel groups can withhold information needed for purposes of collective bargaining.

Over time, as the conflict at the top intensifies, the operating personnel people in fact do begin to exercise this source of power. To a very limited extent they have brought some expertise, related to technical training for instance, into their own shops by hiring appropriate people. But the major consequence is that the staff people within the department have less and less to do and the overall level of personnel practice suffers badly. Outside departments recognize this but are loath to intervene in what is viewed as basically a family argument; yet they are concerned that the industrial relations department is not doing its job. Within that department there is growing discussion as to whether certain staff people should be encouraged

to look for work elsewhere, since they have practically nothing to do here. Some begin to do just that on their own.

Questions
1. What techniques for conflict reduction and resolution or coordination might solve the problem in the industrial relations department?
2. Evaluate each alternative approach against your knowledge of the situation and the technique, and plot out an appropriate course of action to achieve the needed coordination.

Problem 2. A large, diversified company has just acquired a small firm engaged primarily in the manufacture of highly specialized electronic equipment. The smaller firm was owned and managed by a rather eccentric gentleman who believed strongly in the personal touch and who considered control systems, especially those of an accounting nature, as excessively impersonal. Accordingly the company operated for years without budgets or any other types of financial controls, although various quality control procedures were used in connection with production processes. Managers operated pretty much on their own insofar as expenditures were concerned, although on occasion the CEO would question certain items. It was rare that purchases were put out for bids; rather, the managers tended to develop long-standing relationships with preferred suppliers.

The firm is not unionized and compensation levels were largely a matter of individual managerial discretion. Where the same jobs exist in different units, the managers involved are expected to coordinate pay levels directly. It is generally accepted that many people are being paid well above the going rates in the local labor market, but there has never been any coordinated effort to control pay across the firm as a whole. Managers, including the CEO, would view this as an invasion of individual managerial rights.

Unfortunately, although this type of approach to costs proved adequate in the firm's early years when profits were high, increasing competition gradually eroded price levels to the point where the company was in some difficulty. This was the point at which the CEO decided to sell out and retire from the business. It is immediately apparent to the top executive people who have taken over the business that something must be done about costs if their investment is ever to pay off. Yet given the history and traditions of the company they have acquired, that matter is not going to be resolved easily.

Questions

1. What types of control systems could be utilized to bring costs under control in the small firm?

How might those control systems be introduced?

2. What difficulties or dysfunctions would you anticipate arising if these control systems are introduced? How would you go about dealing with these problems?

Additional Sources for More Detailed Study

Anthony, Robert N., and Dearden, John. *Management Control Systems.* Homewood, Ill.: Irwin, 1980.

Bedford, Norton M. "Management Control." In *Contemporary Management: Issues and Viewpoints,* ed. Joseph W. McGuire. Englewood Cliffs, N.J.: Prentice-Hall, 1974.

Filley, Alan C. *Interpersonal Conflict Resolution.* Glenview, Ill.: Scott, Foresman, 1975.

Flamholtz, Eric. *Human Resource Accounting.* Encino, Calif.: Dickenson, 1974.

Jerome, William T. *Executive Control—The Catalyst.* New York: Wiley, 1961.

Kraus, William A. *Collaboration in Organizations: Alternatives to Hierarchy.* New York: Human Sciences Press, 1980.

Lawler, Edward E., and Rhode, John G. *Information and Control in Organizations.* Pacific Palisades, Calif.: Goodyear, 1976.

Likert, Rensis, and Likert, Jane G. *New Ways of Managing Conflict.* New York: McGraw-Hill, 1976.

Newman, William H. *Constructive Control: Design and Use of Control Systems.* Englewood Cliffs, N.J.: Prentice-Hall, 1975.

Robbins, Stephen P. *Managing Organizational Conflict: A Nontraditional Approach.* Englewood Cliffs, N.J.: Prentice-Hall, 1975.

Scott, William G. *The Management of Conflict: Appeal Systems in Organizations.* Homewood, Ill.: Irwin, 1965.

Tricker, R. I. *Management Information and Control Systems.* New York: Wiley, 1976.

Notes

1. L. David Brown, *Managing Conflict at Organizational Interfaces* © 1983, Addison-Wesley, Reading, Massachusetts. Pp. 1–3. Reprinted with permission.

2. Robert R. Blake, Herbert A. Shepard, and Jane S. Mouton, *Managing Intergroup Conflict in Industry* (Houston: Gulf, 1964).

3. D. C. Dearborn and Herbert A. Simon, "Selective Perception: A Note on the Departmental Identifications of Executives," *Sociometry* (June 1958).

4. Kenneth W. Thomas, "Conflict and Conflict Management," in *Handbook of Industrial and Organizational Psychology,* ed. Marvin D. Dunnette (Chicago: Rand McNally, 1976).

5. Muzafer Sherif, *In Common Predicament* (Boston: Houghton Mifflin, 1966).

6. Selwyn W. Becker and Duncan Neuhauser, *The Efficient Organization* (New York: Elsevier, 1975).

7. Linda Argate, "Input Uncertainty and Organizational Coordination in Hospital Emergency Units," *Administrative Science Quarterly* (September 1982).

8. See L. David Brown, *Managing Conflict at Organizational Interfaces* (Reading, Mass.: Addison-Wesley, 1983).

9. Eric Flamholtz, "Behavioral Aspects of Accounting/Control Systems," in *Organizational Behavior,* ed. Steven Kerr (Columbus: Grid, 1979), p. 309.

10. Rensis Likert and David G. Bowers, "Organization Theory and Human Resource Accounting," *American Psychologist* (June 1969); idem, "Improving the Accuracy of P/L Reports by Estimating the Dollar Value

of the Human Organization," *Michigan Business Review* (March 1973).

11. See Pradip N. Khandwalla, "Viable and Effective Organizational Designs of Firms," *Academy of Management Journal* (September 1973); Anant R. Negandhi, *Organization Theory in an Open System* (New York: Dunellen, 1975).

12. Kenneth A. Merchant, "The Control Function of Management," *Sloan Management Review* (Summer 1982): 44.

13. Lawrence G. Hrebiniak and William F. Joyce, *Implementing Strategy* (New York: Macmillan, 1984), chapter 7.

CHAPTER 9

Designs for Organizations

CHAPTER OUTLINE

Open Systems Formulations
Katz and Kahn's Social Psychological Approach
    What Is a System?
    The Operation of Subsystems
    Organizational Environments
Sociotechnical Systems Theory
    Types of Environments
    Postindustrial Society
Thompson's Sociological Approach
    Protecting the Production Subsystem
    Co-optation and Coalition
    Departmentation

Contingency Views of Organization
The Technological Imperative
    Types of Technology
    Implications for Design
    Is Technology an Imperative?
    Mechanistic and Organic Systems
Differentiation and Integration under Uncertainty
    The Role of Environmental Uncertainty
    Extrapolations to Matrix Structures
    What Is Fact and What Is Not
Growth Strategy and Structure
    Chandler's Views and the Lessons of History
    Strategy, Structure, and Performance

Bureaucratic Theory and Professional Systems
Evidence on the Value of Bureaucratic Structures
    Early Conclusions
    The Decentralization Issue
    Bureaucratic and Professional Systems
        Distinguished
The Nature of Professional Systems
    Professional Organizations
    Effects of Increased Size
    Professional Components

OBJECTIVES

To consider some of the more important open systems approaches and how they relate to organizational design.

To develop an increased understanding of aspects of organization structure by considering situational contingency approaches.

To provide information on how bureaucratic systems work and when they are most effective, and to distinguish them from professional systems.

The top level policy making group at one of Scott Paper Company's plants had been meeting over several years to consider various policy matters. Attendance at the meetings was not compulsory, but it was generally accepted that if a subject affecting a particular member of the group was on the agenda for discussion, that member ought to be present. Generally about two-thirds of the total group attended each meeting. Then a decision was reached to carry out an extensive revision of the plant's organization structure. The reorganization was to be accomplished on the basis of the group's planning process, and that planning was to be done in an intensive series of meetings extending over as long a period as might prove necessary. In fact, the group met several times a week for almost six months. During this period, when the discussions were focused on redesigning the plant structure, not one member of the group missed a single meeting.

Why is this matter of organizational design viewed as so important? A major reason is that organizational structuring, and then the process of filling positions once a structure is in place, determines who will wield more power and authority and who will have less. For example, the personnel/human resources function in the company could be a large component, headed by a vice-president who also serves on the company's board of directors, with authority to exercise a broad range of control over hiring, labor relations, compensation, and so on. In this case, all personnel staff would report to personnel managers, except for the vice president, who would report to the chief executive. Alternatively, there could be no personnel vice-president, and no personnel people at or near the top levels of the company at all. Individuals working in this area would be assigned directly to specific units and thus would report to plant managers, regional marketing managers, or another manager lower in the hierarchy. There would be no formal structural ties among these managers, and in fact, the scope of the work performed by the personnel components around the company would be small.

Clearly, whether personnel activities are functionally centralized, as in the first instance, or decentralized, as in the second, makes a great deal of difference in terms of the power, authority, and pay of personnel managers. It is not surprising that, in the situation just described, the plant personnel manager attended all the meetings of the top level group when a new organization structure was being planned. He could have been designed right out of a job. And it was much the same logic that kept the other members of the group in attendance at the meetings.

The discussion in this chapter focuses on the crucial matter of organization structure. What options are available? What factors influence design? What approaches make for a more effective organization? What useful concepts do we have to work with?

| **OPEN SYSTEMS FORMULATIONS** | One approach to understanding organizations and their design takes an open systems perspective as its primary focus, thus utilizing certain concepts discussed in chapter 4. Formulations of this kind view organizations as input–output sys- |

tems, and they place particular stress on interactions and exchanges across the borders of the organization with the environment. Often these theories are not as explicit about specific design aspects as we might desire. But the systems way of thinking is useful in providing an understanding of what parts need to be designed into organizations, and of the role that environmental factors play in the design process.

Katz and Kahn's Social Psychological Approach

One of the most fully developed open systems formulations has come from the University of Michigan. This approach begins with a generalized statement about the nature of open systems and then considers various aspects of organizational structure and process that follow from the concepts.

EXHIBIT 9.1   Characteristics of open systems

1. *Importation of energy*—Open systems take in energy from their environments—the institutions and people around them.

2. *Throughput*—Open systems transform energy; organizations create products, process materials or people, develop services; work is done within.

3. *Output*—Open systems send something back into the environment; this refers to products and services, but it can also include pollutants.

4. *Systems as cycles of events*—Open systems use their output to the environment, or the results of it, as feedback to continually reinitiate the input-throughput-output cycle; thus money received from the sale of a product serves to purchase new energy, etc.

5. *Negative entropy*—Open systems must reverse the natural tendency toward disorganization and death (entropy); organizations accomplish this by taking in more energy than they expend and storing the residual, thus acquiring negative entropy—this energy is consumed to maintain the system.

6. *Information input, negative feedback, and coding process*—Open systems take in information as well as energy; this includes negative feedback from internal functioning to correct deviations from course (control); there is also a coding process that selects from all possible inputs those that are organizationally relevant.

7. *Steady state and dynamic homeostasis*—Open systems contain mechanisms for countering disruptive forces and restoring their previous state (homeostasis); for organizations, this means a tendency to preserve their basic character by adding safety margins and corrective mechanisms, which in turn fosters growth.

8. *Differentiation*—Open systems move toward increasing differentiation; in organizations there is greater division of labor, specialization in work, and elaboration of separate roles.

9. *Integration and coordination*—Open systems tend to bind their differentiated parts together through integration and coordination; integration involves shared norms and values, as with organizational commitment, while coordination involves structuring and regulating.

10. *Equifinality*—Open systems can achieve the same final state from different starting points and by different paths; in organizations the increasing introduction of regulatory mechanisms can severely restrict this equifinality.

SOURCE: Adapted from Daniel Katz and Robert L. Kahn, *The Social Psychology of Organizations* (New York: Wiley, 1978): 23–30.

What Is a System? Exhibit 9.1 sets forth the ten basic characteristics of open systems. The important consideration is that organizations need designs that ensure the carrying out of these ten process characteristics. In accordance with item 10, equifinality, there are various ways that this can be accomplished. What is crucial for organizational survival is that they are accomplished. Exhibit 9.1 therefore serves as a checklist of factors that must be considered in designing organizations.

The Operation of Subsystems In the Katz and Kahn view, energy that goes into an organization may be used for maintenance purposes, for creating negative entropy and sustaining the system, or for purposes of production to yield productive outputs. If the maintenance input is too great, then inefficiency results. Integration of the total system behind operative goals is achieved through the operation of *roles* (standardized behavior patterns required of those who perform a given function), *norms* (expectations of those who work in the roles that serve to indicate and reinforce requirements), and *values* (more general justifications and aspirations for performance).

Organizations tend to structure themselves to carry out the various activities needed. In open systems theory terminology, *subsystems* appear that are in essence major components of the organization. Exhibit 9.2 specifies the basic types of subsystems that should be included. To varying degrees, these subsystems develop their own roles, norms, and values, thus creating the need for coordination by the managerial subsystem.

But managerial subsystems tend not merely to coordinate and maintain a status quo steady state; they tend also to maximize, with the result that there is often continuing growth. This occurs because:

1. Striving for technical proficiency results in increased capabilities, which should be put to use in order to maintain efficiency—excess manufacturing capacity, for example.
2. Expanded size is one of the easiest ways to deal with problems of internal strain—thus several competing managers can all be promoted into an expanded structure.
3. Expansion is the most direct approach to coping with environmental pressures—achieving and stabilizing a large market share makes competitors much less threatening.
4. Bureaucratic structures are by their nature easy to elaborate and expand once the top of the hierarchy is well in place.
5. Many organizations have goals and values that encourage growth.

Organizational Environments Open systems theories are constantly concerned with the process of coping with environmental forces that might threaten organizational goal attainment and survival. In general, structures to facilitate this coping need to be designed into organizations. The specific nature of these environmental coping units will vary with the environmental sectors that are of primary concern. Exhibit 9.3 provides information on what these sectors are.

At their worst, from an organizational viewpoint, environments are turbulent, diverse, random, and scarce. Each of these terms is considered in an

EXHIBIT 9.2 Nature of organizational subsystems

A Particular Type of Subsystem . . .	Has the Function of . . .	With the Motivation to Attain . . .	Through Mechanisms such as . . .
1. *Production*—the primary organizational processes.	Transforming energy within organization.	Technical proficiency.	Division of labor, specifying jobs, setting standards.
2. *Boundary Support*			
Systems to procure resources and dispose of products.	Carrying out exchanges at system boundaries.	Focused manipulation of environment.	Control of sources of supply, creation of image.
Institutional system.	Obtaining support and legitimacy from larger society.	Manipulation of and integration with society.	Contributing to community, influencing social structures.
3. *Maintenance*	Mediating between task demands and human needs to maintain working stucture.	Maintenance of steady state.	Standardized procedures, reward systems, methods of socializing new members.
4. *Adaptive*	Collecting intelligence, carrying out research, planning.	Pressure for change.	Recommending changes to management.
5. *Managerial*	Resolving conflicts within hierarchy.	Control.	Use of authority.
	Coordinating and directing functional units.	Compromise vs. integration.	Alternative concessions and appeal systems.
	Coordinating environmental requirements with organizational resources and needs.	Long-term survival, optimization, improved resource use, increased capabilities.	Increased business volume, added functions, control of environmental forces by absorbing or changing them, organization planning.

SOURCE: Adapted from Daniel Katz and Robert L. Kahn, *The Social Psychology of Organizations* (New York: Wiley, 1978): 84.

upcoming section on sociotechnical systems theory, from which they derive. For the moment, it is sufficient to emphasize that "bad" environments contain a great deal of uncertainty and complexity, occasioned in particular by high turbulence.

The successive levels idea holds that a firm will try to cope initially by focusing on the physical environment (exploration, prospecting, real estate, etc. are emphasized). If this fails, so that the problems posed by environmental complexity and uncertainty remain unresolved, the focus moves to the information and technological environment level (research and development units grow). Next comes the economic environment (with stress on marketing on the output side and recruiting and purchasing on the input). At the next level, the organization will focus on the political environment (with staff size increases in public relations and the legal areas). Finally, the organization will attempt a solution at the cultural level, involving expanded managerial commitments in informational roles such as figurehead and spokesman. This suc-

Designs for Organizations

EXHIBIT 9.3 Dimensions of environmental variation

Environments may be considered in terms of five *sectors*, with solutions to problems of complexity and uncertainty sought at successively higher levels as lower level solutions fail:

Higher Level ↑
1. Value patterns of society and culture
2. Political environment, including laws and legal precedents
3. Economic environment of competitive markets and resource inputs
4. Informational and technological environment
5. Physical environment, including geography, natural resources, and climate
Lower Level ↓

Within each of these sectors, the environments may vary along each of four *dimensions:*

1. Stable ——————— Turbulent
2. Uniform ——————— Diverse
3. Clustered ——————— Random
4. Munificent ——————— Scarce

SOURCE: Adapted from Daniel Katz and Robert L. Kahn, *The Social Psychology of Organizations* (New York: Wiley, 1978): 125.

cessive levels approach perhaps gives insufficient attention to overlapping sector emphasis, but it does point up the ways in which structures depend on environmental forces, and also how different strategies to cope with these environmental forces involve shifts in structures.

Sociotechnical Systems Theory

Chapter 6 discusses sociotechnical systems theory as it relates to group-based systems and autonomous work groups. However, there is more to the theory than that, and the additional aspects have to do with how the environment affects the organization. The theory originated in the idea of a match between technical and social systems, but it expanded quickly to open systems concepts and a concern with environmental factors.

Types of Environments   Four types of organizational environments are posited. Each follows the other in historical sequence, although residuals of past environments persist into the present. The sequence is given in Exhibit 9.4, where turbulent fields are seen as characterizing much of the modern world. The sociotechnical systems within the organization must adjust themselves so as to maintain a steady state, thus permitting work to be done in the face of changing environmental forces.

Post-industrial Society   The basic contention of sociotechnical theory is that organizations of today are still structured along the bureaucratic lines required by a disturbed reactive environment, when in order to maintain a steady state under turbulent field conditions, they should use other structures. Thus, most

EXHIBIT 9.4 Historical perspective of organizational environment types

First:	**Placid Random Environments** Minimal interconnectedness of elements; slow change, if any. Random distribution of factors hindering or helping goal achievement, so that best strategy is doing the best one can locally. Planning not really possible; learning is only by simple conditioning. *Examples:* Pre-agricultural primitive societies; some small jobshops, general stores, typing pools, and assembly lines; old-fashioned mad houses and concentration camps where prediction of events approaches the impossible.
Then:	**Placid Clustered Environments** Although change is slow, there is some logic to the grouping of environmental factors. Consequently, strategies for coping with the environment may be created. Environmental knowledge can be developed and used to position a firm effectively. *Examples:* Traditional agricultural and business societies; in the modern world, these are specialized firms of limited size with a distinctive competence that fills a stable market demand, thus making them relatively invulnerable to business cycles.
Next:	**Disturbed Reactive Environments** Accelerated change based on industrialism and competitive challenge. Organizations must develop strategies to deal with others in the same industry, and counteract power moves of other firms at the same time as they are pursuing their own strategies. *Examples:* Large corporate bureaucracies reacting to other firms within their industries in a competitive free enterprise system.
And finally:	**Turbulent Fields** Change is rampant, characterizing the period since World War II, and occurs not only in response to actions of organizations in the same industry, but also to a host of other environmental forces—governmental actions, new technological research, increased communication, etc. High levels of uncertainty are introduced, to the point that organizations can no longer cope through independent efforts. *Examples:* Huge organizations with impacts beyond individual industries of a kind that project them into a post-industrial society.

SOURCE: Based on Fred E. Emery and Eric L. Trist, "The Causal Texture of Organizational Environments," *Human Relations* (February 1965); idem, *Toward a Social Ecology* (London: Plenum, 1973).

current organizations are outmoded, ineffective, and doomed (because of their failure to generate sufficient negative entropy).

At the organizational level, turbulent environments require a structure with minimal hierarchy and a primary emphasis on autonomous work groups, bound together by overlapping membership networks and matrices.[1] These groups should contain within them a wide repertoire of capabilities so that they can adapt rapidly and flexibly to environmental changes. The binding ethic of the firm should be collaboration, rather than the competitive ethic of bureaucracy. Organizations would thus replace the authority of hierarchy with a set of values or norms, much like the norms that govern a profession such as law or medicine. Management would exist, but the managerial subsystem would be small and limited to dealing with the environment across the boundary of the organization. It would exercise little authority within.

Such organizations would not be merely constrained by the larger society as they are now; they would act in close accord with the needs of society. This requires a move to a new type of social system, here called post-industrial society, that emphasizes such activities as self-actualization, collaboration, participation, conflict confrontation, and innovation. The move to a post-industrial society of the kind needed to cope with turbulent fields is to be achieved through active governmental intervention based on extensive social planning.

Such systems views of organizational (and societal) structuring go well beyond that of Katz and Kahn. The formulations regarding environments and their implications for structure have been seriously questioned.[2] There is good reason to believe that effectively managed bureaucracies can cope with changing environments rather well. They do not necessarily become mired in a bog of excessive controls and innovation-supressing regulations.[3] However, it is important to understand what group-based systems might look like at the organizational level, simply because such matters are being widely discussed among managers. Sociotechnical systems theory is very much an element of this discussion, and many U.S. companies are experimenting with it, including General Motors, General Foods, and Weyerhauser.

| **Thompson's Sociological Approach** | A somewhat different type of systems formulation, characterized less by a strong commitment to humanist values, has been developed by sociologist James Thompson. This approach is primarily concerned with how aspects of the environment and of the basic technology serve to create uncertainty for an organization. Organizations respond to various sources of uncertainty with particular procedures aimed at producing increased certainty—or at least they should do this if they wish to be rational. In the process, they make decisions that have certain implications for organization design. |

Protecting the Production Subsystem   Organizations try to protect the steady state of their core production subsystem so that the subsystem can operate as efficiently as possible. To do this, they invoke procedures such as buffering, leveling, forecasting, and rationing, as described in Exhibit 9.5. According to Thompson, these procedures are brought to bear in a set sequence in dealing with a particular problem; the higher level approaches are less attractive, but they may be needed. The use of each approach requires that the capability to employ it be designed into the organization. Thus units such as production scheduling, forecasting, recruiting and selection, warehousing, training and development, and maintenance may languish, perhaps even disappear, or flourish depending on the particular approaches taken.

Research indicates that the types of approaches noted in Exhibit 9.5 are indeed important in a practical sense. It is not entirely clear whether they always follow the exact sequence Thompson proposed, but they are used to reduce uncertainty.

Co-optation and Coalition   Another problem organizations face is that of becoming overly dependent on a given element in the environment. Thus a small company that manufactures parts which, because of their nature, or plant locations, or other factors, could be sold only to General Motors would be at the mercy of the larger firm. Similarly, a company that is in a situation where only a single bank will lend it needed money is in a highly dependent position, and the bank involved can exert a great deal of influence over the way the company is operated.

Obviously, one method of avoiding such situations is to encourage competition in the environment—among suppliers and customers, for instance. An-

---

EXHIBIT 9.5   Approaches used to protect production subsystems

Higher level ↑

1. *Rationing.* Products or services are provided on the basis of some pre-established system of priorities; this is a less than ideal solution because opportunities are foregone.

   Examples: A manufacturer faced with a sudden fad rations products to wholesalers; a hospital faced with overcrowding rations beds to physicians for non-emergency purposes.

2. *Forecasting.* Fluctuations and peak loads are anticipated in advance, and output of products and services is adjusted accordingly.

   Examples: A manufacturer forecasts variations in product demand accurately and schedules machinery, staffing, shifts etc. accordingly; a bank determines that social security checks and paychecks arrive on certain days and adjusts operations, including teller staffing, to these peak demands.

3. *Leveling.* Steps are taken to spread inputs and outputs so that valleys and peaks can be avoided, or at least reduced.

   Examples: An airline provides reduced fares on late night flights to attract passengers away from heavy traffic hours; a utility varies its rate structure to induce less variation in patterns of use.

4. *Buffering.* Procedures are initiated to create a steady state for the core production subsystem, by placing buffers on the input and output sides to ward off environmental fluctuations.

   Examples: The military builds up a supply of trained personnel against the possibility of war; a manufacturer inventories large supplies of product in warehouses against the possibility of escalating demand.

Lower level ↓

SOURCE: Adapted from James D. Thompson, *Organizations in Action* (New York: McGraw-Hill, 1967): 20–23.

Designs for Organizations

other approach is to negotiate contracts, as companies do with labor unions, so that for a period of time at least, the prospect of facing arbitrary power moves is eliminated. More important from the point of view of organization structure are two approaches known as co-optation and coalition.

Co-optation involves bringing outsiders into the power structure of an organization with the intent of averting threat from that source. Thus, by making the president of a bank a member of its board of directors, a company may hope to neutralize any power the bank might exert over it. The risk here is relatively low because the bank president still has only one vote and can be prevented from exerting great internal influence, while at the same time a degree of common interest between company and bank is created that should make the bank less likely to act against the company's interests.

Although co-optation creates change in the power structure of an organization by some dilution of the control available to insiders, coalition has more profound structural effects. Here, there is an actual combining or merging of organizations. In many cases, one company becomes a division or subsidiary of another. A company may thus find itself in a position where its products are sold exclusively through certain retail outlets. Should these outlets combine in some manner against the company, they would be in a position to exert considerable influence, to the point of affecting profits substantially. To prevent this, the company might attempt to bring as many of these outlets as possible into its own newly established marketing arm. Often the incentive for such coalitions is the payment of a purchase price well above current market value.

As Thompson anticipated, the use of approaches such as co-optation and coalition *is* more frequent in the face of environmental threat. Considerable research has been done to substantiate this conclusion.[4] Furthermore, approaches of this kind have been found effective in contributing to company profits.

Departmentation   In organizations of any size, the units or parts must be grouped in some manner. The basis on which grouping is done varies; the four most common approaches are illustrated in Exhibit 9.6. The term *departmentation* is used to describe this aspect of designing organizations. A major problem arises because, once grouping is done on one basis at the highest level—say by separate products—this usually results in a dispersal of units constituted on other bases. Consequently, units dealing with the same type of customer, located in the same geographical area, and/or in the same functional area may be spread across a number of product line divisions. How should this problem be solved? How should structural priorities be established?

Thompson's solution involves the types of relationships or interdependencies that exist between organizational parts in terms of the work they do. He describes three possible types of interdependence, as defined and illustrated in chapter 8, in Exhibit 8.3. Each of these types carries with it an ideal method of coordinating or adjusting the work of two units that are interdependent. Since mutual adjustment involves some bargaining and a great deal of communication, it is time-consuming and costly. If the nature of the interdependence inherent in the work is reciprocal and calls for mutual adjustment, this should be handled first at the lowest organizational levels. Since planning and scheduling are the next most costly, groupings at the next higher levels should be in terms of any sequential interdependence that is present. Finally, pooled interdependence would govern at the top.

What this means is that if reciprocal interdependence is present in the organization, the structure should place these positions close together in as distinct a unit as possible to facilitate the needed communication. Above these groupings would be those intended to handle any sequential interdependence, because planning and scheduling the relationships between units is easier and less costly to the extent that the units are small. At the top, the structure would be organized on the basis of pooled interdependence. Often this means separate product divisions, as shown in Exhibit 9.6. But it could also mean departmentation by geographical location, *if* each region of the country was a self-contained entity that did not require products, raw materials, or anything else directly from another region in order to function.

Thompson's ideas represent one of the few existing attempts to deal with departmentation issues with enough precision to really help those who design or-

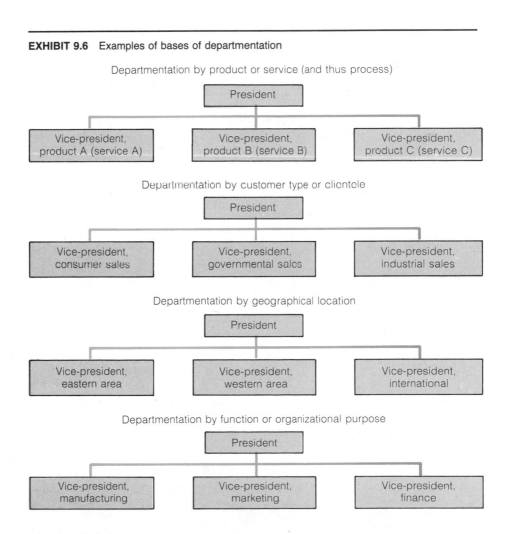

EXHIBIT 9.6 Examples of bases of departmentation

ganizations. Research clearly endorses his views regarding the ties between type of interdependence and method of coordination as set forth in Exhibit 8.3. Beyond this, the evidence is more anecdotal, but what there is supports his concept of grouping at successively higher levels.

CONTINGENCY VIEWS OF ORGANIZATION

Contemporary View

A prevailing theme in the management literature, as early as Fayol and Taylor, but also including many modern contributors such as Likert, is that there is one best way. In this view certain approaches to structure and process are best, regardless of the nature of the organization, the existing situation, and the like. In contrast is the contingency concept, which holds that under one set of circumstances, a particular structure is best, but under opposite conditions, an entirely different structure is required. What one does in designing and operating an organization therefore depends entirely on the situation.

The weight of the evidence would clearly favor some kind of contingency view. Furthermore, contingency thinking is closely aligned with open systems formulations.[5] However, contingency theories have some real difficulty in identifying the key contingency variables. Contingency variables are those on which structure and process depend. Thus, if a certain technology, or environmental condition, or corporate strategy prevails, one approach should be used; if the situation is different, another should be. The question is—what is the nature of the determining contingency variable?

The Technological Imperative

One contingency approach that has shown considerable promise views organization design in relation to the core technology. Technology is the contingency variable and specifies what type of structure will work best. Thus, technology places certain demands on—and provides an imperative for—structure.

Types of Technology Several different ways of classifying technology have been developed, but the approach proposed by Joan Woodward as set forth in Exhibit 9.7 has been the most influential. This approach grew out of a study of a hundred manufacturing firms in England. Originally the study was intended to test classical management views of the kind set forth by Fayol. However, there were so many instances where these views were not supported by research that Woodward decided to seek an explanation for the findings elsewhere. The result was a contingency theory embedded in technology, with technology defined as "the collection of plant, machines, tools, and recipes available at a given time for the execution of the production task."[6]

Implications for Design Certain of the anticipated organizational changes are a direct consequence of increasing technical complexity. Among these consequences are:

More levels in the management hierarchy

More managers reporting to the chief executive, and thus a greater span of control at that point

A greater number of committees

An increase in delegation and decentralization, so that decisions are made at somewhat lower levels

Smaller spans of control at the middle management level

A greater proportion of management personnel relative to total labor force

More industrial relations specialists

Other factors show a relationship to technology such that the extremes of technical complexity are much the same, but the middle-range large batch and mass production technologies demand a different structure. Among these structures for the middle range are:

A greater span of control for first-level production supervisors

More standardization and formalization, with rules and procedures spelled out in advance

Greater use of the traditional line–staff structure wherein staff groups advise and operate control systems for the direct line production units

The theory's basic hypothesis is that companies structured along the lines indicated as appropriate for their technology will be more successful. Those that deviate in either direction—too many levels of management or too few, too large spans of control at each management level or too small, and so on—will be less successful. Technology–structure fit thus becomes the key to organizational effectiveness. In general, the type of organization stressed by Fayol and classical management theorists can be expected to work well only in the middle range of technical complexity. If applied at the extremes, these principles could easily lead to trouble.

EXHIBIT 9.7   Woodward's system for classifying technologies

Degree of Technical Complexity

High

Process Production
Intermittent production of chemicals in multipurpose plants
Continuous flow production of liquids, gases, and crystalline substances

Large Batch and Mass Production
Production of large batches
Production on assembly lines
Mass production

Unit and Small Batch Production
Production of units to customer requirements
Production of prototypes
Fabrication of large equipment in stages

Low   Production of small batches to customer orders

SOURCE: Adapted from Joan Woodward, *Industrial Organization: Theory and Practice* (London: Oxford University Press, 1965): 39.

Is Technology an Imperative? Woodward's ideas focus entirely on manufacturing organizations. Research has since extended them, but even Woodward herself began to have doubts about the technological imperative. Data bearing on the middle range of technical complexity showed certain weaknesses, and there was some reason to believe that type of control might operate alongside technology as a contingency variable. The two together—technical complexity and type of control—would thus combine to yield a degree of uncertainty ranging from high, in unit and small batch production, to low, in process production. Just prior to her death, Woodward clearly was less committed to the technological imperative per se than in her earlier research.[7]

Other researchers have placed technology and structure together in much the way Woodward anticipated, but almost always, the size of the organization, as measured by the number of its employees for instance, has shown at least as strong a relationship to structure, and often stronger. This had led to a proposal that size rather than technology is the important contingency variable.[8] In any event, there is no basis for concluding that technology necessarily has a causal impact on structures throughout an organization. In fact, it appears just as likely that the way a company is structured may influence the nature of its technology. Thus a resort to group-based systems and autonomous work groups appears to preclude the use of mass production technologies with long assembly lines and to favor unit-type production in which each group produces a complete product.

To say that technology does not typically cause the structure of a total organization to take a particular form does not mean that there may not be some immediate local impact. In one instance, changing the technology of a large hospital kitchen from batch to mass production did produce a number of changes in the way jobs were designed within the kitchen itself, but there was no reverberation effect through the hospital as a whole.[9] New technologies can bring in new specialists, and new specialists can mean some decentralization of authority so that expertise is effectively utilized. It would be rare, however, for these technological effects to spread very far.

Given that research has produced no evidence to support the view that the technology–structure fit of the kind Woodward hypothesized leads to more effective organizational performance, we are left with the conclusion that the technological imperative is a rather weak and localized imperative at best. Yet it is also true that the structural features Woodward described are more often found when the technologies are as she anticipated. This does not necessarily make the organization work better, but it is a fact. At present, it is not clear why this outcome occurs as often as it does.

Mechanistic and Organic Systems

A somewhat different view emphasizing the roles of technological and market change as contingency variables is outlined in Exhibit 9.8. These ideas grew out a series of case studies in the electronics industry, again in England, by Burns and Stalker.

The basic concept of these researchers is that, as technological change increases, there is a greater need for people in various parts of the firm to communicate and work together and that an organic form facilitates this. Similarly, as market changes accelerate, a company needs more points of contact with its markets as well as with potential markets, and more organic structures also facilitate this. As Exhibit 9.8 indicates, organic systems are more unstructured and loosely bound together. In certain respects they are more like professional organizations, although they need not actually contain a greater proportion of professionals.

Mechanistic–organic theory is relatively simple and intuitively appealing, factors which have no doubt contributed to its popularity. Yet its dual contingency variable can leave managers feeling uncertain what to do when change is much greater in one area than the other, and there is reason to believe that many managers become anxious and upset when faced with the ambiguity and lack of structure that the organic form can produce. Consequently, the manager may function less well rather than better, as the theory would anticipate.

Although there is reason to believe that rapid technological change may on occasion be associated with more organic systems, this is not always true, and the tie to effectiveness again has not been found. The mechanistic–organic distinction appears to be a useful way of thinking about different organization designs, and it may well be that there are circumstances—stages of contin-

---

EXHIBIT 9.8 Outline of the Burns and Stalker formulations

Stable Technologies and Markets, Mechanistic Systems Characterized by:	Rapidly Changing Technologies and Markets, Organic Systems Characterized by:
1. Highly specialized and separate jobs.	Individuals contribute as appropriate to overall goals.
2. Jobs pursued as distinct from company as a whole.	Jobs relate directly to company's current situation.
3. Coordination by hierarchic supervisory authority.	Coordination by mutual adjustment.
4. Precise definitions of rights and responsibilities.	Wide sharing of responsibility for outcomes.
5. Responsibility and commitment attached only to a single job.	Responsibility and commitment to company as a whole.
6. Hierarchic control, authority, and communication.	Network structure with pressure to serve the common interest.
7. Knowledge focused at top of hierarchy.	Knowledge located anywhere creates its own center of authority.
8. Primarily vertical interaction.	Lateral communication flow resembling consultation.
9. Work behavior governed by superiors' communications.	Communications are in the form of information and advice.
10. Insistence on loyalty and obedience.	Commitment to company goals valued over loyalty and obedience.
11. Local, company knowledge and experience most important.	Knowledge and experience from wider professional and industry arena most important.

Adapted from Tom Burns and G. M. Stalker, *The Management of Innovation* (London: Tavistok, 1961): 120–122.

gency variables—that will tell us when one or the other is more appropriate. But those circumstances have not been precisely identified yet, and neither technological nor market change appear to be promising contingency variable candidates.

Differentiation and Integration under Uncertainty

A more recent and much more sophisticated contingency view has been set forth by two members of the Harvard Business School faculty, Paul Lawrence and Jay Lorsch. These theorists build on the ideas of Woodward, and of Burns and Stalker, incorporating concepts such as uncertainty, technological and environmental change, and the like, but extending them much further. Certain aspects of Lawrence and Lorsch's theory, such as integration and rational confrontation, are considered in the discussions of coordination processes in chapter 8. Here, the concern is with a much broader range of considerations.

The Role of Environmental Uncertainty   Originally the contingency variable of the Lawrence and Lorsch theory was uncertainty. When uncertainty is high, a greater degree of differentiation in the organization's structure is required to cope with the various threats coming from the environment. This means that a large number of distinct functional specialists are, because of their different training and orientations, very likely to conflict with each other. To pull these numerous discrete functional units together, various integrating processes and structures are needed. At the simplest level, this coordination process may be achieved through the use of hierarchic authority, but when uncertainty and differentiation are high, there is a need for a high level of integration also. Typically this requires the creation of positions such as product manager, program coordinator, project leader, planning director, and systems designer to cut across and link the differentiated functional subsystems.

EXHIBIT 9.9   Outline of the Lawrence and Lorsch formulations

When environmental *uncertainty* (defined as the uncertainty perceived by organizational decision makers to exist external to the organization, as well as in the physical machinery and non-human aspects of production; where uncertainty itself is a product of unclear information, uncertain causation, and long feedback on results) is:

This calls for a level of *differentiation* (defined as the difference in cognitive and emotional orientation among managers in different functional departments and the differences in formal structure among these departments) that is:

Which if achieved in turn calls for a level of *integration* (defined as the quality of collaboration among departments that is required by the demands of the environment to achieve unity of effort) that is:

			In order to achieve:
High ⟶	High ⟶	High	High
Low ⟶	Low ⟶	Low	Effectiveness

SOURCE: Adapted from Paul R. Lawrence and Jay W. Lorsch, *Organization and Environment: Managing Differentiation and Integration* (Boston: Harvard Business School, 1967); and Gene W. Dalton, Paul R. Lawrence, and Jay W. Lorsch, *Organizational Structure and Design*. (Homewood, Ill.: Irwin-Dorsey, 1970).

The basic constructs of the theory, their definitions, and their relationships are given in Exhibit 9.9.

In writing about this approach recently, Lorsch has tended to place less emphasis on environmental uncertainty as a contingency variable and has given attention to other aspects of the environment.[10] In particular, he has been concerned with the degree of variety or diversity characterizing the environment. This is similar to uncertainty, and high variety is again said to call for high differentiation and integration, but it is possible to have high variety which, through effective forecasting and intelligence systems, is reduced to a state of considerable certainty. Thus the introduction of this new contingency variable can serve as a source of confusion.

Extrapolations to Matrix Structures One way of achieving both differentiation and integration is by introducing a matrix structure. It is not surprising that Lawrence and Lorsch have embraced this type of organizational design, which they define in terms of the existence of a multiple-command system. Exhibit 9.10 provides examples. In such systems, certain managers have at least two bosses—usually one of a functional nature and one for the product or product group. However, any combination of bases for departmentation could be involved (see Exhibit 9.6), and there can be more than two dimensions to the matrix (and therefore more than two bosses). The distinct managerial roles are: (1) top management, which is outside the matrix, (2) matrix managers sharing subordinates, and (3) subordinate managers with multiple bosses.

Structures of this kind are not recommended under all circumstances. They are complex, difficult to install, and as Exhibit 9.11 indicates, full of potential for things to go wrong. The theory would anticipate that high environmental uncertainty and/or variety would be a necessary condition. More specifically, all three of the following conditions should hold:

1. There should be at least two bases of departmentation that are strong simultaneous contenders for structural emphasis.
2. There is a need to perform uncertain, complex, and interdependent tasks requiring a large capacity to process information.
3. There is a requirement to achieve economies of scale by utilizing scarce human resources as fully as possible.[11]

What Is Fact and What Is Not In Exhibit 8.2, it was noted that the use of integrating structures (such as the matrix) and rational confrontation as coordination devices was closely related to the effectiveness levels of six plastics firms. This industry is one of considerable uncertainty, and so these results fit the theory. The problem is that studies carried out in industries where there is a great deal more certainty produce the same result. Integration looks positive regardless of the state of the contingency variable—whether environmental uncertainty or variety.

Furthermore, these same studies fail to identify a role for differentiation consistent with the theory. Differentiating the structure into more diversely oriented parts does not appear to make much difference in terms of company performance, whether the environment is defined as high or low in uncertainty.

EXHIBIT 9.10 Organization charts depicting matrix design

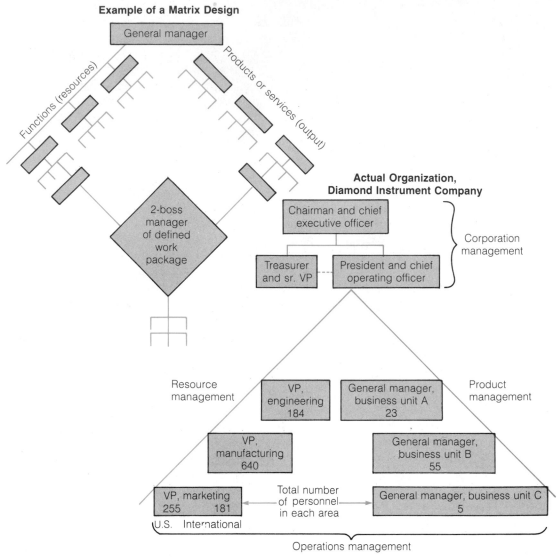

SOURCE: Stanley Davis and Paul Lawrence, *Matrix*, © 1977, Addison-Wesley, Reading, Massachusetts. P. 22, Ex. 2.1, and p. 148, Ex. 6.2. Reprinted with permission.

A major difficulty in this research has been the contingency variable. Uncertainty, and diversity too, has consistently proved difficult to define and measure.[12] Given this fact, it may be that the theory remains correct, and that it merely has not been tested correctly. However, given the evidence available, it seems more likely that integration is important for all organizations, and that differentiation per se, although an important consideration in designing, is not necessarily a source of improved performance (and especially not under con-

EXHIBIT 9.11 What can go wrong with matrix structures

1. *Power Struggles*—Excessive amount of conflict related to states of loose-lying power.
2. *Anarchy*—State of confusion in which no clear lines of authority are recognized and role conflict and ambiguity are pronounced.
3. *Severe Groupitis*—Excessive equating of matrix systems with participative decision making.
4. *Collapse during Economic Crunch*—Elimination of the matrix structure in a period of economic decline because it is blamed for the company's problems, even though the real cause is poor management.
5. *Excessive Overhead*—Costs become excessive because of failure to realize economies of scale.
6. *Decision Strangulation*
7. *Sinking*—Excessive democracy prevents timely action. Gap between matrix and top management becomes excessive or matrix gravitates downward and settles at group level.
8. *Layering*—Power fights, rather than design logic, create matrices within matrices within matrices . . . .
9. *Navel Gazing*—Internal preoccupations divert attention from market realities for too long.

SOURCE: Adapted from Stanley M. Davis and Paul R. Lawrence, *Matrix* (Reading, Mass.: Addison-Wesley, 1977): 129–144.

ditions of uncertainty). This is not to say that particular types of differentiation, intended to cope with specific environmental threats, do not contribute to effectiveness; they almost certainly do, as where a major lobbying unit is created to deal with the threat of potentially adverse legislation.

In any event, the integration results appear to argue for the use of integrating structures such as project managers, coordinators, and liaison personnel and perhaps even for full-scale matrix systems involving widespread use of the two-boss concept. But as indicated by Exhibit 9.11, matrix structures require careful nurturing if they are to survive and prosper. Probably they should not be attempted unless other integrating coordination processes prove inadequate to the task.

Growth Strategy and Structure

A somewhat different contingency approach uses the strategic choices made by top management as its contingency variable. These choices are assumed to be reactive to both technological conditions and environmental circumstances, but the contingency variable itself is a strategic decision related to growth. As a consequence, this approach falls on the borderline between organization theory and the field of business policy/strategy. Yet because it deals with some important types of company structures, it requires discussion here.

Chandler's Views and the Lessons of History The theory of strategy and structure is the creation of Alfred Chandler, a business historian. His theory evolved from analyses of the growth patterns exhibited by a number of firms, but particular attention was given to du Pont, General Motors, Standard Oil of New Jersey (Exxon), and Sears, Roebuck. In the period Chandler studied them, these firms were involved in major expansion. His special concern was with how their strategies for growth influenced their structures. In this context he defined strategy as:

> The determination of the basic long-term goals and objectives of an enterprise, and the adoption of courses of action and the allocation of resources necessary for carrying out these goals. Decisions to expand the volume of activities, to set up distant plants and offices, to move into new economic functions, or become diversified along many lines of business involve the defining of new basic goals.[13]

Growth strategies were adopted in the United States for a variety of reasons—the development of new products, expanding markets here and abroad, economic prosperity, and probably most important, the existence of excess technological capacity. The strategies in turn required the creation of new structures. If growth merely involves expanded volume, the need is for an administrative office to deal with one function in one geographic area. If growth involves geographic dispersion, there is a need for departmental headquarters to handle several such field units. If growth involves expansion into new functions through vertical integration backward into raw materials production and forward into sales, divisional central offices and multidepartmental structure are required. If growth involves the development of new product lines through diversification or major geographic expansion, perhaps internationally, a need is created for a general office to coordinate the divisions.

The major concerns of the general office are long-range planning and allocation of resources. Authority for most aspects of operations is decentralized down to the division level, but not necessarily any further. Structures of this kind became possible with the advent of various methods of coordination, control, and resource allocation, many of them related to accounting.[14] With these methods, it was possible to decentralize authority and still permit top management to keep its hands on the reins. In Exhibit 9.12, CBS Inc. is the general office. There are fifteen product divisions clustered into four product groups. This top level CBS structure is typical of many large corporations today. It is the type of structure Chandler considered most appropriate for implementing growth strategies.

The theory indicates that, although some lag between strategy and structure is inevitable, long delays between adopting a diversified growth strategy and introducing a decentralized, divisionalized structure will be counterproductive. The theory operates best for competitive business enterprise, and to the extent that companies get to the appropriate strategy–structure fit rapidly, they can be expected to benefit over those who do not. On the other hand, in non-competitive, perhaps monopolistic, environments of the kind that existed in Europe for many years, the decentralized form may not be necessary for diversified growth. Also, on the other end of the contingency variable, where no growth or growth within a single business and limited markets are the strategic postures, decentralized divisions are not required and functional forms (see Exhibit 9.6) may be most appropriate.

EXHIBIT 9.12 Top level organization structure at CBS

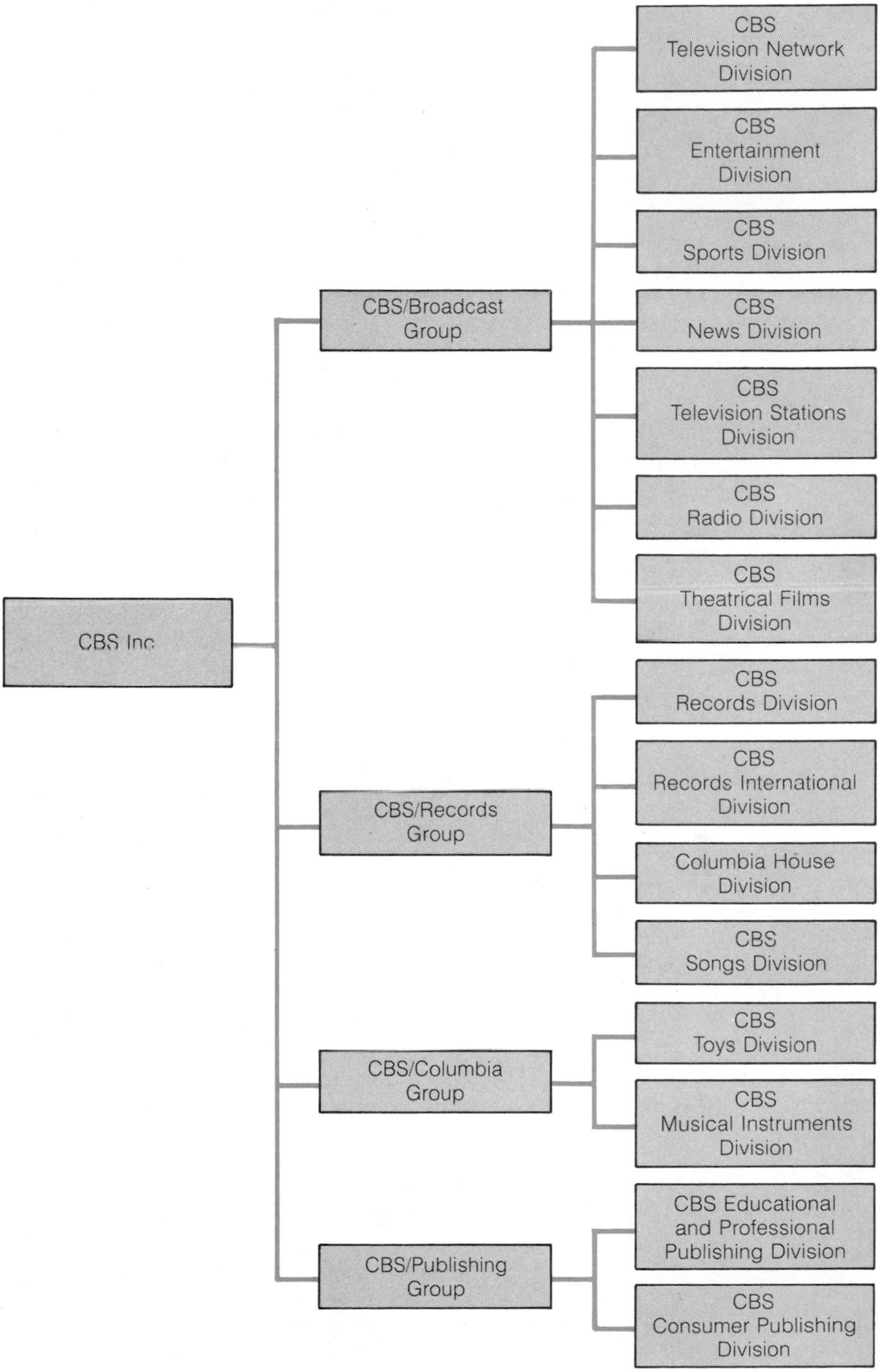

```
CBS Inc
│
├── CBS/Broadcast Group
│       ├── CBS Television Network Division
│       ├── CBS Entertainment Division
│       ├── CBS Sports Division
│       ├── CBS News Division
│       ├── CBS Television Stations Division
│       ├── CBS Radio Division
│       └── CBS Theatrical Films Division
│
├── CBS/Records Group
│       ├── CBS Records Division
│       ├── CBS Records International Division
│       ├── Columbia House Division
│       └── CBS Songs Division
│
├── CBS/Columbia Group
│       ├── CBS Toys Division
│       └── CBS Musical Instruments Division
│
└── CBS/Publishing Group
        ├── CBS Educational and Professional Publishing Division
        └── CBS Consumer Publishing Division
```

Strategy, Structure, and Performance   As indicated in Exhibit 9.13, the 1950s and 1960s in the United States were a period in which large companies increasingly shifted to decentralized divisions, particularly if they were in multiple businesses. This is consistent with Chandler's theory, as is the continuing use of a functional structure by firms pursuing a single business strategy. On this and other evidence, it is apparent that strategy does influence structure; it is an important contingency variable. Furthermore, market competition appears to be a significant catalyst for change.

In spite of these results, however, there has been no consistent demonstration that the process moves through to yield higher profits. A diversification strategy coupled with the decentralized division structure does appear to result in sales growth, but whether it means greater profits is more questionable. What does produce increased profits is a constrained type of growth strategy in multiple businesses that remain "close to home" and within the company's own area of expertise and existing capabilities. Caterpillar Tractor is a good

EXHIBIT 9.13   Emerging relationships between strategy and structure in the 500 largest U.S. companies

Strategic Approach	Percentage of Companies with Each Type of Structure		
	Functional Structure at Top	Decentralized Product Divisions at Top	Other Structural Form
A Single Business			
In 1949	95	3	2
In 1959	96	0	4
In 1969	77	14	9
Multiple Businesses with One Dominant			
In 1949	80	17	3
In 1959	59	34	7
In 1969	38	60	2
Multiple Businesses but Closely Related			
In 1949	57	40	3
In 1959	28	72	0
In 1969	10	89	1
Multiple Businesses Spread Across Multiple Industries			
In 1949	0	61	39
In 1959	0	93	7
In 1969	2	85	13

SOURCE: Adapted from Richard P. Rumelt, *Strategy, Structure, and Economic Performance* (Boston: Harvard Business School, 1974): 71.

example. Given such a strategy, structure does not appear to make a great deal of difference, although it may be that so many large firms are now organized along product division lines that any competitive advantage has been lost.

Bureaucratic theory traces its history to Weber, as discussed in chapter 3. That theory has proved to be of considerable value, and it does tell us a great deal about the structuring of hierarchic organizations, but much is left unexplained. Greater precision is needed than Weber provided, and it has become increasingly evident that Weber did not fully comprehend the relation of education, knowledge, and professionalization to bureaucracy. The professions have produced their own organizational systems, and these are often at variance with bureaucracy.

Evidence on the Value of Bureaucratic Structures

There is a good deal of evidence that bureaucratic systems can be highly effective, if they are operated in close accord with the underlying theory, and if they are viewed as separate and distinct from professional systems. In particular, the bureaucratic form is important because of its ability to handle large size. Bureaucratic hierarchies can serve to control and coordinate organizations that are differentiated into a diverse range of subsystems or parts, and this type of differentiation appears to be a natural consequence of increasing size.[15] No other type of organizational structure is equally suited to coping with the demands of size.

Early Conclusions Exhibit 9.14 summarizes the results of research on essentially bureaucratic organizations carried out through the mid-1960s. A number of organizational processes and structural aspects clearly are related to effective organizational functioning, and most of these are in accord with Weber's theory of bureaucracy. However, the data indicate that certain of these generalizations do not apply when the organization contains a large number of highly educated and knowledgeable specialists or when professionals of one kind predominate.

Weber assumed that knowledge entered a bureaucracy through the top of the pyramid. Experience was greater at the top, and managers at that level could use information control to maintain their authority and to foster rational decision making. The reality, though, is that in a number of organizations, the knowledge needed—of a scientific or legal nature, for instance—comes in laterally at various levels in the hierarchy. The people who bring this knowledge have acquired it through education and experience outside the organization. This kind of situation can create competing power bases vis à vis the existing managerial hierarchy; it also creates major problems for bureaucratic theory. That is why the exceptions are noted in Exhibit 9.14.

The Decentralization Issue Studies conducted since the 1960s have often confirmed the conclusions of Exhibit 9.14, but if anything, they have extended the number of exceptions involving professionalization to the point that it is now clear that bureaucratic and professional systems must be viewed as separate and distinct, even though they may both exist within the same organization.

EXHIBIT 9.14 Characteristics of (essentially bureaucratic) effective organizations

1. Division of labor (tasks are subdivided).
2. Specialized departmentation (functional organization).
   Except with high education levels and knowledge.
3. Mechanization (outputs produced by machines).
   Except where professionalization is high.
4. Continuous systems of assembling outputs (production lines as opposed to batch production).
5. Legitimacy (behavior is socially approved).
6. Rational–legal authority to make decisions (as opposed to charismatic authority, for instance).
7. Centralization with respect to tactical decisions.
   Except with high education levels and knowledge.
8. Centralization with respect to strategic decisions.
9. Autonomy (free to make own decisions).
10. An ideology (for example, the American business creed) with high congruence (logical consistency with the culture), priority (attaching importance to cultural aspects), and conformity (performance corresponds to these norms).
11. Co-optation (including co-optation from the society's major elite).
12. Representation (going out into other organizations of the society, as distinguished from bringing them in via co-optation).
13. A major elite constituency (of stockholders, customers, suppliers, and the like).
14. Use of sanctions (rewards and punishments).
15. Essentially impersonal hierarchic relationships (as in Weber's theory of bureaucracy).
16. Rewards tied to organizational goals and based on group performance.
17. Communication (transmission of information) both vertically and horizontally.
18. Communication that is rational (as opposed to emotional), face-to-face, and formal (official).
19. Size.
   Except where professionalization is high.
20. Transfers to varied jobs in varied locations to promote effectiveness.
   Except where professionalization is high.

Adapted from James L. Price, *Organizational Effectiveness: An Inventory of Propositions* (Homewood, Ill.: Irwin, 1968).

The early studies seemed to indicate that highly centralized decision making at the top of the managerial hierarchy produced greater success. It has become increasingly apparent, however, that this needs qualification. In large organizations, the ideal pattern is one of considerable formalization in that rules and procedures are clearly spelled out. Along with this formalization goes greater division of labor and separation of the work into specialized components, as well as greater standardization of personnel practices, control systems, and the like so that they are applied in essentially the same manner across the diverse array of units. All such division and standardization comes from the top. But given that formalization, specialization, and standardization are firmly in place, there usually is a good deal of decentralization, with decision making moving down from the top of the organization to lower levels. This appears to be a desirable situation.

The type of organization that Chandler described, with decentralized product divisions and sophisticated systems for their coordination and control, fits this model, but so too does a functionally structured firm with a combination of formalization, specialization, standardization, and decentralization. Furthermore, decentralization may extend much further down into the firm than Chandler noted; within established rules and procedures, decisions may in fact be made at quite low levels. As a result, considerable influence is exerted on organization members from a variety of directions. There is ample evidence that, when influence is great throughout the structure for members to act in certain ways consistent with goals, and when that influence comes from varied sources at different levels, organizations are more effective.[16]

Bureaucratic and Professional Systems Distinguished   The ideal pattern described applies only to bureaucracies or to the bureaucratic parts of organizations that contain other systems as well, such as those of a professional or group-based nature. In particular it is important, as Exhibit 9.14 indicates, to distinguish professional systems so that they are not treated as if they were hierarchic—a not infrequent error. Exhibit 9.15 provides information on certain features that distinguish bureaucratic systems (as seen by office and production personnel in large corporations, civil service employees, members of the military, and prison guards) and professional systems (as seen by ministers, physicians, pharmacists, veterinarians, lawyers, dentists, medical technicians, certified public accountants, and college professors). Having considered the design of bureaucratic systems at some length, let us now turn to systems of a professional nature.

The Nature of Professional Systems

The operation of a professional system assumes the existence of some outside reference and membership group beyond the bounds of the organization. Role prescriptions for professionals are influenced much more by this outside source than by the employing organization itself. There are certain things that professionals are supposed to do simply because of the profession they are in, and they are prepared to do these things by their professional training.

Professional Organizations   Purely professional systems start with independent private practice. Such individuals may band together in a group practice. With more professionals involved, a full-scale organization emerges. Professional organizations of particular importance in the business world includ accounting firms, law firms, research organizations, some consulting firms, and architecture firms.

In organizations of this type, many of the activities that managers perform in bureaucratic systems are taken on by the total professional component or by a set of senior, high-status professionals. Influencing, organizing, planning, staffing, and the like thus are professional rather than managerial functions. In contrast to bureaucratic systems, professional organizations tend to use committees extensively and to vote on important issues much more frequently. The structure tends to be quite flat, with status differentiations based on professional expertise and experience. Thus a consulting firm may have its directors, principals, and associates; a university, its full, associate, and assistant professors;

Differentiating Characteristics of Bureaucratic or Hierarchical Systems	Differentiating Characteristics of Professional Systems
Work rules and regulations established by management	A large number of jobs classified as professions
Job results evaluated by superiors	Work satisfaction based on enjoyment of one's profession
Organizational changes carried out by management	Learning of a job based essentially on professional training
Individual competence judged by management	On-the-job training intended primarily for professional development
Pay levels based on seniority or hierarchical position	Long hours due to professional commitment
Freedom of action limited by organizational guidelines	Important day-to-day communication, always with fellow professionals and clients
Organizational leaders appointed by management	Individual efforts devoted to professional goals
Punishments established by management	The benefits of work go to clients or colleagues
Screening and selecting new employees accomplished by a personnel unit	Relationships with clients based on professional knowledge and trust
Counseling of problem employees carried out by superiors	Career development oriented toward professional development
Replacement of absent employees accomplished by superiors	Primary loyalty to the profession
Job changes initiated by management	Leaders selected on the basis of professional competence
Risk of failure assumed by top-level managers	The job is central to one's life and part of one's individual identity
Resources for work accomplishment allocated by management	Professional knowledge more important than any other type
Meetings called and conducted by management	Status based on professional and occupational competence

SOURCE: Based on John E. Oliver, *Scoring Guide for the Oliver Organization Description Questionnaire* (Atlanta, Ga.: Organizational Measurement Systems Press, 1981); and "An Instrument for Classifying Organizations," *Academy of Management Journal* (December 1982).

and a law firm, its senior and junior partners, as well as a group, variously designated, of young lawyers not yet elected to partnership.

Professional organizations do include non-professionals, including clerical and other support staff, usually some finance and accounting people, and perhaps certain personnel specialists, but these individuals are subordinate to the professional group and cannot qualify for professional positions without meeting appropriate training and, in most cases, licensing requirements. Thus individual professionals retain considerable independence and discretion. The major constraints on their behavior come from statements by professional bodies and associations, the existing code of professional ethics and values, and from licensing and certification laws. Discipline, if needed, is administered either by an outside professional group or by the employing firm.

In this type of system, there is considerable participation by professionals in the governance of their organization. As a group, the professionals have the power, and their norms dominate the work situation. Typically, there is strong commitment to both the organization and the profession as a whole, with the two being closely aligned. Furthermore, professional organizations that closely match this model—participation, commitment, support of professional norms, and power primarily in professional hands—tend to be the more effective.

Effects of Increased Size   Problems often arise because successful professional organizations tend to grow. A point is reached at which not all professionals know each other. Local CPA firms grow into national and international organizations, clinics become large hospitals, small colleges become major universities. In most cases, a permanent managerial hierarchy begins to appear, usually a group of professionals turned full-time administrators, or perhaps a non-professional administrative component of the kind presently existing in most hospitals.

The professional system remains, but a bureaucratic overlay is placed on it to coordinate the parts of the growing structure and to allocate resources. As a result, two power centers emerge in the organization, with a very unstable balance between them. Conflict is common, and the consequences detrimental for individuals and for the organization as a whole.[17] Ideally, some agreement is reached early on regarding the kinds of decisions to be made within the professional and bureaucratic systems. But in practice, such agreements are fragile, and there is considerable loose-lying power. Not inappropriately, decision making in large professional organizations has been compared to a garbage can, and a model of the processes involved with that name has been set forth.[18]

Professional Components   Professional systems may develop as components of much larger bureaucratic organizations. Examples of this are government and corporate research and development laboratories, company medical units and legal staffs, and the like. In these situations, there is no uneasy balance; ultimately the bureaucratic system is dominant. However, the organization needs the knowledge provided by the professional system.

Bureaucratic theory gives little guidance regarding how these professional systems should be incorporated within bureaucratic structures. However, the better solutions appear to involve the isolation of the professional system as an enclave or island within the bureaucracy. Under such circumstances, the professionals operate what amounts to a professional organization within the larger, quite differently structured whole. Many scientific research components are in fact geographically separated from other company units for this purpose. But it is not always the case that professional systems can maintain themselves under such circumstances. It is possible to have professionals employed, but working entirely in a bureaucratic system. Usually this alternative is not attractive to capable professionals, and major problems of staffing and turnover result.

Not infrequently, companies create dual hierarchies or ladders, especially in research and development contexts. Scientists are promoted up a ladder containing titles such as Research Associate, Associate Research Scientist, Senior Research Scientist, and the like, while managers move up through a more traditional managerial hierarchy. This dual system permits the payment of high salaries to capable scientists while retaining them in a research capacity. Their skills can then be more fully utilized than would be the case if they were forced into managerial positions in order to pay them at a level required to keep them.

Summary

What is actually known about the effective design of organizations remains considerably less than is desirable. Exhibit 9.16 outlines the contributions of the various theories and concepts. Overall the results are impressive, yet most of our current structures arose not so much as a result of theory, but from trial and error in

EXHIBIT 9.16 Contributions of various viewpoints, concepts, and approaches to organizational design

Source	Major Contributions
Social-psychological open systems concepts	Explaining the importance of environmental forces and the parts that need to be designed into an organization.
Sociotechnical systems theory	Providing a picture of how an organization composed of group-based systems might be achieved.
Sociological open systems concepts	Providing an understanding of various design options available for coping with uncertainty and interdependence.
Technological imperative	Stimulating research that has provided considerable insight into the limited role technology plays in achieving effective designs.
Mechanistic and organic systems	Stating the nature of organic systems, as opposed to more traditional bureaucratic structures.
Differentiation and integration views	Emphasizing the importance of integrating structures and processes, including matrix design.
Strategy and structure theory	Setting forth the relationships between growth strategies and structure, with special emphasis on formation of decentralized product divisions.
Bureaucratic theory	Providing an understanding of how large organizations may be designed and operated effectively.
Professional systems concepts	Specifying a type of organizational structure that differs from both bureaucracy and group-based systems.

practice. Theories such as the differentiation and integration concept, with its matrix design, and the strategy and structure view, with its decentralized product divisions, have tended to clarify existing structures and make them easier to use, but they did not invent them. Furthermore, we know relatively little about designing for organizational effectiveness. As a result, design is a very difficult area, not only for the student, but also for the practitioner.

For managers and others who are involved in the design of organizations, the current state of knowledge can only represent a major source of frustration. It does appear that following existing mandates will permit the design of an effective bureaucracy, or professional organization, or even a group-based system. But organizations of any size are increasingly emerging as composites that incorporate several of these systems, and in some cases other types of systems as well. To date, we do not know how to combine these varied systems in a single whole in such a way that each system will operate optimally. Accordingly, many larger organizations are not very effective.

Faced with these gaps in knowledge, there has been a tendency for companies to play "follow the leader." A successful firm adopts a particular structure, perhaps something new but not necessarily, and others, assuming that the structure caused the success, adopt and adapt it themselves. Consultants are often hired to carry out the restructuring; over time, they may introduce a particular design into hundreds of firms. Before long, they will go back and introduce another design that has achieved popularity. All this is not very good business, except for the consultant. This chapter demonstrates clearly the need for more solid information to guide design decisions.

What Have You Learned?

1. What are some of the major concepts of psychological open systems theory? How do these concepts help to explain organizational functioning?
2. When should matrix structures be used, and what problems can arise in using them?
3. What relationships have been found among standardization, formalization, centralization, specialization, and the effectiveness of bureaucracies?
4. What is the source and meaning of the following?
   a. co-optation
   b. buffering
   c. turbulent environments
   d. leveling
   e. functional departmentation
5. Although the mechanistic–organic systems concept has proved useful in certain respects, it has faced difficulties at the level of the contin-

gency variable. In what ways is the concept useful, and what is the nature of its difficulties?
6. How does growth strategy operate as a contingency variable? In what ways has it proved important?
7. Given what is now known, how would you describe the relationship between technology and structure?
8. How are free-standing professional organizations structured, and how do they differ from bureaucracies?
9. Both social psychological and sociotechnical systems theory consider types and aspects of environments. What are the similarities and differences in the two approaches?
10. What relationships between environmental factors and structural characteristics are proposed by the Lawrence and Lorsch theory? How have these hypotheses fared when subjected to research?

How Well Can You Apply Your Knowledge?

Problem 1. A large retail grocery chain operating in the western states had been experiencing considerable conflict at top levels for some time. This conflict reverberated through the organization and had become so pronounced that the company's fragile profit margin, averaging about 1 percent of sales, was threatened. The conflicts appeared to be perpetuated, rather than resolved, by the existing organizational structure.

One type of structural building block was the system of individual stores, each headed by a store manager. These stores varied consideraly, not only in size, but also in the types of products that sold well and in the degree to which price competition was important. At least three different types of stores could be identified—those in relatively affluent suburban areas, those in urban working-class neighborhoods, and those in rural or small city locations. Managers of some of the larger stores reported directly to the senior vice-president for retail operations, who in turn reported to the president; these reporting relationships typically dated from a period when the chain was much smaller. The more frequent pattern was to form geographical groupings, which typically contained a variety of stores, with a number of store managers reporting to a regional manager who in turn reported to the senior vice-president. Over the years, these regional groupings had changed frequently, so that a single store might have been in three or four different regions over a five-year period.

A second major structural feature was the product organization. At the lower levels, this consisted of buyers and merchandisers who went into the individual stores to provide product and promotional expertise. The product organization was segmented, in large part so as to match the different sources from which products were obtained. As a consequence, there were units for produce, grocery, meat, dairy, frozen foods, and so on. Each of these product units, with its own buyers and merchandisers, was headed by a vice-president. The product vice-presidents reported in turn to their own senior vice-president for purchasing and merchandising, who reported to the president.

The company also included other units such as warehousing, industrial relations, and financial operations, but these did not appear to be major contributors to the firm's difficulties. The real problems revolved around the almost continual conflicts between the store and product organizations and, to a somewhat lesser degree, within the store organization itself. Attempts to solve these problems through top level staffing changes had proven unsuccessful. It seemed that, no matter who held a senior vice-president position, that person inevitably became immersed in controversy. The need for a change in organizational design to reduce this conflict was apparent. In addition, buying, stocking, and pricing decisions were not being adjusted appropriately to differences in store types, with the result that shelf inventories were often not synchronized with demand.

Questions
1. How would you redesign the store and product structures to resolve the existing problems, if you were this company's president?
2. For each instance of change, indicate why you would make that particular alteration and what specific problem it is intended to solve. Do you believe your newly designed organization would prove more profitable? Why?

Problem 2. A large international management consulting firm had grown rapidly by opening new offices in major cities throughout the United States and Europe. The basic strategy was to assign each new office a specific geographical territory and to put a partner in charge of the office who had as a prime mandate the development of new business. Although these managers reported to the managing partner and the firm's central management in Chicago, they were given considerable latitude in building up their offices. How they did this was up to them, but if client billings did not achieve certain predetermined standards for growth, the managers were relieved and a new partner sent in.

The structures within the offices themselves did not permit much discretion below the level of the manager. The consultants were assigned in groups of from four to six to permanent engagement managers. There were rigid guides for various types of client engagements, and the engagement managers watched closely to see that these were followed. In the smaller offices, all engagement managers reported to the individual in charge of the office, but in the larger offices, there were varying levels of management in between, depending on the size of the office. The major concern was to prevent mistakes that might lose clients.

The consultants all had graduate degrees, and many held doctorates in various areas. The firm contained a wide range of expertise. However, consultants were assigned to engagement managers primarily to fill openings and maintain staffing levels, rather than to assure some particular balance of competence. As a result, a group could contain a high proportion of individuals with one type of competence and be totally lacking in individuals with another. There was no formal structure linking those with a particular specialty, either within the offices or across the firm. In general, a consultant was a consultant, in spite of the diverse array of educational and employment backgrounds represented.

Still, the firm carried out engagements in a variety of areas. Among the more frequent contracts were consulting assignments in:

Compensation administration

Organization planning

Market planning

Economic analysis and industry position

Data processing and management information systems

Cost reduction and profit improvement

Product marketing

Acquisitions and mergers

Inventory control

Production planning and control

Client engagements were assigned to engagement managers largely with a view to maintaining a balanced work load. If possible, all the consultants in a group worked on all engagements assigned to that group. In practice, however, some engagements did not require much staffing, and some consultants might end up with little to do for varying periods of time. Large engagements might require the services of two or more groups, and in these cases, actual supervision of the engagement shifted up to the next higher level in the office hierarchy.

An internal audit of this structure carried out by central management and prompted by declining billings in several of the larger and older offices revealed that it was not working very well. The specific problems noted were as follows:

1. Turnover among consultants, and especially among those considered to have the potential to become partners, was too high.
2. Because of excessive administrative overhead and consultants not being fully utilized on engagements, the proportion of time actually billed to clients was well below that for other competing firms.
3. Consultants with certain types of specialized expertise were not remaining current with new developments in their special fields.
4. Clients were often dissatisfied because they believed more consultants were assigned to them than they needed, thus causing over-billing, and because the engagement group often lacked some highly specialized competence needed for the job. These perceptions had negative consequences primarily for repeat business.
5. The practice of servicing clients within strictly defined geographical areas meant that different components of a national or international company would be assigned to different offices. Coordination of these multi-office efforts was poor.

Questions

1. If you were serving on the central management audit group of the firm, what revisions in existing structures and procedures would you propose to correct the problems noted? Outline a new structure for the firm.
2. What arguments would you introduce to support your various proposals? How do these arguments relate to the various concepts and theories discussed in this chapter and summarized in Exhibit 8.18?

Additional Sources for More Detailed Study

Abrahamsson, Bengt. *Bureaucracy or Participation: The Logic of Organization.* Beverly Hills, Calif.: Sage, 1977.

Brown, Warren B., and Moberg, Dennis J. *Organization Theory and Management: A Macro Approach.* New York: Wiley, 1980.

Bucher, Rue, and Stelling, Joan G. *Becoming Professional.* Beverly Hills, Calif.: Sage, 1977.

Chandler, Alfred D. *The Visible Hand: The Managerial Revolution in American Business.* Cambridge, Mass.: Harvard University Press, 1977.

Channon, Derek F. *The Strategy and Structure of British Enterprise.* Boston: Harvard Business School, 1973.

Dyas, Gareth P., and Thanheiser, Heinz T. *The Emerging European Enterprise: Strategy and Structure in French and German Industry.* Boulder, Colo.: Westview Press, 1976.

Franko, Lawrence G. *The European Multinationals: A Renewed Challenge to American and British Big Business.* Stamford, Conn.: Greylock, 1976.

Galbraith, Jay R., and Nathanson, Daniel A. *Strategy Implementation: The Role of Structure and Process.* St. Paul, Minn.: West, 1978.

Hall, Richard H. *Organizations: Structure and Process.* Englewood Cliffs, N.J.: Prentice-Hall, 1977.

Jackson, John H., and Morgan, Cyril P. *Organization Theory: A Macro Perspective for Management.* Englewood Cliffs, N.J.: Prentice-Hall, 1982.

Khandwalla, Pradip N. *The Design of Organizations.* New York: Harcourt Brace Jovanovich, 1977.

Lorsch, Jay W., and Allen, Stephen A. *Managing Diversity and Interdependence—An Organizational Study of Multidivisional Firms.* Boston: Harvard Business School, 1973.

Lorsch, Jay W., and Morse, John J. *Organizations and Their Members—A Contingency Approach.* New York: Harper and Row, 1974.

Miles, Robert H. *Macro Organizational Behavior.* Santa Monica, Calif.: Goodyear, 1980.

Mintzberg, Henry. *The Structuring of Organizations.* Englewood Cliffs, N.J.: Prentice-Hall, 1979.

Perrow, Charles. *Complex Organizations: A Critical Essay.* Glenview, Ill.: Scott, Foresman, 1972.

Rushing, William A., and Zald, Mayer N. *Organizations and Beyond: Selected Essays of James D. Thompson.* Lexington, Mass.: D.C. Heath, 1976.

Steers, Richard M. *Organizational Effectiveness: A Behavioral View.* Santa Monica, Calif.: Goodyear, 1977.

Stogdill, Ralph M. *Individual Behavior and Group Achievement.* New York: Oxford University Press, 1959.

Tosi, Henry L. *Theories of Organization.* New York: Wiley, 1984.

Notes

1. P. G. Herbst, *Alternatives to Hierarchies* (Leiden, Netherlands: Martinus Nijhoff, 1976).

2. Eric Rhenman, *Organization Theory for Long-Range Planning* (London: Wiley, 1973).

3. John B. Miner, *Theories of Organizational Structure and Process* (Hinsdale, Ill.: Dryden, 1982), Chapters 4 and 5.

4. See Jeffrey Pfeffer and Gerald R. Salancik, *The External Control of Organizations: A Resource Dependence Perspective* (New York: Harper and Row, 1978); and Johannes M. Pennings, *Interlocking Directorates* (San Francisco: Jossey-Bass, 1980).

5. Fremont E. Kast and James E. Rosenzweig, *Contingency Views of Organization and Management* (Chicago: Science Research Associates, 1973).

6. Joan Woodward, *Industrial Organization: Behavior and Control* (London; Oxford University Press, 1970).

7. Joan Woodward, "Technology, Material Control, and Organizational Behavior," in *Modern Organizational Theory: Contextual, Environmental, and Socio-Cultural Variables,* ed. Anant R. Negandhi (Kent, Ohio: Kent State University Press, 1973).

8. D. S. Pugh and David J. Hickson, *Organizational Structure in Its Context: The Aston Programme I* (Lexington, Mass.: D. C. Heath, 1976).

9. Robert S. Billings, Richard J. Klimoski, and James A. Breaugh, "The Impact of a Change in Technology on Job Characteristics: A Quasi-Experiment," *Administrative Science Quarterly* (June 1977).

10. Jay W. Lorsch, "Contingency Theory and Organizational Design: A Personal Odyssey," in *The Management of Organizational Design: Strategies and Implementation,* eds. Ralph H. Kilmann, Louis R. Pondy, and Dennis P. Slevin (New York: North-Holland, 1976).

11. Harvey F. Kolodny, "Matrix Organization Designs to Produce Useful Knowledge," in *Producing Useful Knowledge for Organizations,* ed. Ralph H. Kilmann (New York: Praeger, 1983).

12. H. Kirk Downey, Don Hellriegel, and John W. Slocum, "Environmental Uncertainty: The Construct and Its Application," *Administrative Science Quarterly* (December 1975).

13. Alfred D. Chandler, *Strategy and Structure: Chapters in the History of the American Industrial Enterprise* (Cambridge, Mass.: MIT Press, 1962).

14. Alfred D. Chandler and Herman Daems, "Administrative Coordination, Allocation, and Monitoring: Concepts and Comparisons," in *Law and the Formation of the Big Enterprises in the 19th and Early 20th Centuries,* eds. Norbert Horn and Jürgen Kocka (Göttingen, West Germany: Vandenhoeck and Ruprecht, 1979).

15. Peter M. Blau, *On the Nature of Organizations* (New York: Wiley, 1974).

16. Arnold S. Tannenbaum and Robert A. Cooke, "Organizational Control: A Review of Studies Employing the Control Graph Method," in *Organizations Alike and Unlike,* eds. C. J. Lammers and D. Hickson (London: Routledge and Kegan Paul, 1979).

17. James E. Sorensen and Thomas L. Sorensen, "The Conflict of Professionals in Bureaucratic Organizations," *Administrative Science Quarterly* (March 1974).

18. James G. March and Johan P. Olsen, *Ambiguity and Choice in Organizations* (Bergen, Norway: Universitetsforlaget, 1976).

CHAPTER 10

Organizational Change and Development

CHAPTER OUTLINE

Bureaucracy and Change
Direct Hierarchic Change
Consultant-Initiated Change
The Role of Change Units
Resistance to Change
    Rationality and Resistance
    Individual Sources
    Group Sources
    Entrenched Bureaucracy
    Bureaucracy and Innovation

Organization Development
Definitions and Values
Origins in Sensitivity Training and T-Groups
    Argyris's Contributions
    Bennis's Contributions
    Revisions and Results
Sociotechnical Systems Design
    Application Guidelines
    Norwegian and Swedish Projects
    General Foods at Topeka
The Contingency Approach to Organization
    Development
    Grounding in Theory
    Introducing Matrix Structures
The Survey Feedback Approach
    The Role and Use of Data
    Relative Value
Quality Circles
    Japanese Origins
    Introducing the Structure

Growth and Decline
Reasons for Growth
    Survival of the Fittest
    Purposive Action
Stages of Growth
    The Three-Stage Model
    Extended Models
    Acquisitions and Divestitures
Problems of Decline
    Structural Changes
    Managerial Failure

OBJECTIVES

To show how bureaucracies use the hierarchy to bring about changes and how resistance to these changes may develop.

To provide an understanding of what organization development is and how some of its major approaches actually work.

To consider why organizations grow and decline, with emphasis on the process and structure effects.

L ike almost everything else, organizations change over time. Some change rapidly and some slowly. Some change in ways that make them more effective, and some change in ways that make them less so. Organizational change may happen in a variety of dimensions. The most immediately obvious are structural changes—reorganizations. But changes may occur also in organizational processes, procedures, the people who fill key positions, technology, size, and so on. Some changes have a strong "demand character"—that is, they are responses to other changes, either within or outside the organization, that can hardly be avoided. Technological changes, for instance, may force the creation of new specialist positions and the granting of authority to those who fill them, or new computers may require new expertise for their use. Growth in the size of a company seems to force differentiation into more divisions, departments, groups, and units.

In contrast to these "demand character" changes, many changes are made not because they are required, but because they seem desirable. They occur at somebody's discretion. This somebody (or group of somebodies) will vary depending on the type of organizational system. In bureaucratic organizations, which include most companies, changes are typically initiated by key managers; they are top-down changes. But there are also a number of change procedures, grouped primarily under the title of organization development, that are more bottom-up, or at least the source of change is very close to where the change is applied.

BUREAUCRACY AND CHANGE

Top-down changes receive their major support from some level above the point where changes begin to occur. In essence, an announcement is made that a new structure, or set of procedures, or whatever the change will be, will apply as of some specified date. These changes work to the extent that the existing inducement–contributions balance supports the management's right to exercise this type of authority. People say to themselves, "Given what I am getting from the company, it seems right that the company be able to carry out these kinds of changes."

The impetus for changes of this kind may come from somewhere up in the management hierarchy itself, or it may come from a consulting relationship or from an internal unit charged with initiating change. In both of the latter cases, however, the authority for change, the force behind it, still comes from the bureaucratic hierarchy.

Direct Hierarchic Change

Hierarchic changes are typically initiated by some kind of memorandum or written directive. For change to occur exactly as anticipated, there has to be clear and unambiguous support from the top, and clear and unambiguous communication of what is intended as well. The conditions for effective use of hierarchic authority must exist.

Changes carried out in this way can be very effective. Exhibit 10.1 provides an example. In this instance change was limited to one plant that had been suffering major difficulties, with the company's remaining five plants left unchanged. The

EXHIBIT 10.1 Efficiency levels calculated for five unchanged plants and the changed plant—year prior to change and three years later

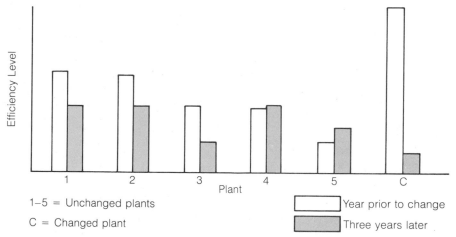

1–5 = Unchanged plants

C = Changed plant

☐ Year prior to change

▨ Three years later

SOURCE: Adapted from Robert H. Guest, *Organizational Change: The Effect of Successful Leadership* (Homewood, Ill.: Irwin-Dorsey, 1962): 99.

changes were initiated by top management and included the installation of a new manager at the changed plant. Previously, power had been highly centralized above the plant level. Management essentially had been running the problem plant on an absentee basis. Now, authority was decentralized to the plant level, and the new plant manager was permitted considerable freedom. The plant manager in turn created a variety of committees and took a number of other steps calculated to foster horizontal communication and integration within the plant. Exhibit 10.1 compares the original problem plant with the other five over a three-year period during which the changes were in effect. Efficiency levels, measured in terms of direct labor costs, at the changed plant went from worst to best in this period. It appears in this instance that the changes initiated by top management did take effect and that their impact was positive.

Consultant-Initiated Change

When management consultants are involved in the change process, the difference is that the specific content of the change is contained in a consulting recommendation. Also, the consultants may participate in implementing the changes once the company's endorsement has been obtained. Again, however, the force for change comes from the legitimized authority vested in the managerial hierarchy. (This approach, which is typical for large management consulting firms, should be clearly distinguished from that of organization development consultants, who usually operate very differently.)

Exhibit 10.2 provides an example of changes initiated by an engagement team from McKinsey and Company in the structure of the personal life sales division of an insurance company. A major objective was to strengthen the branch office organization. The most pronounced structural changes are the creation of the regional manager positions and the movement of the assistant branch managers

EXHIBIT 10.2 Example of organizational change initiated by a consulting firm in a life insurance company

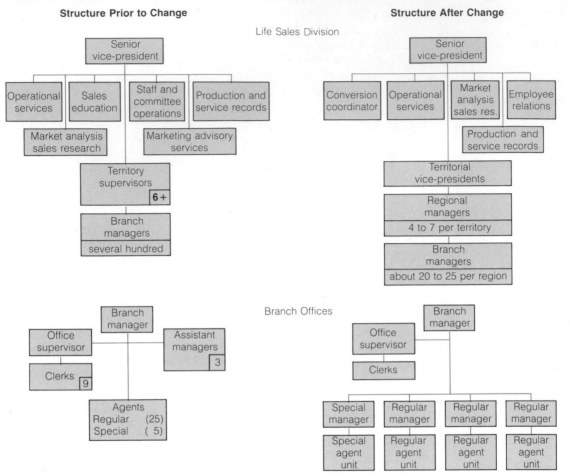

SOURCE: Reprinted by permission from Jeremiah J. O'Connell, *Managing Organizational Innovation* (Hornewood, Ill.: Irwin, 1968): 40–41, 68, 70. Copyright © 1968 by Richard D. Irwin, Inc.

from advisory or supersalesman positions directly into the line chain, as special and regular managers.

The consultants were hired initially by the senior vice president of sales and made their recommendations to top management. Upon acceptance, these recommendations were transmitted down the hierarchy. Procedures for carrying out the changes were specified. The consultants also prepared various guides indicating in detail how the duties of certain positions were to be carried out. The intent of these guides was to ensure that intended shifts in responsibilities and authority actually did occur. Initially the consultants worked directly at the branch level, training personnel and actually implementing the recommendations.

As a result of all this, many changes in behavior patterns did occur. In most cases the results achieved were what the consultants recommended and upper management authorized, although some distortions and departures from design did work their way into the system. Furthermore, after the change, policy lapses decreased, and so did expenses; somewhat later an improvement in net new premiums appeared. Although these contributions to profits could conceivably have been a result of other factors, it appears likely that the changes initiated by the consultants were a major source.

In this particular instance, although the branch manager position changed and may have been weakened, there were numerous new managerial positions created. The overall effect was that many people benefited, and in general the reaction to the changes, once carried out, was positive. But in a period of declining business, during which positions must be eliminated and managers terminated, the reaction might well have been very different. At such times the use of consultants to implement change can be a useful strategy, independent of the expertise the consultants may bring to the problem. The consultants can take the brunt of any opposition or ill-feeling that arises. To a large extent these negative reactions will depart with the consultants. Company management is then left free to carry on without a residual undercurrent of opposition. Some consulting firms attempt to select their clients so as not to be placed in this scapegoat role very often, but all serve in this capacity at one time or another.

The Role of Change Units

In many companies there are internal units that serve in much the same way as outside consultant engagement teams. In fact, these units may on occasion work with the consultants so that a team is formed containing both company and consultant personnel. A common example of this type of unit is an organization planning group, which typically reports at relatively high levels, either within the personnel component or to the chief operating officer of the company. Such groups typically function to:

1. Establish guidelines for analyzing, evaluating, and developing effective organization structures.
2. Perform organization studies and recommend changes.
3. Help clarify the roles of individuals and organizational units.[1]

Resistance to Change

Changes do not always go according to plan. Indeed, some planned changes do not go through at all. Changes can meet resistance of a kind that stops them completely or, more frequently, diverts them in a direction other than that anticipated. Many newly elected U.S. presidents with plans to restructure the federal bureaucracy have seen their terms of office expire without much being accomplished in that direction, despite their best efforts to carry out campaign promises. The same sorts of things happen to company chief executive officers all the time.

Rationality and Resistance   Some theorists imply that resistance to proposed change is irrational, that it arises from personality structures that are rigid, biased, authoritarian, and insecure. This can be true, but there are many instances in which it is not. Some proposed changes are poor ideas and not in the best interests of the organization. In such cases rationality is on the side of the resistors. Change for its own sake has no inherent organizational value; only change that contributes to the organization's goals is organizationally rational.

There is another sense in which resistance to change can be rational as well. Many changes bring about shifts in the power balance. When people resist a change that is perceived as detrimental to their power positions, and perhaps their compensation as well, they may or may not be showing organizational rationality, but they most certainly are being personally rational. Many very capable people initiate this kind of resistance. This does not mean that they become adamant in the face of strong arguments demonstrating that the changes will foster organizational goals. It does mean that they try to establish a bargaining position so that they can come out of the change process with as little loss as possible in their power, status, and earnings.

Individual Sources Exhibit 10.3 summarizes a series of studies that sought to identify characteristics of people who seemed to resist change no matter what the change was, as contrasted with characteristics of people who responded more favorably to change. These and other data indicate clearly some people do seem, by their very nature, to oppose change. Such people are more anxious and worried about their work than others, and they lack confidence in their own capabilities.[2] It appears that their resistance is based on their anticipation of being unable to cope with the changed circumstances.

Many times such individuals simply fail in their resistance efforts and the change occurs anyway. However, if the organization is strongly committed to the status quo and wedded to its successes of the past, if it places a high value on individuals who perpetuate its long-standing traditions, then individual resistance to change gets an assist from the "culture" of the organization. Needed changes may well be blocked under such circumstances, to the ultimate detriment of all concerned.

EXHIBIT 10.3 Individual and managerial characteristics of persons who resist and persons who embrace needed changes

Change Resistors	Change Embracers
Concern for safety and security	Desire for new experiences and some risk
Preoccupied primarily with means, rather than ends	Greater attention to ends, less focus on the means per se
Belief in a "one best way"	Open to alternative courses of action
Aspire to regularity, order, financial security, prestige	Aspire to achievement, interesting work, freedom, personal responsibility
View managers as experts on the work of their subordinates	View managers as generalists, not expert in all areas they supervise
Submissive with superiors and directive with subordinates	Emphasize authority appropriate to individual's contribution
Assume that solutions once successful can be applied to new problems as well	Less stress on prior solutions and more concern with evidence related to specific problem at hand

SOURCE: Adapted from Denis Pym, "Effective Managerial Performance in Organizational Change," *Journal of Management Studies* (February 1966).

Group Sources Resistance can also stem from group sources, as when the change threatens the existence of a cohesive work group. The British coal mining studies discussed in chapter 6 provide a clear example. In that instance, a change to a new technology, the longwall method, did occur, with the result that many long-established work groups were broken up and the miners were forced to perform on an individualized basis. The resistant response thwarted the productive potential of the new technology. Absenteeism became high and productivity low. In cases where work groups were left intact, these signs of resistance to the new technology did not appear. Furthermore, restoration of a group structure appears to have ended resistance where it was occurring.

Entrenched Bureaucracy Several theorists have taken the position that there is something basic in the bureaucratic form of work organization that produces a resistance to change. This view is inherent in sociotechnical systems theory, in the organic-mechanistic distinction, and in many other formulations that have their origins in human relations concepts. The idea is that, in a rapidly changing world, organizations also need to change, to adjust to the changes in their environments. But since bureaucracies are unable to respond to this challenge, they must inevitably disappear, to be replaced by other forms of work organization that are less inherently resistant to change. Certain inadequacies of bureaucracy as an organizational form are listed in Exhibit 10.4. This criticism places strong emphasis on the innovation-resisting characteristics of bureaucracies.

On the basis of previous discussions, we might take issue with a number of the criticisms of bureaucracy contained in Exhibit 10.4. These problems can occur in bureaucracies, and probably in a number of other organizational forms as well, but they do not appear to be so inevitable as the author assumes. However, the

---

EXHIBIT 10.4 "Inherent" problems with bureaucratic systems said to make them unable to change

Bureaucratic systems by nature:

1. Do not adequately allow for personal growth and development of mature personalities.
2. Develop conformity.
3. Do not take into account the informal organization or unanticipated problems.
4. Have systems of control and authority that are hopelessly outdated.
5. Have no adequate judicial process.
6. Do not possess adequate means for resolving differences and conflicts among ranks and, most particularly, among functional groups.
7. Thwart and distort communication and innovative ideas because of hierarchic divisions.
8. Fail to utilize their full human resources because of mistrust or fear of reprisals.
9. Cannot assimilate influx of new technology or personnel entering the organization.
10. Modify the personality structure so that organization members reflect the dull, conditioned "organization man."

SOURCE: Adapted from Warren G. Bennis, *Changing Organizations* (New York: McGraw-Hill, 1966): 6.

crucial question is whether bureaucracy inherently creates a widespread resistance to change.

Bureaucracy and Innovation Historical analyses dealing with strategy and structure, such as those of Alfred Chandler, would seem to say that bureaucracies can change, and very effectively. Conclusions derived from what has now become a sizable body of research appear to support this expectation. For instance, there is evidence that people who work in bureaucratic organizations tend somewhat more than others to embrace change (see Exhibit 10.3) rather than resist it.[3] Other types of organizational systems appear to be very good at generating innovative ideas, but not so good at putting the ideas into effect. When it comes to actual adoption of innovative changes, bureaucratic systems are likely to be superior. It is also not true that bureaucracies are incapable of initiating innovations; under appropriate circumstances, they seem to generate innovative changes as well as adopt them.[4]

The available evidence indicates that any type of organizational system can be innovative or not, depending on factors that have little to do with structure. We know for instance that certain types of entrepreneurial firms can be extremely rigid and resistant to change.[5] Yet other small entrepreneurial companies represent a major source of creative innovation in our society. Professional systems are widely cited as a major source of innovation, and correctly so, but on occasion university faculties will exhibit as much resistance to change as one could find anywhere.

The key factor in an organization's capacity to change appears to be not structure, but the existing culture, climate, or value system. If the organization's values point to change as a good, then people will come up with innovative ideas, and individualized resistance to change will be unlikely to gain much support. In bureaucratic systems, because they are hierarchic, the value for innovation must come from the top. If this is the case, and change-oriented behavior is rewarded as well, then there appears to be no reason to consider the bureaucratic form itself as a source of resistance to change.

ORGANIZATION DEVELOPMENT

A very different approach to change from the traditional bureaucratic "installation" of changes is that of organization development. This approach assumes that resistance, and consequently organizational stagnation, is almost inevitable when hierarchic authority is brought to bear. Accordingly, if a company is to be flexible and adaptive to a rapidly changing environment, the use of hierarchic authority should be minimized. There must be widespread participation in as many phases of the change process as possible so that people feel committed to the change. In this way, resistances are short-circuited. Change is experienced not so much as something that comes down from on high as it is a groundswell that sweeps through the organization.

Definitions and Values

There are a number of organization development methods, several of which are closely associated with some of the theoretical formulations considered in previous chapters. This variety of approaches has created a multiplicity of definitions of organization development itself. Exhibit 10.5 contains an extended statement

EXHIBIT 10.5 A definition of organization development

Organization development is a process of data collection, diagnosis, action planning, intervention and change, and evaluation of results applied to a whole organization or a large component of it. Its aims are to:

1. Enhance the degree of integration or fit among structures, processes, strategies, people, and culture in the organization.
2. Develop creative organizational solutions.
3. Develop the organization's capacity to renew itself so that it continues to cope effectively with external forces.

The organization development process occurs through collaboration of organizational members working with a change agent who possesses relevant knowledge and skills. More specifically, organization development:

1. Seeks to create self-directed change to which people are committed by virtue of their participation in the total process.
2. Is system-wide in nature so that a change in one part inevitably changes other parts.
3. Typically places equal emphasis on solving immediate problems and on the long-term development of an adaptive organization. The latter is achieved by encouraging individuals to confront problems rationally as they occur.
4. Places more emphasis than other approaches on a collaborative, participative process of data collection, diagnosis, and action for arriving at problem solutions.
5. Frequently leads to new organizational arrangements and relationships that break with traditional bureaucratic patterns.
6. Utilizes a change agent who brings two types of competencies to the change effort—skills in working with individuals and groups, and knowledge about organization design, management practice, and interpersonal dynamics.

SOURCE: Adapted from Michael Beer, *Organization Change and Development: A Systems View* (Santa Monica, Calif.: Goodyear, 1980): 10.

that appears to include most of the content in these varied definitions. Characteristically, organization development programs are aimed at moving an organization away from traditional hierarchic, bureaucratic processes and structures toward other more group-based, professional, and/or task-based (as in work redesign) forms. Exactly which among these alternative systems is emphasized depends on the theory underlying the particular organization development effort.

A major part of the considerable controversy that has surrounded organization development since its beginnings over 30 years ago has been concern over the nature of its values. The approach can trace its origins to the Hawthorne studies, and it still carries with it many of the humanistic values that pervaded that research. Accordingly, organization development consultants and practitioners have been accused of being more interested in the personal welfare of organization members than in achieving corporate goals. In this view, the values of organization development place it in direct opposition to managerial goals of profit and growth. The kinds of values represented are those noted in the first two lists of Exhibit 10.6. It is unquestionably true that such values have been associated with organization development since its beginning.

Against this backdrop, the third list of Exhibit 10.6 represents a major departure. The values here are knowledge and rationality, not necessarily humanism. As the author notes, organization development based on these values *could* lead

EXHIBIT 10.6 Three views of the values of organization development

Warren Bennis—A humane and democratic social philosophy
1. Improvement in interpersonal competence.
2. A shift in values so that human factors and feelings come to be considered legitimate.
3. Development of increased understanding among and within work groups.
4. Development of more effective team management.
5. Development of better methods of conflict resolution involving rationality and openness to replace the usual bureaucratic methods (suppression, compromise, unprincipled power).
6. Development of organic systems to replace mechanistic—group emphasis, mutual trust, shared responsibility, multigroup membership, shared control, extensive bargaining.

Newton Margulies and Anthony Raia—A humanistic ethic
1. Providing opportunities for people to function as human beings rather than as resources.
2. Providing opportunities for each organization member, and the organization, to develop to full potential.
3. Seeking to increase the effectiveness of the organization in terms of *all* its goals, not only profit.
3. Creating an environment in which it is possible to find exciting and challenging work.
5. Providing opportunities for people in organizations to influence the way in which they relate to their work, organization, and environment.
6. Treating each human being as a person with a complex set of needs, *all* of which are important.

Michael Beer—The values of informed choice
1. To help organizations generate valid data about the state of the organization in relation to its environment.
2. To help those with a stake in the organization to clarify the outcomes they desire.
3. To help organizations make strategic choices based on a diagnosis of the current situation and desired outcomes.

SOURCES: Adapted from Warren G. Bennis, *Organization Development: Its Nature, Origins and Prospects* (Reading, Mass.: Addison-Wesley, 1969): 15; Newton Margulies and Anthony P. Raia, *Conceptual Foundations of Organizational Development* (New York: McGraw-Hill, 1978): 137; and Michael Beer, *Organization Change and Development: A Systems View* (Santa Monica, Calif.: Goodyear, 1980): 43.

to increased "centralization of decisions, more traditional organizational forms, and more directive management styles."[6] It is unlikely that this viewpoint is held by a majority of organization development practitioners at the present time, but the point made is an important one—many of the concepts and techniques of organization development *can* be divorced from their original humanistic value base. Thus it is possible to consider the various organization development approaches simply as ways to change organizations, and to ask how well the approach does the job.

Origins in Sensitivity Training and T-Groups

The early period of organization development involved a heavy reliance on the techniques of sensitivity or T-group training. People exposed to this type of training learn to function more effectively in small groups, develop interpersonal skills, and acquire humanistic values. The idea was that they would then be better suited to install and operate organizational systems other than those of a bureaucratic nature. The views of Chris Argyris and Warren Bennis are widely associated with this type of emphasis in organization development, and their ideas are given primary attention here.

Argyris's Contributions Argyris's basic idea is that different decision structures should be used under different circumstances, in a manner not unlike the decision tree approaches considered in chapter 6 (see Exhibits 6.13 and 6.14). There is one major difference, however. Instead of managers deciding which structure to use, this decision is made with the widest possible involvement of organization members. Thus, ultimate authority resides in the participative efforts of the membership as a whole, not in the hierarchy. Actually, the decisions made in the traditional hierarchic way, and even those made in the manner of Likert's system 4, are rather trivial. All really important decisions are made so that each person has equal power. The resulting organization is one in which:

1. The direction of core activities is spread throughout, rather than being concentrated in top management.
2. The members are aware of the organization as a totality, rather than as a set of parts.
3. The guiding objectives are those of the whole, rather than of individual components.
4. It is possible to influence goal attainment, rather than lack influence.
5. It is possible to influence activities in the environment, rather than lack influence.
6. Core activities are influenced by past and future considerations, rather than by the present only.

The objective of group training was to change people so that they could adopt this kind of structure and operate it effectively. To this end, Argyris recommended that T-groups be formed extensively throughout the organization. Consultants or internal change agents would work with these groups, seeking to unfreeze commitments to current ideas and values and produce a readiness for, and ultimately acceptance of, the new values of organization development.[7] Thus the intent of the training was to increase:

1. Giving, and receiving from others, feedback on how behavior is perceived by other people.
2. Accepting, and helping others to accept, one's own values, attitudes, and feelings.
3. Openness to new values, attitudes, and feelings, and helping others to be open.
4. Experimenting with new values, attitudes, and feelings, and helping others to do the same.
5. Taking risks with new values, attitudes, and feelings.

Argyris has expanded his views in recent years so that training focuses less on interpersonal processes within a group, and more on real organizational problems outside the group.[8] However, the idea that values, attitudes, and feelings must be changed as a prelude to organizational change remains strong, as does the commitment to using group methods for this purpose.

Bennis's Contributions Although the approaches of Argyris and Bennis are similar in many respects, the basic concepts of the "good" organizations they wished to achieve through sensitivity training and T-groups vary somewhat. Argyris appears to have had in mind some type of group-based system. In contrast, Bennis seems to be more oriented toward models of the professional system, especially the temporary project teams often used in scientific research and development work. His view that bureaucracy is inadequate to the demands of the modern world, as set forth in Exhibit 10.4, is coupled with a prediction that professional employment will expand at an extremely rapid rate.

Given this "professionalization" of society, the need is to change to structures of the following nature:

1. Adaptive, rapidly changing, temporary systems.
2. Systems organized around the problems to be solved.
3. Problem-solving by groups of relative strangers with sets of diverse professional skills.
4. Groups that evolve in response to the particular problem, not to established role prescriptions.
5. Executives who are in fact coordinators or linking pins between project groups; they mediate, but do not arbitrate.
6. Differentiation of people according to skill and professional training, not hierarchic rank.[9]

Since T-groups are also temporary systems, they provide an ideal context for learning the skills and values needed in Bennis's organizations of the future.

Revisions and Results Over time, both Argyris and Bennis have come to question the use of T-groups that concern themselves only with processes internal to the group. In general, this type of training is out of vogue in the business world, and one rarely hears terms such as sensitivity training or T-grouping used favorably. However, terms such as "team-building" and "learning seminars" have a much better reputation. Often they imply much that was inherent in sensitivity training, but they also include a concern with actual tasks and problems of the organization. To the extent that this is true, the values of informed choice as noted by Michael Beer in Exhibit 10.6 come into play. Most current organization development efforts are characterized by a degree of organizational task emphasis and problem-solving.

Studies carried out to evaluate whether organization development with a sensitivity training component—either focused inward on the group or outward on the organization—does bring about change yield mixed results.[10] It is apparent that the approaches pioneered by Argyris and Bennis *can* bring about changes, but they do not always do so, and it is not clear why they work on some occasions and not on others. Overall, some kind of change in values, attitudes, behavior, productive output, or something occurs roughly half the time. Not infrequently these changes are of a kind that would involve a definite positive effect on profits. In comparison with other organization development approaches, the use of traditional sensitivity training or T-groups alone is relatively less effective.

A major problem with these approaches is that they often fail to produce lasting changes in the organization. In particular, the anticipated shifts to less bureaucratic systems fail to occur. This is true of both the older sensitivity training and the more recent team-building approaches. Even when performance and profitability improve, these results typically appear without any change having occurred in group-based or professional types of structures. Other types of organization development approaches, however, do achieve these structural effects.

Sociotechnical Systems Design

Sociotechnical theory is considered in chapter 6 in regard to groups, and again in chapter 9 in regard to broader aspects of organizational design. Applications of these concepts have come to be considered as an approach to organization development, an approach that ensures structural change if carried out in accordance with the theory.

Application Guidelines   Exhibit 10.7 contains a set of guidelines for introducing autonomous work groups. Others have advanced slightly different lists, but this set is characteristic. The emphasis on producing a high quality of work life for organization members (guideline 8) is typical of the sociotechnical approach.

One problem in undertaking sociotechnical organization development projects occurs at the outset. In line with the theory, the decision to move to autonomous work groups should be a group decision. But what if the group decides this is not the structure it wants? Experience indicates that, on occasion, autonomous work groups are resisted at the worker level. In actual practice, most organization development efforts of this kind are introduced through the use of hierarchic authority; the fact, if not the detailed form, of the change is specified by management, and authority is implicitly conveyed to the consultants who help install the new structure. Thus, the usual organization development sequence from value change to process and structure change may not be followed. Accordingly, resistance to change can develop to thwart the program, just as with any other hierarchic change.

This often has proved to be a major obstacle to successful implementation. One solution to this problem is to make participation in the autonomous work groups voluntary. In new plants, only those who want to work in this structure are hired, or only parts of existing operations are changed, and those parts are staffed with volunteers.

Norwegian and Swedish Projects   The problems of imposed work place democracy are well-illustrated by a number of sociotechnical projects undertaken in Norway. These projects stemmed from a concerted effort by industry, the unions, and the Norwegian government to introduce autonomous work groups on a broad scale, with the ultimate objective of transforming the whole society.[11] The plan was to initiate a number of demonstration projects whose visible successes would then foster diffusion of the changes throughout the country.

EXHIBIT 10.7   Guidelines for sociotechnical organization development

1. A structure such as autonomous work groups involving shared decision making requires that organization members share in the design in the first place.
2. Only those aspects of system design that need to be specified at each stage should be specified; thus it is often necessary to specify *what* has to be done, but rarely necessary to say *how* it should be done.
3. Unprogrammed events that constitute problems should be dealt with as close to where they occur as possible; thus, inspection should be incorporated with production so that work is inspected by those who do it, rather than by a distant unit.
4. The organization should be designed to achieve its results in more than one way; through multiskilling, each unit should have a repertoire of performance.
5. Roles that require shared access to knowledge should be within the same grouping.
6. Information systems should be designed to provide information to the organizational grouping that will take action based on the information; thus, work groups can obtain the feedback they need to control their own work.
7. The system of social support should be designed to reinforce the same behaviors as the organization structure; thus, if there are group-based systems, there should be group-based payment.
8. A primary objective should be to provide a high quality of work life to organization members.
9. A transitional structure is required during the changeover period to autonomous groups; thus, there must be a rehearsal of changeover roles.
10. The multifunctional, multilevel, multidisciplinary team required for the original design should be used for its evaluation and review as well.

SOURCE: Adapted from Albert R. Cherns, "Can Behavioral Science Help Design Organizations?" *Organizational Dynamics* (Spring 1977): 55–63.

Overall, the demonstration projects were not so successful as expected, primarily because of resistance from a variety of sources, including often the workers themselves. Even in some successful demonstrations, diffusion did not occur. Thus, the experiment in widespread social change proved to be a failure, although certain organizational changes did result.

In contrast, results obtained in Sweden have been much more impressive.[12] Although hierarchic authority appears to have been a factor in initiating many of the changes, resistance has not been substantial, presumably because the autonomous work groups fit well with the values of Swedish culture. Often new plants were involved at the outset, and then diffusion occurred to other company units. There have been some dramatic shifts away from assembly line technology, as with the much-publicized Volvo automobile plant at Kalmar.

General Foods at Topeka   Another widely publicized application occurred at a newly opened General Foods plant in Topeka, Kansas. Although there have been some problems with the group payment system and sporadic resistance from within the work force, the autonomous work groups have remained in place since the early 1970s.[13] As in other successful applications, production costs have generally been low. In this respect, multiskilling has proved a major advantage.

The problem of diffusion is again apparent, however. The success at Topeka did not create a burst of sociotechnical activity throughout the company. The same situation has occurred repeatedly in other firms. The typical pattern when this type of organization development effort is undertaken is that some plants do in fact become organized as group-based systems, some say they are organized this way even though they really are not, and some retain their bureaucratic form in full.

The Contingency Approach to Organization Development

Chapter 9 considers the Lawrence and Lorsch contingency approach to organization design. This theory, like sociotechnical systems theory, has spawned its own particular approach to organization development that has become increasingly identified with a movement toward some type of matrix structure.

Grounding in Theory   As Exhibit 10.8 shows, the distinguishing characteristic of this approach is the introduction of a degree of differentiation and integration appropriate to environmental demands. Thus, the theory lays down in broad outline the dimensions of the new structure toward which change should occur. In the early days of this approach, questionnaires were used, along with other data-gathering techniques, to establish degrees of environmental uncertainty, existing differentiation levels, integration methods in use, and the like. Then a blueprint for change was developed based on the differences between what was and what should be in terms of the uncertainty faced.

EXHIBIT 10.8   Elements of a contingency approach to organization development

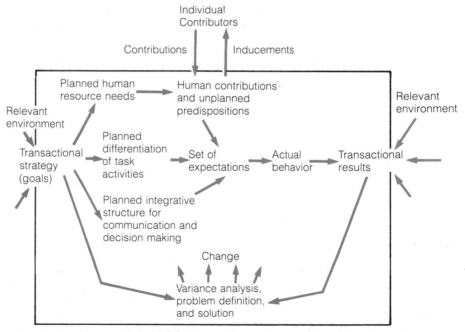

SOURCE: Paul Lawrence and Jay Lorsch, *Developing Organizations*, © 1969, Addison-Wesley, Reading, Massachusets. P. 17, Fig. 3. Reprinted with permission.

More recently this diagnostic phase has become more subjective, based on a consultant's insights as derived from interviews with top managers.[14] In either case, the result has tended to be a change effort directed toward greater differentiation and integration. Changes of any other kind simply are not discussed.

Once a gap between ideal and existing structures has been identified, by whatever means, steps are taken to initiate change. Initially the emphasis is on obtaining the requisite differentiation, by training or by direct structural interventions. The latter can occur at an early phase of organization development, via the use of heirarchic authority. Value change procedures then follow the structural change, or the decision to move toward it. This is a distinct departure from organization development approaches grounded in sensitivity training and T-groups, but it is not unlike the approach often taken in sociotechnical change.

Once the requisite differentiation is achieved, there is a need to install integration mechanisms. This approach places a strong emphasis on rational confrontation. Diagnostic data are fed back to groups of individuals, as in many other organization development approaches. The varying views and values of different units are stressed, with the intent of fostering mutual understanding, trust, and coordination across units. At the same time, there may well be a move toward structural integration devices—project teams, liaison positions, and the like. These may be an outgrowth of confrontation meetings and team-building, but they may also be introduced unilaterally by higher authority.

Introducing Matrix Structures   Increasingly, the primary outcome of the contingency approach has been some kind of matrix structure, introduced via the hierarchy with resistance-reducing efforts following the basic design decision. Team-building is a distinct part of the total effort, but it typically follows a decision by upper management to install a particular structure—the matrix. Exhibit 10.9 sets forth the steps followed from training into change and into continued team-building.

Evidence is lacking as to how effective this approach is. Increasingly it has become a means of changing to more differentiated and more integrated structures, and specifically to matrix systems, just as the sociotechnical approach has become a means to introducing autonomous work groups. In both cases, the other end of the contingency variable has become lost. The use of hierarchic authority to introduce change suggests that resistance can be high. Whether post hoc team-building will adequately defuse this resistance is unknown. On the other hand, approaches of this kind do not suffer from the failure to move through to new designs that has plagued approaches rooted in sensitivity training and T-groups.

| **The Survey Feedback Approach** | Survey feedback, also called survey-guided development, is an outgrowth of Likert's ideas regarding group-based systems, as discussed in chapter 6. As an organization development procedure, the intent is to move companies along the system 1 to system 4 dimension, optimally all the way to system 4 (see Exhibit 6.1). |

The Role and Use of Data.   Exhibit 10.10 describes the process involved in using the survey feedback approach. The primary element is the use of ques-

EXHIBIT 10.9 Steps in a training program to fit managers to new matrix structures

1. Knowledge about the nature of matrix structures and why the company is adopting this design; top management's philosophy in this regard.
2. Lectures, discussion, and exercises dealing with effective communication and group processes.
3. Lectures and exercises dealing with the concepts and techniques of problem-solving in matrix structures.
4. A business game in which the managers play specific roles and make business decisions; trainers facilitate learning from this experience.
5. Bringing the actual work teams together to participate in exercises; the idea is to facilitate self-examination and initial learning in a low-risk context.
6. Team building with the aid of an organization development consultant aimed at dealing with personal and organizational problems related to the conversion to a matrix structure.
7. Change to the matrix
8. Continued team-building with the matrix groups

SOURCE: Adapted from Stanley M. Davis and Paul R. Lawrence, *Matrix* (Reading, Mass.: Addison-Wesley, 1977): 113.

tionnaire data combined to produce measures for work groups and for larger organizational units. The information obtained is given not just to managers, but to the work groups themselves, on the assumption that the groups will make decisions based on the data. The term *survey feedback* refers to the fact that analyzed data are fed back to the groups from which they were obtained

EXHIBIT 10.10 Steps in survey feedback organization development

1. Initial planning sessions involving members of the consultant engagement team, managers who are involved, and representatives from non-managerial groups.
2. Administration of a questionnaire to all members of the organization; topics covered include managerial behavior, organizational climate, group processes, job satisfaction, supervisory needs, job challenge, aversion to bureaucracy, and integration of goals.
3. Training of selected individuals to act as knowledgeable resource persons in the data feedback meetings.
4. Training for organization members in basic concepts of organizatonal functioning; this training presents system 4 in a favorable light.
5. Return of analyzed questionnaire data to group supervisors.
6. Conduct of group feedback meetings.
7. Presentation of a systematic organizational diagnosis.
8. Allocation of resources to carry out change in accordance with the needs indicated by the feedback meetings and the systematic diagnosis.
9. Adminstering and analyzing additional questionnaires to monitor the progress of the change process.
10. Formal reassessment of the organization to evaluate change, again via questionnaires.

SOURCE: Adapted from David A. Bowers and Jerome L. Franklin, *Survey Guided Development I: Data Based Organizational Change* (La Jolla, Calif.: University Associates, 1977): 117.

to identify problems and to permit the groups to develop solutions. A common approach has been to move the questionnaire feedback down through the organization, with each higher level preparing the data for presentation to the groups below. This approach makes it possible to stress the linking pin concept, since each manager of an upper level group can transmit information to members of the group below.

Although the survey feedback approach as originally developed relied almost entirely on questionnaire data obtained from the organization as a whole, there has been a tendency in recent years to draw upon a wider range of data. This latter approach is illustrated in Exhibit 10.11. The result of such an expanded data base is that the work groups obtain a great deal of information for decision making, of a kind that might otherwise be available only to top management.

Relative Value   It is apparent that organization development is not a single entity; it comes in a range of forms. There has now been enough research done about the changes actually produced that it is possible to say something about the relative value of the different approaches.[15]

Overall, it appears that organization development results in meaningful change, although not necessarily structural change, roughly 50 percent of the time. It is not possible to say that one approach is always better than the others, nor is there any certainty about the nature of change that will be produced by a particular intervention. There is evidence, however, that the use of multiple approaches is more likely to yield change—something of a "shotgun ef-

---

EXHIBIT 10.11   Types of data and their use in an expanded feedback system

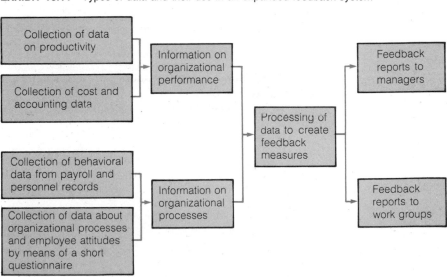

SOURCE: David A. Nadler, *Feedback and Organization Development: Using Data-Based Methods*, © 1977, Addison-Wesley, Reading, Massachusets. P. 37, Fig. 2.2. Reprinted with permission.

fect." For a variety of reasons, isolated organization development interventions frequently fail to have much effect.[16] But then, the same appears to be true of other types of change efforts as well.

Quality Circles

This final approach has very different origins from those previously considered, but has so much in common with other types of organization development, especially team-building, that it seems best considered in that context. It is being used increasingly by organization development consultants in conjunction with other approaches.

Japanese Origins The quality circle idea originated in Japan in the early 1960s as a means of overcoming the poor quality image Japanese products had at that time in world markets. Extensive quality control training was initiated throughout the country, not only for quality control specialists, but also for managers at all levels. Ultimately, foremen who were trained in quality control began to enlist the help of their workers in solving product quality problems. Training was then conducted for small groups of workers who were typically seated around a table—thus the name *quality circle*.

Although quality circles constituted only one aspect of Japan's success in improving its market image in the late 1960s and 1970s, observers in the United States have tended to associate them almost exclusively with Japanese industrial achievements in that period. Furthermore, the origins of the circles in manufacturing and their close ties to engineering, especially the quality control area, has given them broad appeal. As a result, quality circles have become popular in the United States as well.

Quality circles are groups of employees, usually eight to ten, who volunteer to serve. Most commonly the members are from a single work unit, although circles may be formed across units to solve joint problems. The leader of the circle may be the supervisor of the work unit, but workers may also be elected to this role. Problems to be dealt with are selected by the circle and may include not only quality, but productivity, costs, safety, equipment—almost anything germane to the members' work. Meetings typically occur once a week. Members are given training in problem-solving skills and techniques, and they themselves implement the solutions they develop. Where special resources are required, as they often are, the circle itself presents its case to management.

A major objective in this process is to develop practical solutions to work problems. Often this means cost savings, but there may be other goals and results as well. A typical goal is improved communication, particularly between middle and upper management and workers; another is coordination, and yet another is the introduction of participative processes that utilize employee talents and facilitate motivation.

Introducing the Structure The quality circle idea involves not only the individual circles, but also a related structure that operates as an overlay on whatever organization structure is already present. Exhibit 10.12 sets forth the steps involved in introducing the quality circle structure. Note that there are not only circle members and leaders, but facilitators and various committees as well. Evaluation of the concept and its implementation involves attendance at out-

EXHIBIT 10.12 Planning schedule for introducing quality circles

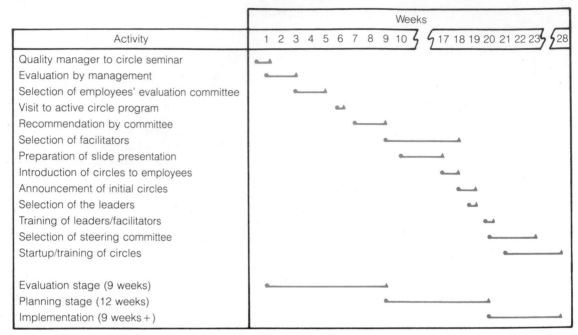

side seminars and visits to active programs, and is carried out by both management and employee groups.

The overlay structure that subsequently appears is shown in Exhibit 10.13. In this structure the facilitators may be either internal or external organization development consultants; they function particularly in relation to the problem-solving training and in a team-building role. The coordinator oversees the program as a whole on a day-to-day basis, but the ultimate responsibility resides in the steering committee. This steering committee may be made up of middle level manufacturing managers only, or it may contain people from diverse levels and functions. Not shown in Exhibit 10.13 is the concept of second-level circles, which some companies have begun to introduce. These are composed of managers only and deal with problems requiring coordination across units.

Although the quality circle idea is relatively new in the United States, it has shown considerable appeal. Research has yet to develop sound evaluations of its success, but a number of organizations have reported successes—Lockheed, Norfolk Naval Shipyard, Motorola, and many more.[17] Whether this approach will develop into a major source of organizational change remains an open question. There may be a gradual merger of the concept into team-building, so that the quality circles concept itself eventually loses its separate identity.

EXHIBIT 10.13   Structure of a quality circles organizational overlay

Circles
Three to thirteen members;
identify, analyze, and resolve
work-related problems;
implement solutions

Leaders
Direct Circles

Facilitators
Make integration of program
easier at all levels

Coordinator
Supervises facilitators
and directs administration
of program

Steering Committee
Five to fifteen members;
oversee and
direct program

SOURCE: From Joseph Hanley, "Our Experience with Quality Circles." Copyright American Society for Quality Control, Inc. Reprinted by permission from *Quality Progress*. February 1980.

GROWTH AND DECLINE

Some of the most significant organizational changes are those of growth and decline. Much more common than a simple rise and fall in the business world is a pattern of successive expansions and contractions. And, although companies do disappear eventually, the length of their functional lives can vary tremendously. Many corporations have been in existence much longer than any human life span.

This topic of the organizational life cycle, with its periods of growth and decline, is closely related to both organizing and organizational process/structure and to planning and management policy/strategy. In many respects it bridges the two areas, as does the Chandler theory of strategy and structure discussed in chapter 9. In fact, the Chandler theory, with its emphasis on growth strategies, has for many years been a major impetus to theories regarding corporate growth processes. Several formulations regarding the stages of growth have emerged from it.

Why do organizations grow? The answer in part, is that sometimes they do not. Many small firms remain small because those who have power over their futures wish to remain closely involved in all phases of their operation. At the same time, many companies do not grow for the simple reason that they cannot. But there are numerous organizations that do grow.

Survival of the Fittest   One view is that organizations survive and grow because they successfully adapt to their environments. This is an ecological view, based on concepts regarding the survival of biological species. Companies that meet the competitive requirements they face are successful and thus grow. Companies that fail to meet these requirements shrivel and die, leaving room for the survivors to grow even more. Such a view says little about how an organization may influence and change its environment—it is all a matter of adaptation. Ecological views also do not address the processes by which organizations adapt, the particular strategies they use. Additionally, there is the question of what "environment" is. Companies may select their environments. Thus, a retail grocery might be anything but the fittest in coping with general retail trade, but be highly successful in the limited environment of gourmet foods and specialty products. Should the company choose to stay with the specialty route, its success and growth would be much different from that in another, broader business environment.

Purposive Action   All of these criticisms suggest that growth is more fully explained in terms of the strategies and intentions of those who have the power in organizations, often top management, even though these strategies must ultimately meet the test of environmental adaptation. Survival of the fittest is not an incorrect explanation, but it is not sufficient to explain how organizations come to survive and grow.

As discussed earlier (see Exhibit 4.1, for instance) growth is an operative goal supported by many managers; its endorsement is particularly strong in Japan. Systems views, such as that of Katz and Kahn discussed in chapter 9, emphasize the need for negative entropy to protect against pervasive forces tending toward organizational decline and death.

Growth is often a defensive strategy. Increasing size enhances a company's capacity to survive because the firm has greater power to influence forces in its environment and because there are more parties with an interest in its continuation.[18] For example, a large automobile manufacturer is able to obtain help from the government in times of difficulty, while a much smaller firm would almost certainly disappear unnoticed. In addition, larger size permits the hiring of a wide range of specialists to handle external and internal problems, again fostering survival. Inherent in much corporate growth is the idea that "the best defense is a good offensive."

Furthermore, growth can make a company easier to manage because more options are available. A large firm is likely to have a diverse array of positions, so that a person who is not working well in one job can be moved to another. In a small company such opportunities rarely exist. Similarly, new positions are continually created during organization growth, with increased horizontal and vertical division of labor. People can then be given a chance to grow and exercise their talents, rather than stagnate as a result of staying in the same position for years. Also, managers need not make as many unpopular decisions as in a company that does not grow. It is not surprising, therefore, that managerial job satisfaction has historically been greater in large firms than in small ones.

Perhaps more important than anything else is the fact that, for highly competitive managers, growth is a way of winning. It is clear evidence of success, often involving high visibility throughout an extended geographical area, listing in sources such as the *Fortune* 500 top industrial firms, and many other business success indicators. In addition, top executives in larger companies are almost universally paid more than those in smaller firms. Consequently, when their firms grow, executives experience a feeling of success not only through their identification with the organization itself, but also at a more personal level.

Stages of Growth

Given that growth frequently does occur, what do we know about how it occurs and how it changes organizations?

The Three-Stage Model   Exhibit 10.14 describes a three-stage growth model extending from the entrepreneurial firm of stage 1, to the managed company with a major product line of stage 2, to the stage 3 firm that has diversified its products as a protection against the vulnerability of operating in a single industry. This model was developed with direct reference to Chandler's theories. There is no implication that companies must necessarily move from stage 2 to

---

EXHIBIT 10.14   Aspects of the three-stage model

Characteristics of the Company	Stage 1	Stage 2	Stage 3
Products	Single line	Single line	Multiple lines
Distribution system	One channel or set	One set of channels	Many different channels
Organization structure	Little structure at all	Functional at the top	Product-line at the top
Research and development	Depends on desires of owner	Formal system to improve products	Formal system to improve products and find new products
Managerial performance appraisal	Highly subjective	Impersonal—against cost and technical criteria	Impersonal—against market criteria such as return on investment
Control system	Personal at all levels	Personal at strategic level and by policies at operating level	Indirect—delegation based on responsibility for results

SOURCE: Adapted from Bruce R. Scott, "The Industrial State: Old Myths and New Realities," *Harvard Business Review* (March–April 1973): 137.

stage 3 as they grow. A firm can stay at stage 2 and become very large. However, vulnerability to changing market circumstances is high under such conditions, and survival is by no means assured. On the average, stage 3 firms have grown to a larger size than those at stage 2.

Historical evidence supports this three-stage model.[19] Still, the model may reflect the specific setting of the past hundred years or so, more than any inevitable pattern of corporate growth. There is a real possibility that the future holds very different patterns with whole new sets of stages.

Extended Models   Even now, a number of models have been proposed that extend beyond the three basic stages. These models seek to deal with such issues as expansion into multinational markets, eventual government ownership, movement through an extended organization development program to a group-based system, and the like. They also consider the role of crises in growth and change, as well as the concern of decline. In general these models deal with specific circumstances. More to the point for illustrative purposes is the model outlined in Exhibit 10.15.

This five-stage approach serves to differentiate the last stage of Exhibit 10.14 much more fully than in previous models. It makes the development of a conglomerate structure of unrelated businesses—usually developed through acquisitions rather than internal growth—a specific part of the model. Although conglomerates of this kind may not be the most profitable, they are an important part of the business scene, both in the United States and internationally.

Acquisitions and Divestitures   Two points need to be made about growth achieved through acquisition of other businesses, as is the case with many unrelated business conglomerates. One is that there tends to be a cyclical pattern of growth and decline, of many acquisitions followed by many divestitures, over time. Secondly, the organization that results from growth by acqui-

---

EXHIBIT 10.15   A five-stage growth model

> **Stage 1: Entrepreneurial Firm**
> A one-person show, lacking formal administrative management
>
> **Stage 2: Single Small Business Firm**
> A single product limited to a particular market. Growth is through expansion in the scale of operations.
>
> **Stage 3: Dominant Business Firm**
> Diversified to some degree, but still having one major product line on which the company relies heavily. Thus there is still a strong tie to the business cycle of one industry.
>
> **Stage 4: Related Business Firm**
> Diversification is extensive, but new products and activities are closely related to the particular knowledge, skills, and strengths of the original firm, as with vertical integration.
>
> **Stage 5: Unrelated Business Firms**
> Diversification into areas not related to original capabilities and strengths.

SOURCE: Adapted from Milton Leontiades, *Strategies for Diversification and Change* (Boston: Little, Brown, 1980): 42.

sition is quite different from one that results from internal expansion into new product areas, even though both strategies may yield a multi-business firm.

The first point is illustrated in Exhibit 10.16. In the late 1960s, Fuqua Industries grew rapidly through one acquisition after another. Then in the early 1970s, difficulties in managing many of the new firms began to surface, with the result that there was a retrenchment involving the sale of several businesses acquired earlier. At the same time, there was some movement back from the unrelated business strategy to a greater stress on related businesses. Later, in the mid-1970s, Fuqua further divested itself in order to build up cash reserves and reduce bank debts for the purpose of purchasing a multi-industry company with sales in the $500 million range. This latter goal was achieved with the acquisition of National Industries in 1978.

Conglomerates like Fuqua Industries are constantly changing in size, in business composition, and in personnel. Not surprisingly, because they may come and go rapidly, divisions acquired through purchase are typically much more independent than those developed through internal growth. Companies employing the acquisition approach to growth tend to provide few corporate services to the divisions and exercise limited control over them. Profit perfor-

---

EXHIBIT 10.16   Patterns of acquisition and divestiture as illustrated by Fuqua Industries

The 1966–69 Acquisition Period
(companies contributing to Fuqua's principal operations)

Entry Company	Industry	$ Sales (in millions)
Fuqua Communications (broadcasting)	Entertainment	26.4
Martin Theatres	Entertainment	
Stormor (agricultural buildings)	Shelter	34.1
Fuqua Homes (mobile homes)	Shelter	
McDonough (snapper)	Lawn & garden	22.2
Colorcraft	Photofinishing	17.9
Interstate (motor freight)	Transportation	113.2
Yarbrough (boat trailers)	Sporting goods	17.1
Other acquisitions subsequently divested		96.9

The 1970–73 Divestiture Period

Company	Sold to	$ Sales (in millions)
Ward (camper trailers)	Ward Interfinancial	11
Varco-Pruden (steel buildings)	Dombrico Inc.	19
Career (vocational schools)	Fortune Enterprises	9
Trojan (seed corn)	Pfizer, Inc.	17
Rome (farm implements)	Wyman, Gordon Co.	10
Scorpion (snowmobiles)	Individuals	8

SOURCE: Adapted from Fuqua Industries and from Milton Leontiades, *Strategies for Diversification and Change* (Boston: Little, Brown 1980): 11–12.

mance of the division is often the sole basis on which division managers are rewarded.[20] Typically, most managers of a given division have not worked elsewhere in the company.

In contrast, a multi-business firm that has achieved this status through internal growth and through research and development expenditures tends to be much more integrated. Ties between corporate headquarters and the various divisions are closer, with more staff advice and more control coming from the top. Rotation of managers across divisions is also more frequent. Thus, the ways in which growth and change occur can make a great deal of difference insofar as organizational processes are concerned.

Problems of Decline

Companies may decline temporarily, for reasons related to the business cycle or because of managerial failures, and still survive and grow. They may also decline permanently, gradually selling off assets or abruptly going into bankruptcy and liquidation. Often, a declining business is acquired by another firm, merges, and loses its identity. In any event, decline—whether permanent or temporary—can produce major changes. Such changes almost always occur in personnel, and often in methods of operation as well.

Structural Changes   Decline tends to produce a reduction in the number of divisions because of divestitures and elimination of unprofitable product lines. Also there is typically a major effort to reduce managerial overhead. Many managerial positions are abolished, with the result that the length of the hierarchy is shortened. As levels of management are eliminated, the spans of control of managers who remain increase. Often, whole staff units disappear. In one instance, a firm in decline eliminated its personnel department completely, although this seems to have done little to stem the tide. In another instance, research and development expenditures were drastically reduced, to a point where the function lacked the capability to do more than provide occasional technical advice to manufacturing.

Patterns of this kind are not limited to the corporate world. Consulting firms with declining business close offices. Universities with declining enrollments eliminate majors and departments. Governments with declining tax revenues curtail services and abandon programs. Yet in all these instances, although the structural effects may be profound, the overall form of the organization tends to remain the same. One rarely sees a movement from decentralized, product-line divisions back to a functional structure at the top in times of decline. The typical structure instead is a shrunken version of what was achieved during growth.

Managerial Failure   In the business world, decline appears to be caused primarily by the failure of top management to develop and implement effective strategies for coping with the external environment. It is not that appropriate strategies could not have been found, only that they were not.[21] In some cases, top management appears to resist change, even when faced with the seemingly unalterable dictates of environmental forces. Old solutions are retained too long, threats are underestimated until too late, forces such as government interventions are resisted to the point of no return. The managers involved simply do not want to change in response to real changes in the organization's environment. Ultimately the change occurs, in the form of decline.

A somewhat different pattern of decline occurs as a consequence of attempts to grow. In this instance, risks are taken on the basis of mistaken forecasts. The company overexpands, expends an excessive amount of resources in a single venture, and information that might lead to questioning the strategy is ignored or suppressed. In short, the decision processes at the top lead to an attempt to achieve more than is possible, and in the final analysis, what results is not the anticipated growth, but as resources are dissipated, an unanticipated decline.

Summary

In considering organizational change, a major distinction needs to be made between approaches that rely heavily on hierarchic authority to produce change and approaches that generate changes out of the whole organization, or at least out of the affected parts. Originally, the latter approaches were what characterized organization development. However, as the theories underlying various organization development approaches have come to endorse specific types of changes, and to have difficulty in getting organizations to actually move toward them, a tendency to utilize hierarchic authority has emerged to some extent.

Matters such as degree of resistance, development of innovative ideas, extent of overall commitment, satisfaction with outcomes, effectiveness of implementation, and specific consequences as they relate to change are all closely tied to this hierarchic-systemic distinction. The ways in which these factors operate in relation to different change procedures are outlined in Exhibit 10.17. The exhibit also attempts to provide an indication of how effective these procedures are. In large part, what will work best, or even if anything will work at all, appears to be a matter of the values or culture of the organization, and perhaps of the surrounding society as well. Changes that go with the culture tend to prosper; changes that go against it are likely to flounder.

What Have You Learned?

1. Is resistance to change always undesirable and irrational? Explain.
2. How do the sociotechnical and contingency approaches in organization development differ from approaches grounded in sensitivity training and T-groups? What advantages and disadvantages are associated with these differences?
3. What are the similarities and differences between the three- and five-stage models of company growth?
4. What are the traditional values of organization development? How might they relate to operative goals involving growth and profit?
5. Under what circumstances and in what ways are bureaucracies likely to prove resistant to change?
6. How may decline affect an organization? What appear to be the major causes of decline?
7. Survey feedback relies heavily on data collection. What types of data are obtained, and how are the data used to bring about change?

8. What roles do external consultants and members of internal organizational change units play in changes based on hierarchic authority?
9. Although many organizations do not grow, there seems to be an overall tendency for organizations that survive to grow. Why is this so?
10. What do quality circles have in common with other organization development approaches?

EXHIBIT 10.17   Types of change procedures and their relative value

Change Procedure	Relative Value
Direct hierarchic change by management	Can be effective if clearly and consistently articulated and supported by organizational values and rewards; may arouse resistance; often better at implementing innovation than creating ideas.
Consultant-initiated hierarchic change	Has the added value of bringing in fresh ideas; also may defuse negative feelings caused by a change.
Hierarchic change initiated by an internal change unit	Primary added value to managerial change is in production of good ideas, well worked out.
Organization development using sensitivity training and T-groups	Good at mobilizing support for certain types of changes, but changes actually occur relatively infrequently; overall, not very effective.
Organization development including team-building and an external, task emphasis	Same pros and cons as the pure sensitivity training approach, but has a better record in producing change.
Sociotechnical systems approach	Can be effective, but to the extent hierarchic authority is involved, resistance may be mobilized; steps need to be taken to align values and motives with the type of change involved.
Development based on contingency views of organization	Effectiveness is unknown; use of team-building to defuse resistance to change appears conceptually sound; may well succeed in producing change to matrix structure.
Survey feedback	Can be effective under the right circumstances; resistance to change is minimized.
Quality circles	Effectiveness in implementing changes is unknown; appears to produce useful ideas for change and to facilitate communication.
Growth through acquisition	Can be more rapid than internally generated growth, but tends to be somewhat unstable and to produce a less integrated organization.

How Well Can You Apply Your Knowledge?

Problem 1. A major medical school and center had been experiencing severe problems for some years. The primary difficulty was that costs had risen sharply at the same time that income limitations had imposed a major burden. The center had a long tradition of service to the community and had for years taken a number of patients with a limited ability to pay. Given the history of the institution and its relation to the community, this situation was almost impossible to change, but it severely restricted the number of beds that could be used to produce income.

As a result of these financial problems, competition began to develop among units and groups within the medical school for the scarce resources available. Considerable polarization occurred, and groups secretly plotted their own strategies without regard to effects on the school as a whole. The overall structure of the school was not clearly defined, but there were a series of departments representing the various specialty areas; each faculty member held an appointment in one, and only one, department. In addition there were the various functions: M.D. education, Ph.D. education, internship and residency education, research, and patient care. Some faculty members were more strongly identified with one of these functions than with the departments to which they nominally belonged, and accordingly devoted their efforts to obtaining funds for that function. The picture was one of marked fragmentation. It was very difficult to get a sizable group of faculty members to support any type of change. But because the system was essentially professional in nature, change could not occur without a concerted faculty effort. Professional values made that very clear.

The dean of the school became increasingly concerned about this situation. The school was part of a large university, but it operated with a good deal of autonomy. As far as the university was concerned, the dean could take whatever steps he saw fit to remedy the situation. This was not the problem; the problem was to get faculty action.

In the dean's opinion, what was needed was some kind of matrix structure in which communication between groups and individuals would be facilitated, and integration of effort behind the goals of the school as a whole, however defined, might be achieved. What the dean had in mind was something like the following:

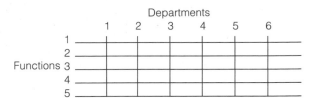

Each faculty member would be a member of a department, or perhaps have a joint appointment in more than one department, and also serve one or more functions.

The dean was convinced that this kind of structure would break down existing provincial loyalties and get the school moving once again out of what was threatening to become total mediocrity. His problem was how to bring the change about. He knew he did not have the authority to simply make it happen.

Questions
1. If you were the dean in this situation, how would you go about attempting to change to the new structure? Which of the procedures noted in Exhibit 10.17 might be used? Which could not be used? Why?
2. Present a specific plan outlining the steps you would follow to achieve the change.
3. What do you see as the strengths and weaknesses of the plan you have developed?

Problem 2. Like its competitors, one of the major U.S. automobile manufacturers had been suffering substantial losses because of the need to correct defects that surfaced after a line of cars had been purchased. In some cases, this occurred because customers exercised their rights under warranties, and in some cases government safety regulations were involved. The net effect was that the company was losing money, and if the situation continued, its carefully nurtured reputation for high quality would almost certainly be severely damaged.

The quality control manager in one of the company's major plants, who felt that in some ways the recalls and repairs reflected on him personally, had been looking for solutions. He became increasingly convinced that the quality circles idea was a good one and had even gone so far as to visit several firms that had introduced them. He was particularly impressed with the extent to which these firms had succeeded in getting the production workers themselves to develop procedures for correcting defects in products or preventing the poor quality work from being done in the first place.

After considerable study, the quality control manager approached the plant manager about introducing quality circles at the plant. At that time he learned that the personnel manager, out of very similar concerns, had been working on a different approach to the problem involving the use of an organization development consultant. The consultant had in fact been contacted and had spent a day at the plant in discussions with the plant manager and personnel manager. This consultant had had long experience working with T-groups, had been associated with the National Training Laboratories, and was an early participant in the work in this area at Bethel, Maine. His credentials were impeccable, and he believed he could help management to deal with its quality control problems more effectively.

The plant manager's preference in this situation, and that of most of the people who reported to him directly, would have been to increase the emphasis on inspection and perhaps expand the size of the quality control staff. He believed the workers should be taught to respect the need to produce a high quality automobile. Yet this type of approach had seemed to accomplish little in the past except to increase the number of grievances filed by the union. Furthermore, the arguments presented by both the quality control manager and the personnel manager did make some sense. In the plant manager's mind, the options available were:

1. Mobilize an all-out effort to make the workers improve quality.
2. Introduce quality circles as the quality control manager recommended.
3. Follow the personnel manager's advice and utilize the organization development consultant.
4. Use some combination of these three approaches.

Questions
1. What are the pros and cons of each of these options in this specific situation? With regard to option 4, which of the alternatives could meaningfully be combined? Why?
2. What do you think is the best thing to do? How exactly should one go about implementing your approach?

Additional Sources for More Detailed Study

Aldrich, Howard E. *Organizations and Environments.* Englewood Cliffs, N.J.: Prentice-Hall, 1979

Argyris, Chris. *Intervention Theory and Methods: A Behavioral Science View.* Reading, Mass.: Addison-Wesley, 1970.

Blake, Robert R., and Mouton, Jane S. *Building a Dynamic Corporation through Grid Organization Development.* Reading, Mass.: Addison-Wesley, 1969.

Burke, W. Warner. *Organization Development: Principles and Practices.* Boston: Little, Brown, 1982.

Cummings, Thomas G., and Srivastva, Suresh. *Management of Work: A Socio-Technical Systems Approach.* Kent, Ohio: Kent State University Press, 1977.

Daft, Richard L., and Becker, Selwyn W. *Innovation in Organizations.* New York: Elsevier, 1978.

Dalton, Gene W.; Barnes, Louis B.; and Zaleznik, Abraham. *The Distribution of Authority in Formal Organizations.* Boston: Harvard Business School, 1968.

Davis, Louis E., and Cherns, Albert B. *The Quality of Working Life—Volume I: Problems, Prospects, and the State of the Art; Volume 2: Cases and Commentary.* New York: Free Press, 1975.

Dyer, William G. *Contemporary Issues in Management and Organization Development.* Reading, Mass.: Addison-Wesley, 1983.

French, Wendell L.; Bell, Cecil H.; and Zawacki, Robert A. *Organization Development: Theory, Practice, and Research.* Dallas: Business Publications, 1978.

Harrigan, Kathryn R. *Strategies for Declining Businesses.* Lexington, Mass.: D. C. Heath, 1980.

Heenan, David A., and Perlmutter, Howard V. *Multinational Organization Development: A Social Architectural Perspective.* Reading, Mass.: Addison-Wesley, 1979.

Huse, Edgar F. *Organization Development and Change.* St. Paul, Minn.: West, 1980.

Kimberly, John R., and Miles, Robert H. *The Organizational Life Cycle: Issues in the Creation, Transformation, and Decline of Organizations.* San Francisco: Jossey-Bass, 1980.

Lippitt, Gordon L. *Organizational Renewal: A Holistic Approach to Organization Development.* Englewood Cliffs, N.J.: Prentice-Hall, 1982.

Miner, John B. *Theories of Organizational Structure and Process.* Hinsdale, Ill.: Dryden, 1982.

Nicholas, John M. "The Comparative Impact of Organization Development Interventions on Hard Criteria Measures." *Academy of Management Review,* October 1982.

Robey, Daniel, and Altman, Steven. *Organization Development: Progress and Perspectives.* New York: Macmillan, 1982.

Rowe, Lloyd A., and Boise, William B. *Organizational and Managerial Innovation: A Reader.* Pacific Palisades, Calif.: Goodyear, 1973.

Thompson, Philip C. *Quality Circles: How to Make Them Work in America.* New York: AMACOM, 1982.

Notes

1. William F. Glueck, "Who Needs an Organization Department?" *California Management Review* (Winter 1972).

2. M. J. Kirton and Glenn Mulligan, "Correlates of Managers' Attitudes Toward Change," *Journal of Applied Psychology* (August 1973).

3. Melvin L. Kohn, "Bureaucratic Man: A Portrait and an Interpretation," *American Sociological Review* (June 1971).

4. Michael Aiken, Samuel B. Bacharach, and J. Lawrence French, "Organizational Structure, Work Process, and Proposal Making in Administrative Bureaucracies," *Academy of Management Journal* (December 1980); Jon L. Pierce and André L. Delbecq, "Organizational Structure, Individual Attitudes, and Innovation," *Academy of Management Review* (January 1977); and Gerald Zaltman and Robert Duncan, *Strategies for Planned Change* (New York: Wiley, 1977).

5. Norman R. Smith, *The Entrepreneur and His Firm: The Relationship Between Type of Man and Type of Company* (East Lansing, Mich.: Michigan State University Bureau of Business and Economic Research, 1967); and Arthur L. Stinchcombe, *Creating Efficient Industrial Administrations* (New York: Academic Press, 1974).

6. Michael Beer, *Organization Change and Development: A Systems View* (Santa Monica, Calif.: Goodyear, 1980).

7. Chris Argyris, *Interpersonal Competence and Organizational Effectiveness* (Homewood, Ill.: Irwin, 1962); *Integrating the Individual and the Organization* (New York: Wiley, 1964).

8. Chris Argyris, *Reasoning, Learning, and Action: Individual and Organizational* (San Francisco: Jossey-Bass, 1982).

9. Warren G. Bennis, *Changing Organizations* (New York: McGraw-Hill, 1966).

10. Jerry I. Porras and Per O. Berg, "The Impact of Organization Development," *Academy of Management Review* (April 1978).

11. Fred E. Emery and Einar Thorsrud, *Democracy at Work* (Leiden, Netherlands: Martinus Nijhoff, 1976); and Einar Thorsrud, Bjorg A. Sorensen, and Bjorn Gustavsen, "Sociotechnical Approach to Industrial Democracy in Norway," in *Handbook of Work, Organization, and Society,* ed. Robert Dubin (Chicago: Rand, McNally, 1976).

12. Richard B. Peterson, "Swedish Experiments in Job Reform," *Business Horizons* (May 1976); Pehr G. Gyllenhammar, "How Volvo Adapts Work to People," *Harvard Business Review* (July–August 1977).

13. Richard E. Walton, "Work Innovations at Topeka: After Six Years," *Journal of Applied Behavioral Science* (October 1977).

14. Jay W. Lorsch, "Organizational Design: A Situational Perspective," *Organizational Dynamics* (Autumn 1977).

15. Jerry I. Porras and Per O. Berg, "The Impact of Organization Development," *Academy of Management Review* (April 1978); and John M. Nicholas, "The Comparative Impact of Organization Development

Interventions on Hard Criteria Measures," *Academy of Management Review* (October 1982).

16. Philip H. Mirvis and David N. Berg, *Failures in Organization Development and Change: Cases and Essays for Learning* (New York: Wiley, 1977).

17. Robert Wood, Frank Hull, and Koya Azumi, "Evaluating Quality Circles: The American Application," *California Management Review* (Fall 1983).

18. Jeffrey Pfeffer and Gerald R. Salancik, *The External Control of Organizations: A Resource Dependence Perspective* (New York: Harper and Row, 1978).

19. Jay R. Galbraith and Daniel A. Nathanson, *Strategy Implementation: The Role of Structure and Process* (St. Paul, Minn.: West, 1978).

20. Robert A. Pitts, "Diversification Strategies and Organizational Policies of Large Diversified Firms," *Journal of Economics and Business* (Spring 1976).

21. John Argenti, *Corporate Collapse* (London: McGraw-Hill, 1976); Max Richards, "An Exploratory Study of Strategic Failure," *Academy of Management Proceedings* (August 1973).

READINGS AND EXECUTIVE PROFILES

**Looking Back at Topeka: General Foods and
the Quality-of-Work-Life Experiment**
David A. Whitsett and Lyle Yorks
California Management Review

Conversation with Charles L. Brown
David A. Nadler
Organizational Dynamics

Ruben F. Mettler and TRW Inc.

These selections are concerned with the organizing function. They deal in particular with the processes of changing organizations and their structures, including both voluntary and involuntary changes.

Whitsett and Yorks provide an objective evaluation of the changes introduced at General Food's Topeka plant, changes that produced a structure not existing previously, nor found since in the company. These changes created a socio-technical organization, a type of organization development, and would now be viewed as representing a quality-of-work-life experiment.

In contrast to the voluntary changes made by General Foods, AT&T is undergoing major involuntary changes as a result of environmental forces, namely court orders. Nadler presents an interview with Charles Brown, AT&T's chief executive officer, that points up the major sources of uncertainty and internal anxiety that face a company undergoing critical changes of this nature.

The executive profile of Ruben Mettler and TRW provides an example of the decentralized, diversified structure that Chandler expected would result from a growth strategy. In the *Fortune* survey, TRW emerged as clearly at the top of the motor vehicle and parts grouping—well ahead of General Motors, Ford, and Chrysler. TRW is a company committed to innovation and change, with all the problems and advantages that accrue to such an approach.

Looking Back at Topeka: General Foods and the Quality-of-Work-Life Experiment

David A. Whitsett and Lyle Yorks

The Topeka Pet Food Plant has been one of the most highly publicized examples of organizational innovation in recent times. However, some of the publicity associated with it has been highly misleading. The authors offer a careful reexamination of the development and operation of the plant, outline the role that publicity has played in its history, and discuss the use of case studies in general.

Some of the better-known theories in the field of management draw much of their support from certain notorious "case studies" which appear to demonstrate the validity of those theories. On occasion, these case studies are used not as sources of hypotheses for future testing but as anecdotal arguments for ideological positions. The story of General Foods' Gaines Pet Food plant located near Topeka, Kansas has been such a case. Often cited as a prototype of what future humanized facilities might be like, the plant has taken a position in many minds as a classic demonstration of the power of systemwide organizational innovation, quality-of-work-life interventions, and sociotechnical systems approaches. Opponents of such approaches have sought to discredit claims made for the plant as part of an effort to reassert the advantages of more traditional approaches to work organization.

The Topeka plant, opened in January of 1971, first received wide exposure in an article by Richard Walton.[1] It subsequently became one of the most widely discussed and written-about business facilities in the United States, the subject of dozens of articles in books, professional journals, maga-

David A. Whitsett is a professor of psychology at the University of Northern Iowa in Cedar Falls and former vice-president of Drake-Beam & Associates, Inc., Psychological Management Consultants, in New York City. He has been a consultant in personnel management and human resource utilization in a wide variety of organizations and is the author of numerous articles on motivation, job design, and human resource utilization.

Lyle Yorks is an associate professor of management sciences at Eastern Connecticut State University and former senior vice-president of Drake Beam Morin, Inc., an international consulting firm, which he currently serves as consultant-to-the-firm. During 1982–83 he was a visiting faculty fellow at Yale University, associated with the School of Organization and Management. He is the author of several books and articles on management and has served as a consultant on human resource issues to companies in North America, Latin America, and Europe.

zines, and newspapers, of a lengthy report on NBC's "First Tuesday" program, and of countless discussions at management conferences and training sessions. The story of what occurred at Topeka has been distorted in many of the reports, and the wide exposure has itself become part of the Topeka story. Now that the plant is over ten years old and much of the original fervor has died down, a reassessment is appropriate. In this article we will present what we feel is an accurate description of the development and operation of the Topeka plant, discuss some of the distortions that have arisen about it, and highlight the lessons that can be learned from Topeka and the way it has been presented.[2]

Development and Operation of the Plant

The Birth of Topeka   Prior to the establishment of the Topeka plant, all Gaines products were produced at a plant located in Kankakee, Illinois. When Lyman Ketchum was appointed manager of the Kankakee operation in 1966, demand for the plant's products was already creating a need for significant overtime. Productivity problems at Kankakee were considered serious. Ketchum's predecessor had initiated a consulting relationship with Professor Richard Walton, then of Purdue and later of Harvard University. Managers of the Kankakee plant had been extensively involved in NTL laboratory experiences and University of Illinois training programs. Ketchum wanted to continue the group and individual development of his staff for both their own and General Foods' benefit. Walton was retained to work with members of the management group.[3]

It became clear by 1968 that the continued increase in demand for Gaines products was going to require additional plant capacity. Both Ketchum and Walton "felt strongly about the need for innovation in the new plant organization."[4] This feeling was based on their desire to design a plant in which alienation, negative attitudes, and behavior problems (existent at Kankakee) would not occur and on their belief that the "evolving expectations of American workers would increasingly come in conflict with the demands, conditions, and rewards of conventional organizations."[5]

The concepts of designing the new plant to maximize the use of knowledge of the behavioral sciences and using the plant as a kind of laboratory or learning model for the corporation were first generated by Ketchum and Walton in mid-1968 during a meeting of General Foods managers at Geneva, Wisconsin.[6] A model for such a plant existed in the General Foods organization in the form of a Post Division carton and container plant in Saratoga Springs, New York. This plant had been operating successfully in an innovative way for several years. In addition, the managers were influenced by what they had heard concerning such innovations in some of Procter and Gamble's newer plants.[7]

Staffing the Operation   Ketchum held an off-site meeting with his staff in the fall of 1968 to address the question of how to manage the new plant. The basic objectives and philosophies to be involved were determined at that meeting, and by June of 1969 Edward R. Dulworth had been selected as project leader. He was an engineer by training and a member of the management group at Kankakee who was therefore familiar with the manufacturing processes to be used at Topeka. Walton described Dulworth as follows:

> His past performance at Kankakee left no doubt about his technical competence. He had in the past established effective and close relationships with his immediate subordinates. Moreover, he had indicated prior interest in the behavioral sciences and had tested some concepts such as openness, team building, participative decision making and cooperative objective setting in his previous jobs. Finally, he evinced an innovative mind.[8]

Dulworth then selected a group of three managers who had worked well together at Kankakee, who were technically competent and open to new ideas, and who had a desire to further develop interpersonal and organizational skills.[9]

When the team was formed in 1969 the basic technology and the physical layout of the new plant had already been decided upon. Dulworth's team did not have the opportunity to design the plant to accomodate the autonomous work groups inherent in a sociotechnical systems approach, but they did their best to build operating worker teams around existing technology. In fact, the engineering design team had virtually no contact with the planning-operating group headed by Dulworth. Ketchum wrote later, "Today I would describe the concepts as a sociotechnical approach although the account will reveal this as an evolution."[10] The sociotechnical emphasis was brought to the project by Professor Eric Trist of the Wharton School, who, according to Ketchum's account, was not involved until at least 1970, long after the physical facilities were established. Dulworth and his team had the opportunity to alter certain features of the plant if they could demonstrate that the type of organization they wanted required it.

The extent to which the physical design of the plant and its technology were altered to accomodate the work groups or to support the planned management innovations was quite limited. There were no "status indicators." There was one entrance for everyone and one lunchroom, one color scheme and decor used throughout. Offices had glass walls facing the plant, and, to facilitate worker involvement in quality control, small quality control labs were placed on several floors of the plant. Dulworth's group chose not to use one of the equipment features that the engineers had provided—the processing equipment's automated control system. Operators would control the processing manually. The planning group also placed a desk and clipboard in the control room and encouraged the operators to use this room as a natural team-gathering point. Other than these features (which, while significant, are clearly "tinkering" as opposed to basic design), Topeka was a plant very much like any other modern processing/packaging facility. To conceive of it as being in the same category as plants designed to accommodate radical work innovation (such as Volvo's facilities) is to misunderstand what took place.

Dulworth's planning team worked for about six months developing what became known as the Topeka System. It included a work and supervisory structure, a reward system, and a social system designed to accomplish their goal of establishing "an operating organization capable of sustaining high levels of production and uniform high quality, low cost and responsive flexibility."[11] The team's next task was to recruit and select supervisors (called

"team leaders"), who were to function primarily as managers of people rather than technical specialists. The team carefully developed a profile of the kind of people wanted as team leaders—secure, interpersonally skilled, open, comfortable in an unstructured environment, intelligent, creative—and then recruited accordingly. An elaborate screening process, including simulations and interviews, resulted in the selection of 6 team leaders from a pool of 30 applicants. These 6 were then involved in extensive managerial development activities, and participated in the recruitment and selection of plant employees. Once again, a profile of the kind of person desired was developed. Characteristics such as good comprehension and communication abilities, openness, disposition to work in groups, and good analytical skills were included. Recruiting resulted in 625 applications. Testing, extensive interviewing, and a "selection weekend" reduced the group to the 63 people who were hired.

Organizing the Work The organization was set up in teams: a processing team, a packaging/warehouse team, and an office team. Processing was a highly automated operation staffed by eight people (per shift), who ran the entire processing operation, beginning with the receipt of raw materials from freight cars. Corn, soya, vitamins, and meat meal were dumped directly into bins from the cars, then conveyed to storage. The incoming material was weighed, moisture levels were adjusted, and the ingredients (in predetermined percentages) were mixed. The process was monitored from an air-conditioned computer control room, with two or three team members usually in the control room at any one time monitoring the process and making adjustments. Their objective was to produce a minimum of one hundred tons of dog food per shift so that the packaging warehouse team would have a steady flow of product with which to work.

The packaging/warehouse team, made up of seventeen people per shift, had the functions of coating the product, placing it in bags and boxes, moving it to the warehouse for storage, and conducting some in-process quality control functions. Much of this work was done at stations and involved positioning bags or boxes to be filled automatically with preweighed amounts of dog food, then placing the container on a conveyer where it was sealed, palletized, and stored.[12]

In addition to performing their basic production tasks, the teams carried out a variety of other functions to achieve the planners' goal of having largely self-managed teams.

> Assignments of individual team members to sets of tasks [were] subject to team consensus. Sets of tasks [could] be redefined by the team in light of individual capabilities and interests. . . . Staff units and job specialties [were] avoided. Activities typically performed by maintenance, quality control, custodial, industrial engineering and personnel units [were] built into an operating team's responsibilities.[13]

Other team responsibilities included coping with manufacturing problems that occurred within or between the teams' areas of responsibility, temporarily redistributing tasks to cover for absent team members, choosing team members to serve on plantwide committees such as safety and recreation, counseling employees who did not perform well, and screening and selecting new team members.[14]

Team Leader's Role All this self-management meant that the role of the supervisor or team leader was significantly different than that in the traditional organization. The planning team's concept was that the team leader's primary role was as a manager of people. In terms of actual responsibilities this role remained a bit unclear but the team leaders were largely responsible for team development and facilitating group decision making. They also played more specific roles in deciding when a team member's pay should be increased and in approving a team member's sick leave. Plant manager Dulworth described the team leader as "a kind of coach. He is a resource person rather than a governing person. He encourages independence, not dependence in team members. The more team members do on their own, the better."[15]

One of the most innovative features at Topeka was its pay system. The plant had a single job classification and starting pay rate ($3.40 per hour in 1971) for all operators. Increases in pay were to be a function of the person's learning. According to Walton, there were four pay rates: the starting rate; the single job rate, received when the employee mastered the job assignment; the team rate, which was paid when a team member learned the jobs of all the team's members; and the plant rate, to be paid when an employee had learned all jobs in the entire plant.[16] In addition, there was the possibility of qualifying for an "add-on" rate if the employee had some special ability, such as electrical maintenance skills. The pay system was designed to encourage employees to develop themselves. In addition, there were no limits placed on the number of operators who could qualify for higher pay brackets, a policy intended to encourage employees to teach other.

Report on the System's Success

Early reports on the Topeka plant's progress were quite positive. The most extensive such report was Walton's 1972 article, in which he reported very positive indications regarding the costs of operation: "Using standard principles, industrial engineers originally estimated that 110 employees should man the plant. Yet the team concept, coupled with the integration of support activities into team responsibilities, has resulted in a manpower level of slightly less than 70 people."[17] He also reported that "after 18 months, the new plant's fixed overhead rate was 33% lower than in the old plant. Reductions in variable manufacturing costs (92% fewer quality rejects and an absenteeism rate 9% below the industry norm) resulted in annual savings of $600,000. The safety record was one of the best in the company and the turnover was far below average."[18]

In regard to the more-difficult-to-measure indicators, such as job attitudes, Walton stated that all members of the plant community, operators, team leaders, and managers had become involved in their work and were deriving high satisfaction from it. He indicated that there was an atmosphere of openness and mutual respect and that the plant's "participatory democracy" was spreading in the sense that team leaders and other plant managers had been unusually active in civic affairs.[19] Finally, he reported that "the apparent effectiveness of the new plant organization has caught the attention of top management and encouraged it to create a new corporate-level unit to transfer the organizational and managerial innovations to other work environments."[20]

Subsequent reports continued to be positive. In a presentation given in March 1974 at a UCLA program, "The Changing World of Work," Dulworth reported savings of about $2 million a year, a quality reject rate 80 percent below that regarded as normal, an absence rate of about 1.5 percent, turnover one-third below the rate for the parent company, and continued positive levels of work attitudes.[21] Walton reported the same figures he had reported in 1972 again in 1974 and in 1975 labeled Topkea "an unqualified success."[22]

In his "after six years" assessment in 1977, Walton reported a continuation of the positive atmosphere, work attitudes, and commitment, along with the now-familiar absence and turnover figures and added that the plant went three years, eight months from start-up (1.3 million man hours) without a single lost time accident.[23] Walton also mentioned here again that General Foods had moved to establish similar restructuring approaches in other plants but noted that the actual diffusion of these ideas to other plants had been slow in coming.

Not only had diffusion of the Topeka system been slow, the plant itself was experiencing rather significant difficulties, including the following:

Some team members and team leaders were having a difficult time fulfilling their expected roles. Tendencies toward traditional supervisor-employee behaviors were quite pronounced in some plant personnel. The openness of the social system created some ambiguities which some people found uncomfortable. In addition, the team leader role was not well understood by General Foods management outside the Topeka plant.

· The unusual pay system became, as Walton put it, "an important source of tension."[24] The extent to which pay was clearly linked to the desired behaviors varied widely. It was closely related to learning and skill development but much less closely tied to participation in group discussion, openness, and trust. There was a tendency toward leniency in making pay decisions

among some groups and there was, in general, significant concern with issues of equity with regard to pay. Finally, there was a continuing feeling among some plant personnel that the pay plan did not provide adequate rewards for the level of involvement required by the Topeka system.

The original intent at Topeka was to make all the jobs in the plant interesting and challenging. This was not accomplished as well as had been hoped for. For example, the processing team jobs quite clearly offered more opportunity for planning and decision making than the packaging/warehouse team jobs. This is particularly important because the packaging/warehouse team involved about twice as many employees as the processing team.

An unfortunate side effect of the development of strong, clearly identified teams was that problem-solving mechanisms at the plantwide level were sometimes quite weak. Plantwide committees formed to handle problems often functioned poorly.

The most serious of the problems experienced at Topeka concerned the movement of management people. Between 1973 and 1976, four managers left the Topeka plant. One went to an adjacent General Foods canned pet food plant and the other three left the organization. The plant manager, Ed Dulworth, left the company in 1975. Most, if not all, of this exodus was, in our opinion, the result of the fact that Lyman Ketchum (Topeka's originator and "protector") moved from his position as Dulworth's boss to a highly visible corporate staff position in organizational development in September of 1971, less than nine months after Topeka's start-up. The impact of Ketchum's move was felt at Topeka in two ways: first, the plant (and more specifically, its manager, Ed Dulworth) lost a crucial buffer between it and the larger organization, and second, Ketchum's rapid rise drew fire from many members of the corporation against himself and Topeka. Ketchum left General Foods in 1975 after four years of trying unsuccessfully to spread the message of Topeka throughout the corporation.

The Topeka plant can perhaps be viewed as an example of the trade-offs involved in the design of social systems. The advantages of this system, such as lower staffing requirements, high productivity, and low absence rates, were achieved as part of a package which included the difficulties listed above. These problems should not be taken as indications that the attempt at innovative design was ill-advised, but they do suggest a situation somewhat less optimistic than some of the very positive reports would indicate.

How Innovative Was/Is Topeka?

Quite apart from any discussion of the success or problems associated with Topeka (but still relevant to the issue of the use of case studies as data) is the question of just how radical a departure from conventional management practice Topeka really has been. The plant has often been described as a "radically innovative" plant,[25] as a "glimpse of what may be the industrial work environment of the future," a prototype of the "more radical, comprehensive and systemic redesign of organizations" which its supporters see as imperative to combat alienation in the work place.[26] Sociologist Robert Schrank has argued that perhaps Topeka is not so radical after all. After an extended visit to the Topeka plant he suggested: that the work of the warehousing and packaging team was "highly repetitive, with little room for autonomy and growth";[27] that the work of the processing team, while much more challenging and interesting than that of the warehousing and packaging team, was that of "a typical operations-maintenance crew where initiative, decision-making and teamwork are essential to the smooth functioning of the process. Nothing is unusual in this type of operation;"[28] that a natural hierarchy of jobs similar to that in more traditional operations existed at Topeka;[29] and that there was not (and, perhaps, could not have been, since it was a new plant start-up) any worker participation in planning the new plant.[30] Walton observed that there was no "procedure for redress outside the existing institutional structure"; and that the Topeka system offered no guarantee of employment security in the event that workers' contributions to improved productivity might result in some of them becoming superfluous.[31] For all of these reasons, Schrank concluded that Topeka did not, in fact, represent a very dramatic departure from conventional modern plants.

How, then, does he explain the very positive early results achieved there? Schrank accounts for them in two ways. First, he suggests that some of the employees (specifically, the processing team members) had a high level of freedom to circulate in the plant and to "schmooze" (socialize). Second, he observed a general "open and humanistic" management style at Topeka, which he describes as simply good human relations—not very radical either.

Under close scrutiny, and when considered in comparison to other production facilities within its parent organization, Topeka emerges both as less conservative than Schrank's picture and less radical than Walton's. Considerable effort when into designing jobs around a largely existing physical plant. The success of this effort was limited in large part to the processing area of the plant. The supervisory role and the compensation approach had truly innovative characteristics, but these factors also created strains on the system. The general personnel policies governing the plant provided a genuinely humanistic climate. This mixed picture provided different writers with the opportunity to emphasize a variety of features of the system.

How Generalizable Is Topeka?

One conclusion seems clear. Under the traditional rules of science, Topeka cannot be offered as a generalizable example of organizational innovation—the conditions there were unusual enough to severely limit the extent to which we can safely generalize. Walton himself has admitted that Topeka operated under a number of "favorable" conditions. His list of those conditions includes the following:

The technology permitted and even called for effective communication between team members as well as providing "room for human attitudes and motivation to affect cost."

Technical and economic conditions permitted the elimination of some of the more boring and disagreeable tasks.

The plant was new, geographically isolated from other parts of the company, had a small work force, and was not unionized.

Pet foods are "socially positive" products and the company had a good image which allowed employees to develop positive attitudes toward the product and the company.

Mitchell Fein has suggested that there was another favorable condition which Walton omitted from his list—that the employees at Topeka were carefully selected from a large group of applicants to be compatible, both in ability and behavior, with the Topeka system. It is Fein's opinion that the quality of the work force was the major factor in Topeka's early success. He asserts that "writers who extoll the GF-Topeka case do not understand, or refuse to see, that this plant is unique not because of the management style, but because of the workers themselves, who were hand picked."[32] William Gomberg of the Wharton School has offered a similar criticism of Walton's representation of Topeka.[33]

Subsequent to the Fein and Gomberg criticisms, Walton commented on the selection process employed at Topeka. He confirmed that approximately one in ten applicants was selected but he maintained that, "because of the limited state of the art in employee selection generally and because the supervisors who screened applicants at Topeka were relatively inexperienced interviewers, it remains an open question whether the final sample of employees differed in any systematic way from that which would have been selected for a new plant with a more conventional work structures."[34]

Whatever the quality of the original employee group at Topeka may have been, Walton, as well as Miles and Rosenberg, has commented on the likelihood that the same human resource surplus that developed at Topeka is likely to characterize other high commitment work systems.[35] When such systems are in the early phases of their development there appears to be a human resource gap between the skills required and those available. Later, when many of the challenges of establishing the system have been overcome, a surplus of human resources may emerge.[36]

Fein and Gomberg focused on the advantage afforded the Topeka experiment due to the quality of its employee group. It should also be noted that the selection and ultimate make-up of the management group constituted still another favorable condition. Ed Dulworth, the plant manager, was, as Walton himself has acknowledged, an extraordinary manager whose talents and interests were exceptionally well suited to an innovative, open plant.[37] In addition, Dulworth was afforded the opportunity to hand pick each member of his management team. He selected individuals that he knew held philosophies of management consistent with the type of organization Topeka was going to be, and moreover, ones with whom he had worked and who had worked well with each other at Kankakee. Add to this the fact that during planning and start-up the operation was protected to a significant extent from corporate intervention by Dulworth's boss, Lyman Ketchum, and you have a set of circumstances which makes it difficult to extrapolate from the Topeka experience to other situations. However, both Walton and Miles and Rosenberg have made significant contributions along these lines to which we will refer again later in this article.[38] However generalizable the conditions at Topeka may be shown to be, we do know that those conditions were not sufficient to insure the success of Topeka itself.

Topeka's success can be evaluated from three perspectives. First, one can consider the extent to which the plant has maintained the levels of productivity, quality, safety, and absence that earlier reports indicated. Our discussions with Don Lafond, the only member of the original planning team still in Topeka and now the manager of the can plant, lead us to believe that, in this regard, Topeka should be judged quite successful. Lafond reports that, as of the end of 1982, all of these indicators are holding up quite well.

A second measure of Topeka's success might be the extent to which the form of the original innovation has been sustained. From this perspective, the results appear mixed. In many ways, the plant still operates in a manner very similar to that established originally. Lafond indicates that the teams still make many of their own decisions concerning personnel, purchasing, and product quality. On the other hand, the plant now has a personnel manager and a quality control coordinator, positions not part of the original plan. Other pressures to add staff have been successfully resisted; for example, there is as yet, no purchasing agent in the plant. It should also be noted that the same pressures that have been brought to bear elsewhere with respect to Equal Employment Opportunity Commission requirements have, of course, affected the freedom with which Topeka's teams can operate in the area of personnel decisions.

A third and very important indicator of Topeka's success is the extent to which it has served as a laboratory or learning model for others in the General Foods organization. Ketchum and Walton had this role in mind for Topeka from the very inception of their planning. Viewed from this perspective, Topeka has clearly not succeeded. There seems to be very little disagreement on this point. Walton has written about why Topeka's success didn't spread, and our discussions with two members of the original planning team, Don Lafond and Philip Simshauser, confirm that little of substance has diffused from Topeka to other General Foods locations. It is, however, probable that Topeka's influence as a model to others outside General Foods has been substantial. Let us turn our attention to that aspect of the Topeka story.

Topeka as a Case Study

There is another aspect of what happened at Topeka that concerns the way in which the events at the plant were reported. While Ketchum hoped the plant would serve as a laboratory for General Foods, Walton was interested in a broader issue, the general reform of America's work institutions. Walton's announced purpose in writing the first, and perhaps most widely read, report on the plant shortly after its opening was "to undertake the major innovations necessary for redesigning work organizations to deal effectively with the root causes of alienation." This point is extremely important in understanding Walton's writings on Topeka and the whole Topeka story. With respect to the type of organizational innovation represented by Topeka, Walton was not an unbiased, scientific observer

and reporter of events. He was, as he himself has asserted, an advocate. In 1975, he wrote, "I do not offer myself as a strictly unbiased observer. Specifically, I was deeply involved in the design effort of the Topeka plant. Moreover, generally I am committed to encouraging and improving upon innovations such as those at Topeka."[39]

Walton sincerely tried to illuminate the difficulties involved in accomplishing work restructuring but maintained his advocacy position by continuing to imply that in spite of these difficulties Topeka was a success. To Dutsch and Hornstein's *Applying Social Psychology,* Walton contributed a chapter called "Using Social Psychology to Create a New Plant Culture."[40] Although serious problems had by this time (1975) emerged at Topeka, Walton chose to describe the process he and the design team originally followed in developing and implementing the Topeka system. He reported that "to date, the innovation is an unqualified success," a clearly overoptimistic assessment.[41] At this point, as he himself asserts, Walton had become "active in diffusing information about this particular innovation and the urgent need for similarly inspired (although perhaps formally different) social experimentation."[42] Walton's footnote to this comment gives a flavor of the widespread exposure that Topeka received:

> As a result of efforts by Ketchum, Dulworth, and myself, the Topeka plant experiment has been on NBC's "First Tuesday" program; discussed in *Newsweek, Atlantic, Harvard Business Review, Innovation, The New York Times* and *Work in America;* has been presented at a symposium on the humanization of work sponsored by the American Association for the Advancement of Science, at conferences on changing work ethics in New York and San Francisco sponsored by the Urban Research Corporation, at a conference on the quality of working life sponsored by the Ford Foundation, at a conference on social indicators of the quality of work life sponsored by the Canadian Ministry of Labor; has been discussed with hundreds of other managers who have a particular interest in how changes might be effected in their own companies; and has been brought before a congressional subcommittee.[43]

Even when Walton was engaged in "explaining why success didn't take," he asserted that "the strong success of the Topeka plant in GF is not matched so far by a high amount of diffusion."[44] The clear implication is that the Topeka innovation itself was highly successful but that it was failing to spread. The issue by this time was more than diffusion of the Topeka system throughout General Foods—the larger system was beginning to diffuse into Topeka. Walton was well aware that this could occur. In 1975, he had written that a "circular relationship exists whereby lack of diffusion can eventually undermine the viability of the initial project."[45] His emphasis, even later, remained on the viability and "robust" nature of the innovation, even though he gave greater attention to its problems.[46]

For Walton, and indeed for most management theorists, the case study serves as an instrument of policy rather than science. Walton's purpose in writing was to persuade managers into action, not advance the basis of scientific knowledge. The case study method of presenting management theory has certain persuasive advantages. Among them are:

The presentation is set in a live work environment, making the discussion seem less theoretical and more practical.

The description of events offers a step-by-step approach for making theory work, meeting a demand continually made of management theorists—"Show me how to use your ideas."

The case provides the reader with something of a vicarious experience. Walton has written about this attribute of the case study.[47]

Once a case study becomes directed toward persuasion, subtle pressures build on the case writer, influencing what gets included in the discussion. In his initial reports Walton downplayed the problems of the plant, dismissin them as insignificant. The selection process of employees was ignored. While freely admitting that there were some conditions favorable to success at Topeka, Walton denied that those factors constituted preconditions for success, asserting they merely facilitated success.[48] He has continued to argue that "the broad principles underlying the Topeka work structure are widely applicable."[49]

This is a political argument, not a scientific one. Nothing in the Topeka experience supports such a generalization. While space does not allow a complete discussion of the role of the case study in science, it is fair to state that the case study provides a very tentative type of knowledge, suggestive of hypotheses, and perhaps supportive of existing paradigms, but by itself is inconclusive. The nature of the case study simply does not permit generalizing to a wider sample of organizations. Walton wrote more confidently than was warranted. Further, the study was lacking in detail. In social situations very small differences are often important, and Walton himself has emphasized the importance of including detail in case studies.[50]

Walton, whose credentials and important reference groups are rooted in social science, has been walking the tightrope walked by most management theorists. He apparently recognizes the potential role conflict involved. He writes (while drawing generalizations from several innovative work systems):

The fact that I was similarly involved in these four plants that were attempting to create high commitment work systems has permitted me to make comparisons among plants with confidence. Thus, if I have not managed to completely avoid bias introduced by my personal involvement, that bias should not affect either the interperiod comparisons of a plant or the comparisons among plants. Naturally I wanted all four work systems to succeed.[51]

It may be true that Walton's biases were spread equally among the plants so that, as he says, they would not have affected his comparisons of the four, but the last line of the above quote is the crucial one. *Of course* he wanted the plants to succeed. He was an active change agent, a consultant being compensated for what was assumed to be his contribution to their success, and, even more compelling, he was and is committed to encouraging the spread of such innovations because of what he believes to be their positive social contributions.

A management theory is ultimately measured by the extent to which it is applied in organizations. Management researchers must gain access to organizations to demonstrate the utility of their ideas.

For theorists, widespread application is a very real measure of professional success. Indeed, business school faculty are repeatedly exposed to this pressure—the question of applicability is raised by students and executives alike. It is here that the case method proves to have high utility as an instrument of policy rather than science.

The leveraging of the plant as an instrument of institutional reform is an important part of the Topeka story. It politicized the Topeka system to the extent that representatives of opposing schools of thought found it necessary to either protect it or repudiate it. Understanding it became a secondary issue. In the process, myths about Topeka became institutionalized into textbooks as case reports became part of the body of knowledge of management.

Most organizational researchers find themselves writing for two audiences, management scientists and management practitioners. The demands of the two audiences are considerably different. Those researchers who are motivated toward reform find themselves especially vulnerable to the pressures of writing to convince their primary audience, the practitioner.

What Can Be Learned From Topeka?

The widespread publicity given Topeka has undoubtedly helped shape the attitudes and beliefs of many managers. Most of these managers have informally integrated their conclusions into their approaches to managing, whether or not they were favorably disposed toward Topeka. Some, however, have developed more formal reponses.

Miles and Rosenberg have recently written about what they call "second-generation" new plants. They suggest that "the defining characteristic of a second-generation plant is its having 'gone to school' and learned the lessons of the first generation."[52] In their terms, Topeka is among the first-generation plants and thus has contributed to the body of knowledge growing out of such innovations. In reviewing Miles and Rosenberg's report, one is struck by the extent to which the managers of the second-generation plants learned both from the success and the problems encountered in the first-generation facilities. The process was not one

of imitation but one of information gathering for purposes of anticipating and avoiding (or at least effectively managing) the inevitable difficulties associated with organizational innovation. With this in mind, we offer the following observations, which we hope contribute to the emerging body of knowledge available to managers of second-generation facilities.

To begin with, many of Topeka's problems were made significantly worse by the fact that Ketchum's superiors never really understood what Topeka was all about. In spite of his, and later Dulworth's, repeated attempts to make clear what they had in mind, they did not succeed in generating the kind of appreciation necessary to allow Topeka to function as a learning model for the General Foods Corporation. This was most evident in top management's choice of a replacement for Ketchum—a man whose personal style and management philosophy were incompatible with those of Dulworth and the Topeka system. In addition, top management consistently responded to proposals concerning management policy innovations at Topeka by saying, "How are we going to handle it if everybody else wants this too?" In the eyes of General Foods' top management, Topeka's payoffs were apparently expected to be much more in terms of output of pet food than output of ideas for innovative management.

A second lesson concerns the extent to which attention was given to integrating Topeka into the total General Foods' organizational culture. There was a strong tendency on the part of Topeka management to emphasize the differences between their system and the corporation's way of doing things. As advocates of the plant discussed Topeka at management meetings with General Foods (and outside the corporation as well), they tended to emphasize the uniqueness in their approach and to deemphasize the similarities to conventional systems. Ultimately, this caused them as well as their system to be shunned. As two examples, the corporation never did allow them to install completely the compensation system they felt they needed and the "graduates" of Topeka were never accepted into other positions in General Foods.

There was, in addition, some confusion over exactly what it was that the Topeka people were selling. In many ways, the plant appeared to outside observers as something less than radical. Thus, many within General Foods reacted to descriptions of the plant's unique features as examples of exaggerated self-importance. It was, more than anything else, a philosophy of management the plant's advocates were promoting, a difficult thing to communicate under the best of circumstances.

A third lesson has to do with the Topeka managers' (and, more particularly, Ketchum's) apparent insensitivity to the realities of the political climate in their company. Ketchum in particular should have known that his meteoric rise to prominence within and outside of the organization was certain to produce hostility and resistance within General Foods to his ideas and the Topeka system in general. It is, of course, impossible to know whether this could have been avoided, but there appears to have been little effort devoted to do so.

We feel that Ketchum became confused, perhaps in part as a result of Walton's influence, between two roles for Topeka. One goal was as a learning model within General Foods; the other was as a learning model for society. Walton was interested in general social change in the work place. He viewed Topeka as a significant, even prototypical, example of the direction in which such change should move. In order to capitalize on the existence of Topeka he wanted to maximize its visibility. Ketchum and, to a certain extent, the other Topeka people as well, became caught up in this excitement and lost sight of their original idea of having Topeka be a model within General Foods. They should have been able to see that the more publicity and exposure their experiment received outside the company, the less viable it became inside their organization. If they could have controlled their own and Walton's zeal for a few years until they had a solid, established plant which had been integrated into the General Foods organization, they might then have been able to offer it as a legitimately successful prototype of things to come. Basically, the plant was an example of a modern processing plant, which could attract a motivated, capable and somwhat atypical work force if managed by principles other than "traditional" industrial management. This lesson was lost as the plant became promoted more and more

widely as an example of radical, sociotechnical system design, which, unfortunately, it was not.

Part of the learning which Topeka can offer concerns the difficulty of modifying existing corporate practices. This may be the most important lesson to emerge from Topeka. Field applications of management principles are always situation specific. As Miles and Rosenberg have pointed out, "What first generation process models (and good road maps) . . . offer those who use them . . . is a sense of control, a basis for planning, increased predictability of distance, dips, tolls and critical intersections along an otherwise harrowing route. What first generation experience does not provide, however, is a set of operational solutions to second generation problems."[53] The important lessons concern the trade-offs to be made in establishing work place innovations. The issue in future applications should not be theoretical purity but organizational effectiveness.

References

1. R. E. Walton, "How to Counter Alienation in the Plant," *Harvard Business Review* (November/December 1972), pp. 70–81.
2. This article is based on information gathered during a five-year research project concerning some of the most widely known case studies in the field of management. Our statements and conclusions here have been assembled from published reports on Topeka, examination of many of the Topeka planning team's original documents, and discussions with members of that team.
3. L. D. Ketchum, "A Case Study of Diffusion," in L. Davis and A. Cherns (eds.), *Quality of Working Life, Vol. II, Cases and Commentary* (New York: Free Press, 1975), pp. 140–141.
4. Ibid.
5. R. E. Walton, "Using Social Psychology to Create a New Plant Culture," in M. Deutsch and H. Hornstein (eds.), *Applying Social Psychology: Implications for Research, Practice and Training* (Hillsdale, NJ: Erlbaum, 1975), p. 140.
6. Ibid., p. 139.
7. Ketchum, op. cit., p. 142.
8. Walton, "Using Social Psychology," p. 147.
9. Ibid.
10. Ketchum, op. cit., p. 139.
11. L. D. Ketchum, "Topeka Organization and Systems Development," an internal General Foods' document

written to explain the Topeka system (30 December 1969).

12. R. Schrank, "On Ending Worker Alienation: The Gaines Pet Food Plant," in R. Fairfield (ed.), *Humanizing the Workplace* (Buffalo, NY: Prometheus, 1974), pp. 124–127; idem, *Ten Thousand Working Days* (Cambridge, MA: MIT Press, 1979), pp. 231–233.

13. Walton, "Using Social Psychology," p. 142.

14. Walton, "How to Counter Alienation," p. 75.

15. "New Way to Run a Plant," *GF News* (February/March 1972), p. 10.

16. Walton, "How to Counter Alienation," p. 76.

17. Ibid., p. 77.

18. Ibid.

19. Ibid., p. 78.

20. Ibid.

21. E. M. Glaser, *Productivity Gains through Worklife Improvement* (New York: Harcourt, 1976), pp. 61–62.

22. R. E. Walton, "Innovative Restructuring of Work," in J. Rosow (ed.), *The Worker and the Job* (Englewood Cliffs, NJ: Prentice-Hall, 1974), p. 162; Walton, "Using Social Psychology," p. 141.

23. R. E. Walton, "Work Innovations at Topeka: After Six Years," *Journal of Applied Behavioral Sciences,* vol. 13 (1977), p. 423.

24. Ibid.

25. Ibid., p. 422; "How to Counter Alienation," p. 70; and idem, "The Topeka Story: Teaching an Old Dog Food New Tricks," *The Wharton Magazine* (Winter 1978).

26. Walton, "How to Counter Alienation," p. 71.

27. Schrank, *Ten Thousand Working Days,* p. 233.

28. Schrank, "Ending Worker Alienation," p. 125.

29. Schrank, *Ten Thousand Working Days,* p. 235.

30. Schrank, "Ending Worker Alienation," p. 124.

31. R. E. Walton, "The Topeka Story, Part II: What's the Bottom Line?" *The Wharton Magazine* (Spring 1978), p. 41.

32. M. Fein, "Job Enrichment Does Not Work," *Atlanta Economic Review,* vol. 25 (1975), p. 52.

33. W. Gomberg, "Job Satisfaction: Sorting Out the Nonsense," *American Federationist* (June 1973), pp. 14–19.

34. R. E. Walton, "Establishing and Maintaining High Commitment Work Systems," in J. R. Kimberly, Robert H. Miles, and Associates (eds.), *The Organizational Life Cycle* (San Francisco: Jossey-Bass, 1980), pp. 220–221.

35. Ibid., pp. 260–261; R. E. Miles and H. R. Rosenberg, "The Human Resources Approach to Management: Second-Generation Issues," *Organizational Dynamics* (Winter 1982), pp. 26–40.

36. Ibid., p. 31.

37. Walton, "Using Social Psychology," p. 147.

38. Walton, "Establishing and Maintaining Commitment"; Miles and Rosenberg, op cit.

39. R. E. Walton, "From Hawthorne to Topeka and Kalmar," in E. Cass and F. Zimmer (eds.), *Man and Work in Society* (New York: Van Nostrand-Reinhold, 1975), p. 117.

40. Walton, "Using Social Psychology."

41. Ibid., p. 141.

42. Ibid., p. 154.

43. Ibid.

44. R. E. Walton, "The Diffusion of New Work Structures: Explaining Why Success Didn't Take," *Organizational Dynamics* (Winter 1975), p. 12.

45. Ibid.

46. Ibid.; idem, "Using Social Psychology"; idem, "Establishing and Maintaining Commitment."

47. R. E. Walton, "Advantages and Attributes of the Case Study," *Journal of Applied Behavioral Sciences,* vol. 3 (1972), p. 77.

48. Walton, "How To Counter Alienation," p. 79.

49. Walton, "The Topeka Story: Part II," p. 41.

50. Walton, "Advantages and Attributes."

51. Walton, "Establishing and Maintaining Commitment," p. 218.

52. Miles and Rosenberg, op. cit., p. 27.

53. Ibid., p. 31.

Conversation with Charles L. Brown

David A. Nadler

The American Telephone & Telegraph Company (AT&T) has been called the "biggest company on earth." In terms of size it is difficult to conceive of, with its more than 1,000,000 employees, approximately 3,000,000 shareholders, and more than $125 billion in assets. AT&T itself is a holding company that includes 21 operating telephone companies. It also holds non-controlling ownership in two other companies (Cincinnati Bell and Southern New England Telephone). The corporate family also includes Western Electric, a wholly owned subsidiary that manufactures and purchases telecommunications products and supplies for the Bell System; Bell Laboratories, which provides research and development services; the AT&T Long Lines Department, which is reponsible for the nationwide telecommunications network; and AT&T International.

The AT&T Company has long been of interest for reasons that go beyond its size. During the last 15 years the company's orientation has shifted away from the exclusively regulated monopoly configuration that had existed for decades. This shift has accelerated in recent years in response to events in the environment. Specifically, in the spring of 1980 the Federal Communications Commission ruled that AT&T could become involved in providing deregulated products and services, but only through a fully separated subsidiary. Planning began to set up that subsidiary as the competitive side of AT&T, but outside pressure continued—with some arguing for the complete breakup of the Bell System. In January 1982, in what many have described as an historic settlement, AT&T and the Justice Department agreed on the future shape of the Bell System, including an agreement for AT&T to divest itself of its operating telephone companies.

Reprinted, by permission of the publisher, from *Organizational Dynamics,* Summer 1982. © 1982 by AMACOM Periodicals Division, American Management Associations, New York.

Since 1979 Charles L. Brown has been chairman of the board of AT&T and, as the most senior manager of the company, has been ultimately responsible for guiding the organization through this period of profound change. As part of *Organizational Dynamics'* special issue on organizational change, Mr. Brown was interviewed with a particular focus on the issues of change management in the Bell System. The first interview was held in late 1981, before the AT&T–Justice Department agreement. Interviewed again in the spring of 1982, Mr. Brown modified some of his comments to reflect some of the key events that had occurred. The interview thus provides some insight into the thoughts of Charles Brown in the midst of a major organizational change, one that is far from complete.

The interview was conducted by David A. Nadler, a member of the editorial board of *Organizational Dynamics.* Dr. Nadler also wrote a commentary article, which follows this interview.

NADLER: As a starting point, I'd be interested in getting a picture of your career path at AT&T.

BROWN: I started in the business climbing telephone poles before World War II. Then I went back to college and into the Navy. I started again after the war with the company as an equipment attendant in Hartford. I went on through a number of assignments, lots of different departments and lots of different geography with the long-lines department. Then I went to Illinois Bell in 1963 and eventually got to be president out there. I came to New York in the job of chief financial officer in 1974. From there, I moved to president and chief operating officer and then, in 1979, to this job of chairman of AT&T.

NADLER: As you look back on your progression, are there any particular events or assignments that stand out as having been particularly formative?

BROWN: I think an early district plant superintendent's job was probably very formative. It was the first time I had supervised a large number of people and had a significant investment to worry about.

NADLER: A lot of people, in both the business and the academic communities, have been watching the changes at AT&T with great interest. Some would say it's probably the biggest single planned organizational change in the country in the second half of the century. From where you sit, what are some of the most critical issues in managing this change?

BROWN: I think the critical issue was and is getting an understanding of what the public expects of this business, and how that expectation either has changed or will change. Once we've decided what it is we think that the public expects of us, then it is crucial to explain that to the organization. It is critical for us to seize the initiative—as opposed to just letting something happen to the organization or submitting to somebody else's design of what the organization should do, or what its aims should be. So I think those are the two critical things—an understanding of what is expected and seizing the initiative to adapt the organization to the new world.

NADLER: The second issue, adaptation, is one of particular interest. What are the biggest things that have to change?

BROWN: The homogeneous job that this organization has done over most of its existence, the end-to-end provision of universal telephone service, has been imbedded in the minds and the actions of its people. It has guided the operating procedures by which the people do their jobs. In a change as vast as this, both the overall objectives of the company and the means by which they're accomplished need to be explained and re-explained, examined and re-examined. And they need to be changed as logic and experience indicate. It is difficult to do that while, at the same time, continuing the service job with the quality of results we've come to expect of ourselves. And, of course, the earnings job must be carried out all along in a way that permits us to have the resources to do the service job. The balancing act is extremely difficult—thinking about the change and what has to happen, while at the same time keeping an eye on the ball in terms of the current business. It's a very, very complex and challenging job.

NADLER: As you think about this juggling act, what are the parts that you've spent the most time thinking about?

BROWN: Well, first of all, I have to spend a great deal of time trying to accelerate decisions in Washington concerning the ground rules under which the business will operate in the future. It's exceptionally important that we get a reasonable, coherent charter from the federal government, and that this limbo in which the telecommunication policy now exists (and has existed for a dozen years) be put behind us. That means that I have to spend a great deal of time planning and attempting to orchestrate our position vis-à-vis the various positions of the different groups in Washington.

It doesn't seem that, in the face of that problem, the internal job is very difficult, and I have to tell you that I think we can do the internal job without fear of failure, once we're given some decent understanding of what is expected of us. But the complexity of trying to change ourselves, when we don't know what the future rules are going to be, injects a degree of uncertainty that creates a lot of anxiety.

NADLER: Some people outside of the Bell System have questioned whether it is possible to bring about such a large and profound change, even if you could get a definition of the future.

BROWN That's what management is all about. And if we can't do it, we're not very good manager. I just don't believe that.

NADLER: Well, then, what do you think is the most critical element in accomplishing it? Some people say that's a pretty tough job—to try to change the culture of the organization, to have people think in a different way and, somehow at the same time, hold on to values that have made it strong and have defined the character of the organization. How does that happen?

BROWN: What we face is a split of the local telephone companies from the parent and from the inventor and the manufacturer. This is not our idea. It stems from an agreement with the Justice Department and was acceded to only because it seemed to coincide with a national consensus that competition rather than regulation should be the dominant force in this industry. The telephone companies will take with them the culture of 100 years in the Bell System. The remaining AT&T, the Bell Labs and Western Electric, is the group organization with real culture shift. It will be partly regulated—the long-distance network—and partly unregulated. It will be freed up from ancient restrictions and it will be riskier. There are a number of committees and panels working on this—to look at every part of the business to see how it will be affected or how we want it to function. It's the job of the senior managers to detect the important things, to push aside the things that are not important, and to go at the former in ways that we know how.

I'd be foolish to brush off the cultural problem, but I don't see it in the magnitude that some outside observers do. Our culture is one of quality service with financial strength. And those qualities form the sine qua non of any successful organization.

NADLER: It seems to me—on the basis of the time I spent out in some of your operating companies—that there are still significant cultural shifts to be made. For example, one frequently sees what appear to be culturally based conflicts between sales groups and the installation organization.

BROWN: I don't know of any organization where the salesmen think that the factory people understand their problem. And I don't know of any factor manager who doesn't harbor in his inner soul the thought that if those salespeople stayed out of cocktail lounges, they'd be able to sell his product at a higher price. So there's always tension between the people in marketing and sales and between those in manufacturing and service.

That type of tension has existed in this business long before this recent series of events. Actually, we have fostered it—by virtue of measuring departments independently. We realize that, in the process, we have erected walls between them. We've tried to mitigate that in various ways over many years—in organizational ways or in measurement plans that avoid departmental barriers.

It's an unusual organization that manages to get rid of this tension completely, but our aim is to try very hard to do so. I think we can be successful, and there's nothing like a little competition to convince individuals in the business that you either get the business or you don't have a job. That is a very compelling motive and it's a good way to get attention—one that will be effective.

NADLER: So you're saying first that the cultural problem may be overstated.

BROWN: Yes.

NADLER: And that perhaps the most compelling device in dealing with it is the presence of competition.

BROWN: No, I think the most compelling device in dealing with people is a clear statement of goals on the part of the management of the business—a clear understanding (as clear as you can get in a large organization) of the strategies and tactics necessary to get us to the objectives. Then the existence of competitive environment helps one with the management of that process. If you lose the business, you don't have to explain the results to very many people. They understand very well. So where we might have had a problem in getting goals across in the past, the competitive environment has helped. But the primary thing is to articulate goals and get employees to agree that the goals are worthwhile and the strategies appropriate.

NADLER: If the cultural issue is knocked out, what do you see as the other critical issues internally?

BROWN: I think the matter of business systems is generally underestimated when one considers the miracles that can be accomplished by mechanization and computerization. A deep and complex problem is posed by the need to change employee work habits and methods that are almost instinctive. In other words, the business procedures that get the job done are going to have to change and it's not easy to do that. I think it's a major problem that almost surmounts most of the others. We have an immense "book" of "correct" procedures that aren't so correct anymore.

NADLER: Part of that is instinctive, you were saying, and that part is a way of working—a way of doing things. What, then, are some of the general management processes that might have to change?

BROWN: We have to work very hard on getting the input and cooperation and assent of the people working with us. We cannot wait for somebody writing a practice somewhere to come up with the best way to get something accomplished. We may revise and institutionalize ways of getting things accomplished over the oncoming years, but we don't have time to write it all out because we're not very sure of what it's going to be like in the new environment. Therefore, we need to get the help and cooperation of the people actually doing the job. We need a managerial style that is somewhat different than it has been in more stable times.

Also, we tend to underestimate the degree to which regulation has overhung this business. We've had to have an immense apparatus to anticipate and comply with the regulators who have dealt with this business over the years and who are dealing with it now. These regulators and their styles and objectives turn over frequently. As a result, the business is very busy trying to outguess what's going to happen next and how the regulators are going to judge one's actions. I think getting into unregulated businesses will be a liberating experience. When that happens, and to whatever degree it happens, we will have to think differently. No longer is it going to be necessary or even feasible to base some actions on what a regulator may think about it. The only thing that will count is what the customer thinks.

I don't mean that we haven't *been* customer-oriented—our record belies that. What I do mean is that it's easy to underestimate the overhang of that regulator presence.

NADLER: You mentioned a change in managerial style. You summarized it as sort of a moving down of decision making, perhaps a less formal style with less waiting for the practice to be written, and more bottom up than top down.

BROWN: I think that's part of it. The other part of it is being more agile in order to be able to react to situations that don't lend themselves to waiting around for comprehensive solutions that suit everybody.

NADLER: There would seem to be problems because you're working with a group of managers who have grown up in the regulated environment. That is, the managers have been raised with that regulatory overhang, which leads to a managerial style aimed at making sure you're in compliance, and being certain to do things the right way, even if it might take longer or cost a little more. How do you feel about changing that?

BROWN: Well, in the first place, we're talking about a small percentage of the business, which is going to change radically toward less regulation. The only way I know how to do it is to make sure the goals are clear and then start selecting people who can understand them and reach for them. And not to select people who can't. I believe our people, given a reasonable understanding of what it is that has to be done, will adapt themselves and do it. Time and time again I've seen them adapt themselves to a situation and do a very creative and effective job. Some of them will take to it much more easily than others, but most people will do what the job calls for.

NADLER: In the last year or two in the Bell System, there has been a lot of thinking, acting, and talking about quality of work life as an initiative. How does that fit into all that we've been talking about? It's a style change, too.

BROWN: It is a style change, and it fits right in, no question about it. I think the extent to which we're successful in changing our style will be a measure of how well we adapt to the new world. We have tried to avoid laying out a BSP (Bell System Practice) for this because it is not something that yields to that treatment. I think that as we continue to press, ask questions, help supervisors, and employ these ideas, we're going to find it's easier to spread the principles than if we were to try it in a highly formal way.

NADLER: So the regulatory change provides the impetus, unfreezes some things, and enables you to start some change in this area.

BROWN: Yes, I think so. If you don't have an urgent need to change, then it's pretty hard sometimes to do it. If, in fact, some of these ideas are workable

and understandable in the new context, I think they'll be adopted more quickly.

NADLER: In the Bell System, you're perceived as personally involved in trying to foster the quality of work life activities. How did you come to get interested in this?

BROWN: I have seen it as a particularly welcome thing, one that will facilitate what I think has to happen in any event in the way of management style changes. I suppose, also, I flatter myself that it is the way that I like to manage, and when I don't do it, I should. What interested me in it? I think the combination of the currentness of the matter in the literature, the experiences of other organizations, and just an inherent feeling that if we can push responsibility lower down, then we should. I was attracted to it because I felt it would be helpful to us in facing our future.

NADLER: Specifically for you, what does it mean to be doing quality of work life activities or managing that way?

BROWN: I think one of my predecessors explained it about as well as I can. People do a superior job when they're first convinced that they have a job that's worth doing. I think that exemplifies a good deal of the thrust of the "quality of work life" idea. As soon as people understand and personally believe that they have a job worth doing, miracles occur in the way they do their job. That's certainly a major part of it—to raise the level of an individual's respect for the job that he or she is doing, as opposed to going in the other direction. Respect for one's job, after all, is one step toward respect for oneself.

I have believed for most of my career that we have not taken enough advantage of this opportunity. We have expected too many supervisors at too many levels to do too much of the wrong thing. I'm glad to have a good reason to get on with it.

NADLER: Again, this involves a lot of change. For example, the supervising job at the first, second, and third level tends to become quite different in the kind of environment where decision making is moving down. Do you think it may be hard to get some people to let go of their previous approaches to their jobs?

BROWN: Sure. People will do whatever they have been brought up to do. By and large, if they've thrived in this organization, it's because they did things the way they thought the organization wanted them to do it. And one means of explaining the "new way" is to reduce the number of levels of supervision. We're in the process of doing that.

NADLER: Still, it's a picture that may be traumatic for some managers—I'm thinking again of middle levels in the organization.

BROWN: Yes, but I wouldn't overestimate that.

NADLER: You've been in this job since 1979. As you look back now, do you have any key insights about how one functions as an effective leader for a large organization?

BROWN: Well, I think a lot remains to be decided as to whether I've been an effective leader or not. So I'm not about to pontificate on it. History will decide whether my style, my attitude, and the objectives we're driving at are appropriate and suitable for the times. But it's possible to learn a lot about how things are going by measuring or listening to the attitudes of the managers in the business. If they were, in any significant numbers, to raise an objection about the way we're headed, then I would have to pause and rethink whether we were making sense.

But as I talk with people at all levels, it seems to me we have been successful in saying, "Here are the circumstances and options, here is what we're trying to do, here is the direction we're going, and here is the initiative we must seize. There are lots of things to do between here and there. But do you see any other route, do you see any slowing down, any accelerating that's advisable? Do you find anything that you object to with respect to the way the organization is now headed?" And I don't find very much dissention or objection, at least not on a broad scale. Mostly I encounter people saying, "For goodness' sake, you've got the right idea here—get going. Don't worry so much about this flywheel of culture that's alleged to be so important. You have the job, you don't have much time, keep going." That's the major kind of reaction I get from the internal side of the business.

I know about the anxieties, and they're mostly personal anxieties. Thus the focal question is, "What's going to happen to me personally?" And we have driven at that problem by repeating many times that, as soon as we can, we need to be specific about how the change will affect each individual. We need to answer that question as quickly as we can and do so without equivocation.

That is the source of most of the anxiety. The top officers and myself have to deal with the corporate anxiety, but much of the rest of the organization is experiencing anxiety on an individual basis. We will try to shake out the individual anxieties as quickly as we can.

NADLER: As a final question, does Charlie Brown have an approach or a specific style or philosophy of managing that guides him in general?

BROWN: I think I have a management style that encourages personal decision making down the line. This is basically so even though under certain circumstances I do tend to supervise in detail to make sure I know what's going on. I place a great deal of responsibility on other people and urge them to do so, too. I hope that's the kind of example that's useful to the organization at this particular time.

Ruben F. Mettler and TRW Inc.

TRW's top level organization chart (Exhibit 1) indicates that the company is headed by a chief executive office. Within that office, Ruben Mettler is the senior individual, with the functions of board chairman and chief executive officer (CEO). At the next level in the chart are a number of corporate staff officers. These positions are structured to deal with the various internal and external problems the company faces and could change as circumstances change. The remainder of the chart is devoted to the line operating divisions.

TRW is a conglomerate, and its diverse array of businesses is grouped into three major industry sectors, each headed by an executive vice president. Note that, in this operating structure, sector officers report directly to the chief executive office, not through the vice presidents as in a functional type of organization. There are in turn functional vice presidents for financial control, law, communications, planning, and human relations at the sector level, but they do not report directly to Allen, Coyle, Fay, Harter, and Knicely at the corporate level; they report to the sector managers. At this top level, the company provides a good example of the decentralized product division structure emphasized by Chandler.

TRW opened operations in Cleveland, Ohio as a manufacturer of screws and bolts. Its early success was in making valves for the automobile industry, and then later for aircraft. Gradually the company expertise branched into other automobile and aircraft components. During much of its early life, it was known as Thompson Products Company.

In 1953, Thompson Products provided financial support to Simon Ramo and Dean Wooldrige to found a small electronics system firm. Ramo and Wooldrige had obtained their doctorates at California Institute of Technology at the same time, and both were with Hughes Aircraft before starting their own company. In 1958 the Ramo-Wooldridge firm merged fully with Thompson Products to form the present TRW, an aerospace company.

What TRW has become insofar as product lines are concerned is indicated by the group designa-

EXHIBIT 1 Top level organization chart at TRW

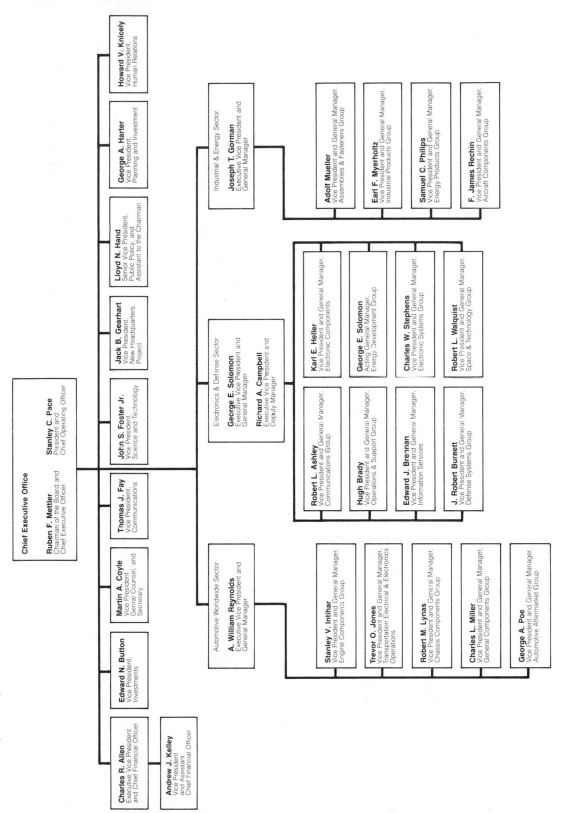

tions in the organization chart. It has grown rapidly, especially in the space technology field. Much of its growth has been internally generated through research, but there have been a large number of acquisitions as well. The common thread has been a strong technological base in products and services.

Innovation and change are essential ingredients to TRW's success. TRW was one of the first corporations to undertake an organization development program, and to use team-building. The company was an early user of the matrix structure. It has pioneered in new methods of administering employee benefits, in the use of salary compensation in its plants, and in the application of systems analysis, which has been used in an attempt to solve some of the problems of its headquarters city, Cleveland, Ohio. Not only have many new businesses been acquired, but also, the company has

divested itself of businesses that were viewed as having little growth potential. Such innovation and change put a strain on the company. It is very important that the mix of businesses at any time be both manageable and profitable.

Technicians install protective cover on TRW's Tracking & Data Relay Satellite No. 2. This satellite will be a key element in NASA's space-based global communications system.

Ruben Mettler

Ruben Mettler's career almost perfectly parallels the growth of TRW. He began his college education at Stanford University with a law degree in mind. However, as a consequence of a Navy enlistment during World War II, he found himself at the California Institute of Technology, where he earned a B.S. in electrical engineering. By 1949 he had a Ph.D. in electrical and aeronautical engineering from the same school.

Mettler then went to work with Simon Ramo and Dean Wooldridge at Hughes Aircraft and began a career in research. After a year as a consultant with the Department of Defense in Washington, D.C., he returned to California with the newly founded Ramo-Wooldridge firm. He took an active role in the ballistic missile and early space programs there, serving as an inventor himself and a manager of technological innovations. With the merger in 1958, he rapidly moved to head the Space Technology Laboratories. From there he stepped steadily up the TRW ladder to become president in 1969 and chairman and CEO in 1977. Ruben Mettler is just as clearly committed to innovation and change as his company is. He has been a technological innovator and is widely respected as an engineer. He appears to understand well the problems TRW has in managing innovation and change.

The Ground-based Electro-Optical Deep Space Surveillance System developed by TRW allows scientists to track and identify satellites and observe more than 6 million stars an hour.

Planning and Management Policy/Strategy

Part Four has as its central concern matters that are normally the province of chief executive officers and boards of directors. Looking at an organization from this top level, internal perspective reveals a very different picture from that of organizational behavior or process/structure. This is the broad landscape of strategic management, as opposed to the more limited operational management that prevails at lower levels.

Strategic management involves dealing with the threats, pressures, and opportunities that loom in the environment. At the very least these considerations include the value patterns of the culture, the political structures and legal processes of the society, the economic forces of competitive markets, the changing technologies of both information and machines, and the physical environment. Strategic management also involves maintaining a balance between the various parts of the organization as they compete with one another for resources. Chief executives are repeatedly called upon for capital outlays to one division or another that they must deny or curtail because it is not in the interests of the *whole* firm to grant the requests as stated.

At times strategic management appears to call for the exercise of charismatic authority of the kind Max Weber discussed. This is particularly true with regard to spelling out the objectives of the organization—both official and operative—and obtaining commitments to them. Somehow, chief executives must achieve a reasonable match between objectives, plans to reach them, and actual performances. Even with all the means of bureaucracy available, this is not easy to accomplish.

It would be reasonable for a student to ask at this point why a knowledge of strategic management is worth obtaining. One answer is that some students will ultimately move to this sphere; for them, this early learning is obviously relevant. A number may found or take over a small business of their own. But an even more important point is that organizations, and among them business corporations, are the essence of our society. A truly liberal education ought to include an understanding of why and how these organizations do what they do. That understanding is the essence of strategic management. Thus, whether one works within an organization or merely has the desire to understand an important aspect of society's functioning, the subject of management policy and strategy is worth knowing about.

Chapter 11 is concerned with the ways in which the strategies and overall policies of a firm are formulated. It deals with the nature of the planning process, identification of policies and strategies to consider, and the evaluation of alternative approaches. In Chapter 12, the decision making processes underlying policy and strategy formulation are addressed. How do individuals and groups function within this process, and how do they function most effectively? Finally, in Chapter 13, a topic of major concern in strategic management is considered. This is the matter of business ethics and social responsibility as they relate to formulating and implementing important decisions in the business world. The chapter also considers the subject of representing the organization within its environment, a topic closely tied to social responsibility.

Planning and Formulating Policy/Strategy

CHAPTER OUTLINE

Strategic Management
Terms and Definitions
    The Place of Strategic Planning
    Strategy and Tactics
    The Policy Role
Types of Policies and Strategies
    Variations in Strategic Stance
    Growth Strategies
The Atlantic Refining Co. (ARCO): Strategy in
    Action

Strategic Planning
The Planning Process
    What Planning Is and Is Not
    Degrees of Sophistication
    Steps in Planning
    Types of Plans
The Organization of Planning
Contributions and Problems
    Comparisons of Planners and Non-planners
    Why Should Planning Help?
    Sources of Problems

Identifying and Evaluating Policies and Strategies
Specific Approaches
    Gap Analysis
    Industry Analysis
    The Product-Market Matrix
    The Product-Portfolio Matrix
    Product Life Cycles
    Profit Impact of Market Strategies (PIMS)
    Experience Curves
    Computer Models
Forecasting
    Economic and Sales Forecasts
    Forecasting Technology and Innovation
    Social and Political Forecasts
    Environmental Scanning

OBJECTIVES

To specify through discussion and examples what strategic management is and how planning fits into the process.

To describe the strategic planning process as it operates in various corporations and to consider some of the reasons why it achieves success and why it fails.

To provide information on the various methods used to identify and evaluate strategies, and to forecast future events of importance to a company.

A student working part-time in a large aeronautics design firm has been watching her supervisors with interest. It seems to her that some unproductive decisions have been made lately, and she feels not only frustrated but also very certain that, in a management position, she could make some positive, profitable changes. The idea fascinates her, and within several weeks, it feels like a real decision—to pursue a career in management, and to be a successful manager.

With this goal in mind, she sets out to collect information by reading and by talking to people who have already achieved that goal. She begins to develop a plan to attain her goal. In the process she considers a variety of ways of getting into management—working her way up, starting her own firm, concentrating on education, and so on. She evaluates each alternative in terms of costs, both personal and financial, time to achieve the goal, probability of successful implementation, and the like. Gradually her plan is filled in as she makes further choices and completes various steps in the process.

Let us assume that what she decides is to obtain an undergraduate degree in management as quickly as possible by borrowing money, taking a heavy course load, and quitting the part-time job. Then she hopes to obtain employment in the manufacturing area with a large multinational firm that would employ her in a location where she could work toward an MBA at night, and pay the costs of her further education. Once she gains the MBA, she could transfer to a plant outside the United States to gain international experience. After 10 years with the company, she would be able to go with a smaller firm in the same industry that would pay well and offer a considerable promotion in order to obtain the competencies and expertise she had developed.

This scenario constitutes strategy formulation and strategic planning at the personal level. The student has developed a long-term strategy to achieve her career goals. Organizations do much the same thing to achieve their goals of profit, growth, prestige, and the like. The ways in which they go about doing this are the focus of this chapter.

STRATEGIC MANAGEMENT

Chapter 9 introduced the concept of strategy in the discussion of Alfred Chandler's views. There, the primary focus was on growth strategy. Now, in a much-expanded perspective, we will look at ongoing strategy and planning.

Terms and Definitions

Strategy may be defined as the creation of missions, the setting of organizational objectives with full consideration of external and internal forces, the formulation of specific policies to achieve objectives, and the assurance of implementation—all with a view to making certain that the purposes and objectives of the organization are accomplished. Accordingly, *strategic management* involves relating an organization to its environment, formulating strategies to cope with that environment, and taking steps to achieve implementation of the strategies. This includes:

1. Constantly watching the environment external to the organization, as well as within the organization.
2. Identifying opportunities to exploit and dangers to avoid within the environment.
3. Evaluating company strengths and weaknesses in the context of its environment.
4. Formulating missions and objectives.
5. Identifying possible strategies to achieve missions and objectives.
6. Evaluating these strategies and choosing among them.
7. Establishing and monitoring implementation processes.

Unfortunately, it is not possible to guarantee other theorists will use these terms in the same way they are used here. In fact, the basic terminology of the policy/strategy field is in a state of confusion at present, for largely historical reasons.[1] Originally the idea of strategy came from the military, where it referred to actions taken to offset what an adversary did or was expected to do. It is only recently that the term has come into general use in the business world. In that context, a major concern has been dealing with competitors, as reflected in various economic concepts of industrial organization.[2] But there are other important factors in the environment besides competitors—governments, for instance, and citizen action groups. Typically, but not always, strategy has come to refer to these other factors as well. In addition, some use the term strategy to apply to only very broad statements at a high level of abstraction; other definitions include much more specific detail. It would appear that, for some time to come, meanings will have to be inferred largely from the contexts in which the terms are used.

The Place of Strategic Planning   In many companies, particularly larger ones, a major vehicle through which strategies are devised is some type of formal planning process. This process is considered in detail in a later section, but it is introduced here to help explain what strategic management is about. Strategic planning is not all of strategic management, and its role varies considerably from firm to firm, but it can be a major component.

Exhibit 11.1 presents an overview of the planning process, starting with a plan as to how and on what schedule company planning will be carried out, and ending with a review and evaluation of what actually happened. The primary phases are initial strategic planning, then medium-range programming and programs, then short-range planning and plans, then implementation, and finally review. There is a gradual narrowing and increasing emphasis on action specification, building on the master strategies and program strategies that result from the strategic planning process. In short, the planning process becomes more tactical.

A master strategy would be the decision to diversify into new industries in order to keep the company from being totally dependent on one line of business—for instance, the vulnerability of the oil companies to possible changes in the way automobiles are powered. A program strategy would be the subsequent decision to acquire a particular company, say, a firm that mines basic metals. Within the master strategy, mission refers to products and markets, the businesses

EXHIBIT 11.1 The nature of companywide planning

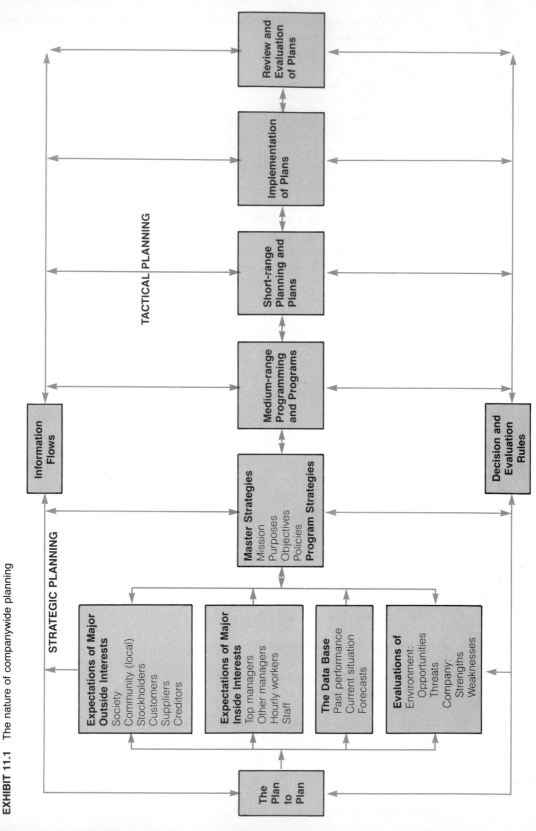

SOURCE: Reprinted with permission of Macmillan, Inc., from *Strategic Planning: What Every Manager Must Know* by George A. Steiner. Copyright © 1979 by The Free Press, a Division of Macmillan Publishing Co., Inc.

a company is in. Purposes are stated in terms of broad generalities dealing with product quality, service to society, ethics, and the like. Objectives are best stated in terms of specific measures such as dollar sales volume and market shares, numerical values, and time spans for achievement. Policies at this level deal with the allocation of resources and the specification of guidelines for establishing more detailed policies of a tactical nature.

Strategy and Tactics Exhibit 11.1 places certain types of planning in the strategic area and others in the tactical. Exhibit 11.2 attempts to make this distinction more clear-cut. At the same time, it is well to recognize that what is involved here is a continuum extending from very broad, and often abstract, company plans to very specific operating plans applicable to the short-term activities of individual employees. Where strategy stops and tactics start, within a rather broad band, is a matter of individual opinion and definition. The extremes are clear enough, but as one moves inward from them, the potential for confusion and misunderstanding increases. Because the term *strategy* carries a more positive value, there is a tendency to extend it further in the tactical direction than might otherwise be useful.

The Policy Role In years past it was common practice to title courses and books in the strategic management area as "business policy," or perhaps "administrative policy," if one wished to take up a broader range of organizations.

EXHIBIT 11.2 Strategy distinguished from tactics

Planning Area	Strategy	Tactics
Organizational Level	At the top—in corporate headquarters and major divisions	Employed at lower management levels
Timing	Continuous, but decisions occur at irregular intervals depending on opportunities and crises	Usually on a periodic cycle—a fixed time schedule
Uncertainty Level	High, because of long time dimension and difficulty of assessing risks	Much less—results become known quickly
Information Requirements	Sizable—mostly with regard to future states of the external environment	Focused more on internal sources—historical data and accounting information
Detail Level	Broad in scope, with regard to future states of the external environment	More detailed—fleshes out strategy in various areas
Ease of Evaluation	Difficult—results usually become known only after years, hard to determine causes	Easier, because of more rapid and specific feedback

SOURCE: Adapted from George A. Steiner and John B. Miner, *Management Policy and Strategy* (New York: Macmillan, 1982): 20–21.

In one sense, what has happened is that the word strategy has replaced policy. In this sense, "policy and strategy" are redundant, introduced as separate terms to make sure that old-timers and new-timers both know what is being considered.

But there is another sense in which the term *policy* is used that differentiates it from strategy, and from tactics as well. This is the sense in which policies serve as guides to carrying out action or channeling thinking in support of strategies and tactics..They act as role prescriptions, although not always without considerable ambiguity. In most cases they substitute for decisions that might otherwise be made at the discretion of an immediate superior. For example, when a district sales manager knows that it is company policy to meet prices set by competitors, she does not need to ask her superiors before taking action in the face of price-cutting by another firm; the policy guides her behavior.

In this view, policies are of the same nature as rules, standing orders, procedures, and the like. All operate to specify at some level of generality what should be done, when, and by whom. Policies apply to groups of people, perhaps to everyone in the company, rather than to individuals and individual jobs. They mediate between plans and implementation.

Types of Policies and Strategies

Policies and strategies may vary in a number of dimensions, only one of which is scope. Thus, what are here called master strategies are of greater scope than program strategies. In the same way, corporate strategies for the company as a whole are of greater scope than strategies for separate product line divisions or business units. In the latter instance there is variation not only in scope, but organizational level as well.

Variations also occur in terms of the type of resources involved—monetary, material, or human (see Exhibit 1.8). Some writers tend to give more attention to monetary and material resource strategies and policies, but those dealing with human beings can be of equal or greater importance. We tend to think of acquisitions, for instance, in terms of financial considerations and physical assets, but many acquisitions are motivated primarily by a need for certain managerial talents, research and development capabilities, and other kinds of expertise that the parent company does not possess.

Also important are the differing personal policies and strategies of managers at the top—chief executive officers primarily, but often other influential managers as well. These policies and strategies tend to be susceptible to strong influence by values. In many cases they are unwritten rules of thumb, such as "the best defense is a good offense." But they are also reflected in formal company creeds dealing with social responsibilities, ethics, consumer service, and the like. These creeds can of course be of an official nature only. Not infrequently, however, they take on an operative character as well.

Finally, strategies may differ in purpose or function, and so may policies. Typically, the latter deal with marketing, procurement, production, personnel and industrial relations, government relations, and other such matters. Growth strategies have been discussed previously. There are also survival strategies, turnaround strategies, diversification strategies, divestiture strategies, and so on.

EXHIBIT 11.3 Three successful types of strategic stance

Defenders

Major concern is to seal off a portion of the total market to create a stable set of products and customers.

Success depends on ability to maintain aggressive prominence in chosen markets, and to ignore developments outside this domain.

Growth is by cautious, incremental penetration deeper into current markets.
  Strength—Invulnerable to being dislodged by competitors.
  Weakness—Vulnerable to major shifts in overall market demand.

Prospectors

Major concern is to locate and exploit new product and market opportunities in a broad and continually developing domain.

Success depends on capacity to monitor a wide range of environmental circumstances and to create change within the industry.

Growth is by location of new markets and development of new products.
  Strength—Well-protected against environmental changes.
  Weakness—Risk of low profits and overextended resources.

Analyzers

Major concern is to locate and exploit new product and market opportunities while still maintaining a stable product and customer base.

Success depends on use of extensive methods of marketing surveillance.

Growth is through penetration of existing markets and through product and market development.
  Strength—Low risk because of minimal research and development investment and imitation of products with demonstrated success.
  Weakness—Difficulty of maintaining optimal balance between flexibility and stability.

SOURCE: Adapted from Raymond E. Miles and Charles C. Snow, *Organizational Strategy, Structure, and Process* (New York: McGraw-Hill, 1978): 37–79.

Variations in Strategic Stance Exhibit 11.3 describes three types of overall strategic positions or stances that have proved successful. These stances were originally developed from an analysis of the college textbook publishing industry, and then extended to other types of organizations, including electronics corporations, food processing firms, and hospitals. Overall, they have been found to produce more effective results than a fourth type of strategic stance called reactors.[3] Reactors are characterized by one or more of the following three problems:

1. Management fails to establish any viable strategy.
2. A strategy is established but is not implemented through appropriate links to organizational process, structure, and technology.
3. Management holds to an existing strategy long after it has lost its value.

Growth Strategies Exhibit 11.4 considers seven different types of growth strategies that can be used effectively. It is apparent that the later ones assume prior use of the earlier ones. It is also true that in practice the later strategies can become very complex and difficult to implement. They require the devel-

EXHIBIT 11.4 Types of growth strategies

Early Growth Stage ↑	1. Hold onto the company's relative position in a high growth, rapidly expanding product/market. In other words grow with the market and product demand.
	2. Increase the company's relative market share in a high growth market with a view to establishing a dominant comparative position.
	3. Increase the company's relative market share in mature, slow growth markets, either through cost leadership or through segmenting the market and moving heavily into still growing segments.
	4. Hold onto the company's relative position in mature markets, and then use the resulting cash flow and capacity to obtain funds to support penetration of multinational markets with existing products.
	5. Hold onto the company's relative position in mature or maturing markets, and then use the resulting cash flow and capacity to obtain funds to support penetration of new product/market areas domestically. This can be done either through acquisitions or through internal generation of new products.
	6. Hold onto the company's relative position in multinational markets with existing product lines, and then use the resulting cash flow and capacity to obtain funds to diversify products.
Advanced Growth Stage ↓	7. Hold onto the company's relative position in multiple product lines domestically, and then use the resulting cash flow and capacity to obtain funds to diversify markets.

NOTE: Assume the company starts with a single product line.

SOURCE: Adapted from William D. Guth, "Corporate Growth Strategies," *Journal of Business Strategy* (Fall 1980): 56–62.

opment of a wide range of plans, program strategies, substrategies, and policies, as well as a great deal of information about markets, products, international environments, and many other considerations. Strategic management is by far the most complex part of the management process because everything comes together at this point.

The Atlantic Refining Co. (ARCO): Strategy in Action

The case of ARCO provides a particularly good opportunity to see how strategies guide large corporations.

In the 1950s and early 1960s, The Atlantic Refining Company was a regional oil company marketing primarily on the highly competitive east coast of the United States, and headquartered in Philadelphia. It lacked the crude oil needed to operate its refineries and therefore bought its oil from other, primarily foreign, sources. The governing strategy at that time was stability rather than growth, but with an emphasis on greater self-sufficiency. To attain this self-sufficiency, the company engaged in explorations overseas, especially in Venezuela, with some success. In large part, exploration costs were bankrolled from the sale of the company's European marketing operations.

In 1963, Atlantic purchased Hondo Oil & Gas Co., a New Mexico firm, for stock. As a result, Robert O. Anderson became the largest stockholder, assumed a position on the board of directors, and eventually took control of the company. He replaced Henderson Supplee, Jr., a Philadelphia native whose experience prior to joining Atlantic had been in the milk business. With this change, the company moved from mainline Philadelphia conservativism to the entrepreneurial enthusiasm of a southwestern wildcatter. Strategic changes followed rapidly.

The major change was from stability to growth. The focus on self-sufficiency continued, but on a much accelerated time-table. Also, the emphasis was on finding oil in the United States, so as not to be dependent on the uncertainties of foreign governments. In addition to domestic self-sufficiency, the new strategy also called for diversification into related businesses, against the possibility that dwindling worldwide oil supplies might ultimately limit the use of oil as a major energy source. These master strategies have been pursued ever since, but with a variety of shifting tactics. The result has been a degree of what many have considered to be opportunism. Indeed, new approaches have been continually explored.

In 1966 Atlantic Refining merged with Richfield Oil, to form Atlantic-Richfield (ARCO), thereby gaining access to attractive west coast markets. Later came the Sinclair Oil acquisition, which actually contributed much less to domestic self-sufficiency than had been hoped originally, because of divestitures forced by governmental anti-trust decisions. There were movements into the production of oil from shale, and then out again as the economics of production appeared less attractive. Perhaps most important was finding oil on the North Slope in Alaska— a development from which ARCO has benefited greatly.

The Sinclair deal did have the advantage of accelerating a move into petrochemicals. Further diversification came with the acquisition of Anaconda (copper and aluminum) in 1977, and with the purchase of several small coal companies. Exhibit 11.5 shows the five-year expenditure plan under which ARCO is currently operating—a very ambitious plan that involves the accumulation of considerable debt. Note the heavy emphasis on domestic exploration and production. Yet this type of strategic position has produced the growth projected. The company is now twelfth in sales among U.S. industrial corporations, while during the 1950s and early 1960s, it was typically between seventieth and eightieth. There has been major movement toward self-sufficiency, almost entirely from domestic production. Profitable diversification now represents almost 20 percent of assets. Over a twenty-five-year period, employment has gone from 14,000 to 54,000.

STRATEGIC PLANNING

Exhibit 11.1 diagrams the planning process, and the foregoing discussion emphasizes the role of planning in strategic management, with particular attention to master and program strategies. Let us look now at other aspects of the model, and matters related to them.

The Planning Process

Planning in the formal sense is a relatively new phenomenon on the corporate scene. Most large companies now engage in it, but they use it to actually manage operations to varying degrees. As one moves down the scale of size, formal planning becomes less and less manifest. Yet, as we shall see, planning can yield major benefits.

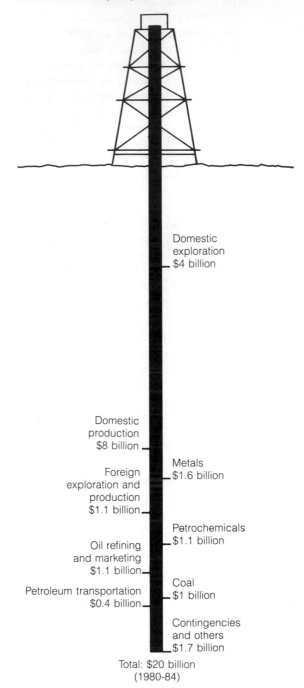

EXHIBIT 11.5 ARCO's current five-year plan

Domestic
exploration
$4 billion

Domestic
production
$8 billion

Metals
$1.6 billion

Foreign
exploration and
production
$1.1 billion

Petrochemicals
$1.1 billion

Oil refining
and marketing
$1.1 billion

Coal
$1 billion

Petroleum transportation
$0.4 billion

Contingencies
and others
$1.7 billion

Total: $20 billion
(1980-84)

SOURCE: Reprinted from the June 2, 1980, issue of *Business Week* by special permission, © 1980 by McGraw-Hill, Inc.

What Planning Is and Is Not   Strategic planning deals with the future, but only as it relates to present decisions. It does not say what decisions will be made in the future; those remain open to varying degrees. It does consider what is likely to happen if certain decisions are made now and evaluates those outcomes as to whether they are desirable. Typically, a number of possible decisions and the paths they put the company on are considered, and choices are made among them. As planning progresses and alternatives are evaluated, certain choices usually look much more attractive than others.

This aspect of planning means that planning should be a continuous process that takes into account both feedback on results as the plan is gradually put into effect and indicators of what is really happening in the environment. Because planning deals with the future of current decisions, plans must often be remade later on to adjust to what really did happen in a given interval. Thus, ARCO originally planned to move into the extremely costly process of obtaining oil from oil shale, and got as far as initiating construction of the necessary facilities. But the company stopped itself and reassigned that budget to domestic exploration and drilling. Present prices for gasoline and current estimates of future prices were not as attractive as when the oil shale operation was originally planned. The future did not look the same, and so the plan was changed.

Contrary to what is often assumed, then, planning, at least at the top level, is far from being a matter of laying out one path and following it no matter what. At various points, it may be appropriate to cut over to another path, even though at some cost. To do this, one needs to be constantly aware of where the other paths are.

Because different firms have different internal and external environments, planning can vary considerably from one application to another. There is no one methodology for planning. Planning contains within it an assortment of possible tools, techniques, and approaches. There is also a variety of types of plans, and each company needs to put together its own combination.

Degrees of Sophistication   Planning can be the intuitive-anticipatory work of one person, usually the chief executive. In such cases, information is incorporated as opportunities arise; plans tend to be short-term, heavily grounded in individual experience and values, and usually not written down. This approach is well illustrated in the development of Steinberg Inc., the Canadian retail chain, and the entrepreneurial vision of its long-time chief, Sam Steinberg.[4] Above this level are increasing degrees of sophistication in formal planning process, as indicated in Exhibit 11.6. At each higher level, the planning process is more rational, more comprehensive in scope, and more correctable.

Large companies tend to be at level 4. This appears to be a reaction to environmental complexity and change. When companies see more problems, they tend to develop more sophisticated planning systems, and they do so at an earlier point. On the other hand, this does not mean that the intuitive-anticipatory plans of a strong-minded chief executive may not guide the company. These views can be incorporated in the formal planning process, so that both approaches work together. Not infrequently such incorporation fails to

EXHIBIT 11.6 Four levels of planning development

Degree of Sophistication	Planning Process
Low	1. No formal strategic planning process. Planning is intuitive-anticipatory at best.
	2. Plans are written, documented, cover three years or more in advance, and include specification of objectives. Strategies are developed.
	3. Determination of cash and physical resources needed to realize the plan. Proforma financial statements and other quantitative projections are included. (Includes level 2.)
	4. An attempt to deal with the extended environment of the firm, beyond the immediately obvious. Also, procedures for anticipating and detecting errors in, or failures of, the plan and for preventing or correcting them on a continuing basis are included. Planning is
High	continuous and highly flexible. (Includes levels 2 and 3.)

SOURCE: Adapted from William M. Lindsay and Leslie W. Rue, *Environmental Complexity in Long-Range Planning,* (Oxford, Ohio: Planning Executives Institute, 1976): 10.

occur, so that the firm is guided by two separate strategic rudders at once. Under such circumstances its course can become highly erratic.

Steps in Planning   Strategic planning starts with a plan to plan. This plan is often contained in a detailed manual. It sets forth a statement of top management commitment to planning, a set of term definitions to head off communication problems, a statement of required information and documentation, a detailed time schedule, and a review of policies to be taken into account in carrying out planning—particularly policies related to price inflation, depreciation, and other financial matters.

Next in the planning process are the four components of the situation audit, as given in Exhibit 11.1. Information is collected on the attitudes and expectations of stockholders, customers, and other relevant groups, including the social responsibilities prescribed by society as a whole. Data for this purpose come from many sources. Secondly, the values and expectations existing inside the firm are considered. Typically, the strongest interest here is with the views of top managers, but there is more to it than that. If there is likely to be resistance to a particular plan from any source, that fact needs to be considered. Thirdly, data are compiled on past performance in areas such as sales, profits, productive outputs, and the like; on the company's current situation, ranging from market shares to employee skills to government regulations; and on the future, in the form of forecasts about markets, competition, economic trends, technological developments, population changes, the stability of governments, and so on.

Finally, the situation audit includes a close look at opportunities and threats in the environment, present and anticipated, and at the strengths and weaknesses of the company in capitalizing on and coping with them. This is a big aspect of the planning process. Out of it the firm's master strategies and program strategies emerge. The result is a document resembling Exhibit 11.7 in broad outline. That

EXHIBIT 11.7 Outline of a typical divisional plan

1. Executive summary
2. Statement of mission, charter
3. The appraisal/situation analysis
   a. Corporate environmental assumptions/guidelines
   b. Corporate financial guidelines
   c. Divisional environmental assumptions
   d. External analysis: the market, competition
   e. Internal analysis: strengths, weaknesses, opportunities, and threats
   f. Product-line analysis
   g. Evaluation of previous plans
4. Objectives, purposes
5. Strategies
6. Action programs/policies
7. Contingency plans, alternative plans

SOURCE: Adapted from Rochelle O'Connor, *Corporate Guides to Long Range Planning* (New York: Conference Board, 1976).

particular outline applies to divisional plans, and accordingly incorporates aspects of corporate plans as part of the external analyses. A corporate plan, on the other hand, would treat aspects of various divisional plans as inside considerations.

Once the strategies are in place, medium-range plans are developed. These focus primarily on major functions or programs—marketing, production, employee levels, research and development, facilities, and the like. Usually the plans are converted to financial terms, and five-year projections are made. The degree of detail depends on how central a role the function has in strategy. Thus, a company that has decided upon a growth strategy grounded in internal product research programs would normally develop very specific middle-range research and development plans.

Short-range plans can vary over a wide spectrum. They grade gradually into implementation and often provide the standards against which control systems compare performance. Many firms link their yearly budgets, which are in themselves short-range plans, closely with middle-range planning, so that the first-year figures of the middle-range plans match with budget figures. Exhibit 11.8 shows how first-year middle-range plans are expanded into the much more detailed budget process.

Implementation itself, of course, includes everything we have considered to this point. It is a matter of carrying out all of the management functions discussed in other parts of this book. There is a tendency to emphasize the close link between planning and controlling, and the tying of budgets tightly to plans reflects this emphasis. Yet, in actuality, plans are implemented through a variety of activities other than the control process. This is not to say, however, the control link is not important in implementation.

The final stage of Exhibit 11.1, review and evaluation, is a continuing process that provides input to new plans. Many companies now go through an annual planning cycle. One value of this approach is that it tends to force an evaluation

EXHIBIT 11.8 Development and structuring of operating budgets from middle-range functional plans

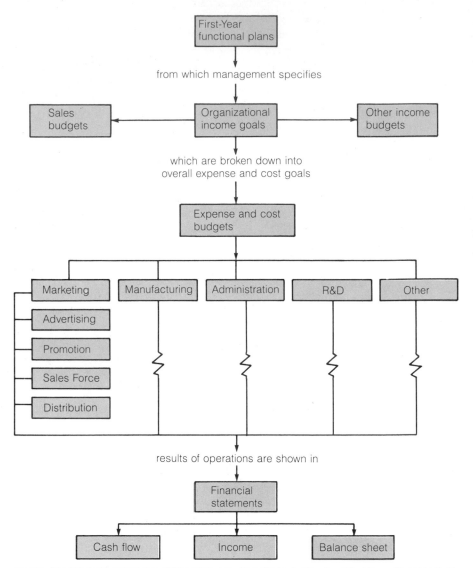

SOURCE: Reprinted with permission of Macmillan, Inc., from *Strategic Planning: What Every Manager Must Know* by George A. Steiner. Copyright © 1979 by The Free Press, a Division of Macmillan Publishing Co., Inc.

of how well the previous year's planning worked. Such feedback on results can produce changes in the plan to plan, and in all other steps in the process.

Types of Plans In addition to the plans already considered, one often hears several other types of plans mentioned. Certain of these are strongly influenced by the chief executive officer: (1) posture or stance plans dealing with basic company missions, purposes, philosophies, or aims, (2) portfolio plans dealing with resource allocations among divisions, subsidiaries, or projects, and (3) ad hoc policy/strategy analyses dealing with top management activities to aid in making strategic decisions. Clearly, all these emanate from the corporate, as opposed to the divisional or strategic business unit, level.

Contingency plans, on the other hand, may be developed at any level. Most strategic planning is done on the basis of the most likely occurrence. Contingency planning branches out and establishes courses of action should other, somewhat less likely alternatives become the reality. Thus, a five-year plan may anticipate the negotiation of a new union contract within the interval. Contingency plans may then be developed to cover the possibilities that substantially more or less desirable contract terms become effective, or even to cover the possibility of a strike. Extensive contingency planning of this kind is costly, and the possible benefits drop off sharply as the alternatives considered become less likely. As a result, companies engage in contingency planning only to the degree they have to. Exactly how and when contingency planning can best be used remains a matter of some uncertainty.[5]

The Organization of Planning

Although in the simplest case, formal strategic planning can occur with only the chief executive and perhaps a small planning committee involved, the more typical structural relationships in a large divisionalized company are as indicated in Exhibit 11.9. In this type of company, four ways of organizing the planning process may be found:

1. *Centralized*—Planning is done at the top, and lower level units are in large part told what their plans are. On occasion, divisions do prepare plans for higher level approval, but within guidelines and restrictions that permit little discretion.
2. *Decentralized*—Plans are prepared by each division, based only on an outline of topics to be covered. These plans are submitted to top management for approval and are also used in developing the corporate plan. Thus the planning process is initiated at the divisional, rather than the corporate, level.
3. *Mixed*—Top management gives broad guidelines to the divisions, and planning then goes on at both levels at the same time. There is often considerable bargaining between the two levels regarding specific objectives.
4. *Team*—The chief executive and a number of senior managers reporting to the top level develop plans as a group. This team often is constituted as an executive committee to meet on a regular basis and deal with various company problems. In such instances, planning is only one of its activities.

It seems apparent that strictly decentralized planning approaches give too little attention to the needs of the firm as a whole.[6] But regardless of which approach is used, planning is an activity that requires a substantial proportion of the chief executives' time. They must create a climate that not only fosters planning, but that also encourages using it in day-to-day operations. They must determine how planning should be organized, including the way in which planning specialists and staff should be incorporated in the process. They must maintain constant

EXHIBIT 11.9 A typical planning structure with corporate and divisional groups

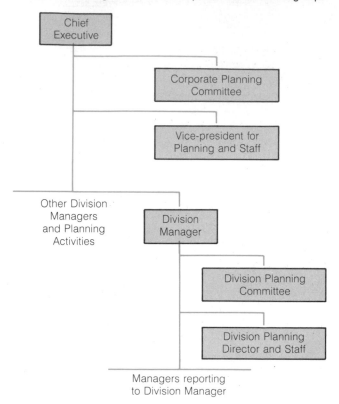

contact with the planning process as it moves through various steps. In a very real sense, the effectiveness of formal strategic planning in a company is a direct reflection of the chief executive's effectiveness.

Most large corporations maintain a sizable planning staff to develop information and assist in the preparation of plans, as noted in Exhibit 11.9. Staff members frequently have advanced degrees, but their areas of specialization can vary considerably. Often these are people with backgrounds in management science, finance and economics, or engineering.[7] Planning is a highly rational process, and there is a tendency to favor disciplines that emphasize rational decision making.

Among the activities carried out by planning staffs are:

Studying ways of entering new markets and acquiring new product lines

Recommending regarding product planning, pricing, and promotion

Collecting information on business and economic conditions bearing on the company

Forecasting future market volume and share

Studying distribution trends

Defining the company's existing markets

Appraising acquisitions and divestitures

Recommending regarding staffing needs

Surveying changing customer actions, attitudes, and views

Collecting information on new scientific developments and technologies

Maintaining information on competitor activities

Studying legal and political trends having significance for the company

Does all this attention to planning really help a company? If and when it does help, how might this occur? What problems are likely to arise to diminish the effectiveness of planning?

Comparisons of Planners and Non-planners   A number of studies have been carried out comparing the profitability and other indexes of success of firms that do not engage in formal strategic planning, or do so at a less sophisticated level, with success levels for more sophisticated planners. The majority of these comparisions support the use of the more sophisticated planning approaches in that the planners subsequently had better records.[8] On the other hand, there are studies that fail to demonstrate that strategic planning makes a contribution.[9]

The disparity in results is difficult to reconcile, but the data make it almost certain that planning *can* make a difference. Whether it *will* make a difference for a particular firm appears to depend on a number of factors, not the least of which is how well the planning is done. In addition, planning should contribute more where it is needed most—under conditions of a complex and unstable environment—and where it can work best. If a company faces an environment in which, because of extreme complexity or inadequacies of forecasting methodology, prediction over any extended time period is impossible, strategic planning is not likely to prove very helpful. Furthermore, it takes time for companies to learn how to plan well and for the results to become apparent. Positive outcomes should not be expected immediately. Finally, research shows that strategic planning need not affect all indexes of success equally. Probably this is a result inherent in the nature of the planning process itself. If planning focuses on market share, then market share will be affected. If it focuses on cost reduction and profits, then they will be affected. Exactly what a company is trying to accomplish is where strategic planning begins. There is no reason to expect it to work for purposes other than those intended.

Why Should Planning Help?   There are at least five reasons why effective planning should contribute positively to a company:

1. Because the company's environment and future are better known and understood, it is less likely to be caught off-guard and more likely to cope effectively.
2. The very process of planning sensitizes managers to a variety of factors they need to consider and thus teaches them to be better managers.
3. The company as a whole is moved toward increasing rationality in pursuit of its goals, with the result that arbitrary actions by individuals are held to a minimum.

4. A greater degree of predictability, and consequently less uncertainty and less ambiguity and conflict in roles, comes to characterize company operations and internal workings.
5. Planning contributes to better performance of other management functions.

These considerations add up to a very strong argument for formal planning. At the same time, it should be recognized that planning can be overdone. It is possible for management to spend so much time in planning that little else gets accomplished. And it is possible to spend so much money on planning that its potential financial benefits are lost.

Sources of Problems   In actuality, not everyone feels positive about formal strategic planning. There are companies that have tried it and found it unworkable for them. Information provided by a number of firms indicates that certain problems are particularly likely to arise. The following list focuses on major pitfalls of the strategic planning process as a whole:

1. Failure to develop throughout the company an understanding of what strategic planning really is, how it is to be done in the company, and the degree of commitment of top management to doing it well.
2. Failure to accept and balance interrelationships among intuition, judgment, managerial values, and the formality of the planning system.
3. Failure to encourage managers to do effective strategic planning by basing performance appraisal and rewards solely on short-range performance measures.
4. Failure to tailor and design the strategic planning system to the unique characteristics of the company and its management.
5. Failure of top management to spend sufficient time on the strategic planning process so that the process becomes discredited among other managers and staff.
6. Failure to modify the strategic planning system as conditions within the company change.
7. Failure to mesh properly the process of management and strategic planning from the highest levels of management and planning through tactical planning and its complete implementation.
8. Failure to keep the planning system simple and to weigh constantly the cost-benefit balance.
9. Failure to secure within the company a climate for strategic planning that is necessary for its success.
10. Failure to balance and link appropriately the major elements of the strategic planning and implementation process.[10]

Exhibit 11.10 is concerned with specific behavioral problems of those involved in doing the planning. As such it supplements, and provides some insight into, the pitfalls noted. Problems do not arise by chance or through oversight. It appears that they occur in part because those involved actively resist the planning or want to avoid using the planning process, including the changes stemming from it. Additional problems appear to arise from stress and ambiguity created by the process and a failure to fully comprehend what is involved. As a potential

EXHIBIT 11.10 Critical behavioral problems encountered in planning process

Managers who resist planning:

1. Project current trends rather than analyze the future for opportunities
2. Primarily bargain for resources rather than identify new resources
3. Pad plan to avoid close measurement
4. Consider the purpose of planning to be the plan itself
5. Resist the discipline that planning requires
6. Resist changes in the status quo
7. Fear making mistakes
8. Avoid thinking beyond short-run, day-to-day activities
9. View their part of the organization as more important than other parts
10. Are uncertain about the expectations of upper-level managers
11. Comply with rather than being committed to goals
12. File their plan until next year and do not look at it
13. Become bored with the planning process
14. Are judged on the basis of their credibility in the organization rather than upon reaching planned objectives

SOURCE: Marjorie A. Lyles and R. T. Lenz, "Managing the Planning Process: A Field Study of the Human Side of Planning," *Strategic Management Journal* (April–June 1982): 113.

source of change, strategic planning can arouse many types of resistances. Chapter 10 discusses in some detail how these resistances may block change.

IDENTIFYING AND EVALUATING POLICIES AND STRATEGIES

Within the situation audit, a wide range of possible strategies is identified and steps are taken to evaluate each in terms of its contribution to goal attainment. This process of identification and evaluation is complex, and numerous techniques have been developed for these purposes.

Many managers prefer to develop the kind of information needed for a situation audit and in strategic decision making through talking to acquaintances, reading, and reflecting on their own experiences—thus in relatively unsystematic, nonquantitative ways.[11] But increasingly, formal models and complex mathematical analyses are being used, especially in the forecasting area. The reason for their growing popularity is that these methods work, and good managers are pragmatic.

Specific Approaches

It is common practice in identifying and evaluating strategies to utilize various accounting ratios, such as return on investment, to project trends from a historical base. Other examples of such ratios are net income/total assets, debt/total capital, net worth/sales, and the like. Although not inherent in strategic management itself, these are powerful tools. Other approaches are more directly part of the policy/strategy area.

Gap Analysis Whenever there is a disparity between stated objectives and forecasts of what is likely to happen in relation to them, a gap is said to exist. Perhaps objectives call for a given sales volume at a particular time in the future, but a realistic forecast based on projected expenditures yields a short-fall of considerable magnitude. Gap analysis seeks out such differences in various areas. Once differences are found, either the objectives themselves must be reconsidered or strategies devised to fill the gap.

Industry Analysis An industry specifies the competitors in a market arena. Competition in such an arena is influenced predominantly by the bargaining power of suppliers, the threat of new entrants, the bargaining power of customers, the threat of substitute products or services, and the jockeying for position of competitors already present.[12] Industry analysis is concerned with obtaining information so that a company can place itself clearly in this competitive arena and, with that information, select strategies to reach desired goals. Data categories used in an industry analysis are:

Product lines

Buyers and their behavior

Complementary and substitute products

Growth rates and patterns, and what determines them

Technology of production and distribution, including such things as cost structures, logistics, and labor

Marketing practices and segmentation

Suppliers

Distribution channels

Innovation types, sources, and rates

Competitor strategies, goals, strengths, and weaknesses

Social, political, and legal environments

Macroeconomic environment

Analyses of this kind are difficult and time-consuming, and of course many diversified companies operate in multiple industries. It is not uncommon for consulting firms that specialize in strategic studies to be brought into the process of carrying out such an industry analysis.

The Product–Market Matrix Exhibit 11.4 sets forth a set of product–market growth strategies. Exhibit 11.11 provides a simple matrix that may be used to specify such strategic alternatives and to evaluate the risks inherent in them. More complex matrices may of course be developed containing a greater number of product and/or market alternatives. Product–market matrices are useful in considering overall growth possibilities, but actual strategies, especially program strategies, require much more specific content.

The Product–Portfolio Matrix Exhibit 11.12 presents a very simple product–portfolio matrix. A number of companies have developed more complex versions, but this example is sufficient to explain what is involved.

The approach is applicable to corporations with multiple product lines, product divisions, or strategic business units. Each of these is placed in a quadrant of the matrix in terms of its market share and growth rate. This placement

EXHIBIT 11.11 A product–market matrix

	Product Strategy		
Market Strategy	**Stay with Present *Products***	**Expand to Related *Products***	**Expand Further to Unrelated *Products***
Stay in Present *Market*	Low risk	Medium risk	High risk
Expand into Related *Markets*	Medium risk	High risk	Very high risk
Expand Further into Unrelated *Markets*	High risk	Very high risk	Excessive risk

itself does not specify an exact strategy for the particular business, but preferred strategic approaches for the various quadrants have been developed. "Stars," with their high market shares and prospects for growth, should be fed with heavy investments of capital, and every effort should be made to consolidate their positions. "Cash cows" should require little capital, and the cash they generate should be diverted to other, growing businesses. "Question marks" require careful attention to find special market niches or to position them for subsequent sale. The conventional wisdom for many years was that "dogs" should be disposed of on the best terms possible. It now appears that this is an overly pessimistic view. However, they do require careful, cost-conscious managing.[13]

Product Life Cycles   Product life cycles have been recognized for some time, but their relevance for strategy formulation has only recently come to be understood. Different stages in the cycle pose different problems and different strategy needs. Exhibit 11.13 indicates various stages and how they relate to investments, sales, profits, and strategies.

The time span for each stage varies sharply with the product. However, it is clear that product life cycles generally have been decreasing from stages 2 through 5, while research and development costs have been increasing, and so has the time for stage 1. Unrecovered investments extending over five years or more at this point are almost inevitable. And there are products that never move beyond stage 2 and that never should have been produced in the first place.

EXHIBIT 11.12 A product–portfolio matrix

	Relative Competitive Position as Reflected in Market Share	
	High	**Low**
Prospective Business Growth Rate — **High**	Stars	Question marks
Prospective Business Growth Rate — **Low**	Cash cows	Dogs

SOURCE: Adapted from Barry Hedley, "Strategy and the Business Portfolio," *Long Range Planning* (February 1977): 12.

Planning and Formulating Policy/Strategy

EXHIBIT 11.13 Stages of the product life cycle

1. Research and development
Investments with no sales and no return
Strategic choices relate to amount of investment, manufacturing technologies, timing of product introduction

2. Market Development
Investments shift to marketing, sales begin, but profits not expected
Strategies relate to product acceptance and minimizing losses

3. Growth
Sales and profits move up sharply and in parallel
Strategies relate increasingly to maintaining customer loyalty in the face of growing competition

4. Maturity
Sales continue to increase, but profit margins peak and decline
Strategies relate to intensified price competition, added services, and maintaining profits

4. Decline
Sales drop off, but profits decline more sharply
Strategies relate to maintaining profits and replacement products

Profit Impact of Market Strategies (PIMS) PIMS is a data base initiated by General Electric, but it has since become established as a separate project supported by some 200 companies. Statistical analyses are carried out on more than 30 factors, with data provided by member companies at regular intervals. The predominant finding has been that, as market share for a product increases, so does pretax return on investment. There are many other findings as well, and the extent to which the market share–return on investment relationship holds depends on a variety of circumstances. This is a rich source of information, but by its nature it is historical. Relationships that have held in the past need not be maintained into the future, although they very well might be. All in all, the PIMS findings say a great deal about where a company might best focus its strategic emphasis.

Experience Curves Companies learn to do better with experience in producing a product. Out of analyses of this process has come the conclusion that specific curves can be plotted for different products showing a decrease in unit costs as more and more units are produced. The general finding is that the unit costs, correcting for inflation, of producing, distributing and selling a product should decline by a constant percentage, typically in the range of 15 to 30 percent, every time total industry unit volume doubles.[14] Assuming that a company can find ways to obtain this effect, and it is not automatic, then pricing and related market share strategies can be adjusted to it. The strategy shows when aggressive pricing is appropriate and when it is not, and shows what advantages might be anticipated from getting into a market early.

Computer Models The preceding discussion covers a few of the better-known approaches to identifying and evaluating policies and strategies. The objective is to provide a general understanding of what is involved. Some of the approaches noted, such as PIMS, do represent computer models. However, the discussion would be incomplete without noting that a wide range of such models now exists. Some are constructed to simulate the economy as a whole, some deal with particular industries such as insurance and oil, and some model individual companies or aspects of them. Typically, these computer models yield forecasts of anticipated future trends on various factors of importance in developing strategies.

<table>
<tr><td>**Forecasting**</td><td>A forecast is only as good as its accuracy, and by its nature, checking the accuracy of forecasts is not a difficult task; all one has to do is wait. Given current forecasting capabilities, it is reasonable to expect quarterly forecasts to be roughly 98 percent accurate and yearly forecasts to be 94 to 95 percent accurate. Strategies are usually developed, at least initially, with somewhat longer projections in mind—the typical corporate five-year plan, for instance. It should be possible in such cases to achieve an average accuracy of at least 85 percent, although forecasts on particular factors may fail to reach this level. Some companies have missed badly in this area. For example, Gerber Products projected in 1958 that birth rates would rise steadily, so that by 1970 there would be almost six million new babies as a market for its baby food. Instead the birth rate decreased; the error was 38 percent.</td></tr>
</table>

If forecasts are not reasonably accurate, and frequent revision is one way to increase accuracy, the forecasting process and ultimately strategic planning itself are discredited. The result is that people do not pay much attention to plans, and any potential value they might have is lost. One of the first things implied by good strategic planning is good forecasting, especially with regard to economic conditions and sales.

Economic and Sales Forecasts Larger corporations usually make forecasts regarding aspects of the economy such as gross national product, inflation, employment levels, and the like. In addition, they will be concerned with factors specifically bearing on their particular businesses. For instance, telephone companies need to predict population shifts into and out of various geographic areas.

Sales forecasts, which project anticipated sales for various products assuming certain price levels, are probably the most widely used of any forecasts. Extensive data on sales, markets, and competition are essential if industry analyses are to be used effectively in planning and strategy formulation.

Traditionally, sales forecasting has relied heavily on information provided by knowledgeable people within and outside the company to develop sales estimates, thus combining the contributions of individuals to reach overall values. The easiest approach, known as the *jury of executive opinion*, solicits forecasts from top-level executives who are supplied with certain basic data on costs, profit margins, and past sales. Simple averages may then be computed, or there may be some weighting to emphasize the views of those perceived as more likely to be right.

The *sales force composite* method is similar in that estimates are obtained from a number of people. Sales personnel complete standard forms dealing with expected sales in the territory served. These estimates subsequently move up

EXHIBIT 11.14 Average reported accuracy of one-year sales forecasts for various techniques

Technique	Accuracy (%)
Product life-cycle analysis	95.5
Leading index	94.6
Input–output models	93.8
Trend projection	93.8
Regression	93.6
Simulation models	93.5
Sales force composite	93.2
Jury of executive opinion	93.0
Users' expectations	91.5

SOURCE: Adapted from Douglas J. Dalrymple, "Sales Forecasting Methods and Accuracy," *Business Horizons* (November–December 1975): 71–73.

through the organization, forming the basis for the projections of larger units. At the corporate level, adjustments are made with reference to advertising expenditures, product life cycles, and other data to yield specific product forecasts. An extension of this approach utilizes survey research procedures to move beyond the sales force and obtain *users' expectations*. Actual or potential customers are asked for information on the extent of present product use and on their intended usage in the future. These data are combined, perhaps weighted to correct for sampling variations, and then used as with the sales force composite to provide forecasts.

In recent years, the larger companies have relied increasingly on various mathematical forecasting aids, often in conjunction with judgmental methods. Several of these have already been mentioned. In time-series analysis, long-term growth trends, cyclical business fluctuations, and seasonal fluctuations are separated on the basis of historical data and used to project future trends. Correlation techniques are used to relate product sales to other leading indexes that can be predicted with good precision: then, given the mathematical relationships established, it is possible to move to sales forecasts, working back from the leading indicators. In the simulation models, a number of factors expected to influence sales are studied and weighted to produce the best possible predictions of the sales themselves. Computers make it possible to handle a large number of factors in this process and to deal with very complex relationships.

Exhibit 11.14 provides information on the accuracy of a number of these sales forecasting approaches. As it happens, the six techniques that are essentially mathematical in nature are also the most accurate, varying among themselves by only two percentage points. It is not surprising that these approaches are being used more often.

Forecasting Technology and Innovation In this area, businesses are concerned with developments related to existing technologies, identification of new technologies, and customer desires related to products. Often, given the trend of events, it happens that science is not far removed from a certain breakthrough. Technological forecasting is concerned with predicting such matters. It is a very important forecasting form to high technology companies, but it is considered important by many others also.

Many of the sales forecasting approaches can be adapted to technological purposes. A widely used procedure is not unlike the jury of executive opinion. In this case, however, forecasts are made not so much by managers as by individuals considered to be experts in the particular type of technology. The panel of experts often extends outside the company itself, and in the particular approach known as the *delphi method,* it involves obtaining successive waves of judgements. In delphi, the experts are first asked to provide forecasts and their reasoning for making them. This may be done by mail or through interviews, but the experts themselves do not talk to each other. Next, the results of the first round are summarized, available data are provided as requested, and the panel is asked for another set of forecasts taking this new information into account. Ideally, the process is repeated until a consensus is achieved. Practically, consensus rarely occurs, but the best estimates are finally averaged to forecast what innovations will occur, and when.

Social and Political Forecasts   The forecasting of social and political trends and events that might affect a company is not as widespread as other approaches—at least, not forecasting of this kind that is fairly sophisticated. Thus a firm like ARCO, having had its properties nationalized often by foreign governments, has adopted a basic domestic strategy that does not require forecasting the stability and economic policies of foreign regimes.

Yet it is becoming increasingly evident that some forecasts in these areas are needed. Shifts in attitudes toward managing in large bureaucratic systems can influence managerial talent supplies. Shifts in government taxation policies can influence profits. Shifts in consumer attitudes can influence product design and distribution. Shifts in societal values and ethical codes can influence a whole host of factors, including the extent to which raw materials are made available and the ways in which labor is utilized. Particularly when a company operates in many countries, forecasts in areas such as these become very important. In this connection, increasing use is being made of opinion survey data obtained from either experts on the particular society or part of the world, or from a cross-section of the population.

Environmental Scanning   Environmental scanning is much more loosely defined than the other forecasting approaches, although it may incorporate certain parts of other approaches. It deals with predicting future events, particularly those that might pose a major crisis for the company; it tends to be rather subjective and unstandardized in approach; and it is a method that is increasingly used.[15]

Most forecasting is focused on the projection of specific factors known to be important to the company, and usually the quantitative relationships involved are well understood. Neither is true of environmental scanning. Here the intent is to monitor a wide range of phenomena, often moving out to the fringes of the organization environment and into the future. Published sources are studied regularly, interviews are conducted with knowledgeable people, data are brought together from diverse sources within the firm. Sometimes specific scenarios considered likely to occur in the future are developed and then deductions are made back to the company in the present. The result may be the identification of something that is likely to become of major concern three, or five, or ten years hence—or the deductions may miss the company entirely, suggesting that even if the particular scenario does become fact, the company would probably be unaffected.

EXHIBIT 11.15 Tests of major strategies—key questions and selected sub-questions

1. *Is the strategy consistent with the company's environment?*
   a. Do you really have an honest and accurate appraisal of your competition? Are you underestimating your competition?
   b. Are the forecasts on which your strategy is based really creditable?
   c. Is your present and/or prospective market share sufficient to be competitive and make an acceptable profit?
   d. Is your strategy in conformance with moral and ethical codes of conduct applicable to your company?

2. *Is the strategy consistent with the company's internal policies, styles of management, philosophy, and culture?*
   a. Does the strategy exploit your strengths and avoid your major weaknesses?
   b. Is your organizational structure consistent with your strategy?
   c. Does your strategy really fit both management and worker values?

3. *Is the strategy appropriate in light of company resources?*
   a. Do you have sufficient capital to see the strategy through to successful implementation?
   b. Is your strategy appropriate with respect to your existing and prospective physical plant? Will the strategy utilize plant capacity? Is equipment obsolete for purposes of implementation?
   c. Do you have the necessary skills among managers and employees to make the strategy successful?

4. *Are the risks in pursuing the strategy acceptable?*
   a. Has your strategy been tested with appropriate analyses such as return on investment?
   b. Do you have too large a proportion of your capital and management tied into the strategy?
   c. Does the strategy take you too far from your current products and markets?

5. *Does the strategy fit product life cycle and product portfolio circumstances?*
   a. Are you rushing a revolutionary product to market?
   b. If your strategy is to fill an unfilled market niche, is that niche likely to remain open long enough to utilize it effectively?

6. *Can the strategy be implemented efficiently and effectively?*
   a. Is there a commitment, a system of communication and control, a managerial and employee capability, that will assure implementation of your strategy?
   b. Is the timing of your implementation appropriate given market conditions, competition, etc.?

7. *Are there any other important considerations that should be taken into account?*

SOURCE: Adapted from Seymour Tilles, "How to Evaluate Corporate Strategy," *Harvard Business Review* (July–August 1963).

Summary

This chapter has considered a whole host of matters related to planning and how it ties in with strategic management. Both strategies and strategic plans come in a variety of forms, and a number of techniques have been developed to help in identifying, evaluating, and constructing them. This is a complex field, and it is no help that existing terms and definitions are often confused and overlapping. Yet when we see strategy in action, as in the ARCO case, there is little question what strategy is and how it operates.

Exhibit 11.15 provides a guide to analyzing and evaluating plans and strategies. It touches upon many of the topics considered at various points in this chapter. These are the kinds of questions that should be asked before settling on a particular strategy. It is easy to choose first a strategy based on one's values, interests, and the like, and then to arrange the existing information to fit the preferred strategy. If questions like these are given high visibility within the organization and answered honestly, the exercise may save the company from taking a disastrous course. One of the reasons that companies get in serious financial trouble is that they bet too much on a single strategic alternative that looks attractive at the time, but which because of delays in implementation or changed circumstances or incorrect forecasts proves to be a sort of black hole, gobbling up resources and returning nothing. At the same time, companies that invest substantial time and effort in the strategy formulation process and in strategic planning can reap major rewards.[16]

What Have You Learned?

1. Planning may be organized in various ways. What are some of these ways and how do various people and groups contribute to them?
2. What are the steps in the strategic planning process? Give examples of each.
3. What is the relative value of the various forecasting techniques, and what standards should be applied in evaluating these techniques?
4. How does strategic planning vary in its degree of sophistication, and what factors appear to influence these variations?
5. Why is it that terms such as *strategy* and *strategic management* are used in so many ways?
6. What are some of the various ways in which strategies can differ? Indicate how the various types of strategic stances relate to these differences.
7. How would you compare and contrast the following?

    a. The delphi method and users' expectations
    b. The product life cycle and the experience curve
    c. Environmental scanning and sales forecasting
    d. The product–market matrix and the product-portfolio matrix
    e. Industry analysis and profit impact of market strategies (PIMS)

8. What are the pros and cons of formal strategic planning? Why should it help, and where can it go wrong?
9. How can strategy, tactics, and policy be differentiated?
10. What exactly is a situation audit, and what factors are involved in it? Note some of the approaches used and why they are helpful.

How Well Can You Apply Your Knowledge?

Problem 1. A major U.S. oil company (not ARCO) is a regional marketer and faces an unusual problem. It has become rich beyond anyone's wildest dreams, but top management does not know what to do with its money, and in fact is a little embarrassed about having it. This situation is a new one for the company and has developed so rapidly that strategic planning and strategy formulation have not kept up with developments.

For many years, the company marketed in a handful of states and operated refineries close to its markets. It bought most of the crude oil to run these refineries in world markets. Although there had been some sporadic efforts at exploration, these had not been very successful. A small proportion of the company's crude requirements was supplied from wells it had drilled; most of these were in the United States. The company had had very little experience in exploration abroad.

Through a series of events, the company acquired major holdings on the North Slope in Alaska. It borrowed heavily to develop these properties and to aid in the construction of the trans-Alaska pipeline. During this period it continued to operate much as before, but with a rapidly expanding debt to be serviced. Until the pipeline was completed, relatively little crude came out of the Alaskan operations. This situation changed dramatically with completion of the pipeline, however. Almost overnight crude began to flow in abundance. There was more than enough to fill the company's total refining and marketing needs. The remainder was available for sale to others, at a time when oil prices were rising rapidly and the federal government was lifting its price controls on oil coming from Alaska. Very quickly the company acquired a cash reserve that would permit it to pay off its debt, and a great deal more.

At various times the company had made moves toward diversification, but with very little success. Like so many other oil firms, it had acquired certain coal operations, but has had trouble making them profitable. Dealing with the United Mine Workers proved to be quite different from dealing with the oil unions, and there have been numer-

ous problems with slowdowns and strikes. A rather hesitant move into petrochemicals came very late, and many other oil companies were far ahead in both know-how and position. At one point the company acquired a retailing firm with outlets in the same geographical area as its service stations. This did not work out well, however, primarily because the oil men who headed the company did not understand their new business, but still wanted to make the strategic decisions. Ultimately the retailing firm was sold off at a loss. The company did have holdings in oil shale in the Rocky Mountains, and had even produced some oil from these holdings at one point for sale to the government. But estimates of the economic future in oil shale were not favorable.

Given current profits, none of these considerations would have mattered much except for two factors. The company was seriously worried about negative attitudes toward the oil industry in the population as a whole and about certain politicians who were making much of such terms as profiteering, windfall profits, and gouging the consumer. There was a real fear that their money would be taken away in some manner, if it were not put to use rapidly. Secondly, the wealth flowing out of the North Slope in crude was not going to continue forever. The extent of the crude oil available there was known, and reserves were being depleted. Another ten years and the bonanza would be over. There would be some production beyond that point, but the company's total self-sufficiency in crude would be a thing of the past unless there was a new find somewhere.

Questions
1. What alternative strategies do you see as available to the company? It may be useful to review the ARCO case in developing this list.
2. How would you evaluate each of these strategies, taking into account the questions in Exhibit 11.15 and the procedures considered in this chapter? What is your strategic choice?

Problem 2. A small, high technology firm headquartered in California had begun to grow rapidly as its inventor-entrepreneur founder made one good decision after another. His capacity to foresee potential markets for products that he himself had a major role in creating had proved uncanny. For a considerable period, these markets remained within the United States, and production increases were achieved by expanding on the California facilities. The company's founder felt comfortable with the U.S. market and was convinced he could guide the firm as well as anyone in its current situation. There were some discussions about introducing more formal planning processes, but these never got anywhere, mainly because the founder kept shelving such ideas as unnecessary.

As growth continued, a number of the company's managers became concerned because they never knew exactly what was going to happen next. To them the situation seemed out of control, and several even left the company because of this. Yet the company's founder was opposed to change, and his record supported him. The real reason he did not want a formal strategic planning process was that he could not explain how and why he made his gut-level decisions, even to himself. He knew that, with more formalized planning, he would have to produce some kind of rational arguments in favor of various strategic choices. He was not sure he could do this, or at least not very well. He felt that he might lose control of company strategy to others who could argue better than he. It was not the idea of losing control itself that bothered him. Rather, it was the possibility that his decisions might no longer guide the firm, and since he had been right so often, that could prove to be catastrophic.

What the company's founder had not anticipated is that product demand would begin to develop outside the country. He had traveled to Mexico a few times, but that was his entire acquaintance with life outside the United States. But it became increasingly clear that there was an enormous market outside the country that was waiting to be tapped. Finally, the company hired a person with considerable international experience, created an international division, and set out to explore that untapped market. The new vice-president was soon asking for authority to establish offices in various countries and even raised the possibility of doing some of the manufacturing in overseas locations. These plans would require some large capital investments, and almost for the first time in his life, the founder did not know what to say. Often he had no real understanding of what his international vice-president was talking about, and there always seemed to be people around speaking in languages whose identity he could not even guess at. Now he was the one who felt things were getting out of control.

The next time the company's treasurer made his periodic proposal that they look into the establishment of a formal planning process, the founder surprised everyone present by agreeing to do so. He even appointed a steering committee on the spot to get things going, and asked the treasurer to chair it. The company was clearly moving into a new era.

Questions

1. How should this company go about establishing a formal planning process? What should be the characteristics of that process? How should it be organized? What steps should be involved, and what types of plans?

2. What particular problems or pitfalls face planning in this company, given its history and situation? How should they be dealt with?

Additional Sources for More Detailed Study

Ansoff, H. Igor. *Strategic Management*. New York: Wiley, 1979.

Ansoff, H. Igor; Declerck, Roger P.; and Hayes, Robert L. *From Strategic Planning to Strategic Management*. New York: Wiley, 1976.

Bates, Donald L., and Eldridge, David L. *Strategy and Policy: Analysis, Formulation, and Implementation*. Dubuque, Iowa: Wm. C. Brown, 1984.

Bright, James R. *Practical Technology Forecasting*. Austin, Texas: Industrial Management Center, 1978.

Grant, John H., and King, William R. *The Logic of Strategic Planning*. Boston: Little, Brown, 1982.

Harrigan, Kathryn R. *Strategies for Declining Businesses.* Lexington, Mass.: D. C. Heath, 1980.

Harvey, Donald F. *Business Policy and Strategic Management.* Columbus, Ohio: Merrill, 1982.

Hrebiniak, Lawrence G., and Joyce, William F. *Implementing Strategy.* New York: Macmillan, 1984.

LeBell, Don, and Krasner, O.J. "Selecting Environmental Forecasting Techniques from Business Planning Requirements." *Academy of Management Review,* July 1977.

Lorange, Peter. *Corporate Planning: An Executive Viewpoint.* Englewood Cliffs, N.J.: Prentice-Hall, 1980.

Naylor, Thomas H. *Corporate Planning Models.* Reading, Mass.: Addison-Wesley, 1979.

Newman, William H., and Logan, James P. *Strategy, Policy, and Central Management.* Cincinnati, Ohio: South-Western, 1981.

Paine, Frank T., and Naumes, William. *Organizational Strategy and Policy.* Hinsdale, Ill.: Dryden, 1982.

Patz, Alan L. *Strategic Decision Analysis.* Boston: Little, Brown, 1981.

Quinn, James B. *Strategies for Change: Logical Incrementalism.* Homewood, Ill.: Irwin, 1980.

Richards, Max D. *Organizational Goal Structures.* St. Paul, Minn.: West, 1978.

Rothschild, William E. *Strategic Alternatives: Selection, Development, and Implementation.* New York: AMACOM, 1979.

Schendel, Dan E., and Hofer, Charles W. *Strategic Management: A New View of Business Policy and Planning.* Boston: Little, Brown, 1979.

Summer, Charles E. *Strategic Behavior in Business and Government.* Boston: Little, Brown, 1980.

Wheelwright, Steven C., and Makridakis, Spyros. *Forecasting Methods for Management.* New York: Wiley, 1980.

Notes

1. See Charles W. Hofer and Dan Schendel, *Strategy Formulation: Analytical Concepts* (St. Paul, Minn.: West, 1978); and Jeffrey Bracker, "The Historical Development of the Strategic Management Concept," *Academy of Management Review* (April 1980).

2. Michael E. Porter, *Competitive Strategy: Techniques for Analyzing Industries and Competitors* (New York: Free Press, 1980).

3. Charles C. Snow and Lawrence G. Hrebiniak, "Strategy, Distinctive Competence, and Organizational Performance," *Administrative Science Quarterly* (June 1980).

4. Henry Mintzberg and James A. Waters, "Tracking Strategy in an Entrepreneurial Firm," *Academy of Management Journal* (September 1982).

5. Rudi K, Bresser and Ronald C. Bishop, "Dysfunctional Effects of Formal Planning: Two Theoretical Explanations," *Academy of Management Review* (October 1983).

6. Peter Lorange, *Implementation of Strategic Planning* (Englewood Cliffs, N.J.: Prentice-Hall, 1982).

7. James K. Brown and Rochelle O'Connor, *Planning and the Corporate Planning Director* (New York: Conference Board, 1974).

8. Major studies include Stanley S. Thune and Robert J. House, "Where Long Range Planning Pays Off," *Business Horizons* (August 1970); Anant R. Negandhi, *Organization Theory in an Open System* (New York: Dunellen, 1975); and Richard B. Robinson, "The Importance of 'Outsiders' in Small Firm Strategic Planning," *Academy of Management Journal* (March 1982).

9. For example, see Ronald J. Kudla, "The Effects of Strategic Planning on Common Stock Returns," *Academy of Management Journal* (March 1980).

10. George A. Steiner, "Evaluating Your Strategic Planning System," in *Implementation of Strategic Planning,* ed. Peter Lorange (Englewood Cliffs, N.J.: Prentice-Hall, 1982).

11. For an early demonstration of this point, see for example Francis J. Aguilar, *Scanning the Business Environment* (New York: Macmillan, 1967); and more recently, Aguilar, "Managing the Quality of Strategic Thinking," in *Implementation of Strategic Planning,* ed. Peter Lorange (Englewood Cliffs, N.J.: Prentice-Hall, 1982).

12. These considerations are developed much more fully in the Porter volume. See note 2.

13. Donald C. Hambrick and Ian C. Macmillan, "The Product Portfolio and Man's Best Friend," *California Management Review* (Fall 1982).

14. Boston Consulting Group Staff, *Perspectives on Experience* (Boston: Boston Consulting Group, 1968).

15. See Jeremiah J. O'Connell and John W. Zimmerman, "Scanning the International Environment," *California Management Review* (Winter 1979); John F. Preble, "Corporate Use of Environmental Scanning," *Michigan Business Review* (September 1978); and

Philip S. Thomas, "Environmental Scanning—The State of the Art," *Long Range Planning* (February 1980).

16. See Donald R. Melville, "Top Management's Role in Strategic Planning," *Journal of Business Strategy* (Spring 1981), regarding Norton Company's experience; and Sandra D. Kresch, "The Impact of Consumer Trends on Corporate Strategy," *Journal of Business Strategy* (Winter 1983), on the experience of General Mills.

CHAPTER 12

Organizational Decision Making

CHAPTER OUTLINE

How Decisions Are Made
The Importance of Decision Making
Bounded and Full Rationality
    Simon's Arguments
    Computers and Decisions
    Evidence on Satisficing
Incremental Decision Making
Variations With Decision Circumstances
Decision Making in the Boardroom
    The Structure of Decisions
    The Role of Outside Directors
    The Board as a Co-optation Mechanism
The Top Level Decision Hierarchy
    People at the Top
    The Office of the President Concept

Individual Decision Making
Entrepreneurial Decision Making
    The Broad Decision Horizon
    Small Business Success
    Types of Entrepreneurs
Factors Influencing Individual Decisions
    Age and Decisions
    Aspects of Personality
Creative Decisions
    Who Are the Creative People?
    Developing Creativity

Group Decision Making
Creativity in Groups
    Overcoming Obstacles
    When Creativity Is Not Needed
    Bargaining and Creativity
Special Problems with Group Decisions
    Groupthink
    Risky Shift
Diversity and Size Considerations
    Varying the Degree of Diversity
    Dialectical Debate
    Group Size

OBJECTIVES

To look at some of the ways decisions are made in corporations, particularly at the top levels.

To consider the factors that may make some people better decision makers than others.

To understand when groups should be used to make decisions and how they might be used best.

S trategic planning, strategy formulation, and the development of policies all involve decision making. Yet decisions may be made that are not related directly to any of these contexts—the decision to fire a high-level executive who has become alcoholic and is unable to implement strategies and policies, for instance.

Decision making, then, is a broader concept than is planning and strategy formulation. A useful definition is the following: *Decision making* is a conscious human process, involving both individual and social (group) phenomena, based upon factual and value premises, that concludes with a choice of one behavioral activity from among one or more alternatives with the intention of moving toward some desired state of affairs.[1]

For the purposes of this discussion, it is important to add that this choice has some significance for organizational goals; that is what is meant by *organizational* decision making. Given this addition, the focus of this chapter is on situations in which:

There is a gap between the existing circumstances and what is desired.

Attention is focused on this gap and there is a desire to reduce it.

There is an expectation that the problem can be solved and the gap reduced.

HOW DECISIONS ARE MADE

Major decisions in corporations generally are an outgrowth of long discussions, extensive data collection, and intermittent bargaining among those with alternative viewpoints. Often decisions take a long time to make, so that the history of who actually did and said what is forgotten. It may not even be possible to pinpoint the exact time at which the decision was made; it becomes a fact as a consensus is gradually reached.

Because corporate decision making is inherently political, and is strongly influenced by the particular cast of characters involved, it tends to vary from one organization to another. It also varies with the nature of the problem, the location in the organization where the decision is made, and numerous other factors. The heroic picture of a lone decision maker, at the very apex of the organization, rattling off major decisions in rapid-fire order is not descriptive of what happens in today's corporations. Organizational decision making, even when strongly influenced by a single individual, is much more complex.

In some cases decisions are sufficiently "programmable" so that various quantitative techniques and mathematical models can be applied. These approaches are considered in the production/operations management chapters (chapters 16–17) because that is the context in which they are most frequently used. The focus in this chapter is on decisions that rarely occur in exactly the same form, and that therefore place the greatest demands on individuals. There are no precise formulas that can be applied. Exhibit 12.1 explains the distinction between such programmed and nonprogrammed decision making.

EXHIBIT 12.1 Programmed and nonprogrammed decision making

Type of Decision	Nature of Decision	Techniques for Making the Decision
Programmed	Repetitive and routine	Habit
	A definite procedure has been worked out—decisions do not have to be handled as if they were new	Standard operating procedures
		Organizational structures
		Operations research
		Electronic data processing
Nonprogrammed	Novel, unstructured, and unusually consequential	Judgment, intuition, and creative thought
	No cut-and-dried method, because the type of decision is new or complex, or because it is important enough to deserve custom treatment	Selection and training of executives
		Complex computer programs that "think" and solve problems in accordance with predetermined rules

SOURCE: Adapted from Herbert A. Simon, *The New Science of Management Decision* (Englewood Cliffs, N.J.: Prentice-Hall, 1977): 46, 48.

The Importance of Decision Making

There has been considerable debate over the extent to which managers, in particular those at the top level, spend time in planning and decision making. Some theorists consider decision making to be the essence of managing, from which everything else flows. The ideas of Herbert Simon as discussed in chapter 3 fall in this category. There are others who hold to the view that managers are so committed to live action that planning and decision making actually get little attention. This latter position has often been substantiated by reference to studies in which top managers were observed in the conduct of their work.[2]

However, observation of managers at work is not a very good way to study decision making. Decision making, insofar as individual managers are concerned, goes on internally and therefore cannot readily be observed. Also it is clear that, whether they should or not, many managers take their problems home with them—and to lunch, and to the golf course as well. Consequently, if we want to know how much time is devoted to decision making, we have to ask the managers to tell us, rather than just watch them. For this reason, some research on the subject clearly underestimates the importance of decision making.

Another consideration is that many managers probably should spend more time in decision making than they do. They would be much more effective if they gave the subject more time. Chapter 3 (and especially Exhibit 3.9) deals with the distinction between full rationality and bounded rationality. It sets forth the view that managers tend primarily to "satisfice," in the manner of administrative man. To the extent that this is true, and a closer approach to full rationality is possible, decision making gets less time than it should.

Satisficing when fuller rationality would be desirable is not the only such factor leading to an underestimation of decision making's importance. Even more significant is a tendency not even to satisfice—to avoid decisions entirely, if at all possible. Avoidance occurs because decisions can be risky. If a few bad decisions become identified with a particular manager, that manager's career can be badly tarnished. And on the other hand, good decisions often tend to get separated from the person who had the greatest influence on them and are viewed as group products. Or, at a later point, they may appear merely to have reinforced the obvious. Given this tendency, many managers avoid decisions in the hope that someone else will make them. Usually someone else *does* have to make them— often too late.

In sum, there are a number of factors that contribute to underestimation of the importance of decision making in management positions, to the perception and belief that managing can be done with little attentions to such matters. In the short run this may be true, but not in the long run. Unmade or poorly made decisions have a way of circling back. Decision making is an extremely important managerial function.

Bounded and Full Rationality

Much of economic theory and many of the quantitative techniques used in decision making assume a highly rational process carried out to maximize the attainment of some stated goal. This model of the decision process has come under increasing attack, sometimes on the grounds that "decisions are not really made that way" and sometimes, furthermore, on the grounds that they should not be made that way. The most widely discussed of these alternative views is that of Herbert Simon, as was set forth in Exhibit 3.9 involving concepts such as bounded rationality, administrative man, and satisficing.

Simon's Arguments   Central to Simon's views is the idea that decision making is bounded by certain aspects of the person, including (1) skills, habits, and reflexes, (2) values and concepts of purpose, and (3) knowledge, particularly of the consequences that would result if various alternatives were chosen. Given these limiting factors, a manager simply cannot make a perfect, maximizing decision; it is not humanly possible. Accordingly, managers satisfice, and accept the first alternative that is good enough. It is not always true, however, that the satisficing decision is the most fully rational that could be obtained. Contrary to some others, Simon argues in favor of rationality in decision making. He simply does not see it happening very often, partly because of human limitations and partly because managers settle for less than they could achieve.

Simon uses the idea of bounded rationality to explain a number of aspects of organizational functioning. Planning operates as it does, moving from the substantive to the more narrowly procedural, and finally to execution—from strategy to tactics—so that each individual can deal with small bits of the total decision process. No one person could possibly handle the details of execution at the highly specific level needed, especially if it were necessary for that person to cope with execution throughout a company containing tens of thousands of people.

Similarly, division of labor exists to break up the decision making task, and decision making is decentralized for the same reason. In this view, hierarchy in organizations is a natural outgrowth of the limitations of human intelligence. Abstract solutions of nonprogrammed problems occur at the top; more specific decisions, which can be programmed within the structure provided by the top level decisions, are made in the middle; and the actual carrying out of decisions is a bottom-level activity.

Computers and Decisions The arguments for division of labor, decentralization of decisions, and hierarchy, which flow from the idea of bounded rationality, have been amended somewhat in recent years as computers have taken on a more important role. Simon now believes that, with the aid of computers, managers can become less bounded.[3] Computers make it possible for those at the top to have access to and handle more information. Upper level jobs can consequently be enlarged to include decisions that previously had to be decentralized. Computers tend to bring about more coordination and planning at the top, with more information available and better feedback on the consequences of decisions. Computers thereby foster centralization, or at the very least they make it possible, and they make decision making more fully rational as well.

In general, research carried out before and after the introduction of computers has tended to substantiate Simon's view.[4] The data in Exhibit 12.2 are typical. Although in the data presented, many managerial jobs did not change, those that did change almost invariably increased in decision making scope. On the other hand, lower level, clerical jobs were more likely to decrease in scope rather than increase. Because of the availability of more information at higher levels, which the advent of computers makes possible, decisions do tend to shift upward, and the result is greater centralization. If anything, the introduction of personal computers should accentuate these trends.

Evidence on Satisficing It remains Simon's basic view that most decisions are made in a satisficing mode, even though computers may move them in the *direction* of fuller rationality. Is he correct?

EXHIBIT 12.2 Impact of introducing computers on the scope of managerial and clerical jobs in 23 life insurance companies

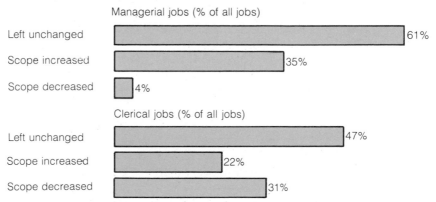

Managerial jobs (% of all jobs)

Left unchanged — 61%
Scope increased — 35%
Scope decreased — 4%

Clerical jobs (% of all jobs)

Left unchanged — 47%
Scope increased — 22%
Scope decreased — 31%

SOURCE: Adapted from Thomas L. Whisler, *The Impact of Computers on Organizations* (New York: Praeger, 1970): 131–132.

EXHIBIT 12.3 Comparison of a bank trust officer's portfolio decisions with decisions from a computer model of satisficing

Account #1—Growth
The trust officer decided to buy shares in five companies.
The computer decided on the same number of shares in the same companies in two instances.
In two more instances the same companies were named, but the number of shares differed slightly.
In one instance the company named was not the same.

Account #2—Income and Growth
The trust officer decided to buy shares in nine companies.
The computer decided on the same number of shares in the same companies in seven instances.
In two instances the companies named were not the same.

Account #3—Income and Growth
The trust officer decided to buy shares in eight companies.
The computer decided on the same number of shares in the same companies in seven instances.
In one instance the company named was not the same.

Account #4—Income
The trust officer decided to buy shares in seven companies.
The computer decided on the same number of shares in the same companies in six instances.
In one instance the company named was not the same.

SOURCE: Adapted from G. P. E. Clarkson, "A Model of Trust Investment Behavior," in *A Behavioral Theory of the Firm,* eds. Richard M. Cyert and James G. March (Englewood Cliffs, N.J.: Prentice-Hall, 1963): 265–266.

One way of answering this question has been to construct computer programs to model decision making that is satisficing in nature and see if that model matches actual decision making. Exhibit 12.3 shows what happens. In general, it appears that the bank trust officer in this case was using something very close to a satisficing approach.

Other studies have been conducted in which an individual's decision process is closely monitored to see whether satisficing is the typical approach.[5] These studies indicate that, although some people do satisfice, a large proportion continue the decision process beyond the point of a choice that is only good enough. They do this for two reasons. Often there is a move toward more rationality, a greater maximization of whatever goals are being sought, than satisficing permits. The other reason for continued search is to confirm or validate a decision that has already been made. In this instance, the individual collects more information, not to make a better decision, but to be able to defend one already made.

Simon was clearly right in pointing out the fact of satisficing. Yet decisions are made in other ways as well, and many approximate, if they do not reach, full rationality. This shift toward rationality is particularly characteristic of corporate managers, and appears to be more characteristic in successful companies. The decision processes found in more, as compared with less, profitable firms are highly formalized, utilize extensive data, and include inputs from many sources. As with formal strategic planning, as described in chapter 11, there is a major concern with rationality. Yet it is interesting to note that the goal is not always the unbridled pursuit of maximum profits; the company's public image is important also. Data on these points are as follows; in more profitable firms there is:

1. A concern over formal steps in decision making—regular meetings, written records, formal routines.
2. Computation of estimated costs and anticipated profits to result from a decision.
3. Discussion that includes all executives affected by the decision, usually in a meeting together.
4. Use of a top level policy or operating committee in the decision process.
5. Detailed information on which to base decisions because this is a major concern of the chief executive.
6. Use of formal communication channels and lines of authority that are followed in making decisions.
7. Satisfaction with decision making processes at a high level.
8. A concern with the company's public image, which serves as a major criterion, often outweighing cost considerations, in reaching decisions.[6]

Incremental Decision Making

A somewhat different concept from satisficing, but still short of full rationality, is that of incrementalism. This idea arose from observations of decision making in the federal government. It seeks not only to simplify the decision process to make it more manageable, but also to accommodate considerable bargaining as well. Its starting point, as indicated in Exhibit 12.4, is not some view of future goals, but the imperfections of current reality. Ultimately, one "muddles through" to change as a result not of one big decision, but a number of small ones.

Something of the same quality is inherent in the logical incrementalism championed by Quinn to describe decision processes in today's corporations. As set forth in Exhibit 12.5, this approach also moves slowly to achieve sufficient consen-

---

EXHIBIT 12.4 Characteristics of disjointed incremental decision making in government

1. Rather than making a comprehensive survey and analysis of alternatives, the decision maker focuses on alternatives that differ incrementally (substantially) from existing policies and strategies.
2. Only a relatively small number of alternatives are considered.
3. For each alternative only a restricted number of consequences considered important are evaluated.
4. The problem is continually redefined, with countless adjustments that make the problem more manageable.
5. There is assumed to be no one right decision; rather there is a series of continuing attacks on immediate issues through a series of analyses and evaluations.
6. In essence the incremental approach is remedial, geared more to the alleviation of current imperfections than the achievement of future goals.

SOURCE: Adapted from Charles E. Lindblom, "The Science of Muddling Through," *Public Administration Review* (Spring 1959); idem, *The Intelligence of Democracy; Decision Making Through Mutual Adjustment* (New York: Free Press, 1965).

EXHIBIT 12.5 Characteristics of logical incremental decision making

1. Top manager recognizes need for change.
2. Top manager seeks to encourage company to acknowledge this need by commissioning study groups, staff members, or consultants to examine context of need.
3. Top manager tries to broaden support through unstructured discussions, probing positions, defining differences of opinion, supporting favorable ideas, discouraging unfavorable ideas.
4. Top manager creates pockets of commitment by building needed skills and technologies, testing options, and utilizing opportunities to build support.
5. Top manager establishes a clear focus by appointing an ad hoc committee to specify a position or specifies this directly as a managerial prerogative.
6. Real commitment is obtained by assigning a manager to champion the goal and assume responsibility for its accomplishment; commitment perhaps also obtained by budget commitments and inclusion in operating plans.
7. Top manager moves on to ensure capacity to respond to new opportunities and threats, so that decision does not become unchanging in changing circumstances.

SOURCE: Adapted from James B. Quinn, "Strategic Goals: Process and Politics," *Sloan Management Review* (Fall 1977); idem, *Strategies for Change: Logical Incrementalism* (Homewood, Ill.: Irwin, 1980).

sus that a decision can be made and implemented. It is highly political, involves a number of other people in the decision, and the very process of decision making becomes the subject of considerable thought; it is something like the "plan to plan."

Unfortunately, although decision making of the kind noted by Lindblom and Quinn clearly does exist, we know little about this kind of complex organizational decision making. Does it reduce or increase error? How frequent are false starts? What are its overall chances for success, as opposed to other approaches? Will the brute force of highly rational confrontation do the job as well, or better? These questions remain unanswered at present.

Variations With Decision Circumstances

How decisions are made depends in large part on the circumstances surrounding the particular decision. Chapter 6 discusses the various decision tree concepts, in which managers share decisions with their subordinates under certain conditions. As indicated in Exhibits 6.12 and 6.13, this kind of decision sharing varies with such factors as the manager's confidence in subordinates, and the like. Clearly there are circumstances in which managers are likely to involve others in the decision process, and at the same time, somewhat different circumstances appear to make this much less attractive.

One of these circumstances appears to be the country or culture in which the decision is made. As indicated in Exhibit 12.6, decisions are much more likely to be shared with subordinates in some countries, such as Sweden, than in others, such as Israel. This same study finds that the extent to which decisions are shared varies among industries, with oil and electronics sharing most, and that turbulent environments bring on more sharing. Rapidly changing technologies and customer requirements lead managers to bring others into the decision process. This is particularly true when the subordinate manager has skills, experience, and ed-

EXHIBIT 12.6 Degree of decision sharing between upper level managers and managers who report to them as described by both in various countries

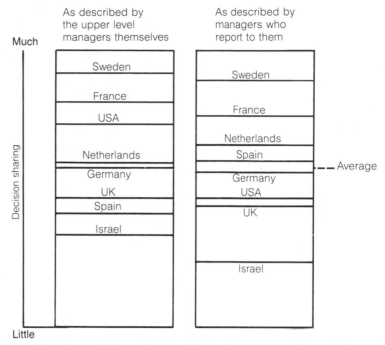

SOURCE: Adapted from Frank A. Heller and Bernhard Wilpert, *Competence and Power in Managerial Decision Making* (New York: Wiley, 1981): 99. Copyright 1981 by John Wiley & Sons, Inc. Reprinted with permission of the publisher.

ucation that might prove useful. In short, decisions are shared when sharing is most likely to produce a more fully rational decision.

Decision Making in the Boardroom

Many important decisions occur within groups variously referred to as regents, trustees, or in the business world, boards of directors. For many years these boards operated largely to rubber-stamp decisions actually made by the company's top executives. In fact, boards tended to be composed primarily of managers working for the same company. These managers simply "put on another hat" when they entered the boardroom.

Increasingly, however, company directors are becoming actively involved in the decision processes of the company. In part this involvement has been a result of changes within companies themselves, but it has also been influenced by pressures from society, actions by government bodies such as the Securities and Exchange Commission, and suits brought against individual board members holding them responsible for company actions.

The Structure of Decisions Legally, corporations must have at least three directors. As Exhibit 12.7 indicates, few companies of any size have boards that small; the average is 13 or 14 members. The larger boards are most characteristic in banking and in the insurance industry. Thus the board at Northwestern Mutual Life, ranked as the top life insurance firm by *Fortune,* numbers a full 30.[7]

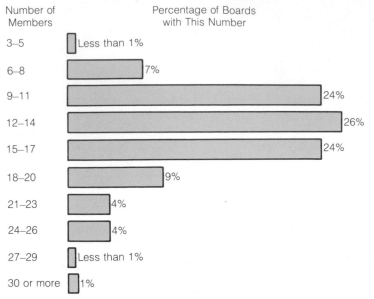

EXHIBIT 12.7 Sizes of boards of directors

Number of Members	Percentage of Boards with This Number
3–5	Less than 1%
6–8	7%
9–11	24%
12–14	26%
15–17	24%
18–20	9%
21–23	4%
24–26	4%
27–29	Less than 1%
30 or more	1%

SOURCE: Adapted from Johannes M. Pennings, *Interlocking Directorates* (San Francisco: Jossey-Bass, 1980): 65.

Many boards are sufficiently large that decision making by the board as a whole can become quite cumbersome. The result has been the creation of committees within which most of the actual work of the board occurs. These committees deal with executive compensation, financial planning, company auditing procedures, corporate structure, top level appointments, the payment of stock dividends, and many other matters. Typically, there is an executive committee that serves as a board within the board to make necessary decisions in the intervals between meetings.

The Role of Outside Directors The proportion of "outside" directors has grown for several reasons.[8] One is a widespread view that these people will keep a watch on the insiders and make the company more socially accountable. This view is reflected in the Securities and Exchange Commission requirement that audit committees be composed of outside directors. In addition, companies themselves have sought outside directors to provide needed know-how on the board and to co-opt organizations and groups that pose potential threats. Most firms have their top level officers as directors, but beyond that norm, there is little consistency in board composition. Exhibit 12.8 provides information on the proportion of outsiders for nonfinancial firms.

Outside directors come from a variety of backgrounds. The great majority hold only the one directorship, at least in larger firms, although there are a few people for whom board service is the major source of employment, and who are members of a number of boards. The greatest proportion of outside directors are executives of other firms or retired executives. Another major source is the finan-

EXHIBIT 12.8 Proportion of board members who are not and never have been employed by the firms on whose boards they serve

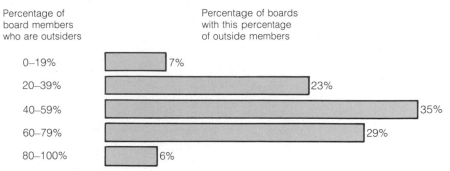

Percentage of
board members
who are outsiders

Percentage of boards
with this percentage
of outside members

0–19% 7%

20–39% 23%

40–59% 35%

60–79% 29%

80–100% 6%

SOURCE: Adapted from Johannes M. Pennings, *Interlocking Directorates* (San Francisco: Jossey-Bass, 1980): 77.

cial community, especially the large banks. A number of professionals, including corporate lawyers, members of accounting firms, and consultants, serve on boards, and so do some university professors and administrators.

In short, outside directors are almost without exception people who know something about business, but what they know varies considerably. They may know very little about the company on whose board they serve, relative to the executives of the firm, who are there every day. The result is mixed. Diverse expertise and experience are brought to bear on behalf of the company, but at the same time, diverse values and perceptions foster conflict and disagreements that may make the board a much less effective decision making body than it should be.

The Board as a Co-optation Mechanism Not all boards are intended to be effective decision making groups. Some clearly are, but when a board is very large and contains a high proportion of outsiders, many of whom actually know very little about the organization, it is more likely that the board's major function is to co-opt and thus neutralize threats in the environment. Many banks and companies in highly regulated industries fall into this category. In Europe laws have been passed that increasingly require companies to place members of outside groups, and in particular labor union representatives, on their boards. Under all of these circumstances, the board of directors becomes heavily politicized, and can become an arena for bargaining.

When a board becomes a co-optation mechanism, it may serve to reduce the organization's dependence on elements in its environment, as James Thompson anticipated (see chapter 9). This is positive. However, such a board is unlikely to function effectively as a top level decision making body for a company. Other provisions often need to be made so that decision processes will be carried out. A frequent result is that many top level decisions are actually made by company management or by a small executive committee of the board.

If in fact the board of directors is not the apex of the decision hierarchy, where is the top, and how is the hierarchy organized? In some cases, the board is the major decision making body and its chairperson is the most influential—the chief executive officer. This is the simplest structure and probably the most common, but it is not the only one, as the co-optation approach would indicate.

People at the Top   The relative status of the board's chairperson and the company president can be a source of confusion. We hear of a president's being "kicked upstairs" for instance, and at the same time of presidents being fired by their superiors. Who is boss? The answer is that it depends on the company. Sometimes chairing the board and serving as president is a one-person job. Sometimes the two positions are separate, and in such cases either one or the other may serve as chief executive. It may be that the two have joint responsibility, with the president having responsibility for operating matters, and the board chairperson, for finance, legal affairs, public relations, stockholder relations, and strategic planning.

The power relationships at the top are diverse, and are influenced by such factors as stock holdings and company seniority. There is no one best way, but it is clear that if lines of responsibility are not clear, role conflict can operate to undermine top level decision making just as much as at lower levels. Free-lying power certainly can exist at the top levels of companies, but until its locus is established, it will be difficult for the organization to get on with its major business decisions.

The Office of the President Concept   Some firms have attempted to deal with ambiguity and conflict at the top by creating an office consisting of several individuals, usually two to five, which operates between the board of directors above and the group vice-presidents or division general managers below. TRW is a case in point. This office may function in a variety of ways. Sometimes those involved meet frequently and arrive at joint decisions; sometimes any member who is present is authorized to make a decision for the group, thus speeding up decision processes. In any event, the office becomes the chief executive officer for many purposes.

The office of the president concept is not new, nor is it necessarily desirable. Some companies have found it unworkable. Others have used it on a transition basis, and yet others have made it their regular approach to top level decision making. It appears to depend very much on the company whether this type of decision making will work.

Organizational decision making is best considered as varying along a continuum that runs from an entirely individual process to an entirely group process. Decisions within a company can occur at various points along this continuum, depending on a variety of factors. This section addresses decision making on the individual end of the continuum; in the following section, the focus is on the more group-based end.

One of the most frequent instances of individual decision making in the modern business world involves the single entrepreneur who heads a relatively small firm that he or she has founded. In a few cases of large companies, major decisions may be made on a primarily individual basis, but this is almost always a development based on entrepreneurial origins. The entrepreneur has been able to retain control, and the firm has survived and prospered. Probably the best examples of this pattern are major conglomerates that are made up of unrelated businesses—James Ling of Ling-Temco-Vought, J. B. Fuqua of Fuqua Industries, Charles Thornton of Litton Industries, for example. Firms following this pattern have not always been able to hold the positions they achieved or even survive in the long run, but they did grow to a large size under a heavy reliance on individual, entrepreneurial decision making.[9]

It is not true, however, that individual decision making and entrepreneurship always go together. Many firms are founded as or soon become partnerships, in order to provide needed skills and achieve sufficient funding. Usually, though, if the firm does well, there comes a point when the decision process moves to a more individual mode. One of the partners asserts dominance, and the stage of shedding partners begins. As one major study found, the dominant entrepreneur:

> . . . must get rid of those people who have . . . either supported him or used his temporary position of weakness to intrude upon him . . . . At the interpersonal level he must get rid of them because they block the further development of the entrepreneur's own career and the development of the firm. At the level of internal dynamics, he must get rid of them because they inhibit him, restricting the autonomy for which he constantly searches.[10]

The Broad Decision Horizon   Small firms by their nature do not have multiple specialists with the expertise to move decisions to a position of high rationality. Furthermore, these firms typically cannot afford consultants and other outside professionals; usually these expenditures are limited to lawyers and accountants. Yet, as indicated in Exhibit 12.9, the range of areas in which decisions must be made, somehow, just to start the business, is sizable. Most of these decisions must be made by one person, on the basis of a limited search for information. This point is where satisficing becomes inevitable, and intuition is used more frequently than formal procedures.

Planning is important. In fact, it is essential if one is to obtain financing from a bank, for instance. But there is little time to plan once the company gets started, because day-to-day operating decisions absorb the available hours. Also, planning can be more difficult in a small firm because there is little opportunity to influence the environment and stabilize it. The entrepreneur often must simply respond as well as possible to what happens. Accordingly, short- and medium-range planning, for up to two years or so, is likely to be most productive.

Whether a new business survives appears to be strongly influenced by what business it got into in the first place.[11] At present, high technology offers a high probability of success; consumer products generally do not. New companies must look for a market niche where the competition is not so rough in the beginning. Retail stores often have difficulty doing this and as a result many fail at an early point. Still, in spite of these industry-level effects, the major reason for most new

EXHIBIT 12.9 Range of decisions an entrepreneur must deal with in starting the business

Factors Incorporated in a Business Plan to Obtain Financing, Projected Over Three to Five Years
1. The objectives of the business
2. The nature of the market
3. Existing competitors and their strengths and weaknesses
4. Anticipated selling prices and their relation to current prices
5. Product or service specifications
6. Patents held
7. Key technologies and required skills
8. Alternative distribution channels
9. Capital equipment needed
10. Additional funds needed in the future
11. Staffing and space requirements
12. Proposed business locations
13. Cash flow positions projected
14. Profit and loss positions projected
15. Ownership positions projected
16. Capabilities and experience of management

Additional Areas in Which Decisions Must be Made
1. Legal assistance
2. Market research
3. Recruiting and selecting personnel
4. Establishing accounting procedures
5. Insurance coverage
6. Establishing information needs
7. Dealing with government regulations and tax laws
8. Research needs
9. Employee compensation

business failures is inefficient management, and that in turn translates to inefficient decision making. Many entrepreneurs simply do not plan enough, or do not plan well enough, and their decisions fall too far short of full rationality.

Small Business Success Many entrepreneurs do succeed, nevertheless, and prosper, often to a substantial degree. How does this happen?

Chapter 5 notes that achievement motivation theory, as set forth by David McClelland, provides good predictions of entrepreneurial success. People with strong achievement motivation like to make decisions themselves and receive clear feedback on how well they have done—to be able to say "I did it myself." They tend to plan for the future and make decisions that will get their plans accomplished. They search out new information whenever possible.[12] This suggests a person who prefers individual to group decision making, but also a person who does plan and seeks rationality. Such individuals are ideally suited to the requirements of entrepreneurial decision making.

Other research findings support this picture of the individual decision maker. Successful entrepreneurs do not appear to make very good subordinates in larger organizations. They are very independent, with little desire to be supported and helped by others; they want to "go it alone." They view the world as something that can be influenced through their own efforts, and conversely they do not see the future as placing them at the mercy of fate. Such people may be overly individualized to succeed in corporate management, and in fact many have failed there. But, they are ideal for founding a new business.

Types of Entrepreneurs   It is apparent that entrepreneurs differ in a variety of respects. The person who starts a small grocery store in his hometown may have little in common with the inventor who develops a high technology firm to produce and market his inventions. Several ways of classifying entrepreneurs have been proposed. One of the more useful is described in Exhibit 12.10.

Opportunistic entrepreneurs usually head highly adaptive firms—firms that change their customers, their products, their facilities, and their markets as the situation requires; accordingly, these entrepreneurs are more likely to bring about

---

EXHIBIT 12.10   Distinction between craftsman and opportunistic entrepreneurs

Craftsman Entrepreneurs	Opportunistic Entrepreneurs
1. Formal education is technical only	1. Formal education includes some nontechnical area
2. Prior jobs were technical only	2. Prior jobs include activities other than technical, such as managing
3. Does not view management as a reference group	3. Views management as a reference group
4. Tends to model behavior on a single person and has never worked closely with any manager	4. Influenced by various people at different times; worked closely with at least one top executive
5. Belongs to professional associations only	5. Involved in community associations not directly related to the business
6. Limited oral and written communication ability	6. Effective in oral and written communication
7. Does not delegate authority	7. Delegates to relieve self of routine
8. Hires employees who will be loyal members of the company family	8. Hires the kind of person who could work for any organization
9. Capital sources are few, usually savings and a loan from a friend	9. More than two sources of capital
10. Customers developed by personal contact based on long-term relationships	10. Customers developed using various marketing methods such as personal selling, space advertising, direct mail, etc.
11. Strategies limited to price, quality, and company reputation	11. Strategies extend to new products and marketing methods, different distribution channels, etc.
12. Plans to form company go back no more than one year	12. Initiation of business planned for more than a year prior to the start
13. No plans for growth and change	13. Desires to grow and has a plan to accomplish
13. Has paternalistic, "family type" relations with employees	14. Employee relations are not paternalistic

SOURCE: Adapted from Norman R. Smith and John B. Miner, "Type of Entrepreneur, Type of Firm, and Managerial Motivation: Implications for Organizational Life Cycle Theory," *Strategic Management Journal* (December 1983).

growth. When this pattern is present, with an opportunistic entrepreneur running an adaptive firm, sales volume tends to be much higher than in the more stable, rigid firms headed by craftsman entrepreneurs. The opportunistic entrepreneur develops more complex strategies and plans more, including planning for growth.

Many of the factors that influence individual decisions are those that influence performance generally, as discussed in chapter 4. More intelligent people tend to be better at reasoning through to rational solutions of complex problems. The more a manager already knows about a problem, the less the need to search out, learn about, and evaluate new alternatives; thus, relevant knowledge makes for quicker decisions and reduces the tendency to satisfice. As indicated in Exhibit 4.3, different cognitive styles are appropriate to different decisions, but rationality is fostered by the hierarchic and integrative approaches.

In addition to these more cognitive processes, motivation, values, feelings, stress, and even physical factors enter into decision making. Satisficing is in certain respects a consequence of lesser motivational effort. Values serve to make certain decision alternatives preferable to others. High emotion and stress can lead to both an avoidance of decisions and a clogging of decision making processes. Physical impairments can restrict the energy available to make decisions.

Age and Decisions   In bureaucratic systems, managers generally rise through the hierarchy. Thus they are not young by the time they reach the strategic level—certainly in their forties in most cases, and usually in their fifties in the largest corporations. What are their decision capabilities likely to be at this point—better or worse than their younger, highly motivated subordinates?

First, it can be assumed that most people at the top are also highly motivated; they really do like to manage.[13] They have experience, and probably some wisdom. In short, they possess a certain kind of knowledge, although whether this is exactly the type needed depends on their educational backgrounds and the extent to which they have kept up to date. Usually they have already proved their capacity to handle stress and keep their emotions under control. Their continued decision making effectiveness assumes certain physical capabilities—freedom from the memory defects and rigidity of senility, for instance. Insofar as intelligence is concerned, the critical verbal abilities appear to increase on the average at least into the fifties. After that they may level off some, but decline among active managers and professionals is rare indeed, at least until after the typical mid-sixties retirement age, and often not even then.[14]

The evidence is that those who are in key decision making positions in their fifties and sixties are very likely to have the characteristics that make for effective decision making. Age itself is no detriment in this type of work; William Paley of CBS and Ronald Reagan are just two examples. Yet individual differences are real, and some will lack the necessary capabilities, for one reason or another.

Aspects of Personality   The most striking finding from studies of how personality characteristics influence decision making is that there are major variations with the type of decision. It takes a different type of person to engage in the lengthy study and search for alternatives that makes for good strategic planning than it does to make the quick decisions needed in keeping a production line going or in adapting to competitive price moves in a local market. Sometimes managers have to move fast with the best information available, and sometimes they need to approximate full rationality. The two are not the same kinds of people.

For example, it has been found that, in spite of the fact that confidence and high self-esteem make for better performance in many aspects of managerial work, this is not true for certain types of decision making. Where lengthy search is desirable, as in strategic planning, those who lack self-esteem do better.[15] They are unsure of themselves, and their knowledge, and so they devote more time to finding and evaluating information. As a result, they do a more effective job than those who are sure of themselves and what they already know.

Many research findings support this disparity in decision and personality types. Risk-takers do well when a decision has to be made quickly, because they do not delay beyond the point where negative consequences occur; a production line could stay down for hours simply because the person in charge would not risk a decision on anything but full information. People who believe that they can influence what happens get better results from planning. Those who feel that they are at the mercy of forces beyond their control plan less effectively. The important point is that all decisions are not the same, and ideally managers should be placed where the decisions to be made fit their personalities best.

Creative Decisions

Exhibit 12.11 provides a working definition of creativity. In practice, managers are not known for this type of thinking, and historically, people who think this way have generally been attracted to other occupations. Yet the need for creative ideas in operating organizations is great. The distinction between programmed and nonprogrammed decision making is important here (see Exhibit 12.1). Pro-

---

EXHIBIT 12.11   Nature of creativity and characteristics of creative people

Creative ideas are original and therefore embody something new. But not all original ideas are creative. For creativity to exist, there must be a close correspondence to reality and some redeeming social value. Outright eccentricity or deluded thinking do not constitute creativity.

Characteristics of people who consistently produce creative ideas are:

1. Self-confidence and courage in resisting pressures to conform to the ideas of others
2. Humility in bowing to rules not of their own making
3. Ability to tolerate disorder and ambiguity
4. Capacity to use intuition
5. Ability to integrate conflicting and opposing tendencies within one's personality
6. Willingness to work hard on a problem
7. Degree of discipline in handling impulses

SOURCE: Based in part on Michael B. McCaskey, *The Executive Challenge: Managing Change and Ambiguity* (Boston: Pitman, 1982): 116.

grammed decisions require knowledge and perhaps a capacity to innovate—to introduce already-known approaches into a different context. Nonprogrammed decisions, on the other hand, can be improved by creative input.

Who Are The Creative People?   Certain characteristics of creative people that have been established by research are noted in Exhibit 12.11. Creativity by its nature is nonconforming, and as a result, those who like to seek creative solutions to problems may not always be popular. They may try to be creative when creativity is not needed. They may stick to problems tenaciously long after others have given up on them and moved to something else. They may be viewed as not very good team players. In short, creative thinking may attract conflict, as noted in chapter 8, and there is always the risk that the methods of coordination employed will serve to stifle it. In fact, it is the decision maker who can develop new ideas while retaining a respect for meaningful limits and rules who is most likely to be both original and realistic—and thus truly creative in the business context.

It is apparent that creative thinkers must tolerate ambiguity. In fact, they rather like it. It presents them with a challenge to bring some kind of order to a situation where disorder prevails. Exhibit 12.12 provides a picture of the types of situations that appear to attract creative decision makers and in which they prove most effective. This exhibit may be used as a kind of check list to determine your own orientation to creative ideas. If you function comfortably and well in this type of environment, you are more likely to be a creative person than if you find such an environment disturbing or unpleasant.

EXHIBIT 12.12   Most troublesome characteristics of ambiguous situations

1. *Differing value orientations with consequent political and emotional clashes.* Given the ambiguity of the situation, people rely more on personal or professional values to make sense of things. Values often clash.
2. *Exact nature of the problem faced is uncertain.* Problem is unclear and shifting. Managers involved have vague, changing, and competing definitions. Problem is intertwined with various other problems.
3. *There are numerous contradictions and paradoxes.* Situation has features, relationships, and demands that initially appear to be inconsistent with one another.
4. *Managers involved make extensive use of symbols and metaphors.* Instead of precise definitions and rational arguments, the situation fosters the use of symbols and metaphors in expressing viewpoints.
5. *Amount and reliability of information is a problem in itself.* Because nature of problem is uncertain, collecting and organizing information is difficult. Information overloads or severe lacks may occur. Questions as to the reliability of data obtained.
6. *Goals to be achieved are either unclear or, if they are clear, several are present that conflict.* Managers involved are unable to work toward clearly defined consistent goals. Either the goals are vague, or they are well-defined and in apparent conflict.

SOURCE: Adapted from Michael B. McCaskey, *The Executive Challenge: Managing Change and Ambiguity* (Boston: Pitman, 1982): 5, 156.

Creativity is not a substitute for hard work, learning, and discipline. In fact, the more knowledge advances, the harder it is to be creative. Creative ideas go beyond what is already known. They are at the leading edge of knowledge, and often they combine existing ideas in some way not previously achieved. One must know what there is to be known in an area before one can aspire to be creative in it. The beginning student in management is unlikely to produce a creative breakthrough in the field for this reason. The odds favor the experienced person who is fully aware of the nature and value of alternatives that already exist.

Developing Creativity   Creative ideas are spawned and thrive in an environment where creative thinking and innovation are valued, rewarded, and encouraged. TRW is a company that appears to have such a climate. Many organizations tend to put out the creative flame, not necessarily intentionally, but because it has become common practice to respond to deviation and nonconformity with ridicule and suppression—or not to respond at all. One method of developing creativity is to introduce a set of values favorable to it. In bureaucracies this means that top management needs to nurture creative thinking not only among its members, but elsewhere as well. In professional systems it means stressing the creativity-supporting norms of the profession, to the extent that they exist. Some professions do tend to foster creativity more than others, however—the sciences as opposed to law, for instance.

Not inconsistent with this idea of creating a favorable value climate are a variety of techniques, training courses, and group procedures for developing creativity. Some of these procedures are considered in the next section. They encourage people to put together ideas and concepts they have not combined before, to look at a wide range of alternatives, and to think freely without fear of ridicule and negative reaction. Counterarguments and practical realities are held in abeyance while ideas come into being. Although these approaches are not in widespread use in the business world, research indicates that they can be valuable in developing individual creative potential.[16]

GROUP DECISION MAKING

Decision making toward the group end of the individual–group continuum occurs in policy groups, committees, project teams, organizational units composed of managers and those who report to them, informal groups, boards of directors, autonomous work groups, and the like. In some cases the group has been in existence for a considerable period and has dealt with a number of previous decisions; in some cases it is brand new. In some cases outsiders such as lawyers or consultants are part of the group; in others they are not. The point is that group decision making can occur with considerable variation. Yet there are some distinctive pluses and minuses associated with the approach overall.

Creativity in Groups

One of the potential problems relates to developing creative solutions to nonprogrammed problems. Creativity can be stifled easily, and groups seem to have some stifling effects. It is apparent that the usual group setting is not the place to generate creative answers to difficult problems. Some of the reasons for this are:

1. Groups often become focused on one train of thought for long periods, with the result that other alternatives are not considered.

2. Group members actively participate in discussions only if they view themselves as equally competent with the others; thus the good ideas of less self-confident people may be lost.

3. Even when more expert members do not criticize, others tend to expect that they will and consequently hold back on their ideas.

4. Lower level individuals often are inhibited and end by endorsing ideas of their superiors, even though in their own minds there are better solutions.

5. Group pressures for conformity, with the implicit threat of ridicule or punishment, are inevitable in group settings.

6. More dominant people speak up more and tend to monopolize discussions so that the ideas of others are lost.

7. Groups tend to devote time to maintaining themselves as groups and to their members getting along with one another; this takes time away from decision making and may serve to limit movement to good decisions.

8. In many cases groups make decisions more quickly than they should if alternatives are to be adequately considered.[17]

Overcoming Obstacles A number of approaches have been developed to overcome group difficulties. One method that has been used is the delphi technique discussed in chapter 11. In this approach, the ideas of many people are tapped but the people involved never actually meet face-to-face; consequently, the negative, inhibitory forces inherent in group discussions are avoided, and the prospects of someone finding a truly creative answer are increased. In the process, considerable communication occurs, however, as questions are formulated, answered, and results fed back to members. These processes are all conducted in writing. In many cases, delphi is carried out by mail, with a large panel of experts, but it is possible to apply the approach within a single locale. In any event, there are two, and possible more, rounds of questions and answers. As a result, a long period of time usually elapses before a solution is obtained.

To overcome this difficulty and still avoid the inhibitory influences of group interaction, various types of so-called *nominal group* procedures have been devised. Here, ideas that might help to solve difficult problems are produced independently by a number of people; usually they are written down. This may be done while the people sit quietly around a table, or over a period of a week or more as each person develops a position paper. In one variation, these ideas are then presented orally in a group situation, but there is a strict rule that no one is to react to the ideas set forth until everyone has had a say.

Similar concepts are inherent in approaches such as *brainstorming*, but in these cases procedures are introduced to reduce inhibitory forces entirely within the group setting itself.[18] Thus, there are rules indicating that evaluative judgments should be withheld, wild ideas should be voiced, and as many ideas as possible should be produced. These attempts to organize group processes to prevent their potential negative effects are not so effective as the approaches where a number of people first work independently. Still, all the approaches considered can be expected to generate more and better new ideas than simply having a committee get together to solve a problem.

When Creativity Is Not Needed Settling on a good solution to a nonprogrammed problem is not simply a matter of generating creative ideas. A choice must also be made among the various alternative ideas so that the solution is in fact a good one to put into action. This choice requires solid, bottom-line arguments evaluating profit potentials, costs, and other practical benefits. Here group discussion does help. It can bring new information to bear and can stimulate sound thinking. Inhibition of creativity is not an issue in this stage. Group discussion is thus the preferred approach when judgments must be made about the value of different alternatives.

Group discussion is also the preferred approach in dealing with programmed problems. In such cases, alternatives tend to be clear at the outset, and there is generally a correct solution. Consequently there is no need to deal with possible answers that might be outlandish or impractical, as when creativity is involved. The need is to develop a method of reaching a decision, to apply sound judgment so as to know when a correct decision has been obtained, and above all to avoid a poor decision. Under the right circumstances, groups can be very effective in this kind of decision making.

Bargaining and Creativity In chapter 7 it was noted that a great many decisions in organizations result from bargaining. When two divisions try to come to an agreement on which division will market a new product that overlaps with both their product groups, the focus is on bargaining; there is usually very little concern with developing a creative solution. The alternatives are two: either one division or the other gets the new product. It would be a rare division manager indeed who would even consider withstanding the pressure from the division management group as a whole to go all out for their division to get the product. These, then, are not conditions under which creative thinking is likely to prosper; bargaining tends to foster group consolidation and to prevent creativity.

Yet many bargaining situations desperately need creative solutions. In the above case, the ideal solution might be the initial establishment of a joint marketing team with a separate budget that could bring the expertise of both divisions to marketing the new product. This might well bring about a sufficiently greater sales volume that both divisions would be better off than either could have been alone. It is difficult even to get such approaches mentioned in bargaining situations. Even a higher level group vice-president might find it politically inexpedient to coordinate the decision process along these lines. In short, bargaining and creativity tend to be directly opposed processes in organizational decision making, even though creative solutions to bargaining dilemmas often appear to be badly needed.

Special Problems with Group Decisions

As we have seen, whether decision processes should be enmeshed in group interaction depends in large part on the degree of creativity desired. Many management decisions do not require much creativity, but some do, and these tend to be the most important strategic decisions. In these decisions, group processes can pose major obstacles, but at the same time, inputs from many creative people are needed. There are additional problems inherent in group decision making, problems that can be overcome, but that need to be recognized clearly.

Groupthink When decision making groups with considerable power experience a sense of cohesion so that they think as one, the conditions are ripe for *groupthink*. To the extent that the following are increasingly present, decisions will become increasingly poorer as a result of the effects of groupthink:

1. An illusion of invulnerability that creates too much optimism and encourages risk taking.
2. Numerous efforts to rationalize so that warnings of possible problems are discounted.
3. An unquestioned belief in the inherent morality of the group and its purposes, so that ethical and moral considerations are in fact ignored.
4. Stereotyped ways of thinking about opposing groups and organizations as evil, weak, and/or stupid.
5. Pressure on members who express dissent to be more loyal to the group.
6. A kind of self-censorship so that doubts about the apparent group position are suppressed by the individual members.
7. A shared illusion that everyone agrees totally with the majority view.
8. The emergence of mindguards who keep information that might shatter the group's shared complacency from reaching members.[19]

These processes can be disastrous for the organization involved. These ideas were originally developed following various top level U.S. government decisions related to wartime or warlike decisions, specifically, the Bay of Pigs invasion of Cuba and the escalation of the Vietnam War. However, they apply equally well to the decision processes of any executive bodies. Such was the case in the Watergate coverup, for instance. Somehow the integrity of the group becomes more important than the integrity of its decisions. The result can be not only very poor decisions, but also decisions that would be ethically unacceptable in the society beyond the group. In fact, they probably would be ethically unacceptable to members of the group as individuals. This process, by which groups develop their own morality, over and above the morality of their members, has been recognized for many years.[20] It is one of the major origins of some of the business ethics problems to be discussed in the next chapter.

Exhibit 12.13 considers some of the approaches that might be used to counteract groupthink, should an awareness arise of its potential existence. The problem is that groups, once they achieve a state of cohesiveness, are unlikely to recognize the groupthink problem. Thus, if the various methods of counteracting groupthink are to work, they probably have to be introduced while a decision making group, such as a board of directors executive committee, is being formed. The best solution seems to be that procedures such as those noted in Exhibit 12.13 become a matter of company policy so that they apply to any group formed, new or old.

Risky Shift A second problem in group decision making is similar in that it is particularly disastrous when the group itself is very powerful. There are some similarities in the dynamics involved, but there are differences as well. This problem is usually referred to as *risky shift,* although more recently it has been called *choice shift*.

EXHIBIT 12.13 Suggested methods of counteracting groupthink

Procedures that may be used within a decision making group

1. Leader assigning a policy-planning mission to a group should be impartial instead of stating preferences and expectations at the outset.
2. Leader of a policy-forming group should assign role of critical evaluator to each member, encouraging the group to give high priority to airing objections and doubts.
3. At every meeting devoted to evaluating policy alternatives, at least one member should be assigned the role of devil's advocate.
4. Throughout the period when the feasibility and effectiveness of policy alternatives are being surveyed, policy-making group should divide into two or more subgroups to meet separately, under different chairpersons, then come together to hammer out differences.
5. Whenever policy issue involves relations with a rival group or organization, a bloc of time should be spent surveying warning signals from the rivals.
6. After reaching preliminary consensus about what seems to be the best policy alternative, the policy-making group should hold a "second chance" meeting at which members are expected to express all residual doubts as vividly as they can.

Procedures that require participation more broadly within the organization

7. One or more outside experts or qualified colleagues within the organization who are not core members of the policy-making group should be invited to each meeting on a staggered basis and should be encouraged to challenge the views of the core members.
8. Members of the policy-making group should discuss periodically the group's deliberations with trusted associates in their own units of the organization and report back their reactions.
9. Organization should routinely follow the administrative practice of setting up several independent policy-planning and evaluation groups to work on the same policy question.

SOURCE: Adapted from Irving L. Janis, *Groupthink* (Boston: Houghton Mifflin, 1982): 262–271.

The nature of risky shift is spelled out in Exhibit 12.14. It should be emphasized that making decisions in the risky shift manner is neither necessarily good nor bad. Young, high-growth firms tend to take high risks, and without them would rarely be successful. On the other hand, one of the major sources of business failure is the commitment of too much of the company's resources to a single endeavor that does not work out as planned. Rolls-Royce, for instance, overcommitted itself to the RB211 engine intended for use in Lockheed's L-1011 airplane, planned and priced its product poorly, and ultimately went into a severe financial reverse.

Risky shift does not appear to be inevitable, in part because it requires at least one person in the group who takes a risky position from the outset. If everyone is conservative, there is no risky shift worth speaking about. But it is also true that, on occasion, groups shift dramatically in a conservative direction, as contrasted with the average position of individual members before the discussion began. This is why the term choice shift is used—to cover both types of results. Risky shift is much more common, but both types of shift can occur. We do not know why.

EXHIBIT 12.14 The nature of risky shift

Risky Shift is the tendency for individuals to be more willing to accept high-risk decisions after participating in group discussion than they would have been before the discussion.

The *Processes and Results* involved are:

1. A shift in a risky direction of the average preferred decision for the group as a whole.
2. A greater agreement in the group centering on the more risky position.
3. A movement toward, but not beyond, the riskiest position taken by any single group member before the discussion began.
4. A tendency to focus comments during the discussion on the desirability of risk.
5. An increasing degree of risk-taking with increases in the amount of time spent in discussion.

SOURCE: Adapted from James H. Davis, Patrick R. Laughlin, and Samuel S. Komorita, "The Social Psychology of Small Groups: Cooperative and Mixed-Motive Interaction," *Annual Review of Psychology* (1976).

Diversity and Size Considerations

When groups exist primarily for purposes of co-optation or are made up of representatives from different organizational components so that each may have its views heard, and bargained for, the result tends to be a rather large assemblage of people who differ considerably one from another. But when groups are established strictly for the purpose of making good decisions—a team to develop ways of dealing with new federal government safety standards, for instance—the group may be small as well as large, and it may be made up of very similar people as well as people who differ substantially. What are the pluses and minuses here?

Varying the Degree of Diversity. Diversity can be introduced in a variety of dimensions—abilities, knowledge, attitudes, values, personality characteristics, race, sex, and so on. A group of young, white, male, protestant manufacturing managers, most of whom went to the same local college and majored in engineering, is not likely to be very diverse in any regard. Groups that include a range of educational levels and backgrounds, women, minorities, various religious persuasions, ages, and the like are often extremely diverse.

The more similar the members, the easier time they will have working together, at least initially; the group can get right to the task at hand. Diversity means that a certain amount of conflict and misunderstanding is inevitable. It is hard for such a group to get itself organized to focus on a task; sometimes internal conflicts never get resolved. Yet diversity also brings varied capabilities and viewpoints to a problem. Many more different ideas are there to be tapped. Groups of very similar people are in many respects comparable to a single individual. Diversity permits a greater range of ideas and more considerations to be brought to bear in evaluating alternatives. In general, it follows that similar groups are better for programmed decisions and diverse groups for nonprogrammed decisions. Yet diverse groups may fail to realize their potential because they cannot cope with internal conflicts and communication problems well enough to get a good decision, or even any decision at all. The nominal group approach is one way of coping with some of these difficulties.

Dialectical Debate.   Recently, procedures have been developed for making nonprogrammed strategic decisions that appear to combine the advantages of both group similarity and diversity. Two groups are formed to reflect conflicting positions within the company. Internally in each group, the people are selected to be as similar as possible. But the two groups themselves are made as different as possible from each other. These groups engage in debate, with the objective of bringing out the assumptions behind each decision alternative. Usually one group espouses the existing strategy and the other an opposing strategy that would best counter the first group's position. As the two sets of underlying assumptions become apparent, it is often possible to obtain agreement on a single specific set, and then to work from there toward a single "best strategy."

Approaches of this kind have been the subject of considerable recent debate.[21] It is not entirely clear that they yield results superior to those obtained by the simple use of a devil's advocate (see item 3 in Exhibit 12.13). However, in utilizing the advantages of group similarity to obtain a concerted internal group effort and of diversity between groups to obtain varied capabilities and viewpoints, these approaches appear to be building some useful ideas. The next step might be to create more than two groups, to reflect a greater range of positions.

Group Size.   When decisions are complex, as they typically are at the policy/strategy level, group size can be critical. Generally, a group of less than five is too small, eight to twelve tends to be optimal, and more than twelve is increasingly less effective. Too few members restrict the range of ideas and views available and also tend to inhibit their expression, while too many create problems of coordination, clique formation, and often lead to considerable dissatisfaction among the members.[22] The optimal range noted is for nonprogrammed decision making by groups working face-to-face. Programmed decisions appear to be best made by somewhat smaller groups—five or six. Approaches such as the delphi technique or nominal procedures, which do not require the members to actually meet together, can use much larger groups.

In many respects the similarity–diversity issue and that of group size are parallel. Small groups invariably limit the range of differences possible. Large groups tend to introduce increasing degrees of diversity unless something is done to restrict the range. In groups such as boards of directors, increasing size almost always means increasing diversity, to the point where decision making becomes unmanageable. As noted, these larger boards usually are intended more as a means of co-opting outsiders than as a means for obtaining good decisions.

Summary

Decision making is an even broader concept than planning and strategy formation, which focuses on reducing the gap between existing and desired states of affairs. Decisions may be distinguished as programmed and nonprogrammed, and it is the latter type that is most important at the policy/strategy level. Nevertheless, decisions of all kinds play a very significant role in managerial work. In addition, aspects of decision making—and in particular human bounded rationality and the tendency to satisfice—serve to determine in large part the forms that organizational structures and processes take. The satisficing mode in decision making is normally set against maximizing or full rationality; people also attempt to validate decisions already made. The concepts of disjointed and logical incrementalism describe highly political types of organizational decision making involving many people and extensive bargaining.

A major factor in top level decision making is the board of directors. Boards are often larger than they should be for effective decision making, and in these cases the board's function is likely to be primarily the co-optation of important forces in the environment. Under these circumstances, important decisions are usually made by committees of the board, by company management with the chief executive officer having major influence, or in some cases by an "office of the president."

Decision making may range from a distinctly individual process to an entirely group process. A prime example of the former occurs in entrepreneurial firms, where satisficing becomes essential because the entrepreneur cannot become an expert in all areas. High achievement motivation appears to contribute to success in this type of endeavor. Opportunistic entrepreneurs tend to do much better than the craftsman type. Generally, entrepreneurs are independent people who are better suited to individual decision making than to the politicized group processes of large bureaucratic organizations.

Factors influencing individual decision making are much the same as those influencing performance generally. Age appears to be no detriment to decision making effectiveness. Personality factors operate differently depending on the nature of the decision. Thus, in spite of the usual positive consequences of high self-esteem, a lack of self-esteem makes for better performance in areas such as strategic planning. Creative decisions require a particular type of person who can cope with ambiguity and resist conformity pressures. In addition, the organization that wishes to foster creative decisions should maintain a climate and value system favorable to it. Various techniques such as the delphi method, nominal groups, and brainstorming have been developed to this end.

Group decision making is most effective in evaluating decision alternatives and in dealing with programmed decisions. However, group decision making may be severely hampered by groupthink and by risky shift unless specific steps are taken to deal with these processes. When groups are used, diversity of membership and a somewhat larger size contribute to better results in dealing with nonprogrammed decisions, but internal conflicts and misunderstandings can present problems. The value of smaller, more homogeneous groups is that they can organize for work more easily. Techniques of dialectical debate are intended to bring the advantages of both similarity and diversity to bear on nonprogrammed strategic decisions.

What Have You Learned?

1. There is a clear tie between ambiguity and creativity. How does this occur, and how does it relate to the characteristics of creative people?

2. How can the concepts of satisficing, validation of past decisions, disjointed incrementalism, and logical incrementalism be differentiated? Why are they important?

3. Why are certain entrepreneurs more successful and others less so? How does success relate to the decision making requirements of the entrepreneurial situation?

4. What is the distinction between programmed and nonprogrammed decision making, and what aspects of decision making are related to it?

5. Why are diversity and size considerations important in putting together decision making groups? How does each factor relate to effectiveness in different circumstances?

6. How may creativity be developed and fostered in both individuals and a group context? What are some of the techniques used?

7. What individual characteristics are most likely to influence decision making, and how do they operate?

8. How are boards of directors constituted, and how does the process of co-optation enter in? What are the consequences for decision making?

9. How do groupthink and risky shift differ? How may the negative consequences of each be avoided?

10. What are the consequences of bounded rationality for organizational functioning, process, and structure? How do computers enter in here?

How Well Can You Apply Your Knowledge?

Problem 1. A woman in her late thirties has held a number of positions in various companies since graduating from college. At present, she is in charge of training at a major plant of an electronics firm. Her career has been marked by a number of ups and downs. She feels that she has been discriminated against as a woman, yet she has never been able to put her finger on anything specific. Somehow she seemed always to get into what turned out to be a dead-end position. Then she would get frustrated and move on to another company. This pattern has repeated itself so often that she is now determined to put an end to it. What she has in mind is to start her own company.

She likes her training work itself and, although she finds it difficult to get along with her boss, she is particularly intrigued by some work they have been doing to develop creativity among research and development personnel. She has in fact created her own training program in this area, and the course has been so successful that she was asked to conduct it at several company locations. Her idea is to market this course to firms around the country.

To do this she will have to hire a number of trainers, train them to conduct the courses, and open offices in various locations. She will also have to implement some kind of business development plan to contact potential users and interest them in creativity training. From what she can tell, the biggest problem is not to get firms to replace their current creativity training with her approach, but to get them to undertake this kind of training at all. Although there are a number of these training programs in existence, none appears to be used very extensively. Thus her marketing efforts will have to be focused on both creating a market and getting her product into it.

All this means that, once she gets started, the firm will need access to considerable capital in order to grow rapidly and take advantage of opportunities. Opening offices, getting people out prospecting for work, paying travel and entertainment expenses—this will cost a lot before the actual training begins to bring in money. This will mean borrowing heavily, since the woman herself is in no position to bankroll such a business. Nevertheless, she is very excited about her prospects as she moves closer to the date set in her own mind for resigning from her training position and starting her new firm.

Questions

1. How would you go about developing a business plan to secure financing for this new business? What factors would you emphasize? What arguments would you make in support of your new business?
2. Assuming that the business got started, what major decisions would you anticipate facing in the early period? How would you go about making these decisions?

Problem 2. The advertising manager of a large corporation has just heard a presentation by the company's agency proposing an expensive campaign for a new product to be introduced within the year. There had been some discussions within the company about this campaign previously, and the advertising manager thought he had heard some ideas then that were just as good as what the agency proposed. Obviously, the agency had worked things out in greater detail, but he was not at all sure that what they wanted to do would really sell the product.

The problem was that the new product was not substantially different from several already on the market. The competing products, already established in the marketplace, were being heavily advertised and were doing well. There were, in fact, several advantages in the company's new product, but they were not of a kind that would be immediately apparent to the consumer. Television advertising seemed best-suited to demonstrating these advantages, and the agency had indeed recognized this fact. Yet the advertising manager feels that their proposed campaign did not bring out these advantages as well as it should. It simply lacked the kind of completely new, creative approach he feels is necessary. The money was there to be spent, since the company had recognized for some time that the new product would require an extensive advertising effort to achieve a meaningful market share, and had budgeted accordingly. Yet new products rarely got more than one campaign, and if the one selected did not work, both the company and the advertising manager would be in trouble.

It would be possible to shift to another agency, of course, but in the manager's experience, such shifts rarely work. His preferred approach is to try to develop the outlines of a really new and original campaign within his own staff and then to go back to the agency with a much more specific set of guidelines from which they could then work out the details. He has a sizable group of people, many of whom have agency experience. At least ten or twelve have had experience in creating campaigns in one capacity or another, and at least an equal number of younger people are in his group who seem to have some good ideas. He wants to tap this talent pool before going any further.

Questions

1. If you were the advertising manager, how would you organize the decision making process to tap the creative potential of your staff? Exactly how would you do this? What would be the sequence of steps involved?
2. Why would you take this approach? What specific problems would the various steps be intended to overcome?

Additional Sources for More Detailed Study

Baumback, Clifford M., and Lawyer, Kenneth. *How to Organize and Operate a Small Business.* Englewood Cliffs, N.J.: Prentice-Hall, 1979.

Brightman, Harvey J. *Problem Solving: A Logical and Creative Approach.* Atlanta: College of Business Administration, Georgia State University, 1980.

Davis, Gary A. *Psychology of Problem Solving: Theory and Practice.* New York: Basic Books, 1973.

Delbecq, André L.; Van de Ven, Andrew H.; and Gustafson, David H. *Group Techniques for Program Planning.* Glenview, Ill.: Scott, Foresman, 1975.

Ebert, Ronald J., and Mitchell, Terence R. *Organizational*

Decision Processes: Concepts and Analysis. New York: Crane, Russak, 1975.

Harrison, E. Frank. *The Managerial Decision-Making Process*. Boston: Houghton Mifflin, 1981.

Heller, Frank A. *Managerial Decision-making: A Study of Leadership Styles and Power-sharing among Senior Managers*. London: Tavistock, 1971.

Hollingsworth, A. Thomas, and Hand, Herbert H. *A Guide to Small Business Management: Text and Cases*. Philadelphia: Saunders, 1979.

Huber, George P. *Managerial Decision Making*. Glenview, Ill.: Scott, Foresman, 1980.

Janis, Irving L., and Mann, Leon. *Decision Making: A Psychological Analysis of Conflict, Choice, and Commitment*. New York: Free Press, 1977.

Kent, Calvin A.; Sexton, Donald L.; and Vesper, Karl H. *Encyclopedia of Entrepreneurship*. Englewood Cliffs, N.J.: Prentice-Hall, 1982.

Mace, Myles L. *Directors: Myth and Reality*. Boston: Harvard Graduate School of Business Administration, 1971.

MacMillan, Ian C. *Strategy Formulation: Political Concepts*. St. Paul, Minn.; West, 1978.

Maier, Norman R. F. *Problem Solving and Creativity: In Individuals and Groups*. Belmont, Calif.: Brooks/Cole, 1970.

Mason, Richard O., and Mitroff, Ian I. *Challenging Strategic Planning Assumptions: Concepts, Methods, and Techniques*. New York: Wiley, 1981.

Mitroff, Ian I. *Stakeholders of the Organizational Mind*. San Francisco; Jossey-Bass, 1983.

Vance, Stanley C. *Corporate Leadership: Boards, Directors, and Strategy*. New York: McGraw-Hill, 1983.

Van Voorhis, Kenneth R. *Entrepreneurship and Small Business Management*. Boston: Allyn and Bacon, 1980.

Notes

1. Fremont A. Shull, André L. Delbecq, and Larry L. Cummings, *Organizational Decision Making* (New York: McGraw-Hill, 1970).

2. Henry Mintzberg, *The Nature of Managerial Work* (New York: Harper and Row, 1973).

3. Herbert A. Simon, *The New Science of Management Decision* (Englewood Cliffs, N.J.: Prentice-Hall, 1977).

4. Studies carried out in the period when most companies were introducing computers, in addition to the study noted in Exhibit 12.2, are Hak C. Lee, "Human Resources Administration in the Computer Age," in *Human Resources Administration: Problems of Growth and Change,* eds. William J. Wasmuth, Rollin H. Simonds, Raymond L. Hilgert, and Hak C. Lee (Boston: Houghton Mifflin, 1970); and William E. Reif, *Computer Technology and Management Organization* (Iowa City: Bureau of Business and Economic Research, University of Iowa, 1968).

5. See for example Peer Soelberg, "Unprogrammed Decision Making," *Academy of Management Proceedings* (December 1966); and William F. Glueck, "Decision Making: Organization Choice," *Personnel Psychology* (Spring 1974).

6. Ross Stagner, "Corporate Decision Making: An Empirical Study," *Journal of Applied Psychology* (February 1969).

7. Claire Makin, "Ranking Corporate Reputations," *Fortune* (January 10, 1983).

8. Robert M. Estes, "The Emerging Solution to Corporate Governance," *Harvard Business Review* (November–December 1977); and Business Roundtable, *The Role and Composition of the Board of Directors of the Large Publicly Owned Corporation* (New York, January 1978).

9. Stanley C. Vance, *Managers in the Conglomerate Era* (New York: Wiley, 1971).

10. Orvis F. Collins and David G. Moore, *The Enterprising Man* (East Lansing, Mich.: Graduate School of Business Administration, Michigan State University, 1964).

11. Karl H. Vesper, *New Venture Strategies* (Englewood Cliffs, N.J.: Prentice-Hall, 1980).

12. David C. McClelland, *The Achieving Society* (Princeton, N.J.: Van Nostrand, 1961); and David C. McClelland and David G. Winter, *Motivating Economic Achievement* (New York: Free Press, 1969).

13. Frederic E. Berman and John B. Miner, "Motivation to Manage at the Top Executive Level: A Test of the Hierarchic Role-Motivation Theory," *Personnel Psychology* (in press).

14. John B. Carroll and Scott E. Maxwell, "Individual Differences in Cognitive Abilities," *Annual Review of Psychology* (1979).

15. Howard M. Weiss and Patrick A. Knight, "The Utility of Humility: Self-Esteem, Information Search, and Problem-Solving Efficiency," *Organizational Behavior and Human Performance* (April 1980).

16. Irvin Summers and David E. White, "Creativity Techniques: Toward Improvement of the Decision Process," *Academy of Management Review* (April 1976);

and Min Basadur, George B. Graen, and Stephen G. Green, "Training in Creative Problem-Solving: Effects on Ideation and Problem Finding and Solving in an Industrial Research Organization," *Organizational Behavior and Human Performance* (August 1982).

17. Andrew Van de Ven and André L. Delbecq, "Nominal Versus Interacting Group Processes for Committee Decision-Making Effectiveness," *Academy of Management Journal* (June 1971); and "The Effectiveness of Nominal, Delphi, and Interacting Group Decision Making Processes," *Academy of Management Journal* (December 1974).

18. Alex F. Osborn, *Applied Imagination* (New York: Scribner's, 1963).

19. Irving L. Janis, *Groupthink* (Boston: Houghton Mifflin, 1982).

20. Sigmund Freud, *Group Psychology and the Analysis of the Ego* (New York: Bantam Books, 1960).

21. See Richard A. Cosier, "Dialectical Inquiry in Strategic Planning: A Case of Premature Acceptance?" and Ian I. Mitroff and Richard O Mason, "The Metaphysics of Policy and Planning: A Reply to Cosier," both in *Academy of Mangement Review* (October 1981).

22. Alvin Zander, "The Psychology of Group Processes," *Annual Review of Psychology* (1979); and Robert J. House and John B. Miner, "Merging Management and Behavioral Theory: The Interaction Between Span of Control and Group Size," *Administrative Science Quarterly* (September 1969).

CHAPTER 13

Social Responsibilities and Ethics

CHAPTER OUTLINE

Whistle-Blowing at the Bay Area Rapid Transit System (BART)

Concepts of Social Responsibility
Conflicting Views of Social Responsibility
    The Purely Economic View
    Expanded Concepts
    Realities and Resolutions
    Relationships to Profits
Humanism and Quality of Work Life
    The Humanistic View
    The *Work in America* View
Ethics, Morality, and the Law
    The Current State of Business Ethics
    International Payoffs
    Theft in Organizations

Corporate Responses to Social Expectations
Types of Response
    The Range of Activities
    Industry Variations
Policies and Their Implementation
    A Suggested Policy Statement
    Planning and Implementing
Social Auditing
    Types of Audits
    The Roles Social Audits Play

Representing and Public Relations
The Scope of Activities
    Coping with Environments
    Specific Public Relations Activities
    Political and Government Relations
Influencing the Corporate Image
    Conflicting Forces
    Different Publics

OBJECTIVES

To understand what social responsibility and ethics are as they relate to organizations, and how viewpoints differ in this area.

To describe what kinds of social actions companies have been engaged in and how these actions may be carried out most effectively.

To provide a general picture of what representing is and the role of public relations in representing.

WHISTLE-BLOWING AT THE BAY AREA RAPID TRANSIT SYSTEM (BART)[1]

On March 2 and 3, 1972, three engineers were fired by the management of the Bay Area Rapid Transit System, a free-standing governmental authority created to develop and operate train service in and around San Francisco. At the time of the firings, BART was under construction. The stated reasons for the firings were:

1. Repeated insubordination.
2. Falsification of information and lying to superiors and to members of BART's board of directors.
3. Perpetuation of actions that created severe staff disruptions and seriously impaired morale.
4. Failure to perform the jobs for which employed in a competent and acceptable manner.
5. Repeated refusal to follow procedures for bringing job-related problems to the attention of management.

These five points refer to events that occurred over a long period. The three engineers had become convinced that the complicated automatic train control system being developed for BART by Westinghouse Electric was not being and would not be adequately tested before being put in use. They saw major problems with the software and other aspects of this system. Given the high speed of the trains, they were concerned that if these problems were not eliminated, severe accidents would result. They considered it a matter of professional ethics and social responsibility to do everything in their power to protect the public from exposure to such a potentially hazardous system.

In order to understand the engineers' actions, it is necessary to know something about BART, how it operated at the time, and the engineers' positions in it. Exhibit 13.1 provides some of this information. As can be seen, the three engineers were low in the BART hierarchy. At the top was a board of directors whose members were appointed by the governments of the counties where BART would operate. However, the California state legislature had sufficient control over related legislation and funding to represent another major power source in BART's environment. Also important was a con-

sortium of three independent engineering firms that had contracted to design the BART system. Direct supervision of subcontractors—including supervision of Westinghouse Electric Company, which was to develop the automatic train control system—was the responsibility of this consortium.

Over a long period, the three engineers individually and collectively expressed their concerns over the system's safety to their superiors—both verbally at meetings and in written memoranda. These actions appeared to have little effect; often there was no reply at all. At the same time, the issues involved were highly technical in nature and did not clearly fall within the direct job jurisdictions of any of the engineers, or of their immediate superiors. Finally they prepared an anonymous memorandum and distributed it widely. It was highly critical of the engineering competence of BART management and of the joint venture consortium. This memorandum proposed the creation of a Systems Engineering Department within BART to deal with train control problems.

At roughly the same time, the three engineers engaged an independent engineering consultant who prepared a report on BART operations, and they began attempts to establish contact with members of the board of directors. These attempts ultimately resulted in the safety issue and the consultant's report, which was not very professionally done and was strongly critical of management, being taken to the board. Several newspaper articles also brought the safety problems and the deficiencies of BART management to public attention. By this time, events were largely beyond the control of the three engineers, but they certainly had put the events in motion.

In the end, the board gave management a vote of confidence on the issue. When questioned by management, the engineers denied their roles and also authorship of the anonymous memorandum (which they did write). There was very good reason to believe that, apart from the ethical issues, at least two of the three were trying to promote a reorganization, the creation of the Systems Department, that could materially advance their own ca-

EXHIBIT 13.1 BART's interorganizational network, internal structure, and the positions of the three engineers

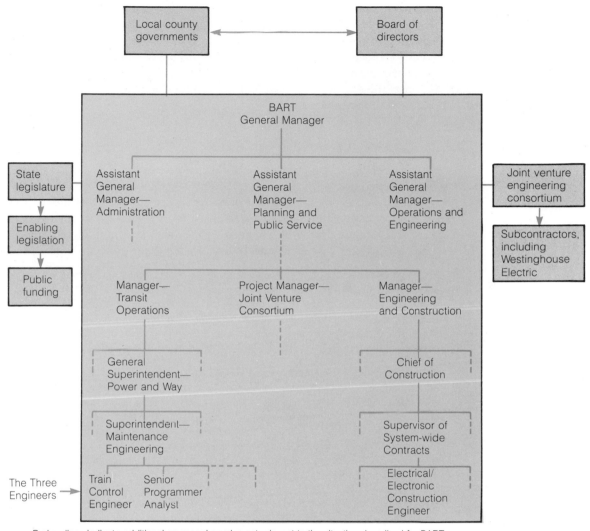

NOTE: Broken lines indicate additional personnel or roles not relevant to the situation described for BART.

SOURCE: Adapted from Robert M. Anderson, Robert Perrucci, Dan E. Schendel, and Leon E. Trachtman, *Divided Loyalties: Whistle-Blowing at BART* (West Lafayette, Ind.: Purdue University, 1980).

reers. Thus, the strength of their ethical position was partially undermined. The now-public attack on the competence and ethics of other engineers in the consortium and in BART management made a number of people very angry. At the same time, the dissenting engineers had lost credibility and become vulnerable. Their firing brought some support from professional engineering societies, but they were not reinstated.

The engineers suffered substantial financial and professional losses as a result of these events. All were unemployed for long periods and when they did obtain jobs, all three were at lower salaries. A suit that they brought against BART for a total of $875,000 in damages was settled out of court for $75,000, of which 40 percent went for legal fees.

But what about the validity of the three engineers' contentions? Was the train control system unsafe? In actual practice, it proved to be one of the safest in the country. But this appears to be because changes were made between the time the engineers were fired and the time full-scale operations began. Many knowledgeable people believe the engineers were substantially correct in what they advocated. A systems engineering group *was* subsequently organized. Whether these changes would have occurred without the three engineers'

actions is impossible to say. It does appear, however, that their concerns were the major spark setting off a legislative investigation that ultimately resulted in positions on the board of directors being made elective rather than appointive, and in bringing about the unseating of all but one board member. BART's general manager was also forced to resign.

A number of aspects of social responsibility and ethics in organizations are illustrated by the BART episode. The engineers felt a societal responsibility to protect the public from an unsafe train system. They had the knowledge, and professional ethics demanded that they act to prevent others from being seriously injured or killed. Yet in advancing their views in the way that they did, they opened the door to charges of unethical behavior on their own part:

> The engineers . . . appear to have taken the position that their ethical imperative was not satisfied until everybody else in the organization had done what they recommended. The position of BART management . . . is that the individual engineer has met his professional criterion for ethical behavior when he has as fully and specifically as possible reported to his supervisor any questions, concerns, or reservations he might harbor.[2]

> If, in the pursuit of some ethical ideal, individuals or groups violate another canon of ethical behavior, they seriously compromise their own position. And in management's view this is precisely what the three engineers did. In pursuit of the admittedly ethical and benevolent goal of improving the effectiveness of the train control system and thereby protecting the public safety, the engineers cast aspersions on the professional integrity of (other) engineers, undercut morale throughout the organization and, then, to compound this behavior, failed to own up to their actions but instead flatly denied their roles in the incident.[3]

In addition there is good reason to believe that these actions were taken, to a degree that varied among the three engineers, out of self-serving as well as ethical motives. The point is that, because differing values are often involved, one person's social responsibility and ethics may not be the same as another's. Additionally, appeals to ethics can be used to cover up underlying motives that are not nearly so worthy and to win support for behavior that would otherwise have little general appeal. As we will see throughout this chapter, issues of social responsibility and organizational ethics can become very slippery.

CONCEPTS OF SOCIAL RESPONSIBILITY

For whatever reasons, BART management ultimately created a train control system that provided extensive protection against accidents. This system was very costly and, because it shut down operation whenever control standards were exceeded, it introduced frequent delays. Nevertheless, BART management clearly viewed the provision of a wide safety margin to be the socially responsible thing to do. Yet others have viewed this same system as a reflection of irresponsibility in spending public funds, as an excessive preoccupation with technical gadgetry, and as a lack of concern for the time needs of the system's riders. Many of the same types of conflicting viewpoints surface in looking at concepts of social responsibility in business.

Conflicting Views of Social Responsibility

Historically, in the United States, concepts of social responsibility have gone through a series of changes. This has meant that managers have had to take differing sets of factors into account in planning and formulating strategies at different points in time. In general the changes have represented an increasing departure from purely economic decision making, with more and more considerations of other types being added. However, the earlier, more strictly economic views have not disappeared entirely.

The Purely Economic View

> There is one and only one social responsibility of business—to use its resources and engage in activities designed to increase its profits so long as it stays within the rules of the game, which is to say, engages in open and free competition, without deception or fraud . . . for corporate officials to make as much money for their stockholders as possible.[4]

The views expressed in this quotation are still held by some business executives today. In its present form, this view holds that it is business' role in society to provide goods and service, and to do this within certain rules established by society. In the vast majority of cases these rules are expressed as laws, thus establishing a moral minimum. Should business move beyond this minimum and do more for the social welfare, it would be usurping social and political activities that are the just province of government. The result would be a dilution of economic efficiency. To the extent that stockholders are deprived of profits, moving beyond the moral minimum is in fact unethical.

As Exhibit 13.2 shows, executives of large corporations see a decreasing commitment over time to the purely economic view of social responsibility, and to views that are close to it. The exhibit provides a scale of increasing departure from, or violation of, the ethics of basic economic concepts, and there is a clear shift up that scale. Yet it remains true that even the future projections do not envisage anything like a majority endorsement of social responsibilities that cut directly into profits. Perhaps this is why most managers prefer to avoid the term "social responsibility," in favor of such designations as public affairs, social action, and community relations.

Expanded Concepts   What are the arguments that might persuade business to go beyond the purely economic view, perhaps even to the point of reducing profits? Three considerations seem particularly important:

1. Corporations exist to serve various purposes for society; thus to the extent that society expects corporations to move beyond the purely economic sphere, and society is increasingly doing just that, corporations must do so.
2. It is in the self-interest of corporations to promote a better society because a better society provides better customers and fewer operating problems.

EXHIBIT 13.2 Reported recent past, present, and future views on social responsibility in 180 large corporations

**Degree of Departure
from Purely
Economic View**

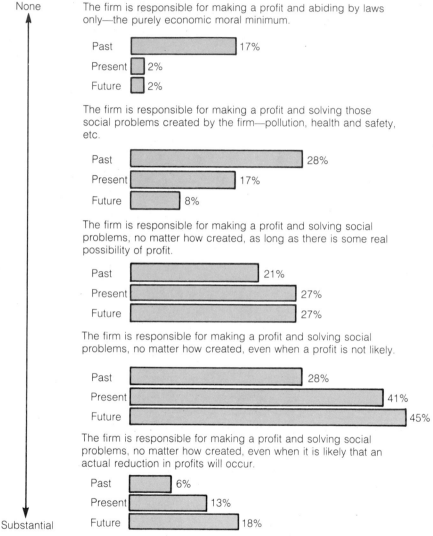

None

The firm is responsible for making a profit and abiding by laws only—the purely economic moral minimum.

Past — 17%
Present — 2%
Future — 2%

The firm is responsible for making a profit and solving those social problems created by the firm—pollution, health and safety, etc.

Past — 28%
Present — 17%
Future — 8%

The firm is responsible for making a profit and solving social problems, no matter how created, as long as there is some real possibility of profit.

Past — 21%
Present — 27%
Future — 27%

The firm is responsible for making a profit and solving social problems, no matter how created, even when a profit is not likely.

Past — 28%
Present — 41%
Future — 45%

The firm is responsible for making a profit and solving social problems, no matter how created, even when it is likely that an actual reduction in profits will occur.

Past — 6%
Present — 13%
Future — 18%

Substantial

SOURCE: Adapted from Sandra L. Holmes, "Executive Perceptions of Corporate Social Responsibility," *Business Horizons* (May–June 1976): 36.

3. The assumption of expanded social responsibilities reduces the pressure for governmental regulation of corporations; this in turn reduces costs and provides for a wider range of discretion in executive decision making.

These are not by any means all the arguments that could be and have been advanced in favor of an expanded business role on the social scene. They do, however, appear to be the most important ones. It should be emphasized that these arguments apply not only to operations within the United States, but to international contexts as well. Many companies operating in the less developed parts of the world have put a great deal of money into building hospitals and schools, for instance; the oil companies in Venezuela provide a case in point. This has occurred partly because the societies involved expected them to, partly because the creation of a healthier and better-educated populace was in the self-interest of the companies, and partly because doing this would serve to reduce governmental interference, including possible expropriation of company assets.

Realities and Resolutions   The various types of decisions potentially subject to social responsibility influences may be summarized as follows:

1. Decisions concerned with the traditional economic and technical activities of the firm.
2. Decisions generated by basically irresistible internal human and organizational pressures within the firm.
3. Decisions responding to government laws, regulations, and other mandates.
4. Decisions responding to demands from powerful groups in the environment, such as labor unions and environmentalists.
5. Decisions regarding socially oriented actions which, at the time they are taken, are voluntary.
   a. Decisions regarding new social programs.
   b. Decisions adding a social dimension to traditional actions in other categories.[5]

The first four types, although somewhat variable from company to company, are part of the realities of the world in which corporations function. These types of social responsibilities ultimately have to be assumed in some way by companies that have grown large enough to become highly visible in society. It is not realistic to say that companies should not assume them; they must if they are to survive.

Decisions falling in the fifth category are voluntary to a much greater degree. They do more than the law requires, although they may well anticipate public expectations and the possibility of future legislation. They often are aimed at generating good will and an image of social leadership for the company. But relative to the other four types of decisions, decisions of this fifth type can be expected to be few in number, and minimal in the dollars attached to them. Realistically, voluntary decisions in this category cannot absorb a high proportion of a company's budget. Because these decisions are widely publicized, there is a tendency to overestimate their magnitude. Thus, although companies cannot ignore social demands, they do not, and in the future are unlikely to, voluntarily expend really large sums on such social actions.

Furthermore, smaller companies can be expected to do less voluntarily than larger ones, and they may also be somewhat less responsive to social demands in making decisions of the first four types. This is in part because there are many more small firms than large ones, and each is less visible in the society as a whole; each is also less powerful and important. Many small firms are struggling to survive. It may not be realistic to expect them to do any more than that, and indeed, this appears to be the view of a sizable portion of the public.

Relationships to Profits As indicated in Exhibit 13.2, the way social responsibility relates to profits is a major concern. The concept of social responsibility used here assumes that what companies do to improve productivity, such as the purchase of more modern equipment, is socially responsible behavior; other things being equal, this type of behavior should have a positive impact on profits. Actions that improve the quality of the work force, provided the benefits exceed the costs, can have the same effect. Yet there are decisions made out of social responsibility considerations that can have the opposite effect. If a company installs expensive pollution control equipment not required by law and not purchased by its competitors in the marketplace, the cost of this equipment almost certainly will have to come out of profits.

There is ample evidence that, even within the same industry, certain companies are much more likely to incorporate social responsibility considerations in their planning and decision making than others.[6] In the paper and wood products industry, for example, pollution control is a major concern; in this industry, companies like Weyerhauser and Owens-Illinois historically have done much more than others, like St. Regis and Potlatch. In the petrochemical industry, Standard Oil of Indiana and Dow Chemical have been among the leaders, while Standard Oil of California and Texaco have come much closer to the purely economic moral minimum. The basic question, however, is how these differences relate to profitability.

Probably the best answer at present is that they are not related at all, at least in a causal sense. A recent review of studies in this area does find some instances in which social responsiveness was associated with *greater* profits, but the most common pattern was no relationship at all.[7] In those studies where a positive relationship was found, it is not possible to rule out the quite plausible hypothesis that profitable firms simply can afford to engage in more social action projects because they have the profits to fund them. There is no basis for concluding that greater social responsibility causes a firm to be more profitable, as some have contended. Nor can we conclude that social responsibility typically harms profits either, as many who endorse the moral minimum have hypothesized. Quite probably, the scale of strictly voluntary actions is so small relative to the scale of other factors that can influence profits that any effects on final results are totally hidden. Also, different types of programs can have differing consequences for profits, thus cancelling each other out in any overall result.

Humanism and Quality of Work Life

Exhibit 13.3 presents a matrix of expectations regarding social responsibilities. Three of the quadrants are covered well by the preceding discussion of conflicting views of social responsibility. To this point, however, the lower right quadrant really has not been considered. Part of an organization's social responsibilities are often said to be to its members—to produce satisfaction at work and a high quality of work life. If this is true, what does it mean?

The Humanistic View One view of internal social responsibilities originates in the writings of the Hawthorne researchers (chapter 3). It foresees and endorses a shift in values as indicated in the now almost classic statements in

EXHIBIT 13.3 Application of social expectation matrix to goals of productive organizations

	Expectations Regarding Task Performance	Expectations Regarding Cultural Performance
Expectations of External Effectiveness		
Nature	High quality, low price utility	Contribution to wide range of cultural values
By whom made	Consumers, clients, resource suppliers	Groups not connected with organization's primary task
Expectations of Internal Efficiency		
Nature	Efficient rationalization of internal resources	Contribution to employee satisfaction, or to quality of work life inside organizations
By whom made	Consumers, clients, resource suppliers	Two groups of internal members—managers and direct labor

SOURCE: Adapted from Charles E. Summer, *Strategic Behavior in Business and Government* (Boston: Little, Brown, 1980): 7.

Exhibit 13.4. The basic idea is that companies should take steps to become more humanistic and equalitarian. Arguments for this concept of social responsibility stem both from the Judeo-Christian ethic and from principles of democratic political process.

Inherent in this view is the belief that management should change its beliefs, attitudes, and behavior so as to move away from hierarchic, bureaucratic systems. On both religious and political grounds, these appeals often have considerable impact; on economic grounds they may not. The result can be conflict, both within and between individuals. Group-based systems and organization development, as discussed in other chapters, tend to reflect this humanistic view of internal social responsibilities.

Many believe that these approaches are truly socially responsible only to the extent that they in fact do make for a better work life for organization members, and also yield at least as large, if not a greater, economic contribution to society. This depends on the approach used, the individuals involved, and the surrounding situation. Merely because an approach is advocated as humanistic does not mean that in a particular application it truly will be. It is very difficult to say what a company's social responsibility is in this area—depending as it does on so many circumstances. Thus it seems wise to tread very gently here; one person's responsibility may well be another person's irresponsibility.

EXHIBIT 13.4   Value shifts inherent in humanistic view of social responsibility

1. Away from a view of people as essentially bad toward a view of them as basically good.
2. Away from avoidance or negative evaluation of individuals toward confirming them as human beings.
3. Away from a view of individuals as fixed toward seeing them as being in process.
4. Away from resisting and fearing individual differences toward accepting and utilizing them.
5. Away from utilizing an individual primarily with reference to his job description toward viewing him as a whole person.
6. Away from walling off the expression of feelings toward making possible both appropriate expression and effective use.
7. Away from maskmanship and game-playing toward authentic behavior.
8. Away from use of status for maintaining power and personal prestige toward use of status for organizationally relevant purposes.
9. Away from distrusting people toward trusting them.
10. Away from avoiding facing others with relevant data toward making appropriate confrontation.
11. Away from avoidance of risk-taking toward willingness to risk.
12. Away from a view of [group] process work as being unproductive effort toward seeing it as essential to effective task accomplishment.
13. Away from a primary emphasis on competition toward a much greater emphasis on collaboration.

SOURCE: Adapted from Robert Tannenbaum and Sheldon A. Davis, "Values, Man, and Organizations," in *Organizational Frontiers and Human Values,* ed. Warren H. Schmidt (Belmont, California: Wadsworth, 1970): 132–144.

The *Work in America* View   The idea that it is a company's social responsibility to provide a high quality of work life to employees is embodied in the human relations movement, various concepts of motivation and leadership, the whole idea of group-based systems, and numerous formulations of the organization development approach. For many this view is best stated in the 1973 report *Work in America,* developed by a task force convened by the Secretary of Health, Education, and Welfare.[8]

This report has received widespread circulation. It endorses various changes in society's approach to work, chief among which is a broad-scale redesign of jobs to make them more satisfying, challenging, and appropriate to the needs of the current work force—in short, job enrichment. According to the task force, changes in the desires, values, and capabilities of the work force have not been matched by changes in job requirements, and as a result the quality of work life has suffered. People have become dissatisfied and alienated at work, and extreme measures are needed to produce reversals of this trend. It is the social responsibility of modern corporations to introduce job enrichment on a massive scale to solve this problem.

Again, however, the difficulty is that employees are individuals, with individual needs and individual concepts of "enrichment." Enrichment programs might make a number of employees happy, given the greater challenge of their work. But others may become dissatisfied because they feel overloaded and overworked. At the very least, this view of internal social responsibility should be modified to incorporate differential application according to the needs and capabilities of the employees involved. Job enrichment does not always work to solve deep-lying problems of dissatisfaction.[9] And not all employees are dissatisfied, in any event.

It is easy for outsiders to say what actions must be taken by companies in the name of humanism and improved quality of work life. It is much more difficult for management to decide what really will accomplish these goals, let alone the extent to which this type of social responsibility should be endorsed. A number of companies have come to believe that the best solution is to design and organize jobs so as to contribute to organizational goals, and then to fill these jobs with people who are the most suited to them in terms of both performance effectiveness and job satisfaction. Humanism thus becomes a side benefit of the pursuit of other, more economic objectives.

Ethics, Morality, and the Law

It is not always a simple matter to distinguish between social responsibility and ethics, as is evident in the BART example. The two are closely related concepts, and in both instances a moral minimum is established by existing legal requirements. However, in practice, ethics tend to refer more often to actions of individuals in organizations, while social responsibility is used with reference to the organization as a whole. Ethics are concepts of right and wrong that stem from the values and expectations of society; or they may derive from some major sector of society. Thus, as in the BART case, we often hear reference to professional ethics. Certain industries over time have evolved codes of ethics dealing with issues like conflict of interest, misrepresentation of products, just pricing, safe operation, truth in advertising, fair competition, and the like.

The Current State of Business Ethics From media reports, it would appear that behavior in business has hit a new ethical low. But evidence supporting this conclusion is lacking. As indicated in Exhibit 13.5, managers in business and government tend to be split about equally as to whether managerial ethics

---

EXHIBIT 13.5 Responses of business and government managers to questions regarding ethics (percent agreeing)

	Business Managers	Government Managers
Present managerial ethics are superior to those of the past.	53	40
Managers feel under pressure to compromise personal standards.	64	60
It is possible to have good ethics in an organization and still have lower level people compromise their beliefs because of pressures for results from the top.	78	76

SOURCE: Adapted from James S. Bowman, "Managerial Ethics in Business and Government," *Business Horizons* (September–October 1976): 50–53.

have improved or not, although government managers are somewhat less optimistic on this score. Both groups recognize that pressures for unethical behavior are present in managerial work, and they are particularly sensitive to the conflicts between ethical standards and pressure for results at lower levels in hierarchic systems.

Data on the views of a cross-section of the U.S. population regarding the extent to which ethics are at a low level in various occupations indicate that sales occupations and elected officials are seen as more unethical, while the professions (with the notable exception of lawyers) receive a more favorable vote. As Exhibit 13.6 shows, business executives are at the average of the occupations considered.

These and other data seem to indicate that management as a group is not either particularly ethical or unethical relative to other groups in society. In all probability there has been little change in this regard over the years, although

EXHIBIT 13.6 Proportion of people viewing the honesty and ethical standards of various occupations as low or very low

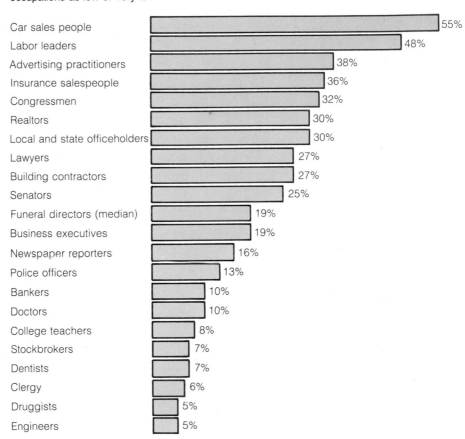

SOURCE: Based on Gallup Poll results as reported in *U.S. News and World Report* (September 6, 1982):29.

society does appear to expect more of business now, probably because its organizations are larger and more powerful. There is good reason to believe that bureaucratic organizations in general tend to arouse conflicts between pressure for results and ethics, and that they are prone to the loss of individual morality inherent in the groupthink phenomenon. This has always been true and will continue to be unless a new way can be found to deal with this type of problem. In any event, a view expressed some years ago based on an extensive study of the subject holds that any manager with a well-defined and reasonable ethical code can act ethically if he or she desires to do so without career damage resulting, and that in fact a great many managers do act in an entirely ethical manner.[10] This view appears equally valid today.

International Payoffs One of the areas in which media criticism has been most pronounced involves payoffs by large corporations that permit or facilitate doing business in various foreign countries; by U.S. standards, such payoffs constitute bribery and extortion. Yet the ethics and legalities involved vary substantially from one society to another. In the Middle East, for instance, political payments are deeply embedded in the fabric of the culture. Such payments may be for the purpose of reducing political risk, avoiding threats and harassment, reducing inflated taxes, inducing government employees to perform their duties, and obtaining or retaining business.

An example of what can be involved in payoff situations is provided by a statement from Castle and Cooke regarding the reasons for payments to military guards and local police to obtain security protection:

> This type of payment dates back more than 20 years and clearly arose from the Company's concern about the risk of physical harm to its personnel and the risk of loss or destruction of Company property. It must be remembered that many of the Company operations in foreign areas are necessarily conducted in rural areas where little or no governmental services exist, and incidents of murder, robbery, and vandalism are not uncommon. In one country where the law requires payment of all wages in cash, the Company is required to handle payrolls in the hundreds of thousands of dollars on a regular basis and therefore needs armed guards to safely fulfill its payroll responsibilities. In at least one country, the Company is prohibited from maintaining a private security force and therefore has no alternative but to look to the military to provide soldiers to serve as security guards for the Company. In countries where civilian police forces existed the Company sometimes felt it necessary to make private payments to police officials to be assured of timely and adequate police protection in emergency situations such as occurred during an unruly labor strike. Although the laws of the various countries varied somewhat, legal opinions from independent attorneys in the principal countries involved have advised the Company that virtually all such payments were lawful and customary in the countries involved.[11]

Exhibit 13.7 provides information as reported to the Securities and Exchange Commission on the prevalence of payoffs in different industries. The data may not be complete, but the large variations from one industry to another appear to be rooted in fact. In part these variations reflect the needs of companies in various industries, their degree of dependence on governmental functionaries, and the social customs of the countries in which they operate. But, as noted previously, there are certain industry-based codes of ethical conduct, and these may play a role as well.

EXHIBIT 13.7 Proportion of companies in various industries reporting foreign payoffs

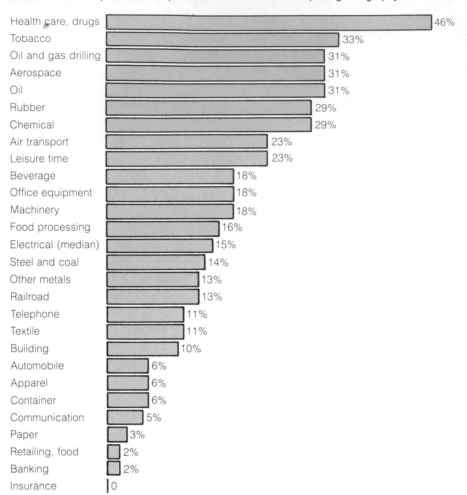

Industry	Percent
Health care, drugs	46%
Tobacco	33%
Oil and gas drilling	31%
Aerospace	31%
Oil	31%
Rubber	29%
Chemical	29%
Air transport	23%
Leisure time	23%
Beverage	18%
Office equipment	18%
Machinery	18%
Food processing	16%
Electrical (median)	15%
Steel and coal	14%
Other metals	13%
Railroad	13%
Telephone	11%
Textile	11%
Building	10%
Automobile	6%
Apparel	6%
Container	6%
Communication	5%
Paper	3%
Retailing, food	2%
Banking	2%
Insurance	0

SOURCE: Adapted from Neil H. Jacoby, Peter Nehemkis, and Richard Eells, *Bribery and Extortion in World Business* (New York: Macmillan, 1977): 141.

Theft in Organizations Another important topic, although not usually given the same degree of publicity as international payoffs, is theft by employees at all levels from their employers. The ethical status of this type of theft is much less clear in U.S. society than, for instance, armed robbery. In some cases, what is taken seems to be viewed as part of just compensation for work performed. Thus, office supplies, tools, food, and certain types of company products may be taken for personal use rather openly in certain firms without much concern being aroused. In some parts of the country, domestic workers have for years been taking food, clothing, and other items home with them at the end of the day, almost by tacit agreement, without employers even mentioning it. It is much easier in such cases to say what is illegal than to say what is unethical. The ethics involved depend on the local culture.

However, there is a great deal of theft in organizations that is both illegal and clearly unethical, much of it planned and operating on a large scale.[12] Banks lose much more money to employees than to holdups. Retail stores lose more to employees than to shoplifting. Scrap dealers systematically send runners into manufacturing plants to solicit metal thefts by employees. Production records are regularly altered to cover thefts made, not for personal use, but for sale in the open market. Managers divert business from their employers to their own private firms, with all the costs of securing the business paid by the employer. This list could be extended indefinitely. Many small companies fail because they cannot protect themselves against internal thefts. It is estimated that about 15 percent of corporate pre-tax profit is normally absorbed in this manner.

Given the financial scale involved, companies need to include consideration of such matters in their planning. It accomplishes nothing to pretend that theft does not exist. If its potential existence is recognized, steps to reduce it can be taken. The money involved can be sufficient to make the difference between the success and failure of a particular strategy.

CORPORATE RESPONSES TO SOCIAL EXPECTATIONS	The preceding discussion provides some ideas regarding the nature and scope of social responsibility and ethical considerations. This is an area of considerable disagreement and controversy, but it is very important to organizations, because they can lose badly should they run afoul of either legal requirements or strong social expectations, as BART ultimately did. This section presents a consideration of some corporate social responses, and how they can be reflected in policy and implemented.

Types of Response

The following statement, which reflects the views of the chief executive officer of Procter & Gamble, is typical of those coming from companies that are actively involved in social responsibility efforts of one kind or another:

> Company management must consistently demonstrate a superior talent for keeping profit and growth objectives as first priorities. However, it also must have enough breadth to recognize that enlightened self-interest requires the company to fill any reasonable expectation placed upon it by the community and the various concerned publics. Keeping priorities straight and maintaining the sense of civic responsibility will achieve important secondary objectives of the firm. Profitability and growth go hand in hand with fair treatment of employees, of direct customers, of consumers, and of the community.[13]

When evidence linking its product to toxic shock syndrome began to emerge, Procter & Gamble not only took its "Rely" tampon off the market, thus negating a $75 million investment and twenty years of research, but also, the company initiated an expensive advertising campaign to retrieve the tampons, offered to buy back unused products including free promotional samples, undertook an educational campaign dealing with toxic shock syndrome, and funded new research on the disease. These efforts went well beyond merely protecting the company against possible liability. Thus, they reflect one kind of social responsibility.

The Range of Activities Exhibit 13.8 lists a number of social responsibility activities in which companies have engaged. This list is by no means all-inclu-

EXHIBIT 13.8 Corporate social responsibility programs in rank order of expected future priorities as indicated by company presidents

Most often of high priority ↑	Response to changing aspirations of minority groups and female employees
	Improvement of physical working environment, including safety
	Job enrichment programs
	Better consumer relations
	Increased employee participation in decision making
	Product safety improvement
	Contributions to urban or community improvements
	Reduction of damaging environmental effects
	Support to education
	Truth in advertising/marketing
	Employee volunteerism programs such as sabbaticals
	Support to the arts
	More purchasing from minority vendors
Less often of high priority ↓	Improved relations with socially oriented investors such as churches and universities

SOURCE: Adapted from John L. Paluszek, *Business and Society: 1976–2000* (New York: AMACOM, 1976): 34.

sive, but there is a clear indication that efforts directed toward employees, often involving humanism and the quality of work life, tend to have very high priorities. Many of the high-priority areas also are ones in which considerable legislation has been enacted and/or the possibility of legal liability exists. This does not necessarily indicate an absence of voluntary efforts, however. Legislation and increasing numbers of court cases typically reflect a focusing of social concern in a particular area. One would expect companies to turn to these same areas in initiating social programs, simply because the companies are subject to the same social forces as are others in society.

Industry Variations The types of social responsibility actions companies take and the directions they emphasize are in many cases associated with the particular industry they are in. In Exhibit 13.9, nine areas are noted, but only one, charities, is considered among the most important in all five industry groupings. Not surprisingly, conservation of resources is uniquely important to the oil and gas companies; urban renewal and development, to a company grouping that contains finance (mortgages), insurance, and real estate companies; and consumer protection, to wholesale and retail trade. Companies clearly tend to focus their efforts in areas that are close to their major endeavors. This appears appropriate. Not only can the firms bring greater expertise to these

EXHIBIT 13.9 Ranked importance of areas of social involvement in various industries

Area of Social Responsibility	Oil and Gas	Finance, Insurance, and Real Estate	Wholesale and Retail	Manufacturing	Transportation, Communication, and Utilities
Pollution control	1	*	*	3	5
Resource conservation	2	*	*	*	*
Education	3	3	*	2	3
Recruitment and development of minorities	4	*	4	4	2
Charities	5	1	2	1	1
Community affairs	*	2	1	5	4
Recruitment and development of females	*	4	3	*	*
Urban renewal and development	*	5	*	*	*
Consumer protection	*	*	5	*	*

NOTE: * indicates not in top five.

SOURCE: Adapted from Sandra L. Holmes, "Adapting Corporate Structure for Social Responsiveness," *California Management Review* (Fall 1978): 51.

areas, and probably greater motivation or energy, but also there is the prospect of achieving both socially responsible actions and a profitable return on these investments at the same time.

Policies and Their Implementation

Experience and research have now accumulated to the point where it is possible to become quite specific about how planning for social actions should be carried out and what types of policies are likely to be most fruitful. This knowledge has not come easily. A number of firms have launched with reckless abandon into areas they know little about, with all best intentions, only to suffer unnecessary losses and accomplish little. It is clearly not enough to want to help. One has to know what one is doing as well.

A Suggested Policy Statement   Exhibit 13.10 contains a comprehensive policy statement appropriate for firms that wish to become involved in social responsibility activities. This is a statement that fits with the views expressed by Procter & Gamble's chief executive officer. It assumes that companies do have a major commitment to contribute to the economic needs of society. It also assumes that, under appropriate circumstances, a company can act in ways that yield both positive economic outcomes and social contributions. It should seek these circumstances wherever possible, but not limit itself to them. Finally,

EXHIBIT 13.10 Policies governing company social actions

It is the policy of this company to:

1. Think carefully about its social responsibilities.
2. Make full use of tax deductibility laws through contributions when profit margins permit.
3. Bear the social costs attendant upon its operations when it is possible to do so without jeopardizing its competitive or financial position.
4. Concentrate action programs on limited objectives, thus limiting and focusing actions.
5. Concentrate action programs on areas strategically related to the present and prospective functions of the business, begin action programs close to home before acting in distant regions, and deal first with what appear to be the most urgent areas of concern to the company.
6. Facilitate employee actions that can be taken as individuals rather than as representatives of the company.
7. Search for product and service opportunities to permit this company and others to make profits while advancing social interests; however, not all social actions should be taken solely for profit.
8. Take actions in the name of social responsibilities, but not at the expense of the level of rising profits needed to maintain the economic strength and dynamism desired by top management.
   This policy expands traditional profit policy so that the overall mission becomes:
   a. To set forth and achieve corporate objectives that meet specified social challenges ranging from product quality to quality of life requirements, both internally and externally.
   b. To increase the company's earnings per share at a rate required to meet shareowner profit expectations and these new requirements as well.
9. Take socially responsive actions on a continuous basis rather than *ad hoc,* one at a time, or for a short duration.
10. Examine carefully the social needs the company wishes to address, the contributions the company can make, the risks involved for the company, and the potential benefits to both company and society—all before proceeding with any program.

SOURCE: Adapted from George A. Steiner and John F. Steiner, *Business, Government, and Society* (New York: Random House, 1980).

policies related to social responsibilities should be based on the same degree of rational planning and effective decision making as any other policies. Social programs have a tendency to elicit emotional responses from managers. It is important, once decisions are made, to handle the program as rationally as one would other types of strategies and policies.

Planning and Implementing   Exhibit 13.11 is addressed to the planning process and implementation; it fits the concept of social responsibility into the overall process of managing. Larger firms have typically created special positions to serve as a focus for activities of this kind. In a few cases, representatives of important social groups in the environment have been co-opted within the board of directors. In other cases, specific individuals have been given responsibility for these programs, on occasion heading up an entire department. This shift to the creation of a separate department has been most com-

EXHIBIT 13.11 Guidelines developed from research for implementing social programs

Management Functions	Specific Activities
Planning	Develop knowledge about environment in which program will operate.
	Set realistic objectives that are not overly ambitious and that can be verified.
	Set realistic timetables for implementation of various program parts.
	Provide for participation of lower level managers in planning.
Organizing	Delegate much of planning function to staff specialists, allowing time for both technical and administrative learning.
	Delegate authority for actual operation of program to line managers.
	Hold line managers responsible for achieving program goals.
Staffing	Select appropriate staff personnel to work with the program, who have a favorable attitude toward social issues involved and are skilled in organizational implementation.
	Replace line personnel who demonstrate they will not support the program.
Influencing	CEO should support the program visibly.
	Communicate purposes and appropriate details of program to employees, using two-way communication procedures wherever changes may be threatening or information easily misinterpreted.
	Establish performance evaluation and reward systems to reinforce desired behaviors.
Controlling	Modify management information system to incorporate information on social performance.
	Feed information into performance evaluation and planning systems.

SOURCE: Adapted from Edmund L. Gray, "Planning for Corporate Social Programs—Problems and Guidelines," *Long Range Planning* (April 1981): 51–53.

mon in industries subject to considerable governmental regulation—for example, transportation, communication, and utilities. In any event, the important point is that once the planning process incorporates a substantial social responsibility commitment, implementation should occur in essentially the same way as with any other commitment. Attention should be given to organizing for the conduct of the activity, staffing, influencing performance, and maintaining carefully developed standards; that is, specific standards of socially responsible behavior must be stated and events continually monitored to see that they are met.

Social Auditing

As a result of the increasing pressures in recent years for companies to take on social responsibilities, a type of report has been developed called the social audit. Social audits are prepared in a variety of ways; they are most likely to be prepared by company personnel, but outside consultants, accounting firms, research organizations, and public action groups may also be involved. The term *social audit* implies a control process with strict enforcement procedures analogous to those in financial auditing. This was originally envisioned when the approach was proposed some forty-five years ago, and there have been proposals to establish comprehensive federal standards and legally required audit procedures.[14] To date, this has happened on only a limited scale, and in fact, many so-called social audits are not technically audits at all.

Types of Audits Exhibit 13.12 sets forth a definition of social auditing and describes a number of types of audits. The definition is all-inclusive, and all the elements are not always present in a specific application.

The first two types of social audits relate to the external control of corporate social performance. In the case of government-mandated audits, the law requires companies to provide certain information, and there are agencies that can go in and check this information as well as obtain other data to see whether legal compliance has occurred. If it has not, the government can bring various sanctions to bear, including enforcement through the courts. Most areas included

---

EXHIBIT 13.12 Social auditing and some approches used

Social Audit.	A systematic attempt to identify, analyze, measure, evaluate, and monitor the effect of an organization's operations on society, including specific social groups, and on the public well-being.

Government-mandated Audits

Content	Analytical or numerical measurement of the organization's performance in certain mandated areas—environmental pollution, employment discrimination, industrial safety and health; also, description of practices, policies, and organizational features related to problem area.
Preparer	Company personnel
Auditor	Respective governmental agencies
Use	Enforcement of governmental requirements in mandated area
Scope	Whole company or division

Social Performance Audit

Content	Critique of company or industry performance in selected areas of social concern—pollution, minority hiring, operations in South Africa.
Preparer	External critics
Audience	Investment community and interested public
Use	Negative publicity for company or industry, with intent of influencing investment decisions and thus inducing company compliance
Scope	Selected companies

Constituency Group Attitudes Audit

Content	Analytic measurement of attitudes and preferences of groups affected by corporate actions regarding various areas and issues of social concern; groups may include employees, stockholders, suppliers, customers, local citizens, and general public.
Preparer	External consultant or research firm
Audience	Company management and interested public
Use	Management review of social impacts and communication to public
Scope	Whole company or divisions, or specific areas of social concern

EXHIBIT 13.12   (continued)

Macro-Micro Social Indicator Audit

Content	Numerical assessment of company performance relative to a set of social indicators developed at a national or regional level; indicators may include health and safety, education, housing, transportation, income levels, cultural activity, citizen participation, and the like.
Preparer	At macro social indicator level—public or private agencies; at micro company performance level—company personnel
Audience	Company management, shareholders, and interested public
Use	Management review of social performance; communication to shareholders and public
Scope	Whole company or divisions, or specific areas of social concern

Social Balance Sheet and Income Statement

Content	Social performance stated in dollar terms, using conventional accounting and financial categories.
Preparer	Expert company personnel
Auditor	Accounting firm
Audience	Company management and interested public
Use	Management review of cost-benefit ratios and communication to stockholders
Scope	Whole company

Social Process/Program Management Audit

Content	Quantitative, descriptive, and analytic assessment of organizational performance in selected programs of social significance.
Preparer	Company personnel or external consultants
Audience	Company management and interested public
Use	Management review of program effectiveness and communication to public
Scope	Specific programs

SOURCE: David H. Blake, William C. Frederick, and Mildred S. Myers, *Social Auditing: Evaluating the Impact of Corporate Programs* (New York: Praeger, 1976): 3–15.

under the social responsibility concept are either not audited in this manner, or if they are, the legal requirements can be viewed as a moral minimum. In the case of social performance audits, corrective action is to be achieved through economic rather than legal pressure. Public action groups conduct the audits using externally available data and then use what they find to attempt to influence potential or present owners of a company's stock. The idea is to punish the company for social transgressions by driving down the value of its stock.

In contrast, constituency group attitudes audits, macro-micro social indicator audits, social balance sheet and income statements, and social process/program management audits are prepared by or for management, for its own purposes. If corrective actions are involved, they occur within the firm; they do not come from the outside. Two other types of reports of this kind are often labeled as social audits; these are not explicitly included in Exhibit 13.12. One is the report derived from human asset accounting procedures as discussed in chapter 8. In this case,

EXHIBIT 13.13 Outline of a social process/program management audit report

> *Introduction*. Identification of audit team; authorization source of audit; dates conducted.
>
> *Summary Statement*. Summary of major findings; summary of recommendations; references to details in the body of the report.
>
> *Presentation of Findings*. History and rationale of audited activity; identification of focal areas of audited activity, including goals, inputs, implementation, outputs; findings related to each focal area.
>
> *Analysis of Program Processes*. Goal achievement, input adequacy, implementation effectiveness, assessment of outputs.
>
> *Problem Identification and Analysis*. With respect to goals, inputs, implementation, outputs, the data base.
>
> *Recommendations*. Actions to be taken with regard to goals, inputs, implementation, outputs, the data base.
>
> *Audit Evaluation*. Limitations of the audit methodology, the auditors, the data-cost considerations.
>
> *Appendixes*. Definition and rationale of social process/program management audit; methods used in conducting audit.

SOURCE: Adapted from David H. Blake, William C. Frederick, and Mildred S. Myers, *Social Auditing: Evaluating the Impact of Corporate Programs* (New York: Praeger, 1976): 81–82.

dollar values are placed on the human assets and external good will developed by the company, in a manner generally comparable to that used in the social balance sheet and income statement approach. In addition many companies develop inventory-type statements listing and describing social programs to be publicized. Often these are added to the annual report to stockholders. There are no criteria or standards for evaluating company performance in most cases, and in fact a question can be raised as to whether the definition given in Exhibit 13.12 is approximated closely enough to use the term *social audit* at all.

Exhibit 13.13 presents a sample outline for a report of a social process/program management audit. A report of this kind is highly analytic and evaluative, not merely descriptive, and consequently seems to justify the use of the audit designation.

The Roles Social Audits Play   One obvious intended purpose of social audits is external control of company performance. To the extent that this is achieved through government-mandated reports and effective auditing by government agencies, audits appear to work. But this is only a small part of organizational social responsibility and ethics. Efforts made by public action groups to depress the stock prices of companies that are viewed as less socially responsible have not proved very effective as an external control. Social performance audits conducted by external critics, and in fact negative evidence regarding company social responsibility and ethics generally, appear to have little impact on the investor community—either in the short or long term.[15]

A second major role is in management's efforts to exercise control internally with regard to social responsibilities. Here the social audit approaches can be very useful in inducing divisions and other units to meet goals and standards for social performance—safety standards or minority hiring requirements, for instance. However, it appears to be necessary to either repeat the audits frequently or monitor performance on a continuing basis to get the desired results. The extent to which social auditing for internal control achieves its objectives depends in any event on how well the control process is designed and administered. The control of social responsibility is no different from any other type of control in this respect.

Social audits, as conducted in practice, have increasingly taken on a third primary role and in doing so have moved from the realm of controlling to representing and public relations. Here the designation *social audit* appears to be a misnomer. The essential objective is to show the public, or some particular group such as stockholders, what the company is doing with regard to social responsibility, thus to neutralize social pressures and generate good will. These are really social reports, and their content and/or the extent to which they are publicized are influenced by a desire to present the company in a favorable manner. Without question, reports of this kind, where a company has made significant contributions, serve a useful purpose in representing that company to its publics. But the designation as an audit may be only part of the representation process, intended to convey an image of authenticity.

REPRESENTING AND PUBLIC RELATIONS

In chapter 1 representing was defined as involving efforts to influence external forces such as laws, societal values and ethics, resources, and customer or client attitudes with the goal of creating a favorable climate for the organization to operate in. Clearly this type of activity is closely allied to matters of social responsibility. In both cases, there are objectives such as creating good will, preventing restrictive legislation, and dealing effectively with ethical and other crises the company may face. How this representing function and public relations generally are conducted has important implications for a company's overall effectiveness.

The Scope of Activities

Activities involving representing and public relations primarily involve the management component, particularly top management, and a public relations function. The latter is often headed by a vice-president. Some firms have created specific departments to handle social responsibility programs; on occasion these departments and public relations are welded into one. In addition, outside public relations firms are often employed, particularly when a company faces a crisis with regard to its public image. The advantage is that these firms may have dealt with a similar problem for another client, and thus may be in a position to provide expertise the company itself does not possess. Generally charitable activities intended to generate good will are handled though a separate tax-exempt foundation created by the company. Activities such as advertising and personnel recruiting also involve an element of representing, as may almost any other task where the company person involved must deal with some external public—from union representatives to stockholders.

Coping with Environments   Representing, then, can occur at many points within an organization, but in each instance its task is to cope with some aspect of the external environment. Often outside forces operate to exert influence or power so that company actions are restricted. Laws passed by government, contracts signed with a union or supplier, boycotts imposed by consumers, evaluations of the firm by financial analysts all serve to limit what a company can do. The degree of discretion possible in making decisions is correspondingly reduced. In a very real sense, corporate decisions are funneled in particular directions by these outside forces.

Representing and public relations are involved in coping with environmental forces in two ways. The first is essentially one of making the most of compliance and adaptation. An effort is made to present the organization in as favorable a light as possible, so that a maximum of good will is generated. Thus, when firms comply with social responsibility pressures, they take steps to make known what they have done, and they attempt to carry out the activities themselves so as to get the maximum mileage from their efforts.

A second type of effort is focused not on adaptation to environmental forces, but on a more direct attempt to alter the environment. The objective is to blunt pressures, change the balance among forces, or promote the emergence of new power sources. For example, laws can be changed so that they are more favorable to a company or permit a greater degree of discretion than existed previously. At one point, Bethlehem Steel Company moved its senior public and government relations executive into the presidency of the company in order to exert maximum pressure in the Washington scene.

Specific Public Relations Activities   In general, public relations personnel are more concerned with the techniques and methods of presenting a message than with formulating the content of the message itself. The public relations function provides expertise in verbally representing an organization to various publics. Exactly what that message is and what the policies are that govern it may be influenced somewhat by public relations specialists, but generally the major decisions are made elsewhere, usually by top management.

Public relations are intended to win people to causes and products, to attract people to the company as a place of employment, to encourage favorable responses from the financial community, and to create a positive image in the local areas where the firm operates. As a result, public relations people become involved in many aspects of company operations. Their job is to generate good will, or at the very least to prevent bad will, wherever contact with some kind of public exists.

Normally a sizable part of the work is focused on press relations. Public relations specialists also draft speeches for managers, prepare stockholder publications, encourage employee participation in community affairs, and conduct tours of company facilities. The scope of the function tends to vary from one company to another, and also, the type of function tends to be influenced strongly by the nature of the business. Public relations for a bank involve a substantial emphasis on community relations to attract depositors and borrowers. In a wood products firm, the major concerns are much more likely to be pollution, perhaps safety, and government relations.

Recently, public relations people in some companies have become involved in preparing and placing so-called advocacy advertising. Here, advertising space is purchased to express a company viewpoint on some issue that is controversial and important to the organization. The major objectives are to:

Counteract public hostility that is rooted in ignorance or misinformation.

Restrict the spread of misleading information by company critics, and explain complex issues that are not widely understood.

Foster the values of the free enterprise system.

Overcome inadequate access to the news media and biases that exist there.[16]

This type of corporate advertising is done on occasion simply to generate good will and associate the company with socially acceptable positions. Thus at one point Young and Rubicam, an advertising agency, ran a magazine ad urging people to vote in an upcoming election, without any reference to particular candidates, parties, or issues. This type of approach is not very common, but it does have a public relations function.

Political and Government Relations. Many companies have become heavily involved in attempts to influence federal and state legislation. They may maintain a staff in Washington, D.C. and in certain state capitals for public relations and lobbying purposes. These staffs also serve to gather information, explain government actions to company management, and support government sales. Activities of this kind may require considerable top management time. Often it has proved more effective for companies of a like mind on an issue to band together through trade associations or other groups to present a unified position. Many top level executives regularly devote a portion of their time to representing the company within and through such groups.

In addition, companies attempt to influence those holding political office by first influencing public opinion via newspapers, magazines, radio, television, films, interviews, speeches, and advertising.[17] The result may be that elections are shifted in a manner consistent with company desires, or a legislator may perceive certain opinions among the voters at home and act accordingly on the floor of the house. Political contributions may be made to candidates who are friendly to a company's views. Mail and telegram campaigns may be mounted to influence legislators. Thus business enters the political arena, along with, and in much the same manner as, numerous other groups that seek to influence legislation in their own interests.

How actively companies seek to influence legislation typically depends on the degree of existing political intervention in the industry. The appropriate relationships, and some typical industries at each point, are depicted in Exhibit 13.14. Here company patterns of action are designated in three categories—sensing, progressive, and aggressive. Sensing involves having an early warning system so that attempts to change legislation in a manner adverse to the company are spotted when they first emerge. A progressive posture goes beyond watching into direct corporate lobbying and involvement in the administrative proceedings for setting forth regulations. For example, McDonald's made a direct, though to date unsuccessful, attempt to exempt part-time teenage employees from the minimum wage law in order to reduce its labor costs. An aggressive stance goes even fur-

EXHIBIT 13.14 Managerial intervention in relation to political intervention in the industry

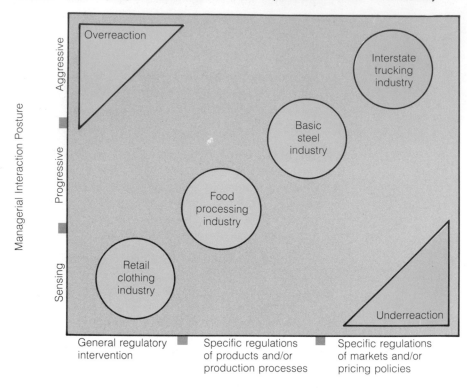

Degree of Political Intervention in the Industry

SOURCE: Marianne M. Jennings and Frank Shipper, "Strategic Planning for Managerial-Political Interaction," *Business Horizons* (July–August 1981): 47. Reprinted by permission of the publisher.

ther and may involve court tests of laws to see how judges will actually interpret them. In the trucking industry, both the companies and the union have combined their lobbying efforts to the same ends, thus producing a particularly effective political coalition.

Influencing the Corporate Image

A corporate or organizational image is the total of all impressions in the minds of various publics—customers, suppliers, bankers, stockholders, potential investors, competitors, government officials, and the general public. These impressions are created by dealings with these groups, by products, services, business transactions, community relations, securities investments, labor relations, employment interviews, and many other factors. This image may be focused on certain symbols such as corporate names, trademarks, emblems, and the like. Yet it may also be influenced by a host of relatively simple things such as the way a telephone call is handled, the decor of a building, the number of typing errors in a letter, and the forms used in billing.

Conflicting Forces A favorable corporate image can contribute to sales and earnings. However, the creation of such an image is not entirely under company control. Public relations efforts can play a positive role, but they can come into conflict with other forces in the environment that serve to tarnish the image. Thus in spite of management's best efforts, BART was not able to prevent a great deal of negative publicity associated with legislative investigation. Ultimately BART's public image become so bad that the organization was totally reorganized and restaffed at the top.

Similarly, Procter & Gamble was initially tarnished by the association of its name and product with toxic shock syndrome, even though the company had no knowledge of the existence of the disease at the time the Rely tampon was put on the market. The cyanide deaths resulting from Johnson & Johnson's Extra Strength Tylenol, the effects on the cigarette companies of research into links between smoking and cancer, and Ralph Nader's charges regarding product safety in the automobile and other industries all involve uncontrolled outside forces that had adverse effects on corporate images.

Many companies lack a meaningful corporate image. Others have outdated images as a consequence of mergers, acquisitions, and divestitures. In both cases, new images must be created. The anonymity or impressions of the past must be overcome and a new set of opinions established. Such image creations present a substantial public relations challenge. Not infrequently, companies mount extensive campaigns around new names or insignia in these cases. A firm may attempt to portray itself as innovative, growing, a good neighbor, well-managed, socially responsible, and the like. Public relations campaigns of this nature can prove highly successful if they build upon real and established strengths of the concern. If other messages coming from the company conflict with their public relations materials, intentional image-building becomes almost impossible. Thus an image of sound management is very difficult to create in the face of frequent revelations in the press that reflect on the ethics, dedication, and organizational commitment of top management.

Different Publics   Exhibit 13.15 presents the results of an attempt to measure an organizational image as reflected in the perceptions of several different publics. These data were obtained as part of a social audit of the organization. It is apparent that the various publics considered have rather different images. In particular, the community leaders tend toward somewhat negative perceptions. It appears that the department falls down most in terms of the community and the social responsibilities these individuals wish it to undertake. On the other hand, the several minor creditors of the department have a very positive image. The data for these external publics can also be contrasted with the perceptions of internal groups. Here, too, there is variation, with the managers being very positive and the employees generally being neutral.

These results appear to be typical. Variations among publics are likely to be present, and it thus becomes crucial to focus public relations efforts where they are needed—on publics that carry a more negative image and on those that are considered to be of greatest importance. It is also characteristic that management has a more positive image of the organization than other groups. This can represent a major problem. Groupthink may well be at work, and management may have a difficult time recognizing the negative realities in its environment. In such cases, public relations and effective representation efforts tend to be minimal.

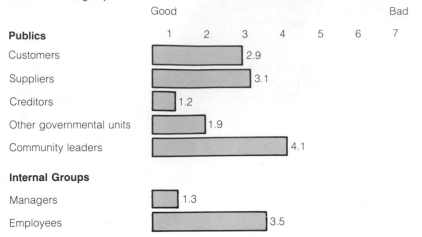

EXHIBIT 13.15 Images of the Fayetteville, Arkansas Sanitation Department held by various publics and internal groups

SOURCE: Adapted from Robert D. Hay, "Social Auditing: An Experimental Approach," *Academy of Management Journal* (December 1975): 874–875.

Little is done until the situation escalates to crisis. Then the typical response is to hire an external public relations firm to put out the fire—something it may or may not be able to do.

Summary

There is no unanimity as to what business's social responsibilities are. Views range from the purely economic to an expectation that firms should engage in extensive social expenditures in a wide range of areas, even if profits are substantially reduced in the process. In support of the expanded concepts, it is argued that companies must serve the expectations of the larger society, that it is in their self-interest to promote a better society, and that assuming social responsibilities reduces the pressure for governmental regulation. In practice many decisions falling in the realm of social responsibility are unavoidable. Voluntary social actions, in contrast, represent a rather small part of overall company operations, even in the larger firms where they are most prevalent. Perhaps as a result of this, studies relating company social responsiveness to profits have failed to establish any consistent relationships.

The social responsibility concept includes not only activities external to the organization, but also the improvement of the quality of work life at home. This latter concern has become associated with democratization of the workplace and with extensive job enrichment. Yet to the extent these approaches are suited to some individuals and not others, companies face a problem; they may improve the quality of work life for some at the same time that they decrease it for others.

While social responsibility is essentially an organizational concept, ethics deal primarily with the actions of individuals. Current business managers appear to be neither more nor less ethical than their predecessors, and also about at the average among occupational groups. Two areas of special ethical concern have been international payoffs by U.S. corporations and thefts by employees at all levels from their companies. In both cases, the ethical issues involved may be clouded by social norms and values that make these behaviors acceptable. Yet both can be very costly to a company, and it is in the company's interest to hold them to as low a level as possible.

Many companies have undertaken a wide range of programs in the name of social responsibility. The specific types selected appear to depend on both the focus of governmental legislation and the particular industry involved. These programs have become increasingly effective as experience has accumulated; it has proved possible to develop policies that integrate them with the traditional profit goals of the firm. Rational planning and decision making are essential, as are implementation procedures that fit with the management process as a whole. Social audits have demonstrated usefulness for maintaining internal control over planned socially responsive activities and for publicizing what a company is doing in this area. They may also be used in connection with efforts by government or public action groups to impose external controls on company behavior related to social issues.

Efforts in the area of social responsibility almost inevitably become associated with representing the firm to its publics and with public relations generally. Not surprisingly, companies want to get as much mileage from their activities as possible—both in influencing external forces such as legislation and in stimulating good will. Much of the work needed to get that mileage is provided by public relations specialists who write speeches, prepare press releases and annual reports, develop advocacy advertisements, and the like. Often the need is to extricate the company from a crisis associated with product safety or perhaps business ethics. Government relations are a major activity for many companies, either involving the direct lobbying of legislators or efforts to change public opinion so as to influence legislative actions indirectly. How aggressively companies pursue this process of influencing government is in large part determined by the extent of political intervention in the industry involved.

A major objective in dealing with outside publics is to foster a favorable corporate image. This is not something that can be accomplished by a public relations campaign alone. But campaigns that build upon real company strengths can prove highly effective. The important thing is that other messages coming from the firm do not contradict the intended image. Also, the campaign must be directed at specific publics—particularly those of great import for the company and those holding the more negative images.

What Have You Learned?

1. Why do companies become involved in political and government relations? How do they do this, and how does the corporate image relate to the degree of success?
2. What types of social programs and activities do companies engage in? Which of these appear to be of the highest priority, and how are industry variations determined?
3. The "quality of work life" concept had its origins in various sources and is reflected in a wide range of company actions. How have these sources operated, and what actions are

advocated? Does the fact of individual differences present any problems for the quality of work life concept? If so, how, and what can be done about it?

4. What is whistle-blowing, and what arguments can be advanced for and against it?

5. Various types of social audits serve varying purposes for different groups. What are these purposes, and how effective is a social audit in achieving them?

6. There appear to be major differences between small and large firms in their handling of social responsibilities. What are these differences, and why do they exist?

7. How are public relations activities carried out, and how do they fit into the strategic and policy processes of a firm?

8. As companies have developed experience with social responsibility programs, what types of policies have proved most fruitful in this area? How may economic and more expanded social goals be coordinated?

9. In what sense may international payoffs and employee thefts be considered illegal, but not unethical? How should companies deal with these matters?

10. What is the purely economic view of business social responsibility, and how does it contrast with other, expanded views? What arguments have been advanced for these expanded views?

How Well Can You Apply Your Knowledge?

Problem 1. A medium-sized bank located in a large southeastern city had grown rapidly as a result of the astute investment policies of its chief executive and principal stockholder. This individual was strongly committed to the free enterprise system. He believed that a bank's primary role in society was to return a profit, and that many banks were less successful than they might be because they had diverted their energies to various community activities and social programs. Investing in the rebuilding of poverty-stricken neighborhoods, hiring inexperienced minorities and women when experienced white males were available, and spending management time on charity campaigns were not what a bank should be doing, in his view. In fact, these activities were really unethical because they diluted the profits—and worse still, the profit drive—of the organization. The chief executive felt strongly enough about this that he had for some time made it a condition for serving on the bank's board of directors that the individual hold similar views to his own.

The only real exception to this policy was his son, who served on the board of directors and who did not share his father's purely economic concept of social responsibility. Apparently, the older man was willing to overlook such a difference from his children, though not from anyone else. Furthermore, the son had proved himself to be a first-class banker, and there was little chance that the board as currently constituted would begin acting like "do-gooders."

Upon the father's death, the son assumed his position as the bank's chief executive, in accordance with long-standing expectations. The transition went smoothly, and by the time a year had passed, the son had established himself firmly in the new position. At that point he began to consider the possibility of reversing existing policies and moving more actively into community activities and other types of social programs. He was aware of the various arguments for improved quality of work life also, and believed something should be done in this regard for the bank's employees. To do anything substantial along these lines, however, he would need the support of the board of directors.

Several factors operated to bring this matter to the forefront. The son was a deeply religious person, and this fact had conditioned his attitudes regarding social responsibility in business for many years. Recently he had held several discussions on the subject with the rabbi at his synagogue and as a result had substantially increased his personal contributions to religious charities. He believed that the bank had grown to a sufficient size and achieved a degree of community visibility that it simply could not continue in its previous, non-involved course. Finally, the composition of the board of directors and its overall viewpoint had changed somewhat, and he believed there was some possibility of getting the board to take a more open view on the matter of social responsibilities than it had in the past.

Questions

1. In this situation, what arguments might the new chief executive use with his board of directors to get them to support an expanded view of the bank's social responsibilities?
2. What basic policy stance might the bank take in this area, given that the board still had a number of members, if not a majority, whose primary allegiance was to the purely economic moral minimum? What specific statements should be included in a revised policy document?
3. What types of activities and programs should the bank become engaged in, both externally in the community and internally among its employees? How should the bank go about planning for and implementing these activities?

Problem 2. The woman in charge of equal employment opportunity compliance for an electric utility in a large metropolitan area had been given a new challenge. In fact, she believed that her job had been enriched to the point where the whole thing might have been overdone. She had been put in charge of a team made up primarily of line managers and public relations people with the task of updating the firm's image in the equal employment area. It had been strongly hinted that one way of contributing to this objective might be to conduct a social audit focused specifically on this topic.

There was no question that the subject was an important one for the firm. For many years there had been practically no blacks or females employed, except in low-paying labor and clerical positions. This had not represented a special problem since it did not violate the social conscience of either the community or the employees at the time. Then, in the late 1960s and early 1970s, the situation changed rapidly. Government compliance officers seemed ever-present. Installations were picketed by minority action groups, discrimination suits

were filed, and the firm became the major local target of feminist activists. The union, which had been equally remiss, moved rapidly to put its house in order; the company, placed on the defensive, did not move as fast, and found itself at a disadvantage by contrast. All of these developments were documented in painful detail by the local media. Almost every day the newspaper discussed some new discrimination problem or a new charge lodged by the National Association for the Advancement of Colored People (NAACP), the Urban League, or the National Organization for Women (NOW).

It was not long before the company had a terrible image as a place to work and in the community generally. Meter readers were beaten up, applicants no longer sought employment with the utility, and problems in collecting utility bills increased sharply. Gradually, the company did improve its performance in the equal employment opportunity area. Minorities and women began to move into better-paying, higher-level jobs. The proportion of women employed actually increased to a point exceeding the proportion in the local labor force, and minorities also achieved at least equal representation. A black man was elected to the board of directors. The company spent a great amount of money advertising for and recruiting minority job applicants in the predominantly black south side of the city. The government compliance officers recognized the efforts, and their visits became less and less frequent. Still the old image lingered on.

The media continued to play up the slightest sign of discrimination, and the social action groups were unrelenting in their pressures. Employee suits against the company for discrimination were no longer joined by the Equal Employment Opportunity Commission, but they continued nevertheless. This is why the team headed by the equal employment opportunity officer had been put together. There was a distinct need to update the firm's image in this area—both in the community generally, which of course included customers, and among employees. The idea of developing a social audit was to focus on company programs in this specific area and bring them to public attention.

Questions

1. How might a social audit for this purpose be carried out, what form should a report take, and how could the audit be used to improve the company's image with regard to discrimination? If you were the person in charge of the team, how would you go about your task in this regard?

2. What other approaches could be used to update and improve the company's image in this area? How might the public relations people contribute to these efforts?

Additional Sources for More Detailed Study

Aram, John D. *Managing Business and Public Policy: Concepts, Issues, and Cases.* Marshfield, Mass.: Pitman, 1983.

Carroll, Archie B. *Managing Corporate Social Responsibility.* Boston: Little, Brown, 1977.

Carroll, Archie B. *Business and Society: Managing Corporate Social Performance.* Boston: Little, Brown, 1981.

Center, Allen H., and Walsh, Frank E. *Public Relations Practices: Case Studies.* Englewood Cliffs, N.J.: Prentice-Hall, 1981.

Corson, John J., and Steiner, George A. *Measuring Business's Social Performance: The Corporate Social Audit.* New York: Committee for Economic Development, 1974.

Davis, Keith; Frederick, William C.; and Blomstrom, Robert L. *Business and Society: Management, Public Policy, Ethics.* New York: McGraw-Hill, 1984.

Elkins, Arthur, and Callaghan, Dennis W. *A Managerial Odyssey: Problems in Business and Its Environment.* Reading, Mass.: Addison-Wesley, 1981.

Fritschler, A. Lee, and Ross, Bernard H. *Business Regulation and Government Decision Making.* Cambridge, Mass.: Winthrop, 1980.

Hay, Robert D. and Gray, Edmund R. *Business and Society: Cases and Text.* Cincinnati, Ohio: South-Western, 1981.

Luthans, Fred; Hodgetts, Richard M.; and Thompson, Kenneth R. *Social Issues in Business: Strategic and Public Policy Perspectives,* New York: Macmillan, 1984.

Miles, Robert H. *Coffin Nails and Corporate Strategies.* Englewood Cliffs, N.J.: Prentice-Hall, 1982.

Post, James E. *Corporate Behavior and Social Change.* Reston, Va.: Reston, 1978.

Preston, Lee E. *Research in Corporate Social Performance and Policy.* Greenwich, Conn.: JAI Press, 1978 and following years.

Preston, Lee E., and Post, James E. *Private Management and Public Policy: The Principle of Public Responsibility.* Englewood Cliffs, N.J.; Prentice-Hall, 1975.

Richards, Max D. *Organizational Goal Structures.* St. Paul, Minn.: West, 1978.

Seitel, Fraser P. *The Practice of Public Relations.* Columbus, Ohio: Merrill, 1984.

Sethi, S. Prakash, and Swanson, Carl L. *Private Enterprise and Public Purpose.* New York: Wiley, 1981.

Sturdivant, Frederick D. *Business and Society: A Managerial Approach.* Homewood, Ill.: Irwin, 1981.

Weidenbaum, Murray L. *Business, Government, and the Public.* Englewood Cliffs, N.J.: Prentice-Hall, 1981.

Notes

1. The following discussion is based on Robert M. Anderson, Robert Perrucci, Dan E. Schendel, and Leon E. Trachtman, *Divided Loyalties: Whistle-Blowing at BART* (West Lafayette, Ind.: Purdue University, 1980).

2. Ibid., p. 235.

3. Ibid., pp. 169–70.

4. Milton Friedman, *Capitalism and Freedom* (Chicago: University of Chicago Press, 1962): 133.

5. George A. Steiner and John B. Miner, *Management Policy and Strategy* (New York: Macmillan, 1982): 62.

6. See Harold L. Johnson, "Ethics and the Executive," *Business Horizons* (May–June 1981).

7. Peter Arlow and Martin J. Gannon, "Social Responsiveness, Corporate Structure, and Economic Performance," *Academy of Management Review* (April 1982).

8. James O'Toole, et al., *Work in America: Report of a Special Task Force to the Secretary of Health, Education, and Welfare* (Cambridge, Mass.: MIT Press, 1973).

9. Edwin A. Locke, David Sirota, and Alan D. Wolfson, "An Experimental Case Study of the Successes and Failures of Job Enrichment in a Government Agency," *Journal of Applied Psychology* (December 1976).

10. Raymond Baumhart, S. J., *An Honest Profit* (New York: Holt, Rinehart and Winston, 1968).

11. Castle and Cooke, Inc., *Report on the Investigation Conducted by the Finance and Audit Committee of the Board of Directors with Respect to Payments to Foreign Governments and Officials* (Honolulu, Hawaii, July 1976): 4.

12. Richard J. Tersine and Roberta S. Russell, "Internal Theft: The Multi-Billion-Dollar Disappearing Act," *Business Horizons* (November–December 1981).

13. Edward G. Harness, "Views of Corporate Responsibility," *Corporate Ethics Digest* (September–October 1980).

14. Archie B. Carroll and George W. Beiler., "Landmarks in the Evolution of the Social Audit," *Academy of Management Journal* (September 1975).

15. See H. Russell Fogler and Fred Nutt, "A Note on Social Responsibility and Stock Valuation," *Academy of Management Journal* (March 1975); and Neil H. Jacoby, Peter Nehemkis, and Richard Eells, *Bribery and Extortion in World Business* (New York: Macmillan, 1977).

16. S. Prakash Sethi, *Advocacy Advertising and Large Corporations* (Lexington, Mass.: Heath, 1977): 57.

17. George Schwartz, "Lobbying Effectively for Business Interests," *Business Horizons* (September–October 1981).

READINGS AND EXECUTIVE PROFILES

Conversation with Reginald H. Jones and Frank Doyle
Charles Fombrum
Organizational Dynamics

Top Management's Role in Strategic Planning
Donald R. Melville
Journal of Business Strategy

The Impact of Consumer Trends on Corporate Strategy
Sandra D. Kresch
Journal of Business Strategy

James E. Burke and Johnson & Johnson Company

Planning, strategy formulation, and decision making at the top levels of large, successful corporations provide the central theme for these selections. How have companies gone about doing strategic planning and making major decisions? It is important to understand how these processes operate and what influences them.

The Fombrum publication reports on an interview with the former chairman and chief executive officer of General Electric and with the senior vice-president of corporate relations employee, public, and government. The selection given here is from the first part of the interview, which primarily concerns the company's experience with strategic planning. Under Reginald Jones, General Electric was widely regarded as the best-managed company in the world. Under John Welch, his successor, the company has done very well, but does not have quite the same stature. Nevertheless, it was rated at the top of the electronics and appliances industry in the *Fortune* survey.

The short piece by Donald Melville, chief executive of the Norton Company of Worcester, Massachusetts, describes some of that company's experiences with strategic planning. Norton is a very different type of firm from General Electric, and accordingly, it has taken a different route.

Sandra Kresch takes a consultant's eye view of strategy formulation at General Mills. The company is a major marketer of consumer products, and the article points up how acquisition and market strategies have been adapted to changing consumers and changing needs. This is a very good example of how consumer analyses can influence strategy. General Mills is ranked first in the food industry by the *Fortune* respondents. Notice that, at all three companies—General Electric, Norton, and General Mills—there were false starts in strategic planning before the systems really began to work well.

The executive profile of James Burke at Johnson & Johnson deals with the overall strategic stance of that company and how it has structured itself to make strategic decisions and carry them out. James Burke's decisions at the time of the Tylenol poisonings demonstrate the effectiveness of the system, while at the same time providing an example of decision making with major social responsibility overtones. Johnson & Johnson is rated top in the pharmaceuticals industry in the *Fortune* survey, and third among all 200 companies in quality of management, long-term investment value, financial soundness, and community and environmental responsibility. It is first in use of corporate assets, and is the third most admired company in the United States, just behind IBM and Hewlett-Packard.

Conversation with Reginald H. Jones and Frank Doyle

Professor Charles Fombrum

When Reginald H. Jones retired as chairman and CEO of the General Electric Company (GE) on April 1, 1981, he left to his hand-picked successor, John F. Welch Jr., an organization widely regarded as the best-managed company in the world (*Fortune,* April 1981). With a record earnings of $1.5 billion on $25 billion in sales, profits have tripled over a ten-year period on a 160 percent increase in sales. No one doubts that much of the credit belongs to Jones.

In a conversation with Professor Charles Fombrun of The Wharton School, University of Pennsylvania, Reginald Jones and Frank Doyle (senior vice-president of corporate relations at GE) describe some of the ideas and systems that have contributed to making GE the best-managed company in the world and Jones perhaps the premier organizational statesman of the decade.

FOMBRUN: GE is particularly noted for its excellence in two core areas: strategic planning and human resources management. GE's strategic business units (SBUs) have become common parlance in the corporate world, and few companies have achieved as much sophistication in either strategic planning or employee management as GE has. How did these ideas evolve, and what kinds of systems did you put in place to link human resources management with strategic management?

JONES: Let me start with a little history to give you some background on how we got at strategic planning. We had been organized on a decentralized basis at GE from about 1951 forward—and the decentralized organization consisted of a number of departments, divisions, and groups on a line basis. There were some 200 or so of these departments, each one a distinct business enterprise. On the staff side, we were organized into what were called services. For example, there was a vice-president of

Excerpted, by permission of the publisher, from "Conversation with Reginald H. Jones and Frank Doyle" by Charles Fombrum, *Organizational Dynamics,* Winter 1982, pp. 42–48 © 1982 by AMA Periodicals Division, American Management Associations, New York. All rights reserved.

manufacturing services, a vice-president of financial services, and one for employee relations—except that, as I recall, we called it employee and community relations.

Now, what would happen when a major business problem or business opportunity developed for General Electric? The operating business closest to the problem or the opportunity—whether it was a department, division, or group—would generate a proposition and a so-called business plan for the chief executive officer. The CEO, in turn, would call on the various services for counsel. Well, counsel from the vice-president of manufacturing services took a manufacturing point of view, engineering gave him a technical point of view, and marketing presented a marketing point of view. All this left the CEO with a number of memoranda—each one addressing a slice of the problem, but none taking an overall business point of view.

None of them asked things like whether the proposition fit with the mission of the General Electric Company, or whether we had the necessary resources—human, physical, or financial—given all the other problems and opportunities facing the corporation as a whole. Frankly, the CEO decided that he could not assume the burden resulting from this procedure. So, in about 1970, he created something we didn't have before: a corporate executive staff. He took three of us and said: "First, I want you three fellows to look at some of our major business problems and some of the significant opportunities available to us, and then come up with a system within General Electric that will give us a basis for doing some business planning. I'm looking for some long-range plans for this company—some vision of where we should be taking it." Our discussion focused on strategic, not tactical, planning.

Our major problem then was a confluence of three very disparate businesses, all requiring enormous investments at the same time. We were entering—or re-entering, really—the commercial aircraft engine business; we had the nuclear business, which was a real problem in those days; and we had the computer business, which was already absorbing just about every spare cent General Electric had, and was going to require very major investments. The CEO suggested that we start by looking at those businesses in considering a planning system for General Electric.

FOMBRUN: You did this in addition to your regular activities?

JONES: No, we were divorced from our normal activities. We set out on this venture by launching three major studies. The results on the study of the computer business led us to sell it because, given the other things we wanted to do, it was going to absorb too much of our resources. Study results of the nuclear business led us to make drastic changes in some of our approaches to it and put it on a more solid footing. And results on the commercial aircraft engine business led us up the road to one of our greatest successes.

At the same time, we brought in the McKinsey people and the Boston Consulting Group people to work on developing a planning system. Of course, the planning system developed then was rudimentary compared with the one we have today. But the concept of a strategic business unit evolved out of all that work. We looked at our company and said we didn't see how it would be feasible for us to develop detailed strategic plans for something like 200 business departments. We argued that there should be a way to look at them that would pull together the businesses that were similar. So we developed a set of criteria for what came to be known as a strategic business unit.

FOMBRUN: What were some of the criteria?

JONES: Oh, such things as a distinct market, a distinct set of competitors, and a distinct mission—that is, distinct from other entities within the company. We found, for example, that a number of departments in the major appliance business—the range department, the refrigerator department, the dishwasher department, the laundry department, and so on—were really one strategic business unit because they had a common set of competitors, a common set of customers, common markets, a common mission.

So we were able to group together a significant number of entities into one strategic business unit from which we would get one strategic plan. Our first cut left us with nearly 50 strategic business units. A few were quite small—for instance one that we called our commercial equipment department, which made commercial cooking equipment sold only to restaurants and fast-food people. Their mission, their competitors, and their markets were distinct from anything else General Electric was doing. Right alongside this was an SBU several hundred times larger; it was responsible for all the white goods, yet it was just one strategic business unit. So a strategic business unit could be anything from a department right up to a division or even a group.

By grouping things in this way, we were able to spend enough time looking at strategic business plans to get a reasonable understanding of them. It required a tremendous amount of effort, even though we kept a corporate executive staff in place to review these plans—review them not from a functional viewpoint (we still had that coming to us from the former services), but from a *business* executive's viewpoint. Well, after we'd developed these strategic business plans and had begun to gain some appreciation of them, we found that, again, we were committing too much of the time of the corporate executive office—the chairman and the vice-chairman. That was when we went to the sector approach.

FOMBRUN: So the sector approach was a structural change provoked by GE's need for more sophisticated planning?

JONES: Yes. We divided the company into six sectors because although the businesses had individually distinct missions, markets, and so on, they also had a lot in common. This presented a great opportunity for all kinds of symbiotic action and planning among the businesses. To test the concept, we first set up one sector for a period of slightly more than a year—and that one consisted of all the businesses that dealt with what we called our consumer markets: businesses like small appliances, television, lamps, radios, and so on.

Again, we found opportunities to do things on a larger scale when we grouped businesses that had a lot in common than when each one handled its own affairs. In corporate advertising, for example, we found not only that we made a greater impact on the consumer, but that we could do so at considerably less expense (or could use the extra money for greater coverage) when we scheduled the advertising of the small appliances, the major appliances, televisions, lamps, and so on to get consistency. Instead of having all their advertising hit in one month, with nothing for the next month, we could get a consistent approach—we could do some scheduling. We also found that, by George, you could get some extra mileage out of putting a small appliance on a counter when you were advertising a kitchen, instead of featuring just the major appliances in the kitchen.

The sector approach brought another dimension to our strategic planning. The real test, of course, was to classify the businesses in such a way that we could apply our available resources most effectively—focusing on those businesses that offered more profitable opportunities for the company.

Sure, we classified our businesses—but we didn't go to the four-box matrix that so many companies use: the stars, the cash-cows, the dogs, and the question marks. Instead, we went to a nine-box matrix. Some situations obviously called for a harvest/divest decision. Some were just as obviously businesses in which you were going to make major investments for growth. In between were a lot of businesses that had to be approached with selectivity—and we graded those on the nine-box matrix, with reasonable success.

FOMBRUN: Did you try to measure your success rate?

JONES: Interestingly, after we'd been doing our strategic planning for a couple of years and trying to allocate our resources on the basis of those plans, we went back to look at our resource allocation and asked: Where did we actually spend our money? Where did we authorize appropriations? Where did we put development funds, and so on? We found that the funds had been going just where they should have been going. That is, the fellows in the upper-left corner of the matrix were getting what they wanted, and those down in the lower-right hand corner were on very short leash. In between, of course, there were gradations. And this relationship has held up ever since then: Our funds have been going where we intended them to go.

The results, over a decade, have been rather startling. When we started all this, the international activities of General Electric accounted for some 16 percent of our net income—and we knew we had tremendous opportunities offshore that we weren't capitalizing on when we went into our strategic planning. (Now, however, the situation is different. Last year the international share of our net income was up to roughly 40 percent of the total.) We knew that the utility businesses had peaked and were not going to continue with the growth we had witnessed over several decades, so we had to do some cutting back on them. The percentage of our net income that came from the electrical equipment businesses, which had been our core for many years, dropped sharply.

FOMBRUN: How far?

JONES: Let me just give you those numbers. As we started in the '70s the electrical core of the business—electrical equipment, supplies, and apparatus—represented 80 percent of net income. At the end of that decade it represented only 47 percent of net income. It hadn't dropped—in fact it was much higher at the end of the decade than at the beginning. What had happened was that our materials businesses, which we saw as great growth opportunities—our new engineered plastics, our man-made diamonds, our carboloids, and the like—grew from some 6 percent of our net income to 27 percent ten years later. Of course, we knew that services in a post-industrial economy were going to grow and they did—moving up from 10 percent to 16 percent of our net. And as we strengthened our commercial aircraft engine business, our locomotive transportation business moved from 4 percent to 10 percent. Obviously, then, we saw our strategic planning pay off.

FOMBRUN: Most of the implications you mention seem to leave off what many would consider a vital aspect of strategic planning, namely the human resources dimension. To what extent were human resources considerations included in the planning process?

JONES: I was getting to that. When we classified these businesses, and when we realized that they were going to have quite different missions, we also realized we had to have quite different people running them. That was where we began to see the need to meld our human resources planning and management with the strategic planning we were doing. If you're going to grow a business, you have to provide it not only with physical resources, but with human resources as well. You have to have specific types of people running those businesses. This is where you need the bold entrepreneurs. When you get to the harvest/divest stage, you've got to have the type of management that really knows how to control costs, and can at the same time be looking for opportunities to sell off a piece of the business or to price a piece of the business so that it becomes more profitable. We found to our great surprise, for example, that some dog businesses which weren't yielding very much for us were more important to our customers than we appreciated. And when we raised our prices to see whether the markets would stand it—a make or break move that would decide whether we'd stay with a business or close it down—people responded and the businesses became more profitable. But, again, it took a manager who was more concerned with cost control than with entrepreneurship.

Frank, why don't you explain the human resources planning systems that we put in place to match what we were doing in strategic planning.

DOYLE: As Reg mentioned, this started with the build-up of a need for specific management and executive talent to run specific businesses—to move people with distinct kinds of personal assets into areas they were suited to. Of course, there are some who can do it all—but they are few. The second need in this regard is that when you begin to take a longer-range look at the business, you have to start taking a much longer-range view of available executive manpower and where that manpower is coming from. So the first pass focused heavily on, not human resources planning as we use it today, but where the system grew in sophistication over the decade: the manpower planning system. And most of that manpower focus was on executive and managerial manpower.

FOMBRUN: It was really the fit with the strategic plan: manpower planning as a requirement for effective strategy implementation.

DOYLE: That, I think, was the lead. But what we found, for a lot of reasons, was that the current availability of managerial manpower or technical manpower was not the total equation. There were several reasons for this. Society began to look at corporations as more than just employers. As the businesses changed more rapidly, as their life cycles altered, the external world began to penetrate the decision process—particularly in the area of human resources management. So we began to consider how to introduce the concept of human resources in conjunction with strategic thinking or strategic management planning, without going back to the days of services and narrow functional views.

The great debate of the mid-'70s focused on how to introduce a more forceful look at human resources, production resources, technical resources planning—without functionalizing the strategic planning system. That was the effort. We found that we needed to get human resources considerations introduced into the planning process at an earlier stage—because if we waited until the plans were formalized and then stepped back, the human resources decisions were already made—and a lot of them were necessarily accommodating, since they were treated as a derivative rather than a primary function.

FOMBRUN: In other words, make the human resources dimension a driving force in the formulation of strategic plans rather than consider it as an implementation issue.

DOYLE: Yes. The decision was clear-cut—that is, human resources strategic planning was not to be conducted as a separate activity. Rather, we were going to have strategic planning with a human resources input at every stage. The reason I mention each stage is that some issues, clearly of a human resources nature, could be identified at the SBU level. For example, a business recognizing that it was moving into a heavy electronics concentration knew it would need a different mix of manpower than its ordinary systems would generate. And a business entering a harvest/divest condition knew that it might have to close plants.

The reason we then took a next-level look is that some problems representing human resources issues were generated by the cumulative impact of several discrete SBU decisions. The biggest, I think (and it also correlated with our emerging electronics issue), is that we needed to change our image on campus in view of our forecast cumulative need for electronics talent. And this was so not in terms of 1978 needs, 1979 needs, or even '81 needs—but '85, '86, and '87 needs. Knowing that our business strategies were going to take us into a different kind of manpower requirement, we began to make investments in a campus presence reflecting '86 needs rather than our '76 needs.

We also began to see that the second major effort we needed was a better quantitative fix on the external environment—to pull together such obvious things as demographics, trends in social legislation, relocation, plant closings. As we looked at what was happening both to General Electric and to the U.S. economy as a whole, it became quite obvious that a major dynamic in the late '70s and on through the '80s would arise from the emergence of new businesses and the need for old businesses to die, or be sloughed off. We had an issue that required us to start doing some early planning—on, for example, what products we put into our plants to make sure we didn't impact the community precipitously.

Top Management's Role in Strategic Planning

Donald R. Melville

The 1970s were a successful decade of growth and diversification for Norton Company. In 1979, sales exceeded $1 billion, ranking Norton 261 on the list of *Fortune*'s 500 industrial companies. Half of Norton's sales were made outside the United States. In 1979, the company's return on equity was 20 percent. Norton maintained a leading market position in its historical business, abrasives, and in half a dozen other industries.

One of Norton's most significant acts in this decade of growth was to disband its corporate planning department. While the planning department was doing a very effective job, top management perceived that the planners were the wrong people to be doing the job.

At Norton Company, strategy is the business of line managers. The line manager's knowledge, experience, skill—even his gut feel—are indispensable to realistic planning. In addition, the best-conceived strategy is worthless if it's not well implemented. People are much more likely to wholeheartedly implement a plan if they have played the leading role in developing it.

Three Key Roles

At Norton, top management plays three important roles—guide, interpreter, and asker of difficult questions—in the planning process. In his guiding role, the top manager must keep an eye on long-range goals for the total corporation, to see that a line manager's strategy fits into the overall direction of the company. He must have a view of the company in general, a concept of what he wants it to be, as well as an understanding of all its particulars.

As an interpreter, he must try to understand, and help others in the company understand, the

Donald R. Melville is President and Chief Executive Officer, Norton Company.

Reprinted by permission from *The Journal of Business Strategy,* Spring 1981, Copyright © 1981, Warren, Gorham & Lamont Inc., 210 South Street, Boston, Mass. All rights reserved.

social, political, and economic trends outside the company and how those trends could influence the company's future.

As an asker of difficult questions, the top manager must continually challenge the prevailing orthodoxy, the conventional wisdom. By its very nature, an organization becomes bureaucratic, and its people will devise the obvious solutions. The top manager must be prepared to ask the probing, the difficult, even the embarrassing questions.

Norton Company uses well-known planning techniques but top management probably spends more time and has greater involvement in both the planning and implementation process than at many other companies.

Managing the Portfolio

The heart of the process is the portfolio management concept. By working with portfolio charts, such as growth/market share matrices, managers answer the questions: What are we now? What are we trying to become? Can we get there and, if so, how will we do it? Every business is, of course, a portfolio of many businesses. At Norton, there are about forty separate strategic business units among seven major businesses. To understand the position of each individual unit, you have to know its position in its industry's life cycle, its rate of growth, and its market share relative to that growth. Then, with knowledge of the experience curve and an evaluation of future trends, perceived competitive patterns, and available resources, one can predict its potential return and the optimum strategic path to follow. To evaluate the unit, one must see it in terms of the direction in which the corporation is moving as a whole. What might be good business for Norton might not fit at all in the plans of another company.

Additionally, it is important to weigh the attractiveness of the industry in which the SBU is operating. There can, after all, be greater differences in profitability between industries than between companies in the same industry.

How the Strategy Guidance
Committee Works

In 1972, Norton formed a top management committee whose job is to continually look at the company's businesses, and to develop and monitor the portfolio, from the viewpoint of achieving Norton's corporate objectives.

At the moment, this committee, the Strategy Guidance Committee, has fourteen members—the CEO, the financial vice-president, eight top vice-presidents in charge of operations, the controller, assistant controller, vice-president for corporate development, and an assistant vice-president. Each of these individuals spends at least 10 to 20 percent of his time on strategic planning. When top managers clearly define strategy with and for the line manager, top managers do not then have to spend as much of their time actually running the business. Consensus has been found and, therefore, delegation will work.

The line manager in charge of each strategic business unit comes before the committee about every two years with a detailed strategy for each major segment of the unit's operations. A review every two years is about right for top management to be assured that the unit's strategy is viable and that it is still in harmony with overall corporate objectives.

The Strategy Guidance Committee looks at a strategic business unit from many viewpoints—return on net assets, return on sales, asset turnover, market share strategy. The committee might test sales growth rate against market growth rate against market share strategy. The committee also looks at competition, relative strengths and weaknesses, and cash generation plotted against market share strategy. It also places the unit on a balloon chart or growth/market share matrix for the entire company, to see how this unit fits in with all the others.

Asking the Right Questions

While looking at the unit from all possible angles, the committee asks a lot of questions:

How does this unit contribute to the overall scheme of things?

Does it help to balance the total?

Does it increase or decrease the cyclical nature of the company?

How does it relate to other Norton technologies, processes, or distribution systems?

How successfully does it compete?

How is it regarded by its customers and by its competitors?

Does it hurt or improve the company's image with the investment community?

What are its mission and mode of operation in terms of build, maintain, or harvest?

Is its current strategy appropriate?

Can we win and, if so, how?

If it has changed its strategy or performance since the last review, why has it changed?

What does our analysis suggest about the unit's profitability in comparison with similar businesses?

The Strategy Guidance Committee meets about twenty-five times a year—an average of about two meetings per month—for two to five hours, to review line managers' strategies and, if necessary, to discuss acquisition candidates. Once a year, the committee updates Norton's regular five-year financial model, which provides a major progress check on planning, and discusses the overall corporate mission and objectives.

While this top management committee is obviously very powerful, it takes no votes, approves no capital expenditures or budgets. Its most important role is to keep everybody moving in the same corporate direction.

The company's overall strategies are presented annually to Norton's Board of Directors to ensure that there is agreement with the general direction being charted by the management of the company. The board, by asking searching questions, provides an important check to ensure objectivity.

Case Study: The Coated Abrasive Division

The recent experience of the Coated Abrasive Division is a good illustration of this process at work. Norton was founded nearly 100 years ago as a grinding wheel manufacturer. In the 1930s, it acquired a coated abrasive business. By 1970, Norton's abrasives businesses had good market share in slow-growth markets. The abrasives businesses were seen as cash generators for Norton's growing portfolio of nonabrasive businesses which would be the key to future growth. The company hoped that the nonabrasive businesses would offset the cycles of abrasives, which follow the ups and downs of the manufacture of durable goods.

In the early 1970s, the Coated Abrasive Division in the United States was having difficulties. Market share and profitability were declining. The company undertook a major restructuring program in 1974 that emphasized substantial cost reductions to make the division more competitive. In spite of this restructuring, market share and profitability continued to decline for another two years.

In 1976, the Strategy Guidance Committee decided to evaluate again the long-term strategy for the Coated Abrasive Division. The corporate objectives were twofold:

Norton intended to remain the worldwide leader in abrasives.

Management wanted to increase overall profitability by diversifying into nonabrasive businesses, using abrasives as the cash generator for this diversification.

It wasn't clear to the Committee that the Coated Abrasive Division could fulfill its corporate role as a cash generator.

Picking the Strategy

The line manager of the division, who thought it could, had developed a strategy for maintaining market share. He wanted to complete the restructuring and cost-reduction programs that had been launched two years before. He thought that with some more time the organization could be consolidated into a coherent team, and a focused marketing effort through segmentation could be pursued on the basis of some strengths that had emerged during the restructuring. He also recommended directing a larger percentage of research resources into an emerging new product line and technology. He thought that this strategy would eventually allow the division to be the cash generator it was intended to be, and also allow it to continue as the technical focal point for coated abrasive operations overseas.

A PIMS (Profit Impact of Marketing Strategies) analysis, which Norton received as a subscriber to the Strategic Planning Institute, suggested a different strategy. It suggested a moderate harvest strategy.

During its discussion, the Strategy Guidance Committee looked at what the future would probably be for the coated abrasive industry. The consensus was:

It would experience low growth and only gradual change.

There would be no major changes in manufacturing technology, but the division could slowly develop some important new abrasive products.

Except for one significant competitor, the return of most companies in the business was below the U.S. industrial average.

The committee studied a summary of the market share strategies for all the businesses in Norton's portfolio. A growth share matrix showed the division to lie well in the undesirable low-growth/smaller-than-competitor quadrant, which meant that it was not a very desirable business. When the committee applied its cash generation versus market share test to the line manager's proposed strategy, it found that the combination of maintaining market share and generating cash was acceptable if the market share could be maintained.

To maintain or to harvest? In the end, the committee decided not to harvest the division, but to take the approach of careful segmentation, building on some strengths, and harvesting only those portions where position was irretrievably weak. There were several reasons for this decision.

First, and most important, coated abrasives complemented Norton's grinding wheel business and therefore strengthened the company's distribution network. It didn't seem wise to harvest, at that time, such an important part of the abrasives business which is still the guts of the company.

Another reason for the decision to maintain was that continuing research and development efforts in the United States would benefit Norton's large overseas coated abrasives operations.

Back on Track

Since that 1976 decision, the restructuring of the division continued with additional emphasis on organization development—getting the right people

into the right positions. Norton is now successfully building some of its coated abrasives businesses and has introduced new products by capitalizing on advances in product development and manufacturing technology. The company is also successfully harvesting parts of the business. The division's line manager has developed the appropriate segmentation and the appropriate strengths.

The repair of the Coated Abrasive Division is still in progress. Since 1976, its profits have at least doubled. It is moving toward a positive cash flow. It seems clearer now that it would have been a mistake five years ago to harvest the whole division. The line manager saw this, from his close knowledge of the strategic segments of the business and the division's strengths relative to its competitors. The top managers on the Strategy Guidance Committee also saw this, from their perspective on overall corporate strategy.

Planning in the 1980s

How will Norton's planning process change in the 1980s? Top management's involvement—and line management's—will remain much as it is. If a planning department is reinstituted, the planners will work closely and intensely with the line people on current planning operations. Top management's role will still be to guide, to interpret, to question, and to challenge.

It is important that top management continues to be involved and to provide leadership to the strategic planning effort. If top managers believe in the process and spend time and effort in making it as effective as possible, then strategic planning will become a way of life throughout the company.

During the 1980s, Norton will put more emphasis on human resource planning as part of its strategic planning. It takes an entrepreneur to build a business, an administrator to maintain one, and an economizer to harvest one. It is important to find the right person for the right job and reward people appropriately for attaining their individual goals. Helping to choose the right people must become part of the top manager's function, along with the continuing role of reconciling all strategies with corporate objectives.

During the 1980s, it will be increasingly important that top managers study public issues and how they will affect planning for the future. At Norton, we already do some scenario building when we review our five-year financial model. In the 1980s, we expect the scenarios to include social and political issues as well as economic ones and to reach out ten or more years rather than the five that has so far seemed appropriate.

During the 1980s, top management will have to ensure that the organization remains sufficiently flexible and resilient to respond effectively to the unforeseen change which produces a discontinuity. None of us foresaw in 1970 the impact that OPEC was to have on every business in every country. Some companies, and some countries, responded to the challenging change in the economic, political, and social climate better than others. We must be prepared to respond appropriately to the next profound discontinuity when it occurs.

In the 1980s, Norton's strategic planning system will rest, as it did in the 1970s, on the premise that the job of planning is the business of line managers. So far, that has been the most important factor in our success.

The Impact of
Consumer Trends on
Corporate Strategy

Sandra D. Kresch

O ver the past few decades, the American
corporate community operated in an
environment of rapid growth, changing
technology, and aggressive expansion into world
markets. Throughout this period, productivity
increased consistently, resulting in an ever-climb-
ing GNP. With this rising tide of economic progress, the material and social rewards available to the American consumer appeared to be unlimited.

Today, this view of the world—and America's
industrial role within it—seems startlingly naive
and nostalgic. Declining economic growth coupled
with increased global competition and a host of
other forces has sent shock waves through the
business community and the consumer environment. As we move into the 1980s, top management finally is coming to grips with the unique
demands of a low-growth, inflationary economy,
increased competition, an unstable political/eco-
nomic environment, the high cost of capital, and
falling productivity.

Beyond these concerns, there is an important,
though often neglected, overlay of consumer issues
that will dramatically affect corporate performance
and profitability in the 1980s. So far-reaching is
their impact that we believe top management must
factor consumer analysis into its planning process
along with traditional economic analysis if its strategic business decisions are to be implemented
successfully. If top management fails to do so, it
runs the risk of being at the wrong place at the
wrong time with the wrong products, as recent
events in the troubled automotive industry graphi-
cally demonstrate.

Without doubt, consumer needs and preferences have always been considered in the planning
of consumer packaged goods firms. Typically, how-

Sandra D. Kresch is Vice-President, Booz-Allen & Hamilton,
Inc.

ever, they have been researched and acted upon at the micro level—in the areas of new product positioning, for instance, or marketing strategy. Today, by contrast, consumer goods firms are seeing the need to understand, anticipate, and capitalize on a changing consumer environment and developing trends as critical components of their strategic planning and implementation. In the 1980s, the need to link technology, competitive positioning, and customer needs will be equally critical for industrial companies.

Why the greater emphasis on a discipline traditionally viewed as "soft" and peripheral? Mainly because consumer trends now surfacing will impinge upon all facets of corporate strategic planning—from new product development, technology management, and the restructuring of corporate portfolios to productivity, management style, internal operating structure, and executive compensation. The heightened importance of consumer issues raises a number of questions for management:

What are the pivotal consumer/customer trends shaping the new marketing environment of the 1980s?

How can top management use consumer analysis as a strategic tool?

What kinds of business decisions will result from an increased emphasis on consumer trend analysis?

With these questions providing the background, the discussion that follows focuses primarily on the experience of one consumer packaged goods firm—General Mills—and the way in which it has consistently used sophisticated consumer trends analysis in planning, implementing and, when necessary, redirecting its corporate strategy.

The New Marketing Environment

Four major trends have converged to radically reshape the U.S. marketplace of the 1980s.

Demographic Shifts

Over the past twenty years, a vast body of statistical research about changing U.S. demographics has been developed, yet there is little evidence that this—or the changing population that it profiles—is being integrated into corporate planning.

As we look to the 1980s, demographic analysis points to the emergence of three dominant population segments:

A record number of aging adults, more active and affluent than ever before;

A huge mid-to-late-thirties segment at the family formation stage; and

An incipient, but modified, baby boom resulting from delays in marriage and childbearing.

The fastest growing population group will be in the twenty-five-to-forty-four-year-old range, the life stage that focuses on establishing new homes, and raising families, providing, as in the past, a market for a broad range of products.

However, this family formation group differs from its predecessors in many respects. Its members, for example, are increasingly more affluent, as two-income families become the norm, higher education levels are achieved, and marriage and children are postponed. Recent analysis suggests that people in this category spend 36 percent more than any other segment on durables. Spending on indulgences during the single years has become a way of life—and young consumers will continue to create a profitable market for products—though the product mix appealing to them is likely to be quite different from that of a generation ago. By 1985, this group will control more than half the nation's wealth.

Economic Instability

Inflation and economic flux have caused sweeping changes in consumer buying patterns by eroding confidence and altering attitudes toward purchasing. As consumers perceive that more money is buying them less, more and more people are beginning to fear that the American dream is no longer "for sale." With inflation cutting into higher disposable incomes, consumers are more inclined than ever to adopt the much publicized "buy now, save later" motto at the expense of future security.

Rapid Social Change

The dramatic recent changes in the structure of the nuclear family and the fabric of American society are familiar and indisputable. First marriages are being delayed, the divorce rate has increased by 96 percent in the last ten years, and the "single head of household" is now a recognized economic and political entity. An unprecedented 42 million women are now in the work force; through the 1990s, experts predict that they will continue to swell the labor ranks at the rate of one million per year. The impact on the corporation, and on virtually every basic service and product—from housing to convenience foods—has been unparalleled.

Value Shifts

Such rapid social upheaval has had its price. Today, consumers no longer believe that technological change, economic growth, and hard work guarantee prosperity—or even a moderately comfortable lifestyle. As the social activists of the 1960s and 1970s move into the traditional family formation stage, some of their behavior patterns appear to reflect or conform to those of previous generations, but the attitudes underlying that behavior are very different.

The 1980s are emerging as a decade in which consumers are preoccupied with maintaining their own economic and emotional stability and with finding personal, not social, fulfillment in an environment that is perceived to be increasingly hostile and uncomfortable.

Receding interest in issues related to social causes has created a new definition of survival: personal comfort and economic security. This has resulted in greater emphasis on successful interpersonal relations, the gratification achieved through leisure time, and social involvement focused largely on the individual. "Quality of life," a rallying principle of the past few decades, has been linked to, or transformed into, a new concept: "quality time." Increasingly, in all forums—from the workplace to the family—emphasis is shifting from the drive to acquire more and "bigger" objects to the search for ways to use limited personal resources—time and money among them—most productively.

As a corollary, there is strong evidence of a continuing decline in the view of work as an expression of identity. With notable exceptions, there appears to be a weaker commitment to the work environment and ethic, more questioning of corporate values and procedures, more job turnover

and "burnout," and more demand for employers to assume social as well as economic functions, from child care to retirement counseling.

All the trends capsulized here have and will continue to affect the corporate bottom line through impact on:

Types of consumer products developed;

Product positioning and marketing;

Business segmentation to optimize profitability;

Corporate portfolio structure; and

Implementation strategies, from new product introductions to organization design and policy.

General Mills' recent expansion into a broad range of businesses offers a prime example of the effective use of consumer trend analysis as a strategic planning tool. Over a ten-to-fifteen-year period, the company undertook a dramatic diversification program built around the concept of a family of complementary, consumer-oriented businesses and based on its in-depth experience in servicing the customers of its core food business.

General Mills: Matching Corporate Strategy to Consumer Demands

During its fifty-year history, General Mills had evolved from a flour milling company into a classic consumer packaged goods firm. In the 1950s, the company launched its first diversification effort, moving into a series of businesses—home appliances, precision instruments, electronics and others—all unrelated to consumer foods. These were divested in the early 1960s when they proved unsuccessful in achieving desired growth and profitability goals because they failed to exploit General Mills' major assets: marketing savvy and consumer goods expertise.

A second diversification program—this one playing to General Mills' strengths—was launched in 1966. Analyzing its approach, a four-step planning strategy emerges:

Step 1: Analysis of existing corporate portfolio and short-term market outlook. As General Mills reviewed its core food business in the late 1960s, it was clear that the food processing industry was maturing and profits were being squeezed by price controls, inflation and a recessionary economy, and that expansion of its food distribution outlets had peaked. In addition, the company's core businesses were fending off antitrust litigation and consumer campaigns against advertising to children. Growing interest in nutrition and "health" foods also threatened sales in General Mills' flour, cake mix, and frosting categories.

At the same time, demographic data suggested that population growth had slowed, and that the number of children—primary consumers of cereals and other core products—was declining. The move of women into the work force indicated a growing demand for convenience foods and other labor-saving products.

Step 2: Analysis of General Mills' corporate strengths. Examined from the consumer perspective, General Mills had a number of formidable assets:

Strong, well-known brand names that cut across consumer and market segments;

A tradition of monitoring consumer attitudes and needs through a sophisticated and well-controlled market research function; and

National distribution channels and a strong marketing organization.

Step 3: Analysis of long-term consumer trends and their potential impact. General Mills identified a variety of long-term consumer shifts that would affect its core operating businesses:

Increased emphasis on "family formation";

A greater proportion of primary market consumers shifting attention from the home to careers;

Changes in spending patterns, including increased financial pressures due to inflation, making discretionary purchasing more difficult, and the need to save time through more costly convenience products;

Increased concern about the quality of food, diet, physical fitness, and "naturalness";

Shifts in food-consumption patterns to increased away-from-home eating and staggered meals in response to more active life-styles, signaling a

decline in the total food dollars spent in the grocery store;

Greater interest in "investment spending" expressed through the purchase of high-quality durables and a shift of discretionary funds from savings to tangibles; and

Increased emphasis on do-it-yourself activities fueled by both the drive to economize and increased leisure time.

Step 4: Matching high-growth market segments to corporate strengths. Using a consumer analysis as a foundation, General Mills embarked on a strategy of aggressive, highly focused diversification. Between 1967 and 1979, it acquired more that forty companies at a cost of $335 million and 3.5 million shares (excluding full business acquisitions). The underlying theme of its acquisition strategy: every business entered would be consumer-oriented and closely tied to the "family market." The result was acquisition of a carefully selected group of businesses in areas ranging from fashion, jewelry, and travel to restaurants, toys, collectibles, and crafts.

Evidence of the strategy's overall success lies in the fact that 33 percent of General Mills' 1980 sales came from products and services introduced in the last five years, representing a dollar volume of about $1.4 billion. Overall, 45 percent of its growth in the same period stems from new products and services developed internally and focused largely on serving changing consumer needs.

Growth in sales has been significantly higher in the new businesses than in the traditional food market: not only have the nonfood operations increased as a proportion of the total business, but all the new units have grown at a substantially faster rate. While consumer foods represented 73 percent of sales and 81 percent of total operating profits in 1971, by 1980 these figures had fallen to 53 percent of sales and 53 percent of profits.

Analysis of several new General Mills businesses illustrates a key reason for this profit picture—the successful interaction between strategic planning and consumer trend analysis.

Fashion

With the acquisition in 1969 of David Crystal and its prestige sportswear line, Izod/LaCoste, General

Mills entered the fashion field—an area in which consumers spend substantial discretionary income. While relatively small when acquired, Izod/LaCoste has become the mainstay of the Crystal business and a major success story. Capitalizing on increased consumer interest in physical fitness, General Mills built Izod's alligator into a highly profitable symbol of quality and broadened its product line to a full range of leisure wear.

Anticipating a trend toward widespread branding in the fashion field, General Mills expanded Izod dramatically through leverage provided to retailers by the use of a consumer pull strategy far more typical of selling cake mix than of the apparel market. The result: a highly profitable business that continues to account for much of the David Crystal Division's growth.

By contrast, other General Mills fashion acquisitions have been less successful in adapting to new consumer demands. The mainstream of the David Crystal line—"dressy" sportswear geared to suburban activities—has proven to be out of tune with apparel market trends. The same is true of Kimberly Knitwear, which suffered from declining consumer interest in knit fabrics, a growing preference for natural textiles, and the changing wardrobe needs of career women.

Restaurant Operations

Foreseeing the trend toward increased away-from-home eating in the 1970s, General Mills began to acquire a variety of restaurant operations. Choosing not to compete in the fast-food market already dominated by McDonald's, the company focused instead on family style, relatively inexpensive restaurants with specific themes. Red Lobster Inns specialized in seafood, York Steak House in mid-price-range steak, and Castle Gallardo in Mexican food. In 1980, General Mills also began development of Good Earth restaurants, specializing in natural foods. Each of these acquisitions has been developed into larger businesses under General Mills' direction and represents an effort to segment away-from-home eating in a way that enables General Mills to achieve high penetration in a well-defined niche: the middle-price family restaurant market.

Specialty Retailing

In developing its Specialty Retailing Group, General Mills used consumer trend analysis to identify new distribution channels for conventional consumer products—chiefly mail-order marketing.

The acquisition of The Talbots, for instance, brought General Mills into the fashion retailing market, while also generating substantial mail-order volume. Built on a reputation for high quality, traditional styles, and durability, The Talbots fashion line proved to be highly compatible with working women's demand for classic, easy-to-care-for "investment" clothing. Initially, General Mills used mail-order marketing to cultivate a strong customer base with a geographic reach beyond The Talbots' original New England locale. Once a strong mail-order operation was established, customer loyalty was easily transferred to additional retail outlets.

Eddie Bauer, another retail acquisition, specializes in high-quality, down-insulated products and outdoor gear. Again, as in the case of The Talbots, a mail-order distribution structure brought Eddie Bauer into the homes of consumers who never would have been exposed to the company through retail outlets and rapidly expanded the business.

In addition, the use of advanced telecommunications and computer technology has streamlined mail-order fulfillment, providing better service to consumers at lower cost. This has an added benefit for General Mills: not only has it tapped into consumer trends related to shopping behavior, it has also positioned itself effectively to move foward into an era of expanded in-home shopping via computer.

Core Convenience Foods

General Mills' core business, convenience food products, was also affected by shifts in its strategy.

References to physical fitness and diet consciousness, for instance, have emerged in product development specifications and advertising. The development of a whole range of Granola-based products, high fiber cereals, and snack products all reflect consumer interest in "naturalness" and nutrition and offer opportunities for highly sophisticated market segmentation. General Mills has effectively segmented the "nutritional" cereal market in a way that allows it to sustain traditional brands that are highly fortified (meeting the needs of vitamin-conscious consumers), "natural" brands (appealing to a different set of consumers concerned with the negative effects of additives and preservatives), and also reach children (through vitamin-enriched cereals with good taste). At the same time, it has sustained traditional brands like Cheerios and Wheaties through communication strategies that focus on contemporary values.

Similarly, General Mills has entered the high growth market with Yoplait and the portable food category with Nature Valley Granola Bars—convenience foods that meet consumer demands for "healthy" eat-on-the-run products.

Consumer Impact Analysis

As the General Mills experience suggests, sensitive analysis of consumer trends can be a powerful strategic tool for determining how and where to allocate scarce and costly resources. It can help identify corporate strengths, unify corporate objectives, and serve as a frame of reference for the management of technology, new product development, acquisitions, and marketing.

A variation on the concept of environmental impact analysis, consumer trend analysis also provides an added dimension to traditional strategic planning, which uses financial and other variables as methods for understanding markets and competitors. It also can help pinpoint appropriate timing for new-product introductions and determine how new technology can be used most effectively to address consumer needs.

However, two factors appear to deflect management's attention—especially in the United States—from consumer trend analysis: the short-term profit perspective and entrancement with technology.

Much has been written about the impact of short-term objectives on innovation. From the consumer perspective, the key problem is that emerging trends usually result in long-term market opportunities that are difficult to assess precisely in terms of potential or to justify in the face of short-term profit constraint.

At the same time, much of the attention given to technology innovation has focused on potential

profits rather than the problems inherent in the process of commercialization. There is a danger—already apparent—that the sheer magnitude of the new technology and applications available will overshadow the need to link product development to consumer needs and benefits. As a result, industrial manufacturers have persisted in introducing technological innovations without regard to their benefits—and have then been baffled when genuinely innovative products based on these technologies have not generated markets as large as expected.

In the consumer appliance industry, for example, manufacturers have electrified household items ranging from crepe pans to vegetable peelers, generating a steady new stream of faddish new products with short-term profit potential rather than sustaining market value. In the process, they have missed early entry into new long-term markets—notably food processors and microwave ovens—which keyed into consumers' changing convenience food needs.

Both consumer and industrial businesses have also failed to pinpoint new buying patterns. In many segments, the demand for middle-price-range products is declining, as economic pressures and value perceptions force buyers into either "investment purchasing"—buying high quality, high-value products with a long life—or the purchase of low-cost, minimum-feature models if a product is perceived to be disposable, easily replaced, or likely to be made obsolete by changing technology.

In some cases, American companies are financially acknowledging these shifts and redirecting their strategies. Increasingly, they are beginning to understand the need to marry careful market planning with technological innovation at profitable levels.

In many cases, industrial companies have been very successful at providing customer input into their planning and product development. As an example, in the early days of Hewlett Packard, the "next bench" approach to product development proved very successful. New product ideas came from customers and/or scientists in the HP laboratories; new products were developed using emerging electronics technologies, but always in response to well-defined objectives based largely on customer needs.

In most industrial markets where this close interaction is not typical, the same sort of monitoring of customer trends must become an important component of strategic planning to offset slow growth and increasing competition.

The home entertainment/information industry provides a very timely example of an area in which balancing technological innovation and real consumer value will be paramount. In many cases, strategists in the burgeoning industry are leaping off into the twenty-first century in terms of technology without effectively analyzing consumer trends and benefits in their market planning. Optimistic projections on markets for personal computers, home electronic information systems, and other ventures are widespread, resulting in huge investments by major corporations in an industry that will have to grow substantially in order to support profitable businesses.

Yet, to date, there is limited evidence of consumer behavior and buying patterns suggesting that the population at large will accept the new products, services, and technologies being developed with anywhere near the rapidity projected. In fact, research indicates that conventional wisdom about the adoption of innovative technology may not be applicable to the consumer environment of the 1980s, driven as it is by rising costs, decreased discretionary income, and smaller families.

Whatever the long-term economic outlook, unfounded and poorly conceived consumer strategies could dramatically affect the size and profitability of the markets for electronic innovations in the next decade.

Building Consumer Trend Analysis Into Corporate Strategy

Even in the companies with the most sophisticated consumer research capabilities, the data developed often are used only in tactical decisions on very narrowly defined projects—often by lower or middle management. To be successful, however, consumer trend analysis must be integrated into planning at the top level of management. Guidelines for effective integration include:

Integrating a consumer impact component into market/competitive analysis in the formal strategic planning process;

Focusing top management attention on consumer/customer trends through periodic updates;

Adding consumer/customer market-oriented professionals to strategic planning project teams;

Providing continuing access to data on consumer/customer trends through a strong market research program; and

Focusing consumer/customer trend analysis on specific business objectives to avoid ethereal, largely useless data with no strategic relevance.

Integrating consumer trends into strategic planning can provide an entirely new dimension to traditional product/market segmentation. To ensure optimal results:

Segment markets based on consumer variables, as well as traditional factors such as product line, price, and distribution channels.

Do not limit consumer segmentation to demographic characteristics. Increasingly, attitudes related to specific product benefits are more important in identifying market potential and changes.

Integrate consumer/customer needs and feedback on existing products into the product development processes.

Consider consumer franchise and brand presence as corporate resources equal in value to physical assets, distribution reach and technology.

Carefully assess trade-offs between technology and consumer benefits. The availability of new technology applications, unless linked to concrete consumer benefits, can provide a springboard not for success but for costly failure.

Look for convergence of market forces; in combination, dramatic social changes, pricing shifts, and technological advances can point to untapped or underexploited markets.

When building consumer trend analysis into the planning process, analyze internal corporate structure to ensure that it supports this process. Often, adding the consumer perspective to planning is difficult for managers used to making strategic decisions based solely on financial or economic criteria.

"The customer is always right" used to be a phrase reserved for salespeople at retail counters. Today, business is finding that it has a new meaning, as consumer attitudes help shape the market-place. Effectively used, consumer trend analysis can be a valuable strategic tool in pinpointing growth markets, identifying new product niches, and developing new technologies. Increasingly in the 1980s, both consumer-oriented and industrial companies will find that it is far more profitable to actively exploit that tool than to have to defend against its use by competitors.

James E. Burke and Johnson & Johnson Company

Johnson & Johnson is an unusual company. It is in fact a composite of 158 companies, 25 operating in the United States, and 133 in fifty-four other countries. These subsidiary companies are coordinated and controlled by a corporate level executive committee, which is the principal management group responsible for operations. Executive committee members typically have responsibility for a group of U.S. and international companies. Presidents of the larger companies may report directly to the appropriate executive committee member, but smaller companies are typically marshalled under a company group chairman who in turn reports to an executive committee member. The resulting structure is highly decentralized and complex as well. It is not easy to manage, and it requires large numbers of talented managers. James E. Burke rose through this system over a twenty-three-year period, during which control of the business shifted from the Johnson family to others.

The major theme characterizing the subsidiary companies is health care. Involvement in product lines outside health care has generally resulted from application of know-how originally developed within the health care field. The largest share of the company's business is in consumer products—toiletries, hygiene products, first-aid products, and non-prescription drugs. Next largest is the professional segment, which sells a wide range of surgical, dental, and other products to hospitals, clinics, and individual practitioners. The company also markets a number of prescription drugs. Finally, there is a relatively small group of industrial products—primarily textiles and chemicals—used by manufacturers in the production of their own end-use products.

Strategic decisions at Johnson & Johnson were for many years made by the executive committee, which met almost daily. When board action was required, these individuals simply "put on another hat"; the board of directors was an entirely inside group. This has now changed, but the eleven executive committee members continue to dominate the twenty-member board. Strategic decision making, whether in the executive committee or the board, is guided by a credo (Exhibit 1) that has much the same function in the company as the constitution does for the United States. This credo has been changed some over the years, but not easily. Its influence is clearly evident in the way the recent Tylenol tragedy was handled.

EXHIBIT 1   Johnson & Johnson: Our Credo

We believe our first responsibility is to the doctors, nurses and patients, to mothers and all others who use our products and services.
In meeting their needs everything we do must be of high quality.
We must constantly strive to reduce our costs in order to maintain reasonable prices.
Customers' orders must be serviced promptly and accurately.
Our suppliers and distributors must have an opportunity to make a fair profit.

We are responsible to our employees, the men and women who work with us throughout the world.
Everyone must be considered as an individual.
We must respect their dignity and recognize their merit.
They must have a sense of security in their jobs.
Compensation must be fair and adequate, and working conditions clean, orderly and safe.
Employees must feel free to make suggestions and complaints.
There must be equal opportunity for employment, development and advancement for those qualified.
We must provide competent management, and their actions must be just and ethical.

We are responsible to the communities in which we live and work and to the world community as well. We must be good citizens—support good works and charities and bear our fair share of taxes.
We must encourage civic improvements and better health and education.
We must maintain in good order the property we are privileged to use, protecting the environment and natural resources.

Our final responsibility is to our stockholders.
Business must make a sound profit.
We must experiment with new ideas. Research must be carried on, innovative programs developed and mistakes paid for.
New equipment must be purchased, new facilities provided and new products launched.
Reserves must be created to provide for adverse times.
When we operate according to these principles, the stockholders should realize a fair return.

Seven Chicago-area residents died because bottles of Johnson & Johnson's Tylenol pain remedy were tampered with, and the capsules inside laced with cyanide. Shortly thereafter, the medicine's share of the market dropped from 35 percent to 7 percent. Tylenol had been the company's best-selling product, by a wide margin. As the deaths increased, Johnson & Johnson had to decide whether to recall the unsold product remaining on the druggists' shelves. The U.S. Food and Drug Administration recommended against recall because it feared increased panic. The Federal Bureau of Investigation took a similar position, on the grounds that recall would encourage terrorism. But the company decided on recall. Two of the bottles that came back were indeed poisoned. The company lost $100 million as a result of the product's withdrawal and lost sales.

At the same time, a decision was made to reestablish Tylenol in the marketplace. Within 10 weeks the product was available again, with newly developed tamper-resistant packaging. Major television and print advertising campaigns were mounted. Nine months later, Tylenol's market share was back up to 29 percent, in spite of the fact that the killer has never been located. The person ultimately responsible for these strategic decisions—to recall, and then not to abandon, Tylenol—was James Burke.

After graduating from Holy Cross College in Worcester, Massachusetts, James Burke earned an MBA from Harvard Business School and went to work for Procter & Gamble, a major Johnson & Johnson competitor in a number of markets. A brief, unsuccessful fling at entrepreneurship followed, and then he joined Johnson & Johnson in 1953 as product director for Band-Aids. He moved up to director of new products and then was put in charge of merchandising and advertising for consumer products. Twelve years after joining the firm, James Burke took over as head of the large Johnson & Johnson Products subsidiary company and at the same time joined the parent firm's executive committee. Later, he assumed the position of vice-chairman of the executive committee, with responsibility for a number of domestic and international companies. In 1973 he became president of the company and chairman of the executive

James E. Burke

committee, and in 1976, chairman of the board and chief executive officer.

James Burke has spent his entire career with the company very close to its New Brunswick, New Jersey headquarters. He has had solid experience in product merchandising and advertising, has worked in the subsidiary company structure, and has long served as a member of the powerful executive committee. Johnson & Johnson relies strongly on decentralized decision making, coupled with a unique brand of group decision making at the strategic level. James Burke clearly understands these decision processes and is able to work with them effectively.

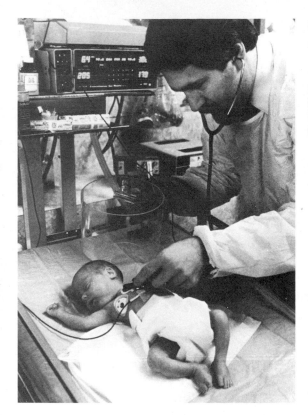

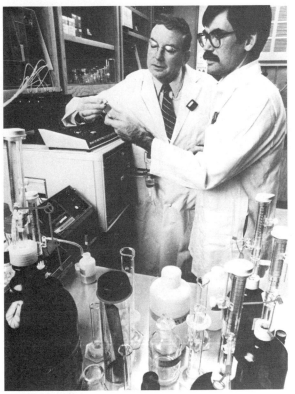

Oxygen content in the blood is an important indicator of the progress of critical care patients like this premature neonate attended by the staff at Albert Einstein Medical Center in Philadelphia. The Transcutaneous Gas Monitor, developed by Critikon, Inc., a Johnson & Johnson subsidiary, provides an accurate reading of this vital sign by analyzing oxygen content through the skin.

In 1982 Johnson & Johnson strengthened its ties with the Research Institute of the Scripps Clinic and Research Foundation in La Jolla, California, to enhance collaborative efforts in biotechnology research designed to produce products for use in both human and veterinary medicine. Dr. James L. Bittle of Johnson & Johnson (left) is shown in a laboratory with Dr. Richard A. Houghten of Scripps, at work on one project that could lead to synthetic vaccines.

Staffing and Personnel/ Human Resources Management

The personnel/human resources function deals with a wide range of activities having to do with bringing employees into the organization, retaining them, influencing their performance and morale, and handling their departures. Chapter 2 considered the nature of careers in personnel management and the opportunities in the field. Chapter 3 traced the historical development of personnel/human resources management. These chapters delve directly into current personnel practice, considering the various activities performed and what is known about performing them well.

In an introductory text such as this, it is not possible to cover personnel practice in great detail, and in fact that is not the intention of this discussion. A wide range of advanced courses deal with the various subject areas, including personnel selection, compensation, personnel research, labor law, training and development, collective bargaining, and others. The objective here is merely to sample the subject matter of the field, and in the process, to provide some of the grounding needed for more advanced work.

Exhibit 1 is a scaled-down version of Exhibit 2.8. It provides a good overview of the material covered in the next two chapters. Chapter 14 is concerned with creating positions within the organization, filling those positions with qualified people, and keeping the positions filled. This is what is meant by *staffing*. Organization planning is essential to the creation of positions, at least management positions, and is considered at length in Part 3, especially in chapters 9 and 10. The remaining staffing activities are treated in chapter 14; this includes the various input processes, job analysis, human resource planning, training, and management development. Also included in the chapter is an

EXHIBIT 1 Activities carried out by personnel departments

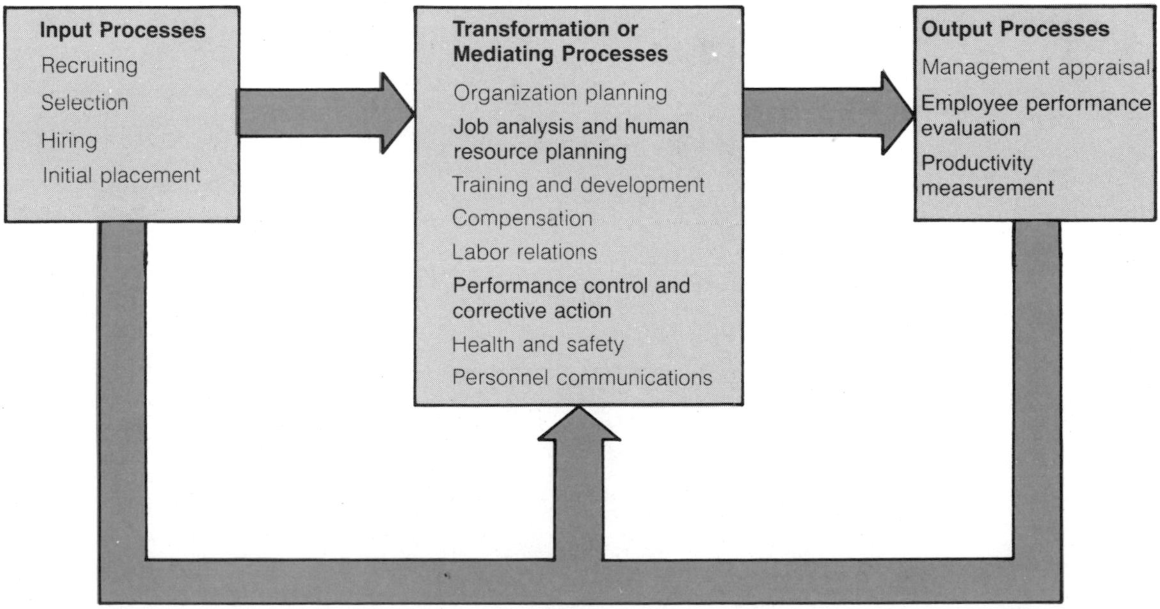

EXHIBIT 2 Corporate level organization structure of Personnel/Human Resources Function at Becton, Dickinson and Company

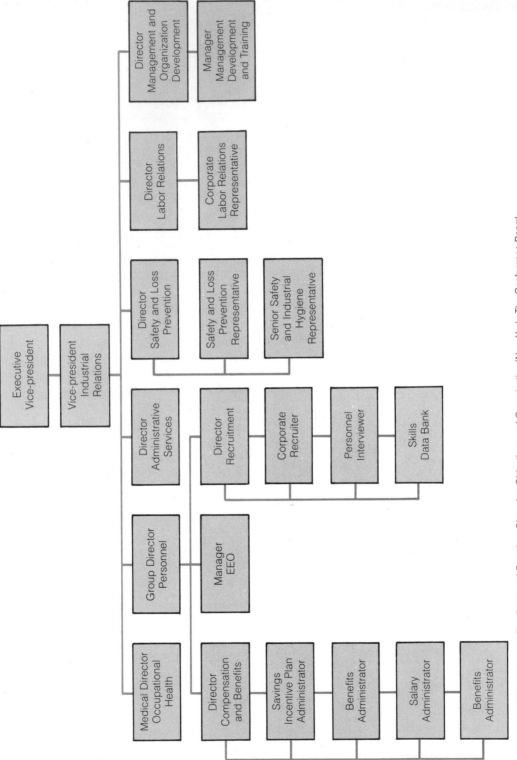

SOURCE: Allen R. Janger, *The Personnel Function: Changing Objectives and Organization* (New York: The Conference Board, 1977):71. Reprinted by permission of the publisher.

introductory treatment of the factors that must be considered in making staffing decisions—human resource availability, the legal structure, and agreements with labor unions. The discussions of laws and unions generally reflect a management viewpoint. It is important that students understand this viewpoint, and an introductory management text seems an appropriate place to present it.

Chapter 15 moves beyond the creation and staffing of positions to the various activities carried out to maintain an effective labor force. Special attention is given to the matter of compensation, including employee benefits, and to the output processes noted in Part 5 Exhibit 1.

Part 5 Exhibit 2 shows how certain of these activities fit into the organization structure of a company at the corporate level. The firm is Becton, Dickinson and Company of Paramus, New Jersey.

CHAPTER 14

Organizations

CHAPTER OUTLINE

Major Constraints: Resource Availability, Laws, and Labor Unions
Availability of Needed Human Resources
    Individual and Group Differences
    Group Differences and the Law
Personnel/Human Resources Laws
    Effects on Personnel Decisions
    Labor Relations Law
Labor Union Activities
    The Unionization Process
    Collective Bargaining
    Contract Administration

Job Analysis and Human Resource Planning
The Role and Nature of Job Analysis
    Analysis Factors
    Analysis Methods
Approaches in Human Resource Planning
    Establishing Future Demand
    Establishing Internal Supply

Recruiting and Selection
The Logic of Selection
Recruiting
    Sources
    College Recruiting
    Affirmative Action Recruiting
Selection Methods
    The Interview
    Application Blanks and Biographical Data
    Reference and Background Checks
    Physical Examinations
    Psychological Tests
    Assessment Centers

Training and Development
The Logic of Training and Development
    Training Needs Analysis
    Evaluation of Training
Training and Development Methods
    Training to Develop Self-Understanding
    Training to Develop Job Skills
    Training to Develop Motivation

OBJECTIVES

To explain how various external forces serve to limit personnel decisions and push them in certain directions.

To show how positions are specified through job analysis and then kept filled over time as a result of human resource planning.

To describe recruiting and selection procedures as they relate to staffing positions with effective employees.

To provide an understanding of the training and development approach in staffing including when it is appropriate and how it can be evaluated.

person reads an advertisement in the classified section of the newspaper and calls the number listed to see if the job is still open. The answer is that applications are still being accepted, and an appointment for interviewing and testing is arranged. This is *recruiting*.

The person arrives at the employment office and spends several hours completing various paper-and-pencil tests and providing an interviewer with information regarding educational qualifications, previous employment, and the like. An application blank is also completed. The person's test scores, interview ratings, educational and experience qualifications, and the like, are then compared with those of other applicants, and being relatively superior, a decision to hire is made. This is *selection*.

The person is contacted, told of the decision, and asked to come in to firm up the details. At this meeting, matters of placement, compensation, and other considerations related to the inducements–contributions balance are worked out, and a mutual decision regarding employment is reached. This is *hiring*.

At the agreed upon time, the person shows up for work and takes over a particular job, the duties of which have previously been specified as a result of some type of job analysis. This is *initial placement*.

Generally, soon after beginning work, the person is provided with orientation information about the company and the work context. Also in this early period, the person is provided with an opportunity to learn any facts, skills, and behaviors needed to perform the job in a satisfactory manner at the least and ideally, in an outstanding way. This is *training*. At this point the job is fully staffed, assuming of course that any training needed is successful and the person achieves an effective performance level.

MAJOR CONSTRAINTS: RESOURCE AVAILABILITY, LAWS, AND LABOR UNIONS

Underlying the staffing process just described are a number of additional activities. Recruiting advertisements must be placed, selection procedures must be studied in relation to performance on the particular job involved, jobs must be analyzed, plans must be established to keep the job filled, and so on. All of these activities may be constrained by various factors which, at the time they operate, are largely beyond the control of the personnel people involved.

Perhaps the job specifications, established after extensive study of people who do and do not succeed at this kind of job, call for a particular combination and level of abilities. For reasons including stiff competition from other employers, it may prove very difficult to find applicants meeting these requirements. As a result of the limited availability of the kind of human resources needed, the company may be forced into a time-consuming and costly recruiting effort that management would much prefer to have avoided.

Difficulties can be compounded if, as a result of previous legal actions, the company finds itself bound to fill a high proportion of its openings with minority group members. Thus, in addition to the low availability of needed human resources, the legal structure within which the company operates also introduces constraints on staffing decisions and the way they are carried out.

Finally, a union contract might be in effect that establishes the amount that the person hired for the position must be paid and the benefits such as health insurance, holidays, and retirement income that the company must provide. Perhaps the local labor situation is such that good people could be hired at a rate well below the union's. Nevertheless, action is constrained by the terms of the contract; it would be very risky for the company to violate them.

Availability of Needed Human Resources

The first of these types of constraints is the one least frequently recognized. It may operate externally to the organization, or internally, or both. The essential constraint is that the company does not possess or cannot find some particular type of person it needs to carry out its activities, thus forcing it into some variation from usual practice if staffing is to be achieved. In this context, "type of person" means an individual with the underlying intellectual, motivational, emotional, or physical characteristics that are needed. Skills, knowledge, and expertise that take years to acquire may be involved. However, if the needed skills can be learned rather rapidly through a training program, the constraint is lessened. Few people may be available who are completely job-ready at the moment of hire, but this need not be a major problem if the needed learning can be provided quickly and at low cost.

Individual and Group Differences An important distinction in considering the availability of human resources is that between individual and group differences. The point can be made with reference to Exhibit 14.1. On this partic-

EXHIBIT 14.1 Distribution of verbal intelligence scores among adults as a whole and in low and high education groups

Test Score Level	Adults in General	Six Years or Less Education	College Graduates
		Percent at Each Score Level	
0–1	0	0	0
2–3	1	5	0
4–5	4	16	0
6–7	11	19	1
8–9	19	27	3
10–11	21	19	10
12–13	19	10	13
14–15	13	3	30
16–17	8	Less than 1	27
18–19	3	0	12
20	Less than 1	0	4

SOURCE: Based on John B. Miner, *Intelligence in the United States* (Westport, Conn.: Greenwood Press, 1973).

ular intellectual measure, which is of a kind that relates strongly to job level and performance, scores in the adult population spread over almost the entire score range; there are large differences between individuals, with scores ranging from 2 to 20 at the extremes. These same individual differences appear within the two education groups as well, but they are less pronounced—the range is from 2 to 17 among those with limited education, and from 7 to 20 among the college graduates.

Clearly, the two education groups differ substantially, with one group clustering toward the low end of the score distribution and the other toward the upper end. On the average, those with six or fewer years of education score a little above 8; college graduates score only slightly below 15. Thus, there is a sizable group difference.

Problems of resource availability occur when the individual–group distinction is not made, and groups are treated as if all members were the same. Thus, a personnel manager might conclude that, because the average person with under six years education has below-average intelligence, such people should not be considered for a certain position. But such a conclusion compounds the problem of limited resource availability. Actually, because of individual differences within the less educated group, over 20 percent of the people composing it do have above average intelligence, and a good number score as high as some of the college graduates. Presumably, many of that group would have the capacity to learn highly skilled jobs. Emphasizing group differences rather than individual differences not only denies talented people opportunities, it severely restricts the resources available to a company.

Group Differences and the Law The previous example is based on verbal intelligence and educational groups. The same type of argument can be developed for a wide range of individual characteristics of an intellectual, emotional, motivational, and physical nature that make a difference in performing one job or another. At the present time, the greatest concern in terms of law is with groupings based on race, color, religion, national origin, sex, age, and handicapped status. These have become important because there was reason to believe that organizations often made employment and other personnel decisions on the basis of these group considerations, rather than on individual capabilities; certain jobs were for women only, others for blacks only, and so on. A number of group differences exist within these categories.[1] For example, studies indicate that men tend to be more aggressive and that women have greater verbal ability. Whites tend to have better mechanical comprehension, but blacks exhibit a more pronounced psychological toughness. Many of these differences could make a difference in job performance, but it is also true that wide individual variations exist within the various groups. Personnel managers need to know about group differences, as well as individual differences, because the laws say they *must* pay attention to them. The best reason to pay attention, though, is that it is individual differences that really matter from a performance viewpoint. Even if a firm is forced to hire primarily within a given group, it pays to select those who will perform best.

Increasingly in the past fifty years, federal and state laws have been passed restricting the alternatives available to a company in dealing with its employees or prospective employees. The initial impetus for this type of legislation came from the depression of the 1930s. The business sector did not perform its economic role in society well in this period, and it lost considerable discretion as a result. A similar wave of restrictive legislation occurred in the 1960s and early 1970s. Some of the recent laws focus directly on personnel decisions. Others focus on labor relations decisions, and specify how management and unions should deal with each other. These latter laws may influence personnel decisions such as hiring and firing also, but they do so through a primary concern for union members.

Effects on Personnel Decisions   Exhibit 14.2 outlines a number of the more comprehensive laws that might influence personnel decisions. Most of these are federal laws, but in many cases the states have their own, often matching, laws applying in circumstances not covered by the federal statutes. The pressure for compliance may come from the threat of court action, if companies do not accept the constraints, or it may come through making non-compliance directly economically unattractive, as with executive orders on discrimination by government contractors and unemployment compensation.

The coverage in Exhibit 14.2 is not complete; there are many other laws that apply to certain types of employers or under a restricted set of circumstances. Furthermore, the meaning of these laws tends to become clarified only after a series of court decisions. Employers may remain uncertain about the exact nature of the legal constraints for a period of years; many provisions of the Civil Rights Act remain uncertain in their interpretation today, after some twenty years of litigation. Exhibit 14.2 also is intended to provide only a general view of the various constraints noted. More detailed treatments occur in advanced texts on personnel, industrial relations, and law. The point that society can use its legal processes to sharply limit personnel decisions should be evident, however.

Labor Relations Law   Exhibit 14.3 outlines major laws dealing with union–management relationships. In effect, these laws make it easier for labor unions to organize a company's work force and engage in collective bargaining with management over conditions of employment. A number of possible management practices, such as firing employees who engage in union activity and requiring new employees to agree not to join a union, are forbidden.

At the same time, certain restrictions are placed on the unions and their officers as well. The net effect is to foster existing federal policy, which is to rely upon collective bargaining between essentially equally powerful parties to resolve disputes whenever possible. One consequence is that continuing union–management conflict has become a major element in practically all personnel decisions in many companies. This conflict serves as a constraint in and of itself because decisions often cannot be made quickly by management on a unilateral basis. They have to be worked out with the union, or they will be appealed to arbitrators and the courts. Consequently, many decision alterna-

EXHIBIT 14.2 U.S. federal laws affecting personnel decisions

Laws	Influence on Personnel Decisions
Civil Rights Act of 1964 (major amendment in 1972)	Prohibits discrimination in hiring, promotion, seniority systems, etc. on the basis of race, color, religion, national origin, or sex, often with the result that priority must be given to protected groups.
Executive Orders, such as #11246 (1965)	Require affirmative action so that discrimination does not exist among those doing business with the government; otherwise they will lose their business.
Social Security Act of 1935 (with numerous amendments and name changes)	Influences retirement ages, originally with the intent of removing employees from the labor force at least by the age of 65; must be considered in company pension planning.
Age Discrimination Act of 1967 (as amended)	Prohibits discrimination in hiring, promotion, mandatory retirement, etc. against those 40 to 70 years old, making this a protected group in personnel decision making.
Rehabilitation Act of 1973	Constrains employers to hire the handicapped.
Credit Reporting Act of 1971	Requires companies to notify individuals who are subjects of investigations regarding this fact.
Fair Labor Standards Act of 1938 (with numerous amendments)	Establishes that a minimum wage must be paid, and requires premium pay for hours beyond 40 per week.
Equal Pay Act of 1963	Requires equal pay for men and women doing the same work.
Wage and Salary Controls (1942, 1951, 1971)	Restrictions on the increases in compensation companies may grant employees. Invoked at intervals.
Employee Retirement Income Security Act of 1974	Introduces controls over company retirement plans.
Worker's Compensation Plans (state laws)	Mandate payments to injured workers with funding of plans based on company's accident record; thus exert pressure to reduce work environment accidents.
Occupational Safety and Health Act of 1970	Establishes safety and health standards in the workplace and provides for their enforcement.
Federal Unemployment Tax Act of 1935 (and amendments) in conjunction with state laws	Require company payments to fund unemployment insurance, with amount of payments based on number of forced separations; thus exerts pressure to reduce separations.

tives involving rapid action simply are not available to management at all. This is why many companies would prefer not to have their employees represented by unions.

EXHIBIT 14.3 Laws affecting labor relations decisions

Laws	Influences on Labor Relations Decisions
Railway Labor Act of 1926 (major amendment in 1936)	Specifies what can and cannot be done in collective bargaining and dispute settlement; applies to railroads and airlines.
Norris–LaGuardia Act of 1932	Severely restricts management's freedom to use courts to limit unionization and strikes.
Wagner Act of 1935	Makes it very difficult for management to prevent union representation and growth by specifying various unfair labor practices that management cannot use.
Taft–Hartley Act of 1947	Further controls labor–management relations, establishing government as an impartial umpire, attempts to ensure power equalization between parties.
Landrum–Griffin Act of 1959	Restricts alternatives open to management in dealing with unions and their officers.
State Labor Laws (since 1937)	To varying degrees, fill in gaps left by federal laws at the state level, thus extending certain of their limitations.

Labor Union Activities

Labor unions introduce a variety of constraints on personnel decision making. There is considerable controversy over whether these constraints are justified, but the practical fact is that where a union exists, constraints are very likely to exist also. The processes by which these constraints come into being, and their nature, are the concern of this section.

The Unionization Process Because of the constraints involved, most companies would prefer not to have unions. To the extent they legally can, many have taken steps to keep unions out or to get rid of them where they already exist. The result has been some reduction in unionization of the labor force over a period extending back to the 1950s. In part, the reduction is a function of changes in the labor force itself. The traditional *craft* unions (carpenters, machinists, etc.) and the *industrial* unions (auto workers, steelworkers, etc.) have suffered losses at the blue collar level because of reduced employment. There have been modest gains, however, among white collar clerical workers, and for the *professional* unions (teachers, engineers, etc.), often as a result of growth in union representation of government employees. In general, the larger the union, the more money from dues it can bring to bear for political action, organizing campaigns, and strike benefits; thus the more influence it can exert.

Certainly unions are still attempting to organize new groups of employees. The impetus may come from a group of dissatisfied employees or from union organizers sent in for this purpose. The initial step is to get 30 percent or more of a group to sign a petition; then an election must be held. If a majority of the employees want a union, this means that the company must engage in collective bargaining in good faith with that union. Not surprisingly, union organizing campaigns and elections produce a great deal of conflict that can influence union–management relations for years to come. So too do decertification campaigns in which companies attempt to convince employees to vote the union out.

Collective Bargaining   Once a union is certified, the company must bargain and ultimately sign a contract on certain issues, including those noted in Exhibit 14.4. Usually there is considerable preparation for bargaining on both sides, and both sides present a series of demands. If agreement cannot be reached, the union may decide to strike. The company may attempt to operate anyway with employees it can retain and with new hires, or it may shut down and lock out all employees.

Relationships in collective bargaining may take many forms. Conflicts are frequent. Communications problems are often produced by faulty perceptions and by the differing personalities, backgrounds, values, and motives of the negotiators. Problems also arise from the ritualistic, legalized formality of the bargaining situation, which serves to stifle new solutions, and from the need to behave in ways that constituencies may desire—thus interpersonal factors may supersede economic.[2] Where these problems predominate and deadlock seems likely, government mediators may enter as third parties to facilitate a resolution. These media-

---

EXHIBIT 14.4   Factors often considered in union–management contracts

Management Rights—Statement of areas in which management can make unilateral decisions. Usually also notes areas in which the contract limits management's freedom.

Union Security—Statement whether all employees must join the union (union shop), or only pay dues (agency shop), or are free to join or not as they choose (often under some type of state "right to work law"). Included are provisions regarding direct deductions of union dues from paychecks (checkoffs).

Regulation of Union Activity—Provisions regarding the use of company property by union representatives, their terms of employment, and the scope of their activities.

Job Security—Conditions under which the company may discipline employees, including grounds for firing. Also seniority provisions as related to promotion, transfers, shift choices, and layoffs.

Wages and Hours—Although the contract usually does not include specific rates (these are contracted separately), general principles of payment are stated, including any cost-of-living escalators, step improvements, and incentive terms.

Employee Benefits and Services—Paid vacations, holidays, insurance plans, retirement pensions, and the like that the company must provide.

Strikes and Lockouts—Factors controlling union strikes and company lockouts, including penalties for unauthorized strikes.

Grievances and Arbitrations—How individual grievances are to be handled.

tors have no power to force a particular outcome. In contrast, some existing contracts, especially those involving government employees, call for arbitration of the issues by a third party whose decisions are binding to varying degrees.[3] In any event, whether negotiated through collective bargaining or imposed by binding arbitration, contract terms become a force on management and constrain its decisions.

Contract Administration The contract provides a guide for management–union relations over the period of its duration—typically one to three years. It does not eliminate conflict, however. Even when the contract contains a no-strike clause, so-called "wildcat" strikes may occur to protest some management action. There may also be slowdowns and certain kinds of sabotage.

The major procedure used to contain and resolve conflict is the grievance machinery. Exhibit 14.5 outlines a typical procedure. The number of steps may vary; sometimes they are fewer than five. The time limits at each level are specified in the contract, and so too is the need to put the complaint in writing. This limit is usually above the first step. The specific individuals involved for both management and union can differ at each step. In most, but not all, contracts the final step is impartial arbitration by an outsider acceptable to both parties. Such arbitration hearings have become increasingly formal over the years, with lawyers representing the union and management, witnesses called and sworn, transcripts prepared, and briefs filed by both sides. Although grievance systems are almost universal in unionized organizations, they also exist

EXHIBIT 14.5 Steps in a full-scale grievance procedure leading to arbitration

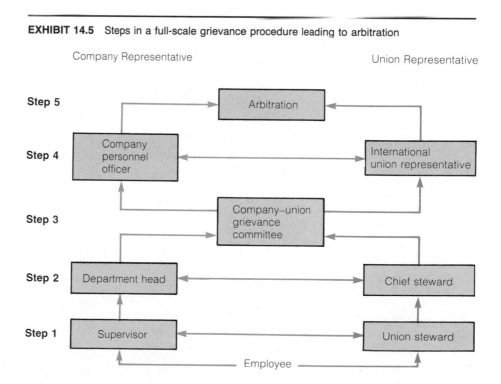

505   Organizations

in many non-union contexts, though generally without a provision for final arbitration.[4]

In many companies the grievance process operates fairly and efficiently. But it can become bottlenecked, with a huge backlog of unresolved cases, and it can be distorted to serve the purposes of one party or the other, with little reference to justice for the individual employee. There is tremendous variation in the grievance filing tendencies of individual stewards at step one, which is closely related to the level and type (company or union) of the steward's organizational commitment.[5] Many stewards push employees to file even when they do not want to, or even file on behalf of the union without the employee's signature. In such cases, the union is directly creating the problem and the grievance procedure becomes a channel for conflict to be voiced much more than a means for resolving it. In any event, the final decision reached, whether in the form of an arbitrator's award or not, becomes a constraint on management and/or the union.

JOB ANALYSIS AND HUMAN RESOURCE PLANNING

The basic building blocks of organizations are positions, ideally constituted so as to maximize attainment of the operative goal structure. In part, how these positions are defined and related one to another, especially at the management level, is an outgrowth of the organizing function as considered in part 3. At lower levels, however, and sometimes well into the ranks of management, positions are specified and tied together through the process of job analysis, and that is a personnel/human resource activity.

Once the position structure is specified, it needs to be staffed. Furthermore it needs to be kept staffed, with people who are likely to perform in ways as closely aligned with what the job analysis says is desirable as possible. As the position structure varies in the future, the staffing process must vary to keep pace with it. This is a matter of human resource planning—a process whose purpose is to ensure that the right number and kinds of people will be at the right places at the right time in the future, capable of performing so that the organization can accomplish its goals.

The Role and Nature of Job Analysis

Exhibit 14.6 sets forth and defines some of the terms used in connection with studying jobs. Not all companies carry out such formal job analyses, although more and more are doing so under pressure from the federal government related to equal employment opportunity legislation. A common reason for not doing formal job analyses is the fear that the jobs thus defined will become locked into the union contract and will be difficult to change. Yet even where this problem exists, companies do in fact study jobs on an informal basis, and there is a general understanding of what tasks different people are expected to perform.

Whether done formally or informally, and whether the resulting job description is written out in detail or is merely a set of ideas in the minds of individuals, job analysis serves to indicate what people *should* do at work—how they should perform, and thus what their role prescriptions are. Job analysis does not necessarily include a description of what people actually do. Poor performers may not behave in ways that are very close at all to what the job description specifies. Good performers will come much closer. Job descriptions serve to guide behav-

EXHIBIT 14.6 Terminology used in job analysis

Task—Distinct work activity carried out for a specific purpose.

Position—Specific set of tasks and duties performed by a given individual in an organization at a particular time.

Job—Very similar positions within an organization; the number depends on the scope of the organization and can be as small as one.

Occupation—Very similar jobs existing in different organizations and at different points in time.

Job Description—Written statement of the tasks, duties, and behaviors required in a given job.

Job Specification—Personal qualifications that candidates for the job must possess; typically appended to the job description.

Job Family—Collection of two or more jobs that require similar worker characteristics or contain parallel tasks.

Position Analysis—Study of the tasks performed by one person.

Job Analysis—Study of two or more positions constituting a job.

ior and provide a basis for evaluating it, but they are not invariably identical with behavior.

Analysis Factors   Exhibit 14.7 describes the various factors considered or elements involved in a comprehensive job analysis. How these factors are woven into the job description varies considerably from company to company. For example, the job specification may be a separate entity or incorporated within the job description. It is important to recognize in any event that the job specification deals not with desired job behaviors, but desired individual character-

EXHIBIT 14.7 Components included in a comprehensive job description

Job Title—What the job is called within the company and outside it, including alternative and slang titles.

Work Activities—What is to be done, including the tasks and duties, materials used, machinery operated, required interaction with others, supervision given and received, and reporting relationships.

Physical Environment—Physical working conditions, including heat, lighting, noise, ventilation, geographical location, and safety hazards.

Social Environment—Number and nature of people in the work environment as well as nearby non-company facilities and recreational opportunities.

Employment Conditions—Place of the job in the organization in such terms as wage structure, working hours, payment method, position permanency, seasonal or part-time nature, benefits, relation to other jobs and job families, and opportunities for transfer and promotion.

Job Specifications—Preferred or required education, experience, knowledge, physical capability, personal characteristics, etc., for performing the job.

istics. It establishes the criteria for staffing positions, and decisions of this kind may be sharply constrained by both human resource availability and the law. The job specification is thus most closely allied with recruiting and selection activities.

Analysis Methods   Various techniques are used in carrying out job analyses, as indicated in Exhibit 14.8. Approaches are selected depending upon suitability to the particular job, cost considerations, geographical dispersion of positions, and other factors. Ideally, more than one analysis method will be employed. If at all possible, data should be collected on experienced workers who are performing well. It is also helpful to have any data that are obtained from incumbents reviewed by their superiors. This can provide a valuable antidote to employee biases, and job descriptions should be corrected accordingly.

EXHIBIT 14.8   Methods for job analysis

Observation of Job Occupants

Approach—Job analyst observes performance of a number of individuals and records performance in narrative form or on a preestablished checklist.

Problems—Worker may act differently when observed. Mental work is difficult to determine by observation. Long job cycles extending over months, as with research studies, are difficult and costly to consider by observation.

Interview of Job Occupants

Approach—Job analyst interviews job incumbents asking them standardized questions about what they do and how they do it.

Problems—Adequate rapport may not be obtained, with the result that information is distorted. Conscious efforts to portray job as something it is not may occur.

Job Occupant Descriptions

Approach—Job occupants complete some type of questionnaire dealing with tasks performed and other factors in job description.

Problems—Similar to those in interviews of job occupants, except that some flexibility in dealing with individual variations and opportunities for rapport are lost.

Examination of Previous Job Descriptions

Approach—Analyst studies previous job descriptions prepared by the company, those of other companies, and occupational descriptions such as those prepared by governmental agencies.

Problems—Data may be incomplete, out of date, or simply erroneous.

Examination of Work Materials

Approach—Job analyst studies raw materials, tools, machines, and equipment used in the job.

Problems—In most cases this is not enough, but it can be of supplementary value.

Performance of Actual Work Activities

Approach—Job analysts actually perform the job, or work in a simulation of it and use information they obtain to prepare job description.

Problems—Where extensive training is required, this may not be feasible because of time needed to learn the job.

Although almost all approaches in job analysis deal with relationships among jobs, and thus with job families, there are some techniques that are particularly suited to this purpose.[6] Detailed questionnaires have been developed so that jobs may be studied on the same dimensions and related to each other accordingly. This facilitates transfers and promotions. Career ladders may be specified, indicating the positions through which people should move during a career in the organization and the training they will need to do so. Upward movement on a career ladder provides an enriched occupational experience, both personally and financially. Similar effects are obtained in some companies through redesigning and enriching the present position along the lines discussed in chapter 5.

Approaches in Human Resource Planning

Formal human resource planning is most characteristic of the larger companies, although even there it is not universally practiced. At its best it requires that a well-developed strategic planning process be in place (see chapter 11). In this context, human resource planning becomes an extension of the overall business planning effort. In many respects it is the most important extension, because if the people are not available when needed, no strategy will achieve implementation.

Human resource planning involves four basic processes:

1. Forecasting future needs for different kinds of skills and types of human resources.
2. Inventorying existing human resources.
3. Projecting present resources into the future and comparing the anticipated future position thus derived against the needs that have been forecast in item 1.
4. Planning the necessary recruiting, selection, training, compensation, placement, and any other personnel activities required to fill any gaps identified in item 3 and thus meet future human resource needs.

A model of the planning process is given in Exhibit 14.9. The overall concept is much the same as that used in discussing managerial careers in chapter 2. It all comes down to a matter of future supply and demand.

Establishing Future Demand The usual approach to forecasting future personnel needs requires the identification of some business factor that is closely tied to the basic nature of the business and also closely related to personnel requirements. Thus projected gross sales volume might be used to predict sales force demand. Different factors may be used with different labor force components, and sometimes multiple factors are combined. A number of sophisticated mathematical approaches have been developed for use in this kind of demand forecasting. Nevertheless, the basic procedure is to project future conditions from a knowledge of historical trends and relationships. These projections are then modified on the basis of judgments from knowledgeable people to take into account anticipated changes in organization structures, technology, and the like. Subjective modification of this kind can contribute substantially to the accuracy of the forecasting process.[7] The final result is a specification of the number of individuals needed at certain times in the future in certain employment categories.

EXHIBIT 14.9 Model of the human resource planning procedure

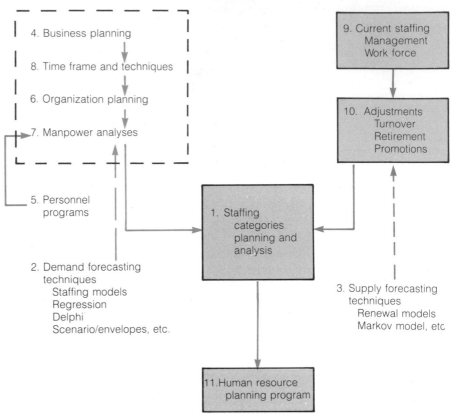

SOURCE: Elmer H. Burack and Nicholas J. Mathys, *Human Resource Planning: A Pragmatic Approach to Manpower Staffing and Development* (Lake Forest, Ill.: Brace-Park, 1980): 115. Reprinted by permission of the publisher.

Establishing Internal Supply   Using the same categories and times as for demand, supply must then be predicted with the assumption that current policies and procedures are retained. The starting point is an inventory of existing personnel. Then attrition is projected, taking into account voluntary separations, dismissals, retirements, layoffs, deaths, and transfers, demotions, or promotions out of the particular job category. These figures must then be adjusted to take into account the anticipated effects of future policies or strategies that may serve to change turnover patterns.[8] Finally, estimated attrition is compared with projected inmovements from hiring and job changes within the company. The result is a specification of what the employment situation will be at certain times in the future if things continue as they are. Note in Exhibit 14.9 that the forecasting techniques applicable to the supply problem differ considerably from those used with demand. With supply in particular, data from computerized employee information systems and skills inventories can prove particularly useful, although it is important to be sure that these systems are up-to-date and accurate.[9]

When supply and demand forecasts are compared, the crucial consideration is whether shortages can be anticipated at certain points in the future in certain categories. Excesses can usually be dealt with more easily, although union and legal considerations are making this a more difficult problem also. The real reason for human resource planning nevertheless is to stimulate additional planning to deal with anticipated shortage situations. A more detailed consideration of this latter type of planning must await discussion of the various approaches in staffing themselves. It is important to recognize, however, that sophisticated human resource planning may not be worth the cost involved unless there is some reason to anticipate possible future shortages. Some companies have experimented with human resource planning and found it wanting.[10]

RECRUITING AND SELECTION

Probably more than any other aspect of personnel management, the input processes of recruiting and selection have become constrained by legalities and government enforcement. The various laws, court decisions, government guidelines, and decisions by compliance officers have combined to produce a very considerable set of recruiting and selection limitations.[11] As a result, a new breed of personnel specialists—part lawyer and part psychologist—has come on the scene to deal with the highly technical problems involved.

The Logic of Selection

The essential requirement for a good selection system is to use predictors that will lead to the staffing of positions with individuals who have a high probability of performing well. To identify these predictors, personnel research studies are conducted. The basic design for such studies is outlined in Exhibit 14.10. This is not only the preferred approach from the viewpoint of accuracy of prediction, but it is also the approach that the courts have considered least likely to produce discrimination.

The problems with the model in Exhibit 14.10 are that it is time-consuming, requires hiring people who may not perform satisfactorily, and necessitates the hiring of a large number of employees. Many approaches have been developed to deal with these problems, usually at some cost to the certainty of prediction.[12] Thus the research may be conducted with current employees rather than new hires, predictor and performance data may be obtained at roughly the same time, groups of jobs may be combined for research purposes, a number of predictors may be used in the same study and combined in various ways, a wide range of statistical analysis techniques may be used, and so on. But the key idea remains the same—to be as certain as possible, within constraints imposed by human resource availability, that the people selected for employment will be the ones most likely to perform well.

Recruiting

For the whole input activity to function well, efforts must be made to ensure that a pool of potential employees is available within which selection processes may operate. Recruiting is the means by which this pool is created. For some purposes, recruiting may occur inside the company, when a job is posted so that all who are interested may apply or when a "promotion from within policy" is in

EXHIBIT 14.10 Basic longitudinal selection model

Step 1. Use job analysis to identify characteristics of incumbents that might be related to effective performance.

Step 2. Determine specific measures of these characteristics—whether from psychological tests, interviews, application blanks—to be used.

Step 3. Obtain measures of these predictor characteristics from a relatively large group of job applicants.

Step 4. Hire from this group, to the degree positions are open, without reference to the scores on predictor measures. The need is that insofar as possible those with both low and high scores will have a chance to perform.

Step 5. After a short period, obtain performance evaluation data to see who has done well and who poorly on the job.

Step 6. Establish relationship between earlier predictor characteristics and subsequent performance data. A possible outcome for a sample of 100 employees is as follows:

Predictor Characteristic		Performance						
		Low	1	2	3	4	5	High
High	80–99				2	4	4	
	60–79			4	2	8	6	
	40–59		4	4	24	8		
	20–39		2	10	8			
Low	0–19		4	2	4			

In this case, high scores on the predictor characteristic do tend to yield high levels of performance.

Step 7. When high scores do correspond to high performance levels, repeat the study to be sure the results hold.

effect. But basically, recruiting is externally oriented, and that is the major thrust of the present discussion.

In large part, what a company does in recruiting is dictated by the results of human resource planning. To this may be added the fact that affirmative action plans, usually legally mandated, may require special efforts to recruit minorities, women, etc. within the staffing requirements of the human resource plan. As a result of these considerations, most growing companies are constantly in the recruiting market; the process is an ongoing one, often operating on a major scale.

In this process, an important consideration is the degree to which the available jobs are portrayed realistically by recruiters. Candidates should be able to accept or turn down offers on the basis of a candid presentation of what the job involves. There is evidence to indicate that, when jobs are portrayed realistically, rather than through a "pie-in-the-sky" approach, those who accept employment are more likely to stay on. Companies thus do well to have their recruiters present an honest, fair, ungarnished picture of what can be expected. It is unclear exactly why this straightforward approach works as well as it does,[13] but the simple fact is that it does.

Sources Companies generally prefer to use the least costly recruiting sources they can, and these sources tend to be those in which the applicants seek out the company. In contrast, when the company has to find job candidates or pay someone else to find them, the costs rise rapidly. Yet for various reasons, most larger firms do have to use these more costly procedures.

The ideal situation from a company viewpoint is one in which good candidates apply directly to the personnel office—so-called walk-ins, people who call or send resumés listing their qualifications. Often these people are in fact referred by friends or relatives who work for the company, and some companies make it a practice to keep their employees informed about job openings in the hope that this type of referral will occur. Although they rarely constitute a primary source, former employees may seek reemployment, or the company may contact them with this end in mind.

Unions as a source are of variable usefulness, even among unionized employers. The *closed shop,* where only union members can be hired, is no longer legal, but in the shipping industry and in construction, the unions certainly can be the major source for recruiting. On the other hand, many companies in other industries would not even consider using union sources.

Advertising in newspapers and other types of publications, or on the radio or television, moves the company into a more applicant-seeking stance. Help-wanted ads are usually sent in by company personnel people, but more extensive display advertising may be prepared by an outside agency. Private employment agencies are used mostly for clerical, professional, and lower managerial employees. The state employment agencies, which operate under the guidance of the U.S. Job Service, tend to provide more blue collar workers. At the upper professional and managerial levels, various executive recruiting firms are widely used. Also there are organizations that maintain computerized files of resumés. Companies can use these job market information systems much as they would their own internal employee information systems to generate a list of candidates for various types of jobs.

Other ways in which candidates may be sought out include using placement services at professional society meetings and sending representatives to geographical locations where numbers of qualified people are known to exist. Canceled government contracts, plant closings, and the like can serve to set this type of activity in motion. A number of firms that are reducing their work force now provide out-placement services through which new employees may be located.[14] Many large companies also devote considerable time and money to recruiting at schools and colleges. High schools and vocational schools near company locations are a major source of lower level employees. Campus recruiting is a primary source for management trainees.

College Recruiting   Recruiting on college campuses is carried on by most large and medium-sized companies on a continuing basis. College graduates are the primary source for staffing many managerial, professional, and sales positions, and companies compete strongly for the best candidates. Almost all colleges maintain placement offices to coordinate these efforts and in some cases, professional schools have their own placement activities as well.

Usually the campus interviews conducted by company recruiters are for the purpose of an initial screening. If candidates impress the interviewer, they are invited to some company location, partly as an extension of the recruiting process, partly to carry out a more extensive selection procedure. The objective is to inform candidates about the company and create a favorable impression so that, if an offer is extended, they will accept. At the same time, data from multiple interviews, tests, and the like are obtained to aid in the selection decision. An offer of employment may be made during a visit, or by telephone or letter at a later date. The types of questions recruiters typically ask are the following:

What are the individual's goals in life, and how do these relate to career objectives?

What type of work is desired, and what types of expectations does the person have regarding this work?

How much does the individual know about the company, and why is he or she interested in it?

What specific strengths and weaknesses exist insofar as employment is concerned?

How well reasoned is the person's career choice?

In what ways does the person's college education relate to the type of work that will be performed if hiring occurs?

Why did the individual choose a particular college and major? Were these well-reasoned decisions?

Are there any geographical preferences, family, or personal factors that might create problems?

What have been the individual's major achievements so far in life?

Affirmative Action Recruiting   Under agreements with various government agencies, often signed under the threat of legal action, many companies have committed themselves to actively seek out minorities and women. Typically this means that walk-ins can no longer be relied upon as primary sources. If the existing labor force is almost entirely white or male, then using this source will only serve to perpetuate that situation. Thus to implement affirmative action plans, companies may have to utilize more costly approaches that require active efforts to find the types of people they have agreed to hire.

For minorities, the best source appears to be community action agencies operating in minority neighborhoods. Also valuable are referrals by current employees (usually minorities themselves) and employment agencies. For women, the best source is advertising, usually in newspapers. Also useful are referrals by current employees and employment agencies. Community agencies have proved particularly helpful in locating qualified handicapped individuals.[15]

Selection Methods

Ideally, a company would generate a sizable list of candidates for a set of openings and then use selection data to choose those most likely to perform well. In actual practice, however, both recruiting and selection are ongoing processes over time. Thus, when a candidate meets certain pre-established requirements, that candidate is hired, without waiting to see if an even better-qualified individual would come along later. Although this procedure may mean a less than optimal return on recruiting and selection system investments, it does protect against losing a good person by waiting too long to make an offer, and it does get openings filled more rapidly.

In any event, it is important to recognize that the various selection methods are of help only to the extent that they can actually be used to select. There have to be enough candidates so that some can be hired and some rejected as unlikely to succeed. If the labor maket is such that few candidates can be located and practically everyone who is located must be hired, then selection is not really meaningful. The following discussion assumes, then, a level of human resource availability sufficient to permit meaningful selection.

The Interview Interviews often combine recruiting and selection components to varying degrees. In addition, interviewer judgments frequently are influenced by information from application blanks, psychological tests, or other written materials made available prior to the interview. The result is that preconceived notions may be more important than the content of the interview itself.[16] When this is the case, the interview becomes a meaningless exercise insofar as selection is concerned.

Perhaps because of considerations of these kinds, the value of the interview as a selection procedure has come into serious question. Often different interviewers do not agree, and interview judgments regarding subsequent performance cannot be relied upon to predict what that performance will be. Yet there are circumstances under which these problems are less likely to occur. If the interviewer is well-informed regarding the job to be performed, if the interview is conducted following a structured format using a pre-established interview questionnaire, and if interview questions have been studied and certain answers designated as highly predictive of subsequent job success, then interviews can work well as a means of selecting employees. Unfortunately, the typical employment interview does not satisfy these requirements. As a result, many interviews do not work well for purposes of selection, although they may serve other purposes such as recruiting, bargaining, and the like.

Application Blanks and Biographical Data Almost all firms have application blanks, and many have several different types for various categories of employment. Used to best advantage, these instruments are scored in accordance with known relationships between the reponses provided and subsequent job performance. Sometimes application blanks scored in this way contain questions dealing with early life experiences, hobbies, health, social relationships, and a number of other factors. Thus they may obtain a wide range of biographical data in addition to the usual application blank questions.

However, the essence of this approach is to focus on questions that have been shown by research to be predictive of subsequent job success. Exhibit 14.11 contains an application blank developed in this way. It was designed to yield data that could be scored to predict success as a management consultant with McKinsey and Company. The responses that yield the maximum scores on various factors are noted. Using application blank and other biographical data in this way can contribute greatly to selection effectiveness. Unfortunately, many application blanks, like selection interviews, are not tied directly to performance outcomes in this manner, and thus fail to achieve their potential.

EXHIBIT 14.11 Application form developed from analysis of biographical data

---

Biographical Information—Consulting Staff
(Brief Form)

Name _____ Date _____
Address _____
Telephone _____
Date of Birth _____ Nationality _____

Work Experience. Please note all regular, full-time employment (not summer)
starting with the most recent position.

1. Name and nature of organization _____
   Dates of employment (month & year) _____
   Titles of positions held _____
   Duties (highest level position) _____
2. Name and nature of organization _____
   Dates of employment (month & year) _____
   Titles of positions held _____
   Duties (highest level position) _____
   (Note additional positions on the back of this sheet using the same format.)

Military Experience. Please note active duty service only.
   Nation _____ Branch (Army, Navy, Air Force, etc.)_____
Dates of service (month & year) _____
Rank at separation _____

Education

Type of School	Name and Location	From	To	Degree	Major
High School					
Prep. School					
College					
Grad. School					

Early Background
Place where spent childhood (longest residence) _____
Father's education (level and type) _____
Father's highest position _____
   Name and nature of organization _____
Other positions held by father _____
Mother's education (level and type) _____

Characteristics Yielding the Highest Score:
1. Less than 1.5 years of prior business experience
2. Business experience with managerial responsibility
3. Military service in the Navy or Marines
4. Active duty military service with commissioned rank
5. Secondary schooling at a private preparatory school.
6. Graduated from a small private college
7. Graduated from the Harvard Business School with an MBA
8. Father did not graduate from high school
9. Father's highest occupational attainment was in small business or corporate
   management below the middle level

SOURCE: Adapted from Mary G. Miner and John B. Miner, *Employee Selection Within the Law*
(Washington, D.C.: Bureau of National Affairs, 1980): 183–184.

Reference and Background Checks Letters of reference, and telephone references as well, suffer from the major problem that most of the responses are so positive that differentiations cannot be made. More extensive field investigations conducted by credit agencies and other sources may unearth more negative information through direct interviews with former employers, neighbors, and the like. However, a question remains whether this information would in fact be of value in predicting job performance. Thus, such an investigation in one instance revealed that a man was living with a woman to whom he was not married, and this information served to prevent an offer of employment. But the company involved had no evidence that circumstances of this kind make for less effective job performance. The point is that, with reference and background checks, as with other selection procedures, it is important to develop research evidence regarding performance effects. It is not sufficient to rely on what seems obvious.

Overall the evidence indicates that, at best, references provide very weak predictions of success in jobs which are similar to those left. There is something of value in the reference process, but care should be taken to ensure that those giving the references are indeed well-informed and unbiased. Again, standardized questionnaires developed from a knowledge of who performs best are most likely to work well.

Physical Examinations As with other techniques, physical examinations may have other objectives than pure selection. They may influence placement decisions so that a person can be placed in a job where any physical limitations are minimized. They can serve to restrict a company's liabilities under workers' compensation when conditions existing prior to employment are identified. They may be required, as with truckers and airline pilots, by existing laws. Nevertheless, physical limitations can serve as a company bar to employment on occasion.

When thus used for selection purposes, physical examinations are no more perfect than other procedures. In particular they can fail to identify physical problems that should be identified, and they can magnify the effects on performance of problems that are identified. Supplementing the examinations with health questionnaires on which the individual reports on his or her own health problems has proved useful. In particular, those who report fewer problems on these questionnaires appear to have less absenteeism.

Some companies have turned to polygraph or lie detection measures as selection instruments to predict honesty and potential theft. Because these instruments utilize records of blood pressure, pulse, respiratory patterns, and sweat gland activity in relationship to specific questions, they are closely allied to physical examinations. In the hands of competent examiners these techniques can work well, and sufficient agreement between examiners can be obtained.[17] But in certain states, legal restrictions make polygraphs unavailable for employment selection purposes. Polygraphs have been used in selection most frequently in wholesale and retail trade and for positions where bonding is required. Obviously, from a recruiting perspective, these approaches can create a negative image, but as selection instruments, in the right hands, they can make a useful contribution.

Psychological Tests The most extensively used psychological tests are those of an intellectual or mental ability nature and, because of current legal requirements, these tests have been widely researched in relation to subsequent job performance. Exhibit 14.12 provides information on the nature of individually

---

EXHIBIT 14.12 Types of mental ability items used in individually administered and paper and pencil tests

Wechsler Adult Intelligence Scale (individually administered)

1. *Information.* Open-ended questions dealing with factual data normally acquired in regular contacts.
2. *Comprehension.* Open-ended questions dealing with understanding of need for social rules.
3. *Arithmetic.* Questions of a story or problem type scored in terms of the correctness of the numerical solutions and the time to respond.
4. *Digit Span.* Group of numbers read off which is to be repeated from memory, sometimes backward.
5. *Similarities.* Pairs of terms read off and a common property or characteristic is to be abstracted.
6. *Vocabulary.* Words of increasing difficulty must be defined.
7. *Picture Completion.* Pictures are presented in which missing components must be identified.
8. *Picture Arrangement.* A series of pictures must be arranged as quickly as possible in an order that makes sense.
9. *Object Assembly.* Jigsaw puzzles to be assembled within a given time limit.
10. *Block Design.* A set of small blocks with faces colored in various ways is to be put together so as to match pre-established designs.
11. *Digit Symbol.* A series of paired symbols and their code numbers are given, and the person writes the appropriate numbers for scrambled sets of symbols within an established time period.

Differential Aptitude Tests (paper-and-pencil)

1. *Verbal Reasoning.* The person must match a series of verbal analogies requiring a good background of general information.
2. *Numerical Ability.* Arithmetic computations are made, with the answer selected from a set of multiple-choice alternatives.
3. *Abstract Reasoning.* Four problem figures are presented in logical sequence, and then a fifth answer figure must be selected from multiple-choice alternatives to complete the sequence.
4. *Space Relations.* Given a series of items requiring visualization of forms in space, the person must match a key pattern with various multiple-choice alternatives.
5. *Mechanical Reasoning.* Pictures depicting various mechanical problems are presented along with question intended to determine whether the mechanical processes involved are understood.
6. *Clerical Speed and Accuracy.* Pairs of numbers or letters are presented in series and then repeated in a different order with the requirement that an originally underlined pair be identified as quickly as possible.
7. *Language Usage, Spelling.* Correctly and incorrectly spelled words must be identified as to their correctness.
8. *Language Usage, Sentences.* Determination of the degree to which the formal rules of grammar are understood.

administered measures, usually used in psychological assessments of managerial and professional candidates, and in the more extensively used paper-and-pencil procedures.

In addition to tests of these kinds, a number of personality and interest measures have proved particularly useful in predicting success in sales, service, and managerial occupations. These instruments vary widely in approach, and some require considerable training to use them well.

Another type of measure focuses not on underlying abilities and personality factors, but on specific job skills and knowledge. Typing and shorthand tests are examples. Much testing of this type uses a job sample or simulation approach and assumes a degree of prior learning of job skills. However, some measures of this type have been developed that tap the ability to learn job skills rapidly. There are also achievement tests that determine how much job knowledge a person has. These are particularly useful as a check on prior work experience. Not infrequently, applicants will claim higher levels of experience and knowledge in skilled trades, computer work, and the like than they actually have. Achievement tests can identify such instances very effectively.

Assessment Centers A procedure that combines several of the selection methods already considered is the assessment center. People are evaluated over a period of time, often as long as three days, during which they complete personal history forms, undergo interviewing, perform various situational exercises of a job sample or simulation nature, fill out personality and other types of tests, and are observed to identify various personal characteristics. Ratings are made either by psychologists, or company managers, or both. These ratings have been shown to have good relationships with subsequent work performance and career success.[18]

When used properly, the assessment center approach is time-consuming and costly. Its use for selecting new hires has been restricted largely to managers or management trainees and sales personnel. A more common application is in the selection of already-employed managers for promotions, special training programs, and the like. In general it has been the larger companies that have considered the results achieved to be worth the investment in the time of company personnel that is necessary.

TRAINING AND DEVELOPMENT	Organizations do a great deal to prepare people for positions as defined by job analysis and other approaches. Pressures on companies to provide increased training have come from a variety of sources. Where trained human resources are not available in the labor market, companies must provide the needed training as a means of overcoming the availability constraint. And with the emergence of many new, highly technical positions, this is an increasing need. Legal pressures have focused on the training of minorities and women, not only to give them initial occupational skills, but also to permit upgrading into higher-level positions. The unions have long emphasized the retraining of their members to cope with changing technologies and shifts in skill requirements within the labor force. The diverse array of approaches noted in Exhibit 14.13 reflects the very substantial organizational response that these forces have elicited.

EXHIBIT 14.13 Training and development methods classified by goals and strategies

Primary Strategy	Intended Goals		
	Improved Self-Understanding	Better Job Skills and Knowledge	Increased Motivation
Cognitive changes in thoughts and ideas	Career development Manageral work roles training Sensitivity or T-group training	Orientation training Lectures and discussion Training in decision tree approach to participation Case study and games	Role motivation training Achievement and power motivation training
Changed behavior		On-the-job training Apprenticeships Programmed instruction Role playing	Goals and performance coaching
Changed environments	Leader match training		Job rotation Behavior modification

SOURCE: Adapted from Kenneth N. Wexley and Gary P. Latham, *Developing and Training Human Resources in Organizations* (Glenview, Ill.: Scott, Foresman, 1981): 7.

The Logic of Training and Development

In staffing positions there is often some trade-off between selection and training. From an economic viewpoint, companies would generally prefer the selection alternative. In that situation, individuals who are hired come into the organization already possessed of the necessary job skills as a result of secretarial training, university coursework, professional education, attendance at vocational schools, prior work experiences, and the like. Selection processes are then used to choose those individuals most likely to succeed on the job.

In the training situation, on the other hand, the company must bear the major costs of training; the person is hired without needed job skills and capabilities, and obtains them while being paid by the employer. Selection enters in here, to choose those likely to acquire the necessary proficiencies with the least investment possible. Because of the investment required, staffing through training tends to occur primarily when other approaches are insufficient.

Training Needs Analysis Following this logic, it is very important to know when people are being hired who lack certain of the requirements for successful performance and to spot already-employed workers who for one reason or another are inadequately prepared for the jobs they hold. When the selection approach to staffing is insufficient, there is always the risk that the training and development approach may not get mobilized. Training needs analysis attempts to deal with this problem by first identifying where performance deficiencies exist or can be anticipated, then determining whether training and development would correct the situation, and finally, specifying the type of approach to be used if training does appear to be called for.

Training needs analysis can use achievement tests and job samples to determine whether people know what they should know. Other approaches involve spotting problem areas in the company through the examination of production records, turnover statistics, performance evaluations, and the like. Training coordinators may use checklists that they complete on the basis of observations, study of company statistics, and discussion with managers. Once problem areas and jobs are identified, needs are gradually narrowed to pinpoint what types of training might be required and who should receive it. Job analysis data can be of considerable value in this process.

Evaluation of Training   The essence of any training or development procedure is that it is intended to transform people in some way so that they are different afterwards. Furthermore, the change must be enduring if it is to have any real influence on performance, and it must be of a kind that has some relevance for the goals of the organization. Thus a course that produced a greater appreciation and understanding of major literary works would not under most circumstances be the type of training a company could justify investing in.

The logic of training and development requires first that these procedures be used with people and in situations where they are needed or where major benefits are likely to be realized. It requires second that anticipated changes actually occur. As with establishing the performance relatedness of selection methods, this is a personnel research question.

Exhibit 14.14 outlines the basic model for training evaluation, although both simpler and more complex approaches are sometimes used. In this model, two comparable groups of individuals are established initially, and both groups take a pre-test. This may in fact be a measure of performance on the job, or it may be a measure related to one of the goals of training—self-understanding, job skills, or motivation—as indicated in Exhibit 14.13. One of the groups then undergoes whatever training is being evaluated, and the other group does not. After the training is completed, both groups take a post-test, which is either identical to or directly comparable to the pre-test. If the average change in the trained group is appreciably greater than any change in the untrained group, then an initial positive evaluation of the training is warranted. The follow-up at time 3 is intended to determine whether change is enduring, and essentially repeats the pre-test–post-test comparison at an appropriate later date. If there is a clear pre-test follow-up superiority for the trained group, then the positive evaluation of training is confirmed.

EXHIBIT 14.14   Basic model for training evaluation

	Time 1	Intervening Period	Time 2	Intervening Period	Time 3
Trained Group	Pre-test ⟶	Training ⟶	Post-test ⟶		⟶Follow-up
Untrained Group	Pre-test ⟶		Post-test ⟶		⟶Follow-up

In Exhibit 14.13, a number of training and development methods are listed. Some seek to improve the level of self-understanding, some to increase job skills and knowledge, and some to change job-related motives. Three strategies are also indicated, involving various focuses of the training process—cognitive changes in thoughts and ideas, behavioral changes, and changes in the work environment. Detailed treatment of the various methods and of the results of evaluation research applying approaches like that of Exhibit 14.14 to these methods is the subject matter of advanced courses in industrial training and management development. The brief coverage provided here follows the framework of Exhibit 14.13 while recognizing that there may be some disagreement with details of these classifications and that a number of additional methods exist.

Training to Develop Self-Understanding Career development is concerned with encouraging people to engage in personal career planning and assisting them to tie this process in with career ladders and other factors within the company. Outside consultants or internal counselors often aid in this process, but others are involved as well, as the model in Exhibit 14.15 indicates. In many respects, career development represents vocational guidance inside the

---

EXHIBIT 14.15 Factors and individuals involved in personal career planning

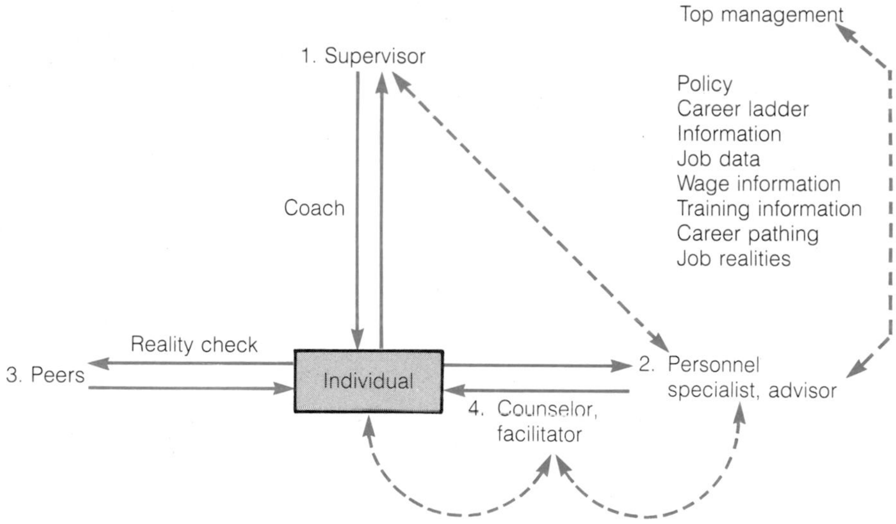

5. Questions to be answered
     Where am I today?
     Where do I want to be in the future?
     What are my goals?
     What skills do I have?
     What skills do I need?
     How do I get to where I want to be?

SOURCE: Elmer H. Burack and Nicholas J. Mathys, *Career Management in Organizations: A Practical Human Resource Planning Approach* (Lake Forest, Ill.: Brace-Park, 1980): 215. Reprinted by permission of the publisher.

company. This occurred originally as a result of legal pressures to improve opportunities for minorities and women, but in many firms it has spread well beyond that initial focus.

Managerial work role training involves an intensive self-study of one's own managerial job and one's performance in it. The framework for this analysis is the managerial work roles approach discussed in chapter 1 (see Exhibit 1.4). The objective is to gain a solid understanding of what a particular position requires of a manager; questions for self-study are provided to this end.

Sensitivity or T-group training was considered in chapter 10 as it related to the origins of organization development. This training approach utilizes learning within a group, with the assistance of a group leader, to increase understanding of oneself, of the nature of group processes, and of interpersonal skills in general. The approach appears best suited to the development of effective group-based systems and least appropriate for bureaucratic management. The usual consequences are a better understanding of others, greater self-awareness, increased competence in handling conflicts, a more pronounced tendency to utilize group processes in dealing with other people, and the acquisition of a more humanistic set of values.

Leader match training is based on the contingency view of leadership, as considered in chapter 6 and outlined in Exhibit 6.9. It teaches people how to understand their primary leadership style and the situations in which that style can be expected to produce the best results. Then they learn to engineer the work environment so as to produce a style–situation match that the theory views as optimal. Thus the person changes the environment based on an increased understanding of the relationships involved. The primary medium used to achieve this result is a self-study workbook developed as a programmed text. The value of the training is of course a direct function of the correctness of the theory; on that score, there has been some question.

Training to Develop Job Skills Orientation training is intended to prepare the new employee to function effectively in the organization. Typically it involves some formal presentation by members of the training staff, study of company handbooks and other materials, and more specifically job-related training by an immediate supervisor. The objective is to provide knowledge of the work and company environment in a condensed form.

Some companies use the traditional classroom lecture format combined with varying amounts of discussion. When this approach is used, it is most likely to be for the purpose of conveying specific job-related knowledge, and the groups involved rarely contain more than twenty to twenty-five people. As a result there tends to be more two-way interaction between instructor and trainees than in a regular educational setting. Audio-visual aids such as slides, films, videotapes, and the like are widely included.

Training in the decision tree approach to participation is an outgrowth of the views considered in chapter 6 (see Exhibit 6.13). Managers are taught how to use the decision tree concepts through case analysis, group discussions, and computerized feedback on the decision processes they are using. In the end, they develop skills in selecting an approach to decision sharing appropriate to the existing situation.

Case analysis is central to the decision tree approach and to a number of other types of management development. Overall, however, it does not appear to be quite as appropriate in the business setting per se as in business school education. The same is true of management games in which trainees make decisions and subsequently receive feedback from a computer on the consequences of those decisions—a case in action over time. Some managers feel that these approaches lack the emotional realism of "real world" decision making. Probably more important, however, is the fact that they want to deal with the actual problems they face in their jobs, not those in a hypothetical case. For these reasons, case study and management games seem most appropriate for those preparing for or just starting out in management.

On-the-job training is the most widely used of all the methods. It is given by a supervisor or an experienced employee and assumes that that person knows how to, wants to, and does train effectively. This is not always the case, and accordingly, on-the-job training can leave many training needs unfulfilled. Yet at its best, this is the least costly and closest to reality of the available methods. Apprenticeships for the various skilled trades generally incorporate a number of hours of on-the-job training and add classroom work, reading, shop instruction, and the like. They are joint union–management activities, but the U.S. Department of Labor acts as a general overseer and administers standards. Completion of an apprenticeship may require four or five years, but many workers receive their essential training in this way without staying on to completion.

Programmed instruction involves the presentation of material to be learned in logical sequence, with the individual required to actively respond at each step of the process and then receive feedback on the effectiveness of this response before progressing. It is highly standardized, permits learning at the person's own pace, and, once the program has been created, it does not require the services of an instructor; people teach themselves. In the business world, programmed instruction is used by a number of companies, and it is almost always used when a large number of people must be taught the same subject matter. Developing programmed materials is a time-consuming and costly process.

Role playing is typically used in conjunction with other management development methods. Trainees are to imagine themselves in a particular role and then act out that role while being observed by others. The role-playing is rotated within the group, and the reactions of observers provide feedback on behavior. This method is very effective in getting people to try out job behaviors they have not used previously, as when a new sales approach is to be learned.

Training to Develop Motivation Managerial role motivation training is conducted using conventional lecture and discussion methods, sometimes supplemented by cases, video-taped role scenes, and readings. The objective is to develop motives of the kind needed to perform effectively in managerial roles in bureaucratic organizations; more specifically, it is to increase motivation to manage, as discussed in chapter 2 and outlined in Exhibit 2.4. The content of the training focuses on methods of dealing with ineffective performance in a subordinate—how to diagnose the causes of performance problems and take appropriate corrective actions. The training covers much the same ground as chapter 4 in this book and uses Exhibit 4.11 as a basic outline.

Achievement motivation training is intended primarily to develop the motives needed to successfully start and operate a business, i.e. become an entrepreneur. It is based on the theory discussed in chapter 5. Trainees learn about their own achievement fantasies and drives and study cases as well as other materials to learn achievement-oriented behaviors. They develop career plans to implement their achievement interests. The training is intended to, and apparently does, make people engage more in entrepreneurial activities of the type discussed in chapter 12. In addition, a similar training procedure has been developed to increase power motivation, especially that of a more mature nature (see Exhibit 5.3). In this case the focus is on producing more effective corporate managers. To date, however, less has been learned regarding the value of power motivation training than about achievement motivation training.

Goals and performance coaching involves the feedback of performance evaluation results by a superior to a subordinate. To some extent this may represent on-the-job training, but when the subordinate is an experienced employee, the objective is not so much to teach job skills and knowledge as to stimulate motivation to behave in ways specified by the role prescriptions for the position. The coaching is intended to result in the establishment of specific, hard goals in accordance with the ideas regarding the motivational effects of goal setting considered in chapter 5. Coaching of this kind may be part of a formal management-by-objectives (MBO) program as outlined in Exhibit 5.10. It may also be carried out on a strictly individual basis between a superior and each subordinate. The goal setting may involve considerable participation on the part of the subordinate, or the goals may be assigned by the superior.

Job rotation provides a person with experience in several different positions, usually following a pre-planned sequence and set time schedule. With management trainees these assignments are usually to specifically created trainee positions in various departments. The intent is to expose the trainee to different departmental environments in order to increase understanding of departmental workings and interrelationships, but more importantly to develop specific career aspirations and organizational commitment (see chapter 5). At more advanced career levels, job rotation schedules are often worked out on an individual basis to meet the requirements of a particular person. In this case, the positions are actual ones, rather than of a trainee nature, and the goal is to stimulate and broaden.

Behavior modification is considered in chapter 5. It involves controlling the work environment and manipulating reinforcements. Although the developers of these views typically deny an important role to internal motivational processes, the results of organizational behavior modification procedures are essentially motivational in nature—people's behavior is changed so that they do (want to do) certain things and not others. Programs of this kind have been widely used to improve performance, including attendance, safety, and productive output. Exhibit 5.7 describes how supervisors may achieve these results.

Summary

The staffing process in organizations is in fact a matter of continuous decision making under conditions in which a set of constraints imposes severe limitations on what can be done. The major external constraints are the availability of human resources, the laws, and the labor unions. Each can be changed so that the constraints operate somewhat differently or are reduced, but the process of change is typically costly, time-consuming, and difficult. Human resource constraints can be influenced by more extensive recruiting and a greater reliance on training and development. Laws can be changed through political action, and their interpretation through engaging in litigation. The influences of labor unions can be shifted or removed through collective bargaining at the time of contract renewal and through decertification elections. But in the near-term, these constraints are binding.

Organizations also create certain additional internal constraints. Past staffing decisions determine the nature of the human resources currently available internally. If these are insufficient to the need, it becomes necessary to go outside— the company is forced to recruit and select externally. Organization planning and job analysis create a structure of jobs and positions that also acts as a constraint. It becomes necessary to fill this specific set of positions, and not others that might have been invented; accordingly, certain types of people must be found, and not others. This structure can be changed by redesigning jobs, but changing one job without considering its relationships to others invites problems, and redesigning whole organizations or major segments of them does not occur quickly. Finally, human resource planning establishes role prescriptions for those working in the personnel area, specifying what they must do in the areas of recruiting, selection, training, and development. These plans also operate as constraints; the plans can be changed, but it is often unwise to do so without an extended reanalysis of the considerations that went into the initial planning, as well as the new considerations that have arisen.

All this does not mean that staffing decisions are made without alternative options. The decisions are restricted, but not completely predetermined. There are trade-offs between emphasizing recruiting and selection only, and placing a greater stress on training and development. Even if it becomes necessary to seek out candidates, there are various recruiting sources that may be used. A wide range of selection methods is available to choose from. The same is true of training and development methods.

In many areas related to staffing, there is also the option of doing very little— of recruiting only enough to find someone, of hiring whoever appears without resorting to selection, of investing practically nothing in training and development, of ignoring the need for job analysis and human resource planning. In such cases there is no need to carry out personnel research to establish performance-relatedness or evaluate training either. In fact, there may not really be a need for a personnel function at all. But if the work to be done is at all demanding, and there are few companies any longer in which it is not, this approach will inevitably result in widespread performance deficiencies. Except under conditions of an extremely favorable market environment, these deficiencies will ultimately add up to corporate failure as well.

What Have You Leaned?

1. What are the problems and disadvantages associated with the different types of selection methods? How can these problems be overcome in each instance?

2. How does the grievance process work, and how does it relate to collective bargaining? In what ways can a formal grievance process serve to reduce conflict? To increase conflict?

3. Training and development methods are carried out to achieve three different types of goals. What are these goals? In each instance, illustrate your response with reference to several specific training methods.

4. How do demand and supply forecasting differ in human resource planning? State your answer in terms of the different techniques used. What type of relationship between demand and supply tends to justify human resource planning?

5. What are individual and group differences, and why is it important to distinguish between them? How do these issues relate to discrimination in employment?

6. Several approaches are used to carry out job analyses. What are these approaches, and how appropriate is each for studying various types of jobs and providing information for different components of the job description?

7. In what ways does one go about establishing the performance-relatedness of a selection procedure? Under what circumstances would such information be worthless?

8. Why are training needs analyses carried out, and how are they conducted? In what sense does evaluation of training research serve to validate or confirm aspects of the training needs analysis?

9. What specific laws serve to impose constraints on what is done in each of the following areas of personnel/human resource management:
   a. separating employees from the company?
   b. selection and hiring?
   c. wage payments and benefits administration?

10. How does affirmative action recruiting differ from the traditional approaches most companies have used in the past? Why, as a recruiting approach per se, is it likely to be relatively unattractive?

How Well Can You Apply Your Knowledge?

Problem 1. At the end of chapter 1, problem 1 describes a manufacturing company that, due to changes in the industry, had come to face a more competitive environment. As a result, a need arose for more advanced personnel practices, and this need had become manifest initially with regard to conducting managerial job analyses and human resource planning. The questions asked at the end of the problem were:

1. How would you approach the problem of writing these three management position descrip-

tions (for a vice-president of manufacturing, quality control supervisor, and industrial relations manager)? What categories would you use in looking into the jobs?

2. Try to draft position descriptions of the kind needed for purposes of recruiting. What would you emphasize, and what would you deemphasize with regard to each position? Be as detailed as you can.

Answering these questions clearly might have seemed a rather large order at the time you first faced them, although this is the sort of challenge the business world often presents. Now, however, you have more knowledge regarding job analysis and how to do it.

Questions

1. How would you answer questions 1 and 2 above now, with the benefit of more knowledge?
2. If you were asked to make recommendations regarding the installation of a human resource planning system that the company could use to guide staffing at the managerial level, what approaches would you advocate? How should the company go about doing this planning? Be as specific as possible.

Problem 2. The company considered in the previous problem did in fact install a human resource planning system. Over time, largely because of certain strategic decisions at the top management level, this system began to indicate a gradually expanding need for management personnel over a twenty-year period. The initial need would be greatest at lower levels, but would extend into middle management toward the end of the planning period. The end result would be a substantial increase in the number of managerial positions to be staffed.

Questions

1. How exactly should the company undertake recruiting for these positions? Consider sources that should be used, approaches to them, and affirmative action considerations.
2. What should the company use in the way of selection procedures? What specific methods seem most suitable, and what should be done to install and use them effectively?
3. How should the matter of training and development be handled? What needs might be anticipated, what methods should be used to deal with them, and what should be done to install and use these methods effectively?

In answering these questions, you will find it helpful to review not only the material in this chapter, but also the discussion of managerial careers in the first section of chapter 2.

Additional Sources for More Detailed Study

Alpander, Guvenc G. *Human Resources Management Planning.* New York: AMACOM, 1982.

Bureau of National Affairs. *Basic Patterns in Union Contracts.* Washington, D.C.: BNA, 1983.

Cascio, Wayne F., and Awad, Elias M. *Human Resources Management: An Information Systems Approach.* Reston, Va.: Reston, 1981.

Crane, Donald P. *Personnel: The Management of Human Resources.* Boston: Kent, 1982.

French, Wendell L. *The Personnel Management Process.* Boston: Houghton Mifflin, 1982.

Goldstein, Irwin L. *Training: Program Development and Evaluation.* Monterey, Calif.: Brooks/Cole, 1974.

Hall, Douglas T. *Careers in Organizations.* Pacific Palisades, Calif.: Goodyear, 1976.

Hamner, W. Clay. *Organizational Shock.* New York: Wiley, 1980.

Heneman, Herbert G.; Schwab, Donald P.; Fossum, John A.; and Dyer, Lee D. *Personnel/Human Resources Management.* Howewood, Ill.: Irwin, 1983.

Herman, E. Edward, and Kuhn, Alfred. *Collective Bargaining and Labor Relations.* Englewood Cliffs, N.J.: Prentice-Hall, 1981.

Kochan, Thomas A.; Mitchell, Daniel J. B.; and Dyer, Lee. *Industrial Relations Research in the 1970s: Review and Appraisal.* Madison, Wisc.: Industrial Relations Research Association, 1982.

London, Manuel, and Stumpf, Stephen A. *Managing Careers.* Reading, Mass.: Addison-Wesley, 1982.

McBurney, William J. *College Recruitment: Effective Programs and Practices.* New York: AMACOM, 1982.

Patten, Thomas H. *Classics of Personnel Management.* Oak Park, Ill.: Moore, 1979.

Sayles, Leonard R., and Strauss, George. *Managing Human Resources.* Englewood Cliffs, N.J.: Prentice-Hall, 1981.

Schein, Edgar H. *Career Dynamics: Matching Individual and Organizational Needs.* Reading, Mass.: Addison-Wesley, 1978.

Sloane, Arthur A., and Witney, Fred. *Labor Relations.* Englewood Cliffs, N.J.: Prentice-Hall, 1981.

Stieber, Jack; McKersie, Robert B.; and Mills, D. Quinn. *U.S. Industrial Relations 1950–1980: A Critical Assessment.* Madison, Wisc.: Industrial Relations Research Association, 1981.

Taylor, Benjamin J., and Witney, Fred. *Labor Relations Law*. Englewood Cliffs, N.J.: Prentice-Hall, 1983.

Walker, James W. *Human Resource Planning*. New York: McGraw-Hill, 1980.

Wanous, John P. *Organizational Entry: Recruitment, Selection and Socialization of Newcomers*. Reading, Mass.: Addison-Wesley, 1980.

Yoder, Dale, and Heneman, Herbert G. *ASPA Handbook of Personnel and Industrial Relations*. Volumes 1–8. Washington, D.C.: Bureau of National Affairs, 1974–1979.

Zima, Joseph P. *Interviewing: Key to Effective Management*. Chicago, Ill.: Science Research Associates, 1983.

Notes

1. John B. Miner and Mary G. Miner, *Personnel and Industrial Relations: A Managerial Approach* (New York: Macmillan, 1985): Chapter 4.

2. See Richard E. Walton and Robert B. McKersie, *A Behavioral Theory of Labor Negotiations* (New York: McGraw-Hill, 1965); Lane Tracy, "The Influence of Noneconomic Factors on Negotiators," *Industrial and Labor Relations Review* (January 1974); and D. Quinn Mills, "Reforming the U.S. System of Collective Bargaining," *Monthly Labor Review* (March 1983).

3. Raymond D. Horton, "Arbitration, Arbitrators, and the Public Interest," *Industrial and Labor Relation Review* (July 1975).

4. See, for example, Robert T. Boisseau and Harvey Caras, "A Radical Experiment Cuts Deep into the Attractiveness of Unions," *Personnel Administrator* (October 1983).

5. Dan R. Dalton and William D. Todor, "Antecedents of Grievance Filing Behavior: Attitude/Behavioral Consistency and the Union Steward," *Academy of Management Journal* (March 1982).

6. See in particular Ernest J. McCormick, *Job Analysis: Methods and Applications* (New York: AMACOM, 1979); and Sidney A. Fine, "Functional Job Analysis: An Approach to a Technology for Manpower Planning," *Personnel Journal* (November 1974).

7. Milton Drandell, "A Composite Forecasting Methodology for Manpower Planning Using Objective and Subjective Criteria," *Academy of Management Journal* (September 1975).

8. Allen C. Bluedorn, "Managing Turnover Strategically," *Business Horizons* (March–April 1982).

9. Edward A. Tomeski and Harold Lazarus, *People-oriented Computer Systems: The Computer in Crisis* (New York: Van Nostrand Reinhold, 1975).

10. Kendrith M. Rowland, Gerald R. Ferris, and Jay L. Sherman, *Current Issues in Personnel Management* (Boston: Allyn and Bacon, 1983).

11. For details, see Richard D. Arvey, *Fairness in Selecting Employees* (Reading, Mass.: Addison-Wesley, 1979); James Ledvinka, *Federal Regulation of Personnel and Human Resource Management* (Boston: Kent, 1982); and Mary G. Miner and John B. Miner, *Employee Selection Within the Law* (Washington, D.C.: Bureau of National Affairs, 1980).

12. For extended treatments of this subject, see Robert M. Guion, *Personnel Testing* (New York: McGraw-Hill, 1965); Benjamin Schneider, *Staffing Organizations* (Pacific Palisades, Calif.: Goodyear, 1976); and John E. Hunter, Frank L. Schmidt, and Gregg B. Jackson, *Meta-Analysis: Cumulating Research Findings Across Studies* (Beverly Hills, Calif.: Sage, 1982).

13. Paul Popovich and John P. Wonous, "The Realistic Job Preview as a Persuasive Communication," *Academy of Management Review* (October 1982); and Bernard L. Dugoni and Daniel R. Ilgen, "Realistic Job Previews and the Adjustment of New Employees," *Academy of Management Journal* (September 1981).

14. Joel A. Bearak, "Termination Made Easier: Is Outplacement Really the Answer," *Personnel Administrator* (April 1982).

15. Bureau of National Affairs, *Recruiting Policies and Practices* (Personnel Policies Forum Survey no. 126, Washington, D.C.: BNA, 1979).

16. Robert L. Dipboye, "Self-Fulfilling Prophecies in the Selection-Recruitment Interview," *Academy of Management Review* (October 1982).

17. Gershon Ben-Shakkar, Israel Lieblich, and Maya Bar-Hillel, "An Evaluation of Polygraphers' Judgments: A Review from a Decision Theoretic Perspective," *Journal of Applied Psychology* (December 1982).

18. Douglas W. Bray, Richard J. Campbell, and Donald L. Grant, *Formative Years in Business: A Long-term AT&T Study of Managerial Lives* (New York: Wiley, 1974); and George C. Thornton and William C. Byham, *Assessment Centers and Mangerial Performance* (New York: Academic Press, 1982).

Maintaining an Effective Work Force

CHAPTER OUTLINE

Performance Appraisal
Management Appraisal
    Judgmental Processes
    Objective Measures
    Feeding Back Results
Problems in Evaluation Systems
    Sources of Error
    Methods of Dealing with Error
    Resistance to Evaluation

Compensation
Wage and Salary Administration
    Wage Levels and Surveys
    Job Evaluation
    Pricing Jobs
    Supplementary Pay
Incentive Systems
Executive Compensation
Employee Benefits
    Direct Monetary Benefits
    Insurance and Retirement Plans
    The Cafeteria Approach

Personnel Communications
The Choice of Media
Company Publications
    Employee Handbooks
    Magazines and Newspapers
    Readership Surveys
Employee Attitude Measurement
    Approaches to Obtaining Information
    Sources of Resistance
Suggestion Programs

Health, Safety, and Performance Control
Preventive Medicine
    Range of Activities
    The Inside vs. Outside Question
Safety Management
    Accident Statistics
    Approaches to Prevention
Reassignment, Discipline, and Counseling
    Promotion, Transfer, and Demotion
    Disciplinary Action
    Employee and Executive Counseling

OBJECTIVES

To describe the roles of performance appraisal, the methods for carrying it out, and the practical problems involved in using it.

To explain the various types of compensation and how they work.

To provide an understanding of the nature and uses of various communications approaches in the personnel field.

To describe various specialized personnel activities, not previously considered, related to maintaining and restoring performance levels.

Organizations are constantly being staffed as people leave and new people come in, and as individuals change and grow. For each person, however, there is a need to introduce procedures that will maintain effective performance levels, after staffing has been accomplished. Such procedures are the subject of this chapter. Of course, training and development can serve to maintain effectiveness, in addition to its role in initial staffing, but there are other procedures that have not yet been introduced.

A key consideration in maintaining an effective labor force is the determination of the degree to which performance is effective or ineffective. Performance appraisal for this purpose constitutes the output processes category in Exhibit 1. Compensation in its various forms can be a major factor in recruiting, of course, but in the long run, it is most important as a means of keeping people in the organization and stimulating them to be effective. Compensation for this purpose includes salaries, wages, incentive payments, and employee benefits.

Personnel communications procedures—both those that communicate downward from management, and those that permit information to flow upward from employees—serve in large part to maintain organizational membership and to deal with conflicts so that cooperation in the work effort may be maintained. However, these procedures can influence the quality and quantity of an individual's performance. Health and safety procedures are intended primarily to maintain employees in good condition so that they are able to work effectively, although some companies go beyond "preventive medicine" to a limited amount of treatment. This emphasis on corrective action and restoring effective performance also is inherent in performance control procedures such as discipline, reassignments, and various types of counseling.

PERFORMANCE APPRAISAL

Performance appraisal may be formal or informal, but one way or another, it is a fact of organizational life. People are evaluated at work whether they wish to be or not, and usually it is to their advantage to be evaluated as part of a formal program that establishes definite criteria for various levels of performance. Evaluations of some kind are needed to make decisions regarding pay, promotions, training and development, continued employment, and human resource planning. They are also needed to carry out personnel research studies to establish the performance-relatedness of selection instruments. If there are no formal procedures for obtaining performance information, managers who have to make these kinds of decisions will find other ways to obtain it.

In some cases, performance appraisals deal only with the minimum acceptable performance standards needed for control purposes. This type of use is discussed in chapter 4. More commonly, especially in the appraisal of managers, a range of performance levels is considered, running from very high to very low. When pay is closely keyed to performance, this type of approach is essential. In many other instances, where performance information is needed to make personnel decisions, the range approach is also very useful.

There are two major methods by which managers are appraised. One uses the judgments of people who should have knowledge of the individual's performance, or of factors related to it. The other uses objective measures of factors that should be under the manager's control, such as budget performance and responsibility accounting data. In this latter case, hard figures are available to indicate how well the manager is doing.

Judgmental Processes Exhibit 15.1 outlines the appraisal process and will serve as a guide for the discussion. Usually the evaluating is done by the immediate superior alone. However, self-evaluations, group or committee appraisals, and appraisals developed by the personnel staff are used with some frequency.[1] It is not uncommon to use several of these procedures for the same overall evaluation.

In many cases the result of these processes is an appraisal summary that provides a general statement, not only of present performance, but also of potential for future performance and developmental actions that might improve upon the present. Such a summary is used by Atlantic Richfield and is outlined in Exhibit 15.2.

Self-appraisals have the value that they are most likely to stimulate managers to improve their performance. There is less likely to be a question in the manager's mind that the appraisal is wrong. Yet, as might be expected, self-appraisals do tend to differ substantially from appraisals by superiors; individuals do rate themselves higher.[2] Thus in using these appraisals, it is necessary to consider both the developmental advantages and the potential biases.

Group approaches generally consider the judgments of various people who have worked with the individual being evaluated—usually managers at a higher level. Ideally, these judgments would be obtained separately and averaged; however, not infrequently they are the result of group consensus from face-to-face discussion.

Appraisals developed by the personnel staff usually involve a field review in which performance data are obtained through interviews with knowledgable persons. Personnel representatives go out to managers rather than waiting for their responses to questionnaires. The situation is much like that in recruiting, in which

---

EXHIBIT 15.1 Performance appraisal process

Step 1. Develop an appraisal form or instrument based on organization planning and job analysis data, taking into account legal constraints. Be sure it will serve the desired purposes.

Step 2. Train those who will use this measure to use it effectively.

Step 3. Obtain appraisals from those selected to do the evaluating.

Step 4. Have these appraisals reviewed by someone else who is knowledgable regarding the individual's performance—a higher level manager, personnel manager, etc.

Step 5. Feed the results back to the employee in some form.

Step 6. Use the appraisals for whatever purposes were envisioned in step 1.

EXHIBIT 15.2 Outline for a management appraisal summary used by Atlantic Richfield

Personal Background
Age
Family background
Education
Work history
Special accomplishments and limitations
Hobbies and recreational activities

Nature of Work
General statement (based on organization plans and job analysis)
Committee assignments
Individuals supervised

Job Performance and Qualifications
General statement (value to the company and probable future contribution)
Technical performance
Motivation in current position
Intelligence manifested in job performance
Emotional stability
Supervisory capabilities
Major strengths and weaknesses

Overall Performance Rating
Individual rating
Ranking vs. others in the same job

Potential for Advancement
Promotability and timetable for progress
Long-range potential rating

Recommended Actions
Changes in placement
Appropriate duration of current placements
Development needs and plans

advertising is replaced by direct contacts. The results tend to be equally favorable. Actively going out and asking questions tends to yield more valid information than sending out requests to complete a form, but it is also more costly. Also in this personnel staff category are various types of assessments. The assessment center approach has been noted in chapter 14, and it can be used for purposes of appraisal as well as for staffing. In addition, psychological assessments are sometimes used in which a clinical write-up is prepared on the basis of test and interview data, as well as reports on performance. These latter are most frequently introduced to predict future performance and thus potential for promotion.

Finally, evaluations can be done by peers or subordinates, but neither of these methods is widely used. Peer ratings have shown considerable value, in part because peers are often in the best position to observe what is going on. Some strong arguments for their use have been advanced.[3] Still, there is no reason to believe that these sources are necessarily less biased than others. Any judgmental appraisal source can produce arbitrary actions and be used for personal ends. The best check against this is to obtain information from multiple and independent sources.

Objective Measures   Objective measures are based primarily on the behavior of the unit under the manager appraised. They may be used to good advantage in conjunction with a judgmental appraisal system. If such a dual approach is not taken, there is considerable risk that more easily measured or quantified factors will be emphasized at the expense of other factors that are equally or more important. Performance may become skewed to what is easily measured, and the company can find itself getting types of behavior it really does not want. Thus managerial accounting systems that stress short-term profits can result in failures to invest in training, new equipment, and the like, which in the long term almost guarantee profit declines.

A number of the types of financial measures that may be used to evaluate managers are considered in the discussion of organizational control in chapter 8. These procedures are most likely to be used toward the top of the organizational hierarchy, although some companies attempt to extend them to lower levels of management. They work less well there because managers at that level have less control over their costs and accordingly may be blamed or praised for things that they really did not do themselves.

In addition, a number of objective measures of unit performance aspects are used as appropriate to the particular context. Examples of these nonfinancial measures are given in Exhibit 15.3. The extent to which factors of this kind are used to appraise managers varies considerably from company to company. In many cases, only extreme negative variations are given consideration. Nevertheless, continuous monitoring in these areas can provide useful data on what managers are doing.

EXHIBIT 15.3   Nonfinancial measures for managerial performance appraisal

Productivity Measures

Manufacturing—units produced, meeting production schedules, machine down time, scrappage

Sales—units sold, changes in sales figures over the preceding year, customer complaints

Research and Development—assigned projects carried to completion, patents obtained

Office—typing output, filing errors, bills processed

Measures Related to Presence on the Job and Cooperative Work

Absenteeism rates
Voluntary and involuntary turnover rates
Accident frequencies, particularly lost time accidents
Visits to the company dispensary
Disciplinary actions taken
Grievance rates
Work stoppages and slowdowns
Employee attitude survey results

NOTE: These are all measures for the total unit supervised over a given time period.

Feeding Back Results   Exhibit 15.1, at step 5, notes the feedback of appraisal results to the manager appraised. In some instances this step is not included, as is often the case when the data are to be used only to establish the performance-relatedness of a selection instrument, for instance. On the other hand, this step is a crucial one when the appraisal process is part of a coaching and goal-setting procedure intended to develop higher levels of motivation. Also, the very fact of feedback tends to produce an element of self-appraisal that can bring new and important information into the evaluation process. Usually this information is favorable to the individual appraised, but it may nevertheless contribute significantly to a final evaluation.

There are, however, certain problems with the use of appraisal feedback that should be recognized. One is that managers resist it, especially if the individual is evaluated negatively. They often tend to avoid conducting the interview or spend very little time on it. Conflicts may be aroused, and people whom the company would nevertheless like to keep may be incited to seek employment elsewhere. A related problem is that, when managers know they will be expected to feed back results, or have gained some experience in doing so, they may very well learn to distort their evaluations in a positive direction to reduce unpleasantness and conflict. This may well make the ratings useless for many purposes.[4]

Several factors appear to make for more positive outcomes from a feedback interview.[5] The result ultimately may be that upward distortion of ratings becomes minimal. For one thing, a thorough knowledge of the subordinate's job on the part of the superior makes for greater credibility of the evaluation. Secondly, if in the interview the superior is in an overall sense supportive and constructive, conflict can be minimized. Finally, it helps to have subordinates express their views, to engage in self-appraisal, as much as possible. These factors are most likely to operate effectively when the superior is given a certain amount of training regarding the feedback process as a whole. This can be done at step 2 in the Exhibit 15.1 outline.

Problems in Evaluation Systems

In many companies, performance appraisal systems have had a rocky history. There are plenty of good arguments for having such systems, and so it is not difficult to get something installed. What gets installed, however, may be a compromise between what would constitute a technically accurate system and the personal preferences of key individuals able to exert influence on decisions in this area. In any event, once in place, the specific system tends to become the target of a continuing series of criticisms. This nit-picking process finally brings the system down. There may then be no system for a few years, often as a committee studies the problem, before another effort is made.

Sources of Error   One reason that judgmental systems fail is that they incorporate sources of error that make them vulnerable. Some of these error sources are described in Exhibit 15.4. There is a common tendency for "halo," constant leniency errors, and errors of range restriction to combine so that the ratings bunch up toward the top of all scales used. Ultimately the evaluation system becomes almost worthless for discriminating between more and less effective performers. There are differences to be sure, but the system does not

EXHIBIT 15.4 Sources of error in performance ratings

Halo. Tendency to evaluate a person in a similar manner, favorably or unfavorably, on all or most of the dimensions of a rating form because a general overall impression colors ratings.

Constant error. Tendency of individual raters to apply different standards so that one is consistently more lenient and another consistently more demanding; difference between easy and difficult graders in the classroom provides another example.

Recency error. Tendency to base ratings on what is most easily remembered, the most recent behavior, even though average performance over a more extended period is intended.

Errors of range restriction and central tendency. Tendency to rate all individuals within a narrow range so that there is little or no difference between best and worst, even though much greater differences actually exist. When this occurs in the middle or center of a scale, it is defined as an error of central tendency.

Personal bias. Tendency to rate not on the basis of actual performance, but on other grounds—favors done for the rater, sex, minority status, social standing, etc.

SOURCE: Adapted from John B. Miner and Mary G. Miner, *Personnel and Industrial Relations: A Managerial Approach* (New York: Macmillan, 1985).

detect them—on paper everyone is performing wonderfully. As a result, feeding back results is no problem at all.

Methods of Dealing with Error   One method of dealing with error, or the potential for error, is to demonstrate to those making the ratings that the company has a genuine interest in the appraisal system, needs valid data, and is willing to invest something to get useful results. Generally this means helping the raters to do a better job. Good training at step 2 (see Exhibit 15.1) is one method of accomplishing this. Another approach is to have a personnel representative actually go out and administer the appraisal forms in an interview, recording answers for the raters. This not only demonstrates that the company cares about obtaining unbiased information, but raters who might have difficulties with the appraisal process can be helped on the spot.

The second major method of dealing with error is to design the appraisal form in such a way as to reduce the likelihood of error occurrence. A great many techniques and procedures have been developed with this objective in mind, some of them quite complicated and technical.[6] As an example, an approach that has been found to help in spreading out ratings (reduce range restriction error) and keep them from bunching at the top (constant leniency error) is to use a number of scale categories and make the majority of them positive. Scales of this type have been used at McKinsey and Company and at Georgia Kaolin Company. The scale for rating a particular factor might be:

Clearly very outstanding	_____
Clearly outstanding	_____
Approaches outstanding	_____
Clearly well above standard	_____
Somewhat above standard	_____

Approaches being above standard _____
Clearly meets the standard _____
Barely up to standard _____
Somewhat below standard _____
Clearly unsatisfactory _____

Another approach that is particularly effective in removing halo and personal bias is to focus on actual job behaviors established through some type of job analysis, rather than on personal traits merely thought to be important in the work. The distinction is made in Exhibit 15.5. This tendency for behavior-oriented scales to serve as a means of reducing bias has been recognized by the courts. Thus companies have been more likely to win discrimination cases if their appraisal system used behavioral items.[7] It also helps to use job analysis in developing the system, to provide specific written instructions to the raters, and to feed back the appraisal results to employees.

Resistance to Evaluation Evaluation system problems derive from a number of sources. Managers, and in particular the not-so-good ones, do not like to go on record with negative evaluations, and they do not like to feed negative

---

EXHIBIT 15.5 Examples of trait and behavioral rating items

Trait Items	Outstanding	Average	Poor
Leadership ability	_____	_____	_____
Decisiveness	_____	_____	_____
Aggressiveness	_____	_____	_____
Dependability	_____	_____	_____
Loyalty	_____	_____	_____

Behavioral Items

Production Foreman

Explains job requirements to new employees in a clear manner

Almost never   1   2   3   4   5   Almost always

Distributes overtime equally

Almost never   1   2   3   4   5   Almost always

Waiter/Waitress

Stops talking to a fellow employee as soon as a customer approaches the counter

Almost never   1   2   3   4   5   Almost always

Keeps counter stools and legs clean

Almost never   1   2   3   4   5   Almost always

Janitor

Empties ashtrays thoroughly before vacuuming carpets

Almost never   1   2   3   4   5   Almost always

Keeps washroom filled with toilet paper

Almost never   1   2   3   4   5   Almost always

SOURCE: Based in part on Gary P. Latham and Kenneth N. Wexley, *Increasing Productivity Through Performance Appraisal* (Reading, Mass.: Addison-Wesley, 1981).

results back to subordinates. They tend accordingly either to fight the appraisal system as a whole or to distort their evaluations in a positive direction. Both approaches may ultimately contribute to abolishing the system.

Similarly, those being evaluated are likely to fight the system, if they are doing a poor job and expect to be rated accordingly, or if they are apprehensive and pessimistic on this score even though the results actually are positive. Putting formal appraisal systems out of business does not solve these problems, and most people know that. But there is a tendency to believe that the more informal evaluations can somehow be influenced in favor of the subordinate, and in any event, with an informal system, there is no written record. Because the informal appraisal process is not out in the open it is easier to ignore it—even though the results ultimately show in terms of salary raises and promotions gained and lost.

These factors have combined with traditional union resistances to make formal performance appraisal relatively infrequent in unionized work forces, even though the same companies typically do have management appraisal systems. Unions almost without exception are opposed to the evaluation of individual employees on the ground that it is inconsistent with the idea of a collective relationship between labor and the company. The union alternative is that personnel decisions regarding layoff, promotion, shift selection, eligibility for overtime, work assignments, and the like should be based on seniority of employment, regardless of performance levels. Where this position has won out and has been incorporated in the union contract through collective bargaining, there in fact may not be much need for a performance evaluation system. A problem arises, however, in selecting employees for promotion from the bargaining unit—to first level supervision, for instance. In the absence of an appraisal system, seniority often comes to govern there also, and that can be disastrous.

All in all, formal performance appraisal faces a rather large number of obstacles in spite of its potential value for many personnel/human resource purposes. These obstacles should not be viewed as reasons to abandon appraisal activities. However, if they are not recognized and dealt with in some manner, they are very likely to undermine even the best-intentioned efforts.

COMPENSATION

Compensation is closely related to the subject of motivation as discussed in chapter 5. It contributes to the desire to join an organization, to behave in ways that yield productive output, and to stay in the organization. At the same time, it must be recognized that other types of motives not involving compensation can operate in all of these areas. Furthermore, various aspects or approaches within the total compensation concept contribute unevenly to the recruitment, productivity, and retention goals—and to their disadvantage, a number of companies appear to operate their compensation programs so that they probably contribute very little to any of these goals.

Exhibit 15.6 notes many of the processes and factors involved in developing compensation systems and the relationships among them. It provides a broad outline for the discussion that follows.

EXHIBIT 15.6 Components of compensation process

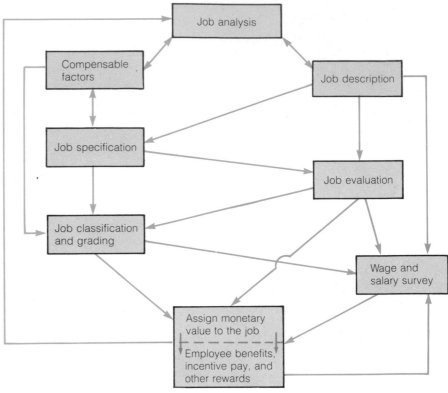

SOURCE: Richard I. Henderson, *Compensation Management: Rewarding Performance,* 1982. Reprinted with permission of Reston Publishing Company, a Prentice-Hall company, 11480 Sunset Hills Road, Reston, Va. 22090.

Wage and Salary Administration

The *wage level* of a firm relates to the overall level of a company's payments to its employees in relationship to the overall payments of other firms; on average, does the firm pay well or not? Information of this kind is obtained from *wage surveys.* The *wage structure* of a firm is established by the relative *grading* or ordering of jobs within the company in terms of their pay. This is typically done through some type of *job evaluation.* Then, finally, jobs are *priced* in terms of specific hourly wages or salaries that reflect both the firm's wage level and the job's position in the structure.

Wage Levels and Surveys Overall, company wage levels tend to be highest when union pressures are greatest, recruiting has become difficult, other employers in the area (for lower level employees) and in the industry (for managerial and professional employees) are paying well, skill levels are high on the average, the company is larger in size, the number of positions to be filled is high, and employee satisfaction is low. Minimum wage laws become important when there are a number of low-skill jobs.

Companies are strongly influenced in their overall wage levels by wage surveys coupled with the particular compensation strategies they have adopted. Wage surveys typically concentrate on certain key jobs that contain large numbers of employees and range over a wide spectrum of job levels. They may be conducted by individual companies, groups of companies banded together for this purpose, industry associations, professional societies, consulting firms, and the like. The U.S. government conducts surveys in many local labor markets. The surveys typically solicit information on a variety of aspects of compensation administration, but are most concerned with base rates for various jobs independent of any supplementary payments.

Job Evaluation Job evaluation is a judgmental process much as is performance appraisal. It can be biased, and there clearly have been enough instances in which bias has intervened to make this an important issue. Bias is a major consideration in many discrimination cases that involve two comparable jobs being filled by persons of different races or sexes and the compensation being unequal. Is the pay difference justified by real differences in job levels established by valid job evaluations? Or are the jobs really the same and the pay differences discriminatory? The values and preferences of the people doing the job evaluations can exert considerable influence on the results obtained in such cases. Thus job evaluation is no more inherently free of error than is performance evaluation. Again, the preferred solution is to obtain judgments from several independent sources.

Exhibit 15.7 lists and describes the basic approaches to job evaluation. In each instance, the level assigned to a job is based on judgments by one or more people, although in some cases the judgmental process is simple and in other cases it is quite complex. There are many variants and combinations of these methods, but some type of point system is most frequently used. Although various complex statistical methods for defining and combining com-

---

EXHIBIT 15.7 Four basic categories of job evaluation methods

Job ranking. Set of jobs is ranked, through use of job descriptions, in terms of each job's overall worth to the company by a panel of evaluators.

Job classification. Jobs are assigned to a pre-established set of job categories by evaluators; categories of worth have been specified previously in considerable detail.

Factor comparison. Jobs are ranked on each of a number of job factors. Factors are then weighed in terms of importance for the particular job, and the two are combined to establish job levels; compensable factors may include skill, effort, responsibility, working conditions, and other considerations.

Point system. Jobs are assigned points in terms of previously established classification systems set up for each of a number of compensable factors. The total points, typically 500 or more, are split up to emphasize certain factors more than others, and a detailed manual specifies both factors and levels of worth within each. Total points define the job level for each job.

pensable factors have been developed, these methods do not appear to be superior to the kinds of approaches noted in Exhibit 15.7[8].

Pricing Jobs   Wage levels and wage structures come together in the actual pricing of jobs. Jobs that are close together in the points assigned to them or on some other basis are put in the same pay grade. The number of pay grades thus created can vary considerably. Each grade is assigned a minimum and maximum pay, and steps are established between the two, representing the amounts of merit increases to be awarded based on performance appraisal results. The ranges of pay for successive steps overlap, and as one goes up the grade scale, and thus the number of points awarded by job evaluation, the dollar values attached to jobs tend to increase in a straight-line progression. This process is depicted in Exhibit 15.8.

Rate ranges and steps within them are almost universal in white collar jobs and in many production jobs. However, in certain heavily unionized industries,

EXHIBIT 15.8   How pay grades overlap and relate to rates of pay

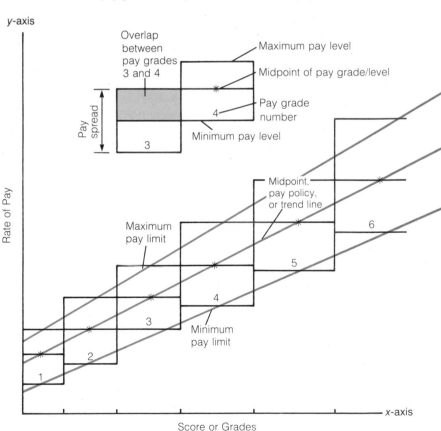

SOURCE: Richard I. Henderson, *Compensation Management: Rewarding Performance,* 1982. Reprinted with permission of Reston Publishing Company, a Prentice-Hall company, 11480 Sunset Hills Road, Reston, Va. 22090.

such as steel and automobile manufacturing, there are single pay rates for all employees in a given job; there are no ranges or steps, and pay increases are based only on cost of living or inflationary factors and collective bargaining agreements.

Supplementary Pay The procedures considered thus far relate primarily to so-called base rates of pay, either involving hourly wages or salaries of a monthly or annual nature. Overtime at a higher rate may be paid based on wage and hour laws or at company discretion. Usually the rate is one and a half times base pay, but it can go as high as three times the base rate under certain circumstances. Premium pay may be awarded for working on weekends or holidays, working undesirable night shifts, reporting for work even though work is not available, and reporting to work on other than a regularly scheduled shift. In many cases, supplementary pay of this kind is a major component of the total compensation package. Under many collective bargaining agreements, opportunities to earn supplementary pay are awarded on the basis of seniority.

Incentive Systems

Incentive aspects may be built into regular wage and salary plans by giving raises for outstanding or improved performance. In such cases, pay is tied to performance, but not fully. The problem is that, if performance subsequently fluctuates downward, the raise still remains in force. Although attractive from an employee viewpoint, this type of incentive loses some of its motivational potential.

In contrast, piece rate plans that pay by the amount of product produced, commissions that pay by the amount sold, and bonuses permit money to come and go. If an employee performs well, total earnings go up; if performance is poor, compensation drops off. Because it provides less security, this approach is usually less attractive to employees, but it does tie pay more closely to performance and thus contributes a greater motivational impact to the organization. It is of course possible to introduce some mix of guaranteed compensation and incentive pay so that a minimum security level is provided.

Exhibit 15.9 indicates the effects of some of these distinctions. Individual approaches relate incentives to the performance of the individual employee, group plans relate them to the performance of the work group as a whole, and organizational plans relate them to overall company performance, usually in terms of profitability. From the total score column in Exhibit 15.9, it appears that differences in approach are not large, but this is because of the trade-offs involved. Organizational bonuses, for instance, do not tie pay to individual performance very well, but they are relatively more effective in fostering cooperation and gaining acceptance. Individual piece rates provide good pay-performance ties, but at some costs in negative side effects such as restriction of output, reduced cooperation, and low employee acceptance. Thus, the approach that should be used depends on the nature of the work and the particular needs of a given company.

In any event, the evidence indicates that incentive systems, especially individual incentives, do tend to exert a motivating effect on performance and to yield increased output.[9] There are many plans of this kind in existence, many of which have been developed by industrial engineers. Installing some of these systems is a very complex process indeed.

EXHIBIT 15.9 Ratings of various incentive pay approaches

Type of Approach	Tying Pay to Performance	Producing Few Negative Effects	Encouraging Cooperation	Gaining Employee Acceptance	Total Score
Changes in wages and salaries					
Individual	3.3	5.0	1.0	3.7	13.0
Group	2.7	5.0	2.0	3.7	13.4
Organizational	2.0	5.0	2.5	4.0	13.5
Bonuses, piece rates and commissions					
Individual	4.3	3.7	1.0	2.0	13.0
Group	3.3	5.0	3.0	3.0	14.3
Organizational	2.7	5.0	3.0	3.7	14.4

NOTE: Low = 1.0; high = 5.0.

SOURCE: Adapted from Edward E. Lawler, *Pay and Organization Development* (Reading, Mass.: Addison-Wesley, 1981): 94.

Executive Compensation

Much of what has been discussed to this point applies at the management level as well as below it. However, there are certain aspects of executive compensation that are different. At the upper levels in particular, tax considerations become much more important. Approaches that defer compensation until after retirement so that lower tax rates will apply, or shift payments so that they become capital gain distributions and thus are taxed at a lower rate, become increasingly attractive. A number of the major consulting firms provide specialized services to companies in these areas, and there are other firms that consult only with regard to compensation or executive compensation matters.

At the top management level, the pay is best in larger firms and in certain industries where profit margins tend to be greater. Thus, overall, the more regulated industries—banks, life insurance, railroads, utilities—do not pay as well. The pay of the chief executive officer tends to govern that of managers below. Thus, the second person in the company will normally receive 50 to 60 percent of what the top person receives. In any event, much of their compensation will be contained in bonuses, averaging from 30 to 50 percent of base salary when the company is profitable. Payments are often made in the form of stock options under which company stock may be purchased at a later date at well below market value, if the stock rises in the interim.

In many companies, bonuses tied to company profits extend well down into the management ranks. However, middle management bonuses also are often tied to gross sales volume, budget performance, and production levels, which are not direct reflections of profit. This is a recognition that at this level, managers may not be able to exert much influence on total company profitability. In first-level supervision, incentive payments such as bonuses are less frequent, and when they do occur, they are often established as a proportion of the piece rate earnings of work group members.

Employee benefits have become a major component of the total compensation package in recent years for most companies. This has occurred because of both legal and union pressures. Since these benefits are usually provided across the board, without reference to employee performance levels, they exert no influence on productivity at all. What they do is assist in recruiting, because people are attracted to firms by liberal benefits, and help to maintain an effective labor force once staffing has occurred.

This lack of relationship to productivity means that, beyond a certain level, benefits probably return very little on the investments companies make in them. A good retirement plan relative to those of other employers may help retain employees and attract some applicants in their middle years, but an outstanding retirement plan is unlikely to do much more. It still will not attract younger workers, and it is unlikely to retain everyone. In fact, such a plan could serve to retain employees the company would just as soon have leave.

Yet companies often do get themselves into a position of providing excess benefits, many of which, though costly, have major appeal only for a small number of employees—or even worse, which provide the greatest payment to those who have already left employment because of retirement, layoff, or other reasons. The major cause of such situations is that employee benefits tend to be negotiated one at a time by unions. An improvement in the retirement plan or addition of another holiday seems to be a good idea when it means the company will have to give less in terms of direct wage increases. But when years of these benefit changes are added together, the company's compensation package can look totally chaotic.

Direct Monetary Benfits Companies pay a great deal of money for time that is not actually worked. Holidays and vacations are the best examples. Almost all firms provide at least six paid holidays a year, and in some cases the number is as high as 16. Vacation time generally varies with the period the person has been employed by the company. In some cases for new employees it may be as low as one week a year, but the amount of paid vacation has been rising steadily for some time, and two weeks is now the most likely minimum. For long-service employees, this amount can be as high as six weeks. Leaves with pay may also be given for illness, death in the family, jury duty, and the like.

There are also a number of payments related to a lack of available work, or to separation. Companies may guarantee a certain amount of working time and, if it is not possible to provide it, will pay for time not worked. A number of unions have negotiated supplemental unemployment benefits with the result that, in times of layoff, the individual receives more than the legally mandated unemployment compensation or is paid over a longer period. Employees who leave the company permanently may receive severance pay or some type of retraining allowance. The amount and duration of these payments are usually tied to length of service, with the maximum being as much as a full year at the base pay rate. At the upper management levels, such payments may be specified in an employment contract. So-called "golden parachutes" may provide for very sizable amounts of compensation if a manager is forced to leave, as William Agee was when his Bendix Corporation was taken over.

There is a wide range of other direct monetary benefits that companies may provide. These include the payment of tuition and other expenses of schooling, sometimes adjusted proportionately to the grade received in a course. Some firms have thrift plans in which the company matches employee contributions to a savings fund. In a number of instances, these monies are invested in company stock. Cash bonuses may be paid for ideas that result in improved company operations, winning sales contests, and for a variety of other reasons.

Insurance and Retirement Plans Probably the major employee benefits are group insurance and retirement plans. Both have grown dramatically in recent years due at least in part to pressures generated by legislation. Insurance benefits available to employees are of three types—life, medical, and disability. The costs of this insurance may be borne entirely by the employee or entirely by the company, or apportioned between the two in some manner. Companies increasingly are paying a greater share. However, even if the employee assumes the total expense, there are benefits involved, because group rates are lower than individual rates, and certain types of coverage are available only through group plans.

Life insurance provides for payments to an employee's family in case of death. The primary concern is with the death of the employee, but coverage can extend to other family members as well. Medical insurance pays for charges by physicians and hospitals in cases of injury or illness to a family member. Federal legislation now encourages the development of Health Maintenance Organizations as a source of these medical services and treatment. These are group medical practices providing a full range of services. Disability insurance pays various amounts in lieu of earnings to employees who are unable to work because of illness or injury. Insurance of this kind becomes of major importance after company sick-leave benefits have been exhausted, particularly in cases of long-term or permanent disability.

Retirement plans provide income to employees and their families after normal retirement. They may also provide for payments in cases of disability if the employee has reached a certain age and has a specified number of years of service. In most instances, there is a provision for early retirement prior to the normal age, although usually this means that payments are at a somewhat reduced level. As with insurance, the extent to which retirement plan costs are paid by the employee and the employer vary considerably. Also, in many plans employees do not obtain a right to company contributions, a process known as *vesting,* until they have worked for a company a certain number of years—now usually ten.

The Cafeteria Approach Originally conceived as an aspect of top executive compensation, the cafeteria approach has now spread to much broader components of the labor force in some companies. In this approach, employees may make certain choices among various straight pay and benefit options, in accordance with their particular needs at the time. How these choices are made, what options are included, and the extent to which a fixed benefit package is retained can vary considerably.[10] The key idea, however, is that costs are attached to various benefits, and employees can make trade-offs between items of equal cost. Each employee's individual benefit package is stored in a computer and administered from that source.

EXHIBIT 15.10 Rank order of preferences for different compensation options in the context of a cafeteria approach

Compensation Alternative	Younger Employees (18–35)	Middle-Aged Employees (36–49)	Older Employees (50–65)
Extra Vacation Time	1	2	2
Pay Increase	2	1	3
Dental Plan	3	4	7
Four-day Week	4	6	6
10 Fridays Off	5	7	5
Pension Increase	6	3	1
Early Retirement	7	5	4
Shorter Workday	8	8	8

NOTE: Values for the alternatives to be considered were established so as to have essentially equal monetary value.

SOURCE: Adapted from J. Brad Chapman and Robert Ottemann, "Employee Preferences for Various Compensation and Fringe Benefit Options." In *Policy Issues in Contemporary Personnel and Industrial Relations,* eds. Mary G. Miner and John B. Miner (New York: Macmillan, 1977): 554.

As indicated in Exhibit 15.10, there are major differences between preference for various types of compensation overall, and also changes associated with age. Marital status, sex, number of dependents, years of service, and job classification have also been found to make a difference. In particular, as highlighted in the exhibit, a preference for a pension increase becomes more important with advancing age. In contrast, inclusion of dental benefits in the medical insurance plan is most desired in the early years. The point is that there are group differences in preferences, and on the evidence, even greater individual differences. Cafeteria approaches that match these needs satisfy them and make employees more willing to remain in their assignments once the positions are staffed.

PERSONNEL COMMUNICATIONS

Personnel communications have a variety of objectives, but a major intent is to foster positive morale, thus reducing turnover, limiting conflict, and helping to maintain an effective labor force. Part of the intent relates to unions and union organizing attempts. Personnel communications are frequently used directly or indirectly to present the company view on labor–management issues. This is the major area in which personnel communications are subject to some legal constraint. Under *free speech* provisions of the law, companies can communicate with employees on such matters, but only if there is no threat of punishment for union activity or promise of benefits for avoiding it. Overall, however, personnel communications are less restricted by legal considerations than by either performance appraisal or compensation activities.

In Exhibit 15.11, a number of communications activities are noted that are intended not only for purposes of maintaining an effective labor force, but to serve other objectives as well. Certain of these activities that are likely to involve

EXHIBIT 15.11 Verbal communication activities within a company and areas of personnel/human resources involvement

Level of Communication Activity Involved	Objectives of Activities			
	Securing Conformity to Plans for Purposes of Productivity	Solving Problems and Producing Innovations	Maintaining the Labor Force and Fostering Morale	Providing Information and Instructing Personnel
Interpersonal— Between Two People	Supervisor directions and requests	Ad hoc problem resolution	President's welcome letter to new employee	*Hiring interview*
	Supervisor– subordinate meetings	Supervisor– subordinate idea development meetings	*Grievance discussion*	*New employee orientation*
	Job descriptions and standards	*Annual goals determination in work planning program*	*Progress review in work planning program*	Memoranda
	Annual appraisal			Oral and written reports
	Special problem sessions	Informal get-togethers as in-house lunch meetings	*Annual appraisal*	Cross-functioning
	Reports on operations	Reports on visits to other organizations, conventions, seminars	Informal meeting of two organization members	
	Memoranda		Superior– subordinate informal conversation on personal matters	
Interpersonal—Small Groups	Meetings: directors, executive committee, departmental; crisis-type meetings as in fire, flood, strike	Meetings: directors, executive committee, departmental, interdepartmental, problem-solving, sales development, crisis-type, budget, group lunch	Meetings: participative work group, inter-departmental, coffee break, group lunch	*Meetings*
				Training in small groups
Intraorganizational	Organization plans	*Suggestion program*	*In-house publications*	*In-house publications*
	Policy statements	Problem-finding program	Holiday social function	*Bulletin board notices*
	Standard procedures	Operations audit reports as to general and specific areas of organization	The grapevine	Staff meetings
	Regulations		*Literature available to personnel concerning plans, etc.*	*Employee handbooks*
	Union contract	*Attitude survey*	President's talk to all employees	*Benefits brochure*
	Staff memos		Supervisory staff meeting	Statement of standard procedures
	Organization chart		*Attitude survey*	*Union contract*
			Grievance system	Organizational policy statements
				The grapevine

NOTE: Italicized activites are those with primary personnel/human resources involvement.

SOURCE: Adapted from Howard H. Greenbaum, "The Audit of Organizational Communication," *Academy of Management Journal* (December 1974): 748.

the personnel/human resources function are so designated. The personnel communications activities operating at an interpersonal level have been considered in chapter 14 or earlier in this chapter in other connections; so too have the intraorganizational activities intended to secure conformity to plans for purposes of productivity. It is therefore those personnel activities at the intraorganizational level that serve the other three objectives—not only labor force maintenance proper, but innovation and information giving or instruction—that concern us here.

The Choice of Media

One of the questions personnel managers face is how to communicate a certain matter to employees. Overall, if it is important to get the message through, a combination of oral and written communication is desirable, but of the two, oral communication is the most effective, ideally at some type of meeting. Meetings for this purpose are often organized by personnel representatives; they work particularly well if there is an opportunity for questions and answers so that possible sources of misunderstanding can be resolved. It is much more difficult to get this two-way interaction into written procedures, and this may be why the latter are somewhat less effective. Even memoranda, letters, and company publications transmit information much better than the posting of things on company bulletin boards. Bulletin boards seem to work better than rumor or the company grapevine.

There is also reason to believe that various media are preferable for different types of communication.[11] Thus changes in employee benefits are best communicated by memoranda or letters to employees, or perhaps through articles in company publications. Group meetings are particularly useful for discussing changes in operations that might cause layoffs and the status of collective bargaining negotiations, although letters to employees have considerable appeal for the latter purpose as well. One of the most important guides to media choice is to select the particular media from which employees *expect* to obtain various kinds of information. If these expectations are frustrated and desired information is not available from an anticipated source, this in and of itself can create dissatisfactions.

Company Publications

As noted in Exhibit 15.11, companies make a variety of publications available to employees. In many cases an editorial staff is maintained within the personnel department for this purpose. Staff editors are generally trained in their discipline and have experience in journalism and publishing.

Employee Handbooks   One of the major company publication activities is the preparation of an employee handbook, or in some cases handbooks. More than one such publication is likely if different employee groups, such as sales and manufacturing, require substantially different information. These handbooks contain company rules, disciplinary procedures, pay practices, benefit information, employee relations policies, and other material dealing with the company and its operation. The objective is to have a permanent reference source that employees can use to obtain needed information.

Handbooks also often prove useful to companies during arbitration and court proceedings because they provide evidence that certain information was made available to employees. If an employee brings suit against the company for an on-the-job injury and claims she never was told she needed to wear protective clothing, reference to a clearly stated safety rule in the handbook dealing with this subject can help the company's case a great deal. To serve this type of function effectively, however, handbooks must be put in the hands of every employee and should be revised and updated frequently.

Magazines and Newspapers Most companies produce at least one in-house publication on a regular basis, usually once a month, that is sent to all employees. In addition there may be various newsletters or even more substantial publications prepared for different company locations, geographical areas, departments, etc. The latter usually deal with local issues and contain more material dealing with the activities of individual employees, recreational events, and the like.

Publications of these kinds provide a valuable medium through which companies can inform employees about changes, plans, policies, and the like while at the same time fostering good will for the organization. It has been evident for some time that employees do look to these publications as a major source of information about their company and what it is doing.[12] Although some firms include considerable material intended to persuade employees to the organization's viewpoints on various political, economic, and labor–management matters, this is done less frequently in company publications than in those published by unions. The reason appears to be a desire to maintain an image in the eyes of employees that focuses on valid information, objective treatment, and legitimacy, rather than advocacy of special positions. In this way, readership levels are maintained and the communication channel remains open for widespread use when it is needed. When there are major difficulties with a union, including strikes, companies tend to use this channel to present the company view.

Readership Surveys It is common practice to conduct surveys to gain information from employees, either as feedback on items that have been published or for guidance on items being considered for publication. These surveys may be conducted internally by the personnel staff or by an outside consulting firm. The approach may be relatively informal—discussions are held with small panels of employees at periodic intervals. On the other hand, it is not uncommon to conduct a formal survey using questionnaires sent to sizable numbers of employees. In either event, the objective is to find out what will and will not be read as well as what is preferred and what is not, and to shape the content of the publication accordingly.

Exhibit 15.12 contains an item used to determine readership levels for *The Atlantic Magazine,* then published by the Atlantic Refining Company. This and other items were contained in a questionnaire mailed to the homes of a cross-section of the company's employees. On the basis of reponses to these questions, the company made major changes in the content of the magazine.

Employee Attitude Measurement

Attitude measures derived directly from employees have much in common with readership surveys. The approaches used to obtain information are much the same, although the uses of the resulting data differ. One use of attitude data involves feeding back the responses to managers and employees as part of an organization development program designed to bring about major changes in company structures and processes. This survey feedback approach is described in more detail in chapter 10. Another use is in the evaluation of managers. In an

EXHIBIT 15.12 Example of a company magazine readership survey item

AS THE YEARS GO BY

Atlantic Congratulates Its Faithful Employees Who Celebrate
Service Anniversaries With the Company

★ ★ ★ ★ ★ ★ ★ **25** YEARS SERVICE ★ ★ ★ ★ ★ ★ ★

Philip Alston	James R. Davis	John A. Fries	Williams E. Harkins	Elmer E. Schmidt	Delbert P. Wynia
Mechanical	Domestic Sales	Domestic Sales	Domestic Sales	Domestic Sales	Refining
Point Breeze Refinery	Pittsburgh, Pa.	Mechanicsburg, Pa.	Gloucester, N. J.	Hartford, Conn.	Point Breeze Refinery

20 YEARS SERVICE

Raymond Esham, Domestic Sales, Salisbury, Md.
George R. Laines, Domestic Sales, Wilkes-Barre, Pa.
Wesley M. Plyler, Domestic Sales, DuBois, Pa.

15 YEARS SERVICE

Lawton Coulbourne, Marine Fleet, S.S. *Atlantic States.*
Ira D. Ellis, Accounting, Odessa, Texas.
Carl W. Feld, South Jersey Sales, 260 S. Broad St.
Leslie J. Healey, Domestic Sales, Binghamton, N. Y.
Leo W. Holton, Operations, St. John, Kansas.
Ollie L. May, Atlantic Pipe Line, Cleveland, Texas.
Patrick J. McCann, Refining, Point Breeze Refinery.
S. Donald McKinstry, Products Pipe Line, Keystone & Buffalo.
John F. McLaughlin, Jr., Domestic Sales, Phila.
...dus F. Morris, Budget...6 Broa...

Jack L. Sanderford, Accounting, Dallas.
Dock Sharpe, Atl. Pipe Line, Mount Enterprise, Texas.
Clifford S. Shipley, Research and Development, Phila.
Pearl B. Sperry, Domestic Sales, New Haven, Conn.
Hugh H. Trager, Exploration, Wichita, Kansas.
Henry F. Traynor, Operations, Plainville, Kansas.
Cleo G. Turner, Operations, Longview, Texas.
Myrle F. Welch, Atl. Pipe Line, Wasson, Texas.
Rollin R. Williams, Domestic Sales, Scranton, Pa.
Samuel Young, Power, Point Breeze Refinery.

Do you usually read items like this completely through when they appear

in The Atlantic Magazine or do you rarely read this type of item?

Comments

approach pioneered by Sears, Roebuck, attitude data obtained from employees working under a particular manager are used to appraise that manager and determine what changes are needed.[13]

Probably the major use of employee attitude measurements is in the area of labor relations. For many years, companies have obtained this type of information largely for the purpose of spotting situations where dissatisfaction is pronounced and thus a potential exists for either union inroads or increased militancy. Based on the information obtained from the attitude measures, it may then be possible not only to take steps to improve the overall employee climate, but also to thwart union objectives. Attitude data can be used effectively to predict labor unrest and to guide efforts to minimize it. Companies are aware of this and they do use the data for this purpose, as well as to deal with other employee problems that are unrelated to union activities.

Approaches to Obtaining Information   Exhibit 15.13 outlines a number of the methods used to obtain employee attitude data and their major features. Although not necessarily best for all purposes, survey questionnaires appear to

EXHIBIT 15.13 Methods of obtaining information regarding employee attitudes

Method	Characteristics	Main Strengths	Main Weaknesses	Structure	Time Involved	Directness
Survey Questionnaires	Most widely used technique to obtain information from a large number of employees	Particularly useful for studies of beliefs, attitudes, values; data lend themselves to quantitative analysis	Impersonal, problems of nonresponse, question validity, misleading questions	Closed-ended: high Open-ended: low	Relatively economical	Relatively indirect
Survey Instruments	Similar to questionnaires but developed around a specific theme or body of theory; preplanned orientation	Validity, pretested	Likely to miss important issues for a particular organization	High	Economical	Relatively indirect
Interviewing	Questions posed directly to employees	Subjective data can be clarified; more in-depth data can be obtained; greater flexibility and deviation than above two methods	Expensive, requires highly skilled interviewers, difficulty ensuring comparability of data, self-report bias	Closed-ended: moderately high Open-ended: low	Lengthy	Highly direct
Organization Sensing	Unstructured group interviews, usually with a cross section of employees; can involve managers or third-party moderators	Group interaction can lead to "richer" ideas, more thoughtful analysis	High dependence on trust, effective listening skills; low degree of statistical rigor	Low	More economical than personal interview	Highly direct

EXHIBIT 15.13 (continued)

Method	Characteristics	Main Strengths	Main Weaknesses	Structure	Time Involved	Directness
Polling	Questioning a particular work group about a certain issue, problem	Since whole group takes part, can lead to increased sense of involvement	Does not lend itself to large groups; not scientific	Low to moderate	Short time span	Direct
Observation	Watching actual behavior of people at work, interacting with each other	Flexibility, insights into working arrangements, collection of data on behavior not reports of behavior	Open to perceptual bias, Hawthorne effect, requires highly trained individuals, sampling problems	Casual to highly structured	Varies	Relatively direct
Unobtrusive Measures	Use of records, such as turnover, absenteeism, and production statistics	Uncontaminated data (no respondent bias)	Measures must be used in their proper context and often must be refined, interpretational coding	High	Varies	Highly indirect
Collages and Drawings	Individuals, subgroups, or groups are asked to do a drawing around a particular theme	Nonverbal way of expressing feelings about an issue, situation, etc.	Often perceived as "child's play," difficult to interpret	Low	Moderate time span	Relatively indirect

SOURCE: James L. Bowditch and Anthony F. Buono, *Quality of Work Life Assessment: A Survey-Based Approach* (Boston: Auburn House, 1982): 32–33. Reprinted by permission of the publisher.

be the most widely used. These questionnaires are often enclosed in paychecks, handed out at work, or mailed to the home. The respondents are not required to provide their names, but they usually can be identified to the extent of their work groups or locations. An increasingly common approach, and the one almost always used when outside consulting firms conduct the survey, is to assemble employees in small groups and have them complete the questionnaires on company time. This approach assures that many more completed measures will be obtained.

The questionnaires themselves may focus on specific local issues of concern, in which case they are devised anew for each survey. There are also standardized instruments available that have been widely used in attitude research. With these measures it is possible to make comparisons against data obtained in other companies—a major advantage. Factors considered in the more comprehensive measures vary, but the aspects noted in Exhibit 4.5 as components of job satisfaction are typical. In some cases, items are devised, selected, and scored using complex scaling techniques that add considerable precision to the measurement process.

Sources of Resistance   Like performance appraisal, attitude measurement has often been met with resistances that make it difficult to maintain a program of repeated measurements over long time periods. Not surprisingly, union leaders prefer to be the primary source of information on what employees think and feel. They do not wish to be confronted with direct information that may conflict with their interpretations, nor do they like to have the company, rather than the union, identify and solve employee problems.

Management, too, may prove a potent source of resistance. The results obtained may not be flattering to a particular manager. Furthermore, many line managers have been taught to believe that only productivity and profit results really count. They do not consider employee attitudes important, and they resent being held accountable for them. Work stoppages, sabotage, excessive turnover, and strikes are seen in this view as acts of nature and beyond human—or at least, managerial—control. Managers of this kind alternate between considering attitude measurement a waste of money and seeing it as an unjustified intrusion on their activities. They can often succeed in having it stopped by resisting any changes based on attitude measurement results and then, after several surveys have yielded the same conclusions (and no changes), arguing that continuing this approach to upward communication is worthless because it does not accomplish anything.

Suggestion Programs

A somewhat different approach to upward communication is intended more for innovation and problem-solving than labor force maintenance. It has much in common with the quality circles concept as discussed in chapter 10. These suggestion systems can differ considerably among themselves, but the basic idea is that employees who would not otherwise do so as part of their normal work assignments contribute ideas for improvements in some aspect of company operations. These ideas are evaluated by a committee in most instances. The committee typically contains at least one personnel representative and a number of rank-and-file employees.

In the majority of cases, cash awards are made for approved suggestions, although this is not always the case. Where measurable savings can be shown, it is common to award a percentage, perhaps 15 percent, of the one-year reduction in company costs. Such awards sometimes run into the thousands of dollars, and some companies, such as General Motors, pay out a great deal of money over the course of a year. When it is not possible to put a monetary value on the idea, even though there is a clear intangible value, the usual procedure is for the committee to use a point system for judgment much like the one used in job evaluation. Thus points are awarded for such things as the nature of the benefit, the scope of its use within the company, the ingenuity of the idea, the degree to which adoption involves little cost, the effort involved, and the completeness of the proposal. The total point award is then keyed into a table of dollar amounts to determine the actual award value.

Some suggestion systems, especially those with a potential for sizable earnings, serve their purpose well. But many do not, largely because a negative image develops around them. Supervisors may feel threatened, jealousies may emerge, and there may be strong group pressure not to participate. These factors can combine to leave a suggestion program practically dormant. Whether this happens or not is largely a function of the general employee relations climate.

HEALTH, SAFETY, AND PERFORMANCE CONTROL

The primary objective of company activities in health and safety is to prevent occurrences that would make an employee unable or less able to contribute as an effective performer. In contrast, performance control activities focus on restoring effective performance where some types of performance failure is apparent.

Preventive Medicine

In-house industrial medicine activities and dispensaries are typically located in a personnel department. Health activities are closely allied with safety functions, an alliance that increasingly has been fostered by the various laws related to employee health and safety considered in chapter 14. However, there are ties to other personnel/human resources activities as well, such as selection, benefits administration, job placement, and aspects of job analysis.

Range of Activities The major activities associated with industrial medicine are the conduct of physical examinations, the elimination of health hazards in the environment, and a degree of treatment appropriate to the situation. In most cases in the United States, this latter means some treatment of minor illnesses that do not necessitate absence from work, and initial emergency treatment in accident cases and in instances of more severe illness.

Physical examinations are often used as part of the staffing process—in selecting employees and in assigning individuals who are partially disabled or otherwise physically limited to appropriate positions. They are also used periodically with regular employees, especially managers, to identify physical problems at an early point and to head off potential disorders. Another use is to establish whether a person should return to work after an illness or accident.

Records from dispensary visits and physical examinations provide a valuable source of information regarding health and safety hazards in the work environment. In addition, environmental health conditions are monitored to establish whether toxic or other detrimental conditions such as excessive noise are present. Such matters as radioactivity levels in nuclear plants are a major concern. Many industrial hygiene activities are required by various state and federal laws. The objective is to identify potential threats to health before they actually can affect employees, and do something about them—including, if necessary, shutting down operations.

In recent years, companies have become increasingly involved in smoking cessation, weight control, physical fitness, and stress management programs—all designed to promote employee health.[14] Some firms provide full-scale exercise facilities. A course designed to improve stress levels might deal with the following topics:

1. Course objectives and ways of assessing stress levels.
2. Sources of stress in the job.
3. Individual differences in stress reactions.
4. Preventive approaches—nutrition, exercise, relaxation, meditation, time management, etc.
5. Goal-setting for stress reduction.

Health promotion of this kind is particularly common in the larger firms.

The Inside vs. Outside Question   In some locations, especially outside the United States, companies provide a full range of medical services for employees and dependents simply because these services are not available in the community. However, under most circumstances, there is a choice between staffing some type of internal medical program and relying on external resources almost entirely. A number of considerations are involved.

Some contend that working full-time for a company compromises the professional integrity of the physician. Although there is considerable evidence that this need not be the case, the possibility exists that the welfare of the company could, under certain circumstances, dominate over that of the patient in cases of conflict. On the other hand, the in-house physician is in a much better position to engage in preventive medicine and to provide emergency treatment.

Many of the larger firms do have their own internal medical staffs at major company locations. Smaller firms and also some large ones tend to rely on outside sources. In many cases, independent industrial medicine clinics are utilized; this is the case with Georgia Power Company, for instance. These may be established by several companies in an area working together. In recent years, health maintenance organizations have often been used in much the same manner. There appears to be no single satisfactory solution, and thus what works for one company in one location may not work for another firm in another location. A major consideration, in any event, is that medical activities be well integrated with the personnel/human resources function as a whole.

Safety Management

Large companies frequently locate a safety division within the personnel/human resources function. This division operates the safety program, relying heavily on a staff with considerable expertise in safety engineering. In order to obtain the widespread involvement needed to achieve a degree of safety consciousness throughout the organization, an extensive committee structure generally is utilized as well. In some cases these committees include union representatives.

At the top of the committee structure is a management policy group that regulates safety expenditures, sets safety rules, and sometimes becomes involved in investigating particularly dangerous conditions. At the unit level, the committees focus more on inspections and the limitation of accident hazards; they contain both management and nonmanagement members. There may be other committees as well concerned with safety training, contests, and the like. The more people that can be involved in some way, the more effective the safety program appears to be, both in preventing accidents and in keeping governmental intervention to a minimum. Minimizing interventions can become a major goal if the legal setting is such that government insists on costly changes or levies fines against the firms.

Accident Statistics   From a company viewpoint, accident statistics have a number of values. One is that they tell how well a company is doing relative to national and industry figures. Thus they say something about what needs to be done in the future. Statistics vary widely among industries, with construction, mining, and manufacturing being the most dangerous; these differences need to be taken into account. Furthermore, intracompany differentials indicate where accident prevention efforts should be concentrated. There is a tendency for rates to remain high in parts of the company where problems have arisen. Thus it is important to identify high frequency accident areas early, and concentrate on them in any prevention effort.

Accident statistics are developed from accident reports, now mandated by federal law. Some of the terms used in these reports and in developing the statistics are given in Exhibit 15.14. Exhibit 15.15 shows an accident report

---

EXHIBIT 15.14   Some terminology of accident reporting

Injury frequency rate—number of disabling injuries times a constant (usually one million) divided by number of hours worked in a unit

Injury severity rate—number of work days lost times a constant (usually one million) divided by number of hours worked in a unit

Lost time injuries—includes deaths, permanent disabilities (both partial and total), and injuries that prevent job performance for at least an entire work shift

Agency—item most closely associated with an injury (hand tools, chemicals, animals, machines, etc.). An agency part is the aspect of the above involved.

Unsafe condition of the agency—aspect of the agency that could have been guarded or corrected (inadequate mechanical guarding, defective condition of agency, unsafe apparel, etc.)

Accident type—type of contact between injured person and agency (struck by, contact with noxious substance, fall against, etc.)

Unsafe act—type of behavior associated with accident (working unsafely, horseplay, failure to use safe attire, removing safety devices, etc.)

Unsafe personal factor—characteristic of individual associated with accident (lack of knowledge, disturbed emotional state, etc.)

EXHIBIT 15.15 Accident report form

Name of employee _____ Location _____

Address _____ Division _____

Sex _____ Age _____ Occupation _____

Married _____ Children _____ Wage rate _____

Date and time of alleged accident _____

Place of alleged accident _____

Description of alleged accident _____

_____

_____

_____

_____

Working on regular job? _____

Agency involved _____

Part of agency _____

Unsafe mechanical or physical condition of agency _____

_____

Accident type _____

Unsafe act _____

Unsafe personal factor _____

Safeguards provided _____

Safeguards in use _____

Nature and extent of injury _____

_____

_____

Days lost _____ Attending physician _____

Recommendations to prevent similar accidents _____

_____

_____

Prepared by _____ Date _____

form. Calculating accident rates, filing the necessary reports with the government, and developing strategies for dealing with identified problem areas are essential roles of the safety function within personnel management.

Approaches to Prevention   Major factors in accident prevention are equipment design and structuring of the work environment to make it safer. Efforts of this kind serve two functions. For one thing they protect people from themselves and from their environments. They simply make it harder to have an accident. Barriers are introduced in the form of guards, clothing, protected areas, and the like. Perhaps equally important, reducing the accident potential of a work environment tends to increase feelings of security and reduce anxiety levels. This in itself makes people less likely to have accidents because they are no longer distracted by their anxieties. Much of accident prevention is an engineering function; it is an important function.

Some controls of this kind are unbeatable. But others can be disregarded or subverted by people, and there are areas in which mechanical and engineering protections are not feasible. Thus at times prevention must move from the environment to the individual. One such approach is to create safety consciousness coupled with a knowledge of potential dangers. This is particularly important in the early period of employment, when people are most vulnerable. Safety training can be very important at this point; so can skill training, which makes the employee more capable of coping with the work environment and gives a feeling of increased confidence as well.

Safety training may also be mobilized to deal with high-accident situations wherever and whenever they are located. A not infrequent circumstance is that off-the-job accidents, in the home and on the streets, assume a more important role than those on the job. Many company programs become successful enough that the major cause of absenteeism, insofar as accidents are concerned, is no longer the work context. Under these circumstances, safety training may focus on off-the-job factors as a primary consideration.

Companies also use publicity campaigns, involving various personnel communications media and contests to promote safety. The contests typically provide financial rewards to members of groups with low accident rates. The focus of these contests and the measures employed can vary considerably, but the essential ingredient is the idea that it pays to be safe. Group pressures are mobilized to this end. The result, as in so many other incentive-type programs, is positive. But, when contests are used, care must be taken to control for possible falsification of accident reporting.

Rather surprisingly, the simple fear of injury and the pain it produces are not enough to keep accident rates at a minimum. Preventive procedures are helpful for this, but the issues involved are complex and the consequences costly from both humanitarian and economic viewpoints. Safety is an area in which further knowledge is desperately needed.

Reassignment, Discipline, and Counseling

Although dealing with people who have fallen below standards of acceptability on some aspect of performance is primarily a supervisory concern, many of the methods for correcting such a situation are basically personnel/human resource activities. Chapter 4, under the subject of controlling individual performance, discusses the processes involved in some detail and notes a number of possible corrective actions that may be used depending on the factors operating to cause the ineffective performance. Certain of these corrective actions, as they relate to the personnel function, have already been considered—job redesign (job analysis), training and development, changes in compensation, medical treatment. Others are dealt with in the following sections.

Promotion, Transfer, and Demotion If a person cannot do one job well, it is always possible that there is some other job within the organization that fits the individual better. Shifting a person to a new job is done for numerous reasons, but one of the most important is to try to improve performance. However, there are serious limits to what can be achieved with this approach. Some individuals will fail at any job. Furthermore, in smaller firms the diversity of jobs often is so limited that there simply is not a position that would match the particular set of capabilities a person possesses. Even in larger firms, appropriate positions may all be filled with employees whose performance is entirely acceptable. Thus there may be no openings of the type needed.

Promotion is not generally associated with ineffective performance; it seems to be rewarding failure. Yet there are instances, as when a person has been underplaced and bitterness over this fact is a cause of failure, in which it is the best thing to do. Usually, though, it is not wise to promote such a person in the same work group. A shift to a new group of people will help to minimize conflicts and jealousies.

Transfer refers to moving an individual laterally to another job that has been placed at the same grade level through job evaluation. It is important in such cases, if a change in work unit is involved, that the new position be one in which there is every reason to believe the individual definitely will succeed. A second failure always raises questions about one supervisor dumping a problem employee on another. Also, in some companies, there is a whole host of barriers that make lateral transfers very difficult. Among these are seniority considerations, separations between crafts, and the unwillingness of supervisors to accept transfers. Usually transfer works best at an early point from an entry level position to another such position more suitable to the individual's abilities.[15]

Demotions can be difficult, but rather surprisingly, they often are not. When employees clearly recognize that they are in serious trouble in their present position and believe they can handle a lower-level position, possibly because they have done so before, the demotion may come as something of a relief. In fact, the greatest resistance may come from management. Managers who feel somewhat guilty about these situations may actually prefer to fire the person rather than authorize demotion. Discharge may be difficult, but once accomplished, the person is gone and can be quickly forgotten. Demotion means the person is still present, and is a constant reminder of the unpleasantness involved. As with promotion and transfer, demotion may not be easy for a personnel manager to carry out. But once a record of success with such reassignments is achieved, and the reassigned people really do become effective performers again, the sources of resistance usually disappear.

Disciplinary Action Some companies use demotion as a part of a formal disciplinary process. However, the usual components of that process are warnings, suspensions, and discharge. Exhibit 15.16 describes the various patterns of actions and the offenses to which they are usually applied. If demotion is used, it is generally introduced just prior to discharge.

Warnings, as part of a disciplinary process, are stated in writing and are to be signed by the employee. Suspensions are without pay and usually do not extend

Disciplinary Action	Offenses
Pattern 1 Immediate Discharge on First Offense	Intoxication at work Theft Possession of narcotics Falsifying employment application Willfully damaging company property Fighting Outside criminal activities Falsifying work records
Pattern 2 First Offense → Second Offense Warning → Discharge	Gambling Sleeping on the job Insubordination Abusive language to superior
Pattern 3 First Offense → Second Offense → Third Offense Warning → Suspension → Discharge	Leaving without permission Failure to use safety devices Slowdown of production Unauthorized smoking
Pattern 4 First Offense → Second Offense → Third Offense → Fourth Offense Warning → Warning → Suspension → Discharge	Chronic absenteeism Unexcused and excessive lateness Carelessness Unexcused absence

beyond a week. When a union is involved, union representatives take part in each stage of the process, and a grievance may be filed at any point. In discharge cases, grievances are frequent, and many of these go through the various steps to arbitration. The arbitrator may put the individual back to work with full pay if there is reason to believe the union contract was violated in some way.

Supervisors generally do not resort to formal discipline nearly so often as they could. Many prefer to use threats or other approaches and reserve formal action for particularly difficult situations. This means that the "first offense" often is not the first offense at all. Evidence indicates that progressive discipline and the threat of discharge are effective in overcoming performance problems. Even if an employee finally is put back to work by an arbitrator, the whole experience can be a sobering one, and the performance problems are unlikely to recur. However, this is less true of individuals with emotional disorders, including drug and alcohol problems.

Employee and Executive Counseling Experience with extensive employee counseling programs such as the one introduced at Western Electric in conjunction with the Hawthorne research (see chapter 3) has not been very positive, and few companies use that type of approach today. Still, counseling that focuses more specifically on performance problems and on career guidance is being used with considerable success. There may be an internal staff of counseling specialists, or outside consultants may be called upon as needed. Usually the counseling is short-term and intended to solve some particular problem inherent in the job or in social relationships at work. More severe emotional disorders are almost without exception treated outside the company. Probably about half of all companies of sufficient size to justify it provide some kind of job-related counseling, usually through a personnel department. A number of these counseling programs are broad employee assistance programs for dealing with alcoholism, drug problems, emotional disorders, family and marital difficulties, financial concerns, and legal assistance.[16]

At the executive level, companies tend to be more active in this area. It is not uncommon for firms to provide for extensive psychological or psychiatric counseling over a long period in the hope of restoring a previously competent manager to former performance levels. When the counseling required is clearly long-term, it is almost always done by an outside practitioner, although often at company expense. In general, companies report considerable success with their counseling efforts. The approach can be a useful method of dealing with certain types of substandard performance.

Summary

Major personnel/human resource functions designed to maintain an effective labor force have been considered. Performance appraisal is at the center of these activities because, first and foremost, it is necessary to know when and where effectiveness—and the lack of it—exist. For managers, these evaluations are obtained either through the personal judgments of individuals who are in a position to know about the person's work or by using objective measures of factors that are under the manager's control. Exhibit 15.1 outlines the judgmental appraisal process. The judgments of superiors are used most frequently in this process, although there are a variety of approaches to obtaining them; Exhibit 15.3 provides examples of some objective measures. Judgmental appraisal systems in particular are subject to considerable criticism and resistance. One problem is that they may incorporate certain types of errors, as indicated in Exhibit 15.4, although these errors can be overcome.

Compensation is closely related to employee motivation and thus can play a significant role in maintaining an effective work force. Exhibit 15.6 provides a general overview of the compensation process and the elements it comprises. A key aspect of wage and salary administration is job evaluation. Methods used for this purpose are noted in Exhibit 15.7. On the basis of job evaluation, jobs are assigned to pay grades. Prices are then placed on them, taking into account both the overall, market-related wage level of the firm and the grade level of the job. Many firms rely heavily on incentive payments, and Exhibit 15.9 lists the major types of incentives, as well as some of the pros and cons associated with their use.

Employee benefits are an important aspect of compensation, although they do little to stimulate productivity. One type of benefit involves payments for time not worked—holidays, vacations, severance pay, and the like. However, the primary employee benefits are the various types of group insurance and retirement plans. A major innovation in the benefits area has been the development of "cafeteria" approaches under which, to varying degrees, employees may select their own benefit packages.

Personnel communications also play an important role in maintaining an effective labor force. The various approaches of a personnel nature are distinguished from organizational communication in general in Exhibit 15.11. Among the various types of downward communications, company handbooks, magazines, and newspapers play a particularly significant role. Major sources of upward communication in the personnel area are readership surveys, employee attitude measurements, and suggestion systems. Exhibit 15.13 outlines approaches used to obtain attitude data and notes some of their strengths and weaknesses.

Company health and safety programs function primarily in a preventive mode so that people can continue as productive members of the organization. Industrial medicine and hygiene programs use both physical examinations and study of the work environment aimed at eliminating health hazards to accomplish this end. Safety management uses accident statistics to guide its efforts and pinpoint problems. Various procedures are then introduced to help keep accident rates down.

In contrast to health and safety efforts, corrective actions in performance control function to restore effective performance once it has been lost. Procedures considered include reassignment, formal disciplinary actions, and personnel counseling. Promotions, transfers, and demotions may all be used for corrective purposes, with the particular alternative among the three depending on the causes of the employee's difficulties. Formal discipline operates on a sequential basis, as described in Exhibit 15.16; it can be a useful type of corrective action in appropriate cases. Counseling works best if it is focused on specific types of performance problems and the employees with these problems.

What Have You Learned?

1. In what ways do the following contribute to establishing what companies pay for different jobs?
   a. wage surveys
   b. pay grades
   c. job evaluation
   d. minimum wage laws
   e. compensable factors
2. How is the industrial medical function carried out? What are its major activities, and how does it relate to the overall personnel process?
3. What are the different sources from which subjective performance appraisal data derive? What are the advantages and disadvantages of these various sources?
4. Employee benefits often result in company payments during a period when the individual is not working. When would this be the case? What is the nature of these benefits?
5. How do the various types of company publications serve the goals of personnel communications? How do they relate to union activities?
6. Why are accident statistics obtained, and in what manner? What preventive procedures may be introduced based on them?
7. How may resistances operate to undermine performance appraisal systems? Do these resistances exert more influence on performance appraisals used for certain purposes than others? Explain.

8. What are the different types of incentive pay systems, and how effective is each for various purposes? How are these systems used in executive compensation?

9. Why are attitude surveys used, and what are the various measurement approaches employed? What advantages are associated with these various approaches?

10. A number of error sources have been noted in subjective performance ratings. What are these types of errors? What steps may be taken to reduce them?

How Well Can You Apply Your Knowledge?

Problem 1. A management appraisal panel had been convened in accordance with standard company procedures to evaluate one of the branch managers. The company was a life insurance firm—the same one discussed in chapter 10. Its structure within the Life Sales Division at the time of the appraisal was that noted for the "after change" period in Exhibit 10.2. The appraisal panel consisted of the branch manager's immediately superior regional manager, his superior—a territorial vice-president, a representative from the life sales division's own employee relations staff, and a member of the corporate management appraisal unit, whose duties were to coordinate the performance evaluation process.

Some background on the vice-president involved is necessary. Under the old organizational structure in effect some years back (see Exhibit 10.2), the branch manager had worked directly for the vice-president, then a territory supervisor. Since the reorganization, however, the two had had practically no direct contact with each other. During the prior period, the two men had been located in the same city along with a number of other managers from the company, and a very active social life had developed among the families in this group. At this time, rumor had it that a very close relationship developed between the branch manager and the wife of the territory supervisor. Apparently, some time after the reorganization, the husband, newly appointed to a vice-presidency, became aware of the situation. As a result of geographical moves, the affair had cooled, and there now seemed to be no actual threat to the vice-president's marriage. On the other hand, it was generally accepted that the relationship still continued, although at a much reduced tempo, and that the vice-president was to some degree aware of this.

The appraisal panel for the branch manager now convened was the first one for this manager in which the vice-president had participated since when he was a territory supervisor. He had asked to be put on the panel on this occasion.

In past appraisals, the branch manager had been rated up toward the top of the 10-point scale, in the outstanding range. In the present instance, as previously, the appraisal summary written by the corporate level personnel representative on the basis of face-to-face discussions among the panel members contained a number of positive statements:

> Pushes aggressively for results, a hard worker who finds challenge in his work.
>
> Has demonstrated substantial managerial ability.
>
> Is very effective in developing his subordinate managers.
>
> Has shown considerable imagination in developing new approaches.
>
> Deals promptly and effectively with subordinates who do not measure up.
>
> Has been successful in meeting budgetary constraints, increasing new premiums, and reducing policy lapses in his area.

However, at the urging of the vice-president, a number of additional statements were also included:

> Is not as attentive to his family and its needs as he probably should be.
>
> Tends to use his substantial knowledge of company policies less to implement them than to break them, although the latter cannot be proved.

In committee work, may tend to dominate the situation beyond the level his authority would warrant, even though his committees produce good work.

Needs counseling on the dangers of discriminating against female employees; at present it cannot be established that he does this.

Deals with those under him too forcefully on occasion, with the result (rumor has it) that the company may be faced with a union organizing attempt among the agents working out of his branch.

As a result of the addition of these statements, the branch manager's overall rating dropped to a point at which he was considered to meet the standard, but not to excel. Whereas he had previously been first in line to fill any openings at the regional manager level, this performance evaluation removed him from consideration for promotion at this time.

Questions

1. What appears to be wrong with this performance appraisal process? Assuming that an error has been made, what is the error, and why has it occurred?
2. What could be done to change and improve the performance appraisal and promotion systems of this company so that this sort of thing would be less likely to happen in the future?

Problem 2. A nationwide firm manufactures products that are sold both directly to retailers such as department stores and indirectly through wholesalers. Its sales force has emerged through a series of historical developments, rather than as a result of detailed planning. In the early years, the major component was a group of housewives who worked part time, before their children came home from school, introducing the products in local stores. These were women who wanted to earn some extra money to supplement the family income, and the pay was at a low level consistent with general practice and markets for such employment.

Over time, as the wholesale part of the business grew, another sales force was added, initially to handle the rapidly expanding wholesale demand as well as some larger retail outlets that needed more than the part-timers could provide. This was a full-time component, and it was staffed almost entirely with males. Because most of these people were hired either from other firms or through college recruiting, the pay scale was forced up by market conditions. In hourly terms, this full-time sales force started at more than twice what the part-time housewives were making.

Initially there was no question regarding the difference between these two sales forces. The volume of accounts, complexity of sales activities, amount of travel, training needed, and many other activities were much greater for the full-time salesmen. However, in some geographical areas, these differences began to blur over time. The part-time saleswomen started to work full-time, encouraged by sales managers who saw this as a method of keeping costs down. Some salesmen focused increasingly on retail service because that was what was needed most in local areas. Nationwide, the differences were still there, but not in every local area.

Not surprisingly, a group of women in one of the areas where the differences had become blurred ultimately filed suit for discrimination under the equal pay act. The group charged that, in terms of the job factors contained in that act, they did the same work as the men and that they were paid less than half as much—unfairly. Furthermore, they contended that this unfair discrimination existed throughout the company's nationwide sales operations, and that therefore the case should be considered as a class action. This meant that any woman who had worked for the company in the recent past should be compensated for the differential between her pay rate and that applied to the full-time male sales force.

The money involved amounted to millions of dollars. Unfortunately, the company had not previously conducted job analyses or job evaluations on these positions. At the time of the suit, the low-paying job was staffed entirely with females, and the high-paying job entirely with males. Although perhaps it should not have been, given changes in the climate of opinion on such matters, the company was caught completely offguard by the court action.

1. What actions on the part of the company in the past could have either protected the company from this type of litigation or made it relatively easy to defend against such a suit?

2. Given the course of events, what could the company do now to show that the pay differential nationwide was justified? What wage and salary procedures could be brought to bear to this end? Be specific.

Additional Sources for More Detailed Study

Baird, Lloyd S.; Beatty, Richard W.; and Schneier, Craig E. *The Performance Appraisal Sourcebook.* Amherst, Mass.: Human Resource Development Press, 1982.

Barrett, Richard S. *Performance Rating.* Chicago, Ill.: Science Research Associates, 1966.

Belcher, David W. *Compensation Administration.* Englewood Cliffs, N.J.: Prentice-Hall, 1974.

Bernardin, H. J., and Beatty, Richard W. *Performance Appraisal: Assessing Human Behavior at Work.* Boston: Kent, 1984.

Cascio, Wayne F. *Costing Human Resources: The Financial Impact of Behavior in Organizations.* Boston: Kent, 1982.

DeVries, David L.; Morrison, Ann M.; Shullman, Sandra L. and Gerlach, Michael L. *Performance Appraisal on the Line.* New York: Wiley, 1981.

Dunham, Randall B., and Smith, Frank J. *Organizational Surveys: An Internal Assessment of Organizational Health.* Glenview, Ill.: Scott, Foresman, 1979.

Ellig, Bruce R. *Executive Compensation: A Total Pay Perspective.* New York: McGraw-Hill, 1982.

Henderson, Richard. *Performance Appraisal: Theory to Practice.* Reston, Va.: Reston, 1984.

Hunt, Raymond G. *Interpersonal Strategies for System Management: Applications of Counseling and Participative Principles.* Monterey, Calif.: Brooks/Cole, 1974.

Lusterman, S. *Industry Roles in Health Care.* New York: The Conference Board, 1974.

Mahoney, Thomas A. *Compensation and Reward Perspectives.* Homewood, Ill.: Irwin, 1979.

Miner, John B. "Management Appraisal: A Capsule Review and Current References." *Business Horizons,* September 1968.

Mobley, William H. *Employee Turnover: Causes, Consequences, and Control.* Reading, Mass.: Addison-Wesley, 1982.

Nash, Allan N., and Carroll, Stephen J. *The Management of Compensation.* Monterey, Calif.: Brooks/Cole, 1975.

Noland, Robert L. *Industrial Mental Health and Employee Counseling.* New York: Behavioral Publications, 1973.

Olson, Richard F. *Performance Appraisal: A Guide to Greater Productivity.* New York: Wiley, 1981.

Root, L. S. *Fringe Benefits: Social Insurance in the Steel Industry.* Beverly Hills, Calif.: Sage, 1982.

Salisbury, Dallas L. *America in Transition: Implications for Employee Benefits.* Washington, D.C.: Employee Benefits Research Institute, 1982.

Wallace, Marc J., and Fay, C. H. *Compensation Theory and Practice.* Boston: Kent, 1983.

Notes

1. Robert I. Lazer and Walter S. Wikstrom, *Appraising Managerial Performance: Current Practices and Future Directions* (New York: The Conference Board, 1977).

2. Paul A. Mabe and Stephen G. West, "Validity of Self-Evaluation of Ability: A Review and Meta-Analysis," *Journal of Applied Psychology,* (June 1982).

3. Gary P. Latham and Kenneth N. Wexley, *Increasing Productivity Through Performance Appraisal* (Reading, Mass.: Addison-Wesley, 1981).

4. Lee Stockford and H. W. Bissell, "Factors Involved in Establishing a Merit-Rating Scale," *Personnel* (January 1949).

5. Douglas Cederblom, "The Performance Appraisal Interview: A Review, Implications, and Suggestions," *Academy of Management Review* (April 1982).

6. See the discussion in Stephen J. Carroll and Craig E. Schneier, *Performance Appraisal and Review Systems* (Glenview, Ill.: Scott, Foresman, 1982).

7. Hubert S. Feild and William H. Holley, "The Relationship of Performance Appraisal System Characteristics to Verdicts in Selected Employment Discrimination Cases," *Academy of Management Journal* (June 1982).

8. Luis R. Gomez-Mejia, Ronald C. Page, and Walter W. Tornow, "A Comparison of the Practical Utility of

Traditional, Statistical, and Hybrid Job Evaluation Approaches," *Academy of Management Journal* (December 1982).

9. Edwin A. Locke, Dena B. Feren, Vickie M. McCaleb, Karyll N. Shaw, and Anne T. Denny, "The Relative Effectiveness of Four Methods of Motivating Employee Performance," in *Changes in Working Life,* eds. K. D. Duncan, M. M. Gruneberg, and D. Wallis (New York: Wiley, 1980).

10. See Albert Cole, "Flexible Benefits Are a Key to Better Employee Relations," *Personnel Journal* (January 1983).

11. Bureau of National Affairs, *Employee Communications,* Personnel Policies Forum, July 1975.

12. See for example John B. Miner and Eugene E. Heaton, "Company Orientation as a Factor in the Readership of Employee Publications," *Personnel Psychology* (Winter 1959).

13. James C. Worthy, "Organizational Structure and Employee Morale," *American Sociological Review* (April 1950).

14. See Andrew J. J. Brennan, "Worksite Health Promotion Can be Cost Effective," *Personnel Administrator* (April 1983); and Michael T. Matteson and John M. Ivancevich, "The How, What and Why of Stress Management Training," *Personnel Journal* (October 1982).

15. For further discussion, see John B. Miner and J. Frank Brewer, "The Management of Ineffective Performance," in *Handbook of Industrial and Organizational Psychology,* ed. Marvin D. Dunnette (Chicago: Rand McNally, 1976).

16. Fred Dickman and William G. Emener, "Employee Assistance Programs: Basic Concepts, Attributes and an Evaluation," *Personnel Administrator* (August 1982).

READINGS AND PROFILES

Managing Turnover Strategically
Allen C. Bluedorn
Business Horizons

A Radical Experiment Cuts Deep Into the Attractiveness of Unions
Robert T. Boisseau and Harvey Caras
Personnel Administrator

David C. Garrett and Delta Air Lines Inc.

The common thread in these selections is the description of highly effective, and often highly innovative, ways of staffing and maintaining organizations. The personnel policies and procedures considered appear to have worked well.

Bluedorn deals with the matter of turnover—how and when it should be discouraged or encouraged. In the process he considers certain applications and aspects of human resource planning, performance appraisal, compensation, and personnel research. These ideas are illustrated with reference to some techniques developed at Merrill, Lynch and Company, a firm designated by *Fortune*'s survey respondents as tops in the diversified financial grouping, and also number two overall, just behind Citicorp, in innovativeness.

The Boisseau and Caras article describes an innovation developed in one of the plants of General Electric Company, top ranked by *Fortune* in the electronics and appliances industry. This short piece provides a good picture of why most managers would prefer not to have labor unions, and why they feel that way. In addition to labor relations, it also considers aspects of training, career development, grievance administration, and employee communications.

The executive profile for this part focuses on the unique personnel programs and policies of Delta Air Lines, how these programs and policies have contributed to Delta's competitive edge, and how David Garrett relates to them. Delta is placed at the top of the transportation industry in the *Fortune* survey. If there had been a separate designation for effectiveness in overall staffing and personnel/human resource management in that survey, there seems little doubt that Delta would have emerged as one of the best firms in that regard.

Managing Turnover Strategically

Allen C. Bluedorn

The major problem with turnover is not the fact that people quit their jobs; it is that managers regard their quitting as a *problem*. For years a popular management response to quitting has been, "We must reduce this turnover." Fifty years ago Henri Fayol listed "stability of tenure of personnel" as management principle number twelve, and this attitude persists today.[1] It is well illustrated in a conversation I had with a vice president of a southern insurance company. He was disturbed that some employees were quitting, and he was very receptive to the suggestion that a turnover study be made in his company. I am sure he thought the study could lead to reduced turnover, and he did need the study. He did not know whether his turnover was high, low, or average for his industry and geographical location. He did not know what impact the turnover was having on his company; and he did not distinguish between "good" and "bad" turnover.

Today, rising labor costs, high inflation, and the loss of cheap sources of energy are systematically removing slack from the American economy. These conditions reduce margins of error for managerial decisions. At the same time the decline in both productivity and the competitive position of American business provides a powerful incentive to improve managerial behavior. In view of present conditions it is important to rethink turnover management.

My purpose here is to begin the rethinking process by addressing several important questions. Why do managers see turnover as a problem? What distinguishes "good" turnover from "bad" turnover? What is an alternative turnover management strategy and how can it be implemented?

Allen C. Bluedorn is an assistant professor of management at the University of Missouri-Columbia. He conducts research on the effects of turnover on organizations and turnover's management. The author would like to acknowledge the assistance of Alice E. Warne, Paul S. Greenlaw, and Robert A. Pitts in the preparation of this article.

Reprinted with permission from *Business Horizons,* March–April 1982, pp. 6–12.

Why Turnover Is a "Problem"

There are three reasons why managers evaluate turnover negatively. Two of these reasons are social, and the third is economic.

Manager Socialization. Managers formally acquire a negative definition of turnover through management education and informally from superiors, colleagues, and consultants. Fayol's prescription to keep turnover rates low has already been mentioned, and Fayol was writing sixty years ago. Scores of textbooks for courses in management, organizational behavior, organizational development, and personnel management have made a cliche of the statement, "Turnover and absenteeism are indications that something is wrong." Thus, even before they begin their first jobs, managers have learned to interpret turnover as a sign of trouble. If they do not learn it in school, they soon pick it up from other managers or consultants employed by their firms. The conclusion that turnover means trouble has become a firm part of management lore.

The Social Meaning of Turnover. Managers do more than merely note the hiring and resignation of their employees. When employees quit, managers develop explanations for their turnover behavior. One of the more common ones is that the employee who quits has *rejected* the organization. Research by Richard Mowday indicates that insecure managers are more likely to interpret turnover as rejection than are managers who feel secure.[2]

When turnover is defined as rejection, it becomes the organizational equivalent of divorce. Since nobody likes to be rejected (even by people we dislike), the interpretation of turnover as rejection is particularly repulsive to managers.

The Economic Reason. Judged by the criterion of profit maximization, there are very real costs associated with turnover. Cawsey and Wedley's recent survey of Canadian businesses revealed that the cost of a single episode of turnover ranged from $400 for a shoe manufacturer to $3,732 for the International Nickel Company.[3] The expenses result from separation costs when an employee quits (exit interview, severance pay, and so on), advertising and recruiting to replace the departed employee, orientation and training for the new employee, idle equipment while the replacement is recruited and trained, lost production while the position is vacant, and lower productivity while the new employee learns the job. The most catastrophic turnover cost I have encountered is the estimated $800,000 the U.S. Air Force spends to train a replacement for each pilot who quits.[4] With over 3,000 pilots quitting each year, pilot turnover costs the Air Force $2.4 billion annually, just for replacement training.

The economic costs of turnover cannot be ignored. They are real and are a genuine reason for managers to be concerned about turnover.

With these powerful social and economic forces operating on managers, it is not surprising that turnover is viewed as a monolithic monster. To manage it properly, it is necessary to realize that turnover is neither always monstrous nor monolithic.

How Much Is Too Much?

Realizing that turnover is not always bad is the first step toward adopting the new strategic view: turnover is either good or bad depending on its net consequences, either economic or behavioral, for the organization.

Economic Criteria. The economic evaluation of turnover forces the manager to weigh the costs of turnover against its benefits. Many common turnover costs have already been identified, but far less attention has been devoted to the organizational benefits of turnover. One economic benefit is the lowering of average labor costs. As the length of an employee's tenure increases, the higher he or she moves up on the organization's wage and salary schedule. In many jobs, the learning curve is short and productivity does not increase with increasing job tenure. In such cases, total organizational productivity would decline as employees are paid higher and higher wages without attendant increases in the quantity and/or quality of production. Turnover in these jobs would reduce labor costs since new job holders would start at the bottom of the wage scale. For example, a recent study by Dan Dalton reveals a 15 percent yearly turnover rate would save a large Western public utility $294,271 annually in wage costs compared to a zero turnover rate, assuming a work force of 200 employees. At a 25 percent turnover rate, the savings would be $484,712 annually.[5]

This economic benefit was recognized by the management of one large national service organization which was interested only in a turnover study of managerial personnel. Its officers did not want to find out how to reduce the turnover of non-exempt employees. Jobs such as stocking vending machines and selling hot dogs at baseball games are easy to learn, and management wanted high turnover in these jobs to keep the average wage of non-exempt employees low. This company is not alone in this policy. Most firms in the fast food industry, for instance, desire high turnover among their non-exempt employees for the same reason.

Another reason an organization would want high turnover in certain jobs is to present a youth-ful image. Amusement parks such as Walt Disney World want their work force in direct contact with the public to project a youthful image, and turnover helps keep the work force young.

Some other benefits of turnover are the introduction of change and innovation. Companies which use turnover to generate these benefits feel they outweigh the costs. Exhibit 1 presents the classic economic scenario for weighing costs against benefits applicable to turnover.

A specific turnover rate should be thought of as a purchasable commodity. Just as a turnover reduction has costs and benefits, so too does an increase in turnover. Managers thinking of changing a turnover rate should think in terms of purchasing the change: the greater the changes, the greater the benefits will have to be to outweight the costs. Since the marginal utility of any commodity decreases as increasing amounts of the commodity are acquired, a point will be reached when another unit of the commodity will not be worth the extra

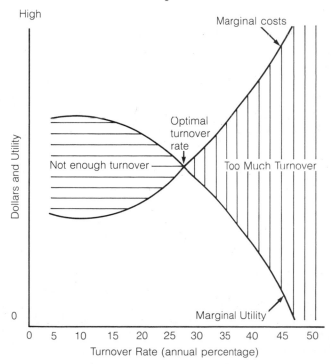

EXHIBIT 1 The economics of turnover management

cost to the purchaser. Like any other commodity, the optimal turnover rate to purchase is the rate at which the marginal costs equal the marginal utility of the turnover rate. As is illustrated in Exhibit 1, a rate below this level is too low and a rate above this point is too high.

The Turnover Intervention Rule compares existing turnover rates with the optimal turnover rate, and recommends that the existing rate be increased, decreased, or maintained to reach the optimal rate.

In 1978 Herbert Simon received the Nobel Prize in economics for his work revealing that people seldom fully perform this type of economic analysis. He concluded that many times it is impossible for a human being to do so because of insufficient information, uncertainty over preferences, limited abilities to process existing information, and so forth.[6] While the exact form of economic analysis just described may not be a ready working tool, it has heuristic value for the manager. The *principle* it reveals is useful to the manager willing to think in terms of return on investment.

I have already used the idea of purchasing a specific turnover rate. Like any other purchase, the return the specific turnover rate is likely to yield must be compared with the likely returns of other investments. For example, will the organization receive a greater return by spending $1 million on a turnover rate 5 percent lower than the existing rate, or would the same money bring a greater return if it were spent on increased advertising or new equipment? Foregone opportunities are part of the costs of purchasing a specific turnover rate. Evaluating which investment will bring the greater return will often be an imprecise comparison, and the manager will have to rely ultimately on experience, advice, intuition, and the information at hand to make the choice.

Behavioral Criteria. It will usually be impossible to perform the formal analysis of marginal costs and utilities just described. The general principle that turnover should be sometimes increased and sometimes decreased leads to a second general idea that it is more beneficial for an organization to retain high performers than low performers. In investment terms, there is a greater return from retaining five high quality employees than five of low quality, everything else being equal. A strategy of reducing turnover among high performers and ignoring or encouraging turnover among poor performers will yield a greater return than an equal investment in an across-the-board turnover reduction.

This strategy can be easily defined with Exhibit 2.[7] Hits are high performers who stay and poor performers who quit. Misses are high performers who leave and poor performers who stay. Success in turnover management is defined by the ratio of hits to misses. The greater the proportion of hits, the more successful the strategy—up to the point where the marginal costs equal the marginal utility of the hit/miss ratio. The economic logic still applies with high performers, even if it will be difficult to use precisely for the reasons noted by Simon. As a practical matter, a manager will actually have to evaluate comparative return on investment potentials rather than marginal cost and utility curves.

Are the Best Employees More Likely to Leave? To implement the strategy being outlined in this article, it would be convenient for management if high performing employees were responsible for most turnover. There are reasons why this would be expected and data which support these reasons. The argument is basically that higher performers are more employable because employers are eager to hire the best personnel. This makes the employee less dependent on any single job and more likely to move. While this is a plausible argument, there are also studies which show that high performers

EXHIBIT 2   Hits and misses in turnover management

		Are the people the ones the organization really wants to keep?	
		No	Yes
Did the people quit?	No	Miss	Hit
	Yes	Hit	Miss

are no more likely to quit than average or low-level performers. One of these is the study I conducted on the southern insurance company.

Because of its potential usefulness for managing turnover, I tested the question of whether employees at any performance level were more likely to quit than those at any other level. Employees were asked to evaluate their own performance on a seven-point scale ranging from "excellent" to "terrible." Because of possible problems with self-evaluations (exaggerations, lack of variance in responses, and so on), each employee was also evaluated by his or her supervisor using the same seven-point scale.

The results were consistent regardless of the measure of performance. Level of performance was not correlated with turnover linearly; it was not true that the better the employee the more likely there was to be turnover (a negative correlation). Nor was there a curvilinear correlation; middle-level employees were neither more likely to quit (a ∩-shaped relationship) or less likely to quit (a ∪-shaped relationship). The exact results are presented in Exhibit 3.

Although some studies have found that better employees are more likely to quit, the results of my study illustrate the danger of making such an assumption. Even if performance and turnover are positively correlated in an organization, this means only that *more* turnover comes from the better performing employees. It does not mean that *all*

turnover comes from the better performers. This means that even when performance and turnover are positively correlated, an across-the-board turnover management strategy will still not optimize the hit/miss ratio since the turnover of some of the poorer performers would also be reduced. It will still be necessary to identify the better performers.

Implementing the New Strategy

A strategy is worthless unless the means for implementing it are developed and utilized. Some companies, such as the large service organization mentioned earlier, have implemented a version of the new strategy by ignoring turnover among non-exempt personnel. In many organizations the exempt/non-exempt distinction will be far too gross to implement the new turnover strategy successfully. Fortunately the Merrill Lynch Pierce Fenner and Smith investment firm has developed a mechanism for implementing the strategy which can be applied to most organizations.[8]

Merrill Lynch's Problem. Like many industry leaders, Merrill Lynch found itself in the position of being the training center for its industry. Individuals would accept a job with Merrill Lynch, and the firm would put them through an extensive training program. After the training was completed, the individual would go to work for Merrill Lynch—for a while.

After a few years, many trainees left to accept good jobs with Merrill Lynch's competitors, who got well-trained and experienced brokers without having to pay the costs of training them.

Management at Merrill Lynch came to realize that many of their brokers came to the firm with the deliberate strategy of receiving the training and experience and then moving on to one of their competitors. The firm decided to make an effort to reduce the turnover rate among its most valuable brokers.

The Merrill Lynch Matrix. Merrill Lynch effectively implemented the strategy I have described in this article. Rather than an across-the-board assault on the broker turnover rate, the decision was made to focus on retaining selected categories of brokers. The method used to identify the brokers to be retained was to classify all brokers within the cells of the matrix presented in Exhibit 4.

EXHIBIT 3 Correlations between job performance and employee turnover in a southern insurance company

Performance Measure	Linear Correlation	Curvilinear Correlation
Self-Evaluation	.05	.09
Evaluation by Supervisor	.03	.14

NOTE: The linear correlation measure is Pearson's product moment correlation coefficient (r). The measure of curvilinear correlation is eta. None of these four coefficients was significant at the .05 level nor were the two tests for curvilinear relationships (eta^2-r^2). $N = 158$.

EXHIBIT 4 The Merrill Lynch matrix used to identify targets for turnover reduction

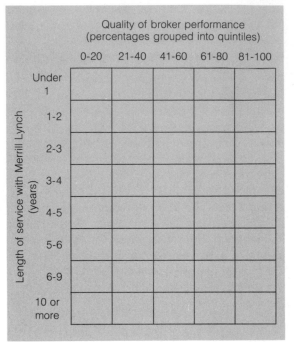

For Merrill Lynch, the two most important broker characteristics were performance level (measured by dollars produced) and length of service with the firm. These two variables were used to form the Merrill Lynch matrix. Each broker's performance and length of service would define the broker's location in the matrix. Management then had to decide which cells of the matrix would be targets for the reduction effort.

Merrill Lynch was most bullish about new brokers (under six years of service) who performed well. The firm was bearish about poor performers who had been with the company a short time. The brokers in bullish cells were targeted for the turnover reduction effort; no changes were made in the treatment of the brokers in the other cells.

The year before the intervention, Merrill Lynch's broker turnover rate was 8 percent *above* the industry average. One year after the intervention (a redesigned compensation system for brokers in targeted cells), the turnover rate had fallen to a level 11 percent *below* the industry average. Compared to the firm's turnover rate a year before the intervention, this was a 24 percent reduction. It was achieved by focusing the effort on the brokers Merrill Lynch most wanted to retain. An across-the-board intervention was neither necessary nor desirable.

The particular variables used to form the matrix at Merrill Lynch were suitable to that company's purposes. Most organizations would want to use the performance variable as one dimension of the matrix, but might want to use a different variable for the other dimension. Length of service is only one possibility. For example, some jobs are more critical to an organization than others. An organization could form a matrix defined by different job categories in one dimension and performance levels in the other. For example, the U.S. military services have had particular difficulty retaining personnel in technical specialties. The Armed Services could form a job category-performance level matrix and target higher performers in the most critical specialties, such as Air Force pilots, for a turnover reduction effort.

Multi-Dimensional Matrices. Merrill Lynch used a two-dimensional matrix successfully. I have described other variables that could be used to form an N-dimensional matrix. Three, four, and five or more variables might be useful to identify precisely the organization's most valuable members. Adding dimensions creates problems, unfortunately, and the more dimensions, the more serious the problems.

With more dimensions, more data must be obtained about each member, which increases both the cost of data collection and the chances of error. The most important drawback to a matrix with three or more dimensions is the complexity of directing the change effort to the targeted cells. For instance, special pay plans for high performing MBA engineers with six to twelve years of service who work the night shift in divisions east of the Rockies would become an administrative nightmare. Other interventions such as team building would often be impossible.

The value of the two-dimensional matrix is its ability to identify precisely the members the organization wants to retain without so much precision that the intervention is either too costly or impossible. Even a one-dimensional matrix based solely on performance level can often be all that is required to target employees for a turnover intervention.

There is an old proverb which says, "A man must be very brave who attempts to kill a porcupine by sitting on it." Too many managers have been sitting on their turnover porcupines for far too long. Managing turnover by assuming it must be continuously reduced is a doctrine best forgotten. There are many times when turnover should be reduced, but it is no longer valid to think that it must always be reduced.

The strategic approach to turnover described here will complement any well-developed management program. A good program of personnel management will have the performance appraisal system which is necessary to implement the strategy. To implement the strategy fully, the manager will be forced to learn more about the organization's work force, learning which will also serve a manager well for making other decisions.

A manager consciously considering an organization's turnover should ask the following four questions: (1) Which members of my organization do I most want to retain? (2) Which members do I least want to retain? (3) At the present time, what is my ratio of hits to misses? (4) Will the return on investment to improve the hit/miss ratio make the effort worthwhile compared to other possible investments? If the answer to question four is "Yes," the manager should make the investment. If the answer is "No," the turnover rates should be left alone, and the investment should be made on something else.

Notes

1. Henri Fayol, *General and Industrial Management* (London: Sir Isaac Pitman, 1949): 38–39.
2. Richard T. Mowday, "Viewing Turnover from the Perspective of Those Who Remain: The Relationship of Job Attitudes to Attributions of the Causes of Turnover," *Journal of Applied Psychology,* February 1981: 120–123.
3. Thomas F. Cawsey and William C. Wedley, "Labor Turnover Costs: Measurement and Control," *Personnel Journal,* February 1979: 90–95.
4. Robert S. Dudney, "What's Really at Stake in Draft Controversy," *U.S. News & World Report,* August 4, 1980: 24–25.
5. Dan R. Dalton, "Turnover: A Hard Dollar Positive Perspective," Paper presented at the 40th Annual meeting of the Academy of Management, Detroit, Michigan, August 10–13, 1980.
6. Herbert A. Simon, "Rational Decision Making in Business Organizations," *American Economic Review,* September 1979: 493–513. This article is the lecture Herbert Simon delivered in Stockholm, Sweden when he received his Nobel Prize in Economic Science. It provides a good review and introduction to his ideas.
7. I would like to thank my colleague Henry P. Sims, Jr., who suggested this figure to me after reading my article, "A Taxonomy of Turnover," *Academy of Management Review,* July 1978: 647–651.
8. I would like to thank George Hollenbeck, Manager of Personnel Planning and Research at Merrill Lynch, for providing me with the details of the Merrill Lynch Matrix and the data about the reduction intervention.

A Radical Experiment Cuts Deep Into the Attractiveness of Unions

Robert T. Boisseau and Harvey Caras

"Are you crazy?" people in our company and in other industrial relations organizations ask when they first hear about the new Grievance Review Panel at GE's Appliance Park-East in Columbia, MD.

They wonder how we, as a non-union facility—one of the largest in the General Electric Co. chain—allow a rotating panel of three hourly employees decide the fate of grievances at third step.

But after they hear the background and results of the new procedure, those employee relations practitioners are less inclined to consider us candidates for an insane asylum.

The facts are that hourly employees—with a 3–2 majority over management—can control the results of most grievances submitted by their peers in our facility.

Other industrial relations people who've contacted us about our program may have another goal, avoiding unionization. That's one of our long-range objectives also.

With much-publicized givebacks and wage freezes, it is very difficult for union organizers to-day to promise non-union employees a big pay raise if they join the union. Likewise, with union companies' closing down and laying off, it is not likely that non-union people will accept promises of job security as something a union could honestly deliver.

So, what then, can the union really guarantee non-union people? What can they do differently? Formal grievance procedures are one of their few remaining lures.

Troubled History

As the second largest non-union plant in GE, located in the highly unionized Baltimore area, we

Robert T. Boisseau is manager of employee and community relations for GE Appliance Park-East, Columbia, MD. Harvey Caras is manager of hourly employee relations at the same plant.

Reprinted from the October 1983 issue of Personnel Administrator, copyright 1983, the American Society for Personnel Administration, 606 North Washington Street, Alexandria, Va. 22314, $30 per year.

576   Readings and Profiles

had been a constant target of union organizers throughout the 1970s.

The production and quality of electric ranges and microwave ovens, as well as good human relations programs, were severely hampered by extensive time devoted to union campaigns—nine of them leading to six elections during our first eight years of operation. Our winning majorities were constantly under 60 percent.

More importantly, each election divided our people into pro- and anti-union camps, causing major morale problems from which it took months to recover.

But in the last three years, we've made major strides toward improving relationships, management credibility, training, policies and practices, supervision and communication in our plant. We're determined to make Columbia the best place to work that we can, and to put an end to the constant union battles.

Both of us had previously worked in unionized plants outside GE and were familiar with how ineffective some union grievance procedures really are.

It was hard at first to believe that it could be attractive to our people. But we also knew that in the hands of a skillful union salesman, the union's grievance procedure could certainly be made to sound like something far greater than it truly is, with its representation, documentation and arbitration.

Grievance Background

For years, the Columbia plant had used a formal, written grievance procedure that allowed employees to go to immediately higher levels of management with their grievances. Even though our history showed a success rate of over 40 percent (considerably higher than at most union plants) we still noticed a steady decline in employee usage each year.

While, in truth, part of the blame for this decline rested with improved supervision and more consistent application of policies, we couldn't run from the fact that some of the decline had to result from lack of faith in the process.

Many employees admitted honestly that they had a low regard for our procedure.

We brainstormed many different ideas, but finally settled on the one recommended by our plant manager, Joe Carando, who was then the decision-maker at the final step in our process. It was he who was willing to give up total authority in recommending the use of the panel of hourly employees to help him make the best possible decisions. This was the framework:

Each panelist has an equal vote.

The authors are the two management panelists, who can be out-voted by three hourly members of the grievance review board.

Review board decisions are final and binding.

Expect Skepticism

We presented our idea to groups of managers, to foremen and hourly employees. Their responses were all about the same—positive about the concept, but skeptical that we were really serious.

Even more skepticism came from personnel managers at local companies and other GE plants: "How can you let yourselves be outnumbered and still maintain your right to run the business?" they invariable asked.

To that question, we had a standard response: "If we have a major issue that truly divides the management and hourly members of the panel—and if we cannot convince one of the hourly people that we are right—then we must be wrong."

We didn't think that was that dangerous, for a number of reasons:

We trust our hourly employees—because they've matured in understanding how a successful business needs to operate.

A growing number of employees have taken part in a two-year self-development program which exposes them to all the major functions of the business. In that forum, they can get answers to questions that bother them, helping them understand why things are done as they are.

In-plant communication about business realities has been brightened and stepped up so that employees know more about what's going on—and why—in their business.

Columbia-GE has a unique workforce, we believe, and they deserve a unique grievance procedure.

Introducing the Process

How the panel would work was discussed for many months as an "informal agenda" at self-development training program classes.

When all the recommended details were in place—based on our research, and also on the ideas from hourly people who were taking those classes—we asked for help.

An after-work review of the new procedure was scheduled in our auditorium. Current class participants were invited to attend on their own time. They came. They listened. They contributed to the thought process and planning. And they (unofficially) endorsed our plan, many of them indicating an interest in a program to train panelists. Thirty-nine employees volunteered.

Each completed an eight-hour program on their own time. Training emphasized the legal and ethical elements of grievance handling—problem solving techniques—effective listening . . . culminating in a realistic role play of an actual grievance.

Response from the panelists was overwhelming. Even some of the most skeptical among them had a totally different perception by the end of the sessions. All were geared up and ready for our first grievance.

Helping introduce the process were communication vehicles at our manufacturing facility:

A tabloid-size special edition of the *GE NEWS*—with full details, and comments from a panel of employees who had prior knowledge of the project—announced the grievance panel idea.

Other special publications and our Management Hotline—a recorded 60-second daily telephone commentary on items of interest in our business—encouraged people to take the training.

The *GE NEWS* covered our first panel case.

A tape/slide program, developed for use at employee roundtable meetings with their foremen, gave testimonials of how people felt after they'd taken the panel training.

Process Works

Shortly after the procedure went into effect, a grievant took our first case to the panel. By policy, the grievant was allowed to choose the names of four panelists at random and put one name back, leaving three panelists to hear the case with the two managers.

The case was an intriguing one. It involved a job promotion, which had been denied, due to a rule prohibiting a person from downgrading and returning to the same classification within six months. The grievant felt that extenuating circumstances should have allowed him to by-pass the six-month rule.

After hearing all the evidence and investigating precedent, the panel ruled against the grievant. One of the hourly members of the panel said: "We sympathize with the guy, but a rule is a rule and it's the same for everyone."

There was a strong message in that statement—one that makes all of us feel good about the future of our new grievance procedure. Each panelist has taken their responsibility seriously.

No Panacea

Is the expanded grievance procedure with the review panel the cure-all and end-all to our union concerns? Perhaps not. But we've proved ourselves correct in our belief that we can trust hourly employees to make wise decisions.

Maybe, in turn, they've learned to trust management a little more, and believe us when we say that we want to have rules to benefit the whole business, and apply them, consistently.

Perhaps people who are trained now to help make important business decisions—as the "last word" in the grievance procedure at Columbia–GE—are realizing how touchy that process becomes. Maybe they're learning, as a by-product of that experience, that it's not unionization that helps employees solve their problems—it's people who care.

In any event, there is little doubt that the Columbia plant is now a better place to work today than it once was thanks to a grievance review panel and the people who make it work.

David C. Garrett and Delta Air Lines Inc.

Delta began operating as a crop dusting service headquartered in Monroe, Louisiana in the 1920s. From those beginnings, it has gradually expanded over the years, moving to Atlanta, Georgia in 1941, and merging with Chicago and Southern in 1953 and with Northeast Airlines in 1972. The greatest expansion has occurred since World War II. The present chief executive officer, David Garrett, has been part of that expansion throughout its duration, having joined the company in 1946. At present, Delta flies to 85 cities in 33 states as well as to Canada, the Caribbean, and Europe. Its fleet totals 219 aircraft. Over the years, it has been a very successful airline—much more so than its major competitor—Eastern.

Delta's success has a number of roots, but a major factor has been a capacity to plan effectively. This proclivity for planning extends into the personnel area and, in fact, the company is noted for the effectiveness of its personnel policies. Personnel is a very important function at Delta, and its chief executive officers typically have had some background in that field. Delta is one of the few major corporations in which a career in personnel management is viewed as appropriate preparation for the corporate top spot.

There are two interrelated reasons that the company stresses the personnel function. One is the fact that training plays a very important role in its operations. The other is a long-standing policy of attempting to defuse any conflict between management and employees, so that all can work together toward common objectives—a concept that spawned the term "the Delta family feeling."

Company training programs emphasize this family feeling, customer service, cooperation, and friendliness. They attempt to build organizational commitment, while at the same time staffing the company with a very effective group of employees. Classroom training is provided for personnel in Maintenance, Quality Control, Materiel Services, Flight Operations, Flight Control, Stations, Traffic, Sales, Computer Services, and In-Flight Service. All new employees go through extensive orientation, and pilots are trained continually on aircraft simulators.

Cooperation and commitment are fostered by a number of techniques besides training. Basically, the company is non-union, with the only unionized group being the pilots. Over 55 percent of the employees have been with the company for ten years or more. Trainees are assessed by a psychologist to determine their sense of teamwork. Almost all positions are filled by promotion from within. Outside consultants are rarely used; needed expertise is obtained through regular employment. A stable work force is emphasized, and layoffs are avoided. Salaries and benefits are excellent. All employees meet with senior management frequently to discuss any problems.

How this commitment-oriented personnel program works can be illustrated by the response to the company's first profitless year since 1947, occasioned by the combination of a recession economy and increased fare competition following deregulation. Unlike other airlines, Delta did not lay off employees. Instead, executive salaries were cut, pilots agreed to fly more hours, and dividends to stockholders were reduced. Employees, however, received raises averaging 8.5 percent at a time when most competitors were bargaining with unions to achieve pay reductions. The employee reaction was to organize a voluntary campaign to buy the company the first of the new Boeing B-767 planes it had on order. Through payroll deductions, contributions from retirees, and other efforts, money was raised for the $30 million plane. Over 77 percent of employees contributed.

In its origins and in much of its current operations, Delta is a southern airline, and David Garrett reflects this fact. He grew up in South Carolina and attended Furman University there. After service in the Air Force during World War II, he joined Delta, working initially in a job handling flight reservations. By 1955 he had earned a masters degree in business from Georgia Institute of Technology in Atlanta, and that same year was placed in charge of Delta's employee training activities. In the late 1950s, he was the company's primary educational planner. Moving from there into operations, he progressed steadily up the line—assistant vice-president in 1963, vice-president in 1965, and senior vice-president in 1967. In 1971 David Garrett became president of the company, and seven years later, the chief executive officer designation was added.

Much of Delta's competitive edge in its industry is attributable to the fact that it has a superior work force that strives to contribute to, rather than fight against, the company. This situation has been created and maintained through very effective personnel policy administration. No one is more aware of this than David Garrett. He helped to create many of these policies, and he has continued to nurture them. By training, experience, and temperament, he is ideally suited to Delta's needs.

Every Delta pilot trains reguarly on the Company's fleet of eight flight simulators. These highly sophisticated devices provide training under virtually every type of weather condition and flying situation.

David C. Garrett

Much of Delta's success is attributable to its superior work force.

David C. Garrett and Delta Air Lines Inc.

Management Process and Production-Operations Management

Part 6 deals with the process of adding value to activities of the organization. Earlier parts have covered the general management functions as well as organization behavior. The basic elements of getting things done were discussed along with influencing and leadership, directing, and motivating members of organizations toward contributing to goals.

In Part 6, the concern is with operations that apply the previous chapter materials in planning, organizing, and controlling those activities important to the purpose of the organization. The heart of the organization consists of those things the organization was established to do. Tasks at the heart of the organization are accomplished by planning, organizing, and controlling the interplay of people and other resources in the organization.

Operations are described here as the heart or core activity of the organization. That activity may be manufacturing, health care delivery, entertainment, or any service function. Manufacturing conventionally was considered to be production, but scholars and practitioners are increasingly concerned about good management in any enterprise that converts organization inputs into outputs. In the process, value is added to input resources, and products and services are rendered to customers and clients. The more productivity and quality rendered by the organization, the more it is successful, whether it is a profit or a not-for-profit organization.

Chapter 16 deals with production operations systems. Previous material on systems is related to the open systems view of the organization seeking to enhance or improve its basic operations.

A strategic approach to operations takes into account the goals and purposes of the organization, in both the long and short run. The relationships of operations functions are discussed with reference to marketing, finance, and other functions in the organization. The role of technology is viewed as assisting the operations of any enterprise by providing tools and options for members of the organization. Then productivity is analyzed. Our national concern for productivity enhancement is related to the productivity of both organizations and participants in the organization.

Chapter 17 discusses designing, planning, and controlling operating systems. A decision approach considers the many decisions involved in designing the intended output of organizations, the planning and organizing of operations to support outcomes, and in controlling outcomes.

Resource planning and allocation are joined with selection of sites, laying out of facilities, designing the job and work flow, and control systems. Using the capacities of the organization to meet forecast demands is seen as a way to match needs and capabilities. Inventories, as precious assets, are to be carefully ordered, protected, and utilized to produce desired output. Many assets of every organization can be tied up in inventory, and careful management is required to reduce waste and loss so as to enjoy the greatest possible efficiency of operations.

Last, quality control is viewed as an important guardian of the organization's attempt to produce the standard of outcome intended, whether in automobiles, health services, or administrative services. Quality has become a catchword in the drive for productivity. The chapter material includes ways of planning for quality, and techniques for assuring quality.

CHAPTER 16

Production-Operations Management Systems

CHAPTER OUTLINE

Production–Operations Management
Major Concepts of Production–Operations
    Management
Systems Approach to Operations Management
Importance of the Operations Approach
Operations and Outputs
Operations Systems

Managing Operations
A Strategic Emphasis
Jobs in Operations
Operations and the Environment
Operations and Other Functions
Managing Operations Functions
    Planning and the Managing of Operations
    Organizing and the Managing of Operations
    Control and the Managing of Operations

Operations Management and Technology
Definition and Concepts
Technology and the Manager
Technology and Society
Managing Technology
Technology Available for Choices
    Factory Technology
    Office Technology
    Service Organizations
Managing Technological Change

Productivity
The Nature of Productivity
Trends in Productivity
Factors Influencing Productivity
Managing Productivity in Operations
Operations Management and the Future

OBJECTIVES

To identify the nature and major concepts of production–operations management, to describe the contribution of the systems approach, and to describe the major contributions of the operations function.

To show the relationship of strategy to managing operations, to describe the kinds of jobs found in the operations field, and to discuss how the environment affects the management of operations.

To understand the concept of technology and how it affects managers and the management of operations, to grasp the nature of high technology and other technologies, and to understand what is involved in managing technological change.

To understand what productivity is, what the relationship is between operations and productivity, the trends in productivity, the factors that influence productivity, and the options for operations managers to enhance the productivity of future operations.

Production–operations management systems are relatively new topics in management theory. While industrial and production management topics have been described and analyzed for decades, only in recent years have production and operations topics received increasing emphasis.

In economics, the production function is concerned with the transformation of inputs of land, labor, capital, and entrepreneurship into goods, products, and services. In the management context, a broader definition is held for production–operations.

Exhibit 16.1 presents some relevant definitions of production–operations management.

**PRODUCTION–
OPERATIONS
MANAGEMENT**

This chapter considers the operations function as the subsystem of the organizational system that converts input resources into output products and services to meet the goals of the organization.

**Major Concepts of
Production–Operations
Management**

A key element of the concept of production–operations is the creation or addition of value. As in the management of any enterprise, the major concern is with effectiveness and efficiency in the adding of value or utility, that is, effectiveness in adding value as intended and efficiency in adding value by prudent use of resources.

The value that is added in the production–operations function is a reflection of utility in the marketplace. In other words, there is no increased value unless the utility is recognized in the marketplace. This factor strongly relates production–operations to the marketing function of the enterprise under consideration.

As in economics, the increased utility may be of several types:

1. *Form utility*—by manufacturing, as in assembly, refining crude oil, cleaning clothes, or water treatment
2. *Time utility*—by providing goods and services when needed, as in delivery services, paying bills on time, or providing emergency services
3. *Place utility*—by providing goods and services where they can be used, as in transportation systems, communication systems, and retail stores. The form is not changed, only the location.

The challenge of the operations manager is to add value to inputs by means of the conversion or transformation process, given that the value is recognized as utility in the marketplace (or by clients of the managerial system). Aggregate value added is a valuable construct to measure the vitality of a city or region or industry. The organization seeks to add value in the same way, by conversion processes (manufacturing, extraction, services, etc.). Note that the operations of the organization include (1) Combining, as in manufacturing, (2) Separating, as in refining, (3) Reforming, as in steel fabrication, (4) Presentation, as in retailing or consulting.

EXHIBIT 16.1 Production–operations management

> *The production or operations function* in an organization consists of the group of persons within the organization who are responsible for producing the goods or services for which the organization exists.[1]
>
> *Operations managers* are responsible for producing the supply of goods or services in organizations . . . making decisions regarding operations functions and the transformation systems used.[2]
>
> *Productive systems* are the means by which we transform resource inputs to create useful goods and services.[3]

A further clarification may be made in the concept of operations. Barndt and Carvey separate the general field of operations management to differentiate between production management (manufacturing) and service management.[4]

Conventional use of the term *production management* is related to manufacturing in which the output is goods and products rendered by conversion or transformation processes. The value of the goods and products is generally indicated by physical properties or characteristics, as in manufactured autos, clothing, or computers. Service organizations and processes involve conversions in which knowledge, information, and assistance need not result in physical outputs, but modify situations that add value, such as real estate, tax services, and social action agencies.

Both production (or manufacturing) and service organizations are subsets of operations management, and are discussed later in the chapter under the "umbrella" of operations management.

Similar techniques and management tools are used in both production and service organizations. This chapter is intended to highlight the operations function in organizations and the managerial role in helping operations activities improve the ability of the enterprise to meet objectives efficiently. A systems approach is especially appropriate to operations management, given the role of inputs applied to processors so as to render outputs. The processor involves operations management.

Some studies of management concentrate on particular features of organizations—finance, marketing, structure, personnel, or decision techniques. The operations management approach integrates functions in the core process of the organization and relates to all the other functions of the organization.

Systems Approach to Operations Management

The systems approach considers the operations subsystem as the subset of the total organization that takes inputs from within the organization and from the environment to become processed. The processor, as the heart of the system, transforms and converts those inputs into goods, products, and services, which become the output of the organization. The output is then distributed (or marketed) to the environment, where the value of the output is recognized and in turn exchanged for resources that may be reapplied as input to the organization for future operations.

Following the discussion of the systems approach in chapter 9, Exhibit 16.2 illustrates these relationships in the flow of resources through the system on the way to becoming outputs with added value. The general management function in the center coordinates the entire organization. The functional managers in resource, operations, and distribution subsystems coordinate their own functions. In true systems fashion, the output of the resource function (finance, accounting, and purchasing) is the input for operations. The output of operations is the input for the distribution (marketing) function. The enterprise output is rendered to the environment for the clients of the organization.

The operations subsystem relates to a number of other subsystems in the organization, as follows:

1. *Purchasing*—for the acquisition of resources
2. *Accounting*—for cost, tax, and financial information
3. *Personnel*—for manpower and human resource assistance
4. *Maintenance*—for upkeep and repair of facilities
5. *Other* units as appropriate to the organization

In the well-run operations system or organization, the systems advantages of integration and perspective are utilized to optimize the performance of the organization.[5] The enterprise works together, and the systems perspective provides the "big picture" of how the individual subsystems contribute to the overall benefit of the organization.

Importance of the Operations Approach

The American Assembly of Collegiate Schools of Business (AACSB), the business school accrediting organization, has stated that operations management and production are one of the required areas for inclusion in business study. This emphasis on the fundamental importance of production–operations management as a functional area was recently endorsed on the basis of the following criteria:[6]

1. The central nature of production in the creation of goods and services that constitute the output of the organization.
2. The control that the production function has over resource flows and asset management in the organization.

EXHIBIT 16.2 The production–operations management system

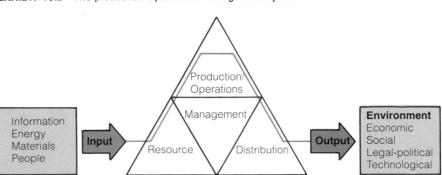

3. The pervasive presence of production functions and their outputs in our industrial society.
4. The direct relationship of the production activities to some of society's most pressing problems.

This support runs the gamut from production–operations involvement in profit generation and goal attainment to productivity and growth of the economy. In spite of the growth of the service sector of the United States economy to over 70 percent of the work force, effective and efficient management requires operations performance in both sectors—manufacturing and service.

In view of the national situation regarding the economy and productivity issues, other researchers have endorsed increased attention to the role of production and operations. Exhibit 16.3 presents some recent viewpoints on the vital role of production and operations.

Not only is production–operations management fundamentally important in an industrial society, but it can support upgrading of operational capability in a wide range of situations and organizations—public, private, profit, and non-profit. This chapter further pursues the capabilities and potential contributions of operations management.

Operations and Outputs

The objective of operations management is to generate outputs, the nature of which depend upon the the type of organization. Product and service production formats are first compared here, and then presented according to the common operations management principles they use.

Product-producing organizations are characterized by outputs that are:

1. Tangible
2. Capable of being inventoried
3. Intended for regional, national, and overseas markets
4. Rendered in complex processes for longer term demand

EXHIBIT 16.3 Testimony for production–operations management

"U.S. companies are beginning to demand that business schools supply them with graduates who have specialized in operations and people—not just numbers." (*Business Week,* August 30, 1982)

"Manufacturing, a subject that long ago fell from favor among graduate students and professors at many business schools, is making a comeback." (*Wall Street Journal,* January 26, 1981)

"Chief executives skimp on research and development and instead expend energy and resources on 'paper entrepreneurialism'—complex financial maneuvers with little real production involved. Most MBA's know all about discounted cash flows, decision trees, and game theory but apallingly little about factory techniques and motivations of live human beings, both of which are essential to keeping a competitive edge. (Robert Reich, *The Next American Frontier,* 1983)

"The key line posts—engineering, manufacturing, and marketing—require the best talent available in a competitive world." (Arch Patton, "Ideas and Trends," *Business Week,* April 5, 1982)

5. Low in customer contact with processor
6. Easy for productivity measurement

Examples of such products are automobiles, computers, or chemicals produced to be shipped or inventoried in distant locations for use over weeks, months, or years.

Service-producing organizations are identified by outputs that are:

1. Intangible, and often perishable
2. Not inventoried, but presented when open for service
3. For local distribution
4. Tied to users in simpler processing, and presented on demand
5. High in customer contact
6. Difficult for productivity measurement

Examples of service products are insurance services, personal hair care, auto repairs, food service, and education and training.

While the service sector of the economy is growing, both product- and service-producing organizations use management processes that are similar. Both plan, organize, and control.

Operations Systems

Operations systems are the heart of the productive organization, whether they provide products or services. Exhibit 16.4 illustrates operations as a transformation unit.

Since the purpose of an operating system is to transform a set of inputs into a desired output, some attention to types of systems is in order. Some transformations that help add value or utility to inputs are classified as:

1. Physical, as in manufacturing or assembly
2. Exchange, as in retailing and sales activity
3. Storage, as in warehousing or stockpiling
4. Locational, as in transportation[7]

Not only the transformation process, but also the type of organization that uses operations management to conduct its business may vary. Exhibit 16.5 reflects a variety of organizations that utilize operations management to execute their missions.

EXHIBIT 16.4 Operations system as a transformation unit

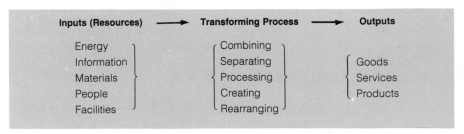

EXHIBIT 16.5 Organizations with transforming operations systems

System	Inputs	Processing	Outputs
Restaurant	Hungry customers	Food, staff	Satisfaction
Auto factory	Materials	Workers, equipment	Autos
Hospital	Sick patients	Staff, facilities	Well patients
School	Students	Faculty	Graduates
Stores	Customers	Staff, stock	Sales
Theater	Patrons	Presentations	Entertainment

One of the chief benefits of using the systems approach in viewing operations management is to derive integration and perspective from the systems process. With an emphasis on outputs that correlate with objectives and effectiveness, the managing process can concentrate on "doing the right things" and also "doing things right." This applies to both the service and production sectors of operations management.

MANAGING OPERATIONS

In looking at the particular features of managing operations, we can use the same principles and concepts found in earlier chapters of this book.

A Strategic Emphasis

Contemporary management literature places a great deal of emphasis on strategic approaches. The focus is on goal-setting and development of strategic guidelines for achieving those goals. In particular, long-term implications are examined rather than over-emphasizing the short term. Preoccupation with short-term accomplishment is blamed for much of the mismanagement and decline in organizations and segments of our economy.

Many very successful companies in both service and manufacturing have adopted the concept of "strategic business units." General Electric is credited with major advances in this area. Strategic business units promote responsibility for the decisions made in an identified area of the enterprise.

A national expert on business operations strategy, Steven C. Wheelright of Stanford, has suggested the following criteria for strategic operations decisions:[8]

1. Quality of products and services
2. Dependability of delivery and product or service
3. Cost efficiency of performance
4. Flexibility to change as needed

Whether for the manager of an engine assembly plant or the manager of a hospital admissions office, these operations criteria should enhance the accomplishment of objectives.

Other opinions on corporate and operations strategy come from Hayes and Abernathy in their classic article, "Managing Our Way To Economic Decline."[9] They cite the mistaken emphasis on short-term analysis rather than the longer

Production–Operations Management Systems

term view needed in genuine strategic planning. They also fault the lack of spending on research and development in the strategic planning of many firms.

Another view comes from Wickham Skinner of Harvard, who has long championed the coordination of corporate planning and operations planning. Skinner is famous for his description of strategy as a set of plans and policies by which a company aims to gain advantages over its competition. He supports three basic concepts in discussing trade-offs between corporate and operations strategy:[10]

1. There are many ways to compete besides producing at low costs, especially in competitive or technologically advanced fields.
2. A factory cannot perform well on every measure. Trade-offs must be made between low training costs and high product quality, or between high production volume and multiple product lines.
3. Simplicity and repetition breed competence. Effort should be concentrated on key activities.

The simple fact is that corporate and operations strategy must be coordinated, and in the process some trade-offs will have to be made.

Jobs in Operations

What do operations managers do? This is a natural question following the explanation of operations management as filling a core function in the firm, as was mentioned in chapter 2. The classic statement of skills required in management applies also to operations. Those skills are technical, human, and conceptual:

1. *Technical skills*—mastering the knowledge and scientific elements of the job. These skills are gained by education, training, and/or experience. Technical aspects relate to computer use, operations research, purchasing regulations, and similar bodies of knowledge.
2. *Human skills*—dealing with people as a valuable resource in the organization. Developing productive work teams and establishing effective interpersonal relationships at work and communications competence are examples of human skills.
3. *Conceptual skills*—improving decision making and awareness of interrelationships of subsystems in the enterprise. This includes the personal and intellectual growth to assume more and higher levels of responsibility.

Some types of jobs commonly found in the operations field are presented in Exhibit 16.6. Each of them involves planning, organizing work, dealing with different levels of the organization, supervising people, and controlling activities to ensure achievement of objectives.

The types of managerial jobs described in Exhibit 16.6 are a few of the most common. At various levels or in different types of operations capacities, the managerial skill requirements remain in technical, human, and conceptual areas.

Every manager does many things that all other managers do, such as planning, communicating, and controlling. Yet special differences exist between jobs of quality supervisors, office managers, and production line supervisors. Mastering the mix in the operations system is the key to success.

Managers need to remember that the criterion for success is always that value is added. This value must be added in the system over and above the cost of inputs and the transformation process. Positive value added provides inputs back

EXHIBIT 16.6 Operations management jobs

Typical Title	Job Components
Operations Manager	Manages operations in stores, hospitals, buildings, banks, offices, factories. Responsible for overall coordination of activities. Often called plant or general manager.
Materials Manager	Manages materials in storage or transit between work stations. Provides the right material at the right place at the right time at lowest cost.
Quality Assurance Manager	Manages programs designed to provide the desired quality of products and services provided. Involved with setting standards and monitoring work activities, as well as testing procedures to verify quality.
Line Manager	Supervises ongoing activities, whether in an office, factory production line, psychiatric ward, or street maintenance crew. Heavily involved with supervision of personnel and monitoring work progress.
Facility Manager	Manages physical facilities such as buildings and equipment to support missions of the enterprise.
Purchasing Manager	Manages the acquisition of materials from vendors. Securing the right kind of input at the right time at least cost is a prime consideration.

into the system that fuel sustained operations and growth. Negative value added means the system will have to dip into its capital for continuation, may go bankrupt, or, in non-profit systems, may suffer budget cuts.

Operations and the Environment

A special word about the environment of the operations manager: despite the temptation to become inward-looking, operations managers must look outward. It is very easy to become preoccupied with processes directly under the responsibility of the operations manager.

In the systems sense, it is important to remember that operations transform and add value on behalf of the enterprise. The enterprise in turn is a part of a larger system—the industry or community. This environmental orientation should remind operations personnel why they transform or process to add value. Again, in the operations systems sense, the emphasis must be on outputs. Those outputs should have value added that supports the objectives of the enterprise in coping with its environment.

Operations and Other Functions

As a subsystem of the enterprise, the operations function interacts with many other functions as subsystems. There is a mutual interaction of inputs and outputs.

The general management function of the enterprise coordinates all the functions. Smooth relationships between functions facilitate activity of the total system. Some of the most common interfaces (relationships) with other functions are with marketing, finance, accounting, personnel, purchasing, and research and development.[11]

Marketing relationships are crucial. Marketing cannot sell and distribute what is not processed or produced. Information on sales forecasts, new products, and customer feedback and requirements are essential to operations' fulfilling its obligations. In turn, production–operations provides input to marketing about how the transformation process is providing desired outputs for distribution.

Finance is involved in resource considerations that affect operations. Information on budgets, investment analyses, and the financial condition of the firm figure strongly in the resource base that sustains operations.

Accounting provides cost data and special reports that support operations decisions. Accounting information is especially important in estimating and giving feedback on performance measures and productivity.

Personnel (human resources) provides information and services dealing with recruitment, training, safety, and labor relations. These activities sustain the human resource in playing its vital role in operations.

Purchasing is commonly an operations activity. It performs a crucial part in determination of purchasing requirements, delivery schedules, and the availability of new products, materials, and processes from vendors.

Research and development is a function not found in every organization. It supports the search for new products, methods, tools, and processes that will keep the enterprise on the leading competitive edge in its business.

Other functions, such as industrial engineering, public relations, security, and legal departments, may have working relationships with operations. The key point here is to develop productive working relationships with other functions that have an impact on the effectiveness and efficiency of operations.

Managing Operations Functions

As was indicated in chapter 2, the role of the operations manager involves many challenges. In a functional sense, operations must be planned, organized, and controlled. This section looks at the responsibilities of operations managers. Most of the challenges revolve around the acquisition and utilization of resources in the conversion role of the organization. Some of the managerial activities and roles include forecasting, purchasing, analysis of work flow, inventory control, job design, and quality control.

The operations management roles work toward harmony between the systems elements of inputs, conversion process, and outputs in order to add value. As previously described, the operations subsystem also seeks balance and order with other functions in the organization, such as marketing and finance. To produce the best results from the entire organization, flexibility may be required in operations planning.

Resource constraints (budget) may suggest changes in the design of the product, or in the production process. Time constraints may indicate a need for overtime or changing priorities to meet deadlines on a particular product. To view the impact of various factors on managing operations, the management of operations is discussed in the following sections in terms of planning and the managing of operations, organizing and the managing of operations, and control and the managing of operations.

Planning and the Managing of Operations   The successful projection of operations to achieve success and results requires decisions to be made about the future. As discussed in earlier chapters on planning, the goals, strategies, and plans of the organization provide the direction and guidance for managing operations. Operations goals, strategies, and plans must fit within the framework of planning for the organizational system. Strengths, weaknesses, opportunities, and threats impact on operations plans as well as organization plans. Operations planning must fit within the strategic planning of the organization. This applies to products, quality, service, and use of human and material resources. The signs of turnaround in the U.S. industrial picture indicate changes of strategy that impact on operations. One vivid example is the increased emphasis on quality in the automobile industry. Such a strategic goal has had considerable impact on operations planning as it affects personnel, quality standards, and purchasing of materials. The concept of quality is represented as having been planned in.

Planning involves a series of decisions by management, and managing operations thus involves the making and executing of decisions about inputs, transformation processes, and outputs. Exhibit 16.7 illustrates a number of key decision areas in managing operations as well as basic questions that stem from those decisions. Strategic decisions may deal with product lines, competitive strengths,

EXHIBIT 16.7 Management decisions impacting on production and operations management

Management Decision	Basic Questions
Business plan	What is our corporate policy and strategic business plan?
Product line and design	What will we produce?
Resource plan	What facilities, materials, equipment, and personnel will be needed?
Site selection and logistics	Where do we locate? How is transportation to and from the location?
Process layout and design	How do we produce our product?
Job design	How do we fit people to jobs and technology?
Inventory policy	What materials should be purchased, and when?
Aggregate production planning and master scheduling	How much do we produce? When?
Capacity planning	What is our capability to produce?
Materials requirements planning	What materials are required? When? Where?
Operations scheduling	How are operations coordinated?
Production control	How are equipment and personnel used?
Material management	How are materials moved and controlled?
Quality control	What are our quality standards? How are we meeting them?

Adapted from J. R. Evans, D. Anderson, D. Sweeney, and T. Williams, *Applied Production and Operations Management* (St. Paul, Minn.: West, 1984): 15.

and service systems. For example, Johnson & Johnson, the renowned producer of Tylenol, Band-Aids, and other health products, has decided to enter the field of high-technology medical products. The introduction of dialysis machines (for assisting reduced kidney function), diagnostic equipment, and biotechnology (using high technology in medicine) as new product lines for Johnson & Johnson requires a serious shifting of priorities and operations for the firm.

Managing operations in the planning function requires product line changes, capacity determination, technology use, and facilities modification to help implement the changes in strategic plans. Johnson & Johnson will undergo some very serious changes in operations to accommodate the strategic decision to become involved in high-technology health products. Needless to say, the new demands for trained personnel will test the company. This example is a dramatic case of strategic shifts producing other major changes in managing operations of the firm.

Exhibit 16.7 addresses a number of decision areas involved in the management of operations. The full array of decisions includes planning, organizing, and control decisions, as well as basic questions that pertain to operations issues falling under the umbrella of strategic decision issues, as discussed in the earlier planning and management policy/strategy chapters. Managing operations fulfills the need for planning, organizing, and controlling operations transformation processes to add value.

Organizing and the Managing of Operations   While the operations function is often described as the heart of the organization, the organizing aspect of operations is crucial to the successful interplay of processes in the organization. Managers should understand the organization of the operations function in terms of structure and relationships.

Organization structure should serve organization function. The same applies to the operations process. Parts of the operations system may be organized on a functional, product, customer, or geographical basis. While the main portion of operations is line activity, product design and quality control may be staff activities. As noted in previous chapters on organizing, the structure is adapted to suit the function of the organization.

Choices made about decentralization, delegation of authority, and use of staff are not made by rules, but by the strategic considerations of the organization and the factors involved in the operations process. Modern methods of operations design and control described in the next chapter require the organization to be flexible and responsive to changing needs of the situation. Individual personnel, technology, and environmental factors will affect design of the organization and the organization of tasks. Often trade-offs must be made in the interests of productivity, economy, control, or worker satisfaction.

Exhibit 16.8 is an organization chart for the operations activity of a toy manufacturer. It has functional vice-presidents, geographical plant managers, operations staff functions, and line supervisors for the functional processes involved in fabricating, assembling, and painting toys.

Product design and operations planning are functionally related to the marketing forecasting unit, and the eastern plant personnel office is related to the office of vice-president for personnel. The vice-president for operations probably would have staff offices that the staff of the eastern plant manager would coordinate with.

EXHIBIT 16.8 Organization chart for toy manufacturer

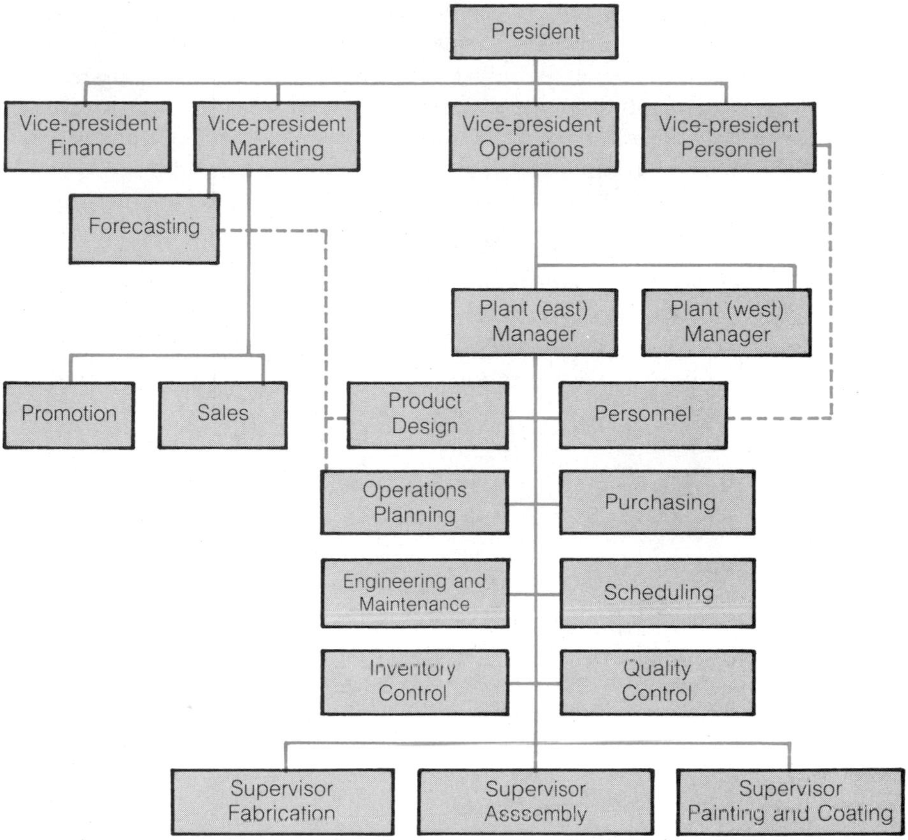

NOTE: Dashed line indicates the existence of a functional relationship.

The purpose is to place the activities in the structure at such a point that each activity can perform in the best interests of the overall operations function. No one arrangement is best. A situational analysis of the tasks, technology, people, and environmental factors should provide guidance for effectively managing the operations organization.

Control and the Managing of Operations   In preceding chapters, we have seen that control is a means of comparing performance to standards. The next chapter will deal with operations control processes in more detail. However, some points about managing operations through control may be made at this point.

One purpose of control is to ensure coordination of operations functions with the other functions of the organization. The operations function is technically only accountable for those activities over which it has decision control. Yet coordination with marketing is important regarding product line and design considerations. Coordination with finance and accounting is important in areas of cost control.

Production–Operations Management Systems

Within operations, good management control ensures that the process utilizes resources, personnel, and facilities to accomplish low unit cost of products or services, on-time deliveries, and desired quality.

Cost control measures the value of resources consumed or converted in the production process. Materials, labor, and facilities all have worth that is used in operations. Cost standards are important as yardsticks against which to measure the actual costs of operations. Significant variances require management control action to bring costs back into line.

Inventory control monitors the investment in materials of the operations process. Types of inventory are:

1. *Raw materials*—purchased to make the product or to provide the service
2. *Work in process*—partially completed products
3. *Finished goods*—completed products available for customers
4. *In-transit goods*—products or services enroute to customers

Modern inventory control methods allow for close control of inventory as a means of lowering costs and investments in the operations process.

Scheduling control checks the arrival and departure of work and services to meet schedules and ensure a smooth flow of operations. Bottlenecks, idle capacity, and erratic schedules waste time and capacity to perform.

Maintenance control ensures that preventive and corrective measures are taken for equipment and facilities, so that they are in shape to do the job expected. Breakdowns are costly, and quality can be adversely affected by lapses in maintenance control.

Quality control begins with standards for performance of products and services. Quality control management begins before operations, continues throughout the operations process, and finishes with verification of quality of the final product or service.

Managing operations truly involves the intelligent functions of planning, organizing, and controlling to ensure that the final output is coordinated so as to meet the objectives of the organization.

A factor that bears heavily on the management of operations is technology. The next section discusses how technology gives the operations manager more power in making decisions. Nevertheless, technology is a troublesome element for many managers today.

OPERATIONS MANAGEMENT AND TECHNOLOGY

Technology has become a forceful element in our lives, its impact seeming to increase at a nearly exponential rate. Much social and political concern is being expressed about the ways that technology touches human life and work, and whether this effect is desirable or controllable. This section takes the position that technology gives us choices, including a choice of technologies.

Definition and Concepts

The definition of technology is a challenge, since there is so much talk and writing about the topic, and such a lack of understanding of it. Technology is defined here as the process of applying science and knowledge to human affairs, especially in transformations, processes, and products used to solve problems. In

EXHIBIT 16.9 Peter Drucker on technology and management

"Technology is no more mysterious or unpredictable than developments in the economy or society."

"Technology is not separate from the business, and cannot be managed as such if it is to be managed."

"The business manager needs to be concerned as much with the impacts and consequences of technology on the individual, society and economy as with any other impacts and consequences of his actions."

"We do have a choice and must learn to become aggressive managers of technology by choosing certain technologies and rejecting others."

SOURCE: Peter F. Drucker, *Toward the Next Economics* (New York: Harper and Row, 1981).

short, technology helps us to do things better. It gives us more options in making decisions and solving problems, and provides tools to accomplish tasks. Technology can be divided into material and non-material sectors:

1. Material technology consists of tangible implements, tools, devices, and equipment, usually developed from a scientific or engineering basis.
2. Non-material technology consists of knowledge, processes, and methods.

Over the centuries, people have learned to cope with the environment by the use of fire, glass, traffic rules, and thousands of procedures that we generally take for granted. Actually, each of these constitutes a technology that has been discovered and improved. Human technological history has come to the point of biotechnology, space shuttles, genetic engineering, and other developments that boggle our minds and will later be taken for granted as well. How has the development of technology affected management?

Technology and the Manager

Certainly technology has had an impact on management. It has helped managers to do their jobs better, but it has inevitably created some questions.

Management scholar Peter Drucker has pointed out that business has increasingly become the creator of technology. He further claims that business managers have to learn that "technology is managerial opportunity and managerial responsibility."[12] Some more of Drucker's thoughts on technology are reflected in Exhibit 16.9.

For years, Drucker has claimed that we need to become "managers of technology" rather than just users of technology. Technology can be anticipated, and to manage it requires an understanding of the process of technology and of its dynamics. For instance, "high tech" is a term much heard today. So-called high technology can be differentiated from other (or lower) technology as follows:

1. High technology is characterized by:
   a. Science and engineering base.
   b. Technical rigor.
   c. Usually a high unit cost.
   d. Less human involvement.

2. Lower technologies usually entail:
   a. A more established and procedural base.
   b. Orientation to operations.
   c. More human involvement in process.
   d. Derivations and applications.

High technology includes such products as integrated circuits in home computers and games, solar panels, fiber-optics, and portable telephones. Lower technology includes items like aluminum bats and webbed gloves in baseball, plastic chairs, ball point pens, and thin-lead mechanical pencils.

Consider the impact on your life from technological applications such as:

Electric typewriters	Paint rollers
Electronic calculators	Direct-dial long distance
Copying machines	telephone calling
Power lawn mowers	Microwave ovens
Hair dryers	Vending machines

Technology and Society

At the same time as technology is viewed as providing valuable options, there are also drawbacks. Herbicides contain toxic poisons, effluents from chemical plants pollute streams, automation affects manual labor, and "wonder drugs" can have undesirable side effects.

Many people are concerned that modern technology has advanced so far in terms of efficiency and mechanization that human and environmental values have been threatened. These effects may be found in absenteeism, low job satisfaction, alienation, pollution, decrease in a sense of meaning in work, and other social and economic ills. People often feel powerless in the face of a burgeoning technology that provides convenience and entertainment but threatens jobs, life style, and a sense of well-being.

The term *appropriate technology* is used to describe the use of enough technology to perform as desired at a reasonable social, economic, and personal cost. Appropriate technology applies to forms of organization, extent of automation, job design, and choice of processes and products by operations managers. So while technology enhances the ability of managers and organizations to be effective and efficient, those choice decisions must be considered carefully in terms of consequences.

Some critics have claimed recently that small is beautiful, that advances are too rapid, and that technology must be held in check. This position is held by some regarding the use of natural resources such as oil, gas, water, and land. Clearly, this concern focuses the need for managers to make wise decisions that incorporate values, long-range thinking, and concerns for the environment.

Changes in technology have social, economic, and political effects. But technology plays a vital role in productivity, which is also a concern of the nation as well as of the organization.

Managing Technology

Technological development creates pressures on society. At the same time, society calls upon technology to help meet its needs and aspirations. The management of technology is the art of reconciling those demands and pressures. This form of

EXHIBIT 16.10 How management views technology

93% Agree that technology importance will grow in the 1980s.
21% Involve technologists in planning
37% Effectively integrate strategy and technology
14% Say that management has an analytic approach to integrating technology and planning

SOURCE: From the Booz Allen & Hamilton study cited in Paul Cathey, "Technology's Input Is Vital to Sound Business Planning," *Iron Age* (September 16, 1981).

management complements other management functions in providing the necessary inputs to the decision making process.[13]

Managing technology should help society and operations managers keep their options open in applying the knowledge and tools of technology to the needs of particular situations. Managers at all levels need to explore issues and concepts that deal with the relationship of technology to society and operations in developing their philosophies and methods of management.

A recent study has been cited as evidence that management is neglecting technological planning in business projections. Some findings from the study are presented in Exhibit 16.10.

This study of 3,000 senior managers concluded that managers need a better understanding of technology in conjunction with its potential for business. Mere technical expertise or business experience is not enough. Individuals or management teams must combine the awareness of technological process and products with business performance. Technological management decisions and choices must include both long- and short-term implications.

Technology Available for Choices

Choosing technologies intelligently requires some knowledge of the technologies that are available. The following brief orientation reviews some aspects of factory, office, and service technologies.[14]

Factory Technology Much is heard today of the "factory of the future." This concept utilizes the latest of manufacturing technology in materials handling, automation, robotics, and Computer-Aided Design/Computer-Aided Manufacturing (CAD/CAM). Processes have progressed from hand operation through machine operations to automated functions.

CAD/CAM has been described as the greatest boon to manufacturing productivity since electricity. Robots operate at a rate of $6 per hour on operations that cost $16 per hour for skilled labor. Robots perform best at "3-D" work—work that is dirty, dull, and dangerous.

For purposes of perspective, a recent study found robotics used in various capacities:

36% Spot and arc welding
35% Material handling (pick and place, machine loading)
15% Coating and painting
14% Processing (assembly, inspection, parts finishing)[15]

Computer-driven, highly automated factories will have profound social and economic impact. Automated factories of the future are predicted to constitute a "second industrial revolution." Highly trained workers will be required, with less qualified workers generally receiving the brunt of technological displacement.

Office Technology   Office technology has not advanced much since the invention of the typewriter. Recent years, however, have brought terms like "the office of the future" and the "automated office."

Given that offices are very labor-intensive (80 percent of office costs are labor), there are great opportunities for technology to make contributions to productivity. A recent study noted that, from 1971 to 1981, business invested some $24,000 per worker in factories. Factory workers' productivity increased 84 percent during that period.[16] During that same decade, business invested about $3,000 per office worker, with an increase of 3 percent for office workers.

The office of the future promises assistance from technology such as the following:

1. Word processing and text editing.
2. Video and teleconferencing.
3. Electronic mail and calendars.
4. Computer graphics.
5. Data processing and data base management systems.
6. Electronic filing and communication networks.

A report on future prospects is shown in Exhibit 16.11.

The use of office technology should result in lower costs (or certain costs avoided), improved quality, and increased capability. This improved output will be achieved at considerable cost in investment, training, and facilities. A premium will be placed upon work design, planning, and supervision to help those upgraded resources produce, receive, store, and analyze information to support the operations and other functions of the business.

Paperwork should be reduced, and personnel operating office "work stations" will have more capability at their disposal. This capability will extend to executives, managers, and other personnel who deal with operational or administrative

---

EXHIBIT 16.11   Future automation of the office

By 1990, there will be 3.1 million secretaries in comparison to 2.5 million in 1980.

By 1986, U.S. business will spend:
   $1 trillion on information processing
   $280 billion on word processing and data processing
   $270 billion on video and teleconferencing and telephones

By 1990, 90 percent of the work force will be in the automated office. White collar workers today account for 53 percent of the work force.

SOURCE: Kelly Services Report in *Office Administration and Automation,* May 1983.

information. Even better, local networks will connect work stations to enhance the total communications of the organization.

Office technology will have a profound impact on the organization and on individuals. A simplistic view of information processing technology sees it as making clerical positions merely more productive. A more enlightened view seeks to capitalize on information technology as an ingredient for finding new and better ways to process information on a cost-effective basis. This change may weaken central bureaucratic control and strengthen local control in organizations and operations.

Service Organizations   The growth of the service sector of the economy suggests use of technology for improvements. Some lessons may be learned by applying production technologies in designing work flows and processes. Even such a device as the scoop for putting french-fries in bags in fast-food restaurants reflects use of lower technology to improve work processes and service in the process.

Technology provides services in such organizations as car washes, fast-food restaurants, banks (automatic tellers), supermarkets, and car rental agencies. Health care, education, and personal service establishements provide a considerable challenge for utilization of technology to improve service while maintaining the individual touch.

Managing Technological Change	The management of technological change ultimately involves choices of technology. Analysis accompanying decisions in this area requires preparation and study.

Donald Schoen has identified three stages of change.

1. *Invention*—the creation of a new product or process
2. *Innovation*—the introduction of that product or process into use
3. *Diffusion*—the spread of the product or process beyond first use[17]

In the complex, dynamic modern world, change is required to enable organizations to survive and compete. Ideally, technological change can work to stabilize the framework of the enterprise and its operations, much like the feedback element in electronic circuits or thermostats. In general, good management principles, if followed, should enable managers and operators to cope with problems and challenges to generate innovative and useful solutions. Technological change is the link between status quo, or the past state-of-the-art, and future states and options.

Recent evidence indicates that the United States was lagging in new high-technology products as late as 1984.[18] The U.S. "high-tech" companies are slow in bringing new products into the marketplace. Firms in Great Britain, West Germany, and Belgium have clearly defined strategies to produce and develop sophisticated technologies. The structure of U.S. companies was claimed to be too rigid to react quickly to international competition. Exhibit 16.12 illustrates the findings of a recent survey that supports this position on technology implementation.

Choice of technology should not depend solely upon return-on-investment principles. Effects of technology on operations objectives, on the environment,

EXHIBIT 16.12 Chief executive officer views on technology implementation

Introduction of significant new products in past year		CEO opinions that their company's products were the world's most technologically advanced	
USA	40%	USA	40%
Germany	49%	Germany	63%
Britain	42%	Britain	50%
Belgium	29%	Belgium	50%

NOTE: U.S. executives were the most satisfied, at 75%, with their research and development activities.

SOURCE: Based on a survey of 411 chief executives and managing directors in Europe and America, conducted by Market Opinion International, reported in *USA Today* (May 4, 1984): B1.

and on the work force should be considered. Choice of technology in technological change should be a well-organized ongoing process. The process includes surveillance of technology, choice of appropriate products or processes, and implementation options. Many changes are poorly executed, which negates the good decision or investment made.

PRODUCTIVITY

Recent years have brought strong attention to the state of productivity in organizations and the economy. Publications and organizations have joined a chorus of concern. Operations management lies at the heart of productivity.

The Nature of Productivity

Productivity can be defined as the relationship between the inputs applied to some transformation process and the output that ensues. Outputs can be any combination of goods, products, or services. Inputs can be human or material resources transformed in the process. Simply put:

$$\text{Productivity} = \text{Output} / \text{Input}$$

Productivity can be increased by raising the quality or quantity of output, or by reducing the inputs applied. Involved here also is the value-added concept introduced earlier. More productivity relates to more value added when the output is increased. The classic measurement of productivity considers the labor hours applied as inputs. Actually, productivity is difficult to measure in a meaningful way. One of the relevant tasks in any enterprise is to determine methods for measuring productivity. The method may vary between factories, hospitals, and colleges, but the concept remains the same—output compared to input applied.

Factors in productivity are reflected in Exhibit 16.13.

Technology in the form of equipment, processes, materials, and methods has been discussed as a factor in productivity. Labor can also contribute significantly to productivity, whether or not the enterprise is labor-intensive. Motivated personnel are assets, especially in service operations. This includes "working smart" as well as working hard.

Capital is a necessary ingredient for investment in all the other factors. Money cannot be simply thrown at productivity problems, but cost-effective innovation and improvements are alternatives that pay off in productivity.

EXHIBIT 16.13   Factors in productivity

> Efficiency of technology +
>   Efficiency of labor +
>   Efficiency of capital +
>   Effectiveness of management =
>   **Productivity**

Management is a key factor in productivity. Management cannot do the job itself, but works through the orchestration of other productivity factors. Still, management has received considerable criticism for failing to anticipate and take actions to deal with productivity dilemmas.

Trends in Productivity

Since its inception, the United States has been the most productive nation on earth, a nation that takes pride in its productivity, which originated from vast natural resources and people. In recent years, changes have occurred, and the typical annual productivity increases of about 3 percent have withered. Recently, other nations have enjoyed larger increases than the United States. Exhibit 16.14 shows U.S. Bureau of Labor statistics for average annual growth.

While the United States is still the most productive nation overall, other nations are catching up, as shown in Exhibit 16.15 from the 1982 report of the American Productivity Institute. This condition represents a challenge to U.S. enterprises to maintain their competitive edge.

It would appear that the United States is not realizing its potential. Factors in improving productivity will be discussed shortly. At this point, it should be noted that productivity is not a simple subject. While the output of the U.S. private

EXHIBIT 16.14   Gross domestic production per employed person by nation: 1950–1980

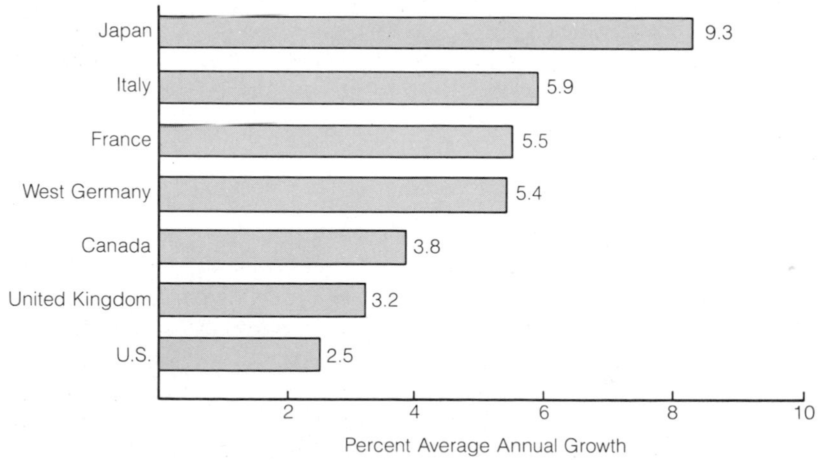

Nation	Percent Average Annual Growth
Japan	9.3
Italy	5.9
France	5.5
West Germany	5.4
Canada	3.8
United Kingdom	3.2
U.S.	2.5

SOURCE: Bureau of Labor Statistics, 1981.

Production–Operations Management Systems

EXHIBIT 16.15 Estimates of real GDP per hour, selected industrial nations[1]

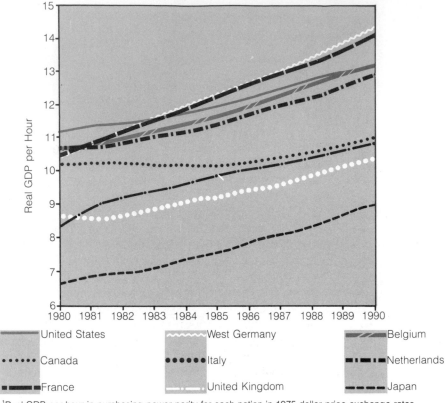

United States

Canada

France

West Germany

Italy

United Kingdom

Belgium

Netherlands

Japan

[1]Real GDP per hour in purchasing power parity for each nation in 1975 dollar price exchange rates.

SOURCE: American Productivity Center, 1982.

business economy has doubled every twenty years, the nation will be sorely pressed to maintain that growth. Still, reports indicated that first quarter 1984 productivity increases were over 3 percent, a hopeful sign of turnaround.[19]

Factors Influencing Productivity

The U.S. Department of Labor reported that forty-two of sixty-nine industries experienced a drop in productivity in 1982.[19] If U.S. productivity has flattened, and if growth is desired, some study of the factors influencing productivity will be needed.

The American Productivity Institute presents this cycle:

1. Falling productivity yields rising labor costs
2. Unit labor cost increases lead to higher prices
3. Higher prices lead to declining sales volumes
4. Declining sales lead to reduced employment and reduced plant capacity utilization
5. Reduced capacity utilization leads to lower productivity
6. Lower productivity leads to more inflation, slackened capital investment, reduced competitive ability, loss of sales and volume, and hence to unemployment[20]

Other sources of slowdown in productivity were suggested as well:

1. Insufficiency of capital investments
2. Slowdown in research and development
3. Growth in government regulation
4. Labor and management inattention
5. Aging industrial plant
6. Increases in energy costs
7. Growth of the service sector
8. Age–sex mix change in the work force

Since the U.S. economy, its organizational performance, and its standard of living are tied to productivity, it appears important to study the productivity situation and devise improvement methods.

Managing Productivity in Operations

One strategy for managing productivity would be to approach the reasons just given for slowdown. Those will be discussed shortly.

Another method is to separate "macro" from "micro" factors. Macro factors are large scale and relate to the society and economy as a whole. Macro factors may be out of the hands of the manager, considering the state of the economy and the work force. Micro factors, on the other hand, are within the realm of the operations manager, within the framework of the determinants of productivity—technology, labor, capital, and management.

Technology will include improvement in products, processes, and equipment. Labor includes dealing with the work force, whatever the mix of age, sex, and skill, with improvements in selection, training, and evaluation. Capital comprises the generation and use of resources to improve productivity. Management constitutes the methods of supervision and dealing with the total situation in converting inputs to outputs.

Some contributions to productivity come from the cooperation of labor and management. Exhibit 16.16 shows how some concessions by unions have been made to support industry's search for improved productivity. The major lesson here is that cooperation of labor and management is essential in the quest for better operations at acceptable costs.

EXHIBIT 16.16 Work changes in industries seeking productivity

Changes Granted by Unions	Industries
Job redesign—enlarging jobs, cutting crew size, eliminating unneeded jobs	Steel, autos, railroads, airlines
Team work—Job rotation, pay by knowledge rather than function, change of crew structure	Autos, steel, rubber
Wages—restricting pay to hours worked rather than miles travelled	Railroads, trucking
Skilled maintenance and construction—combining jobs, permitting operators to run different types of machines	Autos, rubber, steel, petroleum, construction

SOURCE: Adapted from "A Work Revolution in U.S. Industry," *Business Week* (May 16, 1983): 100.

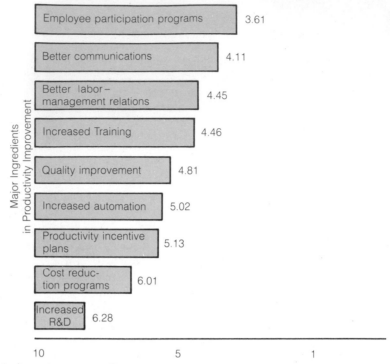

EXHIBIT 16.17 Measures in effectiveness in improving productivity

NOTE: On the scale, 1 = most effective, 10 = least effective.

SOURCE: Adapted from Norman Bodek, ed., *Productivity Newsletter,* Summer 1981.

Exhibit 16.17 shows the results of a study of measures of effectiveness in improving productivity. Notice that the most effective means deal with the management sector of productivity improvement. Lessons from the Japanese experience with productivity are similar.

While the successes of Japanese management cannot be directly translated into American practice, there are lessons to be learned. The popular "Theory Z" approach blends American and Japanese approaches. Adapting the factors in productivity improvement to the American culture and organizational framework provides insight for managers.

Quality circles are one example of management techniques that have been borrowed from the Japanese. The concept of quality circles has been found in many organizations over the years, but the Japanese seem to have perfected their use. Now quality circles have come back to the United States. As noted in chapter 10, a quality circle is a group of people (usually up to fifteen) doing similar work who voluntarily meet on a regular basis to identify, analyze, and solve quality and other work-related problems.[21]

Quality circles are an example of lower-order technology applied to work to support productivity. A quality circle program requires management support and training. Tangible results bring improved quality and work operations. Other intangible results are improved communication, greater employee involvement, a sense of ownership and commitment, as well as improved morale.

Operations Management and the Future

The future effectiveness and efficiency of operations management will depend on many factors. Some of the most important are:

1. *Energy sources and usage.* There is no doubt that operations will depend upon intelligent use of energy, from whatever source derived.
2. *International impacts on operations.* International trade deficits, competition from abroad, and an apparent "shrinking" of the world will demand more attention to relationships with developed and developing countries.
3. *Population dynamics.* These dynamics will cause changes in market demands and the composition of the work force. These dynamics will require sensitivity to the environment and adaption to changes in ages, sex ratios, skills, and readiness to work.
4. *Business, labor, and government relationships.* A stronger form of cooperation will be required for the harmonious blend of influences on operations.
5. *Information systems.* The growth in quantity and quality of information services will provide the opportunity for operations managers to improve functional decisions and activities.
6. *Automation.* Automation has already been discussed and will play an increasingly important role in the future of operations.
7. *Service sector growth.* The increasing relevance of production–operations know-how to service and non-profit activities will grow. This will provide opportunity for increased productivity while maintaining and improving the quality and quantity of services.
8. *Increased emphasis on operations functions.* In the quest for productivity, the crucial role of operations functions in production and service organizations will be more strongly supported.[22]

All in all, the future of operations management faces complexity and uncertainty to a degree never before experienced. Still, the job of the manager is to reduce uncertainty in making and executing decisions to fulfill objectives.

Summary

This chapter portrays production–operations management systems as key elements in the functioning of organizations. Operations management includes both production and service management. Production involves conversion processes that render product outputs. Service organizations provide outputs that satisfy personal needs of clients. The techniques of operations management apply equally to both.

Both production and service systems seek to add value in the conversion process by assembly, breakdown, rearrangement, or presentation of outputs.

A strategic orientation is appropriate in looking at the longer-term implications of both internal and external environmental factors. A variety of positions are involved in operations management. Relationships with other functions, such as marketing and finance, support the interactive role of operations in the organization.

Technology is a vital ingredient in operations management. As a popular, but misunderstood, factor in organizations and the environment, technology is the use of scientific applications and knowledge in human affairs. This includes material and non-material technology. High technology includes rigorous engineering and science-based products and processes that give operations managers options in doing their work. Lower technology is techniques and products that are more knowledge-based to assist operations.

The management of technology should be encouraged to ensure that technology serves human interests in operations applications. The choices available to managers may be examined in areas of factory, office, and service organizations.

Productivity is the ratio of outputs generated from the conversion of inputs. There has been declining annual productivity growth in the American economy. Various factors are available for the improvement of productivity, and these provide options for use by management.

Operations management is a core function in the organization attempting to add value in its contribution to objectives. Nothing can be sold until it is produced in the operations function. In that conversion capacity, operations works closely with marketing and finance, as well as other functions of the organization.

What Have You Learned?

1. What is operations management? How does production management differ from service management?
2. What are some operations functions performed in hospitals, universities, stores, and factories?
3. How does the operations function differ from finance and marketing functions? How are they alike? Is similar management used?
4. What production techniques could be used in:
   a. dentists' offices?
   b. student recreation centers?
   c. university admissions offices?
   d. service stations?
5. Why do we misunderstand technology? What are some good and some undesirable consequences of technology? How has technology affected the jobs of people you know?
6. What are some examples of high and lower technology that you see in the marketplace? What is present that was not available when your parents were your age?
7. How do you feel about productivity? Is productivity worth the cost of its improvement? Compare your personal productivity to that of fellow students or co-workers. What conclusions do you reach from those differences?
8. If you were in charge of productivity for your university, what changes would you encourage? Why?
9. How can college students prepare today for technological change? What do you plan to do to prepare yourself?
10. What types of jobs exist in the production–operations area? How do these different jobs relate to the management functions of the management process framework?

How Well Can You Apply Your Knowledge?

Problem 1. Sandy works in the college book store as a stocker. The bookstore has four checkout aisles, but only two persons work at checkout except for the beginning and ends of semesters. Five persons are working with Sandy as stockers, and three persons work the checkout stands and the office. The bookstore manager has been on the job for twenty years.

Sandy has studied quality circles in class, and is concerned about what she sees as inefficiencies in the bookstore. She has made some suggestions to the manager, but was told that she should do her job and let the manager run the store.

After studying operations management, Sandy is convinced that there are things that could be done to improve both efficiency and effectiveness in the bookstore. Other student workers in the store are also concerned. Every stocker is supposed to be able to break open boxes, stock shelves, price books, and run errands as required.

Questions

1. If jobs were not defined, how could student workers have a better idea of what duties are expected each day?
2. What operations suggestions are relevant to assist the productivity of bookstores?
3. Could a quality circle to generate and evaluate suggestions be productive in the bookstore? How would you go about this?
4. What technology might assist productivity in the bookstore?

Problem 2. Think of a university or college as a system. As a system, it has an operations function.

In that context, and in the sense of the material of this chapter, answer the following questions. Be prepared to discuss different points of view in your answers. You may wish to consult Exhibit 2.12 in developing your answers.

Questions

1. What are the objectives of the system?
2. What are the system outputs?
3. What are the system inputs?
4. Describe the operations function in the university.
5. What conversions or transformations take place in the processing of the operations function?
6. What high and lower technologies are found in the university? How do they contribute to productivity?
7. Describe the resource and distribution functions in the university. How do they relate to the operations function?
8. Describe the environment of the university system. How does your system relate to this environment? How could this be improved?
9. What could be done to make the university system more productive? How could this be worked out with and by management?

Additional Sources for More Detailed Study

Adam, Everett E., and Ebert, Ronald J. *Production and Operations Management*. Englewood Cliffs, N.J.: Prentice-Hall, 1982.

American Productivity Institute. *Productivity Perspectives*. Houston, Texas. Published annually.

Barndt, Stephen E., and Carvey, Davis W. *Elements of Operations Mangement*. Englewood Cliffs, N.J.: Prentice-Hall, 1982.

Buffa, Elwood S. *Elements of Production/Operations Management*. New York: Wiley, 1981.

Business Week. Published weekly.

Chase, Richard B, and Acquilano, Nicholas J. *Production and Operations Management*. Homewood, Ill: Richard D. Irwin, 1981.

Hawthorne, Edward P. *The Management of Technology*. New York: McGraw-Hill, 1978.

Kendrick, John W., and Grossman, Eliot S. *Productivity in the United States*. Baltimore: Johns Hopkins Press, 1980.

Notes

1. James B. Dilworth, *Production and Operations Management* (New York: Random House, 1983).
2. Roger G. Schroeder, *Operations Management* (New York: McGraw-Hill, 1981).
3. Elwood S. Buffa, *Elements of Production/Operations Management* (New York: Wiley, 1981).
4. Stephen E. Barndt and Davis W. Carvey, *Essentials of Operations Management* (Englewood Cliffs, N.J.: Prentice-Hall, 1982).
5. Vincent P. Luchsinger and V. Thomas Dock, *The Systems Approach: An Introduction* (Dubuque, Iowa: Kendall-Hunt, 1982).

6. Charles G. Andrew and George A. Johnson, "The Crucial Importance of Production and Operations Management," *Academy of Management Journal* (January 1982).

7. Richard B. Chase and Nicholas J. Acquilano, *Production and Operations Management* (Homewood, Ill.: Richard D. Irwin, 1981).

8. Steven C. Wheelwright, "Reflecting Corporate Strategy in Manufacturing Decisions," *Business Horizons* (February 1978).

9. R. H. Hayes and William Abernathy, "Managing Our Way to Economic Decline," *Harvard Business Review* (July–August, 1980); see also William J. Abernathy, Kim B. Clark, and Alan M. Kontrow, "The New Industrial Competition," *Harvard Business Review* (September–October 1981).

10. Wickham Skinner, "The Focused Factory," *Harvard Business Review* (May–June 1974).

11. Richard J. Hopeman, *Production and Operations Management* (Columbus, Ohio: Charles E. Merrill, 1980).

12. Peter F. Drucker, *Toward The Next Economics* (New York: Harper and Row, 1981).

13. Edward P. Hawthorne, *The Management of Technology* (New York: McGraw-Hill, 1978).

14. From the technology discussion in Roger G. Schroeder, *Operations Management* (New York: McGraw-Hill, 1981).

15. From the Predicasts report cited in "Robotics," *Automotive Industries* (January 1983).

16. *The Integrated Electronic Office* (San Antonio, Texas: Datapoint Corporation, 1981).

17. Donald R. Schoen, "Managing Technological Change," *Harvard Business Review* (May–June 1969).

18. *Wall Street Journal* (May 21, 1984).

19. *Wall Street Journal* (July 26, 1983).

20. *Productivity Perspectives* (Houston, Texas: American Productivity Institute, 1977).

21. John J. Dailey and Rudolph L. Kagerer, "A Primer on Quality Circles," *Supervisory Management* (June 1982).

22. Everett E. Adam and Ronald J. Ebert, *Production and Operations Management* (Englewood Cliffs, N.J.: Prentice-Hall, 1982).

CHAPTER 17

Designing, Planning, and Controlling Operating Systems

CHAPTER OUTLINE

Design of Operating Systems
Strategic Aspects of Design
Decisions in Design of Operating Systems
   Product/Service Line and Design
   Procurement/Materials Management
   Site Selection and Location
   Facilities Layout
   Process Selection
   Job Design
   Control of Maintenance, Inventory, and Quality

Planning and Control of Operations
Aggregate Planning
Resource Allocation
Activity Scheduling

Inventory Planning and Control
Inventory Economics
Inventory Planning
Economic Order
Inventory Systems
   The ABC Inventory System
   Inventory Cycles
   Material Requirements Planning

Quality Control
Planning for Quality Control
   Costs of Quality
   Quality Control Procedures
Types of Quality Control
   Acceptance Sampling
   Process Control
Quality Control Circles

OBJECTIVES

To describe and relate the decisions, factors, and activities involved in design of the operating system and to discuss the implications for inclusion of innovations and technology in design decisions.

To discuss the activities relevant to the planning of production–operations functions, to show how resources can be allocated to match supply and demand, and to describe how schedules are derived to execute operations plans.

To consider the purpose of inventory, the economics of inventory in terms of benefits and costs, and the various types of inventory systems.

To explain what quality control is, describe how it is planned for in the organization, and discuss the types of quality control.

The operating system is the heart of the production–operations system. It is the operating system that transforms, converts, and processes inputs into the intended outputs of the system and thereby adds value. As described in chapter 9, the operations system is an open system, the essence of which is to increase form, time, and place utility to inputs of the system. This function is performed by operating systems in all successful organizations—insurance companies, hospitals, schools, banks, and manufacturing firms.

Operating systems are best viewed in the context of systems theory, in which a flow of input resources, information, energy, materials, and products in process is operated upon in such a way as to create outputs that help the organization to cope with the systems environment. Exhibit 17.1 illustrates the conversion role of the operating system within various types of organizations.

DESIGN OF OPERATING SYSTEMS

The design of the operating system is crucial to the successful function of the organization. It is very difficult for an organization to perform above the quality of the system design. Peter Drucker has indicated that the two essential tasks of the manager are to make decisions, and to ensure execution of those decisions.[1]

As a subsystem of the organization, operations behaves as shown earlier, in Exhibit 9.2. This chapter reviews the series of decisions involved in operating system design. Those decisions must take into account the opportunities and constraints to be found in the internal and external environments of the organization, whether these involve financial, marketing, service, or manufacturing functions. The internal environment includes the strengths and weaknesses of the organization, the work force, the management, and the nature of the organization. The external environment includes suppliers, customers, the industry, the market, and the prevailing economic and political conditions.

Generally, decisions about operating system design arise from the objectives, alternatives, preferences, and values of the decision makers. Naturally, most of their considerations are heavily tied to the nature of the organization and what "business" it is in. Proposed benefits and costs of the design are usually the strongest driving factors in the decisions.

Strategic Aspects of Design

Strategy is concerned with goals and the means of achieving those goals. In the design of operating systems, strategic considerations are very important. The decisions must conform to the organization strategy. In the planning sense, the overall strategy influences:

1. *What* the company will produce
2. *How much* will be produced
3. *How* the company will produce
4. *Who* will produce
5. *Where* production will occur

EXHIBIT 17.1 The production–operations system

Inputs $\longrightarrow$	Transformation Process $\longrightarrow$	Outputs
Materials	Conversion	Products
Information	Assembly	Services
Purchases	Manufacture	Goods
Labor		

The responses to these strategic points create the guides to courses of action that become the operating system of the enterprise. In effect, the organization will be living with the consequences of those five strategic considerations in the quest for effectiveness and efficiency. In particular the basic strategic decisions will influence the structure and function of the organization. Wickham Skinner, a Harvard production–operations scholar, has long encouraged corporate strategists to consider the production–operations function more seriously.[2] In turn, the production–operations process should closely tie to corporate strategy, goals, and objectives. In the classic sense, structure and function follow strategy.

Decisions in Design of Operating Systems

Seven major decisions constitute the design of the operating system. In the true systems sense, these decisions are highly interdependent. They are:

1. Product/service line and design
2. Procurement and materials management
3. Site selection
4. Facilities layout
5. Process selection
6. Job design
7. Control of maintenance, inventory, and quality

These decisions are described in the following subsections in terms of how they affect what the organization decides to produce, how inputs will be acquired, where the facilities will be located and laid out, what process formats will be used, how jobs will be designed to match personnel, and how control can be accomplished to ensure quality, maintenance, and suitable inventory conditions. The impact of these decisions constitutes the productive state of the system.

Failure or performance loss in any one of the seven decision areas will affect the output of the system, as well as the operation of related functions. Truly, the performance of the enterprise can be no better than the underlying design of the system.

Product/Service Line and Design These decisions determine the intended output of the system. The decisions should relate to the other functions of the organization, since the total product or service mix describes what the organization is all about. In the product/service design phase, the specification of output is the starting point.

In most organizations, this decision is made in coordination with the marketing department, since the marketing activity will put the output in the hands

Designing, Planning, and Controlling Operating Systems

of clients and consumers. This type of interdepartment coordination is in line with the systems approach. Finance experts will also contribute in terms of cost and financial considerations.

Some special areas of consideration in product line and design are makeup and design of output, based upon research, components or materials to be used, and performance specifications of the product.

These concerns require review of basic issues about the product—what it should be like, what will go into it, and what it should be able to do. Successful design work helps ensure the success of the output. Technical and market factors are combined with options for production costs and methodologies. Some of the specific concerns in the design stage are:

1. *Technical feasibility*—Is the technology available?
2. *Human impact*—Is the product appropriate for clients and work force?
3. *Producibility*—Are operations processes, resources, and equipment available?
4. *Reliability*—Will the product be trouble-free?
5. *Legality and Safety*—Will patents, product liability, other factors with the law be a problem?
6. *Maintenance status*—Is the product easy and accessible to repair?

All of these considerations should be reviewed in the product design phase to ensure that the product can be delivered to the satisfaction of the company and customers alike. Much of our contemporary concern with quality indicates that a great deal can be done in the design phase to improve and maintain quality.

The design phase is an area for potential conflict or cooperation. The interests of various parties must be reconciled:

1. Operations managers' work methods and costs
2. Design engineers' work requirements and design
3. Financial managers' work money flows
4. Marketing managers' work product salability

Value analysis and engineering also contribute to product design. Value analysis/engineering involves the rigorous study of cost reduction potential in products or services. The objective is to provide function at the least cost. This can be achieved by an increase in or versatility of function, or by reduction of cost in methods or materials.[3]

Another factor in contemporary operations is computerization in design. Computer-Aided Design/Computer-Aided Manufacturing (CAD/CAM)[4] uses advanced computer software capability to provide flexibility and innovation. Design time can be greatly reduced by the use of CAD cathode ray tube (CRT) displays. These methods will be a prominent part of the "factory of the future."

A 1983 *Industry Week* article elaborated on the automated factory of the future, claiming that CAD/CAM installations costing from $25,000 to $50,000 can simplify planning, reduce parts by 40 percent, cut design time by 65 percent, and reduce costs of assembly.[5] Such are the implications of product design.

Procurement/Materials Management   This very important function involves decisions about securing from outside vendors the materials, supplies, and services to support smooth operations. The procurement function provides inputs from vendors to support organization operations and objectives. Materials management ensures the flow of materials and work-in-process throughout the organization in a cost-effective manner.

The cost of materials amounts to a significant proportion of the sales price of products. The *Annual Survey of Manufacturers* indicates that materials costs of manufactured goods will range from 55 percent to 62 percent. This is a heavy responsibility for productivity and represents a challenge for savings and cost reduction in purchasing (procurement) actions.

The function of procurement is often decentralized by department, especially for high-value items. The functions of the procurement activity include refining needs of the organization, developing sources of supply, maintaining relationships with vendors, and executing purchases in an expeditious, cost-effective manner. The function of procurement has been described as "securing the right material in the right quantity at the right time at the right place from the right source at the right price."[6]

Careful selection of vendors is very important to obtain the best opportunity for:

1. Best quality
2. Best price and terms (discounts, volume buys, etc.)
3. Reliability of product
4. Delivery on schedule and in good condition
5. Service, as required

The logistics of materials management is important, since up to 50 percent of the sales price can involve acquisition and movement of materials.[7] Reduction of work-in-process, and minimizing of movement can greatly lessen the amount of financial resources tied up in operations. Costs are reduced because there is less investment tied up in processing.

Value analysis is practiced in the procurement function to secure the best possible value for the cost. In the area of the purchasing action, value analysis seeks the most function at least cost, compared to the design improvement goal of value engineering. The goals of purchasing are listed in Exhibit 17.2.

The role of materials management deserves some final mention. If procurement acquires materials, the materials management function strives to move ma-

---

EXHIBIT 17.2 Goals of procurement functions

> Provide uninterrupted flow of materials, supplies, and services.
> Minimize inventory investment and loss.
> Maintain quality standards.
> Find or develop competent vendors.
> Where possible, standardize items bought.
> Purchase required items at lowest reasonable prices.
> Achieve harmonious working relationships with other departments of the organization.

SOURCE: Michiel R. Leenders, Harold E. Fearon, and Wilbur B. England, *Purchasing and Materials Management,* 7th ed. (Homewood, Ill.: Irwin, 1980).

terials smoothly throughout the operations. The Japanese "kan-ban" methods, described later in the chapter, are typical of modern techniques of minimizing inventory to make sure that materials are available when needed, but that they are not stored so that inventory is tied up and costs are raised.

Site Selection and Location   One of the most important strategic decisions in operations is site selection. Although it is expensive and troublesome to change locations, correct siting can be very supportive of profitable and competitive operations. A "good" location will help business, and a "bad" location will hurt it.

Site selection includes consideration of regional, community, and site aspects in terms of favorability for establishment or extension of facilities for office, service, or production activities. The following elements are important in the site selection process:

1. Proximity to markets, for reduced transportation costs
2. Proximity to materials and suppliers, for reduced storage transportation costs
3. Access to labor force, for appropriate skills mix and costs
4. Access to utilities, for power, water, communication
5. Access to services, including security, fire, and health protection
6. Availability of transportation as appropriate
7. Climate, considering heat, humidity, cold, dust, and so on
8. Taxes, and special breaks or considerations
9. Land costs, condition, drainage, stability, and so on
10. Community factors, including schools, quality of life, housing, and civic attitudes
11. Legal factors, including zoning and pollution regulations

This general set of factors is found on many location checklists for firms considering sites for new or additional facilities. Many firms have regretted overlooking items that later proved to be critical. Consultants and siting specialists are often used for improving selection decisions. Site location has particular impact on operating costs and investments, productivity of facilities working as intended, ease of maintenance (which cuts overhead and repairs), and flexibility for expansion or contraction of use.

Facilities Layout   Once a site has been established for the organization, layout of the facility is one of the next important decision areas. Arrangements of homes and rooms is something we may take for granted, but layout can substantially help or hinder productive operations. An ideal layout should:

1. Utilize labor and equipment efficiently.
2. Minimize movement and handling of materials.
3. Minimize the use of space.
4. Reduce hazards and danger spots.
5. Keep flexibility for possible changes.
6. Be esthetically appealing and allow for a high quality-of-work life.

Note that the items on this list are related to cost reduction as well as provision of a setting for effective work operations. Two main approaches are available for layouts—process and product layout.

Process layout features the arrangement of work facilities based on grouping similar kinds of equipment (painting, drilling, etc.). Product layout arranges work and equipment so that material flows according to the progressive steps by which the product is made. Process layout deals with the job to be done. In organizations like hospitals, restaurants, and custom-tailoring, layout revolves around the job at hand. The process layout format provides flexibility as the job changes, variety of products that can be handled, and capital costs that are usually lower.

Product layout deals with standardization or continuous flow of activity. This type of layout is found in clinics, cafeterias, and assembly lines. In comparison to process layout, product layout can provide features such as lower costs, less demand on labor, and simplified control.

Layout is a very important element in achieving smooth work flow. Balancing a line of activities is crucial in matching the flow of demands for service to the capability of the system for providing service or operations. College students need to think only of registration and other lines on campus that could be improved by layout so as to smooth the flow. Line balancing seeks to minimize the cost or time involved in conducting operations, preventing costly and aggravating bottlenecks.

Computer-assisted models are available to conduct layout studies to optimize all the factors involved. Although the use of such sophisticated tools is costly, the costs of bottlenecks can often warrant expensive solutions.

Process Selection   Selection of the operations process is related to the layout decision. Layout deals with the "where" of the work, and process with the "how." Process selection is a strategic decision that will commit the organization to a particular form of operation.

Part of the consideration of process depends on the forecast of demand and the capacity of the system. The process, or method, must take into account the goals of the organization, and the way that it intends to reach those goals. The strategic approach has been endorsed by Dr. Wickham Skinner of Harvard, who claims that process planning has been too lightly regarded.[8]

The process selected binds the firm to facilities, equipment, and type of work force. These commitments affect the future options and alternatives of the firm. Further, Reich has claimed in a recent thought-provoking analysis that the fixed continuous production formats of the United States are not adaptable to the advancements of modern technology.[9] He endorses more flexible and tailored applications of process.

Chase and Aquilano indicate that process selection consists of major and minor technological choices.[10] Major technology deals with transformation potential, such as product choice. Minor technology deals with choice of equipment and techniques. Specific choices relate to output levels, routings, and flow patterns.

Process flow patterns also can fall into several categories. *Line flow (or product layout)* has a linear sequence of operations that shape or transform the

EXHIBIT 17.3 Process flow patterns

Format		Characteristic Flow	Volume
Line	Product	Continuous	High
Job shop	Process	Intermittent	Intermediate
Fixed	Project	One-time	Low

product. Examples are assembly lines, cafeterias, or a bottling plant. High volume, continuous operation, and mass production are the chief characteristics. *Job shop flow (or process layout)* deals with the job shop and batch tasking. Examples are hospitals, garages, and department stores that organize around process, rather than product. The job or task is the key. *Fixed (or project) formats* address unique programs, usually quite large. Construction, shipbuilding, and aircraft manufacturing are examples. These flow patterns are summarized in Exhibit 17.3.

Process selection is not only a strategic choice, but also a practical decision about how the work of the organization should be done.

Job Design Job design assembles tasks into jobs that fit the capabilities of workers and the work to be done. This is discussed from a personnel/human resources perspective in chapter 14. A job design companion, human engineering, deals with designing machines, work stations, and work processes to capitalize on the physical and mental capacities of the worker, thereby minimizing human limitations.[11]

Job design accepts the product, process, and layout as given, while specifying the nature and content of tasks and jobs. Designing the job and staffing relates the human input to the operation. The process of job design involves specifying tasks in the job, specifying task performance criteria, describing the identity of the job, and relating the job to the person. The tasks involve the work to be done to achieve the goals of the organization. Exhibit 17.4 shows some factors in job design in the production–operations setting.

EXHIBIT 17.4 Factors in job design

Who—work force physical and mental characteristics
What—tasks to be performed in the job structure
Where—location of organization and work areas
When—point in work flow; point in time
How—techniques and method of performance
Why—organizational rationale for job; motivation and objectives of workers

SOURCE: Adapted from Richard B. Chase and Nicholas J. Aquilano, *Production and Operations Managment* (Homewood, Ill.: Irwin, 1981).

In many of today's jobs, a person–machine interaction is involved. Human engineering (sometimes referred to as human factors) can be extended to design of tools, effects of light, noise, temperature, and other work stresses.

Final determination of job design includes factors such as the following:

1. *Technical feasibility*—the capability of people, often working with machines
2. *Economic feasibility*—the relevance of costs in the various options for job design
3. *Behavioral feasibility*—the interplay of human perception, motivation, and relationships associated with work[12]

A complicating factor in job design is that people are both alike, yet individual. Factors in job design affect different persons differently. Occasionally, job redesign is in order, modifying structure of some sociotechnical factor. This involves use of various work group arrangements or supervisory training, worker training, and methods such as job enrichment. Sociotechnical methods combine aspects of the technical system and social arrangements on the job.

Jobs are important to job holders, and the tasks that constitute the job are those activities deemed necessary to help the organization reach objectives. The content of the job should provide productivity for the organization by adding value in the operations sense. In the job design, it is also important for job holders to find their objectives fulfilled.

Control of Maintenance, Inventory, and Quality Decisions about control affect the levels of quality and quantity that the operation will seek to establish and sustain. Maintenance decisions are dedicated to keeping facilities, assets, and equipment in working order. Though it is commonly overlooked, poor maintenance can become extremely costly to remedy when assets deteriorate to such a condition that much time, effort, and cost will be required to restore them to working condition. Maintenance is costly, but it is intended to prevent more costly investments later. Effective maintenance decisions prevent idle time, accidents, and delays, and ensure preventive and remedial measures to minimize long- and short-term maintenance costs and depreciation.[13] The task of inventory functions is to maintain adequate supplies of materials to sustain operations. The categories of inventory include materials and parts, supplies (expendable and non-expendable), work-in-process, and finished goods and products. All inventory represents a considerable investment. Careful control of inventory can mean substantial savings. Note that inventory may represent up to 25 percent of invested capital.

Inventory and quality control are discussed in more detail in the next section on planning and control of operations. As this point, the emphasis is on decisions to be made about the operations of any type of organization. Choices must be made early in the operations planning to ensure the best function of the organization.

Professor W. Deming, the American expert who helped Japanese industry get on its feet after World War II, indicates that management must make early decisions to improve operations.[14] As an expert on inventory and statistical quality control, Deming claims that after-the-fact control and inspection cannot remedy the lack of good decisions made early about inventory and quality matters. Planning of operations, as well as control, examines further the nature of inventory and quality control issues.

PLANNING AND CONTROL OF OPERATIONS

A major element in planning and controlling operations involves the use of technology, innovation, and analysis to improve operations. The attempts of managers to increase productivity are recognized in a recent *Fortune* article recognizing the "10 best-managed factories in America." The *Fortune* survey of executives, consultants, and analysts provided the listing shown in Exhibit 17.5. The exhibit shows the benefits of automation, improved design, robotics, and worker-management systems. This listing includes high-tech firms and labor-intensive operations. The important point is that planning, design, and control have been incorporated into improved management of operations.

Day-to-day operations are guided and sustained by effective planning and control. The flow of products and services must be allocated, scheduled, and directed through the system. The entire transformation subsystem must be managed. Inventory and quality controls should ensure that the business operates at allowable

EXHIBIT 17.5 Characteristics of best-managed factories

Company	Product	Claim to Fame
AT&T Technologies Richmond, Va.	Circuit boards	Advanced production technology
Chaparral Steel Midlothian, Texas	Steel products	Steel production technology
Dana Corp. Spicer Div. Auburn, Ind.	Truck clutches	High productivity
E. T. Wright & Co. Rockland, Mass.	Men's shoes	High quality
General Electric Erie, Pa.	Locomotives	Highly automated
General Elcctric Louisville, Ky.	Dishwashers	Robotics
Hewlett-Packard Waltham, Mass.	Medical electronics	Product design-engineering cooperation
IBM East Fishkill, N.Y.	Semi-conductors	Advanced production technology
Lincoln Electric Cleveland, Ohio	Welding equipment	Worker involvement, compensation system
Nissan Motor	Pickup trucks	Automation, labor–management cooperation

SOURCE: Adapted from G. Bylinsky, "America's Best Managed Factories," *Fortune* (May 28, 1984).

costs while operations provides the quality sought by the system. "Hidden factory" is a concept used to refer to the amount of excess inventory, scrap, and rework that occupies the energy and resources of many organizations. The "hidden factory" is maintained at great cost to ensure that the organization renders the goods and services that were originally called for.

Several basic concepts of planning control apply very strongly to operations. These include:

1. Bases of future demand forecasts
2. Best allocation of resources for productivity
3. Scheduling to ensure value added as desired
4. Control of inventory and quality to minimize cost, scrap, and rework

Aggregate Planning

Aggregate planning and the ensuing control function begin with forecasting. Forecasts are required throughout the organization to make decisions dealing with the future. In operations management, the principal use of forecasting is in predicting the demand for products and services through time, but forecasts also include predictions of technology as well as predictions of sales. Better forecasting will help correctly anticipate the demand for products and services so that the resources of the organization can be most efficiently allocated to the operations process that will render those products and services.

Long-range forecasting is required to plan facilities and future requirements for personnel and equipment. Long lead times for facilities and expansions place a critical emphasis on long-range forecasting. Intermediate-range forecasts (for six to eighteen months) are important for allocating budgets to product or service divisions, to establish the appropriate purchasing activity, and to plan work force levels. Short range forecasts assist in establishing production and service schedules, as well as to assign human resources to jobs. These forecasts help expedite the flow of operations from receiving docks to processing operations to shipping.

Managers can encounter many different types of forecasting demands. University managers need to forecast students for courses, travel managers need to forecast tourist demand, city managers need to forecast demand for transportation and utilities with growing population, and manufacturing managers must forecast demand for products. This process is complicated by forecasting for new products or services not yet on the market. In addition, forecasts for prices, costs, and delivery schedules complicate the forecasting challenge.

Exhibit 17.6 shows a classification of forecasting methods. Note that the general breakdown is into statistical, or quantitative, methods and judgment methods, which are more qualitative. Statistical methods assume that the future will look like the past. Judgment methods are concerned with factors in the future that will affect demand, such as interest rates, inflation, changing technology, or new markets.

In statistical forecasting, time series methods are used to construct models based upon historical data. By these methods, the demand over time is smoothed or averaged to construct a line (demand function) that can be projected or extrapolated to predict future demand. Regression models attempt to determine some form of causality between two factors such as auto production and demand for tires. A regression equation can be derived that can be used to predict de-

Designing, Planning, and Controlling Operating Systems

EXHIBIT 17.6 Forecasting methods

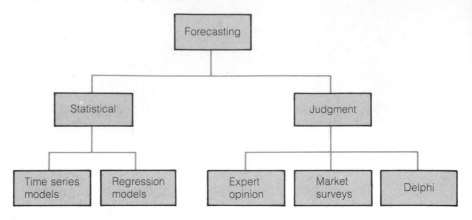

mand for tires based upon best estimates of new autos to be produced, as well as demand for replacement tires.

In judgment forecasting, historical data, which are useful in statistical methods, are often lacking. Expert opinion consists of the judgments and opinions of expert personnel based on experience and knowledge of the particular market. This is important for new markets such as convenience foods or newly developed auto accessories. Market surveys are used in judgment forecasting. Questionnaires and telephone or personal interviews are used to gather data. This method is subject to bias and costly techniques, but may develop useful information regarding consumer behavior. The delphi method utilizes a panel of experts who are individually asked about their expectation of future events, without meeting as a group to avoid group behavior phenomena. The expert responses are summarized and fed back to the experts with additional questions. Over several rounds, the composite of expert opinions is sharpened to the point where a useful forecast is obtained.

Forecasting may be continuous, but at certain points, the forecasts are supplied to planning groups for incorporation into aggregate and capacity planning.

Planning in the aggregate or total sense coordinates and programs the use of overall resources and goals over time in the transformation/conversion function. A key element is capacity planning. Capacity planning attempts to balance the overall system by matching demands for products and services with the organization's resources and capability. Aggregate or capacity planning involves setting goals related to organization strategy, assessing resources available, setting timetables for processes, and forecasting demand for time periods.

Schroeder describes aggregate planning as the link between facilities planning and scheduling of operations.[15] The product or service sequence is planned for six to eighteen months in advance. Seasonal fluctuations in demand create the aggregate planning problem. Work force requirements are anticipated, and rates of production or service are established. Inventory levels are set to provide for fluctuating or constant demands upon the firm. The objective is to level work force requirements (eliminating overtime and layoffs) by planning where possible. Another option might be to "chase" demand with the work force by adapting to demand rather than relying on forecasting or ancitipating it. However, the chase option is a reactive tactic, and good planning for demand, if possible, is preferred.

Examples of aggregate or capacity planning include:

City recreation departments planning for summer programs

Hospitals planning for operating room schedules

Construction planning for cold weather months

Universities planning for commencements

Auto manufacturers planning for anticipated model sales[16]

Another factor considered in aggregate planning is consideration of the product life cycle discussed in chapter 11. Time phasing of demand is greater for growth stages than for declining stages of products.

Time phasing becomes critical in such endeavors as crop growth and harvest, seasonal casual clothing, holiday sales, and convention planning. Capacity is a very expensive commodity to phase into demand without waste, delay, or mismatch.

Resource Allocation

Once capacity has been estimated and planned, the next step is allocation of resources. This allocation involves determination of the mix of capacities and resources: personnel, materials, and facilities. The benefits and costs are projected for each of the options available.

In recent years, resource allocation has become increasingly difficult. As a follow-on to aggregate and capacity planning, resources must be allocated wisely, even though they become most costly and scarce. Competition from domestic and overseas firms has made the allocation of resources more crucial. Mistakes can be very costly.

In some cases, demand can be modified regarding the allocation of capabilities. Demand can change as a result of pricing policies and changes, advertising and promotion, development of complementary products and services, and shifting demand by backlogs. Schroeder notes further that supply can be modified in resource allocation by altering capacity mix by hiring or laying-off employees, using part-time labor, carrying inventory, and subcontracting.

Several quantitative tools have become useful in allocating resources in the organization: linear programming provides perspective on mixes of variables; Critical Path Method (CPM) uses network analysis to study interrelationships of activities in relating time and cost; and simulation uses models of operations to study effects of decisions and alternatives.

Activity Scheduling

The scheduling of activities provides a time-phased plan with milestones for allocating resources or capacity to jobs, customers, or tasks. This schedule is made up following decisions about aggregate planning and facilities. Activity scheduling is related to process selection, as described earlier. Line process scheduling, for example, allocates line capacity to products or services on a continuous basis. Intermittent process scheduling projects inputs and loading of work centers. And individual jobs can use dispatching or sequencing (as with radio-dispatched plumbers). Among the questions which scheduling seeks to answer are: What is

Designing, Planning, and Controlling Operating Systems

the delivery date? How much capacity is needed? When should each activity begin? How can it be ensured that the job is completed on time?

Line balancing is an important consideration in scheduling each activity so that the workers and work stations are occupied with tasks and do not have to wait because of a bottleneck earlier in the process. The objective of balancing the line is to have a smooth flow of operations with no waiting or overloads.

In scheduling projects, the one-time nature of the program permits the use of some techniques such as:

1. *Gantt Charts.* These charts project activities on a bar chart format on a time base. Milestones provide points at which the status of projects can be checked for on-time completion.
2. *Critical Path Method (CPM).* CPM uses a network to show precedence relationships, with times indicated for activities.
3. *Program Evaluation Review Technique (PERT).* PERT is another networking method used for experimental and one-time projects involving expected, pessimistic, and optimistic times.

Computer simulation has also been used to project flows and relationships of activities, and to study the effects of changes and mixes of the variables.

Scheduling is so important in the attempt to minimize time and cost that improving the schedule is worth extra effort. The total scheduling effort will then provide a master schedule and a series of detailed schedules for subsystem activities.

INVENTORY PLANNING AND CONTROL

Inventory planning and control deal with the flow of materials, supplies, and products through the organization. The usual emphasis is on control, but in both the strategic and the operational sense, good planning enhances good control. Both promote the effectiveness and efficiency of the operation.

Simply put, the purpose of inventory planning is to never run out of stock but to have no more than needed. Further, the cost of having—and not having—inventory must be minimized. This is a crucial consideration. What is the cost of being out of stock in losing customers or good will? What is the cost of having extra resources tied up in extra inventory? The answers to these questions are very important to management, which decides the price to pay, either intentionally or unintentionally. Here is another area for cooperation or conflict between marketing and finance deparmments. Finance would like to keep costs down. Marketing is more interested in having goods available.

Inventory Economics

Among the costs to the organization that should be considered are the following:

Acquisition costs—in purchasing and transportation

Order and set-up costs—in processing orders or setting up equipment for production runs

Carrying costs—in storage, materials handling, taxes, insurance, and losses

Stockout costs—in loss of profit or good will from unfilled orders

The benefits to be derived from the above costs include an uninterrupted supply of goods through the organization and the completeness of availability of product and service lines. Given the calculation of benefits, the cost equation emerges as follows:

$$\text{Total Cost} = \text{Purchase Costs} + \text{Carrying Costs}$$

Inventory Planning

Inventory is the commodity that ties the organization together. Whether as products or services, inventory is what the organization has to offer. The operations process transforms and adds value to that inventory as the organization does its work. The inventory thus flows from *Vendors* to *Raw Materials* to *Work-in-Process* to *Finished Goods.*

Again, decisions play a major role in inventory planning. The essential considerations are: Which items or services should be carried in inventory? How much should be ordered and carried in stock? When should orders be placed? What type of inventory control system should be used? The answers to these planning questions provide the basis for an effective control system, a principle discussed in earlier chapters. Product planning and forecasting give some answers to the first question. Economic order methods answer the second question, and inventory control procedures answer the others. Brief discussions of each method type follow.

Economic Order

The goal of an economic order is to obtain the right amount of goods at the minimum cost. There is a necessary tradeoff between ordering large amounts so as to lower order costs and increasing the carrying costs. The investment in inventory can be viewed in terms of opportunity cost. Inventory is expensive, but it is part of the cost of staying in business.

Models of economic orders can become very complex, but a simple model can carry the logic of the economic order. Exhibit 17.7 illustrates the relationships

---

EXHIBIT 17.7 Economic order quantity: order size vs. inventory costs

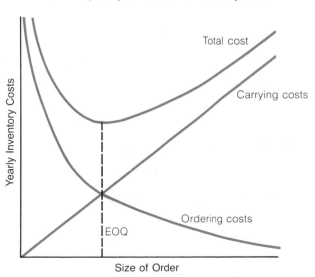

Designing, Planning, and Controlling Operating Systems

between ordering (and acquisition) costs and carrying costs. Mathematics can be used to form an expression of the same concept:

$$\text{Economic order quantity} = \text{Square root of } 2DS/C$$

$$\text{where } D = \text{annual demand}$$
$$S = \text{setup or order costs}$$
$$C = \text{carrying costs (\$/unit/year)}$$

The figure and the equation show that the order size is directly related to annual demand and setup or order costs, and inversely related to carrying costs. Beyond the mathematics, the logic is important in describing the factors that play a role in shaping inventory and economic order (or lot) sizes. Note again that the model is simplistic, and many assumptions are made in the interest of simplicity. However, the complex models carry on from this point. In addition, as in any use of management science models, data that accurately and reliably relate to the real world are difficult to obtain.

Inventory Systems

The ABC Inventory System   Another scheme for inventory decisions carries the intriguing title of ABC system. The ABC system is simple but widely used. It focuses on the important thing—the value of the inventory. By the widely held "law of inverse propositions," the inventory case shows that most inventory items have lesser value than the lesser amount with higher value. The ABC system concentrates on the higher value items.

Exhibit 17.8 gives an example, with the smallest group (A) having the greatest proportion of value, the B group having less value, and the largest group, C, having the least value. The principle for inventory planning and control is to give the greatest attention and care to the A group. Note that the A group either can possess the highest value or be the most critical to operations.

EXHIBIT 17.8   The ABC inventory system

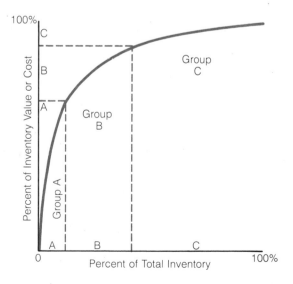

EXHIBIT 17.9 Fixed time period method of reordering

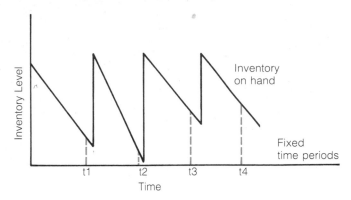

This model involves judgment about concentrating on the significant few rather than the insignificant many. The logic of the model is the key element in guiding decisions about how to manage inventories more intelligently, whether those inventories are electronic components, grocery stocks, or hospital operating room supplies.

Inventory Cycles   Generally the most important feature of inventory planning and control is the inventory cycle. The cycle involves demand that draws on inventory, reorder points at which orders are made for new stock, and safety stock that sustains operations until the new orders arrive. The objective is to have enough inventory for operations, but no excess that incurs extra costs.

Materials and supplies are usually ordered, delivered, and used in cycles. Few flows are constant the way that, for example, electricity and water are. The chief issues are when to order, and how much to order. Basic inventory systems are dependent upon demand. They can be described as either fixed period, variable size order, or fixed order, variable time period.

Exhibit 17.9 shows the fixed period operation. At regular intervals, reorders are made of enough volume to build inventory to the desired level. This method requires periodic inventory monitoring.

The fixed order system is presented in Exhibit 17.10. Here, reorders are placed when stock reaches a certain level. Times may vary, but constant inventory monitoring is needed to determine when the reorder point is met.[17] Both systems are called non-anticipatory systems: they follow demand rather than anticipate it. Examples of such systems are hospitals, wholesale warehouses, and retail businesses. Other, more extensive variations on basic inventory models are available, and many are computerized. An example is Material Requirements Planning (MRP).

Material Requirements Planning   MRP is an anticipatory system that manages inventories by anticipating their use. The basic strategy of the MRP system is to synchronize procurement or fabrication of materials and parts to coincide with the master schedule. MRP is being held as a potent contributor to productivity by minimizing inventory.

EXHIBIT 17.10 Fixed order quantity method of reordering

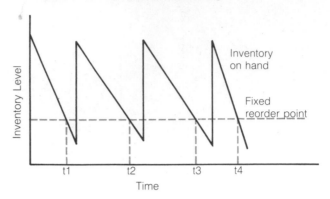

One of the Japanese productivity techniques is their kan-ban system, which minimizes work-in-process and inventories by use of a "just-in-time" regime. This program uses many small deliveries at exact timing. Toyota, for example, considers stock on hand as a collection of trouble and costs.[18] MRP at its best is a finely tuned anticipatory model that is being used increasingly in American industry.

The computerized MRP system operates through:

1. A master production schedule of end products that drives the entire system.
2. A bill of materials for each part.
3. Inventory status of each component part.
4. Lead time status on each part.
5. Product construction schedules.[19]

The MRP system at its best reduces inventory and cost, improves work flow, facilitates capacity planning, minimizes shortages, and generally improves the entire planning and control system. The costs of MRP are considerable investment and training, as well as overhaul of manufacturing policies.

Other computerized inventory systems are in use today in industry. For example, the IBM Production and Information Control System (PICS) is a complete manufacturing information system. It further extends the inventory control system to include scheduling.

QUALITY CONTROL

Quality control is critical in modern industry, but quality is an attribute that is difficult to define. Operations management is very concerned that quality be present in its products and services. The customer or client of the system is more involved with quality in use of products and services. The operations manager is concerned with ways to ensure the proper quality in the transformation process. Our sophisticated society is deeply concerned with quality.

Schroeder describes quality in terms of "fitness for use,"[20] with the customer being the criterion for fitness for use. The operations manager attempts to install that fitness in the productive process. Juran et al. describe fitness on the following quality dimensions:

1. Technological (e.g., strength, hardness)
2. Psychological (e.g., beauty, status, taste, color)
3. Time-oriented (e.g., reliability, ease of maintenance)
4. Contractual (e.g., guarantee, warranty)
5. Ethical (e.g., courtesy of personnel, honesty)[21]

The above qualities may also be present in manufactured products or services provided by non-manufacturing organizations.

Planning for Quality Control

Quality begins with design, and should be specified before the operation begins. Exhibit 17.11 illustrates the aspects of quality that relate to the planning and control process.

In the planning for quality, the specifications for quality generally come from the customer or client. Those needs are refined into product features by the marketing process or product planning. Product features are then interpreted into design concepts and specifications by engineers and designers. This guidance is then the input for operations managers who oversee the transformation, which renders products and services that satisfy the quality needs of the customer/client.

Some writers describe the above relationships as a quality assurance cycle. The cycle from customer/client back through the organization represents a continuing concern for quality. The modern concern for product liability relates strongly to quality assurance. "Caveat emptor"—let the buyer beware!—no longer reigns. Quality assurance recognizes the responsibility of the organization to provide quality.

Quality assurance policy is a term often used to describe the involvement of the total organization in the quest for quality. A typical list of factors for quality assurance is given in Exhibit 17.12.

These activities seek to provide quality of design, conformance, and service, the cornerstones of quality assurance. From such quality policy, objectives can flow that involve raising quality levels, training in quality procedures, or upgrading of quality checks.

EXHIBIT 17.11 Types of quality

Design	Conformance	Availability	Field Service
Market Research	Technology	Reliability	Promptness
Concept	Manpower	Maintainability	Competence
Specification	Management	Logistics	Integrity
		Support	

SOURCE: J. M. Juran, F. Gryna, and R. S. Bingham, eds., *Quality Control Handbook,* 3d ed. (New York, McGraw-Hill, 1974): 2–9.

EXHIBIT 17.12 Quality assurance activities

1. *Reliability Engineering*—for an adequate expected use
2. *Value Engineering*—for best function at minimum cost
3. *Usability Evaluation*—for user convenience and safety
4. *Process Control*—to ensure adequate transformation processes
5. *Product Screening*—to verify quality of goods sold
6. *Service Assurance*—to certify training, parts, and maintenance
7. *Corrective Action*—when field use indicates inadequate quality

SOURCE: James B. Dilworth, *Production and Operations Management,* 2nd ed. (New York: Random House, 1983), pp. 384–85.

Costs of Quality Quality has a price. Poor quality is often the result of neglect or unwise trade-offs. Extra attention to quality does cost in the short run, but the longer term pay-offs should make this cost acceptable. Some costs occur within the organization, and others occur after the product is in the hands of customers. Hospitals, banks, government offices, and factories should decide where they stand in costs related to levels of desired quality. External costs (in customer hands) may lose future sales or good will. Internal costs are the price paid to raise and hold quality in the organization.

A cost of quality equation would then be expressed:

$$\text{Total cost of quality} = \text{Control costs} + \text{Failure costs}$$

$$\text{where Control costs} = \text{Prevention} + \text{appraisal costs}$$

$$\text{Failure costs} = \text{Internal} + \text{external failure cost}$$

A common rule of thumb indicates that quality costs run about 10 percent, similar to many profit margins. If quality costs could be decreased over time, while improving the quality of the product or service, profitablity should increase. Prevention and appraisal efforts have been used by many organizations to improve profitability and quality while gradually reducing the cost of quality. This is an example of "working smart and working hard."

"Zero defects" programs must be mentioned as an example of practice. Used for many years, the principle of "doing it right the first time" is worthy of review. As a matter of philosophy and practice, zero defects programs have been found in many organizations to reduce errors and defects by up to 50 percent. This represents a substantial saving with improved quality, whether in administration, sales, or manufacturing. No clients or customers appreciate mistakes or defects when they think they paid good value.

Some other interesting ideas on quality come from Philip Crosby in his celebrated book *Quality Is Free.*[22] Crosby claims that quality is free when the job is done right the first time, whether in producing a product or rendering a service. He points out that quality really begins with people, not with things. He emphasizes people-intensive programs in evaluation of management style, defect prevention programs, and procedures for quality improvement. The cost of quality is then the expense of doing things wrong. Quality is defined as "conformance to requirements"; it is managed by introducing expectations for quality and simultaneously preventing defects. Interestingly, Mr. Crosby is also credited with originating the "Zero defects" program just described.

Quality Control Procedures A first consideration is where in the operation quality control activities should be implemented. Hopeman has indicated that the checkpoints should be logical:

1. Acceptance checking when materials are received
2. At entry points to transformation processes
3. Before costly or irreversible processes
4. Before processes that may cover defects
5. After the product or process has been completed[23]

The logic of when and where to check starts with inputs. Increasingly, organizations are demanding materials in good condition. Good procurement assists this. Checks before process ensure that defects are absent before the process might alter the appearance or configuration of the product, and thus hide the flaw. Naturally, a check after the processing should determine whether the product or process was completed as desired.

Types of Quality Control

The basic objective of quality control is to verify quality. But how? Can every item be checked in detail as an aircraft is flight-tested before delivery? What about tires, bulbs, and shoes?

If quality control checks the conformance to given product or service specifications, some system design should indicate where, when, and how. The type of quality control should be worth the marginal cost of checking. Two main methods are used today for making the checks for quality: acceptance sampling or process control. Both methods attempt to measure attributes or variables of product quality.

Acceptance Sampling In acceptance sampling, samples are taken from lots of items. If the quality of the sample is acceptable, the lot is accepted. If the sample is not acceptable, a decision is made for rejection of the lot or for further sampling. Sampling is used rather than 100 percent checking when the cost of total checking is excessive. The sampling is random, and conducted on the basis of statistical rules.

The sampling, being cheaper and faster, attempts to verify the true state of the lot. Since it is based on probability, there are risks involved. The producer's risk is the probability of rejecting a good lot or batch, based on high standards for statistical acceptance. The consumer's risk is the probability of accepting a bad lot or batch. The risks are traded off against each other and can only be alleviated by increasing the sample size, at extra cost and time. Decisions must be made about the levels of each risk to face, along with the time and cost to invest in obtaining the desired level of quality. In electronics and drug manufacturing, very high levels of acceptance quality are sought, permitting one defect in tens of thousands of items.

Process Control Process control uses a different approach. Quality is checked while the product or service is being produced, rather than after the fact as in acceptance sampling. Control charts are used to show how the prod-

635   Designing, Planning, and Controlling Operating Systems

uct or service relates to a standard. Periodic samples are taken during processing to see if performance is within control limits. Performance is analyzed for its condition on the control charts, but the reason for the performance is yet to be determined. The control chart is presented as:

The desired level of performance would be the ultimate performance. However, as long as the periodic checks indicate that performance is between the upper and lower control limits, the output may be satisfactory, barring trends that will exceed limits. When limits are exceeded, some cause would be sought for a remedy to bring performance back into limits. Note that the cause of the unsatisfactory output may be attributed to machines, personnel, or material. Again, decisions must be made about how to remedy the situation, just as decisions were made about desired levels of output and upper and lower control limits.

With the process quality control technique, the transformation process can be maintained in a continued state of statistical quality control. The process method presented was simplified. More complex and computerized models are available.

Quality Control Circles

The use of quality circles for productivity has already been discussed. In the area of quality control, we find one of the more powerful applications. Willis reports the first Japanese use of quality control circles (QCC) in 1963, when the Japanese became concerned about their reputation for low-quality goods.[24] The Lockheed Aircraft Company began the use of QCC in 1974.[25]

Both Japan and the United States have made considerable strides with QCC, although Japan enjoys most of the accolades for QCC use. Their implementation requires top management support and the organized effort of workers to study work problems for solutions that contribute to increased quality. In quality control applications, workers are trained to collect and analyze data, to use techniques for creative study (such as brainstorming), and to make recommendations to management about possible initiatives to improve operations. The quality control circles are not a "quick fix" for quality, but another option in a carefully planned and executed program for improvement of quality.

Summary

This chapter covers the heart of the organization—the operating system. This system should operate by design to convert inputs into outputs for optimum effectiveness and efficiency. Accordingly, both design and the production–operations system as a whole assume a strategic role in the organization.

The design of operating systems may be described in the context of decisions guiding the operations system:

1. *Product/service* line and design decisions describe the intended output of the system. The clients and customers of the organization are taken into account so as to provide the attributes of product or service that have value.

2. *Procurement and materials management* decisions govern the acquisition of inputs for the system, as well as the management of materials through the operation. Quality begins with procurement, and the role of acquisition of inputs is a first step in the provision of desired outputs of the organization.

3. *Site selection* governs the investment of operations as to location and other features of the enterprise. The operation will live with the location, for better or worse. Judicious site selection can save money and provide the organization with an improved opportunity for profitability and service.

4. *Facilities layout* decisions determine the configuration of the operation, hence governing smooth flow, cost reduction, and flexibility for operations.

5. *Process selection* decisions govern the type of arrangement for the transformation activity. Depending upon the nature of the firm—product or service—and the transformation, several options for process are available to conserve resources while fulfilling the purpose of the operation.

6. *Job design* decisions match the human resource to the job. Considering the work to be done, and the personnel available, job design provides the setting for detailing tasks into jobs that will generate productivity and satisfaction.

7. *Control of maintenance, inventory, and quality* decisions govern the management of resources that are blended into outputs. Maintenance sustains facilities and equipment. Inventory is guided along the path to becoming products and services. Quality ensures conformance to standards for performance and products.

The planning and control of operations sustain the strategic purpose of the organization. Planning provides guidance for the successful culmination of conversion of resources into the desired outputs.

Aggregate planning studies the needs of customers and clients so as to provide indications of planning of capacity. The entire operations format and subsidiary subsystems blend into a holistic view of the organization coping with its environment.

Resource allocation designates the inputs to be dedicated to the various streams of activity within the organization. Supply and demand factors are considered in feeding the operations in support of transformations.

Scheduling activities consider the various methods of time-phasing desired operations. Continuous, batch, and project operations are appropriately matched to scheduling techniques that smooth the flow of operations while observing allowable costs.

Inventory control seeks to provide the right amount of resource inventory to the right location at the right time. Inventories are considered as raw materials, work-in-process, and finished products. A method for evaluating economic order quantities considers demand, carrying costs, and setup or order costs.

One technique, the ABC method, manages inventory in terms of the relative value of items. Fixed order and fixed period methods are available to determine a decision rule for reordering materials to maintain desired levels of inventory.

Material Requirements Planning (MRP) is a method for anticipating inventory needs. A carefully orchestrated plan then expedites materials so as to reduce lead times and inventory on hand, thus reducing costs.

Quality control determines conformance to product or service specifications. The importance of planning for quality supports the design of quality philosophy and practice. Quality cannot be inspected into products, but must be designed and managed into reality.

The cost of quality indicates internal and external considerations. Internal factors are cost producers in the organization because of faults, rejects, and rework. External factors reflect costs of customer dissatisfaction. There is a trade-off between the cost of quality customers will pay and the desire for high-level performance.

Quality control circles contribute to quality by creative study of quality problems. Considerable attention has been drawn to this inclusion of the work force, operating in groups, into the total plan for quality in organizations.

What Have You Learned?

1. What is the importance of the strategic approach to the design of operating systems?
2. What are the decisions involved in design of operating systems?
3. What factors would guide the decision to locate a hospital, a church, a convention center, an airport?
4. How would facilities layout decisions for restaurants differ from fast food outlets?
5. If you were asked to make some recommendations for aggregate planning for your college, how would you go about it? What information would you need?
6. What cases of inventory stockout have bothered you most recently? How could these have been avoided? If you were in charge of the out-of-stock organization, what price would you be willing to pay to eliminate stockouts?
7. What cases of poor quality have you encountered lately? What can consumers do about this after the fact? What could have been done before the fact? How much are you willing to pay for quality?
8. Define quality for three kinds of products. How does quality for services differ from quality for products?
9. What are the benefits and costs of quality?
10. If inventory is so important, why should MRP go to great expense to reduce inventory levels and lead times for replenishment?

How Well Can You Apply Your Knowledge?

Problem 1. The Pilgrim Furniture Company had been a bastion in the home furnishings industry for over 100 years. Jack Franklin was proud to be president of such an institution. He was most proud of the tradition of excellence and quality in the New England style. Customer service was also important, since the Pilgrim Company had served generations of furniture buyers.

Mr. Franklin had held the presidency for thirty years, and, being of the frugal New England tradition, was conscious of the need to save wherever possible, while not sacrificing quality. In fact, the generations of service convinced him that being able to provide whatever a customer wanted from stock was a strong reason that customers kept coming back.

When Joan joined her uncle's firm following her graduation from business school, she was eager to learn. Being a Franklin herself, she had grown up appreciating the Pilgrim tradition of handiwork. While the firm had 200 employees, and sold $2,500,000 worth of furniture, the small plant style kept the Pilgrim appeal. Craftsmen produced pieces of furniture from start to finish.

Business had grown consistently until five years ago. Then sales leveled out, and profitability declined. Mr. Franklin decided to modernize by almost doubling the furniture line. He claimed, "We've always been able to produce and stock anything our people would want." To economize, Mr. Franklin vigorously sought quantity discounts, usually for the largest lot or a year's supply, whichever was smaller. Stock policy was altered to maintain the largest daily usage, since service was—along with quality—the proudest tradition of the Pilgrim company.

As an expediter, Joan was interested in finance. The office manager showed her that short- and long-term financing was very much in hand. Costs were rising and adversely affecting profits. When Joan looked at marketing, she noticed that, while their sales had merely leveled, the furniture industry in general was in deep trouble in the Northeast. Pilgrim still had a strong share of the market.

Finally, Joan talked her uncle into hiring a consultant who was a professor at a local school of business. After two days of consulting, her boss was livid when he showed the consultant's report to her.

"Your professor may be a smart man, but his report is gobbledy-gook. What's this EOQ, MRP, anticipatory demand, quality circle stuff? Read this report, and tell me in one page how his academic hogwash has anything to do with the Pilgrim Company."

Questions

1. If you were Joan, what would you put in your report to Mr. Franklin?
2. When you next saw the consultant professor, and he asked you how the report for Pilgrim went, what would you say?

Problem 2. The Devil Drill was one of the favorite products of the Blue Demon Tool Company. A dozen persons worked in the Devil Drill department—eight men and four women in three stations. The first station assembled the motor components, and the second station received the motor on a moving belt and installed the motor in the housing of the drill. The moving belt carried the drill to the third station, where the cord, accessories, and labels were added.

The Blue Demon Tool Company used scientific management methods and had carefully balanced the assembly line operations and installed work standards with the aid of the company industrial engineers. Workers were paid a standard hourly wage.

Still, trouble loomed. The inspectors were rejecting 20 percent of the drills for workmanship. Morale was low. Management took pride in quality, but the Devil Drill crew concluded at lunch time that management expected the inspectors to "inspect in" quality.

The concerned foreman realized a change was in order. A suggestion was made to change procedures from the "darned belt driving us" to permitting teams of two to completely assemble a drill.

After two months, productivity increased 45 percent over the previous quarter, and rejects had dropped to 3 percent since each two-person team inspected their own work before the final inspector took over.

Questions.

1. What happened here?
2. Explain the changes in terms of job design and quality control procedures.

Additional Sources for More Detailed Study

Barndt, Stephen E., and Carvey, Davis W. *Essentials of Operations Management.* Englewood Cliffs, N.J.: Prentice-Hall, 1982.

Hopeman, Richard. *Production and Operations Management.* Columbus, Ohio: Merrill, 1980.

Fearon, Harold; Ruch, William; Decker, Patrick; Reck,

Ross; Reuter, Vincent; and Winters, David. *Fundamentals of Production/Operations Management.* St. Paul, Minn.: West, 1981.

Schroeder, Roger, *Operations Management.* New York: McGraw-Hill, 1981.

Notes

1. Peter Drucker, *The Practice of Management* (New York: Harper, 1954).
2. Wickham Skinner, "Manufacturing—Missing Link in Corporate Strategy," *Harvard Business Review* (May–June 1969).
3. Richard Hopeman, *Production and Operations Management,* (Columbus, Ohio: Merrill, 1980).
4. Mikell Groover, *Automation, Production Systems, and Computer Aided Manufacturing* (Englewood Cliffs, N.J.: Prentice-Hall, 1980).
5. John Teresko, "CAD/CAM Goes to Work," *Industry Week* (February 7, 1983).
6. Harold Fearon, William Ruch, Patrick Decker, Ross Reck, Vincent Reuter, and David Winters, *Fundamentals of Production/Operations Management* (St. Paul, Minn.: West, 1981).
7. Norman Gaither, *Production and Operations Management* (Hinsdale, Ill.: Dryden, 1980).
8. Skinner, op. cit.
9. Robert B. Reich, "The Next American Frontier," *The Atlantic* (March 1983).
10. Richard B. Chase and Nicholas J. Aquilano, *Production and Operations Management* (Homewood, Ill.: Irwin, 1981).
11. Stephen E. Barndt and Davis W. Carvey, *Essentials of Operations Management* (Englewood Cliffs, N.J.: Prentice-Hall, 1982).
12. James B. Dilworth, *Production and Operations Management* (New York: Random House, 1983).
13. Joseph G. Monks, *Operations Management: Theory and Problems* (New York: McGraw-Hill, 1982).
14. Edwards Deming, *Quality, Productivity and Competitive Advantage* (Cambridge: MIT Press, 1982).
15. Roger G. Schroeder, *Operations Management* (New York: McGraw-Hill, 1981).
16. Ibid.
17. Roger W. Schmenner, *Production/Operations Management* (Palo Alto, Calif.: Science Research Associates, 1981).
18. James W. Rice and Takeo Yoshikawa, "A Comparison of Kanban and MRP Concepts for the Control of Repetitive Manufacturing Systems," *Production and Inventory Management* (First Quarter, 1982).
19. Schmenner, op. cit.
20. Schroeder, op. cit.
21. J. M. Juran, F. Gryna, and R. S. Bingham, eds., *Quality Control Handbook,* 3d ed. (New York: McGraw-Hill, 1974).
22. Philip Crosby, *Quality Is Free* (New York: McGraw-Hill, 1979); see also Lee A. Iacocca, "The Rescue and Resuscitation of Chrysler," *Journal of Business Strategy* (Summer 1983).
23. Hopeman, op. cit.
24. Judith Willis, "Quality Circles Breed Enthusiasm," *Minneapolis Star* (April 2, 1980).
25. Robert E. Cole, "Made in Japan—Quality Control Circles," *Across the Board* (November 1979).

READINGS AND PROFILES

The New Industrial Competition
William J. Abernathy, Kim B. Clark, and Alan M. Kantrow
Harvard Business Review

The Rescue and Resuscitation of Chrysler
Lee A. Iacocca
The Journal of Business Strategy

Thornton A. Wilson and The Boeing Company

These selections are intended to provide examples of the important role that manufacturing and production–operations management play in company success, and in the success of the society as well. Quality of products clearly emerges as one of the most important considerations.

Abernathy, Clark, and Kantrow take an in-depth look at the U.S. automobile industry, comparing it with the Japanese competition. They calculate the cost advantage to the Japanese and demonstrate the quality advantage as well. Japanese success is attributed to superiority in the manufacturing plant, especially in process systems and work force management.

The article by Lee Iacocca, chief executive officer of Chrysler Corporation since his shift from Ford in 1979, is in fact a reply to Abernathy, Clark, and Kantrow, although it was not specifically written with that goal in mind. Iacocca describes Chrysler's turnaround from almost certain disaster. His emphasis is on the role that manufacturing and quality improvements played in the turnaround process, and on the cost reductions that were achieved. It should be noted that sizable loans from the U.S. government played an important role as well. However, the fact that these loans were paid off in a very short time appears to be due to the events Iacocca describes.

Thornton Wilson achieved much the same results at Boeing in the late 1960s and 1970s that Lee Iacocca did at Chrysler in the late 1970s and 1980s. Boeing reached its current pre-eminence largely through engineering excellence and product quality. The *Fortune* surveys consistently rate it at the top of the aerospace industry. Boeing is also the top manufacturer insofar as quality of products is concerned. As the executive profile notes, Thornton Wilson was a major force in producing these results.

The New Industrial Competition

William J. Abernathy, Kim B. Clark, and Alan M. Kantrow

The results of Japanese competition in U.S. markets are evident to all Americans. Repercussions from competitive pressures exerted by European and Japanese manufacturers have been or are being felt by U.S. producers of cars, machine tools, minicomputers, commercial aircraft, textile machinery, and color TV sets, to name a few traditional businesses. Taking auto manufacture as their case example, the authors of this article attribute the Japanese carmakers' success to superiority in the manufacturing plant, especially in their process systems and work force management.

The authors describe the current dilemma of U.S. car manufacturers, who find themselves at a crossroads because this struggle has changed the rules of the game. Now these producers face a situation in which advancing technology and the momentous changes it wreaks—instead of the incremental changes through styling, marketing, and service to which U.S. manufacturers are accustomed— will determine the winners and losers. As often happens in a mature industry when a new phase of competition appears, the auto industry may well undergo a renewal that transforms it. The challenge for U.S. companies in endangered industries is to recognize the altered situation, adjust to it, and learn to manage change.

It is barely possible that in some remote corner of the United States a latter-day Rip Van Winkle awoke this morning fresh with shining images of American industry in the 1950s still fixed in his head. But it is not very likely. Who, after all, during the past few years could have slept undisturbed through the general chorus of lament about the economy? Who could have remained unaware that much of U.S. industry—especially the mature manufacturing sector—has fallen on hard times?

And who did not have a surefire remedy? Born-again supply-siders argued for the massive forma-

William Abernathy is professor of business administration at the Harvard Business School. A noted expert on the automobile industry, he wrote *The Productivity Dilemma: Roadblock to Innovation in the Automobile Industry* (Johns Hopkins University Press, 1978). Kim Clark, assistant professor of business administration at the Harvard Business School, is author of the National Academy of Sciences' forthcoming report on *The Competitive Status of the U.S. Automobile Industry.* Alan Kantrow, an associate editor at HBR, has written two previous HBR articles, the more recent being "The Strategy-Technology Connection" (July–August 1980).

tion of capital; "new class" advocates of a more systematic industrial policy, for better allocation of existing capital; industrial economists, for enhanced productivity; organized labor, for a coherent effort at reindustrialization; subdued (if unrepentant) Keynesians, for more artful demand management; boisterous Lafferites, for a massive tax cut; congressional experts, for carefully targeted tax breaks on depreciation and investment; Friedmanites, for tight money; and Naderites, for an anticorporate economic democracy.

This loudly divided counsel on the best strategy for managing economic change reflects inadequacy in both perception and understanding: our current industrial malaise defies the usual interpretations and resists the usual prescriptions. Managing change successfully has proved difficult because policymakers in business and government, trained in an old economic calculus, have found it hard to see the new competitive realities for what they are—or to identify the best terms in which to analyze them.

Policymakers fail to understand that the old rules of thumb and worn assumptions no longer hold. Similarly, the traditional structural arrangements in many industries—the familiar relationship between, say, labor and management or producer and supplier—no longer square with the facts of competitive life. As a result, decision makers who continue to act as if nothing has happened are, at best, ineffective and, at worst, inadvertent agents of economic disaster.

Levers of Change

What has happened? The two principal changes have been greater exposure to international competition and technical advances that alter competition. For a start, let's look at two basic major manufacturing industries that have experienced these forces.

One is color television:

This industry was confronted with new competitors who emphasized high productivity, reliability, quality, and competent deisgn (but not innovative design, except for Sony).

Many competitors—Warwick, Motorola, and Admiral among them—did not survive the foreign thrust and were either taken over or went out of business.

Foreign competitors' emphasis on manufacturing, a critical element, was transferred to their U.S. operations—witness Sanyo's management of the previously unsuccessful old Warwick plant, with many of the same employees and U.S. middle managers.

Now technological changes have created a situation of potential renewal of the product life cycle—developments in videocassette recorders; videodiscs; flat, high-resolution screens; telecommunications; and computers may combine to revolutionize the television business.

. . . And another is textile machinery:

Before the 1960s a few U.S. manufacturers (for example, Draper) dominated this business. Conglomerates acquired them (e.g., Rockwell International took over Draper).

The U.S. manufacturers began to lose business primarily because of deterioration in product performance relative to European and Japanese models and failure to remain at the cutting edge of new technology.

Because of insufficient investment (conglomerates treated them as cash cows), the once-dominant U.S. manufacturers have lost technical and market leadership to the Swiss, Germans, and Japanese.

Now consider two other industries that are facing the new forces of international competition. One of them is computers:

Fujitsu has introduced a mainframe computer that attacks IBM where its strength is—service. Fujitsu is doing this by building a high-quality, reliable machine that can *guarantee* 99% uptime. In a test run of strategy, Fujitsu has taken on IBM in Australia with this approach and bested the U.S. giant in obtaining some mainframe contracts. The experience there to date: 99.8% uptime.

In minicomputers and home computers the Japanese are entering the U.S. market. Producers like Mitsubishi, Nippon Electric, and Hitachi will soon offer high-quality products that are cost competitive.

. . . And another is machine tools:

Japanese producers have entered this market with a strategy built around a very reliable, high-quality product. Recently, for instance, a U.S. auto producer ordered transfer lines from an established U.S. machine tool manufacturer and from Toyota. The lines arrived at the U.S. plant at the same time. Toyota sent two engineers who had the equipment running and fully debugged in two weeks, while the competitor's team of eight engineers spent several months getting its line operational.

Developments in new technology—electronics, optical and tactile sensors, lasers, and robotics—are creating opportunities for improved metalworking operations and are opening up new applications in areas like assembly and inspection, where mechanization and automation have hardly played a role. Integration of these advances with computerized design and manufacturing could change the very concepts on which traditional machine tools are founded.

A number of other long-stable U.S. manufacturing industries no doubt will be shaken in the not-distant future by these pressures. One is the air compressor field, which a few companies have dominated. A Japanese producer, Hokuetsu, entered its domestic market five years ago and now rules it. Among the companies left in its wake is Ingersoll-Rand, whose market share in Japan plunged from well over 50% to zero. Hokuetsu offers a dependable, good-quality product at half the cost of the comparable U.S. compressor.

Still another field is major household appliances, which the Japanese have slated for heavy export activity in this decade. Sanyo, Toshiba, and other companies are setting up U.S. plants and distribution systems. General Electric, for one, is worried; GE has begun a program designed to improve greatly the quality and productivity of its Louisville appliance complex.

The list of endangered industries goes on: jet engines, commercial aircraft, small forklift trucks, steel, electric motors, lawnmowers, and chainsaws, to name just a few.

Character of the New Competition

Let us focus on a single industry to show in detail the character of the conditions that the imperiled U.S. industries face. An inkling of these conditions has entered the consciousness of all Americans as they witnessed Japan's extraordinary success in capturing a large share of the automobile market from the entrenched Big Three domestic producers. In this article we go beyond the previously known facts and show exactly how the Japanese implemented their strategy on the plant floor, on the engineers' design boards, and in the executive offices.

Until recently, developments in the U.S. auto industry were determined mostly by government policies and economic forces peculiar to North America. The sheer extent of the U.S. market and its productive base had long guaranteed the industry a largely self-contained posture. Over the past 15 years, however, the competitive boundaries have expanded drastically until now they are virtually worldwide in scope.

Accompanying this expansion has been a rapid increase in the number of healthy competitors. These new international players, moreover, have quite a different approach from that of the U.S. Big Three; their plan consists of radically new strategies, modes of operation, and production experience.

More to the point, the novel competitive challenge they present cannot be overcome by the familiar responses U.S. companies have long used against each other. Strategically, the Big Three are well prepared to fight not this new war, but the last one.

Many observers believe that the perceived low quality of Detroit's vehicles is a simple function of lethargy and past practice. This view ignores the close connection between poor quality and a disadvantage in costs. The productive capacity of some new entrants, notably the Japanese, enjoys a significant cost advantage over that of the Americans. The Japanese have been especially skillful in exploiting this advantage by adding performance and quality to their cars. This combination of competitive price and high quality has proved tremendously successful in reaching consumers in the American market.

What makes this advantage particularly troublesome is that it does not represent primarily an investment problem; if it did, it would be far easier to remedy. Instead, it arises to some extent from differences in wage rates and, more significant, from differences in productivity and management of operations.

In 1973, when Lee A. Iacocca was asked about the competitive advantage of innovation as perceived by Ford, he responded simply, "Give them [American consumers] leather. They can smell it." In Ford's reading of the U.S. market, innovation did not pay; styling did. Things are quite different today: technology matters.

In the 1950s and 1960s, product technology was competitively neutral. No auto company sought a competitive advantage through significant innovation. In the 1980s, however, the necessity for advantage through innovation is steadily growing. In fact, consumer preference for small, fuel-efficient automobiles has developed faster in the United States than it did earlier in Europe or Japan. Beset by unfortunate decisions in the past, the continued absence of a workable long-term energy policy, conflicting regulatory requirements, and the massive financial demands posed by a retooling of production capacity, U.S. producers find themselves at a serious technological disadvantage.

But this is not all. The edge that U.S. companies have long enjoyed in mass production technology and in the resulting economies of scale—an edge long believed essential to competitive success—no longer obtains. Most of the standard U.S. technology is either already widely diffused or easily transferable. Moreover, the process technology for the new, smaller autos is subtly but significantly different from that now in place. In other words, changing market preferences and changing rates of technology diffusion have diluted, perhaps destroyed, the established scale economies of U.S. producers.

Premium on Management

Two main distinctions have largely provided the structure for discussions of manufacturing competitiveness. The first is the division between analysis and prescription of a "macro" sort (that is, having to do with such overarching questions of economic management as fiscal and monetary policy and tax

EXHIBIT 1 Key elements in manufacturing competitiveness

	Macro	**Micro**
Hardware	1. Government fiscal and monetary policies	2. Production capability
	Taxation	Plant
	Capital markets	Equipment
	Savings	
Software	3. Socioeconomic environment	4. Corporate management
	Work ethic	Organization
	Regulation	Administration
	Education	Production systems

incentives) and those of a "micro" sort (that is, having to do with issues relating to the management of particular companies). The second is the division between analysis and prescription based on "hardware" (equipment, buildings, and machinery) and those based on "software" (people management, organizational systems, and corporate strategies).

Considered together, these distinctions form the simple matrix shown in Exhibit 1. Although the distinctions among these quadrants are rough, they are nonetheless useful. In practice, however, they are often neglected, which has left the unfortunate impression in some minds that the current industrial difficulties are composed equally—and indistinguishably—of problems in all the quadrants.

This impression has been mischievous, for these difficulties and their remedies are distributed unevenly about the matrix. In the auto industry the key measures for meeting the new competition fall primarily into Quadrant 4.

Japanese Micromanagement

The Japanese advantage in production costs and product quality in the auto industry, as well as many other established U.S. industries, is not only a fact defining the new competitive reality but also the result of a carefully honed approach to management—the stuff of Quadrant 4. Americans' talk of overregulation, underdepreciation, pervasive national culture, and markedly absent government support is misplaced.

Costs of Production

Several estimates have placed the landed cost advantage in U.S. markets of Japanese-produced subcompact cars in the $400 to $600 range per vehicle. For example, Abraham Katz, then assistant secretary of commerce for international economic policy, testified last year that "the apparent cost advantage to Japanese producers may have been $560 per car in 1979."[1]

These estimates, in our view, seriously understate the advantage. In the first place, they fail to reflect both current rates of labor compensation and, perhaps more important, the great differences in productivity between Japanese and American manufacturers. Furthermore, they are often based on a narrow definition of the productive units to be compared, for they assume that the relevant comparision is between two original equipment manufacturers—say, Ford and Toyota—even though the really meaningful comparison lies between two productive systems, or "confederations"—that is, an OEM and its constellation of suppliers.

To get a truer picture of the Japanese cost advantage, we must therefore produce estimates that account for productivity differentials, labor costs, and industry structure.

The first step in developing these improved estimates is to update assessments of differential labor productivity. We know that in 1974 output per labor hour in the Japanese auto industry—OEMs and suppliers—was 88% of the level in the United States (that is, the ratio of Japanese to U.S. productivity was 0.88). Published data suggest that growth in labor productivity in the Japanese auto industry (motor vehicles and parts) averaged 8% to 9% in the 1970s; the comparable figure for the United States was 3% to 4%. Using a midrange estimate of the difference (5%), we arrive at a 1980 productivity ratio of 1.18. This means that in 1980 Japanese producers operated at a productivity level almost 20% above that of their American competitors.

This rapid growth was offset in part by higher rates of wage increase: in 1974 Japanese hourly compensation rates were about 37% of those in the United States, while in 1980 they were roughly 50%. Dividing the compensation ratio (0.5) by the productivity ratio (1.18) yields a unit labor cost ratio of 0.424—a figure that has remained more or less constant during the entire 1974–1980 period.

Exhibit 7 in the Appendix translates this steady labor cost ratio into a Japanese advantage of $1,673. Subtracting $400 for freight and tariff costs yields a landed cost advantage of $1,273 on a 1980 subcompact that sells in the American market for about $5,500—a cost advantage of 23%.

Although the calculations in Exhibit 7 are based on a number of undocumented assumptions about cost structure and labor content, reasonable adjustment of these assumptions would not affect the order of magnitude of the Japanese cost advantage. Indeed, we were biased conservatively throughout in estimating that cost advantage. Moreover, inclusion of general administrative and selling expenses, as well as the costs of capital and salaried personnel, would leave the Japanese cost advantage intact. So we figure that Japanese producers enjoy a $1,200 landed cost advantage on every small vehicle sold in the United States.

We can to some extent check these numbers against information in the annual reports of major U.S. and Japanese producers. These reports yield data on the costs of nonlabor inputs and salaried personnel but none on the labor embodied in components or materials.

Getting at these data, however, presents several analytic problems. Perhaps the most serious is the great difference between U.S. and Japanese OEMs in their degree of vertical integration and in the nature of their relationships with suppliers. At Toyota, for example, purchases account for almost 80% of the value of sales; but because Toyota holds an equity interest in many of its suppliers, this figure is somewhat misleading. Comparable data for U.S. companies show much less reliance on suppliers; GM, for instance, has a purchase-to-sale ratio of less than 50%.

A second problem is the quite different product mix of U.S. and Japanese OEMs. The data we use come from 1979, when medium-size cars dominated the U.S. Big Three's product lines. The Japanese were producing a much narrower range of vehicles and, of course, were emphasizing the sub-compact segment.

Exhibit 8 in the Appendix shows estimates of total employee costs per vehicle in 1979 at Ford and Toyo Kogyo (Mazda). Our calculations suggest that assembly of the average Ford vehicle required 112.5 employee hours; a Toyo Kogyo vehicle, only 47. Employee costs in building the Ford vehicle were $2,464; for Toyo Kogyo, $491.

As already noted, this sizable cost gap reflects differences in product mix and vertical integration as well as in labor costs and productivity. Information on value added in the annual reports and discussions with industry sources suggest that the Toyo Kogyo results should be increased by 15% to 20% to adjust for vertical integration. Using these higher estimates yields a per-vehicle total of 56 hours instead of 47. (To correct for product mix, we have estimated the cost to Ford of producing the Toyo Kogyo product mix. These calcuations are presented in Exhibit 9 in the Appendix.)

Our analysis of annual report data suggests that in 1979 the difference between Ford and Toyo Kogyo employee costs per small vehicle was about $1,300. Updating this figure to 1980 might increase the absolute dollar amount somewhat, but the evidence we cited on relative growth rates in productivity and compensation implies that the percentage gap would not change much.

Adjustment for changes in exchange rates would also have a negligible effect. Using a rate of 200 yen to the dollar (the approximate rate at the end of 1980) instead of 218 would reduce the gap by only $50. And when we adjust this $1,300 to reflect the U.S. advantage in administrative and selling expenses, the 2.9% tariff with the relevant freight costs for Japanese imports, and the Japanese productivity edge at the supplier level, we emerge

---

EXHIBIT 2 Evidence on assembly quality of U.S. autos vs. certain imports

	Vehicle Category	Condition at Delivery Scale of 1–10 (10 is excellent)		Condition After One Month of Service (Number of Defects Per Vehicle Shipped)
Aggregates		**Domestic**	**Imports**	
	Subcompact	6.4	7.9	
	Compact	6.2	7.7	
	Midsize	6.6	8.1	
	Standard	6.8	—	
Models	**Domestic**			
	Omni	7.4		4.10
	Chevette	7.2		3.00
	Pinto	6.5		3.70
	Rabbit (U.S.)[1]	7.8		2.13
	Horizon	7.5		NA
	Imports			
	Civic	8.0		1.23[2]
	Fiesta	7.9		NA
	Colt	7.8		NA
	Corolla	7.8		0.71[3]

[1]European Rabbit averages 1.42 defects per vehicle shipped.
[2]Honda average.
[3]Toyota average.

SOURCE: Aggregates—Rogers National Research, *Buyer Profiles,* 1979; models—industry sources.

with a landed cost advantage for Japanese OEMs of about $1,400.

Contrasts in Product Quality

It is, of course, true that the competitively important dimensions of auto quality are established not by experts but by the market. And many American consumers, who place a high value on quality of assembly workmanship (what the industry calls "fits and finishes"), on reliability, and on durability, seem to believe that Japanese cars are superior in each of these dimensions.

Exhibit 2, which presents industry data on assembly quality, suggests that consumer perceptions are consistent with experience. Buyers rated the imports as a group superior in quality to the domestically produced cars, while the top Japanese models were ranked first and third among the nine

EXHIBIT 3 Ratings of body and mechanical repair frequency (average = 10; maximum = 20; minimum = 0)

Make (All Models)	Body 1980	Mechanical 1980
Domestic		
Buick	9.3	9.4
Chevrolet	8.4	8.9
Dodge	10.0	10.0
Ford	7.2	9.2
Lincoln	8.1	8.4
Oldsmobile	8.4	9.3
Volkswagen	11.3	8.6
Imports		
Datsun	15.3	10.8
Honda	16.0	11.1
Mazda	17.5	12.7
Toyota	16.9	12.4
Volkswagen	11.3	10.0
Volvo	11.9	10.5

NOTE: The data cover repair frequency of mechanical systems, components, and body (structure and finish). Ratings are given in five categories: average, below average, far below average, above average, and far above average. Beginning with a score of zero for far below average, we have assigned values of 5, 10, 15, and 20 to the other categories. The sum of the scores on body and mechanical systems gives the total score.

SOURCE: *Consumer Reports* annual auto issue, April 1981.

EXHIBIT 4 Customer loyalty (percent who would buy same make/model again)

	Domestic	Imports	Total
Subcompact	77.2	91.6	81.2
Compact	74.2	91.4	72.4
Midsize	75.3	94.5	76.9
Standard	81.8	—	—
Luxury	86.6	94.6	87.2
Weighted average	78.7	91.8	—

SOURCE: Rogers National Research, *Buyer Profiles,* 1979.

rated. Japanese makes also had fewer defects after one month of service.

Similarly, subscribers to *Consumer Reports* gave high ratings to Japanese autos for reliability as measured by the incidence of repairs (see Exhibit 3). Nevertheless, what little evidence exists indicates that U.S.-built vehicles have superior corrosion protection and longer-lived components and systems.

At any rate, American automobiles enjoy much less customer loyalty than do Japanese imports. Exhibit 4, which summarizes the data on loyalty, gives perhaps the clearest evidence of the differential customer perception of product value for each dollar spent.

Lessons of Quadrant 4

Most explanations of this Japanese advantage in production costs and product quality emphasize the impact of automation, the strong support of the central government, and the pervasive influence of national culture. No doubt these factors have played an important role, but the primary sources of this advantage are found instead in the Japanese producers' mastery of Quadrant 4—that is, in their execution of a well-designed strategy based on the shrewd use of manufacturing excellence.

It may seem odd to think of manufacturing as anything other than a competitive weapon, yet the history of the U.S. auto market shows that by the late 1950s manufacturing had become a competitively neutral factor. It was not, of course, unimportant, but none of the major American producers sought great advantage through superior manufacturing performance. Except perhaps for their reliance on economies of scale, they tended to compete by means of styling, marketing, and dealership networks.

The Japanese cost and quality advantage, however, originates in painstaking strategic management of people, materials, and equipment—that is, in superior manufacturing performance. This approach, in our view, arose from the Japanese pattern of domestic competition and the need for an effective strategy to enter the U.S. market.

At that time the Japanese realized it would be foolish to compete head-on with the established domestic producers' competence in making elaborately (and annually) styled large cars with a "boulevard ride." They lacked the experience, the manufacturing base, and the resources. Instead, taking a lesson from Volkswagen's success, the Japanese concentrated on producing a reliable, high-quality, solid-performance small automobile and on backing it up with a responsible network of dealers.

Exhibit 5 outlines the seven factors most responsible for successful productivity performance and compares the Japanese practice in each with the American. On the basis of extensive discussions with U.S. industry executives, engineers, and consultants, we have ranked these factors in the order of their importance in determining the current state of the industry and have given them approximate relative weights.

Surprisingly, the hardware associated with technology—new automation and product design—proves relatively insignificant in assessing the competitive difficulties of the U.S. manufacturers, although its importance for the future of the industry grows ever larger. Despite the publicity given Japan's experimentation with industrial robots and advanced assembly plants like Nissan's Zama facility, the evidence suggests that U.S. producers have so far maintained roughly comparable levels of process equipment. However appealing they may be, Quadrant 2 explanations cannot themselves account for U.S.-Japanese differentials in manufacturing productivity.

Focus on 'Process Yield'

To the contrary, a valid explanation must start with the factor of "process yield," an amalgam of management practices and systems connected with production planning and control. This yield category reflects Japanese superiority in operating processes at high levels of efficiency and output over long periods of time. Although certain engineering considerations (machine cycles, plant layouts, and the like) are significant here, the Japanese advantage has far more to do with the interaction of materials control systems, maintenance practices, and employee involvement. Exhibit 6 attempts to make this interaction clear.

At the heart of the Japanese manufacturing system is the concept of "just in time" production. Often called *Kan-ban* (after the cards or tickets used to trigger production), the system is designed so that materials, parts, and components are produced or delivered just before they are needed. Tight coupling of the manufacturing stages reduces the need for work-in-process inventory. This reduction helps expose any waste of time or materials, use of defective parts, or improper operation of equipment.[2]

Furthermore, because the system will not work if frequent or lengthy breakdowns occur, it creates inescapable pressure for maximizing uptime and minimizing defects. This pressure, in turn, supports a vigorous maintenance program. Most Japanese plants operate with only two shifts, which allows for thorough servicing of equipment during nonproductive time and results in a much lower rate of machine breakdown and failure than in the United States.

Pressure for elimination of defects makes itself felt not in maintenance schedules but in the relationships of producers with suppliers and in work practices on the line. Just-in-time production does not permit extensive inspection of incoming parts. Suppliers must, therefore, maintain consistently high levels of quality, and workers must have the authority to stop operations if they spot defects or other production problems.

Worker-initiated line stoppages are central to the concept of *Jidoka* (making a just-surfaced problem visible to everyone by bringing operations to

EXHIBIT 5 Seven factors affecting productivity: comparison of technology, management, and organization

Factor (with Ranking and Relative Weights)	Definition	Comparative Practice (Japan Relative to United States)
Process Systems		
Process Yield 1 (40%)	Output rate variations in conventional manufacturing lines; good parts per hour from a line, press, work group, or process line. Key determinants are machine cycle times, system uptime and reliability, affected by materials control methods, maintenance practices, and operating patterns.	Production-materials control minimizes inventory, reduces scrap, exposes problems. Line stops highlight problems and help eliminate defects. Operators perform routine maintenance; scheduling of two shifts instead of three leaves time for better maintenance.
Quality Systems 5 (9%)	Series of controls and inspection plans to ensure that products are built to specifications.	Japanese use fewer inspectors. Some authority and responsibility are vested in production worker and supervisor; good relationship with supplier and very high standards lead to less incoming inspection.
Technology		
Process Automation 4 (10%)	Introduction and adaptation of advanced, state-of-the-art manufacturing equipment.	Overall, state of technology is comparable. Japanese use more robots; their stamping facilities appear somewhat more automated than average U.S. facilities.
Product Design 6 (7%)	Differences in the way the car is designed for a given market segment; aspects affecting productivity: tolerances, number of parts, fastening methods, etc.	Japanese have more experience in small car production and have emphasized design for manufacturability (i.e., productivity and quality). Newer U.S. models (Escort, GM J-car) are first models with design/manufacturing specifications comparable to Japanese.
Work Force Management		
Absenteeism 3 (12%)	All employee time away from the workplace, including excused, unexcused, medical, personal, contractual, and other reasons.	Levels of contractual time off are comparable; unexcused absences are much higher in United States.
Job Structure 2 (18%)	Tasks and responsibilities included in job definitions.	Japanese practice is to create jobs with more breadth (more tasks or skill per job) and depth (more involvement in planning and control of operations); labor classifications are broader; regular production workers perform more skilled tasks; management layers are fewer.
Work Pace 7 (4%)	Speed at which operators perform tasks.	Evidence is inconclusive; some lines run faster, some appear to run more slowly.

EXHIBIT 6 Determinants of process yield

| Rated machine speed total parts per hour | × | Uptime hours per year | × | 1-defect rate goods parts/total parts | = | Annual output of good parts |

a halt), which—along with Kan-ban—helps direct energy and attention to elimination of waste, discovery of problems, and conservation of resources.

It is difficult, of course, to separate the effects of Kanban-Jidoka on process yield from the effects of, say, job structure and quality systems—factors given a somewhat lower ranking by the experts we consulted (see Exhibit 5). It is also difficult to separate them from the benefits of having a loyal work force (Japanese factories have little unexcused absenteeism). Taken together, these aspects of work force management clearly account for much of the Japanese advantage in production.

It is sometimes argued, by the way, that the union-management relationship in the United States helps explain the superior Japanese performance in productivity and product quality. There is no doubt that the industrial relations system in the U.S. auto industry is a critical element in its performance. Nor is there any doubt that many aspects of that system do not square with the new facts of competitive life. Yet to lay these problems at the door of the union—and only there—is misleading.

Employment contracts and collective bargaining relationships do not just happen. Indeed, a contract provision that a company today finds dysfunctional often was initiated by management some time in the past. Moreover, the production philosophy embodied in a contract may have had its origins in the very early days of the industry, long before unionization. Finally, many of the systems and practices that inhibit performance have little to do with a collective bargaining agreement.

Superior manufacturing performance, the key to the Japanese producers' competitive success, is therefore not the fruit of government policy, technical hardware, or national culture (Quadrants 1, 2, and 3). Instead it derives simply from the way peo-ple and operations are organized and managed (Quadrant 4).

Technological Renewal

Having looked at causes, we now turn our attention to cures. In a time of expensive energy, by their success in the marketplace Japanese producers have rekindled interest in the automobile—especially the small, fuel-efficient automobile—as a product and thus have opened the way for technology to become the relevant basis of competition in the American market. As one General Motors executive remarked, "We took a look at the Honda Accord and we knew that the game had changed."

But does the American auto industry—or, for that matter, do government bureaucrats, lenders, and suppliers—really understand that the game has changed? Our investigation indicates that it has not—yet. We often hear two interpretations of the current crisis, both of them deeply flawed. By extension, both of these interpretations can apply to other sectors of the U.S. industrial economy.

Misperceptions of Causes

The first of these interpretations, which we call "the natural consequences of maturity," holds that what has happened is the natural consequence of life cycle processes operating internationally on mature industrial sectors. Once an industry reaches the point where its production process has been embodied in equipment available for purchase—that is, once its mode of production is stable and well known—the location of factories becomes a simple matter of exploiting geographic advantages in the relative costs of production. In this view, it makes perfect sense to move these facilities out of the United States as lower cost opportunities become available elsewhere.

Many economists argue that rather than coming to the aid of threatened industries, government and management should follow the path of least resistance, so to speak, and let the life cycle work its will. They recommend a policy not of intervention but, in the phrase of Edward M. Graham, of "positive adjustment." "Government should not," he writes, "protect or subsidize industries that are threatened by imports or [are otherwise] noncompetitive internationally, but should take concrete steps to encourage the transfer of resources from less into more competitive industries."[3]

The question of who is sufficiently infallible to be entrusted with the nasty job of picking winners and losers is, of course, conveniently left unanswered. The evidence to date suggests that no one is.

The second line of interpretation, which we call "transient economic misfortune," is a considerably more optimistic point of view. It holds that the present difficulties with automobiles are temporary, the result of rapid changes in oil prices and consumer preferences. Cost or quality is not the problem, but inappropriate capacity: too many facilities for building big cars.

The forces needed to right the competitive balance are even now locked into place, their happy result merely a matter of time and of bringing the needed capacity on line. Understandably, this view of things appealed strongly to many in the Carter administration, who could use it to rationalize a firm policy of doing nothing.

Both of these interpretive schemes are inadequate—not only because they ignore differences in Quadrant 4 management but also because they count on future stability in technology. Adherents of the maturity thesis assume an irreversible tendency of products to become standardized—that is, technologically stable over time. Adherents of the misfortune thesis, assuming that all outstanding technological problems have been solved, see the industry as needing only to bring the requisite capacity on line to recapture its competitive standing.

Both groups of adherents argue from a set of familiar but outdated assumptions about the relation of technology to industrial development. Looking back on the years since World War II as a period of competition in autos based mainly on economies of scale, styling, and service networks, they persist in viewing the car manufacturers as constituting a typical mature industry, in which any innovation is incremental, never radical, and is thus—in marketing terms—virtually invisible.

Fluidity Versus Stability

Times have changed. Environmental concerns and the escalating price of oil have combined since the oil shock of 1979 to change the structure of market demand fundamentally. Technological innovation—in its radical as well as its incremental forms—again has vital competitive significance.

Changes in product technology have become at once more rapid and more extreme. Unlike most of the postwar period, recent technical advances have spawned a marked diversity in available systems and components. In engines alone, the once dominant V-8 has been joined by engines with four, five, and six cylinders, diesel engines, rotary engines, and engines with turbocharging and computer feedback control.

Moreover, these kinds of product innovation are increasingly radical in their effects on production processes. We have moved from a period in which product innovation focused on the refinement and extension of existing concepts to a period in which completely new concepts are developed and introduced. And this transition from a time of little change in production systems to a time of great turbulence in equipment, processes, skills, and organization is only beginning.

If our assessment is right, this shift in the nature of innovation will have far-reaching implications for the structure of the industry, the strategic decisions of companies, and the character of international trade. The supposedly mature auto industry now has the opportunity to embark on a technology-based process of rejuvenation in which the industry could recover the open-ended dynamics of its youth when competitive advantage was based largely on the ability to innovate.

Research has shown that manufacturing processes, no less than the products turned out, go through a life cycle evolution. As products evolve from low-volume, unstandardized, one-of-a-kind items toward high-volume, standardized, commoditylike items, the associated processes likewise evolve from individual job-shop production toward continuous-flow production. In other words, a product-process configuration, or productive unit that is initially fluid (relatively inefficient, flexible, and open to radical change), gradually becomes stable (relatively efficient, inflexible, and open only to incremental change).

This seemingly inexorable movement toward technological stability has long been the fate of the auto industry. Economies of scale on massive production lines have for more than a generation dictated the search for ever-greater product standardization and more streamlined production. Radical change in the underlying technology of either became competitively dysfunctional; the production unit was too finely tuned to wring out the last increment of marginal cost reduction—and its management too focused on organizational coordination and control—to allow the entrepreneurially fertile disruptions caused by radically new technology.[4]

The new industrial competition, however, has dated this older logic by rewarding the ability to compete on technological grounds. It has precipitated a technological ferment, which has in turn been supported by the market's post-1979 willingness to pay a premium for vehicles boasting new technology.

Consider, for example, the rapid market adoption of General Motors' X-bodies with their transaxle and transverse mounted engines; the popularity of enhanced four-cylinder engines like Ford's compound-valve hemispherical head; or the appeal of such fuel-saving materials as graphite fibers, dual-phased steel, and advanced plastics. As a result, the industry has begun to revitalize itself in a movement back to a more fluid process-product configuration in the companies and a more lively technology-based competition among them.

Technology-Driven Strategies

Three factors are the prime elements in the renewal of the auto industry: (1) an increasing premium in the marketplace on innovation, (2) a growing diversity in the technology of components and production processes, and (3) an increasingly radical effect of factors 1 and 2 on long-established

configurations in the productive unit as a whole. These developments, in turn, have begun to define the structure and competitive dynamics of the industry in the years ahead—and the corporate strategies best suited to both.

The conventional wisdom about industry structure and strategy accepts an implicit equation between concentration and maturity. When technology-based competition heats up, this logic runs, industry concentration loosens. In such a case, car manufacturers will know how to adjust their strategies accordingly.

To be sure, in a capital-intensive industry with great economies of scale, a period of ferment in product technology often allows manufacturers to offer an increasing variety of products at or below the cost of the old product mix. Especially when the production technology is well understood and easily procurable (in the form of equipment or human skills), companies on the fringe of the industry and fresh entrants can identify and exploit new market niches. Technological activity, market growth, and industry deconcentration usually go hand in hand.

When, however, the ferment in product technology is so extreme that it causes fundamental alterations in process technology, the same degree of activity may have very different results. In this case the immediate effect of a process-linked industry renewal may well be to *increase* the degree and the stability of concentration—that is, as many believe, to push industry structure apparently in the direction of *greater* maturity.

Where these observers go wrong is in failing to distinguish concentration from maturity or, said another way, in assuming that all evidence of frozen or rising concentration is evidence of movement toward maturity. This may, but need not, be the case.

In the auto field, for example, some corporate responses to the prospect of radical process innovation probably will take the industry farther along the road to maturity. Because truly radical product changes are still some years off and because commitments to existing process technology are large (especially in the standard model segment), it is reasonable to expect producers with experience in the older technologies to defend their positions through technical alterations that reduce costs or improve performance but do not make their processes obsolete.

Such a strategy requires the high volumes necessary for scale economies. As a result, the strategy may help concentrate production—either through greater use of joint ventures or, if the scale effects are great enough, through mergers and like forms of mature industry consolidation.

Other corporate responses to process-linked renewal may have the opposite effect. Major innovations in products that are linked to innovations in process technology often permit drastic reductions in production costs or improvements in performance, thus making possible the higher volumes necessary to expand market share. These innovations, however, usually involve large capital outlays as well as development of hard-to-acquire skills on the part of workers and management. So they require large increases in volume to offset the greater investment. As a result, only the leading producers may be able to profit from the process innovations and thus, temporarily at least, enhance their market share and reinforce industry concentration.

Though this pattern of concentration may appear identical to the one we have described, noth-

Appendix: The Japanese Cost Advantage

EXHIBIT 7 Calculation of U.S. and Japanese labor costs for a subcompact vehicle

	1 Share in OEM Manufacturing Costs	2 Average OEM Hours Per Vehicle	3 Estimated OEM Employee Cost Per Hour	4 Estimated Cost Per Vehicle	5 Labor Content	6 [4 × 5] Labor Cost Per Vehicle	7 [6 × .575] U.S.–Japan Difference
OEM Labor							
Hourly	.24	65	$18	$1,170	100%	$1,170	$ 673
Salaried	.08	15	21	315	100	315	181
Purchased Components	.39	NA	NA	1,901	66	1,255	721
Purchased Materials	.14	NA	NA	683	25	171	98
Total	—	—	—	$4,875	NA	$2,911	$1,673

NOTES: OEM hourly labor is defined as total nonexempt and includes direct and indirect production workers. The calculations assume an exchange rate of 218 yen per dollar. The method of calculation and sources of data are as follows:

Column 1 contains estimates of the share of total manufacturing cost accounted for by direct and indirect production labor (at the OEM level), purchased components, and materials. These estimates do not reflect the experience of any one company but approximate an industry average. They are based on data prepared for the National Research Council's Committee on Motor Vehicle Emissions as well as on discussions with industry sources. The latter have also provided us with the data in columns 2, 3, and 5.

We made the calculation of U.S.–Japan cost differences in three steps. We first used the data in columns 2 and 3 to get an OEM labor cost per vehicle of $1,170, then extrapolated using the cost shares (column 1) to arrive at a total manufactured cost and the cost of purchased components and materials (column 4). We next multiplied the cost per vehicle in column 4 by an estimate of the labor content to the three categories presented in column 5. The data imply, for example, that $1,255 of the $1,901 cost of components is labor cost. Finally, we calculated the Japan–U.S. labor cost gap by multiplying the U.S. data in column 6 by 0.575, the adjustment factor derived from our estimate of the Japan-to-U.S. unit labor cost ratio.* Thus column 7 provides an estimate of the difference in the cost of producing a subcompact vehicle in the United States and Japan due to differences in unit labor costs, not only at the OEM level but also at the supplier level.

*Let C(US) and C(J) indicate unit labor costs in the United States and Japan. We estimate C(J)/C(US) − 425. We want to know C(US) (CJ). Column 6 gives us C(US). Thus, $C(US) - C(J) = \left(1 - \frac{C(J)}{C(US)}\right) \times$ column 6; this result is in column 7.

EXHIBIT 8 Ford and Toyo Kogyo's estimated per-vehicle employee costs in 1979

	Ford	Toyo Kogyo
Domestic Car and Truck Production[1] (in millions)	3.163	0.983
Total Domestic Employment[2]		
Automotive	219,599	24,318
Nonautomotive	19,876	2,490
Total Domestic Employee Hours[3]		
Automotive in millions	355.75	46.20
Total Employee Cost[4]		
Automotive in millions	$7,794.50	$482.20
Employee hours per vehicle	112.5	47.0
Employee cost per vehicle	$2,464	$491

[1]Ford figure excludes 65,000 imported vehicles; Toyo Kogyo figure is adjusted for production of knock-down assembly kits.

[2]Data on automotive employment and costs were obtained by assuming that the ratio of automotive employment to total employment was the same as the ratio of sales. The same assumption was made to obtain Ford employment costs.

[3]Ford hours were determined by assuming that each employee worked 1,620 hours per year; Toyo Kogyo hours assume 1,900 hours. These adjustments reflect vacations, holidays, leaves, and absences.

[4]Data include salaries, wages, and fringe benefits. Toyo Kogyo compensation data were derived by updating a 1976 figure using compensation growth rates at Toyota. An exchange rate of 218 yen/$ (1979 average) was used to convert yen.

EXHIBIT 9 Product mix adjustment

	Ford	Toyo Kogyo
1. Ratio of Car to Total Vehicle Production	0.645	0.652
2. Production Shares by Size		
Small	0.11	0.83
Medium	0.68	0.17
Large	0.21	—
3. Relative Manufacturing Cost by Size		
Small	1.00	NA
Medium	1.35	NA
Large	1.71	NA
4. Weighted Average of Relative Manufacturing Cost (small = 1.00)	1.38	1.06
5. Production of Toyo Kogyo Mix at Ford Level of Integration		
Employee cost per vehicle	$1,893	$589
Employee hours per vehicle	87	56

NOTES: Line 2 for Ford assumes that only Pinto and Bobcat models are small; Mustang and Capri sales were placed in the medium category.

Line 5 for Ford is obtained by multiplying lines 6 and 7 in *Exhibit 8* by (1.06/1.38).

Table B uses the data on manufacturing costs by vehicle size developed for the Committee on Motor Vehicle Emissions of the National Research Council in 1974. We derived estimates of the cost to Ford of producing the Toyo Kogyo mix by first computing a weighted average of the relative manufacturing cost indices with Ford's 1979 production shares by size as weights. The ratio of the comparable Toyo Kogyo weighted average (1.06) to the Ford weighted average (1.38) was used to adjust both costs and productivity as a means of estimating the effect of product mix on Ford's average cost and labor hours per vehicle. After these adjustments we estimate that Ford would require 87 employee hours to produce the average-size vehicle in the Toyo Kogyo product line, compared with 56 hours in the Japanese company. Labor cost per vehicle is just over $1,300 higher at Ford. These comparisons are based on the average-size vehicle at Toyo Kogyo. For a small vehicle (i.e., Pinto vs. Mazda GLC), the Ford estimate is 82 hours per vehicle, while the comparable Toyo Kogyo figure is 53; the corresponding costs per vehicle are $1,785 (Ford) and $568 (Toyo Kogyo). Even this adjustment may overstate costs and hours required to produce the Toyo Kogyo mix at Ford if the trucks and commercial vehicles produced by the two companies differ substantially.

ing could be further from the truth. Here a consolidation of the market serves to throw the industry into technological ferment that stimulates further technological competition—not to lock it into older process technology.

In time, this upheaval in process technology may even provide the competitive basis for new entrants to the field. Depending on the nature of process advances in auto production, companies in related industries (electronics, for example, or engines or energy) may find invasion of the market an attractive strategic option.[4] But even if a decade from now these new entrants have not materialized, the forces that made their participation possible will have changed the competitive structure of the industry in two fundamental ways:

Whatever its immediate tendency, industry concentration will in the long run have become far less stable than at present.

The basis of competition will have changed to reflect the now-crucial importance of technology-driven strategies.

The Challenge to Management

Once U.S. auto manufacturers understand that energy prices and internationalization of competition have altered the industry's old competitive dynamics, they have to decide how they want to compete under the new rules of the game. It may be best for them to avoid duplicating the Japanese pattern of competition. At any rate, after decades of the maturing process, the basis for competing is in flux for U.S. producers and radical rethinking about strategy—not blind imitation—is in order.

The industrial landscape in America is littered with the remains of once-successful companies that could not adapt their strategic vision to altered conditions of competition. If the automobile producers prove unequal to the new reality that confronts them, their massive, teeming plants will become the ghost towns of late twentieth century America. The same, of course, holds true for all companies, large and small, in those old-line manufacturing industries exposed to assault from abroad. Only those able to see the new industrial competition for what it is and to devise appropriate strategies for participating in it will survive.

Managers must recognize that they have entered a period of competition that requires of them a technology-driven strategy, a mastery of efficient production, and an unprecedented capacity for work force management. They cannot simply copy what others do but must find their own way. No solutions are certain, no strategies assured of success. But the nature of the challenge is clear.

Henry Ford, as Alfred P. Sloan recalled him, was a man who had had ". . . many brilliant insights in [his] earlier years, [but] seemed never to understand how completely the market had changed from the one in which he had made his name and to which he was accustomed. . . . The old master failed to master change."[5] That is still the crucial challenge—and opportunity.

Notes

1. Statement before the Subcommittee on Trade of the House Ways and Means Committee, March 18, 1980.
2. See Robert H. Hayes, "Why Japanese Factories Work," HBR July–August 1981, p. 56.
3. Edward M. Graham, "Technological Innovation and the Dynamics of the U.S. Competitive Advantage in International Trade," in *Technological Innovation for a Dynamic Economy,* edited by Christopher T. Hill and James M. Utterback (Elmsford, N.Y.: Pergamon Press, 1979), p. 152.
4. For a discussion of the evolution toward industrial maturity, see James M. Utterback and William J. Abernathy, "A Dynamic Model of Process and Product Innovation," *Omega,* vol. 3, 1975, p. 639.
5. Alfred P. Sloan, Jr., *My Years with General Motors* (Garden City, N.Y.: Doubleday, 1964), pp. 186–187.

The Rescue and Resuscitation of Chrysler

Lee A. Iacocca

When I came to Chrysler in 1979, the Michigan State Fairgrounds were jammed with thousands of unsold, unwanted, rusting Chryslers, Dodges, and Plymouths. Foreign operations were leeching the lifeblood out of the company. And worst of all, cars were coming off the assembly line with loose doors, chipped paint, and crooked moldings.

The Chrysler experience highlighted some painful realities!

The quality of our products had declined.

Work practices had shortchanged productivity.

The government had become an enemy instead of an ally.

Foreign countries that the United States had defeated in war and rebuilt in peace were beating this country in its own markets.

American managers sat on their laurels while America's lead slowly ebbed away.

Chrysler was faced with a choice. The company could go under—the suggestion of not a few; or efforts could be made to save the company, and with it the American way of doing business—with honesty, pride, ingenuity, and good old-fashioned hard work.

Six Steps to Success

Chrysler took some basic steps to turn the situation around.

First, the company reduced salaried expense dramatically, literally half the work force from about 160,000 to about 80,000. And those 80,000 are now producing a broader range of cars and trucks than they ever did before. That is the simple definition of productivity—more product, more volume, half the people. Part of the medicine was white-collar. The white-collar work force was cut

Lee A. Iacocca is Chairman, The Chrysler Corporation.

Reprinted by permission from *The Journal of Business Strategy*, Summer 1983 67–69. Copyright © 1983, Warren, Gorham & Lamont Inc., 210 South Street, Boston, Mass. All rights reserved.

in half, from 40,000 people to 21,000. Union and nonunion workers made wage and benefit sacrifices, saving $1.2 billion.

Second, the company reduced fixed costs by about $2 billion on an annual basis. Chrysler closed or consolidated twenty obsolete and outmoded plants. More important, the company modernized the remaining forty plants to make them among the most efficient and productive in the industry. This was done well before either GM or Ford got rolling. Walk down the aisle of a Chrysler plant today and you will see state-of-the-art robots and welders, computer-controlled engine and power train test stands, just-in-time inventory feeders, hospital-clean uniprime paint shops, and fully manned quality operations—all of which are the equal of anything in the world, including Japan.

Third, Chrysler simplified operations by reducing the number of different parts in its manufacturing system by one-third—from 75,000 items down to 40,000. And in the process, the company shook $1 billion out of inventory.

Fourth, Chrysler launched an all-out, deadly serious program to improve the quality of both its finished products and the components that go into them. The company worked meticulously both internally and with its suppliers, using the latest methods of preventive surveillance and statistical controls.

Fifth, Chrysler restructured its balance sheet. The company retired its U.S. bank debt by converting $1.3 billion into preferred stock and acquired some financial breathing room. The company also changed preferred into common, which further strengthened Chrysler's capital base.

Sixth, and ultimately most important, management ensured that Chrysler will be a potent force in the years to come by embarking on a five-year $6.6 billion product program—the most ambitious in its entire history.

The results of these striking steps are a matter of public record. Chrysler is now different than it was three years ago: half the size, but twice the company.

Important Strides

Chrysler cut its break-even point to *half* the level of three years ago. It used to be 2.4 million units,
now it's under 1.2 million. (This is the reason for three profitable quarters in 1982, why momentum held despite the costly Canadian strike in the fourth quarter, and for the spectacular first-quarter 1983 results.) Management will never allow this company to balloon up again, no matter how much the economy improves, no matter how successful business becomes.

The company accumulated $1 billion in cash in 1982 in the face of a terrible year in the automotive industry. (This was done by selling off the tank business, tightening bookkeeping, and employing tough management—tough cash controls, tough inventory cuts, tough production coordination. The cash cushion gives the comfort of making normal business decisions in a normal way—especially when the economy still sputters like a wet fuse.)

The company offers better long-term value. It has improved quality by one-third in the past year alone, according to in-plant audits. And the 1981 recall record is far better than General Motors' and Ford's. Chrysler lowered the cost of maintenance. That's why it can back its products better than anyone else.

Chrysler is delivering the highest-technology products in its history. It has taken the lead in front-wheel drive, with 90 percent of productive capacity so geared. Chrysler leads in engines and power trains, with a virtually indestructible 2.2-liter four-cylinder engine and the only five-speed transmission for front-wheel drive made in America. It also leads in electronics, with seek-and-scan electronically tuned radios, multifunction electronic travel computers, and the domestic industry's only talking cars. In addition, the firm leads in computer-aided design and manufacturing, with what is regarded as the most sophisticated CAD/CAM center in the entire automotive world—including Japan.

Chrysler has the best fuel economy in the industry—for the third year in a row—a fleet average of more than twenty-eight miles per gallon. That is not only ahead of the competition, it is two years ahead of federal requirements. Today, about one out of every four compact cars sold in America is a K-car; in Canada, it's one out of two (where the price of gasoline is $2 per gallon). Thanks to the K-cars, Chrysler is back into the lucrative, high-volume fleet business in a big way; sales to leasing groups jumped 60 percent in 1982. These are smart buyers, and Chrysler cars hold their value better than the competition.

Chrysler has a solid 10 percent market share of the car market and 10 percent of the truck market right now. The goal is 12 percent. The company is developing a whole new line of cars—convertibles, the new Town and Country wagon, the sports cars, the new imports, the K-car Specials, and the new small truck built by Mitsubishi. Chrysler has fought for share. Early in 1981 it introduced the interest allowance plan and increased sales. Later in 1981 the company declared war on sticker shock; it introduced its biggest volume 1982 cars at 1981 prices and moved the needle a little further. At the end of the year, the company offered rebates one more time—full factory rebates that did not depend on dealer contributions—and share went over 11 percent.

The Road Back to Profitability

Chrysler reported a genuine operating profit of $107 million in the second quarter of 1982. The first and second quarters of 1982 were the first back-to-back black quarters reported in five and a half years. Then, a $10 million operating profit in the third quarter—traditionally the most difficult quarter, even in the best and healthiest of companies, because of the plant changeovers, the shutdowns, and the retooling. In fact, as the topper, Chrysler—to the best of my knowledge—was the only full-line auto company in the world, outside of Japan, to show a real operating profit from car and truck operations in the third quarter of 1982. And the first quarter of 1983 was among the best in Chrysler's history.

Now that's a strong record of accomplishment— a fantastic turnaround when you compare where the company is with where it was. Against all odds, against the highest unemployment since 1938, against the highest interest rates ever, against a falling gross national product, against the lowest rate of new car sales in a quarter of a century, management has fulfilled its commitment to restore Chrysler as a strong competitor in the automotive marketplace and a substantial company in corporate America.

At Chrysler, management is fully prepared to do whatever is necessary to keep Chrysler on the leading edge of innovative design, production, and marketing.

One foundational pillar upon which the new Chrysler is built is the best automotive quality in the industry—and the company stands behind it with more than slogans and claims.

Over the past few years, Chrysler has developed an intensive program to upgrade quality: to reduce maintenance costs, to reduce warranty costs, to cut the number of demerits in all automobiles, to deliver to customers the kinds of cars that will compete against the best in the world.

Tremendous progress has been made. Since the beginning of the 1982 model year, Chrysler has:

Reduced the number of demerits per car by 35 percent.

Reduced warranty costs per average car by 25 percent.

Reduced repairs in the field by 21 percent.

Reduced scheduled maintenance costs to a level $20 to $200 below the competition.

Effectively removed rust as a problem by building all cars with special galvanized and precoated steels in crucial areas and by doubling the thickness of antirust primers.

Proved the durability of power trains to the point where there have been no engine or drive train recalls. Chrysler offers the best four-cylinder engines in the business today. After twenty-one months of production, K-cars were up to the recall standards of Toyota and Datsun and are superior to Escort/Linx and GM's X-cars on the basis of recalls.

Providing What the Customer Wants

Chrysler dealers report that quality is the best in our history, and our customers tell us we are delivering the best-quality products they have ever driven. The company also took an extensive consumer survey to determine how to meet the demands of today's car buyers. The results were clear: People want *more* than good quality, *more* than good fuel economy, *more* than all-around product value.

Today's customer wants a long-lasting, trouble-free car—and he wants a warranty that is at least as long as his finance contract. He wants cost-free maintenance. And he also wants cars that won't rust.

Beginning on April 11, 1982, Chrysler offered a new, three-part "5 and 50" protection plan for customers at no extra cost.

> Chrysler Corporation provides an extended five-year or 50,000-mile power train protection plan for all domestically built new Chrysler, Plymouth, and Dodge cars. (This program does not cover fleet sales.) Chrysler stands behind the performance of the entire drive train—engine, transmission, transaxles, drive axles—for the average length of time that a first owner keeps his car.

> Chrysler Corporation provides all regularly scheduled maintenance for the new cars it sells under this program for five years or 50,000 miles.

> Chrysler Corporation warrants all the external sheet metal on our automobiles against perforation from rust for five years or 50,000 miles.

With these actions, Chrysler discontinued the rebate programs then in effect. The protection plan is a direct response to the market demands of the 1980s, and a clear reflection of complete confidence in manufacturing quality. And, no Japanese company has yet matched Chrysler's 5/50!

It has become fun to be a Chrysler dealer again. Chrysler signed up about 300 new dealers in the last twelve months—tough, private, entrepreneurial businessmen. And first results look good. The 3,700 Chrysler, Plymouth and Dodge dealers saw their average return on investment increase 100%

in 1982. (Helping dealers is an integral part of the Chrysler strategy. Last fall the company pumped $700 million into Chrysler Financial through the sale of some retail receivables. That allowed the company to give dealers a couple of attractive financing programs.)

What the Future Holds

Chrysler is planning a whole series of new products, including the world's first true front-wheel-drive sports cars: the fuel-injected, turbo-charged Dodge Daytona and Chrysler Laser and the seven-passenger, thirty-mile-per-gallon "Caravans." All will use the same platform—drive train, floor plan, suspension parts—as the entire product line, thus cutting manufacturing expense and inventory carrying costs.

Chrysler is planning to spend $1.5 billion in 1983, mostly on these new products. The company will cover about half that amount through its own depreciation and amortization; the other half is going to have to come from existing cash, from operations, and from continued balance sheet squeezing. (And remember, large net operating loss carryforwards will effectively double any profits earned.)

The future for Chrysler looks bright. The company has come a long way from where it was three years ago when it set out to prove, against all odds, that Chrysler was worth saving.

The company got its financial house in order, got costs in line, cut break-even down to size, and developed an exciting array of new products. Chrysler put strong dealer organization and some tough, experienced people in Detroit in place.

Chrysler is eager to compete and is planning to outrun the best of them in the next few years.

Thornton A. Wilson and the Boeing Company

The Boeing Company was founded 68 years ago in the state of Washington under the original name of Pacific Aero Products Company. Thornton Wilson has been with the company for 41 of those years, not counting several short interruptions for advanced study. The company remains headquartered in Seattle, and many of its plants are located in the surrounding area, but its products are used around the world. In many years, foreign sales have exceeded domestic.

Boeing's major product line is its family of commercial jet airplanes extending from the relatively small 737 to the huge 747. The newest members to go into service are the 757 and 767. Recently, however, this commercial business has been declining somewhat, and at the same time military aircraft sales have increased; so too have missiles and space products. The company produces airplanes, missiles, airborne warning and control systems, spacecraft and satellite components, helicopters, computer software, hydrofoils, and is engaged in the design and management of construction projects of various kinds. At one time, Boeing also manufactured and installed rapid transit systems for cities. However, the company was unable to extend its strong product quality capability into this area, and subsequently ceased operations of this kind.

What is distinctive about Boeing and what has accounted for much of its success over the last fifteen years is its reputation for outstanding quality. Its planes are considered to be the best, safest, and most efficient available. The key to this reputation appears to be the company's excellence in the areas of engineering and design. Products are tested over and over again under all kinds of conditions before being put into service. A great variety of backup systems and tolerances are designed in so that safety is maintained. This is what has made Boeing so attractive to purchasers of commercial aircraft. The planes may be expensive, but they work, and they continue to do so over long periods with a minimum of repair.

It is not surprising that the head of such a company is an aeronautical engineer. Thornton Wilson received his undergraduate degree in that field

Thornton Wilson

Sloan fellow at Massachusetts Institute of Technology studying business subjects.

Rising steadily through the engineering ranks at Boeing, Thornton Wilson had a major impact on the development of the new B-47 swept-wing bomber. He became overall project engineer of the B-52 program during the latter design stages, and then led the proposal team that won the Minuteman intercontinental ballistic missile program for the company. He subsequently took over active management of that program as a vice-president. Next he was placed in charge of operations and planning for corporate headquarters. In 1966 he became executive vice-president and, in 1968, president. The chief executive officer title was added in 1969, and Thornton Wilson has retained it ever since, although he became chairman of the board rather than president in 1972.

The year 1969 is a key one in Boeing's history. With the advent of recession, the company's earnings slumped badly and disaster appeared imminent. Thornton Wilson replaced William Allen, a lawyer, as chief executive and immediately began slashing costs. Thousands of employees were laid off, and corporate headquarter operations were slimmed down substantially. Operating efficiency and productivity began to increase. Thornton Wilson is widely credited with saving the company during that period and with building it back to new highs of success. He has been rewarded handsomely for his efforts. His yearly compensation is among the highest in the business world, totalling over $1.2 million in 1982.

from Iowa State University after previously attending Jefferson City (Missouri) Junior College. He went to work immediately for Boeing, leaving briefly for advanced study at Iowa State and a year at the California Institute of Technology, where he earned an M.S. in aeronautical engineering. Four years later, in 1952–53, he spent another year as a

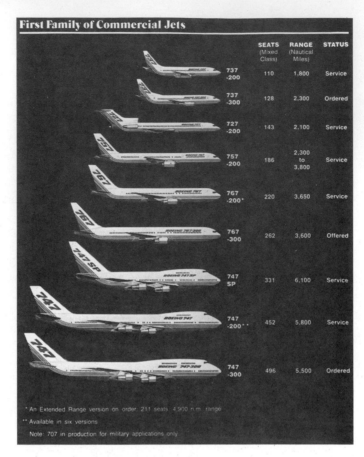

First Family of Commercial Jets

	SEATS (Mixed Class)	RANGE (Nautical Miles)	STATUS
737 -200	110	1,800	Service
737 -300	128	2,300	Ordered
727 -200	143	2,100	Service
757 -200	186	2,300 to 3,800	Service
767 -200*	220	3,650	Service
767 -300	262	3,600	Offered
747 SP	331	6,100	Service
747 -200**	452	5,800	Service
747 -300	496	5,500	Ordered

* An Extended Range version on order: 211 seats, 4,900 n.m. range

** Available in six versions

Note: 707 in production for military applications only

Boeing's major product line

The products of Boeing factories and thousands of subcontractors are joined in the 767 final assembly area.

As part of the 737-300 program, a mockup of the CFM56-3 engine and strut is used for engineering evaluation leading to detailed design.

Thornton A. Wilson and the Boeing Company

The Expanding Arena

Throughout the previous chapters we have considered research and examples extending beyond the borders of the United States into far corners of the world. Among the topics treated have been various conceptions of corporate goals in different societies, common characteristics for managerial success in world businesses, country-to-country differences in achievement motivation and entrepreneurial development, the diversity of values across cultures, similarities and differences at the national level in managers' espousal of theory X and theory Y, and cultural variations in group functioning. At the level of organizing and organizational process, attention has focused on other differences—in bargaining approaches and in receptiveness to sociotechnical systems and autonomous work groups, for instance—as well as on the influence that Japanese origins has had on the use of quality circles as an organization development approach. Also explored have been such matters as the similarities and differences across nations in decision sharing at high corporate levels and variations among cultures in their ethical precepts.

What these discussions indicate is that there are certain areas in which major variations are found around the world, but that diversity is not everywhere; there are similarities also—among certain characteristics needed to manage successfully in hierarchic organizations in different countries, for instance. The matter of the extent of national and cultural variations is given further attention in this final chapter. The chapter helps to provide a perspective on the kinds of problems that the multinational corporations face as they operate in different parts of the world, and on the approaches that they use in conducting their affairs. At least for United States-based companies, this expansion of the business arena is the most significant development of the past few decades. It has seen many U.S. firms go out into new markets around the world, and at the same time it has seen multinationals based in other countries move into the lucrative U.S. markets, creating types of competition that never existed before.

This latter phenomenon is portrayed best by the expansionist thrust of Japanese industry. New approaches have been brought to bear in solving management problems that often have placed U.S. firms on the defensive in recent years. Some contend that we must learn from the Japanese, just as they once learned from us, if the United States' economic system is to prosper. The issues are complex, but one thing is certain. The international perspective will be a major, if not *the* most important, influence on management for some years to come.

CHAPTER 18

Management in International Perspective

CHAPTER OUTLINE

*Dow Chemical Company's International
    Development Process*
National and Cultural Variations
Educational Characteristics
Sociological Characteristics
    The IBM Research
    The Influence of Industrialization
Political and Legal Characteristics
Economic Characteristics

Multinational Corporations
Organizing Multinational Operations
Independence of Decision Making
Strategies for Dealing with National Contexts
    Adaptive Responses
    Cultural Island Strategies
    National and Cultural Change

The Japanese
Evidence of Success
Alternative Interpretations
    Theories A, J, and Z
    Human Resources Management
Research Studies of the Japanese
    Pulling Together Previously Noted Findings
    New Evidence
The Transferability Question

OBJECTIVES

To explain how a wide range of factors may vary around the world and exert different influences on company operations.

To describe how multinationals operate and the structures, processes, and strategies they use.

To provide an understanding of the Japanese approach to management, the reasons for its success, and its relevance for American business.

DOW CHEMICAL COMPANY'S INTERNATIONAL DEVELOPMENT PROCESS[1]

In 1979 Zoltan Merszei, who was born and raised in Hungary, resigned as chief executive of Dow Chemical, the largest U.S. Chemical Company in terms of profits and second largest in terms of sales. Merszei went on to become president of Occidental Petroleum and was replaced at Dow by Paul Oreffice, who was born in Italy. Although Oreffice moved to the United States when he was twelve years old, he spent years of work in Europe and Latin America before becoming Dow's chief executive.

Some observers would argue that this placement of foreign-born persons at the helm of the firm was an indication of the multinationalization process. For example, a leading management authority, Peter Drucker, stated that a really multinational firm "demands of its management people that they think and act as international businessmen in a world in which national passions are as strong as ever." A firm whose top management includes persons from various countries is presumably less likely to place the interests of one country above those of others and will presumably have a more world-wide outlook.

Whether or not nationality or place of birth is sufficient to indicate a world-wide outlook is, of course, debatable. The experience of working abroad under some very different environmental conditions is, however, very useful for grasping some of the problems that are not as prevalent in a purely domestic context. Paul Oreffice described his foreign experience at Dow as follows:

> I would never have risen as far as I have in Dow if it hadn't been for my foreign experience. What I learned in Brazil in the 1960s influenced and advanced my career. Even though my training was technical, my job was about 70 percent a financial job, because that's what management in a high-inflation country is. The only way we could get dollars to import goods from the U.S. was to go to the exchange and bid on how many cruzieros we would pay per dollar for imported goods. It was so important to the job that every Tuesday morning I personally went to the exchange in Sao Paulo and stood there with my

broker. I learned the maintenance of margins or replacement cost pricing which is the only way you can make sufficient profit to buy and build more plants.

That Dow's chief executive had progressed through the ranks with considerable foreign experience was itself an indication of the firm's attitude that international operations would be an integral part of Dow's total commitment. Dow's dependence on foreign activities had increased very rapidly, and, in order to effect that growth, it had been necessary to gain a commitment to international business from a broad spectrum of managers. The actual growth and commitment are illustrated by the fact that until 1954, Dow's only foreign subsidiary was in Canada. The attitude in the late 1950s was expressed by a company historian as follows:

> As for the overseas operations, a majority of the veterans regarded them as a sideline. The foreign market was all right as a place for getting rid of surplus products, but the only truly promising market was in the United States. They questioned the idea of the company becoming too deeply involved in countries whose politics, language, culture, monetary controls and ways of doing business were strange to them.

Although some of the younger managers in Dow did not share this domestic attitude, it was necessary to take some dramatic steps to gain the commitment of the majority of the management ranks. One method employed by the company's president in 1958 was to give international responsibilities to individuals who were widely perceived to be destined for top-level positions in the firm. C. B. Branch, who was managing Dow's fastest-growing department, was appointed head of foreign operations. Herbert "Ted" Dow Doan, who at age thirty-one was already a member of the board of directors, went to Europe on a fact-finding mission. (Ted Doan's father and grandfather were both Dow presidents.) Both Branch and Doan went on quickly to become presidents of Dow; thus the importance of international operations was readily apparent to any manager in the company.

By 1964 Dow's foreign sales accounted for about 20 percent of its total. By 1980 the portion was slightly over 48 percent, and Dow had plants and holdings in twenty-nine foreign countries. Dow had a large cadre of middle- and upper-level managers with foreign work experience. While most of this experience was represented by Americans who had assignments in Europe, there were increasing numbers with experience in more remote areas. The firm estimated, for example, that about fifty senior executives had been moved into Saudi Arabia and Kuwait.

The internationalization of management in U.S.-based companies is clearly evident in the Dow Chemical case. Rotation through positions abroad for purposes of broadening and development is now common practice in many firms. At the same time, foreign nationals come to the United States, assigned here by multinationals around the world as well as transferred here by U.S. multinationals. The managerial mix thus takes on a new cultural character closely related to changing markets, changing manufacturing locations, and new developments of a logistical and communications nature. In short, the world of business and management has grown much smaller quite rapidly. It is important to know how this has happened and what it means for an understanding of management.

NATIONAL AND CULTURAL VARIATIONS

It should be recognized at the outset that cultures are not limited to nations, geographical areas, or populations characterized by certain religious beliefs. Companies, especially multinationals, can develop their own cultures (including values, beliefs, rituals, symbols, etc.), and these company cultures may well compete with cultures of the more traditional types.[2] However, these unique company cultures are little known at present, and from an international perspective, they are of lesser importance.

Exhibit 18.1 sets forth a model, which has received research support, that demonstrates how cultural factors act as constraints on management decisions, and how they ultimately influence corporate outcomes. The constraint process is not unlike that considered in chapter 14 for personnel/human resources management. The model is used in this chapter to consider sources of national and cultural variation that make a difference in company operations.

Educational Characteristics

Educational attainment varies sharply among nations and introduces a constraint in the form of human resource availability on what it is possible for companies to do. This constraint can be substantial in the developing countries where illiteracy rates are high and educational levels consistently low. The educational attainments of a population are a major independent factor contributing to economic development.[3] However, it is not just the level of education that matters. It is also important that the education relate to the needs of business enterprises.

Thus for many years, higher education in Great Britain and in Europe generally tended to focus heavily on the arts, literature, and other subjects intended to produce a "well-rounded," educated person. As a result, people who subsequently became business managers rarely had had any opportunity to acquire

EXHIBIT 18.1 Model of established relationships between culture-based processes and organizational outcomes

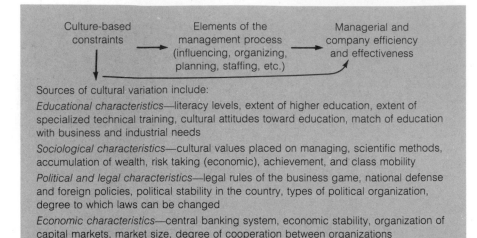

Culture-based constraints → Elements of the management process (influencing, organizing, planning, staffing, etc.) → Managerial and company efficiency and effectiveness

Sources of cultural variation include:

Educational characteristics—literacy levels, extent of higher education, extent of specialized technical training, cultural attitudes toward education, match of education with business and industrial needs

Sociological characteristics—cultural values placed on managing, scientific methods, accumulation of wealth, risk taking (economic), achievement, and class mobility

Political and legal characteristics—legal rules of the business game, national defense and foreign policies, political stability in the country, types of political organization, degree to which laws can be changed

Economic characteristics—central banking system, economic stability, organization of capital markets, market size, degree of cooperation between organizations (companies, unions, government, etc.)

SOURCE: Adapted from Richard N. Farmer and Barry M. Richman, "A Model for Research in Comparative Management," *California Management Review* (Winter 1964); and Lane Kelley and Reginald Worthley, "The Role of Culture in Comparative Management: A Cross-Cultural Perspective," *Academy of Management Journal* (March 1981).

business knowledge, and the companies involved suffered accordingly. For many years, American consulting firms operated extensively in Europe to fill this knowledge gap. Individuals preparing for managerial careers often obtained their business educations in the United States. Now professional schools have sprung up in many countries, especially in Europe, and the problem is much less acute.

Sociological Characteristics

Cultural values as they are held by members of a society can, much like educational characteristics, act as constraints on human resource availability. If the society does not value hard work or innovation, then it will be very difficult to accumulate a labor force that holds these values in high regard. At the same time, cultural values held external to the firm, regarding such matters as economic competition and the accumulation of wealth, for instance, can have a strong influence on what the firm is allowed to do, or what it can do without facing major conflicts. In either case, variations in cultural values can play a major role in how companies operate.

The IBM Research An important study of values around the world has been conducted with employees of IBM who were natives of about forty different countries. The research establishes without question that major national differences exist when company culture is held constant and thus cannot be a factor in the results. Furthermore, it is possible to establish clear groupings of countries into culture clusters containing nations with similar values, as noted in Exhibit 18.2. Values associated with greater economic development, and thus with a more favorable business climate, are: little emphasis on hierarchy, little

EXHIBIT 18.2 Culture clusters around the world

Culture Cluster	Characteristic Value Pattern
More developed Latin (Belgium, France, French-speaking Switzerland, Spain, Italy, Argentina, Brazil)	Strong emphasis on hierarchy Strong emphasis on avoiding risks Above average individualism Average emphasis on masculine behavior
Less developed Latin (Portugal, Colombia, Chile, Peru, Venezuela, Mexico)	Strong emphasis on hierarchy Strong emphasis on avoiding risks Little individualism No particular pattern of emphasis on masculine or feminine behavior
More developed Asian (Japan)	Average emphasis on hierarchy Strong emphasis on avoiding risks Average individualism Strong emphasis on masculine behavior
Less developed Asian (India, Pakistan, Thailand, Hong Kong, Taiwan, Singapore, Phillipines)	Strong emphasis on hierarchy Below average emphasis on avoiding risks Little individualism Average emphasis on masculine behavior
Near Eastern (Yugoslavia, Greece, Iran, Turkey)	Strong emphasis on hierarchy Strong emphasis on avoiding risks Little individualism Average emphasis on masculine behavior
Germanic (Germany, German-speaking Switzerland, Austria, Israel)	Little emphasis on hierarchy Above average emphasis on avoiding risks Average individualism Above average emphasis on masculine behavior
Anglo (USA, Canada, Great Britain, Ireland, Australia, New Zealand, South Africa)	Below average emphasis on hierarchy Below average emphasis on avoiding risks Strong individualism Strong emphasis on masculine behavior
Nordic (Sweden, Norway, Finland, Denmark, the Netherlands)	Little emphasis on hierarchy Below average emphasis on avoiding risks Above average individualism Emphasis on feminine behavior

Adapted from Geert Hofstede, *Culture's Consequences: International Differences in Work-Related Values* (Beverly Hills, Calif.: Sage, 1980): 336.

emphasis on avoiding risks (and thus more risk taking), and strong individualism. Emphases related to masculine or feminine behavior, and thus the degree of social orientation, do not show an association with economic factors one way or the other. A comparison of the more and less economically developed culture clusters in Exhibit 18.2 indicates that substantial differences in values are present.

The Influence of Industrialization A widely held hypothesis among students of international relations is that, with increasing industrialization, societies become more alike—a managerial or business culture takes over.[4] The IBM research demonstrates that this process is far from complete, There are major value differences among the highly industrialized nations—between Great Britain and Sweden, for instance.

Yet the idea of some type of *convergence* toward a single industrialized norm finds some support also. The convergence is only partial, and it appears to be more pronounced in certain areas, such as the sources of job satisfaction and attitudes toward the control of one's own destiny, than in others.[5] But to a degree at least, business development appears to bring about changes in the cultures where it occurs. Thus companies are not entirely constrained by the cultures in which they find themselves. They may also exert some influence on those cultures, even though the time span for these effects to take hold may be long.

Political and Legal Characteristics

Probably the most pronounced differences of a political nature, insofar as business operations are concerned, relate to whether the country is a democracy, communist, or socialist. Receptiveness to free enterprise can vary substantially with the political system. Political stability is also important. Companies are very wary of situations in which a sudden change in governments could result in expropriation and nationalization of company assets located in the country. They tend to avoid major investments in such countries. In the recent past it has been impossible to carry on business as usual in Lebanon because of the political instability there. Atlantic-Richfield and other oil companies generally avoided drilling for oil in Syria because they feared their facilities would be taken over by the government.

The laws discussed in chapter 14 affecting personnel and labor relations decisions are laws of the United States. Other countries have very different laws dealing with the same topics, some of which make it easier to conduct business and some, more difficult. An example of a very different legal context for union–management relations is provided by the *codetermination* laws in Europe.[6] These laws exist in Austria, Denmark, the Netherlands, Norway, Sweden, and Germany. They all require some degree of employee (union) representation in the membership of the senior corporate boards, which are in many respects comparable to boards of directors in this country. In Germany this legally required representation amounts to 50 percent. The law applies to multinationals operating in that country as well as German-based firms. It has had a profound impact not only on personnel/human resources decisions, but also on a broad range of strategic decisions.

Economic Characteristics

Among economic factors that may vary around the world and have a major impact on company behavior, monetary and banking considerations loom large, and so too do the nature and sizes of product markets. If there is very little accumulated wealth in a country, many types of products will lack markets. This is one reason that companies have been inclined to avoid entering into many of the developing countries. If they do enter such countries, they do so with very different strategies than where market conditions are more favorable.

In some parts of the world there is a strong desire to bring multinational corporations in. Within the United States at the present, many state governments are actively trying to attract foreign firms in order to provide jobs and increase tax revenues. Every effort is made to create a favorable economic climate and minimize sources of friction between foreign companies and organizations in the United States. In other parts of the world, cooperation involving government and other institutions with entering firms is minimal at best. The economic climate is strongly favorable to domestic companies, and foreign firms are not welcome because they introduce undesired competition. This has been true of a number of nations in South America. Obviously, the results for multinational corporations are very different under the two sets of circumstances.

MULTINATIONAL CORPORATIONS

Movement into the markets of other countries from a base in one country, such as the United States, can take a number of forms. What varies is the degree of commitment to the foreign investment. This is depicted in Exhibit 18.3. In some cases, the pattern shown may represent a developmental transition. However, this

EXHIBIT 18.3   Degrees of commitment to an international status

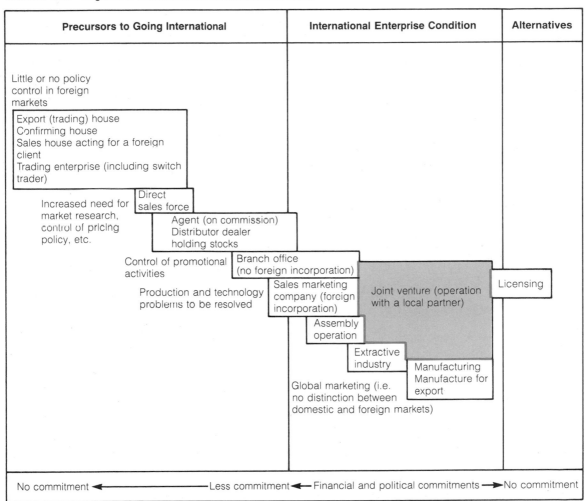

NOTE: ////// indicate overlapping situations.

Adapted from James M. Livingstone, *The International Enterprise* (New York: Wiley, 1975): 57.

need not be the case. Some companies never move beyond the early "precursors" stage. Some move directly to the licensing alternative in conjunction with a local partner. By whatever route, many achieve some aspect of the "international enterprise condition" and stay at that point. These are the situations given primary attention here.

Organizing Multinational Operations

Just as companies vary in their degree of commitment to international activities, they also vary in the structures they develop for this purpose.[7] Exhibit 18.4 portrays some of the alternatives. In part A of the exhibit, international operations are handled out of the marketing function. In part B, in which the company has diversified product lines and has developed product divisions, the export manager reports to the president and handles international marketing for all product divisions. In both of these cases, commitment to an international status tends to be low.

EXHIBIT 18.4 Alternative methods of structuring international operations

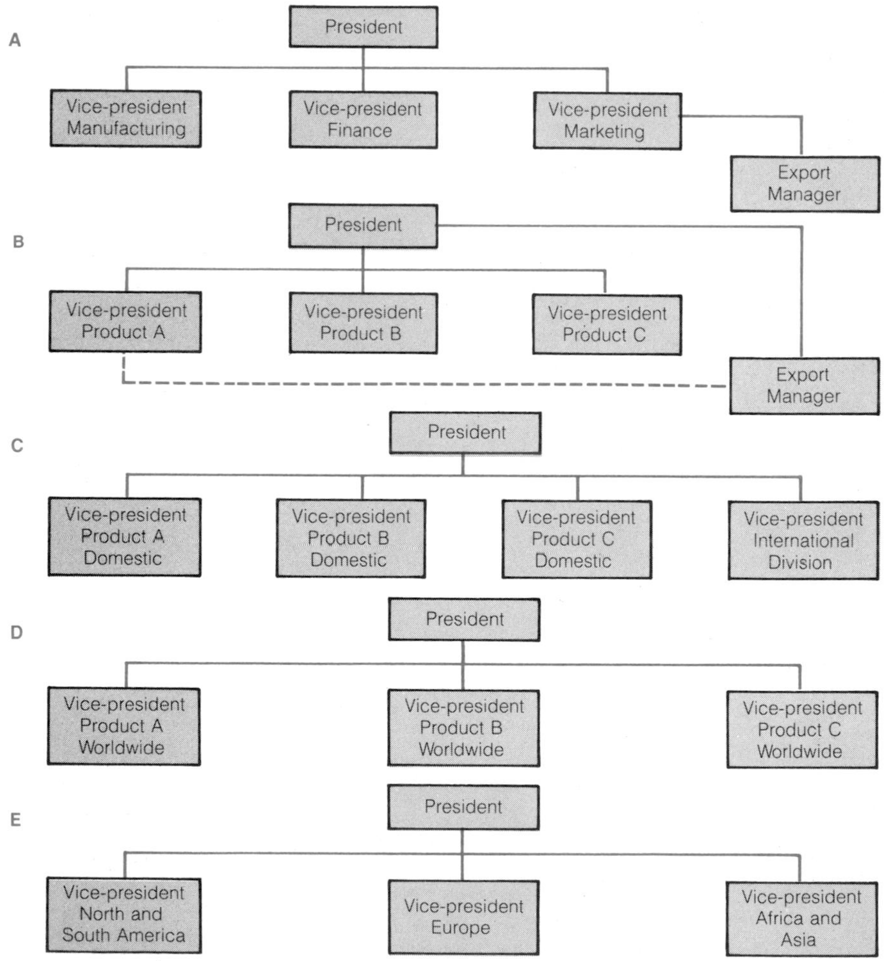

In part C of Exhibit 18.4, commitment is much more pronounced. A full-scale international division is created that is devoted not just to marketing, but to other functions as well. Manufacturing, for instance, may occur outside the domestic country of origin and be handled by this division. Still, international operations are not fully integrated with domestic, and they stand equal only to a single product group. In parts D and E, international and domestic operations become fully integrated. Many of these companies derive more of their earnings from international sales than domestic sales; thus international operations tend actually to dominate. The structure of part D would be characteristic where there is considerable diversification of products, while part E would be more likely to be used with a single product line or one dominant product.

Independence of Decision Making

A major consideration for multinational corporations is how much independence to grant to the various foreign subsidiaries. In part this is influenced by the laws of the various countries. Codetermination laws, for instance, tend to force a greater amount of independence. However, there is still a great deal of variation in this regard from company to company, and much of this variation relates to factors within the company itself.[8] Foreign operations tend to have greater independence if the stock of the subsidiary is owned to a substantial degree in the local country rather than in the parent country, if the subsidiary serves primarily the local market rather than markets outside the country, if the multinational operates in relatively few foreign countries, and if the subsidiary's operations and products are somewhat different from those of other subsidiaries and the parent so that there is less need for interchange with them.

Exhibit 18.5 provides further evidence of the great variation in degree of subsidiary independence and relates this to different functional areas of the business. Independence is greatest for marketing decisions, and production decisions show a very similar pattern. Independence is also great for purchasing decisions, but the pattern is quite different; in this instance, most decisions are made in the subsidiary, but if they are not, authority shifts entirely to headquarters. Financial decisions are most likely to be influenced by headquarters, reflecting the utilization of financial controls on budgets and resource utilization. Certain types of research investment decisions are controlled in the same manner. Overall, the most common pattern is for headquarters to generate solutions, submit them to subsidiary managers for comment and suggestions, and then for the final decision to be made at headquarters. Thus the trend is in the direction of less than equal influence, with the greater power in the hands of headquarters personnel.

Strategies for Dealing with National Contexts

Multinationals use three primary types of strategies in relating foreign operations to various national contexts. These range from the situation in which the primary line of influence is from national context to foreign subsidiary to the situation in which influence flows primarily in the opposite direction—from subsidiary to the particular nation and culture. The same company may use different strategies in different countries.

Adaptive Responses   The most widely used strategy involves a substantial degree of adjustment to local constraints and circumstances. Rather than attempting to change the existing situation, even over the long term, the company

EXHIBIT 18.5 Extent to which decisions in different functional areas are made at corporate headquarters and by foreign subsidiaries

Degree of Subsidiary Independence (1 = low, 5 = high)	Percent of Decisions Made in Each Functional Area					
	Finance	Research	Personnel	Production	Purchasing	Marketing
1. Headquarters personnel generate solutions, make choice, and inform subsidiary management of decision	23	23	18	17	33	15
2. Headquarters personnel generate solutions and submit them to subsidiary manager for suggestions before making decision	20	30	10	17	0	14
3. Headquarters and subsidiary managers share problem and collectively generate alternatives; they attempt to reach consensus and implement decisions having support of both.	25	13	32	13	3	19
4. Subsidiary managers generate alternative solutions, make decisions, and submit them to headquarters for approval	33	33	28	33	3	38
5. Subsidiary managers generate alternative solutions and make decisions themselves.	0	0	12	20	60	15
Mean Degree of Subsidiary Independence	1.7	1.9	2.1	2.2	2.6	2.6

Adapted from Donna G. Goehl, *Decision Making In Multinational Corporations* (Ann Arbor, Mich.: UMI Research Press, 1980): 55, 146–147.

merely attempts to maximize goal attainment within the limits it finds imposed upon it. Usually this means a good deal of independence for the foreign subsidiary so that adjustments can be made on the spot. However, some companies try to orchestrate an adaptive strategy in large part from the parent headquarters and thus keep independence at a minimum. Often this is done by headquarters managers who have had some experience in the country involved and who travel to it frequently.

Generally, the adaptive approach requires staffing as many positions as possible with nationals of the country involved. Initially managers from the parent country may be placed in top positions, or perhaps managers are moved in from other countries in which the multinational firm has been operating for a longer period of time. In the long run, however, the adaptive response tends to be associated with the employment of local nationals at all levels. In a number of countries, this is required to varying degrees by laws created to limit foreign domination and foster domestic employment. Johnson & Johnson, for instance, employs local nationals extensively at all levels in the operation of its network of subsidiary companies around the world.

The use of an adaptive approach does not necessarily mean that the subsidiary of a multinational is managed along the same lines as firms of local origin.

One can adapt to constraints without doing things that are not constrained in exactly the same way as they are in domestic companies. A comparison of subsidiaries of U.S.-based multinationals operating in Latin America and Asia with locally owned firms in the same countries found the subsidiaries generally were managed in a more systematic manner and were more effective, even though they utilized primarily adaptive strategies.[9] The comparison found that various management functions—influencing, organizing, planning, staffing, and the like—were more likely to be handled in some formally established manner, and they were more likely to be performed well. Thus, adaptive strategies can be quite successful.

Cultural Island Strategies   Adaptation clearly works best where constraints are at a minimum. Under conditions of limited education, a value structure that is antithetical to business development, an unfriendly political and legal environment, and a poor economy, adaptation may condemn a company to mediocrity, if that.

Under these latter circumstances, the best approach may be one that isolates the multinational's operations from the culture as a whole, to the degree this is possible. Staffing is carried out using many people from the parent, headquarters country who are better and more appropriately educated; they also provide a more favorable value structure for development of the business. The political, legal, and economic systems of the host country remain intact, but special provisions are secured for the multinational's subsidiary so that it is possible to operate more in line with conditions in the parent country. Typically, independence of decision making is limited because the major focus is not on adaptation, but on maintaining headquarters values and policies and assuring that they will not be eroded by local pressures. Subsidiary personnel and their families may live in something of an enclave, associate relatively little with the local populace, and fail to learn the language or customs of the country in which they are located.

Strategies of this kind carry considerable risk at present. The country involved may not be willing to accept the strategy and may create a political and legal environment that dooms the company to failure. Typically, this cultural island approach is used in developing countries, where adaptation may well be totally inadvisable. It has much in common with the colonialism of an earlier period and is used for many of the same reasons. Mining operations, agricultural production, and the like are often involved. Ideally, the result is a "live and let live" balance that works to the mutual advantage of all parties. However, many countries no longer permit cultural island strategies to work effectively. Out of a desire to improve the foreign exchange position, gain control of new technologies, increase domestic employment, and add to internal wealth, the country imposes constraints that make the approach infeasible. Furthermore, the excesses of colonialism have created a very negative value climate in many parts of the world. At present, then, cultural island approaches can be employed only on a very selective basis, and rarely under conditions of a socialist political system.

Furthermore, the heavy reliance on expatriate personnel from the parent country can present additional problems. Rewards may be insufficient to attract the numbers needed. Problems of adjustment to the new culture, even within the separate environment provided, can present major difficulties so that many expatriates have to be returned home. A certain amount of cultural preparation and training appears to be necessary if the parent country nationals are to function effectively in their new environment. This can work, but it entails some cost, and at the present time, a successful cultural island strategy may only be an invitation to take the additional step to cultural change.[10]

National and Cultural Change   The cultural island approach assumes two different cultures existing in close proximity in unstable equilibrium. Perhaps it is inevitable that the balance eventually will shift one way or the other. Often it is toward enforced adaptation, but it may also be toward major changes in the nation involved and its culture. These changes can take many forms and, in fact, if they are not substantial and broad in scope, the strategy may fail. Thus it may be necessary to take steps to upgrade education and focus it more on business needs. Values may need to be refocused, especially in a manner consistent with the convergence hypothesis—thus away from the values of a rural, agricultural, and perhaps strongly family-oriented society to those of an urban, industrialized society. Political and legal changes may be needed. In a democratic society, this means political action and lobbying, but under other circumstances it may be possible only through more direct political intervention in the affairs of the country. In the economic area, a company may take steps to create needed institutions, such as banks and exchanges.

Such change is a long-term process, and it assumes that a company can exert the necessary influence. Values existing in both the parent country and the country directly involved may play a role in the degree of success. Removal of certain types of constraints, such as improving national educational standards, may be viewed very favorably. Removing others, such as a political administration unfavorable to business development, may be labeled as undue meddling and be very differently received. It is not surprising that this type of strategy has worked best when carried out with little publicity, perhaps even under the guise of adaptation. Yet it can succeed, and the potential rewards for the company, and often for the society too, can be considerable.

THE JAPANESE

The country that, above all others, has taken on the greatest significance for the U.S. business community in recent years is Japan. It is important to understand what has happened in this regard and why it has come about.

At the present, the United States has a two-pronged attitude toward the Japanese and their very real economic success. On the one hand, there is a great deal of respect for the success itself. Americans value success, and pragmatic managers are quick to adopt approaches that they believe will produce it. Thus, there has been considerable urging that U.S. industry introduce many Japanese practices. Because these practices are seen together with success, it is assumed—sometimes rather uncritically—that they cause it.

On the other hand, there is also some resentment of the Japanese and their successes, some feeling that success has been achieved unfairly, thus depriving American workers of jobs and companies of profits. This latter view supports increased legal constraints on Japanese multinationals, which could in the long run bring about major changes in the conduct of international business throughout the world. All in all, it is apparent that an understanding of what the Japanese are doing and how it may affect U.S. management is becoming increasingly important.

What has been most impressive about Japanese economic success is its growth. Productivity increases have been two to three times those of the United States. Japanese trade with other countries has been expanding at about twice the world average rate. Japan's economic growth rate has outdistanced that of any other industrialized nation. Although the total of Japanese foreign investment is still well below the U.S. multinationals, the trend lines were distinctly different through the 1960s and 1970s, with the Japanese line accelerating much more rapidly. Even the Japanese have experienced some fall-off during the recession of the early 1980s, however. Much of the growth has occurred within U.S. markets in industries such as autos, steel, television, machine tools, and computer components. All this has occurred in a nation recently devastated by war, with very limited natural resources, and historically short on investment capital.

Given this situation, it is not surprising that attention has focused on methods of managing human resources in attempting to explain the success. The role that quality circles have played and the general emphasis in Japan on quality control has been noted, in chapter 10. There have also been a number of innovations in technology and production–operations management techniques.[11] However, the greatest concern has been with the broad philosophy and approach that underlies the management of the larger Japanese firms.

Alternative Interpretations

Those who look at the ways that Japanese firms operate do not always come to the same conclusions. This may reflect two factors. One is that the Japanese themselves have long been concerned as a culture with what Westerners call "face." Thus, they may present themselves and their practices in ways intended more to give a positive impression than to describe reality in all of its aspects. Second, outside observers have tended to fit the Japanese system into some model with which they are familiar from their own experience, to view it through their own cultural looking-glass. This too can provide a somewhat distorted picture.

Theories A, J, and Z   One method of looking at the Japanese experience is depicted in Exhibit 18.6. Theory A is said to describe the typical Western firm, including American companies. Theory J describes the larger Japanese firms in Japan. Theory Z is a new form, containing many aspects of Theory J, that is found to some degree among Japanese multinationals operating in the United States, and more importantly among some of the more successful U.S. companies. The results of extensive interviewing conducted in 1978 in companies in both countries were as follows:

> In Japanese companies in Japan were found: almost total inclusion of the employee into the work organization so that the superior concerns himself or herself with the personal and family life of each subordinate; a collective, non-individual approach to work and responsibility; and extremely high identification of the individual with the company. These characteristics are largely the result of the lifetime employment system which

EXHIBIT 18.6   Outline of theories A, J, and Z

	Theory A (American)	Theory J (Japanese)	Theory Z (ideal)
Employment term	Short primarily, but varies	Lifetime for males	Long
Decision making	Individual by managers	Consensus among many	Consensus among many
Responsibility	Resides in the individual	Held collectively by many	Resides in the individual
Evaluation amd promotion	Rapid and based on performance primarily	Slow and based on loyalty primarily	Slow and based on loyalty primarily
Control system	Formally stated and written down	Informal and not explicitly stated	Informal, but with explicit measures
Career path	Within a specialized area	Movement through many areas	Less specialized than in Theory A
Breadth of supervisory concern	Segmented and focused on performance only	The whole person and all aspects of life	The whole person and all aspects of life, including family

Adapted from William G. Ouchi and Alfred M. Jaeger, "Type Z Organization: Stability in the Midst of Mobility," *Academy of Management Review* (April 1978):308–311; and William G. Ouchi, *Theory Z: How American Business Can Meet the Japanese Challenge* (Reading, Mass.: Addison-Wesley, 1981).

characterizes large companies in Japan. . . . Japanese companies with operations in the U.S. are applying a modified form of the pure Japanese type with some success. While they do not provide company housing or large bonuses as in Japan, they attempt to create the same sort of complete inclusion of the employee into the company.[12]

Clearly, Japanese firms operating in the United States are applying something of a culture change strategy. Some differences between the two cultures are highlighted in Exhibit 18.7. To the extent that Japanese multinationals bring their approaches and values to the United States and apply them to U.S. nationals here, they are involved in culture change. The evidence would indicate that they are doing just that, and with some degree of success. It is significant that Japanese multinationals around the world, much more than U.S. or European-based multinationals, staff their management positions with parent country nationals.[13] The tendency to use Japanese nationals predominantly is particularly pronounced at the senior management levels.

Theory Z is reflected primarily in certain United States firms that have studied the Japanese approach, learned from it, and developed a type of organization that fits Theory J into U.S. culture. An example is Hewlett-Packard, manufacturer of minicomputers and precision instruments, which is generally considered to be one of the best-managed U.S. firms.[14] Hewlett Packard's corporate objectives are given in Exhibit 18.8. They are said to represent the essence of a Theory Z philosophy.

Human Resources Management   A view of the Japanese approach that overlaps in many respects with that presented in Exhibit 18.6 is outlined in Exhibit 18.9. Here, the central explanatory role given to lifetime employment is expanded to a broader focus on human resource development generally. It

EXHIBIT 18.7 Some apparent cultural differences between Japan and the United States

In Japan	In the United States
Individuals should subordinate themselves to the group to attain harmony.	Society exists to provide fulfillment for the individual.
People are inherently unequal; each has a proper place in the hierarchy.	All people are created equal, although inequalities may appear later.
Nonconformity is not tolerated.	Diversity and nonconformity are expected and accepted.
Membership in the national family incurs certain duties and obligations.	Citizenship bestows freedom and certain inalienable individual rights.

Japan is a homogenous society that has evolved a unique and highly effective system of management characterized by a pervasive organizational paternalism, a unique group decision-making process, and distinctive interpersonal behavior growing out of deep emotional sensitivity. In the heterogeneous, individualistic culture of the *United States,* a different concept is necessary.

Adapted from William A. Long and K. K. Seo, *Management in Japan and India: With Reference to the United States* (New York: Praeger, 1977): 3, 10, 15.

EXHIBIT 18.8 Corporate objectives of a Theory Z firm—Hewlett Packard

Profit. To achieve sufficient profit to finance our company growth and to provide the resources we need to achieve our other corporate objectives.

Customers. To provide products and services of the greatest possible value to our customers, thereby gaining and holding their respect and loyalty.

Fields of Interest. To enter new fields only when the ideas we have, together with our technical, manufacturing, and marketing skills, assure that we can make a needed and profitable contribution to the field.

Growth. To let our growth be limited only by our profits and our ability to develop and produce technical products that satisfy real customer needs.

Our People. To help Hewlett-Packard people share in the company's success, which they make possible; to provide job security based on their performance; to recognize their individual achievements; and to insure the personal satisfaction that comes from a sense of accomplishment in their work.

Management. To foster initiative and creativity by allowing the individual great freedom of action in attaining well-defined objectives.

Citizenship. To honor our obligations to society by being an economic, intellectual, and social asset to each nation and each community in which we operate.

Fundamental Requirements to Fulfill Objectives
1. The most capable people available should be selected for each assignment within the organization. Moreover, these people should have the opportunity—through continuing programs of training and education—to upgrade their skills and capabilities.
2. Enthusiasm should exist at all levels. There can be no place, especially among people charged with management responsibility, for half-hearted interest or effort.
3. All levels should work in unison toward common objectives and avoid working at cross-purposes if ultimate efficiency and achievement are to be obtained.

Adapted from William G. Ouchi, *Theory Z: How American Business Can Meet the Japanese Challenge* (Reading, Mass.: Addison-Wesley, 1981): 225–232.

should be recognized, however, that in traditional Japanese culture, all of this applies basically to males, and to the larger companies. Women are typically temporary employees, and they are expected to leave the labor force at least by the age of 30. Smaller firms are more vulnerable to economic fluctuations and thus only approximate the pattern shown in Exhibit 18.9.

Something of the "flavor" of this human resource model as it is reflected in Japanese practices can be gained from the following quotations, taken from Hatvany and Pucik:

> Firms invest a great deal in training, and naturally attempt to discourage turnover . . . workers at early stages of their careers are underpaid . . . they are compensated for this at later stages in their tenure with the firm . . . these wages may surpass the pay of new employees by 200–400 percent.

> The basic criteria for hiring are moderate views and a harmonious personality . . . employees are selected on the basis of their perceived ability to fit in with the company values and philosophy.

EXHIBIT 18.9 Human resources model of Japanese management

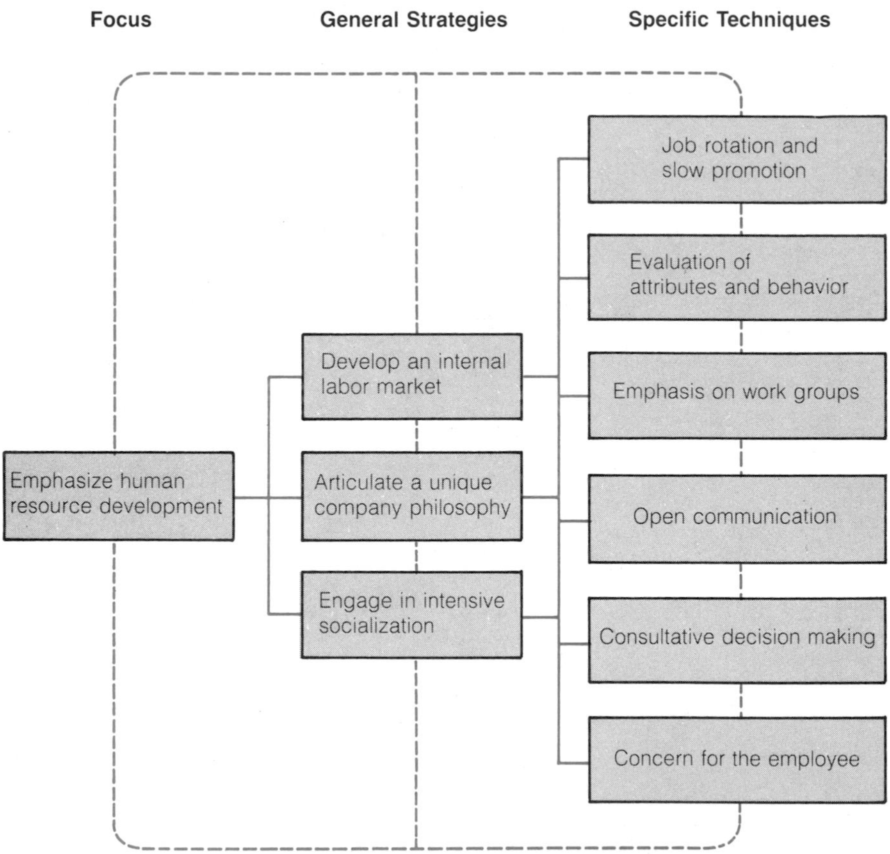

Nina Hatvany and Vladimir Pucik, "An Integrated Management System: Lessons from the Japanese Experience," *Academy of Management Review* (July 1981): 470. Reprinted by permission.

As employees remain in an organization over an extended period of time, they tend to adopt the positive values, attitudes, and performance levels of their co-workers. This is partly a function of conformity in order to avoid rejection as a deviant.

Employee evaluations include not only performance measures on the individual and, especially, the team level, but also desirable personality traits and behaviors.

There are various welfare systems that penetrate into every crack of worker's lives . . . company scholarships for employee's children, credit extension, housing allowances, savings, insurance. (pp. 471–75)

One is tempted to equate this approach with participative management and group-based systems. To a substantial degree, advocates of Theory Z have indeed taken this step. Yet the human resource model does not; a subtle distinction is introduced:

A proposal is initiated by a middle manager, most often under the directive of top management. This middle manager will engage in informal discussion and consultation with peers and supervisors. When all are familiar with the proposal, a request for a decision is made formally and because of the earlier discussions, it is almost inevitably ratified often in a ceremonial group meeting. This does not indicate unanimous approval, but does imply consent to its implementation. . . . This kind of decision making is not participative in the American sense of the word, which implies frequent group meetings and negotiation between manager and subordinates. Nor is it bottom-up; rather it is a top-down or interactive consultative process, especially when long-term planning and strategy are concerned. Although the locus of responsibility may appear ambiguous to outsiders, it is actually quite clear within the organization, especially at the upper levels (p. 473).

The implication is that Japanese firms still are generally hierarchical and rely on top-down authority. There is research to support this conclusion, although it is also true that in certain circumscribed areas, group-based systems are clearly in evidence as well.

Research Studies of the Japanese

The most consistent finding from research is that business in Japan is different from the United States and other western countries. Regardless of the measures used, when a number of countries are studied together and efforts are made to develop culture clusters, Japan stands alone, in its own "cluster." This is true of no other country. The findings given in Exhibit 18.2 are thus typical of other studies in this regard.

Pulling Together Previously Noted Findings At numerous points throughout this book, studies have been reported that compare Japan with other countries. Exhibit 18.2 does this also, but buries the United States in the Anglo culture cluster. Exhibit 18.10 extracts the U.S. data and thus permits a direct comparison of the Japanese and the U.S. findings from the IBM research.

An important conclusion from research has to do with managerial goals. In Exhibit 4.1 it was noted that profit maximization is important in both the United States and Japan, but there is more emphasis on high productivity and, in particular, on company growth in Japan. It would be reasonable to conclude, based on goal-setting theory, that Japan's greater productivity and more rapid economic growth is in large part a function of the types of goals Japanese managers set for themselves. In this respect, it should be noted that employee welfare is not con-

EXHIBIT 18.10   Relative value positions of Japan and the United States

	Rank among 40 Nations			
	Emphasis on Hierarchy	Emphasis on Avoiding Risks	Emphasis on Individualism	Emphasis on Masculine Behavior
Japan	22	4	22.5	1
United States	26	32	1	13

Adapted from Geert Hofstede, *Culture's Consequences: International Differences in Work Related Values* (Beverly Hills, Calif.: Sage, 1980): 315.

sidered an important operative goal. To the extent that it is achieved by the Japanese system, it would appear to be a by-product of the methods used to achieve other goals.

Some of the value differences between American and Japanese workers noted in Exhibit 18.7 are documented also in Exhibit 5.14. There clearly are major differences, and these are reflected in variations in decision making approaches, personnel practices, and the scope of legitimate supervisory concern. It is of course quite possible that these differences may have little to do with company success in either country.

Japan and the United States appear to be rather similar in the extent to which managers hold theory Y assumptions about subordinates and favor theory Y types of administrative practices (see Exhibit 6.8). Relative to many other countries, both tend in a theory Y direction, although in neither case is there evidence of strong positive belief regarding the motives and capabilities of subordinates. It is important to note, however, that any differences between Japanese and American managers found on the theory X vs. theory Y measures in this study are not of the magnitude that the theory A, J, and Z formulations would lead us to anticipate. Japan is not more likely to embrace theory Y.

Research dealing with national variations in characteristics thought to be related to bargaining behavior unearths both similarities and differences (Exhibit 7.3). On the conciliation–belligerence continuum, Japanese and American managers are much the same. However, there are very wide differences in two other characteristics. Americans are much more trusting of others and have a much greater belief in self-determination and individual effort. The Japanese, in contrast, tend to be more suspicious and to exhibit a greater degree of fatalism. Insofar as risks are concerned, American managers emerge as the stronger risk-takers, but the findings do not place the Japanese as sharply in the risk avoidance category as do the IBM findings noted in Exhibit 18.10.

Probably the IBM data should be given the greater emphasis here. Japanese decision processes serve to minimize risk by searching within the organization for problems of decision content and, more importantly, for problems that might arise in implementation. In fact, the consensus process goes a long way toward assuring that implementation problems will not occur. Furthermore, this process helps to reduce uncertainty and to avoid risk to the individual—everyone was consulted, everyone was involved, everyone agreed. If something goes wrong, everyone has a problem. Responsibility may realistically reside at the top, but the process makes it very difficult for anyone to come out and say so. Thus the collective decision process serves to minimize risk for all involved, in particular those at the very highest levels.

The most pronounced differences in Exhibit 18.10 involve individualism and masculine behavior. In the United States, individualism is paramount; in Japan, it is sharply diluted by collectivism and fatalism. There are many other countries that are less individualistic than Japan, but there is a substantial difference in comparison with the United States. This would appear to yield some long-run advantage for the United States. It is much less certain that the masculinity–femininity difference matters in an economic sense. Nevertheless, Japanese culture does appear to focus primarily on masculine behavior patterns; the United States does so to a somewhat lesser degree. This reflects distinct value differences between the two countries; it also suggests that the Japanese might have much more difficulty in effectively utilizing female talent supplies should this become necessary.

A final point from Exhibit 18.10 can be related to emphasis on hierarchy. Not surprisingly, given the results previously discussed, the two countries do not differ much in this regard, and both are in the middle range. Nevertheless, it is significant that Japanese systems are more hierarchical than American systems—not less, as the theory Z concept would imply. This would suggest that top management does retain considerable influence over corporate decisions, in spite of the collective aspects of Japanese decision processes.

New Evidence Additional research suggests that the traditional Japanese approaches, including lifetime employment commitment, are now breaking down in favor of the convergence hypothesis. In short, Japan is becoming more like other industrialized nations. Furthermore, the evidence indicates that many of these traditional approaches, and thus their gradual disappearance, have little relation to the success of Japanese industry:

> The organizational variables most distinctively Japanese—paternalism, company housing, participation by workers in company-sponsored recreational activities, company identification, and lifetime commitment—have *less* causal impact on performance than do the more universal factors . . . . Contrary to the lifetime commitment thesis, the more distinctively Japanese an organizational variable is, the *less* it has to do with performance; performance in Japanese firms appears to have the same causal sources as in Western firms.[15]

Findings of this kind accept culture differences, while contending that they are diminishing, but still assert that many of these differences have little to do with the productivity and growth differentials between Japan and the United States.

Another program of research has found that, objectively, Japanese firms are just as bureaucratic as those in other countries.[16] The basic structures are much the same at the present time. This does not mean that subtle variations in both structure and process might not produce differences. And, indeed, this appears to be the case. At all levels, the Japanese perceive their jobs to involve a *greater* division of labor and specialization, and thus to be *more* routine. Furthermore, they experience a *greater* impact of hierarchic authority, again at all levels. However one computes it, Japanese culture does not appear to be one in which the precepts of human relations, participative management, and group-based decision making have taken strong hold, in spite of superficial signs to the contrary. Japan's organizational culture is different and complex, but contrary to common belief in this country, it is not essentially democratic.

The Transferability Question

What, then, do these conclusions mean to those who argue for transferring Japanese approaches to the United States? Can these approaches solve America's problems of productivity and economic growth? Perhaps a complete answer is not possible, but certain indicators bear noting.

The Japanese approach derives from a very homogeneous culture, and it emphasizes conformity to a single perspective. The United States has a pluralistic, highly diversified set of cultures, and emphasizes individualism and, often, nonconformity. Not very long ago, books entitled *The Organization Man* and *The Man in the Gray Flannel Suit,* which attacked conformity to organizational norms, were among the best sellers in the United States. Today, with the influx of women into companies at all levels, the word "man" in these titles is out of date. But the underlying values the books appealed to are still present.

Given this situation, it seems unlikely that Japanese management will "take" on a broad scale in the United States. It is likely to be condemned as thwarting individual freedoms, being paternalistic, sexist, and perhaps racist as well, among other violations of cultural values. Yet it may be appropriate to a segment of U.S. society, and that is an important consideration. In a diversified culture, there are a great many different kinds of people and thus a diversity of organizational forms is needed to accommodate all. A number of people may work well under the Japanese system and be successful in it. However, Japanese multinationals operating in the United States, and perhaps a limited number of U.S. firms, may well exhaust the available supply of this type of human resource within the United States rather rapidly.

In this view, neither theory J nor theory Z is the one best way for American business. There are a number of problems and unanswered questions regarding the theory Z concepts.[17] Although firms such as Hewlett-Packard, IBM, and General Electric, which are cited as approximating theory Z, are generally considered to be very well managed, others also cited do not enjoy such a favorable reputation in their industries. Among these are International Harvester, Chrysler, and Lockheed. It seems likely that Japanese industry has been as successful as it has been because it has clearly found a way of bringing cohesive, concerted effort behind specific, challenging goals for productivity and growth. This need not be the only way of doing this, or even the best way, but it is an approach that fits well with Japanese culture.

In all likelihood, however, the Japanese approach has also incorporated certain aspects of that culture that really do not matter very much one way or the other in mounting a strong effort behind goals; these aspects simply go along with the system. If the Japanese approach is particularly vulnerable in any specific regard, it would appear to be in its potential for groupthink. Organizations of this kind have few safeguards against making major miscalculations, while retaining a widespread, strong belief in their invincibility.

In the United States, the Japanese approach may work very well on a limited scale for some companies or parts of companies. However, there are other ways of achieving the same types of results, and the United States is not entirely devoid of companies that have found such ways. Certainly in the past a great many American firms prospered and grew to become major multinational corporations without adopting the approaches now being used by the Japanese. Given the cultural diversity of the society and the wide range of individual differences, it seems unlikely that U.S. industry will ever solve its problems by adopting one single approach to organizational management.

Summary

Approaching management from an international perspective adds a new dimension to the various topics considered throughout this text, but the basic building blocks—the management functions and subdisciplines—remain the same. Companies operating within one culture must deal with that culture, but they are less aware of it because it is a constant factor affecting all operations. Multinational firms, on the other hand, deal with many cultures. Culture becomes a variable, and strategies for dealing with it in its various forms assume a more visible role. Differences in educational, sociological, political/legal, and economic characteristics as outlined in Exhibit 18.1 must be taken into account. They impose varying constraints on strategies, policies, and decisions. Thus it becomes necessary to develop a different approach to dealing with each national context in which a multinational firm operates.[18]

One aspect of this strategic stance is the degree of commitment to foreign operations in each country where a multinational becomes involved. Organizational structures vary with this country-by-country commitment and with a company's international commitment as a whole. At minimal levels, international activities are managed by an export manager associated first with the marketing functions and, under more expanded conditions, reporting to the president. At the next step, an international division is formed. In the fully developed multinationals, however, operations outside the host country are incorporated into product or geographical divisions; in many cases, the international operations account for a major share of earnings.

The degree to which subsidiaries in different countries exercise independence in decision making varies with many factors, and it varies from one functional area to another as well. Usually financial controls are retained at headquarters so that resources are not overcommitted. Strategies such as adaptation, cultural islands, and culture change are instituted depending on the constraints existing in the local culture and the philosophies operating on home country top management.

Much of what has been considered in terms of international management and in terms of the field of management as a whole can prove useful in understanding the success that Japanese multinationals have experienced over the past thirty years. Because this success has been achieved in large part in U.S. markets and using managerial approaches differing from those typically used by U.S. firms, few American companies can afford to ignore what has happened. The Japanese success story has been attributed to various factors, and it has been used to support the use of a number of different management approaches. Thus there have been varied interpretations of the core factors in the Japanese system. In the end, as in

Management in International Perspective

other aspects of management, it comes down to conducting careful, controlled research into what is actually happening and what makes for success.

The results of this research suggest that Japan Inc. is in many respects the latest among numerous fads and cure-alls that have come upon the management scene in recent years. There is an element of truth and an element of fantasy, the latter occasioned by the hope of finding the one best way of managing an organization effectively. It seems increasingly improbable that such a way will ever be identified. Different people, different cultures, and different organizational forms appear to combine in a variety of ways to produce the ultimate goal of corporate success.

What Have You Learned?

1. Why is the study of Japanese management approaches important for U.S. managers? Will it continue to be important? Why?

2. What are the major ways in which companies organize multinational operations? Under what conditions is each most appropriate?

3. How do educational characteristics and cultural values operate to produce constraints in the form of availability of needed human resources?

4. When is a culture change strategy particularly attractive to multinational firms? Give some examples of this strategy.

5. What is the convergence hypothesis, and what is the nature of the evidence for and against it?

6. What exactly is theory Z? How valid does it appear to be, and to what extent can it be expected to solve the productivity problems of U.S. industry?

7. Independence in making decisions for foreign subsidiaries appears to vary with the functional area involved. What are these functional differences, and why do they exist?

8. What does comparative research tell us about the differences between Japanese and American cultures and management approaches?

9. How does codetermination serve to produce a very different context for decision making in European countries from the context in the United States?

10. What different approaches are used in staffing management positions in foreign subsidiaries, and how do they relate to the various strategies for dealing with national contexts?

How Well Can You Apply Your Knowledge?

Problem 1. A United States-based consumer goods company had been operating for a number of years in Europe. These European operations included both manufacturing and marketing and had generally been quite profitable, even though the major part of the company's business was still in the United States. In both Europe and the United States, the great preponderance of the business involved a single product line that had been the company's mainstay from the time it was founded. There had been some diversification on a small scale into certain related products recently, but the company's master strategy did not call for substantial diversification. Rather the intention was to grow through international expansion.

The European operations had been handled for some time out of an international division headed by a vice-president. This individual had been born and raised in Great Britain and had previously headed the British subsidiary. This was typical. Most of the European subsidiaries were staffed with nationals of the country involved and this was true even at the very highest levels of management. It is important to note that, although the company's operations outside the United States were assigned to an international division, that division was for all practical purposes a geographical division for Europe.

The international growth strategy called for expansion through the world on a sequential basis. The idea was to move gradually, learn from past experiences, and consolidate the company's position in one area before moving to the next. Africa had been selected as the first target for expansion, largely because the company had several managers within its European subsidiaries who had had experience there in the employ of other firms. Clearly, Africa would represent a very different business environment from those the company had dealt with in the past, but it was not totally unknown.

The initial focus was to be in Nigeria. There had been some consideration given to South Africa, in view of the more advanced state of its economy. However, the company felt that its products could be sold throughout much of Africa, and for this purpose Nigeria represented a more central location. Also, the company's top management had been exposed to some pressure by special interest groups in the United States not to invest in South Africa because of its policies regarding blacks and racial separatism. It simply did not seem wise to initiate a strategic move that would bring the company into contact with diverse cultures throughout the world by stepping directly into the center of one of the world's major culture conflicts. Furthermore, Nigeria represented a sizable market relative to African nations generally. The population was among the largest, and as a result of its oil production, the country did have some wealth.

The company was aware of many of the problems it would face. Educational levels in the Nigerian population were generally low, compared to those in Europe and the United States, and the educational emphasis tended to be on the professions and government rather than on business management. The history of government stability was not appealing, and attitudes toward foreign investment were still tainted by years of colonialism. But these were factors that would have to be faced anywhere in Africa. The company simply had to learn how to cope with them.

Questions

1. The international expansion strategy, beginning now with the move into Nigeria and Africa, introduces certain problems insofar as the company's overall organization is concerned. What steps should be taken to change the existing structure? Why would you recommend these particular structural changes?

2. How should the company go about coping with the educational, sociological, political, and economic constraints in its new environment? What types of strategies are appropriate, and why?

Problem 2. A woman had risen rapidly in the management structure of her company, largely as a result of her ability to sell industrial products in substantial quantities. She had started with the firm as a secretary in marketing while she was going to college. Her intent had been to become a school teacher. However, when an opportunity to join the company sales force came along, she accepted it, even though she knew she would be travelling a great deal. Initially, she intended to finish college somehow and move to an education position, but that did not happen. She was good at selling, she liked the work, and she was very successful. Gradually college and teaching school became less important.

In fact, it was the company that ultimately brought the education issue back into consideration. There came a point when the manager had gone as far as she could go in sales without a more general knowledge of business. She had the potential to ultimately move into top management, but to do that, she needed to learn a great deal that she did not know about business operation in all its aspects. The proposed solution was that she enter the executive M.B.A. program at a local university and obtain the master's degree. A small percentage of students without a college degree were accepted, and courses would be given on alternate Fridays and Saturdays. The company would grant her whatever time off might be needed and would pay her tuition. She was urged to apply, did, and was accepted.

At first the manager found the program difficult going. As time went on, however, she improved and began to like it. The university had an arrangement that executive M.B.A. students could travel to Japan toward the end of their course work if a sufficient number were interested to form a group. The manager wanted very much to do this and in fact was instrumental in putting together such a group when the time came. Although the program of study was largely set so that all students took the same courses, she tried whenever there was an opportunity to focus on international business, and especially on Japan. She wrote several papers on Japanese approaches and did a good deal of reading on the subject on her own.

The trip to Japan provided an opportunity to visit various manufacturing plants, to see at first hand how Japanese human resource policies worked, and talk with both executives and government officials. There were some things she liked and some she did not, but she learned a great deal, and returned home to find herself viewed as something of an expert on Japanese management by other managers in her company. The company had had very few dealings with Japanese managers and little exposure to their business practices, but considerable interest in the subject had developed within the company. This increasing interest and need for information came together with the manager's first-hand exposure and study to create a situation in which more was probably expected of her than could be fully justified.

Nevertheless, she quickly found herself asked to speak to an informal group of company managers on the subject of Japanese management practices. The group met periodically in the evening to hear various speakers and included several vice-presidents. Being asked to speak was something of an honor; a good performance could help one's career.

Question

1. How would you go about meeting this challenge? Develop an outline or set of notes for your talk, focusing on the nature of Japanese management and the potential use of these practices by American companies. Try to bring as many of the concepts and ideas considered previously in this course into your discussion as possible.

Additional Sources for More Detailed Study

Behrman, Jack N., and Wallender, Harvey W. *Transfers of Manufacturing Technology Within Multinational Enterprises.* Cambridge, Mass.: Ballinger, 1976.

England, George W.; Negandhi, Anant R.; and Wilpert, Bernhard. *Organizational Functioning in a Cross-Cultural Perspective.* Kent, Ohio: Kent State University Press, 1979.

Evans, Peter B. "Recent Research on Multinational Corporations." *Annual Review of Sociology,* 1981.

Granick, David. *Managerial Comparisons of Four Developed Countries: France, Britain, United States and Russia.* Cambridge, Mass.: MIT Press, 1972.

Heenan, David A., and Perlmutter, Howard U. *Multinational Organization Development.* Reading, Mass.: Addison-Wesley, 1979.

Hochmuth, Milton S. *Organizing the Transnational: The Experience with Transnational Enterprise in Advanced Technology.* Leiden, the Netherlands: A. W. Sijthoff, 1974.

Hofstede, Geert, and Kassem, M. Sami. *European Contributions to Organization Theory.* Assen, the Netherlands: Van Gorcum, 1976.

Kolde, Endel-Jacob. *Environment of International Business.* Boston: Kent, 1982.

Matheson, Ross. *People Development in Developing Countries.* New York: Wiley, 1978.

Northrup, Herbert R., and Rowan, Richard L. *Multinational Collective Bargaining Attempts.* Philadelphia, Pa.: Industrial Research Unit, University of Pennsylvania, 1979.

Prasad, S. B., and Shetty, Y. Krishna. *An Introduction to Multinational Management.* Englewood Cliffs, N.J.: Prentice-Hall, 1976.

Pascale, Richard T., and Athos, Anthony G. *The Art of Japanese Management.* New York: Simon and Schuster, 1981.

Tannenbaum, Arnold S.; Kavcic, Bogdan; Rosner, Menachem; Vianello, Mino; and Wieser, Georg. *Hierarchy in Organizations: An International Comparison.* San Francisco: Jossey-Bass, 1974.

Triandis, Harry C., and Brislin, Richard W. *Handbook of Cross-Cultural Psychology: Social Psychology.* Boston: Allyn and Bacon, 1980.

Vernon, Raymond, and Wells, Louis T. *Manager in the*

International Economy. Englewood Cliffs, N.J.: Prentice-Hall, 1981.

Vogel, Ezra F. *Japan as Number One: Lessons for America.* Cambridge, Mass.: Harvard University Press, 1979.

Williamson, Harold F. *Evolution of International Management Structures.* Newark, Delaware: University of Delaware Press, 1975.

Notes

1. From J. D. Daniels, E. W. Ogram, and Lee H. Radebaugh, *International Business: Environments and Operations,* © 1982, Addison-Wesley, Reading, Mass., pp. 606-7. Reprinted with permission.

2. See Terrence E. Deal and Allan A. Kennedy, *Corporate Cultures: The Rites and Rituals of Corporate Life* (Reading, Mass.: Addison-Wesley, 1982); Howard Schwartz and Stanley M. Davis, "Matching Corporate Culture and Business Strategy," *Organizational Dynamics* (Summer 1981); and Bro Uttal, "The Corporate Culture Vultures," *Fortune* (October 17, 1983).

3. See for instance David C. McClelland, "Does Education Accelerate Economic Growth?" *Economic Development and Cultural Change,* 1966.

4. Clark Kerr, John T. Dunlop, Frederick Harbison, and Charles A. Myers, *Industrialism and Industrial Man* (Cambridge, Mass.: Harvard University Press, 1960).

5. Uma Sekaran, "Are U.S. Organizational Concepts and Measures Transferable to Another Culture? An Empirical Investigation," *Academy of Management Journal* (July 30); and John B. Miner, "Participation and Management," *International Yearbook of Organizational Democracy,* Vol. II (New York: Wiley, 1984).

6. See Franz-Jürgen Sächer, "The German Model of Codetermination," and Donald V. Nightingale, "Codetermination and Quality of Work Life Movements Compared," both in *Management Under Differing Value Systems: Political, Social, and Economical Perspectives in a Changing World,* eds. Günter Dlugos and Klaus Weiermair (Berlin: deGruyter, 1981).

7. See Robert G. Hawkins and Ingo Walter, "Planning Multinational Operations," in *Handbook of Organizational Design. Volume 1: Adapting Organizations to Their Environments,* eds. Paul C. Nystrom and William H. Starbuck (New York: Oxford University Press, 1981).

8. Gerard H. Garnier, "Context and Decision Making Autonomy in the Foreign Affiliates of U.S. Multinational Corporations," *Academy of Management Journal* (December 1982).

9. Anant R. Negandhi, *Organization Theory in an Open System: A Study of Transferring Advanced Management Practices to Developing Nations* (New York: Dunellen, 1975).

10. John B. Miner, "The Cross-Cultural Perspective to Work Motivation," in *Motivation and Organizational Effectiveness,* ed. S. K. Roy (New Delhi, India: Shri Ram Centre for Industrial Relations and Human Resources, 1974).

11. Richard J. Schonberger, "The Transfer of Japanese Manufacturing Management Approaches to U.S. Industry," *Academy of Management Review* (July 1982).

12. William G. Ouchi and Alfred M. Jaeger, "Type Z Organization: Stability in the Midst of Mobility," *Academy of Management Review* (April 1978).

13. Rosalie L. Tung, "Selection and Training Procedures of U.S., European, and Japanese Multinationals," *California Management Review* (Fall 1982).

14. Claire Makin, "Ranking Corporate Reputations," *Fortune* (January 10, 1983).

15. Robert M. Marsh and Hiroshi Mannari, "Divergence and Convergence in Industrial Organizations: The Japanese Case," in *Management Under Differing Value Systems: Political, Social, and Economical Perspectives in a Changing World,* eds. Günter Dlugos and Klaus Weiermair (Berlin: deGruyter, 1981).

16. Dezso Harvath, Koya Azumi, David J. Hickson, and Charles J. McMillan, "Bureaucratic Structures in Cross-National Perspective: A Study of British, Japanese, and Swedish Firms," in *Management Under Differing Value Systems: Political, Social, and Economical Perspectives in a Changing World,* eds. Günter Dlugos and Klaus Weiermair (Berlin: deGruyter, 1981).

17. Jeremiah J. Sullivan, "A Critique of Theory Z," *Academy of Management Review* (January 1983).

18. For a good example, see Karl Schwarz, "HP-Grenoble: Case Study in Technology Transfer," *California Management Review* (Spring 1982).

READINGS AND PROFILES

The Corporate Culture Vultures
Bro Uttal
Fortune

HP-Grenoble: Case Study in Technology Transfer
Karl Schwarz
California Management Review

John F. Bookout and Shell Oil Company

A number of issues related to international operations and cultures were not fully covered in chapter 18. These selections attempt to fill those gaps.

The article by Uttal deals with corporate, as opposed to national, cultures and with the flourishing consulting business that has sprung up to aid in diagnosing and changing these cultures. Particular attention is given to the work being done by Management Analysis Center headquartered in Cambridge, Massachusetts. Interest in this whole area has been spurred by the various analyses of Japanese business culture and its potential for transfer to American companies.

Schwarz describes how the national and cultural variations considered— educational, sociological, political and legal, and economic—converge in an actual operating situation. He was in charge of the start up of Hewlett-Packard's facility in Grenoble, France. The article is important because it points up the interactions among factors and the various ways in which they can condition decisions in an international context. It brings what was previously a list of factors into perspective as a unified whole.

John F. Bookout heads the thirteenth largest industrial corporation in the United States—Shell Oil. While primarily an oil company, his firm is also one of the country's largest chemical producers. It was rated at the top of the petroleum refining industry in *Fortune*'s surveys and is generally considered to be one of the best-managed U.S. firms. Yet Shell Oil is distinctive because its majority ownership and control reside in Dutch and British corporations. It is, in fact, one subsidiary among five hundred. Dealing with this situation presents John Bookout with certain challenges unique in the field of international management.

The Corporate Culture Vultures

Bro Uttal

U.S. business is in the throes of a cultural revolution. Even some of the hardest-nosed managers have started worrying about the appropriateness of their corporate cultures. Consultants have begun to offer high-priced advice on how to mesh a company's culture with its strategy. The problem is, it isn't clear that most corporations can consciously create a new culture for themselves. Or even that they should try.

The revolutionary concern for the soft, bewilderingly human underpinnings of business has several hard roots. Within the last three years a quartet of hot-selling management books— *Theory Z, The Art of Japanese Management, Corporate Cultures,* and *In Search of Excellence,* now at a million copies in print and still rising—have hammered home the idea that companies with a record of outstanding financial performance often have powerful corporate cultures. The books also helped clarify what culture is: a system of shared values (what is important) and beliefs (how things work) that interact with a company's people, organizational structures, and control systems to produce behavioral norms (the way we do things around here). For example, at IBM customer service is a dominant value that keeps everyone, from the chairman to the factory worker, pulling in the same direction.

These aren't new notions, but recently they've become riveting. What thinking manager can ignore the connections increasingly drawn between, say, Toyota's success and the image of its workers intoning the company song? Or between Hewlett-Packard's long-term growth rate—an average of 25% a year in revenues—and its beliefs, which seem to lead almost everyone at the company to behave like an entrepreneur? The word is out: a survey of 305 chief executives published last month by William M. Mercer Inc., a New York City firm that designs compensation systems, showed that all but a handful think strong corporate values are important to their companies' success. Asked how much their companies had "addressed the issue of corporate values," two-fifths of the group checked off "a great deal."

The idea that culture matters happened along at the right time, just as many managers were learning that corporate strategy alone, no matter how well formulated, can't produce winning results (see

Bro Uttal with Research Associate *Jaclyn Fierman.* Reprinted from *Fortune* (October 17, 1983): 66–72. Copyright © 1983 Time Inc. All rights reserved.

"Corporate Strategists Under Fire," *Fortune,* December 27, 1982). At best, big-league management consultants observe, only one company in ten can successfully carry out a complex new strategy, say, to bring down production costs systematically, cut price, and gain share of market. But the need for devising and executing better strategies has, if anything, grown of late. Recession, deregulation, technological upheavals, foreign competition, and markets that seem to emerge and vanish by the month have cranked up the pressure on companies to adapt.

The fashionable view holds that the biggest stumbling block on the path to adaptation is often an inappropriate corporate culture. A widely cited example is AT&T, which has labored for years to behave like a marketing company, but with scant success. Efforts to serve different market segments in different ways have run afoul of the strong values, beliefs, and norms Bell managers have imbibed since the turn of the century—that it's important to furnish telephone service to everybody, that you do that by not discriminating too much among different kinds of customers. The solution seems obvious: change the culture. As AT&T's dilemma shows, that's not easy.

A number of consultants, however, have sensed and abetted the shift in focus to the soft—they're eager to help the culturally distressed. Most of them have specialized for years in human resource problems such as organizational design. "The pendulum is swinging away from the strategists and toward the social architects," exults Paul V. Croke, vice president of Boston's Forum Corp., which focuses on training salesmen and managers.

The most ambitious of this crew is the Management Analysis Center, or MAC, of Cambridge, Massachusetts. Over the last few years, MAC has encroached on the turf of specialists in corporate strategy such as the Boston Consulting Group by arguing that you can't change strategies without taking heed of culture. Now the firm, with about 120 professionals in eight offices worldwide, sees a "window of opportunity" through which it hopes to squeeze by selling a new product—the "Ceo's Change Agenda," a list of six steps for implementing strategy by massaging the softer side of management. MAC expects revenues—around $20 million in 1982—to grow by more than 25% this year.

The Management Analysis Center began delving into culture six years ago to help Willard C. Butcher, then heir apparent to Chief Executive David Rockefeller at Chase Manhattan Bank. Butcher wanted to execute a plan for regaining industry leadership and avoiding disasters like Chase's $61-million loss in real estate investment trusts in 1976. At his urging, Stanley M. Davis, a research professor at Boston University, and Howard M. Schwartz, a MAC consultant, interviewed Chase's top two dozen managers to collect anecdotes about the way the company worked. The two observed meetings and pored over logs of how executives spent their time.

The objective was to flush out the actual rules of behavior at the bank rather than the ones people professed. The consultants homed in on unwritten laws that governed relations among people when handling six general management tasks: innovating, decision-making, communicating, organizing, monitoring, and appraising and rewarding. Then they laid these norms—for example, "be a gentleman" and "avoid confrontations"—against the elements of Chase's plan for strategic redirection.

The result, naturally enough for consultants, was a matrix—a chart that plots some variable against two yardsticks—in this instance one that described the risk of making organizational changes. Each planned change was arrayed along a horizontal axis running from high to medium to low compatibility with Chase's patterns of behavior, and along a vertical axis indicating high, medium, and low importance to Butcher's strategy. Any change that showed up in this three-by-three matrix as being higher in strategic importance than in cultural compatability was deemed an unacceptable risk. In those cases MAC advised the bank to find less dangerous tactics, rethink its strategy, or, as a last resort, try to change its culture.

Ultimately, the project flopped, as Chase's subsequent record suggests—the bank still is prone to unforeseen disasters, such as the collapse of Drysdale Securities last year. Neither party will discuss the grisly details, but it seems MAC's first report on Chase's unspoken norms was so scathing that it nearly wiped out any audience for the 100 pages of recommendations submitted later on.

The debacle did not, however, prevent Chase and other banks from pursuing cultural change, or keep consultants from going after their business (see box, page 702). It also helped spur MAC to come up this year with the CEO's Change Agenda, a less inflammatory recipe for yoking strategy and culture. The first three steps focus on planning. Honchos are advised to start by having senior managers reexamine the company's history, culture, and skills, as well as the traits of the business they're in. The process is aimed at culling bad strategies and uncovering good ones that the received corporate wisdom has masked. Next, the chief executive is to forge a vision of the new strategy and the shared values needed to make it work, then spread this gospel himself—in speeches, memos, and more informal contacts—and check up regularly on the number of converts.

Ideally, these steps work up enough momentum to whirl a company through the trickiest part of the process—confronting mismatches between present behavior patterns and those the future requires. This may entail designing new organizational arrangements and control systems to encourage different behavior. Getting into cultural issues late in the game presumably makes them easier to face. "You can't change culture by working on it directly," Howard Schwartz says today. "You must have some strategic ground to stand on, then build a vision of what a company wants to be before rubbing their noses in what they are."

The last three items on the list specify methods of creating change. Chief executives are told to promulgate and reinforce the new values in everything they do, from the kinds of people they spend most of their time with to the incidents they choose to magnify to subordinates. They must reshuffle power to elevate exemplars of the new ways, including outsiders hired mainly for their values. The leader should use such levers of change as the budgeting process and internal public relations, constantly varying the pressure to keep people moving toward the right behavior.

MAC's approach is a lot for most companies to buy. Following it can cost up to $1 million a year in fees alone and take several years. But the agenda has appealed to some companies that face radical shake-ups in their circumstances, especially dereg-ulation. Theodore J. Saenger, president of Pacific Telephone, has coped with AT&T's reorganization by redefining his business according to the market segments that his company serves. He thinks MAC helped achieve behavioral changes to further that move: "We get much faster decisions about our lines of business, and I sense a willingness to get on with market positioning as well as clear agreement among middle managers and old hands on the need for a market orientation." Saenger tries to get people to think strategically by his own example: he used to spend 25% of his time on strategy and the rest on operations, but has now reversed that allocation. Pacific has also hatched plans to tie more of its top managers' compensation to corporate performance.

Still, the company has conceded much to a strong, old culture rather than risk changing it radically. Despite talk of marketing, Pacific retains a functional structure—one executive in charge of network operations, another responsible for engineering—and has no managers specifically accountable for attacking particular market segments. Saenger remains the only executive who must answer for profits and losses.

Consultants other than MAC treat culture less globally. They rely on questionnaires to measure organizational climate—how much a company should and actually does encourage individual responsibility, clear standards of behavior, appropriate rewards, and so forth—and on conventional tools for modifying behavior. These include feedback sessions (subordinates tell their supervisor how he's *really* doing) and team-building (getting them to work together).

Forum, for instance, with over 150 professionals in 13 offices, has started stressing the execution of strategy. The firm uses a method generally like MAC's—including the three-by-three matrix of cultural risk—though the names of the steps it recommends and their order differ. Forum concentrates on training people to change their patterns of behavior to fit the kind of culture a strategy implies. Often the company follows on the heels of strategy consultants with a climate survey, then helps managers to develop an ideal of new practices, to find out from subordinates how much current management practices fit the ideal, and to make plans for closing the gap. Smaller firms such as McBer & Co. of Boston, as well as a horde of individual consultants, offer minor variations on the basic trilogy of survey, feedback, and plan for change. Their emphases differ according to whether their traditional specialties are compensation, motivation, or organizational design and development.

Larger, broader-based consulting firms have reservations about the upsurge of concern with culture. Booz Allen & Hamilton, for example, insists that culture is but one aspect of organization. "To assume that the tail wags the dog is inane," says Francis N. Bonsignore, a partner charged with developing organizational concepts for clients. To the extent that Booz Allen has embraced cultural change, he adds, "We're making hay of an issue that's topical."

Paradoxically, McKinsey & Co., the colossus of consulting, is the most reluctant to endorse the new wisdom, even though two McKinseyites, Thomas J. Peters and Robert H. Waterman Jr., wrote *In Search of Excellence* and another, Allan A. Kennedy, was the coauthor of *Corporate Cultures.* Peters and Kennedy subsequently left the firm; Waterman heads up what McKinsey calls the organizational effectiveness group, but it's just a handful of people with a minuscule budget.

The big consulting firms may be right to be skeptical. A review of the evidence suggests that anybody who tries to unearth a corporation's culture, much less change it, is in for a rough time. The values and beliefs people espouse frequently have little to do with the ones they really hold; these tend to be half-hidden and elusive. Diagnosing culture calls for unusual, time-consuming techniques: auditing the content of decision-making, using an anthropologist to code the content of popular company anecdotes, holding open-ended interviews with people ranging from the man working on the loading dock to the executive in the corner office.

Having grown out of a company's history, values are strengthened daily in a myriad of subtle ways, from observation of how people get ahead in the organization to the words employees choose to describe their companies. Moreover, people cling tightly, even irrationally, to their values and beliefs—a popular example among consultants and academics is the religious group that predicted the end of the world, and when the prophecy failed, advanced the date of doomsday, refusing any longer to specify it.

It may be easier to change the people instead. In the long term, according to many human-resource specialists, the key to culture is whom you hire and promote. People often get jobs and move up more for the degree to which they fit prevailing norms than for any objective reason. George G. Gordon, a partner at Hay Associates, which specializes in designing compensation schemes, says, "AT&T at one time had people in personnel who had been there for years hire the new marketing types. Is it any wonder the new hires turned out be a lot like the old guard?" This is not to say that judging people solely on performance—"making the numbers"—is a good way to build a vibrant culture. "Hiring and promoting build culture and weed out incompatibles," notes Richard E. Boyatzis of McBer. "The companies that do the worst job of it have the sink or swim philosophy, and I predict they'll die when their main products do." A corollary, notes Vijay Sathe, who teaches a course on corporate culture at the Harvard Business School, is the importance companies like Minnesota Mining & Manufacturing, IBM, and Procter & Gamble attach to indoctrinating new hires. "The early stages are crucial," he thinks. "It's your greatest chance to make real changes in people's values."

In extreme cases, companies pressed to transform themselves just fire the recalcitrants who harbor fusty, intractable values and norms. As William T. Ylvisaker, chairman of Gould, went on a business-buying-and-selling spree to transform that auto parts and battery company into a power in electronics, he sold off longtime executives along with their operations. Two-thirds of Gould's current senior managers came from acquired businesses or from somewhere else outside. Directors of Burroughs and Prime Computer concluded the best way to change those companies was to bring in a chief executive from elsewhere; in both cases, the new leaders have replaced many of the old guard with recruits from IBM (see "The Blumenthal Revival at Burroughs," *Fortune,* October 5, 1981). Such dramatic measures—in effect, cultural transplants—were deemed necessary to achieve desired financial results.

The clarion message of the culture books is that high-performing corporations foster values beyond simple concern for the numbers. The IBM field engineer doesn't hesitate to use his own money for traveling to soothe a grumpy customer; his devotion to the value of service makes him do it, and the company's devotion to the same value ensures that he'll be reimbursed. Boeing and other "excellent" companies find it easier to assemble and disperse teams that cross organizational lines because shared values are more compelling than the boxes on an organization chart or a department's subculture. When Hewlett-Packard is forced to eliminate jobs and put the displaced workers through sometimes difficult retraining, managers reinterpret the H-P value of secure employment, building a new belief that workers are obliged to keep themselves well trained. Employees still regard H-P as a secure place to work.

If you long to instill such values in your company, can you do it? *Should* you? Most students of culture would answer "Probably not" to both questions. Notes Allan Kennedy: "There are only five reasons to justify large-scale cultural change; if your company has strong values that don't fit a changing environment; if the industry is very competitive and moves with lightning speed; if your company is mediocre or worse; if the company is about to join the ranks of the very largest companies; or if it's smaller but growing rapidly. Otherwise, don't do it." Kennedy's analysis of ten cases of attempted cultural change shows that it will cost you between 5% and 10% of what you already spend on the people whose behavior is supposed to change, and even then you're likely to get only half the improvement you want. He warns, "It costs a fortune and takes forever." Executives who have succeeded in fundamentally transforming a culture put a more precise estimate on how long the process requires: six to 15 years.

It's important to make sure you're not just caught up in a fad. "Corporate culture could be the Hula-Hoop of the 1980s," cracks one consultant. The prospect of a strong culture can seem a panacea for all your problems, much as getting the right corporate strategy did in the 1970s. "The fantasy is of some magic force, some secret ingredient, or some mystical glue that brings together all the people in an organization in a sense of shared purpose, commitment, and direction," notes David A. Nadler, founder of Organizational Research & Consultation Inc., a New York City firm. It's all too easy to pin your company's problems on an amorphous culture, forgetting the closely related, harder aspects of organization—control systems, planning meetings, divisional structures, and so forth—that both shape and express culture.

If you still covet the mystical glue, consider the obvious, low-cost adhesives. A tactic fairly standard by now is to develop a statement of corporate purpose, an awesome list of what the company believes in, and then remind everyone of it constantly. To be consistent, tailor your formal systems, structures, and personnel policies to reflect those declarations. You should reinforce the message by giving special awards for behavior in accordance with key values—inventiveness, say, or customer service—taking care to publicly shower "attaboys" on the folks with the right stuff. You can work your company's informal structures and processes, holding picnics for the elect and spreading stories about what Joe, the star salesman, did to get the big order. Some poetic license will help. Like McDonald's, Apple, and others, you could set up an internal "university" to indoctrinate employees.

These fixes may well change behavior, but they won't do much by themselves to instill the compelling culture you seek. As attentive readers of *In Search of Excellence* recall, the book posits that the great majority of outstanding companies trace their cultures back to an influential founder or other top manager who personified the value system. These revered characters—Robert Wood Johnson, Harley Procter, Thomas J. Watson Sr.—relentlessly hammered at a few basics that became the cultural core of their companies. Subsequent managements perpetuated the legacy. The despair of many corporations is that they can't point to such seeming superhumans in their past.

The lament for the extraordinary man doesn't cut much ice with the culturalists. Many of the stories that grow up around a Watson, they point out, are just legends born of the human tendency to attribute all values to an omnipotent, omniscient, preferably dead person. Legendary leaders, they insist, aren't uniquely charismatic, just savvy. They are smart enough to know what kind of culture is best for the business, persistent enough to harp on values in word and deed for decades, and dedicated enough to tailor all their actions to the value system. The top managers of Walt Disney Productions, for example, are known to instinctively pick up any gum wrappers and cigarette butts they spot defiling Walt's vision of Disneyland. They have followed the advice of IBM's Watson to put the business into their hearts.

Leaders driven by values are, above all, tuned in to symbolism. "They're showmen," says Tom Peters. Rene McPherson, one of the few executives Peters will credit with having transformed a culture, dramatized new values at Dana Corp. by tossing the auto parts company's multi-volume policy manuals into a wastebasket during a staff meeting and replacing them with a one-page statement of beliefs. Renn Zaphiropoulos, the flamboyant co-founder and president of Versatec, a Xerox subsidiary that makes graphics plotters for computers, places a high value on loyalty—understandably, since Versatec sits in the middle of California's high-turnover Silicon Valley. Whenever a Versatec employee reaches his fifth or tenth anniversary with the company, he's invited to lunch with the president, who carries off the feted individual in one of his Rolls-Royces. The main features of Versatec's lobby are two plaques listing the names of five- and ten-year veterans. It comes as no great surprise that as a young man Zaphiropoulos was a three-time winner on Ted Mack's *Original Amateur Hour.*

By the standards of most companies, managers given to such symbolic behavior would be considered near-fanatics who indulge themselves in grandstanding, corny stories, and other sundry foolishness. Indeed, Peters calls them "maniacs who overkill." The corporations they inspire are intolerant, at least when it comes to central values. A chief executive who wants to beef up his culture may well have to hire an extremely forceful, close-to-obsessive new leader or, if he doesn't want to replace himself, become a true believer. It's quite an unlikely transformation, suggests one student of

corporate culture, because the real constituency of most top managers is not their organization at large, but their peers and immediate subordinates. The other fellows at the country club may not be amused.

The importance of management by symbolic behavior makes life awkward for consultants. Since most chief executives lack the theatrical skills to trumpet values powerfully, the hired gun must play drama coach. MAC, for instance, usually meets monthly with clients' chief executives to help them manage their daily behavior and review the kinds of signals they give out at company meetings. But few senior managers are likely to welcome tinkering with their personal styles, and few consultants are likely to be good at doing it. "To help out with cultural change," says Bob Waterman of McKinsey, "you have to be a concerned analyst, a role model, a coach, a counselor, and a catalyst who will help the client's internal teams make their own decisions. Those activities undermine our traditional value—special knowledge—and haven't fallen within the skill sets of most MBAs and consultants." Waterman says that McKinsey can do such cultural consulting, but that his firm and others have good reason to approach the subject gingerly, at least for now.

If they listen to the academics, consultants may never enter the culture biz at all. Theoretically, charismatic founders of companies are ideally situated to shape culture. But according to Joanne Martin, an associate professor of organizational behavior at the Stanford Graduate School of Business Administration, who is studying several nascent Silicon Valley companies, fewer than half of a new company's values are those of the founder and chief executive. The rest develop because of the business environment and employees' need to attach meaning to their work. Says Martin, "Culture may simply exist."

In established firms, conclude experts who don't have a consulting ax to grind, the possibilities for influencing culture may be even slimmer. Says William P. Nilsson, who runs management development for Hewlett-Packard, "I don't think [President] John Young could fundamentally change our values if he wanted to." In sum, says Vijay Sathe of

Harvard, it is exceedingly difficult to transform a culture. Waterman and Peters, he suggests, should have ended *In Search of Excellence* with a boldface warning: Caution—this may be impossible to duplicate.

For all the hype, corporate culture is real and powerful. It's also hard to change, and you won't find much support for doing so inside or outside your company. If you run up against the culture when trying to redirect strategy, attempt to dodge; if you must meddle with culture directly, tread carefully and with modest expectations.

Cultural Therapy for Anxious Bankers

If trying to get a grip on your corporate culture can be compared to undergoing psychotherapy—and it can without much distortion—U.S. banks have good reason to put themselves on the couch. As they look out over the new, deregulated landscape, many are finding that they're not sufficiently adaptive, to use the therapist's favorite encomium, to chart a winning course. Brokers, insurance companies, and foreign institutions are trespassing on their turf, and yesterday's genteel behavior won't stand up to the new competitive pressure.

Not surprisingly, the appointment books of management-consulting firms that help companies work on their cultures are full of bank names. "When the definition of an industry changes, not only do strategies have to be reexamined, but also the fundamental beliefs and principles on which the strategies are premised," says Stanley Davis, 43, an independent consultant and self-described "organizational clinician," whose clients have included a number of money-center banks.

Among them is First Chicago, where personnel turnover was so hectic before and after his arrival that Chairman Barry Sullivan found himself a stranger among strangers. The bank's culture seemed to have been ousted along with its former chairman, A. Robert Abboud. "We needed to develop a standard of shared values, of how to behave to customers and to each other," explains Chief Financial Officer William McDonough, who guided the bank through eight months of soul-searching with Davis and the Management Analysis Center (MAC) of Cambridge, Massachusetts.

In evaluating staff behavior throughout the bank, McDonough and his crew identified one troubling predisposition—an aversion to risk—that was likely to hamper Sullivan's efforts to push First Chicago into the ranks of the nation's top five performers by 1985. "Serious credit losses in the late 1970s had made people gun-shy," McDonough says. "We had to make everyone realize that risk is part of this business." First Chicago has attempted to foster aggressiveness in the staff by implementing incentive plans geared to successful risk-taking. The new spirit seems to be taking hold, though not without risk—nonperforming assets are on the rise.

Bank of America recently engaged Davis and MAC to help it get back to the basics that rapid growth had obscured. "Our course over the last decade was to focus on profits. The customer didn't always come first," concedes Robert Beck, 43, an executive vice president of the bank. The formula began to fail B of A in the mid-1970s, when market share dropped. Return on assets fell soon after.

Still, at an early stage, B of A's battle plan is to reacquaint the bank with the values of its founder, A. P. Giannini. On the then novel conviction that every man deserved a teller, Giannini turned the unassuming Bank of Italy in San Francisco's North Beach area into one of the world's largest commercial banks. Most companies don't have a home-grown hero around whom to rally, and both Davis and MAC agreed Bank of America should capitalize on its past to woo customers. Today this means a commitment to a more aggressive approach to marketing and more widespread use of automatic teller machines. Every man still deserves a teller—even an electronic one.

Too much too fast was also what drove Toronto-Dominion Bank to take a long, slow look at itself. Since 1970, assets at Canada's fifth-largest bank have ballooned eightfold and branches have grown to 1,000. Qualified personnel to handle the challenge were in short supply and union rules made it nearly impossible to fire people. The prescription from Forum Corp, of Boston: have subordinates evaluate their managers to isolate trouble spots. Forum then uses this feedback from the subordinates to train the managers in goal setting, coaching, teamwork, and accountability as needed. "Forum helps us keep our work force current, able, and competitive," says President Robert Korthals, 50. So far, the bank has appraised 375 managers and replaced their cost-of-living raises with bonuses based on individual performance. In phase two, bank customers will critique branch personnel.

While most executives are stuck with managing around an existing corporate culture, David Banks, 40, had the luxury of creating his own when he set up the Global Specialized Industries group at Chase Manhattan Bank. In 1979 Chase summoned the McKinsey & Co. consulting firm to help reorganize international lending. In the process, Banks unabashedly adopted and attempted to instill in his 200 officers the eight "excellent-company qualitites" later celebrated in the book *In Search of Excellence*.

Among the book's more cryptic tenets is that "simultaneous loose-tight properties" are important in handling the troops. Banks's down-to-earth translation of the principle: "I give my managers enough latitude to achieve objectives in their own personal way. If someone closes a good deal, I give him a bottle of champagne. But I crack heads when the objectives aren't being met." Also heartily endorsed: "Stay close to the customer." Banks has cut back office staff and increased the number of lending officers because he believes bankers in the field are better equipped to design the kind of financial deals that his clients are looking for.

Though it's still too early to tell if excellent qualitites ensure excellent results, the global industries group appears healthy. Since 1980 its loans outstanding have grown some 30% a year, to about a quarter of the bank's corporate loan portfolio. The Drysdale fiasco originated elsewhere in the bank. So did Chase's Penn Square loans—after Banks had enough excellent instincts to turn them down.

Jaclyn Fierman

HP-Grenoble: Case Study in Technology Transfer

Karl Schwarz

The transfer of a product or process from one location of an organization to another may be proposed for a variety of reasons. a need to increase corporate presence in a given market area, a desire to spread risks, or a requirement to free congested facilities for other purposes. Technology may be transferred to areas with lower operating costs or tax structures for obvious profit motives. Occasionally, the purpose may be to seed new operations or to simply balance production. Besides these stated considerations, transfers usually involve some interdivisional competition, which often leads to significant innovation. The consequent attitudinal and profit benefits frequently exceed those originally projected and extend to other products, processes, or people. The motives for any two transfers are never quite the same, even within the same company. But in any technology transfer, there are enough common elements to make a single case study instructive.

In the late 1960s, the Hewlett-Packard Company, a then $300 million manufacturer of electronic measuring and computational equipment, began to question the wisdom of continuing to focus all of its European manufacturing growth on its two existing facilities. Would greater benefits accrue if a third factory were opened? The idea did not stem from a lack of confidence in either the ten-year-old

Karl Schwarz was trained as a mechanical engineer, receiving his B.S. from Stanford University in 1955. Following a three-year assignment on a Navy destroyer as an engineering officer, he returned to Stanford for a year of graduate work in mechanical engineering and in 1959 joined the Hewlett-Packard Company in Palo Alto as a development engineer. After holding various research-and-development and manufacturing positions, he was transferred to Hewlett-Packard's Japanese affiliate in Tokyo, where he held management posts in research and development, manufacturing, and marketing. In 1970, following a five-year stay in Japan, he was asked to establish the subsidiary in France, HP-Grenoble. In 1976, he returned to the United States and his present assignment as general manager of the Scientific Instruments Division of Hewlett-Packard.

German factory or the slightly newer unit in Scotland. These European divisions had historically been a great source of pride to HP. By almost every measure, they had consistently shown outstanding performance. But the question as to whether or not a broader presence in the European community would better serve the total European marketing effort was one which had to be objectively answered.

A task force consisting of senior members of the German factory management team studied the issue. For a variety of reasons, they concluded that establishment of a third facility in Europe—specifically, in France—would provide the best balance for marketing and manufacturing Hewlett-Packard electronic products there.

One major virtue of having a European team develop such arguments was that they were bound to be supportive of any new venture resulting from the study. This proved to be a critical element in maintaining harmonious relationships between all the factories under the demands of some subsequent intra-European product line rationalizations.

In 1969, HP contacted the French authorities concerning its interest in establishing a manufacturing facility in France. The company, its products and policies, were well known to the government; a wholly owned sales organization employing over three hundred people had been established in France several years earlier. Within the next year, HP visited several areas in which the French wanted to encourage foreign investment.

None of the products manufactured by HP at that time imposed major geographic constraints. The raw materials were easily transported, as were the finished instruments. Proximity to international airports (one to two hours by truck) and customs clearance facilities were the only logistic considerations. The primary factors in the site selection process involved people: the availability of trained or trainable personnel and the appeal of the region to those who would have to move there. Cultural activities, housing, educational facilities, and recreational opportunities were all important; the quality of life was an issue that was discussed frequently, even at that time. And of course, the site had to be an easy and attractive place for customers to visit! Labor costs were scarcely considered.

Rather quickly, the international vice-president and his staff determined that the city of Grenoble held the greatest appeal for HP. This was in spite of generous government incentives to locate in other parts of France. HP made it clear that investment plans would be developed if a suitable building site could be agreed upon. Grenoble easily met HP's criteria because of the existence of local centers of high technology—academic, governmental, and industrial—which could ensure a good supply of skilled and talented people, and because of its beautiful setting, which would be especially important to professionals and their families.

The city of Grenoble, for its part, was anxious to attract high technology companies and had established a liaison office specifically for that purpose. An excellent, forty-acre parcel of land in the adjoining town of Eybens was made available to the company, and an agreement to purchase this land, enough for a plant site capable of ultimately employing up to three thousand people, sealed HP's commitment to the region.

In mid-1970, I was asked to manage the start-up of HP's factory in France, and the following twelve months were dedicated to working out the details of the program. It was not a propitious year for new investments. A major recession had forced the company to reduce production schedules to a four-and-a-half-day week. Although there were no layoffs, most managers were not enthusiastic about expanding abroad when there was a shortage of work in the American factories.

Nevertheless, it was felt that since a long-term strategy was involved, planning should be continued. An investment proposal was developed by the HP European headquarters in Geneva to meet the requirements of the French government. This outlined, in a general way, the financial nature of the investment, the timetable for such a program, the activities planned, and a manning schedule. Great care was taken to ensure that the company, its philosophy, and its plans were honestly represented and that its need for flexibility in the product program was preserved.

The French government, for its part, wanted a rather specific itemization of products to be produced. However, the very rapid model changes characteristic of the electronics business required that HP forsake none of its product options. After considerable negotiation, the government consented to HP's request for permission to manufacture most items in its line. This proved to be a critically important decision. As it turned out, of the two product technologies actually transferred, one was a commercial failure, the other succeeded beyond anyone's most optimistic projections.

The investment proposal was submitted to the government on February 8, 1971, and approval was granted on April 9, 1971. There was only one major stipulation: that a research activity be started within the year following the commencement of manufacturing operations. This turned a statement of intent in HP's investment proposal into a requirement, but one that was consistent with the company's operating philosophy: to have a product development laboratory associated with each manufacturing division.

In June, in spite of continued concern regarding the unfavorable economic climate, HP gave the final go-ahead for the start-up of operations in leased facilities. Two product lines were selected for transfer to the operation, which was to be known as HP Grenoble. These were products which would complement existing European manufacturing activities and, in addition, would present a good opportunity to train a technical staff. One product was an electronic distance measuring instrument (DMI) for the surveying market. The other was a scientific minicomputer for use in automatic measurement and data systems, systems which were being integrated by the other two European factories. One product, therefore, was destined for direct sale to European customers, the other for sale to HP's existing European factories and subsequent resale. Since the Grenoble production was to be only a small fraction of worldwide requirements, adequate backup for Europe was available should there have been technical difficulties during the start-up or should demand have exceeded the rather tight capacity limits.

Within the general framework of the investment plan, a specific set of one-year targets was developed. The finance manager of HP's Japanese joint venture, Yokogawa-Hewlett-Packard, was in the United States on special assignment, and he volunteered to work out the targets for the new Greno-ble facility. He was an ideal person for this task since he had an excellent grasp of international finance and manufacturing. It was quickly determined that a September 1, 1971 start-up was a realistic goal, and that first-year shipments of about $2 million at 8 percent net profit would be reasonable. This could be accomplished with a total employment of forty-five persons by year's end. Actual unit production would average about ten minicomputers per month and twenty of the distance measuring instruments. An initial capital investment of $1 million had been agreed to with the majority of the capitalization earmarked for the purchase of land.

Later targeting iterations determined what kind of manpower levels could be dedicated to training. It became clear that in order to maintain a good balance between desired profit margins and training investments upon which solid growth could occur, the division could not afford a large team of expatriate trainers. Ultimately, only four expatriates were brought into the operation, two Americans, a Swiss, and a German. In addition to major training responsibility, each of these individuals held a key management assignment. This concept of a working manager/trainer worked well during the first years of operation and evolved naturally into the permanent organizational structure. Research and development and marketing managers were not initially assigned, as these functions were only scheduled to be implemented following the complete transfer of manufacturing technology. Exhibit 1 describes the individuals on the start-up team, their responsibilities, and backgrounds.

The objective in staffing was to ultimately utilize local nationals for the entire operation. In its years of international activities, HP had continually reinforced its good experience in using nationals to operate and manage its overseas facilities. It was with considerable pride that the company pointed out in 1971 that even with an employment level of 17,000 and international sales at over 40 percent of the corporate total of $378 million, less than two dozen U.S. employees worked overseas! Only those who had a particular technical or managerial expertise were given a chance to go abroad and then usually only during the early phases of a new activity.

EXHIBIT 1   HP-Grenoble start-up team

Manufacturing manager. Pierre Ollivier, a French citizen, electrical engineer, nine years experience in HP's R&D labs, responsible for manufacturing systems, production engineering, personnel and community liaison.

Production manager. Gary Mueller, a U.S. expatriate, technician, five years of HP experience in minicomputer fabrication, responsible for all test and technical training, on a two to three year assignment.

Materials manager. Ludwig Ott, a German citizen, ten years international manufacturing with HP, responsible for importation, scheduling of materials, and inventory control, on a nine month assignment.

Finance manager. Christoph Beck, a Swiss citizen, five years experience in HP's Geneva headquarters, assigned to manage all financial systems and financial reports, on a two to three year assignment.

Line leaders. Francois Fouladoux and Jackie Porcher, French citizens, technicians with broad experience in customer service activities in the French sales company, primary recipients of technical training, assigned to build up teams of technicians and assembly personnel, permanent.

General manager. Karl Schwarz, a U.S. citizen, eleven years of HP experience, five years in international, general responsibility for policy and planning on a three to five year assignment.

It was standard HP practice to hire talented, English-speaking nationals and to provide opportunities for them to travel widely to other locations, to learn specific tasks, to interact with their counterparts, and to understand the personality of the company. This supplement to formal on-the-job-training ensured that within a period of two to three years, the culture of the corporation could be successfully transplanted. The fierce local pride that developed as a result of these policies ensured some of the most productive, quality-oriented units in the corporate system.

In June 1971 a 9,000-square-foot building, which had been used to manufacture furniture, was leased. In September the first expatriates (myself and my family) arrived. During the next three months, the leased buildings were cleaned, painted, and outfitted with lights and power. Competitive bidding was carefully managed to gain ex-perience with local subcontractors for the construction of the permanent building. Banking relationships were established, customs clearance procedures worked out, and about ten people were hired. Parts began to arrive in December, and assembly and test work began immediately. In February 1972, five months after the first personnel arrived in Grenoble, the first minicomputers had been completed and shipped. Much of the work was straightforward. The soldering and assembly skills were similar to those required for making the hi-fi kits popular during the 1960s. Transfer of these skills was facilitated by reference to standard practice documentation available generally throughout the company, with interpretational backup provided by the technical managers. Components and many fabricated parts were purchased from the parent U.S. divisions. Some of the electronic modules had been prebuilt, although most of the printed circuit assemblies were made in France.

The real challenge lay in the final test of the product. Unlike the parent division, which relied on highly automated test equipment to locate circuit faults, the Grenoble management elected to use only very simple manual diagnostic tools. This was intended to force the development of high-level troubleshooting skills among the French technicians. They were equal to the task. Rather than have automatic testers to logically trace, identify, and locate faults, the technicians themselves were required to understand the entire circuit function and, by reasoning alone, to find and fix defective components. Because of the complexity of many of the circuits, this game of digital hide-and-seek demanded superb understanding of the operation of the product. The production manager worked alongside the technicians to ensure that their understanding was accurate and complete. Success was easy to measure. Either the computers passed their diagnostic tests or they didn't. More than any other decision, this policy ensured the building of great technical strength within the work force and offered an important reason for the French team's pride in its skills and in its product quality. At the time the first units were shipped, capital equipment costs were a modest $28 thousand.

Shortly after the first assembly work was started, two young engineers were hired to work on the production line as technicians. Both were ultimately destined for production management. But by transferring the technical details to engineers as well as technicians, much greater understanding was transplanted than had only the technicians themselves been exposed to the nuts and bolts of the business. This redundancy in skills, of course, generated widespread management confidence in the operation.

In June, with more technicians on board, and the work beginning to specialize, a training course on the fundamentals of HP minicomputers was started. It was to run about six months at four hours per week. The instructor was the production manager.

Little by little, more complex assemblies were transferred to the operation. All of these subsequent transfers were accompanied by visits to the American parent facility by a key French technician or engineer so that the technology as well as a sense of the process and its problems could be assimilated.

During the same period, but shifted by two months, a similar program was proceeding on the DMI. However, sales soon began to fall well below forecast and it became apparent that the product was not matched to the requirements of the European market. Forecasts had not been based on any European sales history since it was a new instrument. It was a metric version of a successful U.S. model which had made an enormous technical contribution to the surveying art. Sales plans had been based on extrapolating the U.S. experience. However, the Europeans used slightly different measurement methods which neutralized some of the technical advantages of the device, and the primary competition was Swiss, which, because of duties, neutralized HP's price advantage. After a year of effort and some innovative marketing, it became apparent that this particular model of the DMI could not sustain the necessary investment levels in marketing or manufacturing. Although the technology was exciting and had been well mastered, production of the DMI was abandoned in mid-1973.

Meanwhile, the minicomputer production was evolving smoothly. At the end of 1972, the factory employed forty-eight people in the following categories:

Manufacturing: direct labor, twenty; overhead, three; manufacturing, engineering and quality assurance, seven; materials, eight.

Product development, three.

Finance, seven.

Manufacturing efficiency was respectable. Efficiency was simply measured by comparing French labor times to the U.S. times for similar operations. No allowances were made for the production volume differences, but the U.S. volume was normally at least ten times greater than France's. For the minicomputer activities, the French unit-labor times were only 32 percent higher than the U.S. times after twelve months of operation. For the DMI, Grenoble times were 12 percent higher, and for printed circuit assembly and test, 24 percent higher.

Since great stress was placed on quality rather than quantity during the learning phase and since much of the test equipment designed to increase productivity was not available to the French team, the first year's performance was considered remarkable. Profit figures from 1972 and subsequent years corroborated this judgment. Warranty rates were also excellent, with the French warranty costs being 35 percent lower than the U.S. costs for identical products.

During 1973, three peripheral products were added to broaden and balance the operation. The same basic transfer methodology was followed for these products: training of a single technician (in the United States), with emphasis on manual testing and logical troubleshooting. Growth to eighty people was projected, of which thirty-four were to be direct labor (wire, assembly, and test personnel). Twenty-five computers and forty-seven peripheral instruments per month were forecast. By the end of that year, shipments were to have reached an annual rate of about $5 million.

As it turned out, business boomed. Late 1973 saw unit sales at double the forecast, and personnel hiring was obliged to keep pace. The year ended with the divisional payroll standing at 122 employees. The U.S. fabrication backstop was removed, and the French factory acquired full responsibility for meeting the entire European marketing demand.

Although the number of additional people was not large in the absolute sense, growth of over 150 percent in one year represented a significant training challenge. It caused the team to realize that for the first time the division's growth, now being determined exclusively by market factors, would be much more dynamic than the carefully controlled situation which had characterized the first year and a half of its experience. The real world meant that fast footwork was required to manage this kind of business. Although the change of pace was tough on some people, the great majority of the team accepted the frequent scheduling and targeting modifications as natural and normal business challenges.

During the first year, it became clear that the technicians, production engineers, and production managers would easily master the problems of understanding how to manufacture American designed products. Their accelerated apprenticeship, built upon the universal language of electronics and computer engineering, would be soon completed and they had demonstrated that they were capable of adapting their skills to the fabrication of practially any product in the Hewlett-Packard line. But manufacturing of this type still called for great dependence upon the parent U.S. facility. Product improvements, component substitutions, tooling, pricing, marketing strategies were still the responsibility of the parent.

To be a truly viable entity, to complete the transfer of technology, a research and development or product development capability had to be established. The transfer of some technical responsibility along with a clear product line charter was necessary. Such a move would provide tangible evidence to the corporation, to the division's employees, and to the government agencies monitoring the facility's progress of HP's confidence in the completeness of the technology transfer. Manufacturing is the first step in a transfer of technology;

successful research and development is the final one.

The original research and development charter for the division involved development of unique applications software for European customers. As with manufacturing, a nucleus of highly talented people was assembled. It consisted of two French engineers who had recently completed graduate work at the University of California, Berkeley and Stanford, the French manager of the HP Paris Data Center, and two Americans, a computer scientist, and an electrical engineer. The team began to come together in 1972 and started work almost immediately on its first project—an applications program to manage data in a clinical laboratory environment.

After a year's work, a change in U.S. product group management led to a redirection of effort away from the applications software toward a more traditional HP hardware effort. Much of the previous year's work was saved and built upon. The year of focusing Grenoble's development efforts at a specific problem in the clinical laboratory served well to guide the engineers' thinking as a general purpose data collection system was planned. The division's charter was appropriately modified. It would be responsible for the worldwide data collection activity of Hewlett-Packard.

In many ways, this aspect of the research-and-development technology really wasn't transferred; it grew. It was nourished by support from the product group management in the U.S., who also made sure that unnecessary competition didn't develop in domestic U.S. divisions, and it was shaped by the French team working within what they perceived to be the spirit of the company's research-and-development philosophy. Dozens of liaison trips were made in the succeeding several years between France and the U.S. to ensure that the French product would be complementary to and compatible with the other products in the HP computer group family. As the supporting technology evolved, the new product was modified. The process was analogous to the architectural design of a new building: frequent checks with the commissioner to make certain that there were no surprises and that the commissioner's technical ideas were being used and good sense of freedom in the "architect's office," that it might do what was necessary to design and build the structure.

A unique large-scale integrated circuit critical to the project was developed in conjunction with EFCIS, one of the leading custom integrated circuit fabricators in France. Special-purpose mechanical tooling was adapted from other HP products to simplify the design effort, and slowly the team grew in size. In 1976, it numbered fifteen.

Concurrently, full worldwide manufacturing and marketing responsibility for two products which had been produced by other HP divisions but which were related to the data collection area were transferred to Grenoble. This was to encourage growth of the marketing team in preparation for the time when the facility would have its own product. Profits from these two products were to be used to finance the research-and-development efforts of the division. This provided a mechanism to gage and manage the size of the research-and-development budget. The data collection "product line" had to stand on its own feet financially, including the new research-and-development investments. Initial levels would be set by profits of the existing two products in the line. Growth would be possible in proportion to the success of the locally developed product.

Again, an apprenticeship was served by the division and its managers under the eye of the parent division and the product groups. Among the individual engineers, it was more of a weaning and growing process. Four years and thousands of decisions later, the first Grenoble product, the HP 3070 Data Collection Terminal, was announced.

Throughout the rest of the division, other activities were developing. The personnel program had been innovative and marked an extension of HP's established policy of "being among the leaders of the industry." Competitive pay, flexible working hours, liberal vacation, holiday and sick-leave policies keyed to regional standards contributed to excellent employee morale and enthusiasm for the operation. Above all, an interested and supportive top management team (comprised of Hewlett, Packard, the international vice-president, and several executive vice-presidents and group manag-

ers), displayed continued support by frequent visits. They cemented a sense of pride among the new HP Grenoble employees by confirming their importance as contributing members of the HP family. Not only were the managers supportive on every visit, more significantly, they continued to issue positive reports upon their return home.

By the end of 1973, when there were enough statistics to be meaningful, absenteeism was averaging 1.9 percent, and annual attrition was 5 percent. Both of these were considered useful indicators of good employee attitudes. The company's reputation was solidly established. The acceptance rate for employment offers was 95 percent and 3,300 job applications had been made to fill the 122 positions occupied in the fall of 1973. Clearly, HP had had the opportunity to be selective and used it to acquire an outstanding group of men and women.

During the early planning stages in 1971, some top-level concern was expressed that the socialist and communist parties in Grenoble would cause major problems for the operation. The citizens of Grenoble had, after all, played a major part in the beginnings of the French revolution and more recently, in 1968, had elected a socialist mayor. The suburb in which the facilities were located had a communist mayor, and most of the companies in the region were involved with either the communist CGT or the more pragmatic socialist CFDT unions.

The political worries turned out to be only worries. The mayor of Grenoble, in fact, proved to be one of the most articulate supporters of Hewlett-Packard within the local community as well as in Paris where his *savoir faire* proved critical on several occasions.

Concerns about socialist-backed unionism were another matter, however. Two years after the start-up, and in spite of the fact that there were no early problems with leftists, U.S. management once again became anxious about the implications of the government-mandated "committee d'entreprise" (employee council) and the "deleges du personnel" (shop stewards). There was considerable confusion about the union's power and rights to represent the employees. Most U.S. managers imagined the

French system to be similar to that in the U.S. or worse, the U.K. But French law and practice are far more subtle. With reasonable sensitivity, good managers can achieve excellent working relationships with the multifaceted groups that the employees elect to represent them. While French labor law is heavily weighted in favor of the employee, it is pragmatic. If legal recourse is necessary, the mechanism is logical and the outcome usually predictable.

In 1973, the year after the employment level reached fifty, elections were held. By law they had to be structured to give the inside track to union representatives. About three employees sought sanctioning by the local CFDT and a minority of the employees supported them. This minority did so largely out of feelings that it was the norm in France to have a counterbalance, a loyal opposition, to management. The majority of the employees voted for independent candidates. Regardless of whether they were elected from the union or the independent ticket, the individuals who made up the first employee council were remarkably free of doctrinaire or disruptive attitudes. They all worked hard for the improvement of the operation.

Because the benefits program already in place was extremely progressive, there was little leadership that union representatives could offer. During subsequent years, what small interest there was in union-inspired programs withered away. For their part, top management generally came to feel that the elected employee representative structure had made a positive contribution to divisional communications, a contribution that may serve as a model for other facilities in the future.

By 1975 employment had reached 250 people, a new 120,000-square-foot building had been completed, and operations in three rented buildings were consolidated. A metal shop was beginning to fabricate parts for the locally produced instruments and the research-and-development operation had completed its first prototype. In addition, profits of 8.5 percent were close to the corporate average.

In September 1975, the new facility was dedicated, almost exactly four years from the time the first members of the start-up team began their work in France. The division had earned responsibility for the worldwide production and technical support of an important family of minicomputer peripherals. This charter would ensure an opportunity for the division to contribute its own technology to the corporation, and in a sense, it would complete the cycle of the technology transfer. In late 1976, the first new product designed in the Grenoble labs and produced by its manufacturing activities was announced and technology began to flow west across the Atlantic. A different type of technology transfer began. HP-Grenoble embarked upon the most important phase of its existence, a new era of shared rather than simply transferred technical collaboration with the rest of the Hewlett-Packard Company.

John F. Bookout and Shell Oil Company

S hell Oil is an international corporation in two respects. Although it markets in the United States, it carries on exploration activities, produces crude oil, and operates other facilities around the world. More significant, however, is the fact that it is 69 percent foreign-owned. Its parent companies are the Royal Dutch Petroleum Company and The "Shell" Transport and Trading Company headquartered in London, England and The Hague, the Netherlands. It is the largest of a consortium of some five hundred companies operating in a hundred countries.

The nature of the relationship between Shell Oil and this group is complex. The eleven-member board of directors contains two representatives from the parent companies, one of whom is chairman. John Bookout has been president of Shell Oil and its chief executive officer since 1976, but the senior position on the board remains foreign-held. Shell Oil is America's largest foreign-controlled company (Exhibit 1), although it appears in fact to operate with considerable autonomy. The major

areas of involvement with other companies in the consortium are research and development and some exploration ventures.

Unlike many other oil companies, Shell has chosen not to diversify. It has certain coal operations and some scattered holdings outside the industry, but basically it is a petroleum company. Among the oil companies it has long been the leader in petrochemical production. It has characteristically emphasized domestic sources in exploring for oil, but major exploratory drilling operations have been mounted also in Brazil, Cameroon, and Malaysia. Significant production of oil and gas occurs in Cameroon, Canada, Malaysia, and New Zealand. The company is in the process of building a major petrochemical facility in Saudi Arabia.

Shell Oil was started in 1912 by Dutch interests as part of a plan to wrest a share of the U.S. oil market from John D. Rockefeller and his heirs. As it has grown, there has been a continuing need to balance out its relationships with its foreign parent companies, the U.S. government and its regulatory apparatus, and the American public to whom it markets. Generally, the foreign owners have maintained a very low profile. The company retains sizable lobbying and public relations staffs, and John Bookout devotes a substantial amount of his time to dealing with external publics. There has been a continuing effort to create an image of a company that is socially responsible within the United States context.

John Bookout's career reflects Shell Oil's international dimension as well as the nature of its industry. Born and raised in Shreveport, Louisiana in the midst of that state's oil industry, he made an early decision to work in the petroleum field. Service overseas with the U.S. Air Force during World War II delayed his pursuit of this goal, but by 1949, he had obtained a B.S. degree in geology from the University of Texas in Austin. A year later he had a master's degree, also in geology, and a starting job in exploration with Shell Oil Company.

For nine years, John Bookout worked as a petroleum geologist in the Tulsa, Oklahoma area. His first management position was as a division exploration manager in Tulsa. After two years, he went to Denver as area exploration manager and then spent 1963 and 1964 at parent company headquarters in The Hague. This was a clear signal that his career had shifted from practicing scientist to corporate executive. Returning to the United States, he served as manager of the Economics Department within Exploration and Production in New York, and then as vice-president successively of the Denver and New Orleans Exploration and Production areas. In 1970 he took over as president of Shell Canada in Toronto—a separate company within the consortium. Four years later, he moved to Shell Oil headquarters in Houston, Texas as executive vice-president of the company, preparatory to becoming president and CEO in 1976.

John Bookout is widely considered to be the leader of the best management team in the U.S. petroleum business. His career pattern, with its emphasis on both the technical and international aspects of his job, clearly has contributed to his success.

John Bookout

An 80-well drilling platform and a production platform were installed in 1980 in the Beta Field off Long Beach, California.

EXHIBIT 1 Foreign operations of Shell Oil

Foreign Operations

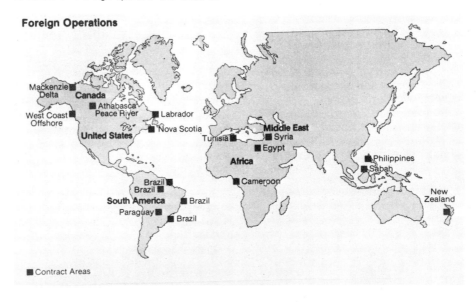

John F. Bookout and Shell Oil Company

At this plant in Norco, Louisiana, Shell produces olefins, ethylene, propylene, and butadiene.

PART EIGHT

Cases

Part One
1. Jack Powers' Morning
2. Choosing a Computing Center Supervisor: Six Candidates
3. Predicting the Future

Part Two
4. ABC Mud Engineering Company
5. Professor Zanuli Goes to Germany
6. Bendix Corporation "As the Boardroom Turns"

Part Three
7. Rodman Motors
8. Wade Jones Company of Illinois
9. Who's on First?
10. AT&T's Entrepreneur

Part Four
11. Texas Air Corporation: Peanuts and Profits
12. The Love Canal Incident

Part Five
13. A Thermos of "Tea" at KWC
14. Survey at Venture Manufacturing
15. Internal Theft at Kline's
16. The Road to Hell . . .

Part Six
17. Production Control at Carbide Products, Inc.
18. Tower Motor and Machine Company

Part Seven
19. John Lockley
20. Which Company Is Truly Multinational?

Jack Powers' Morning

8:23 A.M.

Jack had been with The Phone Company about five years and had reached the level of assistant district traffic superintendent.

He was at his desk on Tuesday morning reflecting on the billing error increases that had been brought to his attention last week. He was concerned about these increases and felt that this was the major problem facing his unit at the current time. He was trying to determine what course of action he should take to correct these problems when the secretary buzzed his office. He answered the phone, and the secretary told him that the union steward wanted to see him on the 2nd floor concerning a problem that she felt was crucial. He left his office wondering what the union steward was so upset about. He walked down the two flights of stairs imagining all sorts of wild stories the steward might have for him.

When he arrived at the unit, the union rep immediately began complaining of her schedule and of the unfair scheduling practices that the Chief Operator and the Assistant Chief Operator were guilty of. Her major complaint was that operators with large amounts of seniority were getting "split shifts," a very undesirable type of schedule. She said that she hadn't received a split shift yet, but she knew of several that had; and she was planning on filing a grievance unless the problem was corrected. After a lengthy discussion, Jack assured her that some action would be taken.

9:11 A.M.

As he walked back up the stairs he thought, "I should be turning this over to the Chief Operator to let her handle it, but it seems to me she's part of the problem, so I'll go ahead and handle it myself."

9:39 A.M.

As he reached the 3rd floor he met Dwayne, also an assistant district traffic superintendent, who was on his way to a coffee break. Dwayne asked him to join him. At the coffee break they discussed several problems that were common to both Dwayne's unit and Jack's unit. It was a comfort to find out that Dwayne was having as many problems as Jack felt that he was having. After the coffee break Jack went back to his office and began looking for the billing error reports that he knew were on his desk somewhere. He just couldn't remember which stack they were in. He had gone through the second stack of work on his desk when the secretary

The research and written case information were presented at a Case Research Symposium and were evaluated by the Case Research Association's Editorial Board. This case was prepared by Ron Thorn of the University of Southwestern Louisiana as a base for class discussion

buzzed him again and said there was a telephone call for him. When Jack answered, he was greeted with a very familiar voice. John had been his golfing partner since he moved to Fort Worth and was always ready to talk about golf. John had simply called to verify that they had tee off time on Saturday morning at 8:30. Jack said, "I'm looking forward to the game because I'll have a chance to work on that horrible slice I've developed. I can't figure out why I'm slicing so badly. Have you got any ideas?"

After about 15 minutes of discussing the possible cause of a left to right curve in a golf ball's flight, Jack hung up and began looking on his desk again for the billing error reports. He couldn't find them in the third stack and decided to work on the union steward's gripe first. It did seem urgent. He called his secretary and asked her to get a seniority list of the unit and last month's schedules, hoping to find out if there was, in fact, truth to the report that senior operators were getting split schedules.

10:04 A.M.
He began again looking for the billing error reports when Bill stuck his head in the door and said, "You got a minute?" Jack said, "Of course, come in." Bill was having trouble with a piece of equipment in his unit on the same floor and asked Jack if he had ever had a similar problem. Jack replied that he had not, but he would be glad to look at it and see if they could work something out. "Can you come now?" Bill asked. "Sure," Jack agreed, and they went down to Bill's unit to check out the piece of recording equipment that was used to check operator courtesy on a sampling basis. After spending over forty minutes with Bill looking at the equipment and not resolving the problem, they decided to call the Plant Manager. The Plant Manager said he'd send someone up immediately. Equipment was the Plant Department's responsibility, and they could usually fix these problems easily. "Thanks anyway, Jack," Bill said as Jack headed back toward his office.

10:51 A.M.
When he arrived at his office he found that his secretary had placed last month's schedules and the employee seniority records on his desk. After analyzing the schedules, Jack discovered that two of

the senior operators had been scheduled split shifts recently and on a regular basis. "Doggone it," he muttered to himself. "The Chief ought to know better than to let this happen." He didn't know whether it had been ordered by the Chief Operator, the Assistant Chief Operator, or whether the clerk had taken it on herself to do this, but he was upset with all of them. This kind of thing makes the union mad as Hell. Senior operators were supposed to have preference in selecting shifts according to the contract. Consistent with his decision to clear this mess up himself he immediately called Jane, the unit clerk. "Jane, this is Jack Powers. I want you to do something about the shift schedule of Mary Albert and Sue Knight. They've got twenty years' seniority and they've been scheduled an early morning-late evening split shift." "Mr. Powers, I was just doing what the Chief Operator told me to do, but I'll change the schedule right now if you say so," replied Jane. "I say so," answered Jack.

11:14 A.M.
Jack sat at his desk proudly reflecting on how easily he had solved the scheduling problem. He was sure that it wouldn't be coming up again for he had been firm and forceful in dealing with the Chief Operator's clerk. He started looking for the billing error report on his desk, but the secretary buzzed before he could find it. "Who is it?" Jack queried. "It's the Chief Operator, Mr. Powers."

The discussion that ensued revealed that the two senior operators who had been given split shifts had requested split shifts. These shifts would allow them to go home mid-day and be with their children who were getting off of school at that time. Obviously, Jack's face was somewhat red. He apologized to the Chief Operator, guaranteed her that next time he wouldn't bypass channels and promised to come to her first to find out if she knew more about any future problems than he did. After hanging up he was somewhat shook and decided to take his daily round of the units to find out if anybody had any major complaints or overwhelming problems that he could help out with. By the time he had returned from his daily round, it was time for lunch. As he was walking down to the cafeteria, he looked at his watch. It was 12:30 p.m. and he still hadn't found those billing error reports.

Choosing a Computing Center Supervisor: Six Candidates

The company was faced with the problem of selecting from among six internal candidates the individual who would serve most effectively as supervisor of a major computing center unit. The candidates were nominated by other computing center unit supervisors and personnel managers throughout the company. The question is which one would you select and why, if you were the primary decisionmaker and had to live with your decision.

The Candidates

George Smith was 24 years old and was a senior computer programmer without supervisory experience. He had been with the company since graduating from high school and had spent four of his six years in computer work. He was completely involved in his work, to the point where he viewed work as his main hobby. He had attended a nearby university intermittently at night since graduating from high school, but had not progressed very far.

At the present time George was viewed very favorably as a programmer; in fact, over the past year his supervisor had rated him at the top of his group in the speed with which he worked, and he was on the same level as one of the other candidates (Zastrow) in his dedication to work and cooperativeness. He was viewed as somewhat less accurate than some of the others, including Zastrow. Overall there was little question that he was a top-flight programmer.

On the other hand, there *had* been some problems in the past. George had been quite resistant early in his career about adjusting his work schedule to company needs, and there had been one occasion when he could not be found in the building when he was supposed to be working on the night shift. He had had some tax problems that had come to the company's attention.

These matters were generally considered over and done with, however. George was presently completely bound up in his work; if anything, he drove himself *too* hard. He was a very competitive person and the kind of individual who made his presence known and took an active part in the affairs of the group.

This is a revision of the case "Choosing a Data Processing Supervisor: Six Candidates," which appeared in John B. Miner, *The Challenge of Managing* (Philadelphia: W. B. Saunders Company, 1975).

These were the qualities that led his supervisor to recommend him for the promotion; in spite of the fact that George was obviously not as bright as some of the others, he made up for his lesser mental ability by his drive and hard work. True, it took him a little longer to learn new things, but once he understood what was involved, he did well. The only questions his boss had were whether he was entirely trustworthy in all respects and whether he was yet mature enough to assume major managerial responsibility. It was a long jump from grade 4 programmer to grade 8 supervisor, and it might take George a while to adjust to the change. Yet his boss thought he could do it.

Louise Zastrow was 29 years old and also a senior programmer. She had some ten years with the company, almost all of it in the same area. Her efforts to obtain a college education had progressed somewhat further than those of George Smith, and among other things she had a year of coursework in accounting. However, she was still a long way from a degree, and family pressures had been such that she had not taken any courses for several years. All her college work was at night.

As previously indicated, Louise and George Smith had been the two top people in the same unit for some time. It was very hard to say who was better, although each was good for a different reason. Whereas Smith worked very rapidly and made a fair number of mistakes, Zastrow worked more slowly and turned out an almost error-free product.

Louise was quite popular with the other workers and with her supervisors; she was also very perceptive in understanding others. People liked to do things for her, and she seemed to enjoy getting them to go along with her ideas. She typically came across as rather easygoing, and her wide range of interests made her easy to talk to. Yet she was a hard worker and never avoided a difficult task. In fact, because she was very bright and caught on to things quickly, her boss typically turned over to her most of the jobs that were new and different in nature.

It was primarily because of her skill in dealing with people and her facility in getting them to do what she wanted that Louise was a candidate for the promotion. She was not really the kind of person who characteristically solved problems herself; it was more her style to find someone else who could provide a solution. But because she was very flexible and rarely got rattled, she was almost invariably successful at getting others to help her. On the few occasions when she could not deal with a difficult situation by calling on others, she did tend to become moody and preoccupied. This was rare, but her boss had to admit that it would probably be her major weak spot as a supervisor.

Unlike several of the other candidates, Louise had not had formal supervisory experience. Like George Smith, she was at grade 4. Yet she had assumed something of a leadership role in the group, and several of the younger employees typically looked to her for guidance. There was no question that she would be conscientious and hard-working as a supervisor and get along well with those around her.

Elliot Corbett was a grade 5 group leader who spent most of his time as a programmer. However, he did perform some supervisory duties, especially when the boss had to be away from the work place. He was 29 years of age and had been with the company for the 10 years since he graduated from high school. However, only about half of this time had been spent in computer work, the rest having been spread over a number of relatively minor clerical positions. He had attended college in the evening throughout his employment and was still going, having just achieved junior standing.

As a programmer Elliot was well above average, but not the best in the group. The supervisor felt that he was capable of doing better, but that he never quite worked hard enough to be outstanding. Yet his overall work record was good. He had been somewhat slow to learn new jobs when he first started, but eventually this problem solved itself as he gained more experience. Certainly he was bright enough to handle the work, and in the numerical aspects of his job he was actually quite quick.

As far as his supervisory duties were concerned, Elliot's major asset was that he knew a great deal about the diverse aspects of the office work in the company, having been assigned to several different departments early in his career. In addition he seemed to enjoy being in a take-charge position and asserting himself with others. All in all he had done well, although the nature of the group leader position was such that only very limited supervisory responsibility was required.

The major problem that his boss had with Elliot was that he did not seem to enjoy work as much as other things—his hobbies, church work, socializing, and the like. He talked a great deal more about these than about his job. Also, he rarely initiated things at work, tending to sit back and wait to be told what to do. Once he was told what to do, there was no problem. The question was how he would react to the greater freedom and discretion in assigning his own time that a supervisory position permitted. Currently, his boss kept a rather close rein on him because that is what seemed to work best. Nobody really knew how he would perform free of this kind of supervision. He might end up doing very little.

On the other hand, there was no question about his being able to handle the promotion in the sense of adjusting to it. Elliot was obviously a very relaxed, well-adjusted person who enjoyed life and had a good time. He was not likely to get "uptight" about things. Because of his group leader status, and because he was currently doing entirely satisfactory work in this position, his candidacy for promotion was almost automatic.

Daniel Turner had had considerable experience in the computing center, having started in the field with another firm. He was now 31 and had joined the company with the expectation of moving into supervision. At the present time he was a grade 6 group leader with somewhat more responsibility than Elliot Corbett; his duties were largely supervisory. Although Dan had not graduated from high school, he had been through several specialized computer training courses. His test scores at hiring were unusually high, and it was clear that his failure to finish high school was not because of insufficient intelligence.

In general Dan's record was a good one. There had been a difficult period several years before, when one of the company's vice-presidents detected an error in some reports he had prepared. The job had to be completely rerun on a rush basis, and as a result Dan was not very popular in the unit involved; nor did he get a raise at the time of his next performance review. However, the situation did blow over, and throughout the whole period Dan retained the confidence and support of his supervisor.

This was largely because Dan was of great help in taking over responsibility for routine supervisory matters, lessening the load on his superior. The unit was growing rapidly both in size and in the extent of demands for its services. The supervisor had all he could do to keep on top of things, and Dan's capacity to handle routine had proved a godsend. He was a very hard worker and extremely conscientious. A little praise or approval for a job well done was sufficient to keep him plugging away for hours on end. Often he would stay late to work on a job himself after the others had left.

However, it was this tendency to do things himself rather than to get others to do them that was the one questionmark in the supervisor's mind about Dan. Dan obviously found it very difficult to tell others what to do, and it was almost impossible for him to criticize anyone for poor work. In fact, the problem went even deeper, because Dan's desire to keep on the good side of the other people in the group and avoid antagonizing them often extended to his keeping things from the supervisor. The supervisor was a good deal more likely to tell his subordinates what he thought of them than Dan was, and apparently Dan wanted to avoid any of the subordinates blaming him for getting a chewing out.

In spite of all this, the supervisor liked Dan and found him a pleasant and helpful person to have around. There was no question that he should be recommended as a candidate for the promotion, especially since he had been hired originally with a view to using him in a supervisory capacity. On the other hand replacing Dan would be a problem, if he were the one selected.

Herman Rosenburg was a night-shift supervisor who was in charge of a reduced force operation that handled overflow work from the day shift. He reported to the day-shift supervisor and was in grade 6, the same grade as Dan Turner. Because the number of people working the night shift was never large, Herman actually spent a good proportion of his time programming and operating the computers. There was not a great deal of supervising to be done.

Herman was 33 years old and had been with the company for two years, all of it as night-shift supervisor with the same unit. After graduating from high school and military service, he had worked for several companies in office positions and had moved into computer work seven years before because that seemed to be where the opportunities were. Although not by any means a brilliant person, his intelligence had always been adequate to the positions he had held.

As a programmer Herman was first-rate. He got along well with others and turned out very accurate work. At times it appeared that he did not work as hard as he might, but he was sufficiently experienced and knowledgeable about his work so that his output did not suffer. The only problems that ever occurred were associated with his partial deafness. There were a few occasions when his failure to hear what someone said interfered with his work. However, he was far from being totally deaf and in general had learned to live with his handicap quite effectively.

On the other hand, no one really knew much about his effectiveness as a supervisor. For one thing, he was on the night shift and there were not many people around to report on his performance; for another, he really did not have very many people to direct. It was clear that Herman found it difficult to tell his people what to do and that he was far from being a forceful person; yet he was well liked. He was a very social individual and being with others buoyed him up. Alone he often became depressed and dejected. His boss, the day-shift supervisor, thought that Herman was more worried about his deafness than he showed, and that being alone brought this out. In any event, it was clear that the night shift as a whole spent a great deal of time in coffee breaks. Also, Herman was very liberal in granting time off to his people. The general impression was that his relationship to his subordinates was more that of a friend than a manager.

Yet he could develop resentments and hold grudges for long periods of time. Personal loyalty was very important to him. His superiors had very mixed feelings about Herman. As a technically competent programmer, he received nothing but favorable comments. As a supervisor who was responsible to the company and was really effective in dealing with subordinates, there was some question. Perhaps he cared more about being popular with his own group than about doing a good job as a supervisor. In any event he, like Dan Turner, was an obvious candidate for the promotion.

Gloria Graham was an assistant supervisor of a large unit and, at grade 7, the senior candidate for the grade 8 opening. She was 30 years old and had attended college for two years before joining the company. Her 10 years of service had included diverse experience in various office functions, including 4 years working in the computer area. Her current duties were about equally split between supervisory activities, programming, and machine operation.

Gloria's performance had been outstanding over a number of years. Yet for some reason she had done much less well for the last couple of years. As a programmer she was now no better than average. She and the people she supervised had been making many errors. Gloria was clearly not following established procedures, and she often failed to follow up on the assignments she gave to subordinates. In many ways her boss felt she was insecure and disorganized. Yet she certainly had the intelligence to do the work and was in fact outstandingly qualified in the mathematical area, both in terms of ability and education.

There is real concern in the company as to what was happening to Gloria. She had been very cooperative and tried hard; she still did. However, her overall performance was no longer impressive. Somehow she was distracted and found it difficult to concentrate on her work. She no longer appeared to enjoy being with people and in fact was clearly more comfortable alone.

This presented a particular problem with regard to her supervisory duties. In many respects she was a good supervisor. She had the expertise, and people respected her; in general they liked her too, and she was quite capable of making her wishes known and getting things done. She appeared to have a normal desire to get ahead and to enjoy being a supervisor. Yet for some reason, in the last few years and for quite some time after she became an assistant supervisor, she had become increasingly anxious and upset, and had also become more and more antisocial.

There were some who felt that Gloria was headed for a nervous breakdown. Others, however, considered her to be underplaced relative to her capabilities and recommended her for the promotion on the grounds that the new challenge involved would bring out her greatest strengths. Her immediate superior, who probably knew her better than anyone, could not make up his mind. He did know that she was currently upset and not performing up to her previous level. In spite of his best efforts, he could not figure out why. But at the same time he could not predict how she would respond to the challenge of a promotion and new responsibilities. He knew she ought to be a candidate, simply because of her current position; but he could not honestly say whether she should be selected. If only she were less preoccupied and distracted.

Predicting the Future

Jed Barket and Bill Thomas, both members of the board of directors of ABC Manufacturing, were discussing a major dilemma—that of deciding which of three men under consideration should be offered the company's presidency. The former president, Will Ziebuld, had been doing an excellent job when he suddenly collapsed at his desk. Suffering an apparent heart attack, Ziebuld was rushed to a nearby hospital. After extensive tests, Ziebuld was told he would have to go easy from then on. Following this advice, he tendered his resignation as president.

This turn of events left the company's top management stunned. However, the board decided to fill the vacancy as quickly as possible. After screening all possible candidates, the board narrowed its list to three men, two outsiders and one insider. The first two individuals were both presidents of competitive firms, but each indicated that he would be willing to change jobs if given the offer. The third man was the company's executive vice-president and the individual Will Ziebuld had been grooming for his job for the past two years.

The board of directors was charged with choosing the new president. However, Jed and Bill were the most senior members and the five other members generally agreed with their recommendations. As a result, the two men were asked to evaluate the three candidates, arrive at a consensus, and present their findings to the board.

The best method of choosing the new president was not clear to either Jed or Bill. Nevertheless, Jed believed strongly that human behavior was predictable from past history.

"You know," he told Bill, "a systematic analysis of an individual can give you a behavioral profile of that person. On the basis of this information, you can predict quite a bit about their behavior. All we really have to do is obtain such a profile of the three men under consideration." Bill, however, was not so sure. "I just don't think you can do it that easily. Give me an illustration."

"I'll do better than that. Let me get you a clipping from a past issue of *Time*, and I'll show you how this idea of a behavioral profile is used." Jed left the office and returned a few minutes later. He opened the magazine to the "law" section

This case was prepared by Richard M. Hodgetts of Florida International University.

and handed it to Bill. The story to which he was referring related to some of the latest techniques used by defense attorneys in choosing jurors. In recent years a system has arisen for screening these jurors. It essentially entails bringing in a special team of individuals skilled in psychology and sociology to work with the defense attorneys. The team identifies those most likely to vote for 'acquittal' or 'not guilty.'

In arriving at a decision of whether or not to oppose the sitting of a particular juror, the group divides its operation into three parts: a) making a sociological profile of the community in which the trial will be held; b) a scrutiny in court of potential jurors; and c) a field investigation of their backgrounds. To indicate how successful this approach has been, *Time* reported that the team helped pick thirty-four of thirty-six jurors who voted for acquittal.

BILL: Are you suggesting that we merely obtain this type of profile of each candidate?

JED: No, that would be too simple; it would only provide us with a brief sketch of the individual. We might be able to determine how he would vote on a given issue. However, that is too limited in scope. We need to obtain behavioral information that will give us an over-all profile of the person.

BILL: How would you suggest we get such information?

JED: Well, I think we ought to hire some qualified people to gather data on the early, formative years of each candidate.

BILL: Why?

JED: Because by the time a person is eighteen years old, his options are limited. He's either capable of being a company president or he isn't. The basic behaviors have already been developed.

BILL: That sounds like a way-out idea to me.

JED: Look, I'll give you an illustration. Is there anyone you went through grade school with whom you can remember?

BILL: Sure, there was a boy named Larry McCracken. He was the smartest kid in the class. Of course, we moved away after seventh grade so I don't know whatever happened to Larry. However, his father was the mayor, so my guess is that the family had roots there and may still be living in the same city.

JED: What do you think Larry is doing today?

BILL: Well, if he's not the mayor there, I'd say he's either a successful businessman or a college professor—maybe in mathematics or accounting.

JED: Why do you say that?

BILL: Because he was both analytical and good at math.

JED: Okay, let's take a wild shot and call your old home city and find out what he's doing today.

BILL: Heck, nobody will remember him. Besides, whom do I call?

JED: Is there any school teacher you had who, if she were still alive, would be living there?

BILL: Probably Miss Anna Dunworthy. She was unmarried in those days and the school was her whole life.

JED: Okay, call the information operator, see if Miss Dunworthy still lives there. If she does, ask her about Larry; maybe she remembers.

Bill placed the call and to his surprise learned that there was indeed an Anna Dunworthy living in the city. Furthermore, upon talking to her he learned that Miss Dunworthy not only remembered him but was able to tell him about Larry—he was the president of the largest bank in the metropolitan area. In fact, at the last annual high school get-together, she and Larry had spent over an hour talking about old times. They wondered what had ever happened to Bill. By the time Bill hung up the telephone, he was amazed.

BILL: I can't believe it. He not only still lives in town but he's in a profession similar to the one I guessed.

JED: Sure, it's like I told you. Tell me something about the person's early years and I'll project the future.

BILL: Okay, but you've got to admit that we had awful skimpy data to go on.

JED: Oh sure, but we could get a lot more information on the candidates for the presidency of the firm. We could have a complete check made on each one.

Bill agreed that the suggestion was a good one and upon hearing of it, the board of directors also agreed. An investigative agency was then hired to obtain the requisite background information. Ten days later the data was in the hands of the two men.

The report revealed that one of the outside candidates, Roger Kenan, was a star pupil in grammar and high school. In addition, he was active in baseball and basketball and was elected president of his high school class. Neighbors and friends remembered him as an easygoing boy who never seemed to get in any trouble. He was fairly well liked although he did not seem to have any close friends. Meanwhile, his grammar school teachers remembered him as industrious and likable. The second outside candidate, William Rheem, was apparently something of a cut-up in both grammar and high school. School reports indicated that he was twice reprimanded for fighting during recess. Nevertheless, he was well remembered by his teachers because of his success in midget, junior varsity, and varsity football. Bill was apparently a superb quarterback. His grammar school and his high school had undefeated seasons while he was there. In fact, he was still affectionately known by his old English teacher as "Touchdown" Bill Rheem, because of a ninety-one-yard winning touchdown he ran from scrimmage in the last minute of the state finals. Old neighbors and friends called him a "likable roughneck." One of his friends said, "We figured he'd either do very well for himself or wind up in jail. There's no in-between with Bill."

The third candidate, Martin McChorder, was the inside man Will Ziebuld had been grooming for the presidency. The investigators learned that Martin's parents had been killed when he was a child and Martin had been raised by an elderly aunt. Around his neighborhood, Martin was regarded as shy and introverted, a marked change from his behavior in the firm where he was outgoing and gregarious. Martin had also been quite sickly as a child and missed quite a few days of school. In the sixth grade he was almost left back because he had been absent so often. While he engaged in no contact sports, he was active in the band, glee club, chess club, and was president of the high school's debating team. One of his old school friends said he was "outstanding in intellectual or noncompetitive endeavors."

Bill was still a bit skeptical. He and Jed must sit down and make their decision.

ABC Mud Engineering Company

Dan Dumestre (pronounced DEW MESS TREE), Technical Director of ABC Mud Engineering Company (see Exhibit 1 for a partial organizational chart), sat relaxed in his office on the top floor of the ABC office building. Dan was discussing with the corporate Personnel Manager some of the changes that had occurred in the management of professional employees during the last 10 years.

Dumestre: "I have one of my biggest jobs trying to convince young men just out of engineering school that their job with ABC of necessity must be service to the customer. Since our competitors can offer about the same "product" our efforts should be directed at presenting ABC as the Vendor most capable of giving the kind of service that sets us apart from all the rest. Perhaps one way to accomplish that goal is to package our services somewhat differently. For example, the data compiled by ABC from some of our old wells probably is some of the most comprehensive data available. This, of course, gives us an advantage in offering our services to our customer."

Dumestre was aware of the fact that ABC's competition could accrue the same data on wells they had serviced. Because of this, Dumestre knew that the initial presentation to potential customers was of primary importance. However, presentation was only the beginning since customers stake their own success rate on the services offered by vendor companies like ABC. It is imperative that the service companies be capable of supplying the proper "mud" in a timely fashion.

As Dumestre pondered the service issue he knew that it was linked somehow to the various functions within ABC. While engineering is a key factor in developing customer information, Dumestre felt that the status relationships of the departments at ABC placed Operations at the top. Engineering, and the other technical assistance departments under Dumestre (see Exhibit 1 for an organizational breakdown) function as service departments for Operations.

This case was prepared by Louis P. White, Assistant Professor, and Dorothy N. Harlow, Visiting Professor, University of Houston at Clear Lake City. It was presented at a Case Research Association Workshop and distributed by the Intercollegiate Case Clearing House, Soldiers Field, Boston, Mass. 02163. All rights reserved to contributors. Printed in U.S.A. All names have been disguised.

EXHIBIT 1 ABC partial organizational chart

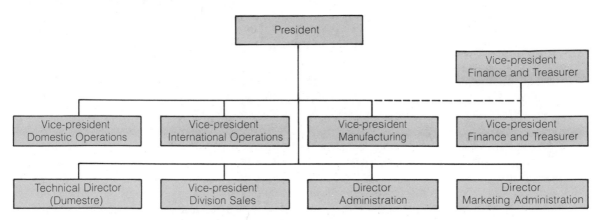

As Technical Director for ABC Dumestre has the following departments under his direction (also see Exhibit 2):

1. Staff Engineering—the manager of this department is a graduate engineer and supervises 6 degreed engineers. They support Operations by preparing mud programs (technical reports generated to prescribe the type of mud to be used on a particular well). These programs are written from data about well depth, soil composition, and customer requests. This section also uses a computer unit that is programmed to do well control program simulations to help predict well blow outs.
2. Technical Training—this department at ABC is headed by a manager who has a degree in geology. He has six people who report to

him, all of them degreed. Their primary responsibility is to train "mud engineers," whose job it is to maintain first-hand contact with customers. These men, and in rare cases, women work on-site to insure the proper kind of mud is supplied relative to site conditions. The major thrust of mud school is to train prospective mud engineers in this craft.

3. Equipment Development Services—the manager for this department is a degreed geologist and has electronic engineers who report to him. The responsibilities of this functional area are research and development of equipment to be used in the drilling services field. Their function includes development of well site monitors and other equipment used in the drilling business.
4. Fluids Development Services—the manager

EXHIBIT 2 ABC Mud Engineering partial organizational chart

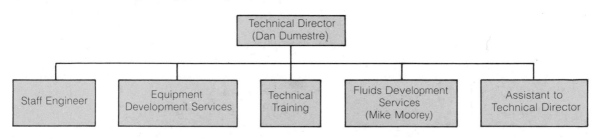

of this department has a Ph.D. in mathematics. He supervises a group of 30 people, some of whom are degreed in petroleum engineering and chemistry. However, not all people in this department have a degree. The function of this department is to conduct research on the fluids that aid in the drilling process. They also perform a quality control function by acting in the role of a field back-up service.

5. Assistant to Technical Director—the department is headed by a graduate engineer. The two primary functions of this functional area are sales support and the supervision of approximately 200 "mud engineers." They are not engineers in the usual sense. Their education is varied coming from many fields—some have degrees and some don't. Almost all, however, have had some university education, and upon joining ABC are sent to training (conducted by the Technical Training Department) called "mud school." These men and some women work "on site" with the customer servicing drilling operations primarily by insuring the use of the specific mud mixture called for by the drilling program. They work seven days "on site" and seven off. Technically they are supposed to report to the office on those off days; however, this practice is not universally enforced or adhered to.

With a sense of pride Dumestre described to the Personnel Manager the Well Control School headed by a graduate engineer. The school is approved by the United States Geodetic Survey and is staffed by two engineers who are also trained as teachers. This school is one of the ways used to attract and keep young engineers, especially if they are single and do not mind foreign travel. They teach customers using the ABC patented well control simulator. ABC gets so many requests for training they cannot fill them. It reminds one of the "link trainer" of the oil industry. The thing that makes ABC's unit unique is that it is portable—one man can carry it. If there is a big rush for the train-

ing, and no other way to get the simulator there, ABC will buy a ticket for it on the airline, strap it in the seat, and take it along with the engineer-teacher. The usual pattern is for 20 to 30 people to want training (these are ABC's customers) in about 4 or 5 locations. The engineer will then go overseas for 30 to 60 days. One had just left for Scotland the week before the conversation with the Personnel Manager.

Turnover, another problem facing ABC, has become a rather serious concern. The men usually leave to go with either ABC's customers or competitors. ABC prefers that if their people are going to leave they go with customers because they have had field training at ABC and it would be natural for them to request ABC equipment in their new job.

Dumestre explained, "One factor contributing to turnover at ABC is our wage policy. We began trying to bring our older employees up faster in terms of dollar increases when we realized that they were out of line with salaries we had to offer new employees. We offered 8% plus merit, a review at six and nine month intervals and we wanted them up even in two years. So our hands are pretty well tied with the current salary guidelines that corporate headquarters is insisting we follow. (See Note 2 for a description of wage allocation system.) The only trouble is that our good people can go anywhere else and make more money than we can pay them. With inflation in the local area so much higher than most areas, buying groceries and paying the rent is a big issue even with relatively high salaries received by engineers. Salary is particularly important for the young people who are having trouble getting enough for a down payment on a home. Once 'home buying' is a reality, then they can start to live. The base salary for the company starts with mud engineers and the salary of everyone else is built up from that. These mud engineers may not have formal engineering training, some even with limited or no college, but the company hires them and trains them. One of the norms of ABC, as with most mud companies, is that everyone should "spend some time in the tank"—out on the rig in the field so they have practical, hands-on experience. Because of this attitude, most managers in this company know what it is like because they have been there.

PERSONNEL MANAGER: What is the answer? How can we possibly continue to attract new people, and more importantly, keep them after a few years along with retaining our experienced people if they can go to our customers or competitors and make two or three times what we pay them?

DUMESTRE: The way we manage these professional people is one answer. You simply cannot give them orders any more. They insist on freedom to explore—to try their wings. Our managers in the field say they are smarter than any we have ever had, but they are a new crop. They don't want to work 24 hours a day like we did in the good old days.

PERSONNEL MANAGER: How are the managers in the field taking all this new philosophy? Bet they would like to just tell the kids off once in a while.

DUMESTRE: In some cases that is true. But I have worked with them and the men have convinced most of them that we really are a service organization staffed by professionals who want to do their own thing—they want freedom to experiment, to learn. But somewhere there is a balance between the freedom the professional employee wants and the ultimate control that management must have if the organizational goals are to be met. One thing we have found that works pretty well if the old timer is too rigid to turn the new engineer loose is to give the "oldtime" manager an assistant. The assistant is the one who then works directly with new engineers and acts as a buffer between the manager and the professional.

PERSONNEL MANAGER: Well, it seems to me we have it cut out for us. Our turnover rate is higher than it has been in some time—about 100% in some areas, raises are limited by our salary policies, and our professional employees want minimum control or direction from management. Morale is not too good right now and probably won't be until everyone gets used to the idea that the recent purchase of ABC by Amalgamated Industries won't be all that bad.

Notes

1. Mud is a term applied to a type of drilling fluid that is used primarily to lower the pressure caused by gas pockets beneath the surface of the earth. It is derived from Barite, a mineral that is mined from beneath the earth's surface. ABC mines its own Barite and does not have to rely on other companies for this basic substance. Once the Barite is mined it is then ground into a fine powder and then mixed with water. Other fluids and chemicals may be added depending upon the geology of the drilling site. The basic purpose of "mud" is to prevent well blowouts or explosion of gas pockets. The proper viscosity of drilling mud is a key factor in the prevention of these explosions. Drilling mud meets other necessities in that it is used to lubricate the drill bit as it cuts through the earth. This results in a longer life with greater efficiency for drill bits, a high priced item used by the drilling company.

   The proper use of the manufacturing output of ABC is the responsibility of the Mud Engineer. Upon completion of Mud Engineering School, which is under the jurisdiction of Dumestre, the new mud engineer is assigned to a district. This district is headed by a District Manager who has as direct subordinates four Senior Engineers, who in turn manage nine Mud Engineers (see Exhibit 3 for partial organizational chart).

   The basic function of a Mud Engineer is to serve customer specifications as prescribed by detailed technical data about soil composition, and knowledge of fluids and chemicals to achieve the proper viscosity of the mud. An equally important role played by the Mud Engineer is maintaining a favorable client relationship as the ABC "on site" representative.

2. The wage allocation system employed at ABC is one that has come into existence since acquisition by the parent company. This system is set up in such a way that ABC is able to participate in the allocation of salary increases.

   The initial step in the wage allocation system is performed by the employee relations department. Its role is to gather wage data from competing companies as well as from companies generally in the oil industry. Subject companies include other drilling service companies as well as the major oil companies such as Exxon and Texaco. These data are compiled into a report and are forwarded along with legal recommendations concerning salary increases to a group called the "Staff Committee."

EXHIBIT 3   ABC partial organizational chart

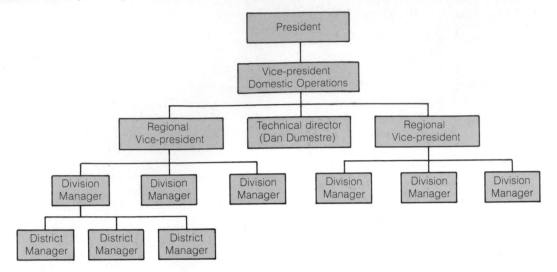

The Staff Committee is comprised of nine members (see Exhibit 1) whose organizational position ranges from Director (at the level of Dumestre) to the President of ABC. The report generated by the Employee Relations Department is studied, along with current salary levels. Along with these two factors, legal aspects are discussed and a recommendation for salary increases is made.

The final recommendation of this staff committee is submitted to the parent company by the President of ABC where the final wage allocation is made.

Professor Zanuli Goes to Germany

The Management Department at Eastern State University had long made a practice of employing several young faculty members who had recently obtained their MBA degrees. The Department offered these individuals the opportunity to see if they would enjoy an academic position before making the personal sacrifice required to pursue a terminal degree. Eastern State also was thought to benefit from this policy in that these faculty members brought a certain youth and vitality to the Department which was otherwise lacking. Following several years of teaching, these individuals would either enter industry or return to a university to pursue a terminal degree. In no case would tenure be granted to any faculty member without a terminal degree. Since a person was considered for tenure during their sixth year, no one was allowed to stay beyond this point. The typical stay was from two to four years.

Jeremiah Zanuli was 25 years old and had just obtained his MBA degree from a highly regarded institution when he joined the faculty at Eastern State. He was told, prior to his accepting employment, that he was not expected to engage in research activities, but instead to concentrate upon the development of his courses and teaching techniques and style. He was also told that he would not be granted tenure and that he would be encouraged to return to school to pursue a terminal degree as soon as possible. The Department Head, Professor Benson, had always stressed to the young MBA faculty that it was in their best interest to return to school and pursue a doctorate as soon as they could make a sound decision.

Young Mr. Zanuli soon developed into a very capable teacher. He received very high ratings by his students and got along well with his colleagues. By the end of his third year at Eastern State, Mr. Zanuli had become involved with several business ventures in the city in which Eastern was located. He had not completely

The research and written case information were presented at a Case Research Symposium and were evaluated by the Case Research Association's Editorial Board. This case was prepared by Roland B. Cousins of the University of Southwestern Louisiana as a base discussion.

Professor Zanuli Goes to Germany

dismissed the idea of returning to graduate school to pursue a terminal degree, although he was leaning toward remaining in town to pursue a business career once he left Eastern State. In order to plan his future, in early April of this year which was his third at Eastern State, he went to see the Dean of the School of Business, Dean Hoffman. He asked the Dean if he would be allowed to remain at Eastern for several more years. Dean Hoffman replied that he would, although it would be in his best interest to return to school as soon as possible.

Zanuli seemed to have developed a good relationship with his Department Head and Dean. However, this relationship appeared about to fall apart by the end of April. Zanuli's problems began when he accepted the opportunity to travel with his parents to Germany for the week preceding Easter Sunday. The university was in session Monday, Tuesday and Wednesday with holidays beginning at the close of school on Wednesday. Zanuli had scheduled an exam to be given to his classes on Monday and Tuesday and he made arrangements for a colleague to cover those classes for him. He had also told the students that there would be no classes on Wednesday. His Wednesday schedule included teaching two classes of Managerial Accounting in the daytime, 50 minutes each, and one graduate class Wednesday evening. When the opportunity arose for Professor Zanuli to take the trip, he gave considerable thought to whether he should request permission for a leave of absence for those three days. Because his Department Head, Dr. Benson, and his Dean, Dr. Hoffman, were both known to be very reluctant to authorize the missing of classes and since he had decided to take the trip, Professor Zanuli figured that his best course of action would be simply not to say anything to any of the university administrators. Since his office was located in a separate building from his Department Head, he assumed that he would not be missed.

All went well with his plans until the Saturday prior to his Sunday departure. On that day he happened to meet his Department Head in a local health club. Much to Professor Zanuli's surprise, Dr. Benson asked if he could make an appointment to see him on Monday morning for his an-nual performance appraisal interview. Since Zanuli was planning on being on a plane bound for Germany at this time, he did not know how to respond to the request. If he told Dr. Benson of his plans now, he was quite confident that Benson would state that he could not go. If that were the decision, then Zanuli figured that he could be in serious trouble if he directly violated his superior's order. On the spur of the moment, the only response which Zanuli could think of was to make the requested appointment for Monday.

On Saturday evening Zanuli agonized over what should be done now. He rejected the idea of telling additional lies and decided to write a letter to Dr. Benson explaining his decision to go to Germany. He would have a friend deliver the letter right before his scheduled appointment. Then he figured he'd face Dr. Benson a week later after the latter had had a chance to cool off.

When Dr. Benson received the letter he was beside himself with rage. He was rather glad that it would be a week before he would see Zanuli again since he was afraid that if Zanuli were in front of him now, he would say something he may regret later.

As he considered how the problem might be handled, he made mental note of the following alternatives:

1. Do nothing, recognizing that other faculty members do miss class occasionally although it is usually for illness or attending professional association meetings.
2. Have a firm discussion with Zanuli and impress upon him the importance of meeting his teaching obligations, but take no disciplinary action.
3. Ask Dean Hoffman to have that discussion with Zanuli, but take no other action.
4. Write a formal letter of reprimand to be included in Zanuli's personnel file.
5. Have Zanuli's pay docked for one day, the Wednesday on which he dismissed classes.
6. Have Zanuli's pay docked for 3 days corresponding to the Monday, Tuesday and Wednesday on which the university was in session but Zanuli was in Germany.

7. Write a letter of termination giving Zanuli one year's notice. Any non-tenured faculty member may be dismissed with no reason given if he is given the one year's notice.

As he pondered these alternatives, Benson was also wondering if the new Department Head should play any role in the decision or even be informed concening the incident. Professor Benson was stepping down as the Department Head at the end of this semester after approximately twenty-five years of service. His replacement has been selected but will not arrive on the Eastern campus until the end of August.

Bendix Corporation: "As the Boardroom Turns"

"Bill (Agee) has a rare combination of talents, including a very nice way with people."—Mike Blumenthal (late 1978)

"She (Mary Cunningham) is the most vital and important person within the company and has played an important part in conceptualizing the strategy."—William Agee (September 1980)

"Now that the Mary and Bill soap opera has run its course, Bill Agee had better get back to work." (*Fortune,* November 1980)

"Moving targets are hard to hit, and never more so than at a company that constantly shifts its goals." (*Business Week,* April 1981)

"A loss of confidence in top management."—Robert Purcell (August 1981)

"Oh God, all those Bendix resumés floating around." (*Fortune,* January 1981)

"Bill (Agee) was my greatest misjudgment."—Mike Blumenthal (*Fortune,* January 1981)

Bendix was one of the few Detroit companies to squeeze profits from industrial business through the severe recession that started in 1979. Net earnings for the 1981 fiscal year were $453 million on sales of $4.4 billion. Bendix's performance was made more incredible because the company derived almost half of its operating revenues from the sale of automotive parts to the auto industry which was especially hard hit by the 1980–1982 recession. The remainder of operating revenues was derived evenly from machine tools and aerospace equipment.

By 1981, Bendix had increased profits for 13 consecutive years; however, the Bendix of 1981 was not the same company as the Bendix of 1968, or even the Bendix of 1976. In 1976, William Agee took control as Chairman of the Board and CEO. Between 1976 and 1981, Bendix was transformed from a conservative industrial concern to what some people referred to as a financial holding company. Fifty percent of the 1981 profits came from short term cash investments.

This case was written by Timothy M. Singleton. The initial research was prepared by Debbie Schneider, Rick Schneider, Mary McGivern, David Horwath, Tom Moore, Charles Simon, and Lou Demaree, a group of MBA students at the University of Houston–Clear Lake, in the Spring of 1982.

Agee Restructures Bendix

Upon graduation from Harvard Business School in 1962, William Agee took a job with Boise Cascade (forest products) in his home state of Idaho. In 1967, at the early age of 32, he was named the Chief Financial Officer at Boise. Agee survived what he refers to as "the greatest testing period," the time between 1969 and 1970, when Boise was near bankruptcy because of some misadventures in the real estate business. In 1972, Mike Blumenthal, Chairman of Bendix, persuaded Agee to join the Bendix team. Their business relationship blossomed and, in 1976, when Blumenthal was named Secretary of the Treasury by then President-Elect Jimmy Carter, Blumenthal nominated Agee as his successor at Bendix.

Initially, William Agee was both a maverick and a golden boy who could do no wrong. His participative management style endeared him to Bendix's competent management cadre. He tried to move top management down to the employee level by abolishing reserved executive parking places and by making the executive dining room accessible to all employees. He also removed the table from the boardroom so that board members assembled in a circle.

Bendix in 1976 had four main businesses: Automotive; Machine Tools (Industrial Systems); Forest Products; and Aerospace. Some parts had dead weight, i.e., operations within the divisions that were pulling profits down. Some of these operations were conceived and molded by previous top management, and the immediate disposal or reduction of these operations was frowned upon by current top management. However, Agee was never one to go along with tradition. Early in his presidency Bendix disposed of Bendix Home Systems (BHS), a manufacturer of recreational vehicles. BHS was one department that had been developed by Agee's predecessors and had been consistently losing money. One of the first headaches Agee faced was DBA, an international subsidiary. DBA, a French company that manufactured electrical and mechanical parts for the European Auto Industry, lost $23 million in 1977. First, Agee sold a portion of DBA. Then he dispatched a new management team under J. Mason Reynolds to re-structure DBA. Eventually the French company was reduced from 19,000 employees at 19 plants to 7500 employees at 9 plants. Inefficient operations were eliminated, and by 1980 DBA earned $15 million.

Agee purchased 20% of Asarco in 1978, reasoning that Bendix should enter the minerals and mining field. Agee stood alone in this decision and met with strong resistance from board members and top management who were hesitant because of Asarco's $30 million loss in 1977. However, Agee got his way and the gamble paid off. Asarco's profits soared to $259 million in 1979, and its stock doubled in price. Bendix also purchased Caradco and Bass & Co. (both retail outlets) to improve the distribution of the Bendix Forest Products Division.

Bendix's 1980 acquisition of Warner & Swasey Company, a machine-tool company manufacturer, represented a horizontal diversification strategy. Bendix was seen as the "white knight" since Warner & Swasey was fighting off a hostile merger offer by Canadian Pacific. Bendix ended up paying $300 million in cash, at approximately $83 per share, for a stock with a book value of only $45. Warner & Swasey had about $65 million in liquid assets including some stock in Wang Laboratories, which Bendix sold in July, 1980 for $40 million. With this merger, Bendix became the second largest machine-tool builder in the United States, immediately behind Cincinnati Milacron.

In 1980, Bendix abruptly divested both the Asarco stock and the Forest Products Division, plus some other smaller units to generate a war chest of $750 million. Agee announced that Bendix was "returning to its technological roots," and would acquire a high technology company that was similar to its existing business. But by early 1982 no purchase had been made. Instead $257 million was used to repurchase Bendix stock; and the remainder was invested in short term high yield securities which provided a large percentage of the 1981 Bendix profits. Bendix, under Agee's control, resembled a financial holding company, and Agee was adamant in his conviction that Bendix would remain a diversified company making three principal products: automotive parts, aerospace equipment, and machine tools.

Agee not only restructured the Bendix operations, he also changed the Bendix management philosophy and organizational structure. William Panney was hired as the Chief Operating Officer. The company was changed from a highly centralized headquarters, having a strong staff, to a decentralized organization in which the divisional presidents (Automotive, Industrial Systems, and Aerospace) wielded strong power. The headquarters staff was reduced and dispersed. Agee increased the amount spent on research and development recognizing that "the short term financial sacrifices" for research were important for a technological company. A new research center was built in Maryland.

Bendix was changed from a centralized, traditional industrial concern to a technological, decentralized company within four years. The remaining businesses were counter cyclical, helping to insure even profits. It is not surprising that the company suffered uncertainty in 1980. What is surprising is the depth of the turmoil that surfaced in September, 1980 and continued throughout 1981. The changes in Agee's image within Bendix as a golden boy hero to a mistrusted opportunist can be partially explained as fear because of the corporate changes. The explosion in 1980 was ignited by Mary Cunningham who seemed to be the focus of the upheaval.

Mary Cunningham

Mary Cunningham joined Bendix in June, 1979, as Agee's Executive Assistant. Her meteoric rise to a Bendix Vice-Presidency and her subsequent resignation under fire, plus her overall effect on Bendix, can only be understood by examining her background and her Bendix history.

Mary was the youngest born to an Irish Catholic family. When Mary was only five years old, her mother, Mimi, who had struggled through an 18 year marriage to a charming man with a drinking problem, took Mary and left. Waiting for them was Father William Nolan (later Chaplain at Dartmouth College). Father Bill had been a very close friend to Mary's mother for over twenty years. In fact, Bill had introduced Mary's mother to her father. Mary's father was very much an extrovert compared to shy Bill Nolan. After Mimi married Mary's father, Bill

Nolan entered a seminary and became a priest. As Mimi's marriage degenerated both Bill and Mimi realized that they had made a mistake. Father Bill's commitment to the Church forbade him from marrying Mimi. However, he did agree to be legal guardian for her children. Father Bill had a profound effect on Mary.

Mary graduated from Wellesley with high grades and a degree in philosophy. She started law school but dropped out to marry Bo Gray. Bo was a distinguished black man 12 years her senior who was a prominent figure with Chase Manhattan Bank in New York. To Mary, "Bo symbolized a man who had overcome many more hardships than Father Bill because he was a Harlem black man who had worked his way up to corporate middle management." She gave up law school to marry him. For a proper white Catholic girl, "this was more of a forbidden partner than a priest."

Six months after her marriage, Mary became a financial analyst at Chase Manhattan Bank. Her position demanded more and more financial and managerial expertise, so Mary decided to attend Harvard Business School where she graduated Cum Laude. At Harvard she was acclaimed by Harvard's Dean, James Heskett, as the woman capable of achieving the Chief Executive Officer position of a *Fortune* 500 company within the next ten years. Because Mary had attended Harvard, she had only lived with her husband Bo for one of the first three years of their marriage.

Mary Meets Bill Agee

The corporate recruiter for Bendix interviewed Mary Cunningham and found her to be an extraordinarily bright, aggressive individual—someone Bendix had to have working for the company, even if it meant creating a position for her. After her visit to Bendix's headquarters in Southfield, Michigan, in which she impressed everyone she met, she was instructed to go to a particular suite at the Waldorf Astoria Hotel in New York at 8 a.m. the following day. There she met Bill Agee who introduced himself as the Chairman of Bendix and quickly asked, "How would you like to be my Executive Assistant?" Mary replied, "Well, let's see how we get along." Mary later described the meeting as four hours of philosophical soul-searching. At the end of the discussion Bill introduced Mary to his wife, Diane, who had been patiently waiting in the next room.

Mary was being pursued by many companies, which promised salaries in excess of $50,000. According to Mary, when she asked for Bo's input into her career decision, he refused to comment. It appears that Bo was somewhat taken back by the number of companies actively pursuing Mary, and the phenomenal salaries they were offering. Bo realized that Mary was attracted to the excitement of Bendix, and if she accepted the position, she would have to move to Detroit, a considerable distance from him in New York. Recognizing Bo's reticence, Mary initially called Bill Agee and declined the offer. Mr. Agee reassured her that the offer would remain available to her for a period of one year. Bo was surprised to hear that Mary had declined Bendix's offer. He instructed her to call Agee back and accept the position. She waited three weeks, then called Bill Agee and accepted the position at Bendix.

Bill Agee was in the process of making a decision on a very important acquisition deal the next day and insisted on sending the corporate jet to pick up Mary so she could be present for the deal.

Mary at Bendix

For the first three months at Bendix Mary spent her time studying Agee's management lifestyle, his actions, and his likes and dislikes. Her duties gradually expanded. As an Executive Assistant Mary did jobs that gave her close contact with Agee. She wrote his speeches. She compiled reports on potential acquisitions. She helped with the strategic planning. She headed a task force that determined Bendix's strengths and weaknesses in the automotive operations. Mary was responsible for negotiating the deal for the Warner & Swasey Company.

In June 1980, one year after she joined Bendix, Mary was appointed Vice-President of Public Affairs. In September, 1980, she was appointed Vice-President of Strategic Planning.

Mary and Bill became personal friends. They were in close contact and developed a deep respect for each other's intellectual achievements. Mary said, "He is intellectually honest. He has courage and takes risks and has a flawless value system," and, "He is the finest human being I have ever met."

Bill and Mary worked long hours together. They made decisions concerning acquisitions worth hundreds of millions of dollars. They traveled extensively and shared hotel suites. She accompanied Agee to many social events (e.g., U.S. Open Tennis Tournament and the 1980 Winter Olympics) and to political events (1980 Republican Convention).

In August, 1980, Agee divorced his wife, Diane, after 23 years of marriage. Mary Cunningham consoled and supported Diane and Agee's daughter Karen. After the divorce Bill moved into the same suburban Detroit apartment complex where Mary resided.

Turmoil at Bendix

Mary Cunningham's associates at Bendix had strong, and generally negative, opinions of her. Mary's task force investigating the automotive division was dubbed "Snow White and the Seven Dwarfs" by other Bendix employees who claim that the report uncovered nothing new or different from what was already known. The task force methods of bypassing local management to interview plant personnel disrupted plant operations and caused much resentment among Bendix's management. Bill Agee alone praised the final report.

Mary used her power. She bruised many managers' feelings with statements like, "last night Bill Agee and I discussed what to do about such and such an executive." Gradually Mary monopolized so much of Bill's time that other executives had less and less contact with him. Insiders no longer knew what Agee's plans were.

Mary's advancement with Bendix raised many eyebrows, and started rumors throughout the company that she was promoted, not because of her ability, but rather because of her romantic involvement with Agee.

In September 1980, William Panney was removed as Bendix President. Agee said that Panney, an operating manager with a "hands-on" style, did not fit in the decentralized organization Agee was developing at Bendix. Other sources close to Bendix claim that Panney was fired because he had "bruised Mary's feelings." The firing occurred the day after Agee and Panney exchanged heated words over the Agee-Cunningham relationship. Feeling that his termination was imminent, and to avoid the fate of his friend William Panney, Jerome Jacobsen, Vice President of Strategic Planning, tendered his resignation. He contended that he had been stripped of his power, following Agee's decision giving Mary power to conduct strategic planning. This made the Vice President of Strategic Planning position available for Mary to assume.

On September 23, 1980, at a meeting of 600 Bendix employees, Bill Agee announced his promotion of Mary Cunningham to the position of Vice President of Strategic Planning. Agee took the opportunity to attempt to dispel the speculations that Mary was being promoted because of a romantic involvement. He stated that her Harvard MBA credentials and work experience at Bendix merited her promotion. At the same meeting he also announced a further change in the organization of top management. Members of the media were present at this meeting which was held annually to allow Agee to learn more about his employees and vice versa. His effort to diminish rumors backfired, and the Agee/Cunningham relationship made the headlines in local and national news. The media attention forced Mary to consider resignation, even though she realized that resignation would probably be construed as an admission of some kind of guilt. On September 28, 1980, she consulted Father Bill Nolan seeking his advice. He instructed her to take a temporary leave of absence to evaluate her situation. She determined that her departure should not be considered as resignation but rather as taking a break because "innuendoes and gossip rendered her ineffective at this point in time." When Mary requested a leave of absence, the Board gave her a full vote of confidence and refused to grant the leave of absence. The furor continued, however, and finally the Board told Agee that Mary must go. She resigned 10 days later.

Another significant event occurred at Bendix while Mary was working closely with Agee. When President Carter dismissed Mike Blumenthal in mid-1979, Agee made it perfectly clear that his old boss was not welcomed back at Bendix, even as a director. Blumenthal represented a potential threat to Agee's empire. After learning that Blumenthal had returned to Detroit and had joined Burroughs, a computer company somewhat larger than Bendix, as the next apparent Chief Executive Officer, Agee's actions appeared to be an attempt to stop Blumenthal's quest for power. Agee suggested that he be elected to serve as Chairman of both Bendix and Burroughs. Burroughs refused Agee's recommendation and elected Blumenthal to fill the slot. Mike and Bill were no longer friends.

Mary Cunningham after Bendix

Mary Cunningham became a "cause célèbre" after her resignation from Bendix. Her relationship with Agee was front page news and remained in the media for months afterward. She received numerous job offers and finally accepted a strategic planning position with Seagrams (wine & liquor) in New York.

Mary's supporters claimed that she was defeated by a group of sexists who opposed a bright, clever woman because she was a woman. Interviews, and at least one book (*The Pathfinders* by Gail Sheehy), emphasized Mary's strong, almost missionary, Catholic faith and a firm adherence to religious principles and values. In all cases, Mary and Bill denied that there was any sexual relationship. Both claimed only a strong personal friendship and bond based on similar values and intellectual accomplishments.

Mary's detractors included the vast majority of former associates at Bendix. The female managers were angry because Mary's performance hurt their chances for promotion. They claimed that the charges of sexism were nothing more than a shrewd smoke screen.

The Bo Gray-Mary Cunningham marriage gradually dissolved because of separation while Mary was at Harvard and in Michigan. Mary was granted an annulment. In an April, 1982 article in *Parade Magazine* the Agee-Cunningham engagement was mentioned. No wedding date was set.

Bendix after Mary Cunningham

Both the Forest Products and Asarco operations were sold in 1981. Bendix reaped $425 million from its sales of Forest Products and about $336 million more from selling back to Asarco the 6.1 million shares of stock Bendix held. This money was originally earmarked for acquisitions. However, Agee turned around and spent $256 million to repurchase 4 million shares of the Bendix stock, approximately 17% of outstanding stock, at $64 per share. This did not seem to fit in with Agee's announced acquisition plans.

Agee claimed that he wanted his company to be more flexible and capable to meet what lay ahead in the eighties. With the recession eating away at the automotive industry, Bendix's course of action was to direct the company into a more diversified enterprise. Agee wanted to move the company into more of a high technology manufacturer through one or more acquisitions and to invest more in research and development. Agee infuriated the auto industry with his remark that the auto industry was in "the winter of its life."

Agee moved from Southfield, Michigan to New York and leased an expensive office space in New York General Motors Building just six blocks away from Joseph E. Seagram & Sons where Ms. Cunningham was employed. Mr. Agee remarked that he wanted to get into the New York circuit.

Although Bendix paid well and the job market around Detroit was very depressed, there seemed to be a great deal of low employee morale. "People are keeping their heads down and figuring that they can hold on until Agee goes," said one manager. Because of growing unemployment in the Detroit area, many Bendix employees were hesitant to change jobs. Many speculated that when the economy turned around, there would be a higher rate of attrition at Bendix.

On February 25, 1981, a special press meeting was held. Agee opened the session by announcing that Bendix planned to acquire a sizable high-technology company and that those Bendix directors who also sat on Burroughs' board could have a conflict of interest. He wanted the committee's approval to ask Mirabito and Schwartz for their resignations. He added that Eklund, also a dual director, had already agreed to resign from the Burroughs board. Then he suggested that Harry Cunningham (no relation to Mary) should also resign. Mr. Cunningham was shocked and retaliated by saying he would gladly leave the board because of the events which had occurred at Bendix over the past few years. When asked what company

Agee was considering as a high technology company, Agee refused to comment.

Mr. Cunningham had second thoughts about his resignation and called Agee to tell him he had reconsidered and had decided not to resign, only to be boldly told by Agee that a verbal resignation was binding and that his membership on the Bendix Board was terminated.

In March of 1981, Agee hired Alonzo McDonald to be President of Bendix and his second in command. McDonald's appointment was poorly received. The employees no longer seemed to have the confidence and trust they once had in Agee.

In August, 1981, Robert Purcell, 70, quit the board citing "a loss of confidence in top management." In fact, prior to his resignation, Purcell wrote a blistering letter to his fellow directors calling attention to Agee's quest for power and his efforts to "axe" those Bendix board members who could present a potential threat to Agee's empire.

After several confrontations with Agee and continual attempts to obtain the names of the high-technology companies Agee was planning to acquire, Purcell decided to solicit support for his cause from other board members. When his efforts failed, Purcell felt he had no other recourse than to resign effective that same day, August 25, 1981.

The next day, Bendix announced in a lengthy press release that the President of Mobil Corporation, William P. Tavoulareaus, was named to the board. Tacked on the end was a postscript announcing that Robert Purcell had resigned from the board, without any recognition or gratitude for his performance with Bendix. This was certainly unlike the postscript given when Mary Cunningham resigned eleven months before, in which it was noted that she made a contribution to the company and was thought of highly by the Board and Bendix's top management.

At a meeting on Monday, March 8, 1982, Agee told RCA executives of his purchase of a substantial amount of RCA's stock, the exact amount he could not disclose at that time. This announcement touched off what seemed to be hostile takeover attempt by Bendix to gain control of RCA. For Agee, he walked right into a hornet's nest. Was RCA the "high technology" company Agee was seeking?

The atmosphere at RCA resembled a mad scramble. Many executives were scurrying around contacting lawyers and other key people in an effort to stop Bendix's takeover.

On Thursday, March 11, 1982, Bendix disclosed that it had purchased 5.5 million shares or 7.3% of RCA. RCA was consoled to learn that Agee, in an effort to smooth ruffled feathers, had agreed not to purchase any more shares of RCA stock for a period of 30 days and that Bendix would give RCA 48 hours prior notice should Bendix decide to purchase more shares.

Some analysts felt that both Bendix and RCA could benefit from a marriage of the two companies. Bendix could get the high technology they had been seeking, and RCA could get the much needed cash cow to feed them for survival.

Postscript

Bill and Mary were married in early June of 1982. At that time Mary was Vice President of Strategic Planning at Seagram. In the fall of 1982, Bendix attempted, first a friendly, then an unfriendly takeover of Martin-Marietta, a high tech conglomerate. Martin-Marietta countered by making tender offers for Bendix stock. For a while it appeared that Bendix and Martin-Marietta would acquire each other, prompting business analysts to describe the situation as "Corporate Pac-Man." By late 1982, Allied Corporation had acquired Bendix—including Agee with his "Golden Parachute." Some believed that the young and ambitious Agee would soon be CEO at Allied. However in the spring of 1983, Agee resigned his position as CEO at Allied.

Mary resigned from Seagram in the fall of 1983, saying that her work had been completed with Seagram's acquisition of the Wine Spectrum from Coca Cola.

In early 1984, Mary and Bill were reported to be living in New England where they were very actively involved in several venture capital firms.

Rodman Motors

When Tom Rodman came to work at Rodman Motors in 1977, he assumed as a matter of course that a spot in management would eventually be his. Tom's father, Peter, was working less now, and about to move out as manager of the Service Department. Tom naturally assumed he would fill the position. To Tom, in his mid-twenties, the family business was to be his career, not just a way station.

Founded by Tom's great grandfather in 1917, Rodman Motors had always been family owned. Peter Rodman, Tom's father, joined the company in 1952, although not yet a stockholder. Peter's mother owned 50% of the company, and his two older brothers, Joe and Ben, owned 25% each, the result of their uncle selling them his half of the shares (see Exhibit 1).

Over the next few years, Peter convinced his mother to sell him bits and pieces of her 50%; however, she did not sell him enough to make him an equal partner. The three brothers took complete control of the business in 1955, with Joe and Ben each holding 40% and Peter 20%. Rodman Motors traditionally kept the num-

---

EXHIBIT 1 Rodman family tree (1979)

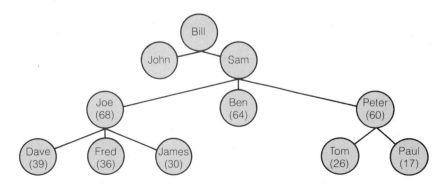

This case was prepared by George Eddy and Kenneth Olm of the University of Texas at Austin as a basis for class discussion. All rights reserved to the authors. Copyright © 1982 by George Eddy and Kenneth Olm.

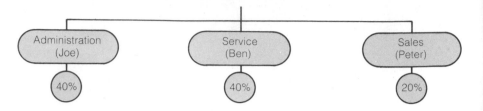

EXHIBIT 2 Organization of Rodman Motors—1977

| Administration (Joe) | Service (Ben) | Sales (Peter) |
| 40% | 40% | 20% |

ber of departments equal to the number of family members available to run them. Consequently, Joe took charge of administrative responsibilities, Ben was in control of the Service Department, and Peter handled Sales, as shown in Exhibit 2.

By the late 1950's, Joe had three sons of his own: Dave, Fred and James. His brother Peter had only one son who was interested in the business, Tom. All three of Joe's sons began their careers at Rodman Motors as salesmen before moving on to management.

In 1971, Fred was promoted to Used Car Manager, a position that had never before existed. Peter was in charge of both new and used cars; thus, Fred's promotion cut Peter's control in half. On top of this, Dave believed the next managerial position should have been his, and he threatened Joe to leave the business. To keep the family order, he was promoted to Assistant Car Sales Manager. Peter fought this restructuring effort all the way. Not only did he believe that it would leave him with less control, but it violated the managerial premise of the past.

By 1975, Ben was ill with cancer and his health forced him to take a less active role in the company. Peter was then persuaded to take over for Ben in the Service Department. This made sense to Peter because of his experience. It also gave him the chance to head his own department again. With his nephew, Dave, taking over new cars, and Fred already in control of used cars, Peter's position in sales had been completely vacated. The net effect was that ¾ of the business was controlled by Joe's family. To Peter, this was a clear indication of where they wanted him in Rodman Motor's—out (see Exhibit 3).

Peter's oldest son, Tom, joined the company in 1977. By this time, Ben's deteriorating health forced him to sell his 40% and retire. This move triggered the first buy-sell agreement since the 1950's and the biggest quarrel yet for control of Rodman Motors.

Under the existing buy-sell agreement, any family manager deciding to sell would split his shares equally with his brothers. Peter, believing this type of sale would eliminate him completely, tried to get Ben to sell him enough shares so his family and Joe's would assume a 50/50 ownership. However, Ben turned the matter over to an attorney who chose to split the stock 50/50 between Joe and Peter. Thus, Peter remained a minority stockholder. Furthermore, he was not in the market to invest money into a minority position.

Peter, feeling vulnerable because of his lack of ownership, subsequently struck a deal with Joe's family. Fred would take charge of the Service Department, with Tom as his assistant, while Peter would become the public relations manager for the firm. Tom would enter training with the objective of becoming the service manager in about 18 months. At that time, Fred would become president upon his father's retirement.

It was with these plans in mind that Peter agreed to relinquish his 20% minority share to his son, Tom, stipulating that his and Joe's three sons would own equal shares and have equal positions in management by 1985. Tom's 25% would come from his father's share plus 5% of Ben's shares now for sale. The agreement organized the dealership in this fashion: Fred would be President and in charge of administrative responsibilities; Dave would manage new cars; Jim would be the used

EXHIBIT 3 Organization of Rodman Motors—1979

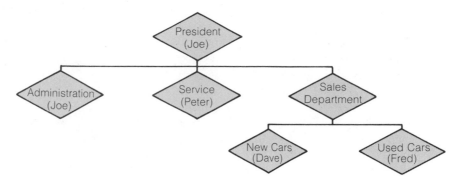

car manager and Tom would manage the Service Department. The new organizational chart is shown in Exhibit 4.

At the same time the new management structure was formulated, incorporation proceedings were also taking place. This would minimize the personal liability of the new owners.

From the beginning of Peter's involvement in the business, he had the reputation as the one willing to take a chance. Being initially in the sales end of the operation, Peter's focus was on increasing sales, and thus profits. He saw a variety of ways to grow, expand, and improve, and he succeeded in forcing a few of his ideas past his brothers. Essentially, Peter's methods were beneficial, especially when he renovated the business by purchasing a separate lot for used cars and remodeling the building. Managers at General Motors were so impressed by the marked increase in sales, up from 1200 to 2000 cars a year, that they wanted to sponsor Peter as a separate dealer. In fact, Peter was practically offered his pick of dealerships in the Southwest. Each time this sort of thing happened, however, his brothers would offer to increase his benefits and Peter agreed to stay on, much to his regret later.

Joe and Ben often disapproved of Peter's improvement ideas, mainly because of their reluctance to spend. Typically, Peter would hire his own contractor and start the job himself until his brothers were sufficiently persuaded by his commitment and the profit potential. Peter kept looking for ways to diversify and strengthen the business. His ideas to get into the financing, leasing, and insur-

EXHIBIT 4 Organization of Rodman Motors—1985

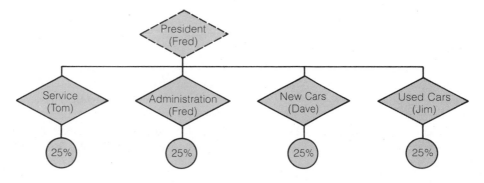

ance end of the automobile market all worked so well that the three brothers began to believe their potential for growth was unlimited.

In the early 1950's, the dealership was a modest business with a healthy, but not overpowering, financial statement. Net profit over a ten year period would have averaged somewhere in the $60,000 range.

It was in the 1960's that Rodman Motors really began to develop. Growth occurred in great surges. Among the many changes that took place, Tom believed that four stand out:

1. The expansion into a new and very sophisticated building complex. Created under Peter's influence.
2. A better trained, more knowledgeable sales team with management of all phases of sales helping to consolidate the sales effort. Created by Peter also.
3. The trade area was beginning a 20 year population boom, and management's good planning reaped the benefits.
4. Extremely strong competition within the family to increase profits and control.

As a result of these changes, Rodman Motors moved to the top of the New Mexico dealerships. Yet in the 1970's, the generation which took the company over was not satisfied with business success. The newcomers wanted to control their own destinies as well.

During the 1970's, sales figures rose to $24 million dollars. Like the sales, net profit ballooned too, and in 1980 profit topped out at nearly one million dollars a year. Exhibit 5 presents the increase in sales and profit experienced by Rodman Motors during the 1970's. Exhibits 6 and 7 show the Balance Sheet and Profit and Loss Statement for the company as of June 30, 1979. Auto sales went from 2,000 total new and used cars in the 1960's to over 5,600 new and used cars in the 1970's. Consequently, Rodman was the number two Oldsmobile dealership in the United States in a city that ranked far below most in total population. The industry average was 7.2% penetration, when Rodman was close to 18%.

EXHIBIT 5

Year	Sales ($000,000)	Net Profit ($000)
1975	$16	$290
1976	17	340
1977	20	650
1978	21	600
1979	24	659
1980	26	996

From the time he began as a new car salesman, Tom thought that he was considered a threat, but not one to be taken too seriously. His select education at a General Motors dealers' school, along with his desire to look for management opportunities, made him a threat. On the other hand, he was not taken seriously because of Joe's determination that his three sons would take over the company. Negative feelings about Peter from Joe's family were transferred to Tom also, and he wondered if there were any measures that could change the situation.

Tom was convinced that he had management potential if only given the chance. After working as a salesman, Tom's big chance was the one he had coveted most: the Parts Department. In handling the Parts Department, Tom thought he could solve some serious management problems and make a mark for himself. His first step was to negotiate with Fred that a percentage of sales would be his basis for pay rather than a salary. Fred agreed, stipulating that $60,000 a month in gross sales had to be achieved first.

Fred gave Tom a free hand and also a good sized budget to revamp the department. Gross sales had only exceeded $40,000 once before and Tom thought the sky was the limit with the right plans and policies. He immediately increased the department's size by 2,600 square feet and moved the entrance to the street side for public access.

Next, he fired the present non-family Parts Manager and several salesmen because of their "you can't do that," "it's just not done that way anywhere else" attitudes. He knew sales come from two sources, internal and external, and that he had no way of making mechanics who are working on automobiles buy more parts, so he had to go outside for additional sales. A telephone Watts line was installed. Local body shops and parts departments were divided into zones by zip code and assigned to each salesperson. He hired an assistant bookkeeper to process the orders by number and then disperse them to the salesmen for ticket writing and billing data.

The bookkeeper also separated the bookkeeping system from the company's main computer. The Parts Department could then get better inventory control by using a weekly method instead of the old monthly way. In less than three months, sales had reached $92,000. Tom then went to Fred with a plan he thought could take the department to a profit level high enough to cover all the overhead in the business. Hence, all New and Used Car sales would represent pure profit, excluding advertising costs. The plan called for these major steps:

1. To hire a parts manager, already found by Tom, who had sold over $214,000 in parts by himself the year before.
2. To go on a complete automatic computer that would locate parts, invoice them, and complete inventory. The system would also have the capacity to prepare a day-to-day inventory report.
3. To not only stock Oldsmobile parts, but also those which were big sellers in other lines.
4. To establish sales quotas and a bonus program tied to direct sales produced.
5. The addition of another 2,000 square feet of storage for sheet metal for the body work industry, an untouched area in the wholesale marketplace at that time.
6. To establish a 2% discount on all parts bought at Rodman's Parts Department by independents.

For two days, Tom and Fred discussed the proposals and their profit potential. The subject of Tom's commission on the $92,000 in gross sales and the net profit came up on the last day.

"My God, I had no idea the potential of the Parts Department was so great," Fred admitted.

"Well, I knew it," said Tom.

"Maybe so," declared Fred, "but no matter, I just don't see how we can afford to pay you a percentage of the sales."

"Are you serious?" Tom asked in disbelief.

"Yes, I am," Fred replied.

"Okay, fine," Tom said and walked out of the office.

EXHIBIT 6

Rodman Motors Inc.

Balance Sheet
<u>June 30, 1979</u>

<u>Current Assets</u>

Cash		$ 86,580
Accounts Receivable	990,000	
Less: Reserve—bad debt	<u>5,490</u>	984,510
Inventory		
New Cars	3,893,544	
Demonstrators	272,547	
Lease & Rentals	92,667	
Used Cars	209,115	
Tires, Batteries, Accessories	42,201	
Paint and other materials	<u>35,190</u>	4,545,264
Prepaid Expense		
Insurance	5,932	
Advertising	<u>6,489</u>	<u>12,421</u>

Total Current Assets $5,628,775

<u>Fixed Assets</u>

Machinery & Equipment	132,106	
Less: Allowance for Depreciation	<u>79,988</u>	
		52,118
Furniture & Fixtures	33,075	
Less: Allowance for Depreciation	<u>27,342</u>	
		5,733
Leasehold Improvements	92,244	
Less: Allowance for Depreciation	<u>23,764</u>	
		<u>68,480</u>

Total Fixed Assets   126,331

<u>Other Assets</u>
Land   <u>119,625</u>

TOTAL ASSETS   <u>$5,874,731</u>

EXHIBIT 6 (*continued*)

Rodman Motors Inc.

Balance Sheet
June 30, 1979

Liabilities & Stockholders' Equity

Current Liabilities

Notes Payable		$4,540,080	
Accounts Payable			
Trade Accounts	265,473		
New Car Deposits	36,801	302,274	

Accrued Liabilities

Interest	3,138		
Insurance	41,300		
Salaries and Bonuses	499,816		
Payroll Tax	4,132		
Sales Tax	27,300		
Property Tax	31,554	607,240	
Total Current Liabilities			5,449,594

Stockholders' Equity

Capital Stock			
Common Stock, 100,000 shares			
issued and outstanding	300,000		
Retained Earnings	125,137		
Total Equity			425,137
TOTAL LIABILITIES AND EQUITY			$5,874,731

EXHIBIT 7

Rodman Motors, Inc.

Profit & Loss Statement
Year Ended June 30, 1979

Gross Sales Revenues	$26,981,110	
Cost of Sales	23,450,000	
Gross Profit		3,501,110
Expenses		
Selling	566,550	
Salaries (Owners)	78,525	
Salaries (Employees)	889,110	
Bonuses	434,610	
Payroll Taxes	111,600	
Vehicle Expense	79,650	
Supplies	39,600	
Advertising	124,740	
Professional Service	106,020	
Travel	25,560	
Memberships	9,450	
Legal	47,880	
Telephone	31,950	
Rent	61,650	
Taxes on Real Estate	78,210	
Utilities	56,610	
Insurance	67,260	
Equipment Repairs	12,330	
Depreciation	19,980	
Miscellaneous	58,410	
Total Expense		2,899,695
NET PROFIT		$601,415

Wade Jones Company of Illinois

The Industry

The segment of the poultry industry served by the firm is the broiler breeder and broiler production operations. Within this segment the firm distributes a line of products devoted to the maintenance of the health of the poultry flocks. Product lines carried include feed additives, water medications, disinfectants and sanitation products, insecticides and rodenticides, and poultry vaccines and antigens. The market for such products in Illinois has attained a firm, established base, and offers potential for growth for a regional supplier. The average price received was for broilers $0.30 per pound, providing a gross income to broiler producers of $278 million. Ten counties in the state were responsible for 93 percent of the total commercial-broilers produced. Of these ten counties, six of the top seven producers were in the market planned to be served by the firm. Central County was the top broiler producer.

The Firm

The Jones Company of Illinois, Inc., serves the poultry industry in Illinois as a jobber distributing antibiotics and feed supplements to the poultry producers. The planned trade territory will cover an area as far west as St. Louis, south to Louisville, north to Chicago, and extending into Indiana and Ohio. The parent, Jones Company, of St. Louis, was founded in 1971 by Wade Jones. To support expansion plans into the Illinois region arrangements were made with AgriGrow, a Central City, Illinois firm, for use of a portion of their warehouse to serve as a base to support local operations. AgriGrow was engaged at that time in the poultry equipment business. When this firm discontinued operations in November, 1980, the Jones Company took over the office and warehouse for their sole use. Mr. Bobby Porter, a former employee of AgriGrow, was employed by the Jones

The research and written case information were presented at a Case Research Symposium and were evaluated by the Case Research Association's Editorial Board. This case was prepared by William E. Wright of the Stephen F. Austin State University as a base for class discussion.

EXHIBIT 1 Main office and warehouse layout—3000 ft² total area

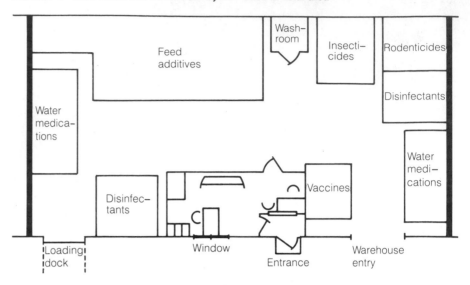

Company to supervise operations in Central City. A reorganization of the activity occurred in June 1981 when Mr. Charles Reynolds joined the firm. The activity in Central City was incorporated as a separate entity from the St. Louis firm, and was named Jones Company of Illinois. Mr. Reynolds, an experienced sales representative of poultry industry products, obtained a forty percent interest in the newly incorporated firm, with the balance held by Jones Company. At that time the one small office and warehouse provided 2500 sq. ft. of space. A second warehouse providing 3000 sq. ft. additional space, approximately one mile away, was leased. Layout facility is shown in Exhibits 1 and 2. A 1½ ton truck and a forklift comprised the delivery and warehouse equipment.

EXHIBIT 2 Subsidiary warehouse layout—2500 ft² total area

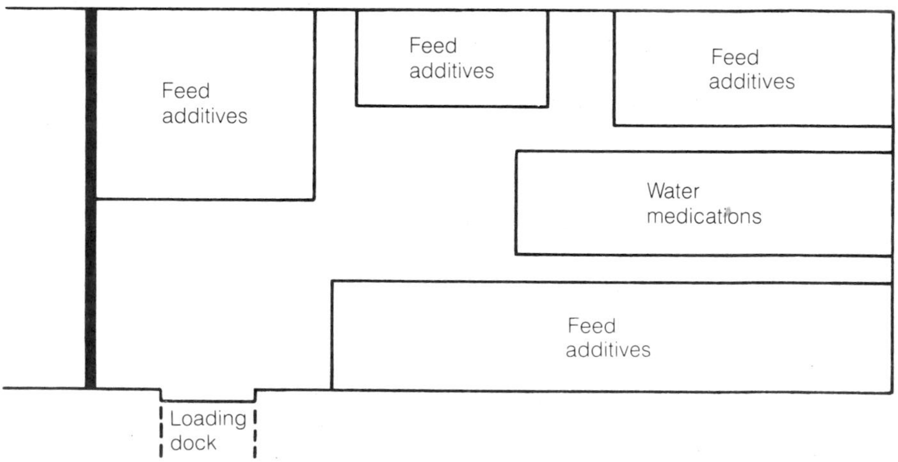

Organization

Mr. Charles Reynolds is President and General Manager of the firm. He has over sixteen years' selling and managerial experience directly related to the Central City operations. Experience just prior to entering the firm was as a regional manager with Brownwood Laboratories, a major supplier to the Jones Company. Mr. Bobby Porter holds the position of Office-Warehouse Manager, and serves as Secretary-Treasure of the Company. Mr. Porter was previously employed by AgriGrow, and brought to the new firm three years' experience in the local poultry industry. Mrs. Tillie Nixon serves the secretarial and bookkeeping function on a part-time basis. Initially she worked 1/2 day, three days per week. This was extended later to 1/2 day, five days per week. Mr. Benny Crownover performed the services of truck driver from the incorporation date until May 1982, when he left the firm to go into business with his father. Mr. Reynolds' son, Bailey, although attending college, took over the delivery function for the summer until a new driver could be obtained.

Objectives

Mr. Charles Reynolds, as 40 percent owner and serving as President and General Manager, established several goals upon entering the firm. His more immediate goals were to develop the capability to maintain the records of Jones Company of Illinois separate from the St. Louis operation, and to consolidate the two warehouse facilities and office at one location. The Jones Company in Illinois at that time was processing certain of the transaction data pertaining to the Central City operation, and subsequent to the incorporation continued to provide inventory and customer information from their data processing facility on an informal accommodation service basis. With regards to facility consolidation, a building site for an approximately 6000 sq. ft. building was purchased in August 1981, and plans developed for new building construction. Longer term goal was to obtain a new delivery vehicle in order to carry heavier loads and reduce the frequency of trips currently being made for merchandise deliveries within the market area served. Mr. Reynolds has steadfastly adhered to the attainment of these goals, awarding in May a contract to begin construction of the new facility, expected to be completed in latter part of August.

Marketing and Distribution

As previously noted, the primary business of the firm is the sale and distribution of antibiotics and food supplements to the poultry industry. Of the ten counties in Illinois which provide most of the state's production of broilers, the majority of the producers are concentrated in Central County and nearby counties. The firm's location in Central City is well suited to servicing the counties and one can avoid overnight travel for deliveries, except in those cases of vehicle emergencies. Sales activity is limited to major accounts and therefore evolves around frequent direct contacts, both personal and through use of telephone calls. At the beginning of each week telephone calls are placed to the customers to develop the necessary deliveries. Frequent calls from customers placing orders during the week are also received. From these activities delivery dates are firmed and the truck routing schedule developed. Experience has proven that several trips may be required during a week due to the limited capacity of the 1½ ton truck, and in many cases has required the use of a pickup truck. For this reason, the purchase of the larger vehicle in the future is planned.

Advertising is somewhat restricted due to the limited customer list which contains the major producers. In March 1982, there were 49 customers served. Customer representatives are provided product lists, and occasionally small promotional items such as pens with the firm's name and telephone number.

Operations

Customers either notify the firm when additional supplement materials are needed, or their needs determined by the marketing activity noted above. In response to the order requests, sales orders are prepared and the materials drawn from the warehouses. The driver delivers the material and secures the necessary customer receipt acknowledging delivery. Merchandise for stocking the warehouse is ordered for a period of one month ahead. The quantity ordered is usually based upon the quantities sold during the previous month, tempered by the experience of the warehouse manager. Shortages noted during frequent surveys of available stocks are immediately reordered. Since the firm in its present form has been in operation for approximately one year, the determination of the reorder requirements is based upon a simple procedure.

The ordering system functions as follows: After review of stock record cards and canvasing stocks through visual inspection, purchase orders to the various vendors are prepared. As of March 1982, twenty-seven vendors served the firm. Upon receipt of merchandise ordered, an inspection is performed, and the shipping documents compared with the original purchase orders to verify amounts, prices, and discount. Damaged materials are noted. The quantities received are recorded on the perpetual inventory cards, adding to the balances on hand.

Pending construction of a new building the material is warehoused in one of the two locations. The forklift is kept in the larger warehouse where the bulkier and larger quantities of materials are stored. By having to keep the forklift in one location considerable manual labor is expended in the other storage area. The warehouse consolidation will alleviate this problem of manually handling bags and containers. Greater use can be made of pallet movements.

In addition to the $1\frac{1}{2}$ ton truck for the large load deliveries, the firm has available two pickup trucks. One is used by Mr. Reynolds for his sales calls, and the other is used by Mr. Porter for local deliveries.

Financial and Accounting

Since the organization of the company in June 1981, Mr. Reynolds has employed essentially five basic accounting and control procedures. These are the recording of transactions involving cash receipts, disbursements, accounts payable, accounts receivable, and inventory. A local accountant is employed to perform monthly write-ups, maintain tax records, and prepare tax reports. The scope of work to be performed by the accountant was never formally established, and as a result some misunderstanding occasionally arose as to the depth of analysis and interpretation of financial statements that should have been forthcoming. The accountant develops the monthly financial statements from the information provided by the secretary. She takes the information from her records. The accountant performs the computations and maintains the record on such account items as depreciation, prepaid income tax, accumulated payroll taxes, and cost of goods sold in his office while the secretary maintains the registers and ledgers noted above. There is no jointly understood or agreed upon chart of accounts. The present methods and procedure have precluded Mr. Reynolds' access to and overview of his current business position. Examples of financial transactions which have given concern in the past are:

1. Discrepancy in the inventory account as a consequence of contributions of inventory to the capital account by Jones Company of St. Louis at the time of the incorporation were not resolved until late August 1981. As a result the beginning inventory in June 1981 was approximately $65,000.00 less on financial statement than that carried in the inventory record, and the ending inventory in July 1981, was approximately $34,000.00 more than shown on the inventory record. The inventory record maintained for the firm by Jones of Illinois and the record maintained locally was subsequently reconciled, yet the variations affected the income statement rendered by the accountant.

2. A problem arose in the computation of the 1981 income tax. The end of the fiscal year had been initially established to be June 26. In December this was changed to be December 26, and the income tax was duly computed for the period. In computation of the tax, certain data provided by the Secretary was misinterpreted by the accountant. An overpayment of the 1981 tax resulted. The January and February financial statements subsequently prepared prior to discovery of the discrepancy were then found to be in error. The problem was resolved in March statements reflecting the overpayment of income tax.

3. The recording of transactions has been rather straightforward. A record of cash receipts and disbursements is maintained in the check register. Occasionally, only dollar amounts of receipts have been recorded which required one to check the deposit slips to determine from whom the money had been received. A running total of receipts during the month is maintained. Disbursements are accounted for through the use of a carbon record of the checks written. While the payee was noted on the stubs, the type or nature of the expense was not always entered.

4. Accounts receivable are kept in alphabetical order by account names. In most cases, the entries are dated as to when the sale was made and when a payment is made on the account. Accounts payable on merchandise purchases are kept in the general ledger along with the accounts receivable. Entries are made noting vendor name, amount of purchase and date of payment. The check number of each payment is recorded in the journal with the purchase payment. Payment for merchandise purchases can be traced through the check register.

5. The inventory record is maintained by Mr. Porter, the warehouse manager. A perpetual form of inventory system is employed with individual cards maintained for each product. The date that merchandise is received or issued from inventory is also noted, along with the quantities involved and a running total of the remaining balance. The price of the goods is not entered on the cards. The product list advertises 184 items, categorized under five product categories. During an examination of selected records, a few instances were noted where computational errors had been made and subsequently corrected.

An indication of activity experienced by the firm can be seen in the transactions relating to the general ledger accounts. A sampling showed 184 transactions in June 1981, 304 in July, 220 in August, 278 in September, and 245 in January 1982. The January transaction details were as follows: 97 sales invoices prepared for a total of $166,483; 63 checks written disbursing $112,499; 29 merchandise orders placed with a total of $169,886; and 56 payments received on accounts totaling $114,471.

Selected financial information pertaining to current position and results of operations are provided in Exhibits 3 and 4.

Management

To achieve his objective in developing a profitable and growing organization, and to realize his

---

EXHIBIT 3 Sales and earnings

Month	Sales	Cost of Sales	Gross Profit	Expenses	Earnings
Jun 1981	$ 90,771	$ 74,483	$ 16,288	$ 8,343	$ 7,945
Jul 1981	137,719	124,482	13,237	12,687	550
Aug 1981	102,902	95,485	7,417	10,518	(3,101)
Sep 1981	122,535	106,762	15,773	9,969	5,804
Oct 1981	124,454	106,491	17,964	11,983	5,981
Nov 1981	104,469	91,049	13,420	10,118	3,302
Dec 1981	108,218	81,137	27,081	17,263	9,818
Jan 1982	169,332	153,892	15,440	13,064	2,376
Feb 1982	137,998	120,119	17,879	11,831	6,047
Mar 1982	121,702	99,007	22,694	12,050	10,645
Apr 1982	102,035	91,032	11,003	12,127	(1,124)
May 1982	130,969	113,241	17,727	13,193	4,535
Jun 1982	143,326	124,318	19,007	13,336	5,672

EXHIBIT 4 Balance sheet items

Month	Current Assets	Fixed Assets	Current Liab.	Notes Payable	Net Worth
Jun 1981	$266,764	$ 50,048	$132,761	$16,105	$167,945
Jul 1981	304,475	49,884	170,608	15,255	168,495
Aug 1981	325,931	49,330	195,462	14,405	165,394
Sep 1981	381,071	55,043	251,360	13,555	171,198
Oct 1981	338,430	54,356	202,902	12,705	177,178
Nov 1981	305,422	53,668	166,754	11,855	180,481
Dec 1981	308,285	47,335	154,316	11,005	190,299
Jan 1982	366,712	46,085	212,876	10,155	189,766
Feb 1982	326,226	44,835	173,359	9,305	188,397
Mar 1982	308,470	43,335	144,308	8,455	199,042
Apr 1982	291,656	41,835	127,969	7,605	197,918
May 1982	343,048	40,335	174,176	6,755	202,452
Jun 1982	342,519	38,835	167,325	5,905	208,124

goals of new building construction for consolidation of warehouse operations and for obtaining the truck replacement, Mr. Reynolds early saw the need for a greater control over the records of his organization. He believed that the records to be maintained in the office should not only reflect the financial condition of the firm more accurately and responsively, but also be in a form suited to analysis of his operations to ascertain performance on a timely basis as well as providing insight into areas where improvements in operations could be made. He believed that through use of a small business computer he could maintain his own records in the office which would be more accurate and in sufficient detail for his needs. With this thought in mind he had begun to look into various systems for possible purchase and installation.

Who's on First?

"I've just got to get some relief from all this paperwork!" Alan Sterling exclaimed, as he looked across his desk to the management consultant, Fred Harvey.

"Well, if you really are serious about it, I'm sure that I can help you," responded Harvey.

"Of course I'm serious about it! Look at all these papers," said Sterling as he swept his hand over the desk, covered with an assortment of documents.

"Few people enjoy paperwork, so your concern is natural and sensible, but there's more to it than just a desire to pass it on to someone else," observed Harvey. As Sterling said nothing, Harvey continued: "What is involved is first to identify what you want to delegate, and then to whom. Sure, this sounds pretty obvious, but it's not as easy as it appears. The difficult part is trying to judge accurately the consequences of whatever you plan to do . . . to you, to others, to the company."

"Sounds like an exercise in physics," Sterling remarked. "Action. Reaction."

"It would be nice if it were that simple!" Harvey replied.

"What do you mean?" Sterling asked, his voice sharp.

"Well, I think it is critical that you recognize that if you want to make any change of real substance that this will mean a change in the complexion of the company," Harvey said mildly. "It will mean a change in the controls that you have grown used to over many years. The company won't be exactly the same any more. That doesn't mean you'll lose overall control, but it does mean that you'll have to give up some control to others. It's easy to pass out responsibilities to others, but it is something else again to also allow others to assume decision making powers that they never possessed before . . . . If you just assign new jobs to others, but keep the decisions to yourself, you've not resolved your workload problem because they'll have to come back to you every time a decision has to

The research and written case information were presented at a Case Research Symposium and were evaluated by the Case Research Association's Editorial Board. This case was prepared by George Eddy of the University of Texas at Austin as a basis for class discussion. Copyright © by George Eddy, 1980.

be made. So, the real question is, are you ready to make a real change?"

When he left a major construction firm in a large metropolitan area of some 2 million persons some 10 years ago to set up his own company, Alan Sterling was convinced that he would be successful. As a graduate mechanical engineer, he had performed well, been commended by his superiors, and had earned the respect of the organization's customers. He expected that because of his reputation for competence and integrity that several of his contacts would switch their business to him when he struck out on his own. His expectations were justified, and while he had ambitious goals, Sterling did not anticipate that his company's performance would be so remarkable. He had hoped to achieve gross receipts of $10 million by the end of his tenth year. When the company sales exceeded $20 million, he was both exhilarated and surprised. However, he did not have time to contemplate the kind of problems that rapid growth would bring.

For years his days, nights and weekends were devoted almost exclusively to company business, and it was typical for him to come to work at three in the morning on a Sunday when he had a critical deadline to meet. This usually entailed putting the finishing touches to a complicated construction bid whose award was essential to the company's survival in the highly competitive construction work.

He drove himself hard, but as he loved his work and was determined to succeed, he did not mind the time he spent on the job. He realized that he would have to scramble to survive, to get established, so he was prepared to put everything he had into his business. As a married man and the father of three children, he recognized and accepted his family responsibilities; nonetheless his business really came first. At the same time, it was true that if his firm prospered, he certainly would be able to support his family handsomely.

Over the years he became accustomed to making difficult decisions by himself, and his ability to develop accurate estimates in large construction jobs in a minimum of time reflected both his insistence on learning rapidly by experience and his perseverance. As his personal reputation grew, the company found itself on an expanding bidders' list

as more and more large petroleum corporations commenced to send him requests for bids on an unsolicited basis. In a relatively short time, the company established itself as a strong competitor for concrete work, such as foundations and platforms for large structures and for process pipe installations of considerable magnitude and complexity.

By the end of the tenth year, Sterling's company had acquired 7 key individuals, not including Sterling's 26 year old son, and a relatively permanent field supervisory group—general superintendents, field foremen and crew chiefs—of approximately 40 men. The numbers of individual craftsmen, electricians, steam fitters, carpenters, and so on—varied with the projects for which the firm received contracts from month to month. Such projects differed in scope and difficulty across a broad spectrum, with some completed in a few weeks to those extending for several years. As a consequence of such ebb and flow, the numbers of field personnel alternated from less than 200 to over 800. Although some construction firms were unionized, Sterling's company was not; he was happy with it that way, and did not regard it as unusual that his work force frequently employed simultaneously both non-union and union workers. He believed that he met the prevailing wages in the area and that the fringe benefits he provided also were comparable. Further, he considered that as a nonunion organization, his company was both more flexible and efficient. His success seemed to bear that out. He had never experienced any major labor difficulty, although from time to time he could not always find locally all the skills needed for a particular project.

While Sterling was pleased with the volume of business his firm had achieved, he was concerned that the administrative procedures had not seemed to have kept pace with the field construction. Field supervisors were beginning to complain that the accounting department was not supporting them properly, thus making it difficult to keep adequate track of progress. It was increasingly hard, they contended, to evaluate physical accomplishment with expenditures; they did not want to be held responsible, for example, for exceeding estimated or targeted costs when they did not always have current reports from accounting on actual costs incurred. Billings to customers were now more complicated as more difficult projects were awarded, and that together with overall increased volume of work created more opportunities for mistakes. This circumstance not only adversely affected cash flow, it also irritated customers when they believed that they had been erroneously charged. It was partly due to these events that Sterling placed Helen Jordan in charge of accounting in addition to her duties as company secretary/treasurer, and gave her the extra title of Office Manager.

Sterling was not pleased with the increased administrative burden he seemed to have inherited with the growth of the firm. True, he had from the outset concentrated on the technical side of the company, making engineering estimates for bids on his own, checking estimates of others, and monitoring work in the field. He depended heavily on Helen to take care of office-type work. He had grown accustomed to personally verifying activities and procedures that he considered to be of significant importance to the company. To keep track of major expenditures, for example, he still continued to sign all payroll checks. Now that these amounted to several hundreds and consumed an appreciable amount of his time, he began to wonder if he could or should begin to divest himself of some of these administrative chores. As he considered various possibilities, he began to think about his organizational arrangement. No organization chart had ever been developed since one had not been needed in his opinion. He thought that it was obvious who did the estimating on bids, for instance, and who supervised the work in the field, overall and on specific projects. If a new project came along and a key individual was not too busy at the time, and it was in his area of general competence, it was assigned to him. The same practice applied to estimating, and if everyone else was busy when a new bid was received, Sterling did not mind tackling it himself—in fact, he rather enjoyed doing it. . . .

Now here he was talking to a consultant, a stranger from another city whom his son Chris knew and had recommended. The consultant, Fred Harvey, was a management professor in a large university who had hired Sterling's son as a student assistant in his senior year. Chris Sterling, a finance major, had worked during the summer in his father's business and was convinced his father needed professional assistance and that Fred Harvey was the one to provide it. Accordingly, Chris persuaded his father to arrange a meeting.

"Are you ready for a change?" repeated Harvey.

"Let's get on with it," Sterling replied.

"One of the first things you should do," Fred said, "is to take a hard look at your goals and then at every key member of the Company."

Alan Sterling agreed that this was a reasonable approach, and when Harvey produced a form for evaluation purposes (see Exhibit 1), Sterling declared he would proceed at once. Within two weeks his appraisal was completed. Selected evaluations of his key personnel are illustrated in Exhibit 2, which also indicates the position each occupied and how long in that capacity. Except Freeman, all had 5 years or more service.

Subsequently and with Sterling's approval, Harvey arranged to discuss the organization with each of the seven who constituted the top management group. During these discussions, Harvey asked each one to sketch his belief about the organizational arrangement. With this action concluded, Harvey began to analyze the results of his conversations, especially those with Freeman, Garrison, Holmes, and Jordan. These four had produced their conceptions of Sterling's firm (shown in Exhibits 3, 4, 5, and 6), which Harvey thought were most revealing.

In the midst of his reflections two quotations from Machiavelli suddenly popped into his mind.

"It must be considered," Machiavelli observed, "that there is nothing more difficult to carry out, nor more doubtful of success, nor more dangerous to handle, than to initiate a new order of things."

On the other hand, Machiavelli also counselled that "Whence it is to be noted, that in taking a state the conqueror must arrange to commit all his cruelties at once, so as not to recur to them every day, and so as to be able, by not making fresh changes, to reassure people and win them over by benefiting them."

EXHIBIT 1   Personal attributes rating scale

Please use the scales on this page to indicate your conclusions about the key persons in your organization. Blacken-in the space corresponding to that position between each pair of terms which best describes your beliefs about the person you are evaluating. For example, if you think that he or she should be moderately interesting, you would blacken in the number two space (2) on the "Interesting–Boring" scale as shown below. Please do this for EACH pair of terms, without skipping any.

	Extremely	Moderately	Neutral	Moderately	Extremely	
Interesting	1 :	2 :	3 :	4 :	5	Boring

1.	Experienced	1 : 2 : 3 : 4 : 5	Inexperienced
2.	Nonenergetic	1 : 2 : 3 : 4 : 5	Energetic
3.	Modest	1 : 2 : 3 : 4 : 5	Vain
4.	Insincere	1 : 2 : 3 : 4 : 5	Sincere
5.	Intelligent	1 : 2 : 3 : 4 : 5	Unintelligent
6.	Unethical	1 : 2 : 3 : 4 : 5	Ethical
7.	Independent	1 : 2 : 3 : 4 : 5	Dependent
8.	Excitable	1 : 2 : 3 : 4 : 5	Calm
9.	Organized	1 : 2 : 3 : 4 : 5	Unorganized
10.	Unconventional	1 : 2 : 3 : 4 : 5	Conventional
11.	Competent	1 : 2 : 3 : 4 : 5	Incompetent
12.	Unreliable	1 : 2 : 3 : 4 : 5	Reliable
13.	Humorous	1 : 2 : 3 : 4 : 5	Humorless
14.	Weak	1 : 2 : 3 : 4 : 5	Strong
15.	Colorful	1 : 2 : 3 : 4 : 5	Colorless
16.	Imitative	1 : 2 : 3 : 4 : 5	Creative
17.	Secure	1 : 2 : 3 : 4 : 5	Insecure
18.	Unhealthy	1 : 2 : 3 : 4 : 5	Healthy
19.	Articulate	1 : 2 : 3 : 4 : 5	Inarticulate
20.	Seeks Responsibility	1 : 2 : 3 : 4 : 5	Avoids Responsibility
21.	Poor Writer	1 : 2 : 3 : 4 : 5	Good Writer
22.	Decisive	1 : 2 : 3 : 4 : 5	Indecisive
23.	Pessimistic	1 : 2 : 3 : 4 : 5	Optimistic
24.	Stable	1 : 2 : 3 : 4 : 5	Unstable
25.	Future-oriented	1 : 2 : 3 : 4 : 5	Present-oriented
26.	Antagonistic	1 : 2 : 3 : 4 : 5	Cooperative
27.	Alert	1 : 2 : 3 : 4 : 5	Dull
28.	Impulsive	1 : 2 : 3 : 4 : 5	Deliberate
29.	Precise	1 : 2 : 3 : 4 : 5	Imprecise
30.	Reactive	1 : 2 : 3 : 4 : 5	Self-Starter

EXHIBIT 2 President's selected evaluations of key personnel

Item Number	Draper (44)	Freeman (38)	Garrison (40)	Holmes (43)	Johnson (47)	Jordan (39)	Wallace (33)
1	2	1	1	1	1	1	1
7	5	1	2	1	2	1	1
8	4	4	2	4	4	1	4
9	2	1	1	1	1	2	1
11	2	1	1	1	1	1	1
14	5	5	5	5	4	5	5
16	4	4	4	5	4	4	5
17	2	2	2	1	4	2	1
19	2	2	1	1	NR	2	2
20	2	2	1	1	2	1	1
22	2	2	2	1	2	2	1
23	4	4	4	4	2	4	1
24	2	2	1	1	2	1	1
25	2	2	1	1	2	4	1
28	4	4	5	5	4	5	4
30	4	5	5	5	5	5	5

NOTE: Number in parentheses represents age; NR = not rated.

Position and time in position are as follows:

Draper	General Superintendent	7 years
Freeman	Purchasing Director	3 years
Garrison	VP, Chief Engineer	3 years
Holmes	VP, Chief Estimator	1 year
Johnson	Project Manager, Estimator	8 years
Jordan	Office Manager	1 month
Wallace	Project Manager	4 years

EXHIBIT 3 The organization as visualized by Freeman

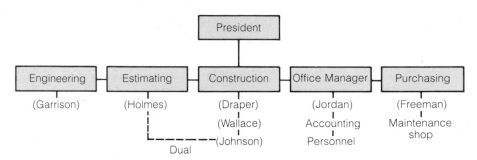

EXHIBIT 4   The organization as visualized by Garrison

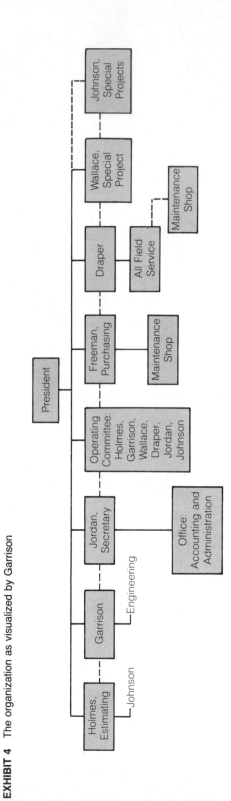

EXHIBIT 5 The organization as visualized by Holmes

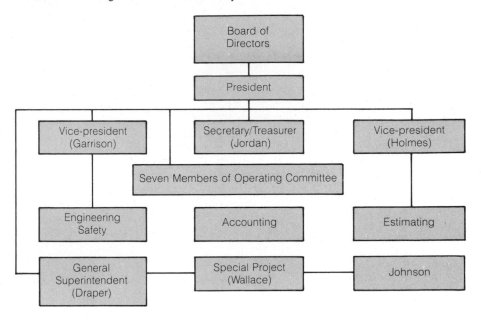

EXHIBIT 6 The organization as visualized by Jordan

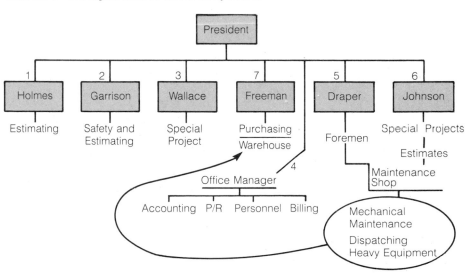

AT&T's Entrepreneur

William F. Buehler looks back on the past year and speaks in elegiac tones about his "noble experiment."

Here he was, 43 years old, just named a vice president at American Telephone & Telegraph Co., given a work force of 3,000 and put in charge of marketing phone systems to small businesses all over the U.S. What's more, his bosses at AT&T gave him considerable freedom to break with the Bell way of doing things.

And that's exactly what he did. In place of Bell's rigmarole of endless memos, interminable meetings and strict chain of command, the boyish-looking Mr. Buehler discarded planning manuals, threw out employee tests, put salespeople on the highest commission-based compensation plan in AT&T history and fired those who couldn't meet his tough quotas.

It worked. Salespeople say they caught "Buehler fever," and sales figures soared off the charts. His boss and the chairman of AT&T Information Systems, Charles Marshall, concedes that the Buehler unit that sold the smaller business systems is outperforming the rival unit selling larger ones.

But today, 12 months later, Mr. Buehler isn't bathing in accolades. Instead, he is being removed from his job and put in an obscure planning position, though he remains a vice president.

"I argued to the management that the system should stay in place and I should continue leading it," he says. "I win most of my arguments around here, but I lost this one."

As a result, the new corporate culture that he created has been weakened, if not snuffed out, and many of his subordinates are apprehensive even though they often found him difficult to work for. "We're all upset and worried that we'll lose our new culture," says James R. Lewis, an AT&T account executive in Southfield, Mich. Moreover, many observers wonder whether AT&T isn't discouraging the kind of competitive zeal it is going to need as it tries to change from a regulated

Monica Langley, "Wrong Number: AT&T Manager Finds His Effort to Galvanize Sales Meets Resistance," *Wall Street Journal* (December 14, 1983). Reprinted by permission of the *Wall Street Journal,* © Dow Jones & Company, Inc. 1983. All rights reserved.

monopoly into a company that can take on the likes of International Business Machines Corp. (AT&T Information Systems said it has received fewer early-retirement volunteers than it had sought.)

Why Mr. Buehler lost his position depends on whom you talk with. If you talk with Robert J. Casale, who ran the rival sales group along traditional lines and recently became his boss, the change was designed "to integrate the two discrete sales staffs in order to eliminate duplication in central support services."

But Mr. Marshall disagrees with that explanation. He says he favored moving Mr. Buehler so that the small-system sales force would report up the same channels as the large-systems division.

To many within the company, however, Mr. Buehler was removed because he was too menacing to the old Ma Bell culture. Despite his bottom-line success, he was viewed more as a maverick than as a visionary, they say.

"Bill Buehler ruffled some feathers at the top. I wouldn't rule out that his different style of leadership caused him to be pushed out of a line position," Mr. Lewis speculates. "In the field, we knew there was a power struggle going on at the top."

Predictable Battle?

That change may have set off a struggle doesn't surprise David A. Nadler, the president of Organizational Research & Consultation Inc., a New York management consulting firm. "Frequently in entrenched organizations where something new and entrepreneurial is tried," he says, "the experiment may not survive because it's too threatening to the old line."

When first meeting Mr. Buehler, you instantly see that he loves the limelight. He deems himself a born leader and constantly postures to dominate conversations, meetings and corporate strategies.

"I am blessed. I am a charismatic leader, I'll just tell you. I've always been able to get up in front of a group of people and motivate them to follow me," Mr Buehler says unabashedly.

But at a recent press briefing in Washington, D.C.—where his superiors and not his subordinates were present—Mr. Buehler was visibly un-

comfortable about taking a back seat. Sitting at the dais with AT&T Information Systems officers, Mr. Buehler was the only one not asked to speak by the chairman, Mr. Marshall. Mr. Buehler fidgeted in his seat throughout the briefing until, finally unable to contain himself, he started waving his arms to get the chairman's attention.

During his 19 years with the Bell System, Mr. Buehler hasn't had any trouble gaining attention as a dynamic manager. Always considered on the fast track by people who have known him over the years, he received promotion after promotion. Some describe him as "Kennedyesque."

When AT&T Information Systems was created last Jan. 1 to become the unregulated equipment-marketing unit for AT&T, which was preparing to divest itself of its Bell operating companies this Jan. 1, Mr. Buehler was tapped as a vice president. He was to head General Business Systems, which would sell smaller systems at high volume, while Mr. Casale would oversee sales of large accounts at National Business Systems.

Not seeing his wife and two sons very much, and putting aside his love for skiing, playing touch football and reading spy novels, Mr. Buehler began working 16-hour days to install a new corporate culture in his unit.

In setting up GBS, Mr. Buehler used as a road map a book "In Search of Excellence: Lessons from American's Best Run Companies." He read the best seller twice and confesses that he "stole from it liberally." Last January, in fact, he handed out to his new force a typewritten sheet of marching orders that was titled "What We Aspire to Be" and contained verbatim phrases from the book. They included such mottoes as "customer is king," "reward results, not process," "staff supports the line" and "keep it simple."

"That little list of points was the only guide I gave my new work force in January—no detailed plans or directives," Mr. Buehler says. "I wanted the team to know from the start that this was an entrepreneurial venture, and they were to abide by these points in a way that worked best for them."

Also from the start, Mr. Buehler was highly visible. He traveled across the country to his 27 branches to meet his people.

"The staffers in my branch have been with Bell for years, but this was the very first time any of them had ever even seen an AT&T vice president," says Robert L. Focazio, the GBS branch manager for New Jersey. "And then he actually sat down with the billing staff and ate hoagie sandwiches. This was radical by AT&T standards, but we came to know it was perfectly natural by Bill Buehler's standards."

Mr. Focazio, who says he is "personally disappointed" that Mr. Buehler won't be his boss after Jan. 1, says Mr. Buehler didn't pay any attention to hierarchical lines. "That's the kind of guy you'd want to kill for," he says. "It almost doesn't matter what Bill Buehler says."

Laying Down the Law

But sometimes Mr. Buehler's managers didn't like what the boss was saying. Mr. Focazio remembers a meeting where the branch managers were complaining about how some nonsales employees were paid. "Bill rejected our proposal," Mr. Focazio recalls, "and we were upset with his decision. So he told us to go outside right then, kick rocks and come back ready to support the decision as if it were our own."

Mr. Buehler minces no words to demonstrate his demand for obedience. "If I found one of my managers trying to sabotage any decision I made, I'd cut his neck off," he says.

He toughness extends to his choice of whom he allows to work for him. Each month, he makes keep or cut determinations based strictly on sales performance. More than one-third of his sales force has quit, been transferred or been fired. "Results are what count," Mr. Buehler says. "If a salesman can't meet quota, he doesn't belong here." Edward R. Hodges, an account executive in Dallas, says, "It's tough to meet Bill's standards, and I've seen a lot of salesmen in Dallas put back in the streets."

The GBS sales force receives compensation based 50% on straight salary and 50% on sales commissions, while the NBS force has a 70%-30% salary-commission mix. In addition, all GBS salespeople have the same quota, while NBS conducts complex, time-consuming quota reviews for each

salesman to allow for differences in sales territories.

Intense Pressure

In this performance-driven regime, Mr. Buehler's salespeople say they feel more competitive pressure from their fellow salesmen than from product competitors such as TIE communications Inc., Mitel Corp. and ITT Corp.

To ensure that peer pressure, not the boss's orders, motivated his salespeople, Mr. Buehler demanded that individual sales results be posted. "One of the few things I insisted on was a sales board to be prominently displayed in every office," Mr. Buehler says. "As hokey as it sounds, when a person comes to work every day and sees his red tab isn't the highest one up there, he will work that much harder."

But some branches worked harder at how the sales board looked than what it said—the "Bell-shaped head" mentality lingered on. "My God, you wouldn't believe it! My managers wanted to know whether the boards should be magnetic or chalk, colored or black and white, large or small," Mr. Buehler complains. "They were so used to detailed corporate orders in the Bell System, they wanted to be led by the hand. Hell, I just wanted any kind of board up there, and then the results."

Mr. Buehler's troops initially had trouble not only picking up his way of thinking but also bringing in the results. GBS made few sales in the first quarter, while the more traditional NBS was meeting its quota. "It was gut-wrenching those first months, watching the results come in," Mr. Buehler says.

Negative Atmosphere

As bad as the initial results were, Mr. Buehler was bothered as much by the reception that his new unit was getting from other AT&T units. "Employees in different parts of the country enjoyed seeing us fail," he recalls.

About the same time, Archie McGill, then the president of AT&T Information Systems and the man who had persuaded Mr. Buehler to leave Pacific Telephone Co., resigned. Insiders said then that Mr. McGill had left rather than be pushed into a less important role because higher-ups found him difficult to control. (He denied this and said it was simply time to move on.) With the departure of the man who had given him autonomy to run his unit, Mr. Buehler was the only one left at AT&T trying to shake up the sleepy giant, some insiders say. (Other inside observers speculate that the recent shake-up concerning Mr. Buehler was a move to expunge the last remnant of Mr. McGill's leadership.)

But shortly after Mr. McGill's resignation, Mr. Buehler's team caught "Buehler fever" and started bringing in the numbers. His salespeople were exceeding quotas and began taking home $40,000 to $45,000 a year.

Helping the Troops

As the salesmen wrote more orders and the managers got the hang of this new free-wheeling atmosphere, they started making more demands on Mr. Buehler—and he responded. When they needed prompter deliveries, Mr. Buehler guaranteed that the phones would be delivered even if a decorative feature was missing. When they refused to spend time filling out contract forms, Mr. Buehler reduced the standard contract to one page from four. When they wanted quicker approvals of customer designs and bids, he organized a small committee to respond within days.

"Decisions that would have taken two years in the Bell System were made in days by Bill Buehler," marvels Diane Allen, an account executive in Monterey, Calif. "Bias for action," an "In Search of Excellence" buzzword, had taken hold. Unlike the tradition-bound AT&T, where planning is often an end in itself, a "try it, fix it, don't study it to death" kind of attitude prevailed.

But many salespeople fear that all this will come to an end when Mr. Buehler moves to his planning job next month. "All of us would have liked to go into 1984 with Bill at the helm," Mr. Hodges says. And Mr. Buehler says, "There were tears around here. But I lost on this, and I can live with that."

An AT&T Mistake?

Mr. Buehler may not be the only loser. Many inside and outside observers say AT&T is making a mistake by stifling Mr. Buehler and the new corporate culture that he tried to create despite the huge bureaucracy. "I would have kept Bill as a leader of the sales force," Mr. McGill says. Mr. Nadler, the consultant, agrees. "Bill Buehler is the kind of leader AT&T needs to develop," he says. And Dennis Lukas, who resigned as marketing director at AT&T Information Systems "in part" because of the recent changes at GBS and has just become an assistant vice president at GTE Corp., predicts "that AT&T will try this kind of experiment again because it was so right."

But for now, this battle between corporate traditionalism and innovation has produced a victory for the old line at AT&T. Yet Bill Buehler makes it clear that his campaign to create a new corporate culture there hasn't ended.

Texas Air Corporation: Peanuts and Profits

Frank Lorenzo, Chairman and Chief Executive Officer of Texas Air Corp. ("TAC"), once said that "by 1990 there will be only six (6) major airlines in the United States. I intend to own one of them."[1] Since coming to the Houston based carrier at the age of thirty in late 1971, most of his efforts have been directed toward that goal. By December, 1980, Texas Air could boast of an operation which generated almost $300 million in revenue on an asset base of almost $400 million, employed 3,500 people, and produced profits in seven of the nine years under Lorenzo's control. In 1981, Texas International acquired controlling interest in the much larger Continental Airlines. These were significant accomplishments for a carrier which eleven years earlier was on the brink of bankruptcy. Some observers believe that the TI-Continental merger is a significant step by Lorenzo to achieve his goal of owning one of the major airlines in the U.S. by 1990.

The Pre-Lorenzo Years: 1947–1971

Trans Texas Airways (TTA), the forerunner of Texas International (TI) and Texas Air Corp. (TAC), began official operations on Saturday, October 11, 1947. It was a rather inauspicious start. R. Earl McKaughan mortgaged everything he owned to purchase two World War II surplus DC-3 aircraft. Each had seating capacity for 21 passengers. Trans Texas employed 96 people and its route structure included eight Texas cities: San Angelo, Brownswood, Fort Worth, Dallas (Love Field), Palestine, Houston (Hobby), Victoria and San Antonio. Due to its size, the nature of the airline industry, governmental regulation, and its regional nature, Trans Texas

The research and written case information were presented at a Case Research Symposium and were evaluated by the Case Research Association's Editorial Board. This case was prepared by Timothy Singleton and Robert McGlashan of the University of Houston at Clear Lake City as a basis for class discussion. The initial research data for the Texas Air Corporation case was gathered in July, 1981 by a group of MBA students as a project for a Business Policy Seminar at the University of Houston at Clear Lake City. The data were taken from the Wall Street Journal, Business Week, Texas Monthly, Texas International employee newsletter and other publications. The student members of the group were Roger A. Barber, Chuck Bigi, Mary Kay Leahy, Frank J. Slaughter and Craig Watson.

Distrbuted by the Case Research Association. All rights reserved to the authors and the Case Research Association. Permission to use the case should be obtained from the Case Research Association.

was besieged by problems from its infancy. Even its airline code letter, TTA, bore the brunt of many remarks such as Tinker Toy Airlines, Tree Top Airways, and Try Try Again.

To really appreciate TTA's position during the pre-Lorenzo years, one must first recognize the regulated condition of the industry. In most business activities, profits are realized by out-performing the competitors. Tactics such as producing a superior product, obtaining patents and better management potential, or reducing costs could be effectively employed. Prior to deregulation in 1978, the Civil Aeronautics Board (CAB) strictly controlled activities within the airline business. Basically, the industry had two types of companies, the trunk or cross-country carriers and the local or intrastate feeder lines.

The trunk carriers were essentially government franchised by the CAB, thus almost guaranteed to make money. Losses occurred due to mismanagement and overzealous acquisition plans for aircraft rather than market forces. The real competition among the trunk carriers took place in the offices of the Civil Aeronautics Board rather than the marketplace. The CAB's major purpose was to control the airline industry through approval of new routes, a process which could take as long as thirty months. The degree of control was remarkable:[2]

1. Sixteen trunk carriers were chartered by the CAB in 1938.
2. By 1975, eleven of these were still operating; the remaining five disappeared through merger.
3. None of the original sixteen had ever been bankrupt.

Life for the local or so called "feeder lines," such as Trans Texas, which were not as regulated by the CAB was radically different. They were "created to lose money, to fly the routes where passengers ain't."[3] With the aid of government subsidies which decreased each year, the feeder lines were relegated to service small cities such as Jonesboro, Arkansas; Big Springs, Texas and the like. Of the original nineteen local airlines authorized in 1945, all but ten were lost through bankruptcy by 1975.

In spite of these conditions, a fleet of aging aircraft, and a route structure composed primarily of small Texas towns, Trans Texas Airways registered revenue growth and modest profits until 1966 when a group of "Minnesota investors" purchased the airline. They immediately embarked upon an ill conceived expansion program from an already highly leveraged financial base which included additional routes into more unprofitable cities and purchase of the Tropicana Hotel in Las Vegas. Net income fell dramatically and a revolving door of presidents followed. The small Texas airline would not have a profitable month from 1966 to 1972. By 1971, Texas International, as it became known in 1969, was $20 million in debt and facing bankruptcy. Its stock, which was traded in the over-the-counter market, fell from $20.25 per share in 1969 to $3.50 per share by 1971. It was then that Frank Lorenzo entered the TI picture.

Francisco A. Lorenzo: Entrepreneur

"My aim is to build the most successful, low fare, airline in the United States."[4] Francisco A. Lorenzo is an enigma, publically quiet and unassuming, yet an energetic and highly ambitious individual. Lorenzo has been described in many terms: a pure entrepreneur, a listener rather than a talker, the maverick of the airways. He seems to be highly regarded in financial circles both in the United States and abroad, but viewed with apprehension by his peers within the industry. When reminded that Wall Street investors had highly acclaimed his financial dealings, his reply was typically modest. "People think we're financial geniuses when all we do is add."[5]

Frank Lorenzo is not unfamiliar with the airline industry. Born in Queens, New York in 1940, to a beauty shop owner, he is a licensed pilot. By the age of twenty-three, his academic credits included a degree in Finance from Columbia University and an MBA from Harvard. Prior to forming Jet Capital Inc. with fellow Harvard classmate, Robert Carney, Frank Lorenzo worked for three years in the financial departments of both Eastern and Trans World Airlines. The latter has been a successful conduit for many of Texas Air Corp.'s top executives.

Lorenzo seems to feel most comfortable when surrounded by highly talented professionals and willing to gamble on creative ideas. Carl R. Pohlad, an investment banker and director at Texas Air describes him as "the initiator who sets the tone (of the board) and provides the broad perspectives."[6] However, Pohlad quickly adds that the company is by no means "a one man show".

Jet Capital Inc. (formerly Lorenzo-Carney Enterprises) was and still is Lorenzo's investment base. He and Carney launched the highly speculative, financial venture in 1966 with the expressed intention of leasing airplanes. However, the underlying implications were clear; Lorenzo wanted an airline. The more official intent was expressed in Jet Capital's charter "to provide a meaningful platform for successful participation in the exciting but beleaguered field of air transportation."[7] They were thwarted by Allegheny in the first acquisition attempt, Mohawk Airlines. Unsuccessful in this effort, Jet Capital shifted gears and acted as a consulting firm to airlines for large New York banks. It was a time when many investment contacts were made on both Wall Street, within the industry, and abroad.

The Early Years: 1971–1974

By the Spring of 1971, Texas International was a financial shambles. Losses were running over one million dollars per month. Employee morale was low and creditors were about to foreclose and liquidate the carrier. These events were viewed as an opportunity by Lorenzo. The Chase Manhattan Bank of New York retained Jet Capital for a $15,000 per month fee to help Texas International out of their dilemma. The Lorenzo-Carney management team went to work. One year later, Frank Lorenzo, at the age of 31, was President and Chief Executive Officer and Robert Carney was Chief Financial Officer of TI. Together, either directly or through ownership of Jet Capital, they controlled 59% of TI's voting stock. The results of their work were dramatic. The carrier's net loss for 1972 was $1.707 million versus a loss of $7.416 million the year before and total debt (current and long term) was reduced by $24.123 million.

The airline industry had caught the first glimpse of Lorenzo's wizardry of debt leverage at work. He worked out a 35 million dollar debt restructuring plan with the Chase Manhattan Bank. This was no small feat considering TI's financial condition. In addition, through reinvesting that $180,000 in consultants' fees and $60,000 in "finder's fees" from Chase for arranging the new loans, he was able to leverage the Jet Capital venture to provide an additional capital infusion of $1.150 million into Texas International.

Lorenzo's expertise went to work in other areas as well. A management housecleaning ensued which formed the nucleus of his new team. Expense reduction areas were identified and plans implemented. The Tropicana operation, a severe drain on profits, was sold. More lucrative routes to large cities such as Denver, Albuquerque, and Mexico City were obtained. The groundwork to replace the aging Convair aircraft with more fuel efficient McDonnell Douglass DC-9's was laid. Productivity improvements were implemented. Route structures were put to the pencil. These were thoroughly analyzed in an attempt to reduce Texas International's dependence on federal subsidies. Through "creative scheduling," service to many of the small, marginal cities which plagued profits was discontinued.

Once again, the tactics produced positive results. In 1973, Lorenzo's first full year, the carrier produced a $121,000 profit, its first in eight years. By 1974, passenger load factor and yield per revenue passenger mile, key profit criteria in the industry, had risen to 50.4% and .0981 from 47.2% and .0796 in 1971. In the process, profits of $257,000 in 1974 more than doubled 1973 levels.

The Strike: December 1, 1974– April 3, 1975

Frank Lorenzo was in his element. Eight years had passed since the formation of Jet Capital and he was finally building his airline. In spite of fierce competition from the major trunks and smaller, regional carriers such as Southwest, his hand picked management team had turned a company from bankruptcy to a profit-generating enterprise in just two short years. However, the storm clouds of change were brewing.

If Lorenzo has a weakness, it is his relationship with Texas International Unions. The Texas carrier has some of the toughest in the industry with which to deal:

A. ALEA—Airline Employees Association (1968–1980) (Clerical/Secretarial)
B. Teamsters—1980 to present (clerical)
C. ALPA—Airline Pilots Association (pilots, stewards and stewardesses)
D. IAM—International Association of Machinists (mechanics)

The friction has always centered around the unions' versus Lorenzo's perception of how the company should be operated in order to allow it to compete within the industry. Pay and benefits have always been competitive and are seldom the root issues involved. On December 1, 1974, the carrier's union personnel walked out in a bitterly contested four month strike which curtailed the momentum gained in the previous two years.

A lawyer representing the union employees expressed resentment concerning the changes made by Lorenzo with the following interview in *Texas Monthly Magazine* in 1975:

Management had to weather the strike to keep the company afloat. It's the easiest thing in the world to avoid a strike, all you have to do is give in. It's harder to make the necessary judgement of what the company can sustain in the long run.

Numerous small issues were involved. However, each side used these merely as negotiating chips. The major areas of concern could be boiled down to two key points of differences.

1. Management's contention that they had the right to hire part-time help in lieu of later furloughing full-time employees in order to handle peak traffic periods.
2. Management's contention that they had the right to have employees work split shifts at premium pay in order to operate the unique flight scheduling requirements at the smaller stations.

On the surface, it may seem that the strike issues were not critical. However, underlying currents of mistrust had grown in the early Lorenzo years. The unions, especially ALEA, viewed these actions as attempts to usurp their authority and weaken them. They had become very apprehensive about the constant changes taking place within the company. Lorenzo, on the other hand, felt that Texas International's survival was at stake. He firmly believed that unless such actions were adopted, the feeder airlines would not be able to compete against the major trunk lines and Southwest Airlines, a non-union, very aggressive regional carrier.

Both sides dug in for the mini-war which followed. It is fair to point out that there was sharp disagreement among union members about the major issues. Management's hand was further strengthened when 19% of the membership refused to honor the picket lines and worked system-wide during the strike. This enraged the pro-union faction and deep bitterness and resentment persisted for a long period after the strike had ended. By April 3, 1975, the unions had exhausted their resources and settled for essentially the same package offered in December 1974. The end was welcomed by both sides. The airline had been kept afloat primarily because of a package called Mutual Aid, which was unique to the airline industry. Mutual Aid was a fund, contributed to by all airlines based upon revenues. Its purpose was to provide capital to maintain skeleton operations during labor difficulties.

Financially, the strike was devastating to Texas International. The net loss for 1975 was $4,249,000 versus income in 1974 of $257,000. More importantly, it had allowed Southwest Airlines to entrench itself as the number one carrier into "The Valley", a group of very lucrative vacation/business routes into the McAllen-Harlingen-Brownsville areas of Texas. Heretofore, these stations represented some of the most profitable in the TI system. The corporate intrigue and court room dealings which followed between Texas International and Braniff against Southwest could fill volumes and was referred to as "The Great Texas Air War." The litigation portion came to an end when Braniff and TI were found guilty of conspiracy and anti-trust violations against Southwest.

On the union front, ALEA, the clerical union, became the real loser. It was the one which initiated the strike and from whom most of the "scab-labor" came. For practical purposes, it was broken and wielded considerably less influence. In 1980, its membership voted to have it replaced by the Teamsters to handle contract negotiations.

Peanuts and Pre-Acquisition: 1976–1978

The concurrent forces of the strike, hints of deregulation, the antitrust suit and recession produced a dismal atmosphere at Texas International. Both morale and profits had reached their lowest ebb under Lorenzo. He needed a gimmick to infuse increased revenue and purpose. It was found in the "Fly for Peanuts" marketing program.

The advantages of the strike concessions were the key ingredients. Lorenzo's management team began a route-by-route analysis of revenues versus costs, an almost unheard of practice in the industry prior to its adoption at TI. The major thrust of the "peanuts campaign" was to attract a new class of traveler, one who would normally drive or take trains and buses. The economics were clear. It requires nearly as much in operating costs to fly a jet 20% full as it does at 60%. TI opted for higher load factors by reducing prices. The results of this innovative marketing ploy were phenomenal. Load factors increased to 53.6% in 1976, 57.7% in 1977, and 60% in 1978. Net income for the same period was $3.479 million, $8.238 million, and $13.151 million. By 1978, Texas International ranked fourth in terms of traffic among the regional lines, experienced thirty-nine consecutive months of record earnings and was heralded as the fastest growing regional airline in the United States. The infusion of profits allowed it to continue its upgrading to a strictly jet fleet and petition the Civil Aeronautics Board for permission to carry its "peanut fares" into twenty-three new markets. Some of the more lucrative included Las Vegas, Baltimore, Kansas City, Salt Lake City, and the Mexican resort communities of Cancun, Cozumel and Merida.

Such expansionist moves were viewed with suspicion by the large trunks such as Delta, Eastern, Continental, Allegheny (U.S. Air), North Central (Republic) and National. Industry-wide fare discounting ensued but they found it difficult to compete against Texas International's cost structure, said to be near the lowest in the industry. TI responded to these competitive threats by reducing prices further. In the highly contested Houston-Baltimore route, its fares were 50% below those charged by Delta on certain late evening flights. By late 1978, "peanuts fares" accounted for 34% of all seats sold.

The mood in Washington toward the airline industry was beginning to change. A more consumerist Congress applauded the fare discounting methods employed by the regionals. By the end of 1978, the regulatory environment which stablized the industry and strangled competition for so many years was being phased out. The major trunks found themselves in a crucial position. Their cost structures could not compete and the regionals were aggressively pursuing their lucrative routes.

"Mr. Peanut" Meets National and TWA: 1978–1979

Either by design or happenstance, Lorenzo had prepared his airline for the deregulatory environment more than any other large regional or major trunk airline. As airlines were still reeling under the effects of the new government regulations and discount fares, Lorenzo took both Wall Street and the industry by surprise. After obtaining major European and South American financial agreements, he announced that Texas International owned 9.2% of National's stock and was intent on merger.

Possessing attractive Sun-Belt routes, a relatively debt-free balance sheet, and a grossly underpriced stock, National was a plum ready to be picked. Other large trunk carriers immediately joined in the bidding. Pan Am desired the domestic routes to complement its international network. Air Florida submitted a plan to liquidate National so that it could buy its planes. Eastern wanted merger so that National's western routes would provide it access to the West Coast. Eastern's proposal came under severe antitrust scrutiny due to the natural competitive nature of Eastern and National on the eastern seaboard and Florida. While recommendations as to what to do about National were bantered about, Lorenzo methodically increased Texas International's holdings of National to 24.5% before it was frozen. By April of 1979, the contestants had been whittled down to Texas International and Pan Am. Bidding had reached $40 per share.

Publicly, Lorenzo was confident and wore his gambler's mask. Internally, things were much different. National's board rejected TI and highly favored Pan Am as their "white knight." In addition, the burden of $400,000 per month in interest charges was beginning to take its toll on profitability. Lorenzo realized his airline probably could not afford the hostile merger attempt and set the stage for one of his patented financial gambles. In mid-May he insinuated in a speech before a group of Wall Street analysts that the book value of National's assets was at least $76 per share rather than the $46.50 indicated by National's board. It was a risk that paid off. Pan Am promptly offered $50 per share which Lorenzo accepted. The after tax profit realized by Texas International was said to be around $46–50 million. TI's stock was selling at eleven times earnings.

The industry was still guessing where Lorenzo would strike next. It didn't take long. On September 13, 1978 Texas International announced that it had acquired 4% of TWA's 16 million shares of stock. Trans World Corporation, the holding company for such diverse ventures as the airline, the Hilton Hotel chain and Century 21 Real Estate, was almost four time Texas International's size and announced on September 19 that it would fight the takeover attempt.

Through complex lending agreements and commitments by Lorenzo to liquidate or sell off the non-airline related venture, he seemed to have adequate financing leverage. Robert J. Joedicke, an analyst from Lehman Bros., remarked:

> Financing such an acquisition would be attractive to lenders primarily because of the reputation of Lorenzo and Texas International. When you have a track record such as his, a lot of people will back you a second time around.

Though hostile toward merger, Trans World Corp. opted to meet with Lorenzo personally rather than fight him in the press. Both factions were very familiar with one another. Some of Texas International's top management had been recruited from the larger airline, Lorenzo had once worked at TWA, and all parties were familiar with his financial dealings. After a series of meetings, Lorenzo, for whatever reason, decided not to press merger talks further. It is said that Texas International realized approximately $6 million in profits from the sale

of TWA stock. It is interesting to note that Continental stock, once mentioned as a possible TI acquisition, fell to $12 per share during the merger talks.

More Peanuts, "TAC" and New York Air: 1979–1980

Primarily due to the sale of National stock, profits in 1979 rose to over $41 million dollars. Only $6.5 million came from operations, down almost $9 million from the year before. The primary factors for decreased earnings from operations were a 68% increase in fuel costs and 30% increase in other expenses. Revenues were up only 30% to offset these increases. Passenger load factor of 62.1% had reached an all time high and yield per passenger mile had decreased slightly.

The company began to utilize its windfall from Pan Am. Contracts were negotiated to purchase twenty used DC-9-30 aircraft, now the standard for the TI fleet. The highly acclaimed peanuts program was expanded. New "stations" such as St. Louis, Tulsa, and Guadalajara were added to the system. Six marginal cities were dropped and the airline operated without a dollar in federal subsidies for the first time since inception. During the period, a common stock dividend ($.04 per share) was paid for the first time in history.

By late 1979, Lorenzo's seven year tenure had produced an airline whose book values assets totaled over $319 million of which approximately $141 million consisted of cash and short term investments which could be utilized for another merger attempt, expansion, or both. To manage such an asset portfolio, the carrier decided to reorganize. In March of 1980, it formed a holding company in the name of Texas Air Corp. In Lorenzo's own words,

> The holding company structure will permit greater business and financial flexibility. For example, the company would be able to raise funds on either the credit of the holding company, the airline, or any subsidiary. We may find it easier to pursue diversification should we find it advisable to enter into either regulated or non-regulated business activities without necessarily being under the jurisdiction of the Federal Aviation Act.[8]

With the formation of the holding company concept in 1980, Texas International was transformed into a subsidiary. In the face of a recessionary environment during 1980, the airline decided to change some fundamental strategic directions.

1. Greater emphasis would be placed on the business traveler who is affected less by a changing economic environment. Efforts were made to raise the ratio to a 60–40 mix in favor of business travel. Prior to that time, the carrier had near the reverse.
2. Consolidate the two major hubs, Dallas/Ft. Worth and Houston. Route expansions would spring from those points only.
3. Re-establish ties with travel agents to expand their marketing network rather than relying solely on incoming calls to their reservation center.

In short, 1980 was a year of consolidation. However, the company remained committed to expansion. Houston's Intercontinental Airport is the eighth busiest in the United States and twentieth in the world according to the Airport Operator's Council International. In June of 1980, Texas Air Corp. announced that fifteen of the twenty-six new gates added upon completion of terminal C would belong to the airline. The other eleven were reserved by Continental. At the time of the announcement, Texas Air was operating fifty-nine flights from five gates in Terminal A at Houston Inter-Continental.

In January of 1980, a "falling out" occurred between Lorenzo and part of his management team concerning among many things the new "Peanuts Payola" marketing plan. The result was the resignation of some key personnel: Don Burr, President of Texas International and a member of TAC's Board; Jerry Gitner, Senior Vice President of Marketing & Planning; and Bob McAdoo, Controller and Vice President of Information Systems. The group left with other Texas Air management personnel to form People's Express, a low cost "commuter line" between New York and Washington.

Not to be outdone, Lorenzo announced his version of People's Express, New York Air, on September 12, 1980. The newly formed subsidiary was formed when $24 million and six DC-9-30's from Texas International's fleet was provided by Texas Air. A public offering of stock was made to raise additional capital. However, Texas Air maintains about an 80% interest in New York Air.

New York Air's system is planned to ultimately span fifteen cities in seven states and the District of Columbia. The hub is planned to be the New York/Newark area with no destination requiring more than two hours in flight time. Cities listed in its initial filing included Detroit, Boston, Newark, Albany, Buffalo, Rochester, Syracuse, New York City, Cincinnati, Cleveland, Columbus, Dayton and Pittsburgh. The airline competes directly with Eastern, the entrenched shuttle system master in the area. Through creative advertising programs such as requiring passengers to take the New York Oath "to never, ever again fly the Eastern shuttle" before receiving the discount fares, the airline has become the darling of the press. Dubbed "Son of Shuttle" by the New York City media, its passenger load factor has been in the 65–70% range.

The venture has not been without its detractors. Being a nonunion subsidiary of Texas Air has caused an uproar from ALPA, Texas International's pilots union. They claim that their contract forbids the use of non-union pilots and that New York Air is in violation. Lorenzo contend that their contract is with Texas International and that New York Air is a subsididary of Texas Air, not TI. Therefore, he sees no justification in their complaints. The issue is crucial in that if TAC wins, a new non-union precedent will be established in a highly unionized industry.

The Attempt to Acquire Continental: 1980–1981

Western and Continental were very near a corporate marriage when Frank Lorenzo announced in early 1981 that Texas International (i.e., *not* Texas Air) had acquired 9.4% of Continental's stock and intended a takeover. Western negotiations terminated and the Los Angeles based carrier was in the fight of its life. On February 9, 1981, Lorenzo announced a tender offer for 4.3 million shares of Continental stock (48% of the outstanding stock) for $13 per share, a quote which bore a 25% premium over the price at which Continental closed

EXHIBIT 1 Update: chronology of events at Texas International, 1981–1983

October 1981	President Reagan approves TI's acquisition of Continental.
March 1982	Lorenzo elected chairman of the Continental board of directors.
June 1982	Continental and TI schedules partially integrated.
October 1982	TI phased out and TI–Continental begins operations as one airline.
January 1983	Continental reports record losses for 1982 of almost $100 million.
February 1983	ALPA union at Continental grants significant wage concessions.
July 1983	Flight attendants union talks of a strike.
July 1983	Continental begins training program for 500 new flight attendants.
August 1983	Continental mechanics union goes on strike. They are replaced by non-striking union members and contract mechanics.
September 1983	Lorenzo asks for an additional $100 million in wage concessions as Continental losses mount.
September 24, 1983	Lorenzo announces that Continental is temporarily suspending operations. This places Continental in Chapter 11 Bankruptcy.
September 28, 1983	Continental resumes operations on a limited basis using about one-third of former Continental employees who were to be paid an average of 50 percent of their former salaries.
October 1983	Continental unions charge that the Chapter 11 was a "union-busting" strategy. Lorenzo announces that the new Continental would become the major low-fare, low-cost airline in the U.S.

on February 5. In a carefully worded statement to Continental shareholders, Texas International reminded them of some facts about the proposed Western merger:

1. There was no guarantee that the merger would either equal or exceed TI's cash offer.
2. The combined loss for Continental and Western in 1980 was $52.7 million.
3. The combination would have produced a net loss of $1.94 per share on Continental Stock versus the .64 per share actually recorded.
4. The combination would have $321.2 million in debt coming due within the next five years.

5. The proposed company would have a total long term debt structure of over $763.8 million, a 132% increase over current levels.

Almost 4.3 million Continental shares were tendered to TI within four days.

By the first week of April, Continental was desperate. It proposed a $185 million ESOP offering in which employees would be able to buy the airline and effectively dilute the ownership of existing shareholders, including Texas International, by 50%. The battle has raged for months. In late June, 1981, the New York Stock Exchange ruled that it would de-list Continental if the ESOP plan was implemented. The California Commissioner of Corporations, the first governmental authority to issue an opinion, ruled that Continental could not issue the additional 15 million ESOP shares without a vote from shareholders and employees. In addition, it acted to neutralize Texas International's voting power by allowing it to vote only in the same proportion as the remaining small investors.

Notes

1. "The Great Texas Air War," *Texas Monthly* (November 1975): 97.
2. "The Great Texas Air War," *Texas Monthly* (November 1975): 92.
3. "The Great Texas Air War," *Texas Monthly* (November 1975): 90.
4. "Texas International's Quiet Pilot," *Business Week* (August 20, 1979): 78.
5. "Texas International's Quiet Pilot," *Business Week* (August 20, 1979): 80.
6. "Who Are The TI Whiz Kids?" *The TI Flyer* (May 1979): 21.
7. "The Great Texas Air War," *Texas Monthly* (November 1975): 94.
8. "Trans World To Fight Takeover," *Aviation Week & Space Technology* (September 24, 1979): 25.

The Love Canal Incident

In 1892, entrepreneur William Love had visions of building a huge hydroelectric plant in the Niagara Falls area that would furnish electrical power to nearby industries and of building a model community for 600,000 people. However, the recession of 1894 and a system for alternating current, which allowed transmission of electricity over long distances, combined to bankrupt the project when only about 1,800 feet of the canal had been dug.

It is in this area that Hooker Chemicals Company (then Hooker Electrochemical Company) purchased and used to bury 21,800 tons of approximately 80 different chemical wastes from 1942 to 1953. These chemicals included polychlorinated biphenyls (PCBs), hexachlorocyclopentadiene benzene, toluene, and tetrachlorodibenzo-paradioxin. Dioxin is considered to be the most toxic compound in existence. These chemical wastes were contained in 55-gallon steel drums and buried in clay which was, and still is, considered an acceptable way to dispose of chemical wastes. Hooker may not be the only agency to have disposed of chemical wastes at Love Canal. According to New York State officials, federal agencies, especially the Army, had used this site for disposing of toxic wastes during and after World War II. This was later denied by the Army.

In November, 1953, Hooker donated (under threat of seizure under eminent domain for the building of a school) this chemical dump landfill site to the Niagara Falls Board of Education. Because the postwar baby boom had produced a need for the construction of more schools and this area was not built up, real estate prices were low. The Niagara Falls Board of Education wanted the Love Canal site very badly.

The research and case information was presented to the Case Research Association for review and evaluation. This case was prepared by Timothy M. Singleton and Robert McGlashan, both of the University of Houston at Clear Lake City, as a basis for class discussion. The initial data for The Love Canal Incident was gathered in April 1981 by a group of MBA students as a project for a Business Policy Seminar at the University of Houston at Clear Lake City. The student members of the group were David McFarland, White Gee, John Gordon, Khawaja Nazimuddin, Tom Nlemch, Elaine Vauthier.

Hooker's legal representative at the time of the sale, Arthur Chambers, informed the board that this property had been used as a chemical dump site. He stated that his company could not prevent the Board from selling the land or doing anything that they wanted to do with it, but Hooker officials felt the land was unsuitable for construction in which basements, water lines or sewers were necessary. Chambers stated that there was four to five feet of fill over the chemicals which made use of

EXHIBIT 1 School site study—Plan A

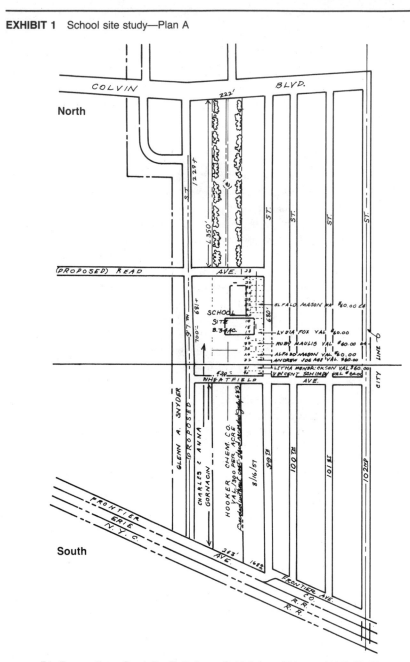

SOURCE: Eric Zuesse, "Love Canal: The Truth Seeps Out," *Reason* (February 1981): 17–33.

the land as a park or a school not dangerous. Exhibit 1 presents the site study plan. In order to protect Hooker from possible future damages, the company would only give a deed with a restriction that no legal claims should ever be made against Hooker. Also, Hooker's Executive Vice President B. J. Klaussen took the School Board president and superintendent to the site where tests had recently been made. Klaussen had a map prepared showing where wastes were deposited, how they were covered, and the results of testing that had recently been completed. On the map provided to the board, he stated that there was

> no evidence of chemicals anyplace digging down 10' right up to within 1' of the excavations. In places where we have dumped chemicals the chemicals are almost unchanged in form and found 4' below top surface. (10)

A chronological list of events surrounding the Love Canal incident are as follows:

May 7, 1953—The School Board voted to accept the Love Canal property with the restrictions that Hooker had placed on the property.

August 6, 1953—The School Board approved the removal of 4,000 cubic yards of soil from the Love Canal for use at the Ninety-third Street School.

January 21, 1954—The School Board approved the removal of up to 3,000 cubic yards of fill from the site.

August 18, 1955—Architectural plans indicated the possibility of the removal of one to 2.88 feet of top soil (approximately 10,000 cubic yards).

November 7, 1957—Mr. Chambers appeared before the School Board warning of the potential health hazards at Love Canal. These warnings came at a time when the School Board was considering the sale of a part of the Love Canal property to private developers. Chambers produced letters between Hooker and the School Board written before the original sale of the land that mentioned the restriction that the property was to be used only for a school and a city park. The School Board finally decided not to sell.

November 8, 1957—The NIAGARA GAZETTA reported that Mr. Chambers had appeared before the School Board, warning that the property was not suitable for uses other than as a park or a school.

1958—The City of Niagara Falls constructed Read and Wheatfield Avenues and installed utilities through the property which broke the cover of the canal (see Exhibit 2). Some chemical wastes were exposed. Three small children received minor chemical burns while playing at the Love Canal property.

1960—The School Board deeded 6.6 acres to the City of Niagara for a park that was never built.

1962—The School Board sold six acres, for $1,200, to Ralph Capone. Mr. Capone planned to subdivide, but after spending nearly $15,000 and being beset with many problems, he finally sold the property to a friend for $100.

1968—Frontier Avenue was relocated through the southern portion of Love Canal because of the construction of LaSalle Expressway by the State of New York. This required removing some buried chemical wastes.

October 1976—There were reports that chemicals had appeared in the basements of some homes near the Love Canal property. (No homes were ever built on Love Canal.) This indicated that chemicals had migrated from the canal into nearby property.

1977—A task force (composed of people from the City of Niagara Falls, the Niagara County Health Department, and Hooker) began a study of the chemical migration problem. Calspan Corporation of Cheektowaga, New York, was to prepare a remedial plan.

March, 1978—The City of Niagara Falls commissioned Conestoga-Rovers of Waterloo, Ontario, Canada, to design a remedial program. Hooker offered to pay one-third of the cost of the work on the south section (estimated at $840,000) because of "moral" rather than "legal" responsibilities.

August 2, 1978—The Health Commissioner of New York State "ordered the temporary closing

EXHIBIT 2 Map showing the location of sewers that pierced the Canal walls and linked up to the neighborhood sewer system

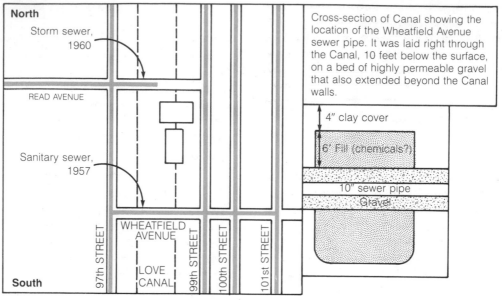

North

Storm sewer, 1960

READ AVENUE

Sanitary sewer, 1957

South

97th STREET

WHEATFIELD AVENUE

LOVE CANAL

99th STREET

100th STREET

101st STREET

Cross-section of Canal showing the location of the Wheatfield Avenue sewer pipe. It was laid right through the Canal, 10 feet below the surface, on a bed of highly permeable gravel that also extended beyond the Canal walls.

4″ clay cover

6′ Fill (chemicals?)

10″ sewer pipe

Gravel

SOURCE: Eric Zuesse, "Love Canal: The Truth Seeps Out," *Reason* (February 1981): 17–33.

of the 99th Street School and recommended the evacuation of pregnant women and children under two living in the first two rings of homes around the canal property." (10) Approximately 20 families were involved.

August 9, 1978—Governor Hugh Carey of New York stated that those families living on both sides of 97th and 99th Streets would be evacuated and their homes purchased. This involved 236 families and would ultimately cost New York State about $37 million. Remedial work was begun several months later.

February, 1979—Beverly Paigen, a biologist at the Roswell Park Memorial Institute in Buffalo, felt the evacuation of more families was necessary as her study indicated a higher rate of birth defects and miscarriages among Love Canal residents than usual. A congressional panel later determined that Ms. Paigen's study was not sound. Also, the New York State Department of Health did not agree with her findings, stating that the additional risk to the remaining people was indeed small.

December 20, 1979—The United States Justice Department filed a lawsuit against Hooker relative to Hooker's use of Love Canal as a dump site. The Environmental Protection Agency's law suit charged that Hooker had not warned people in the area that material there could be injurious. Thus began a flood of personal injury suits.

January, 1980—The City of Niagara Falls issued $6.5 million in bonds to pay for remedial work on the south section of the canal.

May 17, 1980—The Environmental Protection Agency held a press conference to release the results of a preliminary genetic study by Biogenics, Inc., showing chromosome damage in 11 of the 36 Love Canal residents tested. The EPA later indicated that the study could possibly have been biased.

May 21, 1980—President Carter declared a state of emergency at Love Canal. This paved the way for the evacuation of up to 710 families, and was the first time a state of emergency had been declared for other than natural causes.

May 30, 1980—Governor Carey, in an interview with NEWSDAY, charged:

that a costly relocation of more than 700 Love Canal homeowners is medically unnecessary but has to be carried out to assuage the panic caused by the (EPA) report. (10)

June 24, 1980—David Axelrod, M.D., New York State Department of Health Commissioner, issued the department's epidemiologic studies on "Adverse Pregnancy Outcomes in the Love Canal Area." He had not been able to correlate the geographic distributions of adverse pregnancy outcomes with chemical evidence of exposure. Also, blood testing for liver and kidney abnormalities, leukemia and blood diseases showed no pattern of excess abnormality. Computer analyses of the 22-page questionnaire produced no evidence of unusual patterns of illnesses. Cancer incidence was within normal limits.

June 29, 30, and July 1, 1980—The BUFFALO COURIER EXPRESS published the results of its investigation which found the City of Niagara Falls had constructed sanitary and storm sewers at the Love Canal site, despite warnings from Hooker.

A NEW YORK TIMES editorial bemoaned Hooker's "alarming indifference to poisonous practices."

Michael Brown, of the BUFFALO ENTERPRIZE, received a Pulitzer Prize for his book, LAYING WASTE: THE POISONING OF AMERICA BY TOXIC CHEMICALS, which blamed Hooker for the problems at Love Canal.

Ralph Nader and Ronald Brownstein wrote an article which stated that only one pregnancy in 15 had resulted in the birth of a healthy baby in the area around the canal. Also mentioned in the article was the $250,000 spent by Hooker on ads in 23 newspapers disputing articles in THE NEW YORK TIMES and BUSINESS WEEK which were not favorable to Hooker. (12)

In all, approximately 710 families had left the Love Canal area. The possibility of physical harm had been devastating but perhaps even more so had been the psychological stress brought on by

the coverage of this incident. THE NEW YORK TIMES of June 20, 1981, stated:

When all the returns are in, years from now, it may well turn out that the public suffered less from the chemicals there (i.e., at Love Canal) than from the hysteria generated by flimsy research irresponsibly handled.

Hooker's Strategy

There is now a need for companies to develop a plan of response to social needs and responsibilities. This can be integrated into the strategic management plan. When asking the questions of when, should, can, where, etc., there is now need to add "what social responsibilities do we need to meet?" Dealing with social concerns is ever increasing with a more aware public and more alert consumers.

Once a problem has arisen, there are several ways a company can choose to handle it. These are shown in detail in reference 17.

Hooker followed the Davis and Blomstron response strategy of (a) withdrawl, (b) public relations approach, (c) legal approach, (d) bargaining, and (e) problem solving. However, as the Love Canal incident spanned over 25 years, the responses are sometimes slightly out of chronological order due to the complexity of the situation. This is to be expected. Different executives and different state and local officials were involved, also.

Withdrawal

Bruce D. Davis, Executive Vice-President for Hooker's industrial chemicals group, testified that when the company sold the site (for $1) in 1953 to the Niagara Falls Board of Education, Hooker felt no responsibility to advise prospective home-buyers in the area that the site contained hazardous materials. The School Board had been warned about the dangers of excavation and that the site was suitable for a school and a park.

Hooker did offer some technical assistance to the state in planning remedial action but turned down suggestions from the state that Hooker buy some of the homes. After first denying that the state had made such requests, Davis said:

We have indicated that we were not interested in purchasing homes out there. We do not think it would contribute to the revitalization of the Love Canal Area. (12)

In 1957, three children were burned by residue from the site, but Hooker gave no warnings to the public. However, Hooker's legal representative had appeared before the School Board to discourage sale of some of the property to developers.

Hooker spent $250,000 on advertisements in newspapers and magazines regarding the Love Canal incident.

Michael E. Reichgut, Public Relations, Hooker Chemicals, stated:

> One thing our management held the line on, and I think it is an absolute must, is that we did not say anything that we could not document beyond the proverbial shadow of a doubt. This super-imposed policy requiring absolute documentations worked against us in the beginning because the facts were not readily available. The news media struck without getting the full story, but we retained our credibility and the facts show the company acted responsibly in every aspect of the Love Canal issue. (24)

Mr. Reichgut also said that it had been necessary "to develop a plan whereby effective communications are possible even when serious legal problems are involved in public issues. (24)

Legal
The Love Canal property was under the threat of condemnation before Hooker donated it to the School Board. Hooker was only willing to deed the property to the School Board if it were to be used as a school and a park. Otherwise, Hooker would not have given it and would have simply let the land be condemned so that they would not be held legally responsible.

Along with Hooker's competent legal staff (and all indications are that it was competent), Hooker added Louis Nizer who is considered by many to be the finest attorney in the United States.

Mr. Nizer stated that Hooker Chemicals had moved that New York State be joined as a defendent in the federal action. In the personal injury cases, Hooker has cross-claimed against the Niagara Falls School Board and the City of Niagara Falls for the invasion of the protective cover of impermeable clay and should be held responsible if there is any liability found.

Bargaining
In 1977, a year after reports came in that chemicals had seeped into basements of homes on the periphery of Love Canal, a task force was formed, composed of the City of Niagara Falls, the Niagara Falls County Health Department, and Hooker, which began to study the situation. The city commissioned first Calspan Corporation, then Conestoga-Rovers to design a remedial program. Hooker offered to pay one-third of the work which would have been about $840,000. However, the city and the Health Department were unable to furnish the other two-thirds needed, so Hooker's offer was never accepted.

Problem Solving
Hooker has, as of the end of 1980, spent or committed approximately $180 million on environmental programs. More than 200 Hooker employees work on programs involving the safety and health of employees, customers, and neighbors, Hooker's policy has changed "to comply with the spirit as well as the letter of the law and where helpful, in the spirit of a good neighbor, to go beyond the requirements of the law." (22)

Between 1977 and the end of 1980, Hooker had invested close to $1.2 billion to modernize and expand their chemical operations, with a new $75 million Energy-from-Waste facility in operation at the Niagara Falls location.

References
1. "A Deeper Trough," *Wall Street Journal* (June 3, 1980): Sec. E, p. 22.
2. "A Second Look at Love Canal," *New York Times* (June 20, 1981), Sec. L, p. 22.
3. "A Toxic Turnaround," *Fortune* (July 27, 1981): 30.
4. Hank Cox, "Reagan Must Close Credibility Gap," *Regulatory Action Network: Washington Watch* (October 1981), special supplement, pp. 51–54.
5. "Discovery of Dioxin at Montague Could Impede Accord on Hooker Wastes," *Chemical Week* (June 6, 1979): 18.
6. Ken Goldstein, "Hooker Chemical's Nightmarish Pollution Record," *Business and Social Review* (Summer 1979): 25–28.
7. "Heartbreak at Love Canal," *The Economist* (May 24, 1980): 40.
8. "Hooker Tells Its Side of the Story," *Chemical Week* (June 27, 1979): 34–35.

9. "Hooker's Love Canal Warning," *Wall Street Journal* (July 7, 1980): Sec. 1, p. 22.

10. "Love Canal: The Facts (1892–1980)," *Hooker Fact Line.*

11. "Love Canal Residents under Stress," *Science* (June 13, 1980): 1242–3.

12. Ralph Nader and Ronald Brownstein, "Beyond the Love Canal," *Progressive* (May 1980): 28–31.

13. "New York Expands Dumpsite Study," *Chemical Week* (January 17, 1979): 22.

14. "No Demonstrated Health Effects from Love Canal Chemicals, Says Medical Review Study," *Hooker Fact Line.*

15. "Review and Outlook, Love Canal Warnings," *Wall Street Journal* (June 19, 1980): Sec. 1, p. 22.

16. Anthony J. Parish, "Who Pays? Cleaning Up the Love Canal," *New York Times* (June 8, 1980): Sec. 3, pp. 1, 4.

17. Elizabeth Gatewood and Archie B. Carroll, "The Procter & Gamble Rely Case: A Social Response Pattern for the 1980s?" *Proceedings of the Academy of Management,* 1981, pp. 369–372.

18. R. Jeffrey Smith, "Love Canal Reviewed," *Science* (October 31, 1980): 518.

19. "Still More Hassles for Hooker," *Chemical Week* (August 4, 1979): 23.

20. Michael D. Tabris and Michael D. Reichgut, "Love Canal in Perspective," *PR Casebook* (October 1981): 3–8.

21. "The Neighborhood of Fear," *Time* (June 2, 1980): 61–62.

22. "The Other Side of Love Canal," presentation before the Financial Community Representatives from New York, Philadelphia, Boston and Hartford, New York, July 31, 1980.

23. "What Hooker Told Whom, When about Love Canal," *Wall Street Journal* (June 19, 1980): Sec. 1, p. 22.

24. "What Should American Industry Have Learned from the Costly Debacle of Love Canal?" *Trend* 7, no. 3 (1981): 3–8.

25. "What *The Wall Street Journal* Said about Love Canal," *Hooker Fact Line.*

26. Eric Zuesse, "Love Canal: The Truth Seeps Out," *Reason* (February 1981): 17–33.

A Thermos of "Tea" at KWC

"Mr. Smith, I think Wells, the relief crew leader of A Assembly Line, is drinking on the job," stated the voice over the phone. Smith, the shift supervisor of the Ball Valve Assembly Department, was momentarily speechless, but quickly recovered. "What makes you think so," he inquired. Jones, the relief supervisor for Assembly Line A, stated, "When I went to relieve him for his break I smelled alcohol on his breath. After he left on his break I checked his thermos bottle. It had alcohol in it." "This is serious," replied Smith. "I think we better tell your story to the General Superivor."

Smith and Jones went directly to Mr. Jackson, the General Supervisor of Ball Valve Assembly. At Jackson's request, Jones told of the sequence of events leading up to his phone call to Smith.

"Wells requested I relieve him for a few minutes so he could take a break. I told him I would as soon as I got a chance. About one half-hour later, I approached the Crew Leader's office and noticed Wells was inside. As I went in he was drinking from his thermos cup. When I told him I was relieving him for his break I noticed the smell of alcohol. Wells said he wanted to finish his 'iced tea' so I stepped outside the office to observe the assembly line. As I stood outside I glanced through the office window and observed Wells finish his drink, put the cup back on the thermos bottle and place the bottle on his desk. He then left the office and went on his break. After he left I walked down the assembly line to make sure everything was okay and then returned to the Crew Leader's Office. I opened Well's thermos and observed and smelled alcohol. Bourbon, I believe. I then called Mr. Smith."

The research and written case information were presented at a Case Research Symposium and were evaluared by the Case Research Association's Editorial Board. This case was prepared by Robert McGlashan, Professor of Management; William V. Rice, Jr., Associate Professor of Economics and Management; and Gerard V. Hayden, Lecturer in Management, University of Houston at Clear Lake City, as a basis for class discussion.

Jackson knew he had a potentially messy problem on his hands. Jones was normally a member of the bargaining unit. He was currently stepped-up to relief supervisor replacing the regular supervisor who was on vacation. Wells was the Assembly Line A Shop Steward and had 26 years of service with the Company. While Wells had been somewhat troublesome to supervision, his official record was unblemished. Jackson had suspected him of alcoholism but could never prove it or get Wells to admit to it. Jackson decided to call the Labor Relations Manager and let him handle it.

Assembly Line A

Assembly Line A was one of 6 assembly lines at the KWC Valve Company. KWC had been founded 29 years previously by Messrs. Kalisky, Wayne and Corbin as a small machine shop manufacturing specialized valves for the petroleum industry. Over the years the company had grown from the original 12 employees to the present 1300 employees. Mr. Wells' father was one of the first employees of the new company. He had an excellent record until his tenth year of service when he was fired for several instances of drinking on the job. Mr. Wells had joined the firm shortly after his father and had been troublesome to supervision during the 18 years since his father was fired. The periodic problems had never been serious enough, however, to justify formal disciplinary action. During his 26 years of service Wells had worked his way up from starting assembler, the entry level job at KWC, to Senior Assembler, the highest production job at KWC, except for Crew Leader.

Wells had been instrumental in an eventually successful drive to unionize the production workers at KWC. Following unionization, Wells had been appointed the Shop Steward for Assembly Line A and had used this position to file numerous grievances against management. Many employees believed he held a grudge against the Company for the firing of his father.

Assembly Line Crew Leader

As Jones had been stepped-up to relief supervisor for two weeks to replace the vacationing regular supervisor, Wells had stepped-up to Crew Leader to replace Jones. As a Crew Leader, Wells was expected to watch over the whole assembly line which was approximately 100 feet long and had eight assemblers. This responsibility required him to frequently leave the Crew Leader's office, located at one end of the assembly line, and walk the 100 feet to the other end. During some of this time he was out of sight of the Crew Leader's office. In addition, the Crew Leader's office was frequently entered by supervisors, quality control inspectors and various technicians who would leave or pick up reports with regard to the assembly line.

Retrieving the Thermos

When the Labor Relations Manager arrived at the Assembly Line A General Supervisor's office it was decided to confront Wells with the suspicion he was drinking on the job. Jackson directed Jones to go to the Crew Leader's office, relieve Wells and ask him to report to Jackson's office. During the interim, a Shop Steward, from Assembly Line B, was asked to come to Jackson's office. This steward was told of what had happened and requested to remain in the office to represent Wells and the Union.

When Wells came into the office, Jackson confronted him with the company's suspicion that he was drinking on the job and requested permission to inspect Wells' thermos bottle. Wells appeared surprised and stated, "If there is any alcohol in my thermos someone 'planted' it there." Wells agreed to the inspection of his thermos bottle and Jackson, Wells and the Assembly Line B Shop Steward went to the Crew Leader's office to retrieve it. Upon arrival at the Crew Leader's office Jackson again asked Wells if he could inspect the thermos bottle. Wells readily agreed. Jackson opened the thermos and observed what he believed to be whiskey. Wells again stated that someone was trying to "frame" him.

The three men then returned to Jackson's office where Jones confirmed that the contents of the thermos were the same as he had previously observed. The Labor Relations Manager observed the contents of the thermos bottle and agreed it appeared to be whiskey. Wells was asked to explain. Wells stated that he had last poured the contents of the thermos into his cup about one hour before Jones relieved him. He stated that he had left the office several times during that hour, leaving the cup and thermos bottle on the desk. "When Jones came to relieve me I finished the contents in the cup," said Wells, "and it was definitely iced tea. I replaced the cup on the thermos but I didn't check the contents of the thermos. The thermos bottle was open when Jones entered the office and if someone had placed liquor in the thermos while I was gone, Mr. Jones had probably smelled that liquor. I certainly hadn't consumed any." When asked to explain how the iced tea in his thermos could become alcohol Wells suggested that one of his fellow employees was playing a trick on him, someone who was mad at him because he hadn't processed a grievance they wanted to file might have done it or it could have been one of the supervisors he had frequently argued with.

Based on the evidence available, the Labor Relations Manager suspended Wells pending review of the facts and possible disciplinary action. The next day Wells was informed he would be given a 5 day lay-off without pay for violating company rules regarding the possession of intoxicants on Company property. The union filed a grievance under the Labor Agreement requesting Wells receive full pay for the 5 days he did not work and that his record be cleared of any reference to the incident. During the grievance meeting the Company stated it would send the thermos to an independent laboratory for analysis. This was done and the laboratory report confirmed the presence of alcohol in the thermos and no presence of iced tea. Based on this additional evidence the Company denied the grievance at all steps of the grievance procedure. The last step of the grievance procedure is arbitration by a neutral third party. The arbitration hearing was held on April 5, 1978.

Provision of the Contract
"Article XX" Working Rules

The plant working rules are designed to fairly and impartially regulate the actions of employees to assure the orderly and efficient plant operations and to make reasonable provision for employee safety and health. Recognizing this responsibility, the Company will revise and add working rules in Ap-

pendix 'B' as necessary provided, however, that such changes shall not be in conflict with any provision of this agreement.

The Union will be furnished a copy of any published revisions or additions to existing plant working rules. An employee shall have the right to have the question of the reasonableness of any new or revised rules submitted to the Grievance Procedure.

"Appendix 'B' Working Conditions"

Violation of plant working rules, which include but are not limited to those listed below, is cause for discipline and/or discharge, either after a warning or without warning, dependent on the character of the offense.

(K) Bringing intoxicants into the plant, consuming intoxicants on company premises, or reporting for work under the influence of intoxicants.

Position of the Parties

Position of the Company. The Company contended that there were many undisputed facts.

1. Mr. Jones, who is normally a bargaining unit employee, upon entering the Crew Leader's office observed Wells drinking from his thermos cup.
2. Jones, in the absence of Wells, checked the thermos.
3. Jackson, Wells and the Steward from Assembly Line B inspected the thermos together, with Wells' permission, and all three agreed the contents smelled like and appeared to be alcohol.
4. The thermos was returned to Jackson's office and Jones and the Labor Relations Manager confirmed this observation.

Based on these facts the Company felt it was reasonable to conclude Wells did, in fact, knowingly have an intoxicant in his thermos in violation of plant rules. A supervisor of the Company believed he observed Wells drinking an alcoholic beverage. Upon checking Wells' thermos that supervisor confirmed his belief that the grievant was in possession of an alcoholic beverage. Shortly thereafter Jackson, Wells and a Union Steward retrieved the thermos, which Wells offered as his, and all three confirmed the presence of alcohol. The thermos was returned to Jackson's office where Jones and the Labor Relations Manager also confirmed the presence of alcohol. The thermos and its contents were later sent to an independent laboratory where analysis confirmed the presence of alcohol and found no trace of tea. Finally, while Wells offered many hypothetical ways the alcohol could have gotten into his thermos, not one factual proof was offered to substantiate these hypotheses.

Position of the Union. The Union contended that Wells had 26 years of service with the Company and a clean record. The Union further stated that the Crew Leader's job took him away from, and out of sight of, the Crew Leader's office on several occasions between the last time Wells poured the "iced tea" from his thermos and the inspection of the thermos of Jones. These absences allowed ample opportunity for anyone to substitute alcohol for iced tea in Wells' thermos. In addition, the union contended that Mr. Jones checked the thermos after Wells had left the area, thereby violating his right to be there, or have a steward present, when the inspection took place. It was pointed out that Wells readily admitted to Jackson the thermos appeared to contain alcohol when they checked it together, that Wells had nothing to hide as he had no previous knowledge of alcohol in his thermos.

Survey at Venture Manufacturing

Background

Venture Manufacturing produces high-technology flight equipment. It is located in a small city in the Midwest and employs 500 to 550 people. The company has experienced a stable, yet modest, growth over the past three decades.

Venture employees are envied by their peers in the local community. Their salary, benefit package, and working conditions are among the highest, if not the highest, in the area. Several reasons contribute to this situation: 1) high company profits in the past; 2) long-term government contracts; 3) a local wage rate slightly below the national average; and 4) the presence of a strong union (Venture is located in a non-right-to-work state).

The US Armed Forces represents more than seventy percent of Venture's current sales. These government sales are in the form of five year contracts. Venture has successfully bid for these contracts for the past twenty years. The current contract is up for renewal in August, the following month.

Productivity Decline

Production efficiency at Venture has been progressively declining for the past three years. Management is convinced that the majority of this decreased productivity is caused by internal organizational factors. They attribute it primarily to a "morale" problem.

Management, to date, had not been able to reverse this trend. Although the decline could be considered minor (86% efficiency three years ago, 84% 2 years ago, and 79.5% last year), it has particular importance because of the upcoming government contract. Venture wants to be in a favorable competitive position in its bid to retain the government contract.

Bill Jones has been with Venture for the past fifteen years, for the last five years

The research and written case information were presented at a Case Research Symposium and were evaluated by the Case Research Association's Editorial Board. This case was prepared by Dr. James L. Harbin of Missouri Southern State Callege as a basis for class discussion.

EXHIBIT 1 Employee survey questions

1. What are the problems at Venture? What recommendations would you make in light of these problems?
2. Can you improve your performance? If so, by what amount?

as Plant Manager. He is knowledgeable, well-liked, and respected at Venture.

An open door policy has long been maintained by Jones. He feels this provides every employee with the opportunity to "talk" with him. Recently he established a suggestion box and the suggestions go directly to him.

In an effort to identify the efficiency problems and solutions, a series of meetings between and among all Venture employees were conducted. In mid-June, Bill held a meeting with the hourly employees. In an emotional, inspired speech he had tried to impress upon them the importance of improving their efficiency.

The Survey

Bill announced at this meeting that a survey, in the form of a written questionnaire, would be distributed to every hourly employee and their supervisors in an attempt to get their direct input on improving the situation. This survey questionnaire was for all practical purposes a first for the company. It was designed by Jones and took a simplistic form (see Exhibit 1). Of the company's 350 supervisory and hourly employees, 197 filled out the questionnaire. These were completed on the employees' own time and were deposited in the suggestion box. This was done to insure the confidentially of the respondents and also to insure their ideas would be read directly by Jones.

The results of the survey proved perplexing to Jones. Not only did the large number of completed forms prove unwieldy, but the diversity of the responses proved confusing. Some employees had written only a few words on each question, and some had written several pages.

Jones decided to engage the services of a management consulting firm to aid him in the interpretation of the survey. He felt that the consultants could also assist him in proposing recommendations.

The two consultants first met with Bill in mid-July, to learn more about Venture, Bill Jones, and the survey. After the meeting the consultants decided to read the questionnaires independently first, then together they would attempt to interpret them and make recommendations.

This task also proved perplexing to the consultants, and they decided to try to condense the responses in the questionnaire to see if that would make their job easier (see Exhibits 2 and 3).

The consultants had not completed their examination of the survey by August. It was announced on the 2nd of August that Venture had lost in their bid to obtain another five year government contract. Their chief competitor had submitted a lower bid. This meant that the Venture workforce would have to be reduced by some fifty percent in the coming weeks, with possible further reductions.

The loss of the contract would not mean the demise of the company. They could now concentrate their efforts on other projects that had been declined in the past. It would mean, however, that for the short run the company would experience some difficult and uncertain times. Bill Jones felt that efficiency would be just as important, if not more so, in the future. The short run would call for increased cost efficiency, and if they could regain their production efficiency of past years they could possibly regain the government contract five years from now.

EXHIBIT 2 Problems cited by employees

	Frequency	Percent
Problems With Supervision	68	18%
Problems of Parts Availability	35	9%
Coordination Between Departments and Staff	32	9%
Inspection Problems	27	7%
Concerns Over the Front Office	18	5%
Need for Training	18	5%
Problems with Job Classification, Bids, and Seniority	16	4%
Technical Suggestions	14	4%
Need for Regular Meetings Between Management and Workers	14	4%
Abuse of Coffee Drinking	13	4%
Lack of Personal Dedication	13	4%
Abuse of Overtime	12	3%
Problems with Tooling	12	3%
Willing to Forego Wage Increases	11	3%
Contract Violations	10	3%
Need for More Discipline	8	2%
Concern Over Job Security	6	
Poor Hiring Practices	5	
Need for a Better Suggestion System	5	
Need for an Incentive Program	5	
Need for Leadmen	5	
Need to Abide by the Rules	5	
Need to Improve Morale	5	
Concern Over the Personnel Manager	4	
Need for Socials	1	
Need for New Suppliers	1	
Conserve Utilities	1	
Need for Better Equipment	1	
Too Much Job Overload	1	
Too Many Fire Drills	1	
A Better Shop Plan	1	
Too Long Lunch Breaks	1	
Too Many Supervisors	1	
Union-Management Conflict	1	
Total Comments	371	

NOTE: Question 2 of the survey yielded the following: 109 affirmative, 53 nonaffirmative, and 35 no answers. Amounts of improvement varied widely.

EXHIBIT 3 Sample comments from employee survey

1. To increase productivity in the company you need people with background knowledge of the operation, and a willingness to work with the people, and not against the people.
2. You need a better relationship between the front offices and the working people.
3. You shouldn't have to fear your company's manager.
4. Another real problem in this company is the way they hire people. Wives, husbands, brothers, sisters, and etc., but only depending on who's buddy you are.
5. I believe that if the foremen and engineering would not fight with each other so much they could get more done.
6. I believe we need a comprehensive training program for our people.
7. Some place down the line we of management have lost the personal contact with people.
8. We can look for minutes to save in some areas, but if we motivate people to work through good honest leadership we can save hours.
9. Another problem we have, is employee morale. This is something that could be greatly improved with better communication between management and salaried employees.
10. People of Venture are our greatest asset, and we of management should realize this and strive for a better working relationship with them.
11. I feel that there is a very bad communications and working relationship problem in supervision.
12. There is too much competition from the aspect of making each other look bad.
13. Each of us needs to personally evaluate our job performance.
14. I think supervisors and management should work with their people and not give the idea that they are better than the people who work for them.
15. Most people will do a good job for someone they like and respect.
16. Work habits and productivity are affected when employees notice the misuse of funds in the addition of management personnel.
17. General supervisors that harass employees on petty little things.
18. If you would open the lines of communication to the working people on the floor and use their talent more, you could improve things.
19. Make the men feel they are more than just a number.
20. One way would be to have regular meetings between management and shop people to work on problems.
21. I personally would be willing to forego any wage increases that I may get for a period of time.
22. I would be willing to work any overtime work that may be required at straight time only.
23. They never seem to see the good in your work, but they see the bad.
24. You have a good bunch of men, and if personnel would get off our back and get the parts in like they should, you would see a big difference.
25. I think the work habits and quality would improve if the Union and Management both would make a greater effort to stay within the contract.
26. If we all work as a team, both Union and Company, we can increase productivity by quite a bit.
27. There is too much horse-play at times.
28. I would suggest more recognition for the people who are getting the work out.
29. When the work is going good everyone receives praise, when it is going bad everyone gets chewed.
30. They won't listen to the worker when he finds a problem with a certain machine.
31. The flow of parts through the departments is too slow.

EXHIBIT 3 (continued)

32. I think the coffee machines are used too much not only by the working employee but the foremen and salaried people also.
33. My hangup is the out of proportion of blue-badgers (nonproduction) to production people.
34. No tricky moves by labor relations.
35. When a man or woman does a good job very few supervisors tell him.
36. Hiring too many people in the wrong places.
37. I would like to suggest that there be lots of POSITIVE feedback especially on a personal basis.
38. We need more information on how our programs are going, profit or loss.
39. Accept peoples' ideas on how to do something and to admit when we are wrong.
40. Some method of keeping all employees informed of company goals.
41. Every time you turn around a foreman is looking down your shirt size or is going to write someone up.
42. The men on the floor just can't get any cooperation from the floor supervisors to help solve their problems.
43. No one wants to take any responsibility.
44. There is a lot of buck passing.
45. There is too much dissention between departments.
46. The people have gotten a "I just don't care anymore" attitude.
47. The most abused part is job bidding.
48. The company representative never awards jobs the same way.
49. One time its seniority, the next experience.
50. At least 10–15% of all employees seem to be walking around.
51. I think we need working leadmen.
52. We must re-work our parts time and time again.
53. If our parts could be inspected completely the first time it would save a lot of time and frustration.
54. Rules are not enforced by supervision.
55. We need to start an incentive plan for all people.
56. A better working relation between departments.
57. Reduce all overtime to minimum requirements.
58. Make them feel like they were a part of the company not just workers in the plant.
59. Excessive time spent at the vending machine.
60. Supervisors all seem to fear their supervisors.
61. There needs to be a consistent standard for all.

Internal Theft at Kline's

Jack and Marie Lassifer were thoroughly enjoying their Memorial Day weekend in the wilderness area north of the White Mountain Apache Indian Reservation in Arizona. This area was becoming their favorite location for combining a weekend camping experience, hiking and wildlife photography for Marie, and many fine trout fishing opportunities for Jack.

After a busy winter and spring for both Jack and Marie, this trip was their first real opportunity in a long while to forget their active schedules and relax. However, the last day of the trip found Jack less involved with pursuing his fishing exploits and spending many reflective moments thinking about a current work assignment. Jack was absorbed in his thoughts about this project during the five-hour drive home that evening as Marie slept beside him in the car. Jack realized that his boss had provided him with a challenging problem that might require greater sensitivity and creativity than his other personnel assignments over the last few years. The research and thought that Jack had given to the problem were beginning to produce some ideas, and this was welcomed relief, since Silvio Melindez had asked for at least a tentative proposal by mid-week.

Personal and Company

Jack Lassifer had lived in the Midwest most of his life and had graduated with a major in personnel administration from a large, state-supported university. His first job upon graduation was as a job analyst for a large, national insurance company. His ambitious nature and practical intelligence has resulted in Jack's having obtained good grades in college and an enviable record in his first job. Opportunities for a better job and a chance to enroll in a part-time MBA program at another large university had caused Jack to move to a large Southwestern city. He met Marie there 3 years ago at approximately the same time that he started his new job and entered the MBA program. As one of the two assistant personnel managers at the headquarters location, Jack worked for Kline's, a building construction supply firm with outlets in fifteen cities in three states. Kline's operations

Prepared by Stephen L. Payne, University of Southwestern Louisiana, as a basis for classroom discussion. Presented at the Case Workshop of the Case Research Association, New Orleans, 1982.

included two lumber and plywood processing plants that partially supplied the fifteen retail outlets. The company had enjoyed considerable growth since its founding by the original owner after World War II. Still independently operated, the firm had grown to approximately 400 employees. Firm employees were almost evenly grouped among each of the two plant operations, all of the retail outlets, and headquarters. The non-unionized firm had weathered tough economic periods in the past with few or no reductions in workforce, but recent conditions had forced some necessary streamlining at all firm's locations. Kline's management anticipated improving market potentials and hoped that further reductions in manpower would be unnecessary.

Jack Lassifer's job with Kline's had evolved over the last 3 years to include greater responsibilities. The challenges of the job to Jack were less in the administrative routines and controls that represented much of his time and effort. Jack had experienced greater success and praise from his superiors for his handling of special assignments. He was beginning to get some small reputation among Kline's personnel staff for creative problem identification and problem solving. Silvio Melindez, the personnel manager for Kline's, increasingly drew Jack away from his normal duties to consult with Melindez and others on special projects.

The Assignment

Jack's current concentration was directed toward an assignment that Melindez had introduced in mid-April for Jack's study and recommendations. Melindez was concerned that a fairly serious drain on the firm's resources might be associated with increasing employee theft and pilferage. In his initial discussions with Jack, Melindez reported the following observations:

1. Overhead costs associated with replacement of equipment, tools, and supplies had increased beyond inflationary expectations in recent years at plant, outlet, and headquarters locations.
2. Inventory shrinkage figures had likewise shown substantial increases beyond trade associations norms.

3. Comparisons of the expense and effort placed on technical security protection showed Kline's using more modern and extensive techniques than industry or trade standards.
4. Personnel policy statements about internal theft, while very limited, specifically state that theft behavior will result in firing and/or prosecution.
5. Firm experience with internal theft seemed limited. Eleven employees over the history of the firm had been fired upon proof of theft, but none had been prosecuted. Five of these employees had been fired in the last two years. Several employees had agreed to reimburse the firm for their theft to avoid prosecution.
6. Petty pilferage seemed endemic at Kline's. Work group norms appeared to support at least a small degree of theft. Fifteen years ago, each plant had instituted a video monitoring device at its exits to discourage workers' removing company property. About five years ago, Melindez had been similarly concerned about pilferage and unauthorized employee use of company property. He had fired one plant supervisor who had been using plant employees, supplies, and time to construct personal conveniences, such as kennel doghouses and a duckblind. Melindez had hoped that this quick termination of a supervisory employee would get a message across to other employees that this behavior was dangerous.

Silvio Mclindez's assignment for Jack was to study this problem in more detail and present recommendations concerning the necessity for any changes in policy and training. Melindez told Jack that he had assigned Herb Scott in the accounting department and Jerry Washington, one of several security consultants permanently with the firm, to take a special look at accounting, inventory, and security controls. According to Melindez, however, Jack should approach his assignment by focusing on employee attitudes, norms, and behaviors and suggesting possible ways to change these. Jack recalled that he had never read or studied much specific discussion concerning internal business theft. His strategy for undertaking this assignment was a three-pronged one that would provide him with the background information necessary to draw upon for a thorough, careful analysis. Jack believed that his most valuable resources for gaining more information about this problem were 1) discussions with individuals within the company, 2) discussions with personnel representatives in similar business operations about their experiences, and 3) library and secondary source review about internal business theft and pilferage.

Jack's interviews with plant, outlet, and headquarters employees at Kline's gave him the following two overall inputs:

1. Some of the employees that Jack interviewed were also concerned about attitudes and actions taken by others at Kline's. Almost all employees claimed to be more ethical in their use of company supplies, tools, and services than the typical employee. A few employees openly admitted using the company copying machines and taking inexpensive supply items for personal use. Such employees saw these minor conveniences as a form of implied fringe benefit.

2. Many of the 15 supervisors in retail locations, and also the 12 plant supervisors and six headquarter supervisors, were surprised at Jack's attention to this problem. Several stated that this was not a significant problem in their location. Others thought little practically could be done to reduce this expense. Two supervisors agreed on the very same conclusion. They objected to any role expectations of their playing policeman and seriously questioning their workers' honesty. One older supervisor in one of the plants pointedly suggested that Jack's assignment would be another witch hunt followed shortly afterward by a return to normal operations.

Jack's telephone calls to personnel staff in other firms in his trade association produced little assistance. Of the ten contacts, six were sympathetic and at least somewhat concerned about the problem. The six had not been able to formulate any real solutions, though two of these contacts stated that they had instituted tough policy and discipline procedures with little or only a modest improvement in conditions seen. Two other contacts reported increasing security expenses recently. Three firms claimed to not have any real problems with internal theft or pilferage, and two of the three thought that worker satisfaction with the company was one reason. Several personnel managers asked Jack to let them know if he was able to suggest anything new or innovative that might assist their companies. At this point though, Jack was certainly not confident that there would be any easy solutions.

In mid-May Jack believed that more research and thought would be necessary to view this complex problem more accurately. Days of library research by Jack and his personnel assistant produced the following major findings:

1. The Chamber of Commerce estimated in 1974 that 50 percent of office and factory workers steal, and that 5 to 8 percent steal in large volume. Other reference sources indicated manufacturing and retail operations where even larger percentages of employees admitted pilferage.[1]

2. A study by the American Management Associations and the University of Minnesota in 1980 of 5,000 employees in 35 companies reported that younger, unmarried workers do most of the stealing and dissatisfied workers are more likely to steal.[2]

3. Characteristic in the security literature concerning causation of employee theft is mention of perceived economic or psychological needs as a trigger and of rationalizations to sustain behavior and a positive self image.[3]

4. Normative influences of worker pilferage and theft and their subsequent reinforcement can present vicarious learning opportunities to other workers.[4]

5. Work groups maintain norms as relatively loose guidelines to an acceptable level of pilferage and the type of company property that may be taken. The work group protects members acting within these guidelines; otherwise personal gains are jeopardized by increased risk.[5]

6. Jaspan credits some employee theft to supervisory attitudes concerning reporting and punishment. Since theft may involve friends as well as subordinates, the supervisor may be criticized for even admitting theft problems; as reporting results in other hassles and paperwork, the supervisor may easily avoid the "distasteful" situation.[6]

7. Managerial attitudes and practices are commonly blamed as contributors to an unhealthy organizational climate where employee theft prevails. Management is criticized for often failing to create a motivating and satisfying work environment, providing inappropriate controls, allowing expedience to govern its discipline, and acting itself in an inconsistent and hypocritical manner.

After taking the time to assimilate these points and his own interviews with firm and industry sources, Jack began to see the outline of a program that he would propose to Silvio Melindez.

Notes

1. U.S. Chamber of Commerce, *Handbook on White Collar Crime,* 1974, p. 35.
2. B. Mass, "Thefts by Employees Jump during Recession," *The Arizona Republic* (January 27, 1980): C1.
3. M. J. Comer, *Corporate Fraud* (London: McGraw-Hill Book Company, 1977): 12.
4. S. L. Payne, "Organization Ethics and Antecedents to Social Control Processes," *Academy of Management Review* 5 (1980): 414–415.
5. D. N. M. Horning, "Blue Collar Theft: Conceptions of Property, Attitudes Toward Pilfering, and Work Group Norms in a Modern Industrial Plant," in E. O. Smigel and H. L. Ross (Eds.), *Crimes Against Bureaucracy* (New York: Van Nostrand Reinhold, 1970), pp. 63–64.
6. N. Jaspan, *Mind Your Own Business* (Englewood Cliffs, N.J.: Prentice-Hill, 1974), pp. 19–21.

The Road to Hell ...

John Baker, chief engineer of the Caribbean Bauxite Company of Barracania in the West Indies, was making his final preparations to leave the island. His promotion to production manager of Keso Mining Corporation near Winnipeg—one of Continental Ore's fast-expanding Canadian enterprises—had been announced a month earlier and now everything had been tidied up except the last vital interview with his successor—an able young Barracanian, Matthew Rennalls. It was vital that this interview be a success and that Rennalls should leave the office uplifted and encouraged to face the challenge of his new job. A touch on the bell would have brought Rennalls walking into the room but Baker delayed a moment and gazed thoughtfully through the window considering just exactly what he was going to say and, more particularly, how he was going to say it.

John Baker, an English expatriate, was 45 years old and had served his 23 years with Continental Ore in many different places: the Far East; several countries of Africa; Europe; and, for the last two years, in the West Indies. He hadn't cared much for his previous assignment in Hamburg and was delighted when the West Indian appointment came through. Climate was not the only attraction. Baker had always preferred working overseas (in what were termed the developing countries) because he felt he had an innate knack—better than most other expatriates working for Continental Ore—of knowing just how to get on with regional staff. Twenty-four hours in Barracania, however, made him realize that he would need all of this "innate knack" if he was to deal effectively with the problems in this field that now awaited him.

At his first interview with Hutchins, the production manager, the whole problem of Rennalls and his future was discussed. There and then it was made quite clear to Baker that one of his most important tasks would be the "grooming" of Rennalls as his successor. Hutchins had pointed out that not only was Rennalls one of the brightest Barracanian prospects on the staff of Caribbean Bauxite—at London University he had taken first-class honors in the B.Sc. Engineering Degree—but, being the son of the Minister of Finance and Economic Planning, he also had no small political pull.

This case was prepared by Mr. Gareth Evans and is reproduced with his permission and the permission of the Harvard Business School.

The company had been particularly pleased when Rennalls decided to work for them rather than for the government in which his father had such a prominent post. They ascribed his action to the effect of their vigorous and liberal regionalization program which, since World War II, had produced 18 Barracanians at mid-management level and given Caribbean Bauxite a good lead in this respect over all other international concerns operating in Barracania. The success of this timely regionalization policy has led to excellent relations with the government—a relationship which had been given an added importance when Barracania, three years later, became independent, an occasion that encouraged a critical and challenging attitude toward the role foreign interests would have to play in the new Barracania. Hutchins therefore had little difficulty in convincing Baker that the successful career development of Rennalls was of the first importance.

The interview with Hutchins had been held two years earlier, and Baker, leaning back in his office chair, reviewed just how successful he had been in the "grooming" of Rennalls. Which aspects of Rennalls' character had helped and which had hindered? The first item to go on the credit side would, without question, be the abiltiy of Rennalls to master the technical aspects of his job. From the start he had shown keenness and enthusiasm and had often impressed Baker with his ability in tackling new assignments and the constructive comments he invariably made in departmental discussions. He was popular with all ranks of Barracanian staff and had an ease of manner which stood him in good stead when dealing with his expatriate seniors. These were all assets, but what about the debit side?

First and foremost, there was his racial consciousness. His four years at London University had accentuated this feeling and made him sensitive to any sign of condescension on the part of expatriates. It may have been to give expression to this sentiment that, as soon as he returned home from London, he threw himself into politics on behalf of the United Action Party, which was later to win the preindependence elections and provide the country with its first Prime Minister.

The ambitions of Rennalls—and he certainly was ambitious—did not, however, lie in politics for, staunch nationalist as he was, he saw that he could serve himself and his country best by putting his engineering talent to the best use possible, for was not bauxite responsible for nearly half the value of Barracania's export trade? On this account, Hutchins found that he had a unexpectedly easy task in persuading Rennalls to give up his political work before entering the production department as an assistant engineer.

It was, Baker knew, Rennalls' well-repressed sense of race consciousness that had prevented their relationship from being as close as it should have been. On the surface, nothing could have seemed more agreeable. Formality between the two men was at a minimum; Baker was delighted to find that his assistant shared his own peculiar "shaggy dog" sense of humor so that jokes were continually being exchanged; they entertained each other at their houses and often played tennis together—and yet the barrier remained invisible, indefinable, but ever present. The existence of this "screen" between them was a constant source of frustration to Baker since it indicated a weakness he was loath to accept. If successful with all other nationalities, why not with Rennalls?

But at least he had managed to "break through" to Rennalls more successfully than any other expatriate. In fact, it was the young Barracanian's attitude—sometimes overbearing, sometimes cynical—toward other company expatriates that had been one of the subjects Baker had raised last year when he discussed Rennalls' staff report with him. He knew, too, that he would have to raise the same subject again in the forthcoming interview because Jackson, the senior draftsman, had complained only yesterday about the rudeness of Rennalls. With this thought in mind, Baker leaned forward and spoke into the intercom. "Would you come in Matt, please? I'd like a word with you," and later, "Do sit down," proffering the box, "Have a cigarette." He paused while he held out his lighter and then went on.

"As you know, Matt, I'll be off to Canada in a few days' time, and before I go, I thought it would be useful if we could have a final chat together. It is indeed with some deference that I suggest I can be of help. You will shortly be sitting in this chair doing the job I am now doing, but I, on the other hand, am 10 years older, so perhaps you can accept the idea that I may be able to give you the benefit of my longer experience."

Baker saw Rennalls stiffen slightly in his chair as he made this point so added in explanation, "You and I have attended enough company courses to remember those repeated requests by the personnel manager to tell people how they are getting on as often as the convenient moment arises and not just the automatic 'once a year' when, by regulation, staff reports have to be discussed."

Rennalls nodded his agreement so Baker went on. "I shall always remember the last job performance discussion I had with my previous boss back in Germany. He used what he called the "plus and minus" technique. His firm belief was that when a senior, by discussion, seeks to improve the work performance of his staff, his prime objective should be to make sure that the latter leaves the interview encouraged and inspired to improve. Any criticism must, therefore, be constructive and helpful. He said that one very good way to encourage a man—and I fully agree with him—is to tell him about his good points—the plus factors—as well as his weak ones—the minus factors—so I thought, Matt, it would be a good idea to run our discussion along these lines."

Rennalls offered no comment, so Baker continued. "Let me say, therefore, right away, that, as far as your own work performance is concerned, the plus far outweighs the minus. I have, for instance, been most impressed with the way you have adapted your considerable theoretical knowledge to master the practical techniques of your job—that ingenious method you used to get air down to the fifth-shaft level is a sufficient case in point—and at departmental meetings I have invariably found your comments well taken and helpful. In fact, you will be interested to know that only last week I reported to Mr. Hutchins that, from the technical point of view, he could not wish for a more able man to succeed to the position of chief engineer."

"That's very good indeed of you, John," cut in Rennalls with a smile of thanks. "My only worry now is how to live up to such a high recommendation."

"Of that I am quite sure," returned Baker, "especially if you can overcome the minus factor which I would like now to discuss with you. It is one which I have talked about before so I'll come straight to the point. I have noticed that you are more friendly and get on better with your fellow Barracanians than you do with Europeans. In point of fact, I had a complaint only yesterday from Mr. Jackson, who said you had been rude to him—and not for the first time either.

"There is, Matt, I am sure, no need to tell you how necessary it will be for you to get on well with expatriates because until the company has trained sufficient men of your calibre, Europeans are bound to occupy senior positions here in Barracania. All this is vital to your future interests, so can I help you in any way?"

While Baker was speaking on this theme, Rennalls had sat tensed in his chair and it was some seconds before he replied. "It is quite extraordinary, isn't it, how one can convey an impression to others so at variance with what one intends? I can only assure you once again that my disputes with Jackson—and you may remember also Godson—have had nothing at all to do with the color of their skins. I promise you that if a Barracanian had behaved in an equally peremptory manner I would have reacted in precisely the same way. And again, if I may say it within these four walls, I am sure I am not the only one who has found Jackson and Godson difficult. I could mention the names of several expatriates who have felt the same. However, I am really sorry to have created this impression of not being able to get on with Europeans—it is an entirely false one—and I quite realize that I must do all I can to correct it as quickly as possible. On your last point, regarding Europeans holding senior positions in the company for some time to come, I quite accept the situation. I know that Caribbean Bauxite—as they have been doing for many years now—will promote Barracanians as soon as their experience warrants it. And, finally, I would like to assure you, John—and my father thinks the same too—that I am very happy in my work here and hope to stay with the company for many years to come."

Rennalls had spoken earnestly and, although not convinced by what he had heard, Baker did not think he could pursue the matter further except to say, "All right, Matt, my impression *may* be wrong, but I would like to remind you about the truth of that old saying, 'What is important is not what is true but what is believed.' Let it rest at that."

But suddenly Baker knew that he didn't want to "let it rest at that." He was disappointed once again at not being able to "break through" to Rennalls and having yet again to listen to his bland denial that there was any racial prejudice in his makeup. Baker, who had intended ending the interview at this point, decided to try another tack.

"To return for a moment to the 'plus and minus technique' I was telling you about just now, there is another plus factor I forgot to mention. I would like to congratulate you not only on the calibre of your work but also on the ability you have shown in overcoming a challenge which I, as a European, have never had to meet.

"Continental Ore is, as you know, a typical commercial enterprise—admittedly a big one—which is a product of the economic and social environment of the United States and Western Europe. My ancestors have all been brought up in this environment for the past 200 or 300 years and I have, therefore, been able to live a world in which commerce (as we know it today) has been part and parcel of my being. It has not been something revolutionary and new which has suddenly entered my life. In your case," went on Baker, "the situation is different because you and your forebears have only had some 50 or 60 years' experience of this commercial environment. You have had to face the challenge of bridging the gap between 50 and 300 years. Again, Matt, let me congratulate you—and people like you—on having so successfully overcome this particular hurdle. It is for this very reason that I think the outlook for Barracania—and particularly Caribbean Bauxite—is so bright."

Rennalls had listened intently and when Baker finished, replied, "Well, once again, John, I have to thank you for what you have said, and, for my part, I can only say that it is gratifying to know that my own personal effort has been so much appreciated.

I hope that more people will soon come to think as you do."

There was a pause and, for a moment, Baker thought hopefully that he was about to achieve his long-awaited "breakthrough," but Rennalls merely smiled back. The barrier remained unbreached. There remained some five minutes' cheerful conversation about the contrast between the Caribbean and Canadian climate and whether the West Indies cricket team had any hope of beating England in the Fifth Test March before Baker drew the interview to a close. Although he was as far as ever from knowing the real Rennalls, he was nevertheless glad that the interview had run along in this friendly manner and, particularly, that it had ended on such a cheerful note.

This feeling, however, lasted only until the following morning. Baker had some farewells to make, so he arrived at the office considerably later than usual. He had no sooner sat down at his desk than his secretary walked into the room with a worried frown on her face. Her words came fast. "When I arrived this morning I found Mr. Rennalls already waiting at my door. He seemed very angry and told me in quite a peremptory manner that he had a vital letter to dictate which must be sent off without any delay. He was so worked up that he couldn't keep still and kept pacing the room, which is most unlike him. He wouldn't even wait to read what he had dictated. Just signed the page where he thought the letter would end. It has been distributed and your copy is in your in-basket."

Puzzled and feeling vaguely uneasy, Baker opened the "Confidential" envelope and read the following letter:

14 August 19xx
From: Assistant Engineer
To: The Chief Engineer, Caribbean Bauxite Limited
Assessment of Interview Between Messrs. Baker and Rennalls

It has always been my practice to respect the advice given me by seniors, so after our interview, I decided to give careful thought once again to its main points and so make sure that I had understood all that had been said. As I promised you at the time, I had every intention of putting your advice to the best effect.

It was not, therefore, until I had sat down quietly in my home yesterday evening to consider the interview objectively that its main purport became clear. Only then did the full enormity of what you said dawn on me. The more I thought about it, the more convinced I was that I had hit upon the real truth—and the more furious I became. With a facility in the English language which I—a poor Barracanian—cannot hope to match, you had the audacity to insult me (and through me every Barracanian worth his salt) by claiming that our knowledge of modern living is only a paltry 50 years old whilst yours goes back 200–300 years. As if your materialistic commercial environment could possibly be compared with the spiritual values of our culture. I'll have you know that if much of what I saw in London is representative of your most boasted culture, I hope fervently that it will never come to Barracania. By what right do you have the effrontery to condescend to us? At heart, all you Europeans think us barbarians, or, as you say amongst yourselves, we are "just down from the trees."

Far into the night I discussed this matter with my father, and he is as disgusted as I. He agrees with me that any company whose senior staff think as you do is no place for any Barracanian proud of his culture and race—so much for all the company "clap-trap" and specious propaganda about regionalization and Barracania for the Barracanians.

I feel ashamed and betrayed. Please accept this letter as my resignation which I wish to become effective immediately.

cc   Production Manger
     Managing Director

Production Control at Carbide Products, Inc.

Mr. Robert Bartlett, production control manager for Carbide Products, Inc., sat pondering the company's delivery performance problem and the preliminary reports he had recently received from the consultant (Aaron Thompson) hired to investigate the problem (see Exhibits 1 and 2). As he contemplated the contents of the reports, he was doubly concerned because he knew that the situation in the forming operation was probably typical of jobs processed elsewhere in the plant.

EXHIBIT 1

11-6-80

Mr. R. Bartlett:

Bob,

    The results of the delivery performance study on the forming shop are as follows:

        Sample size = 100
        Number and percent of jobs late = 62
        Number and percent of jobs on time = 38
        Average number of days late for late jobs = 6 days
        Number of these that were 1–3 days late = 37
            "   "   "   "   "   4–6   "   " = 8
            "   "   "   "   "   7-10 "   " = 7
            "   "   "   "   "   10–20 "   " = 2
        Number that were more than 20 days late = __8__
        Total   62

                                 Aaron

The research and written case information were presented at a Case Research Symposium and were evaluated by the Case Research Association's Editorial Board. This case was prepared by Taylor Cox, Jr. (with the assistance of Mrs. Brenda Campbell) of Johnson C. Smith University as a base for class discussion. The identity of the company has been disguised.

EXHIBIT 2

11-6-80

Mr. R. E. Bartlett

Bob,

I am currently conducting a study which has the objective of providing some data on the reasons for missed delivery dates for jobs routed through the forming area.

The sample is composed of 25 jobs with various originations and routings. Specifically, the sample is composed as follows:

Description	Number in sample
Press & form-press room 2 (type 1 job)	10
Press & form-press room 1 (type 2 job)	5
Issue from pre-sintered stock (type 3 job)	10

While a sample of larger size would have been desirable, more than 25 jobs would be difficult to keep track of with the available time and force.

My intent is to track these jobs from the first operation right through to charge-out. Daily notations will be made as to each job's whereabouts. Some of the jobs are not scheduled to start until 12-1 so it may be the end of the year before all results are available.

At the conclusion of the study, I will provide you with a report which summarizes the major causes of late jobs in the forming area of responsibility. Attached is a preliminary report from the first week of observation.

Type 1 jobs
Number under study = 10
Number pressed *on time* = 1
Number for which powder not available = 1

Type 2 jobs
Number under study = 5
Number started on time = 4
Number for which stock not available = 0

Type 3 jobs
Number under study = 10
Number started on time in forming = 3
Number or which stock not available = 0

Aaron

Background Information

Carbide Products, Inc. is a manufacturer of cutting tools, gun-drill bits and numerous other products made from carbide powder. The company employs 500 people, roughly three fourths of whom are associated with production operations. The manufacturing facility has a single site located in a near suburb of a large city in the midwestern United States. Most of the company's products are manufactured in-house using raw material (powder) purchased from independent mining firms. The company has its own sales force which handles all sales of the product, and distribution is direct from producer to users (such as firearms manufacturers). Marketing personnel are located in a building adjacent to the manufacturing plant. Other operations which are part of the same complex include personnel, data processing and engineering.

Carbide Products has been among the leading firms in the industry for many years and has witnessed a strong upward sales trend and more than adequate profitability. In recent years however, competition has intensified and the company has been losing market share. Although the slip in competitive position is undoubtedly due to multiple factors, top management feels that more than

EXHIBIT 3   Partial organization chart showing the production control section

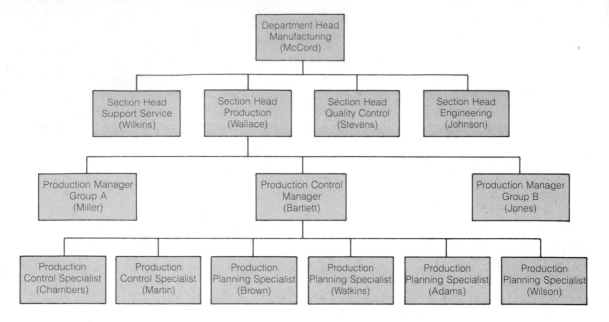

Department Head
Manufacturing
(McCord)

Section Head
Support Service
(Wilkins)

Section Head
Production
(Wallace)

Section Head
Quality Control
(Stevens)

Section Head
Engineering
(Johnson)

Production Manager
Group A
(Miller)

Production Control
Manager
(Bartlett)

Production Manager
Group B
(Jones)

Production
Control Specialist
(Chambers)

Production
Control Specialist
(Martin)

Production
Planning Specialist
(Brown)

Production
Planning Specialist
(Watkins)

Production
Planning Specialist
(Adams)

Production
Planning Specialist
(Wilson)

any other single cause, the company's poor delivery performance is responsible. Details of the manufacturing department of the firm, and more specifically the production control section, are provided below.

Organization Structure

The reporting relationships, basis of departmentalization, degree of decentralization and other fundamental aspects of organization structure of manufacturing have not changed significantly at Carbide since the late 1950's. At that time, the preference for a centralized decision making structure gave way to a much more decentralized structure in which managers down through second level received considerable autonomy for decision making within their own areas. Departments and sections were organized around functions performed. In addition, in 1959, the practice of promoting from within became firmly entrenched, and since then numerous production foremen have been promoted to higher level line positions (and also many staff positions including several in production control).

Exhibit 3 is an organization chart of the production control function of Carbide Products.

Production Technology

The production operation of Carbide utilizes a jobshop type of technology with virtually all products made to order. About 90 percent of the products are repeat orders and made to standard production specifications, with the other 10 percent custom made on a one-time-only basis. A typical order consists of several hundred to several thousand relatively small pieces (weighing less than a half a pound each). There are two basic types of job flows with numerous variations depending upon the specific product to be made. Most products are made by first processing the carbide powder on a press machine (press room 1 or 2) after which they are sent to pre-sinter for preliminary hardening. After pre-sinter, the product goes to forming where it is changed to the desired shape. Next the product goes to the sintering operation for final hardening in large furnaces, and from there products are cleaned, inspected and shipped to the customer. The most basic deviation from the routing just described occurs on products that are made from "crib" stock. The routing on these jobs is the same except that they are started by pulling carbide stock, already in solid form (called ingots), from a stock-bin thereby making the press operation unnecessary. Only certain products can be made sans the press operation. When products do not pass inspection on the first round they frequently wind up in the hot press (HP) or hot iso press (HIP) operations which are shop areas with specialized equipment and extra large furnaces. While in the shop, jobs are identified by colored envelopes which contain copies of the orders complete with routing and due-date information for each work center.

While in process, products are transported from one work station to another by placing them on large metal trays and then manually pushing them on metal carts. The carts are shelved to accomodate 8–10 trays each. Most jobs are contained on a single cart although a very small percentage of the jobs require 3 or 4 carts. Only in the inspection and sandblast areas are conveyors employed. Exhibit 4 is a diagram of the shop floor.

Scheduling

The production control specialists are responsible for job scheduling and expediting and for inventory control. They have no formal authority over line personnel but at Carbide their "requests" are typically honored by production management. For scheduling purposes, the weeks of the year are numbered 1–52 and work days are numbered 1–999. Thus, for example, the current date, November 23rd, is production week 48 and day 674. These numbers are used to plan the start and completion (due) dates of each operation performed in processing the order. The due date given to the customer by marketing is taken directly from the dates put on the order by the PC specialist. Dick Chambers (one of the PC specialists) approaches scheduling in the following manner. A job order form stating the type of product, quantity ordered and necessary routing (the sequence of work stations it must pass through) is sent to Chambers from the planning specialist. The number of orders received each day varies from as few as 6 to as many as 50 or more. Also, the amount of time necessary to schedule orders varies greatly in accordance with the size of the order, number of work stations it must pass through and so on. Chambers schedules the job by first computing the number of hours that it needs on each work center, then checking records of each center to determine when it will be able to accommodate additional

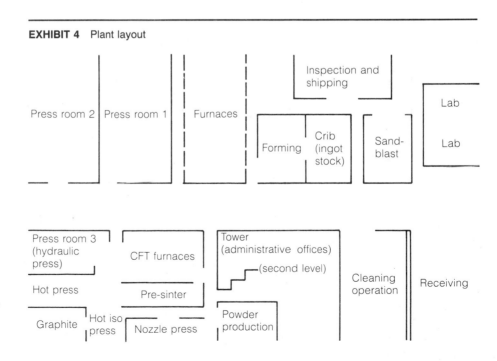

EXHIBIT 4   Plant layout

Production Control at Carbide Products, Inc.

work, and finally by writing the *planned* start and complete dates on the order form itself. The order is then passed on to production where it is placed in a file until the date scheduled to enter production. Exhibits 5 and 6 illustrate recent control records maintained by Chambers for the orders he schedules. Exhibit 5 is a record of the hours scheduled in for work center 1230 (a forming station). Each time a job is scheduled in for that station an entry is made here, and every work station has a similar sheet. To illustrate, you will note on Exhibit 5 that for the current week (week 48) the first three jobs scheduled to begin will require 12, 14 and 19 hours respectively to complete on work station 1230.

Exhibit 6 is a record for the three primary manufacturing areas of the hours scheduled in to hours output comparison for the third quarter of 1980. The "in" columns show total hours of the jobs scheduled to be completed in that area for the week indicated. The "out" columns show the total hours of work actually completed in the area during that week. For any given week, the *out* figures do not necessarily refer to the same *jobs* as the "in" figures because (for various reasons) jobs are not always worked on in the particular week that they are scheduled to be worked on.

Job Prioritizing & Expediting

As mentioned, a second major responsibility of the production control specialist is to handle job expediting and priority changes. Primarily, this entails responding to marketing requests for improved delivery dates or for special treatment on certain orders. The normal policy on job prioritizing is FIFO (First in, First out). On the shop floor, large signs are posted which are intended to display the number of the current production week (in this case 48). This was designed to serve as a reminder for production personnel to work on jobs in accordance with their scheduled due dates. Theoretically, this means working only on jobs which carry due dates that are the same as or earlier than the week posted. However, an inspection of work sta-

EXHIBIT 5   Control form-hours, work station 1230 (assumed capacity = 500 HPW)[1]

Week 47	Week 48*	Week 49	Week 50
8	12	44	102
12	14	39	60
14	19	42	72
19	90	102	
36	16	70	
105	60	76	
90	8	86	
14	36	45	
16	45	64	
45	50		
50	85		
60	105		
85	14		
10	25		
6	20		
4	4		
	6		
	2		

* = current week. HPW = hours per week.

NOTE: [1]This capacity is based on the current work time standards. The practice of using formal work times for each type of job task was initiated in 1962 and they have been updated twice since, most recently in 1970.

EXHIBIT 6 Input/output report, code E, F jobs—third quarter 1980

| | Press Room 1 | | Press Room 2 | | Forming | |
Week	In	Out	In	Out	In	Out
32	2214	2278	3908	2205	7228	6444
33	2280	2295	3620	2615	7964	6201
34	2200	2205	4012	2029	8221	6714
35	2320	2315	3817	1991	8000	6554
36	2276	2272	3912	2012	7198	5999
37	2217	2202	4105	2217	7004	6000
38	2220	2298	4005	2617	7874	6221
39	2202	2196	3642	2246	7762	6105
40	2200	2188	3555	2011	7918	6221
41	2225	2298	3776	1919	8331	6014
42	2210	2214	4012	2044	7842	6332
43	2279	2280	3818	2000	7241	6000

NOTE: Codes E and F identify jobs scheduled by Dick Chambers.

tions reveals that many of the date signs carry numbers of past weeks (at present, signs showing weeks 43 and 44 are not unusual) and that jobs frequently are not worked in accordance with the FIFO rule. When asked about this, the shop foremen explain that the necessary decisions about priorities are made informally between themselves and the production control specialists in daily conversation. Besides, they say, "re-work and crash jobs frequently change normal prioritizing to the point that the posted dates don't mean much anyway." The issue of re-work is taken up in the quality control section. More on crash jobs follows here.

Crash Jobs. A crash job is a job that has been given special priority by production control (often in response to pressure from marketing). These jobs go in a special colored (red) envelope to facilitate identification on the floor, and most are scheduled in for immediate attention regardless of current work loads or due dates of jobs already in the system. Carbide management acknowledges the potentially disruptive effect of job crashing, but defends it on the basis of a need for flexibility in production control. At present, there are roughly 200 "crash" jobs on the floor out of approximately 8,000 total jobs (3,000 of which are in the active

production stage). In addition to priority changes occasioned by job crashing, there are always additional jobs receiving special direct attention of the production control specialists after they enter production. At any point in time there are 1–300 of such additional exception cases in the system.

Inventory Control

The types of inventories of most critical importance to smooth production at Carbide are raw material inventories and W.I.P. inventories. As implied previously, minimal finished good inventories are maintained. Production control has the responsibility to see that adequate supplies of raw materials (essentially carbide powder) and ingots (powder formed into a cylinder shape and chemically treated for certain production uses) are available to meet production needs. Records are maintained of the amount of powder and number of ingots of various types on hand. Although the availability of needed materials has a direct bearing on delivery performance, management does not believe this to be a significant cause of the delivery performance problem.

The W.I.P. The work-in-progress inventory is monitored by production control by means of a computer printout which shows by job number the current work center (or other status), scheduled start and completion dates and other pertinent information of each job. The W.I.P. inventory record has just recently been computerized and many bugs are not yet worked out. The report is issued daily to marketing as well as production control personnel. In spite of the availability of this report, most salesmen have reverted back to the old jobs. Because there are more than a dozen salesmen but only two full-time PC specialists, a significant part of the PC specialist's day is spent handling these calls. More on the situation with the W.I.P. report is revealed in the memo in Exhibit 7.

Quality Control

QC at Carbide is handled by a separate section (from line production) but is housed within the manufacturing department. There are two primary points of inspection; the first is done on materials prior to the start of the production cycle. A sample of jobs have the powder checked via chemical analysis to verify its suitability for production use. Although the powder checked represents only a small fraction of that used, QC personnel report that the system is effective in minimizing most material quality problems.

The other major inspection is a finished goods inspection. A sample of the products from every job are checked against specifications to ensure compliance. A special study done by Mr. Thompson revealed that the rate of reject at this inspection has been running 15–20%.

As a hedge against missed deliveries due to insufficient "good" units to meet the order requirements, jobs are routinely started with more units than the order calls for (in some cases, considerably more). In those instances where more than enough "good" units survive the production process, the overage is either held for a subsequent order or (in the case of one-time-only runs) shipped on to the customer at no additional charge.

Rejected products are returned to appropriate work stations for reprocessing or to HIP or HP for special corrective action. Some jobs are uncorrectable and must be scrapped. This is the basis for the only formally reported quality measure currently available to management. The weight and ratio of scrap (to good product) is recorded and published on a monthly performance report.

Delivery Performance

Robert Bartlett continued to ponder the question of what to do about his substandard delivery results. Performance data indicate that the delivery measure (percent on-time) has been averaging

---

EXHIBIT 7

Date: 10-24-80

To: Mr. Robert Bartlett

From: Richard Chambers

Re: The W.I.P. report

On the basis of my investigation, I would say the following conclusions are warranted.

1. Less than half of the customer promise dates shown on the W.I.P. *agree* with the same dates on the customer status report (summary report used by management to monitor progress of pending jobs).
2. About 10% of the jobs shown as late on the customer status report are *not* on the W.I.P. This probably holds true also for all jobs on the customer status report (i.e. whether late or not).
3. About one fourth of the jobs listed on the W.I.P. have no customer promise (due) date entered.
4. A sizeable proportion of the data listed on the W.I.P. report is obsolete (e.g. showing jobs that have already shipped as not yet entered into production).

around 70 percent. This is 25% below the formal objective of 95 percent. In the past this rather poor performance was tolerated because sales and profits continued to be strong, and the feeling was that Carbide's 70% was probably still better than their competitors. Also, for some products, Carbide had enjoyed a virtual monopoly as the only firm in the industry with the technical capability to produce them. Recently, however, competition has stiffened and management is convinced that better service will be mandatory in the future. Bartlett knows that he will be expected to have some answers or at least a plan of action at the next staff meeting scheduled for two weeks from today.

Tower Motor and Machine Company

Gus Heffington was perplexed and somewhat frustrated when he left Kirk Brommer's office that afternoon. Mr. Brommer, the President of Tower Motor and Machine Company, a large manufacturer of compressors used in residential central air conditioning units, seemed to be asking the impossible. At least it appeared that way to Gus who had only recently been appointed to the new position of materials manager for Tower Motor and Machine Company.

Mr. Brommer had asked Gus to "try to come up with a method for estimating the number of compressors by type and model number that are being held in the distributor's (wholesaler's) warehouses." Mr. Brommer wanted a report with this information sent to him on a monthly basis. He further asked Gus to "have some of your thoughts together on this for next week's staff meeting." The meeting was the regular weekly staff meeting attended by Mr. Brommer; Frank Ryan, the plant operations manager; George Simpson, the sales manager; and Gus. Also attending this particular meeting would be the vice president of manufacturing from the corporate headquarters in Boston.

Gus had been rather excited when he received Mr. Brommer's call that morning asking that he come to his office at 2:00 that afternoon to discuss an important matter dealing with inventories. Since Gus normally received such requests through his own boss, Frank Ryan, Gus had wondered what "important matter" would cause Brommer to alter the normal channel of communication. Now that he knew, he was a little apprehensive about this new assignment. Most of Gus's work had been with inventory management models, and particularly with the materials requirements planning system under development within the company.

What prompted this request by Mr. Brommer was his concern that the demand for compressors might be leveling out, or perhaps even turning down. Forecasts

The research and written case information were presented at a Case Research Symposium and were evaluated by the Case Research Assocation's Editorial Board. The case was prepared by Roy H. Willams and Thomas R. Miller of Memphis State University as a basis for class discussion.

of a general recession were appearing with greater frequency, and Tower was in the early stages of planning for a new factory to be built in Statesboro, Georgia. He believed that changes in the distributors' inventory levels, assuming these could be accurately estimated and monitored, might provide a leading indicator of possible changes in demand for the company's products. Frank Ryan, the plant operations manager, believed that the information obtained from the system could also be used to smooth out production schedules and eliminate many unnecessary production line changes. The management team at Tower had for some time considered the development of an inventory system that would track compressors throughout the entire channel of distribution. Also, Mr. Brommer was expecting this project to be the first phase of a model of the total distribution system of the company.

When Gus returned to his office, he began to jot down what he considered to be some of the major problems facing him in his efforts to fulfill Mr. Brommer's assignment.

1. Gus had no idea how he was to obtain complete inventory data from the distributors, since they were neither owned nor operated by Tower, but acted as agents completely independent of the manufacturer.
2. Gus believed that it would be highly improbable or impossible to get even half of the distributors to report their inventory levels back to the factory. If the distributors were company owned, it would be no trouble to get the necessary information on each model and size in the distributors' warehouse, but this was not the case.
3. Even if Tower could get inventory reports from the distributors, the accuracy would be questionable, especially if there were no incentive for the distributors to supply the requested data.
4. If Tower could somehow obtain the sales of the distributors to their customers, the retail dealers, then Gus might be able to approximate the distributor inventory by subtracting the distributors' sales to their dealers from Tower's factory shipments to the distributors. But even with this data, Gus would need a starting point for the distributor inventory level.

As he reflected on his meeting with Mr. Brommer, Gus seemed to recall that some mention had been made of sampling the distributor warehouses, or something to that effect. He found written in the margin of the meeting notes that he had taken when he met with Mr. Brommer, "check on the possibility of using some kind of sampling procedure . . . our sales people could perhaps collect the sample data from some of the distributor accounts by actually going in and counting the number of compressors in their warehouse."

As Gus continued to think about his new assignment of estimating the number of compressors in distributors' warehouses, he knew he would need to have his thoughts well organized and some definite means of dealing with the problem by the next staff meeting. Also, he realized he would have primary responsibility for the design and development and probably for testing the estimating model.

Background

Tower Motor and Machine Company, a division of a large diversified corporation headquartered in Boston, is located in a small Midwestern community. Tower's sales force sells compressors nationally to independently owned distributors. The United States is divided into seven sales districts, each headed by a district sales manager. The salesmen in each district report to the district manager, who in turn reports to the company sales manager.

The distribution channel is a two-step system, with compressors moving from the factory to the distributor and from the distributor to the retail dealer (see Exhibit 1). The product moves by rail and by truck line to the distributors, and predominantly by truck from distributors to dealers. Approximately 90 percent of the factory's shipments move through the traditional two-phase distribution network, that being from factory to distributor to dealer. There are two special situations, how-

EXHIBIT 1 Schematic of Tower's distribution system

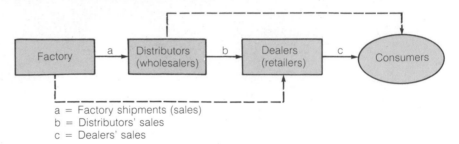

a = Factory shipments (sales)
b = Distributors' sales
c = Dealers' sales

ever, in which shipments may flow directly from the factory to the retail level, or directly from the distributor to the final consumer (shown in Exhibit 1). These latter channels, represented as dashed lines in Exhibit 1, make up less than 10 percent of the total sales.

Over the years, Tower's air conditioning compressors have gained wide acceptance as a quality product. They are widely recognized as being sturdy, dependable, and durable, a fact largely responsible for the strong product demand over the past four years. Demand has been so strong that inventory levels have been consistently low throughout the entire distribution network, forcing the factory to adopt an allocation policy for the distribution of compressors. Of course, the factory has not been able to accumulate an inventory of finished goods, since the completed compressors are shipped as soon as they are crated. In response to this heavy demand for compressors, Tower recently gave up the production of other products to concentrate exclusively on compressors.

The compressors are manufactured in two types, 24,000 BTUs and 36,000 BTUs, with three product models in each size category. Exhibit 2

EXHIBIT 2 Compressor models manufactured by Tower Motors

24,000 BTUs	36,000 BTUs
product #843	product #916
product #852	product #944
product #858	product #972

lists the models in current production. Periodically, models are added to the line, but no new models are anticipated for at least two years.

The Modeling Experience

In recalling his past projects, Gus could not remember an assignment similar to this one. He realized that quantitative methods would play a role in reaching a solution to the problem. While Gus had gained some familiarity with sampling and statistical models from his college work and from meetings with Tower's quality assurance personnel, he had not had an opportunity to use them in his projects until now.

After considering all feasible means by which he might gather the data needed for the project, Gus settled on the sampling approach suggested earlier by Mr. Brommer. After considerable study and analysis and drawing on training from his college courses in statistics, operations research, and production management, Gus was able to develop a conceptual model. In the model he would use inventory and other data from a sample of several of Tower's "key" customers to project the inventory amounts of all the distributors.

The sample of distributor accounts was composed of fourteen "key" accounts selected from the largest volume distributors. An attempt was made to get accounts that were dispersed geographically throughout the major trade areas, which ran from California across the Southwest through the Southeast to Florida. Some distributors had refused to participate in the sampling effort, but Gus continued his search until he had fourteen confirmations for the sample which he believed met the criteria.

EXHIBIT 3   Distributor ranking by volume (in dollars)

Value of Annual Shipments	Number of Distributors	Actual Value (in $1,000)
Less than $5,000	313	$ 782.5
$5,000 – $9,999	172	1,290.0
10,000 – 14,999	128	1,600.0
15,000 – 19,999	102	1,785.0
20,000 – 24,999	64	1,440.0
25,000 – 29,999	49	1,347.5
30,000 – 39,999	39	1,365.0
40,000 – 49,999	27	1,215.0
50,000 – 99,999	11	825.0
over 100,000	5	1,435.0*
Total	910	$13,085.0

* = actual amount shipped to these five accounts.

Thus, the distributors who agreed to take part in the project were some of the largest accounts, representing approximately 15 percent of the total dollar volume of compressors handled. The fourteen accounts came from the last three classes of Exhibit 3. Gus was not entirely satisfied that no medium or small volume distributors were included in the sample, but it seemed to him that there was no feasible way to obtain the necessary data on a timely basis.

In an effort to obtain accurate sample data, Tower's own company salesmen visited the fourteen sample accounts on the first of each month and literally counted the number of units of each product number that was in stock in each distributor's warehouse. It was believed that this method of data collection would produce the best results. In fact, Gus overheard George Simpson, Tower's sales manager, tell a district sales manager in a long distance conversation: "Those inventory figures had better be correct!"

The first report that Gus submitted to Mr. Brommer was for the month of October, 1981 (see Exhibit 4). In generating the report, Gus determined a ratio from the inventory amounts and the shipments to the sample group (column 4) and extended the total factory shipments by applying that ratio. This procedure was followed for each line item, or product number, and was then totaled in column 6. The 9,111 units represented an estimate of the total number of compressors of all product numbers that was in wholesale inventory in October of 1981. While Mr. Brommer seemed pleased with the initial report, he asked Gus if he could estimate the extent of possible error in these projections. Gus responded that he would need to study this issue further.

After reviewing the November report (Exhibit 5) that Gus had submitted, Mr. Brommer was quite concerned when he saw that the estimate of total distributor inventory had grown to 19,212 units. This was more than double the October estimate of 9,111 units. He had expected some increase due to the normal seasonal slowdown of orders, but he was shocked by the indicated size of that increase. His attention was particularly drawn to the total for product number 944, which showed an increase of 6,689 units, growing from 1,152 in October to 7,841 in November. This was especially puzzling to him since the total factory shipments for that product number were only 1,010 units for November.

Mr. Brommer immediately put in a call to Gus to "see me as soon as possible regarding the latest estimate of distributor inventory." As Gus walked rapidly toward Mr. Brommer's office, the tone of the president's message gave him an uneasy feeling that something might be wrong with his inventory estimating model.

EXHIBIT 4 Total distributor inventory—October 1981

Product Number (1)	Factory Shipments to 14 Distributors (2)	Inventory of 14 Distributors (3)	Ratio of Inventory to Shipments (3) ÷ (2) (4)	Factory Shipments to All Distributors (5)	Estimated Inventory of All Wholesalers (4) × (5) (6)
24K BTU					
843	275	418	1.52	786	1,195
852	314	500	1.59	1,570	2,496
858	57	210	3.68	570	2,098
36K BTU					
916	203	310	1.53	594	909
944	435	506	1.16	993	1,152
972	342	210	0.63	2,001	1,261
				Total	9,111

EXHIBIT 5 Total distributor inventory—November 1981

Product Number (1)	Factory Shipments to 14 Distributors (2)	Inventory of 14 Distributors (3)	Ratio of Inventory to Shipments (3) ÷ (2) (4)	Factory Shipments to All Distributors (5)	Estimated Inventory of All Wholesalers (4) × (5) (6)
24K BTU					
843	125	473	3.78	970	3,666
852	223	518	2.32	1,693	3,928
858	122	275	2.25	490	1,103
36K BTU					
916	253	375	1.48	614	909
944	93	722	7.76	1,010	7,841
972	195	353	1.81	975	1,765
				Total	19,212

John Lockley

In June, 1974, John Lockley was a very happy young man. After four years in college the breaks were coming his way. During the Spring term, he had been assigned to write a term paper analyzing the international strategy of a company. Because of his interest in construction, he chose to analyze the Move-It Corporation, a manufacturer and distributor of a specialized line of construction equipment that marketed its products on all continents. By chance, an executive of Move-It was scheduled to speak to Lockley's international business class. Following a discussion after class, Lockley arranged to meet with executives to gather data for the paper. He agreed to provide Move-It with a copy of his analysis. The International Manager was impressed with the analysis and asked whether John had a position following graduation. Since the answer was "no," the company and John began a discussion that led to his employment in the International Division.

Mark Wilson, International Manager for Move-It, was interested in expanding the division to take advantage of the many export and licensing opportunities abroad. Until recently the division had accounted for only a small share of total company revenue. Wilson planned to bring in several people and establish an international training program. In a sense, John would have the chance to pioneer the program. Upon successful completion, he would be assigned abroad with the goal of becoming an international sales manager with responsibility for a designated market. John realized that he would need considerable product knowledge and experience, in addition to learning how to function in different cultures if he was to succeed. He had always been interested in international marketing, but assumed any company would want him to work in its domestic operations for a year or two before the company would be willing to assume the costs of transferring him overseas. The opportunity to start with the International Division seemed ideal, but maybe was possible because of its relatively small size in the total organization.

According to John's agreement with Mark Wilson, the initial training period would last eight months, after which John would receive an overseas assignment.

This case was prepared by Ruel Kahler, professor of Marketing and Director of International Business Programs, The University of Cincinnati. Reprinted by permission of South-Western Publishing Company.

The initial eight months would consist of a familiarization with the company, and visits to company factories to learn the technical aspects of Move-It products. John would participate in several company product sales training programs designed for domestic personnel. Various assignments in the home office would enable him to interact with international personnel and learn company procedures. For an overseas orientation, John would be assigned two weeks to an operating subsidiary.

John began work with Move-It on July 6. For the first three months he performed some general office duties to learn the routines and personalities. The International Marketing Manager and others spent time with John, but they frequently were pressed by immediate administrative responsibilities. John also attended two brief sales training sessions. During this time, he was assigned to develop a dealer manual to show overseas dealers what promotions, advertising, and technical services were available from Move-It. To prepare the manual, John had to learn the company's export policies plus the process by which an order is received and distributed. He also learned the terms under which the product is financed, shipped, and insured. In a second project, John developed a control chart so management could tell at a glance the status of each order and shipment.

Management was impressed with John's performance. He projected a high level of achievement and maturity. Management believed John was capable of accepting more responsibility than the original training schedule.

Three months into the program, John was informed that some adjustments would have to be made. The Belgian subsidiary, where he was to receive indoctrination in a foreign environment, had special problems. But at the same time, an opportunity had opened up in Australia. (Australia was an important market for Move-It that also was serviced by a nationwide sales subsidiary.) The opportunity arose because the company had decided to "Australiaize" the subsidiary by placing it under the management of a local who currently served as Move-It sales manager in Australia's second largest city. John would be the only U.S. citizen in the subsidiary. The present manager, a U.S. citizen, would be returning to the home office in mid-November,

about 20 days after John would arrive. John would spend one week at headquarters and then proceed to the largest city in his assigned district. There he would work with a local dealer to develop his sales presentation and become familiar with his territory. Since Australia was an English speaking country there would be no language problem. The International Manager believed John would have very little difficulty adjusting to the environment.

John was eager to accept the new responsibility, but had some qualms about the change. In Australia, he would be responsible for the development of his territory. That meant generating sales and improving the dealer organization at the same time he was learning. Others at the home office pointed out, however, that he had little to lose and, if successful, he would be well ahead of his planned schedule. One thing that bothered John was that his knowledge of operations in Australia was very sketchy. He had heard that the Australia manager was not very enthused about the arrangement. To provide himself with some security, John asked Mark for some written guidelines so he and the subsidiary would know his function. These guidelines said he was to gain insight and experience in retail programs, develop and execute professional sales presentation, develop budget and financial planning perspectives by organizing his district, conduct a market survey of potential in Australia for the next five years, and produce 5 percent of Australian sales next year. These guides were rather general, but Mark Wilson would clarify them when he visits Australia in December.

Upon arriving in Australia, John was charmed by the lifestyle of the people and by the proximity of both mountains and sea. At the office, he met with both the present and the new manager. The first week was a general orientation. At his first dinner with Ben Taylor, the Australian who would become manager, John was surprised by one question. Taylor asked what function John would be performing in Australia. John reviewed the guidelines from the home office. John also learned that his salary was higher than that of the Australian sales managers, even though they had more experience.

John was placed in a dealership for a month to learn the business, Australian style. Located in Victoria, the territory to which Mark Wilson wanted

John assigned, the dealership was relatively low volume. John knew that the dealer owed Move-It a fair amount of money for inventory sent on consignment. John was concerned because he was not getting much practice in developing his sales presentation, nor could he accomplish the other goals set forth in the guidelines.

At the end of the month, Ben wrote John telling him to stay at the dealership and not worry about the rest of the territory. John wrote back reminding Ben of the guidelines and of his feeling that Mark Wilson would not be satisfied with his program unless he did more than sell in the dealership. In response, Ben asked John to come to the home office in Sydney and make a survey of towns along the way getting the names and locations of potential dealers. Upon presenting this information, Ben told John that the results were very similar to what he (Ben) had found the previous year.

Ben sent John back to Victoria, but told him to begin visiting other towns and lining up dealers. When sufficient dealers were established, they would hold a dealer training program. The dealer organization should be in place by the end of April.

Later Ben became irritated when John had not visited one or two places Ben had suggested. John said he had checked the phone directories and found no construction dealers in those towns and thought he could be more effective by concentrating on areas with greater potential.

During this same time, John was to work with a promotion developed by International in the States and used effectively by other subsidiaries. Unfortunately, Ben felt the time could better be devoted to direct selling.

By March John was uneasy. He felt that in a sense he was caught in a difference of opinion between the Australian manager and the home office. Much of this could have been resolved, he thought, if Mark Wilson had arrived as planned. Other problems and opportunities, however, had led Mark to postpone his trip to Australia. John also was concerned because his work permit had not yet been approved. (A visit to the Immigration office revealed that no sponsoring letter had been sent from the subsidiary.) John realized that Ben's needs were different from the guidelines set by Mark. But John thought this was a larger issue that would have to be settled between Ben and Mark. John had tried to work hard and do what was expected.

Finally, in April, Mark arrived. Ben told him that John was not working out. According to Ben, John did not follow orders and wasted time. Furthermore, it would be impossible for John to continue because he had no work permit.

Which Company Is Truly Multinational?

Four senior executives of the world's largest firms with extensive holdings outside the home country speak:

Company A. "We are a multinational firm. We distribute our products in about 100 countries. We manufacture in over 17 countries and do research and development in three countries. We look at all new investment projects—both domestic and overseas—using exactly the same criteria."

The executive from company A continues, "Of course most of the key posts in our subsidiaries are held by home-country nationals. Whenever replacements for these men are sought, it is the practice, if not the policy, to look next to you at the head office and pick someone (usually a home-country national) you know and trust."

Company B. "We are a multinational firm. Only 1 percent of the personnel in our affiliate companies are nonnationals. Most of these are U.S. executives on temporary assignments. In all major markets, the affiliate's managing director is of the local nationality."

He continues, "Of course there are very few non-Americans in the key posts at headquarters. The few we have are so Americanized that we usually don't notice their nationality. Unfortunately, you can't find good foreigners who are willing to live in the United States, where our headquarters is located. American executives are more mobile. In addition, Americans have the drive and initiative we like. In fact, the European nations would prefer to report to an American rather than to some other European."

Company C. "We are a multinational firm. Our product division executives have worldwide profit responsibility. As our organizational chart shows, the United States is just one region on a par with Europe, Latin America, Africa, etc., in each division."

© 1971, 1984 by Warren J. Keegan, Professor of Marketing and International Business, Lubin Graduate School of Business, Pace University, New York, NY 10038. This case is adapted with permission from Howard V. Perlmutter, "The Tortuous Evolution of the Multinational Corporation." *Columbia Journal of World Business*, January-February 1969.

The executive from Company C goes on to explain, "The worldwide product division concept is rather difficult to implement. The senior executives in charge of these divisions have little overseas experience. They have been promoted from domestic posts and tend to view foreign consumer needs as really basically the same as ours. Also, product division executives tend to focus on the domestic market because the domestic market is larger and generates more revenue than the fragmented foreign markets. The rewards are for global performance, but the strategy is to focus on domestic. Most of our senior executives simply do not understand what happens overseas and really do not trust foreign executives, even those in key positions."

Company D (non-American). "We are a multinational firm. We have at least 18 nationalities represented at our headquarters. Most senior executives speak at least two languages. About 30 percent of our staff at headquarters are foreigners."

He continues by explaining that "since the voting shareholders must by law come from the home country, the home country's interest must be given careful consideration. But we are proud of our nationality; we shouldn't be ashamed of it. In fact, many times we have been reluctant to use home-country ideas overseas, to our detriment, especially in our U.S. subsidiary. Our country produces good executives, who tend to stay with us a long time. It is harder to keep executives from the United States."

Author Index

Abernathy, William, 591, 643–57
Adams, Stacy, 147–48
Alderfer, Clayton P., 176
Allen, Robert W., 237
Anderson, D., 595
Anderson, Robert M., 437
Aquilano, Nicholas J., 621, 622
Argyris, Chris, 323–24

Barnard, Chester I., 4, 5, 8, 56, 57, 67–70, 72, 80
Bass, Bernard M., 164
Beer, Michael, 321, 322
Bell, Eugene C., 43
Bennis, Warren, 319, 322, 324
Bingham, R. S., 633
Blake, David H., 455, 456
Bluedorn, Allen C., 569–75
Boisseau, Robert T., 576–78
Bookout, John F., 711–13
Bowditch, James L., 552–53
Bowers, David A., 329
Bowman, James S., 445
Bray, Douglas W., 86–93
Brown, Charles L., 358–63
Bryan, Judith F., 156
Buchanan, Bruce, 162
Buono, Anthony, 552–53
Burack, Elmer H., 510, 522
Burger, Philip C., 164
Burke, James E., 488–90
Burns, Tom, 292–94
Buskirk, Richard H., 238
Bylinsky, G., 624

Caras, Harvey, 576–78
Carroll, Stephen J., 6
Cartledge, Norman, 155
Cartwright, Dorwin, 175–76
Cathey, Paul, 601
Cattell, James McKeen, 74
Chandler, Alfred, 297–98, 333
Chapman, J. Brad, 546
Chase, Richard B., 621, 622
Chemers, Martin M., 191
Clark, Kim B., 643 57
Connor, Patrick, 5
Coons, Alvin E., 192
Cousins, Roland B., C17–19
Cox, T., 120
Cox, Taylor, Jr., C86–93
Crosby, Philip, 634
Cummings, Larry L., 234

Dalrymple, Douglas J., 394
Davidson, William H., 205–15
Davis, James H., 426
Davis, Ralph C., 4, 5, 8
Davis, Sheldon A., 444
Davis, Stanley M., 297, 329
Dawson, J. A., 121
Deming, Edwards, 623
Dickson, William J., 66
Dilworth, James B., 634
Doyle, Frank, 470–74
Driver, Michael J., 117
Drucker, Peter, 599, 612
Dubrin, Andrew J., 239
Dunbar, Roger L. M., 9

Eddy, George, C27–34, C41–47
Eells, Richard, 448
Emery, Fred E., 285
England, George W., 32, 114
England, Wilbur B., 619
Evans, Gareth, C81–85
Evans, J. R., 595

Farmer, Richard N., 672
Farrell, Dan, 240
Fayol, Henri, 4–10 passim, 61–64, 71, 77, 80, 229, 242
Fearon, Harold E., 619
Fiedler, Fred, 191–92
Fierman, Jaclyn, 695
Filley, Alan C., 230
Follett, Mary Parker, 56, 57, 67
Fombrum, Charles, 470–74
Ford, Henry, 56, 57
Franklin, Jerome L., 329
Frederick, William C., 455, 456
French, John R. P., 230
French, Wendell L., 73

Gantt, Henry L., 56, 57, 60
Garrett, David C., 579–80
Ghiselli, Edwin E., 190
Gilbreth, Frank, 56, 57, 59, 60
Gilbreth, Lillian, 56, 57, 59, 60–61
Goehl, Donna G., 678
Gould, Sam, 50
Graen, George, 198
Gray, Edmund L., 453
Greenbaum, Howard H., 548

Green, Thad B., 42
Grimes, A. J., 230
Gryna, Fran, J. M., 332, 633
Guest, Robert H., 315
Gulowsen, Jon, 182
Guth, William D., 378

Hackman, J. Richard, 158
Haimann, Theo, 5
Haire, Mason, 190
Hammer, W. Clay, 153
Hanley, Joseph, 333
Harbin, James L., C72–76
Harlow, Dorothy N., C12–16
Harnett, Donald L., 234
Hatvany, Nina, 684
Hayden, Gerard V., C68–71
Hayes, R. H., 591
Hay, Robert D., 56, 462
Hedley, Barry, 391
Heller, Frank A., 411
Henderson, Richard I., 540, 542
Henzberg, Frederick, 121, 159
Hodgetts, Richard M., C9–11
Hofstede, Geert, 673, 686
Holmes, Sandra L., 440, 451
Hopeman, Richard, 635
Howard, Ann, 85, 86–93

Iacocca, Lee A., 658–61

Jacoby, Neil H., 448
Jaeger, Alfred M., 682
Janger, Allen, 494
Janis, Irving L., 425
Jennings, Marianne M., 460
Jerdee, Thomas H., 6
Jones, Reginald, 470–74
Jones, S. Roland, 42
Juran, J. M., 633

Kahler, Ruel, C99–101
Kahn, Robert L., 281–84, 334
Kantrow, Alan M., 643–57
Katz, Daniel, 281–84, 334
Keegan, Warren J., C102–103
Kelly, Lane, 672
Knerr, Claramae, 155
Komorita, Samuel S., 426
Koontz, Harold, 5, 58
Kreitner, Robert, 152
Kresch, Sandra D., 480–87

Langley, Monica, C48–51
Latham, Gary P., 520, 538
Laughlin, Patrick R., 426
Lawler, Edward E., 150, 270, 544
Lawrence, Paul R., 262, 294, 297, 327, 329
Leavitt, Harold, 177
Leenders, Michiel R., 619
Lenz, R. T., 389
Leontiades, Milton, 336, 337
Likert, Rensis, 178–79, 269

Lindblom, Charles E., 409–10
Lindsay, William M., 382
Livingstone, James M., 675
Locke, Edwin, 154–56
Long, William A., 683
Lorsch, Jay W., 262, 294, 295, 327
Luthans, Fred, 152
Lyles, Marjorie A., 389

McClaskey, Michael B., 419, 420
McClelland, David, 145–46
McFarland, Dalton, 5
McGlashan, Robert, C52–60, C61–67, C68–71
McGregor, Douglas, 143, 188–90
McMurry, Robert N., 238
Mahoney, Thomas A., 6
Makin, Claire, 85, 94–103
March, James G., 260
Margulies, Newton, 322
Maslow, Abraham H., 56, 57, 143–45
Mathys, Nicholas, 510, 522
Mausner, Bernard, 121
Mayo, George Elton, 56, 57, 64–67, 80
Melohn, Thomas H., 216–20
Melville, Donald R., 475–79
Mettler, Ruben F., 364–67
Miles, Raymond, 189–90, 377
Miller, Thomas R., C94–98
Miner, John B., 30, 41, 48, 375, 417, 516, 537, C4–8
Miner, Mary G., 516, 537
Mintzberg, Henry, 9
Mobley, William H., 123
Morgan, Lee L., 221–23
Morse, Nancy C., 181
Muensterberg, Hugo, 74
Myers, Mildred S., 455, 456

Nadler, David A., 330, 358–63
Nehemkis, Peter, 448
Newman, William, 5
Newsom, Walter B., 42
Novak, Jerry V., 42

O'Connell, Jeremiah J., 316
O'Connor, Rochelle, 383
O'Donnell, Cyril, 5
Oliver, John E., 304
Olm, Kenneth, C27–34
O'Reilley, Charles A., 241
Ottemann, Robert, 547
Ouchi, William, 682, 683

Paluszek, John L., 450
Payne, Stephen L., C77–80
Pennings, Johannes M., 412, 413
Perrucci, Robert, 437
Petersen, James C., 240
Pondy, Louis R., 241
Price, James L., 302
Pucik, Vladimir, 684
Pym, Denis, 318

Quinn, James B., 409–10
Quinn, R. P., 122

Raia, Anthony P., 156, 322
Raven, Bertram, 230
Reich, Robert B., 621
Reimer, Everett, 181
Rice, William V., Jr., C68–71
Richman, Barry M., 672
Roethlisberger, Fritz J., 56, 57, 64–67, 80
Rowe, Alan J., 117
Rue, Leslie W., 382
Rumelt, Richard P., 300

Satow, Roberta, 230
Sayles, Leonard, 185
Schein, Edgar H., 176
Schendel, Dan E., 437
Schnee, Jerome, 5
Schoen, Donald, 603
Schroeder, Roger G., 626, 627, 632
Schwarz, Karl, 703–10
Scott, Bruce R., 335
Scott, William, 5
Seo, K. K., 683
Shapiro, Zur, 9
Shipper, Frank, 460
Simon, Herbert A., 67–70, 72, 80, 260, 405–7
Singleton, Timothy M., C20–26, C52–60, C61–67
Skinner, Wickham, 592, 617, 621
Sloan, Alfred P., Jr., 56, 57
Smith, Norman R., 417
Snow, Charles C., 377
Snydermann, Barbara S., 121
Staines, G. L., 122
Stalker, G. M., 292–94
Steiner, George A., 246, 374, 375, 384, 452
Steiner, John F., 452
Stogdill, Ralph M., 193
Summer, Charles E., 443
Sweeney, D., 595

Takezawa, S., 165
Tannenbaum, Robert, 444
Taylor, Frederick W., 56, 57, 58–61, 70, 80
Thompson, James D., 229, 264, 286–90
Thompson, Victor, 184
Thorn, Ron, C2–3
Tilles, Seymour, 396
Trachtman, Leon E., 437
Trist, Eric L., 285

Uttal, Bro, 695–701

Vroom, Victor H., 196–98

Warren, Kirby, 5
Weber, Max, 56, 62–64, 67, 71, 80, 175, 229–32, 301
Weihrich, Heinz, 5
Wexley, Kenneth N., 520, 538
Wharton, Joseph, 56, 57
Whisler, Thomas L., 407
Whitehill, Arthur M., 165
White, Louis P., C12–16

Whitsett, David A., 346–57
Wild, Ray, 121
Williams, Roy H., C94–98
Williams, T., 595
Wilpert, Bernhard, 411
Wilson, Thornton A., 662–63
Woodward, Joan, 291–92
Worthley, Reginald, 672
Wren, Daniel A., 56

Wright, William E., C35–40

Yetton, Philip W., 197
Yorks, Lyle, 346–57
Young, John A., 85, 104–6

Zander, Alvin, 175–77

Subject Index

Absenteeism, 115
Academy of Management, 15, 56–57
Acceptance theory, 68
Accidents
    and health and safety, 557–59
    prevention training, 558–59
    statistics and reporting, 557–58
Accounting
    and budgets, 267
    control systems for, 267-68, C35–40
    cost center system for, 268
    human asset, 268–69
    investment center system for, 267
    Likert's human asset, 269
    profit center system for, 268
Achievement motivation theory, 145–47
    importance of, in entrepreneurship, 145
    major contribution of, 166
    development, relation of, to economic 145–46
Acquisition, organizational, 336–38
Administration. See also Management; Supervision
    contract, for labor unions, 505–6
    wage and salary, 540–43
Administrative behavior, 68–70
Advertising, 457, 459. See also Public relations
Affiliation needs, 146–47
Affirmative action, 91, 514
Aggregate planning, 625–27
Applications, job, 515

Apprenticeships, 524
Aptitude tests, 518
Assessment centers, 519
Attachment, motivational, 160–61
Attitude, employee
    measurement of, 550–54
    origins of surveys for, 67
    resistance to measurement of, 554
    and role in performance, 65
Audits
    in organizational control systems, 267, C35–40
    situation, and planning process, 382–83
    social, 453–57
Authority
    Barnard's acceptance theory of, 68
    bases and definition of, 228–32
    formal and acceptance views of, 229
    and hierarchic change, 314–15
    and managerial motivation, 33
    and mindless obedience, 231–32
    rational-legal, 230, 231
    use of, in organizations, 226–53
    Weber's concept of, 63–64
Automation, 609, 624. See also Technology
Autonomous groups, 182

Bargaining
    as basic management function, 5–6, 8, 17
    collective, 232, 501, 504–5
    and creativity, 423
    definition and factors of, 233–36

Bargaining (cont'd)
    and organizational politics, 232–40
    strategies in, 235–36
Behavior
    leader, 193–94
    organizational. See Organizational behavior
    structure, aspects of, 192–94
Behavior modification
    ethical consideration of, 154
    major contribution of, 166
    and operant learning, 151–54
    roots in Hawthorne studies, 152
Benefits, employee, 545–47
Boards of directors
    as co-optation mechanism, 413
    and decision making, 411–14, C20–26
    legal size requirements for, 412
    role of outside directors in, 412–13
Bonuses, incentive, 543
Bounded rationality, 69–70, 406–9
Brainstorming, 422
Budgets, 267, 384. See also Accounting
Bureaucracy. See also Hierarchy
    decentralization issues in, 301–3
    distinction of, from professional systems, 303
    efficiency of, 64
    and innovative change, 320
    and organizational change, 314–20
    role of, in sociotechnical systems, 284
    and social responsibility, 443

Bureaucracy (cont'd)
and value of bureaucratic
structures, 301–3
Weber's theory of, 62–64
Bureaucratic theory, 302–6
Burnout, job, 119

Capacity planning, 625–27
Career development, 522–26. *See also*
Training, employee
Careers, management, 26–48
characteristics needed for, 28–33
on college faculties, 46–48
in functional areas of organizations,
37–44
in personnel/human resources, 38–
40
in production-operations, 40–44
in the professions, 44–49
in research and development, 49
Case analysis, 524
Change, organizational. *See*
Organizational change
Change units, 317
Choice shift, 424
Classical management, Fayol's
principles of, 61–64
Coalition, 287–88
Codetermination laws, 674, 677
Cognitive style, 117–18, C48–51
Collective bargaining, 232, 501, 504–5
Commitment, organizational, 160–63
Communication, 240–49
as basic management function, 5–6,
8, 17
and conflict management, 263, 547
effectiveness of written, 248
and effects on job performance,
128–29
as emphasis in early management
practice, 67
informal systems and networks of,
243–45
personnel, 547–55
and power in organizations, 226–53
problems in, 128, 245–47, C81–85
role of, in organizing, 241–43
skills in, 247–49
Compensation, 539–47. *See also*
Salary; Pay
at executive levels, 544
incentive systems, 543–44
and insurance plans, 546
and retirement plans, 546
unemployment, 545
Competition
behavior patterns in, 259–60
Japanese–U.S., 643–57
Computers
and decision making, 407
and feedback overload, 129
and inventory systems, 631–32
and operating systems design, 618

Computers (cont'd)
and performance control systems,
131
and production/operations, 43–44,
76
and simulation models, 628
strategy evaluation models for, 392–
93
Conflict
and confrontation in mediation,
263
and coordination, 256–64
effects of, on performance, 258
intergroup, 258–60
management of, by goals, 262–63
nature and sources of, 256–57
role of communications in
managing, 263, 547
union-management, 501, 504
Consulting, management
career opportunities in, 46
and consultant-initiated change,
315–17
firms specializing in, 45–46
Consumer trends, 485–87
Contingencies, strategic, 232
Contingency approach
and differentiation and integration,
294–97
growth strategy as, 297–300
and leader match training, 523
and matrix structures, 327–28
to organization design, 290–301
to organization development, 327–
28
Contingency planning, 385
Contingency theory, 200
Contracts, union-management, 504–6
Control. *See also* Controlling
inventory, 623–24, 628–32, C77–80,
C86–93, C94–98
maintenance, 623–24
open-loop model for performance,
131–34
performance, 555–62
planning, 624
quality, 598, 617, 623–24, 632–36
timing of, for performance, 134–35
Control group, 78
Controlling. *See also* Control;
Influencing; Supervision
as basic management function, 5–7,
17
and operating systems design, 623–
24
and operations management, 597–
98, C86–93
of organizational components, 254–
77
Control systems
accounting, 267–68
characteristics of effective, 269–73
dysfunctions of, 269–71

Control systems (cont'd)
measures and standards for, 266
open-loop model of, 265
Convergence hypothesis, 680, 687
Cooperation, 115
Co-optation, 287–88
Coordinating
as basic management function, 5–7,
17
and conflict management, 256–64
guidelines for, 263–64
by hierarchy, 261
by horizontal integration, 261–62
of organizational components, 254–
77
and unit interdependence, 264
Corporations, *Fortune's* ranking of,
94–103
Cost center system, 268
Costs
and inventory economics, 628–29
of quality, 634–35
and resource allocation, 627
value analysis of, 618
Creativity
and bargaining, 423
characteristics of, 419–20
in decision making, 419–20
development of, 421
in groups, 421–23
and practicality, 423
Critical Path Method (CPM), 627, 628
Cultural island strategies, 679–80
Culture
as constraint on management, 671,
672
and influence on performance, 130
and international management,
671–80, C81–85
of organizations, 671, C48–51
revolution of, in U.S. corporations,
695–701
and variations of ethics, 447–48
Culture clusters, 673

Data base systems, 245–46
Decision making. *See also* Planning;
Policy; Strategy
Barnard-Simon formulations of, 67–
70
as basic management function, 5–6,
8, 17
and choice shift, 424
and computers, 407
at corporate board level, 411–14
creativity in, 419–20
criteria for, in operations systems,
591
cultural factors as constraints on,
671
defined, 404
and effects of circumstance, 410–11
effects of, on performance, 126–28

Decision making (cont'd)
  entrepreneurial, 415–18
  experience at General Electric,
    470–74
  group, 421–27
  and groupthink, 424
  importance of, 405–6
  incremental, 409–10
  individual, 414–21
  in Japanese management, 685–86
  and laws affecting personnel, 502
  and "office of the president"
    concept, 414
  in operating systems design, 617–24
  organizational, 402–33
  personality factors in, 418–19
  programmed and nonprogrammed,
    404–5
  and risk-taking, 419
  and risky shift, 424–26
  and satisficing, 405
  and social responsibility, 441
  and technology, 601–3
  top-level hierarchy of, 414
Decision tree, 200
  concept of leadership, 195–98
  methods of job skill training, 523
Delphi technique, 395, 422, 626
Demand
  forecasting of, for human resources,
    509
  and supply for managerial work,
    33–38
  time phasing of, 627
Demotion, 560
Departmentation, 288–90
Design, operating systems. See
    Operating systems, design of
Design, organization. See Organization
    design
Development, employee, 519–26. See
    also Training
Development, organization. See
    Organization development
Dialectical debate, 427
Differentiation
  and matrix structures, 295–97
  as open systems characteristic, 281
  under uncertainty, 294–97
Disabilities, 124
Discipline, employee, 560–61
Discrimination, 541
Divestiture, 336–38

Economics. See also Costs
  and forecasting, 393–96
  and internationalization, 674–75
  inventory, 628–29
  and social responsibility, 439
  and values associated with
    development, 672–73
Education, 31, 671–72. See also
    Intelligence

Emotions, and performance, 118–19
Employee benefits, 545–47
Entrepreneurship
  and achievement motivation theory,
    145
  case illustration, C48–51, C52–60
  decision making in, 415–18
  and environmental scanning, 395–
    96
  types of, 417–18
Environment, external
  effect of, on performance, 130
  and new factors in marketing, 481–
    82
  and operations design decisions,
    616
  and organizational change at AT&T,
    358–63
  and performance, 129–30
  and representing, 458
  uncertainty in, 294–95
Environment, internal, 125–29
  effect of, on performance, 130
  and health and safety, 555–56
  in historical perspective of
    organization, 285
  as job description component, 507
  open systems view of, 124–25, 282–
    84
  and operations design decisions,
    616
  and operations manager, 593
  and organizational growth, 334
  and performance, 124–30
  and social responsibility, 441
  in sociotechnical systems, 284–85
Equal opportunity, 506
Equifinality, 281
Equity theory
  implications of, for management,
    148
  major contributions of, 166
  and management motivation, 147–
    49
Ethics, 434–67. See also Social
    responsibility
  corporate responses toward, 449–
    57, C61–67
  current state of, 445–47
  and international payoffs, 447
  and the law, 445–49
  and employee motivation, 142
  in organizational politics, 238–40
  and theft by employees, 448–49,
    C77–80
  and values, 164–66
Evaluation, performance. See
    Performance appraisal
Exception principle, 60
Executives
  decision making by, 414
  functions of, 67–68
  personality characteristics, C9–11

Expectancy theory
  and extrinsic outcome, 149
  major contributions of, 166
  of motivation, 149–51
  zone of application of, 150–51
Experience curves, 392
Extrinsic outcome, 149

"Factory of the future," 601, 618
Factory system, 75, 80
Faculty careers, management
  motivation needed for, 47–48
  nature of work in, 47, C17–19
  opportunities in, 48
  salaries for, 48
  training required for, 46–48
Family, and job performance, 129
Feedback
  as communication technique, 128
  in employee readership surveys,
    550
  in performance appraisal, 536
Fixed format process, 622
Forecasting, 393–96
  classification of methods for, 625–
    26
  of demand for managers, 34
  economic and sales, 393–94, C94–
    98
  environmental scanning, 395–96
  for human resource needs, 509–10,
    C9–11
  in operating systems planning, 625–
    27
  social and political, 395
  as method for subsystem
    protection, 287
  and technology and innovation,
    394–95
Fortune
  corporate rankings by, 94–103
  featured companies, 85, 204, 345,
    468–69, 568, 642, 694
Full rationality, 70, 406–9
Functional foremanship, 59
Future, the, 609, 625. See also
    Forecasting

Games, management, 524
Gantt charts, 628
Gap analysis, 389–90
Goals
  official and operative, 112–13
  personal and recruiting, 514
  variation of, within industries and
    cultures, 113, 685–86
Goal-setting. See also Planning
  Locke's concept of, 154–56
  major contributions of, 166
  and motivation training, 525
  as negative influence on teamwork,
    155

Goal-setting (cont'd)
  and operations management, 591
  and relation to performance, 155
Government. *See also* Law
  and corporate public relations,
    459–60
  regulations and social
    responsibility, 440–41
Grievance procedures, 505–6
Group-based systems, 175–83
  factors favorable to success of, 183
  and Japanese management, 685
  Likert's theory of, 178–79
Groups, 173–203
  aspects of functioning, 183–87
  autonomous, and sociotechnical
    theory, 179–83
  and cohesiveness, 186–87
  and decision making, 421–27
  defined, 175–77
  effectiveness of, in Likert's theory,
    180
  formal and informal, 183–85
  implementation of small, 206–8
  Leavitt's view of, as basic building
    blocks, 177
  open systems character of, 176
  power of, in organizations, 175
  reference, 176–77
  types of, 184–85
  and Weber's concept of power, 175
Groupthink, 424, 461, 688
Growth, organizational
  through acquisitions and
    divestitures, 336–38
  and decline, 333–39
  models for, 335–36
  stages of, 335–38
  as strategy, 334–35

"Halo," 536, 538
Handbooks, employee, 549–50
Handicaps, 124
Hawthorne studies
  chronology of, 65
  evaluation of influence of, 71
  methodological shortcomings of, 78
  and productivity, 66
  and role of social conditions in
    workplace, 65
  as roots of behavior modification,
    152
  and social responsibility, 442–43
Health and safety, 555–62. *See also*
    Accidents
"Hidden factory," 625
Hierarchy. *See also* Bureaucracy
  creation of, from goals, 113
  cultural value comparisons of, 673
  in Japanese management, 685, 687
  and job performance, 126
  Maslow's need theory of, 143–45
  and organizational change, 314–15

Hierarchy (cont'd)
  and social responsibility, 443
  within work groups, 126
Hiring error, 115
Human asset accounting, 455–56
Human engineering, 622–23
Human needs, 142–46
Human relations. *See also*
    Communication; Personnel
  developmental concepts of, 64–67
  Miles' categorization theory of, 189
  and quality of work life, 444–45
  and sensitivity training, 322–25
Human resources management. *See
    also* Personnel; Staffing
  availability and staffing, 499–500
  careers in, 38–40
  and communications, 547–55
  defined, 12
  Japanese approach to, 682–85
  planning approaches to, 509–11
  planning model for, 510
  recruiting and selecting in, 511–19
  as subdiscipline of management
    framework, 12
  and employee turnover, 569–75
Humanism, 442–45

Image, corporate, 460–62
Incentive systems, 543–44
Inducements-contributions balance,
  232
Industrialization, and international
  management, 673–74
Industrial management. *See also*
    Production-operations
    management
  as origin of production
    management, 75–76
  and social responsibility, 450–51
Industrial medicine
  as component of personnel
    management, 75
  in-house activities of, 555–56
Industrial organizations, 61
Industrial psychology, 60, 74
Industry analysis, 390
Influencing. *See also* Leadership;
    Supervision
  as basic management function, 5–7
  as inclusive of leadership and
    supervision, 187
  and organizational behavior, 108–
    23
Information
  processing of, 43–44
  systems for management of, 245–47
Instrumentality, 149
Insurance plans, 546
Integration
  and matrix structures, 295–97
  and uncertainty, 294–97

Intelligence
  as factor in supply and demand, 35
  and job performance, 116–18
  and management potential, 29–30
  and relation to occupational level,
    29–30
  as staffing consideration, 499–500
  tests for, in personnel selection,
    518
  and type required for management,
    29–30
Interviews, personnel selection, 515
Intrinsic outcome, 149
Inventory
  computerized systems for, 631–32
  control systems, 630–32, C94–98
  and Japanese "kan-ban" methods,
    620
  and operating system design, 617,
    623–24
Investment center system, 267

Japanese, the
  and competition in world markets,
    643–57
  and cultural differences from U.S.,
    682–83
  and micromanagement, 646–47
  and productivity approaches, 608
  and quality circles, 331
  and research on management
    practices, 685–88
  and theories A, J, and Z, 681–82
  and transferability of approach, 688
Jobs
  characteristics theory, 157–59
  and components of job
    descriptions, 507
  design of, 154, 157–60, 617, 622–23
  enrichment of, 444–45
  evaluation of, 541–42
  and job analysis, 506–9
  and organization goals, 113
  pricing of, 542–43
  redesign of, 166, 159–60, 623
  requirements of, 115
  rotation of, 525
  and satisfaction, 119–23
Job shop flow process, 622
Journals, management, 77
Jury of executive opinion, 393

"Kan-ban," 620, 632
Knowledge, managerial, 30–31

Labor availability, 499–500. *See also*
    Human resources management;
    Personnel; Staffing
Labor law, 72
Labor relations. *See also* Human
    relations
  and development of personnel

Labor relations (cont'd)
  management, 74
  and employee attitude measures,
    551
  as external force in personnel
    management, 39
  and intergroup conflict, 259
  and international laws, 674
Labor unions
  activities of, 503–6
  and changes toward productivity,
    607
  and codetermination laws, 674
  and collective bargaining, 504–5
  and contract administration, 505–6
  and grievance procedures, 505–6,
    C68–71
  international legal contexts for, 674
  job pricing in, 542–43
  and labor relations law, 501–3
  managers' views of, 576–78
  and personnel management, 73–74
  as recruiting source, 513
  role of, in staffing process, 499, 501
  and strikes, 505
  and view of performance appraisal,
    539
Law
  codetermination, 674, 677
  and ethics, 445–49
  labor relations, 72, 501–3
  and international management, 674
  and minority staffing, 499
  personnel/human resources, 501–3
Leader behavior, 193–94
Leader match training, 523
Leadership, 173–203, C9–11. See also
    Influencing; Supervision
  as basic management function, 5
  cognitive style, C48–51
  boss-centered, 196
  decision-tree concept of, 195–98
  Fiedler's contingency view of, 191–
    92
  and leader behavior, 192–94
  and leader match training, 523
  path-goal views of, 193–95
  situational theory of, 193
  and structure, 192–93
  subordinate-centered, 196
  and supervision, 197–98
Learning
  defined, 117
  and job performance, 116–18
  operant, 151–54
Least preferred coworker score,
    (LPC), 191–92
Life cycle, organizational, 333–39
Line flow process, 621–22
Linking pin, Likert's, 179
Lobbies, 459–60
Logical incrementalism, 409–10
LPC Score, 191–92

Maintenance, operating system, 617–
    18, 623–24
Management. See also Individual
    topics
  in business hierarchies, 85–107
  characteristics needed for, 28–33
  courses in, 13–14
  and current business ethics, 445–47
  definition of field of, 2–23
  Fayol's classical theory of, 61–64
  functions of, 4–9
  historical development of, 54–83
  international perspective on, 668–
    93
  motivational factors in, 140–70
  origins of production-operations,
    75–76
  participative, 179, C20–26
  personnel. See Personnel
    management
  procurement/materials, 617–20
  production-operations. See
    Production-operations
    management
  professional associations in, 14–15
  as a science, 76–80
  and staffing, 469–529
  study of, 24–52
  theory, schools approach to, 57–58
  strategic, 372–79
Management by Objectives (MBO)
  as goal-setting approach, 156–57
  major contributions of, 166
  and standard-setting processes, 132
Management consulting, 45–46
Management Continuity Study, 86
Management process framework, 4–
    10
Management Progress Study, 86
Management strategy, 10–15. See also
    Strategy
Managerial careers, 26–48
Managerial work roles, 8–9
Manufacturing, 40. See also
    Production-operations
    management
Marketing
  in international organizations, 676–
    77, C99–101
  new factors in, 481–82
  relation to production-operations,
    587
  and selection of product/service
    line, 617–18
  surveys for judgment forecasting,
    626
Material Requirements Planning
    (MRP), 631–32
Matrix structures
  and contingency approaches, 327–
    28
  differentiation and integration in,
    295

Matrix structures (cont'd)
  problems with, 297
Mechanistic systems, 292–94
Medicine, industrial, 555–56
Micromanagement, Japanese, 646–47
Minorities
  and affirmative action recruiting,
    514
  entering managerial positions, 34–
    35
  and training and development, 519
Models
  of culture-based processes, 672
  economic order, 629
  for human resources planning, 510
  of input-output systems, 20
  longitudinal employer selection,
    512
  open-loop control, 130, 265
  for organizational growth, 336
  for personal career planning, 522
  of scientific method, 79
  for training evaluation, 521
Motivation, 140–70
  achievement theory, 145–46
  and Adams' equity theory, 147–48
  commitment as factor in, 160, 161–
    63
  and compensation incentives, 543
  contribution of concepts of, 166
  ethical considerations, 142
  and expectancy theory, 149–51
  and expectations, 87–89
  in faculty management careers, 47–
    48
  generational differences, 86–93
  goal-setting approaches to, 154–60
  influencing performance, 118
  job redesign approaches to, 157–60
  to manage, as a trend, 33, 35–36
  and men's management aspirations,
    87–90
  and minorities' management
    aspirations, 91
  "need" theories of, 142–46
  role of values in, 160, 163–66
  training to develop, 524–26
  and women's management
    aspirations, 90–91
  work redesign approaches to, 157–
    60
Motivation-hygiene theory, 159–60
Multinational operations
  case illustration, C81–85, C102–103
  and cultural island strategies, 679–
    80
  decision making in, 677
  organization of, 676–77
  and values refocusing, 680
Multiskilling, 181

Need hierarchy theory, 143–45, 166
Negative entropy, 281, 334

Networks, communication, 243–44
Noise, environmental, 130
Nominal group procedures, 422, 427
Nonmanagerial work, 9
Norms, open systems, 282

"Office of the president" concept, 414
Open-loop control model, 131–34
Open systems
　and approaches to organization
　　design, 280–89
　characteristics, 281
　and definition of groups, 176
　Katz and Kahn's social psychology
　　of, 281–84
　organizational environments in,
　　282–84
　origins of approach, 67–68
　subsystems within, 282–83
　Thompson's sociological approach
　　to, 286–90
　view of environment and
　　performance, 124–25
Operant learning theory, 166
Operating systems, 614–40
　design decisions for, 617–24
　and facilities layout, 620–21
　and forecasting, 625–27
　and inventory planning, 628–32
　job design in, 617, 622–23
　and process selection, 621–22
　and product/service line, 617–18
　and quality control, 632–36
　relation of, to other functions, 593–
　　94
　structure and organization, 596–97
　types of, 590
Operations management. See also
　　Operating systems; Production-
　　operations management
　controlling functions of, 597–98
　defined, 12
　importance of training in, 588
　jobs included in, 592–93
　and planning, 594–96
　of productivity, 607–9
　resource inputs and outputs, 587–
　　88
　role of, 40–43
　strategic approach to, 591–92
　and technology, 598–604
　and the work environment, 593
Organic systems, 292–94
Organizational behavior
　defined, 11
　and influencing functions, 108–223
　and origins in human relations
　　concepts, 64, 66–67
Organizational change, 312–44
　and bureaucracy, 314–20
　consultant-initiated, 315–17, 340,
　　C41–47
　direct hierarchic, 314–15

Organizational change (cont'd)
　and growth through acquisition,
　　340
　and innovation, 320
　procedures and relative values in,
　　340
　resistances to, 317–20
　and shifts in power balance, 317
　and value of contingency approach,
　　340
Organizational goals, 112–15
Organizational politics, 236–40
Organization design. See also Open
　　systems
　and bureaucratic theory, 301–6
　contingency views of, 290–301
　differentiation and integration in,
　　294–97
　and growth strategy, 297–300
　and matrix structures, 295–97
　open systems approaches to, 280–
　　89
Organization development, 312–44
　applications of sociotechnical
　　systems in, 325–27
　Argyris' contributions to, 323–24
　and Beer's values of informed
　　choice, 322
　Bennis' contributions to, 322, 324
　contingency approach to, 327–28
　definitions and values of, 320–22
　Margulies' and Raia's humanistic
　　ethic of, 322
　origins of, in sensitivity training,
　　322–25
　quality circles approach to, 331–33
　survey feedback approach to, 328–
　　31
Organizations. See also Individual
　　topics
　careers in functional areas of, 37–
　　44
　designs for, 278–311
　motivation in, 140–70
　performance in, 110–38
　politics of, 236–40
　power and communication in, 226–
　　53
Organizing, 5–7, 241–43
Outputs, operational, 589–90, 616–18

Parkinson's Law, 155–56
Path-goal theory
　basic propositions of, 194
　evaluation of, 194–96, 200
　leadership behaviors in, 193–94
Pay. See also Compensation; Salary
　and expectancy theory, 149–51
　role of, in equity theory, 147–49
　supplementary, 543
Payoffs, 447
Performance, 110–38

Performance (cont'd)
　appraisal of. See Performance
　　appraisal
　and behavior modification, 151–53
　and compensation incentives, 543
　control activities, 130–35, 559–62
　corrective actions for failing, 132
　cultural influences on, 130
　defined, 114
　diagnosis of failure in, 132
　and disciplinary action, 560–61
　economic influences on, 130
　effects of communications on, 128–
　　29
　effects of conflict on, 258
　effects of decision making on, 126–
　　28
　effect of goal-setting on, 155
　effects of group cohesiveness on,
　　186–87
　effects of motivation training on,
　　525
　effects of sociotechnical theory on,
　　182–83
　and employee counseling, 561–62
　and employee reassignment, 559–
　　60
　environmental influences on, 124–
　　30
　and expectancy theory, 151
　and health and safety, 555–62
　and hierarchical structure, 126
　individual, 115–18
　and quality control, 636
　relation of, to learning, 151–53
　relation of, to strategy, 300–301
　role of values in, 163–66
　setting standards for, 132
　and staffing, 449–500
　Taylor's measurement and
　　evaluation of, 60
　and training evaluation methods,
　　521
Performance appraisal, 532–39
　feedback in, 536
　judgmental processes for, 533–34
　labor union view of, 539
　for managers, 533–36
　measures for, 535–36
　problems in systems for, 536–39
　rating scales, 537–38
　resistance to, 538–39
Personality, managerial, 31–33
Personnel. See also Human resources;
　　Staffing
　activities in management of, 38–39
　and communications, 547–55
　and labor relations law, 501–3
　and medical/health functions, 555–
　　56
　recruiting of, 511–19, C4–8
　and safety management functions,
　　556–59

Personnel (cont'd)
selection of. *See* Personnel selection
Personnel management
defined, 12
factors of success in, 40
historical development of, 72–75
and job analysis, 506–11
and labor relations, 39
Personnel selection
case illustration of, C4–8
methods for, 514–19
and recruiting, 511–19
role of interviews in, 515
use of assessment centers in, 519
use of physical exams in, 517
use of psychological testing in, 518–19
Plan to plan, 382
Planning, 370–401. *See also* Decision making; Human resources planning; Policy; Strategy
aggregate or capacity, 625–27
approaches to human resources, 509–11
as basic management function, 5–7
behavioral problems encountered in, 388–89
centralized organization of, 385
contingency, 385
contribution of, to organizations, 387–88
decentralized organization of, 385
human resources, 506–11
inventory, 628–32
long-range, 383
mixed organization of, 385
and operations management, 594–96, 624–98
organization of, 385–87
overview of process of, 374
problems in, 388–89
process of, 379–85
quality control, 633–35
role of policy in, 375–76
for social responsibility programs, 452–53
strategic, 7, 373–75, 382–85, C20–26
team organization of, 385
Policy, 370–401. *See also* Decision making; Planning; Strategy
distinction of, from strategy, 376
and effects on performance, 127–28
identifying and evaluating, 389–96
and management framework, 11
role of, in planning, 375–76
for social responsibility, 451–53
types of, 376–79
Politicians, characteristics of, 237
Politics
and corporate representing, 459–60
and ethics, 238, 240
and international management, 674

Politics (cont'd)
tactics and characteristics in, 237–38
organizational, 236–40
and bargaining, 232–40
Polygraphs, 517
Positions. *See* Jobs
Post-industrial society, 284–86
Power
and bargaining politics, 232–40
bases of, 229–232
and communication in organizations, 226–53
definition of organizational, 228
need for, as motivational, 146–47
and organizational change, 318
strategic contingencies concept of, 232
uses of, 231
Process selection, 621–22
Product life cycles, 391–92, 627
Product-market matrix, 390
Product-portfolio matrix, 390–91
Production-operations management, 584–612. *See also* Operations management; Operating systems
case illustration, C86–93
and conversion of inputs, 586–87
courses in, 42
defined, 12
educational requirements for, 41
and evolution of factory system, 75–76
and historical tie with manufacturing, 40
major concepts of, 586–87
organizational role of, 40–43
and Taylor's scientific management, 59
Productivity
definition and nature of, 604–5
factors influencing, 606–7
increasing employee, 216–20
international comparison of GDPs, 606
and Japanese management, 608, 685
measures in performance appraisal, 535
measures of improvements in, 608
operations management of, 607–9
problems and methods for, 204–23
and relation to social conditions, 65–66
and small groups, 205–15
strategies at Chrysler, 658–61
and technology, 624
U.S.–Japanese comparative practices, 651
U.S. trends in, 605–6
Professional associations, 14–15
Professional careers, 44–49
Professional systems
authority bases in, 231
bureaucratic structures in, 301–3

Professional systems (cont'd)
and bureaucratic theory, 302–6
distinction of, from bureaucracy, 303
Profit
center system for accounting control, 268
and social responsibility, 439, 442
Profit Impact of Market Strategies (PIMS), 392
Program Evaluation Review Technique (PERT), 628
Program strategy, 373, 376
Promotion, employee, 560
Psychological testing, 518–19
Public, the
and corporate image, 461
and corporate representing, 460–62, C61–67
Public relations. *See also* Representing
activities involved in, 457–60
in advertising, 457
and coping with environments, 458
and corporate image, 460–62
and government, 459–60
and representing, 457–62, C61–67

Quality circles
approach to organization development, 331–33
definition and Japanese origins of, 331
and productivity improvement, 608, 636
and team-building, 332
Quality control, 598, 617, 623–24, 632–36
Quality-of-work-life
and humanism, 442–45
and job enrichment, 444–45
and the *Work in America* view, 444–45

Rating scales, performance, 537–38
Rationality
bounded and full, 68–70, 406–9
and resistance to change, 317–18
Simon's formulations of, 68–70
Rational-legal authority, 63–64
Recruiting, personnel
affirmative action, 514
on college campuses, 513–14
legal constraints on, 511, 514
sources for, 512–13
for staff positions, 498
Reference groups, 176–77
Regulation. *See* Law
Reinforcement, behavior, 151–53
Representing. *See also* Public relations
activities involved in, 457–60
as basic management function, 6, 8, 17
defined, 8

Representing (cont'd)
and government relations, 459–60
and public relations, 457–62
Retirement plans, 546
Risk-taking
cultural value comparison of, 673
in decision makers, 419
Risky shift, 424
Role playing, 524
Role prescriptions, 113–14, 262
Roles
defined, in open systems, 282
managerial, 8–9

Safety, 555–62
Salary. *See also* Compensation; Pay
case illustration, C12–16
and expectancy theory, 151
and job pricing, 542–43
and wage administration, 540–43
Sales force composite, 393–94
Satisfaction, job
and influence on performance,
119–23
and productivity, 121–22
Satisficing
and bounded rationality, 69–70,
406–7
in decision making, 405
and expectancy theory, 150
Simon's concept of, 69–70, 407–408
Scalar chain, Fayol's, 62, 64
Scientific management
as developed by Taylor, 58–61
Gantt's contribution to, 60
Gilbreth's contribution to, 60
and nonscientific knowledge, 76–77
Scientific method, 78
"Schools" approach, 57–58
Selection, personnel. *See* Personnel
selection
Self-actualization, 143, 145
Sensitivity training
and employee development, 523
as origins of organization
development, 322–25
Site selection, 617, 620
Skills training, job, 523–24
Small business, 416–17. *See also*
Entrepreneurships
Small groups, 208–10
Social auditing, 453–57
Social responsibility, 434–67. *See also*
Ethics
conflicting views of, 439–42
corporate activities in, 449–50
corporate responses toward, 449–
57, C61–67
and decision making, 441
economic view of, 439
and job enrichment, 444–45
planning for programs in, 452–53
policies for, 451–53

Social responsibility (cont'd)
and quality of work life, 442–45
and social auditing, 453–57
Social work, 74
Sociological systems
co-optation and coalition in, 287–88
departmentation in, 288–90
protection of production subsystem
in, 286–87
Sociotechnical systems
applications of, 325–27
and autonomous work groups,
179–83
importance of multiskilling in, 181
and job redesign, 623
major contribution of, 200
and organization development,
325–27
theory of, 284–86
and work group emphasis, 325–27
Staffing, 469–529. *See also* Human
resources management;
Personnel
as basic management function, 5–7
in cultural island strategies, 679–80
and job analysis, 506–9
major constraints in, 498–506
and personnel turnover, 569–75
and recruiting and selection, 511–
19
and training and development,
519–26
Standard-setting, 132
Stealing, 448–49
Stewards, union, 506, C2
Stock options, 544
Strategic business units, 591
Strategic contingencies, 232
Strategic management, 372–73. *See
also* Strategy
Strategic planning, 379–85. *See also*
Strategy
Strategy. *See also* Decision making;
Planning; Policy
adaptive response, 677–78
cultural island, 679–80
defined, 372, 375
and design of operating systems,
616–17
for growth, 297–300, 377
identifying and evaluating, 389–96
and management framework, 11
of multinationals, 677–80
and policy formulation, 370–401
program, 373, 376
relation of, to performance, 300–
301
relation of, to structure, 297–300
tests for evaluation of, 396
types of, 376–79
and variations in strategic stance,
377
Stress, 119–20, 556

Structures, 301–6, C12–16. *See also*
Hierarchy; Organization design
Subsystems, 282–83, 286–87
Supervision, 173–203. *See also*
Influencing; Leadership
Supply and demand, 33–38
Survey feedback, 328–31, C72–76
System 4, Likert's, 178–79, 200
Systems
bureaucratic, 301–6
mechanistic and organic, 292–94
natural and artificial, 184
professional, 303–6
open. *See* Open systems
types of operating, 590
Systems approach, 587–88
Systems model, input-output, 20

Tactics, 375
Teaching, 46–48. *See also* Faculty
careers
Team-building, 332
Technological imperative, 290
Technology
"appropriate," 600
and decision making, 601–3
definitions of, 598–99
factory, 601–2
impact of, on management, 599–
600
major and minor, 621
management of, 600–601, 603–4
and mechanistic and organic
systems, 292–94
office, 602–3
and operations management, 598–
604
and productivity, 624
and service organizations, 603
transfer of, 703–10
types of, 290
Woodward's classification of, 291–
92
T-groups, 322–25, 523
Theft, 448–49, C77–80
Theory A, 681–82, 686
Theory J, 681–82, 686
Theory X and theory Y, 190, 200
Theory Z, 608, 681–82, 686–87
Three-way categorization, 189–90
Training, employee, 519–26
to develop motivation, 520, 524–26
effectiveness of on-the-job, 524
evaluation procedures for, 521
and job skill development, 523–24
leader match, 523
needs analysis, 520
Transfer, employee, 560
Transformation process, 617, 621, 624
Turnover, personnel, 569–75, C12–16

Unemployment compensation, 545
Unionization process, 503–4

Unions, labor. *See* Labor unions
U.S. Job Service, 513

Valence, 149
Value analysis, 618–19
Values
   and bureaucratic change, 320
   cultural variations in, 672–73
   definition of, in open systems, 282
   influencing job performance, 118,
     130

Values (cont'd)
   international comparison of, 164–
     65
   and managerial success, 32–33
   in organization development, 320–
     22
   refocusing of, in multinationals, 680
   role of, in motivation, 160, 163–66
Vertical dyad linkages, 198, 200

Wage, minimum, 540–41
Wages. *See* Compensation; Pay; Salary

Women
   and managerial aspirations, 90–91
   entering managerial positions, 34–
     35
   and role in Japanese work force,
     684
Work groups, 126, 325–27
Work redesign. *See* Jobs, redesign of
Workers' compensation, 517

Zone of indifference, 68, 113–14